Human Development

Human Development
Tenth Edition

Diane E. Papalia

Sally Wendkos Olds

Ruth Duskin Feldman

Boston   Burr Ridge, IL   Dubuque, IA   Madison, WI   New York   San Francisco   St. Louis
Bangkok   Bogotá   Caracas   Kuala Lumpur   Lisbon   London   Madrid   Mexico City
Milan   Montreal   New Delhi   Santiago   Seoul   Singapore   Sydney   Taipei   Toronto

Higher Education

HUMAN DEVELOPMENT

Published by McGraw-Hill, a business unit of The McGraw-Hill Companies, Inc., 1221 Avenue
of the Americas, New York, NY, 10020. Copyright © 2007, 2004, 2001, 1998, 1995,
1992, 1989, 1986, 1981, 1978 by The McGraw-Hill Companies, Inc. All rights reserved. No part of
this publication may be reproduced or distributed in any form or by any means, or stored in a
database or retrieval system, without the prior written consent of The McGraw-Hill Companies,
Inc., including, but not limited to, in any network or other electronic storage or transmission, or
broadcast for distance learning.

Some ancillaries, including electronic and print components, may not be available to customers outside the
United States.

This book is printed on acid-free paper.
Printed in China

2 3 4 5 6 7 8 9 0 CTP/CTP 0 9 8 7

ISBN-13: 978-0-07-110714-3 (ISE)
ISBN-10: 0-07-110714-2 (ISE)

About the Authors

As a professor, **Diane E. Papalia** taught thousands of undergraduates at the University of Wisconsin–Madison. She received her bachelor's degree, majoring in psychology, from Vassar College and both her master's degree in child development and family relations and her Ph.D. in life-span developmental psychology from West Virginia University. She has published numerous articles in such professional journals as *Human Development, International Journal of Aging and Human Development, Sex Roles, Journal of Experimental Child Psychology,* and *Journal of Gerontology.* Most of these papers have dealt with her major research focus, cognitive development from childhood through old age. She is especially interested in intelligence in old age and factors that contribute to the maintenance of intellectual functioning in late adulthood. She is a Fellow in the Gerontological Society of America. She is the coauthor of *A Child's World,* now in its tenth edition, with Sally Wendkos Olds and Ruth Duskin Feldman; of *Adult Development and Aging,* now in its second edition, with Harvey L. Sterns, Ruth Duskin Feldman, and Cameron J. Camp; of *Psychology* with Sally Wendkos Olds; and of *Child Development: A Topical Approach* with Dana Gross and Ruth Duskin Feldman.

Sally Wendkos Olds is an award-winning professional writer who has written more than 200 articles in leading magazines and is the author or coauthor of seven books addressed to general readers, in addition to the three textbooks she has coauthored with Dr. Papalia. Her newest book, *A Balcony in Nepal: Glimpses of a Himalayan Village,* describes her encounters with the people and way of life in a remote hill village in eastern Nepal. The updated and expanded third edition of her classic book *The Complete Book of Breastfeeding* was published in 1999. She is also the author of *The Working Parents' Survival Guide* and *The Eternal Garden: Seasons of Our Sexuality* and the coauthor of *Raising a Hyperactive Child* (winner of the Family Service Association of America National Media Award) and *Helping Your Child Find Values to Live By.* She has spoken widely on the topics of her books and articles to both professional and lay audiences, in person and on television and radio. She received her bachelor's degree from the University of Pennsylvania, where she majored in English literature and minored in psychology. She was elected to Phi Beta Kappa and was graduated summa cum laude.

Ruth Duskin Feldman is an award-winning writer and educator. With Diane E. Papalia and Sally Wendkos Olds, she coauthored the fourth, seventh, eighth, ninth, and tenth editions of *Human Development* and the eighth, ninth, and tenth editions of *A Child's World.* She also is coauthor of *Adult Development and Aging* and of *Child Development: A Topical Approach.* A former teacher, she has developed educational materials for all levels from elementary school through college and has prepared ancillaries to accompany the Papalia-Olds books. She is author or coauthor of four books addressed to general readers, including *Whatever Happened to the Quiz Kids? Perils and Profits of Growing Up Gifted,* republished in 2000 as an Authors Guild Back-in-Print edition of iUniverse. She has written for numerous newspapers and magazines and has lectured extensively and made national and local media appearances throughout the United States on education and gifted children. She received her bachelor's degree from Northwestern University, where she was graduated with highest distinction and was elected to Phi Beta Kappa.

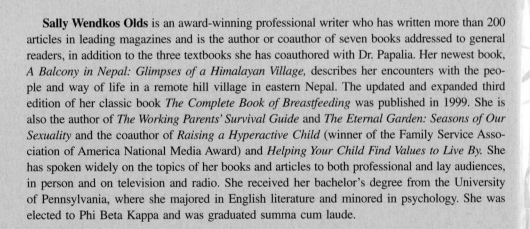

v

To all those who have had an impact
on our own development—
our families and friends and teachers
who have nurtured us, challenged us,
taught us by their example,
provided support and companionship,
and been there for us through the years.

Contents in Brief

Table of Contents

PART 3
Early Childhood

PART 4
Middle Childhood

Chapter 9
Physical and Cognitive
Development in Middle
Childhood

PART 8
Late Adulthood

Chapter 17
Physical and Cognitive Development in Late Adulthood

Chapter 18
Psychosocial Development in Late Adulthood

PART 9
The End of Life

Chapter 19
Dealing with Death and Bereavement

Preface

I n the nearly three decades since the first publication of *Human Development,* the field of human development has increasingly come into its own as a rigorous scientific enterprise. This book, too, has "grown up." Like a child reaching maturity, it has gained in depth, breadth, and objectivity while retaining its unique "personality": the engaging tone and accessible style that have contributed to its popularity over the years.

Our Aims for This Edition

In recent editions of *Human Development* our author team has completely revamped the entire book—its design, content, and pedagogical features. In this tenth edition our primary aim is to build on these foundations by revising and adding much new material.

Cutting-Edge Research

We have sifted through the plethora of literature published each year to select cutting-edge research that will add significantly to students' understanding. For example, in Chapter 3 we present new research findings on the prevalence of multiple births and on hazards of the prenatal environment. As another example, in Chapter 5 we present Kaiser Family Foundation research in a new Practically Speaking box, "Do Babies Watch Too Much Television?" In Chapter 11 we cover new research on adolescent brain development. Our coverage of adult development in Chapters 13 and 14 begins with extensive discussions of the newly defined life stage of emerging adulthood. Our treatment of midlife development in Chapters 15 and 16 includes analyses of data from comprehensive surveys by the MacArthur Foundation's Research Institute on Midlife Development. In Chapters 18 and 19 we present findings of the Changing Lives of Older Couples Study, including grief patterns after the death of a spouse.

We have broadened the research base of each chapter and have updated throughout, using the most current statistics available. We have striven to make our coverage as concise and readable as possible while still doing justice to the vast scope and significance of current theoretical and research work.

Cultural and Historical Influences

In this edition we have expanded our coverage of *cultural* and *historical* influences on development. Reviewers have praised our emphasis on culture as a particular strength of this book. Cross-cultural research is fully integrated throughout the text as well as highlighted in Window on the World boxes, reflecting the diversity of the population in the United States and in other societies. For example, in Chapter 1 we have expanded coverage of ethnic gloss. In Chapter 6 we discuss racial/ethnic minorities' special needs with regard to child care. In Chapter 9 we examine Sternberg's suggestion that culture and intelligence are inextricably linked. In Chapter 18 we have expanded the Window on the World box that discusses aging in Asia. We also include new or enhanced discussions of such topics as acculturation and how culture affects various aspects of development, from memory to the self-concept and from marriage and cohabitation to life expectancy. Our photo illustrations, too, show an ever greater commitment to depicting cultural diversity.

Our strengthened attention to historical influences begins with Chapter 1, which introduces the concept of historical generations, expands our treatment of the history of the study of human development, and updates Elder's work on studying the life course. Discussions in other parts of the book place in a historical context such topics as childbirth customs, infant feeding, the comprehensive high school, and treatment of the dead and dying. Many of our chapter opening Focus vignettes provide historical background as they profile the lives of such figures as Marian Anderson, Margaret Mead, and Charles Darwin's son "Doddy."

As always, we seek to emphasize the continuity of development, highlight interrelationships among the physical, cognitive, and psychosocial domains, and integrate theoretical, research-related, and practical concerns.

The Tenth Edition at a Glance

Following is a brief overview of our tenth edition, including its organization, pedagogical features, and most important content changes.

Organization

This book takes a *chronological* approach, describing all aspects of development at each period of the life span. With this approach students gain a sense of the multifaceted sweep of human development. The 19 chapters fall into nine parts:

- Part 1 summarizes the history, basic concepts, theories, and research tools of the field of human development.

- Part 2 describes the beginnings of life, including the influences of heredity and environment, prenatal development, birth, and physical, cognitive, and psychosocial development during the first three years.

- Parts 3 through 8 are divided into two chapters each, one covering physical and cognitive development and the other covering psychosocial development during infancy and toddlerhood, early childhood, middle childhood, adolescence, young adulthood, middle adulthood, and late adulthood.

- Part 9 deals with the end of life: death and bereavement.

In this edition, as in each of the previous ones, we have carefully assessed and improved the organization of material within and among chapters. For example, in Chapter 5 we have reorganized material on infant cognition to show more clearly the connections between research arising from the Piagetian and information-processing perspectives. Because we believe that all parts of life are important, challenging, and full of opportunities for growth and change, we provide evenhanded treatment of all periods of the life span, taking care not to overemphasize some and slight others.

Pedagogical Features

We are gratified by the overwhelmingly favorable response to the pedagogy we have developed for *Human Development,* which includes the following features.

Our comprehensive *Learning System* is a unique, coordinated set of elements that work together to foster active learning.

- Guideposts for Study: This list of questions at the beginning of each chapter highlights the key concepts to learn. Each Guidepost appears again to introduce the related text section.

- Checkpoints: These questions placed in the margins throughout each chapter serve to help students assess how well they grasp the concepts in the preceding text sections.

- What's Your View? These critical thinking questions, placed in the margins throughout each chapter and in the boxed features, encourage students to examine their own thoughts about the information presented in the text.

- Summary and Key Terms: Concluding each chapter, these resources, organized under each Guidepost, guide students as they review the chapter and check their learning.

Focus vignettes introduce each chapter by highlighting a famous or remarkable person in the stage of development covered by the chapter. Refocus questions at the end of each chapter refer back to the opening Focus vignettes, encouraging students to apply the chapter's concepts to the life of the person profiled.

Each part of the book begins with a distinctive, illustrated two-page spread containing:

- a Part Preview table outlining highlights of each chapter,

- a Part Overview introducing important themes, and, for Parts 2 through 9,

- a list of Linkups to Look for, examples of interaction among the physical, cognitive, and psychosocial domains of development.

Three types of boxes enhance our text by highlighting topics related to the main text. Each chapter contains two of the three types of boxed material, with a total of 38 boxes for the 19 chapters. Each box also contains a "Check It Out" section referring the student to relevant Internet links where further information can be found.

- "Digging Deeper" boxes provide an in-depth examination of research topics briefly mentioned in the text. In our tenth edition you will find new Digging Deeper boxes on "Homelessness" (Chapter 7), "Is Marriage a Dying Institution?" (Chapter 14), and "Centenarians" (Chapter 17).

- "Practically Speaking" boxes deal with a variety of practical applications of research. Our tenth edition offers new Practically Speaking boxes on "Shaken Baby Syndrome" (Chapter 4), "Talking to Children about Terrorism and War" (Chapter 10), and "Should Adolescents Be Exempt from the Death Penalty?" (Chapter 11).

- "Window on the World" boxes explore the way an issue in the chapter is treated or experienced in one or more foreign cultures, or in a United States minority group. New or expanded Window on the World boxes include "Are Struggles with Toddlers Necessary?" (Chapter 6) and "Aging in Asia" (Chapter 18).

For a detailed preview of the book's pedagogical features, see the Visual Walk-Through following this preface.

The following features are new to our tenth edition.

- A Landmark Table in the endpapers helps students "find" the whole human being at each period of development, as well as to trace various domains of development across the life span.

- Marginal links point to relevant segments of our Lifemap CD, a learning tool that is packaged with each copy of the book. The LifeMap CD includes video interviews with child development experts as well as video of children and teens discussing issues and engaged in behaviors covered in the text. It also offers interactive quizzes.

Content Changes

Among the important topics given new or greatly revised, expanded, or updated coverage, chapter by chapter, are the following:

Chapter 1

- New discussions of ethnic gloss and historical generations

- Elaboration of the concept of social construction, especially as applied to adolescence

- Updated and expanded discussions of influences of SES, culture, and race/ethnicity on development

Chapter 2

- Revised discussion of qualitative versus quantitative research methods

Chapter 3

- New section on prenatal impact of maternal stress

- New table of prenatal assessment techniques

- Revised discussions of determination of sex, influences on obesity, and autistic spectrum disorders

- Updated information on multiple births; Down syndrome; hazards of the prenatal environment, including paternal and external influences; and prenatal care. Updated box on fetal welfare and mothers' rights

Chapter 4

- New Practically Speaking box: "Shaken Baby Syndrome"

- New discussions of stillbirth, kangaroo care, and state regulation in infancy

- Expanded cross-cultural and historical information on childbirth customs

- Updated information on cesarean deliveries, use of anesthesia during labor, outcomes for low-birth-weight babies, trends in infant mortality, prevalence and causes of sudden infant death syndrome (SIDS), accidental deaths, infant nutrition, and vaccine safety

Chapter 5

- New section on estimation of scale

- New Practically Speaking box: "Do Infants and Toddlers Watch Too Much Television?"

- Updated discussions of the Bayley Scales (Bayley-III), symbolic development, elicited imitation, language development, and the relationship between SES and IQ

Chapter 6

- New Window on the World box: "Are Struggles with Toddlers Necessary?"

- New material on racial/ethnic minorities' use of child care

- Updated reports of National Institute of Child Health and Development (NICHD) studies of effects of early child care

Chapter 7

- New Digging Deeper box: "Homelessness"

- New material on effects of air pollution on health

- Revised discussions of SES, ethnicity, poverty, and health; theory of mind research; factors influencing memory; delayed language development; and compensatory preschool programs

- Updated discussions of overweight and nutrition and of sleep patterns and problems

Chapter 8

- New material on cultural differences in self-concept

- Revised discussions of gender development, play, corporal punishment, and psychological aggression

Chapter 9

- New material on estimating ability and on educational innovations such as charter schools, home schooling, and the No Child Left Behind Act

- Revised material on sports participation, the Kaufman Assessment Battery for Children (K-ABC-II), and entering first grade

- Updated information on obesity, hypertension, asthma, HIV-AIDS; Robert Sternberg's contributions; mental retardation, learning disabilities, and attention deficit-hyperactivity disorder (ADHD)

Chapter 10

- New Practically Speaking Box: "Talking to Children about Terrorism and War"

- Revised discussions of emotional regulation, impact of poverty on parenting, diverse family structures, impact of the peer group, and childhood aggression

- Updated information on use of drug therapy to treat emotional disorders

Chapter 11

- New Practically Speaking box: "Should Teens Be Exempt from the Death Penalty?"

- Updated information on physical activity, sleep patterns and needs, overweight and eating disorders, trends in drug use and abuse, treatment of depression, adolescent suicide, gender and academic achievement, and dropping out of high school

- Material on working part time moved from box to text

Chapter 12

- New discussions of adolescent cliques and crowds and romantic relationships

- Updated information on sexual orientation, sexual attitudes and behaviors, sexual risk taking, sexually transmitted diseases (STDs), teenage pregnancy and child rearing, and juvenile delinquency

Chapter 13

- New sections on emerging adulthood and reflective thinking

- Updated information on health statistics, genetic and lifestyle influences on health, higher education, and work

Chapter 14

- New Digging Deeper box: "Is Marriage a Dying Institution?"

- New discussion on changing paths to adulthood

- Updated information on Sternberg's Duplex Theory of Love, sexuality, marital and nonmarital lifestyles, parenthood, dual-earner marriages, divorce, remarriage, and stepparenthood

Chapter 15

- Updated information on the meaning and timing of middle age; menopause and hormone replacement therapy (HRT); male sexuality; health trends and influences on health; Schaie's Seattle Longitudinal Study; and work and early retirement

Chapter 16

- New discussions of emotionality and social well-being

- Updated information on the midlife transition; life satisfaction and well-being; importance of social relationships; marriage, cohabitation, and divorce at midlife; relationships with adolescent and adult children, including the revolving door syndrome; and relationships with aging parents, including caregiving issues

Chapter 17

- New Digging Deeper box: "Centenarians"

- New material on the relationship between cognitive abilities, health, and mortality and on speech and aging

- Revised material on anti-aging treatments; brain changes; sensory and psychomotor functioning; lifestyle influences on health and longevity; and depression and dementia, including Alzheimer's disease

- Updated information on the graying of the population; factors in life expectancy; why people age; life extension research; health status and disabilities; Seattle Longitudinal Study; processing abilities, neurological change, and memory

Chapter 18

- New section on emotionality and well-being

- Expanded Window on the World box: "Aging in Asia"

- Revised discussions of coping styles; religion/spirituality and well-being; successful aging; selective optimization with compensation model; retirement trends; volunteer activity; and importance of social support

- Updated information on finances and living arrangements

Chapter 19

- Revised discussions on patterns of grieving; children's understanding of death; coping with loss of a spouse; losing a child; and end-of-life issues, such as advanced directives, aid in dying, and cultural attitudes

- Updated information on suicide trends and organ donation

Supplementary Materials

Human Development, tenth edition, is accompanied by a complete learning and teaching package, keyed into the Learning System. Each component of this package has been thoroughly revised and expanded to include important new course material.

For the Student

LifeMap CD-ROM This helpful study tool is organized by chapter and keyed to the text by means of callouts in the book's margins. The CD features video segments available through McGraw-Hill's exclusive Discovery Channel™ licensing arrangement and from other sources, all chosen to illustrate key concepts in human development. Each video includes a pretest, posttest, and Web resources. LifeMap also includes chapter quizzes, a student research guide, and an interactive timeline that brings the phases of human development to life.

Student Study Guide Peggy Skinner, South Plains College

This comprehensive study guide (ISBN 0-07-322167-8) is organized by chapter and integrates the Guideposts for Study found in the main text. It is designed to help students make the most of their time when reviewing the material in the text and studying for exams. The study guide includes a variety of self-tests, including true/false, multiple-choice, and essay questions.

Online Learning Center for Students The official Web site for the text (*http://www.mhhe.com/papaliah10*) contains chapter outlines, practice quizzes, key term flashcards, Web links to relevant psychology sites, and more.

PowerWeb A PowerWeb access card is packaged FREE with each new copy of the text—be sure to save this as you'll need the password on it to access this unique online tool. Here you'll find current articles, *New York Times* news feeds, curriculum-based materials, weekly updates with assessment, informative and timely world news, refereed Web links, research tools, study tools, and interactive exercises. This is a great way to hone critical thinking skills and stay up to date on current events related to core concepts in the course.

For the Instructor

Instructor's Manual Tammy B. Lochridge, Itawamba Community College

Available on the instructor side of the Online Learning Center and on the Instructor's Resource CD-ROM, this manual provides many useful tools to enhance your teaching. Organized around the Guideposts for Study in the textbook, the Instructor's Manual offers Total Teaching Package outlines and detailed chapter outlines with key terms, suggested lecture openers, critical thinking exercises, essay questions, activities, ideas for independent study, video and multimedia resources, suggested readings, and Web resources for each chapter.

Test Bank   Diane L. Powers, Iowa Central Community College

McGraw-Hill's EZ Test is a flexible and easy-to-use electronic testing program. The program allows instructors to create tests from book-specific items. It accommodates a wide range of question types, and instructors may add their own questions. Multiple versions of the test can be created, and any test can be exported for use with course management systems such as WebCT, BlackBoard, or PageOut. EZ Test Online is a new service and gives you a place to easily administer your EZ Test–created exams and quizzes online. The program is available for Windows and Macintosh environments.

Consonant with the integrative nature of our supplements package, all Test Bank questions are keyed to the Guideposts for Study in the text and can be customized for instructor control and convenience.

The *Human Development* tenth-edition test bank offers more than 2,000 questions, including multiple-choice and essay questions. Question types include not only factual but also applied and conceptual.

PowerPoint Lectures   Cathleen Hunt, South Plains College

Available on the instructor side of the Online Learning Center and on the Instructor's Resource CD-ROM, these presentations cover the key points of each chapter and include charts and graphs from the text. They can be used as-is or modified to meet your needs.

Online Learning Center for Instructors   The password-protected instructor side of the Online Learning Center at *http://www.mhhe.com/papaliah10* contains the Instructor's Manual, PowerPoint presentations, Image Gallery, and other useful teaching resources. Ask your McGraw-Hill representative for your password.

- **PowerWeb.** This unique online reader provides readings, *New York Times* news feeds, weekly updates, curriculum-based materials, refereed Web links; tools for research, study, and assessment; and interactive exercises. This powerful tool will help keep your lectures up-to-date and timely.

Course Management Systems

- **WebCT and Blackboard.** Populated **WebCT** and **Blackboard** course cartridges are available for free upon adoption of a McGraw-Hill textbook. Contact your McGraw-Hill sales representative for details.

- **PageOut.** Build your own course Web site in less than an hour. You don't have to be a computer whiz to create a Web site, especially with an exclusive McGraw-Hill product called PageOut. Best of all, it's FREE! Visit us at www.pageout.net to find out more.

- **Knowledge Gateway.** McGraw-Hill service is second to none. We offer help at a special Web site called Knowledge Gateway. For more information, call 1-888-851-2372. For larger adoptions, if hands-on training is necessary, we have a team of experts ready to train you on campus. This FREE service is available to support PageOut, WebCT, and BlackBoard users.

Image Gallery These files include all of the figures, tables, and photos from this textbook (more than 150 images in all) for which McGraw-Hill holds copyright.

Classroom Performance System (CPS) by eInstruction This revolutionary system brings ultimate interactivity to the lecture hall or classroom. It is a wireless electronic response system that gives the instructor and students immediate feedback from the entire class. CPS is a superb way to give interactive quizzes, maximize student participation in class discussions, and take attendance. Book-specific questions for CPS use are found on the Instructor side of the Online Learning Center and on the Instructor's Resource CD-ROM.

Instructor's Resource CD-ROM This CD-ROM (ISBN 0-07-313381-7) conveniently contains the Instructor's Manual, PowerPoint slides, CPS content, and Test Bank and EZ Test system.

McGraw-Hill Media Resources for Teaching Psychology McGraw-Hill and The Discovery Channel™ have formed an exclusive partnership to bring you video segments and interactivities for use in your psychology course. The 48 video segments and 17 interactivities were chosen especially to support the introductory psychology course. The majority of the video segments are timed at 5 minutes or less; the longest at 12 minutes. They are available either as a DVD + CD-ROM set (ISBN 0-07-293885-4) or as a set of two VHS videocassettes + CD-ROM (ISBN 0-07-293884-6).

Multimedia Courseware for Child Development Charlotte J. Patterson, University of Virginia

This interactive CD-ROM (ISBN 0-07-254580-1) covers central phenomena and classic experiments in the field of child development. Included are hours of video footage of classic and contemporary experiments, detailed viewing guides, challenging follow-up and interactive feedback, graduated developmental charts, a variety of hands-on projects, and related Web sites and navigation aids.

Multimedia Courseware for Adult Development Carolyn Johnson, Pennsylvania State University

This interactive CD-ROM (ISBN 0-07-251761-1) showcases video clips central to phenomena in adult development. The CD-ROM includes hours of video footage of classic and contemporary experiments, detailed viewing guides, challenging follow-up and interactive feedback, graphics, graduated developmental charges, a variety of hands-on projects, and related Web sites and navigation aids.

Visual Asset Database (VAD) Jasna Jovanovic, University of Illinois—Urbana-Champaign

McGraw-Hill's password-protected Visual Asset Database offers hundreds of multimedia resources for use in classroom presentations, including original video clips, audio clips, photographs, and illustrations—all designed to bring to life concepts in developmental psychology. In addition to providing ready-made multimedia presentations for every stage of the lifespan, the VAD search engine and unique "My Modules" program allows instructors to select from the database's resources to create customized presentations, or "modules." Instructors can save these customized presentations in specially marked "module" folders on the McGraw-Hill site, and then run presentations directly from VAD to the Internet-equipped classroom. Contact your McGraw-Hill representative for a password to this valuable resource.

McGraw-Hill Contemporary Learning Series

Taking Sides: Clashing Views on Controversial Issues in Lifespan Development This reader presents current controversial issues in a debate-style format designed to stimulate student interest and develop critical thinking skills. Each issue is thoughtfully framed with an issue summary, an issue introduction, and a postscript. An instructor's manual with testing material is available for each volume. *Using Taking Sides in the Classroom* is also an excellent instructor resource with practical suggestions on incorporating this effective approach in the classroom. Each *Taking Sides* reader features an annotated listing of selected World Wide Web sites and is supported by a student Web site, *www.dushkin.com/online.*

Annual Editions: Human Development This annually updated reader is a collection of articles on topics related to the latest research and thinking in human development. These editions are updated regularly and contain useful features, including a topic guide, an annotated table of contents, unit overviews, and a topical index. An instructor's guide, containing testing materials, is also available.

Notable Sources in Human Development This book is a collection of articles, book excerpts, and research studies that have shaped the study of human development and our contemporary understanding of it. The selections are organized topically around major areas of study within human development. Each selection is preceded by a headnote that establishes the relevance of the article or study and provides biographical information on the author.

Film Clips from Films for the Humanities and Social Sciences Based on adoption size, you may qualify for FREE videos from this resource. View their more than 700 psychology-related videos at *http://www.films.com.*

As a full-service publisher of quality educational products, McGraw-Hill does much more than just sell textbooks to your students. We create and publish an extensive array of print, video, and digital supplements to support instruction on your campus. Orders of new (versus used) textbooks help us to defray the cost of developing such supplements, which is substantial. We have a broad range of other supplements in psychology that you may wish to tap for your introductory psychology course. Ask your local McGraw-Hill representative about the availability of these and other supplements that may help you with your course design.

Acknowledgments

We, the authors, would like to express our gratitude to the many friends and colleagues who, through their work and their interest, helped us clarify our thinking about human development. We are especially grateful for the valuable help given by those who reviewed the ninth edition of *Human Development* and the manuscript drafts of this tenth edition, whose evaluations and suggestions helped greatly in the preparation of this new edition. These reviewers, who are affiliated with both two- and four-year institutions, are as follows:

Mike Arpin,
Coffeyville Community College

Renée L. Babcock,
Central Michigan University

Alan Bates,
Snead State Community College

Dan Bellack,
Trident Technical College

Deneen Brackett,
Prairie State College

Amy Carrigan,
University of St. Francis

Perle Slavik Cowen,
College of Nursing, University of Iowa

Nicole Gendler,
University of New Mexico

Arthur Gonchar,
University of La Verne

Lori Harris,
Murray State University

Jutta Heckhausen,
University of California, Irvine

Henrietta Hestick,
Baltimore County Community College

Kelly Jarvis,
University of California, Irvine

Jyotsna Kalavar,
Pennsylvania State University– New Kensington

Deborah Laible,
Southern Methodist University

Sonya Leathers,
University of Illinois at Chicago

Tammy B. Lochridge,
Itawamba Community College

Karla Miley,
Black Hawk College

Kaelin Olsen,
Utah State University

Randall Osborne,
Texas State University– San Marcos

Lori K. Perez,
California State Univeristy–Fresno

Diane Powers,
Iowa Central Community College, Catonsville

Jennifer Redlin,
Minnesota State Community and Technical College

Stephanie J. Rowley,
University of Michigan

Pamela Schuetze,
Buffalo State College

Peter Segal,
York College of the City University of New York

Jack Shilkret,
Anne Arundel Community College

Peggy Skinner,
South Plains College

J. Blake Snider,
East Tennessee State University

Mary-Ellen Sollinger,
Delaware Technical and Community College

Monique L. Ward,
University of Michigan

Kristin Webb,
Alamance Community College

Colin William,
Columbus State Community College

Lois Willoughby,
Miami-Dade College–Kendall

We appreciate the strong support we have had from our publisher through the years. We would like to express special thanks to Mike Sugarman, executive editor; Elsa Peterson, senior developmental editor; Laura Edwards, freelance development editor; Rick Hecker, project manager; Sheralee Connors, who coordinated the supplements package; our research assistant, Bill Cabin; and our bibliographic assistant, Patricia Klitzke. Toni Michaels used her sensitivity, her interest, and her good eye to find outstanding photographs. Srdj Savanovic produced a strikingly attractive book design.

As always, we welcome and appreciate comments from readers, which help us continue to improve *Human Development*.

Diane E. Papalia
Sally Wendkos Olds
Ruth Duskin Feldman

Visual Walk-Through

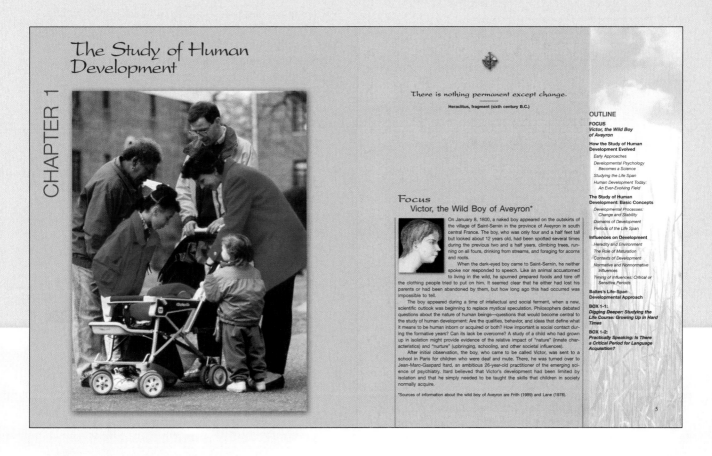

A special goal for this edition, like the previous one, has been to increase its pedagogical value. The single-column format has made it possible to introduce a comprehensive, unified Learning System, which will help students focus their reading and review and retain what they learn.

As always, we seek to make the study of human development come alive by telling illustrative stories about actual incidents in the lives of real people. In this edition, each chapter opens with a fascinating biographical vignette from a period in the life of a well-known person (such as Isabel Allende, Anne Frank, Jackie Robinson, Ingrid Bergman, John Glenn, and Mahatma Gandhi) or a classic case (such as the Wild Boy of Aveyron and Charles Darwin's diary of his son's first year). The subjects of these vignettes are people of diverse national and ethnic origins, whose experiences dramatize important themes in the chapter. We believe students will enjoy and identify with these stories, which lead directly into the body of each chapter, are woven into its fabric, and are revisited in the Refocus feature at the end of the chapter. These vignettes, along with the shorter true anecdotes that appear throughout the book—some of them about the authors' own children and grandchildren—underline the fact that there is no "average" or "typical" human being, that each person is an individual with a unique personality and a unique set of life circumstances. They are reminders that whenever we talk about human development, we talk about real people in a real world.

Learning System

The Learning System forms the conceptual framework of each chapter and is carried through all text supplements. It has the following four parts.

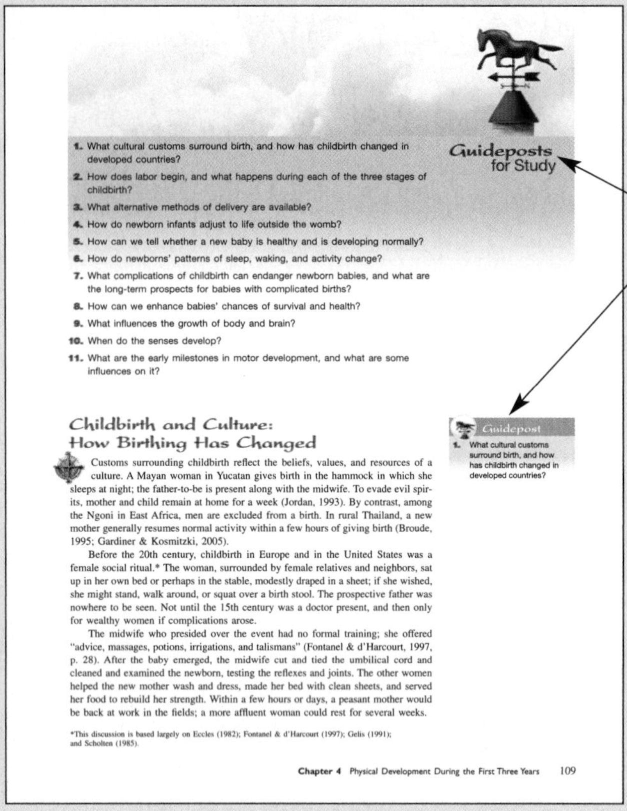

Guideposts for Study

These topical questions, similar to Learning Objectives, are first posted near the beginning of each chapter to capture students' interest and motivate them to look for answers as they read. The questions are broad enough to form a coherent outline of each chapter's content, but specific enough to invite careful study. Each Guidepost is repeated in the margin at the beginning of the section that deals with the topic in question and is repeated in the Chapter Summary to facilitate study.

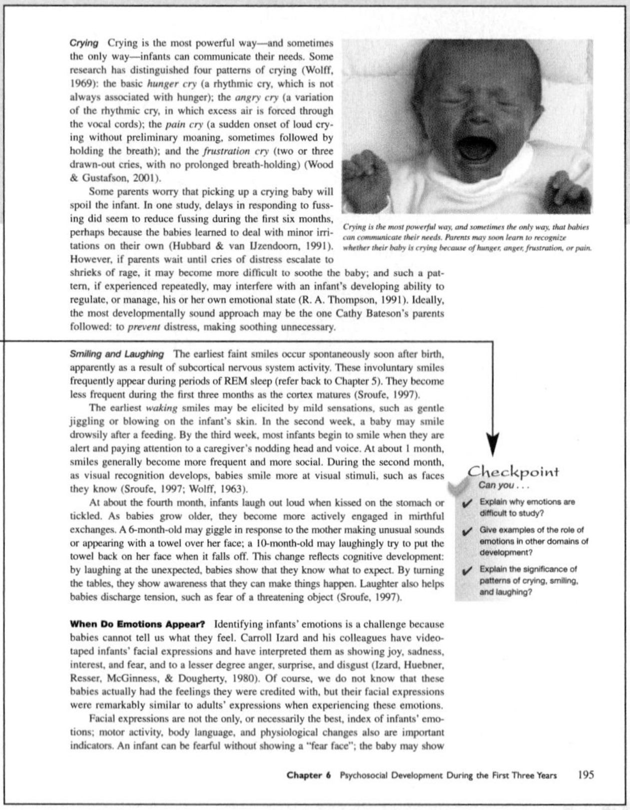

[Textbook page excerpt, top left]

Guideposts for Study

1. What cultural customs surround birth, and how has childbirth changed in developed countries?
2. How does labor begin, and what happens during each of the three stages of childbirth?
3. What alternative methods of delivery are available?
4. How do newborn infants adjust to life outside the womb?
5. How can we tell whether a new baby is healthy and is developing normally?
6. How do newborns' patterns of sleep, waking, and activity change?
7. What complications of childbirth can endanger newborn babies, and what are the long-term prospects for babies with complicated births?
8. How can we enhance babies' chances of survival and health?
9. What influences the growth of body and brain?
10. When do the senses develop?
11. What are the early milestones in motor development, and what are some influences on it?

Childbirth and Culture: How Birthing Has Changed

Customs surrounding childbirth reflect the beliefs, values, and resources of a culture. A Mayan woman in Yucatan gives birth in the hammock in which she sleeps at night; the father-to-be is present along with the midwife. To evade evil spirits, mother and child remain at home for a week (Jordan, 1993). By contrast, among the Ngoni in East Africa, men are excluded from a birth. In rural Thailand, a new mother generally resumes normal activity within a few hours of giving birth (Broude, 1995; Gardiner & Kosmitzki, 2005).

Before the 20th century, childbirth in Europe and in the United States was a female social ritual.* The woman, surrounded by female relatives and neighbors, sat up in her own bed or perhaps in the stable, modestly draped in a sheet; if she wished, she might stand, walk around, or squat over a birth stool. The prospective father was nowhere to be seen. Not until the 15th century was a doctor present, and then only for wealthy women if complications arose.

The midwife who presided over the event had no formal training; she offered "advice, massages, potions, irrigations, and talismans" (Fontanel & d'Harcourt, 1997, p. 28). After the baby emerged, the midwife cut and tied the umbilical cord and cleaned and examined the newborn, testing the reflexes and joints. The other women helped the new mother wash and dress, made her bed with clean sheets, and served her food to rebuild her strength. Within a few hours or days, a peasant mother would be back at work in the fields; a more affluent woman could rest for several weeks.

*This discussion is based largely on Eccles (1982); Fontanel & d'Harcourt (1997); Gelis (1991); and Scholten (1985).

Chapter 4 Physical Development During the First Three Years 109

Checkpoints

These more detailed marginal questions, placed at or near the end of major sections of text, enable students to test their understanding of what they have read. Students should be encouraged to stop and review any section for which they cannot answer one or more Checkpoints.

[Textbook page excerpt, lower right]

Crying is the most powerful way, and sometimes the only way, that babies can communicate their needs. Parents may soon learn to recognize whether their baby is crying because of hunger, anger, frustration, or pain.

Crying Crying is the most powerful way—and sometimes the only way—infants can communicate their needs. Some research has distinguished four patterns of crying (Wolff, 1969): the basic *hunger cry* (a rhythmic cry, which is not always associated with hunger); the *angry cry* (a variation of the rhythmic cry, in which excess air is forced through the vocal cords); the *pain cry* (a sudden onset of loud crying without preliminary moaning, sometimes followed by holding the breath); and the *frustration cry* (two or three drawn-out cries, with no prolonged breath-holding) (Wood & Gustafson, 2001).

Some parents worry that picking up a crying baby will spoil the infant. In one study, delays in responding to fussing did seem to reduce fussing during the first six months, perhaps because the babies learned to deal with minor irritations on their own (Hubbard & van IJzendoorn, 1991). However, if parents wait until cries of distress escalate to shrieks of rage, it may become more difficult to soothe the baby; and such a pattern, if experienced repeatedly, may interfere with an infant's developing ability to regulate, or manage, his or her own emotional state (R. A. Thompson, 1991). Ideally, the most developmentally sound approach may be the one Cathy Bateson's parents followed: to *prevent* distress, making soothing unnecessary.

Smiling and Laughing The earliest faint smiles occur spontaneously soon after birth, apparently as a result of subcortical nervous system activity. These involuntary smiles frequently appear during periods of REM sleep (refer back to Chapter 5). They become less frequent during the first three months as the cortex matures (Sroufe, 1997).

The earliest *waking* smiles may be elicited by mild sensations, such as gentle jiggling or blowing on the infant's skin. In the second week, a baby may smile drowsily after a feeding. By the third week, most infants begin to smile when they are alert and paying attention to a caregiver's nodding head and voice. At about 1 month, smiles generally become more frequent and more social. During the second month, as visual recognition develops, babies smile more at visual stimuli, such as faces they know (Sroufe, 1997; Wolff, 1963).

At about the fourth month, infants laugh out loud when kissed on the stomach or tickled. As babies grow older, they become more actively engaged in mirthful exchanges. A 6-month-old may giggle in response to the mother making unusual sounds or appearing with a towel over her face; a 10-month-old may laughingly try to put the towel back on her face when it falls off. This change reflects cognitive development: by laughing at the unexpected, babies show that they know what to expect. By turning the tables, they show awareness that they can make things happen. Laughter also helps babies discharge tension, such as fear of a threatening object (Sroufe, 1997).

When Do Emotions Appear? Identifying infants' emotions is a challenge because babies cannot tell us what they feel. Carroll Izard and his colleagues have videotaped infants' facial expressions and have interpreted them as showing joy, sadness, interest, and fear, and to a lesser degree anger, surprise, and disgust (Izard, Huebner, Resser, McGinness, & Dougherty, 1980). Of course, we do not know that these babies actually had the feelings they were credited with, but their facial expressions were remarkably similar to adults' expressions when experiencing these emotions.

Facial expressions are not the only, or necessarily the best, index of infants' emotions; motor activity, body language, and physiological changes also are important indicators. An infant can be fearful without showing a "fear face"; the baby may show

Checkpoint
Can you...

✔ Explain why emotions are difficult to study?

✔ Give examples of the role of emotions in other domains of development?

✔ Explain the significance of patterns of crying, smiling, and laughing?

Chapter 6 Psychosocial Development During the First Three Years 195

What's Your View?

These periodic marginal questions challenge students to interpret, apply, or critically evaluate information presented in the text.

One area in which the NICHD study did find independent effects of child care was in interactions with peers. Between ages 2 and 3, children whose caregivers were sensitive and responsive tended to become more positive and competent in play with other children (NICHD Early Child Care Research Network, 2001a).

To sum up, the NICHD findings so far give high-quality child care good marks overall, especially for its impact on cognitive development and interaction with peers. Some observers say that the areas of concern the study pinpointed—stress levels in infants and toddlers and possible behavior problems related to amounts of care—might be counteracted by activities that enhance children's attachment to caregivers and peers, emphasize child-initiated learning and internalized motivation, and focus on group social development (Maccoby & Lewis, 2003).

Impact on Disadvantaged Children and Minorities Children from low-income families or stressful homes especially benefit from care that supplies cognitive stimulation and emotional support, which may otherwise be lacking in their lives (Scarr, 1997b; Spieker, Nelson, Petras, Jolley, & Barnard, 2003). In a five-year longitudinal study of 451 poor, urban families in California and Florida with single mothers who were moving from welfare to work, children demonstrated stronger cognitive growth in center care than in home-based care (Loeb, Fuller, Kagan, & Carrol, 2004).

As we have mentioned, the NICHD study found that the more time a young child spends in nonmaternal care, the greater the risk of problem behavior (NICHD Early Childhood Research Network, 2003). But data from a study of 2,400 randomly selected low-income children in Boston, Chicago, and San Antonio suggest that extensive child care does *not* harm *poor* children's development unless it is of low quality (Votruba-Drzal, Coley, & Chase-Lansdale, 2004). Unfortunately, children from low-income families tend to be placed in lower-cost and lower-quality care than children from more affluent families (Marshall, 2004). The vast majority of children eligible for federal child care subsidies do not receive them (USDHHS, 2000b).

Studies of ethnically and socioeconomically mixed samples and of low-income children may fail to reveal specific factors in minority experience with child care (Johnson et al., 2003). Many minority families live in extended-family households and historically relied on family and friends for child care. Today, although African American and Latina women increasingly choose center care, they are more likely to use family-based care (in the caregiver's home) or to rely on grandmothers. Minority women are more likely to work night shifts or long hours, to hold seasonal, nonoffice jobs, and to be laid off periodically. Thus, child care settings designed for regular daytime employment may not meet their needs.

What's Your View?

- In the light of findings about effects of early child care, what advice would you give a new mother about the timing of her return to work and the selection of child care?

Checkpoint

Can you . . .

✓ Evaluate the impact of a mother's employment on her baby's well-being?

✓ List at least five criteria for good child care?

✓ Compare the impact of child care and of family characteristics on emotional, social, and cognitive development?

✓ Point out special considerations regarding child care for low-income and minority children?

Guidepost

10. What are the causes and consequences of child abuse and neglect, and what can be done about it?

Maltreatment: Abuse and Neglect

Although most parents are loving and nurturing, some cannot or will not take proper care of their children, and some deliberately hurt or kill them. *Maltreatment* is deliberate or avoidable endangerment of a child, either by *abuse*, action that inflicts harm, or *neglect*, inaction that causes harm (U.S. Department of Health and Human Services [USDHHS], 1999a).

Maltreatment takes several specific forms, and any one form is likely to be accompanied by one or more of the others (Belsky, 1993). **Physical abuse**

The normal developmental changes in the early years of life are obvious and dramatic signs of growth. The infant lying in the crib becomes an active, exploring toddler. The young child enters and embraces the worlds of school and society. The adolescent, with a new body and new awareness, prepares to step into adulthood.

Growth and development do not screech to a stop after adolescence. People change in many ways throughout early, middle, and late adulthood, as we will see in the remaining chapters of this book.

SUMMARY AND KEY TERMS

The Search for Identity

Guidepost 1: How do adolescents form an identity?

- A central concern during adolescence is the search for identity, which has occupational, sexual, and values components. Erik Erikson described the psychosocial conflict of adolescence as *identity versus identity confusion*. The "virtue" that should arise from this conflict is *fidelity*.
- James Marcia, in research based on Erikson's theory, described four identity statuses: identity achievement, foreclosure, moratorium, and identity diffusion.
- Researchers differ on whether girls and boys take different paths to identity formation. Although some research suggests that girls' self-esteem tends to fall in adolescence, later research does not support that finding.
- Ethnicity is an important part of identity. Minority adolescents seem to go through stages of ethnic identity development much like Marcia's identity statuses.

identity *(437)*
identity versus identity confusion *(437)*
identity statuses *(439)*
identity achievement *(439)*
foreclosure *(439)*
moratorium *(439)*
identity diffusion *(439)*
crisis *(439)*
commitment *(439)*

Sexuality

Guidepost 2: What determines sexual orientation, and how do people become aware of their sexual identity?

- Sexual orientation appears to be influenced by an interaction of biological and environmental factors and to be at least partly genetic.
- The course of homosexual identity and relationship development may vary with cohort, gender, and ethnicity.

sexual orientation *(443)*

Guidepost 3: What sexual practices are common among adolescents, and what leads some teenagers to engage in risky sexual behavior?

- Teenage sexual activity is more prevalent than in the past but involves risks of pregnancy and sexually transmitted disease. Adolescents at greatest risk are those who begin sexual activity early, have multiple partners, do not use contraceptives, and are ill-informed about sex.
- Regular condom use is the best safeguard for sexually active teens.
- Comprehensive sex education programs delay sexual initiation and encourage contraceptive use. Abstinence-only programs have not been as effective.

Guidepost 4: How common are sexually transmitted diseases and teenage pregnancy, and what are their usual outcomes?

- Rates of sexually transmitted diseases (STDs) in the United States are among the highest in the industrialized world. STDs can be transmitted by oral sex as well as intercourse. They are more likely to develop undetected in girls than in boys.
- Teenage pregnancy and birthrates in the United States have declined. Most of the births are to unmarried mothers.
- Teenage childbearing often has negative outcomes. Teenage mothers and their families tend to suffer ill health and financial hardship, and the children often suffer from ineffective parenting.

sexually transmitted diseases (STDs) *(448)*

Relationships with Family, Peers, and Adult Society

Guidepost 5: How typical is "adolescent rebellion"?

- Although relationships between adolescents and their parents are not always smooth, full-scale adolescent rebellion is unusual. For the majority of teens, adolescence is a fairly smooth transition. For the minority who seem more deeply troubled, it can predict a troubled adulthood.

adolescent rebellion *(453)*

Summary and Key Terms

As in previous editions, the Chapter Summaries are organized by the major topics in the chapter. The Guidepost questions appear under the appropriate major topics. Each Guidepost is followed by a series of brief statements restating the most important points that fall under it, thus creating a self-testing question-answer format. Students should be encouraged to try to answer each Guidepost question before reading the summary material that follows. Key Terms are listed under each Guidepost summary with the pages on which their definitions can be found.

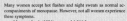

Window on the World

Japanese Women's Experience of Menopause

BOX 15-1

Many women accept hot flashes and night sweats as normal accompaniments of menopause. However, not all women experience these symptoms.

Margaret Lock (1994) surveyed 1,316 Japanese women ages 45 to 55 and compared the results with data on 9,376 women in Massachusetts and Manitoba, Canada. Japanese women's experience of menopause turned out to be quite different from the experience of western women.

Fewer than 10 percent of Japanese women whose menstruation was becoming irregular reported having had hot flashes during the previous two weeks, compared with about 40 percent of the Canadian sample and 35 percent of the U.S. sample. In fact, fewer than 20 percent of Japanese women had *ever* experienced hot flashes, compared with 65 percent of Canadian women, and most of the Japanese women who had experienced hot flashes reported little or no physical or psychological discomfort. (Indeed, so little importance is given in Japan to what in western cultures is considered the chief symptom of menopause that there is no specific Japanese term for "hot flash," even though the Japanese language makes many subtle distinctions about body states.) Furthermore, only about 3 percent of the Japanese women said they experienced night sweats, and Japanese women were far less likely than western women to suffer from insomnia, depression, irritability, or lack of energy (Lock, 1994).

The Japanese women were more likely to report stiffness in the shoulders, headaches, lower back pain, constipation, and other complaints that, in western eyes, do not appear directly related to the hormonal changes of menopause (Lock, 1994). Japanese physicians link such symptoms with the decline of the female reproductive cycle, which they believe is associated with changes in the autonomic nervous system (Lock, 1998).

The symptoms physicians noted were quite similar to those the women reported. Hot flashes were not at the top of the doctors' lists and in some cases did not appear at all. However, very few Japanese women consult doctors about menopause or its

This middle-aged Japanese woman working in her garden seems the picture of health. Japanese women rarely experience hot flashes, discomfort, or other physical symptoms that some western women associate with menopause.

prostate cancer. However, its long-term risks and benefits have not been sufficiently studied; and results of research now under way will not be available for at least a decade (Asthana et al., 2004). Meanwhile, testosterone therapy is medically advisable only for men with clear hormonal deficiencies (Whitbourne, 2001).

Sexual Activity Frequency of sexual activity and satisfaction with sex life tend to diminish gradually during the forties and fifties. In the MIDUS study, 61 percent of married or cohabiting premenopausal women but only 41 percent of postmenopausal women reported having sex once a week or more. This decline was related, not to menopause per se, but to age and physical condition (Rossi, 2004). Possible physical causes include chronic disease, surgery, medications, and too much food or alcohol. Often, however, a decline in frequency has nonphysiological causes: monotony in a relationship, preoccupation with business or financial worries, mental or physical fatigue, depression, failure to make sex a high priority, fear of failure to attain an

What's Your View?

- How often, and in what ways, do you imagine your parents express their sexuality? When you are their age, do you expect to be more or less sexually active than they seem to be?

Other Special Features in This Edition

This edition includes three kinds of boxed material.

"Window on the World" Boxes

This boxed feature offers focused glimpses of human development in societies other than our own or in U.S. minority groups (in addition to the cultural coverage in the main body of the text). These boxes highlight the fact that people grow up, live, and thrive in many different kinds of cultures, under many different influences. Among the new, significantly updated, or expanded topics are struggles with toddlers and aging in Asia.

Digging Deeper

Development of Faith Across the Life Span

BOX 13-2

Can faith be studied from a developmental perspective? Yes, according to James Fowler (1981, 1989). Fowler defined faith as a way of seeing or knowing the world. To find out how people arrive at this knowledge, Fowler and his students at Harvard Divinity School interviewed more than 400 people of all ages with various ethnic, educational, and socioeconomic backgrounds and various religious or secular identifications and affiliations.

Fowler's theory focuses on the *form* of faith, not its content or object; it is not limited to any particular belief system. Faith can be religious or nonreligious: People may have faith in a god, in science, in humanity, or in a cause to which they attach ultimate worth and which gives meaning to their lives.

According to Fowler, faith develops—as do other aspects of cognition—through interaction between the maturing person and the environment. As in other stage theories, Fowler's stages of faith progress in an unvarying sequence, each building on those that went before. New experiences—crises, problems, or revelations—that challenge or upset a person's equilibrium may prompt a leap from one stage to the next. The ages at which these transitions occur are variable, and some people never leave a particular stage.

Fowler's stages correspond roughly to those described by Piaget, Kohlberg, and Erikson. The beginnings of faith, says Fowler, come at about 18 to 24 months of age, after children become self-aware, begin to use language and symbolic thought, and have developed what Erikson called *basic trust:* the sense that their needs will be met by powerful others.

- *Stage 1: Intuitive-projective faith* (ages 18–24 months to 7 years). As young children struggle to understand the forces that control their world, they form powerful, imaginative, often terrifying, and sometimes lasting images of God, heaven, and hell, drawn from the stories adults read to them. These images are often irrational, since preoper-

ational children tend to be confused about cause and effect and may have trouble distinguishing between reality and fantasy. Still egocentric, they have difficulty distinguishing God's point of view from their own or their parents'. They think of God mainly in terms of obedience and punishment.

- *Stage 2: Mythic-literal faith* (ages 7 to 12 years). Children are now more logical and begin to develop a more coherent view of the universe. Not yet capable of abstract thought, they tend to take religious stories and symbols literally, as they adopt their family's and community's beliefs and observances. They can now see God as having a perspective beyond their own, which takes into account people's effort and intent. They believe that God is fair and that people get what they deserve.

- *Stage 3: Synthetic-conventional faith* (adolescence or beyond). Adolescents, now capable of abstract thought, begin to form ideologies (belief systems) and commitments to ideals. As they search for identity, they seek a more personal relationship with God. However, their identity is not yet firm ground; they look to others (usually peers) for moral authority. Their faith is unquestioning and conforms to community standards. This stage is typical of followers of organized religion; about 50 percent of adults may never move beyond it.

- *Stage 4: Individuative-reflective faith* (early to middle twenties or beyond). Adults who reach this postconventional stage examine their faith critically and think out their own beliefs, independent of external authority and group norms. Because young adults are deeply concerned with intimacy, movement into this stage is often triggered by divorce, the death of a friend, or some other stressful event.

issues "from the standpoint of the universe as a whole" (Kohlberg & Ryncarz, 1990, pp. 191, 207). The achievement of such a perspective is so rare that Kohlberg himself had questions about calling it a stage of development. Kohlberg did note that it parallels the most mature stage of faith that the theologian James Fowler (1981) identified (see Box 13-2), in which "one experiences a oneness with the ultimate conditions of one's life and being" (Kohlberg & Ryncarz, 1990, p. 202).

Culture and Moral Reasoning

Kohlberg proposed that his stages of moral development are universal. To test that proposition, researchers have tested Kohlberg's moral dilemmas in several nonwestern cultures. In India, Buddhist monks scored lower than laypeople, apparently because Kohlberg's model was inadequate for rating postconventional Buddhist principles of cooperation and nonviolence (Gielen & Kelly, 1983).

Heinz's dilemma was revised for use in Taiwan. In the revision, a shopkeeper will not give a man *food* for his sick wife. This version would seem unbelievable to Chinese villagers, who are more accustomed to hearing a shopkeeper in such a

"Digging Deeper" Boxes

These boxes explore in depth important, cutting-edge, or controversial research-related issues mentioned more briefly in the text. Some of these include new or significantly expanded or updated discussions of homelessness, centenarians, and marriage as a possibly dying institution.

"Practically Speaking" Boxes

These boxes build bridges between academic study and everyday life by showing ways to apply research findings on various aspects of human development. Among the new, expanded, or substantially updated topics are shaken baby syndrome, whether infants and toddlers watch too much television, talking to children about terrorism and war, and whether teenagers should be exempt from the death penalty.

BOX 14-2

Practically Speaking
Partner Violence

Partner violence, or *domestic violence,* is the physical, sexual, or psychological maltreatment of a spouse, a former spouse, or an intimate partner. Nearly 9 out of 10 victims of partner violence in the United States are women, typically young, poor, uneducated and single, divorced, or separated. According to one estimate, about 1 woman in 5 has been physically assaulted by a partner or mate at some time in her life; about 40 percent of domestic assaults cause injury, and 10 percent are serious enough to require medical care. However, the true extent of domestic violence is hard to ascertain, in large part because the victims are often too ashamed or afraid to report what has happened. In one survey, only 8 percent of abused women had told a doctor about the abuse, and less than half had told anyone (Harvard Medical School, 2004).

Two distinct types of partner violence have been identified. One type is *situational couple violence*—physical confrontations

Most victims of domestic violence are women, and they are more likely to be seriously hurt. Men who abuse their partners often seek to control or dominate. Many were brought up in violent homes themselves.

that develop in the heat of an argument. This type of violence may be initiated by either partner and is unlikely to escalate in severity. The other, and more serious, type is *intimate terrorism*—a man's systematic use of emotional abuse, coercion, and, sometimes, threats and violence to gain or enforce power or control over a female partner. This type of partner abuse tends to become more frequent and severe as time goes on, but its most important distinguishing characteristic is its underlying control-seeking motivation (DeMaris, Benson, Fox, Hill, & Van Wyk, 2003; Leone, Johnson, Cohan, & Lloyd, 2004). Victims of intimate terrorism are more likely than those involved in situational couple violence to experience physical injuries, time lost from work, poor health, and psychological distress (Leone et al., 2004).

Intimate terrorism may be a way to assert masculine identity. Interviews and diaries of 22 men with a history of violence found that such men tend to have difficulty expressing feelings. If a relationship becomes tense or they feel psychologically threatened, they may lose control and take out their repressed feelings on their partners or wives. Some men rationalize their violent acts as having been provoked by their wives or partners (Umberson, Anderson, Williams, & Chen, 2003).

Couples are at greater risk for either type of partner violence if they have been together a relatively short time, are both in their first union, formed it at an early age, or have frequent or hostile disagreements. Anything that places strains on a relationship—for example, one or both partners being substance abusers or only one of the two being employed (especially if it is the woman)—can heighten the risk (DeMaris et al., 2003).

Emotional abuse may occur either with or without physical violence. A survey of 25,876 Canadian men and women found that about 12 percent of married or cohabiting couples experience partner violence or emotional abuse, or both. About 8 percent of the women who had *not* been physically victimized (as well as more than half of those who had) experienced tactics of emotional control, such as

time doing things together. Those conclusions come from two national surveys of married individuals, one in 1980 and the other in 2000. Marital happiness was positively affected by increased economic resources, equal decision making, nontraditional gender attitudes, and support for the norm of lifelong marriage but was negatively affected by premarital cohabitation, extramarital affairs, wives' job demands, and wives' longer working hours. Increases in husbands' share of housework appeared to lower marital satisfaction among husbands but improve it among wives (Amato, Johnson, Booth, & Rogers, 2003). In a study of 197 Israeli couples, a tendency toward emotional instability and negativity in either spouse was a strong predictor of marital unhappiness (Lavee & Ben-Ari, 2004).

Factors in Marital Success or Failure Can the outcome of a marriage be predicted before the couple tie the knot? In one study, researchers followed 100 mostly European American couples for 13 years, starting when they were not yet married. Such factors as premarital income and education levels, whether a couple cohabited before marriage or had premarital sex, and how long they had known each other or dated before marriage had no effect on marital success. What did matter were the

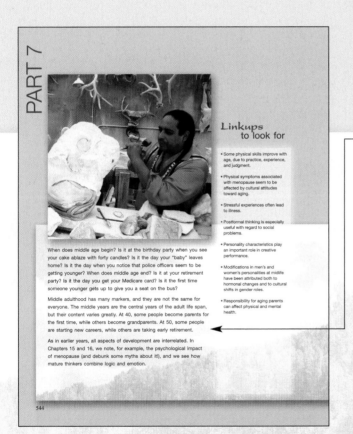

PART 7

When does middle age begin? Is it at the birthday party when you see your cake ablaze with forty candles? Is it the day your "baby" leaves home? Is it the day when you notice that police officers seem to be getting younger? When does middle age end? Is it at your retirement party? Is it the day you get your Medicare card? Is it the first time someone younger gets up to give you a seat on the bus?

Middle adulthood has many markers, and they are not the same for everyone. The middle years are the central years of the adult life span, but their content varies greatly. At 40, some people become parents for the first time, while others become grandparents. At 50, some people are starting new careers, while others are taking early retirement.

As in earlier years, all aspects of development are interrelated. In Chapters 15 and 16, we note, for example, the psychological impact of menopause (and debunk some myths about it), and we see how mature thinkers combine logic and emotion.

544

Linkups
to look for

- Some physical skills improve with age, due to practice, experience, and judgment.

- Physical symptoms associated with menopause seem to be affected by cultural attitudes toward aging.

- Stressful experiences often lead to illness.

- Postformal thinking is especially useful with regard to social problems.

- Personality characteristics play an important role in creative performance.

- Modifications in men's and women's personalities at midlife have been attributed both to hormonal changes and to cultural shifts in gender roles.

- Responsibility for aging parents can affect physical and mental health.

Part Overviews

At the beginning of each part, an overview introduces the period of life discussed in the chapters that follow.

Linkups to Look for

The part overviews include bulleted lists that point to examples of the interaction of physical, cognitive, and psychosocial aspects of development.

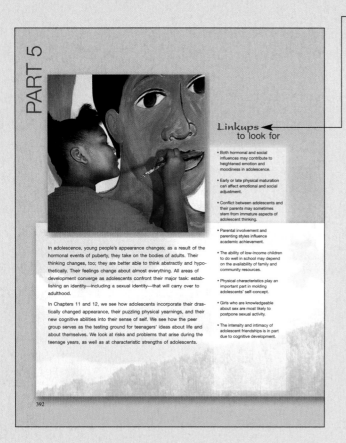

Part Preview Tables

These tables, visually keyed to each chapter of the text, preview the main features of each period of development. The contents of the part preview tables are coordinated with Table 1-1 in Chapter 1, which summarizes major developments of each period of the life span.

Chapter-Opening Outlines

At the beginning of each chapter, an outline previews the major topics included in the chapter.

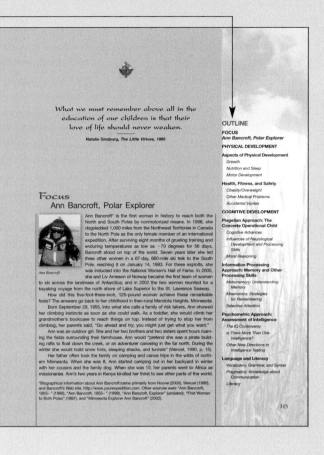

What we must remember above all in the education of our children is that their love of life should never weaken.

Natalia Ginzburg, *The Little Virtues*, 1985

Focus
Ann Bancroft, Polar Explorer

Ann Bancroft

Ann Bancroft* is the first woman in history to reach both the North and South Poles by nonmotorized means. In 1986, she dogsledded 1,000 miles from the Northwest Territories in Canada to the North Pole as the only female member of an international expedition. After surviving eight months of grueling training and enduring temperatures as low as −70 degrees for 56 days, Bancroft stood on top of the world. Seven years later she led three other women in a 67-day, 660-mile ski trek to the South Pole, reaching it on January 14, 1993. For these exploits, she was inducted into the National Women's Hall of Fame. In 2000, she and Liv Arneson of Norway became the first team of women to ski across the landmass of Antarctica; and in 2002 the two women reunited for a kayaking voyage from the north shore of Lake Superior to the St. Lawrence Seaway.

How did this five-foot-three-inch, 125-pound woman achieve these remarkable feats? The answers go back to her childhood in then-rural Mendota Heights, Minnesota. Born September 29, 1955, into what she calls a family of risk takers, Ann showed her climbing instincts as soon as she could walk. As a toddler, she would climb her grandmother's bookcase to reach things on top. Instead of trying to stop her from climbing, her parents said, "Go ahead and try; you might just get what you want."

Ann was an outdoor girl. She and her two brothers and two sisters spent hours roaming the fields surrounding their farmhouse. Ann would "pretend she was a pirate building rafts to float down the creek, or an adventurer canoeing in the far north. During the winter she would build snow forts, sleeping shacks, and tunnels" (Wenzel, 1990, p. 15).

Her father often took the family on camping and canoe trips in the wilds of northern Minnesota. When she was 8, Ann started camping out in her backyard in winter with her cousins and the family dog. When she was 10, her parents went to Africa as missionaries. Ann's two years in Kenya kindled her thirst to see other parts of the world.

*Biographical information about Ann Bancroft came primarily from Noone (2000), Wenzel (1990), and Bancroft's Web site, http://www.yourexpedition.com. Other sources were "Ann Bancroft, 1955– " (1998), "Ann Bancroft, 1955– " (1999), "Ann Bancroft, Explorer" (undated), "First Woman to Both Poles" (1997), and "Minnesota Explorer Ann Bancroft" (2002).

315

If . . . happiness is the absence of fever then I will never know happiness. For I am possessed by a fever for knowledge, experience, and creation.

Diary of Anaïs Nin (1931–1934), written when she was between 28 and 31

Focus
Arthur Ashe, Tennis Champion*

Arthur Ashe

The tennis champion Arthur Ashe (1943–1993) was one of the most respected athletes of all time. "Slim, bookish and bespectacled" (Finn, 1993, p. B1), he was known for his quiet, dignified manner on and off the court; he did not dispute calls, indulge in temper tantrums, or disparage opponents.

The first African American to win the Wimbledon tournament and the United States and Australian Opens, Ashe grew up in Richmond, Virginia, where he began playing on segregated public courts and was barred from a city tennis tournament because of his race. As a young adult, the only black star in a white-dominated game, Ashe was a target for bigotry; but he maintained his composure and channeled his aggressive impulses into the game.

Ashe used his natural physical gifts and stellar reputation to combat racism and increase opportunity for disadvantaged youth. He conducted tennis clinics and helped establish tennis programs for inner-city youngsters. Twice refused a visa to play in the South African Open, he was finally allowed to compete in 1973 and again in 1974 and 1975. Despite South Africa's rigid apartheid system of racial separation, he insisted on nonsegregated seating at his matches.

Ashe continued to work against apartheid, for the most part quietly, behind the scenes. Accused of being an "Uncle Tom" by angry militants who shouted him down while he was giving a speech, he politely rebuked them: "What do you expect to achieve when you give in to passion and invective and surrender the high moral ground that alone can bring you to victory?" (Ashe & Rampersad, 1993, pp. 117, 118). Several years later, he was arrested in a protest outside the South African embassy in Washington, D.C. He felt tremendous pride when he saw Nelson Mandela, the symbol of opposition to apartheid, released from prison in 1990, riding in a ticker-tape

*Sources of biographical information about Arthur Ashe were Ashe and Rampersad (1993), Finn (1993), and Witteman (1993).

471

Chapter-Opening "Focus" Vignettes

Biographical vignettes from the lives of remarkable people illustrate chapter themes.

Bergman began to see her husband—whom she had always leaned on for help and decisions—as overprotective, controlling, jealous, and critical. The couple spent long hours, days, and weeks apart—she at the studio or on tour, he at the hospital.

Meanwhile, Bergman was becoming dissatisfied with filming on studio lots. When she saw Rossellini's award-winning *Open City,* she was stunned by its power and realism and by Rossellini's artistic freedom and courage. She wrote to him, offering to come to Italy and work with him. The result was *Stromboli*—and the end of what she now saw as a constrictive, unfulfilling marriage. "It was not my intention to fall in love and go to Italy forever," she wrote to Lindstrom apologetically. "But how can I help it or change it?"

At 33, Bergman, who had been number one at the box office, became a Hollywood outcast. Her affair with Rossellini made headlines worldwide. So did the illegitimate birth of Robertino in 1950, Bergman's hurried Mexican divorce and proxy marriage there to Rossellini (who had had his own marriage annulled), the birth of twin daughters in 1952, and the struggle over visitation rights with Pia, who took her father's side and did not see her guilt-ridden mother for six years.

The tempestuous Bergman-Rossellini love match did not last. Every picture they made together failed, and finally, so did the marriage. But their mutual bond with their children, to whom Bergman gave Rossellini custody to avoid another bitter battle, made these ex-spouses a continuing part of each other's lives. In 1958, at the age of 43, Ingrid Bergman—her career, by this time, rehabilitated and peace made with her eldest daughter—began her third marriage, to Lars Schmidt, a Swedish-born theatrical producer. It lasted sixteen years, despite constant work-related separations, and ended in an amicable divorce. Schmidt and Bergman remained close friends for the rest of her life.

Ingrid Bergman's story is a dramatic reminder of the impact of cultural change on personal attitudes and behavior. The furor over her affair with Rossellini may seem strange today, when cohabitation, extramarital sex, divorce, and out-of-wedlock birth have become more common. Yet, now as then, personal choices made in young adulthood establish a framework for the rest of life. Bergman's marriages and divorces, the children she bore and loved, her passionate pursuit of her vocation, and her agonizing over the conflicting demands of work and family were akin to the life events and issues that confront many young women today.

Did Bergman change with maturity and experience? On the surface, she seemed to keep repeating the same cycle again and again. Yet, in her handling of her second and third divorces, she seemed calmer, more pragmatic, and more in command. Still, her basic approach to life remained the same: She did what she felt she must, come what may.

Does personality stop growing when the body does, or does it keep developing throughout life? How have paths to adulthood and intimate relationships changed in recent decades? In this chapter, we explore questions such as these. We examine the choices that frame personal and social life: adopting a sexual lifestyle; marrying, cohabiting, or remaining single; having children or not; and establishing and maintaining friendships.

After you have read and studied this chapter, you should be able to answer each of the Guidepost questions that follow. Look for them again in the margins, where they point to important concepts throughout the chapter. To check your understanding of these Guideposts, review the end-of-chapter summary. Checkpoints located at periodic spots throughout the chapter will help you verify your understanding of what you have read.

Chapter Overviews

Near the beginning of each chapter, a brief overview of topics to be covered leads the reader smoothly from the opening vignette into the body of the chapter.

Key Terms

Whenever an important new term is introduced in the text, it is highlighted in boldface and defined, both in the text and, sometimes more formally, in the end-of-book glossary. Key terms and their definitions appear in the margins near the place where they are introduced in the text, and all key terms are listed in the Chapter Summaries and **boldfaced** in the subject index.

Figure 3-5
Sex-linked inheritance.

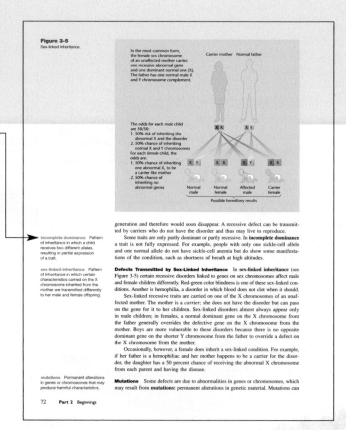

In the most common form, the female sex chromosome of an unaffected mother carries one recessive abnormal gene and one dominant normal one (X). The father has one normal male X and Y chromosome complement.

Carrier mother   Normal father

The odds for each *male* child are 50/50:
1. 50% risk of inheriting the abnormal X and the disorder
2. 50% chance of inheriting normal X and Y chromosomes

For each *female* child, the odds are:
1. 50% chance of inheriting one abnormal X, to be a carrier like mother
2. 50% chance of inheriting no abnormal genes

Normal male   Normal female   Affected male   Carrier female

Possible hereditary results

incomplete dominance Pattern of inheritance in which a child receives two different alleles, resulting in partial expression of a trait.

sex-linked-inheritance Pattern of inheritance in which certain characteristics carried on the X chromosome inherited from the mother are transmitted differently to her male and female offspring.

generation and therefore would soon disappear. A recessive defect can be transmitted by carriers who do not have the disorder and thus may fail to reproduce.

Some traits are only partly dominant or partly recessive. In **incomplete dominance** a trait is not fully expressed. For example, people with only one sickle-cell allele and one normal allele do not have sickle-cell anemia but do show some manifestations of the condition, such as shortness of breath at high altitudes.

Defects Transmitted by Sex-Linked Inheritance In sex-linked inheritance (see Figure 3-5) certain recessive disorders linked to genes on sex chromosomes affect male and female children differently. Red-green color blindness is one of these sex-linked conditions. Another is hemophilia, a disorder in which blood does not clot when it should.

Sex-linked recessive traits are carried on one of the X chromosomes of an unaffected mother. The mother is a *carrier;* she does not have the disorder but can pass on the gene for it to her children. Sex-linked disorders almost always appear only in male children; in females, a normal dominant gene on the X chromosome from the father generally overrides the defective gene on the X chromosome from the mother. Boys are more vulnerable to these disorders because there is no opposite dominant gene on the shorter Y chromosome from the father to override a defect on the X chromosome from the mother.

Occasionally, however, a female does inherit a sex-linked condition. For example, if her father is a hemophiliac and her mother happens to be a carrier for the disorder, the daughter has a 50 percent chance of receiving the abnormal X chromosome from each parent and having the disease.

mutations Permanent alterations in genes or chromosomes that may produce harmful characteristics.

Mutations Some defects are due to abnormalities in genes or chromosomes, which may result from **mutations:** permanent alterations in genetic material. Mutations can

72   **Part 2** Beginnings

Art Program

Many points in the text are underscored pictorially through carefully selected drawings, graphs, and photographs. The illustration program includes new figures and many full-color photographs.

Alexander, & Horne, 1995). Impairment seems to be selective, mainly affecting dull, monotonous tasks (Horne, 2000). However, high-level decision making can be impaired, especially in emergency situations that require innovation, flexibility, avoidance of distraction, realistic risk assessment, metamemory, and communication skills (Harrison & Horne, 2000a).

Compensatory changes in the brain can help maintain initial cognitive performance after short-term loss of sleep (Drummond et al., 2000). However, chronic sleep deprivation (less than six hours' sleep each night for three or more nights) can seriously worsen cognitive performance even when a person is not aware of it (Van Dongen, Maislin, Mullington, & Dinges, 2003).

Smoking Smoking has become less common in the United States since 1964, when the U.S. Surgeon General reported a link between cigarette smoking and lung cancer, but the decline has slowed since 1990. Smoking is still the leading preventable cause of death among U.S. adults, linked not only to lung cancer, but also to increased risks of heart disease, stroke, and chronic lung disease (NCHS, 2004). Smoking is also associated with cancer of the stomach, liver, larynx, mouth, esophagus, bladder, kidney, pancreas, and cervix; gastrointestinal problems, such as ulcers; respiratory illnesses, such as bronchitis and emphysema; and osteoporosis (Hopper & Seeman, 1994; International Agency for Cancer Research, 2002; National Institute on Aging [NIA], 1993; Slemenda, 1994; Trimble et al., 2005).

Secondhand, or passive, smoke exposes nonsmokers to the same carcinogens that active smokers inhale (International Agency for Cancer Research, 2002). Exposure to passive smoke—even for only 30 minutes—has been shown to cause circulatory dysfunction and increase the risk of cardiovascular disease (Otsuka et al., 2001). Passive smoke also may increase the risk of cervical cancer (Trimble et al., 2005).

Despite these risks, about 1 in 4 men and 1 in 5 women over 18 in the United States are current smokers (NCHS, 2004). Emerging adults ages 18 to 25 are more likely to smoke than any other age group (see Figure 13-1); nearly 45 percent report using tobacco products, mostly cigarettes (Substance Abuse and Mental Health Services Adminstration (SAMHSA), 2004b). American Indians are most likely and Asian Americans least likely to smoke (Lethbridge-Cejku et al., 2004; SAMHSA, 2004b).

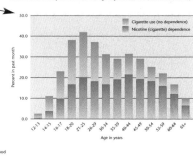

Because smoking is addictive, it is hard for some smokers to quit despite knowledge of the health risks. Smoking is especially harmful to African Americans, who metabolize more nicotine in their blood and are more subject to lung cancer than white Americans.

Figure 13-1
Current (past month) cigarette use and nicotine dependence by age: U.S., 2003. Cigarette use peaks in emerging adulthood, but the proportion of users who are nicotine-dependent generally increases with age. (Source: SAMHSA, 2004b, Figure 4.7.)

478   **Part 6**   Young Adulthood

---

to deal not only with a sense of guilt because the adult children they raised have failed their own children, but with the rancor they feel toward this adult child. For some caregiver couples, the strains produce tension in their own relationship. If one or both parents later resume their normal roles, it may be emotionally wrenching to return the child (Crowley, 1993; Larsen, 1990–1991).

Grandparents providing **kinship care** who do not become foster parents or gain custody have no legal status and no more rights than unpaid baby-sitters. They may face many practical problems, from enrolling the child in school and gaining access to academic records to obtaining medical insurance for the child. Grandchildren are usually not eligible for coverage under employer-provided health insurance even if the grandparent has custody. Like working parents, working grandparents need good, affordable child care and family-friendly workplace policies, such as time off to care for a sick child. The federal Family and Medical Leave Act of 1993 does cover grandparents who are raising grandchildren, but many do not realize it.

kinship care Care of children living without parents in the home of grandparents or other relatives, with or without a change of legal custody.

Checkpoint
Can you . . .
✔ Tell how parents' divorce and remarriage can affect grandparents' relationships with grandchildren?
✔ Discuss the challenges involved in raising grandchildren?

Refocus

Thinking back to the Focus vignette about Madeleine Albright at the beginning of this chapter:

- In what ways did Albright's life course in middle age reflect the points discussed in this chapter?

- How would each of the theories discussed in this chapter describe and explain the changes Albright went through in her middle years?

- Did Albright show the changes in gender identity described by either Jung or Gutmann or in the Mills Longitudinal Study?

- How do you think Albright would score herself on Ryff's six dimensions of well-being?

- What aspects of the discussions on changing relationships at midlife seem to apply to Albright?

Grandparents can be sources of guidance, companions in play, links to the past, and symbols of family continuity. They express generativity, a longing to transcend mortality by investing themselves in the lives of future generations. Men and women who do not become grandparents may fulfill generative needs by becoming foster grandparents or volunteering in schools or hospitals. By finding ways to develop what Erikson called the "virtue" of care, adults prepare themselves to enter the culminating period of adult development, which we discuss in Part 8.

SUMMARY AND KEY TERMS

Looking at the Life Course in Middle Age

Guidepost 1: How do developmental scientists approach the study of psychosocial development in middle adulthood?

- Developmental scientists view midlife psychosocial development both objectively, in terms of trajectories or pathways, and subjectively, in terms of people's sense of self and the way they actively construct their lives.
- Change and continuity must be seen in context and in terms of the whole life span.

Change at Midlife: Classic Theoretical Approaches

Guidepost 2: What do classic theorists have to say about psychosocial change in middle age?

- Although some theorists hold that personality is essentially formed by midlife, there is a growing consensus that midlife development shows change as well as stability. Change can be maturational (normative) or nonnormative.
- Humanistic theorists such as Maslow and Rogers saw middle age as an opportunity for positive change.

Chapter 16   Psychosocial Development in Middle Adulthood   619

Refocus

This series of interpretive questions encourages students to think back over major chapter themes and their application to the famous person described in the chapter-opening "Focus" vignette.

Part I of this book is a guide map to the field of human development. It traces routes that investigators have followed in the quest for information about what makes people develop as they do. It also points out the main directions students of development follow today and poses questions about the best way to reach the destination: knowledge.

In Chapter 1, we describe how the study of human development has evolved and introduce its goals and basic concepts. We look at the many influences that help make each person a unique individual.

In Chapter 2, we introduce some of the most prominent theories about human development—theories that will come up in more detail later in this book. We explain how developmental scientists study people, what research methods they use, and what ethical standards govern their work.

About Human Development

PREVIEW

CHAPTER 1

The Study of Human Development

CHAPTER 2

Theory and Research

Our understanding of human development has evolved from studies of children to studies of the full life span.

Developmental scientists study change and stability in the physical, cognitive, and psychosocial domains.

Development is subject to internal and external influences.

Important contextual influences on development are family, neighborhood, socioeconomic status, race/ethnicity, culture, and history.

The timing of certain influences on the developing person may be critical.

Theoretical perspectives on human development differ on two key issues: (1) whether people contribute actively to their own development, and (2) whether development occurs continuously or in stages.

Major theoretical perspectives are psychoanalytic, learning, cognitive, evolutionary/sociobiological, and contextual.

Research may be qualitative or quantitative and may include case studies, ethnographic studies, correlational studies, and experiments.

To study development, people may be followed over a period of time to see how they change or people of different ages may be compared to see how they differ.

The Study of Human Development

CHAPTER 1

There is nothing permanent except change.

Heraclitus, fragment (sixth century B.C.)

Focus
Victor, the Wild Boy of Aveyron*

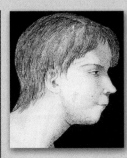

On January 8, 1800, a naked boy appeared on the outskirts of the village of Saint-Sernin in the province of Aveyron in south central France. The boy, who was only four and a half feet tall but looked about 12 years old, had been spotted several times during the previous two and a half years, climbing trees, running on all fours, drinking from streams, and foraging for acorns and roots.

When the dark-eyed boy came to Saint-Sernin, he neither spoke nor responded to speech. Like an animal accustomed to living in the wild, he spurned prepared foods and tore off the clothing people tried to put on him. It seemed clear that he either had lost his parents or had been abandoned by them, but how long ago this had occurred was impossible to tell.

The boy appeared during a time of intellectual and social ferment, when a new, scientific outlook was beginning to replace mystical speculation. Philosophers debated questions about the nature of human beings—questions that would become central to the study of human development: Are the qualities, behavior, and ideas that define what it means to be human inborn or acquired or both? How important is social contact during the formative years? Can its lack be overcome? A study of a child who had grown up in isolation might provide evidence of the relative impact of "nature" (innate characteristics) and "nurture" (upbringing, schooling, and other societal influences).

After initial observation, the boy, who came to be called Victor, was sent to a school in Paris for children who were deaf and mute. There, he was turned over to Jean-Marc-Gaspard Itard, an ambitious 26-year-old practitioner of the emerging science of psychiatry. Itard believed that Victor's development had been limited by isolation and that he simply needed to be taught the skills that children in society normally acquire.

*Sources of information about the wild boy of Aveyron are Frith (1989) and Lane (1976).

Itard took Victor into his home and, during the next five years, gradually "tamed" him. Itard first awakened his pupil's ability to discriminate sensory experience through hot baths and dry rubs. He then moved on to painstaking, step-by-step training of emotional responses and instruction in moral and social behavior, language, and thought. The methods Itard used—based on principles of imitation, conditioning, and behavior modification, all of which we discuss in Chapter 2—were far ahead of their time, and he invented many teaching devices used today.

However, the education of Victor was not an unqualified success. Without question, the boy did make remarkable progress. He learned the names of many objects and could read and write simple sentences. He could express desires, obey commands, and exchange ideas. He showed affection, especially for Itard's housekeeper, Madame Guérin, as well as such emotions as pride, shame, remorse, and the desire to please. Still, aside from uttering some vowel and consonant sounds, he never learned to speak. Furthermore, he remained focused on his own wants and needs and never seemed to lose his yearning "for the freedom of the open country and his indifference to most of the pleasures of social life" (Lane, 1976, p. 160). When the study ended, Victor—no longer able to fend for himself, as he had done in the wild— went to live with Madame Guérin until his death in his early forties in 1828.

W hy did Victor fail to fulfill Itard's hopes for him? The boy may have been a victim of brain damage, autism (a brain disorder involving lack of social responsiveness), or severe early maltreatment. Itard's instructional methods, advanced as they were for his time, may have been inadequate. Itard himself came to believe that the effects of long isolation could not be fully overcome, and that Victor may have been too old, especially for language learning.

Although Victor's story does not yield definitive answers to the questions Itard set out to explore, it is important because it was one of the first systematic attempts to study human development. Since Victor's time we have learned much about how people develop, but developmental scientists are still investigating such fundamental questions as the relative importance of nature and nurture and how they work together. Victor's story dramatizes the challenges and complexities of the scientific study of human development—the study on which you are about to embark.

In this introductory chapter, we describe how the field of human development has itself developed. We present the goals and basic concepts of the field today. We identify aspects of human development and show how they interrelate. We summarize major developments during each period of life. We look at influences on development and the contexts in which it occurs.

After you have studied this chapter, you should be able to answer each of the Guidepost questions that follow. Look for them again in the margins, where they point to important concepts throughout the chapter. To check your understanding of these Guideposts, review the end-of-chapter Summary. Checkpoints located at periodic spots throughout the chapter will help you verify your understanding of what you have read.

Guideposts
for Study

1. What is human development, and how has its study evolved?

2. What are the four goals of the scientific study of human development, what disciplines does it draw upon, and how are research methods changing?

3. What do developmental scientists study?

4. What are three major domains and eight periods of human development?

5. What kinds of influences make one person different from another?

6. What are six principles of the life-span developmental approach?

How the Study of Human Development Evolved

Guidepost

1. What is human development, and how has its study evolved?

From the moment of conception, human beings undergo processes of development. The field of **human development** is the scientific study of those processes. Developmental scientists—people engaged in the professional study of human development—look at ways in which people change throughout life, such as in physiological size and shape, as well as at characteristics that remain fairly stable, such as temperament.

human development Scientific study of processes of change and stability throughout the human life span.

The formal study of human development is a relatively new field of scientific inquiry. Since the early nineteenth century, when Itard studied Victor, efforts to understand children's development have gradually expanded to include the whole life span.

Early Approaches

Forerunners of the scientific study of development were *baby biographies,* journals kept to record the early development of a child. One such journal, published in 1787 in Germany, contained Dietrich Tiedemann's (1897/1787) observations of his son's sensory, motor, language, and cognitive behavior during the first 2½ years. These observations were highly speculative. For example, after watching the infant suck more on a cloth tied around something sweet than on a nurse's finger, Tiedemann concluded that sucking appeared to be "not instinctive, but acquired" (Murchison & Langer, 1927, p. 206).

It was Charles Darwin, originator of the theory of evolution, who first emphasized the *developmental* nature of infant behavior as an orderly process of change. He believed that human beings could better understand themselves, both as a species and as individuals, by studying their early development. In 1877 Darwin published notes on his son Doddy's sensory, cognitive, and emotional development during his first twelve months (see Focus vignette at the beginning of Chapter 5). Darwin's journal gave "baby biographies" scientific respectability; about thirty more were published during the next three decades (Dennis, 1936).

Developmental Psychology Becomes a Science

By the end of the nineteenth century, several important trends in the western world were preparing the way for the scientific study of development. Scientists had unlocked the mystery of conception. Influenced by the writings of the philosophers John Locke and

Jean Jacques Rousseau (see Chapter 2), philosophers and scientists were arguing about the relative importance of "nature" and "nurture" (inborn characteristics and experiential influences)—the question Itard had investigated in his work with Victor. The discovery of germs and immunization made it possible for many more children to survive infancy. Laws protecting children from long workdays let them spend more time in school, and parents and teachers became more concerned with identifying and meeting children's developmental needs. The new science of psychology taught that people could better understand themselves by learning what had influenced them as children.

Still, this new discipline had far to go. For example, adolescence was not considered a separate period of development until the early twentieth century, when G. Stanley Hall, a pioneer in child study, published a popular (though unscientific) book called *Adolescence* (1904/1916). The twentieth century also saw the publication of seminal works by such theorists as Sigmund Freud and Jean Piaget (see Chapter 2). Arnold Gesell's (1929) work on stages in motor development provided research-based information about developments that normally occur at various ages. The establishment of research institutes in the 1930s and 1940s at such universities as Iowa, Minnesota, Columbia, Berkeley, and Yale marked the emergence of child psychology as a true science with professionally trained practitioners.

Hall was one of the first psychologists to become interested in aging. In 1922, at age 78, he published *Senescence: The Last Half of Life*. The first major scientific research unit devoted to aging opened at Stanford University in 1928. Since the late 1930s, long-term studies such as those of K. Warner Schaie, George Vaillant, Daniel Levinson, and Ravenna Helson, which are discussed in the second half of this book, have focused on intelligence and personality development in adulthood and old age.

Studying the Life Span

Today most developmental scientists recognize that development goes on throughout life. This concept of a lifelong process of development that can be studied scientifically is known as **life-span development.**

life-span development Concept of human development as a lifelong process, which can be studied scientifically.

Life-span studies in the United States grew out of research designed to follow children through adulthood. The Stanford Studies of Gifted Children, begun in 1921 under the direction of Lewis M. Terman, trace the development of people (now in old age) who were identified as unusually intelligent in childhood. Other major studies that began around 1930, such as the Berkeley Growth and Guidance Studies and the Oakland (Adolescent) Growth Study, have given us much information on long-term development. More recently, Paul B. Baltes's life-span developmental approach, discussed at the end of this chapter, has provided a comprehensive conceptual framework for the study of life-span development.

Checkpoint

Can you . . .

✔ Trace highlights in the evolution of the study of human development?

Guidepost

2. What are the four goals of the scientific study of human development, what disciplines does it draw upon, and how are research methods changing?

Human Development Today: An Ever-Evolving Field

As the field of human development became a scientific discipline, its goals evolved to include *description, explanation, prediction,* and *modification* of behavior. For example, to *describe* when most normal children say their first word or how large their vocabulary typically is at a certain age, developmental scientists observe large groups of children and establish norms, or averages, for behavior at various ages. They then attempt to *explain* how children acquire and learn to use language, and why a child like Victor did not learn to speak. This knowledge may make it possible to *predict* later behavior, such as the likelihood that such a child could still be taught to speak. Finally, understanding of how language develops may be used to *modify* behavior, as Itard attempted to do in tutoring Victor.

Because human beings are complex, students of human development draw from a wide range of disciplines, or fields of study, including psychology, psychiatry,

The study of human development has such practical applications as helping people deal with life transitions, such as a job or career change.

sociology, anthropology, biology, genetics (the study of inherited characteristics), family science (the interdisciplinary study of family relations), education, history, philosophy, and medicine. This book includes findings from research in all these fields.

The scientific study of human development is an ever-evolving endeavor. The questions that developmental scientists seek to answer, the methods they use, and the explanations they propose are more sophisticated and more eclectic than they were even twenty-five years ago (Parke, 2004). These shifts reflect progress in understanding as new investigations build on or challenge those that went before. They also reflect technological change. Sensitive instruments that measure eye movements, heart rate, blood pressure, muscle tension, and the like are turning up intriguing connections between biological functions and childhood intelligence. Cameras, videocassette recorders, and computers allow investigators to scan infants' facial expressions for early signs of emotions and to analyze how mothers and babies communicate. Advances in imaging make it possible to probe the mysteries of temperament, to pinpoint the sources of logical thought, and to compare a normally aging brain with the brain of a person with dementia.

Increasingly, research findings have direct application to child rearing, education, health, and social policy (Parke, 2004). For example, learning about childhood memory has helped determine the weight to be given children's courtroom testimony, and identifying factors that increase the risks of antisocial behavior has suggested ways to prevent it. An understanding of adult development, too, has practical implications. It can help people deal with their own or others' life transitions: a woman returning to work after maternity leave, a person making a career change or about to retire, a widow or widower dealing with loss, someone coping with a terminal illness.

The Study of Human Development: Basic Concepts

The processes of change and stability that developmental scientists study occur in all aspects of development and throughout all periods of the life span.

What's Your View?

- What reasons do you have for studying human development?

Checkpoint
Can you . . .

✔ Name four goals of the scientific study of human development?

✔ Name at least six disciplines involved in the study of human development?

✔ Give examples of practical applications of research on human development?

Guidepost

3. What do developmental scientists study?

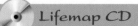
Developmental Processes: Change and Stability

Developmental scientists study two kinds of change: *quantitative* and *qualitative*. **Quantitative change** is a change in number or amount, such as growth or loss in height or weight, gains in vocabulary, or an increase or decrease in frequency of aggressive behavior or social interaction. **Qualitative change** is a change in kind, structure, or organization. It is marked by the emergence of new phenomena that cannot easily be anticipated on the basis of earlier functioning, such as the change from a nonverbal child to one who understands words and can communicate verbally, a change of careers, or the learning of a new skill, such as the use of a computer.

Despite such changes, people show an underlying *stability,* or constancy, of personality and behavior. For example, about 10 to 15 percent of children are consistently shy, and another 10 to 15 percent are very bold. Although various influences can modify these traits somewhat, they seem to persist to a moderate degree, especially in children at one extreme or the other (see Chapter 6). Broad dimensions of personality, such as conscientiousness and openness to new experience, seem to stabilize during young adulthood (see Chapter 14).

Which characteristics are most likely to endure? Which are likely to change, and why? These are among the questions that the study of human development seeks to answer.

Domains of Development

Change and stability occur in various *domains,* or dimensions, of the self. Developmental scientists talk separately about *physical development, cognitive development,* and *psychosocial development.* Actually, though, these domains are interrelated. Throughout life, each affects the others.

Growth of the body and brain, sensory capacities, motor skills, and health are part of **physical development** and may influence other domains of development. For example, a child with frequent ear infections may develop language more slowly than a child without this problem. During puberty, dramatic physical and hormonal changes affect the developing sense of self. In contrast, physical changes in the brains of some older adults may lead to intellectual and personality deterioration.

Change and stability in mental abilities, such as learning, attention, memory, language, thinking, reasoning, and creativity, constitute **cognitive development.** Cognitive advances and declines are closely related to physical, emotional, and social factors. The ability to speak depends on the physical development of the mouth and brain. A child who is precocious in language development is likely to evoke positive reactions in others and gain in self-worth. Memory development reflects gains or losses in physical connections in the brain. An adult who has trouble remembering people's names (a common problem) may feel awkward and reticent in social situations.

Change and stability in emotions, personality, and social relationships together constitute **psychosocial development,** and this can affect cognitive and physical functioning. Anxiety about taking a test can impair performance. Social support can help people cope with the potentially negative effects of stress on physical and mental health. As we report in Chapter 18, researchers even have identified possible links between personality and length of life. Conversely, physical and cognitive capacities can affect psychosocial development. They contribute greatly to self-esteem and can affect social acceptance and choice of occupation.

Although we will be looking separately at physical, cognitive, and psychosocial development, a person is more than a bundle of isolated parts. Development is a unified process. Throughout the text, we will highlight links among the three major domains of development.

These children examining snails on a sand table illustrate the interrelationship of domains of development: sensory perception, cognitive learning, and emotional and social interaction.

Periods of the Life Span

Any division of the life span into periods is a **social construction:** an idea about the nature of reality that is widely accepted by members of a society at a particular time, on the basis of shared subjective perceptions or assumptions. There is no objectively definable moment when a child becomes an adult or a young person becomes old. Indeed, the concept of childhood itself can be viewed as a social construction. Some evidence indicates that children in earlier times were regarded and treated much like small adults. However, this suggestion has been disputed (Ariès, 1962; Elkind, 1986; Pollock, 1983). Archaeological finds from ancient Greece show children playing with clay dolls and "dice" made of bones of sheep and goats. Pottery and tombstones depict children sitting on high chairs and riding goat-pulled carts (Mulrine, 2004).

In industrial societies, as we have mentioned, the concept of adolescence as a period of development is quite recent. Until the early 20th century, young people in the United States were considered children until they left school (often well before age 13), married or got a job, and entered the adult world. By the 1920s, with the establishment of comprehensive high schools to meet the needs of a growing industrial and commercial economy and with more families able to support extended formal education for their children, the teenage years came to be seen as a distinct period of development. In some preindustrial societies, such as that of the Chippewa Indians, the concept of adolescence still does not exist. The Chippewa have only two periods of childhood: from birth until the child walks, and from walking to puberty. What we call *adolescence* is part of adulthood (Broude, 1995). As we report in Chapter 16, the Gusii of Kenya have no concept of middle age.

In this book, we follow a sequence of eight periods generally accepted in western industrial societies. After describing the crucial changes that occur in the first period, before birth, we trace all three domains of development through infancy and toddlerhood, early childhood, middle childhood, adolescence, young adulthood, middle adulthood, and late adulthood (see Table 1-1). For each period after infancy and toddlerhood (when change is most dramatic), we have combined physical and cognitive development into a single chapter.

social construction Concept about the nature of reality based on societally shared perceptions or assumptions.

What's Your View?

- Why do you think various societies divide the periods of development differently?

Table 1-1   Typical Major Developments in Five Periods of Child Development

Age Period	Physical Developments	Cognitive Developments	Psychosocial Developments
Prenatal Period (conception to birth)	Conception occurs by normal fertilization or other means The genetic endowment interacts with environmental influences from the start. Basic body structures and organs form: brain growth spurt begins. Physical growth is the most rapid in the life span. Vulnerability to environmental influences is great.	Abilities to learn and remember and to respond to sensory stimuli are developing.	Fetus responds to mother's voice and develops a preference for it.
Infancy and Toddlerhood (birth to age 3)	All senses and body systems operate at birth to varying degrees. The brain grows in complexity and is highly sensitive to environmental influence. Physical growth and development of motor skills are rapid.	Abilities to learn and remember are present, even in early weeks. Use of symbols and ability to solve problems develop by end of second year. Comprehension and use of language develop rapidly.	Attachments to parents and others form. Self-awareness develops. Shift from dependence to autonomy occurs. Interest in other children increases.
Early Childhood (3 to 6 years)	Growth is steady; appearance becomes more slender and proportions more adultlike. Appetite diminishes, and sleep problems are common. Handedness appears; fine and gross motor skills and strength improve.	Thinking is somewhat egocentric, but understanding of other people's perspectives grows. Cognitive immaturity results in some illogical ideas about the world. Memory and language improve. Intelligence becomes more predictable. Preschool experience is common, and kindergarten experience is more so.	Self-concept and understanding of emotions become more complex; self-esteem is global. Independence, initiative, and self-control increase. Gender identity develops. Play becomes more imaginative, more elaborate, and usually more social. Altruism, aggression, and fearfulness are common. Family is still the focus of social life, but other children become more important.
Middle Childhood (6 to 11 years)	Growth slows. Strength and athletic skills improve. Respiratory illnesses are common, but health is generally better than at any other time in the life span.	Egocentrism diminishes. Children begin to think logically but concretely. Memory and language skills increase. Cognitive gains permit children to benefit from formal schooling. Some children show special educational needs and strengths.	Self-concept becomes more complex, affecting self-esteem. Coregulation reflects gradual shift in control from parents to child. Peers assume central importance.

The age divisions shown in Table 1-1 are approximate and somewhat arbitrary. This is especially true of adulthood, when there are no clear-cut social or physical landmarks, such as starting school or entering puberty, to signal a shift from one period to another. Individual differences exist in the way people deal with the characteristic events and issues of each period. One toddler may be toilet trained by 18 months; another, not until 3 years. One adult may eagerly anticipate retirement while another may dread it.

Despite these differences, however, developmental scientists suggest that certain basic developmental needs must be met and certain developmental tasks mastered during each period for normal development to occur. Infants, for example, are dependent on adults to meet their basic needs for food, clothing, and shelter as well as for human contact and affection. They form attachments to parents or caregivers, who also become attached to them. With the development of speech and self-locomotion, toddlers become

Age Period	Physical Developments	Cognitive Developments	Psychosocial Developments
Adolescence (11 to about 20 years)	Physical growth and other changes are rapid and profound. Reproductive maturity occurs. Major health risks arise from behavioral issues, such as eating disorders and drug abuse.	Ability to think abstractly and use scientific reasoning develops. Immature thinking persists in some attitudes and behaviors. Education focuses on preparation for college or vocation.	Search for identity, including sexual identity, becomes central. Relationships with parents are generally good. Peer group may exert a positive or negative influence.
Young Adulthood (20 to 40 years)	Physical condition peaks, then declines slightly. Lifestyle choices influence health.	Thought and moral judgments become more complex. Educational and occupational choices are made.	Personality traits and styles become relatively stable, but changes in personality may be influenced by life stages and events. Decisions are made about intimate relationships and personal lifestyles. Most people marry, and most become parents.
Middle Adulthood (40 to 65 years)	Slow deterioration of sensory abilities, health, stamina, and strength may begin, but individual differences are wide. Women experience menopause.	Mental abilities peak; expertise and practical problem-solving skills are high. Creative output may decline but improve in quality. For some, career success and earning powers peak; for others, burnout or career change may occur.	Sense of identity continues to develop; midlife transition may occur. Dual responsibilities of caring for children and parents may cause stress. Launching of children leaves empty nest.
Late Adulthood (65 years and over)	Most people are healthy and active, although health and physical abilities generally decline. Slowing of reaction time affects some aspects of functioning.	Most people are mentally alert. Although intelligence and memory may deteriorate in some areas, most people find ways to compensate.	Retirement from workforce may offer new options for use of time. People develop more flexible strategies to cope with personal losses and impending death. Relationships with family and close friends can provide important support. Search for meaning in life assumes central importance.

more self-reliant; they need to assert their autonomy but also need parents to help them keep their impulses in check. During early childhood, children develop more self-control and more interest in other children. Control over behavior gradually shifts from parent to child during middle childhood, when the peer group becomes increasingly important. A main task of adolescence is the search for identity—personal, sexual, and occupational. As adolescents become physically mature, they deal with sometimes conflicting needs and emotions as they prepare to separate from the parental nest.

The developmental tasks of young adulthood include the establishment of independent lifestyles, occupations, and, usually, families. During middle adulthood, most people need to deal with some decline in physical capabilities. At the same time, many middle-aged people find excitement and challenge in life changes—launching new careers and adult children—while some face the need to care for elderly parents.

Checkpoint
Can you . . .

✔ Identify three domains of development and give examples of how they are interrelated?

✔ Name eight periods of human development (as defined in this book) and list several key issues or events of each period?

In late adulthood, people cope with losses in their faculties, the loss of loved ones, and preparations for death. If they retire, they must deal with the loss of work-based relationships but may get increased pleasure out of friendships, family, volunteer work, and the opportunity to explore previously neglected interests. Many older people become more introspective, searching out the meaning of their lives.

Influences on Development

Guidepost

5. What kinds of influences make one person different from another?

normative Characteristic of an event that occurs in a similar way for most people in a group.

individual differences Differences in characteristics, influences, or developmental outcomes.

Students of development are interested in universal processes of development, which are experienced by all human beings. They also are interested in **normative** influences experienced in a similar way by most people in a group. Finally, students of development want to know about **individual differences,** both their influences on development and their outcomes. People differ in sex, height, weight, and body build; in constitutional factors such as health and energy level; in intelligence; and in personality characteristics and emotional reactions. The contexts of their lives and lifestyles differ too: the homes, communities, and societies they live in, the relationships they have, the schools they go to (or whether they go to school at all), the work they do, and the ways they spend their free time.

Why does one person turn out unlike any other? Because development is complex and the factors that affect it cannot always be measured precisely, scientists cannot answer that question fully. However, they have learned much about what people need to develop normally, how they react to the many influences upon and within them, and how they can best fulfill their potential.

Heredity and Environment

heredity Inborn characteristics inherited from the biological parents.

environment Totality of nonhereditary, or experiential, influences on development.

Some influences on development originate primarily with **heredity:** inborn traits or characteristics inherited from the biological parents. Other influences come largely from the inner and outer **environment:** the world outside the self beginning in the womb, and the learning that comes from experience. Which of these two factors has more impact on development? This issue (dramatized by our Focus on the Wild Child of Aveyron) once aroused intense debate. Theorists differed in the relative importance they gave to *nature* (heredity) and *nurture* (environmental influences both before and after birth).

Today, scientists in the field of behavioral genetics have found ways to measure more precisely the roles of heredity and environment in the development of specific traits within a population. When we look at a particular person, however, research with regard to almost all characteristics points to a blend of inheritance and experience. Thus, even though intelligence has a strong hereditary component, parental stimulation, education, peer influence, and other variables also affect it. Although there still is considerable dispute about the relative importance of nature and nurture, many contemporary theorists and researchers are more interested in finding ways to explain how they work together.

The Role of Maturation

maturation Unfolding of a natural sequence of physical and behavioral changes, including readiness to master new abilities.

Many typical changes of infancy and early childhood, such as the emergence of the abilities to walk and talk, seem to be tied to **maturation** of the body and brain—the unfolding of a natural sequence of physical changes and behavior patterns, including readiness to master new abilities such as walking and talking. As children grow into adolescents and then into adults, individual differences in innate characteristics and life experience play a greater role as people adapt to the internal and external conditions in which they find themselves. Still, maturation may continue to influence certain biological processes.

Even in processes that all people undergo, rates and timing of development vary. Throughout this book, we talk about average ages for the occurrence of certain events, such as the first word, the first step, the first menstruation or "wet dream," the development of logical thought, and menopause. But these ages are *merely* averages. Only when deviation from the average is extreme should we consider development exceptionally advanced or delayed.

In trying to understand human development, then, we need to look at the *inherited* characteristics that give each person a special start in life. We also need to consider the many *environmental,* or experiential, factors that affect people, especially such major contexts as family, neighborhood, socioeconomic status, ethnicity, and culture. We need to consider how heredity and environment interact; this will be discussed in Chapter 3. We need to understand which developments are primarily maturational and which are more subject to individual differences. We need to look at influences that affect many or most people at a certain age or a certain time in history and also at those that affect only certain individuals. Finally, we need to look at how timing can accentuate the impact of certain influences.

Contexts of Development

Human beings are social beings. Right from the start, they develop within a social and historical context. For an infant, the immediate context normally is the family, but the family in turn is subject to the wider and ever-changing influences of neighborhood, community, and society.

Family *Family* may mean something different in different times and places. The **nuclear family** is a two-generational kinship, economic, and household unit consisting of one or two parents and their biological children, adopted children, or stepchildren. Historically, the two-parent nuclear family has been the dominant family unit in the United States and other western societies. Parents and children typically worked side by side on the family farm. Today most U.S. families are urban; they have fewer children, and both parents are likely to work outside the home. Children spend much of their time in school or child care. Children of divorced parents may live with one or the other parent or may move back and forth between them. The household may include a stepparent and stepsiblings or a parent's live-in partner. There are increasing numbers of single and childless adults, unmarried parents, and gay and lesbian households (Hernandez, 1997, 2004; Teachman, Tedrow, & Crowder, 2000; see Chapter 10).

In today's nuclear family, unlike the typical U.S. family of 150 years ago, both parents are likely to work outside the home. Families are smaller than in the past, and children spend more of their time in school.

In many societies in Asia, Africa, and Latin America and among some U.S. families that trace their lineage to those countries, the **extended family**—a multigenerational kinship network of grandparents, aunts, uncles, cousins, and more distant relatives—is the traditional family form. Many or most people live in *extended-family households,* where they have daily contact with kin. Adults often share breadwinning and child raising responsibilities, and children are responsible for younger brothers and sisters. Often these minority households are headed by women (Aaron, Parker, Ortega, & Calhoun, 1999; Johnson et al., 2003). Today the extended-family household is becoming less typical in developing countries due to industrialization and migration to urban centers (Brown, 1990; Gorman, 1993), particularly among groups that have achieved upward mobility (Peterson, 1993). At the same time, with the aging of the population, multigenerational family bonds are becoming increasingly important in western societies (Bengtson, 2001).

Socioeconomic Status and Neighborhood Socioeconomic status (SES) includes income, education, and occupation. Throughout this book, we examine many studies

nuclear family Two-generational kinship, economic, and household unit consisting of one or two parents and their biological children, adopted children, or stepchildren.

extended family Multigenerational kinship network of parents, children, and other relatives, sometimes living together in an extended-family household.

socioeconomic status (SES) Combination of economic and social factors describing an individual or family, including income, education, and occupation.

Table 1-2 Poverty Hurts Children

Outcomes	Low-Income Children's Higher Risk
Health	
Death in infancy	1.6 times more likely
Premature birth (*under 37 weeks*)	1.8 times more likely
Low birth weight	1.9 times more likely
Inadequate prenatal care	2.8 times more likely
No regular source of health care	2.7 times more likely
Having too little food sometime in the last 4 months	8.0 times more likely
Education	
Lower math scores at ages 7 to 8	5 test points lower
Lower reading scores at ages 7 to 8	4 test points lower
Repeating a grade	2.0 times more likely
Being expelled from school	3.4 times more likely
Being a dropout at ages 16 to 24	3.5 times more likely
Finishing a four-year college	50 percent as likely

Source: Children's Defense Fund, 2004.

that relate SES to developmental processes (such as mothers' verbal interactions with their children) and to developmental outcomes (such as health and cognitive performance; see Table 1-2). SES affects these processes and outcomes indirectly, through such associated factors as the kinds of homes and neighborhoods people live in and the quality of nutrition, medical care, and schooling available to them.

As we discuss in Chapter 10, poverty can be harmful to the physical, cognitive, and psychosocial well-being of children and families. The harm done by poverty may be indirect, through its impact on where families can live, on parents' emotional states and parenting practices, and on the home environment they create. Threats to well-being multiply if, as often happens, several **risk factors**—conditions that increase the likelihood of a negative outcome, such as lack of health care access and educational opportunity—coexist. Children in affluent families may be at risk for other reasons (Evans, 2004). Under pressure to achieve and often left on their own by busy parents, these "low-risk" children have high rates of substance abuse, anxiety, and depression (Luthar & Latendresse, 2005).

The composition of a neighborhood can affect the way children develop. The most powerful factors seem to be average neighborhood *income* and *human capital*—the presence of educated, employed adults who can build the community's economic base and provide social support and models of what a child can hope to achieve (Black & Krishnakumar, 1998; Brooks-Gunn et al., 1997; Leventhal & Brooks-Gunn, 2000). Still, the resilience of such people as Oprah Winfrey and former President Bill Clinton, who rose from poverty and deprivation to high achievement, shows that positive development can occur despite serious risk factors (Kim-Cohen, Moffitt, Caspi, & Taylor, 2004).

Culture and Ethnicity **Culture** refers to a society's or group's total way of life, including customs, traditions, laws, knowledge, beliefs, values, language, and physical products, from tools to artworks—all of the behavior and attitudes that are learned, shared, and transmitted among members of a social group. Culture is constantly changing, often through contact with other cultures. For example, when Europeans arrived on American shores, they soon learned from the native Indians how to grow corn. Today cultural contact is enhanced by computers and telecommunications, and American music is downloaded around the world.

risk factors Conditions that increase the likelihood of a negative developmental outcome.

culture A society's or group's total way of life, including customs, traditions, beliefs, values, language, and physical products—all learned behavior passed on from parents to children.

An **ethnic group** consists of people united by a distinctive culture, ancestry, religion, language, and/or national origin, all of which contribute to a sense of shared identity and shared attitudes, beliefs, and values. Most ethnic groups trace their roots to a country of origin, where they or their forebears shared a common culture that continues to influence their way of life. Ethnic and cultural patterns affect development by their influence on the composition of a household, its economic and social resources, the way its members act toward one another, the foods they eat, the games children play, the way they learn, how well they do in school, the occupations adults engage in, and the way family members think and perceive the world (Parke, 2004). For example, children of immigrants in the United States are nearly twice as likely as native-born children to live with extended families and are less likely to have mothers who work outside the home (Hernandez, 2004; Shields & Behrman, 2004).

The United States always has been a nation of immigrants and ethnic groups, but the ethnic origins of the immigrant population have shifted from Europe and Canada to Asia and Latin America (Hernandez, 2004). In 2003, 31 percent of the U.S. population belonged to an ethnic minority—African American, Hispanic, American Indian, or Asian and Pacific Islander—representing a threefold increase since the 1930s (U.S. Census Bureau, 1930, 2003); and more than 20 percent were immigrants or children of immigrants (Fuligni & Witkow, 2004). By about 2040 the minority population is projected to rise to 50 percent (Hernandez, 2004; see Figure 1-1).

Furthermore, there is wide diversity within broad ethnic groups. The European-descended "white majority" consists of many distinct ethnicities—German, Belgian, Irish, French, Italian, and so on. Cuban Americans, Puerto Ricans, and Mexican Americans—all Hispanic Americans—have different histories and cultures and may be of African, European, Native American, or mixed descent (Johnson et al., 2003; Sternberg, Grigorenko, & Kidd, 2005). African Americans from the rural South differ from those of Caribbean ancestry. Asian Americans hail from a variety of countries with distinct cultures, from modern, industrial Japan to communist China to the

ethnic group A group united by ancestry, race, religion, language, and/or national origins, which contribute to a sense of shared identity.

KEY:

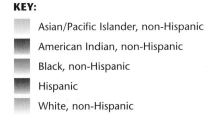

- Asian/Pacific Islander, non-Hispanic
- American Indian, non-Hispanic
- Black, non-Hispanic
- Hispanic
- White, non-Hispanic

Figure 1-1

Past and projected percentages of U.S. children in specified racial/ethnic groups. (Source: Hernandez, 2004, p. 18, Fig. 1. Data from Population Projections Program, Population Division, U.S. Census Bureau, issued January 13, 2000.)

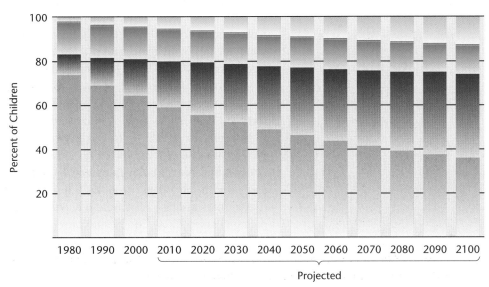

remote mountains of Nepal, where many people still practice their ancient way of life. American Indians consist of hundreds of recognized nations, tribes, bands, and villages (Lin & Kelsey, 2000).

What's Your View?

• How might you be different if you had grown up in a culture other than your own?

Race and Ethnicity: Problems of Definition The term *race,* historically and popularly viewed as an identifiable biological category, is now agreed by most scholars to be a social construct, with no clear scientific consensus on its definition and impossible to reliably measure (American Academy of Pediatrics Committee on Pediatric Research, 2000; Bonham, Warshauer-Baker, & Collins, 2005; Helms, Jernigan, & Mascher, 2005; Lin & Kelsey, 2000; Smedley & Smedley, 2005; Sternberg et al., 2005). Human genetic variation occurs along a broad continuum, and 90 percent of such variation occurs *within* rather than among socially defined races (Bonham et al., 2005; Ossorio & Duster, 2005). Nevertheless, race as a social category remains a factor in much research because it makes a difference in "how individuals are treated, where they live, their employment opportunities, the quality of their health care, and whether [they] can fully participate" in their society (Smedley & Smedley, 2005, p. 23). As one research team suggests, "Race may be a *consequence* of differential treatment and experiences rather than an independent cause of differential outcomes" (Ossorio & Duster, 2005, p. 116; italics added).

Categories of race and ethnicity are fluid (Bonham et al., 2005; Sternberg et al., 2005), "continuously shaped and redefined by social and political forces" (Fisher et al., 2002, p. 1026). Geographic dispersion and intermarriage together with adaptation to varying local conditions have produced a great heterogeneity of characteristics within populations (Smedley & Smedley, 2005; Sternberg et al., 2005). Thus, a person such as the golf champion Tiger Woods, who has a black father and an Asian-American mother, may fall into more than one racial/ethnic category and may identify more strongly with one or another at different times (Lin & Kelsey, 2000). A term such as *black* or *Hispanic* can be an **ethnic gloss**—an overgeneralization that obscures cultural differences within a group (Parke, 2004; Trimble & Dickson, in press).

ethnic gloss Overgeneralization about an ethnic or cultural group that obscures differences within the group.

The dynamic nature of cultural change further confounds ethnic identity (Parke, 2004). In large, multiethnic societies such as the United States, immigrant or minority groups *acculturate,* or adapt, by learning the language, customs, and attitudes needed to get along in the dominant culture while trying to preserve some of their own cultural practices and values (Johnson et al., 2003). Individuals acculturate at different rates depending on such factors as how long they have lived in the majority culture, how old they were when they immigrated, their treatment by the dominant community, and how closely they want to maintain ties with their native culture (Chun, Organista, & Marin, 2002; Johnson et al., 2003).

Although researchers today are paying much more attention to ethnic and cultural differences than in the past, it is difficult, if not impossible, to present a truly comprehensive picture of these differences. Minorities still are underrepresented in developmental research, and minority samples are often unrepresentative, in part because of wariness about participating (Parke, 2004). Many studies reported in this book are limited to the dominant group within a culture, and others compare only two groups, such as white Americans and African

Golf champion Tiger Woods (here, with his proud parents, holding the trophy he won at the Johnnie Walker Classic in 1998) is one of many Americans with dual or multiple ethnic backgrounds.

Americans. When multiple groups *are* studied, often only one or two yield results that are noticeably different and therefore worth noting. Even cross-cultural studies cannot capture all of the variations within and among cultures.

The Historical Context   At one time developmental scientists paid little attention to the historical context—the time in which people live. Then, as the early longitudinal studies of childhood extended into the adult years, investigators began to focus on how certain experiences, tied to time and place, affect the course of people's lives. The Terman sample, for example, reached adulthood in the 1930s, during the Great Depression; the Oakland sample, during World War II (see Box 1-1); and the Berkeley sample, around 1950, the postwar boom period. What did it mean to be a child in each of these periods? To be an adolescent? To become an adult? The answers differ in specific and important ways. Today, as we will discuss in the next section, the historical context is an important part of the study of human development.

Checkpoint
Can you . . .

✔ Explain why individual differences tend to increase with age?

✔ Give examples of the influences of family and neighborhood composition, socioeconomic status, culture, race/ethnicity, and historical context?

Normative and Nonnormative Influences

To understand similarities and differences in development, then, we must look at influences of time and place. We also need to consider influences that impinge on many or most people and at those that touch only certain individuals (Baltes, Reese, & Lipsitt, 1980).

Normative age-graded influences are highly similar for people in a particular age group. They include *maturational* events (such as puberty and menopause) and *social* events (such as entry into formal education, marriage, parenthood, and retirement). The timing of biological events is fairly predictable within a normal range. For example, people don't experience puberty at age 35 or menopause at 12. The timing of social events is more flexible and varies in different times and places. Children in western industrial societies generally begin formal education around age 5 or 6, but in some developing countries schooling begins much later if at all.

Normative history-graded influences are significant events (such as the Great Depression or World War II) that shape the behavior and attitudes of a **historical generation:** a group of people who experience the event at a formative time in their lives. For example, the generations that came of age during the Depression and World War II tend to show a strong sense of social interdependence and trust that has declined among more recent generations (Rogler, 2002). Depending on when and where they live, entire generations may feel the impact of famines, nuclear explosions, or terrorist attacks and of such cultural and technological developments as the changing roles of women and the impact of television and computers. A historical generation is not quite the same as an age **cohort:** a group of people born at about the same time. A historical generation may contain more than one cohort, but not all cohorts are part of historical generations unless they experience major, shaping historical events at a formative point in their lives (Rogler, 2002).

Nonnormative influences are unusual events that have a major impact on *individual* lives. They are either typical events that happen at an atypical time of life (such as marriage in the early teens or the death of a parent when a child is young) or atypical events (such as having a birth defect or being in an airplane crash). They can also, of course, be happy events (such as winning the lottery). People often help create their

Widespread use of computers is a normative history-graded influence on children's development, which did not exist in earlier generations.

historical generation   A group of people strongly influenced by a major historical event during their formative period.

cohort   A group of people born at about the same time.

nonnormative   Characteristic of an unusual event that happens to a particular person or a typical event that happens at an unusual time of life.

BOX 1-1

Digging Deeper
Studying the Life Course: Growing Up in Hard Times

Our awareness of the need to look at the life course in its social and historical context is indebted in part to Glen H. Elder, Jr. In 1962, Elder arrived on the campus of the University of California at Berkeley to work on the Oakland Growth Study, a longitudinal study of social and emotional development in 167 urban young people born around 1920, about half of them from middle-class homes. The study had begun at the outset of the Great Depression of the 1930s, when the participants, who had spent their childhoods in the boom years of the Roaring '20s, were entering adolescence. Elder observed how societal disruption can alter family processes and, through them, children's development (Elder, 1974).

Glen Elder's studies of children growing up during the Great Depression showed how a major sociohistorical event can affect children's current and future development.

As economic stress changed parents' lives, it changed children's lives, too. Deprived families reassigned economic roles. Fathers, preoccupied with job losses and irritable about their loss of status within the family, sometimes drank heavily. Mothers found outside jobs and took on more parental authority. Parents argued more. Adolescents tended to show developmental difficulties.

Still, for boys, particularly, the long-term effects of the ordeal were not entirely negative. Boys who obtained jobs to help out became more independent and were better able to escape the stressful family atmosphere than were girls, who helped at home. As men, these boys were strongly work oriented but also valued family activities and cultivated dependability in their children.

Elder noted that effects of a major economic crisis depend on a child's stage of development. The children in the Oakland sample were already teenagers during the 1930s. They could draw on their own emotional, cognitive, and economic resources. A child born in 1929 would have been entirely dependent on the family. On the other hand, the parents of the Oakland children, being older, may have been less resilient in dealing with the loss of a job, and their emotional vulnerability may well have affected the tone of family life and their treatment of their children.

Fifty years after the Great Depression, in the early 1980s, steep increases in interest rates combined with a precipitous drop in the value of midwestern agricultural land and in prices of farm products pushed many farm families into debt or off the land. This farm crisis gave Elder the opportunity to replicate his earlier research, this time in a rural setting. In 1989, he and his colleagues (Conger & Elder, 1994; Conger et al., 1993) interviewed 451 Iowa farm and small-town families, each with two parents in the household, a seventh grader, and a sibling no more than four years younger. The researchers also videotaped family interactions. Because there were virtually no minorities living in Iowa at the time, all the participating families were white.

As in the Depression-era study, many of these rural parents, under pressure of economic hardship, developed emotional problems. Depressed parents were more likely to fight with each other and to mistreat or withdraw from their children. The children, in turn, tended to lose self-confidence, to become unpopular, and to do poorly in school. In the 1930s this pattern of parental behavior had been less true of mothers, whose economic role before the collapse had been more marginal, but in the 1980s similar patterns fit both fathers and mothers (Conger & Elder, 1994; Conger et al., 1993; Elder, 1998).

This study, now called the Family Transitions Project, continues. The family members have been reinterviewed yearly, with a focus on how a family crisis experienced in early adolescence affects the transition to adulthood. For both boys and girls, a self-reinforcing cycle appeared. Such negative events as economic crisis, illness, and getting in trouble at school tended to intensify sadness, fear, and antisocial conduct, which, in turn, led to further adversity, such as the divorce of parents (Kim, Conger, Elder, & Lorenz, 2003).

Elder's work, like other studies of the life course, gives researchers a window into processes of development and their links with socioeconomic change. Eventually it may enable us to see long-term effects of early hardship on the lives of people who experienced it at different ages and in varying family situations.

Source: Unless otherwise referenced, this discussion is based on Elder, 1998.

What's Your View?

Can you think of a major cultural event within your lifetime that shaped the lives of families and children? How would you go about studying such effects?

Check It Out

For more information on this topic, go to http://www.sos.state.mi.us/history/museum/techstuf/depressn/teacup.html. This Web site contains reminiscences of the Great Depression, originally published in *Michigan History Magazine,* January–February, 1982 (Vol. 66, No. 1). Read one of the oral histories and consider how the Great Depression seems to have affected the person whose story is told.

own nonnormative life events—say, by applying for a challenging new job or taking up a risky hobby such as skydiving—and thus participate actively in their own development. (Normative and nonnormative events are further discussed in Chapter 14.)

What's Your View?

- Can you think of a historical event that has molded your own life? If so, in what ways?

Timing of Influences: Critical or Sensitive Periods

In a well-known study, Konrad Lorenz (1957), an Austrian zoologist, waddled, honked, and flapped his arms—and got newborn ducklings to follow him as they would the mother duck. Lorenz showed that newly hatched ducklings will instinctively follow the first moving object they see, whether or not it is a member of their own species. This phenomenon is called **imprinting,** and Lorenz believed that it is automatic and irreversible. Usually, this instinctive bond is with the mother; but if the natural course of events is disturbed, other attachments, like the one to Lorenz—or none at all—can form. Imprinting, said Lorenz, is the result of a *predisposition toward learning:* the readiness of an organism's nervous system to acquire certain information during a brief *critical period* in early life.

A **critical period** is a specific time when a given event, or its absence, has a specific impact on development. Critical periods are not absolutely fixed; if ducklings' rearing conditions are varied to slow their growth, the usual critical period for imprinting can be lengthened, and imprinting itself may even be reversed. The window of opportunity, some scientists now believe, may never completely shut (Bruer, 2001).

Do human beings experience critical periods? One example occurs during gestation. As we point out in Chapter 3, if a woman receives X rays, takes certain drugs, or contracts certain diseases at certain times during pregnancy, the fetus may show specific ill effects, depending on the nature of the "shock" and on its timing. Critical periods also occur early in childhood. A child deprived of certain kinds of experience during a critical period is likely to show permanent stunting of physical development. For example, if a muscle problem interfering with the ability to focus both eyes on the same object is not corrected early in life, the brain mechanisms necessary for binocular depth perception probably will not develop (Bushnell & Boudreau, 1993).

The concept of critical periods is controversial. Because many aspects of development, even in the biological/neurological domain, have been found to show **plasticity,** or modifiability of performance, it may be more useful to think about **sensitive periods,** when a developing person is especially responsive to certain kinds of experiences (Bruer, 2001). Further research is needed to discover "which aspects of behavior are likely to be altered by environmental events at specific points in development and which aspects remain more plastic and open to influence across wide spans of development" (Parke, 2004, p. 8). Box 1-2 discusses how the concepts of critical and sensitive periods apply to language development.

imprinting Instinctive form of learning in which, during a critical period in early development, a young animal forms an attachment to the first moving object it sees, usually the mother.

critical period Specific time when a given event or its absence has the greatest impact on development.

plasticity Modifiability of performance.

sensitive periods Times in development when a person is particularly open to certain kinds of experiences.

Newly hatched ducklings will follow and become attached to the first moving object they see, as the ethologist Konard Lorenz showed. He called this behavior imprinting.

Checkpoint

Can you . . .

✔ Give examples of normative age-graded, normative history-graded, and nonnormative influences? (Include some normative history-graded influences that impacted different generations.)

✔ Contrast critical and sensitive periods and give examples?

BOX 1-2

Practically Speaking

Is There a Critical Period for Language Acquisition?

In 1970, a 13-year-old girl called Genie (not her real name) was discovered in a suburb of Los Angeles (Curtiss, 1977; Fromkin, Krashen, Curtiss, Rigler, & Rigler, 1974; Pines, 1981; Rymer, 1993). The victim of an abusive father, she had been confined for nearly 12 years to a small room in her parents' home, tied to a potty chair and cut off from normal human contact. She weighed only 59 pounds, could not straighten her arms or legs, could not chew, had no bladder or bowel control, and did not speak. She recognized only her own name and the word *sorry*.

Only three years before, Eric Lenneberg (1967, 1969) had proposed that there is a critical period for language acquisition, beginning in early infancy and ending around puberty. Lenneberg argued that it would be difficult, if not impossible, for a child who had not yet acquired language to do so after that age.

The discovery of Genie offered the opportunity for a test of Lenneberg's hypothesis. Could Genie be taught to speak, or was it too late? The National Institutes of Mental Health (NIMH) funded a study, and a series of researchers took over Genie's care and gave her intensive testing and language training.

Genie's progress during the next few years (before the NIMH withdrew funding and her mother regained custody and cut her off from contact with the professionals who had been teaching her) both challenges and supports the idea of a critical period for language acquisition. Genie did learn some simple words and could string them together into primitive, but rule-governed, sentences. She also learned the fundamentals of sign language. But she never used language normally, and "her speech remained, for the most part, like a somewhat garbled telegram" (Pines, 1981, p. 29). When her mother, unable to care for her, turned her over to a series of abusive foster homes, she regressed into total silence.

What explains Genie's initial progress and her inability to sustain it? The fact that she was just beginning to show signs of puberty at age 13 may indicate that she was still in the critical period, though near its end. The fact that she apparently had learned a few words before being locked up at the age of 20 months may mean that her language-learning mechanisms were triggered early in the critical period, allowing later learning to occur. On the other hand, her extreme abuse and neglect may have retarded her so much—emotionally, socially, and cognitively—that, like Victor, the wild boy of Aveyron, she could not be considered a true test of the critical period (Curtiss, 1977).

Case studies like those of Genie and Victor dramatize the *difficulty* of acquiring language after the early years of life, but, because there are too many complicating factors, they do not permit conclusive judgments about whether such acquisition is *possible*. Brain imaging research has found that even if the parts of the brain best suited to language processing are damaged early in childhood, nearly normal language development can continue as other parts of the brain take over (Boatman et al., 1999; Hertz-Pannier et al., 2002; M. H. Johnson, 1998). In fact, shifts in brain organization and utilization occur throughout the course of normal language learning (M. H. Johnson, 1998; Neville & Bavelier, 1998). Neuroscientists

also have observed different patterns of brain activity during language processing between people who learned American Sign Language (ASL) as a native language and those who learned it as a second language, after puberty (Newman, Bavelier, Corina, Jezzard, & Neville, 2002). It is possible to learn a second language, signed or spoken, even in adulthood but typically not as easily or as well as in early childhood (Newport, 1991).

Because of the brain's plasticity, some researchers consider the prepubertal years a *sensitive* rather than *critical* period for learning language (Newport, Bavelier, & Neville, 2001; Schumann, 1997). But if either a critical or a sensitive period for language learning exists, what explains it? Do the brain's mechanisms for acquiring language decay as the brain matures? That would seem strange, since other cognitive abilities improve. An alternative hypothesis is that this very increase in cognitive sophistication interferes with an adolescent's or adult's ability to learn a language. Young children acquire language in small chunks that can be digested readily. Older learners, when they first begin learning a language, tend to absorb a great deal at once and then may have trouble analyzing and interpreting it (Newport, 1991).

Learning a second language in adulthood, as these Korean immigrants are doing, is generally not as easy as learning a language in childhood.

What's Your View?

Do you see any ethical problems in the studies of Genie and Victor? Is the knowledge gained from such studies worth any possible damage to the individuals involved?

Check It Out

For more information on this topic, go to http://www.facstaff.bucknell.edu/rbeard/acquisition.html. This Web site was developed by Professor Robert Beard of the Linguistics Program at Bucknell University. The page at that URL gives a brief, accurate overview of the nature-nurture question as it concerns language acquisition. Links to other related sites of interest are also given.

Baltes's Life-Span Developmental Approach

6. What are the six principles of the life-span developmental approach?

Paul B. Baltes and his colleagues (1987; Baltes, Lindenberger, & Staudinger, 1998; Staudinger & Bluck, 2001) have identified six key principles of his life-span developmental approach that sum up many of the concepts discussed in this chapter. Together these principles serve as a widely accepted conceptual framework for the study of life-span development:

1. *Development is lifelong.* Development is a lifelong process of change in the ability to adapt to the situations one selects or in which one finds oneself. Each period of the life span is affected by what happened before and will affect what is to come. Each period has its own unique characteristics and value; none is more or less important than any other. Even very old people can grow emotionally and intellectually. The experience of dying can be a final attempt to come to terms with one's life—in short, to develop.

2. *Development involves both gain and loss.* Development is multidimensional and multidirectional. It occurs along multiple interacting dimensions—biological, psychological, and social—each of which may develop at varying rates. Development also proceeds in more than one direction. As people gain in one area, they may lose in another, sometimes at the same time. Children grow mostly in one direction—up—both in size and in abilities. Then the balance gradually shifts. Adolescents typically gain in physical abilities but lose their facility in learning language. Some abilities, such as vocabulary, typically continue to increase throughout most of adulthood; others, such as the ability to solve unfamiliar problems, may diminish; and some new attributes, such as expertise, may develop in midlife. People seek to maximize gains by concentrating on doing things they do well and to minimize losses by learning to manage or compensate for them—for example, by writing "to-do" lists when memory flags.

3. *Relative influences of biology and culture shift over the life span.* The process of development is influenced by both biology and culture, but the balance between these influences changes. Biological influences, such as sensory acuity and muscular strength and coordination, become weaker with age, but cultural supports, such as education, relationships, and technologically age-friendly environments, may help compensate.

4. *Development involves a changing allocation of resources.* Individuals choose to "invest" their resources of time, energy, talent, money, and social support in varying ways. Resources may be used for growth (for example, learning to play an instrument or improving one's skill), for maintenance or recovery (practicing to maintain or regain proficiency), or for dealing with loss when maintenance and recovery are not possible. The allocation of resources to these three functions changes throughout life as the total available pool of resources decreases. In childhood and young adulthood, the bulk of resources typically goes to growth; in old age, to regulation of loss. In midlife, the allocation is more evenly balanced among the three functions.

5. *Development shows plasticity.* Many abilities, such as memory, strength, and endurance, can be improved significantly with training and practice, even late in life. However, as Itard learned, even in children plasticity has limits. One of the tasks of developmental research is to discover to what extent particular kinds of development can be modified at various ages.

Checkpoint

Can you . . .

✔ Summarize the six principles of Baltes's life-span developmental approach?

6. *Development is influenced by the historical and cultural context.* Each person develops within multiple contexts—circumstances or conditions defined in part by maturation and in part by time and place. In addition to age-graded and nonnormative influences, human beings not only influence but also are influenced by their historical-cultural context. As we will discuss throughout this book, developmental scientists have found significant cohort differences in intellectual functioning, in women's midlife emotional development, and in the flexibility of personality in old age.

Refocus

Thinking back to the Focus vignette about Victor, the wild boy of Aveyron, at the beginning of this chapter, in what way does Victor's story illustrate the following chapter themes:

- How the study of human development has become more scientific?
- The interrelationship of domains of development?
- The influences of heredity, environment, and maturation?
- The importance of contextual and historical influences?
- The roles of nonnormative influences and critical or sensitive periods?

Now that you have had a brief introduction to the field of human development and some of its basic concepts, it's time to look more closely at the issues developmental scientists think about and how they do their work. In Chapter 2, we discuss some influential theories of how development takes place and the methods investigators commonly use to study it.

SUMMARY AND KEY TERMS

How the Study of Human Development Evolved

Guidepost 1: What is human development, and how has its study evolved?

- Human development is the scientific study of processes of change and stability.
- The scientific study of human development began with studies of childhood during the nineteenth century.
- As researchers became interested in following development through adulthood, life-span development became a field of study.

human development *(7)*

life-span development *(8)*

Guidepost 2: What are the four goals of the scientific study of human development, what disciplines does it draw upon, and how are research methods changing?

- The study of human development seeks to describe, explain, predict, and modify development.
- Students of human development draw upon such disciplines as psychology, psychiatry, sociology, anthropology, biology, genetics, family science, education, history, philosophy, and medicine.

- Methods of studying human development are still evolving, making use of advanced technologies.
- Developmental research has important applications in various fields.

The Study of Human Development: Basic Concepts

Guidepost 3: What do developmental scientists study?

- Developmental scientists study age-related physical, cognitive, and psychosocial change, both quantitative and qualitative, as well as stability of characteristics such as personality.

quantitative change *(10)*

qualitative change *(10)*

Guidepost 4: What are three major domains and eight periods of human development?

- The three major domains of development are physical, cognitive, and psychosocial. Each affects the others.
- The concept of periods of development is a social construction. In this book, the life span is divided into eight periods: the prenatal period, infancy and toddler-

hood, early childhood, middle childhood, adolescence, young adulthood, middle adulthood, and late adulthood. In each period, people have characteristic developmental needs and tasks.

physical development *(10)*

cognitive development *(10)*

psychosocial development *(10)*

social construction *(11)*

Influences on Development

Guidepost 5: What kinds of influences make one person different from another?

- Influences on development come from both heredity and environment. Many typical changes during childhood are related to maturation. Individual differences tend to increase with age.
- In some societies, the nuclear family predominates; in others, the extended family.
- Socioeconomic status (SES) affects developmental processes and outcomes through the quality of home and neighborhood environments, nutrition, medical care, and schooling. The most powerful neighborhood influences seem to be neighborhood income and human capital. Multiple risk factors increase the likelihood of poor outcomes.
- Important environmental influences stem from culture, ethnicity, and historical context. Race is viewed by most scholars as a social construction. Ethnic and cultural boundaries are fluid and are affected by immigration, intermarriage, and acculturation of minority groups.
- Influences may be normative (age-graded or history-graded) or nonnormative.
- There is evidence of critical or sensitive periods for certain kinds of early development.

normative *(14)*

individual differences *(14)*

heredity *(14)*

environment *(14)*

maturation *(14)*

nuclear family *(15)*

extended family *(15)*

socioeconomic status (SES) *(15)*

risk factors *(16)*

culture *(16)*

ethnic group *(17)*

ethnic gloss *(18)*

historical generation *(19)*

cohort *(19)*

nonnormative *(19)*

imprinting *(21)*

critical period *(21)*

plasticity *(21)*

sensitive periods *(21)*

Baltes's Life-Span Developmental Approach

Guidepost 6: What are six principles of the life-span developmental approach?

- The principles of Baltes's life-span developmental approach include the assumptions that (1) development is lifelong, (2) development involves both gain and loss, (3) the relative influences of biology and culture shift over the life span, (4) development involves a changing allocation of resources, (5) development shows plasticity; and (6) development is influenced by the historical and cultural context.

CHAPTER 2

Theory and Research

> *There is one thing even more vital to science than intelligent methods; and that is, the sincere desire to find out the truth, whatever it may be.*
>
> Charles Sanders Peirce, *Collected Papers*, vol. 5

Focus
Margaret Mead, Pioneer in Cross-Cultural Research

Margaret Mead

Margaret Mead (1901–1978) was a world-famous American anthropologist. In the 1920s, at a time when it was rare for a woman to expose herself to the rigors of fieldwork with remote, preliterate peoples, Mead spent nine months on the South Pacific island of Samoa, studying girls' adjustment to adolescence. Her best-selling first book, *Coming of Age in Samoa* (1928), challenged accepted views about the inevitability of adolescent rebellion.

An itinerant childhood built around her parents' academic pursuits prepared Mead for a life of roving research. In New Jersey, her mother, who was working on her doctoral thesis in sociology, took Margaret along on interviews with recent Italian immigrants—the child's first exposure to fieldwork. Her father, a professor at the University of Pennsylvania's Wharton School of Business, taught her respect for facts and "the importance of thinking clearly" (Mead, 1972, p. 40). He stressed the link between theory and application—as Margaret did when, years later, she applied her theories of child rearing to her daughter. Margaret's grandmother, a former schoolteacher, sent her out in the woods to collect and analyze mint specimens. "I was not well drilled in geography or spelling," Mead wrote in her memoir *Blackberry Winter*, "but I learned to observe the world around me and to note what I saw" (1972, p. 47).

Margaret took copious notes on the development of her younger brother and two younger sisters. Her curiosity about why one child in a family behaved so differently from another led to her later interest in temperamental variations of individuals within a culture.

How cultures define male and female roles was another research focus. Margaret saw her mother and her grandmother as educated women who had managed to have husbands, children, and professional careers, and she expected to do the same. She was dismayed when, at the outset of her career, the distinguished anthropologist Edward Sapir told her she "would do better to stay at home and have children than to go off to the South Seas to study adolescent girls" (Mead, 1972, p. 11).

Margaret's choice of anthropology as a career was consistent with her homebred respect for the value of all human beings and their cultures. Recalling her father's insistence that the only thing worth doing is to add to the store of knowledge, she saw an urgent need to document once-isolated cultures now "vanishing before the onslaught of modern civilization" (Mead, 1972, p. 137).

"I went to Samoa—as, later, I went to the other societies on which I have worked—to find out more about human beings, human beings like ourselves in everything except their culture," she wrote. "Through the accidents of history, these cultures had developed so differently from ours that knowledge of them could shed a kind of light upon us, upon our potentialities and our limitations" (Mead, 1972, p. 293). The ongoing quest to illuminate those "potentialities and limitations" is the business of theorists and researchers in human development.

Margaret Mead's life was all of a piece. The young girl who filled notebooks with observations about her siblings became the scientist who traveled to distant lands and studied cultures very different from her own.

Mead's story underlines several important points about the study of human development. First, the study of people is not dry, abstract, or esoteric. It deals with the substance of real life.

Second, a cross-cultural perspective can reveal which patterns of behavior, if any, are universal and which are not. Most studies of human development have been done in Western, developed societies, using white, middle-class participants. Today developmental scientists are increasingly conscious of the need to expand the research base, as Mead and her colleagues sought to do.

Third, although the goal of science is to obtain verifiable knowledge through open-minded, impartial investigation, observations about human behavior are products of very human individuals whose inquiries and interpretations may be influenced by their own backgrounds, values, and experiences. As Mead's daughter, Mary Catherine Bateson (1984), herself an anthropologist, noted in response to methodological criticism of Mead's early work in Samoa (see Chapter 12), a scientific observer is like a lens, which may introduce some distortion into what is observed. This is why scientists have others check their results. In striving for greater objectivity, investigators must scrutinize how they and their colleagues conduct their work, the assumptions on which it is based, and how they arrive at their conclusions. In studying the results of research, it is important to keep these potential biases in mind.

Fourth, theory and research are two sides of the same coin. As Mead reflected on her own experiences and observed the behavior of others, she formed tentative explanations, or theories, to be tested by additional research. Because theory and research are so closely interrelated, we introduce in this chapter an overview both of major theories of human development and of research methods used to study it.

In the first part of this chapter, we present major issues and theoretical perspectives that underlie much research in human development. In the remainder of the chapter, we look at how researchers gather and assess information so that, as you read further in this book, you will be better able to judge whether research findings and conclusions rest on solid ground.

After you have studied this chapter, you should be able to answer each of the Guidepost questions that appear at the top of the next page. Look for them again in the margins, where they point to important concepts throughout the chapter. To check your understanding of these Guideposts, review the end-of-chapter summary. Checkpoints located at periodic spots throughout the chapter will help you verify your understanding of what you have read.

1. What purposes do theories serve?
2. What are two basic theoretical issues on which developmental scientists differ?
3. What are five theoretical perspectives on human development, and what are some theories representative of each?
4. How do developmental scientists study people, and what are some advantages and disadvantages of each research method?
5. What ethical problems may arise in research on humans?

Basic Theoretical Issues

Developmental scientists have come up with many theories about why people develop as they do. A **theory** is a set of logically related concepts or statements, which seeks to describe and explain development and to predict what kinds of behavior might occur under certain conditions. A theory is not just a guess. It is a way to organize data, the information gathered by research, and is a source of **hypotheses**—tentative explanations or predictions that can be tested by further research.

Theories are dynamic—they change to incorporate new findings. Sometimes research supports a hypothesis and the theory on which it was based. At other times, as with Mead's findings challenging the inevitability of adolescent rebellion, scientists must modify their theories to account for unexpected data. Research findings, in addition to having practical applications, often suggest additional questions and hypotheses to be examined.

The way theorists explain development depends in part on the way they view two basic issues: (1) whether people are active or passive in their own development, and (2) whether development is continuous or occurs in stages. A third issue, whether development is more influenced by heredity or by environment, was introduced in Chapter 1 and will be discussed more fully in Chapter 3.

Issue 1: Is Development Active or Passive?

Are people active or passive in their development? This controversy goes back to the eighteenth century. The English philosopher John Locke held that a young child is a *tabula rasa*—a "blank slate"—on which society "writes." In contrast, the French philosopher Jean Jacques Rousseau believed that children are born "noble savages" who would develop according to their own positive natural tendencies if not corrupted by a repressive society. We now know that both views are too simplistic. Children have their own internal drives and needs that influence development, but children also are social animals who cannot achieve optimal development in isolation.

The debate over Locke's and Rousseau's philosophies led to two contrasting models, or images, of development: *mechanistic* and *organismic*. Locke's view was the forerunner of the **mechanistic model** of development. In this model, people are like machines that react to environmental input (Pepper, 1942, 1961). If we know enough about how the human "machine" is put together and about the internal and external

Guidepost

1. What purposes do theories serve?

theory Coherent set of logically related concepts that seeks to organize, explain, and predict data.

hypotheses Possible explanations for phenomena, used to predict the outcome of research.

Guidepost

2. What are two basic theoretical issues on which developmental scientists differ?

mechanistic model Model that views human development as a series of passive, predictable responses to stimuli.

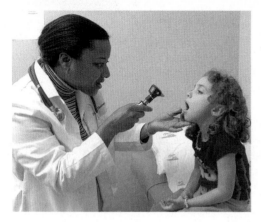

Are more women becoming physicians today because of inner motivation or environmental influences? Mechanistic and organismic theorists might give different answers to that question.

organismic model Model that views human development as internally initiated by an active organism and as occurring in a sequence of qualitatively different stages.

forces acting on it, we can predict what the person will do. Mechanistic research seeks to identify and isolate the factors that make people behave as they do. For example, in seeking to explain why some college students drink too much alcohol, a mechanistic theorist might look for environmental influences, such as advertising and whether the person's friends drink to excess.

Rousseau was the precursor of the **organismic model** of development. This model sees people as active, growing organisms that set their own development in motion (Pepper, 1942, 1961). They initiate events; they do not just react. The impetus for change is internal. Environmental influences do not cause development, though they can speed or slow it. Human behavior is an organic whole; it cannot be predicted by breaking it down into simple responses to environmental stimulation. An organismic theorist, in studying why some students drink too much, would be likely to look at what kinds of situations they choose to participate in, and with whom. Do they choose friends who like to party or who like to study?

Issue 2: Is Development Continuous, or Does It Occur in Stages?

The mechanistic and organismic models also differ on the second issue: Is development continuous, or does it occur in stages?

Mechanistic theorists see development as continuous, like walking or crawling up a ramp. Development, in mechanistic models, is always governed by the same processes, allowing prediction of earlier behaviors from later ones. Mechanistic theorists focus on *quantitative* change, such as changes in the frequency with which a response is made rather than changes in the kind of response.

Organismic theorists emphasize *qualitative* change (Looft, 1973). They see development as occurring in a series of distinct stages, like stair steps. At each stage, people cope with different kinds of problems and develop different kinds of abilities. Each stage builds on the previous one and prepares the way for the next.

Table 2-1 Five Perspectives on Human Development

Perspective	Important Theories	Basic Principles
Psychoanalytic	Freud's psychosexual theory	Behavior is controlled by powerful unconscious urges.
	Erikson's psychosocial theory	Personality is influenced by society and develops through a series of crises.
Learning	Behaviorism, or traditional learning theory (Pavlov, Skinner, Watson)	People are responders; the environment controls behavior.
	Social-learning (social-cognitive) theory (Bandura)	Children learn in a social context by observing and imitating models. Children are active contributors to learning.
Cognitive	Piaget's cognitive-stage theory	Qualitative changes in thought occur between infancy and adolescence. Children are active initiators of development.
	Vygotsky's sociocultural theory	Social interaction is central to cognitive development.
	Information-processing theory	Human beings are processors of symbols.
Evolutionary/ sociobiological	Bowlby's attachment theory	Human beings have the adaptive mechanisms to survive; critical or sensitive periods are stressed; evolutionary and biological bases for behavior and predisposition toward learning are important.
Contextual	Bronfenbrenner's bioecological theory	Development occurs through interaction between a developing person and five surrounding, interlocking contextual systems of influences, from microsystem to chronosystem.

An Emerging Consensus

As the study of human development has evolved, the mechanistic and organismic models have shifted in influence (Parke, Ornstein, Rieser, & Zahn-Waxler, 1994). Most of the early pioneers in the field, including Sigmund Freud, Erik Erikson, and Jean Piaget, favored organismic or stage approaches. The mechanistic view gained support during the 1960s with the popularity of learning theories derived from the work of John B. Watson. (We discuss all these theorists in the next section.) Today much theory and research attention is focused on the biological bases of behavior. Instead of looking for broad stages, there is an effort to discover what specific kinds of behavior show continuity or lack of continuity and what processes are involved in each.

Many developmental scientists are coming to a more balanced view of active versus passive development. There is wide agreement that influence is *bidirectional:* People change their world even as it changes them. A baby boy born with a cheerful disposition is likely to get positive responses from adults, which strengthen his trust that his smiles will be rewarded and motivate him to smile more. A manager who offers constructive criticism and emotional support to her subordinates is likely to elicit greater efforts to produce. Improved productivity, in turn, is likely to encourage her to keep using this managerial style.

Theoretical Perspectives

Despite the growing consensus on the basic issues just discussed, many investigators view development from differing theoretical perspectives. Theories generally fall within these broad perspectives, each of which emphasizes different kinds of developmental processes. These perspectives may influence the questions researchers ask, the methods they use, and the ways they interpret data. Therefore, to evaluate and interpret research, it may be important to recognize the theoretical perspective on which it is based.

Five major perspectives (summarized in Table 2-1) underlie much influential theory and research on human development: (1) *psychoanalytic* (which focuses on

Checkpoint
Can you . . .

✔ Explain the relationship between theories, hypotheses, and research?

✔ State two basic issues regarding the nature of human development?

✔ Contrast the mechanistic and organismic models of development?

Guidepost
3. What are five theoretical perspectives on human development, and what are some theories representative of each?

Technique Used	Stage-Oriented	Causal Emphasis	Active or Passive Individual
Clinical observation	Yes	Innate factors modified by experience	Passive
Clinical observation	Yes	Interaction of innate and experiential factors	Active
Rigorous scientific (experimental) procedures	No	Experience	Passive
Rigorous scientific (experimental) procedures	No	Experience modified by innate factors	Active and passive
Flexible interviews; meticulous observation	Yes	Interaction of innate and experiential factors	Active
Cross-cultural research; observation of child interacting with more competent person	No	Experience	Active
Laboratory research; technological monitoring of physiologic responses	No	Interaction of innate and experiential factors	Active and passive
Naturalistic and laboratory observation	No	Interaction of innate and experiential factors	Active and passive (theorists vary)
Naturalistic observation and analysis	No	Interaction of innate and experiential factors	Active

unconscious emotions and drives); (2) *learning* (which studies observable behavior); (3) *cognitive* (which analyzes thought processes); (4) *evolutionary/sociobiological* (which considers evolutionary and biological underpinnings of behavior); and (5) *contextual* (which emphasizes the impact of the historical, social, and cultural context). Here is a general overview of the assumptions, central focus, and methods of each of these perspectives and some leading theorists within each perspective, who will be referred to throughout this book.

Perspective 1: Psychoanalytic

Sigmund Freud (1856–1939), a Viennese physician, originated the **psychoanalytic perspective,** which views development as shaped by unconscious forces that motivate human behavior. *Psychoanalysis,* the therapeutic approach Freud developed, seeks to give patients insight into unconscious emotional conflicts by asking them questions designed to summon up long-buried memories. Other theorists and practitioners, including Erik H. Erikson, have expanded and modified Freud's theory.

Sigmund Freud: Psychosexual Development Freud (1953, 1964a, 1964b) believed that people are born with biological drives that must be redirected to make it possible to live in society. He proposed three hypothetical parts of the personality: the *id,* the *ego,* and the *superego.* Newborns are governed by the *id,* which operates under the *pleasure principle*—the drive to seek immediate satisfaction of its needs and desires. When gratification is delayed, as it is when infants have to wait to be fed, they begin to see themselves as separate from the outside world. The *ego,* which represents reason, develops gradually during the first year or so of life and operates under the *reality principle.* The ego's aim is to find realistic ways to gratify the id that are acceptable to the *superego,* which develops at about age 5 or 6. The *superego* includes the conscience and incorporates socially approved "shoulds" and "should nots" into the child's own value system. The superego is highly demanding; if its standards are not met, a child may feel guilty and anxious. The ego mediates between the impulses of the id and the demands of the superego.

Freud proposed that personality forms through unconscious childhood conflicts between the inborn urges of the id and the requirements of civilized life. These conflicts occur in an unvarying sequence of five maturationally based stages of **psychosexual development** (see Table 2-2), in which sensual pleasure shifts from one body zone to another—from the mouth to the anus and then to the genitals. At each stage, the behavior that is the chief source of gratification (or frustration) changes—from feeding to elimination and eventually to sexual activity.

Freud considered the first three stages—those of the first few years of life—to be crucial for personality development. He suggested that if children receive too little or too much gratification in any of these stages, they are at risk of *fixation*—an arrest in development that can affect adult personality. Babies whose needs are not met during the *oral stage,* when feeding is the main source of sensual pleasure, may grow up to become nail-biters or smokers or to develop "bitingly" critical personalities. A person who, as a toddler, had too-strict toilet training may be fixated at the *anal stage,* when the chief source of pleasure was moving the bowels. Such a person may be obsessively clean, rigidly tied to schedules and routines, or defiantly messy.

According to Freud, a key event in psychosexual development occurs in the *phallic stage* of early childhood. Boys develop sexual attachment to their mothers, and girls to their fathers, and they have aggressive urges toward the same-sex parent, whom they regard as a rival. Freud called these developments the *Oedipus* and *Electra complexes.* Children eventually resolve their anxiety over these feelings by

psychoanalytic perspective View of human development as being shaped by unconscious forces.

The Viennese physician Sigmund Freud developed an original, influential, and controversial theory of psychosexual development in childhood, based on his adult patients' recollections. His daughter, Anna, shown here with her father, followed in his professional footsteps and constructed her own theories of personality development.

psychosexual development In Freudian theory, an unvarying sequence of stages of personality development during infancy, childhood, and adolescence, in which gratification shifts from the mouth to the anus and then to the genitals.

Table 2-2 Developmental Stages According to Various Theories

Psychosexual Stages (Freud)	Psychosocial Stages (Erikson)	Cognitive Stages (Piaget)
Oral (birth to 12–18 months). Baby's chief source of pleasure involves mouth-oriented activities (sucking and feeding).	*Basic trust versus mistrust (birth to 12–18 months).* Baby develops sense of whether world is a good and safe place. Virtue: hope.	*Sensorimotor (birth to 2 years).* Infant gradually becomes able to organize activities in relation to the environment through sensory and motor activity.
Anal (12–18 months to 3 years). Child derives sensual gratification from withholding and expelling feces. Zone of gratification is anal region, and toilet training is important activity.	*Autonomy versus shame and doubt (12–18 months to 3 years).* Child develops a balance of independence and self-sufficiency over shame and doubt, Virtue: will.	*Preoperational (2 to 7 years).* Child develops a representational system and uses symbols to represent people, places, and events. Language and imaginative play are important manifestations of this stage. Thinking is still not logical.
Phallic (3 to 6 years). Child becomes attached to parent of the other sex and later identifies with same-sex parent. Superego develops. Zone of gratification shifts to genital region.	*Initiative versus guilt (3 to 6 years).* Child develops initiative when trying out new activities and is not overwhelmed by guilt. Virtue: purpose.	
Latency (6 years to puberty). Time of relative calm between more turbulent stages.	*Industry versus inferiority (6 years to puberty).* Child must learn skills of the culture or face feelings of incompetence. Virtue: skill.	*Concrete operations (7 to 11 years).* Child can solve problems logically if they are focused on the here and now but cannot think abstractly.
Genital (puberty through adulthood). Reemergence of sexual impulses of phallic stage, channeled into mature adult sexuality.	*Identity versus identity confusion (puberty to young adulthood).* Adolescent must determine own sense of self ("Who am I?") or experience confusion about roles. Virtue: fidelity.	*Formal operations (11 years through adulthood).* Person can think abstractly, deal with hypothetical situations, and think about possibilities.
	Intimacy versus isolation (young adulthood). Person seeks to make commitments to others; if unsuccessful, may suffer from isolation and self-absorption. Virtue: love.	
	Generativity versus stagnation (middle adulthood). Mature adult is concerned with establishing and guiding the next generation or else feels personal impoverishment. Virtue: care.	
	Integrity versus despair (late adulthood). Elderly person achieves acceptance of own life, allowing acceptance of death, or else despairs over inability to relive life. Virtue: wisdom.	

Note: All ages are approximate.

identifying with the same-sex parent and move into the *latency stage* of middle childhood, a period of sexual calm. They become socialized, develop skills, and learn about themselves and society. The *genital stage*, the final one, lasts throughout adulthood. The sexual urges repressed during latency now resurface to flow in socially approved channels, which Freud defined as heterosexual relations with persons outside the family of origin.

Freud's theory made historic contributions, and several of his central themes have been validated by research. Others have not been supported (Emde, 1992; Westen, 1998) or cannot readily be tested. Freud made us aware of the importance of unconscious thoughts, feelings, and motivations; the role of childhood experiences in forming personality; the ambivalence of emotional responses, especially to parents; and ways in which early relationships affect later ones. Freud also opened our eyes to the presence from birth of sexual urges. Although many psychoanalysts today reject his narrow emphasis on sexual and aggressive drives, his psychoanalytic method greatly influenced modern-day psychotherapy.

The psychoanalyst Erik H. Erikson departed from Freudian theory in emphasizing societal influences on personality.

psychosocial development In Erikson's eight-stage theory, the socially and culturally influenced process of development of the ego, or self.

Checkpoint

Can you . . .

✔ Identify the chief focus of the psychoanalytic perspective?

✔ Name Freud's five stages of development and three parts of the personality?

✔ Tell two ways in which Erikson's theory differs from Freud's?

learning perspective View of human development that holds that changes in behavior result from experience, or adaptation to the environment.

behaviorism Learning theory that emphasizes the predictable role of environment in causing observable behavior.

We need to remember that Freud's theory grew out of his place in history and in society. Freud based his theories about normal development, not on a population of average children, but on a clientele of upper-middle-class adults, mostly women, in therapy. His concentration on the influence of early emotional experience does not take into account other and later influences on personality, including the influences of society and culture, which are stressed by many heirs to the Freudian tradition, notably Erikson.

Erik Erikson: Psychosocial Development   Erik Erikson (1902–1994), a German-born psychoanalyst who originally was part of Freud's circle in Vienna, modified and extended Freudian theory by emphasizing the influence of society on the developing personality. Erikson also was a pioneer in taking a life-span perspective. Whereas Freud maintained that early childhood experiences permanently shape personality, Erikson contended that ego development is lifelong.

Erikson's (1950, 1982; Erikson, Erikson, & Kivnick, 1986) theory of **psychosocial development** covers eight stages across the life span (refer to Table 2-2), which we will discuss in the appropriate chapters throughout this book. Each stage involves what Erikson originally called a *crisis* in personality—a major psychosocial theme that is particularly important at that time and will remain an issue to some degree throughout the rest of life. These issues, which emerge according to a maturational timetable, must be satisfactorily resolved for healthy ego development. (Erikson later dropped the term "crisis" and referred instead to conflicting or competing tendencies.)

Each stage requires the balancing of a positive tendency and a corresponding negative one. The positive quality should predominate, but some degree of the negative is needed as well. The critical theme of infancy, for example, is *basic trust versus basic mistrust.* People need to trust the world and the people in it, or they will be "stuck" in mistrust. However, they also need some mistrust to protect themselves from danger. The successful outcome of each stage is the development of a particular *virtue,* or strength—in this case, the virtue of *hope.*

Erikson's theory has held up better than Freud's, especially in its emphasis on the importance of social and cultural influences and on development beyond adolescence. However, some of Erikson's concepts, like Freud's, do not lend themselves to rigorous testing.

Perspective 2: Learning

The **learning perspective** maintains that development results from *learning,* a long-lasting change in behavior based on experience or adaptation to the environment. Learning theorists seek to discover objective laws that govern changes in observable behavior. They see development as continuous (not occurring in stages) and emphasize quantitative change.

Learning theorists have helped to make the study of human development more scientific. Their terms are defined precisely, and their theories can be tested in the laboratory. Two important learning theories are *behaviorism* and *social learning theory.*

Learning Theory 1: Behaviorism   **Behaviorism** is a mechanistic theory; it describes observed behavior as a predictable response to experience. Behaviorists hold that human beings at all ages learn about the world the same way other organisms do: by reacting to aspects of their environment that they find pleasing, painful, or threatening. Behaviorists look for events that determine whether a particular behavior will be repeated.

Behavioral research focuses on *associative learning,* in which a mental link is formed between two stimuli, or sensory events. Two kinds of associative learning are *classical conditioning* and *operant conditioning.*

Classical Conditioning   The Russian physiologist Ivan Pavlov (1849–1936) devised experiments in which dogs learned to salivate at the sounds of a bell, buzzer, metronome, and other signals that went off at feeding time. These experiments were the foundation for the concept of **classical conditioning,** in which a natural response (salivation) to a stimulus (food) is transferred to a second stimulus (the sounds) through repeated association of one stimulus with the other.

The American behaviorist John B. Watson (1878–1958) applied stimulus-response theories to children, claiming that he could mold any infant in any way he chose. In one of the earliest and most famous demonstrations of classical conditioning in human beings (Watson & Rayner, 1920), Watson set out to teach an 11-month-old baby known as "Little Albert" to fear furry white objects. In this study, Albert was exposed to a loud noise just as he was about to stroke a furry white rat. The noise frightened him, and he began to cry. After repeated pairings of the rat with the loud noise, Watson reported, Albert whimpered with fear whenever he saw the rat. Although such research would be considered unethical today, the study did show that a baby could be conditioned to fear things he had not been afraid of before.

Classical conditioning is a natural form of learning that occurs even without intervention. By learning what events go together, children can anticipate what is going to happen, and this knowledge makes their world a more orderly, predictable place.

Operant Conditioning   Baby Terrell lies quietly in his crib. When he happens to smile, his mother goes over to the crib and plays with him. Later his father does the same thing. As this sequence is repeated, Terrell learns that his behavior (smiling) can produce a desirable consequence (loving attention from a parent); and so he keeps smiling to attract his parents' attention. An originally accidental behavior (smiling) has become a conditioned response.

This kind of learning is called **operant conditioning** because the individual learns from the consequences of "operating" on the environment. Like classical conditioning, operant conditioning involves associative learning, but in operant conditioning the association is between a behavior and its consequences. Also, unlike classical conditioning, operant conditioning involves voluntary behavior, such as Terrell's smiling.

The American psychologist B. F. Skinner (1904–1990), who formulated the principles of operant conditioning, worked primarily with rats and pigeons, but Skinner (1938) maintained that the same principles apply to human beings. He found that an organism will tend to repeat a response that has been reinforced by desirable consequences and will suppress a response that has been punished. Thus, **reinforcement** is the process by which a behavior is strengthened, increasing the likelihood that the behavior will be repeated. In Terrell's case, his parents' attention reinforces his smiling. **Punishment** is the process by which a behavior is weakened, *decreasing* the likelihood of repetition. If Terrell's parents frowned when he smiled, he would be less likely to smile again. Whether a consequence is reinforcing or punishing depends on the person. What is reinforcing for one person may be punishing for another. For a child who likes being alone, being sent to his or her room could be reinforcing rather than punishing.

Reinforcement can be either positive or negative. *Positive reinforcement* consists of *giving* a reward, such as food, a bonus, or praise—or playing with a baby. *Negative reinforcement* consists of *taking away* something a person does not like (known as an *aversive event*), such as changing a baby's wet diaper. Negative reinforcement is sometimes confused with punishment, but they are different. Punishment *suppresses* a behavior by *bringing on* an aversive event (such as spanking a child or jailing a lawbreaker), or by *withdrawing* a positive event (say, by taking away a teenager's use

classical conditioning   Learning based on association of a stimulus that does not ordinarily elicit a particular response with another stimulus that does elicit the response.

What's Your View?

- In an experiment with classical conditioning, what standards would you suggest to safeguard participants' rights?

operant conditioning   Learning based on association of behavior with its consequences.

reinforcement   In operant conditioning, a process that strengthens and encourages repetition of a desired behavior.

punishment   In operant conditioning, a process that weakens and discourages repetition of a behavior.

Punishment can be verbal as well as physical. According to Skinner's principles of operant conditioning, this father's scolding reduces the likelihood that his daughter will repeat her transgression.

of the family car). Negative reinforcement *encourages* repetition of a behavior by *removing* or *avoiding* an aversive event. A driver who takes a side street to avoid a busy thoroughfare is likely to do so again if that route shortens the trip.

Reinforcement is most effective when it immediately follows a behavior. If a response is no longer reinforced, it will eventually be *extinguished,* that is, return to its original (baseline) level. If, after a while, no one plays with Terrell when he smiles, he may not stop smiling but will smile far less than if his smiles still brought reinforcement.

Behavior modification, or behavior therapy, is a form of operant conditioning used to gradually eliminate undesirable behavior or to instill positive behavior. It is particularly effective among people with special needs, mental or emotional disabilities, or eating disorders. However, Skinnerian psychology is limited in application because, in its focus on broad principles of development, it does not adequately address individual differences in behavior (Parke, 2004).

Learning Theory 2: Social Learning (Social Cognitive) Theory   The American psychologist Albert Bandura (b. 1925) developed many of the principles of **social learning theory.** Whereas behaviorists see the environment acting upon the person as the chief impetus for development, social learning theorists (Bandura, 1977, 1989) hold that the impetus for development comes from the person.

Classic social learning theory maintains that people learn appropriate social behavior chiefly by observing and imitating models—that is, by watching other people. This process is called *modeling* or **observational learning.** People initiate or advance their own learning by choosing models to imitate—say, a parent or a popular sports hero. Imitation of models is the most important element in how children learn a language, deal with aggression, develop a moral sense, and learn gender-appropriate behaviors. Adults learn by observation and imitation of coaches, mentors, and colleagues. Observational learning can occur even if a person does not imitate the observed behavior.

The specific behavior people imitate and the models they choose may depend on what they perceive as valued in their culture. If all the teachers in Carlos's school are women, he probably will not copy their behavior, which he may consider "unmanly." However, if he meets a male teacher he likes, he may change his mind about the value of teachers as models.

Bandura's (1989) newest version of social learning theory is *social cognitive theory.* The change of name reflects a greater emphasis on cognitive processes as central to development. Cognitive processes are at work as people observe models, learn "chunks" of behavior, and mentally put the chunks together into complex new behavior patterns. Rita, for example, imitates the toes-out walk of her dance teacher but models her dance steps after those of Carmen, a slightly more advanced student. Even so, she develops her own style of dancing by putting her observations together into a new pattern.

Through feedback on their behavior, children gradually form standards for judging their own actions and become more selective in choosing models who exemplify those standards. They also begin to develop a sense of **self-efficacy,** the confidence that they have what it takes to succeed.

social learning theory   Theory that behaviors are learned by observing and imitating models. Also called *social cognitive theory.*

observational learning   Learning through watching the behavior of others.

self-efficacy   Sense of one's own capability to master challenges and achieve goals.

Checkpoint

Can you . . .

✔ Identify the chief concerns, strengths, and weaknesses of the learning perspective?

✔ Tell how classical conditioning and operant conditioning differ?

✔ Distinguish among positive reinforcement, negative reinforcement, and punishment?

✔ Compare behaviorism and social learning (or social cognitive) theory?

Perspective 3: Cognitive

The **cognitive perspective** focuses on thought processes and the behavior that reflects those processes. This perspective encompasses both organismic and mechanistically influenced theories. It includes the cognitive-stage theory of Piaget and Vygotsky's sociocultural theory of cognitive development. It also includes the information-processing approach and neo-Piagetian theories, which combine elements of information-processing theory and Piagetian theory.

Jean Piaget's Cognitive-Stage Theory   Much of what we know about how children think comes from the work of the Swiss theoretician Jean Piaget (1896–1980). Piaget's **cognitive-stage theory** was the forerunner of today's "cognitive revolution" with its emphasis on mental processes. Piaget, a biologist and philosopher by training, took an organismic perspective. He viewed cognitive development as the product of children's efforts to understand and act on their world.

Piaget's *clinical method* combined observation with flexible questioning. To find out how children think, Piaget followed up their answers with more questions. In this way he discovered that a typical 4-year-old believed that pennies or flowers were more numerous when arranged in a line than when heaped or piled up. From his observations of his own and other children, Piaget created a comprehensive theory of cognitive development.

Piaget suggested that cognitive development begins with an inborn ability to adapt to the environment. By rooting for a nipple, feeling a pebble, or exploring the boundaries of a room, young children develop a more accurate picture of their surroundings and greater competence in dealing with them.

Piaget described cognitive development as occurring in four universal, qualitatively different stages (listed in Table 2-2 and discussed in detail in later chapters). At each stage a child's mind develops a new way of operating. From infancy through adolescence, mental operations evolve from learning based on simple sensory and motor activity to logical, abstract thought. At each stage, cognitive growth occurs through three interrelated processes: *organization, adaptation,* and *equilibration.*

Organization is the tendency to create increasingly complex cognitive structures: systems of knowledge or ways of thinking that incorporate more and more accurate images of reality. These structures, called **schemes,** are organized patterns of behavior that a person uses to think about and act in a situation. As children acquire more information, their schemes become more and more complex. An infant has a simple scheme for sucking but soon develops varied schemes for how to suck at the breast, a bottle, or a thumb.

Adaptation is Piaget's term for how children handle new information in light of what they already know. Adaptation occurs through two complementary processes: (1) **assimilation,** taking in new information and incorporating it into existing cognitive structures, and (2) **accommodation,** adjusting one's cognitive structures to fit the new information.

Equilibration—a constant striving for a stable balance, or equilibrium—dictates the shift from assimilation to accommodation. When children cannot handle new

The Swiss psychologist Jean Piaget studied children's cognitive development by observing and talking with them in many settings, asking questions to find out how their minds worked.

cognitive perspective   View that thought processes are central to cognitive development.

cognitive-stage theory   Piaget's theory that children's cognitive development advances in a series of four stages involving qualitatively distinct types of mental operations.

organization   Piaget's term for the creation of systems of knowledge.

schemes   Piaget's term for organized patterns of behavior used in particular situations.

adaptation   Piaget's term for adjustment to new information about the environment.

assimilation   Piaget's term for incorporation of new information into an existing cognitive structure.

accommodation   Piaget's term for changes in a cognitive structure to include new information.

equilibration   Piaget's term for the tendency to seek a stable balance among cognitive elements.

experiences within their existing cognitive structures and thus experience disequilibrium, they organize new mental patterns that integrate the new experience, thus restoring a more comfortable state of equilibrium. A breast- or bottle-fed baby who begins to suck on the spout of a "sippy" cup is showing *assimilation*—using an old scheme to deal with a new situation. When the infant discovers that sipping from a cup requires different tongue and mouth movements from those used to suck on a breast or bottle, she *accommodates* by modifying the old scheme. She has adapted her original sucking scheme to deal with a new experience: the cup. Thus, assimilation and accommodation work together to produce equilibrium. Throughout life, the quest for equilibrium is the driving force behind cognitive growth.

Piaget's observations have yielded much information and some surprising insights. Who, for example, would have thought that most children younger than age 7 do not realize that a ball of clay that has been rolled into a "worm" before their eyes still contains the same amount of clay? Or that an infant might think that a person who has moved out of sight may no longer exist? Piaget has shown us that children's minds are not miniature adult minds. Knowing how children think makes it easier for parents and teachers to understand and teach them. Piaget's theory has provided rough benchmarks for what to expect of children at various ages and has helped educators design curricula appropriate to varying levels of development.

Yet, as we will see in subsequent chapters, Piaget seems to have seriously underestimated the abilities of infants and young children. Some contemporary psychologists question his distinct stages, pointing instead to evidence that cognitive development is more gradual and continuous (Flavell, 1992). Research beginning in the late 1960s has challenged Piaget's idea that thinking develops in a single, universal progression of stages leading to formal thought. Instead, children's cognitive processes seem closely tied to specific content (what they are thinking *about*) as well as to the context of a problem and the kinds of information and thought a culture considers important (Case & Okamoto, 1996). Further, research on adults suggests that Piaget's focus on formal logic as the climax of cognitive development is too narrow. It does not account for the emergence of such mature abilities as practical problem solving, wisdom, and the capacity to deal with ambiguous situations and competing truths.

sociocultural theory Vygotsky's theory of how contextual factors affect children's development.

Lev Vygotsky's Sociocultural Theory   The Russian psychologist Lev Semenovich Vygotsky (1896–1934) focused on the social and cultural processes that guide children's cognitive development. Vygotsky's (1978) **sociocultural theory,** like Piaget's theory, stresses children's active engagement with their environment; but, whereas Piaget described the solo mind taking in and interpreting information about the world, Vygotsky saw cognitive growth as a *collaborative* process. Children, said Vygotsky, learn through social interaction. They acquire cognitive skills as part of their induction into a way of life. Shared activities help children internalize their society's modes of thinking and behaving and make those folkways their own.

According to Vygotsky, adults or more advanced peers must help direct and organize a child's learning before the child can master and internalize it. Responsibility for directing and monitoring learning gradually shifts to the child—much as, when an adult teaches a child to float, the adult first supports the child in the water and then lets go gradually as the child's body relaxes into a horizontal position.

Vygotsky's theory has important implications for education and for cognitive testing. Tests that focus on a child's potential for learning provide a valuable alternative to standard intelligence tests that assess what the child has already learned; and many children may benefit from the sort of expert guidance Vygotsky prescribes.

According to the Russian psychologist Lev Semenovich Vygotsky, children learn through social interaction.

The Information-Processing Approach The **information-processing approach** attempts to explain cognitive development by analyzing the processes involved in perceiving and handling information. The information-processing approach is not a single theory but a framework that undergirds a wide range of theories and research.

Some information-processing theorists compare the brain to a computer. Sensory impressions go in; behavior comes out. But what happens in between? How does the brain use sensations and perceptions, say, of an unfamiliar face, to recognize that face again? Information-processing researchers *infer* what goes on between a stimulus and a response. For example, they may ask a person to recall a list of words and then observe any difference in performance if the person repeats the list over and over before being asked to recall the words. Through such studies, some information-processing researchers have developed *computational models* or flow charts that analyze the specific steps people go through in gathering, storing, retrieving, and using information.

Despite the use of the "passive" computer model, information-processing theorists, like Piaget, see people as active thinkers about their world. Unlike Piaget, they generally do *not* propose stages of development. Instead, they view development as continuous. They note age-related increases in the speed, complexity, and efficiency of mental processing and in the amount and variety of material that can be stored in memory. Brain imaging research, discussed later in this chapter, supports important aspects of information-processing models, such as the existence of separate physical structures to handle conscious and unconscious memory (Schacter, 1999; Yingling, 2001).

The information-processing approach has practical applications. It enables researchers to estimate an infant's later intelligence from the efficiency of sensory perception and processing. It enables parents and teachers to help children learn by making them more aware of their own mental processes and of strategies to enhance them. Psychologists use information-processing models to test, diagnose, and treat learning problems (R. M. Thomas, 1996; Williams, 2001).

Neo-Piagetian Theories Since the 1980s, in response to criticisms of Piaget's theory, some developmental psychologists have sought to integrate elements of his theory with the information-processing approach. Instead of describing a single, general system of increasingly logical mental operations, these neo-Piagetians focus on *specific* concepts, strategies, and skills, such as number concepts and comparisons of "more" and "less." They suggest that children develop cognitively by becoming more efficient at processing information. Because of this emphasis on efficiency of processing, the neo-Piagetian approach helps account for individual differences in cognitive ability and for uneven development in various domains.

Perspective 4: Evolutionary/Sociobiological

The **evolutionary/sociobiological perspective** proposed by E. O. Wilson (1975) is concerned with evolutionary and biological bases of social behavior. It looks beyond immediate behavior to its function in promoting the survival of the group or species. Influenced by Darwin's theory of evolution, it draws on findings of anthropology, ecology, genetics, ethology, and evolutionary psychology to explain the adaptive, or survival, value of behavior for an individual or species.

According to Darwin, all animal species have developed through the related processes of *survival of the fittest* and *natural selection*. Individuals with traits better adapted to their environments survive; those less adapted do not. Through reproduction, more adaptive characteristics are selected (passed on to future generations), and less adaptive characteristics die out.

information-processing approach Approach to the study of cognitive development by observing and analyzing the mental processes involved in perceiving and handling information.

Checkpoint
Can you . . .

✔ Contrast Piaget's assumptions and methods with those of classical learning theory?

✔ List three interrelated principles that bring about cognitive growth, according to Piaget, and give an example of each?

✔ Explain how Vygotsky's theory differs from Piaget's?

✔ Tell how Vygotsky's theory applies to educational teaching and testing?

✔ Describe what information-processing researchers do, and tell three ways in which such research can be applied?

✔ Give an example of how neo-Piagetian theory draws from both Piaget and the information-processing approach?

evolutionary/sociobiological perspective View of human development that focuses on evolutionary and biological bases of social behavior.

BOX 2-1

Digging Deeper
The Adaptive Value of Immaturity

In comparison with other animals, and even with other primates, human beings take a long time to grow up. Chimpanzees reach reproductive maturity in about eight years, rhesus monkeys in about four years, and lemurs in only two years or so. Human beings, by contrast, do not mature physically until the early teenage years

From an evolutionary perspective, the prolonged period of immaturity known as childhood *permits human beings to develop adaptive skills. One important way this happens is through " pretend" play. This girl playing "doctor" with her teddy bear is developing her imagination and experimenting with social roles.*

and, at least in modern industrialized societies, typically reach cognitive and psychosocial maturity even later.

From the point of view of Darwinian theory, this prolonged period of immaturity is essential to the survival and well-being of the species. Human beings, more than any other animal, live by their intelligence. Human communities and cultures are highly complex, and children have much to learn in order to "know the ropes." A long childhood serves as essential preparation for adulthood.

Some aspects of immaturity serve immediate adaptive purposes. For example, some primitive reflexes, such as rooting for the nipple, are protective for newborns and disappear when no longer needed. The development of the human brain, despite its rapid prenatal growth, is much less complete at birth than the development of brains of other primates; if the fetus's brain attained full human size before birth, its head would be too big to go through the birth canal. Instead, the human brain continues to grow throughout childhood, eventually far surpassing the brains of our simian cousins in the capacities for language and thought.

The human brain's slower development gives it greater flexibility, or *plasticity,* as not all connections are "hard wired" at an early age. One theorist has called this plasticity "the human species's greatest adaptive advantage" (Bjorklund, 1997, p. 157).

The extended period of immaturity and dependency during infancy and childhood allows children to spend much of their time in play, and, as Piaget maintained, it is largely through play that

---

ethology Study of distinctive adaptive behaviors of species of animals that have evolved to increase survival of the species.

evolutionary psychology Application of Darwinian principles of natural selection and survival of the fittest to individual behavior.

Checkpoint

Can you . . .

✔ Identify the chief focus of the evolutionary/sociobiological perspective, and explain how Darwin's theory of evolution underlies this perspective?

✔ Tell what kinds of topics ethologists and evolutionary psychologists study?

contextual perspective View of human development that sees the individual as inseparable from the social context.

Ethology is the study of the distinctive adaptive behaviors of animal species. Ethologists suggest that, for each species, certain innate behaviors, such as squirrels' burying of nuts in the fall and spiders' spinning of webs, have evolved to increase the odds of survival. Another example, studied by the Austrian ethologist Konrad Lorenz, is newborn ducklings' instinct to follow their mother (refer back to Chapter 1). By observing animals, usually in their natural surroundings, ethologists seek to identify which behaviors are universal and which are specific to a particular species or are modified by culture. The British psychologist John Bowlby applied ethological principles to human development. He viewed infants' attachment to a caregiver as a behavior that evolved to promote survival.

Evolutionary psychology applies Darwinian principles to individual behavior. According to this theory, people unconsciously strive not only for personal survival, but also to perpetuate their genetic legacy. The result for the species is the development of mechanisms to solve problems. Sudden aversion to certain foods during pregnancy may be an evolved mechanism for protecting the vulnerable fetus from toxic substances. However, such evolved mechanisms are not as universal or automatic as the innate mechanisms found in animals (Bjorklund & Pellegrini, 2000, 2002). Evolutionary *developmental* psychologists seek to identify behaviors that are adaptive at different ages (see Box 2-1). For example, an infant needs to stay close to the mother, but for an older child independent exploration is important.

Perspective 5: Contextual

According to the **contextual perspective,** development must be understood in its social context. Contextualists see the individual, not as a separate entity interacting with the environment, but as an inseparable part of it. Vygotsky's sociocultural

—continued

cognitive development occurs. Play also enables children to develop motor skills and experiment with social roles. It is a vehicle for creative imagination and intellectual curiosity, the hallmarks of the human spirit.

Research on animals suggests that the immaturity of early sensory and motor functioning may protect infants from overstimulation. By limiting the amount of information they have to deal with, their rudimental sensory and motor abilities may help babies make sense of their world and focus on experiences essential to survival, such as feeding and attachment to the mother. Their limited memory capacity may simplify the processing of linguistic sounds and thus facilitate early language learning.

The immaturity of young children's thought also may have adaptive value. For example, Piaget observed that young children are *egocentric;* they tend to see things from their own point of view. This tendency toward egocentrism may actually help children learn. In one study (Ratner & Foley, 1997), 5-year-olds took turns with an adult in placing furniture in a doll house. In a control group, the adult had already placed half of the items, and the children were then asked to place the other half. When questioned afterward, the children who had taken turns with the adult remembered more about the task and were better able to repeat it. It may be that an "I did it!" bias helps young children's recall by avoiding the need to distinguish between their own actions and the actions of others. Young children also tend to be unrealistic in assessing their own abilities, believing they can do more than they actually can. This immature self-judgment can encourage children to try new things by reducing their fear of failure.

Overall, evolutionary theory and research suggest that immaturity is not necessarily equivalent to deficiency and that some attributes of infancy and childhood have persisted because they are appropriate to the tasks of a particular time of life.

Source: Bjorklund, 1997; Bjorklund & Pellegrini, 2000, 2002.

What's Your View?

Can you think of additional examples of the adaptive value of immaturity? Can you think of ways in which immaturity may *not* be adaptive?

Check It Out

For more information on this topic, go to http://www.brazelton-institute.com. This is the Web site for the Brazelton Institute at Harvard Medical School. Follow the link *The Brazelton Scale: What Is It?* to learn about the scale. The scale shows how much such immature creatures as human newborns can do in responding to the world. This Web site also offers a preview of the discussion of the Brazelton Scale in Chapter 4.

---

theory, which we discussed as part of the cognitive perspective, can also be classified as contextual.

The American psychologist Urie Bronfenbrenner's (1917–2005) **bioecological theory** (1979, 1986, 1994; Bronfenbrenner & Morris, 1998) describes the range of interacting processes that affect a developing person. Every biological organism develops within the context of ecological systems that support or stifle its growth. Just as we need to understand the ecology of the ocean or the forest if we wish to understand the development of a fish or a tree, we need to understand the ecology of the human environment to understand how people develop.

> **bioecological theory** Bronfenbrenner's approach to understanding processes and contexts of human development.

According to Bronfenbrenner, development occurs through increasingly complex processes of regular, active, two-way interaction between a developing person and the immediate, everyday environment—processes that are affected by more remote contexts of which the individual may not even be aware. To understand these processes, we must study the multiple contexts in which they occur. These begin with the home, classroom, workplace, and neighborhood; connect outward to societal institutions, such as systems of education and transportation; and encompass broad cultural and historical patterns that affect the family, the school, and virtually everything else in a person's life. By highlighting the interrelated contexts of, and influences on, development, Bronfenbrenner's theory provides a key to understanding the processes that underlie such diverse phenomena as antisocial behavior and academic achievement.

Bronfenbrenner identified five interlocking contextual systems, from the most intimate to the broadest: the *microsystem, mesosystem, exosystem, macrosystem,* and *chronosystem.* The first four systems are like hollow cylinders that fit inside one another, encasing the developing person. The fifth, the chronosystem, adds the

Figure 2-1

Bronfenbrenner's bioecological theory. Concentric circles show four levels of environmental influence on the individual, from the most intimate environment (innermost circle) to the broadest—all within the dimension of time. (Source: Adapted from Cole & Cole, 1989.)

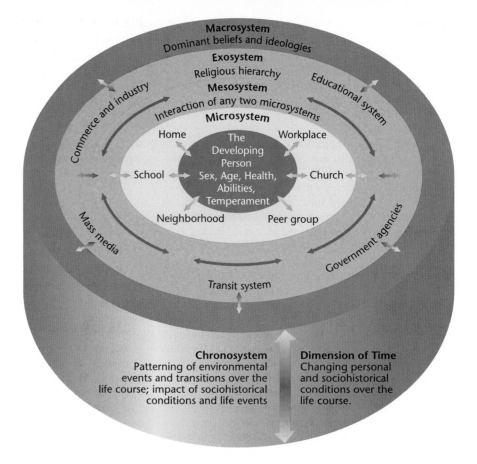

Macrosystem
Dominant beliefs and ideologies

Exosystem
Religious hierarchy

Commerce and industry

Educational system

Mesosystem
Interaction of any two microsystems

Microsystem

Home   Workplace

School   The Developing Person Sex, Age, Health, Abilities, Temperament   Church

Neighborhood   Peer group

Mass media

Government agencies

Transit system

Chronosystem
Patterning of environmental events and transitions over the life course; impact of sociohistorical conditions and life events

Dimension of Time
Changing personal and sociohistorical conditions over the life course.

---

dimension of time. Figure 2-1 shows what we would see if we sliced the nested cylinders across the middle. Keep in mind that the boundaries between the systems are fluid; although we separate the various levels of influence for purposes of illustration, in reality they continually interact.

A **microsystem** is a pattern of activities, roles, and relationships within a setting, such as the home, school, workplace, or neighborhood, in which a person functions on a firsthand, day-to-day basis. A microsystem involves personal, face-to-face relationships, and bidirectional influences flow back and forth. Studying the microsystem can shed light, not only on how a new baby affects the parents' feelings and attitudes, but on how their feelings and attitudes affect the baby. It can reveal how an employer's treatment of employees affects their productivity and how their productivity affects the employer's treatment of them. It is through the microsystem that more distant influences, such as social institutions and cultural values, reach the developing person.

A **mesosystem** is the interaction of two or more microsystems that contain the developing person. It may include linkages between home and school (such as parent-teacher conferences) or between the family and the peer group. Attention to mesosystems can alert us to differences in the ways the same person acts in different settings. For example, a child who can satisfactorily complete a school assignment at home may become tongue-tied when asked a question about the assignment in class. An adult who is outgoing and gregarious among friends and acquaintances may be preoccupied and self-absorbed at home.

An **exosystem,** like a mesosystem, consists of linkages between two or more settings. However, in an exosystem, unlike a mesosystem, at least one of these settings, such as parents' workplaces or parents' social networks, does *not* contain the developing person and thus affects him or her only indirectly. For example, a mother whose employer encourages breast-feeding by providing pumping and milk storage facilities may be more likely to continue nursing her baby.

microsystem Bronfenbrenner's term for a setting in which a child interacts with others on an everyday, face-to-face basis.

mesosystem Bronfenbrenner's term for linkages between two or more microsystems.

exosystem Bronfenbrenner's term for linkages between two or more settings, one of which does not contain the child.

The **macrosystem** consists of overall cultural patterns, like those Margaret Mead studied: dominant values, beliefs, customs, and economic and social systems of a culture or subculture, which filter down in countless ways to individuals' daily lives. Whether a person lives in a nuclear or extended-family household is strongly influenced by a culture's macrosystem.

The **chronosystem** represents the degree of stability or change in a person's world. This can include changes in family composition, place of residence, or parents' employment, as well as larger events such as wars, economic cycles, and waves of migration. Changes in family patterns (such as the increase in working mothers in western industrial societies and the decline of the extended-family household in developing countries) are factors of the chronosystem.

According to Bronfenbrenner, a person is not merely an outcome of development, but a shaper of it. People effect their own development through their biological and psychological characteristics, talents and skills, disabilities, and temperament.

A major contribution of the contextual perspective has been its emphasis on the social component of development. Research attention has shifted from the individual to larger interactional units: parent and child, sibling and sibling, the entire family, the neighborhood, and broader societal institutions. The contextual perspective also reminds us that findings about the development of people in one culture or one group within a culture (such as white, middle-class Americans) may not apply equally to people in other societies or cultural groups.

How Theory and Research Work Together

No one theory of human development is universally accepted, and no one theoretical perspective explains all facets of development. Lacking a widely accepted "grand" theory (as those of Freud and Piaget once were regarded), the trend today is toward smaller "minitheories" aimed at explaining specific research findings, such as how poverty influences family relations and how aging affects social interaction. A number of these theories will be discussed at appropriate points in this book.

As we mentioned at the beginning of this chapter, theories of human development grow out of, and are tested by, research. Although most researchers are eclectic, drawing from a variety of theoretical perspectives, research questions and methods often reflect a researcher's particular theoretical orientation. In trying to understand how a child develops a sense of right and wrong, a behaviorist would examine the way the parents respond to the child's behavior: what kinds of behavior they punish or praise. A social learning theorist would focus on imitation of moral examples, possibly in stories or in movies. An information-processing researcher might do a task analysis to identify the steps a child goes through in determining the range of moral options available and then in deciding which option to pursue.

With this vital connection between theory and research in mind, let's look at the methods developmental researchers use.

Research Methods

Two key issues at the outset of a scientific investigation are how the participants will be chosen and how the data will be collected. These decisions often depend on what questions the researcher wants to answer. All these issues play a part in a research design, or plan.

Researchers in human development work within two methodological traditions: *quantitative* and *qualitative*. **Quantitative research** deals with objectively measurable data. Quantitative researchers may study, for example, how much fear or anxiety patients feel before surgery as measured by standardized tests, physiological

---

macrosystem Bronfenbrenner's term for a society's overall cultural patterns.

chronosystem Bronfenbrenner's term for effects of time on other developmental systems.

Checkpoint
Can you . . .

✔ State the chief assumptions of the contextual perspective?

✔ Differentiate Bronfenbrenner's five systems of contextual influence?

*What's
Your View?*

• Which of the theoretical perspectives would be most useful for (a) a mother trying to get her child to say "please," (b) a teacher interested in stimulating critical thinking, (c) a researcher studying siblings' imitation of one another?

Guidepost
4. How do developmental scientists study people, and what are the advantages and disadvantages of each research method?

quantitative research Research that focuses on "hard" data and numerical or statistical measures.

changes, or statistical analysis. **Qualitative research** involves the interpretation of nonnumerical data, such as the nature or quality of participants' subjective experiences, feelings, or beliefs. Qualitative researchers may study how patients describe their emotions before surgery (Morse & Field, 1995) or, as in Margaret Mead's research, how girls in the South Sea islands describe their experience of puberty.

Quantitative research is based on the **scientific method,** which generally characterizes scientific inquiry in any field. Its usual steps are (1) *identifying a problem* to be studied, often on the basis of a theory or of previous research; (2) *formulating hypotheses* to be tested by research; (3) *collecting data;* (4) *analyzing the data* to determine whether they support the hypothesis; (5) *forming tentative conclusions;* and (6) *disseminating findings* so that other observers can check, learn from, analyze, repeat, and build on the results.

Although most developmental scientists have been trained in quantitative methods, the need for qualitative research is increasingly recognized (Parke, 2004). Qualitative research is open-ended and exploratory. Instead of generating hypotheses from previous research, qualitative researchers gather and examine data to see what hypotheses may emerge. Qualitative research cannot yield general conclusions, but it can be a rich source of insights into individual attitudes and behavior.

The selection of quantitative or qualitative methods depends on the topic for study, how much is already known about it, the researcher's expertise and theoretical orientation, and the setting. Quantitative research is often done in laboratory settings under controlled conditions. Qualitative research is conducted in everyday settings to investigate topics about which little is known.

Often qualitative research yields findings that point the way to quantitative research. For example, surgical patients' descriptions of their experience may suggest means of reducing stress before surgery, which can then be tested and compared for effectiveness (Morse & Field, 1995). Computerized statistical analysis can be applied to verbal reports generated by focus groups (Parke, 2004).

Checkpoint

Can you . . .

✔ Compare quantitative and qualitative research, and give an example of each?

✔ Summarize the six steps in the scientific method and tell why each is important?

Sampling

To be sure that the results of their research are true generally and not just for specific participants, quantitative researchers need to control who gets into the study. Because studying an entire *population* (a group to whom the findings may apply) is usually too costly and time-consuming, investigators select a **sample,** a smaller group within the population. The sample should adequately represent the target population; that is, it should show relevant characteristics in the same proportions as in the entire population. Otherwise the results cannot properly be *generalized,* or applied to the population as a whole. To judge how generalizable the findings are likely to be, researchers need to compare the characteristics of the people in the sample with those of the population as a whole.

Often researchers seek to achieve representativeness through *random selection,* in which each person in a population has an equal and independent chance of being chosen. If we wanted to study the effects of an educational program, one way to select a random sample would be to put all the names of participating children into a large bowl, stir it, and draw out a certain number of names. A random sample, especially a large one, is likely to represent the population well. Unfortunately, a random sample of a large population is often difficult to obtain. Instead, many studies use samples selected for convenience or accessibility (for example, children born in a particular hospital or patients in a nursing home). The findings of such studies may not apply to the population as a whole.

In qualitative research, samples tend to be small and need not be random. Participants in this kind of research may be chosen for their ability to communicate the nature of a certain experience, such as how it feels to undergo a particular type of surgery.

Table 2-3   Characteristics of Major Methods of Data Collection

Type	Main Characteristics	Advantages	Disadvantages
Self-report: diary, interview, or questionnaire	Participants are asked about some aspect of their lives; questioning may be highly structured or more flexible.	Can provide firsthand information about a person's life, attitudes, or opinions.	Participant may not remember information accurately or may distort responses in a socially desirable way; how question is asked or by whom may affect answer.
Naturalistic observation	People are observed in their normal setting, with no attempt to manipulate behavior.	Provides good description of behavior; does not subject people to unnatural settings that may distort behavior.	Lack of control; observer bias.
Laboratory observation	Participants are observed in the laboratory, with no attempt to manipulate behavior.	Provides good descriptions; offers greater control than naturalistic observation, since all participants are observed under same controlled conditions.	Observer bias; controlled situation can be artificial.
Behavioral measures	Participants are tested on abilities, skills, knowledge, competencies, or physical responses.	Provides objectively measurable information; avoids subjective distortions.	Cannot measure attitudes or other nonbehavioral phenomena; results may be affected by extraneous factors.

Forms of Data Collection

Common ways of gathering data (see Table 2-3) include (1) self-reports (verbal reports by study participants), (2) observation of participants in natural or laboratory settings, and (3) behavioral or performance measures. Researchers may use one or more of these data collection techniques in any research design. Qualitative research tends to depend heavily on interviews and on observation in natural settings, whereas quantitative research makes use of more structured methods. A current trend is to combine self-reports and observation with more objective measures.

Self-Reports: Diaries, Interviews, Questionnaires   The simplest form of self-report is a *diary* or log. Participants may be asked, for example, to record what they eat each day or the times when they feel depressed. In studying young children, *parental self-reports*—diaries, journals, interviews, or questionnaires—are commonly used, often together with other methods such as videotaping or audio recording. Parents may be videotaped playing with their babies and then may be shown the tapes and asked to explain why they reacted as they did.

In a face-to-face or telephone *interview,* researchers ask questions about attitudes, opinions, or behavior. In a *structured* interview, each participant is asked the same set of questions. An *open-ended* interview, often used in qualitative research, is more flexible; the interviewer can vary the topics and order of questions and can ask follow-up questions based on the responses. To reach more people and protect their privacy, researchers sometimes distribute a printed *questionnaire,* which participants fill out and return.

By questioning a large number of people, investigators can get a broad picture— at least of what the respondents *say* they believe or do or have done. However, people willing to participate in interviews or fill out questionnaires tend to be unrepresentative of the population. Furthermore, heavy reliance on self-reports may be unwise because people may not have thought about what they feel and think or honestly may not know. Some people forget when and how events actually took place, and others consciously or unconsciously distort their replies to fit what is considered socially desirable.

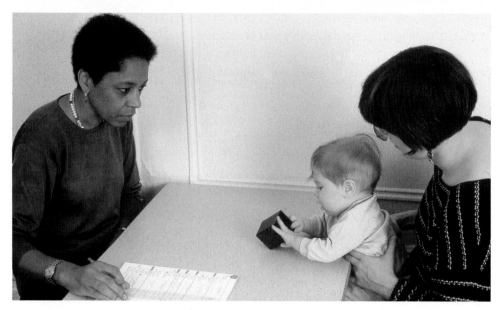

A child under laboratory observation may or may not behave the same way as in a naturalistic setting, such as at home or at school, but both kinds of observation can provide valuable information.

How a question is asked, and by whom, can affect the answer. When questioned about potentially risky or socially disapproved behavior, such as sexual habits and drug use, respondents may be more candid in responding to a computerized survey than to a paper-and-pencil one (Turner et al., 1998).

Naturalistic and Laboratory Observation   Observation takes two forms: *naturalistic observation* and *laboratory observation*. In **naturalistic observation,** researchers look at people in real-life settings. The researchers do not try to alter behavior or the environment; they simply record what they see. In **laboratory observation,** researchers observe and record behavior in a controlled environment, such as a laboratory. By observing all participants under the same conditions, investigators can more clearly identify any differences in behavior not attributable to the environment.

Both kinds of observation can provide valuable descriptions of behavior, but they have limitations. For one, they do not explain *why* people behave as they do, though the observers may suggest interpretations. Then, too, an observer's presence can alter behavior. When people know they are being watched, they may act differently. Finally, there is a risk of *observer bias:* the researcher's tendency to interpret data to fit expectations or to emphasize some aspects and minimize others.

During the 1960s, laboratory observation was used most commonly to achieve more rigorous control. Now such technological devices as portable videotape recorders and computers enable researchers to analyze moment-by-moment changes in behavior, for example, in interactions between spouses (Gottman & Notarius, 2000). Such methods make naturalistic observation more accurate and objective than it otherwise would be.

Behavioral and Performance Measures   For many kinds of research, investigators use more objective measures of behavior or performance instead of, or in addition to, self-reports or observation. Tests and other behavioral and neuropsychological measures, including mechanical and electronic devices, may be used to assess abilities, skills, knowledge, competencies, or physiological responses, such as heart rate and brain activity. Although these measures are less subjective than self-reports or personal observation, such factors as fatigue and self-confidence can affect results.

naturalistic observation   Research method in which behavior is studied in natural settings without intervention or manipulation.

laboratory observation   Research method in which all participants are observed under the same controlled conditions.

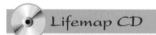

Lifemap CD

Why do scientists sometimes insist on observing people in real-life environments to conduct their research? To find out, watch the video, "The Importance of Naturalistic Observation in Study Young Children," in Chapter 2 of your CD.

Some written tests, such as intelligence tests, compare performance with that of other test-takers. Such tests can be meaningful and useful only if they are both *valid* (that is, the tests measure the abilities they claim to measure) and *reliable* (that is, the results are reasonably consistent from one time to another). (The validity of intelligence tests is in question, as we discuss in Chapter 9.) To avoid bias, tests must be *standardized,* that is, given and scored by the same methods and criteria for all test-takers.

When measuring a characteristic such as intelligence, it is important to define exactly what is to be measured in a way that other researchers will understand so that they can comment on the results. For this purpose, researchers use an **operational definition**—a definition stated solely in terms of the operations or procedures used to produce or measure a phenomenon. Intelligence, for example, can be defined as the ability to achieve a certain score on a test covering logical relationships, memory, and vocabulary recognition. Some people may disagree with this definition, but no one can reasonably claim that it is not clear.

For most of the history of psychology, theorists and researchers studied cognitive processes apart from the physical structures of the brain in which these processes occur. Now, sophisticated imaging instruments, such as magnetic resonance imaging (MRI) and positron emission tomography (PET), make it possible to see the brain in action, and the new field of **cognitive neuroscience** is linking our understanding of cognitive functioning with what happens in the brain (Gazzaniga, 2000; Humphreys, 2002; Posner & DiGirolamo, 2000). *Developmental cognitive neuroscience* focuses on how cognitive growth occurs as the brain interacts with the environment (Johnson, 1999, 2001), why some children do not develop normally, and what happens to cognition as adults age (Posner & DiGirolamo, 2000). This new branch of science may shed light on whether intelligence is general or specialized, what influences readiness for formal learning (Byrnes & Fox, 1998), and why common memory failures occur (Schacter, 1999).

Social cognitive neuroscience is an emerging interdisciplinary field that bridges brain, mind, and behavior, bringing together data from cognitive neuroscience, social psychology, and the information-processing approach. Social cognitive neuroscientists use brain imaging and studies of people with brain injuries to figure out how neural pathways control such behavioral processes as memory and attention, which in turn influence attitudes and emotions, and to identify the brain systems involved in schizophrenia, anxiety, phobias, and learning disorders (Azar, 2002a; Ochsner & Lieberman, 2001).

Checkpoint

Can you . . .

✔ Explain the purpose of random selection and tell how it can be achieved?

✔ Compare the advantages and disadvantages of various forms of data collection?

✔ Explain how brain research contributes to the understanding of cognitive processes and social behaviors and attitudes?

Basic Research Designs

A research design is a plan for conducting a scientific investigation: what questions are to be answered, how participants are to be selected, how data are to be collected and interpreted, and how valid conclusions can be drawn. Four of the basic designs used in developmental research are case studies, ethnographic studies, correlational studies, and experiments. Each design has advantages and drawbacks, and each is appropriate for certain kinds of research problems (see Table 2-4).

Case Studies A **case study** is a study of an individual, such as the research done with Genie, the 13-year-old girl who had been confined to her room and never learned to talk (refer back to Box 1-2 in Chapter 1). A number of theories, such as Freud's, have grown out of clinical case studies, which include careful observation and interpretation of what patients say and do. Case studies also may use behavioral or neuropsychological measures and biographical, autobiographical, or documentary materials.

Table 2-4   Basic Research Designs

Type	Main Characteristics	Advantages	Disadvantages
Case study	Study of single individual in depth.	Flexibility; provides detailed picture of one person's behavior and development; can generate hypotheses.	May not generalize to others; conclusions not directly testable; cannot establish cause and effect.
Ethnographic study	In-depth study of a culture or subculture.	Can help overcome culturally based biases in theory and research; can test universality of developmental phenomena.	Subject to observer bias.
Correlational study	Attempt to find positive or negative relationship between variables.	Enables prediction of one variable on basis of another; can suggest hypotheses about causal relationships.	Cannot establish cause and effect.
Experiment	Controlled procedure in which an experimenter controls the independent variable to determine its effect on the dependent variable; may be conducted in the laboratory or field.	Establishes cause-and-effect relationships; is highly controlled and can be repeated by another investigator; degree of control greatest in the laboratory experiment.	Findings, especially when derived from laboratory experiments, may not generalize to situations outside the laboratory.

Case studies offer useful, in-depth information. They can explore sources of behavior and can test treatments, and they can suggest directions for further research. A related advantage is flexibility: The researcher is free to explore avenues of inquiry that arise during the course of the study. However, case studies have shortcomings. From studying Genie, for instance, we learn much about the development of a single child, but not how the information applies to children in general. Furthermore, case studies cannot explain behavior with certainty because there is no way to test their conclusions. Even though it seems reasonable that Genie's severely deprived environment contributed to or even caused her language deficiency, it is impossible to know how she would have developed with a normal upbringing.

ethnographic study In-depth study of a culture, which uses a combination of methods including participant observation.

participant observation Research method in which the observer lives with the people or participates in the activity being observed.

Ethnographic Studies   An **ethnographic study** seeks to describe the pattern of relationships, customs, beliefs, technology, arts, and traditions that make up a society's way of life. Ethnographic research can be qualitative, quantitative, or both. It uses a combination of methods, including **participant observation.** Participant observation is a form of naturalistic observation in which researchers live or participate in the societies or smaller groups they observe, as did Margaret Mead (1928, 1930, 1935)—often for long periods of time.

Because of ethnographers' involvement in the events or societies they are observing, their findings are especially open to observer bias. On the positive side, ethnographic research can help overcome cultural biases in theory and research (see Box 2-2). Ethnography demonstrates the error of assuming that principles developed from research in western cultures are universally applicable.

correlational study Research design intended to discover whether a statistical relationship between variables exists.

Correlational Studies   A **correlational study** is an attempt to find a *correlation,* or statistical relationship, between *variables,* phenomena that change or vary among people or can be varied for purposes of research. Correlations are expressed in terms of direction (positive or negative) and magnitude (degree). Two variables that are correlated *positively* increase or decrease together. As we report in Chapter 10, studies show a positive, or direct, correlation between televised violence and aggressiveness; that is, children who watch more violent television tend to fight more than

Purposes of Cross-Cultural Research

When David, an American child, was asked to identify the missing detail in a picture of a face with no mouth, he said, "The mouth." But Ari, an Asian immigrant child in Israel, said that the *body* was missing. Since art in his culture does not present a head as a complete picture, he thought the absence of a body was more important than the omission of "a mere detail like the mouth" (Anastasi, 1988, p. 360).

By looking at children from different cultural groups, researchers can learn in what ways development is universal (and thus intrinsic to the human condition) and in what ways it is culturally determined. For example, children everywhere learn to speak in the same sequence, advancing from cooing and babbling to single words and then to simple combinations of words. The words vary from culture to culture, but around the world toddlers put them together to form sentences similar in structure. Such findings suggest that the capacity for learning language is universal and inborn.

On the other hand, culture can exert a surprisingly large influence on early motor development. African babies, whose parents often prop them in a sitting position and bounce them on their feet, tend to sit and walk earlier than U.S. babies (Rogoff & Morelli, 1989). The society in which children grow up also influences the skills they learn. In the United States, children learn to read, write, and, increasingly, to operate computers. In rural Nepal, they learn how to drive water buffalo and find their way along mountain paths.

One important reason to conduct research among different cultural groups is to recognize biases in traditional western theories and research that often go unquestioned until they are shown to be a product of cultural influences. Since so much research in child development has focused on Western industrialized societies, many people have defined typical development in these societies as the norm, or standard of behavior. Measuring against this "norm" leads to narrow—and often wrong—ideas about development. Pushed to its extreme, this belief can cause the development of children in other ethnic and cultural groups to be seen as deviant (Rogoff & Morelli, 1989).

Barriers exist to our understanding of cultural differences, particularly those involving minority subcultures. As with David and Ari in our opening example, a question or task may have different conceptual meanings for different cultural groups. Sometimes the barriers are linguistic. In a study of children's understanding of kinship relations among the Zinacanta people of Chiapas, Mexico (Greenfield & Childs, 1978), instead of asking "How many brothers do you have?" (as they might in the United States), the researchers—knowing that the Zinacantas have separate terms for older and younger siblings—asked, "What is the name of your older brother?" Using the same question across cultures might have obscured, rather than revealed, cultural differences and similarities (Parke, 2004).

Results of observational studies of ethnic or cultural groups may be affected by the ethnicity of the researchers. For example, in one study European American observers noted more conflict and restrictiveness in African American mother-daughter relationships than African American observers saw (Gonzales, Cauce, & Mason, 1996).

In this book we discuss several influential theories developed from research in Western societies that do not hold up when tested on people from other cultures—theories about gender roles, abstract thinking, moral reasoning, and a number of other aspects of human development. Throughout this book, we consistently look at children in cultures and subcultures other than the dominant one in the United States to show how closely development is tied to society and culture and to add to our understanding of normal development in many settings. In so doing, however, we need to keep in mind the pitfalls involved in cross-cultural comparisons.

What's Your View?

Can you think of a situation in which you made an incorrect assumption about a person because you were unfamiliar with her or his cultural background?

Check It Out

For more information on this topic, go to http://zzyx.ucsc.edu/Psych/psych.html. This is the Web site for the Department of Psychology at the University of Santa Cruz. Select the *Faculty* link and read about the work of faculty members who conduct cross-cultural research in human development: Barbara Rogoff, David Harrington, Ronald Tharp, and Stephen Wright.

---

children who watch less violent television. Two variables have a *negative,* or inverse, correlation if, as one increases, the other decreases. Studies show a negative correlation between amount of schooling and the risk of developing dementia (mental deterioration) due to Alzheimer's disease in old age. In other words, the less education, the more dementia (Katzman, 1993).

Correlations are reported as numbers ranging from -1.0 (a perfect negative relationship) to $+1.0$ (a perfect positive relationship). Perfect correlations are rare. The closer a correlation comes to $+1.0$ or -1.0, the stronger the relationship, either positive or negative. A correlation of zero means that the variables have no relationship.

Correlations enable us to predict one variable in relation to another. On the basis of the positive correlation between watching televised violence and aggression, we can predict that children who watch violent shows are more likely to get into fights than children who do *not* watch such shows. The greater the magnitude of the correlation between two variables, the greater the ability to predict one from the other.

Although strong correlations suggest possible cause-and-effect relationships, these are merely hypotheses and need to be examined and tested very critically. We cannot be sure from a positive correlation between televised violence and aggressiveness that watching televised violence *causes* aggressive play; we can conclude only that the two variables are related. It is possible that the causation goes the other way: Aggressive play may lead children to watch more violent programs. Or a third variable—perhaps an inborn predisposition toward aggressiveness or a violent living environment—may cause a child both to watch violent programs and to act aggressively. Similarly, we cannot be sure that schooling protects against dementia; it may be that another variable, such as socioeconomic status, might explain both lower levels of schooling and higher levels of dementia. The only way to show with certainty that one variable causes another is through experimentation—a method that, when studying human beings, is not always possible for practical or ethical reasons.

Experiments   An **experiment** is a controlled procedure in which the experimenter manipulates variables to learn how one affects another. Scientific experiments must be conducted and reported in such a way that another experimenter can *replicate* them, that is, repeat them in exactly the same way with different participants to verify the results and conclusions.

Groups and Variables   A common way to conduct an experiment is to divide the participants into two kinds of groups. An **experimental group** consists of people who are to be exposed to the experimental manipulation or *treatment*—the phenomenon the researcher wants to study. Afterward, the effect of the treatment will be measured one or more times to find out what changes, if any, it caused. A **control group** consists of people who are similar to the experimental group but do not receive the experimental treatment or may receive a different treatment. An experiment may include one or more of each type of group. If the experimenter wants to compare the effects of different treatments (say, of two methods of teaching), the overall sample may be divided into *treatment groups,* each of which receives one of the treatments under study.

One team of researchers (Whitehurst et al., 1988) wanted to find out what effect *dialogic reading,* a special method of reading picture books to very young children, might have on their language and vocabulary skills. The researchers compared two groups of middle-class children ages 21 to 35 months. In the *experimental group,* the parents adopted the new read-aloud method (the treatment), which consisted of encouraging children's active participation and giving frequent, age-based feedback. In the *control group,* parents simply read aloud as they usually did. After 1 month, the children in the experimental group were 8.5 months ahead of the control group in level of speech and 6 months ahead in vocabulary; 9 months later, the experimental group was still 6 months ahead of the control group. It is reasonable to conclude, then, that this read-aloud method improved the children's language and vocabulary skills.

In this experiment, the type of reading approach was the *independent variable,* and the children's language skills were the *dependent variable.* An **independent variable** is something over which the experimenter has direct control. A **dependent variable** is something that may or may not change as a result of changes in the independent variable; in other words, it *depends* on the independent variable. In an experiment, a researcher manipulates the independent variable to see how changes in it will affect the dependent variable.

experiment   Rigorously controlled, replicable procedure in which the researcher manipulates variables to assess the effect of one on the other.

experimental group   In an experiment, the group receiving the treatment under study.

control group   In an experiment, a group of people, similar to those in the experimental group, who do not receive the treatment under study.

independent variable   In an experiment, the condition over which the experimenter has direct control.

dependent variable   In an experiment, the condition that may or may not change as a result of changes in the independent variable.

Random Assignment   If an experiment finds a significant difference in the performance of the experimental and control groups, how do we know that the cause was the independent variable, in other words, that the conclusion is valid? For example, in the read-aloud experiment, how can we be sure that the reading method and not some other factor (such as intelligence) caused the difference in language development of the two groups? The best way to control for effects of such extraneous factors is *random assignment:* assigning the participants to groups in such a way that each person has an equal chance of being placed in any group. (Random assignment differs from random selection, which determines who gets into the full sample.)

If assignment is random and the sample is large enough, differences in factors not intended as variables, such as age, sex, ethnicity, IQ, and socioeconomic status, will be evenly distributed so that the groups initially are as alike as possible in every respect except for the variable to be tested. Otherwise, unintended differences between the groups might *confound*, or contaminate, the results, and any conclusions drawn from the experiment would have to be viewed with suspicion. To control for confounds, the experimenter must make sure that everything except the independent variable is held constant during the course of the experiment. For example, in the read-aloud study, parents of the experimental and control groups must spend the same amount of time reading to their children. When participants in an experiment are randomly assigned to treatment groups and conditions other than the independent variable are carefully controlled, the experimenter can be reasonably confident that a causal relationship has (or has not) been established—that any differences between the reading skills of the two groups are due to the reading method and not some other factor.

Of course, with respect to some variables we might want to study, such as age, gender, and race/ethnicity, random assignment is not possible. We cannot assign Terry to be 5 years old and Brett to be 10, or one to be a boy and the other a girl, or one to be African American and the other Asian American. When studying such a variable—for example, whether boys or girls are stronger in certain abilities—researchers can strengthen the validity of their conclusions by randomly selecting participants and by trying to make sure that they are statistically equivalent in other ways that might make a difference in the study.

Because *race* (as discussed in Chapter 1) has no widely agreed meaning, some researchers argue that racial categories should not be used as independent variables in psychological research, for example, on intergroup variations in intelligence. Instead, researchers can substitute meaningful underlying variables that are often masked by racial categories, such as socioeconomic status and test-taking skills (Helms, Jernigan, & Mascher, 2005).

Laboratory, Field, and Natural Experiments   The control necessary for establishing cause and effect is most easily achieved in *laboratory experiments*. In a laboratory experiment the participants are brought to a special place where they experience conditions manipulated by the experimenter. The experimenter records the participants' reactions to these conditions, perhaps comparing them with their own or other participants' behavior under different conditions.

However, not all experiments can be readily done in the laboratory. A *field experiment* is a controlled study conducted in an everyday setting, such as home or school. The experiment in which parents tried out a new way of reading aloud was a field experiment.

Laboratory and field experiments differ in two important respects. One is the *degree of control* exerted by the experimenter; the other is the degree to which findings can be *generalized* beyond the study situation. Laboratory experiments can be more rigidly controlled and thus are easier to replicate; however, the results may be

Did additional income from a casino on an impoverished Indian reservation cause improvements in mental health? Because this was a natural experiment, we cannot be certain.

less generalizable to real life. Because of the artificiality of the laboratory situation, participants may not act as they normally would. Thus, if children who watch violent television shows in the laboratory become more aggressive in that setting, we cannot be sure that children who watch violent shows at home hit their little brothers or sisters more often than children who do not watch such shows or watch fewer of them.

When, for practical or ethical reasons, it is impossible to conduct a true experiment, a *natural experiment* may provide a way of studying certain events. A natural experiment compares people who have been accidentally "assigned" to separate groups by circumstances of life—one group who were exposed, say, to famine or AIDS or a birth defect or superior education, and another group who were not. A natural experiment, despite its name, is actually a correlational study because controlled manipulation of variables and random assignment to treatment groups are not possible.

One natural experiment dealt with what happened when a casino opened on an Indian reservation in North Carolina, raising the income of tribal members (Costello, Compton, Keeler, & Angold, 2003). The study found a decline in behavioral disorders among children in these families as compared with children in the same area whose families did not receive increased income. Still, because it was correlational, the study could not prove that the increased income *caused* improvements in mental health.

Experiments have two important advantages over other research designs: They can establish cause-and-effect relationships, and they permit replication. However, experiments can be too artificial and too narrowly focused. In recent decades, therefore, many researchers have concentrated less on laboratory experimentation or have supplemented it with a wider array of methods.

Developmental Research Designs

The two most common research strategies used to study development are *longitudinal* and *cross-sectional* studies (see Figure 2-2). Longitudinal studies reveal how people change or stay the same as they grow older; cross-sectional studies show similarities and differences among age groups. Because each of these designs has drawbacks, researchers also have devised *sequential* designs.

Figure 2-2

Developmental research designs. In this *cross-sectional* study, groups of 2-, 4-, 6-, and 8-year-olds were tested in 2004 to obtain data about age-related differences. In the *longitudinal* study, a sample of children were first measured in 2004, when they were 2 years old; follow-up testing is done when the children are 4, 6, and 8, to measure age-related changes. (Note: Dots indicate times of measurement.)

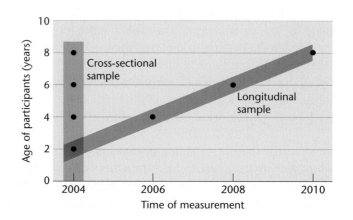

Longitudinal, Cross-Sectional, and Sequential Studies In a **cross-sectional study,** people of different ages are assessed at one time. In one cross-sectional study, researchers asked 3-, 4-, 6-, and 7-year-olds such questions as what a pensive-looking woman was doing. These researchers found a striking increase with age in children's awareness of thinking as mental activity (J. H. Flavell, Green, & Flavell, 1995). These findings strongly suggest that, as children become older, their understanding of mental processes improves. However, we cannot draw such a conclusion with certainty. We don't know whether the 7-year-olds' awareness of mental activity when they were 3 years old was the same as that of the current 3-year-olds in the study. The only way to see whether change occurs with age is to conduct a longitudinal study of a particular person or group.

In a **longitudinal study,** researchers study the same person or group of people more than once, sometimes years apart. They may measure a single characteristic, such as vocabulary size, height, or aggressiveness, or they may look at several aspects of development to find relationships among them. The Oakland (Adolescent) Growth Study, mentioned in Chapter 1, initially was designed to assess social and emotional development from the preteen through the senior high school years; ultimately, many of the participants were followed into old age. The study found that participants who as teenagers showed self-confidence, intellectual commitment, and dependable effectiveness made good choices in adolescence and early adulthood, which often led to promising opportunities (scholarships, good jobs, and competent spouses). Less competent teenagers made poorer early decisions and tended to lead crisis-ridden lives (Clausen, 1993).

Both cross-sectional and longitudinal designs have strengths and weaknesses (see Table 2-5). Advantages of cross-sectional research include speed and economy; data can be gathered relatively quickly from large numbers of people. And, because participants are assessed only once, there is no problem of either attrition (participants dropping out) or repeated testing. One drawback of cross-sectional studies is that they may obscure individual differences by focusing on group averages alone. Their major disadvantage, however, is that the results may be affected by cohort differences—the differing experiences of people born at different times, for example, before and after the advent of the Internet (refer back to Chapter 1). Cross-sectional studies are sometimes interpreted as yielding information about developmental changes, but such information is often misleading. Thus, although cross-sectional studies still dominate the field—no doubt because they are so much easier to do—the proportion of research devoted to longitudinal studies, especially short-term ones, is increasing (Parke et al., 1994).

cross-sectional study Study designed to assess age-related differences, in which people of different ages are assessed on one occasion.

longitudinal study Study designed to assess changes in a sample over time.

Table 2-5	Longitudinal, Cross-Sectional, and Sequential Research: Pros and Cons			

Type of Study	Procedure	Advantages	Disadvantages
Longitudinal	Data are collected on same person or persons over a period of time.	Can show age-related change or continuity; avoids confounding age with cohort effects.	Is time-consuming, expensive; presents problems of attrition, bias in sample, and effects of repeated testing; results may be valid only for cohort tested or sample studied.
Cross-sectional	Data are collected on people of different ages at the same time.	Can show similarities and differences among age groups; speedy, economical; presents no problem of attrition or repeated testing.	Cannot establish age effects; masks individual differences; can be confounded by cohort effects.
Sequential	Data are collected on successive cross-sectional or longitudinal samples.	Can avoid drawbacks of both cross-sectional and longitudinal designs.	Requires large amount of time and effort and analysis of very complex data.

Longitudinal research, in repeatedly studying the same people, can track individual patterns of continuity and change. However, a longitudinal study done on one cohort may not apply to another. (The results of a study of children born in the 1920s, such as the Oakland Growth Study, may not apply to children born in the 1990s.) Furthermore, longitudinal studies generally are more time-consuming and expensive than cross-sectional studies; it is hard to keep track of a large group of participants over the years, to keep records, and to keep the study going despite possible turnover in research personnel. Then there is the problem of attrition; participants may die, move away, or drop out. Longitudinal studies also tend to be biased; those who stay with the study tend to be above average in intelligence and socioeconomic status. Finally, results can be affected by repeated testing; participants may do better on later tests because of familiarity with test procedures.

A current trend is toward very large, multicentered longitudinal studies with governmental or large institutional support, which can trace development within a population on a very broad scale. The planned 21-year National Children's Study (2004) under auspices of the U.S. Department of Health and Human Services and other government agencies aims to follow some 100,000 U.S. children across the country from conception to adulthood. The study is *prospective:* It will include couples of childbearing age who are not yet expecting a child. By following these families, researchers hope to measure how biology and environmental factors interact in influencing children's health.

A **sequential study**—a sequence of cross-sectional and/or longitudinal studies—is a complex strategy designed to overcome the drawbacks of longitudinal and cross-sectional research (again see Table 2-5). Researchers may assess a cross-sectional sample on two or more occasions (that is, in sequence) to find out how members of each age cohort have changed. This procedure permits researchers to separate age-related changes from cohort effects. Another sequential design consists of a sequence of longitudinal studies, running concurrently but starting one after another. This design enables researchers to compare individual differences in the course of developmental change. A combination of cross-sectional and longitudinal sequences (as shown in Figure 2-3) can provide a more complete picture of development than would be possible with longitudinal or cross-sectional research alone. The major drawbacks of sequential studies relate to time, effort, and complexity. Sequential designs require large numbers of participants and the collection and analysis of huge amounts of data over a period of years. Interpreting their findings and conclusions can demand a high degree of sophistication.

sequential study Study design that combines cross-sectional and longitudinal techniques.

Checkpoint
Can you . . .

✔ List advantages and disadvantages of longitudinal, cross-sectional, and sequential research?

Figure 2-3

A sequential design. Two successive cross-sectional groups of 2-, 4-, 6-, and 8-year-olds are tested in 2006 and 2008. Also, a longitudinal study of a sample of children first measured in 2006, when they are 2 years old, is followed by a similar longitudinal study of another group of children who are 2 years old in 2008.

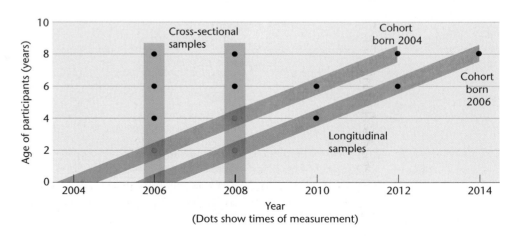

Ethics of Research

Should research that might harm its participants ever be undertaken? How can we balance the possible benefits against the risk of mental, emotional, or physical injury to individuals?

Objections to the study of "Little Albert" (mentioned earlier in this chapter) as well as several other early studies gave rise to today's more stringent ethical standards. Federally mandated committees at colleges, universities, and other institutions review proposed research from an ethical standpoint. Guidelines of the American Psychological Association (2002) and the Society for Research in Child Development (1996) cover such issues as *informed consent, avoidance of deception,* protection of participants from *harm and loss of dignity,* guarantees of *privacy and confidentiality,* the *right to decline or withdraw* from an experiment at any time, and the responsibility of investigators to *correct any undesirable effects.*

In resolving ethical dilemmas, researchers are expected to be guided by three principles: (1) *beneficence,* the obligation to maximize potential benefits to participants and minimize possible harm; (2) *respect* for participants' autonomy and protection of those who are unable to exercise their own judgment; and (3) *justice,* inclusion of diverse groups together with sensitivity to any special impact the research may have on them. In evaluating risks and benefits, researchers should consider children's developmental needs (Thompson, 1990) and be sensitive to cultural issues and values (Fisher et al., 2002).

Let's look more closely at a few ethical considerations that can present problems.

Right to Informed Consent   Informed consent exists when participants voluntarily agree to be in a study, are competent to give consent, are fully aware of the risks as well as the potential benefits, and are not being exploited. The National Commission for the Protection of Human Subjects of Biomedical and Behavioral Research (1978) recommends that children age 7 or over be asked to give their own consent to take part in research and that children's objections should be overruled only if the research promises direct benefit to the child, as in the use of a new experimental drug.

However, some ethicists argue that young children cannot give meaningful, voluntary *consent* because they cannot fully understand what is involved. They can merely *assent,* that is, agree to participate. The usual procedure, therefore, when children under 18 are involved, is to ask the parents or legal guardians and sometimes school personnel to give consent.

Some studies rely on participants who may be especially vulnerable. For example, studies that seek the causes and treatments for Alzheimer's disease need participants whose mental status may preclude their being fully or even partially aware of what is involved. What if a person gives consent and later forgets having done so? Current practice, to be on the safe side, is to ask both participants and caregivers for consent.

Avoidance of Deception   Can informed consent exist if participants are deceived about the nature or purpose of a study, or about the procedures they will be subjected to? Suppose participants are told they are trying out a new game when they are actually being tested on their reactions to success or failure? Experiments like these, which cannot be carried out without deception, have been done—and they have added significantly to our knowledge—but at the cost of the participants' right to know what they were getting involved in.

Ethical guidelines call for withholding information *only* when it is essential to the study; and then investigators should avoid methods that could cause pain, anxiety, or harm. Participants should be debriefed afterwards to let them know the true nature of the study and why deception was necessary and to make sure they have not suffered as a result.

Guidepost

5. What ethical problems may arise in research on humans?

Lifemap CD

What is the basic purpose of all ethical guidelines for research in human development? To consider this question, watch the video, "The Essence of Ethics," in Chapter 2 of your CD.

What's Your View?

- What steps should be taken to protect children and other vulnerable persons from harm due to involvement in research?

Right to Privacy and Confidentiality Not all ethical issues have clear answers; some hinge on researchers' judgment and scruples. In this gray area are issues having to do with privacy and with protecting the confidentiality of personal information that participants may reveal in interviews or questionnaires.

What if, during the course of research, an investigator notices that a person seems to have a learning disability or some other treatable condition? Is the researcher obliged to share such information with the participant or with parents or guardians or to recommend services that may help, when sharing the information might contaminate the research findings? Such a decision should not be made lightly, since sharing information of uncertain validity may create damaging misconceptions about a child. On the other hand, researchers need to know and inform participants of their legal responsibility to report abuse or neglect or any other illegal activity of which they become aware.

Checkpoint

Can you . . .

✔ Identify three principles that should govern inclusion of participants in research?

✔ Discuss three rights of research participants?

Ref⊕cus

Thinking back to the Focus vignette about Margaret Mead at the beginning of this chapter:

- What position do you think Mead might have taken on the issue of the relative influences of heredity and environment?

- Does Mead seem to fit within any of the five theoretical perspectives described in this chapter?

- What research methods described in the chapter did she use? What advantages and disadvantages existed because her research was done in the field, rather than in a laboratory?

- What ethical issues might be relevant to cross-cultural research such as Mead's?

Our final word in these introductory chapters is that this entire book is far from the final word. Although we have tried to incorporate the most important and the most up-to-date information about how people develop, developmental scientists are constantly learning more. As you read this book, you are certain to come up with your own questions. By thinking about them and perhaps eventually conducting research to find answers, it is possible that you yourself, now just embarking on the study of human development, will some day add to our knowledge about the interesting species to which we all belong.

SUMMARY AND KEY TERMS

Basic Theoretical Issues

Guidepost 1: What purposes do theories serve?

- A theory is used to organize and explain data and generate hypotheses that can be tested by research.

theory *(29)*

hypotheses *(29)*

Guidepost 2: What are two basic theoretical issues on which developmental scientists differ?

- Developmental theories differ on two basic issues: the active or passive character of development and the existence of stages of development.

- Some theorists subscribe to a mechanistic model of development, others to an organismic model.

mechanistic model *(29)*

organismic model *(30)*

Theoretical Perspectives

Guidepost 3: What are five theoretical perspectives on human development, and what are some theories representative of each?

- The psychoanalytic perspective sees development as motivated by unconscious emotional drives or conflicts. Leading examples are Freud's and Erikson's theories.

psychoanalytic perspective *(32)*

psychosexual development *(32)*

psychosocial development *(34)*

- The learning perspective views development as a result of learning based on experience. Leading examples are Watson's and Skinner's behaviorism and Bandura's social learning (social cognitive) theory.

learning perspective *(34)*

behaviorism *(34)*

classical conditioning *(35)*

operant conditioning *(35)*

reinforcement *(35)*

punishment *(35)*

social learning theory *(36)*

observational learning *(36)*

self-efficacy *(36)*

- The cognitive perspective is concerned with thought processes. Leading examples are Piaget's cognitive-stage theory, Vygotsky's sociocultural theory, and the information-processing approach.

cognitive perspective *(37)*

cognitive-stage theory *(37)*

organization *(37)*

schemes *(37)*

adaptation *(37)*

assimilation *(37)*

accommodation *(37)*

equilibration *(37)*

sociocultural theory *(38)*

information-processing approach *(39)*

- The evolutionary/sociobiological perspective, represented by E. O. Wilson, focuses on the adaptiveness, or survival value, of behavior. A leading example is Bowlby's attachment theory.

evolutionary perspective *(39)*

ethology *(40)*

evolutionary psychology *(40)*

- The contextual perspective focuses on the individual in a social context. A leading example is Bronfenbrenner's bioecological theory.

contextual perspective *(40)*

bioecological theory *(41)*

microsystem *(42)*

mesosystem *(42)*

exosystem *(42)*

macrosystem *(43)*

chronosystem *(43)*

Research Methods

Guidepost 4: How do developmental scientists study people, and what are some advantages and disadvantages of each research method?

- Research can be either quantitative or qualitative, or both.
- To arrive at sound conclusions, quantitative researchers use the scientific method.
- Random selection of a research sample can ensure generalizability.
- Three forms of data collection are self-reports, observation, and behavioral and performance measures.

quantitative research *(43)*

qualitative research *(44)*

scientific method *(44)*

sample *(44)*

naturalistic observation *(46)*

laboratory observation *(46)*

operational definitions *(47)*

cognitive neuroscience *(47)*

- Two basic qualitative designs used in developmental research are the case study and the ethnographic study. Cross-cultural research can indicate whether certain aspects of development are universal or culturally influenced.
- Two quantitative designs are the correlational study and experiment. Only experiments can firmly establish causal relationships.
- Experiments must be rigorously controlled so as to be valid and replicable. Random assignment of participants can ensure validity.
- Laboratory experiments are easiest to control and replicate, but findings of field experiments may be more generalizable. Natural experiments may be useful in situations in which true experiments would be impractical or unethical.
- The two most common designs used to study age-related development are longitudinal and cross-sectional. Cross-sectional studies compare age groups; longitudinal studies describe continuity or change in the same participants. The sequential study is intended to overcome the weaknesses of the other two designs.

case study *(47)*

ethnographic study *(48)*

participant observation *(48)*

correlational study *(48)*

experiment *(50)*

experimental group *(50)*

control group *(50)*

independent variable *(50)*

dependent variable *(50)*

cross-sectional study *(53)*

longitudinal study *(53)*

sequential study *(54)*

Guidepost 5: What ethical problems may arise in research on humans?

- Researchers seek to resolve ethical issues on the basis of principles of beneficence, respect, and justice.
- Ethical issues in research include the rights of participants to informed consent, avoidance of deception, protection from harm and loss of dignity and self-esteem, and guarantees of privacy and confidentiality.

PART 2

From the moment of conception to the moment of death, human beings undergo complex processes of development. The changes that occur during the earliest periods of the lifespan are broader and faster-paced than any a person will ever experience again. Because human beings are whole persons, all aspects of development are interconnected, even in the womb. As we look at prenatal development in Chapter 3, at physical development of infants and toddlers in Chapter 4, at their cognitive development in Chapter 5, and at their psychosocial development in Chapter 6, we will see, right from the beginning, how these aspects of development are linked.

- The physical growth of the brain before and after birth makes possible a great burst of cognitive and emotional development. Fetuses whose ears and brains have developed enough to hear sounds from the outside world seem to retain a memory of these sounds after birth.

- An infant's earliest smiles arise from central nervous system activity and may reflect nothing more than a pleasant physiological state, such as drowsiness and a full stomach. As the infant becomes cognitively aware of the warm responses of caregivers, and as vision becomes sharp enough to recognize a familiar face, the infant's smiles become more emotionally expressive and more socially directed.

- Infants learn through their physical movements where their bodies end and everything else begins. As they drop toys, splash water, and hurl sand, their minds grasp how their bodies can change their world, and their sense of self begins to flourish.

- Without the vocal structures and motor coordination to form sounds, babies would not be able to speak. Physical gestures precede and often accompany early attempts to form words. The acquisition of language dramatically advances cognitive understanding and social communication.

Beginnings

PREVIEW

CHAPTER 3

Forming a New Life

Conception occurs.

The genetic endowment interacts with environmental influences from the start.

Basic body structures and organs form.

Brain growth spurt begins.

Physical growth is the most rapid in the life span.

Vulnerability to environmental influences is great.

Abilities to learn and remember and to respond to sensory stimuli are present.

Fetus responds to mother's voice and develops a preference for it.

CHAPTER 4

Physical Development During the First Three Years

A method and setting for childbirth are chosen, and the progress of the birth is monitored.

The newborn emerges and is assessed for immediate health, developmental status, and any complications of childbirth.

All senses and body systems operate at birth to varying degrees.

The brain grows in complexity and is highly sensitive to environmental influence.

Physical growth and development of motor skills are rapid.

CHAPTER 5

Cognitive Development During the First Three Years

Abilities to learn and remember are present, even in early weeks.

Use of symbols and ability to solve problems develop by the end of the second year.

Comprehension and use of language develop rapidly.

CHAPTER 6

Psychosocial Development During the First Three Years

Attachments to parents and others form.

Self-awareness develops.

Shift from dependence to autonomy occurs.

Interest in other children increases.

Forming a New Life

CHAPTER 3

If I could have watched you grow
as a magical mother might,
if I could have seen through my magical
transparent belly,
there would have been such ripening within. . . .

Anne Sexton, 1966

Focus
Abel Dorris and Fetal Alcohol Syndrome

Abel Dorris

Fetal alcohol syndrome (FAS), a cluster of abnormalities shown by children whose mothers drank alcohol heavily during pregnancy, is a leading cause of mental retardation. But in 1971, when the writer Michael Dorris adopted a 3-year-old Sioux boy whose mother had been a heavy drinker, the facts about FAS were not widely publicized or scientifically investigated, though the syndrome had been observed for centuries. Not until eleven years later, as Dorris related in *The Broken Cord* (1989), did he discover the source of his adopted son's developmental problems.

The boy, named Abel ("Adam" in the book), had been born almost seven weeks premature, with low birth weight, and had been abused and malnourished before being removed to a foster home. His mother had died at 35 of alcohol poisoning. His father had been beaten to death in an alley after a string of arrests. The boy was small for his age, was not toilet-trained, and could speak only about twenty words. Although he had been diagnosed as mildly retarded, Dorris was certain that with a positive environment he would catch up.

Abel did not catch up. When he turned 4, he was still in diapers and weighed only 27 pounds. He had trouble remembering names of playmates. His activity level was unusually high, and the circumference of his skull was unusually small. He suffered severe, unexplained seizures.

As the months went by, Abel had trouble learning to count, identify primary colors, and tie his shoes. Before entering school, he was labeled "learning disabled." His IQ was, and remained, in the mid-60s. Thanks to the efforts of a devoted first-grade teacher, Abel did learn to read and write, but his comprehension was low. When the boy finished elementary school in 1983, he "still could not add, subtract, count money, or consistently identify the town, state, country, or planet of his residence" (Dorris, 1989, pp. 127–128).

61

By then, Michael Dorris had solved the puzzle of what was wrong with his son. As an associate professor of Native American studies at Dartmouth College, he was acquainted with the cultural pressures that contribute to heavy drinking among American Indians. In 1982, the year before Abel's graduation, Michael visited a treatment center for chemically dependent teenagers at a Sioux reservation in South Dakota. There he was astonished to see three boys who "could have been [Abel's] twin brothers" (Dorris, 1989, p. 137). They not only looked like Abel but acted like him.

Fetal alcohol syndrome had been identified during the 1970s, while Abel was growing up. Once alcohol enters a fetus's bloodstream, it remains there in high concentrations for long periods of time, causing brain damage and harming other body organs. There is no cure. As one medical expert wrote, "for the fetus the hangover may last a lifetime" (Enloe, 1980, p. 15).

For the family, too, the effects of FAS can be devastating. The years of constant attempts first to restore Abel to normality and then to come to terms with the damage irrevocably done in the womb may well have been a factor in the later problems in Michael Dorris's marriage to the writer Louise Erdrich, which culminated in divorce proceedings, and in his suicide in 1997 at age 52. According to Erdrich, Dorris suffered from extreme depression, possibly exacerbated by the difficulties he faced as a father (L. Erdrich, personal communication, March 1, 2000).

As for Abel Dorris, at the age of 20 he had entered a vocational training program and had moved into a supervised home, taking along his collections of stuffed animals, paper dolls, newspaper cartoons, family photographs, and old birthday cards. At 23, five years before his father's death, he was hit by a car and killed (Lyman, 1997).

The story of Abel Dorris is a devastating reminder of the awesome responsibility prospective parents have for the development of the new life they have set in motion. First comes the hereditary endowment they provide. Then come environmental influences—starting with the mother's body. In addition to what the mother does and what happens to her, there are other environmental influences, from those that affect the father's sperm to the technological, social, and cultural environment, which may affect the kind of care a woman gets in the months before giving birth.

In this chapter, we describe how conception normally occurs, how the mechanisms of heredity operate, and how the biological inheritance interacts with environmental influences within and outside the womb. We trace the course of prenatal development, describe influences upon it, and report on ways to monitor and intervene in it.

After you have studied this chapter, you should be able to answer each of the Guidepost questions that appear at the top of the next page. Look for them again in the margins, where they point to important concepts throughout the chapter. To check your understanding of these Guideposts, review the end-of-chapter summary. Checkpoints located at periodic spots throughout the chapter will help you verify your understanding of what you have read.

1. How does conception normally occur?

2. What causes multiple births?

3. How does heredity operate in determining sex and transmitting normal and abnormal traits?

4. How do scientists study the relative influences of heredity and environment, and how do heredity and environment work together?

5. What roles do heredity and environment play in physical health, intelligence, and personality?

6. What are the three stages of prenatal development, and what happens during each stage?

7. What environmental influences can affect prenatal development?

8. What techniques can assess a fetus's health, and why is prenatal care important?

Guideposts
for Study

Conceiving New Life

Guidepost
1. How does conception normally occur?

During the seventeenth and eighteenth centuries, a debate raged between two schools of biological thought. The *animalculists* (so named because male sperm were then called *animalcules*) claimed that fully formed "little people" were contained in the heads of sperm, ready to grow when deposited in the nurturing environment of the womb. The *ovists,* inspired by the influential work of the English physician William Harvey, held an opposite but equally incorrect view: that a female's ovaries contained tiny, already formed humans whose growth was activated by the male's sperm. Finally, in the late eighteenth century, the German-born anatomist Kaspar Friedrich Wolff demonstrated that embryos are not preformed in either parent and that both contribute equally to the formation of a new being.

How Fertilization Takes Place

Fertilization, or conception, is the process by which sperm and ovum—the male and female *gametes,* or sex cells—combine to create a single cell called a **zygote,** which then duplicates itself again and again by cell division to produce all the cells that make up a baby. But conception is not as simple as it sounds. Several independent events need to coincide to conceive a child. And, as we will discuss later in this chapter, not all conceptions end in birth.

At birth, a girl is believed to have about 2 million immature ova in her two ovaries, each ovum in its own small sac, or *follicle.* According to research in mice, new ova continue to develop during adulthood from stem cells in the ovary, and this may be true of adult women as well (Johnson, Canning, Kaneko, Pru, & Tilly, 2004). In a sexually mature woman, *ovulation*—rupture of a mature follicle in either ovary

fertilization Union of sperm and ovum to produce a zygote; also called *conception*.

zygote One-celled organism resulting from fertilization.

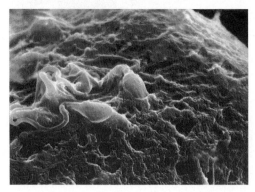

Fertilization occurs when a sperm cell unites with an ovum by fusing with its nucleus. This color-enhanced scanning electron micrograph (SEM) shows two sperm (orange) attracted to an ovum's furry surface (blue). A sperm's long tail enables it to swim through the cervix and up the fallopian tubes; only a few sperm reach the ovum. The sperm's rounded head releases enzymes that help it penetrate the ovum's thick surface and fertilize the ovum. Only one sperm can penetrate an ovum; immediately afterward, the ovum's outer membrane thicknes, forming a barrier to competing sperm.

and expulsion of its ovum—occurs about once every 28 days until menopause. The ovum is swept along through the fallopian tube by tiny hair cells, called *cilia,* toward the uterus, or womb. Fertilization normally occurs during the two to three days when the ovum is passing through the fallopian tube.

Sperm are produced in the testicles (testes), or reproductive glands, of a mature male at a rate of several hundred million a day and are ejaculated in the semen at sexual climax. Deposited in the vagina, they try to swim through the *cervix* (the opening of the uterus) and into the fallopian tubes, but only a tiny fraction make it that far. As we will see, which sperm meets which ovum has tremendous implications for the new person.

Fertilization is most likely if sperm are introduced into the vagina on the day of ovulation or during the five days before (Wilcox, Weinberg, & Baird, 1995). If fertilization does not occur, the ovum and any sperm cells in the woman's body die. The sperm are absorbed by the woman's white blood cells, and the ovum passes through the uterus and exits through the vagina. (In Chapter 13, we'll discuss techniques of artificially assisted reproduction often used when one or both prospective parents are infertile.)

2. What causes multiple births?

dizygotic twins   Twins conceived by the union of two different ova (or a single ovum that has split) with two different sperm cells; also called *fraternal twins.*

monozygotic twins   Twins resulting from the division of a single zygote after fertilization; also called *identical twins.*

temperament   Characteristic disposition, or style of approaching and reacting to situations.

Checkpoint
Can you . . .

✔ Explain how and when fertilization normally takes place?

✔ Distinguish between monozygotic and dizygotic twins, and tell how each comes about?

✔ Give reasons for the increase in multiple births in the United States?

What Causes Multiple Births?

Multiple births occur in two ways. Most commonly, the mother's body releases two ova within a short time (or sometimes a single unfertilized ovum splits) and then both are fertilized. The resulting babies are **dizygotic twins** ("di" means "two"), commonly called *fraternal twins.* The second way is for a single *fertilized* ovum to split into two. The babies that result from this cell division are **monozygotic twins** ("mono" means "one"), commonly called *identical twins.* Triplets, quadruplets, and other multiple births can result from either of these processes or a combination of both.

Monozygotic twins have the same hereditary makeup and are the same sex, but—in part because of differences in prenatal as well as postnatal experience—they differ in some respects. They may not be identical in **temperament** (disposition, or style of approaching and reacting to situations). In some physical characteristics, such as hair whorls, dental patterns, and handedness, they may be mirror images of each other; one may be left-handed and the other right-handed. Dizygotic twins, who are created from different sperm cells and usually from different ova, are no more alike in hereditary makeup than any other siblings and may be the same sex or different sexes.

The incidence of multiple births in the United States has grown rapidly. Between 1980 and 2002, the twin birth rate increased by 65 percent, from 19 to 31 twin births per 1,000 live births (about 3 percent of all live births). Birth rates for triplets and larger multiples increased by 13 percent each year between 1990 and 1998 (Martin, Kochanek, Strobino, Guyer, & MacDorman, 2005) but still, in 2001, represented less than 1 percent of live births (National Center for Education Statistics, 2005). Two related factors in the rise in multiple births are (1) the trend toward delayed childbearing; and (2) the increased use of fertility drugs, which spur ovulation, and assisted reproductive techniques such as in vitro fertilization, which tend to be used more by older women (Martin et al., 2005).

The explosion of multiple births, especially triplets and higher-order multiples, is of concern because such births are associated with increased risks: complications of pregnancy, premature delivery, low birth weight, and disability or death of the infant. In light of these concerns, the proportion of artificial procedures involving three or more embryos declined between 1997 and 2001, and the birth rate for triplets and higher multiples has taken a slight downturn (Jain, Missmer, & Hornstein, 2004; Martin et al., 2003; Martin et al., 2005; Wright, Schieve, Reynolds, & Jeng, 2003).

Mechanisms of Heredity

The science of genetics is the study of *heredity*—the inborn factors, inherited from the biological parents, that affect development. When ovum and sperm unite, they endow the baby-to-be with a genetic makeup that influences a wide range of characteristics from color of eyes and hair to health, intellect, and personality.

The Genetic Code

The basis of heredity is a chemical called **deoxyribonucleic acid (DNA).** The double-helix structure of DNA resembles a long, spiraling ladder whose steps are made of pairs of chemical units called *bases* (see Figure 3-1). The bases—adenine (A), thymine (T), cytosine (C), and guanine (G)—are the "letters" of the **genetic code,** which cellular machinery "reads."

Chromosomes are coils of DNA that consist of smaller segments called **genes,** the functional units of heredity. Each gene is located in a definite position on its chromosome and contains thousands of bases. The sequence of bases in a gene tells the cell how to make the proteins that enable it to carry out specific functions.

Every cell in the normal human body except the sex cells (sperm and ova) has 23 pairs of chromosomes—46 in all. Through a type of cell division called *meiosis,* which the sex cells undergo when they are developing, each sex cell ends up with only 23 chromosomes—one from each pair. Thus, when sperm and ovum fuse at conception, they produce a zygote with 46 chromosomes, 23 from the father and 23 from the mother (see Figure 3-2).

At conception, then, the single-celled zygote has all the biological information needed to guide its development into a human baby. Through *mitosis,* a process by which the nonsex cells divide in half over and over again, the DNA replicates itself, so that each newly formed cell has the same DNA structure as all the others. Thus, each cell division creates a genetic duplicate of the original cell, with the same hereditary information. When development is normal, each cell (except the sex cells) continues to have 46 chromosomes identical to those in the original zygote. As the cells

Guidepost

3. How does heredity operate in determining sex and transmitting normal and abnormal traits?

deoxyribonucleic acid (DNA) Chemical that carries inherited instructions for the development of all cellular forms of life.

genetic code Sequence of bases within the DNA molecule; governs the formation of proteins that determine the structure and functions of living cells.

chromosomes Coils of DNA that consist of genes.

genes Small segments of DNA located in definite positions on articular chromosomes; functional units of heredity.

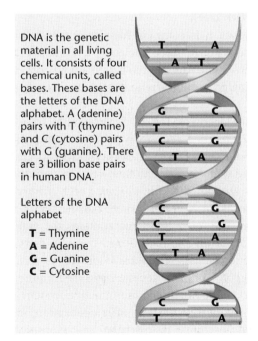

DNA is the genetic material in all living cells. It consists of four chemical units, called bases. These bases are the letters of the DNA alphabet. A (adenine) pairs with T (thymine) and C (cytosine) pairs with G (guanine). There are 3 billion base pairs in human DNA.

Letters of the DNA alphabet

T = Thymine
A = Adenine
G = Guanine
C = Cytosine

Figure 3-1

DNA: The genetic code. (Source: Ritter, 1999.)

Figure 3-2

Hereditary composition of the zygote. (a) Body cells of women and men contain 23 pairs of chromosomes, which carry the genes, the basic units of inheritance. (b) Each sex cell (ovum and sperm) has only 23 single chromosomes because of a special kind of cell division (meiosis) in which the total number of chromosomes is halved. (c) At fertilization, the 23 chromosomes from the sperm join the 23 from the ovum so that the zygote receives 46 chromosomes, or 23 pairs.

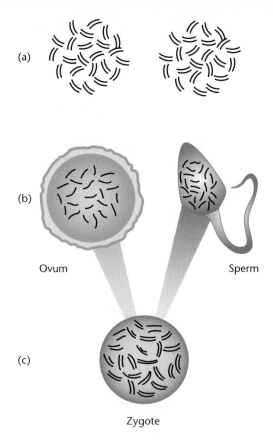

(a)

(b)

Ovum

Sperm

(c)

Zygote

divide, they differentiate, specializing in a variety of complex bodily functions to enable the child to grow and develop.

Genes spring into action when conditions call for the information they can provide. Genetic action that triggers growth of body and brain is often regulated by hormonal levels—both in the mother and in the developing baby—that are affected by such environmental conditions as nutrition and stress. Thus, from the start, heredity and environment are interrelated.

What Determines Sex?

In many villages in Nepal, it is common for a man whose wife has borne no male babies to take a second wife. In some societies, a woman's failure to produce sons is justification for divorce. The irony in the beliefs about conception underlying these customs in male-dominated societies is that it is the father's sperm that determines a child's sex.

At the moment of conception, the 23 chromosomes from the sperm and the 23 from the ovum form 23 pairs. Twenty-two pairs are **autosomes,** chromosomes that are not related to sexual expression. The twenty-third pair are **sex chromosomes**—one from the father and one from the mother—that govern the baby's sex.

Sex chromosomes are either *X chromosomes* or *Y chromosomes.* The sex chromosome of every ovum is an X chromosome, but the sperm may contain either an X or a Y chromosome. The Y chromosome contains the gene for maleness, called the SRY gene. When an ovum (X) is fertilized by an X-carrying sperm, the zygote formed is XX, a genetic female. When an ovum (X) is fertilized by a Y-carrying sperm, the resulting zygote is XY, a genetic male (see Figure 3-3).

Initially, the embryo's rudimentary reproductive system is almost identical in males and in females. About 6 to 8 weeks after conception, male embryos normally start producing the male hormone testosterone, and exposure of a genetically male

autosomes In humans, the 22 pairs of chromosomes not related to sexual differentiation.

sex chromosomes Pair of chromosomes that determine sex: XX in the normal human female, XY in the normal human male.

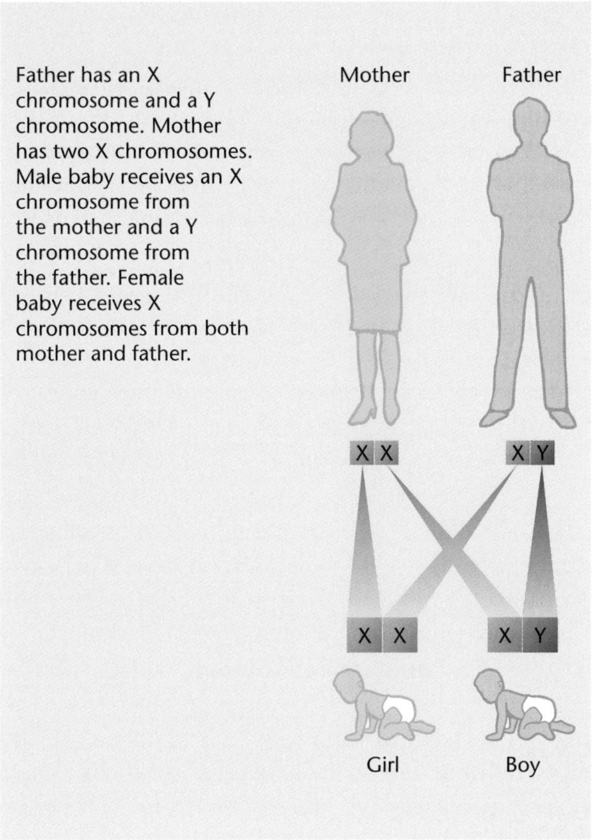

Father has an X chromosome and a Y chromosome. Mother has two X chromosomes. Male baby receives an X chromosome from the mother and a Y chromosome from the father. Female baby receives X chromosomes from both mother and father.

Mother   Father

X X   X Y

X X   X Y

Girl   Boy

Figure 3-3

Determination of sex. Since all babies receive an X chromosome from the mother, sex is determined by whether an X or Y chromosome is received from the father.

embryo to steady, high levels of testosterone ordinarily results in the development of a male body with male sexual organs. However, the process is not automatic. Research with mice has found that hormones must first signal the SRY gene, which then triggers cell differentiation and formation of the testes. Without this signaling, a genetically male mouse will develop female genitals instead of male ones (Hughes, 2004; Meeks, Weiss, & Jameson, 2003; Nef et al., 2003). It is likely that a similar mechanism occurs in human males. Conversely, the development of the female reproductive system is controlled by a signaling molecule called *Wnt-4,* a variant form of which can "masculinize" a genetically female fetus (Biason-Lauber, Konrad, Navratil, & Schoenle, 2004; Hughes, 2004; Vainio, Heikkiia, Kispert, Chin, & McMahon, 1999). Thus, sexual differentiation appears to be a more complex process than simple genetic determination.

Further complications arise from the fact that women have two X chromosomes, whereas men have only one. For many years researchers believed that the "dupli-cate" genes on one of a woman's two X chromosomes are inactivated, or "turned off." Recently, however, researchers sequencing the X chromosome discovered that only 75 percent of the genes on the extra X chromosome are inactive. About 15 percent remain active, and 10 percent are active in some women but not in others (Carrel & Willard, 2005). This variability in levels of gene activity could help explain gender differences both in normal traits and in disorders linked to the X chromosome, which are discussed later in this chapter.

Patterns of Genetic Transmission

During the 1860s, Gregor Mendel, an Austrian monk, laid the foundation for our understanding of patterns of inheritance by cross-breeding pea plants that produced only yellow seeds with pea plants that produced only green seeds. The resulting

Checkpoint
Can you . . .

✔ Describe the structure of DNA and its role in the inheritance of characteristics?

✔ Distinguish between meiosis and mitosis?

✔ Explain why it is the sperm that normally determines a baby's sex and discuss possible complicating factors?

hybrid plants produced only yellow seeds, meaning, he said, that yellow was *dominant* over green. Yet when he bred the yellow-seeded hybrids with each other, only 75 percent of their offspring had yellow seeds, and the other 25 percent had green seeds. This showed that a hereditary characteristic (in this case, the color green) can be *recessive,* that is, carried by an organism that does not express, or show, it.

Today we know that the genetic picture in humans is far more complex than Mendel imagined. Most human traits fall along a continuous spectrum (for example, from light skin to dark). It is hard to find a single normal trait that people inherit through simple dominant transmission other than the ability to curl the tongue lengthwise. Let's look at various forms of inheritance.

Dominant and Recessive Inheritance Can you curl your tongue? If so, you inherited this ability through *dominant inheritance*. If your parents can curl their tongues but you cannot, *recessive inheritance* occurred. How do these two types of inheritance work?

Genes that can produce alternative expressions of a characteristic (such as ability or inability to curl the tongue) are called **alleles.** Every person receives a pair of alleles for a given characteristic, one from each parent. When both alleles are the same, the person is **homozygous** for the characteristic; when they are different, the person is **heterozygous.** In **dominant inheritance,** when a person is heterozygous for a particular trait, the dominant allele governs. In other words, when an offspring receives contradictory alleles for a trait, only one of them, the dominant one, will be expressed. **Recessive inheritance,** the expression of a recessive trait, occurs only when a person receives two recessive alleles, one from each parent.

If you inherited one allele for tongue-curling ability from each parent (see Figure 3-4), you are homozygous for tongue curling and can curl your tongue. If, say, your mother passed on an allele for the ability and your father passed on an allele lacking it, you are heterozygous. Since the ability is dominant (D) and its lack is recessive (d), you, again, can curl your tongue. But if you received the recessive allele from both parents, you would not be a tongue-curler.

alleles Two or more alternative forms of a gene that can occupy the same position on paired chromosomes and affect the same trait.

homozygous Possessing two identical alleles for a trait.

heterozygous Possessing differing alleles for a trait.

dominant inheritance Pattern of inheritance in which, when a child receives different alleles, only the dominant one is expressed.

recessive inheritance Pattern of inheritance in which a child receives identical recessive alleles, resulting in expression of a nondominant trait.

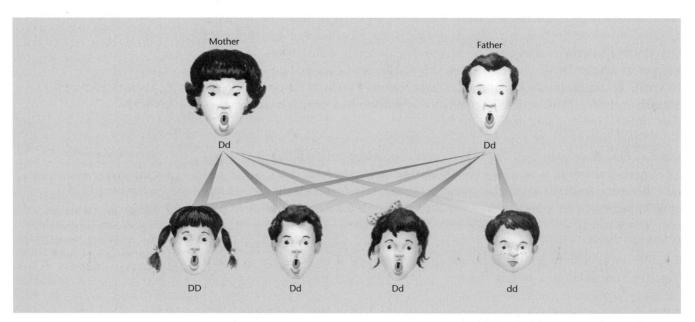

Figure 3-4
Dominant and recessive inheritance. Because of dominant inheritance, the same observable phenotype (in this case, the ability to curl the tongue lengthwise) can result from two different genotypes (DD and Dd). A phenotype expressing a recessive characteristic (such as inability to curl the tongue) must have a homozygous genotype (dd).

Most traits result from **polygenic inheritance,** the interaction of several genes. Skin color is the result of three or more sets of genes on three different chromosomes. These genes work together to produce different amounts of brown pigment, resulting in hundreds of shades of skin color. Intelligence may be affected by fifty or more genes. Indeed, whereas more than a thousand rare genes individually determine abnormal traits, there is no known single gene that, by itself, significantly accounts for individual differences in any complex normal behavior. Instead, such behaviors are likely to be influenced by many genes with small but sometimes identifiable effects. In addition, **multifactorial transmission,** a combination of genetic and environmental factors, plays a role in the expression of most traits.

Genotypes and Phenotypes: Multifactorial Transmission   If you can curl your tongue, that ability is part of your **phenotype,** the observable characteristics through which your **genotype,** or underlying genetic makeup, is expressed. Except for monozygotic twins, no two people have the same genotype. The phenotype is the product of the genotype and any relevant environmental influences. The difference between genotype and phenotype helps explain why a clone (a genetic copy of an individual) or an identical twin can never be an exact duplicate of another person.

As Figure 3-4 shows, the same phenotypical characteristic may arise from different genotypes: either a homozygous combination of two dominant alleles or a heterozygous combination of one dominant allele and one recessive allele. If you are heterozygous for tongue curling, and you and a mate who is also heterozygous for the trait have four children, the statistical probability is that one child will be homozygous for the ability, one will be homozygous lacking it, and the other two will be heterozygous. Thus, three of your children will likely have phenotypes that include tongue curling (they will be able to curl their tongues), but this ability will arise from two different genotypical patterns (homozygous and heterozygous).

Tongue curling has a strong genetic base; but for most traits, experience modifies the expression of the genotype. Imagine that Steven has inherited musical talent. If he takes music lessons and practices regularly, he may delight his family with his performances. If his family likes and encourages classical music, he may play Bach preludes; if the other children on his block influence him to prefer popular music, he may eventually form a rock group. However, if from early childhood he is not encouraged and not motivated to play music, and if he has no access to a musical instrument or to music lessons, his genotype for musical ability may not be expressed (or may be expressed to a lesser extent) in his phenotype. Some physical characteristics (including height and weight) and most psychological characteristics (such as intelligence and personality traits, as well as musical ability) are products of multifactorial transmission. Many disorders arise when an inherited predisposition (an abnormal variant of a normal gene) interacts with an environmental factor, either before or after birth. Attention deficit disorder with hyperactivity (ADHD), discussed in Chapter 9, is one of a number of behavioral disorders thought to be transmitted multifactorially (Price, Simonoff, Waldman, Asherson, & Plomin, 2001).

Later in this chapter we discuss in more detail how environmental influences work together with the genetic endowment to influence development.

Genetic and Chromosomal Abnormalities

Babies born with serious birth defects are at high risk of dying at or shortly after birth or during infancy or childhood. Although most birth disorders are fairly rare (see Table 3-1), they were the leading cause of infant death in the United States in 2003, according to preliminary data, accounting for 20 percent of all deaths in the first year of life (Hoyert, Kung, & Smith, 2005). Most of the serious malformations involve the circulatory or central nervous systems.

The ability to curl the tongue lengthwise, as this girl is doing, is unusual in that it is inherited through simple dominant transmission. Most normal traits are influenced by multiple genes, often in combination with environmental factors.

polygenic inheritance   Pattern of inheritance in which multiple genes at different sites on chromosomes affect a complex trait.

multifactorial transmission Combination of genetic and environmental factors to produce certain complex traits.

phenotype   Observable characteristics of a person.

genotype   Genetic makeup of a person, containing both expressed and unexpressed characteristics.

Checkpoint
Can you . . .

✔ Tell how dominant inheritance and recessive inheritance work and why most normal traits are *not* the products of simple dominant or recessive transmission?

Table 3-1 Some Birth Defects

Problem	Characteristics of Condition	Who Is at Risk	What Can Be Done
Alpha₁ antitrypsin deficiency	Enzyme deficiency that can lead to cirrhosis of the liver in early infancy and emphysema and degenerative lung disease in middle age.	1 in 1,000 white births	No treatment.
Alpha thalassemia	Severe anemia that reduces ability of the blood to carry oxygen; nearly all affected infants are stillborn or die soon after birth.	Primarily families of Malaysian, African, and Southeast Asian descent	Frequent blood transfusions.
Beta thalassemia (Cooley's anemia)	Severe anemia resulting in weakness, fatigue, and frequent illness; usually fatal in adolescence or young adulthood.	Primarily families of Mediterranean descent	Frequent blood transfusions.
Cystic fibrosis	Overproduction of mucus, which collects in the lung and digestive tract; children do not grow normally and usually do not live beyond age 30; the most common inherited *lethal* defect among white people.	1 in 2,000 white births	Daily physical therapy to loosen mucus; antibiotics for lung infections; enzymes to improve digestion; gene therapy (in experimental stage).
Duchenne muscular dystrophy	Fatal disease usually found in males, marked by muscle weakness; minor mental retardation is common; respiratory failure and death usually occur in young adulthood.	1 in 3,000 to 5,000 male births	No treatment.
Hemophilia	Excessive bleeding, usually affecting males rather than females; in its most severe form, can lead to crippling arthritis in adulthood.	1 in 10,000 families with a history of hemophilia	Frequent transfusions of blood with clotting factors.
Neural-tube defects: Anencephaly	Absence of brain tissues; infants are stillborn or die soon after birth.	1 in 1,000	No treatment.
Spina bifida	Incompletely closed spinal canal, resulting in muscle weakness or paralysis and loss of bladder and bowell control; often accompanied by hydrocephalus, an accumulation of spinal fluid in the brain, which can lead to mental retardation.	1 in 1,000	Surgery to close spinal canal prevents further injury; shunt placed in brain drains excess fluid and prevents mental retardation.
Phenylketonuria (PKU)	Metabolic disorder resulting in mental retardation.	1 in 15,000 births	Special diet begun in first few weeks of life can prevent mental retardation.
Polycystic kidney disease	*Infantile form;* enlarged kidneys, leading to respiratory problems and congestive heart failure. *Adult form;* kidney pain, kidney stones, and hypertension resulting in chronic kidney failure.	1 in 1,000	Kidney transplants.
Sickle-cell anemia	Deformed, fragile red blood cells that can clog the blood vessels, depriving the body of oxygen; symptoms include severe pain, stunted growth, frequent infections, leg ulcers, gallstones, susceptibility to pneumonia, and stroke.	1 in 500 African Americans	Painkillers, transfusions for anemia and to prevent stroke, antibiotics for infections.
Tay-Sachs disease	Degenerative disease of the brain and nerve cells, resulting in death before age 5.	Historically found mainly in eastern European Jews	No treatment.

Source: Adapted from AAP Committee on Genetics, 1996; NIH Consensus Development Panel, 2001; Tisdale, 1988, pp. 68–69.

Not all genetic or chromosomal abnormalities are apparent at birth. Symptoms of Tay-Sachs disease (a fatal degenerative disease of the central nervous system that at one time occurred mostly among Jews of eastern European ancestry) and sickle-cell anemia (a blood disorder most common among African Americans) may not appear until at least 6 months of age; cystic fibrosis (a condition, especially common in children of northern European descent, in which excess mucus accumulates in the lungs and digestive tract), not until age 4; and glaucoma (a disease in which fluid pressure builds up in the eye) and Huntington's disease (a progressive degeneration of the nervous system) usually not until middle age.

It is in genetic defects and diseases that we see most clearly the operation of dominant and recessive transmission, and also of a variation, *sex-linked inheritance,* discussed in a subsequent section.

Defects Transmitted by Dominant or Recessive Inheritance   Most of the time, normal genes are dominant over those carrying abnormal traits, but sometimes the gene for an abnormal trait is dominant. When one parent has a dominant abnormal gene and one recessive normal gene and the other parent has two recessive normal genes, each of their children has a 50-50 chance of inheriting the dominant abnormal gene. Among the 1,800 disorders known to be transmitted by dominant inheritance are achondroplasia (a type of dwarfism) and Huntington's disease.

Recessive defects are expressed only if a child receives the same recessive gene from each biological parent. Some defects transmitted recessively, such as Tay-Sachs disease and sickle-cell anemia, which interferes with the transport of oxygen in the blood, are more common among certain ethnic groups, which, through inbreeding (marriage and reproduction within the group), have passed down recessive characteristics (see Table 3-2).

Defects transmitted by recessive inheritance are more likely to be lethal at an early age than those transmitted by dominant inheritance. If a dominantly transmitted defect killed before the age of reproduction, it could not be passed on to the next

Table 3-2	Chances of Genetic Disorders for Various Ethnic Groups	
If You Are	**The Chance Is About**	**That**
African American	1 in 12	You are a carrier of sickle-cell anemia.
	7 in 10	You will have milk intolerance as an adult.
African American and male	1 in 10	You have a hereditary predisposition to develop hemolytic anemia after taking sulfa or other drugs.
African American and female	1 in 50	You have a hereditary predisposition to develop hemolytic anemia after taking sulfa or other drugs.
White	1 in 25	You are a carrier of cystic fibrosis.
	1 in 80	You are a carrier of phenylketonuria (PKU).
Jewish (Ashkenazic)	1 in 100	You are a carrier of familial dysautonomia.
Italian American or Greek American	1 in 10	You are a carrier of beta thalassemia.
Armenian or Jewish (Sephardic)	1 in 45	You are a carrier of familial. Mediterranean fever.
Afrikaner (white South African)	1 in 330	You have porphyria.
Asian	almost 100%	You will have milk intolerance as an adult.

Source: Adapted from Milunsky, 1992, p. 122.

Figure 3-5

Sex-linked inheritance.

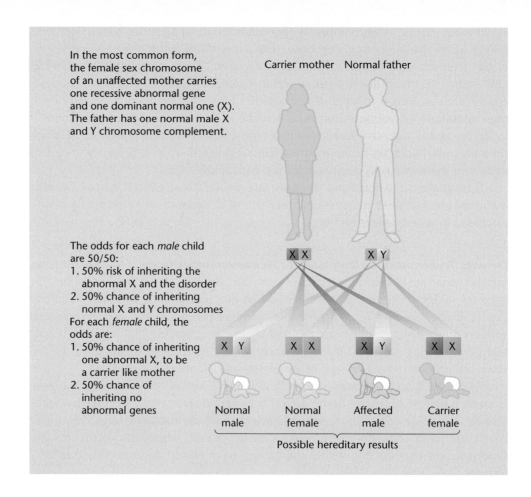

In the most common form, the female sex chromosome of an unaffected mother carries one recessive abnormal gene and one dominant normal one (X). The father has one normal male X and Y chromosome complement.

Carrier mother   Normal father

The odds for each *male* child are 50/50:
1. 50% risk of inheriting the abnormal X and the disorder
2. 50% chance of inheriting normal X and Y chromosomes

For each *female* child, the odds are:
1. 50% chance of inheriting one abnormal X, to be a carrier like mother
2. 50% chance of inheriting no abnormal genes

Normal male   Normal female   Affected male   Carrier female

Possible hereditary results

generation and therefore would soon disappear. A recessive defect can be transmitted by carriers who do not have the disorder and thus may live to reproduce.

Some traits are only partly dominant or partly recessive. In **incomplete dominance** a trait is not fully expressed. For example, people with only one sickle-cell allele and one normal allele do not have sickle-cell anemia but do show some manifestations of the condition, such as shortness of breath at high altitudes.

Defects Transmitted by Sex-Linked Inheritance   In **sex-linked inheritance** (see Figure 3-5) certain recessive disorders linked to genes on sex chromosomes affect male and female children differently. Red-green color blindness is one of these sex-linked conditions. Another is hemophilia, a disorder in which blood does not clot when it should.

Sex-linked recessive traits are carried on one of the X chromosomes of an unaffected mother. The mother is a *carrier;* she does not have the disorder but can pass on the gene for it to her children. Sex-linked disorders almost always appear only in male children; in females, a normal dominant gene on the X chromosome from the father generally overrides the defective gene on the X chromosome from the mother. Boys are more vulnerable to these disorders because there is no opposite dominant gene on the shorter Y chromosome from the father to override a defect on the X chromosome from the mother.

Occasionally, however, a female does inherit a sex-linked condition. For example, if her father is a hemophiliac and her mother happens to be a carrier for the disorder, the daughter has a 50 percent chance of receiving the abnormal X chromosome from each parent and having the disease.

Mutations   Some defects are due to abnormalities in genes or chromosomes, which may result from **mutations:** permanent alterations in genetic material. Mutations can

incomplete dominance   Pattern of inheritance in which a child receives two different alleles, resulting in partial expression of a trait.

sex-linked-inheritance   Pattern of inheritance in which certain characteristics carried on the X chromosome inherited from the mother are transmitted differently to her male and female offspring.

mutations   Permanent alterations in genes or chromosomes that may produce harmful characteristics.

occur spontaneously or can be induced by environmental hazards, such as radiation. It has been estimated that the human species undergoes at least 1.6 harmful mutations per person in each generation. Eventually, these mutations may be eliminated from the human genome by **natural selection,** the failure of affected individuals to survive and reproduce (Crow, 1999; Eyre-Walker & Keightley, 1999; Keightley & Eyre-Walker, 2001).

Genome (Genetic) Imprinting *Genome,* or *genetic, imprinting* is the differential expression of certain genetic traits, depending on whether the trait has been inherited from the mother or the father. In a few specific regions of the genome, genetic information is activated when inherited from the parent of one sex but not from the other. If imprinting is disturbed, abnormal fetal growth and development may result (Hitchins & Moore, 2002).

Problems in genome imprinting may explain why the child of a diabetic father but not of a diabetic mother is likely to develop diabetes and why the opposite is true for asthma (Day, 1993). Imprinting problems also may explain why children who inherit Huntington's disease from their fathers are far more likely to be affected at an early age than children who inherit the Huntington's gene from their mothers (Sapienza, 1990) and why children who receive a certain allele from their mothers are more likely to have autism than those who receive that allele from their fathers (Ingram et al., 2000).

Chromosomal Abnormalities Chromosomal abnormalities typically occur because of errors in cell division, resulting in an extra or missing chromosome. Some of these errors happen in the sex cells during meiosis. For example, Klinefelter syndrome is caused by an extra sex chromosome (shown by the pattern XXY). Turner syndrome results from a missing sex chromosome (XO). The likelihood of errors in meiosis may increase in women age 35 or older. (University of Virginia Health System, 2004). Characteristics of the most common sex chromosome disorders are shown in Table 3-3.

Other chromosomal abnormalities occur in the autosomes during cell division (University of Virginia Health System, 2004). **Down syndrome,** the most common

natural selection According to Darwin's theory of evolution, process by which characteristics that promote survival of a species are reproduced in successive generations, and characteristics that do not promote survival die out.

Checkpoint
Can you . . .

✔ Explain the operation of dominant inheritance, recessive inheritance, incomplete dominance, sex-linked inheritance, mutuations, and genome imprinting in transmission of birth defects?

Down syndrome Chromosomal disorder characterized by moderate-to-severe mental retardation and by such physical signs as a downward sloping skinfold at the inner corners of the eyes.

Table 3-3	Sex Chromosome Abnormalities		
Pattern/Name	**Characteristics***	**Incidence**	**Treatment**
XYY	Male; tall stature; tendency to low IQ, especially verbal.	1 in 1,000 male births	No special treatment
XXX (triple X)	Female; normal appearance, menstrual irregularities, learning disorders, mental retardation.	1 in 1,000 female births	Special education
XXY (Kleinfelter)	Male; sterility, underdeveloped secondary sex characteristics, small testes, learning disorders.	1 in 1,000 male births	Hormone therapy, special education
XO (Turner)	Female; short stature, webbed neck, impaired spatial abilities, no menstruation, infertility, underdeveloped sex organs, incomplete development of secondary sex characteristics.	1 in 1,500 to 2,500 female births	Hormone therapy, special education
Fragile X	Minor-to-severe mental retardation; symptoms, which are more severe in males, include delayed speech and motor development, speech impairments, and hyperactivity; the most common *inherited* form of mental retardation.	1 in 1,200 male births; 1 in 2,000 female births	Educational and behavioral therapies when needed

*Not every affected person has every characteristic.

This boy shows the chief identifying characteristic of Down syndrome: a downward sloping skinfold at the inner corner of the eye. Although Down syndrome is a major cause of mental retardation, children with this chromosomal abnormality have a good chance of living productive lives.

of these, is responsible for about 40 percent of all cases of moderate-to-severe mental retardation (Pennington, Moon, Edgin, Stedron, & Nadel, 2003). The condition is also called *trisomy-21,* because it is usually caused by an extra 21st chromosome or the translocation of part of the 21st chromosome onto another chromosome. The most obvious physical characteristic associated with the disorder is a downward-sloping skin fold at the inner corners of the eyes.

Approximately 1 in every 600 babies born alive has Down syndrome. About 94 percent of these babies are born to normal parents (Pennington et al., 2003). The risk is greatest with older parents; when the mother is under age 35, the disorder is more likely to be hereditary. The extra chromosome seems to come from the mother's ovum in 95 percent of cases (Antonarakis & Down Syndrome Collaborative Group, 1991); the other 5 percent of cases seem to be related to the father.

The brains of these children appear normal at birth but shrink in volume by young adulthood, particularly in the hippocampal area, resulting in cognitive dysfunction (Pennington et al., 2003). The prognosis for children with Down syndrome is brighter than was once thought. As adults, many live in small group homes and support themselves; they tend to do well in structured job situations. More than 70 percent of people with Down syndrome live into their 60s, but they are at elevated risk of early death from various causes, including leukemia, cancer, Alzheimer's disease, and cardiovascular disease (Hayes & Batshaw, 1993; Hill et al., 2003).

Genetic Counseling and Testing

genetic counseling Clinical service that advises couples of their probable risk of having children with hereditary defects.

Genetic counseling can help prospective parents assess their risk of bearing children with genetic or chromosomal defects. People who have already had a child with a genetic defect, who have a family history of hereditary illness, who suffer from conditions known or suspected to be inherited, or who come from ethnic groups at higher-than-average risk of passing on genes for certain diseases can get information about their likelihood of producing affected children.

Geneticists have made great contributions to avoidance of birth defects. For example, since so many Jewish couples have been tested for Tay-Sachs genes, the disease has been virtually eliminated from this population (Kolata, 2003). Similarly, screening and counseling of women of childbearing age from Mediterranean countries, where beta thalassemia (refer back to Table 3-1) is common, has brought a decline in births of affected babies and greater knowledge of the risks of being a carrier (Cao, Saba, Galanello, & Rosatelli, 1997).

A genetic counselor takes a family history and gives the prospective parents and any biological children physical examinations. Laboratory investigations of blood, skin, urine, or fingerprints may be performed. Chromosomes from body tissues may be analyzed and photographed, and the photographs enlarged and arranged according to size and structure on a chart called a *karyotype.* This chart can show chromosomal abnormalities and can indicate whether a person who appears normal might transmit genetic defects to a child (see Figure 3-6). The counselor tries to help clients understand the mathematical risk of a particular condition, explains its implications, and presents information about alternative courses of action.

Today, researchers are rapidly identifying genes that contribute to many serious diseases and disorders, as well as those that influence normal traits. Their work is

Checkpoint

Can you . . .

✔ Tell three ways chromosomal disorders occur?

✔ Explain the purposes of genetic counseling?

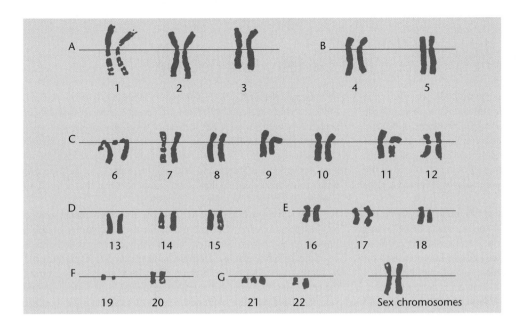

Figure 3-6

A karyotype is a photograph that shows the chromosomes when they are separated and aligned for cell division. We know that this is a karyotype of a person with Down syndrome because there are three chromosomes instead of the usual two on chromosome 21. Because pair 23 consists of two X's, we know that this is the karyotype of a female. (Source: Babu & Hirschhorn, 1992; March of Dimes, 1987.)

likely to lead to widespread genetic testing to reveal genetic profiles—a prospect that involves dangers as well as benefits (see Box 3-1).

Nature and Nurture: Influences of Heredity and Environment

As we discussed in Chapters 1 and 2, the relative importance of heredity and environment was a major issue among early psychologists and the general public. Today it has become clear that, although certain rare physical disorders are virtually 100 percent inherited, phenotypes for most normal traits, such as those having to do with intelligence and personality, are subject to a complex array of hereditary and environmental forces. Let's see how scientists study and explain the influences of heredity and environment and how these two forces work together.

Studying Heredity and Environment

One approach to the study of heredity and environment is quantitative: it seeks to measure *how much* heredity and environment influence particular traits. This is the traditional goal of the science of **behavioral genetics.**

Measuring Heritability   **Heritability** is a statistical estimate of how great a contribution heredity makes toward variability of a specific trait at a certain time *within a given population.* Heritability does *not* refer to the relative influence of heredity and environment between populations or in a particular individual; those influences may be virtually impossible to separate. Nor does heritability tell us how traits develop or to what extent they can be modified. It merely indicates the statistical extent to which genes contribute to individual differences in a trait in a certain population (Sternberg, Grigorenko, & Kidd, 2005).

Heritability is expressed as a number ranging from 0.0 to 1.0; the greater the number, the greater the heritability of a trait, with 1.0 meaning that genes are 100 percent responsible for differences in the trait. Because heritability cannot be measured directly, researchers in behavioral genetics rely chiefly on three types of correlational research: family, adoption, and twin studies. Such studies are based on the

Guidepost

4. How do scientists study the relative influences of heredity and environment, and how do heredity and environment work together?

behavioral genetics   Quantitative study of relative hereditary and environmental influences on behavior.

heritability   Statistical estimate of contribution of heredity to individual differences in a specific trait within a given population.

BOX 3-1

Practically Speaking
Genetic Testing and Genetic Engineering

The complete sequence of genes in the human body constitutes the *human genome.* Scientists have now completed the mapping of the human genome, which is estimated to contain between 20,000 and 25,000 genes (International Human Genome Sequencing Consortium, 2004). Among the interesting findings are that all but 300 human genes have counterparts in mice (Wade, 2001), and the genomes of humans and chimpanzees are nearly 99 percent alike (Clark et al., 2003).

The mapping of the human genome has greatly advanced our ability to identify which genes control specific traits or behaviors and the developmental unfolding of these traits (Parke, 2004). A new field of science, *genomics,* the study of the functions and interactions of the various genes, will have untold implications for *medical genetics,* the application of genetic information to therapeutic purposes (McKusick, 2001; Patenaude, Guttmacher, & Collins, 2002). As efforts shift from finding genes to understanding how they affect behavior (behavioral genomics), scientists will be able to identify genes that cause, trigger, or increase susceptibility to particular disorders (Plomin & Crabbe, 2000) so as to screen at-risk population groups (Khoury, McCabe, & McCabe, 2003).

The genetic information gained from such research could increase our ability to predict, prevent, control, treat, and cure disease—even to pinpoint specific drug treatments to specific individuals (McGuffin et al., 2001; McKusick, 2001; Patenaude et al., 2002; Rutter, 2002; Subramanian, Adams, Venter, & Broder, 2001). Already, genetic screening of newborns is saving lives and preventing mental retardation by permitting identification and treatment of infants with such disorders as sickle-cell anemia

and phenylketonuria (PKU) (Holtzman, Murphy, Watson, & Barr, 1997; Khoury et al., 2003). Genetic screening for breast cancer probably would identify 88 percent of all high-risk persons, significantly more than are identified by currently used risk factors (Pharoah et al., 2002). Genetic information can help people decide whether to have children and with whom, and it can help people with family histories of a disease to know the worst that is likely to happen (Post, 1994; Wiggins et al., 1992).

Gene therapy (repairing or replacing abnormal genes), once a bright hope, appears to have dimmed for the time being. In 2000, French researchers reversed severe combined immunodeficiency, a serious immune disease, in three babies from 1 to 11 months old by taking bone marrow cells from the babies, genetically altering the cells, and then injecting them into the babies. At follow-up one year later, the patients remained healthy (Cavazanna-Calvo et al., 2000). But three of the children have since developed leukemia, and one of the three has died, leading a U.S. drug advisory panel to consider suspending three major gene therapy trials. In 1999 another death occurred in a gene therapy experiment at the University of Pennsylvania (Harris, 2005).

Genetic testing itself involves such ethical and political issues as privacy and fair use of genetic information (Clayton, 2003; Jeffords & Daschle, 2001; Patenaude et al, 2002). Although medical data are supposed to be confidential, it is almost impossible to keep such information private. Some courts have ruled that blood relatives have a legitimate claim to information about a patient's genetic health risks that may affect them, even though such disclosures violate confidentiality (Clayton, 2003).

assumption that immediate family members are more genetically similar than more distant relatives, monozygotic twins are more genetically similar than dizygotic twins, and adopted children are genetically more like their biological families than their adoptive families. Thus, if heredity is an important influence on a particular trait, siblings should be more alike than cousins with regard to that trait, monozygotic twins should be more alike than dizygotic twins, and adopted children should be more like their biological parents than their adoptive parents. By the same token, if a shared environment exerts an important influence on a trait, persons who grew up together in the same household should be more similar than persons who did not.

In *family studies,* researchers measure the degree to which biological relatives share certain traits and whether the closeness of the familial relationship is associated with the degree of similarity. If the correlation is strong, the researchers infer a genetic influence. However, family studies cannot rule out environmental influences. A family study alone cannot tell us whether obese children of obese parents inherited the tendency or whether they are fat because their diet is like that of their parents. For that reason, researchers do adoption studies, which can separate the effects of heredity from those of a shared environment.

Adoption studies look at similarities between adopted children and their adoptive families and also between adopted children and their biological families. When adopted children are more like their biological parents and siblings in a particular trait (say, obesity), we see the influence of heredity. When they resemble their adoptive families more, we see the influence of environment.

What's Your View?

- In what ways are you like your mother and in what ways like your father? How are you similar and dissimilar to your siblings? Which differences would you guess come chiefly from heredity and which from environment? Can you see possible effects of both?

Practically Speaking

—continued

A major concern is *genetic determinism:* the misconception that a person with a gene for a disease is bound to get the disease. All genetic testing can tell us is the *likelihood* that a person will get a disease. Most diseases involve a complex combination of genes or depend in part on lifestyle or other environmental factors (Clayton, 2003; Plomin & Rutter, 1998; Rutter, 2002). Job and insurance discrimination on the basis of genetic information has occurred—even though tests may be imprecise and unreliable and people deemed at risk of a disease may never develop it (Clayton, 2003; Khoury et al., 2003; Lapham, Kozma, & Weiss, 1996). Federal and state antidiscrimination laws provide some protection, but it is not consistent or comprehensive (Clayton, 2003). Policies protecting confidentiality of research also are needed (Jeffords & Daschle, 2001).

The psychological impact of test results is another concern (Patenaude et al, 2002). Predictions are imperfect; a false positive result may cause needless anxiety, and a false negative result may lull a person into complacency. And what if a genetic condition is incurable? Is there any point in knowing you have the gene for a potentially debilitating condition if you cannot do anything about it? A panel of experts has recommended against genetic testing for diseases for which there is no known cure (Institute of Medicine [IOM], 1993).

Additional concerns involve the testing of children. Should a child be tested to benefit a sibling or someone else? How will a child be affected by learning that he or she is likely to develop a disease 20, 30, or 50 years later? The American Academy of Pediatrics Committee on Bioethics (2001) recommends against genetic testing of children for conditions that cannot be treated in childhood.

Particularly chilling is the prospect that genetic testing could be misused to justify sterilization of people with "undesirable" genes or abortion of a normal fetus with the "wrong" genetic makeup (Plomin & Rutter, 1998). Gene therapy has the potential for similar abuse. Should it be used to make a short child taller or a chubby child thinner? To improve an unborn baby's appearance or intelligence? The path from therapeutic correction of defects to genetic engineering for cosmetic or functional purposes may well be a slippery slope (Anderson, 1998), leading to a society in which some parents could afford to provide the "best" genes for their children and others could not (Rifkin, 1998).

Within the next 15 years, genetic testing "will almost certainly revolutionize the practice of medicine" (Anderson, 1998, p. 30). It is not yet clear whether the benefits will outweigh the risks.

What's Your View?

Would you want to know that you had a gene predisposing you to lung cancer? To Alzheimer's disease? Would you want your child to be tested for these genes?

Check It Out

For more information on this topic, go to http://www.ornl.gov/hgmis/resource/medicine.html. This is the Human Genome Project Web site. Information about disease diagnosis and prediction, disease intervention, genetic counseling, and ethical, legal, and social issues is presented.

Studies of twins compare pairs of monozygotic twins and same-sex dizygotic twins. (Same-sex twins are used so as to avoid any confounding effects of gender.) Monozygotic twins are twice as genetically similar, on average, as dizygotic twins, who are no more genetically similar than other same-sex siblings. When monozygotic twins are more **concordant** (that is, have a statistically greater tendency to show the same trait) than dizygotic twins, we see the likely effects of heredity. Concordance rates, which may range from 0.0 to 1.0, estimate the probability that a pair of twins in a sample will be concordant for that trait.

concordant Term describing tendency of twins to share the same trait or disorder.

When monozygotic twins show higher concordance for a trait than do dizygotic twins, the likelihood of a genetic factor can be studied further through adoption studies. Studies of monozygotic twins separated in infancy and reared apart have found strong resemblances between the twins. Twin and adoption studies support a moderate to high hereditary basis for many normal and abnormal characteristics (McGuffin et al., 2001).

To learn more about how twin studies can help researchers understand the interactions of heredity and environment, watch the video, "Nature and Nurture: The study of Twins," in Chapter 3 of your CD.

Critics of behavioral genetics claim that its assumptions and methods tend to maximize the importance of hereditary effects and minimize environmental ones. Also, there are great variations in the findings, depending on the source of the data. For example, twin studies generally come up with higher heritability estimates than adoption studies do. This wide variability, critics say, "means that no firm conclusions can be drawn about the relative strength of these influences on development" (Collins, Maccoby, Steinberg, Hetherington, & Bornstein, 2000, p. 221).

Monozygotic twins separated at birth are sought after by researchers who want to study the impact of genes on personality. These twins, adopted by different families and not reunited till age 31, both became firefighters. Was this a coincidence, or did it reflect the influence of heredity?

Checkpoint
Can you . . .

✔ State the basic assumption underlying studies of behavioral genetics and how it applies to family studies, twin studies, and adoption studies?

✔ Cite criticisms of the behavioral genetics approach?

Even behavioral geneticists recognize that the effects of genetic influences, especially on behavioral traits, are rarely inevitable: Even in a trait strongly influenced by heredity, the environment can have substantial impact (Rutter, 2002), as much as 50 percent. In fact, environmental interventions sometimes can overcome genetically "determined" conditions. For example, a special diet begun soon after birth often can prevent mental retardation in children with the genetic disease phenylketonuria (PKU) (Plomin & DeFries, 1999; refer back to Table 3-1).

How Heredity and Environment Work Together

Today many developmental scientists have come to regard a solely quantitative approach to the study of heredity and environment as simplistic (Collins et al., 2000). They see these two forces as fundamentally intertwined (Parke, 2004). Instead of looking at genes and experience as operating directly on an organism, they see both as part of a complex *developmental system* (Gottlieb, 1991). From conception on, throughout life, a combination of constitutional factors (related to biological and psychological makeup), and social, economic, and cultural factors help shape development. The more advantageous these circumstances and the experiences to which they give rise, the greater is the likelihood of optimum development (Horowitz, 2000).

Let's consider several ways in which inheritance and experience work together.

Reaction Range and Canalization Many characteristics vary, within limits, under varying hereditary or environmental conditions. The concepts of *reaction range* and *canalization* can help us visualize how this happens.

reaction range Potential variability, depending on environmental conditions, in the expression of a hereditary trait.

Reaction range refers to a range of potential expressions of a hereditary trait. Body size, for example, depends largely on biological processes, which are genetically regulated. Even so, a range of sizes is possible, depending on environmental opportunities and constraints and a person's own behavior. In societies in which nutrition has dramatically improved, an entire generation has grown up to tower over the generation before. The better-fed children share their parents' genes but have responded to a healthier world. Once a society's average diet becomes adequate for more than one generation, however, children tend to grow to heights similar to their parents'. Ultimately, height has genetic limits: We don't see people who are only a foot tall, or any who are 10 feet tall.

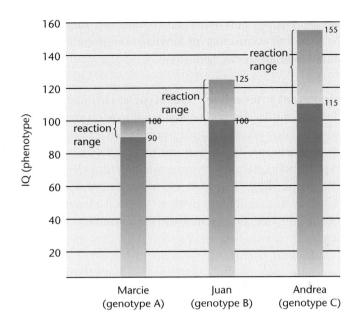

Figure 3-7

Intelligence and reaction range. Children with different genotypes for intelligence will show varying reaction ranges when exposed to a restricted (blue portion of bar) or enriched (entire bar) environment.

Heredity can influence whether a reaction range is wide or narrow. For example, a child born with a defect producing mild retardation is more able to respond to a favorable environment than a child born with more severe limitations. Likewise, a child with greater native intelligence is likely to benefit more from an enriched home and school environment than a child with normal ability (see Figure 3-7).

Instead of a reaction range, advocates of a developmental system model prefer to talk about a *norm of reaction*. Although they recognize that heredity does set some limits, they argue that, because development is so complex, these limits are unknowable and their effects unpredictable (Gottlieb, 1991).

The metaphor of **canalization** illustrates how heredity restricts the range of development for some traits. After a heavy storm, the rainwater that has fallen on a pavement has to go somewhere. If the street has potholes, the water will fill them. If deep canals have been dug along the edges of the street, the water will flow into the canals instead. Some human characteristics, such as eye color, are so strongly programmed by the genes that they are said to be highly canalized: There is little opportunity for environmental influence on their expression.

Certain *behaviors* also develop along genetically "dug" channels; it takes an extreme change in environment to alter their course. Behaviors that depend largely on maturation seem to appear when a child is ready. Normal babies follow a typical sequence of motor development: crawling, walking, and running, in that order, at certain approximate ages. However, this development is not completely canalized; experience can affect its pace and timing. Cognition and personality are more subject to variations in experience: the kinds of families children grow up in, the schools they attend, and the people they encounter. Consider language. Before children can talk, they must reach a certain level of neurological and muscular maturation. No 6-month-old could speak this sentence, no matter how enriched the infant's home life might be. Environment too plays a large part in language development. If parents encourage babies' first sounds by talking back to them, children are likely to start to speak earlier than if their early vocalizing is ignored.

Recently scientists have begun to recognize that a usual or typical *experience* can dig canals, or channels for development (Gottlieb, 1991). For example, infants who hear only the sounds peculiar to their native language soon lose the ability to perceive sounds characteristic of other languages (see Chapter 5). Throughout this book you will find many examples of how socioeconomic status, neighborhood

canalization Limitation on variance of expression of certain inherited characteristics.

conditions, and educational opportunity can powerfully shape developmental outcomes, from the pace and complexity of language development to the likelihood of early sexual activity and antisocial behavior.

genotype-environment interaction The portion of phenotypic variation that results from the reactions of genetically different individuals to similar environmental conditions.

Genotype-Environment Interaction   **Genotype-environment interaction** usually refers to the effects of similar environmental conditions on genetically different individuals. To take a familiar example, many people are exposed to pollen and dust, but people with a genetic predisposition are more likely to develop allergic reactions. Interactions can work the other way as well: Genetically similar children often develop differently depending on their home environment (Collins et al., 2000). As we discuss in Chapter 6, a child born with a "difficult" temperament may develop adjustment problems in one family and thrive in another, depending largely on parental handling.

genotype-environment correlation Tendency of certain genetic and environmental influences to reinforce each other; may be passive, reactive (evocative), or active. Also called *genotype-environment covariance.*

Genotype-Environment Correlation   Sometimes genetic and environmental influences act in the same direction, that is, environmental characteristics reflect or reinforce genetic differences. This is called **genotype-environment correlation,** or *genotype-environment covariance,* and it works in three ways to strengthen the phenotypic expression of a genotypic tendency (Bergeman & Plomin, 1989; Scarr, 1992; Scarr & McCartney, 1983):

- *Passive correlations:* Parents, who provide the genes that predispose a child toward a trait, also tend to provide an environment that encourages the development of that trait. For example, a musical parent is likely to create a home environment in which music is heard regularly, to give a child music lessons, and to take the child to musical events. If the child inherited the parent's musical talent, the child's musicality will reflect a combination of genetic and environmental influences. This type of correlation is called *passive* because the child has no control over it. It is most applicable to young children, whose parents, the source of their genetic legacy, also have a great deal of control over their early experiences.

Musical ability is one of many characteristics passed on from parents to children through a combination of genetic and environmental influences. This father playing the guitar with this daughter may be more motivated to do so because she shows interest and ability in music. In turn, the enjoyable experience with her father is likely to strengthen the little girl's natural inclination toward music.

- *Reactive, or evocative, correlations:* Children with differing genetic makeups evoke different responses from adults. Parents who are *not* musically inclined may make a special effort to provide musical experiences to a child who shows interest and ability in music that they might not otherwise provide. This response, in turn, strengthens the child's genetic inclination toward music.

- *Active correlations:* As children get older and have more freedom to choose their own activities and environments, they actively select or create experiences consistent with their genetic tendencies. A child with a talent for music will probably seek out musical friends, take music classes, and go to concerts if such opportunities are available. A shy child is more likely than an outgoing child to spend more time in solitary pursuits. This tendency to seek out environments compatible with one's genotype is called **niche-picking;** it helps explain why identical twins reared apart tend to have similar lifestyles.

niche-picking Tendency of a person, especially after early childhood, to seek out environments compatible with his or her genotype.

What Makes Siblings Different? The Nonshared Environment Although some children in the same family bear a striking physical resemblance, siblings can be very different in intellect and especially in personality. One reason may be genetic or temperamental differences, which lead children to respond differently to a similar home environment. A child with a high IQ may be more stimulated by a roomful of books and puzzles than a child with a markedly lower IQ—an example of genotype-environment interaction. One child may be more affected by family discord than another (Rutter, 2002). In addition, studies in behavioral genetics suggest that many of the experiences that strongly affect development are different for different children in a family (McGuffin et al., 2001; Plomin & Daniels, 1987; Plomin & DeFries, 1999).

These **nonshared environmental effects** reflect the unique environment in which each child in a family grows up. Children in a family have a shared environment, but they also, even if they are twins, have experiences that are not shared by their brothers or sisters. Parents and siblings treat each child differently. Certain events, such as illnesses and accidents, and experiences outside the home (for example, with teachers and peers) affect one child and not another. Indeed, some behavioral geneticists have claimed that heredity accounts for most of the similarity between siblings and the nonshared environment accounts for most of the difference (McClearn et al., 1997; Plomin, 1996; Plomin & Daniels, 1987; Plomin & DeFries, 1999; Plomin, Owen, & McGuffin, 1994). However, methodological challenges and additional empirical evidence point to the more moderate conclusion that nonshared environmental effects do not greatly outweigh shared ones; rather, there seems to be a balance between the two (Rutter, 2002).

Genotype-environment correlations may play an important role in the nonshared environment. Children's genetic differences may lead parents and siblings to react to them differently and treat them differently, and genes may influence how children perceive and respond to that treatment and what its outcome will be. Children also mold their own environments by the choices they make—what they do and with whom—and their genetic makeup influences these choices. A child who has inherited artistic talent may spend a great deal of time creating "masterpieces" in solitude, while a sibling who is athletically inclined spends more time playing ball with others. Thus, not only will the children's abilities (in, say, painting or soccer) develop differently, but their social lives will be different as well. These differences tend to be accentuated as children grow older and have more experiences outside the family (Bergeman & Plomin, 1989; Bouchard, 1994; Plomin, 1990, 1996; Plomin et al., 1994; Scarr, 1992; Scarr & McCartney, 1983).

The old nature-nurture puzzle is far from resolved; we know now that the problem is more complex than previously thought. A variety of research designs can augment and refine our understanding of the forces affecting human development.

Some Characteristics Influenced by Heredity and Environment

Keeping in mind the complexity of unraveling the influences of heredity and environment, let's look at what is known about their roles in producing certain characteristics.

Obesity/Overweight **Obesity** (sometimes called *overweight*) is usually defined in childhood as having a body mass index, or BMI (comparison of weight to height), at or above the 95th percentile for age and sex and in adulthood as having a BMI of 30 or more. Another criterion is percentage of body fat: more than 25 percent for men and more than 30 percent for women. Obesity is a multifactorial condition; twin studies, adoption studies, and other research suggest that 40 to 70 percent of the risk

nonshared environmental effects The unique environment in which each child grows up, consisting of distinctive influences or influences that affect one child differently than another.

Checkpoint

Can you . . .

✔ Explain and give at least one example of reaction range, canalization, genotype-environment interaction, and genotype-environment correlation?

✔ List three types of influences that contribute to nonshared environmental effects?

✔ List three types of studies that highlight effects of parenting?

✔ Cite criticisms of behavioral genetics research?

Guidepost

5. What roles do heredity and environment play in physical health, intelligence, and personality?

obesity (1) Extreme overweight in relation to age, sex, height, and body type.

- If overweight runs in families, either because of heredity or lifestyle, how can parents who have not been able to control their own weight help their children?

is genetic (Chen et al., 2004). As many as 250 genes or chromosome regions are associated with obesity (Pérusse, Chagnon, Weisnagel, & Bouchard, 1999). One key gene on chromosome 10 normally controls appetite, but an abnormal version of this gene can stimulate hunger and overeating (Boutin et al., 2003). A longitudinal study of risk factors for heart disease has linked specific genes to body mass measurements taken over several decades (Chen et al., 2004).

The kind and amount of food eaten in a particular home or in a particular social or ethnic group and the amount of exercise that is encouraged can increase or decrease the likelihood that a person will become overweight. The rise in the prevalence of obesity in western countries seems to result from the interaction of a genetic predisposition with overeating and inadequate exercise (Leibel, 1997; see Chapters 7, 9, 11, and 13).

Intelligence and School Achievement   Although no specific genes for intelligence have been conclusively identified (Sternberg et al., 2005), heredity seems to exert a strong influence on general intelligence (as measured by intelligence tests) and also on specific abilities (McClearn et al., 1997; Petrill et al., 2004; Plomin et al., 1994; Plomin & DeFries, 1999). Still, experience counts, too; an enriched or impoverished environment can substantially affect the development and expression of innate ability (Neisser et al., 1996; refer back to Figure 3-7).

Evidence of the role of heredity in intelligence comes from adoption and twin studies. Adopted children's IQs are consistently closer to the IQs of their biological mothers than to those of their adoptive parents and siblings, and monozygotic twins are more alike in intelligence than dizygotic twins. This is also true of performance on elementary school achievement tests and on National Merit Scholarship examinations given to high school students. The studies yield a consistent estimate of heritability of about 50 percent for spatial abilities, meaning that genetic differences explain about half of the observed variation among members of a population. A close correlation between verbal and spatial abilities suggests a genetic link among the components of intelligence (Petrill et al., 2004; Plomin & DeFries, 1999).

Furthermore, the genetic influence, which is primarily responsible for stability in cognitive performance, increases with age. The shared family environment seems to have a dominant influence on young children but almost *no* influence on adolescents, who are more apt to find their own niche by actively selecting environments compatible with their hereditary abilities and related interests (Bouchard, 2004; Petrill et al., 2004). On the other hand, the nonshared environment is influential throughout life and is primarily responsible for changes in cognitive performance (Petrill et al., 2004).

Personality   Scientists have identified genes directly linked with specific personality traits, such as neuroticism (see Chapter 14), which may contribute to depression and anxiety (Lesch et al., 1996). Heritability of personality traits appears to be between 40 and 50 percent, and there is little evidence of shared environmental influence (Bouchard, 2004).

Temperament (discussed in detail in Chapter 6) appears to be largely inborn and is often consistent over the years, though it may respond to special experiences or parental handling (A. Thomas & Chess, 1984; A. Thomas, Chess, & Birch, 1968). Siblings—both twins and nontwins—tend to be similar in temperament, though parents often see them as more different than they actually are (Saudino, Wertz, Gagne, & Chawla, 2004). An observational study of 100 pairs of 7-year-old siblings (half of them adoptive siblings and half siblings by birth) found significant genetic influences on activity, sociability, and emotionality (Schmitz, Saudino, Plomin, Fulker, & DeFries, 1996).

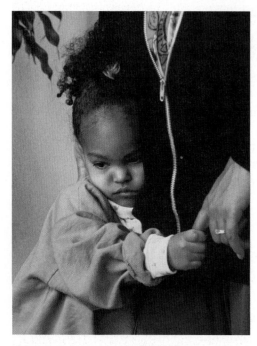

This 2½-year-old girl clinging to her mother may be "just in a phase," but more likely her shyness is an inborn aspect of her temperament, according to research reported in Chapter 6.

Psychopathology There is evidence for a strong hereditary influence on such conditions as schizophrenia, autism, alcoholism, and depression. All tend to run in families and to show greater concordance between monozygotic twins than between dizygotic twins. However, heredity alone does not produce such disorders; an inherited tendency can be triggered by environmental factors. For example, researchers have linked a gene or genes on chromosome 1 to vulnerability to alcoholism or depression, or both, depending on circumstances (Nurnberger et al., 2001). (Alcoholism and depression are discussed later in this book.)

Schizophrenia, a disorder characterized by loss of contact with reality and by such symptoms as hallucinations and delusions, has a strong genetic component (Berry, Jobanputra, & Pal, 2003; Tuulio-Henriksson et al., 2002; Vaswani & Kapur, 2001). The risk of schizophrenia is ten times greater among siblings and offspring of schizophrenics than among the general population; and twin and adoption studies suggest that this increased risk comes from shared genes, not shared environments. The estimated genetic contribution is between 63 and 85 percent (McGuffin, Owen, & Farmer, 1995).

However, because not all monozygotic twins are concordant for the illness, its cause cannot be purely genetic. A controlled study of a large birth cohort examined 30 to 38 years later found a sevenfold increased risk of schizophrenia and related disorders in persons prenatally exposed to influenza during the first trimester of gestation (Brown, Begg, et al., 2004).

Advanced paternal age is a risk factor for schizophrenia. In large population-based studies in Jerusalem and Denmark, the risk of the disorder was greatly increased when the father was 50 years old or more (Byrne, Agerbo, Ewald, Eaton, & Mortenson, 2003; Malaspina et al., 2001). A study of 7,086 persons born in Helsinki, Finland, between 1924 and 1993 found indications that fetal undernutrition increases the risk of schizophrenia (Wahlbeck, Forsen, Osmond, Barker, & Eriksson, 2001).

A postmortem examination of the brains of schizophrenics suggests that the disorder may originate in a lack of a chemical called *reelin*. Reelin helps to correctly position and align nerve cells in the developing brain (Impagnatiello et al., 1998). A defective gene for reelin may result in misplacement of nerve cells, and this may create a predisposition, or vulnerability, to schizophrenia.

Autism a severe disorder of brain functioning, is characterized by lack of normal social interaction, impaired communication and imagination, and a highly restricted range of activities and interests. It usually appears within the first 3 years and continues to varying degrees throughout life (AAP Committee on Children with Disabilities, 2001; National Institute of Neurological Disorders and Stroke, 1999; Rapin, 1997; Rodier, 2000). Its onset appears to be preceded by abnormal brain growth: a small head size at birth followed by a sudden, excessive spurt in size during the first year (Courchesne, Carper, & Akshoomoff, 2003). Four out of five autistic children are boys (Yeargin-Allsopp et al., 2003).

Autism is one of a group of *autistic spectrum disorders (ASDs)* ranging from mild to severe, which may be more common than previously thought. Estimates are that as many as 6 children in 1,000 may have one of these disorders (Yeargin-Allsopp et al., 2003). The most common of these is *Asperger's disorder,* which affects about 1 in 500 children. Preschoolers with ASDs tend to focus on separate bits of information instead of on the total picture. They are weak in verbal ability and in *joint attention*—pointing to an object to call attention to it or looking at another person to see whether the two of them are paying attention to the same

schizophrenia Mental disorder marked by loss of contact with reality; symptoms include hallucinations and delusions.

autism Pervasive developmental disorder of the brain, characterized by lack of normal social interaction, impaired communication and imagination, and a highly restricted range of activities and interests.

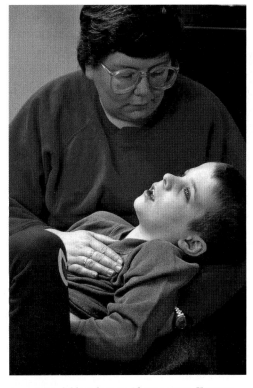

An autistic child tends to avoid eye contact. However, these children often can learn basic social skills through behavior therapy.

event. Lack of joint attention may underlie delayed development of *theory of mind,* awareness of the mental processes of oneself and others (Morgan, Mayberry, & Durkin, 2003; see Chapter 7).

Autistic disorders run in families and seem to have a strong genetic basis (Bailey, Le Couteur, Gottesman, & Bolton, 1995; Constantino, 2003; National Institute of Neurological Disorders and Stroke, 1999; Ramoz et al., 2004; Rodier, 2000; Szatmari, 1999; Trottier, Srivastava, & Walker, 1999). Family members of an autistic child may show symptoms too mild to qualify for a diagnosis of ASD (Constantino, 2003). Monozygotic twins are more concordant for autism than dizygotic twins. Several genes may be involved in cases of varying symptoms and severity (Bespalova & Buxbaum, 2003; Cook et al., 1997; Ingram et al., 2000; Ramoz et al., 2004; Rodier, 2000; Szatmari, 1999).

Environmental factors, such as exposure to certain viruses or chemicals, may trigger an inherited tendency toward autism (National Institute of Neurological Disorders and Stroke, 1999; Rodier, 2000; Trottier et al., 1999). Certain complications of pregnancy, such as uterine bleeding and vaginal infection seem to be associated with a higher incidence of the condition (Juul-Dam, Townsend, & Courchesne, 2001). So are advanced parental age, first births, threatened fetal loss, epidural anesthesia, induced labor, and cesarean delivery (Glasson et al., 2004). Major stress during the 24th to 28th weeks of pregnancy may deform the developing brain (Beversdorf et al., 2001). The prevalence of autism has increased since the mid-1970s (Newschaffer, Falb, & Gurney, 2005) due to broadened diagnostic criteria and greater awareness (Gernsbacher, Dawson, & Goldsmith, 2005). The claim that this increase is related to administration of the measles-mumps-rubella vaccine has not been substantiated (AAP Committee on Children with Disabilities, 2001; Fombonne, 2001, 2003; Madsen et al., 2003).

Some theorists suggest that autism results from a failure of connections within the brain. In a brain imaging study, adults with autism used different parts of the brain than did adults without autism in a simple memory task involving letters of the alphabet. The group with autism tended to use the right side of the brain, normally used to process visual information, rather than the left side, which is normally more active in processing verbal information, suggesting that they remembered the letters as shapes rather than by name. They also showed less activation in the front of the brain, which is involved in higher-level thinking, than in the rear section, which is involved in perceiving details (Just, Cherkassky, Keller, & Minshew, 2004).

Autism has no known cure, but improvement, sometimes substantial, can occur. Some autistic children can be taught to speak, read, and write. Behavior therapy can help them learn such basic social skills as paying attention, sustaining eye contact, and feeding and dressing themselves (AAP Committee on Children with Disabilities, 2001). However, only about 2 percent of autistic children grow up to live independently; most need some degree of care throughout life. Children with Asperger's syndrome generally fare better ("Autism—Part II," 2001).

Prenatal Development

If you had been born in China, you would probably celebrate your birthday on your estimated date of conception rather than your date of birth. This Chinese custom recognizes the importance of *gestation,* the approximately 9-month (or 266-day) period of development between conception and birth. Scientists, too, date *gestational age* from conception.

In this section we trace the course of gestation, or prenatal development. We discuss environmental factors that can affect the developing person-to-be, assess

Checkpoint

Can you . . .

✔ Assess the evidence for genetic and environmental influences on obesity, intelligence, and temperament?

✔ Name and describe two mental disorders that show a strong genetic influence?

techniques for determining whether development is proceeding normally, and explain the importance of prenatal care.

Stages of Prenatal Development

 *Guidepost*

6. What are the three stages of prenatal development, and what happens during each stage?

What turns a fertilized ovum, or zygote, into a creature with a specific shape and pattern? Research suggests that an identifiable group of genes is responsible for this transformation in vertebrates, presumably including human beings. These genes produce molecules called *morphogens,* which are switched on after fertilization and begin sculpting arms, hands, fingers, vertebrae, ribs, a brain, and other body parts (Echeland et al., 1993; Krauss, Concordet, & Ingham, 1993; Riddle, Johnson, Laufer, & Tabin, 1993).

Prenatal development takes place in three stages: *germinal, embryonic,* and *fetal.* (Table 3-4 gives a month-by-month description.) During these three stages of gestation, the original single-celled zygote grows into an *embryo* and then a *fetus.* Both before and after birth, development proceeds according to two fundamental principles. Growth and motor development occur from top to bottom and from the center of the body outward.

The **cephalocaudal principle** (from Latin, meaning "head to tail") dictates that development proceeds from the head to the lower part of the trunk. An embryo's head, brain, and eyes develop earliest and are disproportionately large until the other parts catch up. At 2 months of gestation, the embryo's head is half the length of the body. By the time of birth, the head is only one-fourth the length of the body but is still disproportionately large. According to the **proximodistal principle** (from Latin, "near to far"), development proceeds from parts near the center of the body to outer ones. The embryo's head and trunk develop before the limbs, and the arms and legs before the fingers and toes.

cephalocaudal principle Principle that development proceeds in a head-to-tail direction; that is, that upper parts of the body develop before lower parts of the trunk.

proximodistal principle Principle that development proceeds from within to without; that is, that parts of the body near the center develop before the extremities.

Germinal Stage (Fertilization to 2 Weeks) During the **germinal stage,** from fertilization to about 2 weeks of gestational age, the zygote divides, becomes more complex, and is implanted in the wall of the uterus (see Figure 3-8), marking the beginning of pregnancy.

germinal stage First 2 weeks of prenatal development, characterized by rapid cell division, blastocyst formation, and implantation in the wall of the uterus.

Within 36 hours after fertilization, the zygote enters a period of rapid cell division and duplication, or *mitosis.* Seventy-two hours after fertilization, it has divided first into 16 and then into 32 cells; a day later it has 64 cells. This division will continue until the original single cell has developed into the 800 billion or more specialized cells that make up the human body—a process that continues well after birth.

While the fertilized ovum is dividing, it is also making its way down the fallopian tube to the uterus, a journey of 3 or 4 days. Its form changes from a ball of cells into a fluid-filled sphere, a *blastocyst,* which floats freely in the uterus for a day or two and then begins to implant itself in the uterine wall. Only about 10 to 20 percent of fertilized eggs complete this crucial task of implantation and become embryos.

Before implantation, as cell differentiation begins, some cells around the edge of the blastocyst cluster on one side to form the *embryonic disk,* a thickened cell mass from which the embryo begins to develop. This mass will differentiate into three layers. The upper layer, the *ectoderm,* will become the outer layer of skin, the nails, hair, teeth, sensory organs, and the nervous system, including the brain and spinal cord. The lower layer, the *endoderm,* will become the digestive system, liver, pancreas, salivary glands, and respiratory system. A middle layer, the *mesoderm,* will develop and differentiate into the inner layer of skin, muscles, skeleton, and excretory and circulatory systems.

Other parts of the blastocyst begin to develop into organs that will nurture and protect the embryo: the *amniotic cavity,* or *amniotic sac,* with its outer layers, the

Table 3-4   Prenatal Development

Month	Description

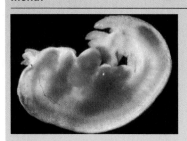

1 month

During the first month, growth is more rapid than at any other time during prenatal or postnatal life; the embryo reaches a size 10,000 times greater than the zygote. By the end of the first month, it measures about ½ inch in length. Blood flows through its veins and arteries, which are very small. It has a minuscule heart, beating 65 times a minute. It already has the beginning of a brain, kidneys, liver, and digestive tract. The umbilical cord, its lifeline to the mother, is working. By looking very closely through a microscope, it is possible to see the swellings on the head that will eventually become eyes, ears, mouth, and nose. Its sex cannot yet be detected.

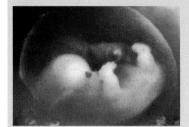

7 weeks

By the end of the second month, the fetus is less than 1 inch long and weighs only ⅓ ounce. Its head is half its total body length. Facial parts are clearly developed, with tongue and teeth buds. The arms have hands, fingers, and thumbs, and the legs have knees, ankles, and toes. The fetus has a thin covering of skin and can make handprints and footprints. Bone cells appear at about 8 weeks. Brain impulses coordinate the function of the organ system. Sex organs are developing; the heartbeat is steady. The stomach produces digestive juices; the liver, blood cells. The kidneys remove uric acid from the blood. The skin is now sensitive enough to react to tactile stimulation. If an aborted 8-week-old fetus is stroked, it reacts by flexing its trunk, extending its head, and moving back its arms.

3 months

By the end of the third month, the fetus weighs about 1 ounce and measures about 3 inches in length. It has fingernails, toenails, eyelids (still closed), vocal cords, lips, and a prominent nose. Its head is still large—about one-third its total length—and its forehead is high. Sex can easily be detected. The organ systems are functioning, and so the fetus may now breathe, swallow amniotic fluid into the lungs and expel it, and occasionally urinate. Its ribs and vertebrae have turned into cartilage. The fetus can now make a variety of specialized responses: it can move its legs, feet, thumbs, and head; its mouth can open and close and swallow. If its eyelids are touched, it squints; if its palm is touched, it makes a partial fist; if its lip is touched, it will suck; and if the sole of the foot is stroked, the toes will fan out. These reflexes will be present at birth but will disappear during the first months of life.

4 months

The body is catching up to the head, which is now only one-fourth the total body length, the same proportion it will be at birth. The fetus now measures 8 to 10 inches and weighs about 6 ounces. The umbilical cord is as long as the fetus and will continue to grow with it. The placenta is now fully developed. The mother may be able to feel the fetus kicking, a movement known as *quickening,* which some societies and religious groups consider the beginning of human life. The reflex activities that appeared in the third month are now brisker because of increased muscular development.

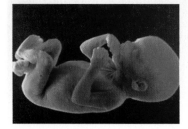

5 months

The fetus, now weighing about 12 ounces to 1 pound and measuring about 1 foot, begins to show signs of an individual personality. It has definite sleep-wake patterns, has a favorite position in the uterus (called its *lie*), and becomes more active—kicking, stretching, squirming, and even hiccuping. By putting an ear to the mother's abdomen, it is possible to hear the fetal heartbeat. The sweat and sebaceous glands are functioning. The respiratory system is not yet adequate to sustain life outside the womb; a baby born at this time does not usually survive. Coarse hair has begun to grow for eyebrows and eyelashes, fine hair is on the head, and a woolly hair called *lanugo* covers the body.

Month	Description

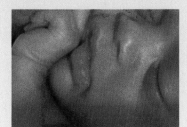

6 months

The rate of fetal growth has slowed down a little—by the end of the sixth month, the fetus is about 14 inches long and weighs 1¼ pounds. It has fat pads under the skin; the eyes are complete, opening, closing, and looking in all directions. It can hear, and it can make a fist with a strong grip. A fetus born early in the sixth month has only a slight chance of survival, because the breathing apparatus has not matured. However, medical advances have made survival increasingly likely if birth occurs near the end of the sixth month.

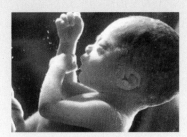

7 months

By the end of the seventh month, the fetus, about 16 inches long and weighing 3 to 5 pounds, now has fully developed reflex patterns. It cries, breathes, and swallows, and it may suck its thumb. The lanugo may disappear at about this time, or it may remain until shortly after birth. Head hair may continue to grow. The chances that a fetus weighing at least 3½ pounds will survive are fairly good, provided it receives intensive medical attention. It will probably need to be kept in an isolette until a weight of 5 pounds is attained.

8 months

The 8-month-old fetus is 18 to 20 inches long and weighs between 5 and 7 pounds. Its living quarters are becoming cramped, and so its movements are curtailed. During this month and the next, a layer of fat is developing over the fetus's entire body, which will enable it to adjust to varying temperatures outside the womb.

9 months—newborn

About a week before birth, the fetus stops growing, having reached an average weight of about 7½ pounds and a length of about 20 inches, with boys tending to be a little longer and heavier than girls. Fat pads continue to form, the organ systems are operating more efficiently, the heart rate increases, and more wastes are expelled through the umbilical cord. The reddish color of the skin is fading. At birth, the fetus will have been in the womb for about 266 days, although gestational age is usually estimated at 280 days because most doctors date the pregnancy from the mother's last menstrual period.

Note: Even in these early stages, individuals differ. The figures and descriptions given here represent averages.

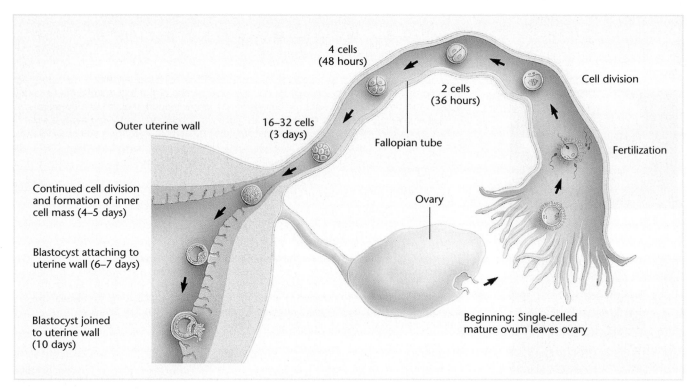

Figure 3-8

4 cells
(48 hours)

2 cells
(36 hours)

Cell division

16–32 cells
(3 days)

Outer uterine wall

Fallopian tube

Fertilization

Continued cell division
and formation of inner
cell mass (4–5 days)

Ovary

Blastocyst attaching to
uterine wall (6–7 days)

Blastocyst joined
to uterine wall
(10 days)

Beginning: Single-celled
mature ovum leaves ovary

Figure 3-8

Early development of a human embryo. This simplified diagram shows the progress of the ovum as it leaves the ovary, is fertilized in the fallopian tube, and then divides while traveling to the lining of the uterus. Now a blastocyst, it is implanted in the uterus and becomes an embryo. It will continue to grow larger and more complex until it is ready to be born.

Figure 3-9

The developing embryo (approximately 6 weeks gestational age). Throughout its development, the embryo is enclosed and cushioned by the expandable, fluid-filled amniotic cavity. The umbilical cord develops to contain the embryonic blood vessels that carry blood to and from the placenta. Diffusion across the chorionic villi removes wastes from the embryonic blood and adds nutrients and oxygen without commingling of maternal and embryonic blood.

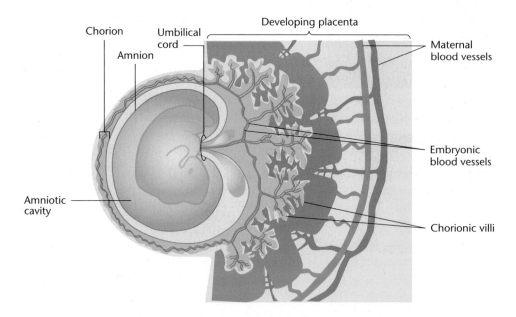

Chorion

Umbilical cord

Amnion

Developing placenta

Maternal blood vessels

Embryonic blood vessels

Amniotic cavity

Chorionic villi

amnion and *chorion;* the *placenta;* and the *umbilical cord* (see Figure 3-9). The *amniotic sac* is a fluid-filled membrane that encases the developing baby, protecting it and giving it room to move. The *placenta,* which contains both maternal and embryonic tissue, will be connected to the embryo by the *umbilical cord.* Nutrients from the mother pass from her blood to the embryonic blood vessels, which are then carried, via the umbilical cord, to the embryo. In turn, embryonic blood vessels in the umbilical cord carry embryonic wastes to the placenta, where they can be eliminated by maternal blood vessels. The mother's and embryo's circulatory systems are not directly linked; instead, this exchange occurs by diffusion across the blood vessel

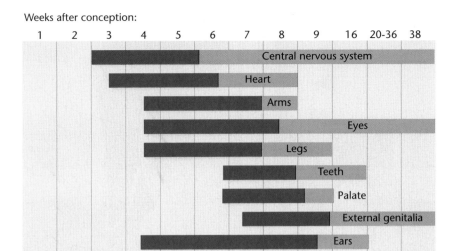

Weeks after conception:

1 2 3 4 5 6 7 8 9 16 20-36 38

Central nervous system
Heart
Arms
Eyes
Legs
Teeth
Palate
External genitalia
Ears

Figure 3-10
When birth defects occur. Body parts and systems are most vulnerable to damage during critical periods when they are developing most rapidly (*darkly shaded areas*), generally within the first trimester of pregnancy. (Source: J. E. Brody, 1995; data from March of Dimes.) *Note:* Intervals of time are not all equal.

walls. The placenta also helps to combat internal infection and gives the unborn child immunity to various diseases. It produces the hormones that support pregnancy, prepare the mother's breasts for lactation, and eventually stimulate the uterine contractions that will expel the baby from the mother's body.

Embryonic Stage (2 to 8 Weeks)   During the **embryonic stage,** the second stage of gestation, from about 2 to 8 weeks, the organs and major body systems—respiratory, digestive, and nervous—develop rapidly. This is a critical period (refer back to Chapter 1), when the embryo is most vulnerable to destructive influences in the prenatal environment (see Figure 3-10). An organ system or structure that is still developing at the time of exposure is most likely to be affected. Defects that occur later in pregnancy are likely to be less serious.

The most severely defective embryos usually do not survive beyond the first *trimester,* or 3-month period, of pregnancy. A **spontaneous abortion,** commonly called a *miscarriage,* is the expulsion from the uterus of an embryo or fetus that is unable to survive outside the womb. As many as 50 percent of all pregnancies, but only about 15 percent of recognized pregnancies, end in miscarriage; the vast majority of spontaneous abortions occur before a woman knows she is pregnant (American College of Obstetricians and Gynecologists, 2001; Wilcox et al., 1988). Most miscarriages result from abnormal pregnancies, most commonly due to chromosomal abnormalities (Hogge, 2003). Smoking, drinking alcohol, and drug use increase the risks of miscarriage (American College of Obstetricians and Gynecologists, 2000a).

Males are more likely than females to be spontaneously aborted or to be *stillborn* (dead at birth). Thus, although about 125 males are conceived for every 100 females—a fact that has been attributed to the greater mobility of sperm carrying the smaller Y chromosome—only 105 boys are born for every 100 girls. Males' greater vulnerability continues after birth: More of them die early in life, and at every age they are more susceptible to many disorders. As a result, there are only 96 males for every 100 females in the United States (Martin, Hamilton, et al., 2002; U.S. Department of Health and Human Services, USDHHS, 1996a).

Fetal Stage (8 Weeks to Birth)   The appearance of the first bone cells at about 8 weeks signals the beginning of the **fetal stage,** the final stage of gestation. During this period, the fetus grows rapidly to about 20 times its previous length, and organs and body systems become more complex. Right up to birth, "finishing touches" such as fingernails, toenails, and eyelids develop.

embryonic stage   Second stage of gestation (2 to 8 weeks), characterized by rapid growth and development of major body systems and organs.

spontaneous abortion   Natural expulsion from the uterus of an embryo that cannot survive outside the womb; also called *miscarriage.*

Checkpoint
Can you . . .

✔ Identify two principles that govern physical development and give examples of how they apply prenatally?

✔ Describe how a zygote becomes an embryo, and explain why defects and miscarriages most often occur during the embryonic stage?

fetal stage   Final stage of gestation (from 8 weeks to birth), characterized by increased differentiation of body parts and greatly enlarged body size.

Ultrasound, the procedure this woman is undergoing, is a diagnostic tool that presents an immediate image of the fetus in the womb. High-frequency sound waves directed at the woman's abdomen reveal the fetus's outline and movements. Ultrasound is widely used to monitor fetal development and detect any abnormalities.

ultrasound Prenatal medical procedure using high-frequency sound waves to detect the outline of a fetus and its movements, so as to determine whether a pregnancy is progressing normally.

Fetuses are not passive passengers in their mothers' wombs. Fetuses breathe, kick, turn, flex their bodies, do somersaults, squint, swallow, make fists, hiccup, and suck their thumbs. The flexible membranes of the uterine walls and amniotic sac, which surround the protective buffer of amniotic fluid, permit and even stimulate limited movement.

Scientists can observe fetal movement through **ultrasound,** using high-frequency sound waves to detect the outline of the fetus. Other instruments can monitor heart rate, changes in activity level, states of sleep and wakefulness, and cardiac reactivity. In one study, fetuses monitored from 20 weeks of gestation until term had increasingly slower but more variable heart rates, possibly in response to the increasing stress of the mother's pregnancy, and greater cardiac response to stimulation. They also showed less—but more vigorous—activity, perhaps a result of the increasing difficulty of movement for a growing fetus in a constricted environment as well as of maturation of the nervous system (DiPietro, Hodgson, Costigan, Hilton, & Johnson, 1996).

A significant "jump" in all these aspects of fetal development seems to occur between 28 and 32 weeks; it may help explain why infants born prematurely at this time are more likely to survive and flourish than those born earlier (DiPietro et al., 1996). This "jump" occurred among fetuses observed in two contrasting cultures, Baltimore and Lima, Peru, suggesting that this aspect of fetal neurological development is universal. On the other hand, there were significant differences in the course of this development, with the Lima fetuses lagging behind the Baltimore fetuses. These differences may have been related to differences in maternal nutrition (DiPietro et al., 2004).

The movements and activity level of fetuses show marked individual differences, and their heart rates vary in regularity and speed. Male fetuses, regardless of size, are more active and tend to move more vigorously than female fetuses throughout gestation. Thus, infant boys' tendency to be more active than girls may be at least partly inborn (DiPietro et al., 1996).

Beginning at about the 12th week of gestation, the fetus swallows and inhales some of the amniotic fluid in which it floats. The amniotic fluid contains substances that cross the placenta from the mother's bloodstream and enter the fetus's own bloodstream. Partaking of these substances may stimulate the budding senses of taste and smell and may contribute to the development of organs needed for breathing and digestion (Mennella & Beauchamp, 1996a; Ronca & Alberts, 1995; Smotherman & Robinson, 1995, 1996). Mature taste cells appear at about 14 weeks of gestation.

The olfactory system, which controls the sense of smell, also is well developed before birth (Bartoshuk & Beauchamp, 1994; Mennella & Beauchamp, 1996a).

Fetuses respond to the mother's voice and heartbeat and the vibrations of her body, suggesting that they can hear and feel. Responses to sound and vibration seem to begin at 26 weeks of gestation, rise, and then reach a plateau at about 32 weeks (Kisilevsky, Muir, & Low, 1992).

Fetuses seem to learn and remember. In one experiment, 3-day-old infants sucked more on a nipple that activated a recording of a story their mother had frequently read aloud during the last 6 weeks of pregnancy than they did on nipples that activated recordings of two other stories. Apparently, the infants recognized the pattern of sound they had heard in the womb. A control group, whose mothers had not recited a story before birth, responded equally to all three recordings (DeCasper & Spence, 1986). Similar experiments have found that newborns 2 to 4 days old prefer musical and speech sequences heard before birth. They also prefer their mother's voice to those of other women, female voices to male voices, and their mother's native language to another language (DeCasper & Fifer, 1980; DeCasper & Spence, 1986; Fifer & Moon, 1995; Lecanuet, Granier-Deferre, & Busnel, 1995; Moon, Cooper, & Fifer, 1993).

How do we know that these preferences develop before rather than after birth? When 60 fetuses heard a female voice reading, their heart rate increased if the voice was their mothers' and decreased if it belonged to a stranger (Kisilevsky et al., 2003). In another study, newborns were given the choice of sucking to turn on a recording of the mother's voice or a "filtered" version of her voice as it might sound in the womb. The newborns sucked more often to turn on the filtered version, suggesting that fetuses develop a preference for the kinds of sounds they hear before birth (Fifer & Moon, 1995; Moon & Fifer, 1990).

Environmental Influences: Maternal Factors

Because the prenatal environment is the mother's body, virtually everything that impinges on her well-being, from her diet to her moods, may alter her unborn child's environment and affect its growth. Prospective mothers' feelings of attachment to their fetuses seem to have increased in the past three or four decades as infant and maternal mortality have decreased. Technology that permits a woman to view images of her fetus early in her pregnancy may motivate her to engage in nurturing behaviors, such as eating properly and abstaining from alcohol and drugs (Salisbury, Law, LaGasse, & Lester, 2003).

Not all environmental hazards are equally risky for all fetuses. Some factors that are **teratogenic** (birth defect–producing) in some cases have little or no effect in others. The timing of exposure (refer back to Figure 3-10), the dose, duration, and interaction with other teratogenic factors may make a difference. Sometimes vulnerability may depend on a gene either in the fetus or in the mother. For example, fetuses with a particular variant of a growth gene, called *transforming growth factor alpha,* have six times more risk than other fetuses of developing a cleft palate if the mother smokes while pregnant (Hwang et al., 1995).

Nutrition and Maternal Weight   Pregnant women typically need 300 to 500 additional calories a day, including extra protein. Those who gain 26 or more pounds are less likely to bear babies whose weight at birth is dangerously low. However, desirable weight gain depends on individual factors, such as weight and height before pregnancy (Martin, Hamilton et al., 2002).

Malnutrition during fetal growth may have long-range effects. In rural Gambia, in western Africa, people born during the "hungry" season, when foods from the

Checkpoint
Can you . . .

✔ List several changes that occur during the fetal stage?

✔ Describe findings about fetal activity, sensory development, and memory?

Guidepost

7. What environmental influences can affect prenatal development?

teratogenic   Capable of causing birth defects.

previous harvest are badly depleted, are ten times more likely to die in early adulthood than people born during other parts of the year (Moore et al., 1997). Psychiatric examinations of Dutch military recruits whose mothers had been exposed to wartime famine during pregnancy suggest that severe prenatal nutritional deficiencies in the first or second trimesters affect the developing brain, increasing the risk of antisocial personality disorders at age 18 (Neugebauer, Hoek, & Susser, 1999). And, as we have already reported, a Finnish study found a link between fetal undernutrition and schizophrenia (Wahlbeck et al., 2001).

In a large-scale randomized study of low-income households in 347 Mexican communities, women who took nutrient-fortified dietary supplements while pregnant or lactating tended to have infants who grew more rapidly and were less likely to be anemic (Rivera, Sotres-Alvarez, Habicht, Shamah, & Villalpando, 2004). However, certain vitamins (including A, B_6, C, D, and K) can be harmful in excessive amounts. Iodine deficiency, unless corrected before the third trimester of pregnancy, can cause cretinism, which may involve severe neurological abnormalities or thyroid problems (Cao et al., 1994; Hetzel, 1994).

Only recently have we learned of the critical importance of folic acid, or folate (a B vitamin), in a pregnant woman's diet. For some time, scientists have known that China has the highest incidence in the world of babies born with anencephaly and spina bifida (refer back to Table 3-1), but it was not until the 1980s that researchers linked that fact with the timing of the babies' conception. Traditionally, Chinese couples marry in January or February and try to conceive as soon as possible. That means pregnancies often begin in the winter, when rural women have little access to fresh fruits and vegetables, important sources of folic acid.

After medical detective work established the lack of folic acid as a cause of anencephaly and spina bifida, China embarked on a massive program to give folic acid supplements to prospective mothers. The result was a large reduction in the prevalence of these defects (Berry et al., 1999). Addition of folic acid to enriched grain products has been mandatory in the United States since 1998, and the incidence of these defects has fallen by 19 percent (Honein, Paulozzi, Mathews, Erickson, & Wong, 2001). Women of childbearing age are urged to take folate supplements and to include this vitamin in their diets by eating plenty of fresh fruits and vegetables even before becoming pregnant, since damage from folic acid deficiency can occur during the early weeks of gestation (American Academy of Pediatrics [AAP] Committee on Genetics, 1999; Mills & England, 2001). In addition, the more fruits, vegetables, and proteins sources a mother eats during the year before becoming pregnant, the lower the risk of having a child who develops leukemia, the most common childhood cancer in the United States (Jensen et al., 2004).

Physical Activity and Strenuous Work Moderate exercise does not seem to endanger the fetuses of healthy women (Committee on Obstetric Practice, 2002; Riemann & Kanstrup Hansen, 2000). Regular exercise prevents constipation and improves respiration, circulation, muscle tone, and skin elasticity, all of which contribute to a more comfortable pregnancy and an easier, safer delivery (Committee on Obstetric Practice, 2002). Employment during pregnancy generally entails no special hazards. However, strenuous working conditions, occupational fatigue, and long working hours may be associated with a greater risk of premature birth (Luke et al., 1995).

The American College of Obstetrics and Gynecology (1994) recommends that women in low-risk pregnancies be guided by their own abilities and stamina. The safest course seems to be for pregnant women to exercise moderately, not pushing themselves and not raising their heart rate above 150, and, as with any exercise, to taper off at the end of each session rather than stop abruptly.

Moderate exercise can contribute to a more comfortable pregnancy and an easier, safer delivery. A woman in a low-risk pregnancy should be guided by her own ability and stamina.

Drug Intake   Everything an expectant mother takes in makes its way to the uterus. Drugs may cross the placenta, just as oxygen, carbon dioxide, and water do. Vulnerability is greatest in the first few months of gestation, when development is most rapid.

What are the effects of the use of specific drugs during pregnancy? Let's look first at medical drugs; then at alcohol, nicotine, and caffeine; and finally at some illegal drugs: marijuana, opiates, and cocaine.

Medical Drugs   In the early 1960s, the tranquilizer thalidomide was banned after it was found to have caused stunted or missing limbs, severe facial deformities, and defective organs in some 12,000 babies. The thalidomide disaster sensitized medical professionals and the public to the potential dangers of taking drugs while pregnant. Today, nearly thirty drugs have been found to be teratogenic in clinically recommended doses. Among them are the antibiotic tetracycline; certain barbiturates, opiates, and other central nervous system depressants; several hormones, including diethylstilbestrol (DES) and androgens; certain anticancer drugs, such as methotrexate; Accutane, a drug often prescribed for severe acne; and aspirin and other nonsteroidal anti-inflammatory drugs, which should be avoided during the third trimester (Koren, Pastuszak, & Ito, 1998). A review of data from eight health maintenance organizations in diverse geographic areas found that nearly 40 percent of women who were given medications during pregnancy received drugs whose safety for the fetus has not been established, and an additional 10 percent received drugs for which evidence of risk to a fetus has been found (Andrade et al., 2004).

Infants whose mothers took antidepressants such as Prozac during pregnancy tend to show tremors, drowsiness, erratic movements, and startles during sleep—all signs of disrupted neurobehavioral activity (Zeskind & Stephens, 2004). Certain antipsychotic drugs used to manage severe psychiatric disorders may have serious potential effects on the fetus, and withdrawal symptoms may occur at birth. It is advisable to taper off and then discontinue the use of such drugs as the delivery date approaches, or, if necessary, to prescribe the lowest dose possible (AAP Committee on Drugs, 2000). The American Academy of Pediatrics (AAP) Committee on Drugs (1994) recommends that *no* medication be prescribed for a pregnant or breast-feeding woman unless it is essential for her health or her child's. Pregnant women should not take over-the-counter drugs without consulting a doctor (Koren et al., 1998).

Alcohol   Like Abel Dorris, as many as 5 infants in 1,000 born in the United States suffer from **fetal alcohol syndrome (FAS),** a combination of retarded growth, face and body malformations, and disorders of the central nervous system—and its incidence seems to be increasing. Problems related to the central nervous system can include, in infancy, reduced responsiveness to stimuli and slow reaction time and, throughout childhood, short attention span, distractibility, restlessness, hyperactivity, learning disabilities, memory deficits, and mood disorders (Sokol, Delaney-Black, & Nordstrom, 2003).

FAS and other, less severe alcohol-related conditions—all classified under the umbrella of *fetal alcohol spectrum disorder (FASD)*—are estimated to occur in nearly 1 in every 100 births. Prenatal alcohol exposure is the most common cause of mental retardation and the leading preventable cause of birth defects in the United States (Sokol et al., 2003). It is also a risk factor for the development of drinking problems in young adulthood (Baer, Sampson, Barr, Connor, & Streissguth, 2003). Yet about 10 percent of pregnant women in the United Stats report using alcohol, 2 percent heavily or frequently. Furthermore, more than half of women of childbearing age who do not use birth control (and therefore could become pregnant) report alcohol use (Tsai & Floyd, 2004).

What's Your View?

- Once banned for causing birth defects, thalidomide has since been found to be effective in many illnesses, from mouth ulcers to brain cancer. Should its use for these purposes be permitted even though there is a risk that pregnant women might take it? If so, what safeguards should be required?

---

fetal alcohol syndrome (FAS) Combination of mental, motor, and developmental abnormalities affecting the offspring of some women who drink heavily during pregnancy.

A mother who drinks during pregnancy risks having a child born with fetal alcohol syndrome, as this 4-year-old boy was.

Even small amounts of social drinking may harm a fetus (Sokol et al., 2003), and the more the mother drinks, the greater the effect. Moderate or heavy drinking during pregnancy seems to disturb an infant's neurological and behavioral functioning, and this may affect early social interaction with the mother, which is vital to emotional development (Nugent, Lester, Greene, Wieczorek-Deering, & Mahony, 1996). In a longitudinal study of 501 women at an urban university's maternity clinic, women who consumed even small amounts of alcohol during pregnancy tended to have children who were unusually aggressive at ages 6 to 7, and prospective mothers who drank moderately to heavily tended to have problem or delinquent children (Sood et al., 2001). Because there is no known safe level of drinking during pregnancy, it is best to avoid alcohol from the time a woman begins *thinking* about becoming pregnant until she stops breast-feeding (AAP Committee on Substance Abuse and Committee on Children with Disabilities, 1993; Sokol et al., 2003).

Some FAS problems recede after birth; others, such as retardation, behavioral and learning problems, and hyperactivity, tend to persist. As with Abel Dorris, enriching these children's education or general environment does not seem to enhance their cognitive development (Kerns, Don, Mateer, & Streissguth, 1997; Spohr, Willms, & Steinhausen, 1993; Streissguth et al., 1991; Strömland & Hellström, 1996), but they may be less likely to develop behavioral and mental health problems if they are diagnosed early and are reared in stable, nurturing environments (Streissguth et al., 2004).

Nicotine Women who smoke during pregnancy are more than one and a half times as likely as nonsmokers to bear low-birth-weight babies (weighing less than 5½ pounds at birth). Even light smoking (fewer than five cigarettes a day) is associated with a greater risk of low birth weight (Martin et al., 2002; Shankaran et al., 2004; Ventura, Hamilton, Mathews, & Chandra, 2003). Indeed, maternal smoking has been identified as the single most important factor in low birth weight in developed countries (DiFranza, Aligne, & Weitzman, 2004). The percentage of U.S. women who smoke during pregnancy has been declining since 1989; 11 percent reported doing so in 2003 (Martin et al., 2005).

Tobacco use during pregnancy also brings increased risks of miscarriage, growth retardation, stillbirth, small head circumference, infant death, colic in early infancy, and long-term respiratory, neurological, cognitive, and behavioral problems (American Academy of Pediatrics Committee on Substance Abuse, 2001; DiFranza et al., 2004; Martin et al., 2002; Shankaran et al., 2004; Sondergaard, Henriksen, Obel, & Wisborg, 2001). An analysis of fetal cells from the amniotic fluid of pregnant women who had smoked at least 10 cigarettes a day for 10 years and continued to smoke during pregnancy found chromosomal instability and abnormalities not found in amniotic fluid of nonsmoking women (de la Chica, Ribas, Giraldo, Egozcue, & Fuster, 2005).

In another controlled study, newborns whose mothers had smoked during pregnancy (but had not used drugs and had taken no more than three alcoholic drinks per month) showed more evidence of neurological toxicity (such as overexcitability and stress) than infants of nonsmoking mothers (Law et al., 2003). The effects of prenatal exposure to secondhand smoke on cognitive development tend to be worse when the child also experiences socioeconomic hardships, such as substandard housing, malnutrition, and inadequate clothing during the first two years of life (Rauh et al., 2004).

Women who smoke during pregnancy also tend to smoke after giving birth, and each type of exposure seems to have independent effects (DiFranza et al., 2004).

One study separated the effects of prenatal and postnatal exposure by examining 500 newborns about 48 hours after birth, while they were still in the hospital's non-smoking maternity ward and thus had not been exposed to smoking outside the womb. Newborns whose mothers had smoked during pregnancy were shorter and lighter and had poorer respiratory functioning than babies of nonsmoking mothers (Stick, Burton, Gurrin, Sly, & LeSouëf, 1996).

Smoking during pregnancy seems to have some of the same effects on children when they reach school age as drinking during pregnancy: poor attention span, hyperactivity, anxiety, learning and behavior problems, perceptual-motor and linguistic problems, poor IQ scores, low grade placement, and neurological problems (Landesman-Dwyer & Emanuel, 1979; Milberger, Biederman, Faraone, Chen, & Jones, 1996; Naeye & Peters, 1984; Olds, Henderson, & Tatelbaum, 1994a, 1994b; Streissguth et al., 1984; Thapar et al., 2003; Wakschlag et al., 1997; Weitzman, Gortmaker, & Sobol, 1992; Wright et al., 1983). A 10-year longitudinal study of 6- to 23-year-old offspring of women who reported having smoked heavily during pregnancy found a fourfold increase in risk of conduct disorder in boys, beginning before puberty, and a fivefold increased risk of drug dependence in girls, beginning in adolescence, in comparison with young people whose mothers had not smoked during pregnancy (Weissman, Warner, Wickramaratne, & Kandel, 1999).

Caffeine   Can the caffeine a pregnant woman swallows in coffee, tea, cola, or chocolate cause trouble for her fetus? For the most part, the answer is no (Leviton & Cowan, 2002). It does seem clear that caffeine is *not* a teratogen for human babies (Christian & Brent, 2001; Hinds, West, Knight, & Harland, 1996). A controlled study of 1,205 new mothers and their babies showed no effect of reported caffeine use on low birth weight, premature birth, or retarded fetal growth (Santos, Victora, Huttly, & Carvalhal, 1998). On the other hand, four or more cups of coffee a day during pregnancy may dramatically increase the risk of sudden death in infancy (Ford et al., 1998). Studies of a possible link between caffeine consumption and spontaneous abortion have had mixed results (Cnattingius et al., 2000; Dlugosz et al., 1996; Infante-Rivard, Fernández, Gauthier, David, & Rivard, 1993; Klebanoff, Levine, DerSimonian, Clemens, & Wilkins, 1999; Mills et al., 1993; Signorello et al., 2001).

Marijuana and Cocaine   Studies of marijuana use by pregnant women are sparse (Fried & Smith, 2001) and the findings mixed (Dreher, Nugent, & Hudgins, 1994). Their interpretation is burdened by confounding factors, such as the unreliability of self-reports and, often, the concurrent use of other substances besides marijuana (Fried & Smith, 2001). However, some evidence suggests that heavy marijuana use can lead to birth defects, low birth weight, withdrawal-like symptoms (excessive crying and tremors) at birth, and increased risk of attention disorders and learning problems later in life (Fried, Watkinson, & Willan, 1984; March of Dimes Birth Defects Foundation, 2004b). In two longitudinal studies, one of low-risk white, predominantly middle-class families and the other of high-risk, low-SES, largely African American families, prenatal use of marijuana was associated with impaired attention, impulsivity, and difficulty in use of visual and perceptual skills after age 3, suggesting that the drug may affect functioning of the brain's frontal lobe (Fried & Smith, 2001). Also, an analysis of blood samples from the umbilical cords of 34 newborns found a greater prevalence of cancer-causing mutations in the infants of mothers who smoked marijuana and did not use tobacco, cocaine, or opiates (Ammenheuser, Berenson, Babiak, Singleton, & Whorton, 1998).

Cocaine use during pregnancy has been associated with spontaneous abortion, delayed growth, premature labor, low birth weight, small head size, birth defects,

BOX 3-2

Digging Deeper
Fetal Welfare versus Mothers' Rights

A South Carolina hospital routinely tested the urine of pregnant women suspected to be using illegal drugs and reported the evidence to police. Ten women were arrested, some of them in their hospital rooms almost immediately after childbirth. They sued, arguing that the urine tests constituted an unconstitutional search of their persons without their consent (Greenhouse, 2000a). In March 2001 the U.S. Supreme Court invalidated the hospital's drug testing policy (Harris & Paltrow, 2003).

In another South Carolina case, a young woman who had a stillbirth was convicted of homicide after an autopsy revealed evidence of cocaine in the baby's body. The woman was sentenced to 12 years in prison. The South Carolina Supreme Court upheld the conviction, and the U.S. Supreme Court declined to hear an appeal (Drug Policy Alliance, 2004).

In both these cases the issue was the conflict between protection of a fetus and a woman's right to privacy or to make her own decisions about her body. It is tempting to require a pregnant woman to adopt practices that will ensure her baby's health or to stop or punish her if she does not. But what about her personal freedom? Can civil rights be abrogated for the protection of the unborn?

The argument about the right to choose abortion, which rests on similar grounds, is far from settled. But the examples just given deal with a different aspect of the problem. What can or should society do about a woman who does *not* choose abortion but instead goes on carrying her baby while engaging in behavior destructive to it or refuses tests or treatment that medical providers consider essential to the baby's welfare?

Ingesting Harmful Substances   Does a woman have the right to knowingly ingest a substance, such as alcohol or another drug, which can permanently damage her unborn child? Some advocates for fetal rights think such behavior should be against the law even though it is legal for other adults. Other experts argue that incarceration for substance abuse is unworkable and self-defeating. They say that expectant mothers who have a drinking or drug problem need education and treatment, not prosecution (Drug Policy Alliance, 2004; Marwick, 1997, 1998).

Since 1985, at least 240 women in 35 states have been prosecuted for using illegal drugs or alcohol during pregnancy, even though no state legislature has specifically criminalized such activity (Harris & Paltrow, 2003; Nelson & Marshall, 1998). Instead, these women have been charged with the broader crimes of child endangerment or abuse, illegal drug delivery to a minor, murder, or manslaughter. In all states except South Carolina, courts have refused to expand these existing laws to cover claims of fetal rights. Only in South Carolina has drug use during pregnancy been held to be a crime (Harris & Paltrow, 2003).

Intrusive Medical Procedures   In January 2004, Melissa Ann Rowland of Salt Lake City was charged with the murder of one of her newborn twins, who was born dead. Until it was too late, Rowland had refused doctors' urgent recommendation that she have a cesarean section. The second child, a girl, was born alive with cocaine and alcohol in her system and was subsequently adopted.

---

and impaired neurological development (Bunikowski et al., 1998; Chiriboga, Brust, Bateman, & Hauser, 1999; Macmillan et al., 2001; March of Dimes Birth Defects Foundation, 2004a; Scher, Richardson, & Day, 2000; Shankaran et al., 2004). In some studies, cocaine-exposed newborns show acute withdrawal symptoms and sleep disturbances (O'Brien & Jeffery, 2002; Wagner, Katikaneni, Cox, & Ryan, 1998). So great has been the concern about "crack babies" that some states have taken criminal action against expectant mothers suspected of using cocaine (see Box 3-2).

More recent studies found no specific connection between prenatal cocaine exposure and physical, motor, cognitive, emotional, or behavioral deficits that could not also be attributed to other risk factors, such as low birth weight, exposure to tobacco, alcohol, marijuana, or a poor home environment (Frank, Augustyn, Knight, Pell, & Zuckerman, 2001; Messinger et al., 2004; Singer et al., 2004). In one study, 2-year-olds prenatally exposed to cocaine whose cocaine-using mothers had given up their care to others had more positive home environments and did better on developmental tests than cocaine-exposed toddlers who were still in their mothers' care (Brown, Bakeman, Coles, Platzman, & Lynch, 2004).

Checkpoint

Can you . . .

✔ Summarize recommendations concerning an expectant mother's diet and physical activity?

✔ Describe the short-term and long-term effects on the developing fetus of a mother's use of medical drugs, alcohol, tobacco, caffeine, marijuana, opiates, and cocaine during pregnancy?

acquired immune deficiency syndrome (AIDS)   Viral disease that undermines effective functioning of the immune system.

HIV/AIDS   **Acquired immune deficiency syndrome (AIDS)** is a disease caused by the human immunodeficiency virus (HIV), which undermines functioning of the immune system. If an expectant mother has the virus in her blood, it may cross over to the fetus's bloodstream through the placenta. After birth, the virus can be transmitted through breast milk. About 600,000 children worldwide are infected annually, most of them by mother-to-child transmission (UNAIDS, 2000). Infants born to HIV-infected

—continued

Rowland, who had a history of mental health problems, pleaded guilty to a reduced charge of child endangerment, agreed to enter a drug treatment program, and was sentenced to 18 months of probation (Associated Press, 2004b; Johnson, 2004).

Should a woman be forced to submit to intrusive procedures that pose a risk to her, such as a surgical delivery or intrauterine transfusions, when doctors say such procedures are essential to the delivery of a healthy baby? Should a woman from a fundamentalist sect that rejects modern medical care be taken into custody until she gives birth? Such measures have been defended as protecting the rights of the unborn, but women's rights advocates claim that they reflect a view of women as mere vehicles for carrying offspring and not as persons in their own right (Greenhouse, 2000b). Also, forcing intrusive measures on a pregnant woman may jeopardize the doctor-patient relationship. If failure to follow medical advice could bring forced surgery, confinement, or criminal charges, some women might avoid doctors altogether and thus deprive their fetuses of needed prenatal care (Nelson & Marshall, 1998).

Courts have held that "neither fetal rights nor state interests on behalf of the fetus supersede women's rights as ultimate medical decision maker" (Harris & Paltrow, 2003, p. 1698). Yet, the U.S. Congress in March 2004, in response to the notorious murder of a pregnant woman that also took the life of her unborn son, made it a federal crime to harm or kill an unborn child (Reuters, 2004b). That law, if not overturned by the courts, for the first time establishes a fetal right to life separate from the mother's and could have repercussions in cases in which fetal welfare conflicts with women's rights.

What's Your View?

- Does society's interest in protecting an unborn child justify coercive measures against pregnant women who ingest harmful substances or refuse medically indicated treatment?

- Should pregnant women who refuse to stop drinking or get treatment be incarcerated until they give birth? Should mothers who repeatedly give birth to children with FAS be sterilized?

- Should liquor companies be held liable if adequate warnings against use during pregnancy are not on their products?

- Would your answers be the same regarding smoking or use of cocaine or other potentially harmful substances?

Check It Out

For more information on this topic, go to http://www.nofas.org. You will find information on behaviors of those affected by Fetal Alcohol Syndrome and Fetal Alcohol Effects, including national statistics and contacts. Resources include newsletters, support groups, audiovisual materials, and information packets.

---

mothers tend to have small heads and slowed neurological development (Macmillan et al., 2001).

In the United States, new pediatric AIDS cases have declined steadily since 1994 due to routine testing and treatment of pregnant women and newborn babies (NCHS, 2004) and to advances in the prevention, detection, and treatment of HIV infection in infants. These include prenatal administration of the drug zidovudine (formerly called *azidothymidine*), commonly known as AZT, together with other antiretroviral drugs, to curtail transmission (Peters et al., 2003; Watts, 2002). Between 1992 and 1997, when zidovudine therapy became widespread, the number of U.S. babies who got AIDS from their mothers dropped by about two-thirds, raising the hope that mother-to-child transmission of the virus can be virtually eliminated (Lindegren et al., 1999). The risk of transmission also can be reduced by choosing cesarean delivery, especially when a woman has not received antiretroviral therapy; by careful management of vaginal delivery to avoid rupture of the membranes and episiotomy, which could bring the infant into contact with the mother's blood; and by promotion of alternatives to breast-feeding (Watts, 2002).

Other Maternal Illnesses Both prospective parents should try to prevent all infections—common colds, flu, urinary tract and vaginal infections, as well as sexually transmitted diseases. If the mother does contract an infection, she should have it treated promptly. Pregnant women also should be screened for thyroid deficiency, which can affect their children's future cognitive performance (Haddow et al., 1999).

Rubella (German measles), if contracted by a woman before her eleventh week of pregnancy, is almost certain to cause deafness and heart defects in her baby. Chances

Watch the video, "Long-Term Effects of Maternal Diabetes," in Chapter 3 of your CD for a compelling description of the troubling research findings on mothers who have diabetes during pregnancy.

of catching rubella during pregnancy have been greatly reduced in Europe and the United States since the late 1960s, when a vaccine was developed that is now routinely administered to infants and children. However, rubella is still a serious problem in developing countries where inoculations are not routine (Plotkin, Katz, & Cordero, 1999).

A diabetic mother's metabolic regulation, especially during the second and third trimesters of pregnancy, unless carefully managed, may affect her child's long-range neurobehavioral development and cognitive performance (Rizzo, Metzger, Dooley, & Cho, 1997). These risks can be greatly reduced by screening pregnant women for diabetes, followed by careful monitoring and a controlled diet (Kjos & Buchanan, 1999). Use of multivitamin supplements during the three months before conception and the first three months of pregnancy can reduce the risk of birth defects in offspring of diabetic mothers (Correa, Botto, Lin, Mulinare, & Erickson, 2003).

An infection called *toxoplasmosis,* caused by a parasite harbored in the bodies of cattle, sheep, and pigs and in the intestinal tracts of cats, typically produces either no symptoms or symptoms like those of the common cold. In a pregnant woman, however, especially in the second and third trimesters of pregnancy, it can cause brain damage, severely impaired eyesight or blindness, seizures, or miscarriage, stillbirth, or death of the baby. Although as many as 9 out of 10 of these babies may appear normal at birth, more than half of them have later problems, including eye infections, hearing loss, and learning disabilities. To avoid infection, expectant mothers should not eat raw or very rare meat, should wash hands and all work surfaces after touching raw meat, should peel or thoroughly wash raw fruits and vegetables, and should not dig in a garden where cat feces are buried. Women who have a cat should have it checked for the disease, should not feed it raw meat, and, if possible, should have someone else empty the litter box (March of Dimes, 2002) or should do it often, wearing gloves (Kravetz & Federman, 2002).

Maternal Stress   Prenatal stress in animal mothers increases the risk of a wide variety of psychological disorders in their offspring (Dingfelder, 2004; Huizink, Mulder, & Buitelaar, 2004), and limited research on prenatal stress in humans suggests negative effects as well (Gitau, Cameron, Fisk, & Glover, 1998; Sjostrom, Valentin, Thelin, & Marsal, 1997). In one study, women whose partners or children died or were hospitalized for cancer or heart attacks were at elevated risk of giving birth to children with certain deformities, such as cleft lip, cleft palate, and heart malformations (Hansen, Lou, & Olsen, 2000).

A mother's self-reported anxiety during pregnancy has been associated with 8-month-olds' inattentiveness during a developmental assessment (Huizink, Robles de Medina, Mulder, Visser, & Buitelaar, 2002) and preschoolers' negative emotionality or behavioral disorders in early childhood (Martin, Noyes, Wisenbaker, & Huttunen, 2000; O'Connor, Heron, Golding, Beveridge, & Glover, 2002). Other studies have found links between expecant mothers' perceptions of stress and their fetuses' activity levels (DiPietro, Hilton, Hawkins, Costigan, & Pressman, 2002) as well as between maternal stress and the synchrony of fetal movements and heart rates (DiPietro, Hodgson, Costigan, Hilton, & Johnson, 1996).

Moderate maternal stress is not necessarily bad for fetuses; in fact, some stress at certain times during gestation may spur organization of the formative brain. In a follow-up study of 100 two-year-olds who as fetuses had participated in studies of maternal stress, those whose mothers had shown greater anxiety midway through pregnancy scored higher on measures of motor and mental development (DiPietro, 2004).

Maternal Age   On January 17, 2005, in Giulesti Maternity Hospital in Bucharest, Adriana Iliescu at age 66 became the oldest woman on record to give birth. Iliescu had become pregnant after fertility treatments. The baby girl's twin sister was stillborn.

Births to U.S. women in their thirties and forties—and, to a lesser extent, even in their fifties—have nearly doubled since 1980, from 19 percent to 38 percent of all births (Martin et al., 2005)—an example of a history-graded influence. How does delayed childbearing affect the risks to mother and baby? Pregnant women over 35 are more likely to suffer complications due to diabetes, high blood pressure, or severe bleeding. Although most risks to the infant's health are not much greater than for babies born to younger mothers, there is more chance of miscarriage or stillbirth. There is also more likelihood of premature delivery, retarded fetal growth, other birth-related complications, and birth defects, such as Down syndrome. However, due to widespread screening for fetal defects among older expectant mothers, fewer malformed babies are born nowadays (Berkowitz, Skovron, Lapinski, & Berkowitz, 1990; P. Brown, 1993; Cunningham & Leveno, 1995).

Women age 40 and over are at increased risk of needing operative deliveries (Gilbert, Nesbitt, & Danielsen, 1999). Women who give birth after age 50 are two to three times more likely than younger women to have babies who are very small, born prematurely, or stillborn (Salihu, Shumpert, Slay, Kirby, & Alexander, 2003).

Although multiple births generally tend to be riskier than single births, twins and triplets born to older mothers do as well or better than those born to younger mothers—unless the mothers have low socioeconomic status. Many multiple births to older women with higher SES are conceived through assisted reproductive technology, and these pregnancies tend to be monitored closely (Zhang, Meikle, Grainger, & Trumble, 2002).

Adolescents also tend to have premature or underweight babies—perhaps because a young girl's still-growing body consumes vital nutrients the fetus needs (Fraser, Brockert, & Ward, 1995). These newborns are at heightened risk of death in the first month, disabilities, or health problems. Risks of teenage pregnancy are discussed further in Chapter 17.

This pregnant woman shopping for fruits and vegetables at an open-air market on a busy street is probably unaware of the potential danger to her fetus from traffic-related air pollution.

Outside Environmental Hazards Air pollution, chemicals, radiation, extremes of heat and humidity, and other hazards of modern life can affect prenatal development. Blood samples taken from 265 New York City mothers and their newborns showed as much DNA damage from combustion-related pollutants in the infants as in the mothers, even though the infants had received a tenfold lower dose in the womb due to the protection of the placenta (Perera, Tang, et al., 2004). Women who work with chemicals used in manufacturing semiconductor chips have about twice the rate of miscarriage as other female workers (Markoff, 1992), and women exposed to DDT tend to have more preterm births (Longnecker, Klebanoff, Zhou, & Brock, 2001). Two common insecticides, chlorpyrifos and diazinon, apparently cause stunting of prenatal growth. Infants born in New York City after a U.S. ban on household use of these substances were heavier and longer and had substantially less insecticide in blood drawn from their umbilical cords than babies born before the ban (Whyatt et al., in press).

Children born to mothers who live near toxic landfills may be at elevated risk for various types of birth defects. Research in the United Kingdom reported a 33 percent increase in risk of nongenetic birth defects among families living within two miles of certain hazardous-waste sites (Vrijheld et al., 2002). Childhood cancers, including leukemia, have been linked to pregnant mothers' drinking chemically contaminated ground water (Boyles, 2002) and to emissions from engine exhausts and industrial processing plants (Knox, 2005).

The principal source of human exposure to organic mercury—and of possible harm to the developing fetal brain—is through high levels of fish consumption.

Breast-fed infants also may be exposed if the mother's diet is heavy on ocean fish. More research is needed to determine what is a safe level of exposure (Davidson, Myers, & Weiss, 2004).

Radiation can cause genetic mutations. Prenatal radiation exposure (for example, through X-rays of a mother's abdomen) can lead to stunted growth, birth defects, abnormal brain function, or cancer later in life. The impact depends on the dose and the timing; risks are greatest before the 15th week of gestation (CDC, undated). Women who have routine dental X-rays during pregnancy triple their risk of having low birth-weight babies (Hujoel, Bollen, Noonan, & del Aguila, 2004).

Environmental Influences: Paternal Factors

A man's exposure to lead, marijuana or tobacco smoke, large amounts of alcohol or radiation, DES, or certain pesticides (Swan et al., 2003) may result in abnormal or poor quality sperm. Offspring of male workers at a British nuclear processing plant were at elevated risk of being born dead (Parker, Pearce, Dickinson, Aitkin, & Craft, 1999). Babies whose fathers had diagnostic X-rays within the year prior to conception or had high lead exposure at work tended to have low birth weight and slowed fetal growth (Lin, Hwang, Marshall, & Marion, 1998; Shea, Little, & the ALSPAC Study Team, 1997). Among nearly 238,000 infants born in Singapore over a four-year period, birth defects were more strongly linked to fathers' occupations—especially such jobs as plant and machine operation and assembly—than to mother's occupations (Chia et al., 2004).

A man's use of cocaine can cause birth defects in his children. The cocaine seems to attach itself to his sperm, and this cocaine-bearing sperm then enters the ovum at conception. Other toxins, such as lead and mercury, may "hitchhike" onto sperm in the same way (Yazigi, Odem, & Polakoski, 1991).

Men who smoke have an increased likelihood of transmitting genetic abnormalities (AAP Committee on Substance Abuse, 2001). A pregnant woman's exposure to the father's secondhand smoke has been linked with low birth weight, infant respiratory infections, sudden infant death, and cancer in childhood and adulthood (Ji et al., 1997; D. H. Rubin, Krasilnikoff, Leventhal, Weile, & Berget, 1986; Sandler, Everson, Wilcox, & Browder, 1985; Wakefield, Reid, Roberts, Mullins, & Gillies, 1998). In a study of 214 nonsmoking mothers in New York City, exposure to *both* paternal smoking and urban air pollution resulted in a 7 percent reduction in birth weight and a 3 percent reduction in head circumference (Perera, Rauh, et al., 2004).

Older fathers may be a significant source of birth defects (Crow, 1993, 1995). A later paternal age (averaging in the late 30s) is associated with increases in the risk of several rare conditions, including Marfan's syndrome (deformities of the head and limbs) and dwarfism (G. Evans, 1976). Advanced age of the father may be a factor in about 5 percent of cases of Down syndrome (Antonarakis & Down Syndrome Collaborative Group, 1991) and in a disproportionate number of cases of schizophrenia (Byrne et al., 2003; Malaspina et al., 2001).

Monitoring Prenatal Development

Not long ago, almost the only decision parents had to make about their babies before birth was the decision to conceive; most of what happened in the intervening months was beyond their control. Now scientists have developed an array of tools to assess an unborn baby's progress and well-being and even to intervene to correct some abnormal conditions (see Table 3-5).

Screening for treatable defects and diseases is only one reason for the importance of prenatal care. Early, high-quality prenatal care, which includes educational, social, and nutritional services, can help prevent maternal, prenatal, and infant death and other complications of birth. It can provide first-time mothers with information

What's Your View?

• Since cocaine, marijuana, tobacco, and other substances can produce genetic abnormalities in a man's sperm, should men of childbearing age be forced to abstain from them? How could such a prohibition be enforced?

Checkpoint

Can you . . .

✔ Summarize the risks of maternal illnesses and stress, delayed childbearing, and exposure to chemicals and radiation?

✔ Identify at least three ways in which the father can influence environmentally caused defects?

Guidepost

8. What techniques can assess a fetus's health, and why is prenatal care important?

Table 3-5 Prenatal Assessment Techniques

Technique	Description	Uses and Advantages	Risks and Notes
Ultrasound (sonogram), sonoembryology	High-frequency sound waves directed at the mother's abdomen produce a picture of fetus in uterus. Sonoembryology uses high-frequency transvaginal probes and digital image processing to produce a picture of embryo in uterus.	Monitor fetal growth, movement, position, and form; assess amniotic fluid volume; judge gestational age; detect multiple pregnancies Detect major structural abnormalities or death of a fetus Guide amniocentesis and chorionic villus sampling Help diagnose sex-linked disorders Sonoembryology can detect unusual defects during embryonic stage	No known risks; done routinely in many places. Can be used for sex-screening of unborn babies.
Embryoscopy, fetoscopy	Tiny viewing scope is inserted in woman's abdomen to view embryo or fetus. Can assist in diagnosis of nonchromosomal genetic disorders.	Can guide fetal blood transfusions and bone marrow transplants	Embryoscopy is still in research stage. Riskier than other prenatal diagnostic procedures
Amniocentesis	Sample of amniotic fluid is withdrawn and analyzed under guidance of ultrasound. Most commonly used procedure to obtain fetal cells for testing.	Can detect chromosomal disorders and certain genetic or multifactorial defects; more than 99 percent accuracy rate. Usually performed in women ages 35 and over; recommended if prospective parents are known carriers of Tay-Sachs disease or sickle-cell anemia or have family history of Down syndrome, spina bifida, or muscular dystrophy. Can help diagnose sex-linked disorders.	Normally not performed before 15 weeks' gestation Results usually take 1 to 2 weeks Small (0.5 percent to 1 percent) added risk of fetal loss or injury; early amniocentesis (at 11 to 13 weeks' gestation) is more risky and not recommended Can be used for sex-screening of unborn babies.
Chorionic villus sampling (CVS)	Tissues from hairlike chorionic villi (projections of membrane surrounding fetus) are removed from placenta and analyzed	Early diagnosis of birth defects and disorders. Can be performed between 10 and 12 weeks' gestation; yields highly accurate results within a week	Should not be performed before 10 weeks' gestation. Some studies suggest 1 to 4 percent more risk of fetal loss than amniocentesis
Preimplantation genetic diagnosis	After in vitro fertilization, a sample cell is removed from the blastocyst and analyzed	Can avoid transmission of genetic defects or predispositions known to run in the family; a defective blastocyst is *not* implanted in uterus	No known risks
Umbilical cord sampling (cordocentesis, or fetal blood sampling)	Needle guided by ultrasound is inserted into blood vessels of umbilical cord	Allows direct access to fetal DNA for diagnostic measures, including assessment of blood disorders and infections, and therapeutic measures such as blood transfusions	Fetal loss or miscarriage is reported in 1% to 2% of cases; increases risk of bleeding from umbilical cord and fetal distress
Maternal blood test	A sample of the prospective mother's blood is tested for alpha fetoprotein (AFP)	May indicate defects in formation of brain or spinal cord (anencephaly or spina bifida); also can predict Down syndrome and other abnormalities Permits monitoring of pregnancies at risk for low birth weight or stillbirth	No known risks, but false negatives are possible Ultrasound and/or amniocentesis needed to confirm suspected conditions

Sources: Chodirker et al., 2001; Cicero, Curcio, Papageorghiou, Sonek, & Nicolaides, 2001; Cuniff & Committee on Genetics, 2004; Kurjak, Kupesic, Matijevic, Kos, & Marton, 1999; Verlinsky et al., 2002.

about pregnancy, childbirth, and infant care. Poor women who get prenatal care benefit by being put in touch with other needed services, and they are more likely to get medical care for their infants after birth (Shiono & Behrman, 1995).

In the United States prenatal care is widespread but not universal, as in many European countries, and it lacks uniform national standards and guaranteed financial

What's
Your View?

• Can you suggest ways to
encourage more pregnant
women to seek early prenatal
care?

coverage. Use of early prenatal care (during the first three months of pregnancy) has risen since 1970 from about 68 percent to 84 percent of pregnant women. In 2003, 3.5 percent of expectant mothers received no care until the last trimester or no care at all (Hamilton et al., 2004; Martin et al., 2005; NCHS, 2004).

Although prenatal care has increased, so have rates of low birth weight and premature birth (Kogan et al., 1998; Hamilton, Martin, & Sutton, 2004; Martin et al., 2003). Why? One answer is the increasing number of multiple births (Martin et al., 2003), which require especially close prenatal attention. Twin pregnancies often end, for precautionary reasons, in early births, either induced or by cesarean delivery. Intensive prenatal care may permit early detection of problems requiring immediate delivery, as, for example, when one or both fetuses are not thriving. This may explain why a U.S. government study of twin births between 1981 and 1997 found parallel upward trends in use of prenatal care and rates of preterm birth—along with a decline in mortality of those twin infants whose mothers obtained intensive prenatal care (Kogan et al., 2000).

A second answer is that the benefits of prenatal care are not evenly distributed. Although usage of prenatal care has grown, especially among ethnic groups that tend *not* to receive early care, the women most at risk of bearing low-birth-weight babies—teenage and unmarried women, those with little education, and some minority women—are still least likely to receive it (Martin et al., 2003; National Center for Health Statistics, 1994a, 1998, 2001, 2004; U.S. Department of Health and Human Services, 1996a). Although nearly 89 percent of white expectant mothers and 85 percent of Asian or Pacific Islanders received prenatal care in the first trimester in 2002, only about 76 percent of African Americans, 77 percent of Hispanic Americans, and 70 percent of American Indians and Alaska Natives did (NCHS, 2004). (Figure 3-11 shows percentages of various ethnic groups that receive late or no prenatal care.) A related concern is an ethnic disparity in fetal mortality. Although fetal

Figure 3-11

Proportion of U.S. mothers with late or no prenatal care, according to race or ethnicity, 2002. Late prenatal care begins in the last 3 months of pregnancy. (Source: Martin et al., 2003.)

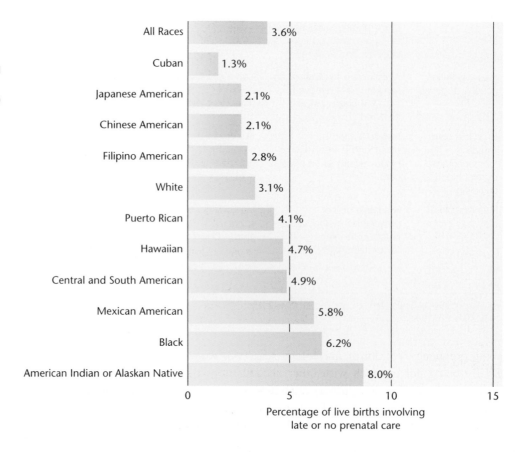

deaths declined substantially between 1990 and 2000 among almost all racial/ethnic groups, the fetal mortality rate in 2000 was nearly twice as high among non-Hispanic blacks as in the rest of the population—12.1 as compared to 6.6 fetal deaths per 1,000 live births (Barfield & Martin, 2004).

Merely increasing the quantity of prenatal care does not address the *content* of care (Misra & Guyer, 1998). Most prenatal care programs in the United States focus on screening for major complications and are not designed to attack the causes of low birth weight. A national panel has recommended that prenatal care be restructured to provide more visits early in the pregnancy and fewer in the last trimester. In fact, care should begin *before* pregnancy. Prepregnancy counseling could make more women aware, for example, of the importance of getting enough folic acid in their diet and could make sure that they are immune to rubella. In addition, care needs to be made more accessible to poor and minority women (Shiono & Behrman, 1995).

Checkpoint
Can you . . .

✔ Describe seven techniques for identifying defects or disorders prenatally?

✔ Tell why early, high-quality prenatal care is important, and how it could be improved?

Refocus

Thinking back to the Focus vignette about Abel Dorris and fetal alcohol syndrome at the beginning of this chapter:

- What light does Abel Dorris's case shed on the role of the prenatal environment in a child's development?

- Why did Michael Dorris's belief that his son Abel would "catch up" given a positive adoptive home environment prove unfounded?

- Does Abel's story illustrate the concept of reaction range? Of canalization? Of critical periods? If so, how?

- What sorts of information might be helpful in counseling prospective parents on adoption of a child whose prenatal history is unknown?

Good prenatal care can give every child the best possible chance for entering the world in good condition to meet the challenges of life outside the womb—challenges we discuss in the next three chapters.

SUMMARY AND KEY TERMS

Conceiving New Life

Guidepost 1: How does conception normally occur?

- Fertilization, the union of an ovum and a sperm, results in the formation of a one-celled zygote, which then duplicates itself by cell division.

  fertilization *(63)*

  zygote *(63)*

Guidepost 2: What causes multiple births?

- Multiple births can occur either by the fertilization of two ova (or one ovum that has split) or by the splitting of one fertilized ovum. Larger multiple births result from either one of these processes or a combination of the two.

- Dizygotic (fraternal) twins have different genetic make-ups and may be of different sexes; monozygotic (identical) twins have the same genetic makeup. Because of differences in prenatal and postnatal experience, "identical" twins may differ in temperament and other respects.

  dizygotic twins *(64)*

  monozygotic twins *(64)*

  temperament *(64)*

Mechanisms of Heredity

Guidepost 3: How does heredity operate in determining sex and transmitting normal and abnormal traits?

- The basic functional units of heredity are the genes, which are made of deoxyribonucleic acid (DNA). DNA carries the biochemical instructions, or genetic code, that governs the development of cell structure and functions. Each gene seems to be located by function in a definite position on a particular chromosome.

  deoxyribonucleic acid (DNA) *(65)*

  genetic code *(65)*

  chromosomes *(65)*

  genes *(65)*

- At conception, each normal human being receives 23 chromosomes from the mother and 23 from the father. These form 23 pairs of chromosomes— 22 pairs of autosomes and 1 pair of sex chromosomes. A child who receives an X chromosome from each parent is genetically female. A child who receives a Y chromosome from the father is genetically male.

- The simplest patterns of genetic transmission are dominant and recessive inheritance. When a pair of alleles are the same, a person is homozygous for the trait; when they are different, the person is heterozygous.

  autosomes *(66)*

  sex chromosomes *(66)*

  alleles *(68)*

  homozygous *(68)*

  heterozygous *(68)*

  dominant inheritance *(68)*

  recessive inheritance *(68)*

- Most normal human characteristics are the result of polygenic or multifactorial transmission. Except for monozygotic twins, each child inherits a unique genotype. Dominant inheritance and multifactorial transmission explain why a person's phenotype does not always express the underlying genotype.

  polygenic inheritance *(69)*

  multifactorial transmission *(69)*

  phenotype *(69)*

  genotype *(69)*

- Birth defects and diseases may result from simple dominant, recessive, or sex-linked inheritance, from mutations, or from genome imprinting. Chromosomal abnormalities also can cause birth defects.

- Through genetic counseling, prospective parents can receive information about the mathematical odds of bearing children with certain defects.

- Genetic testing involves risks as well as benefits.

  incomplete dominance *(72)*

  sex-linked inheritance *(72)*

  mutations *(72)*

  natural selection *(73)*

  Down syndrome *(73)*

  genetic counseling *(74)*

Nature and Nurture: Influences of Heredity and Environment

Guidepost 4: How do scientists study the relative influences of heredity and environment, and how do heredity and environment work together?

- Research in behavioral genetics is based on the assumption that the relative influences of heredity and environment can be measured statistically. If heredity is an important influence on a trait, genetically closer persons will be more similar in that trait. Family studies, adoption studies, and studies of twins enable researchers to measure the heritability of specific traits.

- The concepts of reaction range, canalization, genotype-environment interaction, genotype-environment correlation (or covariance), and niche-picking describe ways in which heredity and environment work together.

- Siblings tend to be more different than alike in intelligence and personality. According to some behavior geneticists, heredity accounts for most of the similarity, and nonshared environmental effects account for most of the difference. Critics claim that this research, for methodological reasons, minimizes the role of parenting and the complexity of developmental systems.

  behavioral genetics *(75)*

  heritability *(75)*

  concordant *(77)*

  reaction range *(78)*

  canalization *(79)*

  genotype-environment interaction *(80)*

  genotype-environment correlation *(80)*

  niche-picking *(80)*

  nonshared environmental effects *(81)*

Guidepost 5: What roles do heredity and environment play in physical health, intelligence, and personality?

- Obesity, longevity, intelligence, and temperament are influenced by both heredity and environment.

- Schizophrenia and autism are highly heritable psychopathological disorders that also are influenced by environment.

  obesity *(81)*

  schizophrenia *(83)*

  autism *(83)*

Prenatal Development

Guidepost 6: What are the three stages of prenatal development, and what happens during each stage?

- Prenatal development occurs in three stages of gestation: the germinal, embryonic, and fetal stages.

- Growth and development both before and after birth follow the cephalocaudal principle (head to tail) and the proximodistal principle (center outward).

- Severely defective embryos often are spontaneously aborted during the first trimester of pregnancy.

  cephalocaudal principle *(85)*

  proximodistal principle *(85)*

  germinal stage *(85)*

  embryonic stage *(89)*

  spontaneous abortion *(89)*

  fetal stage *(89)*

- As fetuses grow, they move less, but more vigorously. Swallowing amniotic fluid, which contains substances from the mother's body, stimulates taste and smell. Fetuses seem able to hear, exercise sensory discrimination, learn, and remember.

  ultrasound *(90)*

Guidepost 7: What environmental influences can affect prenatal development?

- The developing organism can be greatly affected by its prenatal environment. The likelihood of a birth defect may depend on the timing and intensity of an environmental event and its interaction with genetic factors.

- Important environmental influences involving the mother include nutrition, physical activity, smoking, intake of alcohol or other drugs, transmission of maternal illnesses or infections, maternal stress, maternal age, and external environmental hazards, such as chemicals and radiation. External influences also may affect the father's sperm.

  teratogenic *(91)*

  fetal alcohol syndrome (FAS) *(93)*

  acquired immune deficiency syndrome (AIDS) *(96)*

Guidepost 8: What techniques can assess a fetus's health, and why is prenatal care important?

- Ultrasound, amniocentesis, chorionic villus sampling, fetoscopy, preimplantation genetic diagnosis, umbilical cord sampling, and maternal blood tests can be used to determine whether an unborn baby is developing normally.

- Early, high-quality prenatal care is essential for healthy development. It can lead to detection of defects and disorders and, especially if begun early and targeted to the needs of at-risk women, may help reduce maternal and infant death, low birth weight, and other birth complications.

Physical Development During the First Three Years

The experiences of the first three years of life are almost entirely lost to us, and when we attempt to enter into a small child's world, we come as foreigners who have forgotten the landscape and no longer speak the native tongue.

Selma Fraiberg, *The Magic Years*, 1959

Focus
Helen Keller and the World of the Senses*

"What we have once enjoyed we can never lose," the author Helen Keller (1880–1968) once wrote. "A sunset, a mountain bathed in moonlight, the ocean in calm and in storm—we see these, love their beauty, hold the vision to our hearts. All that we love deeply becomes a part of us" (Keller, 1929, p. 2).

This quotation is especially remarkable—and especially poignant—in view of the fact that Helen Keller never saw a sunset or a mountain or moonlight or an ocean or anything else after the age of 19 months. It was then that she contracted a mysterious fever, which left her deaf and with inexorably ebbing sight.

From her birth in an annex of her parents' estate in Tuscumbia, Alabama, until her illness, Helen had been a normal, healthy baby—lively, affectionate, and precocious, with excellent vision. After her illness, she became expressionless and unresponsive. At one year, she had begun to walk; after her illness, she clung to her mother's skirts or sat in her lap, endlessly rubbing her face. She had also begun to talk; one of her first words was *water*. After her illness, she continued to say, "wahwah," but not much else.

Her distraught parents first took her to a mineral spa and then to medical specialists, but there was no hope for a cure. At a time when physical and cognitive development normally enter a major growth spurt, the sensory gateways to the exploration of Helen's world had slammed shut—but not entirely. Deprived of two senses, she leaned more heavily on the other three, especially smell and touch. She later explained that she could tell a doctor from a carpenter by the odors of ether or wood that came from them. She used her ever-active fingertips to trace the "delicate tremble of a butterfly's wings . . . , the soft petals of violets . . . , the clear, firm outline of face and limb, the smooth arch of a horse's neck and the velvety touch of his nose"

*Sources of information about Helen Keller include Keller (1903/1905, 1920, 1929, 2003), Herrmann (1999), Lash (1980), and Ozick (2003).

107

(Keller, 1920, pp. 6–7). Memories of the daylight world she had once inhabited helped her make sense of the unrelieved night in which she now found herself.

Helen realized that she was not like other people, but at first she had no clear sense of who or what she was. She later wrote, "I lived in a world that was a no-world. . . . I did not know that I knew [anything], or that I lived or acted or desired" (1920, p. 113). Sometimes, when family members were talking to each other, she would stand between them and touch their lips and then frantically move her own—but nothing happened. Her frustration found its outlet in violent, inconsolable tantrums; she would kick and scream until she was exhausted.

Out of pity, her parents indulged her whims. Finally, more in desperation than in hope, they engaged a teacher for her: a young woman named Anne Sullivan, who herself had limited vision and who had been trained in a school for the blind. Arriving at the Keller home, Sullivan found 6-year-old Helen to be "wild, wilful, and destructive" (Lash, 1980, p. 348). Upon meeting her new teacher, the child knocked out one of Sullivan's front teeth. Once, after figuring out how to use a key, she locked her mother in the pantry. Another time, she overturned her baby sister's cradle. Frustrated by her teacher's attempts to spell the word *doll* into her palm, Helen hurled her new doll to the floor, smashing it to bits.

Yet, that same day, the little girl made her first linguistic breakthrough. As she and her teacher walked in the garden, they stopped to get a drink at the pump. Sullivan placed Helen's hand under the spout, at the same time spelling "w-a-t-e-r" over and over into her other hand. "I stood still," Keller later wrote, "my whole attention fixed upon the motions of her fingers. Suddenly I felt a misty consciousness as of something forgotten—a thrill of returning thought; and somehow the mystery of language was revealed to me. I knew then that 'w-a-t-e-r' meant the wonderful cool something that was flowing over my hand. That living word awakened my soul, gave it light, hope, joy, set it free!" (Keller, 1905, p. 35).

The story of how Anne Sullivan tamed this unruly child and brought her into the light of language and thought is a familiar and inspiring one. One lesson we can draw from the story of Helen Keller's early development is the central importance of the senses—the windows to a baby's world—and their connection with all other aspects of development. Had Helen Keller not lost her vision and hearing or had she been born without one or the other, or both, her physical, cognitive, and psychosocial development undoubtedly would have been quite different.

Helen Keller is just one of many well-known people—including almost all the presidents of the United States—who were born at home. Today, the overwhelming majority of births in the United States occur in hospitals. However, there is a small but growing movement back to home birth—still the norm in many developing countries.

In this chapter, we describe how babies come into the world, how newborn babies look, and how their body systems work. We discuss ways to safeguard their life and health. We explore how sensory perception goes hand in hand with an infant's growing motor skills and shapes the astoundingly rapid development of the brain. We see how infants become busy, active toddlers and how parents and other caregivers can foster healthy growth and development.

After you have read and studied this chapter, you should be able to answer each of the Guidepost questions that follow. Look for them again in the margins, where they point to important concepts throughout the chapter. To check your understanding of these Guideposts, review the end-of-chapter summary. Checkpoints located at periodic spots throughout the chapter will help you verify your understanding of what you have read.

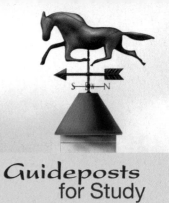

Guideposts for Study

1. What cultural customs surround birth, and how has childbirth changed in developed countries?

2. How does labor begin, and what happens during each of the three stages of childbirth?

3. What alternative methods of delivery are available?

4. How do newborn infants adjust to life outside the womb?

5. How can we tell whether a new baby is healthy and is developing normally?

6. How do newborns' patterns of sleep, waking, and activity change?

7. What complications of childbirth can endanger newborn babies, and what are the long-term prospects for babies with complicated births?

8. How can we enhance babies' chances of survival and health?

9. What influences the growth of body and brain?

10. When do the senses develop?

11. What are the early milestones in motor development, and what are some influences on it?

Childbirth and Culture: How Birthing Has Changed

Customs surrounding childbirth reflect the beliefs, values, and resources of a culture. A Mayan woman in Yucatan gives birth in the hammock in which she sleeps at night; the father-to-be is present along with the midwife. To evade evil spirits, mother and child remain at home for a week (Jordan, 1993). By contrast, among the Ngoni in East Africa, men are excluded from a birth. In rural Thailand, a new mother generally resumes normal activity within a few hours of giving birth (Broude, 1995; Gardiner & Kosmitzki, 2005).

Before the 20th century, childbirth in Europe and in the United States was a female social ritual.* The woman, surrounded by female relatives and neighbors, sat up in her own bed or perhaps in the stable, modestly draped in a sheet; if she wished, she might stand, walk around, or squat over a birth stool. The prospective father was nowhere to be seen. Not until the 15th century was a doctor present, and then only for wealthy women if complications arose.

The midwife who presided over the event had no formal training; she offered "advice, massages, potions, irrigations, and talismans" (Fontanel & d'Harcourt, 1997, p. 28). After the baby emerged, the midwife cut and tied the umbilical cord and cleaned and examined the newborn, testing the reflexes and joints. The other women helped the new mother wash and dress, made her bed with clean sheets, and served her food to rebuild her strength. Within a few hours or days, a peasant mother would be back at work in the fields; a more affluent woman could rest for several weeks.

Guidepost

1. What cultural customs surround birth, and how has childbirth changed in developed countries?

*This discussion is based largely on Eccles (1982); Fontanel & d'Harcourt (1997); Gelis (1991); and Scholten (1985).

Childbirth in those times was "a struggle with death" for both mother and baby (Fontanel & d'Harcourt, 1997, p. 34). In 17th- and 18th-century France, a woman had a 1 in 10 chance of dying while or shortly after giving birth. Thousands of babies were stillborn, and 1 out of 4 who were born alive died during their first year.

The development of the science of obstetrics early in the 19th century and of maternity hospitals after the turn of the 20th century revolutionized childbirth. In 1900, 20 years after Helen Keller's birth, only 5 percent of U.S. deliveries occurred in hospitals; by 1920, in some cities, 65 percent did (Scholten, 1985). A similar trend took place in Europe. In the United States today, about 99 percent of babies are born in hospitals, and more than 91 percent of births are attended by physicians (Martin et al., 2003).

The dramatic reductions in risks surrounding pregnancy and childbirth, particularly during the past 50 years, are largely due to the availability of antibiotics, blood transfusions, safe anesthesia, improved hygiene, and drugs for inducing labor. In addition, improvements in prenatal assessment and care make it far more likely that a baby will be born healthy.

However, the "medicalization" of childbirth has had social and emotional costs, some commentators claim (Fontanel & d'Harcourt, 1997). Today a small but growing percentage of women in developed countries are going back to the intimate, personal experience of home birth, which can involve the whole family. Home births usually are attended by a trained nurse-midwife, with the resources of medical science close at hand. Previous arrangements need to be made with a physician and a nearby hospital in case an emergency arises for which their services may be needed. Freestanding, homelike birth centers provide another option. Studies suggest that births in both of these settings can be as safe and much less expensive than those in hospitals when deliveries are low-risk and are attended by skilled practitioners (Anderson & Anderson, 1999; Durand, 1992; Guyer, Strobino, Ventura, & Singh, 1995; Korte & Scaer, 1984).

Hospitals, too, are finding ways to "humanize" childbirth. Labor and delivery may take place in a homelike birthing room, under soft lights, with the father or partner present as a "coach" and older siblings invited to visit after the birth. Rooming-in policies allow a baby to stay in the mother's room much or all of the time so that

Checkpoint

Can you . . .

✔ Identify at least two ways in which childbirth has changed in developed countries?

✔ Give reasons for the reduction in risks of pregnancy and childbirth?

✔ Weigh the comparative advantages of various settings and attendants for childbirth?

In many hospitals, a woman can deliver in a homelike birthing room with all the resources of medical science at hand. Here a doctor and nurse attend the birth while the prospective father rubs the woman's back and gives her support.

mothers can feed their newborns when they are hungry rather than when an arbitrary schedule allows. By "demedicalizing the experience of childbirth, some hospitals and birthing centers are seeking to establish—or reestablish—an environment in which tenderness, security, and emotion carry as much weight as medical techniques" (Fontanel & d'Harcourt, 1997, p. 57).

The Birth Process

Labor is an apt term for the process of giving birth. Birth is hard work for both mother and baby. What brings on labor is a series of uterine, cervical, and other changes called **parturition.** Parturition typically begins about two weeks before delivery, when sharply rising estrogen levels stimulate the uterus to contract and the cervix to become more flexible. The uterine contractions that expel the fetus begin—typically, 266 days after conception—as mild tightenings of the uterus. A woman may have felt similar "false" contractions at times during the final months of pregnancy, but she may recognize birth contractions as the "real thing" because of their greater regularity and intensity.

Stages of Childbirth

Labor takes place in three overlapping stages (see Figure 4-1). The *first stage,* the longest, typically lasts 12 hours or more for a woman having her first child. In later births the first stage tends to be shorter. During this stage, regular and increasingly frequent uterine contractions cause the cervix to dilate, or widen.

During the *second stage,* which typically lasts up to 1 hour, the contractions become stronger and closer together. The second stage begins when the baby's head begins to move through the cervix into the vaginal canal, and it ends when the baby emerges completely from the mother's body. If this stage lasts longer than 2 hours, signaling that the baby needs help, a doctor may grasp the baby's head with forceps or, more often, use vacuum extraction with a suction cup to pull it out of the mother's body (Curtin & Park, 1999). At the end of this stage, the baby is born; but it is still attached to the placenta in the mother's body by the umbilical cord, which must be cut and clamped. During the *third stage,* which lasts about 5 to 30 minutes, the placenta and the remainder of the umbilical cord are expelled from the mother.

Methods of Delivery

The primary concern in choosing a method for delivering a baby is the safety of both mother and baby. Also of concern is the mother's comfort.

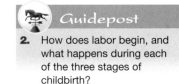

Guidepost

2. How does labor begin, and what happens during each of the three stages of childbirth?

parturition Process of uterine, cervical, and other changes, usually lasting about two weeks preceding childbirth.

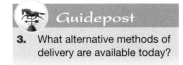

Lifemap CD

What's it like to give birth in a home setting? To find out, view the real-life video, "Childbirth" in Chapter 4 of your CD.

Guidepost

3. What alternative methods of delivery are available today?

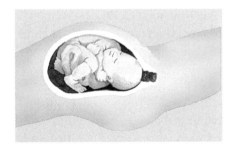

(*a*) First stage

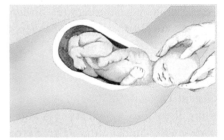

(*b*) Second stage

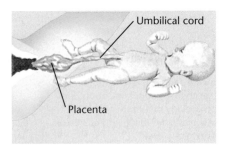

(*c*) Third stage

Figure 4-1

The first three stages of childbirth. (a) During the first stage of labor, a series of stronger and stronger contractions dilates the cervix, the opening to the mother's womb. (b) During the second stage, the baby's head moves down the birth canal and emerges from the vagina. (c) During the brief third stage, the placenta and umbilical cord are expelled from the womb. Then the cord is cut. (Source: Adapted from Lagercrantz & Slotkin, 1986.)

cesarean delivery Delivery of a baby by surgical removal from the uterus.

Vaginal versus Cesarean Delivery The usual method of childbirth, just described, is vaginal delivery. **Cesarean delivery** is a surgical procedure to remove the baby from the uterus by cutting through the abdomen. In 2003, according to preliminary data, 27.6 percent of U.S. births occurred this way, a record high and a 31 percent increase since 1996 (Martin et al., 2005). Cesarean birthrates in the United States are among the highest in the world, despite increased rates in European countries during the 1990s (International Cesarean Awareness Network, 2003; Sachs et al., 1999).

The operation is commonly performed when labor progresses too slowly, when the mother is bleeding vaginally, when the baby seems to be in trouble, when the baby is in the breech position (feet first) or transverse position (lying crosswise in the uterus), or when the head is too big to pass through the mother's pelvis. Surgical deliveries are more likely when the birth involves a first baby, a large baby, an older mother, or a mother who has had a previous cesarean. Thus, the increase in cesarean rates is in part a reflection of a proportional increase in first births, a rise in average birth weight, and a trend toward later childbirth. Other suggested explanations are the increased use of induced labor and of **electronic fetal monitoring** to track the fetus's heartbeat during labor and delivery to alert the physician that a fetus needs help; physicians' fear of malpractice litigation; and mothers' desire to avoid a difficult labor (Guyer et al., 1999; Martin et al., 2003, 2005; Parrish, Holt, Easterling, Connell, & LeGerfo, 1994; Sachs, Kobelin, Castro, & Frigoletto, 1999).

electronic fetal monitoring Mechanical monitoring of fetal heartbeat during labor and delivery.

Along with the sharp increase in cesarean births, the rate of vaginal births after a previous cesarean (VBAC) has fallen by 63 percent since 1996 as risks of such deliveries have become known (Martin et al., 2005). Among 313,238 Scottish women giving birth after previous cesareans, the risk of the infant's dying during delivery was about 11 times higher in vaginal births than in planned repeat cesareans (Smith, Pell, Cameron, & Dobbie, 2002). In the United States, a comparison of 17,898 women who attempted VBAC with 15,801 women who elected a repeat cesarean found greater (though still low) risks of uterine rupture and brain damage associated with VBAC (Landon et al., 2004).

Medicated versus Unmedicated Delivery In the mid-19th century, England's Queen Victoria became the first woman in history to be put to sleep during delivery, that of her eighth child. Sedation with ether or chloroform became common practice as more births took place in hospitals (Fontanel & d'Harcourt, 1997).

Today, general anesthesia, which renders the woman unconscious, is rarely used, even in cesarean births. Usually the woman is given regional anesthesia if she wants and needs it, but she remains fully alert and can participate in the birth process and hold her newborn immediately afterward. Regional anesthesia blocks the nerve pathways that would carry the sensation of pain to the brain. Alternatively, the mother can receive a relaxing analgesic (painkiller).

natural childbirth Method of childbirth that seeks to prevent pain by eliminating the mother's fear through education about the physiology of reproduction and training in breathing and relaxation during delivery.

prepared childbirth Method of childbirth that uses instruction, breathing exercises, and social support to induce controlled physical responses to uterine contractions and reduce fear and pain.

All these drugs pass through the placenta to enter the fetal blood supply and tissues and thus may potentially pose dangers to the baby. Alternative methods of childbirth were developed to minimize the use of drugs while maximizing both parents' active involvement. In 1914, a British physician, Dr. Grantly Dick-Read, suggested that pain in childbirth was caused mostly by fear. To eliminate fear, he advocated **natural childbirth:** educating women about the physiology of reproduction and training them in physical fitness and in breathing and relaxation during labor and delivery. By midcentury, Dr. Fernand Lamaze was using the **prepared childbirth** method to prepare expectant mothers for giving birth. This technique substitutes voluntary, or learned, physical responses to the sensations of uterine contractions for the old responses of fear and pain.

Advocates of natural methods argue that use of drugs poses risks for babies and deprives mothers of what can be an empowering and transforming experience.

In Rajasthan, India, as in many other traditional societies, a doula, or experienced helper, stays at a woman's bedside throughout labor and provides emotional support. Research has found that women attended by doulas tend to have shorter labor and easier deliveries.

What's Your View?

- If you or your partner were expecting a baby, and the pregnancy seemed to be going smoothly, would you prefer (a) hospital, birth center, or home birth, (b) attendance by a physician or midwife, and (c) medicated or nonmedicated delivery? Give reasons.

- If you are a man, would you choose to be present at the birth?

- If you are a woman, would you want your partner present?

However, improvements in medicated delivery have led many mothers to choose pain relief. Today approximately 60 percent of women in labor have regional (epidural or combined spinal-epidural) injections. The combined treatment provides almost immediate relief while enabling a woman to move around and fully participate in the birth with *no* increased risk of adverse outcomes for the fetus (Eltzschig et al., 2003). In a randomized trial of 750 women, those who asked for and received epidurals early in labor had shorter labor and no greater risk of cesarean delivery than those whose pain relief was delayed (Wong et al., 2005).

Pain relief should not be the only consideration in a decision about whether a woman should have anesthesia. More important to her satisfaction with the childbirth experience may be her involvement in decision making, her relationship with the professionals caring for her, and her expectations about labor.

Social and cultural attitudes and customs also may play a part (Eltzschig et al., 2003). In many traditional cultures, childbearing women are attended by a *doula,* an experienced helper who can furnish emotional support and can stay at a woman's bedside throughout labor. In eleven randomized, controlled studies, women attended by doulas had shorter labor, less anesthesia, and fewer forceps and cesarean deliveries than mothers who had not had doulas (Klaus & Kennell, 1997).

The Newborn Baby

The first four weeks of life, the **neonatal period,** is a time of transition from the uterus, where a fetus is supported entirely by the mother, to an independent existence. What are the physical characteristics of newborn babies, and how are they equipped for this crucial transition?

Size and Appearance

An average newborn, or **neonate,** in the United States is about 20 inches long and weighs about 7½ pounds. At birth, 95 percent of full-term babies weigh between 5½

Checkpoint
Can you . . .

✔ Describe the four stages of vaginal childbirth?

✔ Discuss the uses and disadvantages of cesarean births?

✔ Compare medicated delivery, natural childbirth, and prepared childbirth?

Guidepost

4. How do newborn infants adjust to life outside the womb?

neonatal period First 4 weeks of life, a time of transition from intrauterine dependency to independent existence.

neonate Newborn baby, up to 4 weeks old.

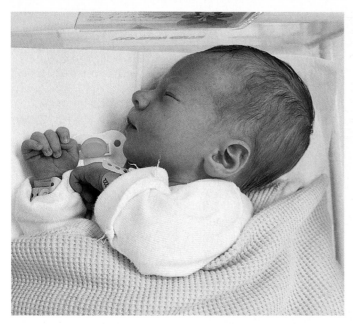

This 1-day-old boy's head is temporarily elongated from its passage through the birth canal. This "molding" of the head during birth occurs because the bones of the skull have not yet fused.

and 10 pounds and are between 18 and 22 inches long. Boys tend to be slightly longer and heavier than girls, and a firstborn child is likely to weigh less at birth than laterborns. In their first few days, neonates lose as much as 10 percent of their body weight, primarily because of a loss of fluids. They begin to gain weight again at about the fifth day and are generally back to birth weight by the tenth to the fourteenth day.

New babies have distinctive features, including a large head (one-fourth the body length) and a receding chin (which makes it easier to nurse). At first, a neonate's head may be long and misshapen because of the "molding" that eased its passage through the mother's pelvis. This temporary molding was possible because an infant's skull bones are not yet fused; they will not be completely joined for 18 months. The places on the head where the bones have not yet grown together—the soft spots, or *fontanels*—are covered by a tough membrane.

Many newborns have a pinkish cast; their skin is so thin that it barely covers the capillaries through which blood flows. During the first few days, some neonates are very hairy because some of the *lanugo,* a fuzzy prenatal hair, has not yet fallen off. All new babies are covered with *vernix caseosa* ("cheesy varnish"), an oily protection against infection that dries within the first few days.

Body Systems

Before birth, blood circulation, respiration, nourishment, elimination of waste, and temperature regulation were accomplished through the mother's body. After birth, all of the baby's systems and functions must operate on their own. Most of the work of this transition occurs during the first 4 to 6 hours after delivery (Ferber & Makhoul, 2004).

The fetus and mother have separate circulatory systems and separate heartbeats; the fetus's blood is cleansed through the umbilical cord, which carries "used" blood to the placenta and returns a fresh supply. A neonate's blood circulates wholly within the baby's own body; the heartbeat at first is fast and irregular, and blood pressure does not stabilize until about the 10th day of life.

The fetus gets oxygen through the umbilical cord, which also carries away carbon dioxide. A newborn needs much more oxygen than before and now must get it alone. Most babies start to breathe as soon as they are exposed to air. If breathing has not begun within about 5 minutes, the baby may suffer permanent brain injury caused by **anoxia,** lack of oxygen. Because infants' lungs have only one-tenth as many air sacs as adults' do, infants (especially those born prematurely) are susceptible to respiratory problems.

In the uterus, the fetus relies on the umbilical cord to bring food from the mother and to carry fetal body wastes away. At birth, babies instinctively suck to take in milk, and their own gastrointestinal secretions digest it. During the first few days infants secrete *meconium,* a stringy, greenish-black waste matter formed in the fetal intestinal tract. When the bowels and bladder are full, the sphincter muscles open automatically; a baby will not be able to control these muscles for many months.

Three or four days after birth, about half of all babies (and a larger proportion of babies born prematurely) develop **neonatal jaundice:** Their skin and eyeballs look

anoxia Lack of oxygen, which may cause brain damage.

neonatal jaundice Condition in many newborn babies, caused by immaturity of liver and evidenced by yellowish appearance; can cause brain damage if not treated promptly.

yellow. This kind of jaundice is caused by the immaturity of the liver. Usually it is not serious, does not need treatment, and has no long-term effects. However, because healthy U.S. newborns usually go home from the hospital within 48 hours or less, jaundice may go unnoticed and may lead to complications (AAP Committee on Quality Improvement, 2002). Severe jaundice that is not monitored and treated promptly may result in brain damage.

The layers of fat that develop during the last two months of fetal life enable healthy full-term infants to keep their body temperature constant after birth despite changes in air temperature. Newborn babies also maintain body temperature by increasing their activity when air temperature drops.

Medical and Behavioral Assessment

The first few minutes, days, and weeks after birth are crucial for development. It is important to know as soon as possible whether a baby has any problem that needs special care.

The Apgar Scale One minute after delivery, and then again five minutes after birth, most babies are assessed using the **Apgar scale** (see Table 4-1). Its name, after its developer, Dr. Virginia Apgar (1953), helps us remember its five subtests: *appear-ance* (color), *pulse* (heart rate), *grimace* (reflex irritability), *activity* (muscle tone), and *respiration* (breathing). The newborn is rated 0, 1, or 2 on each measure, for a maximum score of 10. A 5-minute score of 7 to 10—achieved by 98.6 percent of babies born in the United States—indicates that the baby is in good to excellent con-dition (Martin et al., 2003). A score below 7 means the baby needs help to establish breathing; a score below 4 means the baby needs immediate lifesaving treatment. If resuscitation is successful, bringing the baby's score to 4 or more at 10 minutes, no long-term damage is likely to result (AAP Committee on Fetus and Newborn and American College of Obstetricians and Gynecologists Committee on Obstetric Prac-tice, 1996). In general, Apgar scores reliably predict survival during the first month of life (Casey, McIntire, & Leveno, 2001).

Assessing Neurological Status: The Brazelton Scale The **Brazelton Neonatal Behavioral Assessment Scale (NBAS)** is used in high-risk situations to help parents, health care providers, and researchers assess neonates' responsiveness to their

Checkpoint
Can you . . .

✔ Describe the normal size and appearance of a newborn, and list several changes that occur within the first few days?

✔ Compare four fetal and neonatal body systems?

✔ Identify two dangerous conditions that can appear soon after birth?

Guidepost

5. How can we tell whether a new baby is healthy and is developing normally?

Apgar scale Standard measure-ment of a newborn's condition; it assesses appearance, pulse, grimace, activity, and respiration.

Brazelton Neonatal Behavioral Assessment Scale (NBAS) Neurological and behavioral test to measure neonate's responses to the environment.

Table 4-1	Apgar Scale		
Sign*	**0**	**1**	**2**
Appearance (color)	Blue, pale	Body pink, extremities blue	Entirely pink
Pulse (heart rate)	Absent	Slow (below 100)	Rapid (over 100)
Grimace (reflex irritability)	No response	Grimace	Coughing, sneezing, crying
Activity (muscle tone)	Limp	Weak, inactive	Strong, active
Respiration (breathing)	Absent	Irregular, slow	Good, crying

*Each sign is rated in terms of absence or presence from 0 to 2; highest overall score is 10.

Source: Adapted from V. Apgar, 1953.

physical and social environment, to identify strengths and possible vulnerabilities in neurological functioning, and to predict future development. The test, suitable for infants up to two months old, is named for its designer, Dr. T. Berry Brazelton (1973, 1984; Brazelton & Nugent, 1995). It assesses *motor organization* as shown by such behaviors as activity level and the ability to bring a hand to the mouth; *reflexes; state changes,* such as irritability, excitability, and ability to quiet down after being upset; *attention and interactive capacities,* as shown by general alertness and response to visual and auditory stimuli; and indications of *central nervous system instability,* such as tremors and changes in skin color. The NBAS takes about 30 minutes, and scores are based on a baby's best performance. A newer version, the Newborn Behavioral Observations system (NBO) (Nugent, Keefer, O'Brien, Johnson, & Blanchard, 2005) was developed specifically for clinicians caring for newborns in hospital, clinic, or home settings.

Neonatal Screening for Medical Conditions   Children who inherit the enzyme disorder phenylketonuria, or PKU (refer back to Table 3-1), will become mentally retarded unless they are fed a special diet beginning in the first three to six weeks of life (National Institutes of Health [NIH] Consensus Development Panel, 2001). Screening tests administered soon after birth often can discover this and other correctable defects.

Routine screening of all newborn babies for such rare conditions as PKU (1 case in 15,000 births), congenital hypothyroidism (1 in 3,600 to 5,000), galactosemia (1 in 60,000 to 80,000), and other, even rarer disorders is expensive. Yet the cost of testing thousands of newborns to detect one case of a rare disease may be less than the cost of caring for one mentally retarded person for a lifetime. Now, with tandem mass spectrometry, a test in which a single blood specimen can be screened for 20 or more disorders, about half of all states have expanded their mandatory screening programs. In a study of newborns in several New England states, infants identified by screening were less likely to become retarded or to need hospitalization than those identified by clinical diagnosis. However, the tests can generate false-positive results, suggesting that a problem exists when it does not, and may trigger anxiety and costly, unnecessary treatment (Waisbren et al., 2003).

States of Arousal

Babies have an internal "clock" that regulates their daily cycles of eating, sleeping, and elimination and perhaps even their moods. These periodic cycles of wakefulness, sleep, and activity, which govern an infant's **state of arousal,** or degree of alertness (see Table 4-2), seem to be inborn and highly individual. Changes in state are coordinated by multiple areas of the brain and are accompanied by changes in the functioning of virtually all body systems (Ingersoll & Thoman, 1999).

Most new babies spend about 75 percent of their time—up to 18 hours a day—asleep but wake up every three to four hours, day and night, for feeding (Ferber & Makhoul, 2004; Hoban, 2004). Newborns' sleep alternates between quiet (regular) and active (irregular) sleep. Active sleep is probably the equivalent of rapid eye movement (REM) sleep, which in adults is associated with dreaming. Active sleep appears rhythmically in cycles of about one hour and accounts for up to 50 percent of a newborn's total sleep time. The amount of REM sleep declines to less than 30 percent of daily sleep time by age 3 and continues to decrease steadily throughout life (Hoban, 2004).

Beginning in the first month, nighttime sleep periods gradually lengthen as babies grow more wakeful in the daytime and need less sleep overall. Some infants begin to sleep through the night as early as three months of age. By six months, an infant typically sleeps for six hours straight at night, but brief nighttime waking

Checkpoint

Can you . . .

✔ Discuss the uses of the Apgar test, the Brazelton scale, and routine screening for rare disorders?

Guidepost

6. How do infants' patterns of sleep, waking, and activity change?

state of arousal   An infant's physiological and behavioral status at a given moment in the periodic daily cycle of wakefulness, sleep, and activity.

Table 4-2 States of Arousal in Infancy

State	Eyes	Breathing	Movements	Responsiveness
Regular sleep	Closed; no eye movement	Regular and slow	None, except for sudden, generalized startles	Cannot be aroused by mild stimuli.
Irregular sleep	Closed; occasional rapid eye movements	Irregular	Muscles twitch, but no major movements	Sounds or light bring smiles or grimaces in sleep.
Drowsiness	Open or closed	Irregular	Somewhat active	May smile, startle, suck, or have erections in response to stimuli.
Alert inactivity	Open	Even	Quiet; may move head, limbs, and trunk while looking around	An interesting environment (with people or things to watch) may initiate or maintain this state.
Waking activity and crying	Open	Irregular	Much activity	External stimuli (such as hunger, cold, pain, being restrained, or being put down) bring about more activity, perhaps starting with soft whimpering and gentle movements and turning into a rhythmic crescendo of crying or kicking, or perhaps beginning and enduring as uncoordinated thrashing and spasmodic screeching.

Source: Adapted from information in Prechtl & Beintema, 1964; P. H. Wolff, 1966.

is normal even during late infancy and toddlerhood. A 2-year-old typically sleeps about 13 hours a day, including a single nap, usually in the afternoon (Hoban, 2004).

Babies' sleep rhythms and schedules vary across cultures. Among the Micronesian Truk and the Canadian Hare peoples, babies and children have no regular sleep schedules; they fall asleep whenever they feel tired. Neither do infants necessarily have special places to sleep. Gusii infants in Kenya fall asleep in someone's arms or on a caregiver's back. In many cultures, an infant sleeps in the parents' or mother's bed (see Box 4-1), and this practice may continue into early childhood. Some U.S. parents try to time the evening feeding to encourage nighttime sleep. Mothers in rural Kenya allow their babies to nurse as they please, and their 4-month-olds continue to sleep only four hours at a stretch (Broude, 1995).

Checkpoint

Can you . . .

✔ Explain how states of arousal reflect neurological status, and discuss variations in newborns' states?

✔ Tell how sleep patterns change, and how cultural practices can affect these patterns?

Survival and Health

Although the great majority of births result in normal, healthy babies, some do not. What complications of birth can cause damage? How many babies die during infancy, and why? What can be done to prevent debilitating childhood diseases? How can we ensure that babies will live, grow, and develop as they should?

Complications of Childbirth and Their Aftermath

"It must be a boy," say some mothers whose labor and delivery prove long and difficult. This old adage bears some truth: boys' deliveries are more likely to involve complications than girls', in part because boy babies tend to be larger (Bekedam, Engelsbel, Mol, Buitendijk, & van der Pal-de Bruin, 2002; Eogan, Geary, O'Connell, & Keane, 2003).

Although most babies are born healthy, some are injured in the birth process. Some remain in the womb too long or too briefly or are born very small, and some are born dead or die soon after birth. Let's look at these potential complications of

Guidepost

7. What complications of childbirth can endanger newborn babies, and what are the long-term prospects for babies with complicated births?

BOX 4-1

Window on the World

Sleep Customs

Newborns' sleeping arrangements vary considerably across cultures. In many societies, infants normally sleep in the same room with their mothers for the first few years of life and frequently in the same bed, making it easier to nurse at night (Broude, 1995; Hoban, 2004). In the United States, it is customary in middle-class families to have a separate bed or a separate room for the infant, but bed sharing, or cosleeping, is common in low-income inner-city families (Brenner et al., 2003). In fact, cosleeping occurs to some extent among half of U.S. families with young children (Hoban, 2004).

In interviews, middle-class U.S. parents and Mayan mothers in rural Guatemala revealed their societies' child rearing values and goals in their explanations about sleeping arrangements (Morelli, Rogoff, Oppenheim, & Goldsmith, 1992). The U.S. parents, many of whom kept their infants in the same room but not in the same bed for the first 3 to 6 months, said they moved the babies to separate rooms because they wanted to make them self-reliant and independent. The Mayan mothers kept infants and toddlers in the maternal bed until the birth of a new baby, when the older child would sleep with another family member or in a bed in the mother's room. The Mayan mothers valued close parent-child relationships and expressed shock at the idea that anyone would put a baby to sleep in a room all alone.

Some investigators find health benefits in the shared sleeping pattern. One research team that monitored sleep patterns of mothers and their 3-month-old infants found that those who sleep together tend to wake each other up during the night. The researchers suggested that this may prevent the baby from sleeping too long and too deeply and having long breathing pauses that might be fatal (McKenna & Mosko, 1993).

Bed sharing also promotes breast-feeding. Infants who sleep with their mothers breast-feed about three times longer during the night than infants who sleep in separate beds (McKenna, Mosko, & Richard, 1997). By snuggling up together, mother and baby stay oriented toward each other's subtle bodily signals. Mothers can respond more quickly and easily to an infant's first whimpers of hunger, rather than having to wait until the baby's cries are loud enough to be heard from the next room.

However, under certain conditions such as the use of soft bedding or maternal smoking or drug use, bed sharing can increase the risk of sudden infant death syndrome (American Academy of Pediatrics Task Force on Infant Positioning and SIDS, 1997; Hauck et al., 2003; Malloy, 2004). There is also the possibility that a parent may roll over onto the baby while asleep. In a review of medical examiners' investigations of SIDS deaths in the St. Louis area between 1994 and 1997, a shared sleep surface was the site of death in nearly half (47.1 percent) of the cases investigated (Kemp et al., 2000). And, in an investigation of 84 SIDS cases in Cleveland, Ohio, bed sharing was associated with a younger age at death, especially when the mother was large (Carroll-Pankhurst & Mortimer, 2001).

Adult beds are not designed to meet safety standards for infants, as cribs are (NICHD, 1997, updated 2000; Scheers et al., 2003). Japan, where mothers and infants commonly sleep in the same bed, has one of the lowest SIDS rates in the world (Hoffman & Hillman, 1992), but this may be because Japanese families—as in many developing countries where bed sharing is practiced—generally sleep on thin mats on the floor.

Societal values influence parents' attitudes and behaviors. Throughout this book we will see many ways in which such culturally determined attitudes and behaviors affect children.

What's Your View?

In view of preliminary medical evidence that bed sharing between mother and infant may contribute to SIDS, should mothers from cultures in which sharing a bed is customary be discouraged from doing so?

Check It Out

For more information on this topic, go to http://www .zerotothree.org/0-3_1198.htm [an article from *Zero to Three* that explores "the complex developmental and relational issues surrounding infant sleep"].

---

birth and how they can be avoided or treated so as to maximize the chances of favorable outcomes.

birth trauma   Injury to newborn sustained at the time of birth.

Birth Trauma   **Birth trauma** (injury sustained at the time of birth), which occurs in about 2 in 1,000 births (Wegman, 1994), may be caused by anoxia (oxygen deprivation), diseases or infections, or physical injury. Sometimes the trauma leaves permanent brain damage, causing mental retardation, behavior problems, or even death.

Electronic fetal monitoring can be used to detect any lack of oxygen that could cause brain damage. The procedure was used in 85.2 percent of live births in the United States in 2002 (Martin et al., 2003). Electronic fetal monitoring can provide valuable information in high-risk deliveries, including those in which the fetus is very small or seems to be in distress. Yet monitoring has drawbacks when used routinely in low-risk pregnancies. It is costly; it restricts the mother's movements during labor; and, most important, it has an extremely high "false positive" rate, suggesting that fetuses are in trouble when they are not. Such warnings may prompt doctors to deliver by the riskier cesarean method rather than vaginally (Nelson, Dambrosia, Ting, & Grether, 1996).

Postmaturity   Close to 7 percent of pregnant women have not gone into labor after 42 or more weeks' gestation (Martin et al., 2003). At that point, a baby is considered **postmature.** Postmature babies tend to be long and thin, because they have kept growing in the womb but have had an insufficient blood supply toward the end of gestation. Possibly because the placenta has aged and become less efficient, it may provide less oxygen. The baby's greater size also complicates labor. Because postmature fetuses are at risk of brain damage or even death, doctors sometimes induce labor with drugs or perform cesarean deliveries.

postmature   Referring to a fetus not yet born as of 2 weeks after the due date or 42 weeks after the mother's last menstrual period.

Low Birth Weight   In 2003, 7.9 percent of babies born in the United States had **low birth weight,** weighing less than 2,500 grams (5½ pounds) at birth—the highest rate of low birth weight in three decades. *Very* low-birth-weight babies, who weigh less than 1,500 grams (about 3½ pounds), accounted for 1.4 percent of births. Low birth weight is the second leading cause of death in infancy, after birth defects (Martin et al., 2005), so preventing and treating low birth weight can greatly increase the number of babies who survive the first year of life.

low birth weight   Weight of less than 5½ pounds (2,500 grams) at birth because of prematurity or being small for date.

Although the United States is more successful than any other country in the world in *saving* low-birth-weight babies, the rate of such births to U.S. women is higher than in 21 European, Asian, and Middle Eastern nations (UNICEF, 2002). The increased prevalence of low birth weight in the United States since 1990 is largely attributed to the rise in multiple births (Martin et al., 2005).

Low-birth-weight babies may be *preterm* or *small for gestational age.* Babies born before completing the 37th week of gestation are called **preterm (premature) infants;** they may or may not be the appropriate size for their gestational age. In 2003, 12.3 percent of infants were born preterm, 16 percent more than in 1990 (Martin et al., 2005). **Small-for-gestational-age infants,** who may or may not be preterm, weigh less than 90 percent of all babies of the same gestational age. Their small size is generally the result of inadequate prenatal nutrition, which slows fetal growth.

preterm (premature) infants Infants born before completing the thirty-seventh week of gestation.

small-for-date (small-for-gestational age) infants   Infants whose birth weight is less than that of 90 percent of babies of the same gestational age, as a result of slow fetal growth.

As many as 50 percent of preterm births are associated with uterine infection, which does not seem to respond to antibiotics once labor has begun. Other causes are maternal or fetal stress, placental hemorrhaging, and overstretching of the uterus, usually in multiple pregnancies. Enhanced prenatal care, nutritional interventions, home monitoring of uterine activity, and administration of drugs, bed rest, and hydration for women who go into early labor have proved unable to stem the tide of premature births (Goldenberg & Rouse, 1998; Lockwood, 2002). One promising treatment is a form of the hormone progesterone, called *hydroxyprogesterone caproate,* or *17P.* In a two-and-a-half-year trial at 13 major medical research centers, giving 17P to women who had previously borne premature babies reduced repeat preterm births by as much as one-third (Meis et al., 2003).

Who Is Likely to Have a Low-Birth-Weight Baby?   Factors increasing the likelihood that a woman will have an underweight baby include (1) *demographic and socioeconomic factors,* such as being African American, under age 17 or over 40, poor, unmarried, or undereducated; (2) *medical factors predating the pregnancy,* such as having no children or having more than four, being short or thin, having had previous low-birth-weight infants or multiple miscarriages, having had low birth weight oneself, or having genital or urinary abnormalities or chronic hypertension; (3) *prenatal behavioral and environmental factors,* such as poor nutrition, inadequate

A girl under age 17 who smokes while pregnant has two risk factors for bearing a low-birth-weight baby.

prenatal care, smoking, use of alcohol or other drugs, or exposure to stress, high altitude, or toxic substances; and (4) *medical conditions associated with the pregnancy,* such as vaginal bleeding, infections, high or low blood pressure, anemia, and too little weight gain (Arias, MacDorman, Strobino, & Guyer, 2003; S. S. Brown, 1985; Chomitz, Cheung, & Lieberman, 1995; Nathanielsz, 1995; Shiono & Behrman, 1995; Wegman, 1992; Zhu, Rolfs, Nangle, & Horan, 1999). The safest interval between pregnancies is 18 to 23 months (Zhu et al., 1999).

The high proportion (13.4 percent) of low-birth-weight babies in the African American population—more than twice as high as among white and Hispanic babies—is the major factor in the high mortality rates of African American infants (Martin et al., 2005; see Table 4-3). The higher risks of low birth weight and of preterm births among African American babies seem to be independent of socioeconomic status and may reflect higher levels of stress and of vaginal infections in that population. Babies of African- or Caribbean-born black women are not at such high risk (David & Collins, 1997).

Immediate Treatment and Outcomes The most pressing fear regarding very small babies is that they will die in infancy. Because their immune systems are not fully developed, they are especially vulnerable to infection, which has been linked to slowed growth and developmental delays (Stoll et al. 2004). Feeding them mothers' milk can help prevent infection (AAP Section on Breastfeeding, 2005; Furman, Taylor, Minich, & Hack, 2003). Also, these infants' nervous systems may not be mature enough for them to perform functions basic to survival, such as sucking, and they may need to be fed intravenously (through the veins). Because they do not have enough fat to insulate them and to generate heat, it is hard for them to stay warm. Respiratory distress syndrome is common. Low Apgar scores in preterm newborns are a strong indication of heightened risk and of the need for intensive care (Weinberger et al., 2000).

Table 4-3 Birth Weight, Mortality, and Race, 2003

	Low Birth Weight (less than 5.5 pounds, or 2,500 grams), % of births	Very Low Birth Weight (less than 3.3 pounds, or 1,500 grams), % of births	Infant Mortality Rate* per 1,000	Neonatal Mortality Rate** per 1,000	Postneonatal Mortality Rate*** per 1,000
Black (non-Hispanic) infants	13.4	3.1	13.9	9.3	4.6
White (non-Hispanic) infants	6.9	1.2	5.8	3.9	1.9
Hispanic infants	6.5	1.2	5.6	3.8	1.8

Note: Black infants are more likely than white or Hispanic infants to die in the first year from birth defects or disorders, sudden infant death syndrome, respiratory distress syndrome, disorders related to short gestation and low birth weight and as a result of maternal complications of pregnancy.

*Deaths during the first year of life
**Deaths during first 4 weeks
***Deaths between 4 weeks and 11 months

Source: Martin et al., 2005.

A low-birth-weight baby is placed in an *isolette* (an antiseptic, temperature-controlled crib) and fed through tubes. To counteract the sensory impoverishment of life in an isolette, hospital workers and parents are encouraged to give these small babies special handling. Gentle massage seems to foster growth, weight gain, motor activity, alertness, and behavioral organization, as assessed by the Brazelton NBAS (T. M. Field, 1986, 1998b; T. Field, Hernandez-Reif, & Freedman, 2004; Schanberg & Field, 1987), and can shorten the hospital stay (T. Field, Hernandez-Reif, & Freedman, 2004; Standley, 1998).

Premature infants tend to be uneven in their state development compared with full-term infants the same age. They are more alert and wakeful, have longer stretches of quiet sleep, and show more REMs in active sleep. On the other hand, their sleep is more fragmented, and they have more transitions between sleeping and waking (Ingersoll & Thoman, 1999). Kangaroo care, a method of skin-to-skin contact in which a newborn is laid face down between the mother's breasts for an hour or so after birth, can help preemies—and full-term infants—make the adjustment from fetal life to the jumble of sensory stimuli in the outside world. This soothing maternal contact seems to reduce stress on the central nervous system and help with self-regulation of sleep and activity (Ferber & Makhoul, 2004).

Many very small preterm babies lack surfactant, an essential lung-coating substance that keeps air sacs from collapsing; they may breathe irregularly or stop breathing altogether. Administering surfactant to high-risk preterm newborns has dramatically increased their survival rates (Corbet et al., 1995; Goldenberg & Rouse, 1998; Horbar et al., 1993; Stoelhorst et al., 2005). Currently, survival rates are greater than 90 percent among very low-birth-weight infants weighing between 1,000 and 1,500 grams (about 2 to 3½ pounds) and more than 70 percent among *extremely* low-birth-weight infants weighing between 500 and 999 grams (about 1 to 2 pounds) (Msall, 2004). However, increased chances of survival leave a growing proportion of these infants with respiratory problems (Stoelhorst et al., 2005) and neurological and developmental deficits (Hack, Friedman, & Fanaroff, 1996; Msall, 2004; Stoll et al., 2004).

Long-Term Outcomes   Even if low-birth-weight babies survive the dangerous early days, there is concern for their future. Preterm and small-for-gestational-age infants may be at increased risk of adult-onset diabetes (Hofman et al., 2004; Sperling, 2004). Small-for-gestational-age infants also appear to be at increased risk of cardiovascular disease (Sperling, 2004).

Among *very* low-birth-weight babies, cognitive deficits, especially in memory and processing speed, have been noted by 5 or 6 months of age, continuing through childhood (Rose & Feldman, 2000; Rose, Feldman, & Jankowski, 2002). In longitudinal studies of *extremely* low-birth-weight infants, those who survived tended to be smaller than full-term children and were far more likely to have neurological cognitive, educational, and behavioral problems (Anderson, Doyle, and the Victorian Infant Collaborative Study Group, 2003; Saigal, Stoskopf, Streiner, & Burrows, 2001). Similarly, infants born before 26 weeks of gestation tend to show neurological and cognitive deficits at age 6 in comparison with full-term classmates (Marlow, Wolke, Bracewell, & Samara for the EPICure Study Group, 2005).

As teenagers, the less these children weighed at birth, the lower their IQs and achievement test scores tend to be and the more likely they are to require special education or to have repeated a grade (Saigal, Hoult, Streiner, Stoskopf, & Rosenbaum, 2000). Adults who had very low birth weight tend to have brain abnormalities, neurosensory deficits and illnesses, higher blood pressure, lower IQs, and poorer educational achievement than adults who had normal birth weight

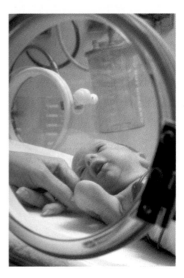

The antiseptic, temperature-controlled crib, or isolette, in which this premature baby lies has holes through which the infant can be examined, touched, and massaged. Frequent human contact helps low-birthweight infants thrive.

What's Your View?

- In view of the long-term out-look for very low-birth-weight babies and the expense involved in helping them survive, how much of society's resources should be put into rescuing these babies?

On the other hand, in a longitudinal study of 296 infants who weighed, on average, just over 2 pounds at birth and were considered borderline retarded, most showed cognitive improvement in early childhood and intelligence in the normal range by age 8. Children in two-parent families, those whose mothers were highly educated, those who had not suffered significant brain damage, and those who did not need special help did best (Ment et al., 2003). Birth weight alone, then, does not necessarily determine the outcome. Environmental factors make a difference, as we discuss further in a subsequent section.

Stillbirth A stillbirth is a tragic union of opposites—birth and death. Death after 23 to 24 weeks of gestation, the earliest age of viability outside the womb, is considered stillbirth. Sometimes fetal death is diagnosed prenatally; in other cases, the death is discovered during labor or delivery.

Checkpoint

Can you . . .

✔ Explain the risks attending birth trauma and postmaturity, and discuss the use and value of electronic fetal monitoring?

✔ Discuss the risk factors, treatment, and outcomes for low-birth-weight babies?

✔ Give reasons for the reduction in stillbirths in the United States?

Stillbirth accounts for more than half of perinatal deaths (deaths that occur during or within 24 hours after childbirth) in developing countries; 3 to 4 babies per 1,000 are born dead in Sweden and in the United States (Surkan, Stephansson, Dickman, & Cnattingius, 2004). Although the cause of stillbirth is not clearly understood, fetal growth restriction seems to be a major factor. Many stillborn infants are small for gestational age, indicating malnourishment in the womb. A woman whose first baby was small for gestational age is at elevated risk of a stillbirth in a second pregnancy, especially if the first baby was preterm (Surkan et al., 2004).

The number of third-trimester stillbirths in the United States has been substantially reduced during the past two decades. This improvement may be due to electronic fetal monitoring, ultrasound, and other measures to identify fetuses at risk for preeclampsia (a toxic condition) or restricted growth. Fetuses believed to have these problems can then be delivered prematurely (Goldenberg & Rouse, 1998).

Can a Supportive Environment Overcome Effects of Birth Complications?

Prospects for overcoming the early disadvantage of birth complications depend on two interrelated factors: the family's socioeconomic circumstances and the quality of the early environment (Aylward, Pfeiffer, Wright, & Verhulst, 1989; McGauhey, Starfield, Alexander, & Ensminget, 1991; Ross, Lipper, & Auld, 1991). Two major studies, the Infant Health and Development Program and the Kauai Study, show that positive development can occur under favorable conditions.

The Infant Health and Development Program The Infant Health and Development Program [IHDP] (1990) has successfully enhanced cognitive development for low-birth-weight children in a variety of family situations, especially those in which the family was poor and the mother had no more than a high school education (Brooks-Gunn, 2003). The study followed 985 preterm, low-birth-weight babies, most of them from disadvantaged families, from birth to age 3. One-third of the heavier (but still low-birth-weight) babies and one-third of the lighter ones were randomly assigned to "intervention" groups. Their parents received home visits, counseling, information about children's health and development, and instruction in children's games and activities; at 1 year, these babies entered an educational day care program.

When the program stopped, the 3-year-olds in both the lower and higher birth weight intervention groups were doing better on cognitive and social measures, were much less likely to show mental retardation, and had fewer behavioral problems than those in control groups of similar birth weight who had received only pediatric follow-up (Brooks-Gunn, Klebanov, Liaw, & Spiker, 1993). However, by age 5, the lower birth weight intervention group had lost their cognitive edge (Brooks-Gunn et al., 1994), and by age 8, the higher birth weight intervention group averaged only four IQ points more than the controls. All groups had substantially below-average IQs and vocabulary scores (McCarton et al., 1997; McCormick, McCarton, Brooks-Gunn, Belt, & Gross, 1998). Perhaps, for such an intervention to have lasting effects, it needs to continue beyond age 3 (Blair, 2002).

Additional studies of the full IHDP sample underline the importance of what goes on in the home. Children whose mothers reported having experienced stressful events—illnesses, deaths of friends or family members, moves, or changes in schooling or work—during the second half of the child's first year showed less cognitive benefit from the intervention at age 3 (Klebanov, Brooks-Gunn, & McCormick, 2001). Children who got little parental attention and care were more likely to be undersized and to do poorly on cognitive tests than children from more favorable home environments (Kelleher et al., 1993; McCormick et al., 1998). Those whose cognitive performance stayed high had mothers who scored high themselves on cognitive tests and who were responsive and stimulating. Babies who had more than one risk factor (such as poor neonatal health combined with having a mother who did not receive counseling or was less well educated or less responsive) fared the worst (Liaw & Brooks-Gunn, 1993).

The Kauai Study For nearly five decades, Emmy E. Werner (1987, 1995; Werner & Smith, 2001) and a team of pediatricians, psychologists, public health workers, and social workers have followed 698 children born in 1955 on the Hawaiian island of Kauai from gestation to middle adulthood. The researchers interviewed the mothers-to-be, monitored their pregnancies, and interviewed them again when the children were 1, 2, and 10 years old. They observed the children at home, gave them aptitude, achievement, and personality tests in elementary and high school, and obtained progress reports from their teachers. The young people themselves were interviewed periodically after they reached adulthood.

The physical and psychological development of children who had suffered low birth weight or other birth complications were seriously impaired *only* when the children grew up in persistently poor environmental circumstances. Unless the early damage was so serious as to require institutionalization, those children who had a stable and enriching environment did well (E. E. Werner, 1985, 1987). They had fewer language, perceptual, emotional, and school problems than did children who had *not* experienced unusual stress at birth but who had received little intellectual stimulation or emotional support at home (E. E. Werner, 1989; E. E. Werner et al., 1968). The children who had been exposed to *both* birth-related problems and later stressful experiences had the worst health and the most delayed development (E. E. Werner, 1987).

Most remarkable is the resilience of children who escaped damage despite *multiple* sources of stress. Even when birth complications were combined with chronic poverty, family discord, divorce, or parents who were mentally ill, many children came through relatively unscathed. Of the 276 children who at age 2 had been identified as having four or more risk factors, two-thirds developed serious learning or behavior problems by the age of 10 or, by age 18, had become pregnant, gotten in trouble with the law, or become emotionally disturbed. Yet by age 30, one-third of these highly at-risk children had managed to become "competent, confident, and caring adults (E. E. Werner, 1995, p. 82). Of the full sample, about half of those on

Thanks to their own resilience, fully a third of the at-risk children studied by Emmy Werner and her colleagues developed into self-confident, successful adults. These children had a positive and active approach to problem solving, the abilities to see some useful aspects of even painful experiences and to attract positive responses from other people, and faith in an optimistic vision of a fulfilling life.

Checkpoint

Can you . . .

✔ Discuss the effectiveness of the home environment and of intervention programs in overcoming effects of low birth weight and other birth complications?

✔ Name three protective factors identified by the Kauai study?

Guidepost

8. How can we enhance babies' chances of survival and health?

whom the researchers were able to obtain follow-up data successfully weathered the age-30 and age-40 transitions. Women tended to be better adapted than men (E. Werner & Smith, 2001).

Protective factors, which tended to reduce the impact of early stress, fell into three categories: (1) individual attributes, such as energy, sociability, and intelligence; (2) affectionate ties with at least one supportive family member; and (3) rewards at school, work, or place of worship that provide a sense of meaning and control over one's life (E. E. Werner, 1987). Although the home environment seemed to have the most marked effect in childhood, in adulthood the individuals' own qualities made a greater difference (E. E. Werner, 1995).

These studies underline the need to look at child development in context. They show how biological and environmental influences interact, making resiliency possible even in babies born with serious complications. (Characteristics of resilient children are further discussed in Chapter 14.)

Reducing Infant Mortality

Infancy and toddlerhood are risky times of life, though far less so than they were when Helen Keller contracted her mysterious illness. How many babies die during the first year, and why? What can be done to prevent dangerous or debilitating childhood diseases? How can we ensure that infants and toddlers live, grow, and develop as they should?

Trends in Infant Mortality Worldwide, in 2000 about 8 million infants—more than 1 in 20 born alive—died before their first birthday (Population Reference Bureau, 2005; UNICEF, 2002). Of these deaths, nearly half—3.9 million—occurred during the neonatal period (Black, Morris, & Bryce, 2003). Infant deaths are much more frequent in many developing countries; as many as 193.8 Angolan infants die for every 1,000 born alive, and life expectancy at birth is only 37 years (U.S. Census Bureau, 2003b). Most infant deaths are preventable, resulting from a combination of poverty, poor maternal health and nutrition, infection, and poor medical care (UNICEF, 2003).

In the United States, the **infant mortality rate**—the proportion of babies who die within the first year—rose slightly in 2002 from 6.8 to 7.0 deaths for every 1,000 live births, after falling steadily for more than 40 years. The upturn seems due primarily to the increasing proportions of multiple births and of infants born with extremely low birth weight (Martin et al., 2005). More than half of all infant deaths take place in the first week of life, and two-thirds occur during the neonatal period (Kochanek & Smith, 2004; Kochanek, Murphy, Anderson, & Scott, 2004). Most likely to die in infancy are boy babies, those who were born preterm or of low birth weight, and those whose mothers are teenagers or in their 40s, did not finish high school, are unmarried, smoked during pregnancy, had late or no prenatal care, or had multiple births (Arias, MacDorman, Strobino, & Guyer, 2003; Mathews, Menacker, & MacDorman, 2003).

Birth defects (congenital abnormalities) are the leading cause of infant deaths in the United States, followed by disorders related to prematurity or low birth weight, sudden infant death syndrome (SIDS), maternal complications of pregnancy, and complications of the placenta, umbilical cord, and membranes. These five causes together account for more than half of all infant deaths (Martin et al., 2005).

The improvement in U.S. infant mortality rates since 1990, even at a time when more babies were born perilously small, is attributable largely to prevention of SIDS (discussed in the next section) as well as to effective treatment for respiratory distress and medical advances in keeping very small babies alive (Arias et al., 2003). Another factor is a striking reduction in air pollution in some cities due to permanent losses of manufacturing (Greenstone & Chay, 2003). Still, mainly because of the

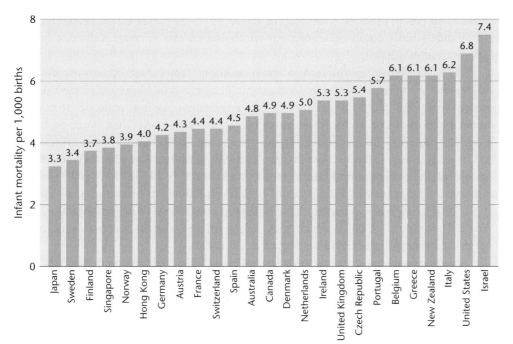

Figure 4-2

Infant mortality rates in industrialized countries, 2003. The United States has a higher infant mortality rate than 19 other industrialized countries, largely because of its very high mortality rate for African American babies. In recent years most nations, including the United States, have shown dramatic improvement. (Source: U.S. Census Bureau, 2003.)

prevalence of low birth weight, U.S. babies have a poorer chance of reaching their first birthday than do babies in many other developed countries (Arias et al., 2003; U.S. Census Bureau, 2003b; see Figure 4-2).

Racial/Ethnic Disparities in Infant Mortality   Although infant mortality has declined for all races and ethnic groups in the United States, large disparities remain (Hesso & Fuentes, 2005). Non-Hispanic black babies are nearly two and a half times as likely to die in their first year as are white and Hispanic babies (Martin et al., 2005; refer back to Table 4-3), largely reflecting the greater prevalence of low birth weight and SIDS among African Americans (Kochanek & Smith, 2004; Kochanek et al., 2004). Infant mortality among American Indians and Alaska Natives is almost twice that among white babies, mainly due to SIDS and fetal alcohol syndrome (American Public Health Association, 2004).

Intragroup variations are often overlooked. Hispanic infants, as a group, die at a slightly lower rate than non-Hispanic white babies, but the rate is higher for Puerto Rican infants. Asian Americans, overall, are least likely to die in infancy, but Pacific Islander infants are 31 percent more likely to die than white babies (American Public Health Association, 2004; Mathews et al., 2003).

Racial or ethnic disparities in access to and quality of health care for minority children (Flores, Olson, & Tomany-Korman, 2005) may help account for differences in mortality, but behavioral factors also may play a part. Obesity, smoking, and alcohol consumption are factors in poor outcomes of pregnancy. African Americans have the highest obesity rates, and American Indians and Alaska Natives tend to be heavy smokers and drinkers. Rates of prenatal care vary from 85 percent of white expectant mothers down to 69 percent of American Indians and Alaska Natives (American Public Health Association, 2004). Because causes and risk factors for infant mortality vary among ethnic groups, efforts to further reduce infant deaths need to focus on factors specific to each ethnic group (Hesso & Fuentes, 2005).

Sudden Infant Death Syndrome (SIDS)   Sudden infant death syndrome (SIDS), sometimes called *crib death,* is the sudden death of an infant under one year of age in which the cause of death remains unexplained after a thorough investigation that

sudden infant death syndrome (SIDS) Sudden and unexplained death of an apparently healthy infant.

includes an autopsy. SIDS is the leading cause of postneonatal infant death (NCHS, 2003) and is most common among American Indian and African American babies (Mathews et al., 2003).

SIDS most likely results from a combination of factors. An underlying biological defect may make some infants vulnerable during a critical period in their development to certain contributing or triggering experiences, such as exposure to smoke, prenatal exposure to caffeine, or sleeping on the stomach (AAP Task Force on Infant Sleep Position and Sudden Infant Death Syndrome, 2000; Cutz, Perrin, Hackman, & Czegledy-Nagy, 1996; R. P. Ford et al., 1998; Kadhim, Kahn, & Sebire, 2003). An elevated level of alpha-fetoprotein in the mother's blood during the second trimester of pregnancy is a predictor of both unexplained stillbirth and SIDS (Smith et al., 2004). SIDS also seems to have a genetic component (Ackerman et al., 2001; Weese-Mayer et al., 2003), which may help explain its greater prevalence among African American babies (Weese-Mayer et al., 2004).

An important clue to what often happens in SIDS has emerged from the discovery of defects in chemical receptors, or nerve endings, in the brain stem, which receive and send messages that regulate breathing, heartbeat, body temperature, and arousal. These defects, which may originate early in fetal life, may prevent SIDS babies from waking or turning their heads when they are breathing stale air containing carbon dioxide trapped under their blankets while sleeping face down (AAP Task Force, 2000; Kinney et al., 1995; Panigrahy et al., 2000; Waters, Gonzalez, Jean, Morielli, & Brouillette, 1996). Even in normal, healthy infants, "tummy" sleeping inhibits the swallowing reflex, which protects the airways from choking due to infusion of nasal and digestive fluids (Jeffery, Megevand, & Page, 1999).

Research strongly supports a relationship between SIDS and sleeping on the stomach. Side sleeping is not safe either, because infants put to bed on their sides often turn onto their stomachs (AAP Task Force, 2000). SIDS rates declined in the United States by more than 50 percent between 1992 and 2001 (Malloy, 2004) and in some other countries by as much as 70 percent following recommendations that healthy babies be put to sleep on their backs (Dwyer, Ponsonby, Blizzard, Newman, & Cochrane, 1995; C. E. Hunt, 1996; Skadberg et al., 1998; Willinger, Hoffman, & Hartford, 1994). However, this reduction may in part reflect attempts to more clearly define SIDS, resulting in the reclassification of some deaths that previously would have been identified as SIDS (Hoyert et al., 2005; Kochanek & Smith, 2004; Malloy, 2004).

Doctors recommend that infants *not* sleep on soft surfaces, such as pillows, quilts, or sheepskin, or under loose covers, which, especially when the infant is face down, may increase the risk of overheating or rebreathing (breathing the infant's own exhaled waste products) (AAP Task Force, 2000; Hauck et al., 2003). The risk of SIDS is increased twentyfold when infants sleep in adult beds, sofas, or chairs, or on other surfaces not designed for infants (Scheers, Rutherford, & Kemp, 2003). Breast-feeding and use of pacifiers are associated with lower risk of SIDS (Hauck et al., 2003).

Sleeping on the back does tend to result in a slight temporary delay in the development of motor skills requiring upper-body strength, such as rolling over, sitting, crawling, and standing. However, these milestones are still attained within the normal age range (Davis, Moon, Sachs, & Ottolini, 1998), and no difference is detectable by 18 months. It is important for infants to have plenty of "tummy time" while awake and supervised, for development of shoulder strength (AAP Task Force, 2000).

Death from Injuries Unintentional injuries are the seventh leading cause of death in infancy in the United States and the third leading cause of death after the first

BOX 4-2

Practically Speaking

Shaken Baby Syndrome

The scenario is all too common. A baby, usually 6 weeks to 4 months old, is brought to the emergency room by a parent or caregiver. The infant may show symptoms ranging from lethargy, tremors, or vomiting to seizures, convulsions, stupor, or coma and may be unable to suck or swallow, make sounds, or follow an object with his or her eyes. However, there is no visible sign of injury, and the parent or caregiver denies knowledge of what caused the condition or claims that the child fell. Closer examination may or may not reveal bruises indicative of abuse, but radiological studies (a CT scan, possibly followed by an MRI) find hemorraghing of the brain or retina—a result of the infant's having been violently shaken (AAP Committee on Child Abuse and Neglect, 2001; National Center on Shaken Baby Syndrome, 2000).

Shaken baby syndrome (SBS) is a form of maltreatment (see Chapter 6), found mainly in children under 2 years and especially in infants, that usually results in serious, irreversible brain trauma. Because it is frequently misdiagnosed and underreported, its true incidence is unknown (AAP Committee on Child Abuse and Neglect, 2001; King, MacKay, Sirnick, & The Canadian Shaken Baby Study Group, 2003), but estimates range from 600 to 1,400 cases each year in the United States alone. Often these children have suffered previous abuse. About 20 percent die within a few days of being shaken. Survivors may be left with a range of disabilities, from learning and behavioral disorders to neurological injuries, mental retardation, cerebral palsy, paralysis, or blindness, or in a permanent vegetative state (Conway, 1998; King et al., 2003; National Center on Shaken Baby Syndrome, 2000).

Why would an adult bring such harm upon a helpless baby? A caregiver who is unable to handle stress or has unrealistic expectations for infant behavior may lose control and shake a crying baby in a desperate attempt to quiet the child. If the injured infant becomes drowsy or loses consciousness, the caregiver may think the shaking "worked" and may do it again when the crying resumes. Or the caregiver may put an unconscious baby to bed, hoping the infant will recover, thus missing the opportunity for early treatment (AAP Committee on Child Abuse and Neglect, 2001; National Center on Shaken Baby Syndrome, 2000).

Adults need to know that a baby's crying is normal and is not a reflection on their caregiving skills, that shaking is *never* "okay," and that help is available. (One resource is the National Center on Shaken Baby Syndrome, 888-273-0071.) Parents also need to know that age-appropriate physical play with a baby is *not* injurious (National Center on Shaken Baby Syndrome, 2000).

What's Your View?

- Why do you think Shaken Baby Syndrome is frequently misdiagnosed and underreported?

- What can be done to raise awareness of this problem?

Check It Out

For more information on Shaken Baby Syndrome, visit http://aboutshakenbaby.com. This Web site sponsored by the Epilepsy Association of Central Florida provides facts about SBS, lists of symptoms and warning signs, and tips for prevention (including ways to soothe a crying baby), as well as a video presentation.

---

four weeks of life, following SIDS and birth defects (Kochanek & Smith, 2004; Anderson, 2002). Black infants are two and a half times as likely to die of injuries as white infants and more than three times as likely to be victims of homicide (Tomashek, Hsia, & Iyasu, 2003).

Many accidental injuries occur at home. In a study of 990 infants brought to emergency rooms in Kingston, Ontario, by far the most injuries were caused by falls (61.1 percent), followed by ingesting harmful substances (6.6 percent), and then by burns (5.7 percent) (Pickett, Streight, Simpson, & Brison, 2003).

Some injuries reported as accidental may actually be inflicted by caregivers unable to cope with a crying baby (see Box 4-2).

Immunization for Better Health

Such once-familiar and sometimes fatal childhood illnesses as measles, pertussis (whooping cough), and infantile paralysis (polio) are now largely preventable, thanks to the development of vaccines that mobilize the body's natural defenses. Unfortunately, many children still are not adequately protected.

In the developing world, 18 percent of deaths of children under age 5 are from vaccine-preventable diseases (Wegman, 1999). A five-year global Measles Initiative,

What's Your View?

- Should parents have the right to refuse to immunize their children? If not, how can they be compelled to do so?

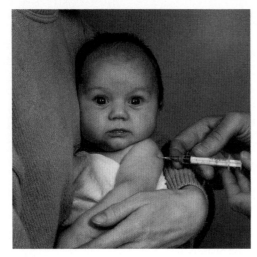

Thanks to widespread immunization of infants and toddlers, rates of infectious diseases have plummeted in the United States. However, many children, especially in low-income urban areas, do not get all required shots or receive them late. Nearly 1 out of 5 deaths of young children in the developing world are from vaccine-preventable diseases.

Checkpoint

Can you . . .

✔ Summarize trends in infant mortality, and explain why black infants are less likely to survive than white infants?

✔ Discuss risk factors for, causes of, and prevention of sudden infant death syndrome and shaken baby syndrome?

✔ Explain why full immunization of all infants and preschoolers is important?

currently focused on Africa, seeks to save lives by immunizing 200 million children. Between 1990 and 2000, such mass campaigns reached approximately 80 percent of the world's infants under 1 year old, and deaths from measles dropped to zero in Latin America. However, in 18 countries, 14 of them in Africa, less than 50 percent of eligible children are immunized (UNICEF Press Centre, 2002).

In the United States, thanks to a nationwide immunization initiative, vaccine-preventable infectious diseases have dropped more than 95 percent since 1993 (AAP Committee on Infectious Diseases, 2000) and immunization rates are at an all-time high. In 2003, 79.4 percent of 19- to 35-month-olds completed a series of childhood vaccinations. Still, many children, especially those in urban, low-income areas, lack one or more of the required shots (Centers for Disease Control and Prevention [CDC], 2004), and about 3 out of 4 children are delayed in receiving one or more vaccines, often by many months (Luman et al., 2005). The immunization gaps between white children and black and Hispanic children widened between 1996 and 2001 (Chu, Barker, & Smith, 2004).

Some parents hesitate to immunize their children because of speculation that certain vaccines—particularly the diphtheria-pertussis-tetanus (DPT) and measles-mumps-rubella (MMR) vaccines—may cause autism or other neurodevelopmental disorders. Much of the concern is over the preservative thimerosal, which contains a form of mercury and was widely used before the development of thimerosal-free vaccines. However, multiple studies in the United States and United Kingdom have found *no* credible evidence for any causal connection between vaccines and autism or other disorders (Andrews et al., 2004; DeStefano, Bhasin, Thompson, Yeargin-Allsopp, & Boyle, 2004; Heron, Golding, and the ALSPAC Study Team, 2004; Mitka, 2004; Parker, Schwartz, Todd, & Pickering, 2004). Some parents worry that infants receive too many vaccines for their immune system to handle safely. (Today's children routinely receive 11 vaccines and as many as 20 shots by age 2.) Actually, the opposite is true. Multiple vaccines fortify the immune system against a variety of bacteria and viruses and reduce related infections (Offit et al., 2002).

Early Physical Development

Fortunately, most infants do survive, develop normally, and grow up healthy. What principles govern their development? What are the typical growth patterns of body and brain? How do babies' needs for nourishment and sleep change? How do their sensory and motor abilities develop?

Principles of Development

As before birth, physical growth and development follow the *cephalocaudal principle* and *proximodistal principle.*

Guidepost

9. What influences the growth of body and brain?

According to the *cephalocaudal principle,* growth occurs from the top down. Because the brain grows rapidly before birth, a newborn baby's head is disproportionately large. The head becomes proportionately smaller as the child grows in height and the lower parts of the body develop (see Figure 4-3). Sensory and motor development proceed according to the same principle: Infants learn to use the upper parts of the body before the lower parts. They see objects before they can control their trunk, and they learn to do many things with their hands long before they can crawl or walk.

According to the *proximodistal principle* (inner to outer), growth and motor development proceed from the center of the body outward. In the womb, the head

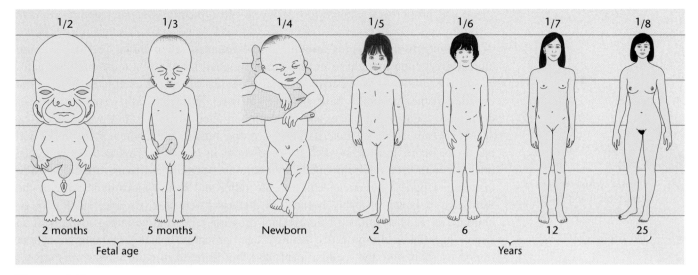

Figure 4-3

Changes in proportions of the human body during growth. The most striking change is that the head becomes smaller relative to the rest of the body. The fractions indicate head size as a proportion of total body length at several ages. More subtle is the stability of the trunk proportion (from neck to crotch). The increasing leg proportion is almost exactly the reverse of the decreasing head proportion.

and trunk develop before the arms and legs, then the hands and feet, and then the fingers and toes. During infancy and early childhood, the limbs continue to grow faster than the hands and feet. Similarly, children first develop the ability to use their upper arms and upper legs (which are closest to the center of the body), then the forearms and forelegs, then hands and feet, and finally, fingers and toes.

Physical Growth

Children grow faster during the first three years, especially during the first few months, than ever again. At five months, the average baby boy's birth weight has doubled to 16 pounds, and, by one year, it has nearly tripled to 23 pounds. This rapid growth rate tapers off during the second and third years (see Figure 4-4). A boy typically gains about 5 pounds by his second birthday and 3½ pounds by his third, when he tips the scales at 31½ pounds. A boy's height typically increases by 10 inches during the first year, by almost 5 inches during the second year, and by a little more than 3 inches during the third year, to top 37 inches. Girls follow a parallel pattern but are slightly smaller. At three years, the average girl weighs a pound less and is half an inch shorter than the average boy (Kuczmarski et al., 2000). Of course, individual growth rates vary greatly, as Figure 4-4 shows. As a baby grows, body

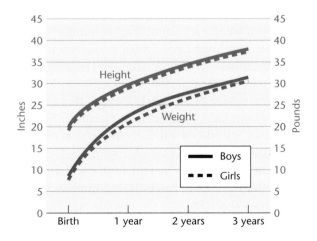

Figure 4-4

Growth in height and weight during infancy and toddlerhood. Babies grow most rapidly in both height and weight during the first few months of life, then taper off somewhat by age 3. Baby boys are slightly larger, on average, than baby girls. *Note:* Curves shown are for the 50th percentiles for each sex. (Source: Kuczmarski et al., 2000.)

shape and proportions change too; a 3-year-old typically is slender compared with a chubby, potbellied 1-year-old.

Teething usually begins around 3 or 4 months, when infants begin grabbing almost everything in sight to put into their mouths; but the first tooth may not actually arrive until sometime between 5 and 9 months of age, or even later. By the first birthday, babies generally have six to eight teeth. By age 3, all twenty primary, or deciduous, teeth are in place, and children can chew any food they want to.

The genes an infant inherits have a strong influence on whether the child will be tall or short, thin or stocky, or somewhere in between. This genetic influence interacts with such environmental influences as nutrition and living conditions. For example, Japanese American children are taller and weigh more than children the same age in Japan, probably because of dietary differences (Broude, 1995). Today, children in many developed countries are growing taller and maturing sexually at an earlier age than children did a century ago, probably because of better nutrition, improved sanitation and medical care, and the decrease in child labor.

Checkpoint

Can you . . .

✔ Summarize typical patterns of physical growth and change during the first three years?

✔ Identify several factors that affect growth?

Nutrition

Proper nutrition is essential to healthy growth. Feeding needs change rapidly during the first three years of life.

Breast milk has been called the "ultimate health food" because it offers so many benefits to babies—physical, cognitive, and emotional.

Breast or Bottle? Feeding a baby is an emotional as well as physical act. Warm contact with the mother's body fosters emotional linkage between mother and baby. Such bonding can take place through either breast- or bottle-feeding and through many other caregiving activities, most of which can be performed by fathers as well as mothers. The quality of the relationship between parent and child and the provision of abundant affection and cuddling may be at least as important as the feeding method.

Nutritionally speaking, however, breast milk is almost always the best food for infants. The only acceptable alternative is an iron-fortified formula that is based on either cow's milk or soy protein and contains supplemental vitamins and minerals. The American Academy of Pediatrics Section on Breastfeeding (2005) recommends that babies be exclusively breast-fed for six months. (If direct breast-feeding is not possible, the baby should receive expressed human milk.) Breast-feeding should begin immediately after birth and should continue for at least the first year of life or longer if mother and baby wish. Infants weaned during the first year should receive iron-fortified formula. At one year, babies can switch to cow's milk.

The health advantages of breast-feeding are striking (AAP Section on Breastfeeding, 2005). Among the illnesses prevented or minimized by breast-feeding are diarrhea, respiratory infections (such as pneumonia and bronchitis), otitis media (an infection of the middle ear), and staphylococcal, bacterial, and urinary tract infections (AAP Work Group on Breastfeeding, 1997; Black, Morris, & Bryce, 2003; A. S. Cunningham et al., 1991; Dewey, Heinig, & Nommsen-Rivers, 1995; J. Newman, 1995; Scariati, Grummer-Strawn, & Fein, 1997). Breast-feeding may reduce the risk of SIDS (AAP Section on Breastfeeding, 2005) and of postneonatal death (death that occurs between 28 days and one year) (Chen & Rogan, 2004). Resistance to some illnesses (influenza, diphtheria, and diarrhea) can be enhanced in bottle-fed babies by fortifying their formula with nucleotides, components of human milk that stimulate the immune system; but babies breast-fed more than six months do better overall (Pickering et al., 1998).

Breast-feeding seems to have benefits for visual acuity (Makrides, Neumann, Simmer, Pater, & Gibson, 1995), neurological development (Lanting, Fidler, Huisman, Touwen, & Boersma, 1994), and long-term cardiovascular health (Owen, Whincup, Odoki, Gilg, & Cook, 2002), including cholesterol levels (Singhal, Cole, Fewtrell, & Lucas, 2004). It may help prevent obesity, asthma, diabetes, lymphoma, leukemia, and Hodgkin disease (AAP Section on Breastfeeding, 2005). Studies also have shown slight benefits for cognitive development (AAP Section on Breastfeeding, 2005), even into young adulthood (Mortensen, Michaelson, Sanders, & Reinisch, 2002). In a randomized clinical trial, when two fatty acids present in breast milk were added to infant formula, infants fed the fortified formula had better cognitive scores at 18 months than infants who had been fed unfortified formula (Birch, Garfield, Hoffman, Uauy, & Birch, 2000).

Since 1971, when only 25 percent of U.S. mothers even tried to nurse (Ryan, 1997), recognition of the benefits of breast milk has brought about a striking reversal of this pattern. In 2002, according to a national random survey, more than two-thirds (71.4 percent) of children in the United States (the highest proportion ever recorded) had been breast-fed. However, only about 35 percent were still breast-fed at 6 months, only about 13 percent exclusively so. At one year, only 16 percent of infants received some breast milk (Li, Darling, Maurice, Barker, & Grummer-Strawn, 2005). Worldwide, only about one-half of all infants are ever breast-fed (UNICEF, 2002).

Since 1991, 16,000 hospitals and birthing centers worldwide have been designated as "Baby-Friendly" under a United Nations initiative for encouraging institutional support of breast-feeding. These institutions offer new mothers rooming-in, tell them of the benefits of breast-feeding, help them start nursing within one hour of birth, show them how to maintain lactation, encourage on-demand feeding, give infants nothing but breast milk (even pacifiers) unless medically necessary, and establish ongoing breast-feeding support groups. At Boston Medical Center, breast-feeding increased substantially after the program went into effect (Philipp et al., 2001). In a French study, mothers who, within two weeks after giving birth, visited a physician specially trained to support breast-feeding were more likely than a control group to report breast-feeding exclusively at four weeks. They were less likely to report difficulties with breast-feeding and tended to continue it longer (Labarere et al., 2005).

Increases in breast-feeding in the United States are most notable in socioeconomic groups that historically have been less likely to breast-feed: black women, teenage women, poor women, working women, and those with no more than high school education, but many of these women do not continue breast-feeding. Flexible scheduling and privacy for nursing mothers at work and at school, as well as education about the benefits of breast-feeding and availability of breast pumping facilities might increase its prevalence in these groups (Ryan et al., 2002; Taveras et al., 2003).

Nursing mothers need to be as careful as pregnant women about what they take into their bodies. Breast-feeding is inadvisable if a mother is infected with the AIDS virus or any other infectious illness, if she has untreated active tuberculosis, if she has been exposed to radiation, or if she is taking any drug that would not be safe for the baby (AAP Section on Breastfeeding, 2005). The risk of transmitting HIV infection to an infant continues as long as an infected mother breast-feeds (The Breastfeeding and HIV International Transmission Study Group, 2004).

Nutritional Concerns Pediatric experts recommend that iron-enriched solid foods—usually beginning with cereal—be introduced gradually during the second half of the first year. At this time, too, fruit juice may be introduced (AAP Section on Breastfeeding, 2005). Unfortunately, many parents do not follow these guidelines. According to random telephone interviews with parents and caregivers of more than 3,000 U.S. infants and toddlers, 29 percent of infants are given solid food before 4 months,

What's
Your View?
• "Every mother who is physically able should breast-feed." Do you agree or disagree? Give reasons.

A child under age 3 with an obese mother (or father) is likely to become obese as an adult, regardless of the child's own weight.

Checkpoint

Can you . . .

✔ Summarize pediatric recommendations regarding early feeding and the introduction of cow's milk, solid foods, and fruit juices?

✔ Cite factors that contribute to obesity in later life?

central nervous system Brain and spinal cord.

17 percent drink juice before 6 months, and 20 percent drink cow's milk before 12 months. Furthermore, like older children and adults, infants and toddlers eat too much, especially of the wrong kinds of food. From 7 to 24 months, the median food intake is 20 to 30 percent over normal daily requirements. Up to one-third of these children eat no fruits and vegetables; but large percentages regularly consume hot dogs, sausage, bacon, dessert or candy, salty snacks, French fries, sugary fruit drinks, and soda (Fox, Pac, Devaney, & Jankowski, 2004).

In many low-income communities around the world, malnutrition in early life is widespread—and often fatal. Undernourished children who survive their first five years are at high risk for stunted growth and poor health and functioning throughout life. In a longitudinal study of a large-scale government-sponsored nutritional program in 347 poor rural communities of Mexico (mentioned in Chapter 3), infants who received fortified nutrition supplements—along with nutrition education, health care, and financial assistance for the family—showed better growth and lower rates of anemia than did infants not yet assigned to the program (Rivera, Sotres-Alvarez, Habicht, Shamah, & Villalpando, 2004).

Overweight is not usually a problem in infancy. Two factors seem to influence most strongly the chances that an overweight child will become an obese adult: whether the child has an obese parent and the age of the child. Before 3 years of age, parental obesity is a stronger predictor of a child's obesity as an adult than is the child's own weight. Having one obese parent increases the odds of obesity in adulthood by 3 to 1, and if both parents are obese, the odds increase to more than 10 to 1 (AAP Committee on Nutrition, 2003). Among 70 children followed from 3 months to 6 years of age, little difference in weight and body composition appeared by age 2 between children with overweight mothers and children with lean mothers. However, by age 4, those with overweight mothers tended to weigh more and, by age 6, also had more body fat than those with lean mothers (Berkowitz, Stallings, Maislin, & Stunkard, 2005). Thus, a 1- or 2-year-old who has an obese parent—or especially two obese parents—may be a candidate for preventive efforts.

The Brain and Reflex Behavior

What makes newborns respond to a nipple? What tells them to start the sucking movements that allow them to control their intake of fluids? These are functions of the **central nervous system**—the brain and *spinal cord* (a bundle of nerves running through the backbone)—and of a growing peripheral network of nerves extending to every part of the body. Through this network, sensory information travels to the brain, and motor commands travel outward to muscles throughout the body.

Building the Brain The growth of the brain both before birth and during the childhood years is fundamental to future physical, cognitive, and emotional development. Through brain-imaging tools, researchers are gaining a clearer picture of how brain growth occurs (Behrman, 1992; Casaer, 1993; Gabbard, 1996).*

The brain at birth weighs only about 25 percent of its eventual adult weight of 3½ pounds. It reaches nearly 90 percent of that weight by age 3. By age 6, it is almost adult size; but growth and functional development of specific parts of the brain continue into adulthood. The brain's growth and development depend on proper nutrition, including such nutrients as proteins, iron, iodine, zinc, vitamin A, vitamin B6, and folic acid (Rao & Georgieff, 2000). The brain's growth occurs in fits and

*Unless otherwise referenced, the discussion in this section is largely based on Gabbard (1996).

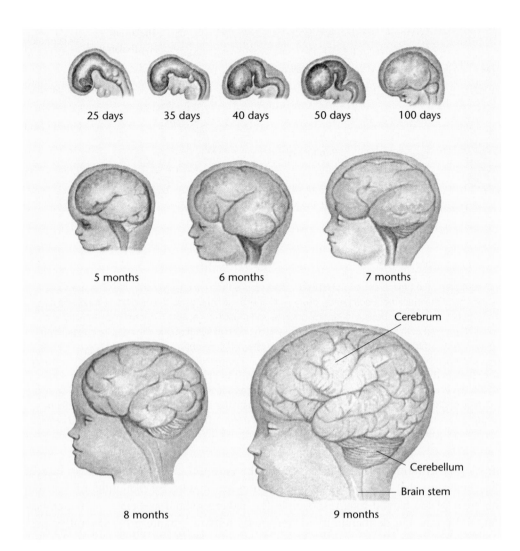

25 days   35 days   40 days   50 days   100 days

5 months   6 months   7 months

Cerebrum

Cerebellum

Brain stem

8 months   9 months

Figure 4-5

Fetal brain development from 25 days of gestation through birth. The *brain stem,* which controls basic biological functions such as breathing, develops first. As the brain grows, the front part expands greatly to form the *cerebrum* (the large, convoluted upper mass). Specific areas of the gray outer covering of the brain have specific functions, such as sensory and motor activity; but large areas are "uncommitted" and thus are free for higher cognitive activity, such as thinking, remembering, and problem solving. The brain stem and other structures below the cortical layer handle reflex behavior and other lower-level functions. The *cerebellum,* which maintains balance and motor coordination, grows most rapidly during the first year of life.
(Source: Casaer, 1993; Restak, 1984.)

starts, and different parts of the brain grow more rapidly at different times. **Brain growth spurts,** periods of rapid growth and development, coincide with changes in cognitive behavior (Fischer & Rose, 1994, 1995).

Beginning about two weeks after conception, the brain gradually develops from a long hollow tube into a spherical mass of cells (see Figure 4-5). By birth, the growth spurt of the spinal cord and *brain stem* (the part of the brain responsible for such basic bodily functions as breathing, heart rate, body temperature, and the sleep-wake cycle) has almost run its course. The *cerebellum* (the part of the brain that maintains balance and motor coordination) grows fastest during the first year of life (Casaer, 1993).

The *cerebrum,* the largest part of the brain, is divided into right and left halves, or hemispheres, each with specialized functions. This specialization of the hemispheres is called **lateralization.** The left hemisphere is mainly concerned with language and logical thinking, the right hemisphere with visual and spatial functions, such as map reading and drawing. Language lateralization increases with age, peaking between ages 25 and 35 (Szaflarski, Holland, Schmithorst, & Weber-Byars, 2004). The two hemispheres are joined by a tough band of tissue called the *corpus callosum,* which allows them to share information and coordinate commands. The corpus callosum grows dramatically during childhood, reaching adult size by about age 10.

Each cerebral hemisphere has four lobes, or sections: the *occipital, parietal, temporal,* and *frontal* lobes, which control different functions (see Figure 4-6) and

brain growth spurts Periods of rapid brain growth and development.

lateralization Tendency of each of the brain's hemispheres to have specialized functions.

Chapter 4 Physical Development During the First Three Years   133

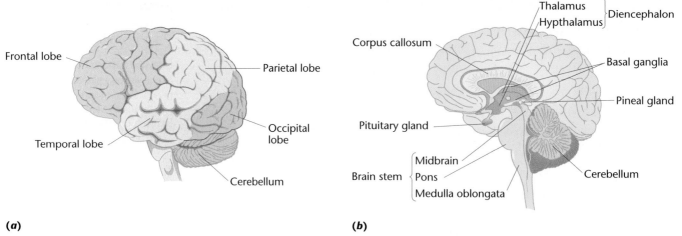

(a)

Frontal lobe

Parietal lobe

Temporal lobe

Occipital lobe

Cerebellum

(b)

Thalamus
Hypthalamus } Diencephalon

Corpus callosum

Basal ganglia

Pineal gland

Pituitary gland

Brain stem { Midbrain
Pons
Medulla oblongata

Cerebellum

Figure 4-6

Parts of the brain. The brain consists of three main parts: the *brain stem,* the *cerebellum,* and, above those, the large *cerebrum.* The brain stem, an extension of the spinal cord, is one of the regions of the brain most completely developed at birth. It controls such basic bodily functions as breathing, circulation, and reflex behavior. The cerebellum, at birth, begins to control balance and muscle tone; later it coordinates sensory and motor activity. The cerebrum constitutes almost 70 percent of the weight of the nervous system and handles thought, memory, language, and emotion, as well as sensory input and conscious motor control. **(a)** *Exterior view of left side of brain:* The cerebrum is divided into two halves, or hemispheres, each of which has four sections, or lobes: the *occipital lobe,* which processes visual information; the *temporal lobe,* which helps with hearing and language; the *parietal lobe,* which receives touch sensations and spatial information and facilitates eye-hand coordination; and the *frontal lobe,* which develops gradually during the first year and permits such higher-level functions as speech and reasoning. The cerebral cortex, the outer surface of the cerebrum, consists of gray matter; it is the seat of thought processes and mental activity. **(b)** *Interior view of right hemisphere (left hemisphere removed).* Several important structures deep within the cerebrum—the thalamus, hippocampus (not shown), and basal ganglia, all of which affect control of basic movements and functions—are largely developed at birth.

develop at different rates. The regions of the *cerebral cortex* (the outer surface of the cerebrum) that govern vision and hearing are mature by 6 months of age, but the areas of the frontal lobe responsible for making mental associations, remembering, and producing deliberate motor responses remain immature for several years.

The brain growth spurt that begins at about the third trimester of gestation and continues until at least the fourth year of life is important to the development of neurological functioning. Smiling, babbling, crawling, walking, and talking—all the major sensory, motor, and cognitive milestones of infancy and toddlerhood—are made possible by the rapid development of the brain, particularly the cerebral cortex.

Brain Cells The brain contains two kinds of cells: *neurons* and *glial cells.* **Neurons,** or nerve cells, send and receive information. *Glial cells* support and protect the neurons.

neurons Nerve cells.

At first the neurons are essentially cell bodies with a nucleus, composed of deoxyribonucleic acid (DNA), which contains the cell's genetic programming. These rudimentary cells migrate to various parts of the growing brain. There they sprout *axons* and *dendrites*—narrow, branching extensions. Axons send signals to other neurons, and dendrites receive incoming messages from them, across *synapses,* the nervous system's communication links. The synapses are tiny gaps, which are bridged with the help of chemicals called *neurotransmitters.* Eventually a particular neuron may have anywhere from 5,000 to 100,000 synaptic connections to and from the body's sensory receptors, its muscles, and other neurons within the central nervous system.

The multiplication of dendrites and synaptic connections, especially during the last two and a half months of gestation and the first six months to two years of life (see Figure 4-7), accounts for much of the brain's growth in weight and permits the emergence of new perceptual, cognitive, and motor abilities. Most of the neurons in

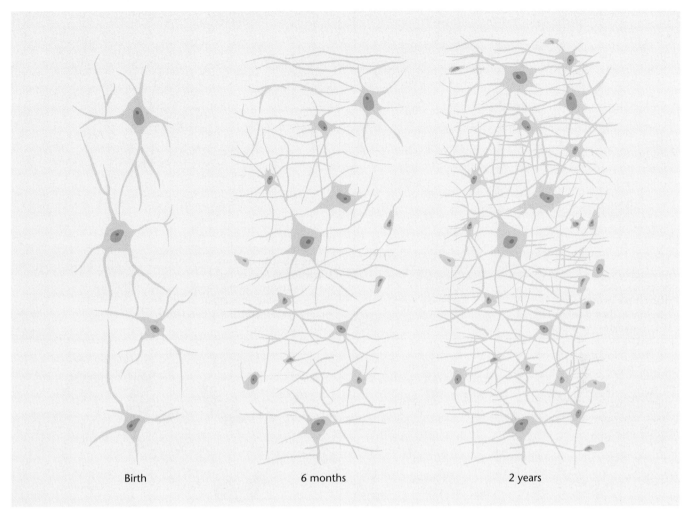

Birth	6 months	2 years

Figure 4-7

Growth of neural connections during the first two years of life. The rapid increase in the brain's density and weight is due largely to the formation of dendrites, extension of nerve cell bodies, and the synapses that link them. This mushrooming communications network sprouts in response to environmental stimulation and makes possible impressive growth in every domain of development. (Source: Conel, 1959.) Reprinted by permission from *The Postnatal Development of the Human Cerebral Cortex,* Vol X. I-VIII by Jesse LeRoy Conel, Cambridge, Mass.: Harvard University Press, Copyright © 1939, 1975 by the President and Fellows of Harvard College.

the cortex, which is responsible for complex, high-level functioning, are in place by twenty weeks of gestation, and its structure becomes fairly well defined during the next twelve weeks. Only after birth, however, do the cells begin to form connections that allow communication to take place.

As the neurons multiply, migrate to their assigned locations, and develop connections, they undergo the complementary processes of *integration* and *differentiation.* Through **integration,** the neurons that control various groups of muscles coordinate their activities. Through **differentiation,** each neuron takes on a specific, specialized structure and function.

In the beginning, the brain produces more neurons and synapses than it needs. Those that are not used or do not function well die out. This process of **cell death,** or pruning of excess cells, begins during the prenatal period and continues after birth (see Figure 4-8), helping to create an efficient nervous system. The number of synapses seems to peak at about age 2, and their elimination continues well into adolescence. Even as some neurons die out, others may continue to form, even during adult life (Eriksson et al., 1998; Gould, Reeves, Graziano, & Gross, 1999). Connections among cortical cells also continue to improve into adulthood, allowing more flexible and more advanced motor and cognitive functioning.

integration Process by which neurons coordinate the activities of muscle groups.

differentiation Process by which cells acquire specialized structure and function.

cell death In brain development, the normal elimination of excess brain cells to achieve more efficient functioning.

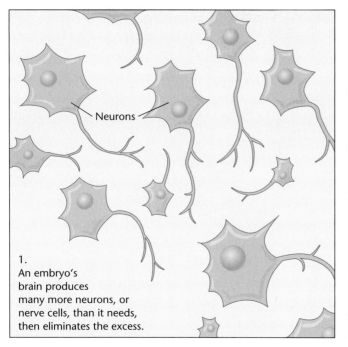

1.
An embryo's
brain produces
many more neurons, or
nerve cells, than it needs,
then eliminates the excess.

Neurons

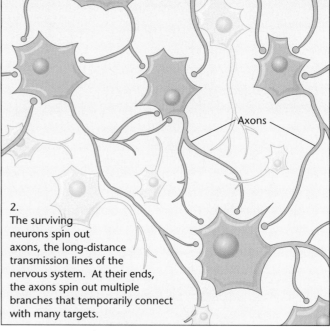

Axons

2.
The surviving
neurons spin out
axons, the long-distance
transmission lines of the
nervous system. At their ends,
the axons spin out multiple
branches that temporarily connect
with many targets.

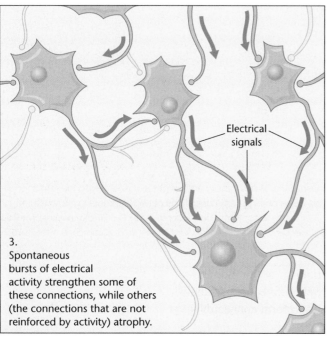

Electrical
signals

3.
Spontaneous
bursts of electrical
activity strengthen some of
these connections, while others
(the connections that are not
reinforced by activity) atrophy.

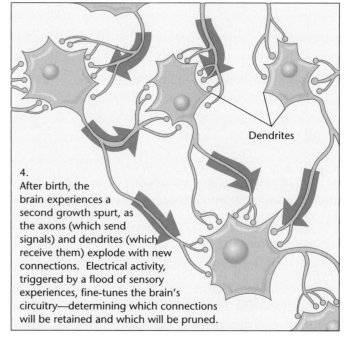

Dendrites

4.
After birth, the
brain experiences a
second growth spurt, as
the axons (which send
signals) and dendrites (which
receive them) explode with new
connections. Electrical activity,
triggered by a flood of sensory
experiences, fine-tunes the brain's
circuitry—determining which connections
will be retained and which will be pruned.

Figure 4-8

Wiring the brain: development of neural connections before and after birth. (Source: Nash, 1997, p. 51.) From "Fertile Lands" by J.M. Nash, *TIME*, 2/3/97.
© 1997 TIME Inc. reprinted by permission.

Myelination   Much of the credit for efficiency of neural communication goes to the glial cells, which coat the neural pathways with a fatty substance called *myelin*. This process of **myelination** enables signals to travel faster and more smoothly, permitting the achievement of mature functioning.

Myelination begins about halfway through gestation in some parts of the brain and continues into adulthood in others. The pathways related to the sense of touch—the first sense to develop—are myelinated by birth. Myelination of visual pathways, which are slower to mature, begins at birth and continues during the first 5 months of life. Pathways related to hearing may begin to be myelinated as early as the fifth month of gestation, but the process is not complete until about age 4. The parts of

myelination   Process of coating neural pathways with a fatty substance (myelin) that enables faster communication between cells.

the cortex that control attention and memory are not fully myelinated until young adulthood. Myelination of the *hippocampus,* a structure deep in the temporal lobe that plays a key role in memory, continues to increase until at least age 70 (Benes, Turtle, Khan, & Farol, 1994).

Myelination of sensory and motor pathways before birth in the spinal cord and after birth in the cerebral cortex may account for the appearance and disappearance of early reflexes.

Early Reflexes When you blink at a bright light, your eyelids are acting involuntarily. Such an automatic, innate response to stimulation is called a **reflex behavior.** Reflex behaviors are controlled by the lower brain centers that govern other involuntary processes, such as breathing and heart rate. These are the parts of the brain most fully myelinated at birth. Reflex behaviors play an important part in stimulating the early development of the central nervous system and muscles.

reflex behaviors Automatic, involuntary, innate responses to stimulation.

Human infants have an estimated 27 major reflexes, many of which are present at birth or soon after (Gabbard, 1996; see Table 4-4 for examples). *Primitive reflexes,* such as sucking, rooting for the nipple, and the Moro reflex (a response to being startled or beginning to fall), are related to instinctive needs for survival and protection or may support the early connection to the caregiver. Some primitive reflexes may be part of humanity's evolutionary legacy; one example is the grasping reflex, which enables infant monkeys to hold on to the hair of their mothers' bodies.

As the higher brain centers become active during the first two to four months, infants begin to show *postural reflexes:* reactions to changes in position or balance. For example, infants who are tilted downward extend their arms in the parachute reflex, an instinctive attempt to break a fall. *Locomotor reflexes,* such as the walking and swimming reflexes, resemble voluntary movements that do not appear until months after the reflexes have disappeared.

Most of the early reflexes disappear during the first six to twelve months. Reflexes that continue to serve protective functions—such as blinking, yawning, coughing, gagging, sneezing, shivering, and the pupillary reflex (dilation of the pupils in the dark)—remain. Disappearance of unneeded reflexes on schedule is a sign that motor pathways in the cortex have been partially myelinated, enabling a shift to voluntary behavior. Thus, we can evaluate a baby's neurological development by seeing whether certain reflexes are present or absent.

Checkpoint
Can you . . .

✔ Describe important features of early brain development?

✔ Explain the functions of reflex behaviors and why some drop out during the early months?

Molding the Brain: The Role of Experience Until the middle of the twentieth century, scientists believed that the brain grew in an unchangeable, genetically determined pattern. This does seem to be largely true before birth. However, it is now widely believed, largely on the basis of animal studies, that the postnatal brain is "molded" by experience, especially during the early months of life when the cortex is still growing rapidly and organizing itself. The technical term for this malleability, or modifiability, of the brain is **plasticity.** Early synaptic connections, some of which depend on sensory stimulation, refine and stabilize the brain's genetically designed "wiring." Thus, early experience can have lasting effects on the capacity of the central nervous system to learn and store information (J. E. Black, 1998; Chugani, 1998; Pally, 1997). It has been suggested that individual differences in intelligence result from differences in neural plasticity—in the brain's ability to develop neural connections in response to experience (Garlick, 2003).

plasticity Modifiability, or "molding," of the brain through experience.

During this formative period, the brain is especially vulnerable. We know that exposure to hazardous drugs, environmental toxins, and maternal stress before and after birth can threaten the developing brain and that malnutrition can interfere with normal cognitive growth (Rose, 1994; Thompson, 2001). Early sensory impoverishment also may leave an imprint on the brain (J. E. Black, 1998). In one classic

Table 4-4 Early Human Reflexes

Reflex	Stimulation	Baby's Behavior	Typical Age of Appearance	Typical Age of Disappearance
Moro	Baby is dropped or hears loud noise.	Extends legs, arms, and fingers, arches back, draws back head.	7th month of gestation	3 months
Darwinian (grasping)	Palm of baby's hand is stroked.	Makes strong fist; can be raised to standing position if both fists are closed around a stick.	7th month of gestation	4 months
Tonic neck	Baby is laid down on back.	Turns head to one side, assumes "fencer" position, extends arms and legs on preferred side, flexes opposite limbs.	7th month of gestation	5 months
Babkin	Both of baby's palms are stroked at once.	Mouth opens, eyes close, neck flexes, head tilts forward.	Birth	3 months
Babinski	Sole of baby's foot is stroked.	Toes fan out; foot twists in.	Birth	4 months
Rooting	Baby's cheek or lower lip is stroked with finger or nipple.	Head turns; mouth opens; sucking movements begin.	Birth	9 months
Walking	Baby is held under arms, with bare feet touching flat surface.	Makes steplike motions that look like well-coordinated walking.	1 month	4 months
Swimming	Baby is put into water face down.	Makes well-coordinated swimming movements.	1 month	4 months

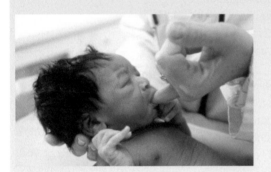
Rooting reflex

Darwinian reflex

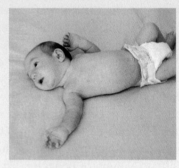
Tonic neck reflex

Moro reflex

Babinski reflex

Walking reflex

experiment, kittens fitted with goggles that allowed them to see only vertical lines grew up unable to see horizontal lines and bumped into horizontal boards in front of them. Other kittens, whose goggles allowed them to see only horizontal lines, grew up blind to vertical columns (Hirsch & Spinelli, 1970). This did not happen when the same procedure was carried out with adult cats. Apparently, neurons in the visual cortex became programmed to respond only to lines running in the direction the kittens were permitted to see. Thus, if certain cortical connections are not made early in life, and *if no further intervention occurs,* these circuits may "shut down" forever (Bruer, 2001). This is why the sensory and cognitive stimulation Anne Sullivan provided was so important to Helen Keller's development.

Sometimes, though, corrective experience can make up for past deprivation (J. E. Black, 1998). Plasticity continues throughout life as neurons change in size and shape in response to environmental experience (M. C. Diamond, 1988; Pally, 1997; Rutter, 2002). Such findings have sparked successful efforts to stimulate the brain development of premature infants (Als et al., 2004) and children with Down syndrome and to help victims of brain damage recover function.

Ethical constraints prevent controlled experiments on the effects of environmental deprivation or enrichment on human infants. However, the discovery of thousands of infants and young children who had spent virtually their entire lives in overcrowded Romanian orphanages offered an opportunity for a natural experiment (Ames, 1997). Discovered after the fall of the dictator Nicolae Ceausescu in December 1989, these abandoned children appeared to be starving, passive, and emotionless. They had spent much of their time lying quietly in their cribs or beds, with nothing to look at. They had had little contact with one another or with their caregivers and had heard little conversation or even noise. Most of the 2- and 3-year-olds did not walk or talk, and the older children played aimlessly. PET scans of their brains showed extreme inactivity in the temporal lobes, which regulate emotion and receive auditory input.

Many of these children were adopted by Canadian families. At the time of adoption, all the children adopted into Canada showed delayed motor, language, or psychosocial development, and nearly eight out of ten were behind in all these areas. Three years later, when compared with children left behind in the Romanian institutions, many of the adopted children showed significant progress. However, one-third—generally those who had been in institutions the longest—still had serious developmental delays (Ames, 1997; Morison, Ames, & Chisholm, 1995).

Age of adoption made a difference. At 4½, those who had spent eight months or more in the orphanages and had been adopted into Canada by age 2 had average IQs and verbal comprehension. However, the orphanage group as a whole had not caught up either with Canadian-born nonadopted children or with a control group of Romanian children adopted by 4 months of age, who had not been in orphanages (Morison & Ellwood, 2000). In preschool, the previously institutionalized children showed poorer social skills and more problems with social interaction than did Canadian-born children or early Romanian adoptees (Thompson, 2001); and at age 8½, PET scans found persistent underactivity in portions of their brains (Chugani et al., 2001).

Similarly, among 111 Romanian children adopted in England before age 2, those adopted before 6 months of age had largely caught up physically and had made a complete cognitive recovery by age 4, as compared with a control group of English adopted children. However, 85 percent of the English adoptees were more cognitively advanced than the average Romanian child adopted *after* 6 months of age (Rutter & the English and Romanian Adoptees [ERA] Study Team, 1998). By age 6, although the Romanian adoptees as a group showed a remarkable degree of recovery, many continued to exhibit substantial cognitive and social deficits (Rutter, O'Connor, & the English and Romanian Adoptees [ERA] Study Team, 2004). Apparently, then, it may take very early environmental stimulation to fully overcome the effects of extreme deprivation.

What's Your View?

- In view of what is now known about the plasticity of the infant brain, how can we make sure that every baby has access to an appropriately stimulating environment?

Checkpoint

Can you . . .

✔ Discuss how early experience can affect brain growth and development both positively and negatively, and give examples?

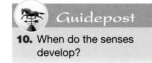
Early Sensory Capacities

The developing brain enables newborn infants to make fairly good sense of what they touch, see, smell, taste, and hear; and their senses develop rapidly in the early months of life.

Touch and Pain Touch seems to be the first sense to develop. Early signs of the rooting reflex (refer back to Table 4-4) occur two months after conception. By thirty-two weeks of gestation, all body parts are sensitive to touch (Haith, 1986).

In the past, physicians performing surgery on newborn babies often used no anesthesia because of a mistaken belief that neonates could not feel pain, or could feel it only briefly. Actually, even on the first day of life, newborns can and do feel pain; and they become more sensitive to it during the next few days. The American Academy of Pediatrics and Canadian Paediatric Society (2000) maintain that prolonged or severe pain can do long-term harm to newborns and that pain relief is essential.

Smell and Taste The senses of smell and taste also begin to develop in the womb. The flavors and odors of foods an expectant mother consumes may be transmitted to the fetus through the amniotic fluid (Mennella & Beauchamp, 1996b).

A preference for pleasant odors seems to be learned in utero and during the first few days after birth, and the odors transmitted through the mother's breast milk may further contribute to this learning (Bartoshuk & Beauchamp, 1994). Six-day-old breast-fed infants prefer the odor of their mother's breast pad over that of another nursing mother, but 2-day-olds do not, suggesting that babies need a few days' experience to learn how their mothers smell (Macfarlane, 1975).

Certain taste preferences seem to be largely innate (Bartoshuk & Beauchamp, 1994). Newborns prefer sweet tastes to sour or bitter ones (Haith, 1986). Sweetened water calms crying newborns, whether full-term or two to three weeks premature—evidence that the mechanisms that produce this calming effect are functional before normal term (B. A. Smith & Blass, 1996). An inborn "sweet tooth" may help a baby adapt to life outside the womb because breast milk is quite sweet (Harris, 1997). Newborns' rejection of bitter tastes is probably another survival mechanism, as many bitter substances are toxic (Bartoshuk & Beauchamp, 1994).

Taste preferences developed in infancy may last into early childhood. In one study, 4- and 5-year-olds who, as infants, had been fed different types of formula had differing food preferences (Mennella & Beauchamp, 2002).

Hearing Hearing, too, is functional before birth. As we discussed in Chapter 3, babies less than 3 days old respond differently to a story heard while in the womb than to other stories; can tell their mother's voice from a stranger's; and prefer their native language to a foreign tongue (DeCasper & Fifer, 1980; DeCasper & Spence, 1986; C. Moon, Cooper, & Fifer, 1993). Early recognition of voices and language heard in the womb may lay the foundation for the relationship between parents and child.

Auditory discrimination develops rapidly after birth. Three-day-old infants can tell new speech sounds from those they have heard before (L. R. Brody, Zelazo, & Chaika, 1984). At 1 month, babies can distinguish sounds as close as *ba* and *pa* (Eimas, Siqueland, Jusczyk, & Vigorito, 1971).

Because hearing is a key to language development, hearing impairments should be identified as early as possible. Hearing loss occurs in 1 to 3 of 1,000 live births and, if left undetected, can lead to developmental delays (Gaffney et al., 2003). Among 10,372 infants born in Honolulu during a five-year period, hearing screening within the first three days followed by hearing aids and aural therapy before six months for those found to have hearing problems enabled those infants to achieve normal speech and language development (Mason & Herrmann, 1998).

Sight Vision is the least developed sense at birth. The eyes of newborns are smaller than those of adults, the retinal structures are incomplete, and the optic nerve is underdeveloped. A neonate's eyes focus best from about one foot away—just about the typical distance from the face of a person holding a newborn. This may be an adaptive measure to promote bonding with the mother.

Newborns blink at bright lights. Their peripheral vision is very narrow; it more than doubles between 2 and 10 weeks of age (E. Tronick, 1972). The ability to follow a moving target also develops rapidly in the first months, as does color perception (Haith, 1986). Four-month-old babies can discriminate among red, green, blue, and yellow (M. Bornstein, Kessen, & Weiskopf, 1976; Teller & Bornstein, 1987).

Visual acuity at birth is approximately 20/400 but improves rapidly, reaching the 20/20 level by about 8 months (Kellman & Arterberry, 1998; Kellman & Banks, 1998). (This means that a person can read letters on a specified line on a standard eye chart from 20 feet away.) *Binocular vision*—the use of both eyes to focus, enabling perception of depth and distance—usually does not develop until 4 or 5 months (Bushnell & Boudreau, 1993). Early screening is essential to detect any problems that may interfere with vision (AAP Committee on Practice and Ambulatory Medicine and Section on Ophthalmology, 1996, 2002).

Motor Development

Babies do not have to be taught such basic motor skills as grasping, crawling, and walking. They just need room to move and freedom to see what they can do. When the central nervous system, muscles, and bones are ready and the environment offers the right opportunities for exploration and practice, babies keep surprising the adults around them with new abilities.

Milestones of Motor Development Motor development is marked by a series of milestones: achievements that develop systematically, each newly mastered ability preparing a baby to tackle the next. Babies first learn simple skills and then combine

Checkpoint
Can you . . .

✔ Give evidence for early development of the senses of touch, smell, and taste, and tell how breast-feeding plays a part in the latter two senses?

✔ Tell how auditory discrimination in newborns is related to fetal hearing?

✔ List three ways newborns' vision is underdeveloped?

Guidepost

11. What are the early milestones in motor development, and what are some influences on it?

Lifting and holding up the head from a prone position, crawling along the floor to reach something enticing, such as a furry cat's tail, and walking well enough to push a wagon full of blocks are important early milestones of motor development.

Table 4-5	Milestones of Motor Development	
Skill	**50 Percent**	**90 Percent**
Rolling over	3.2 months	5.4 months
Grasping rattle	3.3 months	3.9 months
Sitting without support	5.9 months	6.8 months
Standing while holding on	7.2 months	8.5 months
Grasping with thumb and finger	8.2 months	10.2 months
Standing alone well	11.5 months	13.7 months
Walking well	12.3 months	14.9 months
Building tower of two cubes	14.8 months	20.6 months
Walking up steps	16.6 months	21.6 months
Jumping in place	23.8 months	2.4 years
Copying circle	3.4 years	4.0 years

Note: This table shows the approximate ages when 50 percent and 90 percent of children can perform each skill, according to the Denver Training Manual II.

Source: Adapted from Frankenburg et al., 1992.

systems of action Increasingly complex combinations of motor skills, which permit a wider or more precise range of movement and more control of the environment.

Denver Developmental Screening Test Screening test given to children 1 month to 6 years old to determine whether they are developing normally.

gross motor skills Physical skills that involve the large muscles.

fine motor skills Physical skills that involve the small muscles and eye-hand coordination.

them into increasingly complex **systems of action,** which permit a wider or more precise range of movement and more effective control of the environment. In developing the precision grip, for example, an infant first tries to pick things up with the whole hand, fingers closing against the palm. Later the baby masters the *pincer grasp,* in which thumb and index finger meet at the tips to form a circle, making it possible to pick up tiny objects. In learning to walk, an infant first gains control of separate movements of the arms, legs, and feet before putting these movements together to take that momentous first step.

The **Denver Developmental Screening Test** (Frankenburg, Dodds, Fandal, Kazuk, & Cohrs, 1975) is used to chart progress between the ages of 1 month and 6 years and to identify children who are not developing normally. The test measures **gross motor skills** (those using large muscles), such as rolling over and catching a ball, and **fine motor skills** (using small muscles), such as grasping a rattle and copying a circle. It also assesses language development (for example, knowing the definitions of words) and personality and social development (such as smiling spontaneously and dressing without help). The newest edition, the Denver II Scale (Frankenburg et al., 1992), includes revised norms (see Table 4-5 for examples).

When we talk about what the "average" baby can do, we refer to the 50 percent Denver norms. Actually, normality covers a wide range; about half of all babies master these skills before the ages given, and about half afterward. Also, the Denver norms were developed with reference to a Western population and are not necessarily valid in assessing children from other cultures.

As we trace typical progress in head control, hand control, and locomotion, notice how these developments follow the *cephalocaudal* (head to tail) and *proximodistal* (inner to outer) principles outlined earlier. Note, too, that although boy babies tend to be a little bigger and more active than girl babies, there are no gender differences in infants' motor development (Mondschein, Adolph, & Tamis-LeMonda, 2000).

Head Control At birth, most infants can turn their heads from side to side while lying on their backs. While lying chest down, many can lift their heads enough to turn them. Within the first 2 to 3 months, they lift their heads higher and higher—sometimes to the point where they lose their balance and roll over on their backs.

By 4 months of age, almost all infants can keep their heads erect while being held or supported in a sitting position.

Hand Control Babies are born with a grasping reflex. If the palm of an infant's hand is stroked, the hand closes tightly. At about 3½ months, most infants can grasp an object of moderate size, such as a rattle, but have trouble holding a small object. Next, they begin to grasp objects with one hand and transfer them to the other, and then to hold (but not pick up) small objects. Some time between 7 and 11 months, their hands become coordinated enough to pick up a tiny object, such as a pea, using the pincer grasp. By 15 months, the average baby can build a tower of two cubes. A few months after the third birthday, the average toddler can copy a circle fairly well.

Locomotion After three months, the average infant begins to roll over deliberately (rather than accidentally, as before)—first from front to back and then from back to front. The average baby can sit without support by 6 months of age and can assume a sitting position without help about two and a half months later.

Between 6 and 10 months, most babies begin to get around under their own power by means of creeping or crawling. This new achievement of *self-locomotion* has striking cognitive and psychosocial ramifications (Bertenthal & Campos, 1987; Bertenthal, Campos, & Barrett, 1984; Bertenthal, Campos, & Kermoian, 1994; J. Campos, Bertenthal, & Benson, 1980). Crawling infants become more sensitive to where objects are, how big they are, whether they can be moved, and how they look. Crawling helps babies learn to judge distances and perceive depth. As they become more mobile, they begin to hear such warnings as "Come back!" and "Don't touch!" as adult hands pick them up and turn them in a safer direction—and to remember such instructions when tempted to head for a forbidden object. They learn to look to caregivers for clues as to whether a situation is secure or frightening—a skill known as *social referencing* (Hertenstein & Campos, 2004; see Chapter 6).

By holding onto a helping hand or a piece of furniture, the average baby can stand at a little past 7 months of age. A little more than four months later, most babies let go and stand alone. The average baby can stand well about two weeks or so before the first birthday.

All these developments lead up to the major motor achievement of infancy: walking. Humans begin to walk later than other species, possibly because babies' heavy heads and short legs make balance difficult. For some months before they can stand without support, babies practice "cruising" while holding onto furniture. Soon after they can stand alone well, at about 11½ months, most infants take their first unaided steps. Within a few weeks, shortly after the first birthday, the average child is walking fairly well, as Helen Keller did, and thus achieves the status of toddler.

Many U.S. parents put their babies in mobile walkers in the belief that the babies will learn to walk earlier. Actually, by restricting babies' motor exploration, and sometimes their view of their own movements, walkers may *delay* motor skill development (Siegel & Burton, 1999). Furthermore, walkers can be dangerous. The American Academy of Pediatrics has called for a ban on their manufacture and sale (AAP Committee on Injury and Poison Prevention, 2001b). In 2004, Canada became the first country to ban their sale, advertising, and importation (Reuters, 2004a).

During the second year, children begin to climb stairs one at a time, putting one foot after another on the same step; later they will alternate feet. Walking down stairs comes later. In their second year, toddlers run and jump. By age 3½, most children can balance briefly on one foot and begin to hop.

How Motor Development Occurs: Maturation in Context The sequence just described was traditionally thought to be genetically programmed—a largely

Lifemap CD

To see how one baby's gross motor skills progress from rolling over at 10 weeks to standing and walking at 12 months, watch the video, "Gross Motor Development During the First Year," in Chapter 4 of your CD.

automatic, preordained series of steps directed by the maturing brain. Today, many developmental scientists consider this view too simplistic. Instead, according to Esther Thelen (1995), motor development is a continuous process of interaction between baby and environment.

Thelen points to the *walking reflex:* stepping movements a neonate makes when held upright with the feet touching a surface (refer back to Table 4-4). This behavior usually disappears by the fourth month. Not until the latter part of the first year, when a baby is getting ready to walk, do such movements appear again. The usual explanation is a shift to cortical control: An older baby's deliberate walking is seen as a new skill that reflects the brain's development. But, Thelen observes, a newborn's stepping involves the same kinds of movements the neonate makes while lying down and kicking. Why would stepping stop, only to reappear months later, whereas kicking continues? The answer, she suggests, may be that babies' legs become thicker and heavier during the early months, but not yet strong enough to carry the increased weight (Thelen & Fisher, 1982, 1983). In fact, when young infants are held in warm water, which helps support their legs, stepping reappears. Their ability to produce the movement has not changed—only the physical and environmental conditions that inhibit or promote it.

Maturation alone cannot explain such an observation, says Thelen. Infant and environment form an interconnected system, and development has interacting causes. One is the infant's motivation to do something (say, pick up a toy or get to the other side of the room). The infant's physical characteristics and his or her position in a particular setting (for example, lying in a crib or being held upright in a pool) offer opportunities and constraints that affect whether and how the baby can achieve the goal. Ultimately, a solution emerges as the baby tries out behaviors and retains those that most efficiently do the job. Rather than being solely in charge of this process, the maturing brain is only one contributor to it.

According to Thelen, normal babies develop the same skills in the same order because they are built approximately the same way and have similar physical challenges and needs. Thus they eventually discover that walking is more efficient than crawling in most situations. Thelen's hypothesis—that this discovery arises from each particular baby's experience in a particular context—may help explain why some babies learn to walk earlier than others do.

What's Your View?

- Is it advisable to try to teach babies skills such as walking before they develop them on their own?

Motor Development and Perception Early motor development is an excellent example of the interrelationship between the physical and cognitive domains. Sensory perception enables infants to learn about themselves and their environment so they can make better judgments about how to navigate in it. Motor experience, together with awareness of their changing bodies, sharpens and modifies their perceptual understanding of what is likely to happen if they move in a certain way. This bidirectional connection between perception and action, mediated by the developing brain, gives infants much useful information about themselves and their world (Adolph & Eppler, 2002).

Sensory and motor activities seem to be fairly well coordinated from birth (Bertenthal & Clifton, 1998). Infants begin reaching for and grasping objects at about 4 to 5 months. By 5½ months, they can adapt their reach to moving or spinning objects (Wentworth, Benson, & Haith, 2000). Piaget and other researchers long believed that reaching depended on **visual guidance:** the use of the eyes to guide the movement of the hands (or other parts of the body). Now, research has found that 4- to 5-month-olds can use other sensory cues: They can locate an unseen rattle by its sound, and they can reach for a glowing object in the dark even though they cannot

visual guidance The use of the eyes to guide the movement of the hands (or other parts of the body).

see their hands (Clifton, Muir, Ashmead, & Clarkson, 1993). In fact, they can reach for an object based only on their memory of its location (McCarty, Clifton, Ashmead, Lee, & Goubet, 2001). Slightly older infants, 5 to 7½ months old, can grasp a moving, fluorescent object in the dark—a feat that requires awareness, not only of how their own hands move but also of the object's path and speed, so as to anticipate the likely point of contact (Robin, Berthier, & Clifton, 1996).

Depth perception, the ability to perceive objects and surfaces in three dimensions, depends on several kinds of cues that affect the image of an object on the retina of the eye. These cues involve not only binocular coordination but also motor control (Bushnell & Boudreau, 1993). Kinetic cues come from movements of either the object or the observer. To find out which is moving, a baby might hold his or her head still for a moment, an ability that is well established by about 3 months.

Sometime between 5 and 7 months, after babies can reach for and grasp objects, they develop **haptic perception,** the ability to acquire information by handling objects rather than by simply looking at them. Haptic perception enables babies to respond to such cues as relative size and differences in texture and shading (Bushnell & Boudreau, 1993).

Eleanor and James Gibson's Ecological Theory In a classic experiment by Richard Walk and Eleanor Gibson (1961), 6-month-old babies were placed on a plexiglass tabletop over a checkerboard pattern that created the illusion of a vertical drop in the center of the table—a **visual cliff.** Would the infants perceive the illusion of depth? The babies did see a difference between the "ledge" and the "drop." They crawled freely on the "ledge" but avoided the "drop," even when they saw their mothers beckoning on the far side of the table.

How do babies decide whether to move across a "ledge" or down a hill? According to Eleanor Gibson's and James J. Gibson's **ecological theory of perception** (E. J. Gibson, 1969; J. J. Gibson, 1979; Gibson & Pick, 2000), infants size up the "fit," or **affordance,** between their own changing physical attributes or capabilities (such as arm and leg length, endurance, balance, and strength) and the changing characteristics of their environment. Knowledge of affordances enables babies to make moment-to-moment decisions about what they can and cannot do in a given situation (Adolph, 2000; Adolph & Eppler, 2002). (Is the ground too rough to walk on? Can I keep my balance if I try?) According to the Gibsons, perceptual learning occurs through a growing ability to detect and differentiate the many features of a rich sensory environment. It is this ability that permits infants and toddlers to recognize affordances and thus to successfully negotiate a terrain.

Locomotor development depends on increasing sensitivity to affordances and is an outcome of both perception and action (Adolph & Eppler, 2002). With experience, babies become better able to gauge the environment in which they move and to adapt their movements accordingly (Adolph, 2000; Adolph et al., 2003; Adolph & Eppler, 2002). In visual cliff experiments, infants who have been crawling for some time are more likely than novices to avoid the "cliff." Similarly, when faced

No matter how enticing a mother's arms are, this baby is staying away from them. As young as she is, she can perceive depth and wants to avoid falling off what looks like a cliff.

depth perception Ability to perceive objects and surfaces three-dimensionally.

haptic perception Ability to acquire information about properties of objects, such as size, weight, and texture, by handling them.

visual cliff Apparatus designed to give an illusion of depth and used to assess depth perception in infants.

ecological theory of perception Theory developed by Eleanor and James Gibson, which describes developing motor and perceptual abilities as interdependent parts of a functional system that guides behavior in varying contexts.

affordances In the Gibsons' ecological theory of perception, the fit between a person's physical attributes and capabilities and characteristics of the environment.

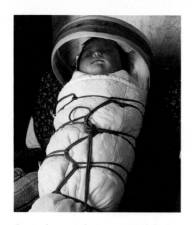

Some observers have suggested that babies from the Yucatan develop motor skills later than American babies because they are swaddled. However, Navajo babies like this one also are swaddled for most of the day, and they begin to walk at about the same time as other American babies, suggesting a hereditary explanation.

Checkpoint

Can you . . .

✔ Trace a typical infant's progress in head control, hand control, and locomotion, according to the Denver norms?

✔ Discuss how maturation, perception, and cultural influences relate to early motor development?

with actual downward slopes of increasing steepness, infants' judgments become more accurate and their explorations more efficient as they gain practice in crawling. They do not seem to learn from fear of heights or of falling or from trial and error. What they apparently learn from experience is how far they can push their limits without losing their balance (Adolph & Eppler, 2002).

This learning is flexible but posture-specific. Babies who learn how far they can reach for a toy across a gap while in a sitting position must acquire this knowledge anew when they begin to crawl (Adolph, 2000; Adolph & Eppler, 2002). Likewise, when crawling babies who have mastered slopes begin to walk, they have to learn to cope with slopes all over again (Adolph, 1997; Adolph & Eppler, 2002).

Cultural Influences on Motor Development   Although motor development follows a virtually universal sequence, its *pace* does seem to respond to certain contextual factors. A normal rate of development in one culture may not be in another.

African babies tend to be more advanced than U.S. and European infants in sitting, walking, and running. In Uganda, for example, babies typically walk at 10 months, as compared with 12 months in the United States and 15 months in France (Gardiner & Kosmitzki, 2005). Asian babies tend to develop these skills more slowly. Such differences may in part be related to ethnic differences in temperament (H. Kaplan & Dove, 1987; see Chapter 6) or may reflect a culture's childrearing practices (Gardiner & Kosmitzki, 2005).

Some cultures actively encourage early development of motor skills. In many African and West Indian cultures in which infants show advanced motor development, adults use special "handling routines," such as bouncing and stepping exercises, to strengthen babies' muscles (Hopkins & Westra, 1988). In one study, Jamaican infants, whose mothers used such handling routines daily, sat, crawled, and walked earlier than English infants, whose mothers gave them no such special handling (Hopkins & Westra, 1990).

On the other hand, some cultures discourage early motor development. Children of the Ache in eastern Paraguay do not begin to walk until 18 to 20 months of age (H. Kaplan & Dove, 1987). Ache mothers pull their babies back to their laps when the infants begin to crawl away. The Ache mothers closely supervise their babies to protect them from the hazards of nomadic life. Yet, as 8- to 10-year-olds, Ache children climb tall trees, chop branches, and play in ways that enhance their motor skills (H. Kaplan & Dove, 1987). Normal development, then, need not follow the same timetable to reach the same destination.

Ref⊕cus

Thinking back to the Focus vignette about Helen Keller at the beginning of this chapter:

- What connections does Keller's story show among physical health, sensory capabilities, cognition, and pyschosocial development?

- How would a cognitive neuroscientist explain why Keller's senses of smell and touch became unusually sharp when she lost her hearing and sight?

- What hypotheses might explain why Keller's language development regressed but not her motor development?

- Would the "mysterious fever" that Helen contracted likely be as damaging today? Why or why not?

By the time small children can run, jump, and play with toys requiring fairly sophisticated coordination, they are very different from the neonates described at the beginning of this chapter. The cognitive changes that have taken place are equally dramatic, as we discuss in Chapter 5.

SUMMARY AND KEY TERMS

Childbirth and Culture: How Birthing Has Changed

Guidepost 1: **How do customs surrounding birth reflect culture, and how has childbirth changed in developed countries?**

- In Europe and the United States, childbirth before the 20th century was not much different from childbirth in some developing countries today. Birth was a female ritual that occurred at home and was attended by a midwife. Pain relief was minimal, and risks for mother and baby were high.
- The development of the science of obstetrics professionalized childbirth. Births took place in hospitals and were attended by physicians. Medical advances dramatically improved safety.
- Today, delivery at home or in birth centers attended by midwives can be a relatively safe alternative to physician-attended hospital delivery for women with normal, low-risk pregnancies.

The Birth Process

Guidepost 2: **How does labor begin, and what happens during each of the three stages of childbirth?**

- Birth normally occurs after a preparatory period of parturition.
- The birth process consists of three stages: (1) dilation of the cervix; (2) descent and emergence of the baby; and (3) expulsion of the umbilical cord and the placenta.

  parturition *(111)*

Guidepost 3: **What alternative methods of delivery are available?**

- More than one-fourth of births in the United States are by cesarean delivery.
- Electronic fetal monitoring can detect signs of fetal distress, especially in high-risk births.
- Natural or prepared childbirth can minimize the need for pain-killing drugs and maximize parents' active involvement. Modern epidurals can give effective pain relief with smaller doses of medication than in the past.

- The presence of a doula can provide physical benefits as well as emotional support.

  cesarean delivery *(112)*

  electronic fetal monitoring *(112)*

  natural childbirth *(112)*

  prepared childbirth *(112)*

The Newborn Baby

Guidepost 4: **How do newborn infants adjust to life outside the womb?**

- The neonatal period is a time of transition from intrauterine to extrauterine life. During the first few days, the neonate loses weight and then regains it; the lanugo (prenatal hair) falls off and the protective coating of vernix caseosa dries up. The fontanels (soft spots) in the skull close within the first 18 months.
- At birth, the circulatory, respiratory, gastrointestinal, and temperature regulation systems become independent of the mother's. If a newborn cannot start breathing within about 5 minutes, brain injury may occur.
- Newborns have a strong sucking reflex and secrete meconium from the intestinal tract. They are commonly subject to neonatal jaundice due to immaturity of the liver.

  neonatal period *(113)*

  neonate *(113)*

  anoxia *(114)*

  neonatal jaundice *(114)*

Guidepost 5: **How can we tell whether a new baby is healthy and is developing normally?**

- At 1 minute and 5 minutes after birth, a neonate's Apgar score can indicate how well he or she is adjusting to extrauterine life. In high-risk situations, the Brazelton Neonatal Behavioral Assessment Scale can assess responses to the environment and predict future development.
- Neonatal screening is done for certain rare conditions, such as PKU and congenital hypothyroidism.

  Apgar scale *(115)*

  Brazelton Neonatal Behavioral Assessment Scale (NBAS) *(115)*

Guidepost 6: How do newborns' patterns of sleep, waking, and activity change?

- A newborn's state of arousal is governed by periodic cycles of wakefulness, sleep, and activity. Sleep takes up the major, but a diminishing, amount of a neonate's time. By the second half of the first year, babies do most of their sleeping at night.
- Cultural customs affect sleep patterns.

state of arousal *(116)*

Survival and Health

Guidepost 7: What complications of childbirth can endanger newborn babies, and what are the long-term prospects for babies with complicated births?

- A small number of infants suffer lasting effects of birth trauma. Other complications include postmature birth, low birth weight, and stillbirth.
- Low-birth-weight babies may be either preterm (premature) or small for gestational age. Low birth weight is a major factor in infant mortality and can cause long-term physical and cognitive problems. Very low-birth-weight babies have a less promising prognosis than those who weigh more.

birth trauma *(118)*

postmature *(119)*

low birth weight *(119)*

preterm (premature) infants *(119)*

small-for-date (small-for-gestational-age) infants *(119)*

Guidepost 8: How can we enhance babies' chances of survival and health?

- A supportive postnatal environment and other protective factors often can improve the outcome for babies suffering from birth complications.
- Although infant mortality has diminished in the United States, it is still disturbingly high for African American babies. Birth defects are the leading cause of death in infancy; for black infants, low birth weight is the leading cause.
- Sudden infant death syndrome (SIDS) is the third leading cause of death of U.S. infants. Major risk factors include exposure to smoke and, prenatally, to caffeine, and sleeping in the prone position.
- Injuries are the third leading cause of death of U.S. infants after the first month.
- Shaken baby syndrome (SBS) is an underdiagnosed and underreported form of abuse, mainly of children under 2. It can cause severe, irreversible brain injury or death.
- Vaccine-preventable diseases have declined as rates of immunization have improved, but many preschoolers are not fully protected.

protective factors *(124)*

infant mortality rate *(124)*

sudden infant death syndrome (SIDS) *(125)*

Early Physical Development

Guidepost 9: What influences the growth of body and brain?

- Normal physical growth and sensory and motor development proceed according to the cephalocaudal and proximodistal principles.
- A child's body grows most dramatically during the first year of life; growth proceeds at a rapid but diminishing rate throughout the first 3 years.
- Breast-feeding offers many health advantages and sensory and cognitive benefits and should be done exclusively at least for the first six months.
- Overweight babies are *not* at special risk of becoming obese adults, unless they have obese parents.
- The central nervous system controls sensorimotor activity. Lateralization enables each hemisphere of the brain to specialize in different functions.
- The brain grows most rapidly during the months before and immediately after birth as neurons migrate to their assigned locations, form synaptic connections, and undergo integration and differentiation. Cell death and myelination improve the efficiency of the nervous system.
- Reflex behaviors—primitive, locomotor, and postural—are indications of neurological status. Most early reflexes drop out during the first year as voluntary, cortical control develops.
- Especially during the early period of rapid growth, environmental experience can influence brain development positively or negatively.

central nervous system *(132)*

brain growth spurts *(133)*

lateralization *(133)*

neurons *(134)*

integration *(135)*

differentiation *(135)*

cell death *(135)*

myelination *(136)*

reflex behaviors *(137)*

plasticity *(137)*

Guidepost 10: When do the senses develop?

- Sensory capacities, present from birth and even in the womb, develop rapidly in the first months of life. Very young infants show pronounced abilities to discriminate between stimuli.
- Touch seems to be the first sense to develop and mature. Newborns are sensitive to pain. Smell, taste, and hearing also begin to develop in the womb.
- Vision is the least well developed sense at birth. Peripheral vision, color perception, acuteness of focus, binocular vision, and the ability to follow a moving object with the eyes all develop within the first few months.

Guidepost 11: What are the early milestones in motor development, and what are some influences on it?

- Motor skills develop in a certain sequence, which may depend largely on maturation but also on context, experience, and motivation. Simple skills combine into increasingly complex systems.
- Self-locomotion brings about changes in all domains of development.
- Perception is intimately related to motor development. Depth perception and haptic perception develop in the first half of the first year.
- According to Eleanor and James Gibson's theory of ecological perception, awareness of affordances helps infants and toddlers determine their ability to traverse a terrain.

- Cultural practices may influence the pace of early motor development.

systems of action *(142)*
Denver Developmental Screening Test *(142)*
gross motor skills *(142)*
fine motor skills *(142)*
visual guidance *(144)*
depth perception *(145)*
haptic perception *(145)*
visual cliff *(145)*
ecological theory of perception *(145)*
affordances *(145)*

CHAPTER 5

Cognitive Development During the First Three Years

So runs my dream; but what am I?
An infant crying in the night;
An infant crying for the light,
And with no language but a cry.

————

Alfred, Lord Tennyson, *In Memoriam*, Canto 54

Focus
Doddy Darwin, Naturalist's Son

*Charles and "Doddy"
Darwin*

On December 27, 1839, when the naturalist Charles Darwin was 30 years old, his first baby, William Erasmus Darwin, affectionately known as Doddy, was born. That day—20 years before the publication of Charles Darwin's *Origin of Species,* which outlined his theory of evolution based on natural selection—the proud father began keeping a diary of observations of his newborn son. It was these notes, published in 1877,* that first called scientific attention to the developmental nature of infant behavior.

What abilities are babies born with? How do they learn about their world? How do they communicate, first nonverbally and then through language? These were among the questions Darwin sought to answer—questions still central to the study of cognitive development.

Darwin's keen eye illuminates how coordination of physical and mental activity helps an infant adapt to the world—as in this entry written when Doddy was 4 months old:

Took my finger to his mouth & as usual could not get it in, on account of his own hand being in the way; then he slipped his own back & so got my finger in.—This was not chance & therefore a kind of reasoning. (Diary, p. 12; quoted in Keegan & Gruber, 1985, p. 135.)

In Darwin's notes, we can see Doddy developing new cognitive skills through interaction not only with his father's finger, but with other objects as well. The diary depicts a series of encounters with reflected images. In these episodes Doddy gains knowledge, not in sudden bursts or jumps, but through gradual integration of new experience with existing patterns of behavior. In Darwin's view—as, later, in Piaget's—this was not merely a matter of piling new knowledge upon old; it involved an actual transformation of the way the mind is organized.

*The source for analysis of Darwin's diary was Keegan and Gruber (1985).

151

When Doddy, at 4½ months, saw his likeness and his father's in a mirror, Darwin noted that the baby "seemed surprised at my voice coming from behind him, my image being in front" (Diary, p. 18; quoted in Keegan & Gruber, 1985, p. 135). Two months later, Doddy apparently had solved the mystery: now, when his father, standing behind him, made a funny face in the mirror, the infant "was aware that the image . . . was not real & therefore . . . turned round to look" (Diary, pp. 21–22; quoted in Keegan & Gruber, 1985, pp. 135–136).

At first, this newfound understanding did not generalize to other reflective materials. Two weeks later, Doddy seemed puzzled to see his father's reflection in a window. By 9 months, however, the boy realized that "the shadow of a hand, made by a candle, was to be looked for behind, in [the] same manner as in [a] looking glass" (Diary, p. 23; quoted in Keegan & Gruber, 1985, p. 136). His recognition that reflections could emanate from objects behind him now extended to shadows, another kind of two-dimensional image.

Darwin was particularly interested in documenting his son's progress in communication. He believed that language acquisition is a natural process, akin to earlier physical expressions of feelings. Through smiling, crying, laughing, facial expressions, and sounds of pleasure or pain, Doddy managed to communicate quite well with his parents even before uttering his first word. One of his first meaningful verbal expressions was "Ah!"—uttered when he recognized an image in a glass.

Darwin made these observations more than 160 years ago, at a time when infants' cognitive abilities were widely underestimated. We now know—as Darwin inferred from his observations of Doddy—that normal, healthy infants are born with the ability to learn and remember and with a capacity for acquiring and using speech. They use their growing sensory and cognitive capacities to exert control over their behavior and their world.

In this chapter we look at infants' and toddlers' cognitive abilities from three classic perspectives—behaviorist, psychometric, and Piagetian—and then from three newer perspectives: information processing, cognitive neuroscientific, and social-contextual. We trace the early development of language and discuss how it comes about.

After you have studied this chapter, you should be able to answer each of the Guidepost questions that appear at the top of the next page. Look for them again in the margins, where they point to important concepts throughout the chapter. To check your understanding of these Guideposts, review the end-of-chapter summary. Checkpoints located at periodic spots throughout the chapter will help you verify your understanding of what you have read.

Guideposts
for Study

1. How do infants learn, and how long can they remember?

2. Can infants' and toddlers' intelligence be measured, and can it be improved?

3. How did Piaget explain early cognitive development, and how well have his claims stood up?

4. How can we measure infants' ability to process information, and how does this ability relate to future intelligence?

5. When do babies begin to think about characteristics of the physical world?

6. What can brain research reveal about the development of cognitive skills?

7. How does social interaction with adults advance cognitive competence?

8. How do babies develop language?

9. What influences contribute to linguistic progress?

Studying Cognitive Development: Classic Approaches

How and when do babies begin to learn, to think, and to solve problems? How and when does memory develop? Are some babies smarter than others? Many investigators have taken one of three classic approaches to the study of such questions, which fall in the domain of *cognitive development:*

- The **behaviorist approach** studies the basic *mechanics* of learning. It is concerned with how behavior changes in response to experience.

- The **psychometric approach** seeks to *measure quantitative differences* in cognitive abilities by using tests that indicate or predict these abilities.

- The **Piagetian approach** looks at changes, or stages, in the *quality* of cognitive functioning. It is concerned with how the mind structures its activities and adapts to the environment.

All three approaches, as well as the three newer ones we discuss in the following section—the information-processing, cognitive neuroscience, and social-contextual approaches—help us understand cognitive development.

behaviorist approach Approach to the study of cognitive development that is concerned with basic mechanics of learning.

psychometric approach Approach to the study of cognitive development that seeks to measure the quantity of intelligence a person possesses.

Piagetian approach Approach to the study of cognitive development that describes qualitative stages in cognitive functioning.

Behaviorist Approach: Basic Mechanics of Learning

Babies are born with the ability to learn from what they see, hear, smell, taste, and touch, and they have some ability to remember what they learn. Although learning theorists recognize maturation as a limiting factor, their main interest is in mechanisms of learning. Let's look first at two learning processes (introduced in Chapter 2) that behaviorists study: *classical conditioning* and *operant conditioning.* Later we will consider *habituation,* a form of learning that information-processing researchers study.

Classical and Operant Conditioning Eager to capture Anna's memorable moments on film, her father took pictures of the infant smiling, crawling, and showing off her

Guidepost

1. How do infants learn, and how long can they remember?

An Indian snake charmer's son eagerly plays with a snake the father has trained, showing that fear of snakes is a learned response. Children can be conditioned to fear animals that are associated with unpleasant or frightening experiences, as "Little Albert" was in a classic study by John B. Watson and Rosalie Rayner, introduced in Chapter 2.

classical conditioning Learning based on associating a stimulus that does not ordinarily elicit a particular response with another stimulus that does elicit the response.

operant conditioning Learning based on reinforcement or punishment.

other achievements. Whenever the flash went off, Anna blinked. One evening when Anna was 11 months old, she saw her father hold up the camera to his eye—and she blinked *before* the flash. She had learned to associate the camera with the bright light, so that the sight of the camera alone activated her blinking reflex.

Anna's blinking at the sight of the camera is an example of **classical conditioning,** in which a person learns to make a reflex, or involuntary, response (in this case, blinking) to a stimulus (the camera) that originally did not provoke the response (see Figure 5-1). Classical conditioning enables infants to anticipate an event before it happens by forming associations between stimuli (such as the camera and the flash) that regularly occur together. Classically conditioned learning will fade, or become *extinct,* if it is not reinforced by repeated association. Thus, if Anna frequently saw the camera without the flash, she eventually would stop blinking.

In classical conditioning, the learner is passive, absorbing and automatically reacting to stimuli. By contrast, in **operant conditioning**—as when a baby learns that smiling brings loving attention—the learner acts, or operates, on the environment. The infant learns to make a certain response to an environmental stimulus (smiling at the sight of her or his parents) in order to produce a particular effect (parental attention). Researchers often use operant conditioning to study other phenomena, such as memory.

Infant Memory Can you remember anything that happened to you before you were about two years old? The chances are you can't. This inability to remember early events is called *infantile amnesia.* One explanation, held by Piaget (1969) and others, is that early events are not stored in memory because the brain is not yet developed enough. Freud, in contrast, believed that early memories are stored but are repressed

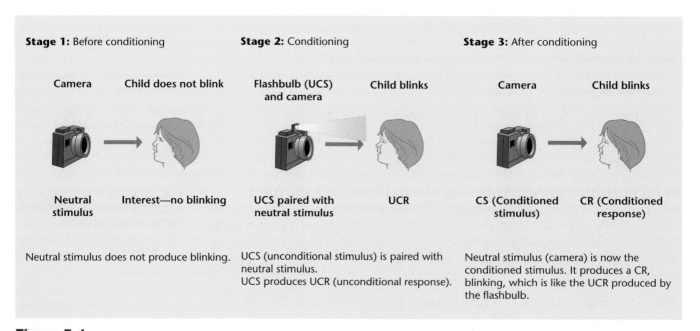

Figure 5-1
Three steps in classical conditioning.

because they are emotionally troubling. Other researchers suggest that children cannot store events in memory until they can talk about them (Nelson, 1992).

Today, research using operant conditioning with nonverbal, age-appropriate tasks suggests that infants' memory processes may not differ fundamentally from those of older children and adults except that infants' retention time is shorter. These studies have found that babies will repeat an action days or weeks later—*if* they are periodically reminded of the situation in which they learned it (Rovee-Collier, 1999).

In a series of experiments by Carolyn Rovee-Collier and her associates, infants were operantly conditioned to kick to activate a mobile attached to one ankle by a ribbon. Babies 2 to 6 months old, when again shown the mobiles days or weeks later, repeated the kicking, even though their legs were no longer attached to the mobiles, showing that recognition of the mobiles triggered a memory of their initial experience with them (Rovee-Collier, 1996, 1999). Similarly, older infants and toddlers were conditioned to press a lever to make a miniature train go around a track. The length of time a conditioned response can be retained increases with age, from two days for 2-month-olds to 13 weeks for 18-month-olds (Hartshorn et al., 1998; Rovee-Collier, 1996, 1999; see Figure 5-2).

Young infants' memory of a behavior seems to be linked specifically to the original cue. Two- to 6-month-olds repeated the learned behavior only when they saw the original mobile or train. However, older infants, between 9 and 12 months, would "try out" the behavior on a different train if no more than two weeks had gone by since the training (Rovee-Collier, 1999).

Context can affect recollection when a memory has weakened. Three-, 9-, and 12-month-olds make the conditioned response to the mobile or train even in a different setting from the one in which they were trained, but not after long delays. Periodic brief exposure to the original stimulus can sustain a memory from early infancy through 1½ to 2 years of age (Rovee-Collier, 1999).

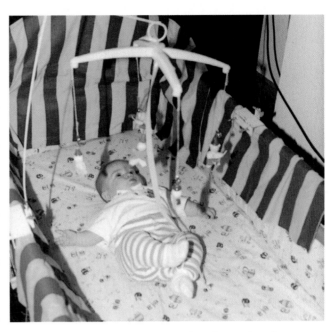

Babies 2 to 6 months old can remember, after a hiatus of two days to two weeks, that they were able to activate a mobile by kicking; they show this by kicking as soon as they see the mobile.

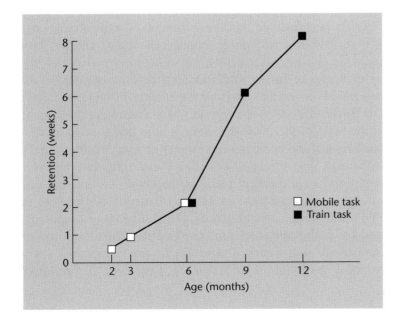

Figure 5-2

Maximum number of weeks that infants of varying ages show retention of how to operate either a mobile or a miniature train. Regardless of the task, retention improves with age. (Source: Rovee-Collier, 1999, Fig. 4, p. 83.)

If infants can remember, why don't their early memories last? One researcher suggests that only after the development of *self-recognition,* around 18 to 24 months (see Chapter 6), can memories be retained as personally experienced events (Howe, 2003). Later in this chapter we will discuss brain research that sheds light on the development of long-term memory.

Guidepost

2. Can infants' and toddlers' intelligence be measured, and can it be improved?

intelligent behavior Behavior that is goal oriented and adaptive to circumstances and conditions of life.

IQ (intelligence quotient) tests Psychometric tests that seek to measure intelligence by comparing a test taker's performance with standardized norms.

Psychometric Approach: Developmental and Intelligence Testing

When Doddy Darwin, at 4 months, figured out how to get his father's finger into his mouth by moving his own hand out of the way, he showed **intelligent behavior.** Although there is no clear scientific consensus on a definition of intelligence (Sternberg et al., 2005), most professionals agree that intelligent behavior is *goal-oriented* and *adaptive:* directed at adjusting to the circumstances and conditions of life. Intelligence, as ordinarily understood, enables people to acquire, remember, and use knowledge; to understand concepts and relationships; and to solve everyday problems.

The goals of psychometric testing are to measure quantitatively the factors that are thought to make up intelligence (such as comprehension and reasoning), and, from the results of that measurement, to predict future performance (such as school achievement). **IQ (intelligence quotient) tests** consist of questions or tasks that are supposed to show how much of the measured abilities a person has, by comparing that person's performance with that of other test takers.

For school-age children, intelligence test scores can predict academic performance fairly accurately and reliably. Testing infants' and toddlers is another matter. Because babies cannot tell us what they know and how they think, the most obvious way to gauge their intelligence is by assessing what they can do. But if they do not grasp a rattle, it is hard to tell whether they do not know how, do not feel like doing it, do not realize what is expected of them, or have simply lost interest.

Bayley Scales of Infant and Toddler Development Standardized test of infants' development.

Checkpoint

Can you . . .

✔ Contrast the goals of the behaviorist, psychometric, and Piagetian approaches to the study of cognitive development?

✔ Give examples of classical and operant conditioning in infants?

✔ Summarize what studies of operant conditioning have shown about infant memory?

✔ Tell why developmental tests are sometimes given to infants and toddlers and describe one such widely used test?

Developmental Testing for Infants and Toddlers Although it is virtually impossible to measure infants' intelligence, it *is* possible to test their cognitive development. If parents are worried because a baby is not doing the same things as other babies the same age, developmental testing may reassure them that development is normal—or may alert them to a problem. Developmental tests compare a baby's performance on a series of tasks with norms established on the basis of observation of what large numbers of infants and toddlers can do at particular ages.

The **Bayley Scales of Infant and Toddler Development** (Bayley, 1969, 1993, 2005) are designed to assess the developmental status of children from 1 month to 3½ years. The Bayley-III has been renormed with a representative sample of 1,700 children, on the basis of the 2000 U.S. census. It is designed to indicate a child's strengths, weaknesses, and competencies in each of five developmental domains—*cognitive, language, motor, social-emotional,* and *adaptive behavior*—to help parents and professionals properly plan for the child. An optional *behavior rating scale* can be completed by the examiner, in part on the basis of information from the child's caregiver. Separate scores, called *developmental quotients* (DQs), are calculated for each scale; they are based on deviation from the mean established by comparison with a normal sample. DQs are most useful for early detection of emotional disturbances and sensory, neurological, and environmental deficits.

Assessing the Impact of the Early Home Environment Intelligence was once thought to be fixed at birth; we now know that it is influenced by both inheritance and experience. What characteristics of the early home environment may influence intelligence? Using the **Home Observation for Measurement of the Environment (HOME)** (R. H. Bradley, 1989; Caldwell & Bradley, 1984), trained observers rate on a checklist the resources and atmosphere in a child's home.

Home Observation for Measurement of the Environment (HOME) Instrument to measure the influence of the home environment on children's cognitive growth.

One important factor that HOME assesses is parental responsiveness. HOME gives credit to the parent of an infant or toddler for caressing or kissing the child during an examiner's visit, to the parent of a preschooler for spontaneously praising the child, and to the parent of an older child for answering the child's questions. A longitudinal study found positive correlations between parents' responsiveness to their 6-month-olds and the children's IQ, achievement test scores, and teacher-rated classroom behavior through age 13 (Bradley, Corwyn, Burchinal, McAdoo, & Coll, 2001).

HOME also assesses the number of books in the home, the presence of playthings that encourage the development of concepts, and parents' involvement in children's play. In an analysis of HOME assessments of 29,264 European American, African American, and Hispanic American children, learning stimulation was consistently associated with kindergarten achievement scores, as well as with language competence and motor and social development (Bradley, Corwyn, Burchinal et al., 2001).

Of course, some HOME items may be less culturally relevant in nonwestern than in western families (Bradley, Corwyn, McAdoo, & Coll, 2001). Also, we cannot be sure on the basis of HOME and correlational findings that parental responsiveness or an enriched home environment actually increases a child's intelligence. All we can say is that these factors are associated with high intelligence. Intelligent, well-educated parents may be more likely to provide a positive, stimulating home environment; and since they also pass their genes on to their children, there may be a genetic influence as well. (This is an example of a *passive genotype-environment correlation,* described in Chapter 3.)

The Home Observation for Measurement of the Environment (HOME) gives positive ratings to a parent who praises a child or answers his or her questions.

Other research has identified six aspects of the early home environment that facilitate cognitive and psychosocial development and help prepare children for school. These six conditions are (1) encouragement to explore the environment; (2) mentoring in basic cognitive and social skills, such as labeling, sequencing, sorting, and comparing; (3) celebration of accomplishments; (4) guidance in practicing and expanding skills; (5) protection from inappropriate punishment, teasing, or disapproval for mistakes or unintended consequences of exploring and trying out skills; and (6) stimulation of language and other symbolic communication. The consistent presence of all six of these conditions early in life may be essential to normal brain development (C. T. Ramey & S. L. Ramey, 1998a, 1998b; S. L. Ramey & C. T. Ramey, 1992). (Table 5-1 lists specific suggestions for helping babies develop cognitive competence.)

What's Your View?

- On the basis of the six essential aspects of the early home environment listed in the text, can you suggest specific ways to help infants and toddlers get ready for schooling?

Early Intervention **Early intervention,** as defined under the Individuals with Disabilities Education Act, is a systematic process of planning and providing therapeutic and educational services for families that need help in meeting infants', toddlers', and preschool children's developmental needs. Two randomly assigned, controlled studies, among others, have tested the effectiveness of early intervention (C. T. Ramey & S. L. Ramey, 1998b).

early intervention Systematic process of providing services to help families meet young children's developmental needs.

Table 5-1 Fostering Competence

Findings from the Harvard Preschool Project, from studies using the HOME scales, and from neurological studies and other research suggest the following guidelines for fostering infants' and toddlers' cognitive development:

1. In the early months, *provide sensory stimulation* but avoid overstimulation and distracting noises.

2. As babies grow older, *create an environment that fosters learning*—one that includes books, interesting objects (which do not have to be expensive toys), and a place to play.

3. *Respond to babies' signals.* This establishes a sense of trust that the world is a friendly place and gives babies a sense of control over their lives.

4. *Give babies the power to effect changes,* through toys that can be shaken, molded, or moved. Help a baby discover that turning a doorknob opens a door, flicking a light switch turns on a light, and opening a faucet produces running water for a bath.

5. *Give babies freedom to explore.* Do not confine them regularly during the day in a crib, jump seat, or small room and only for short periods in a playpen. Baby-proof the environment and let them go!

6. *Talk to babies.* They will not pick up language from listening to the radio or television; they need interaction with adults.

7. In talking to or playing with babies, *enter into whatever they are interested in* at the moment instead of trying to redirect their attention to something else.

8. *Arrange opportunities to learn basic skills,* such as labeling, comparing, and sorting objects (say, by size or color), putting items in sequence, and observing the consequences of actions.

9. *Applaud new skills and help babies practice and expand them.* Stay nearby but do not hover.

10. *Read to babies in a warm, caring atmosphere from an early age.* Reading aloud and talking about the stories develop preliteracy skills.

11. *Use punishment sparingly.* Do not punish or ridicule results of normal trial-and-error exploration.

Sources: R. R. Bradley & Caldwell, 1982; R. R. Bradley, Caldwell, & Rock, 1988; R. H. Bradley et al., 1989; C. T. Ramey & Ramey, 1998a, 1998b; S. L. Ramey & Ramey, 1992; Staso, quoted in Blakeslee, 1997; J. H. Stevens & Bakeman, 1985; B. L. White, 1971; B. L. White, Kaban, & Attanucci, 1979.

Project CARE (Wasik, Ramey, Bryant, & Sparling, 1990) and the Abecedarian Project (C. T. Ramey & Campbell, 1991) involved a total of 174 North Carolina babies from at-risk homes. In each project, from 6 weeks of age until kindergarten, an experimental group was enrolled in Partners for Learning, a full-day, year-round early childhood education program at a university child development center. The program had a low child-teacher ratio and used learning games to foster specific cognitive, linguistic, perceptual-motor, and social skills. Control groups received pediatric and social work services, formula, and home visits, as the experimental groups did, but were not enrolled in Partners for Learning.

In both projects, the children who received the early intervention showed a widening advantage over the control groups in developmental test scores during the first 18 months. By age 3, the average IQ of the Abecedarian children was 101 and of CARE children, 105—equal to or better than average for the general population—as compared with only 84 and 93 for the control groups (C. T. Ramey & S. L. Ramey, 1998b).

As often happens with early intervention programs, these early gains were not fully maintained. IQs dropped between ages 3 and 8, especially among children from the most disadvantaged homes. Still, scores tended to be higher and more stable among children who had been in Partners for Learning than in the control groups (Burchinal et al., 1997). From then on into adulthood, both the experimental and control groups' IQs and math scores increasingly fell below national norms while reading scores held steady but below average. However, the children in the Abecedarian Project who had been enrolled in Partners for Learning continued to outdo the control group by all measures and were less likely to repeat a grade in school (Campbell, Pungello, Miller-Johnson, Burchinal, & Ramey, 2001; C. T. Ramey et al., 2000).

These findings and others like them show that early educational intervention can help protect against environmental risks (Brooks-Gunn, 2003). The most effective early interventions are those that (1) start early and continue throughout the preschool years; (2) are highly time-intensive (i.e., occupy more hours in a day or more days in a week, month, or year); (3) provide direct educational experiences, not just parental training; (4) include health, family counseling, and social services; and (5) are tailored to individual differences and needs. As in the two North Carolina projects, initial gains tend to diminish unless there is enough ongoing environmental support for further progress (Brooks-Gunn, 2003; C. T. Ramey & S. L. Ramey, 1996, 1998a).

Early Head Start, a federally funded intervention for low-income families, is discussed in Chapter 7.

Checkpoint
Can you . . .

✔ Identify aspects of the early home environment that may influence intelligence, according to HOME, and tell why such influence is hard to demonstrate?

✔ Identify six characteristics of the early home environment that contribute to normal cognitive development?

✔ Summarize findings about the value of early intervention?

Piagetian Approach: The Sensorimotor Stage

The first of Piaget's four stages of cognitive development is the **sensorimotor stage.** During this stage (birth to approximately age 2), infants learn about themselves and their world through their developing sensory and motor activity. Babies change from creatures who respond primarily through reflexes and random behavior into goal-oriented toddlers. In Darwin's diary, for example, we saw Doddy progress from simple exploration of the sucking potential of his father's finger to purposeful attempts to solve the mystery of mirrors and shadows.

Substages of the Sensorimotor Stage The sensorimotor stage consists of six substages (see Table 5-2), which flow from one to another as a baby's **schemes,** organized patterns of behavior, become more elaborate. During the first five substages, babies learn to coordinate input from their senses and organize their activities in relation to their environment. They do this by the processes of *organization, adaptation,* and *equilibration,* discussed in Chapter 2. During the sixth and last substage, they progress from trial-and-error learning to the use of symbols and concepts to solve simple problems.

Much of this early cognitive growth comes about through **circular reactions,** in which an infant learns to reproduce pleasurable or interesting events originally discovered by chance. Initially, an activity produces a sensation so enjoyable that the baby wants to repeat it. The repetition again produces pleasure, which, in turn, motivates another repetition (see Figure 5-3). The originally chance behavior has been consolidated into a new scheme.

In the *first substage* (birth to about 1 month), neonates begin to exercise some control over their inborn reflexes, engaging in a behavior even when its normal stimulus is not present. For example, newborns suck reflexively when their lips are touched. But they soon learn to find the nipple even when they are not touched, and they suck at times when they are not hungry. These newer behaviors illustrate how infants modify and extend the scheme for sucking.

In the *second substage* (about 1 to 4 months), babies learn to repeat a pleasant bodily sensation first achieved by chance (say, sucking their thumbs, as in the first part of Figure 5-3). Also, they begin to turn toward sounds, showing the ability to coordinate different kinds of sensory information (vision and hearing).

Guidepost

3. How did Piaget explain early cognitive development, and how well have his claims stood up?

sensorimotor stage In Piaget's theory, first stage in cognitive development, during which infants learn through senses and motor activity.

schemes Piaget's term for organized patterns of behavior used in particular situations.

circular reactions Piaget's term for processes by which an infant learns to reproduce desired occurrences originally discovered by chance.

Table 5-2   Six Substages of Piaget's Sensorimotor Stage of Cognitive Development*

Substage	Ages	Description	Behavior
1. Use of reflexes	Birth to 1 month	Infants exercise their inborn reflexes and gain some control over them. They do not coordinate information from their senses. They do not grasp an object they are looking at.	Dorri begins sucking when her mother's breast is in her mouth.
2. Primary circular reactions	1 to 4 months	Infants repeat pleasurable behaviors that first occur by chance (such as thumb sucking). Activities focus on the infant's body rather than the effects of the behavior on the environment. Infants make first acquired adaptations; that is, they suck different objects differently. They begin to coordinate sensory information and grasp objects.	When given a bottle, Dylan, who is usually breast-fed, is able to adjust his sucking to the rubber nipple.
3. Secondary circular reactions	4 to 8 months	Infants become more interested in the environment; they repeat actions that bring interesting results (such as shaking a rattle) and prolong interesting experiences. Actions are intentional but not initially goal directed.	Alejandro pushes pieces of dry cereal over the edge of his high chair tray one at a time and watches each piece as it falls to the floor.
4. Coordination of secondary schemes	8 to 12 months	Behavior is more deliberate and purposeful (intentional) as infants coordinate previously learned schemes (such as looking at and grasping a rattle) and use previously learned behaviors to attain their goals (such as crawling across the room to get a desired toy). They can anticipate events.	Anica pushes the button on her musical nursery rhyme book, and "Twinkle, Twinkle, Little Star" plays. She pushes this button over and over again, choosing it instead of the buttons for the other songs.
5. Tertiary circular reactions	12 to 18 months	Toddlers show curiosity and experimentation; they purposefully vary their actions to see results (for example, by shaking different rattles to hear their sounds). They actively explore their world to determine what is novel about an object, event, or situation. They try out new activities and use trial and error in solving problems.	When Bjorn's big sister holds his favorite board book up to his crib bars, he reaches for it. His first efforts to bring the book into his crib fail because the book is too wide. Soon, Bjorn turns the book sideways and hugs it, delighted with his success.
6. Mental combinations	18 to 24 months	Since toddlers can mentally represent events, they are no longer confined to trial and error to solve problems. Symbolic thought enables toddlers to begin to think about events and anticipate their consequences without always resorting to action. Toddlers begin to demonstrate insight. They can use symbols, such as gestures and words, and can pretend.	Jenny plays with her shape box, searching carefully for the right hole for each shape before trying—and succeeding.

*Note: Infants show enormous cognitive growth during Piaget's sensorimotor stage, as they learn about the world through their senses and their motor activities. Note their progress in problem solving and the coordination of sensory information. All ages are approximate.

The *third substage* (about 4 to 8 months) coincides with a new interest in manipulating objects and learning about their properties. Babies intentionally repeat an action not merely for its own sake, as in the second substage, but to get results *beyond the infant's own body.* For example, a baby this age will repeatedly shake a rattle to hear its noise, or (as in the second part of Figure 5-3) coo when a friendly face appears, so as to make the face stay longer.

By the time infants reach the *fourth substage,* (about 8 to 12 months), they have learned to generalize from past experience to solve new problems. They will crawl to get something they want, grab it, or push away a barrier to it (such as someone else's hand). They modify and coordinate previous schemes, such as the schemes for crawling, pushing, and grabbing, to find one that works. This substage marks the development of complex, goal-directed behavior.

In the *fifth substage* (about 12 to 18 months), babies will *vary* an action to get a similar result. For example, a toddler may squeeze a rubber duck that squeaked when stepped on, to see whether it will squeak again (as in the third part of Figure 5-3).

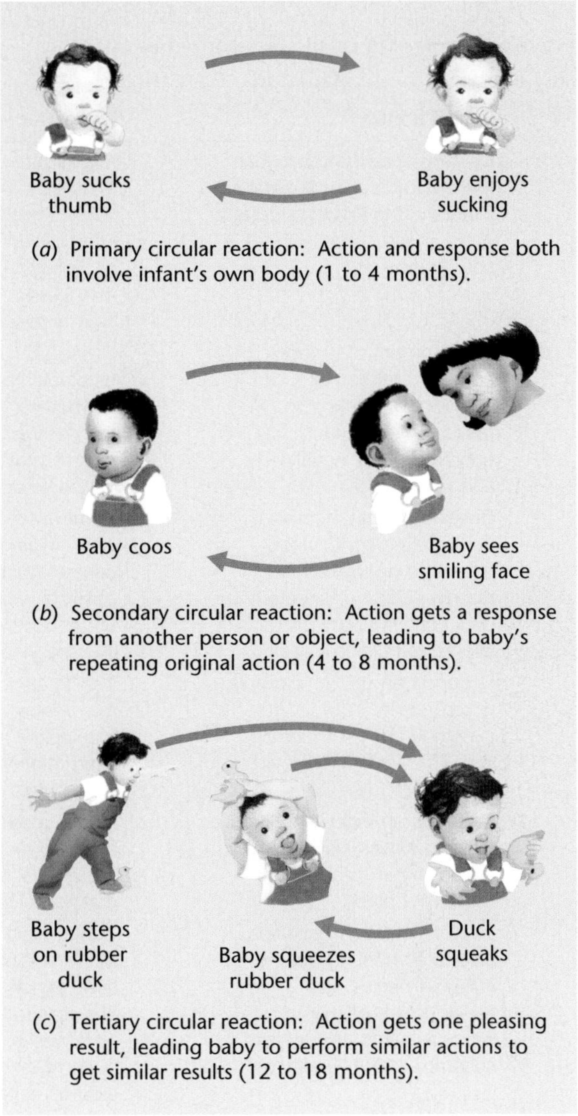

Figure 5-3
Primary, secondary, and tertiary circular reactions.

(a) Primary circular reaction: Action and response both involve infant's own body (1 to 4 months).

(b) Secondary circular reaction: Action gets a response from another person or object, leading to baby's repeating original action (4 to 8 months).

(c) Tertiary circular reaction: Action gets one pleasing result, leading baby to perform similar actions to get similar results (12 to 18 months).

For the first time, children show originality in problem solving. By trial and error, they try out new behaviors until they find the best way to attain a goal.

The *sixth substage* (about 18 months to 2 years) is a transition to the preoperational stage of early childhood. **Representational ability**—the ability to mentally represent objects and actions in memory, largely through symbols such as words, numbers, and mental pictures—frees children from immediate experience. They can pretend, and their representational ability affects the sophistication of their pretending (Bornstein, Haynes, O'Reilly, & Painter, 1996). They can think about actions before taking them. They no longer have to go through laborious trial and error to solve problems. Piaget's daughter Lucienne seemed to show representational ability when, in figuring out how to pry open a partially closed matchbox to remove a watch chain, she opened her mouth wider to represent her idea of widening the opening in the box (Piaget, 1936/1952).

During these six substages, infants develop the abilities to think and remember. They also develop knowledge about certain aspects of the physical world, notably, about objects and spatial relationships. Researchers following in Piaget's footsteps have found that some of these developments conform fairly closely to his observations, but others, including representational ability, may occur earlier than Piaget believed

representational ability Piaget's term for capacity to store mental images or symbols of objects and events.

Table 5-3 Key Developments of the Sensorimotor Stage

Concept or Skill	Piaget's View	More Recent Findings
Object permanence	Develops gradually between the third and sixth substage. Infants in the fourth substage (8–12 months) make the A, not-B error.	Infants as young as 3½ months (second substage) seem to show object knowledge, though interpretation of findings is in dispute. The A, not-B error may persist into the second year or longer.
Spatial knowledge	Development of object concept and spatial knowledge is linked to self-locomotion and coordination of visual and motor information.	Research supports Piaget's timetable and the relationship of spatial judgments to the decline of egocentrism. Link to motor development is less clear.
Causality	Develops slowly between 4–6 months and 1 year, based on an infant's discovery, first of effects of own actions and then of effects of outside forces.	Some evidence suggests early awareness of specific causal events in the physical world, but general understanding of causality may be slower to develop.
Number	Depends on use of symbols, which begins in the sixth substage (18–24 months).	Infants as young as 5 months may recognize and mentally manipulate small numbers, but interpretation of findings is in dispute.
Categorization	Depends on representational thinking, which develops during the sixth substage (18–24 months).	Infants as young as 3 months seem to recognize perceptual categories, and 7-month-olds categorize by function.
Imitation	Invisible imitation develops around 9 months; deferred imitation begins after development of mental representations in the sixth substage (18–24 months).	Controversial studies have found invisible imitation of facial expressions in newborns and deferred imitation as early as 6 weeks. Deferred imitation of complex activities seems to exist as early as 6 months.

possible. (Table 5-3 compares Piaget's views on these and other topics with more recent findings; refer back to this table as you read on.)

Do Imitative Abilities Develop Earlier Than Piaget Thought? Piaget maintained that **invisible imitation**—imitation using parts of the body that a baby cannot see, such as the mouth—develops at about 9 months, after **visible imitation,** the use of hands or feet, for example, which babies can see. Yet in a series of studies by Andrew Meltzoff and M. Keith Moore (1983, 1989), babies less than 72 hours old appeared to imitate adults by opening their mouths and sticking out their tongues, as well as by duplicating adults' head movements.

However, a review of Meltzoff's and Moore's work and of attempts to replicate it found clear, consistent evidence of only one apparently imitative movement— sticking out the tongue (Anisfeld, 1996)—and that response disappears by about 2 months of age. Since it seems unlikely that an early and short-lived imitative capacity would be limited to one gesture, some researchers have instead suggested that the tongue thrust may serve other purposes, perhaps as an early attempt to interact with the mother or simply as exploratory behavior aroused by the intriguing sight of an adult tongue (Bjorklund, 1997; S. S. Jones, 1996). Pending further research, then, the age when invisible imitation begins remains in doubt.

invisible imitation Imitation with parts of one's body that one cannot see.

visible imitation Imitation with parts of one's body that one can see.

Piaget also held that children under 18 months cannot engage in **deferred imitation** of an act they saw some time before because they have not yet developed the ability to retain mental representations. However, Piaget may have underestimated infants' and toddlers' representational ability because of their limited ability to talk about what they remember. Babies as young as 6 *weeks* have imitated an adult's facial movements after a 24-hour delay, in the presence of the same adult, who this time was expressionless. This suggests that very young babies can retain a mental representation of an event (Meltzoff & Moore, 1994, 1998). Deferred imitation of novel or complex events seems to begin by 6 to 9 months (Meltzoff & Moore, 1998; Bauer, 2002). Thus, the findings on deferred imitation agree with those on operant conditioning (Rovee-Collier, 1999); infants do seem capable of remembering after a delay.

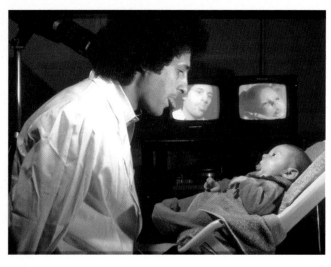

Is this infant imitating the researcher's stuck-out tongue? Studies by Andrew N. Meltzoff suggest that infants as young as 2 weeks are capable of invisible imitation. But other researchers found that only the youngest babies make this response, suggesting that the tongue movement may merely be exploratory behavior.

In **elicited imitation,** researchers induce infants and toddlers to imitate a specific series of actions they have seen but not necessarily done before. The initial demonstration may be accompanied by a simple verbal explanation (Bauer, 1996, 2002; Bauer, Wenner, Dropik, & Wewerka, 2000; Bauer, Wiebe, Carver, Waters, & Nelson, 2003). After a one-month delay, with no further demonstration or explanation, 42 to 45 percent of 9-month-olds can reproduce a simple two-step procedure, such as dropping a toy car down a vertical chute and then pushing the car with a rod to make it roll to the end of a track and turn on a light (Bauer, 2002; Bauer et al., 2003). One study reliably predicted individual differences in performance of this task from scans of the infants' brains as they looked at photos of the same procedure a week after first seeing it. The memory traces of infants who could not repeat the procedure in the right order were less robust, indicating that they had failed to consolidate the memory for long-term storage (Bauer et al., 2003).

Elicited imitation is much more reliable during the second year of life; nearly 8 out of 10 toddlers 13 to 20 months old can repeat an unfamiliar, multistep sequence (such as putting together a metal gong and causing it to ring) as much as a year later (Bauer, 1996; Bauer et al., 2000). Prior practice helps to reactivate children's memories, especially if some new items have been substituted for the original ones (Hayne, Barr, & Herbert, 2003). Four factors seem to determine young children's long-term recall: (1) the number of times a sequence of events has been experienced, (2) whether the child actively participates or merely observes, (3) whether the child is given verbal reminders of the experience, and (4) whether the sequence of events occurs in a logical, causal order (Bauer et al., 2000).

Development of Knowledge about Objects and Space The *object concept—* the idea that objects have their own independent existence, characteristics, and locations in space—is fundamental to an orderly view of physical reality. The object concept is the basis for children's awareness that they themselves exist apart from objects and other people. It is essential to understanding a world full of objects and events. Doddy Darwin's struggle to understand the existence and location of reflective images was part of his development of an object concept.

When Does Object Permanence Develop? One aspect of the object concept is **object permanence,** the realization that an object or person continues to exist when out of sight. The development of this concept in many cultures can be seen in the game of peekaboo (see Box 5-1).

deferred imitation Piaget's term for reproduction of an observed behavior after the passage of time by calling up a stored symbol of it.

elicited imitation Research method in which infants or toddlers are induced to imitate a specific series of actions they have seen but not necessarily done before.

object permanence Piaget's term for the understanding that a person or object still exists when out of sight.

BOX 5-1

Window on the World

Playing Peekaboo

In rural South Africa, a Bantu mother smiles at her 9-month-old son, covers her eyes with her hands, and asks, "Uphi?" (Where?) After 3 seconds, the mother says, "Here!" and uncovers her eyes to the baby's delight. In Tokyo, a Japanese mother plays the same game with her 12-month-old daughter, who shows the same joyous response. In suburban Connecticut, a 15-month-old boy who sees his grandfather for the first time in two months raises his shirt to cover his eyes—as Grandpa did on his previous visit.

Peekaboo is played across diverse cultures, using similar routines (Fernald & O'Neill, 1993). In all cultures in which the game is played,* the moment when the mother or other caregiver reappears is exhilarating. It is marked by exaggerated gestures and voice tones. Infants' pleasure from the immediate sensory stimulation of the game is heightened by their fascination with faces and voices, especially the high-pitched tones the adult usually uses.

The game serves several important purposes. Psychoanalysts say that it helps babies master anxiety when their mother disappears. Cognitive psychologists see it as a way babies play with developing ideas about object permanence. It may also be a social routine that helps babies learn rules that govern conversation, such as taking turns. It may provide practice in paying attention, a prerequisite for learning.

As babies develop the cognitive competency to predict future events, the game takes on new dimensions. Between 3 and 5 months, the baby's smiles and laughter as the adult's face moves in and out of view signal the infant's developing expectation of what will happen next. At 5 to 8 months, the baby shows anticipation by looking and smiling as the adult's voice alerts the infant to the adult's imminent reappearance. By 1 year, babies are no longer merely observers but usually initiate the game, actively engaging adults in play. Now it is the adult who generally responds to the baby's physical or vocal cues, which can become quite insistent if the adult doesn't feel like playing.

To help infants who are in the process of learning peekaboo or other games, parents often use *scaffolding* (see Chapter 2). In an 18-month longitudinal study at the University of Montreal, 25 mothers were videotaped playing peekaboo with their babies, using a doll as a prop (Rome-Flanders, Cronk, & Gourde, 1995). The amount and type of scaffolding varied with the infant's age and skill. Mothers frequently tried to attract a 6-month-old's attention to begin the game; this became less and less necessary as time went on. Modeling (performing the peekaboo sequence to encourage a baby to imitate it) also was most frequent at 6 months and decreased significantly by 12 months, when there was an increase in direct verbal instruction ("Cover the doll") as babies became more able to understand spoken language. Indirect verbal instruction ("Where is the doll?"), used to focus attention on the next step in the game, remained constant throughout the entire age range.

"Peekaboo!" This game, played the world over, helps babies to overcome anxiety about a parent's disappearance and to develop cognitive concepts, such as anticipation of future events.

Reinforcement (showing satisfaction with the infant's performance, for example, by saying "Peekaboo!" when the infant uncovered the doll) was fairly constant from 9 months on. The overall amount of scaffolding dropped substantially at 24 months, by which time most babies have fully mastered the game.

*The cultures included in this report are found in Malaysia, Greece, India, Iran, Russia, Brazil, Indonesia, Korea, and South Africa.

What's Your View?

Have you ever played peekaboo periodically with the same infant? If so, did you notice changes with age in the child's participation, as described in this box?

Check It Out

For more information on this topic, go to http://www.zerotothree.org/dynamic.html [an article by Steve Harvey, Ph.D., from *Zero to Three,* "Dynamic Play Therapy: Integrated Expressive Arts Approach to the Family Treatment of Infants and Toddlers"].

Piaget believed that infants develop knowledge about objects by watching the results of their own actions, in other words, by coordinating visual and motor information. In this way, he observed, object permanence develops gradually during the sensorimotor stage. At first, infants have no such concept. By the third substage, from about 4 to 8 months, they will look for something they have dropped, but if they cannot see it, they act as if it no longer exists. In the fourth substage, about 8 to 12 months, they will look for an object in a place where they first found it after seeing it hidden, even if they later saw it being moved to another place. In the fifth substage, 12 to 18 months, they no longer make this error; they will search for an object in the *last* place they saw it hidden. However, they will *not* search for it in a place where they did *not* see it hidden. By the sixth substage, 18 to 24 months, object permanence is fully achieved; toddlers will look for an object even if they did not see it hidden.

This baby seems to be showing some concept of object permanence by searching for an object that is partially hidden. The age when object permanence begins to develop is in dispute.

Recent research suggests that Piaget may have underestimated young infants' grasp of object permanence because of his testing methods. Babies may fail to search for hidden objects because they cannot yet carry out a two-step or two-handed sequence of actions, such as moving a cushion or lifting the cover of a box before grasping the object. When given repeated opportunities, over a period of one to three months, to explore, manipulate, and learn about such a task, infants in the last half of their first year can do it (Bojczyk & Corbetta, 2004).

Furthermore, when object permanence is tested with a more age-appropriate procedure, in which the object is hidden only by darkness and thus can be retrieved in one motion, infants in the third substage (4 to 8 months) perform surprisingly well. In one study, 6½-month-olds saw a ball drop down a chute and land in one of two spots, each identifiable by a distinctive sound. When the light was turned off and the procedure was repeated, the babies reached for the ball in the appropriate location, guided only by the sound (Goubet & Clifton, 1998). This showed that they knew the ball continued to exist and could tell where it had gone.

Methods based only on infants' looking behavior eliminate the need for *any* motor activity and thus can be used at very early ages. As we will discuss in the next major section of this chapter, recent, controversial research using information-processing methodology suggests that infants as young as 3 or 4 months old seem not only to have a sense of object permanence but also to understand causality and categorization, to have a rudimentary concept of number, and to know other principles governing the physical world.

Symbolic Development, Pictorial Competence, and Spatial Thinking As Piaget suggested, the growth of representational thinking enables children to make more accurate judgments about objects and spatial relationships. One manifestation of this development is the growth of *pictorial competence,* the ability to understand the nature of pictures (De Loache, Pierroutsakos, & Uttal, 2003).

In studies carried out in both the United States and Africa's Ivory Coast, infants were observed using their hands to explore pictures as if they were objects—feeling, rubbing, patting, or grasping them or attempting to lift a depicted object off the page. This manual exploration of pictures diminishes by 15 months, but not until about 19 months—according to Piaget, the dawn of representational thought—do children show, by pointing at a picture of a bear or telephone while saying its name ("beh" or "teltone"), an understanding that a picture is a representation of something else. Even at 18 months, children are as likely to look at a picture upside down as

According to the **dual representation hypothesis,** pictorial competence develops slowly because it is difficult for young children to mentally represent both a picture (or other representation of reality) and the object or objects it stands for (DeLoache et al., 2003). Although 2-year-olds can use representational understanding to guide them to the actual location of something shown in a photograph (Suddendorf, 2003), they have difficulty using scale models. Apparently they tend to think of the model as an object in itself, rather than a representation of something else (DeLoache, 2000). In one experiment, 2½-year-olds who were told that a "shrinking machine" had shrunk a room to the size of a miniature model were more successful in finding a toy hidden in the room on the basis of its position in the model than were children the same age who were told that the "little room" was just like the "big room." What makes the second task harder, according to the dual representation hypothesis, is that it requires a child to mentally represent both the symbol (the "little room") and its relationship to the thing it stands for (the "big room") at the same time. With the "shrinking machine," children do not have to perform this dual operation, because they are told that the room and the model are one and the same. Three-year-olds do not seem to have this problem with models (DeLoache, Miller, & Rosengren, 1997).

Although toddlers may spend a good deal of time watching television, they may not at first realize that what they are seeing is a representation of reality. In one experiment, 2- and 2½-year-olds watched on a video monitor as an adult hid an object in an adjoining room. When taken to the room, the 2½-year-olds found the hidden object easily, but 2-year-olds could not. Yet the younger children did find the object if they had watched through a window as it was being hidden (Troseth & DeLoache, 1998). Apparently, what the 2-year-olds lacked was representational understanding of screen images. In a follow-up experiment, 2-year-olds watched themselves "live" on home videos while their parents pointed out that what they saw was actually happening. After two weeks of this training, the children were able to find an object after seeing it hidden on video (Troseth, 2003).

The dual representation hypothesis has practical implications. It means that preschool teachers should not assume that children will understand when they use concrete objects, such as blocks of varying sizes, to stand for abstract concepts, such as numerical relationships.

Evaluating Piaget's Sensorimotor Stage According to Piaget, the journey from reflex behavior to the beginnings of thought is a long, slow one. For a year and a half or so, babies learn only from their senses and movements; not until the last half of the second year do they make the breakthrough to conceptual thought. Now, as we have seen, research using simplified tasks and modern tools suggests that certain limitations Piaget saw in infants' early cognitive abilities may instead have reflected immature linguistic and motor skills.

In some ways, then, infants and toddlers seem to be more cognitively competent than Piaget imagined. This does not mean that infants come into the world with minds fully formed. As Piaget observed, immature forms of cognition precede more mature forms. We can see this, for example, in the errors young infants make in searching for hidden objects. However, Piaget may have been mistaken in his emphasis on motor experience as the primary "engine" of cognitive growth. Infants' perceptions are far ahead of their motor abilities, and today's methods enable researchers to make observations and inferences about those perceptions. The relationship between perception and cognition is a major area of investigation, as we will discuss in the next section.

---

dual representation hypothesis Proposal that children under the age of 3 have difficulty grasping spatial relationships because of the need to keep more than one mental representation in mind at the same time.

What's Your View?

- What comments might Piaget have made about Darwin's diary entries on his son's early cognitive development?

- On the basis of observations by Piaget and the research they inspired, what factors would you consider in designing or purchasing a toy for an infant or toddler?

Checkpoint

Can you . . .

✔ Summarize major developments during the six substages of the sensorimotor stage?

✔ Explain how primary, secondary, and tertiary circular reactions work?

✔ Tell why the development of representational ability is important?

✔ Summarize Piaget's views on object permanence and spatial knowledge?

✔ Explain why Piaget may have underestimated some of infants' cognitive abilities, and discuss the implications of more recent research?

Studying Cognitive Development: Newer Approaches

During the past few decades, researchers have turned to three new approaches to add to our knowledge about infants' and toddlers' cognitive development:

- The **information-processing approach** focuses on the processes involved in perception, learning, memory, and problem solving. It seeks to discover what people do with information from the time they encounter it until they use it.

- The **cognitive neuroscience approach** examines the "hardware" of the central nervous system. It attempts to identify what brain structures are involved in specific aspects of cognition.

- The **social-contextual approach** examines environmental aspects of the learning process, particularly the role of parents and other caregivers.

information-processing approach Approach to the study of cognitive development by analyzing processes involved in perceiving and handling information.

cognitive neuroscience approach Approach to the study of cognitive development that links brain processes with cognitive ones.

social-contextual approach Approach to the study of cognitive development by focusing on environmental influences, particularly parents and other caregivers.

Information-Processing Approach: Perceptions and Representations

Like the psychometric approach, information-processing theory is concerned with individual differences in intelligent behavior. Unlike the psychometric approach, it aims to describe the mental processes involved when people acquire and remember information or solve problems, rather than merely inferring differences in mental functioning from answers given or problems solved.

Information-processing research uses new methods to test ideas about cognitive development that sprang from earlier approaches. For example, information-processing researchers analyze the separate parts of a complex task, such as Piaget's object search tasks, to figure out what abilities are necessary for each part of the task and at what age these abilities develop. Information-processing researchers also measure, and draw inferences from, what infants pay attention to, and for how long.

Guidepost

4. How can we measure infants' ability to process information, and how does this ability relate to future intelligence?

Habituation At about 6 weeks, Stefan lies peacefully in his crib near a window, sucking a pacifier. It is a cloudy day, but suddenly the sun breaks through, and an angular shaft of light appears on the end of the crib. Stefan stops sucking for a few moments, staring at the pattern of light and shade. Then he looks away and starts sucking again.

We don't know what was going on in Stefan's mind when he saw the shaft of light, but we can tell by his sucking and looking behavior at what point he began paying attention and when he stopped. Much information-processing research with infants is based on **habituation,** a type of learning in which repeated or continuous exposure to a stimulus (such as the shaft of light) reduces attention to that stimulus. In other words, familiarity breeds loss of interest. As infants habituate, they transform the novel into the familiar, the unknown into the known.

habituation Type of learning in which familiarity with a stimulus reduces, slows, or stops a response.

Researchers study habituation in newborns by repeatedly presenting a stimulus (usually a sound or visual pattern) and then monitoring such responses as heart rate, sucking, eye movements, and brain activity. A baby who has been sucking typically stops when the stimulus is first presented, orients his or her attention to the new stimulus (as Stefan did), and does not start sucking again until after it has ended. After the same sound or sight has been presented again and again, it loses its novelty and no longer causes the baby to stop sucking. Resumption of uninterrupted sucking shows that the infant has *habituated* to the stimulus. A new sight or sound, however, will capture the baby's attention and the baby will again stop sucking. This increased response to a new stimulus is called **dishabituation.**

dishabituation Increase in responsiveness after presentation of a new stimulus.

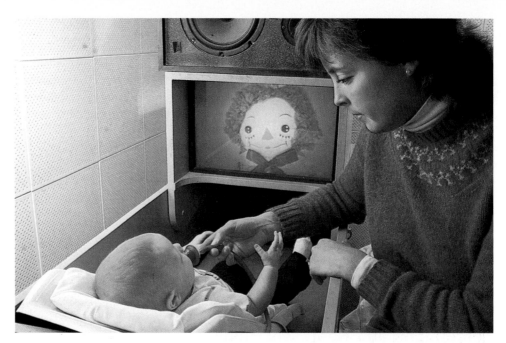

Can this baby tell the difference between Raggedy Ann and Raggedy Andy? This researcher may find out by seeing whether the baby has habituated—gotten used to one face— and then stops sucking on the nipple when a new face appears, showing recognition of the difference.

Researchers gauge the efficiency of infants' information processing by measuring how quickly babies habituate to familiar stimuli, how fast their attention recovers when they are exposed to new stimuli, and how much time they spend looking at the new and the old. Efficiency of habituation correlates with later signs of cognitive development, such as a preference for complexity, rapid exploration of the environment, sophisticated play, quick problem solving, and the ability to match pictures. Indeed, as we will see, speed of habituation and other information-processing abilities show promise as predictors of intelligence (Bornstein & Sigman, 1986; Colombo, 1993; McCall & Carriger, 1993).

Visual and Auditory Perceptual and Processing Abilities The amount of time a baby spends looking at different kinds of sights is a measure of **visual preference,** which is based on the ability to make visual distinctions. Babies less than 2 days old seem to prefer curved lines to straight lines, complex patterns to simple patterns, three-dimensional objects to two-dimensional objects, pictures of faces (or facelike configurations) to pictures of other things, and new sights to familiar ones (Fantz, 1963, 1964, 1965; Fantz, Fagen, & Miranda, 1975; Fantz & Nevis, 1967; Turati, Simion, Milani, & Umilta, 2002). The latter tendency is called *novelty preference.*

Visual recognition memory can be measured by showing an infant two stimuli side by side, one familiar and one novel. A longer gaze at the new stimulus indicates that the infant recognizes the other stimulus as something seen before. Visual recognition memory depends on comparing incoming information with information the infant already has—in other words, on the ability to form and refer to mental representations (P. R. Zelazo, Kearsley, & Stack, 1995).

Contrary to Piaget's view, habituation and novelty preference studies suggest that at least a rudimentary representational ability exists at birth or very soon after and quickly becomes more efficient. Individual differences in efficiency of information processing reflect the speed with which infants form and refer to such mental images. When shown two sights at the same time, infants who quickly shift attention from one to another tend to have better recognition memory and stronger novelty preference than

visual preference Tendency of infants to spend more time looking at one sight than another.

visual recognition memory Ability to distinguish a familiar visual stimulus from an unfamiliar one when shown both at the same time.

infants who take longer looks at a single sight (Jankowski, Rose, & Feldman, 2001; Rose, Feldman, & Jankowski, 2001; Stoecker, Colombo, Frick, & Allen, 1998).

Auditory discrimination studies also are based on attentional preference. Such studies have found that newborns can tell sounds they have already heard from those they have not. In one study, infants who heard a certain speech sound one day after birth appeared to remember that sound 24 hours later, as shown by a reduced tendency to turn their heads toward the sound and even a tendency to turn away (Swain, Zelazo, & Clifton, 1993). Indeed, as we discussed in Chapters 3 and 4, newborns even seem to remember sounds they heard in the womb.

Piaget believed that the senses are unconnected at birth and are only gradually integrated through experience. If so, this integration begins almost immediately. The fact that neonates will look at a source of sound shows that they associate hearing and sight. A more sophisticated ability is **cross-modal transfer,** the ability to use information gained from one sense to guide another—as when a person negotiates a dark room by feeling for the location of familiar objects or identifies objects by sight after feeling them with eyes closed. In one study, 1-month-olds showed that they could transfer information gained from sucking (touch) to vision. When the infants saw a rigid object (a hard plastic cylinder) and a flexible one (a wet sponge) being manipulated by a pair of hands, the infants looked longer at the object they had just sucked (Gibson & Walker, 1984). The use of cross-modal transfer to judge some other properties of objects, such as shape, seems to develop a few months later (Maurer, Stager, & Mondloch, 1999). By 5 to 7 months, infants can link the feeling of their legs kicking to a visual image of that motion (Schmuckler & Fairhall, 2001).

Researchers also study how attention itself develops (Colombo, 2001). From birth to 8 or 10 weeks, the amount of time infants typically gaze at a new sight increases. Between about 2 and 9 months, looking time shortens as infants learn to scan objects more efficiently and shift attention. Later in the first year and into the second, when sustaining attention becomes more voluntary and task oriented, looking time plateaus or increases (Colombo, 2002; Colombo et al., 2004). Five-month-olds have been trained to distribute attention more efficiently and thus to improve processing (Jankowski et al., 2001). The capacity for *joint attention,* or *joint perceptual exploration*—which may contribute to social interaction, language acquisition, and the understanding of others' mental states—develops by 12 months, when babies respond to adults' gaze by looking or pointing in the same direction (Brooks & Meltzoff, 2002). Watching television in infancy and toddlerhood (see Box 5-2) may impede attentional development. In a nationally representative longitudinal study, the more hours children spent viewing television at ages 1 and 3, the more likely they were to have attentional problems at age 7 (Christakis, Zimmerman, DiGiuseppe, & McCarty, 2004).

Speed of processing increases rapidly during the first year of life. It continues to increase during the second and third years, as toddlers become better able to separate new information from information they have already processed (P. R. Zelazo et al., 1995). Children born preterm or with very low birth weight tend to process information more slowly than those born full term (Rose & Feldman, 2000; Rose, Feldman, & Jankowski, 2002).

Information Processing as a Predictor of Intelligence Because of a weak correlation between infants' scores on developmental tests and their later IQ, many psychologists believed that the cognitive functioning of infants had little in common with that of older children and adults—in other words, that there was a discontinuity in cognitive development. Piaget believed this too. However, when researchers assess how infants and toddlers process information, some aspects of mental development seem to be fairly continuous from birth (McCall & Carriger, 1993).

cross-modal transfer Ability to use information gained by one sense to guide another.

BOX 5-2

Practically Speaking
Do Infants and Toddlers Watch Too Much Television?

Six-month-old Jenny reclines in her bouncy seat, watching a Baby Einstein DVD. She bounces up and down, claps, and laughs out loud as bright images flash across the screen. Jenny has been watching Baby Einstein videos since she was 5 weeks old.

Jenny is neither precocious nor unusual, according to a nationally representative random-dialed survey of 1,000 parents of preschoolers, sponsored by the Henry J. Kaiser Family Foundation. On a typical day, 59 percent of children under 2 watch television, 42 percent watch a video or DVD, 5 percent use a computer, and 3 percent play video games. These children spend an average of two hours and five minutes a day in front of a screen, more than twice as much time as they spend being read to (see figure).

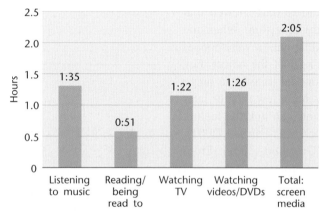

Average amount of time children under 2 spend on media and other activities in a typical day, according to mothers' reports. Note: These data include only children who participate in these activities. (Source: Rideout et al., 2003.)

An avalanche of media geared to infants and toddlers has occurred since the late 1990s: the first television show targeting children as young as 12 months, computer games with special keyboard toppers for infants as young as 9 months, and educational videotapes and DVDs (with accompanying books, flashcards, and puppets) aimed at infants from 1 to 18 months old.

According to the Kaiser survey, 74 percent of children under 2 watch television, and 26 percent have TV sets in their bedrooms. Two-thirds (66 percent) of children 3 and younger turn on the TV by themselves, 52 percent change channels with a remote device, and 30 percent put in a video or DVD by themselves.

Babies in whose households television is frequently on are more likely to start watching before their first birthday than babies not exposed to such heavy doses of TV. The "heavy watchers" are more likely to watch every day, watch for a longer time, and spend less time being read to. They also are less likely to learn to read by age 6.

All of this flies in the face of recommendations by the American Academy of Pediatrics Committee on Public Education (2001) that children under 2 be discouraged from watching television and instead be engaged in interactive activities that promote brain development, such as talking, playing, singing, and reading with parents. Most parents in the Kaiser survey expressed faith in the educational value of the media and said their children were more likely to imitate positive behaviors, such as sharing and helping, than aggressive behaviors. Parents who value and exhibit positive behavior tend to steer children toward stories, films, and television programs that depict such behavior (Singer & Singer, 1998).

Further study is needed to find out how heavy exposure to television affects infants and toddlers. Researchers need to investigate such questions as whether the constant presence of background media interferes with the development of physical coordination and language; whether time spent with media takes away from time playing outdoors, reading, or interacting with parents; whether it contributes to a sedentary lifestyle; whether video and computer games help visual and spatial skills or risk eyestrain and ergonomic problems; how various types of media impact cognitive development and attention span; and what is the extent and effect of young children's exposure to noneducational content.

Source: Unless otherwise referenced, this box is based on Rideout, Vandewater, & Wartella, 2003.

What's Your View?

At what age would you let a baby watch television or a videotape or play a computer game, and what restrictions, if any, would you place on such activities?

Check It Out

For more information on this topic, go to http://www.kff.org/entmedia102803nr.cfm [the Kaiser Foundation report discussed in this box].

Children who, from the start, are efficient at taking in and interpreting sensory information later score well on intelligence tests.

In many longitudinal studies, habituation and attention-recovery abilities during the first 6 months to 1 year of life were moderately useful in predicting childhood IQ. So was visual recognition memory (Bornstein & Sigman, 1986; Colombo, 1993; McCall & Carriger, 1993). In one study, a combination of visual recognition memory at 7 months and cross-modal transfer at 1 year predicted IQ at age 11 and also showed a modest (but nonetheless remarkable after 10 years!) relationship to processing speed and memory at that age (Rose & Feldman, 1995, 1997).

Visual reaction time and *visual anticipation* can be measured by the *visual expectation paradigm.* In this research design, a series of computer-generated pictures briefly appears, some on the right and some on the left sides of an infant's peripheral visual field. The same sequence of pictures is repeated several times. The infant's eye movements are measured to see how quickly his or her gaze shifts to a picture that has just appeared (reaction time) or to the place where the infant expects the next picture to appear (anticipation). These measurements are thought to indicate attentiveness and processing speed, as well as the tendency to form expectations on the basis of experience. In a longitudinal study, visual reaction time and visual anticipation at 3½ months correlated with IQ at age 4 (Dougherty & Haith, 1997). Reaction time and anticipation seem to improve up to 8 or 9 months of age (Reznick, Chawarska, & Betts, 2000).

All in all, there is much evidence that the abilities infants use to process sensory information are related to the cognitive abilities intelligence tests measure. Still, we need to be cautious in interpreting these findings. Most of the studies used small samples. Also, the predictability of childhood IQ from measures of habituation and recognition memory is only modest; it is no higher than the predictability from parental educational level and socioeconomic status and not as high as the predictability from some other infant behaviors, such as early vocalization. Furthermore, predictions based on information-processing measures alone do not take into account the influence of environmental factors (Colombo & Janowsky, 1998; Laucht, Esser, & Schmidt, 1994; McCall & Carriger, 1993). For example, maternal responsiveness in early infancy seems to play a part in the link between early attentional abilities and cognitive abilities later in childhood (Bornstein & Tamis-LeMonda, 1994) and even at age 18 (Sigman, Cohen, & Beckwith, 1997).

Checkpoint
Can you . . .

✔ Summarize three newer approaches to the study of cognitive development?

✔ Explain how habituation measures the efficiency of infants' information processing?

✔ Identify several early perceptual and processing abilities that serve as predictors of intelligence?

Information Processing and the Development of Piagetian Abilities As we mentioned in a previous section, new evidence suggests that several of the cognitive abilities Piaget described as developing toward the end of the sensorimotor stage actually arise much earlier. Research based on infants' visual processing has given developmental scientists a new window into the timing of such cognitive developments as causality, categorization, object permanence, and number, all of which depend on formation of mental representations (refer back to Table 5-3).

Guidepost

5. When do babies begin to think about characteristics of the physical world?

Causality An understanding of *causality,* the principle that one event causes another, is important because it "allows people to predict and control their world" (L. B. Cohen, Rundell, Spellman, & Cashon, 1999). Piaget believed that this understanding develops slowly during the first year of life. At about 4 to 6 months, as infants become able to grasp objects, they begin to recognize that they can act on their environment. Thus, said Piaget, the concept of causality is rooted in a dawning awareness of the power of one's own intentions. However, according to Piaget, infants do not yet know that causes must come before effects, and not until close to one year do they realize that forces outside of themselves can make things happen.

Some information-processing research suggests that a mechanism for recognizing causality may exist much earlier (Mandler, 1998). Infants 6½ months old have shown by habituation and dishabituation that they seem to see a difference between events that are the immediate cause of other events (such as a brick striking a second brick,

This 5-month-old baby is discovering that he can make a dangling chain rattle and swing by pulling it. As infants this age become able to grasp objects, said Piaget, they become aware of the power of their own intentions—a first step toward understanding causality.

which is then pushed out of position) and events that occur with no apparent cause (such as a brick moving away from another brick without having been struck by it). The researcher who conducted these experiments proposed that babies have an innate "brain module" for detecting causal motion or may develop it at an early age (Leslie, 1982, 1984).

Other researchers replicated these findings with 6½-month-olds but not with younger infants, casting doubt on the brain module hypothesis (L. B. Cohen & Amsel, 1998). On the basis of additional experiments with infants of different ages looking at a variety of objects moving at varying trajectories, these investigators attribute the growth of causal understanding to a gradual improvement in information-processing skills. By 7 months, infants may make causal interpretations of a particular set of objects and simple events, but not until 10 to 15 months do they perceive causality in more complex circumstances involving a chain of several events. As infants accumulate more information about how objects behave, they are better able to see causality as a general principle operating in a variety of situations (L. B. Cohen & Amsel, 1998; L. B. Cohen & Oakes, 1993; L. B. Cohen et al., 1999; Oakes, 1994).

Categorization Dividing the world into meaningful categories is vital to thinking about objects or concepts and their relationships. According to Piaget, the ability to classify, or group things into categories, does not appear until the sixth substage, around 18 months. Yet, by looking longer at items in a new category, even 3-month-olds seem to know, for example, that a dog is not a cat (Quinn, Eimas, & Rosenkrantz, 1993).

At first infants seem to categorize on the basis of perceptual features (such as shape, color, and pattern); but toward the end of the first year their categories become more conceptual, based on real-world knowledge (Oakes, Coppage, & Dingel, 1997), particularly of function (Mandler, 1998; Mandler & McDonough, 1993, 1996, 1998). Seven- to 11-month-olds seem to realize that a bird with wide wings is not in the same category as an airplane, even though they may look somewhat similar and both can fly (Mandler & McDonough, 1993). In one series of experiments, 10- and 11-month-olds recognized that chairs with zebra-striped upholstery belong in the category of furniture, not animals (Pauen, 2002).

Results vary depending on the methodology of the study, the perceptual similarity of the items shown to the infant, and the context in which they are presented (Oakes, Coppage, & Dingel, 1997; Oakes & Madole, 2000). Infants who are allowed to touch and manipulate objects rather than just look at them are more likely to form functional categories (Madole, Oakes, & Cohen, 1993).

In the second year, language becomes a factor. Hearing an experimenter name an object and/or point out its function can help 14- to 18-month-olds with category formation (Booth & Waxman, 2002).

violation-of-expectations Research method in which dishabituation to a stimulus that conflicts with experience is taken as evidence that an infant recognizes the new stimulus as surprising.

Object Permanence **Violation-of-expectations** research begins with a familiarization phase, in which infants see an event or series of events happen normally. After the infant is habituated to this procedure, the event is changed in a way that conflicts with (violates) normal expectations. An infant's tendency to look longer at the changed event is interpreted as evidence that the infant recognizes it as surprising.

Using the violation-of-expectations method, Renée Baillargeon and her colleagues claim to have found evidence of object permanence in infants as young as 3½ months. The babies appeared surprised by the failure of a tall carrot that slid behind a screen of the same height to appear in a large notch in the upper part of the screen before reappearing again on the other side (Baillargeon & DeVos, 1991; see Figure 5-4).

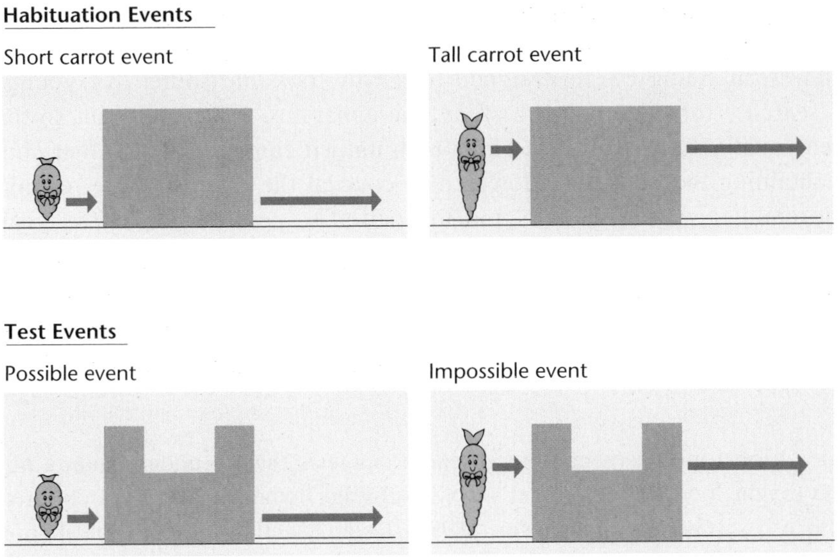

Habituation Events

Short carrot event

Tall carrot event

Test Events

Possible event

Impossible event

Figure 5-4

How early do infants show object permanence? In this experiment, 3½-month-olds watched a short carrot and then a tall carrot slide along a track, disappear behind a screen, and then reappear. After they became accustomed to seeing these events, the opaque screen was replaced by a screen with a large notch at the top. The short carrot did not appear in the notch when passing behind the screen; the tall carrot, which should have appeared in the notch, also did not. The babies looked longer at the tall than at the short carrot event, suggesting that they were surprised that the tall carrot did not reappear in the notch. (Source: Baillargeon & DeVos, 1991.)

In other research, the ability to visually follow the path of a ball that briefly passed behind a box was present at 4 months and more firmly established at 6 months (Johnson et al., 2003). Of course, the perception that an object that disappears on one side of a visual barrier looks the same as the object that reappears on the other side need not imply cognitive knowledge that the object continues to exist behind the barrier (Meltzoff & Moore, 1998). Still, such research raises the possibility that at least a rudimentary form of object permanence may be present in the early months of life.

On the basis of such findings, it has been proposed that infants are born with reasoning abilities—*innate learning mechanisms* that help them make sense of the information they encounter—or may acquire these abilities very early (Baillargeon, 1994a). Some investigators go further, suggesting that infants at birth may already have intuitive *knowledge* about basic physical principles—knowledge that then develops further with experience (Spelke, 1994, 1998). These interpretations and conclusions are highly controversial.

The violation-of-expectations method also has been used with toddlers in object search tests, with puzzling results. In one study, children watched a cylinder roll down a ramp and disappear behind a wall containing a row of four doors. A barrier jutting up from behind the wall could be placed so that the cylinder would have to stop behind one of the doors (see Figure 5-5). When asked to find the cylinder, most 3-year-olds opened the correct door, but most 2½-year-olds did not. Yet, when watching an experimenter open the doors, the 2½-year-olds, like infants in violation-of-expectations experiments, looked longer when the cylinder appeared in an "impossible" location, indicating that they knew it could not be found there. Failure to physically open the correct door may have stemmed from

Figure 5-5

Apparatus for testing young children's object search abilities. When a movable barrier is placed behind the wall and the cylinder is set rolling, most 3-year-olds will open the right door to find where the cylinder stops. Most 2½-year-olds will open a different door. (Source: Hood, Cole-Davies, & Dias, 2003, Figure 1.)

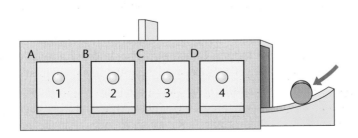

A   B   C   D

1   2   3   4

the younger children's tendency to open the door where the cylinder had been found on previous trials (Hood, Cole-Davies, & Dias, 2003).

Additional studies were designed to narrow possible sources of young children's search errors. In one such study, the apparatus was translucent so that the children could visually follow a ball's path until it came to rest. At that point the wall containing the doors was lowered to conceal the ramp and the resting ball, and the children were asked to find the ball. The performance of 2½-year-olds improved in this situation, but 2-year-olds did little better than chance would predict—in part, it seems, because they did not keep their eyes on the point where the ball had landed. Also, it may be that the younger children could not translate their knowledge of what is physically possible into appropriate action (Keen, 2003).

Number Violation-of-expectations research suggests that an understanding of number may begin long before Piaget's sixth substage, when he claimed children first begin to use symbols. Karen Wynn (1992) tested whether 5-month-old babies can add and subtract small numbers of objects. The infants watched as Mickey Mouse dolls were placed behind a screen, and a doll was either added or taken away. The screen then was lifted to reveal either the expected number or a different number of dolls. In a series of experiments, the babies looked longer at surprising "wrong" answers than at expected "right" ones, suggesting (according to Wynn) that they had mentally "computed" the right answers. Other researchers who replicated these experiments got similar results (Baillargeon, 1994b; Koechlin, Dehaene, & Mehler, 1997; Simon, Hespos, & Rochat, 1995; Uller, Carey, Huntley-Fenner, & Klatt, 1999). Wynn (1996) also found that 6-month-olds seemed to know the difference between a puppet jumping twice in a row and three times in a row—numerical comparisons that could not be taken in at a glance.

According to Wynn (1992, 1996, 2000), this research raises the possibility that numerical concepts are inborn—that when parents teach their babies numbers, they may only be teaching them the names ("one, two, three") for concepts the babies already know. However, this is mere speculation, since the infants in these studies were already 5 and 6 months old. Furthermore, infants may simply be responding perceptually to the puzzling presence of a doll they saw removed from behind the screen or the absence of a doll they saw placed there (Haith, 1998; Haith & Benson, 1998). Other studies suggest that, although infants do seem to discriminate visually between sets of, say, two and three objects, they merely notice differences in the overall contours, area, or collective mass of the sets of objects rather than compare the *number* of objects in the sets (Clearfield & Mix, 1999; Mix, Huttenlocher, & Levine, 2002).

The Piraha, an isolated Amazonian people, do not count. They have only three number-words that translate as "one," "two," and "many," and even the first two words are imprecise. In matching tasks with sticks, nuts, or other small objects, they can perform fairly accurately, but only with very small quantities of items up to two or three. When tested on larger quantities, they can estimate, but only roughly. These observations suggest, contrary to Wynn's hypothesis, that the formation of exact numerical concepts is dependent on language (Gelman & Gallistel, 2004; Gordon, 2004).

Evaluating Violation-of-Expectations Research The interpretation of violation-of-expectations studies is controversial. Does an infant's visual interest in an "impossible" condition reveal a *conceptual* understanding of the way things work or merely a *perceptual* awareness that something unusual has happened? The fact that an infant looks longer at one scene than at another may show only that the infant can see a

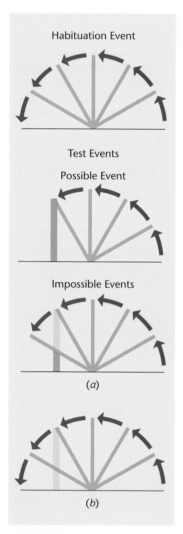

Figure 5-6

Test for infants' understanding of how a barrier works. Infants first become accustomed to seeing a "drawbridge" rotate 180 degrees on one edge. Then a box is placed beside the drawbridge. In the possible event, the drawbridge stops when it reaches the edge of the box. In the impossible events, the drawbridge rotates through part or all of the space occupied by the box. On the basis of how long they stare at each event, 4½-month-old infants seem to know that the drawbridge cannot pass through the entire box (b); but not until 6½ months do infants recognize that the drawbridge cannot pass through 80 percent of the box (a). (Source: Adapted from Baillargeon, 1994a.)

difference between the two. It does not show what the infant knows about the difference or that the infant is actually surprised. The "mental representation" the infant refers to may be no more than a brief sensory memory of something just seen. It's also possible that an infant, in becoming accustomed to the habituation event, develops the expectations that are then violated by the "surprising" event and did not have such knowledge or expectations before (Goubet & Clifton, 1998; Haith, 1998; Haith & Benson, 1998; Mandler, 1998; Munakata, 2001; Munakata, McClelland, Johnson, & Siegler, 1997).

Defenders of this research insist that a conceptual interpretation best accounts for the findings (Baillargeon, 1999; Spelke, 1998), but a recent variation on one of Baillargeon's experiments suggests otherwise. In her original research, Baillargeon (1994a) showed infants of various ages a "drawbridge" rotating 180 degrees. When the infants became habituated to the rotation, a barrier was introduced in the form of a box. At 4½ months, infants seemed to show (by longer looking) that they understood that the drawbridge could not move through the entire box (see Figure 5-6). Later investigators replicated the experiment but eliminated the box. Five-month-olds still looked longer at the 180-degree rotation than at a lesser degree of rotation, even though no barrier was present—suggesting that they simply were demonstrating a preference for greater movement (Rivera, Wakeley, & Langer, 1999). Until further research clarifies these issues, we must be cautious about inferring the existence of adultlike cognitive abilities from data that may have simpler explanations or may represent only partial achievement of mature abilities (Haith, 1998).

Cognitive Neuroscience Approach: The Brain's Cognitive Structures

Brain research bears out Piaget's belief that neurological maturation is a major factor in cognitive development. Brain growth spurts (refer back to Chapter 4) coincide with changes in cognitive behavior similar to those Piaget described (Fischer & Rose, 1994, 1995).

Some researchers have recorded shifts in brain activity to determine which brain structures affect which cognitive functions and to chart developmental changes (Nelson & Monk, 2001). Studies of normal and brain-damaged adults point to two separate long-term memory systems—*explicit* and *implicit*—that acquire and store different kinds of information. **Explicit memory** is conscious or intentional recollection, usually of facts, names, events, or other things that people can state, or declare. **Implicit memory** refers to remembering that occurs without effort or even conscious awareness; it generally pertains to habits and skills, such as knowing how to throw a ball or ride a bicycle. Brain scans provide direct physical evidence of the location of these systems (Squire, 1992; Vargha-Khadem et al., 1997).

In early infancy, when the structures responsible for memory storage are not fully formed, memories are relatively fleeting (Seress, 2001). The maturing of the hippocampus, a structure deep in the temporal lobes, along with the development of cortical structures coordinated by the hippocampal formation, makes longer-lasting memories possible (Bauer, 2002; Bauer et al., 2000, 2003). The hippocampal system continues to develop at least through the fifth year (Seress, 2001).

The *prefrontal cortex* (the large portion of the frontal lobe directly behind the forehead) is believed to control many aspects of cognition. This part of the brain develops more slowly than any other (M. H. Johnson, 1998). During the second half of the first year, the prefrontal cortex and associated circuitry develop the capacity

Checkpoint
Can you . . .

✔ Describe the violation-of-expectations research method, tell how and why it is used, and list some criticisms of it?

✔ Discuss four areas in which information-processing research challenges Piaget's account of development?

Guidepost
6. What can brain research reveal about the development of cognitive skills?

explicit memory Intentional and conscious memory, generally of facts, names, and events.

implicit memory Unconscious recall, generally of habits and skills; sometimes called *procedural memory*.

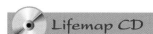
Lifemap CD

Watch the video on "Brain Development and Cognition" in Chapter 5 in your CD to see how researchers combine brain research techniques with studies of behavior.

working memory Short-term storage of information being actively processed.

for **working memory**—short-term storage of information the brain is actively processing, or working on. It is in working memory that mental representations are prepared for, or recalled from, storage.

The relatively late appearance of working memory may be largely responsible for the slow development of object permanence, which seems to be seated in a rearward area of the prefrontal cortex (Nelson, 1995). By 12 months, this region may be developed enough to permit an infant to avoid search errors by controlling the impulse to search in a place where an object previously was found (Bell & Fox, 1992; Diamond, 1991).

Although memory systems continue to develop beyond infancy, the emergence of the brain's memory structures during that period underlines the importance of environmental stimulation during the early months of life. Social-contextual theorists and researchers pay particular attention to the impact of environmental influences.

Checkpoint

Can you . . .

✔ Identify the brain structures apparently involved in explicit, implicit, and working memory, and mention a task made possible by each?

Guidepost

7. How does social interaction with adults advance cognitive competence?

guided participation Participation of an adult in a child's activity in a manner that helps to structure the activity and to bring the child's understanding of it closer to that of the adult.

Lifemap CD

View the video, "Parent-Infant Interaction," in Chapter 5 of your CD, for an example of how guided participation and cultural influences can help us understand cognitive development.

Social-Contextual Approach: Learning from Interactions with Caregivers

Researchers influenced by Vygotsky's sociocultural theory study how the cultural context affects early social interactions that may promote cognitive competence. **Guided participation** refers to mutual interactions with adults that help structure children's activities and bridge the gap between a child's understanding and an adult's. This concept was inspired by Vygotsky's view of learning as a collaborative process. Guided participation often occurs in shared play and in ordinary, everyday activities in which children learn informally the skills, knowledge, and values important in their culture.

In one cross-cultural study (Rogoff, Mistry, Göncü, & Mosier, 1993), researchers visited the homes of 14 one- to two-year-olds in each of four places: a Mayan town in Guatemala, a tribal village in India, and middle-class urban neighborhoods in Salt Lake City and Turkey. The investigators interviewed caregivers about their child rearing practices and watched them help the toddlers learn to dress themselves and to play with unfamiliar toys.

Cultural differences affected the types of guided participation the researchers observed. In the Guatemalan town, where toddlers normally saw their mothers sewing and weaving at home to help support the family, and in the Indian village, where they accompanied their mothers at work in the fields, the children customarily played alone or with older siblings while the mother worked nearby. After initial demonstration and instruction, mostly nonverbal, in, for example, how to tie shoes, the children took over, while the parent or other caregiver remained available to help. The U.S. toddlers, who had full-time homemaker mothers or were in day care, interacted with their parents in the context of child's play rather than in the parents' work or social worlds. Caregivers spoke with the children as peers and managed and motivated their learning with praise and excitement. Turkish families, who were in transition from a rural to an urban way of life, showed a pattern somewhere between the other two.

The cultural context, then, influences the way caregivers contribute to cognitive development. Direct adult involvement in children's play and learning may be better adapted to a middle-class urban community, in which parents or caregivers have more time, greater verbal skills, and possibly more interest in children's play and learning, than in a rural community in a developing country, in which children frequently observe and participate in adults' work activities (Rogoff et al., 1993).

In a cross-cultural observational study of middle-class families in Washington, D.C., and Buenos Aires, 20-month-olds playing at home with their mother engaged in similar activities in both cultures. However, the U.S. children and mothers tended to engage in more exploratory play with toys (such as dialing a telephone); Argentine children and mothers engaged in more symbolic and social play (such as feeding a doll or putting it to bed), and the mothers praised their children more. These differences seem to reflect cultural variations in goals of child raising; U.S. society is highly individualistic and stresses autonomy and assertiveness, whereas Argentine society places greater emphasis on social interdependence and connectedness (Bornstein, Haynes, Pascual, Painter, & Galperin, 1999).

Language Development

Doddy Darwin's exclamation "Ah!" to express recognition of an image in a glass is a striking example of the connection between **language,** a communication system based on words and grammar, and cognitive development. Once children know words, they can use them to represent objects and actions. They can reflect on people, places, and things; and they can communicate their needs, feelings, and ideas in order to exert control over their lives.

The growth of language illustrates the interaction of all aspects of development. As the physical structures needed to produce sounds mature and the neuronal connections necessary to associate sound and meaning become activated, social interaction with adults introduces babies to the communicative nature of speech. Let's look at the typical sequence of milestones in language development (see Table 5-4)

Checkpoint

Can you . . .

✔ Give examples of how cultural patterns affect caregivers' contributions to toddlers' learning?

Guidepost

8. How do babies develop language?

language Communication system based on words and grammar.

Table 5-4	Language Milestones from Birth to 3 Years

Age in Months	Development
Birth	Can perceive speech, cry, make some response to sound.
1½ to 3	Coos and laughs.
3	Plays with speech sounds.
5 to 6	Makes consonant sounds, trying to match what she or he hears.
6 to 10	Babbles in strings of consonants and vowels.
9	Uses gestures to communicate and plays gesture games.
9 to 10	Begins to understand words (usually "no" and baby's own name); imitates sounds.
9 to 12	Uses a few social gestures.
10 to 12	No longer can discriminate sounds not in own language.
10 to 14	Says first word (usually a label for something).
10 to 18	Says single words.
13	Understands symbolic function of naming.
13	Uses more elaborate gestures.
14	Uses symbolic gesturing.
16 to 24	Learns many new words, expanding vocabulary rapidly, going from about 50 words to as many as 400; uses verbs and adjectives.
18 to 24	Says first sentence (2 words).
20	Uses fewer gestures; names more things.
20 to 22	Has comprehension spurt.
24	Uses many two-word phrases; no longer babbles; wants to talk.
30	Learns new words almost every day; speaks in combinations of three or more words; understands very well; makes grammatical mistakes.
36	Says up to 1,000 words, 80 percent intelligible; makes some mistakes in syntax.

Source: Bates, O'Connell, & Shore, 1987; Capute, Shapiro, & Palmer, 1987; Lalonde & Werker, 1995; Lenneberg, 1969.

and at some characteristics of early speech. Then we'll consider how babies acquire language, how brain growth is linked to language development, and how parents and other caregivers contribute to it.

Sequence of Early Language Development

Before babies can use words, they make their needs and feelings known—as Doddy Darwin did—through sounds that progress from crying to cooing and babbling, then to accidental imitation, and then deliberate imitation. These sounds are known as **prelinguistic speech.** Infants also grow in the ability to recognize and understand speech sounds and to use meaningful gestures. Babies typically say their first word around the end of the first year, and toddlers begin speaking in sentences about eight months to a year later.

Early Vocalization *Crying* is a newborn's only means of communication. Different pitches, patterns, and intensities signal hunger, sleepiness, or anger (Lester & Boukydis, 1985). Between 6 weeks and 3 months, babies start *cooing* when they are happy—squealing, gurgling, and making vowel sounds like "ahhh." At about 3 to 6 months, babies begin to play with speech sounds, matching the sounds they hear from people around them.

Babbling—repeating consonant-vowel strings, such as "ma-ma-ma-ma"—occurs between 6 and 10 months of age and is often mistaken for a baby's first word. Babbling is not real language, since it does not hold meaning for the baby, but it becomes more wordlike. Language development continues with accidental *imitation of language sounds* babies hear and then imitation of themselves making these sounds. At about 9 to 10 months, infants deliberately imitate sounds without understanding them. Once they have a repertoire of sounds, they string them together in patterns that sound like language but seem to have no meaning.

Recognizing Language Sounds The ability to perceive differences between sounds is essential to language development. As we have seen, this ability is present from or even before birth, and it becomes more refined during the first year of life. In getting ready to understand and use speech, infants first become familiar with the sounds of words and phrases and later attach meanings to them (Jusczyk & Hohne, 1997).

The process apparently begins in the womb. In one experiment, two groups of Parisian women in their thirty-fifth week of pregnancy each recited a different nursery rhyme, saying it three times a day for 4 weeks. At the end of that time, researchers played recordings of both rhymes close to the women's abdomens. The fetuses' heart rates slowed when the rhyme the mother had spoken was played but not for the other rhyme. Since the voice on the tape was not that of the mother, the fetuses apparently were responding to the linguistic sounds they had heard the mother use. This suggests that hearing the "mother tongue" before birth may "pretune" an infant's ears to pick up its sounds (DeCasper, Lecanuet, Busnel, Granier-Deferre, & Maugeais, 1994).

Before infants can connect sounds to meanings, they seem to recognize sound patterns they hear frequently, such as their own names. Four-and-a-half-month-olds listen longer to their own names than to other names, even names with stress patterns similar to theirs (Mandel, Jusczyk, & Pisoni, 1995). Six-month-olds look longer at a video of their mothers when they hear the word *mommy* and of their fathers when they hear *daddy,* suggesting that they are beginning to associate sound with meaning—at least with regard to special people (Tincoff & Jusczyk, 1999). Babies this age can learn to recognize words that follow their own name or another familiar word (Bortfield, Morgan, Golinkoff, & Rathbun, 2005).

By 6 months of age, babies have learned to recognize the basic sounds, or *phonemes,* of their native language and to adjust to slight differences in the way different speakers form those sounds. In one study, 6-month-old Swedish and U.S. babies routinely ignored variations in sounds common in their own language but noticed variations in an unfamiliar language (Kuhl, Williams, Lacerda, Stevens, & Lindblom, 1992). The ability to discriminate sounds at this age predicts individual differences in language abilities at 13, 16, and 24 months, suggesting that phonetic perception plays an important part in language acquisition (Tsao, Liu, & Kuhl, 2004).

By about 10 months, babies lose their earlier sensitivity to sounds that are not part of the language they hear spoken. For example, Japanese infants no longer make a distinction between "ra" and "la," a distinction that does not exist in the Japanese language. Although the ability to perceive nonnative sounds is not entirely lost—it can be revived, with effort, in adulthood—the brain no longer routinely discriminates them (Bates, O'Connell, & Shore, 1987; Lalonde & Werker, 1995; Werker, 1989).

During the second half of the first year, as babies become increasingly familiar with the sounds of their language, they begin to become aware of its phonological rules—how sounds are arranged in speech. In one series of experiments (Marcus, Vijayan, Rao, & Vishton, 1999), 7-month-olds listened longer to "sentences" containing a different order of nonsense sounds (such as "wo fe wo," or ABA) from the order to which the infants had been habituated (such as "ga ti ti," or ABB). The sounds used in the test were different from those used in the habituation phase, so the infants' discrimination must have been based on the patterns of repetition alone. In another series of experiments based on listening time, 9-month-olds appeared to discern patterns of syllabification and pronunciation of initial and final consonants and to apply those patterns to new words that fit or violated them (Saffran & Thiessen, 2003).

Gestures At 9 months Maika *pointed* to an object, sometimes making a noise to show that she wanted it. Between 9 and 12 months, she learned some *conventional social gestures:* waving bye-bye, nodding her head to mean *yes,* and shaking her head to signify *no.* By about 13 months, she used more elaborate *representational gestures;* for example, she would hold an empty cup to her mouth to show that she wanted a drink or hold up her arms to show that she wanted to be picked up.

Symbolic gestures, such as blowing to mean *hot,* or sniffing to mean *flower,* often emerge around the same time as babies say their first words, and they function much like words. By using them, children show an understanding that symbols can refer to specific objects, events, desires, and conditions. Gestures usually appear before children have a vocabulary of 25 words and drop out when children learn the word for the idea they were gesturing and can say it instead (Lock, Young, Service, & Chandler, 1990).

This toddler is communicating with his father by pointing at something that catches his eye. Gesturing seems to come naturally to young children and may be an important part of language learning.

Gesturing seems to come naturally. In an observational study, blind children and adolescents used gestures while speaking as much as sighted children did and even while speaking to blind listeners. Apparently, then, the use of gestures does not depend on having either a model or an observer but seems to be an inherent part of the speaking process (Iverson & Goldin-Meadow, 1998).

Learning gestures seems to help babies learn to talk. In one experiment (Goodwyn & Acredolo, 1998), 11-month-olds learned gestures by watching their parents perform them while saying the corresponding words. Between 15 and 36 months, when tested on vocal language development, these children outperformed two other groups—one whose parents had only said words and another who had received neither vocal nor gestural training.

First Words   Doddy Darwin, at 11 months, said his first word ("ouchy"), which he attached to a number of objects. Doddy's development was typical in this respect. The average baby says a first word sometime between 10 and 14 months, initiating **linguistic speech**—verbal expression that conveys meaning. At first, an infant's total verbal repertoire is likely to be "mama" or "dada." Or it may be a simple syllable that has more than one meaning depending on the context in which the child utters it. "Da" may mean "I want that," "I want to go out," or "Where's Daddy?" A word like this, which expresses a complete thought, is called a **holophrase.**

linguistic speech   Verbal expression designed to convey meaning.

holophrase   Single word that conveys a complete thought.

Babies understand many words before they can use them. The first words most babies understand (*passive* vocabulary) are the ones they are likely to hear most often: their own names and the word *no.* By 13 months, most children understand that a word stands for a specific thing or event, and they can quickly learn the meaning of a new word (Woodward, Markman, & Fitzsimmons, 1994). Addition of new words to the *expressive* (spoken) vocabulary is slower at first. As children come to rely more on words than on gestures to express themselves, the sounds and rhythms of speech become more elaborate.

Sometime between 16 and 24 months, a "naming explosion" is generally thought to occur. Within a few weeks, a toddler may go from saying about 50 words to saying about 400 (Bates, Bretherton, & Snyder, 1988). These rapid gains in spoken vocabulary may reflect the increase in speed and accuracy of word recognition during the second year of life (Fernald, Pinto, Swingley, Weinberg, & McRoberts, 1998). However, in a longitudinal study of 38 U.S. children, only 5 of them showed a spurt in vocabulary learning, suggesting that this phenomenon is far from universal (Ganger & Brent, 2004).

Nouns are easier to learn than verbs (Childers & Tomasello, 2002). In a cross-cultural study, it did not matter whether a family's native language was Spanish, Dutch, French, Hebrew, Italian, Korean, or American English; in all these languages, parents reported that their 20-month-old children knew more nouns than any other class of words (Bornstein & Cote et al., 2004). At 24 to 36 months, children can figure out the meaning of unfamiliar adjectives from context or from the nouns they modify (Mintz, 2005).

First Sentences   The next important linguistic breakthrough comes when a toddler puts two words together to express one idea ("Dolly fall"). Generally, children do this between 18 and 24 months, about 8 to 12 months after they say their first word. However, this age range varies greatly. Although prelinguistic speech is fairly closely tied to chronological age, linguistic speech is not. Most children who begin talking fairly late catch up eventually—and many make up for lost time by talking nonstop to anyone who will listen! (True delayed language development is discussed in Chapter 7.)

A child's first sentences typically deal with everyday events, things, people, or activities (Braine, 1976; Rice, 1989; Slobin, 1973). Darwin noted instances in which

Doddy expressed his developing moral sense in words. At 27 months the boy gave his baby sister the last bit of his gingerbread, exclaiming, "Oh, kind Doddy, kind Doddy!"

At first children typically use **telegraphic speech,** consisting of only a few essential words. When Rita says, "Damma deep," she seems to mean "Grandma is sweeping the floor." Children's use of telegraphic speech, and the form it takes, vary, depending on the language being learned (Braine, 1976; Slobin, 1983). Word order generally conforms to what a child hears; Rita does not say "Deep Damma" when she sees her grandmother pushing a broom.

Does the omission of functional words such as *is* and *the* mean that a child does not know these words? Not necessarily; the child may merely find them hard to reproduce. Even infants are sensitive to the presence of functional words; at 10½ months, they can tell a normal passage from one in which the functional words have been replaced by similar-sounding nonsense words (Jusczyk, 2003).

Sometime between 20 and 30 months, children show increasing competence in **syntax,** the rules for putting sentences together in their language. They become somewhat more comfortable with articles (*a, the*), prepositions (*in, on*), conjunctions (*and, but*), plurals, verb endings, past tense, and forms of the verb *to be* (*am, are, is*). They also become increasingly aware of the communicative purpose of speech and of whether their words are being understood (Shwe & Markman, 1997)—a sign of growing sensitivity to the mental lives of others. By age 3, speech is fluent, longer, and more complex. Although children often omit parts of speech, they get their meaning across well.

telegraphic speech Early form of sentence use consisting of only a few essential words.

syntax Rules for forming sentences in a particular language.

Characteristics of Early Speech

Early speech has a character all its own—no matter what language a child is speaking (Slobin, 1971).

As we have seen, children *simplify.* They use telegraphic speech to say just enough to get their meaning across ("No drink milk!").

Children *understand grammatical relationships they cannot yet express.* At first, Nina may understand that a dog is chasing a cat, but she cannot string together enough words to express the complete action. Her sentence comes out as "Puppy chase" rather than "Puppy chase kitty."

Children *underextend word meanings.* Lisa's uncle gave her a toy car, which the 13-month-old called her "koo-ka." Then her father came home with a gift, saying, "Look, Lisa, here's a little car for you." Lisa shook her head. "Koo-ka," she said, and ran and got the one from her uncle. To her, *that* car—and *only* that car—was a little car, and it took some time before she called any other toy cars by the same name. Lisa was underextending the word *car* by restricting it to a single object.

Children also *overextend word meanings.* At 14 months, Eddie jumped in excitement at the sight of a gray-haired man on the television screen and shouted, "Gampa!" Eddie was overgeneralizing, or *overextending,* a word; he thought that because his grandfather had gray hair, all gray-haired men could be called "Grandpa." As children develop a larger vocabulary and get feedback from adults on the appropriateness of what they say, they overextend less. ("No, honey, that man looks a little like Grandpa, but he's somebody else's grandpa, not yours.")

Children *overregularize rules:* They apply them rigidly, not knowing that some rules have exceptions. When Delilah, looking out the window with her father on a gloomy day, repeats after him "Windy . . . cloudy . . . rainy . . ." and then adds "coldy," this represents progress. When children first learn the rules for, in this instance, forming adjectives from nouns, they apply them universally. The next step is to learn the exceptions to the rules, which they generally do by early school age.

Checkpoint

Can you . . .

✔ Trace the typical sequence of milestones in early language development, pointing out the influence of the language babies hear around them?

✔ Describe five ways in which early speech differs from adult speech?

Classic Theories of Language Acquisition: The Nature-Nurture Debate

Is linguistic ability learned or inborn? In the 1950s, a debate raged between two schools of thought: one led by B. F. Skinner, the foremost proponent of learning theory, the other by the linguist Noam Chomsky.

Skinner (1957) maintained that language learning, like other learning, is based on experience. According to classic learning theory, children learn language through operant conditioning. At first, babies utter sounds at random. Caregivers reinforce the sounds that happen to resemble adult speech with smiles, attention, and praise. Infants then repeat these reinforced sounds. Sounds that are not part of the native language are not reinforced, and the child gradually stops making them. According to social-learning theory, babies imitate the sounds they hear adults make and, again, are reinforced for doing so. Word learning depends on selective reinforcement; the word *kitty* is reinforced only when the family cat appears. As this process continues, children are reinforced for speech that is more and more adultlike. Sentence formation is a more complex process: The child learns a basic word order (subject-verb-object—"I want ice cream"), and then learns that other words can be substituted in each category ("Daddy eats meat").

Observation, imitation, and reinforcement probably do contribute to language development, but, as Chomsky (1957) persuasively argued, they cannot fully explain it (Flavell, Miller, & Miller, 1993; Owens, 1996). For one thing, word combinations and nuances are so many and so complex that they cannot all be acquired by specific imitation and reinforcement. Then, caregivers often reinforce utterances that are not strictly grammatical, as long as they make sense. ("Gampa go bye-bye.") Adult speech itself is an unreliable model to imitate, as it is often ungrammatical, containing false starts, unfinished sentences, and slips of the tongue. Also, learning theory does not account for children's imaginative ways of saying things they have never heard—as when 2-year-old Anna described a sprained ankle as a "sprangle" and said she didn't want to go to sleep yet because she wasn't "yawny."

nativism Theory that human beings have an inborn capacity for language acquisition.

Chomsky's own view is called **nativism.** Unlike Skinner's learning theory, nativism emphasizes the active role of the learner. Since language is universal among human beings, Chomsky (1957, 1972) proposed that the human brain has an innate capacity for acquiring language; babies learn to talk as naturally as they learn to walk. He suggested that an inborn **language acquisition device (LAD)** programs children's brains to analyze the language they hear and to figure out its rules. More recently, Chomsky (1995) has sought to identify a simple set of universal principles that underlie all languages, and a single multipurpose mechanism for connecting sound to meaning.

language acquisition device (LAD) In Chomsky's terminology, an inborn mechanism that enables children to infer linguistic rules from the language they hear.

Support for the nativist position comes from newborns' ability to differentiate similar sounds, suggesting that they are born with perceptual "tuning rods" that pick up characteristcs of speech. Nativists point out that almost all children master their native language in the same age-related sequence without formal teaching. Furthermore, the brains of human beings, the only animals with fully developed language, contain a structure that is larger on one side than on the other, suggesting that an inborn mechanism for sound and language processing may be localized in the larger hemisphere—the left for most people (Gannon, Holloway, Broadfield, & Braun, 1998). Still, the nativist approach does not explain precisely how such a mechanism operates. It does not tell us why some children acquire language more rapidly and efficiently than others, why children differ in linguistic skill and fluency, or why (as we'll see) speech development appears to depend on having someone to talk with, not merely on hearing spoken language.

Aspects of both learning theory and nativism have been used to explain how deaf babies learn sign language, which is structured much like spoken language and is acquired in the same sequence. Deaf babies of deaf parents seem to copy the sign language they see their parents using, just as hearing babies copy vocal utterances. Using hand motions more systematic and deliberate than those of hearing babies, deaf babies first string together meaningless motions and repeat them over and over in what has been called *hand-babbling* (Petitto & Marentette, 1991). As parents reinforce these gestures, the babies attach meaning to them.

However, some deaf children make up their own sign language when they do not have models to follow—evidence that imitation and reinforcement alone cannot explain the emergence of linguistic expression (Goldin-Meadow & Mylander, 1998). Since the 1970s, successive waves of Nicaraguan deaf schoolchildren who were being taught only lip-reading in Spanish have developed a true sign language, which has gradually evolved from simple gestures into words and sentences that follow linguistic rules (Senghas & Coppola, 2001; Senghas, Kita, & Ozyürek, 2004). Likewise, Al-Sayyid Bedouin Sign Language, which evolved spontaneously in an isolated village in Israel's Negev desert, has a distinct, systematic grammatical structure unlike that of Israeli Sign Language or of the Arabic dialect spoken by hearing members of the community (Sandler, Meir, Padden, & Aronoff, 2005). Furthermore, learning theory does not explain the correspondence between the ages at which linguistic advances in both hearing and nonhearing babies typically occur (Padden, 1996). Deaf babies begin hand-babbling before 10 months of age, about the age when hearing infants begin voice-babbling (Petitto & Marentette, 1991). Deaf babies also begin to use sentences in sign language at about the same time that hearing babies begin to speak in sentences (Meier, 1991; Newport & Meier, 1985). These examples suggest that an inborn language capacity may underlie the acquisition of both spoken and signed language and that advances in both kinds of language are tied to brain maturation.

Most developmental scientists today believe that language acquisition, like most other aspects of development, depends on an intertwining of nature and nurture. Children, whether hearing or deaf, probably have an inborn capacity to acquire language, which may be activated or constrained by experience.

According to classical learning theory, babies learn speech through operant conditioning. By repeating the speech-like sounds his baby happens to make, this father reinforces the likelihood that the baby will repeat those sounds.

Checkpoint

Can you . . .

✔ Summarize how learning theory and nativism seek to explain language acquisition, and point out strengths and weaknesses of each theory?

✔ Discuss implications of how deaf babies acquire language?

Influences on Early Language Development

What determines how quickly and how well children learn to understand and use language? Research has focused on influences both within and outside the child.

Guidepost

9. What influences contribute to linguistic progress?

Neurological Factors The tremendous brain growth and reorganization during the early months and years is closely linked with language development. A newborn's cries are controlled by the *brain stem* and *pons,* the most primitive parts of the brain and the earliest to develop (refer back to Figure 4-6). Repetitive babbling may emerge with the maturation of parts of the *motor cortex* that control movements of the face and larynx. Not until early in the second year, when most children begin to talk, do the pathways that link auditory and motor activity mature (Owens, 1996). Cortical regions associated with language continue to develop until at least the late preschool years or beyond—some, not even until adulthood.

Lateralization of linguistic functions in the brain apparently takes place very early in life (Holowka & Petitto, 2002). In about 98 percent of people, the left hemisphere is dominant for language, though the right hemisphere participates as well (Nobre & Plunkett, 1997; Owens, 1996). Videotapes of babbling babies show that, as in adult speech, the mouth opens more on the right side, which is controlled by the left hemisphere, than on the left (Holowka & Petitto, 2002).

Studies of brain-damaged children suggest that a sensitive period exists before lateralization of language is firmly fixed. The plasticity of the infant brain seems to allow functions to be transferred from damaged areas to other regions. Thus, whereas an adult whose left hemisphere is removed or injured will be severely language impaired, a young child who undergoes this procedure may eventually have nearly normal speech and comprehension (Nobre & Plunkett, 1997; Owens, 1996).

Brains of *normal* infants also show plasticity. In one study, researchers measured brain activity at various places on the scalp as babies listened to a series of words, some of which they did not understand. Between ages 13 and 20 months, a period of marked vocabulary growth, the infants showed increasing lateralization and localization of comprehension (Mills, Cofley-Corina, & Neville, 1997). Other evidence of neural plasticity comes from findings that the upper regions of the temporal lobe, which are involved in hearing and understanding speech, can be activated by a born-deaf person's use of sign language (Nishimura et al., 1999). Such findings suggest that the assignment of language functions to brain structures may be a gradual process linked to verbal experience and cognitive development (Nobre & Plunkett, 1997).

Social Interaction: The Role of Parents and Caregivers Language is a social act. Parents or other caregivers play an important role at each stage of language development.

Prelinguistic Period At the babbling stage, adults help an infant advance toward true speech by repeating the sounds the baby makes. The baby soon joins in the game and repeats the sounds back. Parents' imitation of babies' sounds affects the pace of language learning (Hardy-Brown & Plomin, 1985; Hardy-Brown, Plomin, & DeFries, 1981). It also helps babies experience the social aspect of speech, the sense that a conversation consists of taking turns, an idea most babies seem to grasp at about 7½ to 8 months of age. Even as early as 4 months, babies in a game of peekaboo show sensitivity to the structure of social exchange with an adult (Rochat, Querido, & Striano, 1999; refer back to Box 5-1). In one longitudinal study, mothers' responsiveness to 9-month-olds' and, even more so, to 13-month-olds' vocalization and play predicted the timing of language milestones, such as first spoken words and sentences (Tamis-LeMonda, Bornstein, & Baumwell, 2001).

Vocabulary Development Babies learn by listening to what adults say. When babies begin to talk, parents or caregivers often help them by repeating their first

Checkpoint

Can you . . .

✔ Name areas of the brain involved in early language development, and tell the function of each?

✔ Give evidence of plasticity in the brain's linguistic areas?

words and pronouncing them correctly. Vocabulary gets a boost when an adult seizes an appropriate opportunity to teach a child a new word. If Jordan is looking at a ball and his mother says, "This is a ball," he is more likely to remember the word than if he were playing with something else and she tried to divert his attention to the ball (Dunham, Dunham, & Curwin, 1993). Infants who have not yet begun to talk apparently can learn new words in the same way. In one laboratory experiment, 9-month-olds whose parents had taught them the names of simple objects at home by repeatedly pointing at pictures of the objects and saying their names were shown two images at a time: one of an object, say, a ball, whose name they had been taught and another of an object, say, a car, whose name they had not been taught. When verbally prompted "Look at that!" the infants showed novelty preference—they tended to look at the object whose name they had *not* been taught. But when prompted to look at a specific named object ("Ball! Ball! Look at the ball!" or "Car! Car! Look at the car!") they tended to look at the object whose name they had been taught (Schafer, 2005).

Despite controversy over the value of child-directed speech, or "parentese," this simplified way of speaking does appeal to babies.

A strong relationship has appeared between the frequency of various words in mothers' speech and the order in which children learn these words (Huttenlocher, Haight, Bryk, Seltzer, & Lyons, 1991) as well as between mothers' talkativeness and the size of toddlers' vocabularies (Huttenlocher, 1998). Mothers with higher socioeconomic status tend to use richer vocabularies and longer utterances, and their 2-year-olds tend to have larger spoken vocabularies (Hoff, 2003). However, sensitivity and responsiveness to a child's level of development count more than the number of words a mother uses. In one longitudinal study in which toddlers were observed interacting with their mothers at 13 and 20 months, the mothers increased their vocabulary use to match their children's growing language abilities; and the children with the biggest vocabularies had mothers who were most responsive (Bornstein, Tamis-LeMonda, & Haynes, 1999).

In households where more than one language is spoken, babies achieve similar milestones in each language on the same schedule as children who hear only one language. Bilingual children often use elements of both languages, sometimes in the same utterance—a phenomenon called **code mixing.** But this does not mean that they confuse the two languages (Petitto, Katerelos et al., 2001; Petitto & Kovelman, 2003). A naturalistic observation in Montreal (Genesee, Nicoladis, & Paradis, 1995) suggests that children as young as 2 in dual-language households differentiate between the two languages, using French, for example, with a predominantly French-speaking father and English with a predominantly English-speaking mother. This ability to shift from one language to another is called **code switching.** (Chapter 9 discusses second-language education.)

Child-Directed Speech   You do not have to be a parent to speak "parentese." If, when you talk to an infant or toddler, you speak slowly in a high-pitched voice with exaggerated ups and downs, simplify your speech, exaggerate vowel sounds, and use short words and sentences and much repetition, you are using **child-directed speech**

code mixing Use of elements of two languages, sometimes in the same utterance, by young children in households where both languages are spoken.

code switching Changing one's speech to match the situation, as in people who are bilingual.

child-directed speech (CDS) Form of speech often used in talking to babies or toddlers; includes slow, simplified speech, a high-pitched tone, exaggerated vowel sounds, short words and sentences, and much repetition; also called *parentese*.

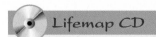

Look at the video, "Infant-Directed Speech," in Chapter 5 of your CD, to discover how parents of a four-month-old use child-directed speech to help their baby learn language.

(CDS) (sometimes called *parentese* or *motherese*). Most adults and even children do it naturally. Such "baby talk" has been documented in many languages and cultures (Kuhl et al., 1997).

Many researchers believe that CDS helps infants learn their native language or at least pick it up faster by helping them hear the distinguishing features of speech sounds. In one cross-cultural observational study, mothers in the United States, Russia, and Sweden were audiotaped speaking to their 2- to 5-month-old infants. Whether the mothers were speaking English, Russian, or Swedish, they produced more exaggerated vowel sounds when talking to the infants than when talking to other adults. At 20 weeks, the babies' babbling contained distinct vowels that reflected the phonetic differences to which their mothers' speech had alerted them (Kuhl et al., 1997).

Some investigators challenge the value of CDS. They contend that babies speak sooner and better and discover the rules of language faster if they hear and can respond to more complex adult speech (Gleitman, Newport, & Gleitman, 1984; Oshima-Takane, Goodz, & Derevensky, 1996). Nonetheless, infants themselves prefer simplified speech. This preference is clear before 1 month of age, and it does not seem to depend on any specific experience (Cooper & Aslin, 1990; Kuhl et al., 1997; Werker, Pegg, & McLeod, 1994).

Preparing for Literacy: The Benefits of Reading Aloud

Reading to an infant or toddler offers opportunities for emotional intimacy and fosters parent-child communication. The frequency with which parents or caregivers read to babies as well as the way they do it can influence the development of **literacy,** the ability to read and write. Children who learn to read early tend to be those whose parents read to them frequently when they were very young.

literacy Ability to read and write.

Adults tend to have one of three styles of reading to children: the *describer style, comprehender style,* and *performance-oriented style.* A *describer* focuses on describing what is going on in the pictures and inviting the child to do so ("What are the Mom and Dad having for breakfast?"). A *comprehender* encourages the child to look more deeply at the meaning of a story and to make inferences and predictions ("What do you think the lion will do now?"). A *performance-oriented* reader reads the story straight through, introducing the main themes beforehand and asking questions afterward. An adult's read-aloud style is best tailored to the needs and skills of the child. In an experimental study of 50 four-year-olds in Dunedin, New Zealand, the describer style resulted in the greatest overall benefits for vocabulary and print skills, but the performance-oriented style was more beneficial for children who started out with large vocabularies (Reese & Cox, 1999).

A promising technique, similar to the describer style, is *dialogic,* or *shared, reading.* In this method (mentioned in Chapter 2), "the child learns to become the storyteller" while the adult acts as an active listener (Whitehurst & Lonigan, 1998, p. 859). Parents ask

By reading aloud to his young daughter and asking questions about the pictures in the book, this father is helping her build language skills and learn how letters look and sound.

challenging, open-ended questions rather than those calling for a simple yes or no ("What is the cat doing?" instead of "Is the cat asleep?"). They follow up the child's answers with more questions, repeat and expand on what the child says, correct wrong answers and give alternative possibilities, help the child as needed, and give praise and encouragement. They encourage the child to relate a story to the child's own experience ("Have you ever seen a duck swimming? What did it look like?").

Children who are read to often, especially in this way, when they are 1 to 3 years old show better language skills at ages 2½, 4½, and 5 and better reading comprehension at age 7 (Crain-Thoreson & Dale, 1992; Wells, 1985). In one study, 21- to 35-month-olds whose parents used this method scored six months higher in vocabulary and expressive language skills than a control group. The experimental group also got a boost in *prereading skills,* the competencies helpful in learning to read, such as learning how letters look and sound (Arnold & Whitehurst, 1994; Whitehurst et al., 1988).

Checkpoint
Can you . . .

✔ Give examples of how caregivers help babies learn to talk?

✔ Assess arguments for and against child-directed speech (CDS)?

✔ Tell why reading aloud to children at an early age is beneficial?

✔ Describe an effective way of reading aloud to infants and toddlers?

Refocus

Thinking back to the Focus vignette about Charles and Doddy Darwin at the beginning of this chapter:

- Which approach to cognitive development seems closest to the one Darwin took in observing and describing his son's development? Why?

- How might a behaviorist, a Piagetian, a psychometrician, an information-processing researcher, a cognitive neuroscientist, and a social-contextual theorist attempt to study and explain the developments Darwin described?

- Did Doddy's early linguistic development seem more consistent with Skinner's theory of language development or Chomsky's? How does it illustrate the role of social interaction?

Social interaction in reading aloud, play, and other daily activities is a key to much of childhood development. Children call forth responses from the people around them and, in turn, react to those responses. In Chapter 6, we will look more closely at these bidirectional influences as we explore early psychosocial development.

SUMMARY AND KEY TERMS

Studying Cognitive Development: Classic Approaches

behaviorist approach *(153)*

psychometric approach *(153)*

Piagetian approach *(153)*

Guidepost 1: How do infants learn, and how long can they remember?

- Two types of learning that behaviorists study are classical conditioning and operant conditioning.

- Rovee-Collier's research suggests that infants' memory processes are much like those of adults, and their memories can be jogged by periodic reminders.

classical conditioning *(154)*

operant conditioning *(154)*

Guidepost 2: Can infants' and toddlers' intelligence be measured, and can it be improved?

- Psychometric tests measure factors presumed to make up intelligence.

- Developmental tests, such as the Bayley Scales of Infant Development, can indicate current cognitive functioning but are generally poor predictors of later intelligence.
- The early home environment may affect measured intelligence.
- If the early home environment does not provide the necessary conditions for cognitive competence, early intervention may be needed.

  intelligent behavior *(156)*

  IQ (intelligence quotient) tests *(156)*

  Bayley Scales of Infant and Toddler Development *(156)*

  Home Observation for Measurement of the Environment (HOME) *(157)*

  early intervention *(157)*

Guidepost 3: How did Piaget explain early cognitive development, and how well have his claims stood up?

- During Piaget's sensorimotor stage, infants' schemes become more elaborate. They progress from primary to secondary to tertiary circular reactions and finally to the development of representational ability.
- Research suggests that a number of abilities develop earlier than Piaget described. He may have underestimated young infants' imitative abilities and their grasp of object permanence.
- The dual-representation hypothesis may explain the slow development of pictorial competence.

  sensorimotor stage *(159)*

  schemes *(159)*

  circular reactions *(159)*

  representational ability *(161)*

  invisible imitation *(162)*

  visible imitation *(162)*

  deferred imitation *(163)*

  elicited imitation *(163)*

  object permanence *(163)*

  dual representation hypothesis *(166)*

Studying Cognitive Development: Newer Approaches

information-processing approach *(167)*

cognitive neuroscience approach *(167)*

social-contextual approach *(167)*

Guidepost 4: How can we measure infants' ability to process information, and how does this ability relate to future intelligence?

- Information-processing researchers measure mental processes through habituation and other signs of visual and perceptual abilities. Contrary to Piaget's ideas, such research suggests that representational ability is present virtually from birth.

- Indicators of the efficiency of infants' information processing, such as speed of habituation, tend to predict later intelligence.

  habituation *(167)*

  dishabituation *(167)*

  visual preference *(168)*

  visual recognition memory *(168)*

  cross-modal transfer *(169)*

Guidepost 5: When do babies begin to think about characteristics of the physical world?

- Such information-processing research techniques as habituation, novelty preference, and the violation-of-expectations method have yielded evidence that infants as young as 3½ to 5 months may have a rudimentary grasp of such Piagetian abilities as causality, categorization, object permanence, a sense of number, and an ability to reason about characteristics of the physical world.
- Some researchers suggest that infants may have innate learning mechanisms for acquiring such knowledge. However, the meaning of these findings is in dispute.

  violation-of-expectations *(172)*

Guidepost 6: What can brain research reveal about the development of cognitive skills?

- Explicit memory and implicit memory are located in different brain structures.
- Working memory emerges between 6 and 12 months of age.
- Neurological developments help explain the emergence of Piagetian skills and memory abilities.

  explicit memory *(175)*

  implicit memory *(175)*

  working memory *(176)*

Guidepost 7: How does social interaction with adults advance cognitive competence?

- Social interactions with adults contribute to cognitive competence through shared activities that help children learn skills, knowledge, and values important in their culture.

  guided participation *(176)*

Language Development

Guidepost 8: How do babies develop language?

- The acquisition of language is an important aspect of cognitive development.
- Prelinguistic speech includes crying, cooing, babbling, and imitating language sounds. By 6 months, babies have learned the basic sounds of their language and have begun to link sound with meaning.
- Before they say their first word, babies use gestures.
- The first word typically comes sometime between 10 and 14 months, initiating linguistic speech. A "naming

explosion" typically occurs sometime between 16 and 24 months of age.

- The first brief sentences generally come between 18 and 24 months. By age 3, syntax and communicative abilities are fairly well developed.
- Early speech is characterized by simplification, under-extending and overextending word meanings, and overregularizing rules.
- Two classic theoretical views about how children acquire language are learning theory and nativism. Today, most developmentalists hold that an inborn capacity to learn language may be activated or constrained by experience.

language *(177)*

prelinguistic speech *(178)*

linguistic speech *(180)*

holophrase *(180)*

telegraphic speech *(181)*

syntax *(181)*

nativism *(182)*

language acquisition device (LAD) *(182)*

Guidepost 9: What influences contribute to linguistic progress?

- Influences on language development include brain maturation and social interaction.
- Family characteristics, such as socioeconomic status, adult language use, and maternal responsiveness, affect a child's vocabulary development.
- Children who hear two languages at home generally learn both at the same rate as children who hear only one language, and they can use each language in appropriate circumstances.
- Child-directed speech (CDS) seems to have cognitive, emotional, and social benefits, and infants show a preference for it. However, some researchers dispute its value.
- Reading aloud to a child from an early age helps pave the way for literacy.

code mixing *(185)*

code switching *(185)*

child-directed speech (CDS) *(185)*

literacy *(186)*

CHAPTER 6

Psychosocial Development During the First Three Years

> J'm like a child
> trying to do everything
> say everything
> and be everything
> all at once
>
> ───────
>
> **John Hartford, "Life Prayer," 1971**

Focus
Mary Catherine Bateson, Anthropologist

Mary Catherine Bateson

Mary Catherine Bateson (b. 1939) is an anthropologist, the daughter of two famous anthropologists: Margaret Mead (refer back to Chapter 2 Focus vignette) and Gregory Bateson, Mead's third husband and research partner. Cathy's was probably one of the most documented infancies on record—her mother taking notes, her father behind the camera. Margaret Mead's memoir, *Blackberry Winter* (1972), and Mary Catherine Bateson's *With a Daughter's Eye* (1984) together provide a rare and fascinating dual perspective on a child's emotional development.

Cathy—Mead's only child—was born when her mother was 38 years old. Her parents divorced when she was 11. Their work during World War II often necessitated long absences and separations. But during her infancy and toddlerhood, when they were still together, Cathy was the focus of their love and wholehearted attention. Her early recollections include sitting with her parents on a blanket outdoors, being read to on her mother's lap, and watching the two of them hold up their breakfast spoons to reflect the morning light, making a pair of "birds" flash across the walls for her amusement.

To avoid subjecting her to frustration, her parents tried to respond quickly to her needs. Mead arranged her professional commitments around breast-feeding and nursed "on demand," like the mothers in the island cultures she had studied.

Like their friend Erik Erikson, Mead and Bateson placed great importance on the development of trust. They never left Cathy in a strange place with a strange person; she always met a new caregiver in a familiar place. As an adult, Catherine observed that, during difficult periods in her life, she often found "resources of faith and strength, a foundation that must have been built in those [first] two years" (Bateson, 1984, p. 35). Yet, as Mead wrote, reflecting on the contributions of nature and nurture, "How much was temperament? How much was felicitous accident? How much could be attributed to upbringing? We may never know" (1972, p. 268).

191

When Cathy was 2 and her parents' need to be away for wartime work increased, they merged households and moved in with a friend and colleague, Lawrence Frank, in New York City. The decision fit in with Mead's belief, gleaned from her studies, that children benefit from having multiple caregivers and learning to adapt to different situations.

The ménage in Frank's brownstone in Greenwich Village included his infant son, Colin and five older children. "Thus," Catherine writes, "I did not grow up in a nuclear family or as an only child, but as a member of a flexible and welcoming extended family . . . , in which five or six pairs of hands could be mobilized to shell peas or dry dishes." Her summertime memories are of a lakeside retreat in New Hampshire, where "each child was cared for by enough adults so that there need be no jealousy, where the garden bloomed and the evenings ended in song. . . . I was rich beyond other children . . . and yet there were all those partings. There were all those beloved people, yet often the people I wanted most were absent" (Bateson, 1984, pp. 38–39).

In Margaret Mead's and Mary Catherine Bateson's complementary memoirs, we can see how Mead put into practice the beliefs she had developed about child rearing, in part from memories of her own childhood and in part from observations of distant cultures. We see her seeking solutions to a problem that has become increasingly common: child care for children of working parents. And we see a bidirectionality of influence: How early experiences with parents help shape a child's development, and how a child's needs can shape parents' lives.

This chapter is about the shift from the dependence of infancy to the independence of childhood. We first examine foundations of psychosocial development: emotions, temperament, and early experiences with parents. We consider Erikson's views about the development of trust and autonomy. We look at relationships with caregivers, at the emerging sense of self, and at the foundations of conscience. We explore relationships with siblings and other children. Finally, we consider the increasingly widespread impact of parental employment and early child care.

After you have studied this chapter, you should be able to answer each of the following Guidepost questions. Look for them again in the margins, where they point to important concepts throughout the chapter. To check your understanding of these Guideposts, review the end-of-chapter summary. Checkpoints located at periodic spots throughout the chapter will help you verify your understanding of what you have read.

Guideposts
for Study

1. When and how do emotions develop, and how do babies show them?

2. How do infants show temperamental differences, and how enduring are those differences?

3. What roles do mothers and fathers play in early personality development?

4. How do infants gain trust in their world and form attachments?

5. How do infants and caregivers "read" each other's nonverbal signals?

6. When and how does the sense of self arise?

7. How do toddlers develop autonomy and standards for socially acceptable behavior?

8. How do infants and toddlers interact with siblings and other children?

9. How do parental employment and early child care affect infants' and toddlers' development?

10. What causes child abuse and neglect, and what are the effects of maltreatment?

Foundations of Psychosocial Development

Although babies share common patterns of development, each, from the start, shows a distinct *personality:* the relatively consistent blend of emotions, temperament, thought, and behavior that makes each person unique (Eisenberg, Fabes, Guthrie, & Reiser, 2000). One baby is usually cheerful; another is easily upset. One toddler plays happily with other children; another prefers to play alone. Such characteristic ways of feeling, thinking, and acting, which reflect both inborn and environmental influences, affect the way children respond to others and adapt to their world. From infancy on, personality development is intertwined with social relationships (see Table 6-1); and this combination is what is meant by *psychosocial development.*

Let's look first at emotions, the building blocks of personality; then at temperament, or disposition; and finally, at an infant's earliest social experiences in the family.

Emotions

Emotions, such as sadness, joy, and fear, are subjective reactions to experience that are associated with physiological and behavioral changes (Sroufe, 1997).* Fear, for example, is accompanied by a faster heartbeat and, often, by self-protective action. People differ in how often they feel a particular emotion, in the kinds of events that may produce it, in the physical manifestations they show (such as heart rate changes), and in how they act as a result. One child may be easily angered; another is not. Culture influences the way people feel about a situation and the way they show their emotions. For example, some Asian cultures, which stress social harmony, discourage expression of anger but place much importance on shame. The opposite

Guidepost

1. When and how do emotions develop, and how do babies show them?

emotions Subjective reactions to experience that are associated with physiological and behavioral changes.

*The discussion in this section is largely indebted to Sroufe (1997).

Table 6-1	Highlights of Infants' and Toddlers' Psychosocial Development, Birth to 36 Months

Approximate Age, Months	Characteristics
0–3	Infants are open to stimulation. They begin to show interest and curiosity, and they smile readily at people.
3–6	Infants can anticipate what is about to happen and experience disappointment when it does not. They show this by becoming angry or acting warily. They smile, coo, and laugh often. This is a time of social awakening and early reciprocal exchanges between the baby and the caregiver.
6–9	Infants play "social games" and try to get responses from people. They "talk" to, touch, and cajole other babies to get them to respond. They express more differentiated emotions, showing joy, fear, anger, and surprise.
9–12	Infants are intensely preoccupied with their principal caregiver, may become afraid of strangers, and act subdued in new situations. By 1 year, they communicate emotions more clearly, showing moods, ambivalence, and gradations of feeling.
12–18	Toddlers explore their environment, using the people they are most attached to as a secure base. As they master the environment, they become more confident and more eager to assert themselves.
18–36	Toddlers sometimes become anxious because they now realize how much they are separating from their caregiver. They work out their awareness of their limitations in fantasy and in play and by identifying with adults.

Source: Adapted from Sroufe, 1979.

is often true in American culture, which stresses self-expression, self-assertion, and self-esteem (Cole, Bruschi, & Tamang, 2002).

Emotional development is an orderly process; complex emotions unfold from simpler ones. A person's characteristic pattern of emotional reactions begins to develop during infancy and is a basic element of personality. However, as children grow older, some emotional responses may change. A baby who, at 3 months of age, smiled at a stranger's face may, at 8 months, show wariness, or *stranger anxiety.* Researchers disagree about how many emotions there are, when they arise, and how they should be defined and measured.

Emotion is closely tied to other aspects of development. For example, a newborn baby who is emotionally neglected—not hugged, caressed, or talked to—may show *nonorganic failure to thrive,* that is, failure to grow and gain weight despite adequate nutrition. The baby often will improve when moved to a hospital and given emotional support. Such emotions as anger and fear, and especially shame, guilt, and empathy, may motivate moral behavior (Ben-Ze'ev, 1997; Eisenberg, 2000; Eisenberg, Guthrie et al., 1999; Kochanska, 1997a).

First Signs of Emotion Newborns plainly show when they are unhappy. They let out piercing cries, flail their arms and legs, and stiffen their bodies. It is harder to tell when they are happy. During the first month, they become quiet at the sound of a human voice or when they are picked up, and they may smile when their hands are moved together to play pat-a-cake. As time goes by, infants respond more to people—smiling, cooing, reaching out, and eventually going to them.

These early signals or clues to babies' feelings are important indicators of development. When babies want or need something, they cry; when they feel sociable, they smile or laugh. When their messages bring a response, their sense of connection with other people grows. Their sense of control over their world grows, too, as they see that their cries bring help and comfort and that their smiles and laughter elicit smiles and laughter in return. They become more able to participate actively in regulating their states of arousal and their emotional life.

Crying Crying is the most powerful way—and sometimes the only way—infants can communicate their needs. Some research has distinguished four patterns of crying (Wolff, 1969): the basic *hunger cry* (a rhythmic cry, which is not always associated with hunger); the *angry cry* (a variation of the rhythmic cry, in which excess air is forced through the vocal cords); the *pain cry* (a sudden onset of loud crying without preliminary moaning, sometimes followed by holding the breath); and the *frustration cry* (two or three drawn-out cries, with no prolonged breath-holding) (Wood & Gustafson, 2001).

Some parents worry that picking up a crying baby will spoil the infant. In one study, delays in responding to fussing did seem to reduce fussing during the first six months, perhaps because the babies learned to deal with minor irritations on their own (Hubbard & van IJzendoorn, 1991). However, if parents wait until cries of distress escalate to shrieks of rage, it may become more difficult to soothe the baby; and such a pattern, if experienced repeatedly, may interfere with an infant's developing ability to regulate, or manage, his or her own emotional state (R. A. Thompson, 1991). Ideally, the most developmentally sound approach may be the one Cathy Bateson's parents followed: to *prevent* distress, making soothing unnecessary.

Crying is the most powerful way, and sometimes the only way, that babies can communicate their needs. Parents may soon learn to recognize whether their baby is crying because of hunger, anger, frustration, or pain.

Smiling and Laughing The earliest faint smiles occur spontaneously soon after birth, apparently as a result of subcortical nervous system activity. These involuntary smiles frequently appear during periods of REM sleep (refer back to Chapter 5). They become less frequent during the first three months as the cortex matures (Sroufe, 1997).

The earliest *waking* smiles may be elicited by mild sensations, such as gentle jiggling or blowing on the infant's skin. In the second week, a baby may smile drowsily after a feeding. By the third week, most infants begin to smile when they are alert and paying attention to a caregiver's nodding head and voice. At about 1 month, smiles generally become more frequent and more social. During the second month, as visual recognition develops, babies smile more at visual stimuli, such as faces they know (Sroufe, 1997; Wolff, 1963).

At about the fourth month, infants laugh out loud when kissed on the stomach or tickled. As babies grow older, they become more actively engaged in mirthful exchanges. A 6-month-old may giggle in response to the mother making unusual sounds or appearing with a towel over her face; a 10-month-old may laughingly try to put the towel back on her face when it falls off. This change reflects cognitive development: by laughing at the unexpected, babies show that they know what to expect. By turning the tables, they show awareness that they can make things happen. Laughter also helps babies discharge tension, such as fear of a threatening object (Sroufe, 1997).

When Do Emotions Appear? Identifying infants' emotions is a challenge because babies cannot tell us what they feel. Carroll Izard and his colleagues have videotaped infants' facial expressions and have interpreted them as showing joy, sadness, interest, and fear, and to a lesser degree anger, surprise, and disgust (Izard, Huebner, Resser, McGinness, & Dougherty, 1980). Of course, we do not know that these babies actually had the feelings they were credited with, but their facial expressions were remarkably similar to adults' expressions when experiencing these emotions.

Facial expressions are not the only, or necessarily the best, index of infants' emotions; motor activity, body language, and physiological changes also are important indicators. An infant can be fearful without showing a "fear face"; the baby may show

Checkpoint
Can you . . .

✔ Explain why emotions are difficult to study?

✔ Give examples of the role of emotions in other domains of development?

✔ Explain the significance of patterns of crying, smiling, and laughing?

At 6 months, butting heads with his grandfather makes Jackson laugh. Laughter at unusual or unexpected occurrences reflects growing cognitive understanding.

fear by turning away or averting the gaze, or by a faster heartbeat. Different indicators may point to different conclusions about the timing of emergence of specific emotions. In addition, this timetable shows a good deal of individual variation (Sroufe, 1997).

Basic Emotions According to one model of emotional development (Lewis, 1997; see Figure 6-1), soon after birth babies show signs of contentment, interest, and distress. These are diffuse, reflexive, mostly physiological responses to sensory stimulation or

Figure 6-1

Differentiation of emotions during the first three years. The primary, or basic, emotions emerge during the first 6 months or so; the self-conscious emotions develop beginning in the second half of the second year, as a result of the emergence of self-awareness (consciousness of self) together with accumulation of knowledge about societal standards and rules. *Note:* There are two kinds of embarrassment. The earlier form does not involve evaluation of behavior and may simply be a response to being singled out as the object of attention. The second kind, evaluative embarrassment, which emerges during the third year, is a mild form of shame. (Source: Adapted from Lewis, 1997, Figure 1, p. 120.) Adapted from Lewis, M. (1997) "The Development of Self. Comments on the Paper of Neisser." In S. G. Snodgrass and R. L. Thompson (eds.), "The Self Across Psychology: Self-Recognition, Self-Awareness, and the Self-Concept," *Annals of the New York Academy of Sciences,* Vol. 818. Copyright © 1997 New York Academy of Sciences, U.S.A. Reprinted with permission.

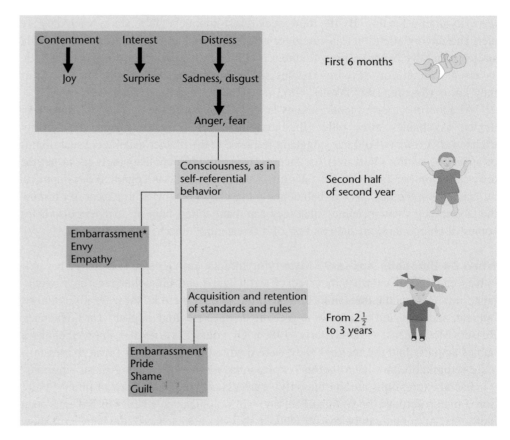

internal processes. During the next six months or so, these early emotional states differentiate into true emotions: joy, surprise, sadness, disgust, and last, anger and fear—reactions to events that have meaning for the infant. As we'll discuss in a subsequent section, the emergence of these basic, or primary, emotions is related to the biological "clock" of neurological maturation.

Emotions Involving the Self **Self-conscious emotions,** such as embarrassment, empathy, and envy, arise only after children have developed **self-awareness:** the cognitive understanding that they have a recognizable identity, separate and different from the rest of their world. This consciousness of self seems to emerge between 15 and 24 months, when, according to Piaget, infants become able to make mental representations—of themselves as well as of other people and things. Self-awareness is necessary before children can be aware of being the focus of attention, identify with what other "selves" are feeling, or wish they had what someone else has. By about age 3, having acquired self-awareness plus a good deal of knowledge about their society's accepted standards, rules, and goals, children can evaluate their own thoughts, plans, desires, and behavior against what is considered socially appropriate. Only then can they demonstrate the **self-evaluative emotions** of pride, guilt, and shame (Lewis, 1995, 1997, 1998).

Guilt and shame are distinct emotions, even though both may be responses to wrongdoing. Children who fail to live up to behavioral standards may feel guilty (that is, regret their behavior), but they do not necessarily feel a lack of self-worth, as when they feel ashamed. Their focus is on a bad *act,* not a bad *self.* A guilty child will often try to make amends, say, by trying to put together a broken dish that the child knocked off the table; an ashamed child is more likely to try to hide the results of a misdeed (Eisenberg, 2000).

Empathy: Feeling What Others Feel **Empathy**—the ability to "put oneself in another person's place" and feel what that person feels, or would be expected to feel, in a particular situation—is thought to arise during the second year. Like guilt, empathy increases with age (Eisenberg, 2000; Eisenberg & Fabes, 1998). As toddlers become increasingly able to differentiate their own mental state from that of another person, they can respond to another child's distress as if it were their own (Hoffman, 1998). Empathy differs from *sympathy,* which merely involves sorrow or concern for another person's plight. Both empathy and sympathy may give rise to *prosocial behavior,* such as giving back a toy (see Chapter 9).

Empathy depends on **social cognition,** the cognitive ability to understand that others have mental states and to gauge their feelings and intentions. Piaget believed that **egocentrism** (inability to see another person's point of view) delays the development of this ability until the concrete operational stage of middle childhood. Other research suggests that social cognition begins so early that it may be "an innate potential, like the ability to learn language" (Lillard & Curenton, 1999, p. 52).

Brain Growth and Emotional Development The development of the brain after birth is closely connected with changes in emotional life. This is a bidirectional process: emotional experiences not only are affected by brain development but also can have long-lasting effects on the structure of the brain (Mlot, 1998; Sroufe, 1997). A newborn has only a diffuse sense of consciousness and is easily overstimulated by sounds, lights, and other sources of sensory arousal. As the structures of the central nervous system develop and sensory pathways become myelinated, the baby's reactions become more focused and tempered.

There appear to be four major shifts in brain organization, which roughly correspond to changes in emotional processing (Schore, 1994; Sroufe, 1997; refer back to

self-conscious emotions Emotions, such as embarrassment, empathy, and envy, that depend on self-awareness.

self-awareness Realization that one's existence and functioning are separate from those of other people and things.

self-evaluative emotions Emotions, such as pride, shame, and guilt, that depend on both self-awareness and knowledge of socially accepted standards of behavior.

empathy Ability to "put oneself in another person's place" and feel what the other person feels.

social cognition Ability to understand that other people have mental states and to gauge their feelings and intentions.

egocentrism Piaget's term for inability to consider another person's point of view; a characteristic of young children's thought.

Figure 4-6). During the first three months, differentiation of basic emotions begins as the *cerebral cortex* becomes functional, bringing cognitive perceptions into play. REM sleep and reflexive behavior, including the spontaneous neonatal smile, diminish.

The second shift occurs around 9 or 10 months, when the *frontal lobes* begin to interact with the *limbic system,* a seat of emotional reactions. At the same time, limbic structures such as the *hippocampus* become larger and more adultlike. Connections between the frontal cortex and the *hypothalamus* and limbic system, which process sensory information, may facilitate the relationship between the cognitive and emotional spheres. As these connections become denser and more elaborate, an infant can experience and interpret emotions at the same time. The development of recognition and recall, object permanence, and other cognitive advances makes it possible to coordinate past and present events and future expectations. A baby this age may become upset when a ball rolls under a couch and may smile or laugh when it is retrieved. Fear of strangers often develops at this time.

The third shift takes place during the second year, when infants develop self-awareness, self-conscious emotions, and a greater capacity for regulating their own emotions and activities. These changes, which coincide with greater physical mobility and exploratory behavior, may be related to myelination of the frontal lobes.

The fourth shift occurs around age 3, when hormonal changes in the autonomic (involuntary) nervous system coincide with the emergence of evaluative emotions. Underlying the development of such emotions as shame may be a shift away from dominance by the *sympathetic system,* the part of the autonomic system that prepares the body for action, and the maturation of the *parasympathetic system,* the part of the autonomic system that is involved in excretion and sexual excitation.

Neurological factors also may play a part in temperamental differences (Mlot, 1998), the topic to which we turn next.

Checkpoint
Can you . . .

✔ Trace a typical sequence of emergence of the basic, self-conscious, and evaluative emotions, and explain its connection with cognitive and neurological development?

Guidepost

2. How do infants show temperamental differences, and how enduring are those differences?

temperament Characteristic disposition, or style of approaching and reacting to situations.

Temperament

Temperament is sometimes defined as a person's characteristic, biologically based way of approaching and reacting to people and situations. Temperament has been described as the *how* of behavior: not *what* people do, but how they go about doing it (Thomas & Chess, 1977). Two toddlers, for example, may be equally able to dress themselves and may be equally motivated, but one may do it more quickly than the other, be more willing to put on a new outfit, and be less distracted if the cat jumps on the bed. Some researchers look at temperament more broadly. A child may not act the same way in all situations. Also, temperament may affect not only the way children approach and react to the outside world, but also the way they regulate their own mental, emotional, and behavioral functioning (Rothbart, Ahadi, & Evans, 2000).

Temperament has an emotional dimension; but unlike emotions such as fear, excitement, and boredom, which come and go, temperament is relatively consistent and enduring. Individual differences in temperament, which are thought to derive from a person's basic biological makeup, form the core of the developing personality.

Studying Temperamental Patterns: The New York Longitudinal Study In the New York Longitudinal Study (NYLS), a pioneering study on temperament, researchers followed 133 infants into adulthood. The researchers looked at how active the children were; how regular they were in hunger, sleep, and bowel habits; how readily they accepted new people and situations; how they adapted to changes in routine; how sensitive they were to noise, bright lights, and other sensory stimuli; how intensely they responded; whether their mood tended to be pleasant, joyful, and friendly or unpleasant, unhappy, and unfriendly; and whether they persisted at tasks or were easily distracted

Table 6-2 Three Temperamental Patterns (according to the New York Longitudinal Study)

"Easy" Child	"Difficult" Child	"Slow-to-Warm-Up" Child
Has moods of mild to moderate intensity, usually positive.	Displays intense and frequently negative moods; cries often and loudly; also laughs loudly.	Has mildly intense reactions, both positive and negative.
Responds well to novelty and change.	Responds poorly to novelty and change.	Responds slowly to novelty and change.
Quickly develops regular sleep and feeding schedules.	Sleeps and eats irregularly.	Sleeps and eats more regularly than the difficult child, less regularly than the easy child.
Takes to new foods easily.	Accepts new foods slowly.	Shows mildly negative initial response to new stimuli (a first encounter with a new person, place, or situation).
Smiles at strangers.	Is suspicious of strangers.	
Adapts easily to new situations.	Adapts slowly to new situations.	
Accepts most frustrations with little fuss.	Reacts to frustration with tantrums.	
Adapts quickly to new routines and rules of new games.	Adjusts slowly to new routines.	Gradually develops liking for new stimuli after repeated, unpressured exposures.

Source: Adapted from A. Thomas & Chess, 1984. Adapted from Thomas, A. and S. Chess, "Genesis and evolution of behavioral disorders: From infancy to early adult life." *American Journal of Psychiatry,* 141 (1) 1984, pp. 1–9. Copyright © 1984 by the American Psychiatric Association. Reproduced with permission.

(A. Thomas, Chess, & Birch, 1968). The children differed in all these characteristics, almost from birth, and the differences tended to continue.

Almost two-thirds of the children fell into one of three categories (see Table 6-2). Forty percent were **"easy" children:** generally happy, rhythmic in biological functioning, and accepting of new experiences. This is how Margaret Mead described the infant Cathy. Ten percent were what the researchers called **"difficult" children:** more irritable and harder to please, irregular in biological rhythms, and more intense in expressing emotion. Fifteen percent were **"slow-to-warm-up" children:** mild but slow to adapt to new people and situations (A. Thomas & Chess, 1977, 1984).

Many children (including 35 percent of the NYLS sample) do not fit neatly into any of these three groups. A baby may eat and sleep regularly but be afraid of strangers. A child may be easy most of the time, but not always. Another child may warm up slowly to new foods but adapt quickly to new baby-sitters (A. Thomas & Chess, 1984). A child may laugh intensely but not show intense frustration, and a child with rhythmic toilet habits may show irregular sleeping patterns (Rothbart et al., 2000). All these variations are normal.

Seven-month-old Daniel's ready smile and willingness to try a new food are signs of an easy temperament.

How Is Temperament Measured? Many researchers have found the complex interviewing and scoring procedures used in the NYLS too cumbersome and have resorted to short-form questionnaires. A parental self-report instrument, the Rothbart Infant Behavior Questionnaire (IBQ) (Gartstein & Rothbart, 2003; Rothbart et al., 2000) focuses on several dimensions of infant temperament similar to those in the NYLS: activity level, positive emotion (smiling and laughing), fear, frustration, soothability, and duration of orienting (a combination of distractibility and attention span) as well as such additional factors as intensity of pleasure, perceptual sensitivity, and attentional shifting. Parents rate their infants with regard to recent concrete events and behaviors ("How often during the past week did the baby smile or laugh when given a toy?" rather than "Does the baby respond positively to new events?").

"easy" children Children with a generally happy temperament, regular biological rhythms, and a readiness to accept new experiences.

"difficult" children Children with irritable temperament, irregular biological rhythms, and intense emotional responses.

"slow-to-warm-up" children Children whose temperament is generally mild but who are hesitant about accepting new experiences.

Although parental ratings are the most commonly used measures of children's temperament, their reliability is in question. Studies of twins have found that parents tend to rate a child's temperament by comparison with other children in the family—for example, labeling one child inactive in contrast to a more active sibling (Saudino, 2003a). Still, not all types of parent-report instruments show this tendency (Hwang & Rothbart, 2003); and observations by researchers may reflect biases as well (Seifer, 2003). Parents see their children in a variety of day-to-day situations, whereas a laboratory observer sees only how the child reacts to particular standardized situations. Thus, a combination of methods may provide a more accurate picture of how temperament affects child development (Rothbart & Hwang, 2002; Saudino, 2003a, 2003b).

How Stable Is Temperament? Temperament appears to be largely inborn, probably hereditary (Braungart, Plomin, DeFries, & Fulker, 1992; Emde et al., 1992; Schmitz et al., 1996; A. Thomas & Chess, 1977, 1984), and fairly stable. Newborn babies show different patterns of sleeping, fussing, and activity, and these differences tend to persist to some degree (Korner, 1996; Korner et al., 1985). Studies using the IBQ have found strong links between infant temperament and childhood personality at age 7 (Rothbart et al., 2000, 2001). Other researchers, using temperamental types similar to those of the NYLS, have found that temperament at age 3 closely predicts personality at ages 18 and 21 (Caspi, 2000; Caspi & Silva, 1995; Newman, Caspi, Moffitt, & Silva, 1997).

That does not mean temperament is fully formed at birth. Temperament develops as various emotions and self-regulatory capacities appear (Rothbart et al., 2000) and can change in response to parental attitudes and treatment (Belsky, Fish, & Isabella, 1991; J. V. Lerner & Galambos, 1985). As Margaret Mead observed, temperament may be affected by culturally influenced childraising practices. Infants in Malaysia, an island group in Southeast Asia, tend to be less adaptable, more wary of new experiences, and more readily responsive to stimuli than U.S. babies. This may be because Malay parents do not often expose young children to situations that require adaptability, and they encourage infants to be acutely aware of sensations, such as the need for a diaper change (Banks, 1989).

goodness of fit Appropriateness of environmental demands and constraints to a child's temperament.

Temperament and Adjustment: "Goodness of Fit" According to the NYLS, the key to healthy adjustment is **goodness of fit**—the match between a child's temperament and the environmental demands and constraints the child must deal with. If a very active child is expected to sit still for long periods, if a slow-to-warm-up child is constantly pushed into new situations, or if a persistent child is constantly taken away from absorbing projects, trouble may occur.

Parents' responses to their children may reflect the amount of control the parents think they have over a child's behavior. In a home observation, parents who saw themselves as having little control over their 12-month-olds were more likely than other parents to play directively with their babies—urging, reminding, restraining, questioning, and correcting them; and mothers who felt and acted this way were more likely to consider their infants "difficult." Similar patterns have been found among parents of older children (Guzell & Vernon-Feagans, 2004).

When parents recognize that a child acts in a certain way, not out of willfulness, laziness, or stupidity or to spite the parents, but largely because of inborn temperament, they may be less likely to feel guilty, anxious, or hostile, to feel a loss of control, or to be rigid or impatient. They can anticipate the child's reactions and help the child adapt—for example,

A "difficult" child may find it hard to take "no" for an answer—and is likely to make his feelings known loudly, as this boy is doing. A parent who understands and accepts a child's temperament may be better able to help the child adjust to parental rules and expectations.

by giving early warnings of the need to stop an activity or, as Mead and Bateson did, by gradually introducing a child to new situations.

Shyness and Boldness: Influences of Biology and Culture   As we have mentioned, temperament seems to have a biological basis. In longitudinal research with about 400 children starting in infancy, Jerome Kagan and his colleagues have studied an aspect of temperament called *inhibition to the unfamiliar,* or shyness, which has to do with how sociable a child is with unfamiliar children and how boldly or cautiously the child approaches unfamiliar objects and situations. When asked to solve problems or learn new information, the shyest children (about 15 percent of the sample) showed higher and less variable heart rates than bolder children, and the pupils of their eyes dilated more. The boldest children (about 10 to 15 percent) tended to be energetic and spontaneous and to have very low heart rates (Arcus & Kagan, 1995).

Four-month-olds who were highly reactive—that is, who showed much motor activity and distress, or who fretted or cried readily in response to new stimuli— were likely to show the inhibited pattern at 14 and 21 months. Babies who were highly inhibited or uninhibited seemed to maintain these patterns to some degree during childhood and adolescence (Kagan, 1997; Kagan & Snidman, 1991a, 1991b). However, behavioral distinctions between these two types of children tend to "smoothe out" by preadolescence, even though the physiological distinctions remain (Woodward et al., 2001).

Again, experience can moderate or accentuate early tendencies. Male toddlers who were inclined to be fearful and shy were more likely to remain so at age 3 if their parents were highly accepting of the child's reactions. If parents encouraged their sons to venture into new situations, the boys tended to become less inhibited (Park, Belsky, Putnam, & Crnic, 1997).

Culture may influence parental handling. In western countries such as Canada, shy, inhibited children tend to be seen as incompetent or immature, whereas in China, shyness and inhibition are socially approved. In a cross-cultural study of Chinese and Canadian 2-year-olds, Canadian mothers of inhibited children tended to be punitive or overprotective, whereas Chinese mothers of shy children were warm and accepting. The Chinese toddlers were significantly more inhibited than the Canadian ones. However, because this was a correlational study, we don't know whether the children's temperament was a consequence or a cause of their mothers' treatment, or perhaps a bidirectional effect (Chen et al., 1998).

Earliest Social Experiences: The Infant in the Family

Infant care practices and patterns of interaction vary greatly around the world, depending on the culture's view of infants' nature and needs. In Bali, infants are believed to be ancestors or gods brought to life in human form and thus must be treated with utmost dignity and respect. The Beng of West Africa think that young babies can understand all languages, whereas people in the Micronesian atoll of Ifaluk believe that babies cannot understand language at all, and therefore adults do not speak to them (DeLoache & Gottlieb, 2000).

In some societies, as Margaret Mead found in the South Seas, infants have multiple caregivers. Among the Efe people of central Africa, infants typically receive care from five or more people in a given hour and are routinely breast-fed by other women besides the mother (Tronick, Morelli, & Ivey, 1992). Among the Gusii in western Kenya, where infant mortality is high, parents keep their infants close to them, respond quickly when they cry, and feed them on demand (LeVine, 1974, 1989, 1994). The same is true of Aka foragers (hunter-gatherers)

What's Your View?

- In the United States, many people consider shyness undesirable. How should a parent handle a shy child? Do you think it is best to accept the child's temperament or try to change it?

Checkpoint
Can you . . .

✔ List and describe nine aspects and three patterns of temperament identified by the New York Longitudinal Study?

✔ Assess evidence for the stability of temperament?

✔ Discuss how temperament can affect adjustment, and explain the importance of "goodness of fit"?

✔ Give evidence of biological influences on temperament, of the role of parental handling, and of cultural differences?

Guidepost
3. What roles do mothers and fathers play in early personality development?

in central Africa, who move around frequently in small, tightly knit groups marked by extensive sharing, cooperation, and concern about danger. However, Ngandu farmers in the same region, who tend to live farther apart and to stay in one place for long periods of time, are more likely to leave their infants alone and to let them fuss or cry, smile, vocalize, or play (Hewlett, Lamb, Shannon, Leyendecker, & Schölmerich, 1998).

We need to remember, then, that patterns of adult-infant interaction we take for granted may be culture-based. With that caution in mind, let's look first at the roles of the mother and father—how they care for and play with their babies, and how their influence begins to shape personality differences between boys and girls. Later in this chapter, we will look more deeply at relationships with parents and then at interactions with siblings. In Chapter 10 we will examine such nontraditional families as those headed by single parents and those formed by gay and lesbian couples.

The Mother's Role   In a series of pioneering experiments by Harry Harlow and his colleagues, rhesus monkeys were separated from their mothers six to twelve hours after birth and raised in a laboratory. The infant monkeys were put into cages with one of two kinds of surrogate "mothers": a plain cylindrical wire-mesh form or a form covered with terry cloth. Some monkeys were fed from bottles connected to the wire "mothers"; others were "nursed" by the warm, cuddly cloth ones. When the monkeys were allowed to spend time with either kind of "mother," they all spent more time clinging to the cloth surrogates, even if they were being fed only by the wire ones. In an unfamiliar room, the babies "raised" by cloth surrogates showed more natural interest in exploring than those "raised" by wire surrogates, even when the appropriate "mothers" were there.

Apparently, the monkeys also remembered the cloth surrogates better. After a year's separation, the "cloth-raised" monkeys eagerly ran to embrace the terry-cloth forms, whereas the "wire-raised" monkeys showed no interest in the wire forms (Harlow & Zimmerman, 1959). None of the monkeys in either group grew up normally, however (Harlow & Harlow, 1962), and none were able to nurture their own offspring (Suomi & Harlow, 1972).

It is hardly surprising that a dummy mother would not provide the same kinds of stimulation and opportunities for positive development as a live mother. These experiments show that feeding is not the only, or even the most important, thing babies get from their mothers. Mothering includes the comfort of close bodily contact and, at least in monkeys, the satisfaction of an innate need to cling.

Human infants also have needs that must be satisfied if they are to grow up normally. Later in this chapter we will discuss the mutual attachment that develops during infancy, with far-reaching effects on psychosocial and cognitive development. We will also examine the emotional signals that enable nonverbal communication between mothers and babies.

In a series of classic experiments, Harry Harlow and Margret Harlow showed that food is not the most important way to a baby's heart. When infant rhesus monkeys could choose whether to go to a wire surrogate "mother" or a warm, soft terry-cloth "mother," they spent more time clinging to the cloth mother, even if they were being fed by bottles connected to the wire mother.

The Father's Role   The fathering role is essentially a social construction (Doherty, Kouneski, & Erickson, 1998), having different meanings in different cultures. The role may be taken or shared by someone other than the biological father: the mother's brother, as in Botswana (where young mothers remain with their own childhood family until their partners are in their forties), or a grandfather, as in Vietnam (Engle & Breaux, 1998; Richardson, 1995; Townsend, 1997). In some societies, fathers are more involved in their young children's lives—economically, emotionally, and in time spent—than in other cultures. In many parts of the world, what it means to be a father has changed—and is changing (Engle & Breaux, 1998).

Among the Huhot of Inner Mongolia, a province of China, fathers traditionally are responsible for economic support and discipline and mothers for nurturing (Jankowiak, 1992). Fathers are stern and aloof, and their children respect and fear them. Men almost never hold infants. Fathers interact more with toddlers but perform child care duties only if the mother is absent. However, urbanization and maternal employment are changing these attitudes. Fathers—especially college-educated ones—now seek more intimate relationships with children, especially sons. China's official one-child policy has accentuated this change, leading both parents to be more deeply involved with their only child (Engle & Breaux, 1998).

Among the Aka of central Africa, in contrast with the Huhot, fathers are as nurturant and emotionally supportive as mothers. In fact, "Aka fathers provide more direct infant care than fathers in any other known society" (Hewlett, 1992, p. 169). In Aka families, husbands and wives frequently cooperate in subsistence tasks and other activities (Hewlett, 1992). Thus, the father's involvement in child care is part and parcel of his overall role in the family.

Fathers around the world differ in the way they play with their infants. A highly physical style of play, characteristic of many fathers in the United States, is not typical of fathers in all cultures. Swedish and German fathers usually do not play with their babies this way (Lamb, Frodi, Frodi, & Hwang, 1982; Parke, Grossman, & Tinsley, 1981). African Aka fathers (Hewlett, 1987) and those in New Delhi, India, also tend to play gently with small children (Roopnarine, Hooper, Ahmeduzzaman, & Pollack, 1993; Roopnarine, Talokder, Jain, Josh, & Srivastav, 1992). Such cross-cultural variations suggest that rough play is *not* a function of male biology, but instead is culturally influenced.

In the United States, fathers' involvement in caregiving and play has greatly increased since 1970 as more mothers have begun to work outside the home and concepts of fathering have changed (Cabrera et al., 2000; Casper, 1997; Pleck, 1997). A father's frequent and positive involvement with his child, from infancy on, is directly related to the child's well-being and physical, cognitive, and social development (Cabrera et al., 2000; Kelley, Smith, Green, Berndt, & Rogers, 1998; Shannon, Tamis-LeMonda, London, & Cabrera, 2002). Nonetheless, among a nationally representative sample of 10,221 children born in the United States in 2001, at 9 months of age 20 percent of the children lived in households with no father, and 13 percent had never seen their father. Poor children and black and Hispanic children were most likely to have no father in the home (NCES, 2005).

What's Your View?

- "Despite the increasingly active role many of today's fathers play in child raising, a mother will always be more important to babies and young children than a father." Do you agree or disagree?

- How do you think your relationship with your father might have been different if you had grown up among the Huhot of Inner Mongolia? Among the Aka people?

"Up-p-ee!" This father obviously enjoys lifting his toddler daughter in the air, and the child obviously enjoys it too. Rough play between fathers and young children is typical in the United States but not in some other cultures.

How Parents Shape Gender Differences   Being male or female affects how people look, how they move their bodies, and how they work, play, and dress. It influences what they think about themselves and what others think of them. All these characteristics—and more—are included in the word **gender:** what it means to be male or female.

gender   Significance of being male or female.

By encouraging his son to "shave like Daddy," this father is engaging in gender-typing: encouraging the boy to adopt behaviors and attitudes his culture regards as masculine. Fathers tend to do more gender-typing than mothers do.

What's Your View?

- Should parents try to treat male and female babies alike?

gender-typing Socialization process by which children, at an early age, learn appropriate gender roles.

Checkpoint

Can you . . .

✔ Give examples of cultural differences in care of infants?

✔ Compare the roles of fathers and mothers and how they influence gender-typing?

Guidepost

4. How do infants gain trust in their world and form attachments?

Measurable differences between baby boys and baby girls are few, at least in U.S. samples. Boys are a bit longer and heavier and may be slightly stronger, but, as we mentioned in Chapter 4, they are physically more vulnerable from conception on. Girls are less reactive to stress and more likely to survive infancy (Davis & Emory, 1995; Keenan & Shaw, 1997). The two sexes are equally sensitive to touch and tend to teethe, sit up, and walk at about the same ages (Maccoby, 1980). They also achieve the other motor milestones of infancy at about the same times.

However, U.S. parents tend to *think* baby boys and girls are more different than they actually are. In a study of 11-month-old infants who had recently begun crawling, mothers consistently had higher expectations for their sons' success in crawling down steep and narrow slopes than for their daughters. Yet, when tested on the slopes, the baby girls and boys showed identical levels of performance (Mondschein, Adolph, & Tamis-LeMonda, 2000).

One of the earliest *behavioral* differences between boys and girls, appearing between 1 and 2 years of age, is in preferences for toys and play activities and for playmates of the same sex (Campbell, Shirley, Heywood, & Crook, 2000; Serbin et al., 2001; Turner & Gervai, 1995). Between ages 2 and 3, boys and girls tend to say more words pertaining to their own sex (such as "necklace" versus "tractor") than to the other sex (Stennes, Burch, Sen, & Bauer, 2005).

Parental shaping of boys' and girls' personalities appears to begin very early. Fathers, especially, promote **gender-typing,** the process by which children learn behavior that their culture considers appropriate for each sex (Bronstein, 1988). Fathers treat boys and girls more differently than mothers do, even during the first year (M. E. Snow, Jacklin, & Maccoby, 1983). During the second year, fathers talk more and spend more time with sons than with daughters (Lamb, 1981). Mothers talk more, and more supportively, to daughters than to sons (Leaper, Anderson, & Sanders, 1998), and girls at this age tend to be more talkative than boys (Leaper & Smith, 2004). Fathers of toddlers play more roughly with sons and show more sensitivity to daughters (Kelley et al., 1998).

We will discuss gender-typing and gender differences in more depth in Chapter 8.

Developmental Issues in Infancy

How does a dependent newborn, with a limited emotional repertoire and pressing physical needs, become a child with complex feelings and the abilities to understand and control them? Much of this development revolves around issues regarding relationships with caregivers.

Developing Trust

For a far longer period than the young of other mammals, human babies are dependent on others for food, for protection, and for their very lives. How do they come to trust that their needs will be met? According to Erikson (1950), early experiences are the key.

The first of Erikson's eight stages in psychosocial development (refer back to Table 2-2 in Chapter 2) is **basic trust versus basic mistrust.** This stage begins in infancy and continues until about 18 months. In these early months, babies develop a sense of the reliability of the people and objects in their world. They need to develop a balance between trust (which lets them form intimate relationships) and mistrust (which enables them to protect themselves). If trust predominates, as it should, children develop the "virtue" of *hope:* the belief that they can fulfill their needs and obtain their desires (Erikson, 1982). If mistrust predominates, children will view the world as unfriendly and unpredictable and will have trouble forming relationships.

The critical element in developing trust is sensitive, responsive, consistent caregiving. Erikson saw the feeding situation as the setting for establishing the right mix of trust and mistrust. Can the baby count on being fed when hungry, and can the baby therefore trust the mother as a representative of the world? Trust enables an infant to let the mother out of sight "because she has become an inner certainty as well as an outer predictability" (Erikson, 1950, p. 247). This inner trust, in Cathy Bateson, may have formed a solid foundation for more difficult periods ahead.

basic trust versus basic mistrust Erikson's first crisis in psychosocial development, in which infants develop a sense of the reliability of people and objects.

Checkpoint

Can you . . .

✔ Explain the importance of basic trust and identify the critical element in its development?

Developing Attachments

Attachment is a reciprocal, enduring emotional tie between an infant and a caregiver, each of whom contributes to the quality of the relationship. Attachments have adaptive value for babies, ensuring that their psychosocial as well as physical needs will be met. According to ethological theory, infants and parents are biologically predisposed to become attached to each other, and attachment promotes a baby's survival.

attachment Reciprocal, enduring tie between two people, especially between infant and caregiver, each of whom contributes to the quality of the relationship.

Patterns of Attachment The study of attachment owes much to the ethologist John Bowlby (1951), a pioneer in the study of bonding in animals. From his animal studies and from observations of disturbed children in a London psychoanalytic clinic, Bowlby became convinced of the importance of the mother-baby bond and warned against separating mother and baby without providing good substitute care. Mary Ainsworth, a student of Bowlby's in the early 1950s, went on to study attachment in African babies in Uganda through naturalistic observation in their homes (Ainsworth, 1967). Ainsworth later devised the **Strange Situation,** a nowclassic laboratory-based technique designed to assess attachment patterns between an infant and an adult. Typically, the adult is the mother (though other adults have taken part as well), and the infant is 10 to 24 months old.

Both Anna and Diane contribute to the attachment between them by the way they act toward each other. The way the baby molds herself to her mother's body shows her trust and reinforces Diane's feelings for her child, which she displays through sensitivity to Anna's needs.

Strange Situation Laboratory technique used to study infant attachment.

The Strange Situation consists of a sequence of eight episodes and takes less than half an hour. During that time, the mother twice leaves the baby in an unfamiliar room, the first time with a stranger. The second time she leaves the baby alone, and the stranger comes back before the mother does. The mother then encourages the baby to explore and play again and gives comfort if the baby seems to need it (Ainsworth, Blehar, Waters, & Wall, 1978). Of particular concern is the baby's response each time the mother returns.

When Ainsworth and her colleagues observed 1-year-olds in the Strange Situation and at home, they found three main patterns of attachment. These are *secure attachment* (the most common category, into which about 60 to 75 percent of low-risk North American babies fall) and two forms of anxious, or insecure, attachment: *avoidant* (15 to 25 percent) and *ambivalent, or resistant* (10 to 15 percent) (Vondra & Barnett, 1999).

Babies with **secure attachment** cry or protest when the mother leaves and greet her happily when she returns. They use her as a secure base, leaving her to go off and explore but returning occasionally for reassurance. They are usually cooperative and relatively free of anger. Babies with **avoidant attachment** rarely cry when the mother leaves but avoid her on her return. They tend to be angry and do not reach out in time of need. They dislike being held but dislike being put down even more. Babies with **ambivalent (resistant) attachment** become anxious even before the mother leaves and are very upset when she goes out. When she returns, they show their ambivalence by seeking contact with her while at the same time resisting it by kicking or squirming. Resistant babies do little exploration and are hard to comfort.

These three attachment patterns are universal in all cultures in which they have been studied—cultures as different as those in Africa, China, and Israel—though the percentage of infants in each category varies (True, Pisani, & Oumar, 2001; van IJzendoorn & Kroonenberg, 1988; van IJzendoorn & Sagi, 1999). Attachment *behaviors,* however, vary across cultures. Among the Gusii of east Africa, on the western edge of Kenya, infants are greeted with handshakes, and Gusii infants reach out for a parent's hand much as western infants cuddle up for a hug (van IJzendoorn & Sagi, 1999).

Other research (Main & Solomon, 1986) has identified a fourth attachment pattern, **disorganized-disoriented attachment.** This pattern is often subtle and difficult to observe, but it has been validated by more than 80 studies (van IJzendoorn, Schuengel, & Bakermans-Kranenburg, 1999). Babies with the disorganized pattern seem to lack an organized strategy to deal with the stress of the Strange Situation. Instead, they show contradictory, repetitive, or misdirected behaviors (seeking closeness to the stranger instead of the mother). They may greet the mother brightly when she returns but then turn away or approach without looking at her. They seem confused and afraid. This may be the least secure pattern. It is most likely to occur in babies whose mothers are insensitive, intrusive, or abusive or have suffered unresolved loss. The child's temperament does not seem to be a factor (Carlson, 1998; van IJzendoorn et al., 1999). Disorganized attachment is thought to occur in at least 10 percent of low-risk infants but in much higher proportions in certain at-risk populations, such as premature children, those with autism or Down syndrome, and those whose mothers abuse alcohol or drugs (Vondra & Barnett, 1999). This attachment pattern tends to remain fairly stable and seems to be a risk factor for later behavioral problems, especially aggressive conduct (van IJzendoorn et al., 1999). (Table 6-3 describes how babies with each of the four patterns of attachment react to the Strange Situation.)

How Attachment Is Established On the basis of a baby's interactions with the mother, proposed Ainsworth and Bowlby, the baby builds a "working model" of what can be expected from her. As long as the mother continues to act the same way, the model holds up. If her behavior changes—not just once or twice but consistently—the baby may revise the model, and security of attachment may change.

A baby's working model of attachment is related to Erikson's concept of basic trust. (Margaret Mead and Gregory Bateson's success as new parents reflected their grasp of this concept.) Secure attachment reflects trust; insecure attachment, mistrust. Securely attached babies have learned to trust not only their caregivers but their own

---

secure attachment Pattern in which an infant cries or protests when the primary caregiver leaves and actively seeks out the caregiver upon his or her return.

avoidant attachment Pattern in which an infant rarely cries when separated from the primary caregiver and avoids contact upon his or her return.

ambivalent (resistant) attachment Pattern in which an infant becomes anxious before the primary caregiver leaves, is extremely upset during his or her absence, and both seeks and resists contact on his or her return.

disorganized-disoriented attachment Pattern in which an infant, after separation from the primary caregiver, shows contradictory behaviors upon his or her return.

Table 6-3 Attachment Behaviors in the Strange Situation

Attachment Classification	Behavior
Secure	Gloria plays and explores freely when her mother is nearby. She responds enthusiastically when her mother returns.
Avoidant	When Sam's mother returns, Sam does not make eye contact or greet her. It is almost as if he has not noticed her return.
Ambivalent (Resistant)	James hovers close to his mother during much of the Strange Situation, but he does not greet her positively or enthusiastically during the reunion episode. Instead, he is angry and upset.
Disorganized/Disoriented	Erica responds to the Strange Situation with inconsistent, contradictory behavior. She seems to fall apart, overwhelmed by the stress.

Source: Based on Thompson, 1998, pp. 37–39.

ability to get what they need. Thus, babies who cry a lot and whose mothers respond by soothing them tend to be securely attached (Del Carmen, Pedersen, Huffman, & Bryan, 1993). Mothers of securely attached infants and toddlers tend to be sensitive and responsive (Ainsworth et al., 1978; Braungart-Rieker et al., 2001; De Wolff & van IJzendoorn, 1997; Isabella, 1993; NICHD Early Child Care Research Network, 1997a). Equally important are mutual interaction, stimulation, a positive attitude, warmth and acceptance, and emotional support (De Wolff & van IJzendoorn, 1997; Lundy, 2003). Contrary to Ainsworth's original findings, babies seem to develop attachments to both parents at about the same time, and security of attachment to father and mother is usually quite similar, as it seems to have been with Cathy Bateson (Fox, Kimmerly, & Schafer, 1991).

Newer Methods to Study Attachment Although much research on attachment has been based on the Strange Situation, some investigators have questioned its validity. The Strange Situation *is* strange; it is also artificial. It asks mothers not to initiate interaction, exposes babies to repeated comings and goings of adults, and expects the infants to pay attention to them. Also, the Strange Situation may be less valid in some nonwestern cultures. Research on Japanese infants, who are less commonly separated from their mothers than U.S. babies, showed high rates of resistant attachment, which may reflect the extreme stressfulness of the Strange Situation for these babies (Miyake, Chen, & Campos, 1985).

Because attachment influences a wider range of behaviors than are seen in the Strange Situation, some researchers have begun to supplement it with methods that enable them to study children in natural settings. The Waters and Deane (1985) Attachment Q-set (AQS) has mothers or other home observers sort a set of descriptive words or phrases ("cries a lot"; "tends to cling") into categories ranging from most to least characteristic of the child and then compare these descriptions with expert descriptions of the prototypical secure child. An analysis of 139 studies found the observer version (but not the maternal report version) a valid measure of attachment security, correlating well with results from the Strange Situation and with measures of maternal sensitivity. The AQS also seems to have cross-cultural validity (van IJzendoorn, Bereijken, Bakermans-Kranenburg, & Riksen-Walraven, 2004). In a study using the AQS, mothers in China, Colombia, Germany, Israel, Japan, Norway, and the United States decribed their children as behaving more like than unlike the "most secure child." Furthermore, the mothers' descriptions of "secure-base" behavior were about as similar across cultures as within a culture. These findings suggest that the tendency to use the mother as a secure base is universal, though it may take somewhat varied forms (Posada et al., 1995). However, because the AQS measures only the *degree* of security of attachment, researchers may need to use the Strange Situation for discriminating between different forms of insecure attachment (avoidant and ambivalent) or when disorganized attachment is suspected (van IJzendoorn et al., 2004).

The Role of Temperament How much does temperament influence attachment and in what ways? Findings vary (Susman-Stillman, Kalkoske, Egeland, & Waldman, 1996; Vaughn et al., 1992). In a study of 6- to 12-month-olds and their families, both a mother's sensitivity and her baby's temperament influenced attachment patterns (Seifer, Schiller, Sameroff, Resnick, & Riordan, 1996).

A baby's temperament may have not only a direct impact on attachment but also an indirect impact through its effect on the parents. In a series of studies in the Netherlands (van den Boom, 1989, 1994), 15-day-old infants classified as irritable were much more likely than nonirritable infants to be insecurely (usually avoidantly) attached at 1 year. However, irritable infants whose mothers received home visits with instruction on how to soothe their babies were as likely to be rated securely attached as the nonirritable infants. Thus, an infant's irritability may prevent the development of secure attachment but not if the mother has the skills to cope with the baby's temperament (Rothbart et al., 2000). "Goodness of fit" between parent and child may well be a key to understanding security of attachment.

Stranger Anxiety and Separation Anxiety Sophie used to be a friendly baby, smiling at strangers and going to them, continuing to coo happily as long as someone—anyone—was around. Now, at 8 months, she turns away when a new person approaches and howls when her parents try to leave her with a baby-sitter. Sophie is experiencing both **stranger anxiety,** wariness of a person she does not know, and **separation anxiety,** distress when a familiar caregiver leaves her.

Separation anxiety and stranger anxiety used to be considered emotional and cognitive milestones of the second half of infancy, reflecting attachment to the mother. However, newer research suggests that although stranger anxiety and separation anxiety are fairly typical, they are not universal. Whether a baby cries when a parent leaves or when someone new approaches may say more about the baby's temperament or life circumstances than about security of attachment (R. J. Davidson & Fox, 1989).

Babies rarely react negatively to strangers before 6 months of age but commonly do so by 8 or 9 months (Sroufe, 1997). This change may reflect cognitive development. Sophie's stranger anxiety involves memory for faces, the ability to compare the stranger's appearance with her mother's, and perhaps the recollection of situations in which she has been left with a stranger. If Sophie is allowed to get used to the stranger gradually in a familiar setting, she may react more positively (Lewis, 1997; Sroufe, 1997). (As we've mentioned, Margaret Mead and Gregory Bateson made sure that Cathy always met a new caregiver in a familiar place.)

Separation anxiety may be due not so much to the separation itself as to the quality of substitute care. When substitute caregivers are warm and responsive and play with 9-month-olds *before* they cry, the babies cry less than when they are with less responsive caregivers (Gunnar, Larson, Hertsgaard, Harris, & Brodersen, 1992).

stranger anxiety Wariness of strange people and places, shown by some infants during the second half of the first year.

separation anxiety Distress shown by someone, typically an infant, when a familiar caregiver leaves.

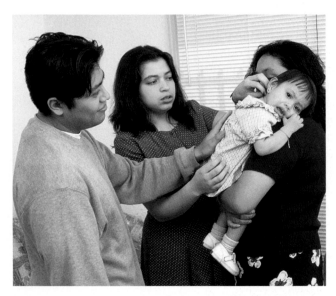

This baby is showing separation anxiety about her parents' leaving her with a baby-sitter. Separation anxiety is common in the last half of the first year.

Stability of care is important. Pioneering work by René Spitz (1945, 1946) on institutionalized children emphasizes the need for substitute care to be as close as possible to good mothering. Research has underlined the value of continuity and consistency in caregiving, so children can form early emotional bonds with their caregivers. As Mead observed in southeast island cultures, bonds can be formed with multiple caregivers, as long as the caregiving situation is stable.

Today, neither intense fear of strangers nor intense protest when the mother leaves is considered to be a sign of secure attachment. Researchers measure attachment more by what happens when the mother returns than by how many tears the baby sheds at her departure.

Long-Term Effects of Attachment As attachment theory proposes, security of attachment seems to affect emotional, social, and cognitive competence (van IJzendoorn & Sagi, 1997). The more secure a child's attachment to a nurturing adult, the easier it seems to be for the child to develop good relationships with others.

If children, as infants, had a secure base and could count on parents' or caregivers' responsiveness, they are likely to feel confident enough to be actively engaged in their world (Jacobsen & Hofmann, 1997). In a study of 70 fifteen-month-olds, those who were securely attached to their mothers, as measured by the Strange Situation, showed less stress in adapting to child care than did insecurely attached toddlers (Ahnert, Gunnar, Lamb, & Barthel, 2004).

Securely attached toddlers tend to have larger, more varied vocabularies than those who are insecurely attached (Meins, 1998). They have more positive interactions with peers, and their friendly overtures are more likely to be accepted (Fagot, 1997). Insecurely attached toddlers tend to show more negative emotions (fear, distress, and anger), whereas securely attached children are more joyful (Kochanska, 2001).

Between ages 3 and 5, securely attached children are likely to be more curious, competent, empathic, resilient, and self-confident, to get along better with other children, and to form closer friendships than children who were insecurely attached as infants (Arend, Gove, & Sroufe, 1979; Elicker et al., 1992; J. L. Jacobson & Wille, 1986; Waters, Wippman, & Sroufe, 1979; Youngblade & Belsky, 1992). They interact more positively with parents, preschool teachers, and peers and are better able to resolve conflicts (Elicker et al., 1992). They tend to have a more positive self-image (Elicker et al., 1992; Verschueren, Marcoen, & Schoefs, 1996).

Their advantages continue. In a French-Canadian laboratory observation, attachment patterns and the emotional quality of 6-year-olds' interactions with their mothers

Lifemap CD

How do early attachments influence social life, both in infancy and onward through early adulthood? View the "Importance of Attachment Theory" video in Chapter 6 of your CD to find out.

Children who were securely attached as infants tend to get along well with other children and form close friendships.

predicted the strength of the children's communicative skills, cognitive engagement, and mastery motivation at age 8 (Moss & St-Laurent, 2001).

Secure attachment seems to prepare children for the intimacy of friendship (Carlson, Sroufe, & Egeland, 2004). In middle childhood and adolescence, securely attached children (at least in western cultures, where most studies have been done) tend to have the closest, most stable friendships (Schneider, Atkinson, & Tardif, 2001; Sroufe, Carlson, & Shulman, 1993).

Insecurely attached infants, by contrast, often have inhibitions and negative emotions in toddlerhood, hostility toward other children at age 5, and dependency during the school years (Calkins & Fox, 1992; Kochanska, 2001; Lyons-Ruth, Alpern, & Repacholi, 1993; Sroufe, Carlson et al., 1993). Those with disorganized attachment tend to have behavior problems at all levels of schooling and psychiatric disorders at age 17 (Carlson, 1998).

Intergenerational Transmission of Attachment Patterns The *Adult Attachment Interview (AAI)* (George, Kaplan, & Main, 1985; Main, 1995; Main, Kaplan, & Cassidy, 1985) is a semistructured interview that asks adults to recall and interpret feelings and experiences related to their childhood attachments. Studies using the AAI have found that the clarity, coherence, and consistency of the responses reliably predict the security with which the respondent's own child will be attached (van IJzendoorn, 1995).

The way adults recall early experiences with parents or caregivers affects their emotional well-being and may influence the way they respond to their own children (Adam, Gunnar, & Tanaka, 2004; Dozier, Stovall, Albus, & Bates, 2001; Pesonen, Raïkkönen, Keltikangas-Järvinen, Strandberg, & Järvenpää, 2003; Slade, Belsky, Aber, & Phelps, 1999). A mother who was securely attached to *her* mother or who understands why she was insecurely attached can accurately recognize the baby's attachment behaviors, respond encouragingly, and help the baby form a secure attachment to her (Bretherton, 1990). Mothers who are preoccupied with their past attachment relationships tend to show anger and intrusiveness in interactions with their children. Depressed mothers who dismiss memories of their past attachments tend to be cold and unresponsive to their children (Adam et al., 2004). Parents' attachment history also influences their perceptions of their baby's temperament, and those perceptions may affect the parent-child relationship (Pesonen et al., 2003).

Mothers' mental representations of their babies begin to form during pregnancy, in part reflecting memories of their own attachment experience. In a prospective longitudinal study of 206 pregnant women of varied ethnicity and SES, these prenatal mental representations predicted the security of the infants' attachment to their mothers at one year of age (Huth-Bocks, Levendosky, Bogat, & von Eye, 2004).

Checkpoint

Can you . . .

✔ Describe four patterns of attachment?

✔ Discuss how attachment is established, including the role of the baby's temperament?

✔ Discuss factors affecting stranger anxiety and separation anxiety?

✔ Describe long-term behavioral influences of attachment patterns and intergenerational transmission of attachment?

Guidepost

5. How do infants and caregivers "read" each other's nonverbal signals, and what happens when communication breaks down?

mutual regulation Process by which infant and caregiver communicate emotional states to each other and respond appropriately.

Emotional Communication with Caregivers: Mutual Regulation

Infants are communicating beings; they have a strong drive to interact with others (Striano, 2004). Interactions that influence the security of attachment depend on the ability of both infant and caregiver to respond appropriately and sensitively to each other's mental and emotional states—a process known as **mutual regulation.** Parents may contribute to these reciprocal, mutually rewarding interactions by making comments that show recognition of what is on an infant's mind (Lundy, 2003). Infants take an active part in the process by sending behavioral signals that influence the way caregivers behave toward them.

Healthy interaction occurs when a caregiver "reads" a baby's signals accurately and responds appropriately. When a baby's goals are met, the baby is joyful or at least interested (E. Z. Tronick, 1989). If a caregiver ignores an invitation to play or insists on playing when the baby has signaled "I don't feel like it," the baby may feel frustrated or sad. When babies do not achieve desired results, they keep on sending signals to repair the interaction. Normally, interaction moves back and forth between well-regulated and poorly regulated states, and babies learn from these shifts how to send signals and what to do when their initial signals do not result in a comfortable emotional balance. Mutual regulation helps babies learn to "read" others' behavior and to develop expectations about it. Even very young infants can perceive emotions expressed by others and can adjust their own behavior accordingly (Legerstee & Varghese, 2001; Montague & Walker-Andrews, 2001; Termine & Izard, 1988), but they are disturbed when someone—whether the mother or a stranger, and regardless of the reason—breaks off interpersonal contact (Striano, 2004).

The **"still-face" paradigm** (Tronick, Als, Adamson, Wise, & Brazelton, 1978) is a research procedure used to measure mutual regulation in 2- to 9-month-old infants. In the *still-face* episode, which follows a normal face-to-face interaction, the mother suddenly becomes stony-faced, silent, and unresponsive. Then, a few minutes later, she resumes normal interaction (the *reunion* episode). During the still-face episode, infants tend to stop smiling and looking at the mother. They may make faces, sounds, or gestures or may touch themselves, their clothing, or a chair, apparently to comfort themselves or to relieve the emotional stress created by the mother's unexpected behavior (Cohn & Tronick, 1983; E. Z. Tronick, 1980, 1989; Weinberg & Tronick, 1996).

How do infants react during the reunion episode? In one study, 6-month-olds showed even more positive behavior during that episode—joyous expressions and utterances and gazes and gestures directed toward the mother—than before the still-face episode. Nonetheless, the persistence of sad or angry facial expressions, "pick-me-up" gestures, distancing, and indications of stress as well as an increased tendency to fuss and cry suggested that the negative feelings stirred by a breakdown in mutual regulation were not readily eased (Weinberg & Tronick, 1996). The way a mother sees and responds to her infant affects the infant's reaction to the still-face procedure (Rosenblum, McDonough, Muzik, Miller, & Sameroff, 2002; Tarabulsy et al., 2003).

The still-face reaction seems to be similar in Eastern and Western cultures and in interactions with both fathers and mothers (Braungart-Rieker, Garwood, Powers, & Notaro, 1998; Kisilevsky et al., 1998). Infants whose parents are normally sensitive and responsive to their emotional needs seem better able to comfort themselves and show less negative emotion during the still-face episode and recover more readily during the reunion episode (Braungart-Rieker et al., 2001; Tarabulsy et al., 2003). (Box 6-1 discusses how a mother's depression may contribute to developmental problems in her baby.)

Social Referencing

In the last quarter of the first year, as infants begin to get around on their own and initiate complex behaviors, they experience an important developmental shift: the ability to participate in person-to-person communication about an external event. They can now engage in *affective sharing,* letting a caregiver know how they feel about a situation or object and reacting to the emotions they discern in the caregiver. These developments are the necessary underpinnings of **social referencing,** the ability to seek out emotional information to guide behavior (Hertenstein & Campos, 2004). In social referencing, one person forms an understanding of how to act in an ambiguous, confusing, or unfamiliar situation by seeking out and interpreting another person's perception of it. Babies seem to use social referencing when they look at their caregivers upon encountering a new person or toy.

"still-face" paradigm Research procedure used to measure mutual regulation in infants 2 to 9 months old.

What's Your View?

- Do you see any ethical problems with the still-face paradigm or the Strange Situation? If so, do you think the benefits of these kinds of research are worth any potential risks?

social referencing Understanding an ambiguous situation by seeking out another person's perception of it.

BOX 6-1

Digging Deeper
How a Mother's Depression Affects Mutual Regulation

Postpartum depression affects about 13 percent of new mothers—including the actress Brooke Shields, who has written a book about it. Unless treated promptly, it may have a negative impact on the way a mother interacts with her baby and on the child's future cognitive and emotional development (Gjerdingen, 2003).

Depressed mothers are less sensitive and less engaged with their infants than nondepressed mothers, and their interactions with their babies are generally less positive (NICHD Early Child Care Research Network, 1999b). Depressed mothers are less able to interpret and respond to an infant's cries (Donovan, Leavitt, & Walsh, 1998) and are less likely to comment on an infant's mental state (Lundy, 2003).

Babies of depressed mothers may give up on sending emotional signals and try to comfort themselves by sucking or rocking. If this defensive reaction becomes habitual, babies learn that they have no power to draw responses from other people, that their mothers are unreliable, and that the world is untrustworthy. They also may become depressed themselves (Ashman & Dawson, 2002; Gelfand & Teti, 1995; Teti et al., 1995).

We cannot be sure, however, that such infants become depressed through a failure of mutual regulation. They may inherit a predisposition to depression or acquire it prenatally through exposure to hormonal or other biochemical influences (Lundy, Field, & Pickens, 1996). Infants of depressed mothers tend to show unusual patterns of brain activity, similar to the mothers' own patterns. Within 24 hours of birth, they show relatively less activity in the left frontal region of the brain, which seems to be specialized for "approach" emotions such as joy and anger, and more activity in the right frontal region, which controls "withdrawal" emotions, such as distress and disgust (G. Dawson et al., 1992, 1999; T. Field, 1998a, 1998c; T. Field, Fox, Pickens, Nawrocki, & Soutollo, 1995; N. A. Jones, Field, Fox, Lundy, & Davalos, 1997). Newborns of depressed mothers also tend to have higher levels of stress hormones (Lundy et al., 1999), lower scores on the Brazelton Neonatal Behavior Assessment Scale, and lower vagal tone, which is associated with attention and learning (T. Field, 1998a, 1998c; N. A. Jones et al., 1998). These findings suggest that a woman's depression *during pregnancy* may contribute to her newborn's neurological and behavioral functioning.

It may be that a combination of genetic, prenatal, and environmental factors puts infants of depressed mothers at risk. A bidirectional influence may be at work; an infant who does not respond normally may further depress the mother, and her unresponsiveness may in turn increase the infant's depression (T. Field, 1995, 1998a, 1998c; Lundy et al., 1999). Some depressed mothers do maintain good interactions with their infants, and these infants tend to have better emotional regulation than other infants of depressed mothers. These infants' characteristics may evoke more positive responses from their mothers (Field, Diego, Hernandez-Reif, Schanberg, & Kuhn, 2003). Interactions with a nondepressed adult—the father or a child care worker or nursery school teacher—can help infants compensate for the effects of depressed mothering (T. Field, 1995, 1998a, 1998c).

Both as infants and as preschoolers, children with depressed mothers tend to be insecurely attached to them (Gelfand & Teti, 1995; Teti et al., 1995). They are less motivated to explore than are other infants and more apt to prefer relatively unchallenging tasks (Hart, Field, del Valle, & Pelaez-Nogueras, 1998; Redding, Harmon, & Morgan, 1990). They are likely to grow poorly, to perform poorly on cognitive and linguistic measures, and to have behavior problems (T. Field, 1998a, 1998c; T. M. Field et al., 1985; Gelfand & Teti, 1995; NICHD Early Child Care Research Network, 1999b; B. S. Zuckerman & Beardslee, 1987). As toddlers these children tend to have trouble suppressing frustration and tension (Cole, Barrett, & Zahn-Waxler, 1992; Seiner & Gelfand, 1995). They are at risk of antisocial behavior at age 7 (Kim-Cohen, Moffitt, Taylor, Pawlby, & Caspi, 2005) and violent behavior in early adolescence (Hay, 2003); a combination of genetic and environmental factors may be involved (Kim-Cohen et al., 2005).

Techniques that may help improve a depressed mother's mood include listening to music, visual imagery, aerobics, yoga, relaxation, and massage therapy (T. Field, 1995, 1998a, 1998c). Massage also can help depressed babies (T. Field, 1998a, 1998b; T. Field et al., 1996), possibly through effects on neurological activity (N. A. Jones et al., 1997). In one study, such mood-brightening measures—plus social, educational, and vocational rehabilitation for the mother and day care for the infant—improved their interaction behavior. The infants showed faster growth and had fewer pediatric problems, more normal biochemical values, and better developmental test scores than a control group (T. Field, 1998a, 1998b).

What's Your View?

Can you suggest ways to help depressed mothers and babies, other than those mentioned here?

Check It Out

For further information on this topic, go to http://www.nimh.nih.gov/publicat/depwomenknows.cfm. This is a National Institute of Mental Health Web resource called "Depression: What Every Woman Should Know." Or go to http://www.nimh.nih.gov/publicat/depresfact.cfm. This is a general fact sheet about depression, located on the Web site of the National Institute of Mental Health.

The idea that infants engage in social referencing has been challenged. When infants spontaneously look at caregivers in ambiguous situations, it is not clear that they are looking for information; they may be seeking comfort, attention, sharing of feelings, or simply reassurance of the caregiver's presence—typical attachment behaviors (Baldwin & Moses, 1996).

However, more recent research provides experimental evidence of social referencing at 1 year (Moses, Baldwin, Rosicky, & Tidball, 2001). When exposed to jiggling or vibrating toys fastened to the floor or ceiling, both 12- and 18-month-olds moved closer to or farther from the toys depending on the experimenters' expressed emotional reactions ("Yecch!" or "Nice!"). In a pair of studies, 12-month-olds (but not 10-month-olds) adjusted their behavior toward certain unfamiliar objects according to nonvocal emotional signals given by an actress on a television screen (Mumme & Fernald, 2003). In another pair of experiments (Hertenstein & Campos, 2004), whether 14-month-olds touched plastic creatures that dropped within their reach was related to the positive or negative emotions they had seen an adult express about the same objects an hour before. Eleven-month-olds responded to such emotional cues if the delay was very brief (3 minutes).

Social referencing—and the ability to retain information gained from it—may play a role in such key developments of toddlerhood as the rise of self-conscious emotions (embarrassment and pride), the development of a sense of self, and the processes of *socialization* and *internalization,* to which we turn in the remainder of this chapter.

Checkpoint
Can you . . .

✔ Describe how mutual regulation works and explain its importance?

✔ Discuss how a mother's depression can affect her baby?

✔ Give examples of how infants seem to use social referencing?

Developmental Issues in Toddlerhood

About halfway between their first and second birthdays, babies become toddlers. This transformation can be seen not only in such physical and cognitive skills as walking and talking, but in the ways children express their personalities and interact with others. A toddler becomes a more active, intentional partner in interactions and sometimes initiates them. Caregivers can now more clearly "read" the child's signals. Such "in sync" interactions help toddlers gain communicative skills and social competence and motivate compliance with a parent's wishes (Harrist & Waugh, 2002).

Let's look at three psychological issues that toddlers—and their caregivers—have to deal with: the emerging *sense of self;* the growth of *autonomy,* or self-determination; and *socialization,* or *internalization of behavioral standards.*

 Lifemap CD

What are some of the distinct feelings we develop about ourselves as infants and toddlers? To find out, watch the "Self-Awareness Test" video in Chapter 6 of your CD.

The Emerging Sense of Self

The **self-concept** is our image of ourselves—our total picture of our abilities and traits. It describes what we know and feel about ourselves and guides our actions (Harter, 1996, p. 207). Children incorporate into their self-image the picture that others reflect back to them.

When and how does the self-concept develop?* From a jumble of seemingly isolated experiences (say, from one breast-feeding session to another), infants begin to extract consistent patterns that form rudimentary concepts of self and other. Depending on what kind of care the infant receives and how she or he responds, pleasant or unpleasant emotions become connected with sensorimotor experiences (such as sucking) that play an important part in the growing organization of the self.

Between 4 and 10 months, when infants learn to reach, grasp, and make things happen, they experience a sense of personal *agency,* the realization that they can control external events. The sense of agency is a forerunner of what Bandura (1994) calls **self-efficacy,** a sense of being able to master challenges and achieve goals. At about this time infants develop *self-coherence,* the sense of being a physical whole with boundaries within which agency resides. These developments occur in interaction with caregivers in games such as peekaboo (refer back to Box 5-1 in Chapter 5), in which the infant becomes increasingly aware of the difference between self and other ("I see you!").

Guidepost

6. When and how do the self and self-concept arise?

self-concept Sense of self; descriptive and evaluative mental picture of one's abilities and traits.

self-efficacy Sense of one's own capability to master challenges and achieve goals.

*The discussion in this section is indebted to Harter, 1998.

This toddler shows self-awareness by touching the spot on her face where she sees in the mirror that experimenters have placed a dot of rouge. According to this research, toddlers come to recognize their own image between 18 and 24 months of age.

The emergence of *self-awareness*—conscious knowledge of the self as a distinct, identifiable being—builds on this dawning of perceptual discrimination between self and others. In an experiment with 96 four- and nine-month-olds, the infants showed more interest in images of others than of themselves (Rochat & Striano, 2002). This early *perceptual* discrimination may be the foundation of the *conceptual* self-awareness that develops between 15 and 18 months. In a classic line of research, investigators dabbed rouge on the noses of 6- to 24-month-olds and sat them in front of a mirror. Three-fourths of 18-month-olds and all 24-month-olds touched their red noses more often than before, whereas babies younger than 15 months never did. This behavior suggests that these toddlers knew they did not normally have red noses and recognized the image in the mirror as their own (Lewis, 1997; Lewis & Brooks, 1974). Once children can recognize themselves, they show a preference for looking at their own video image over an image of another child the same age (Nielsen, Dissanayake, & Kashima, 2003).

By 20 to 24 months, toddlers begin to use first-person pronouns, another sign of self-awareness (Lewis, 1997). Between 19 and 30 months, they begin to apply descriptive terms ("big" or "little"; "straight hair" or "curly hair") and evaluative ones ("good," "pretty," or "strong") to themselves. The rapid development of language enables children to think and talk about the self and to incorporate parents' verbal descriptions ("You're so smart!" "What a big boy!") into their own emerging self-image (Stipek, Gralinski, & Kopp, 1990).

What's Your View?

- Given the integral importance of relationships with caregivers to infants' self-development, what kinds of caregiving practices do you think would lead to a healthy sense of self?

Guidepost

7. How do toddlers develop autonomy and standards for socially acceptable behavior?

autonomy versus shame and doubt Erikson's second stage in psychosocial development, in which children achieve a balance between self-determination and control by others.

Development of Autonomy

Erikson (1950) identified the period from about 18 months to 3 years as the second stage in personality development, **autonomy versus shame and doubt,** which is marked by a shift from external control to self-control. Having come through infancy with a sense of basic trust in the world and an awakening self-awareness, toddlers begin to substitute their own judgment for their caregivers'. The "virtue" that emerges during this stage is *will.* Toilet training, which in most children is completed most rapidly if begun after 27 months (Blum, Taubman, & Nemeth, 2003), is an important step toward autonomy and self-control. So is language; as children are better able to make their wishes known, they become more powerful. Because unlimited freedom is neither safe nor healthy, said Erikson, shame and doubt have a necessary place. Toddlers need adults to set appropriate limits, and shame and doubt help them recognize the need for those limits.

In the United States, the "terrible twos" are a normal manifestation of the drive for autonomy. Toddlers have to test the notions that they are individuals, that they have some control over their world, and that they have new, exciting powers. They are driven to try out their own ideas, exercise their own preferences, and make their own decisions. This drive typically shows itself in the form of *negativism,* the tendency to shout, "No!" just for the sake of resisting authority. Almost all U.S. children show negativism to some degree; it usually begins before 2 years of age, tends to peak at about 3½ to 4, and declines by age 6. Caregivers who view children's expressions of self-will as a normal, healthy striving for independence, not as stubbornness, can help them learn self-control, contribute to their sense of competence, and avoid excessive conflict. (Table 6-4 gives specific, research-based suggestions for dealing with the "terrible twos.")

Many U.S. parents might be surprised to hear that the "terrible twos" are not universal. In some developing countries, the transition from infancy to early childhood is relatively smooth and harmonious (Mosier & Rogoff, 2003; see Box 6-2).

According to Erikson, toilet training is an important step toward autonomy and self-control.

Moral Development: Socialization and Internalization

Socialization is the process by which children develop habits, skills, values, and motives that make them responsible, productive members of society. Compliance with parental expectations can be seen as a first step toward compliance with societal standards of behavior. Socialization rests on **internalization** of these standards. Children who are successfully socialized no longer merely obey

Checkpoint

Can you . . .

✔ Trace the early development of the self-concept?

✔ Describe the conflict of autonomy versus shame and doubt?

✔ Explain why the "terrible twos" is considered a normal phenomenon, and suggest reasons this transition may not exist in some cultures?

socialization Development of habits, skills, values, and motives shared by responsible, productive members of a society.

internalization During socialization, process by which children accept societal standards of conduct as their own.

Table 6-4	Dealing with the "Terrible Twos"

The following research-based guidelines can help parents of toddlers discourage negativism and encourage socially acceptable behavior.

- *Be flexible.* Learn the child's natural rhythms and special likes and dislikes.
- *Think of yourself as a safe harbor,* with safe limits, from which a child can set out and discover the world and to which the child can keep coming back for support.
- *Make your home "child-friendly."* Fill it with unbreakable objects that are safe to explore.
- *Avoid physical punishment.* It is often ineffective and may even lead a toddler to do more damage.
- *Offer a choice*—even a limited one—to give the child some control. ("Would you like to have your bath now or after we read a book?")
- *Be consistent* in enforcing necessary requests.
- *Don't interrupt an activity unless absolutely necessary.* Try to wait until the child's attention has shifted.
- *If you must interrupt, give warning.* ("We have to leave the playground soon.")
- *Suggest alternative activities* when behavior becomes objectionable. (When Ashley is throwing sand in Keiko's face, say, "Oh, look! Nobody's on the swings now. Let's go over and I'll give you a good push!")
- *Suggest; don't command.* Accompany requests with smiles or hugs, not criticism, threats, or physical restraint.
- *Link requests with pleasurable activities.* ("It's time to stop playing so that you can go to the store with me.")
- *Remind the child of what you expect:* "When we go to this playground, we *never* go outside the gate."
- *Wait a few moments before repeating a request* when a child doesn't comply immediately.
- Use *"time out"* to end conflicts. In a nonpunitive way, remove either yourself or the child from a situation.
- *Expect less self-control during times of stress* (illness, divorce, the birth of a sibling, or a move to a new home).
- *Expect it to be harder for toddlers to comply with "dos" than with "don'ts."* "Clean up your room" takes more effort than "Don't write on the furniture."
- *Keep the atmosphere as positive as possible.* Make your child *want* to cooperate.

Sources: Haswell, Hock, & Wenar, 1981; Kochanska & Aksan, 1995; Kopp, 1982; Kuczynski & Kochanska, 1995; Power & Chapieski, 1986.

BOX 6-2

Window on the World

Are Struggles with Toddlers Necessary?

Are the "terrible twos" a normal phase in child development? Many western parents and psychologists think so. Actually, though, this transition does not appear to be universal.

In Zinacantan, Mexico, toddlers do not typically become demanding and resistant to parental control. Instead, toddlerhood in Zinacantan is a time when children move from mama's babies toward the new status of "mother's helpers," responsible children who tend a new baby and help with household tasks (Edwards, 1994). A similar developmental pattern seems to occur in Mazahua families in Mexico and among Mayan families in San Pedro, Guatemala. San Pedro parents "do not report a particular age when they expect children to become especially contrary or negative" (Mosier & Rogoff, 2003, p. 1058).

One arena in which issues of autonomy and control appear in western cultures is in sibling conflicts over toys and the way children respond to parental handling of these conflicts. To explore these issues, a cross-cultural study compared 16 San Pedro families with 16 middle-class European-American families in Salt Lake City. All of the families had toddlers 14 to 20 months old and older siblings 3 to 5 years old. The researchers interviewed each mother about her child-raising practices. They then handed the mother a series of attractive objects (such as nesting dolls and a jumping-jack puppet) and, in the presence of the older sibling, asked the mother to help the toddler operate them, with no instructions about the older child. Researchers who observed the ensuing interactions found striking differences in the way siblings interacted in the two cultures and in the way the mothers viewed and handled sibling conflict.

The older siblings in Salt Lake City often tried to take and play with the objects, but this did not generally happen in San Pedro. Instead, the older San Pedro children would offer to help their younger siblings work the objects, or the two children would play with them together. When there was a conflict over possession of the objects, the San Pedro mothers almost always favored the toddlers (94 percent of the time), even taking an object away from the older child if the younger child wanted it; and the older siblings tended to go along, willingly handing the objects to the toddlers or letting them have the objects from the start. By contrast, in more than one-third of the interactions in Salt Lake City, the mothers tried to treat both children equally, negotiating with them or suggesting that they take turns or share. These observations were consistent with reports of mothers in both cultures as to how they handled such issues at home. San Pedro children are

given a privileged position until age 3; then they are expected to willingly cooperate with social expectations.

What explains these cultural contrasts? A clue emerged when the mothers were asked at what age children can be held responsible for their actions. Most of the Salt Lake mothers maintained that their toddlers understood the consequences of touching prohibited objects; several said this understanding arises as early as 7 months. Yet all but one of the San Pedro mothers placed the age of understanding social consequences of actions much later—between 2 and 3 years. Whereas the Salt Lake mothers regarded their toddlers as capable of intentionally misbehaving, most San Pedro mothers did not. More than half of the Salt Lake mothers reporting punishing toddlers for such infractions; none of the San Pedro mothers did. Whereas all of the Salt Lake preschoolers were under direct caregiver supervision, much like their toddler siblings, 11 of the 16 San Pedro preschoolers were on their own much of the time and had more mature household responsibilities.

The researchers suggest that the "terrible twos" may be a phase specific to societies that place individual freedom before the needs of the group. Ethnographic research suggests that, in societies that place higher value on group needs, freedom of choice does exist, but it goes hand in hand with interdependence, responsibility, and expectations of cooperation. Salt Lake parents seem to believe that responsible behavior develops gradually from engaging in fair competition and negotiations. San Pedro parents seem to believe that responsible behavior develops rapidly when children are old enough to understand the need to respect others' desires as well as their own.

What's Your View?

From your experience or observation of toddlers, which of the two ways of handling sibling conflict would you expect to be more effective?

Check It Out

For more information on this topic, go to http://www.zerotothree.org. Here you will find links to a survey of 3,000 parents and other adults about commonly asked questions regarding the handling of young children and a downloadable article on "Cultural Models for Early Caregiving."

rules or commands to get rewards or avoid punishment; they have made society's standards their own (Grusec & Goodnow, 1994; Kochanska & Aksan, 1995; Kochanska, Tjebkes, & Forman, 1998).

Developing Self-Regulation Katy, age 2, is about to poke her finger into an electric outlet. In her "child-proofed" apartment, the sockets are covered, but not here in her grandmother's home. When Katy hears her father shout, "No!" the toddler pulls her arm back. The next time she goes near an outlet, she starts to poke her finger, hesitates, and then says, "No." She has stopped herself from doing something she remembers she is not supposed to do. She is beginning to show **self-regulation:** control of her own behavior to conform to a caregiver's demands or expectations, even when the caregiver is not present.

Self-regulation is the foundation of socialization, and it links all domains of development—physical, cognitive, emotional, and social. Until Katy was physically able to get around on her own, electric outlets posed no hazard. To stop herself from poking her finger into an outlet requires that she consciously understand and remember what her father told her. Cognitive awareness, however, is not enough; restraining herself also requires emotional control. By "reading" their parents' emotional responses to their behavior, children continually absorb information about what conduct their parents approve of. As children process, store, and act upon this information, their strong desire to please their parents leads them to do as they know their parents want them to, whether or not the parents are there to see.

Before they can control their own behavior, children may need to be able to regulate, or control, their *attentional processes* and to modulate negative emotions (Eisenberg, 2000). Attentional regulation enables children to develop willpower and cope with frustration (Sethi, Mischel, Aber, Shoda, & Rodriguez, 2000).

The growth of self-regulation parallels the development of the self-conscious and evaluative emotions, such as empathy, shame, and guilt (Lewis, 1995, 1997, 1998). It requires the ability to wait for gratification. It is correlated with measures of conscience development, such as resisting temptation and making amends for wrongdoing (Eisenberg, 2000). In most children, the full development of self-regulation takes at least three years (Kopp, 1982).

Origins of Conscience: Committed Compliance **Conscience** includes both emotional discomfort about doing something wrong and the ability to refrain from doing it. Before children can develop a conscience, they need to have internalized moral standards. Conscience depends on willingness to do the right thing because a child believes it is right, not (as in self-regulation) just because someone else said so. However, *inhibitory control*—conscious, or effortful, holding back of impulses, a mechanism of self-regulation that emerges during toddlerhood—may contribute to the development of conscience by first enabling the child to comply voluntarily with parental dos and don'ts (Kochanska, Murray, & Coy, 1997).

Grazyna Kochanska (1993, 1995, 1997a, 1997b) and her colleagues have looked for the origins of conscience in a longitudinal study of a group of toddlers and mothers in Iowa. Researchers videotaped 103 children ages 26 to 41 months and their mothers playing together with toys for two to three hours, both at home and in a homelike laboratory setting (Kochanska & Aksan, 1995). After a free-play period, a mother would give her child 15 minutes to put away the toys. The laboratory had a special shelf with other, unusually attractive toys, such as a bubble gum machine, a walkie-talkie, and a music box. The child was told not to touch anything on the shelf. After about an hour, the experimenter asked the mother to go into an adjoining room, leaving the child alone with the toys. A few minutes later, a woman entered, played with several of the forbidden toys, and then left the child alone again for eight minutes.

Children were judged to show **committed compliance** if they willingly followed the orders to clean up and not to touch the special toys, without reminders or lapses.

self-regulation A person's independent control of behavior to conform to understood social expectations.

conscience Internal standards of behavior, which usually control one's conduct and produce emotional discomfort when violated.

committed compliance Kochanska's term for wholehearted obedience of a parent's orders without reminders or lapses.

Children showed **situational compliance** if they needed prompting; their compliance depended on ongoing parental control. Committed compliance is related to internalization of parental values and household rules (Kochanska & Aksan, 1995; Kochanska, Coy, & Murray, 2001).

Committed compliance and situational compliance can be distinguished in children as young as 13 months, but their roots go back to infancy. Committed compliers, who are more likely to be girls than boys, tend to be those who, at 8 to 10 months, could refrain from touching when told, "No!" Committed compliance tends to increase with age, whereas situational compliance decreases (Kochanska, Tjebkes, & Forman, 1998). Mothers of committed compliers, as contrasted with mothers of situational compliers, tend to rely on gentle guidance rather than force, threats, or other forms of negative control (Eisenberg, 2000; Kochanska & Aksan, 1995; Kochanska et al., 2004).

Factors in the Success of Socialization The way parents go about the job of socializing a child, together with a child's temperament and the quality of the parent-child relationship, may help predict how hard or easy socialization will be (Kochanska, 1993, 1995, 1997a, 1997b, 2002). Factors in the success of socialization may include security of attachment, observational learning from parents' behavior, and the mutual responsiveness of parent and child (Kochanska, Aksan, Knaack, & Rhines, 2004; Maccoby, 1992). All these as well as socioeconomic and cultural factors (Harwood, Schoelmerich, Ventura-Cook, Schulze, & Wilson, 1996) may play a part in motivation to comply.

Secure attachment and a warm, mutually responsive parent-child relationship seem to foster committed compliance and conscience development, according to observational studies of more than 200 mothers and children. Starting in the child's second year and extending until early school age, researchers observed mothers and children in lengthy, naturalistic interactions: caregiving routines, preparing and eating meals, playing, relaxing, and doing household chores. Children who were judged to have mutually responsive relationships with their mothrs tended to show *moral emotions* such as guilt and empathy; *moral conduct* in the face of strong temptation to break rules or violate standards of behavior; and *moral cognition,* as judged by their response to hypothetical, age-appropriate moral dilemmas (Kochanska, 2002).

Constructive conflict over a child's misbehavior—conflict that involves negotiation, reasoning, and resolution—can help children develop moral understanding by enabling them to see another point of view. In one observational study, 2½-year-olds whose mothers gave clear explanations for their requests, compromised, or bargained with the child were better able to resist temptation at age 3 than children whose mothers had threatened, teased, insisted, or given in. Discussion of emotions in conflict situations ("How would you feel if . . .") also led to conscience development, probably by fostering the development of moral emotions (Laible & Thompson, 2002).

What's Your View?

• In view of Kochanska's research on the roots of conscience, what questions would you ask about the early socialization of antisocial adolescents and adults?

Checkpoint

Can you . . .

✔ Tell when and how self-regulation develops and how it contributes to socialization?

✔ Explain the importance of attentional regulation and inhibitory control?

✔ Distinguish between committed and situational compliance?

✔ Discuss how temperament, attachment, and parenting practices affect socialization?

Contact with Other Children

Although parents exert a major influence on children's lives, relationships with other children—both in the home and out of it—are important from infancy on.

Guidepost

8. How do infants and toddlers interact with siblings and other children?

Siblings

Sibling relationships play a distinct role in socialization (Vandell, 2000). Sibling conflicts can become a vehicle for understanding social relationships (Dunn & Munn, 1985; Ram & Ross, 2001). Lessons and skills learned from interactions with siblings carry over to relationships outside the home (Brody, 1998).

Babies usually become attached to their older brothers and sisters. Although rivalry may be present, so is affection. The more securely attached siblings are to their parents, the better they get along with each other (Teti & Ablard, 1989).

Nevertheless, as babies begin to move around and become more assertive, they inevitably come into conflict with siblings—at least in U.S. culture (refer back to Box 6-2). Sibling conflict increases dramatically after the younger child reaches 18 months of age (Vandell & Bailey, 1992). During the next few months, younger siblings begin to participate more fully in family interactions and become more involved in family disputes. As they do, they become more aware of others' intentions and feelings. They begin to recognize what kind of behavior will upset or annoy an older brother or sister and what behavior is considered "naughty" or "good" (Dunn & Munn, 1985).

As this cognitive and social understanding grows, sibling conflict tends to become more constructive, and the younger sibling participates in attempts to reconcile. As with parent-child conflict, constructive conflict with siblings helps children recognize each other's needs, wishes, and point of view, and it helps them learn how to fight, disagree, and compromise within the context of a safe, stable relationship (Vandell & Bailey, 1992).

In many nonwestern cultures, it is common to see older siblings caring for younger siblings, as with these Chinese children.

Sociability with Nonsiblings

Infants and—even more so—toddlers show interest in people outside the home, particularly people their own size. During the first few months, they look, smile, and coo at other babies (T. M. Field, 1978). During the last half of the first year, they increasingly smile at, touch, and babble to them (Hay, Pedersen, & Nash, 1982). At about 1 year, when the biggest items on their agenda are learning to walk and to manipulate objects, babies pay less attention to other people (T. M. Field & Roopnarine, 1982). This stage does not last long, though; from about 1½ years of age to almost 3, children show growing interest in what other children do and an increasing understanding of how to deal with them (Eckerman, Davis, & Didow, 1989; Eckerman & Stein, 1982).

Toddlers learn by imitating one another. Such games as follow-the-leader help toddlers connect with other children and pave the way for more complex games during the preschool years (Eckerman et al., 1989). Verbal communication (such as "You go in playhouse," "Don't do it!" or "Look at me") helps peers coordinate joint activity (Eckerman & Didow, 1996). As with siblings, conflict too can have a purpose: helping children learn how to negotiate and resolve disputes (Caplan, Vespo, Pedersen, & Hay, 1991).

Some children, of course, are more sociable than others, reflecting such temperamental traits as their usual mood, readiness to accept new people, and ability to

Checkpoint

Can you . . .

✔ Explain how sibling relationships play a part in socialization?

✔ Describe changes in sibling interactions during toddlerhood?

✔ Trace changes in sociability during the first 3 years, and state two influences on it?

adapt to change. Sociability is also influenced by experience; babies who spend time with other babies, as in child care, become sociable earlier than those who spend almost all their time at home.

Children of Working Parents

9. How do parental employment and early child care
affect infants' and toddlers'
development?

Parents' work determines more than the family's financial resources. Much of adults' time, effort, and emotional involvement goes into their occupations. How do their work and their child care arrangements affect infants and toddlers?

Most research on this subject pertains to mothers' work. More than half (52.9 percent) of mothers of infants in their first year of life and 57.5 percent of women with children under 3 were in the labor force in 2004 (Bureau of Labor Statistics, 2005b). We'll discuss the impact of parents' work on older children in later chapters.

Effects of Parental Employment

The National Longitudinal Survey of Youth (NLSY) is an annual survey of some 12,600 women, accompanied by assessments of their children. An analysis of 1994 NLSY data (Harvey, 1999) found little or no effect of early maternal employment on children's compliance, behavior problems, self-esteem, cognitive development, or academic achievement. As in a number of other studies, early maternal employment did seem to benefit children in low-income families by increasing the family's resources. The study found no significant effects of fathers' working hours.

On the other hand, longitudinal data on 900 European American children from the National Institute of Child Health and Human Development (NICHD) Study of Early Child Care, discussed in the next section, showed negative effects on cognitive development at 15 months to 3 years when mothers went to work 30 or more hours a week by a child's ninth month. Maternal sensitivity, the quality of the home environment, and quality of child care made a difference but did not fully account for the findings (Brooks-Gunn, Han, & Waldfogel, 2002).

Early Child Care

By 9 months of age, about 50 percent of U.S. infants are in some kind of regular nonparental child care arrangement, and 86 percent of these infants enter child care before they are 6 months old, according to a nationally representative study of children born during 2001. More than half of these babies are in child care more than 30 hours a week (NCES, 2005a). With an average cost upwards of $4,000 to $6,000 a year, affordability and quality of care are becoming a pressing issue (Gardner, 2002), especially for low-income families (Marshall, 2004) and parents of children with disabilities (Shonkoff & Phillips, 2000).

Bronfenbrenner's bioecological theory (refer back to Chapter 2) affords a broad perspective on how early child care can affect children's development. Both the family and the child care setting are microsystems directly affecting the child, but their influences are not fully independent; they are linked through the mesosystem. Parents affect children's child care experience through their selection of particular child care arrangements, which is largely dependent on their means. Child care also may affect family life, for example, when a child learns a new song or game in child care and wants to sing or play it at home. The family-child care mesosystem operates within the exosystem of government policies, subsidies, and regulations that affect the quality and affordability of child care. Above and beyond those specific influences are "the macrosystem of societal beliefs about the desirability of maternal employment and the desired outcomes for children" (Marshall, 2004, p. 167).

Factors in Impact of Child Care   The impact of early child care may depend on the type, amount, quality, and stability of care as well as the family's income and the age at which children start receiving nonmaternal care. Temperament and gender may make a difference (Crockenberg, 2003). Shy children in child care experience greater stress, as shown by cortisol levels, than sociable children (Watamura, Donzella, Alwin, & Gunnar, 2003), and insecurely attached children undergo greater stress than securely attached children when introduced to full-time child care (Ahnert et al., 2004). Boys are more vulnerable to stress, in child care and elsewhere, than are girls (Crockenberg, 2003).

Quality of care contributes to cognitive and psychosocial competence (Marshall, 2004; Peisner-Feinberg et al., 2001). Quality of care can be measured by *structural* characteristics, such as staff training and the ratio of children to caregivers. These features are easier to regulate and measure than such *process* characteristics as the warmth, sensitivity, and responsiveness of caregivers and the developmental appropriateness of activities. Structural quality and process quality may be related; in one study discussed in the next section, well-trained caregivers and low child-staff ratios were associated with higher process quality, which, in turn, was associated with better cognitive and social outcomes (Marshall, 2004). Unfortunately, most child care centers do not meet all recommended guidelines for quality care (Bergen, Reid, & Torelli, 2000; NICHD Early Child Care Research Network, 1998c, 1999a; see Table 6-5).

Table 6-5   Checklist for Choosing a Good Child Care Facility

- Is the facility licensed? Does it meet minimum state standards for health, fire, and safety? (Many centers and home care facilities are not licensed or regulated.)
- Is the facility clean and safe? Does it have adequate indoor and outdoor space?
- Does the facility have small groups, a high adult-to-child ratio, and a stable, competent, highly involved staff?
- Are caregivers trained in child development?
- Are caregivers warm, affectionate, accepting, responsive, and sensitive? Are they authoritative but not too restrictive, and neither too controlling nor merely custodial?
- Does the program promote good health habits?
- Does it provide a balance between structured activities and free play? Are activities age appropriate?
- Do the children have access to educational toys and materials, which stimulate mastery of cognitive and communicative skills at a child's own pace?
- Does the program nurture self-confidence, curiosity, creativity, and self-discipline?
- Does it encourage children to ask questions, solve problems, express feelings and opinions, and make decisions?
- Does it foster self-esteem, respect for others, and social skills?
- Does it help parents improve their child-rearing skills?
- Does it promote cooperation with public and private schools and the community?

Sources: American Academy of Pediatrics [AAP], 1986; Belsky, 1984; K. A. Clarke-Stewart, 1987; NICHD Early Child Care Research Network, 1996; S. W. Olds, 1989; Scarr, 1998.

These children in a high-quality group day care program are likely to do at least as well cognitively and socially as children cared for full time at home. The most important element of day care is the caregiver or teacher, who exerts a strong influence on the children in her care.

The most important element in quality of care is the caregiver; stimulating interactions with responsive adults are crucial to early cognitive, linguistic, and psychosocial development. Low staff turnover is important; infants need consistent caregiving in order to develop trust and secure attachments (Burchinal, Roberts, Nabors, & Bryant, 1996; Shonkoff & Phillips, 2000). Stability of care facilitates coordination between parents and child care providers, which may help protect against any negative effects of long hours of care (Ahnert & Lamb, 2003).

The NICHD Study: Isolating Child Care Effects Because child care is an integral part of a child's ecological system, it is difficult to measure its influence alone. The most comprehensive attempt to separate child care effects from such other factors as family characteristics, the child's characteristics, and the care the child receives at home is an ongoing study sponsored by the National Institute of Child Health and Human Development (NICHD).

This longitudinal study of 1,364 children and their families began in 1991 in 10 university centers across the United States, shortly after the children's birth. The sample was diverse socioeconomically, educationally, and ethnically; nearly 35 percent of the families were poor or near poor. Most infants entered nonmaternal care before 4 months of age and received, on average, 33 hours of care each week. Child care arrangements varied widely in type and quality. Through observation, interviews, questionnaires, and tests, researchers measured the children's social, emotional, cognitive, and physical development at frequent intervals from 1 month of age through the first seven years of life. What do the findings show?

The amount and quality of care children received as well as the type and stability of care influenced specific aspects of development (see Table 6-6). The more time a child spent in child care up to age 4½, the more likely that child was to be seen by adults as aggressive, disobedient, and hard to get along with, then and in

	Attachment	Parent-Child Relationships	Cooperation	Problem Behaviors	Cognitive Development and School Readiness	Language Development
Quality	•	•		+	+	+
Amount	•	•		•		
Type			•	•	+	+
Stability	•		•			

Table 6-6 Aspects of Development Affected by Characteristics of Early Child Care*

*Results after taking into account all family and child variables.

Source: Peth-Pierce, 1998, summary table of findings, p. 15.

+ Consistent effects

• Effects under some conditions

kindergarten—though this effect was limited in size. Long days in child care have been associated with stress for 3- and 4-year-olds; and some children that age in the NICHD sample spent up to 92 hours a week in center care (NICHD Early Child Care Research Network, 2003).

High-quality child care had a positive influence on cognitive development. Children in child care centers with low child-staff ratios, small group sizes, and trained, sensitive, responsive caregivers who provided positive interactions and language stimulation scored higher on tests of language comprehension, cognition, and readiness for school. Their mothers also reported fewer behavior problems (NICHD Early Child Care Research Network, 1999a, 2000, 2002). Furthermore, quality of care predicted cognitive performance in early childhood (NICHD Early Child Care Research Network & Duncan, 2003).

However, factors related to child care seem less influential than family characteristics, such as income, the home environment, the amount of mental stimulation the mother provides, and the mother's sensitivity to her child. These characteristics strongly predict developmental outcomes, regardless of how much time children spend in outside care (Marshall, 2004; NICHD Early Child Care Research Network, 1998b, 2000, 2003). For example, the quality of the family environment is more strongly predictive than is the quality of child care of individual differences in attention and memory in first grade (NICHD Early Child Care Research Network, 2005).

Although a caregiver's sensitivity and responsiveness influence a toddler's socialization, the mother's sensitivity has a greater influence, according to the NICHD research (NICHD Early Child Care Research Network, 1998a). Maternal sensitivity also is the strongest predictor of attachment. Child care had no direct effect on attachment, no matter how early infants entered care or how many hours they spent in it. Neither did the stability and quality of care affect attachment in and of themselves. However, when unstable, poor quality, or more-than-minimal amounts of child care (10 or more hours a week) were combined with insensitive, unresponsive mothering, insecure attachment was more likely. On the other hand, high-quality care seemed to help offset insensitive mothering (NICHD Early Child Care Research Network, 1997, 2001b).

It should not be surprising that what look like effects of child care often may be related to family characteristics. After all, stable families with favorable home environments are more able and therefore more likely to place their children in high-quality care.

One area in which the NICHD study did find independent effects of child care was in interactions with peers. Between ages 2 and 3, children whose caregivers were sensitive and responsive tended to become more positive and competent in play with other children (NICHD Early Child Care Research Network, 2001a).

To sum up, the NICHD findings so far give high-quality child care good marks overall, especially for its impact on cognitive development and interaction with peers. Some observers say that the areas of concern the study pinpointed—stress levels in infants and toddlers and possible behavior problems related to amounts of care—might be counteracted by activities that enhance children's attachment to caregivers and peers, emphasize child-initiated learning and internalized motivation, and focus on group social development (Maccoby & Lewis, 2003).

Impact on Disadvantaged Children and Minorities Children from low-income families or stressful homes especially benefit from care that supplies cognitive stimulation and emotional support, which may otherwise be lacking in their lives (Scarr, 1997b; Spieker, Nelson, Petras, Jolley, & Barnard, 2003). In a five-year longitudinal study of 451 poor, urban families in California and Florida with single mothers who were moving from welfare to work, children demonstrated stronger cognitive growth in center care than in home-based care (Loeb, Fuller, Kagan, & Carrol, 2004).

As we have mentioned, the NICHD study found that the more time a young child spends in nonmaternal care, the greater the risk of problem behavior (NICHD Early Childhood Research Network, 2003). But data from a study of 2,400 randomly selected low-income children in Boston, Chicago, and San Antonio suggest that extensive child care does *not* harm *poor* children's development unless it is of low quality (Votruba-Drzal, Coley, & Chase-Lansdale, 2004). Unfortunately, children from low-income famlies tend to be placed in lower-cost and lower-quality care than children from more affluent families (Marshall, 2004). The vast majority of children eligible for federal child care subsidies do not receive them (USDHHS, 2000).

Studies of ethnically and socioeconomically mixed samples and of low-income children may fail to reveal specific factors in minority experience with child care (Johnson et al., 2003). Many minority families live in extended-family households and historically relied on family and friends for child care. Today, although African American and Latina women increasingly choose center care, they are more likely to use family-based care (in the caregiver's home) or to rely on grandmothers. Minority women are more likely to work night shifts or long hours, to hold seasonal, nonoffice jobs, and to be laid off periodically. Thus, child care settings designed for regular daytime employment may not meet their needs.

Maltreatment: Abuse and Neglect

Although most parents are loving and nurturing, some cannot or will not take proper care of their children, and some deliberately hurt or kill them. *Maltreatment* is deliberate or avoidable endangerment of a child, either by *abuse,* action that inflicts harm, or *neglect,* inaction that causes harm (U.S. Department of Health and Human Services [USDHHS], 1999a).

Maltreatment takes several specific forms, and any one form is likely to be accompanied by one or more of the others (Belsky, 1993). **Physical abuse**

What's Your View?

• In the light of findings about effects of early child care, what advice would you give a new mother about the timing of her return to work and the selection of child care?

Checkpoint

Can you . . .

✔ Evaluate the impact of a mother's employment on her baby's well-being?

✔ List at least five criteria for good child care?

✔ Compare the impact of child care and of family characteristics on emotional, social, and cognitive development?

✔ Point out special considerations regarding child care for low-income and minority children?

Guidepost

10. What are the causes and consequences of child abuse and neglect, and what can be done about it?

involves injury to the body through punching, beating, kicking, or burning. It is generally distinguished from corporal (physical) punishment, such as spanking, though this distinction is debatable (see Box 8-1 in Chapter 8); but harsh physical discipline, such as shaking a very young child, can be equivalent to physical abuse. **Neglect** is failure to meet a child's basic needs, such as food, clothing, medical care, protection, and supervision. **Sexual abuse** is sexual activity or sexual touching involving a child and an older person. **Emotional maltreatment** refers to acts of abuse or neglect that may cause behavioral, cognitive, emotional, or mental disorders. It may include rejection, terrorization, isolation, exploitation, degradation, ridicule, or failure to provide emotional support, love, and affection (USDHHS, 1999a).

physical abuse Action taken deliberately to endanger another person, involving potential bodily injury.

neglect Failure to meet a dependent's basic needs.

sexual abuse Physically or psychologically harmful sexual activity, or any sexual activity involving a child and an older person.

emotional maltreatment Action or inaction that may cause behavioral, cognitive, emotional, or mental disorders.

Maltreatment: Facts and Figures

Since its peak in 1993, the rate of reported child abuse and neglect in the United States has declined by about 20 percent. Still, state and local child protective services agencies investigated and confirmed some 896,000 cases in 2002, and the actual number was undoubtedly far higher (USDHHS, 2004). An anonymous telephone survey of a random sample of mothers in North and South Carolina suggests that physical abuse may be 40 times more prevalent and sexual abuse 15 times more prevalent than officially reported (Theodore et al., 2005). On the other hand, some reported claims filed in the context of divorce proceedings, for example, turn out to be false.

More than 60 percent of children identified as maltreated are neglected, and almost 20 percent are physically abused. About 10 percent are sexually abused and 7 percent emotionally maltreated. American-Indian, Alaska-Native, and African American children have the highest rates of maltreatment, about twice as high as those of white children (USDHHS, 2004). Girls are four times more likely than boys to be sexually abused (NCANDS, 2001).

Children are abused and neglected at all ages, but the highest rates of *deaths* from maltreatment (76 percent) are for ages 3 and younger (USDHHS, 2004; see Figure 6-2; refer back to the discussion of shaken baby syndrome in Box 4-2). An estimated 1,400 U.S. children died of abuse or neglect in 2002—38 percent from neglect, 30 percent from physical abuse, and 29 percent from more than one type of maltreatment (USDHHS, 2004).

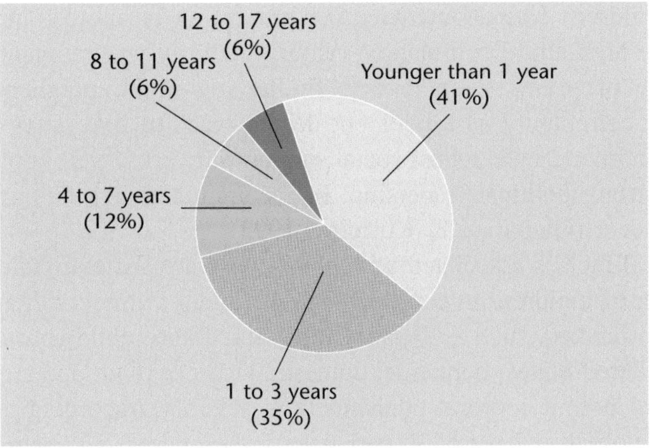

Figure 6-2

Child abuse and neglect fatality victims by age, United States, 2002. (Source: NCCANI, 2004a.)

Contributing Factors: An Ecological View

Abuse and neglect reflect the interplay of multiple layers of contributing factors involving the family, the community, and the larger society (USDHHS, 1999a).

Characteristics of Abusive and Neglectful Parents and Families In more than 8 out of 10 cases of physical abuse or neglect, the perpetrators are the child's parents, usually the mother (USDHHS, 2004). Maltreatment by parents is a symptom of extreme disturbance in child rearing, usually aggravated by other family problems, such as poverty, lack of education, alcoholism, depression, or antisocial behavior. A disproportionate number of abused and neglected children are in large, poor, or single-parent families, which tend to be under stress and to have trouble meeting children's needs (Sedlak & Broadhurst, 1996; USDHHS, 2004). Yet what pushes one parent over the edge, another may take in stride. Although most neglect cases occur in very poor families, most low-income parents do not neglect their children.

The likelihood that a child will be physically abused has little to do with the child's own characteristics and more to do with the household environment, according to a nationally representative longitudinal study of twins (Jaffee et al., 2004). Abuse may begin when a parent who is already anxious, depressed, or hostile tries to control a child physically but loses self-control and ends up shaking or beating the child (USDHHS, 1999a). Parents who abuse children tend to have marital problems and to fight physically. Their households tend to be disorganized, and they experience more stressful events than other families (Reid et al., 1982; Sedlak & Broadhurst, 1996).

Parents who are neglectful distance themselves from their children. They may be critical or uncommunicative. Many of the mothers were neglected themselves as children and are depressed or feel hopeless. Many of the fathers have deserted or do not give enough financial or emotional support. The family atmosphere tends to be chaotic, with people moving in and out (Dubowitz, 1999).

Abuse and neglect often occur in the same families. Such families tend to have no one to turn to in times of stress and no one to see what is happening (Dubowitz, 1999). Substance abuse is a factor in at least one-third of cases of abuse and neglect (USDHHS, 1999a).

Community Characteristics and Cultural Values What makes one low-income neighborhood a place where children are highly likely to be maltreated and another, matched for ethnic population and income levels, safer? In one inner-city Chicago neighborhood, the proportion of children who died from maltreatment (1 death for every 2,541 children) was about twice the proportion in another inner-city neighborhood. In the high-abuse community, criminal activity was rampant, and facilities for community programs were dreary. In the low-abuse neighborhood, people described their community as a poor but decent place to live. They painted a picture of a neighborhood with robust social support networks, well-known community services, and strong political leadership. In a community like this, maltreatment is less likely to occur (Garbarino & Kostelny, 1993).

Two cultural factors associated with child abuse are societal violence and physical punishment of children. In countries where violent crime is infrequent and children are rarely spanked, such as Japan, China, and Tahiti, child abuse is rare (Celis, 1990). In the United States, homicide, domestic violence, and rape are common, and many states still permit corporal punishment in schools. According to a representative sampling, more than 9 out of 10 parents of preschoolers and about half of parents of school-age children report using physical punishment at home (Straus & Stewart, 1999; see Box 8-1 in Chapter 8).

Helping Families in Trouble or at Risk

Because maltreatment is a multifactorial problem, it needs many-pronged solutions. Effective community prevention and intervention strategies should be comprehensive, neighborhood based, centered on protecting children, and aimed at strengthening families if possible and removing children if necessary (USDHHS, 1999a).

In 2003, the U.S. Department of Health and Human Services launched a Child Abuse Prevention Initiative to raise consciousness of this issue and coordinate preventive efforts in communities across the nation (National Clearinghouse on Child Abuse and Neglect Information [NCCANI], 2004a). Some abuse-prevention programs teach basic parenting skills. Other programs offer subsidized day care, volunteer homemakers, home visitors, and temporary "respite homes" or "relief parents" to take over occasionally (USDHHS, 1999a; Wolfe, Edwards, Manion, & Koverola, 1988).

A longitudinal study of 913 preschool-age participants in the Chicago Child-Parent Centers, an early intervention that provides educational and family support services in high-poverty areas, found significantly lower rates of maltreatment by age 17 than for children who participated in other interventions. Children who stayed in the program longer, whose parents were more involved, and whose families did not move were less likely to be maltreated (Reynolds & Robertson, 2003).

State and local child protective services agencies investigate reports of maltreatment. They determine what steps, if any, need to be taken and marshal community resources to help. Agency staff may try to help the family resolve their problems or arrange for alternative care for children who cannot safely remain at home (Larner, Stevenson, & Behrman, 1998).

Services for children who have been abused and their parents include shelters, education in parenting skills, and therapy. Parents Anonymous and other organizations offer free, confidential support groups. Children may receive play or art therapy and day care in a therapeutic environment. However, availability of services is often limited. In a nationally representative survey, nearly half (47.9 percent) of 2- to 14-year-olds investigated by child welfare agencies after reported maltreatment had clinically significant emotional or behavioral problems, but only one-fourth of those with such problems received mental health care (Burns et al., 2004).

When authorities remove children from their homes, the usual alternative is foster care. More than 500,000 children were in foster care in 2001, more than one-fourth of them under age 5 (Chipungu & Bent-Goodley, 2004). Foster care removes a child from immediate danger, but it is often unstable, further alienates the child from the family, and may turn out to be another abusive situation. Often a child's basic health and educational needs are not met (David and Lucile Packard Foundation, 2004; NRC, 1993b).

Due in part to a scarcity of traditional foster homes and an increasing caseload, a growing proportion of placements (31 percent), especially of African American children, are in kinship foster care—under the care of grandparents or other family members (Berrick, 1998; Geen, 2004). Although most foster children who leave the system are reunited with their families, about 28 percent reenter foster care within the next 10 years (Wulczyn, 2004). Children who have been in foster

This adult volunteer uses dolls to help young children realize that they have control over their bodies and need not let anyone—even friends or family members—touch them. Such programs for preventing sexual abuse need to walk a fine line between alerting children to danger and frightening them or discouraging appropriate affection.

care are more likely than other children to become homeless, to become involved in criminal activity, and to become teenage mothers (David and Lucile Packard Foundation, 2004).

Long-Term Effects of Maltreatment

Society needs more effective remedies for the plight of maltreated children. Without help, these children often grow up with serious problems, at great cost to themselves and to society, and may continue the cycle of maltreatment when they have children of their own (USDHHS, 1999a). An estimated one-third of adults who were abused and neglected in childhood victimize their own children (NCCANI, 2004b).

Consequences of maltreatment may be physical, emotional, cognitive, and social, and these types of consequences are often interrelated. For example, a physical blow to a child's head can cause brain damage resulting in cognitive delays and emotional and social problems. Long-term consequences of maltreatment may include poor physical, mental, and emotional health; impaired brain development; cognitive, language, and academic difficulties; problems in attachment and social relationships (NCCANI, 2004b); and, in adolescence, heightened risks of poor academic achievement, delinquency, teenage pregnancy, alcohol and drug use, and suicide (Dube et al., 2003; Dube et al., 2001; Lansford et al., 2002; NCCANI, 2004b).

In a study that followed 68 sexually abused children for five years, these children showed more disturbed behavior, had lower self-esteem, and were more depressed, anxious, or unhappy than a control group (Swanston, Tebbutt, O'Toole, & Oates, 1997). Sexually abused children may become sexually active at an early age (Fiscella, Kitzman, Cole, Sidora, & Olds, 1998). Adults who were sexually abused as children tend to be anxious, depressed, angry, or hostile; to mistrust people; to feel isolated and stigmatized; to be sexually maladjusted (Browne & Finkelhor, 1986); and to abuse alcohol or drugs (NRC, 1993b; USDHHS, 1999a).

Still, many maltreated children show remarkable resilience. Consequences of abuse or neglect may depend on the child's age and developmental status; the type, frequency, duration, and severity of the maltreatment; the relationship between the victim and perpetrator; and the child's personal characteristics. Optimism, self-esteem, intelligence, creativity, humor, and independence are protective factors, as is the social support of a caring adult (NCCANI, 2004b). See Chapter 10 for a further discussion of factors that affect resilience.

Ref⊕cus

Thinking back to the Focus vignette about Cathy Bateson at the beginning of this chapter:

- Which of the four types of temperament did Cathy show? Was there goodness of fit in her relationship with her parents?

- Did Cathy appear to be securely or insecurely attached?

- How did the child-raising practices Cathy's parents followed seem to contribute to her psychosocial development?

- How did her mother's professional life affect Cathy as an infant? As a toddler? On balance, as an only child, did she seem to benefit from her family's unusual child care arrangement with the Frank family?

Checkpoint
Can you...

✔ Define four types of child abuse and neglect?

✔ Discuss the incidence of maltreatment and explain why it is hard to measure?

✔ Identify contributing factors having to do with the family, the community, and the culture?

✔ Cite ways to prevent or stop maltreatment and help its victims?

✔ Give examples of long-term effects of child abuse and neglect and factors that promote resilience?

The experiences of the first 3 years lay the foundation for future development. In Part 4, we'll see how young children build on that foundation.

SUMMARY AND KEY TERMS

Foundations of Psychosocial Development

Guidepost 1: When and how do emotions develop, and how do babies show them?

- Emotional development is orderly; complex emotions seem to develop from earlier, simpler ones.
- Crying, smiling, and laughing are early signs of emotion. Other indices are facial expressions, motor activity, body language, and physiological changes.
- Brain development is closely linked with emotional development.
- Self-conscious and evaluative emotions arise after the development of self-awareness.

emotions *(193)*

self-conscious emotions *(197)*

self-awareness *(197)*

self-evaluative emotions *(197)*

empathy *(197)*

social cognition *(197)*

egocentric *(197)*

Guidepost 2: How do infants show temperamental differences, and how enduring are those differences?

- Many children seem to fall into one of three categories of temperament: "easy," "difficult," and "slow-to-warm-up."
- Temperamental patterns appear to be largely inborn and to have a biological basis. They are generally stable but can be modified by experience.
- Goodness of fit between a child's temperament and environmental demands aids adjustment.
- Cross-cultural differences in temperament may reflect child raising practices.

temperament *(198)*

"easy" children *(199)*

"difficult" children *(199)*

"slow-to-warm-up" children *(199)*

goodness of fit *(200)*

Guidepost 3: What roles do mothers and fathers play in early personality development?

- Child raising practices and caregiving roles vary around the world.
- Infants have strong needs for maternal closeness and warmth as well as physical care.
- Fatherhood is a social construction. Fathering roles differ in various cultures.
- Although significant gender differences typically do not appear until after infancy, U.S. fathers, especially, promote early gender-typing.

gender *(203)*

gender-typing *(204)*

Developmental Issues in Infancy

Guidepost 4: How do infants gain trust in their world and form attachments?

- According to Erikson, infants in the first 18 months are in the first stage of personality development, basic trust versus basic mistrust. Sensitive, responsive, consistent caregiving is the key to successful resolution of this conflict.
- Research based on the Strange Situation has found four patterns of attachment: secure, avoidant, ambivalent (resistant), and disorganized-disoriented.
- Newer instruments measure attachment in natural settings and in cross-cultural research.
- Attachment patterns may depend on a baby's temperament as well as on the quality of parenting and may have long-term implications for development.
- Separation anxiety and stranger anxiety may arise during the second half of the first year and appear to be related to temperament and circumstances.
- A parent's memories of childhood attachment can influence his or her own child's attachment.

basic trust versus basic mistrust *(205)*

attachment *(205)*

Strange Situation *(205)*

secure attachment *(206)*

avoidant attachment *(206)*

ambivalent (resistant) attachment *(206)*

disorganized-disoriented attachment *(206)*

stranger anxiety *(208)*

separation anxiety *(208)*

Guidepost 5: How do infants and caregivers "read" each other's nonverbal signals?

- Mutual regulation enables babies to play an active part in regulating their emotional states.

- A mother's depression, especially if severe or chronic, may have serious consequences for her infant's development.
- The belief that babies display social referencing is in dispute, but there is evidence that 1-year-olds do so.

mutual regulation *(210)*

"still-face" paradigm *(211)*

social referencing *(211)*

Developmental Issues in Toddlerhood

Guidepost 6: When and how does the sense of self arise?

- The sense of self arises between 4 and 10 months, as infants begin to perceive a difference between self and others and to experience a sense of agency and self-coherence.
- The self-concept builds on this perceptual sense of self and develops between 15 and 18 months with the emergence of self-awareness and self-recognition.

self-concept *(213)*

self-efficacy *(213)*

Guidepost 7: How do toddlers develop autonomy and standards for socially acceptable behavior?

- Erikson's second stage concerns autonomy versus shame and doubt. Negativism is a normal manifestation of the shift from external control to self-control.
- Socialization, which rests on internalization of societally approved standards, begins with the development of self-regulation.
- A precursor of conscience is committed compliance to a caregiver's demands; toddlers who show committed compliance tend to internalize adult rules more readily than those who show situational compliance.
- Parenting practices, a child's temperament, the quality of the parent-child relationship, and cultural and socioeconomic factors may affect the ease and success of socialization.

autonomy versus shame and doubt *(214)*

socialization *(215)*

internalization *(215)*

self-regulation *(217)*

conscience *(217)*

committed compliance *(217)*

situational compliance *(218)*

Contact with Other Children

Guidepost 8: How do infants and toddlers interact with siblings and other children?

- Sibling relationships play a distinct role in socialization; what children learn from relations with siblings carries over to relationships outside the home.

- Between 1½ and 3 years of age, children tend to show more interest in other children and increasing understanding of how to deal with them.

Children of Working Parents

Guidepost 9: How do parental employment and early child care affect infants' and toddlers' development?

- In general, mothers' workforce participation during a child's first three years seems to have little impact on development, but cognitive development may suffer when a mother works 30 or more hours a week by her child's ninth month.
- Substitute child care varies in quality. The most important element in quality of care is the caregiver.
- Although quality, quantity, stability, and type of care influence psychosocial and cognitive development, the influence of family characteristics seems greater overall.
- Low-income children, especially, benefit from good child care. Minority children may benefit from care that meets their special needs and is consistent with their family upbringing.

Maltreatment: Abuse and Neglect

Guidepost 10: What are the causes and consequences of child abuse and neglect, and what can be done about it?

- Forms of maltreatment are physical abuse, neglect, sexual abuse, and emotional maltreatment.
- Characteristics of the abuser or neglecter, the family, the community, and the larger culture all contribute to child abuse and neglect.
- Maltreatment can interfere with physical, cognitive, emotional, and social development, and its effects can continue into adulthood. Still, many maltreated children show remarkable resilience.
- Preventing or stopping maltreatment may require multifaceted, coordinated community efforts.

physical abuse *(225)*

neglect *(225)*

sexual abuse *(225)*

emotional maltreatment *(225)*

PART 3

• As muscles come under more conscious control, children can tend to more of their own personal needs, such as dressing and toileting, and thus gain a greater sense of competence and independence.

• Eating and sleep patterns are influenced by cultural attitudes.

• Even the common cold can have emotional and cognitive implications. Occasional minor illnesses not only build immunity, they also help children learn to cope with physical distress and understand its causes.

• Social interaction plays a major role in the development of preliteracy skills, memory, and measured intelligence.

• Cognitive awareness of gender has far-reaching psychosocial implications, affecting children's sense of self and their attitudes toward the roles the two sexes play in their society.

• Environmental influences, including the parents' life circumstances, affect health and safety.

During the years from 3 to 6, often called the *preschool years,* children make the transition from toddlerhood to childhood. Their bodies become slimmer, their motor and mental abilities sharper, and their personalities and relationships more complex.

The 3-year-old is no longer a baby, but a sturdy adventurer, at home in the world and eager to explore its possibilities as well as the developing capabilities of his or her own body and mind. A child of this age has come through a relatively dangerous time of life—the years of infancy and toddlerhood—to enter a healthier, less threatening phase.

Growth and change are less rapid in early childhood than in infancy and toddlerhood, but, as we see in Chapters 7 and 8, all aspects of development—physical, cognitive, emotional, and social—continue to intertwine.

Early Childhood

PREVIEW

CHAPTER 7

Physical and Cognitive Development in Early Childhood

CHAPTER 8

Psychosocial Development in Early Childhood

Growth is steady; appearance becomes more slender and proportions more adultlike.

Appetite diminishes, and sleep problems are common.

Handedness appears; fine and gross motor skills and strength improve.

Thinking is somewhat egocentric, but understanding of other people's perspectives grows.

Cognitive immaturity leads to some illogical ideas about the world.

Memory and language improve.

Intelligence becomes more predictable.

Preschool experience is common, and kindergarten more so.

Self-concept and understanding of emotions become more complex; self-esteem is global.

Independence, initiative, and self-control increase.

Gender identity develops.

Play becomes more imaginative, more elaborate, and usually more social.

Altruism, aggression, and fearfulness are common.

Family is still the focus of social life, but other children become more important.

CHAPTER 7

Physical and Cognitive Development in Early Childhood

Children live in a world of imagination and feeling. . . . They invest the most insignificant object with any form they please, and see in it whatever they wish to see.

Adam G. Oehlenschlager

Focus
Wang Yani, Self-Taught Artist

Wang Yani

Wang Yani (b. 1975)* is a gifted young Chinese artist. She had her first exhibit in Shanghai at the age of 4 and had produced 4,000 paintings by the age of 6. Since she turned 10, her work has been shown throughout Asia and in Europe and the United States.

Yani (her given name)** began painting at 2½. Her father, Wang Shiqiang, was a professional artist and educator. He gave her big brushes and large sheets of paper to permit bold strokes. Rather than teach her, he let her learn in her own way and always praised her work. In contrast with traditional Chinese art education, which emphasizes conformity and imitation, he allowed his daughter's imagination free rein.

Yani went through the usual stages in preschoolers' drawing but far more quickly than usual. Her early paintings were made up of dots, circles, and lines, which represented

people, birds, or fruit. By the age of 3, she could paint recognizable but highly original forms. Yani's father encouraged her to paint what she saw outdoors near their home in the scenic riverside town of Gongcheng. Like traditional Chinese artists, she did not paint from life but constructed her brightly colored compositions from mental images of what she had seen. Her visual memory has been called astounding. When she was only 4, her father taught her Chinese characters (letters) of as many as 25 strokes by "writing" them in the air with his finger. Without hesitation, Yani would put them down on paper from memory.

Her father helped her develop powers of observation and imagery by carrying her on his shoulders as he hiked in the fields and mountains or lying with her in the grass and telling stories about the passing clouds. The pebbles along the riverbank

*Sources of biographical information about Wang Yani are Bond (1989), Costello (1990), Ho (1989), Stuart (1991), and Zhensun & Low (1991).

**In Chinese custom, the given name follows the family name.

235

reminded her of the monkeys at the zoo, which she painted over and over between the ages of 3 and 6. Yani made up stories about the monkeys she portrayed. They often represented Yani herself—eating a snack, refereeing an argument among friends, or trying to conquer her fear of her first shot at the doctor's office. Painting, to Yani, was not an objective representation of reality; it was a mirror of her mind, a way to transform her sensory impressions into simple but powerful semiabstract images onto which she projected her thoughts, feelings, and dreams.

Because of her short arms, Yani's brush strokes at first were short. Her father trained her to hold her brush tightly by trying to grab it from behind when she was not looking. She learned to paint with her whole arm, twisting her wrist to produce the effect she wanted. As her physical dexterity and experience grew, her strokes became more forceful, varied, and precise: broad, wet strokes to define an animal's shape; fuzzy, nearly dry ones to suggest feathers, fur, or tree bark. The materials she used—bamboo brushes, ink sticks, and rice paper—were traditional, but her style, popularly called *xieyi,* "idea writing," was not. It was and remains playful, free, and spontaneous.

With quick reflexes, a fertile imagination, remarkable visual abilities, strong motivation, and her father's sensitive guidance, Yani's artistic progress has been swift. As a young adult, she is considered an artist of great promise. Yet she herself finds painting very simple: "You just paint what you think about. You don't have to follow any instruction. Everybody can paint" (Zhensun & Low, 1991, p. 9).

Although Wang Yani's artistic growth has been unusual, it rested on typical developments of early childhood: rapid improvement in muscular control and eye-hand coordination, accompanied by a growing understanding of the world around her—an understanding guided by her powers of observation and memory and her verbal interactions with her father. Together these physical, cognitive, and social influences helped her express her thoughts and emotions through art.

In this chapter, we look at physical and cognitive development during the years from 3 to 6. Children in this age group grow more slowly than before, but still at a fast pace; and they make so much progress in muscle development and coordination that they can do much more. Children also make enormous advances in the abilities to think, speak, and remember. In this chapter, we trace all these developing capabilities and consider several health concerns. We also discuss an experience increasingly common in many places: early childhood education.

After you have read and studied this chapter, you should be able to answer each of the following Guidepost questions. Look for them again in the margins, where they point to important concepts throughout the chapter. To check your understanding of these Guideposts, review the end-of-chapter summary. Checkpoints located at periodic spots throughout the chapter will help you verify your understanding of what you have read.

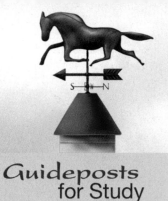

Guideposts for Study

1. How do children's bodies change between ages 3 and 6, and what are their nutritional and dental needs?

2. What sleep patterns tend to develop during early childhood, and what sleep problems may occur?

3. What are the main motor achievements of early childhood?

4. What are the major health and safety risks for young children?

5. What are typical cognitive advances and immature aspects of preschool children's thinking?

6. What memory abilities expand in early childhood?

7. How is preschoolers' intelligence measured, and what are some influences on it?

8. How does language improve during early childhood, and what happens when its development is delayed?

9. What purposes does early childhood education serve, and how do children make the transition to kindergarten?

PHYSICAL DEVELOPMENT

Aspects of Physical Development

In early childhood, children slim down and shoot up. They need less sleep than before and are more likely to develop sleep problems. They improve in running, hopping, skipping, jumping, and throwing balls. They also become better at tying shoelaces, drawing with crayons, and pouring cereal; and they begin to show a preference for either the right or left hand.

Guidepost

1. How do children's bodies change between ages 3 and 6, and what are their nutritional and dental needs?

Bodily Growth and Change

Children grow rapidly between ages 3 and 6, but less quickly than before. At about 3, children normally begin to lose their babyish roundness and take on the slender, athletic appearance of childhood. As abdominal muscles develop, the toddler potbelly tightens. The trunk, arms, and legs grow longer. The head is still relatively large, but the other parts of the body continue to catch up as body proportions steadily become more adultlike.

The pencil mark on the wall that shows Eve's height is 37 inches from the floor, and this "average" 3-year-old now weighs about 30 pounds. Her twin brother Isaac, like most boys this age, is a little taller and heavier and has more muscle per pound of body weight, whereas Eve, like most girls, has more fatty tissue. Both boys and girls typically grow 2 to 3 inches a year during early childhood and gain 4 to 6 pounds annually (see Table 7-1). Boys' slight edge in height and weight continues until the growth spurt of puberty.

Muscular and skeletal growth progresses, making children stronger. Cartilage turns to bone at a faster rate than before, and bones become harder, giving the child

Table 7-1	Physical Growth, Ages 3 to 6 (50th percentile)*			
	Height, Inches		**Weight, Pounds**	
Age	Boys	Girls	Boys	Girls
3	37½	37	32	30
3½	39	38½	34	32½
4	40½	39½	36	35
4½	41½	41	38	37
5	43	42½	40	40
5½	44½	44	43	42
6	45½	45½	46	45

*Fifty percent of children in each category are above this height or weight level, and 50 percent are below it.

Source: Kuczmarski et al., 2000.

Checkpoint

Can you . . .

✔ Describe typical physical changes between ages 3 and 6, and compare boys' and girls' growth patterns?

a firmer shape and protecting the internal organs. These changes, coordinated by the still-maturing brain and nervous system, promote the development of a wide range of motor skills. The increased capacities of the respiratory and circulatory systems build physical stamina and, along with the developing immune system, keep children healthier.

Nutrition: Preventing Obesity/Overweight

Obesity (sometimes called *overweight*) is becoming a problem among U.S. preschoolers. In 1999–2002, more than 10 percent of 2- to 5-year-olds were overweight by 1963–1994 standards, as compared with 7 percent in 1994 (Hedley et al., 2004; Ogden, Flegal, Carroll, & Johnson, 2002). About 12 percent more were considered at risk for overweight. The greatest increase in prevalence of overweight is among children in low-income families (Ritchie et al., 2001), cutting across all ethnic groups (AAP Committee on Nutrition, 2003; Center for Weight and Health, 2001). Mexican-American boys are especially prone to overweight (Hedley et al., 2004). Even at age 5, overweight is associated with behavioral problems (Datar & Sturm, 2004a) and low reading and math scores (Datar, Sturm, & Magnabosco, 2004).

Worldwide, an estimated 22 million children under age 5 are obese (Belizzi, 2002). As "junk food" spreads through the developing world, as many as 20 to 25 percent of 4-year-olds in some countries, such as Egypt, Morocco, and Zambia, are overweight or obese—a larger proportion than are malnourished.

A tendency toward obesity can be hereditary, but the main factors driving the obesity epidemic are environmental (AAP, 2004). Excessive weight gain hinges on caloric intake and lack of exercise (AAP Committee on Nutrition, 2003). As growth slows, preschoolers need fewer calories in proportion

An obese child is likely to find it hard to keep up with slimmer peers, both physically and socially. Obesity among preschool and school-age children is more common than in the past.

to their weight than they did before. According to a representative sampling in Glasgow, Scotland, many 3- to 5-year-olds have mostly sedentary lifestyles (Reilly et al., 2004).

As children move through the preschool period, their eating patterns become more environmentally influenced. Whereas 3-year-olds will eat only until they are full, 5-year-olds tend to eat more when a larger portion is put in front of them. Thus, a key to preventing obesity may be to make sure older preschoolers are served appropriate portions—and not to admonish them to clean their plates (Rolls et al., 2000).

What children eat is as important as how much they eat. To avoid overweight and prevent cardiac problems, young children should get only about 30 percent of their total calories from fat, and no more than one-third of fat calories should come from saturated fat. Lean meat and dairy foods should remain in the diet to provide protein, iron, and calcium. Milk and other dairy products can now be skim or low fat (AAP Committee on Nutrition, 1992a). Studies have found no negative effects on height, weight, body mass, or neurological development from a moderately low-fat diet (Rask-Nissilä et al., 2000; Shea et al., 1993).

Prevention of obesity in the early years, when excessive weight gain usually begins, is critical; the long-term success of treatment, especially when it is delayed, is limited (AAP Committee on Nutrition, 2003; Quattrin, Liu, Shaw, Shine, & Chiang, 2005). Overweight children, especially those who have overweight parents, tend to become obese adults (AAP Committee on Nutrition, 2003; Whitaker et al., 1997), and excess body mass is a threat to health. Early childhood is a good time to treat overweight, when a child's diet is still subject to parental influence or control (Quattrin et al., 2005; Whitaker et al., 1997). According to a nationally representative longitudinal study, one additional hour of physical education per week in kindergarten and first grade could reduce by half the number of overweight girls that age (Datar & Sturm, 2004b).

What's Your View?

- Much television advertising aimed at young children fosters poor nutrition by promoting fats and sugars rather than proteins and vitamins. How might parents counteract these pressures?

Malnutrition

Nearly half (46 percent) of young children in south Asia, 30 percent in sub-Saharan Africa, 8 percent in Latin America and the Caribbean, and 27 percent worldwide are moderately or severely underweight (UNICEF, 2002). In the United States, in 1998, 1 child in 5 did not get enough to eat (U.S. Department of Agriculture, 1999).

Because undernourished children usually live in extremely deprived circumstances, the specific effects of malnutrition may be hard to isolate. However, taken together, these deprivations may negatively affect not only growth and physical well-being but cognitive and psychosocial development as well. In an analysis of data on a nationally representative sample of 3,286 six- to 11-year-olds, those whose families had insufficient food were more likely to do poorly on arithmetic tests, to have repeated a grade, to have seen a psychologist, and to have had difficulty getting along with other children (Alaimo, Olson, & Frongillo, 2001). Moreover, cognitive effects of malnutrition may be long lasting. Among 1,559 children born on the island of Mauritius in a single year, those who were undernourished at age 3 had poorer verbal and spatial abilities, reading skills, scholastic ability, and neuropsychological performance than their peers at age 11 (Liu, Raine, Venables, Dalais, & Mednick, 2003).

Effects of malnutrition on growth can be largely reversed with improved diet (Lewit & Kerrebrock, 1997), but the most effective treatments go beyond physical care. A longitudinal study (Grantham-McGregor, Powell, Walker, Chang, & Fletcher, 1994) followed two groups of Jamaican children with low developmental levels who had been hospitalized for severe undernourishment in infancy or toddlerhood and who came from extremely poor, often unstable homes. Health care paraprofessionals played with an experimental group in the hospital and, after discharge, visited them at home every week for three years, showing the mothers how to make toys and encouraging them to interact with their children. Three years after the program stopped, the experimental group's IQs were well above those of a control group who had received only standard medical care (though not as high as those of a third, well-nourished group). Furthermore, the IQs of the experimental group remained higher than those of the control group as much as 14 years after leaving the hospital.

Early education may help counter the effects of undernourishment. In the Jamaican study, the mothers in the experimental group enrolled their children in preschools at earlier ages than did the mothers in the control group. In another Mauritian study, 100 three- to 5-year-olds received nutritional supplements and medical examinations and were placed in special preschools with small classes. At age 17, these children had lower rates of antisocial behavior and mental health problems than a control group. The effects were greatest among those who had been undernourished to begin with (Raine et al., 2003).

Oral Health

By age 3, all the primary, or deciduous, teeth are in place, and the permanent teeth, which will begin to appear at about age 6, are developing. Thus, parents usually can safely ignore the common habit of thumb sucking in children under 4. If children stop sucking thumbs or fingers by that age, their permanent teeth are not likely to be affected (Herrmann & Roberts, 1987; Umberger & Van Reenen, 1995).

Use of fluoride and improved dental care have dramatically reduced the incidence of tooth decay since the 1970s, but disadvantaged children still have more untreated cavities than other children (Bloom, Cohen, Vickerie, & Wondimu, 2003; Brown, Wall, & Lazar, 2000). Tooth decay in early childhood often stems from overconsumption of sweetened milk and juices in infancy together with a lack of regular dental care. In a longitudinal study of 642 Iowa children followed from ages 1 through 5, consumption of regular (nondiet) soda pop, powdered beverages, and, to a lesser extent, 100 percent juice increased the risk of tooth decay (Marshall et al., 2003).

Sleep Patterns and Problems

Sleep patterns change throughout the growing-up years (Hoban, 2004; Iglowstein, Jenni, Molinari, & Largo, 2003; see Figure 7-1), and early childhood has its own distinct rhythms. Young children sleep more deeply at night than they will later in life. Most U.S. children average about 11 hours of sleep at night by age 5 and give up daytime naps (Hoban, 2004). In some other cultures the timing of sleep may vary. Among the Gusii of Kenya, the Javanese in Indonesia, and the Zuni in New Mexico, young children have no regular bedtime and are allowed to stay up watching adult activities until they are sleepy. Among the Canadian Hare people, 3-year-olds take no naps but are put to sleep right after dinner and sleep as long as they wish in the morning (Broude, 1995).

Bedtime may bring on a form of separation anxiety, and the child may do all she or he can to avoid it. Young children may develop elaborate routines to put off retiring, and it may take them longer than before to fall asleep. Regular, consistent sleep routines can help minimize this common problem. Young children who have become accustomed to being put to sleep by feeding or rocking may find it hard to fall asleep on their own (Hoban, 2004).

Sleep Disturbances A child who experiences a *sleep* (or *night) terror* appears to awaken abruptly from a deep sleep in a state of agitation. The child may scream and

What's Your View?

• In view of childhood malnutrition's apparent long-term effects on physical, social, and cognitive development, what can and should be done to combat it?

Checkpoint

Can you . . .

✔ Summarize preschoolers' dietary needs and explain why overweight and tooth decay can become concerns at this age?

✔ Identify effects of malnutrition and factors that may influence its long-term outcome?

Guidepost

2. What sleep patterns tend to develop during early childhood, and what sleep problems may occur?

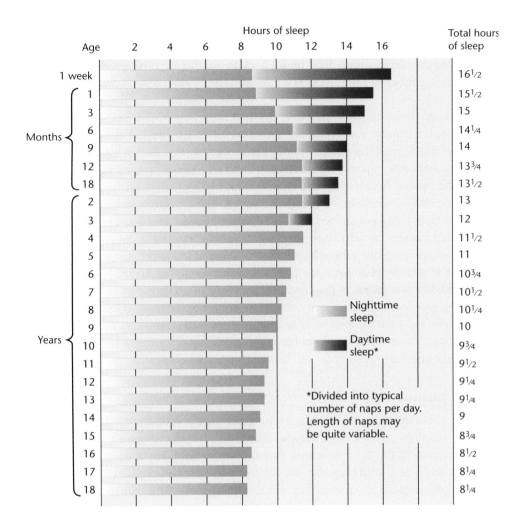

Figure 7-1

Typical sleep requirements in childhood. Unlike infants, who sleep about as long day and night, preschoolers get all or almost all their sleep in one long nighttime period. The number of hours of sleep steadily decreases throughout childhood, but individual children may need more or fewer hours than shown here. (Source: Ferber, 1985; similar data in Iglowstein et al., 2003.)

sit up in bed, breathing rapidly and staring or thrashing about. Yet he is not really awake, quiets down quickly, and the next morning remembers nothing about the episode. Night terrors occur mostly between ages 3 and 13 (Laberge, Tremblay, Vitaro, & Montplaisir, 2000) and affect boys more often than girls (AACAP, 1997; Hobson & Silvestri, 1999).

Walking and talking during sleep are fairly common in early and middle childhood. Although sleepwalking itself is harmless, sleepwalkers may be in danger of hurting themselves (AACAP, 1997; Hoban, 2004; Vgontzas & Kales, 1999). However, it is best not to interrupt sleepwalking or night terrors, as interruptions may confuse and further frighten the child (Hoban, 2004; Vgontzas & Kales, 1999).

Sleep disturbances may be caused by accidental activation of the brain's motor control system (Hobson & Silvestri, 1999) or by incomplete arousal from a deep sleep (Hoban, 2004) or may be triggered by disordered breathing or restless leg movements (Guilleminault, Palombini, Pelayo, & Chervin, 2003). These disturbances tend to run in families (AACAP, 1997; Hobson & Silvestri, 1999; Hoban, 2004). In most cases they are only occasional and usually are outgrown. Persistent sleep problems may indicate an emotional, physiological, or neurological condition that needs to be examined.

Nightmares are quite common, affecting nearly 58 percent of Swedish 5- to 7-year-olds, according to parental reports (Smedje, Broman, & Hetta, 1999). They are often brought on by staying up too late, eating a heavy meal close to bedtime, or overexcitement—for example, from watching an overstimulating television program, seeing a terrifying movie, or hearing a frightening bedtime story (Vgontzas & Kales, 1999). An occasional bad dream is no cause for alarm, but frequent or persistent nightmares, especially those that make a child fearful or anxious during waking hours, may signal excessive stress (Hoban, 2004).

Bed-Wetting Most children stay dry, day and night, by 3 to 5 years of age. Children this age normally recognize the sensation of a full bladder while asleep and awaken to empty it in the toilet. Children who wet the bed do not have this awareness. Thus, **enuresis,** repeated urination in clothing or in bed, occurs mainly at night. About 7 percent of 5-year-old boys and 3 percent of girls that age wet the bed regularly (American Psychiatric Association [APA], 1994; Schmitt, 1997).

Fewer than 1 percent of bed-wetters have a physical disorder, though they may have a small bladder capacity. Nor is persistent enuresis primarily an emotional, mental, or behavioral problem—though such problems can develop because of the way bed-wetters are treated by playmates and family (National Enuresis Society, 1995; Schmitt, 1997). Heredity is a factor in the condition, possibly in combination with slow motor maturation, reduced bladder capacity, and slow arousal from sleep (Hoban, 2004).

Children and their parents need to be reassured that enuresis is not serious. The child is not to blame and should not be punished. Generally parents need not do anything unless children themselves see bed-wetting as a problem.

Motor Skills

Preschool children make great advances in **gross motor skills,** such as running and jumping, which involve the large muscles (see Table 7-2). Development of the sensory and motor areas of the cerebral cortex permits better coordination between what children want to do and what they can do. Because their bones and muscles are stronger and their lung capacity is greater, they can run, jump, and climb farther and faster.

Children vary in adeptness, depending on their genetic endowment and their opportunities to learn and practice motor skills. Only 20 percent of 4-year-olds can throw a ball well, and only 30 percent can catch well (AAP Committee on Sports Medicine and Fitness, 1992). Most children under age 6 are *not* ready to take part in any organized sport. Physical development flourishes best in active, unstructured free play.

Fine motor skills, such as buttoning shirts and drawing pictures, involve eye-hand and small-muscle coordination, skills in which Wang Yani clearly excelled. Gains in these skills allow young children to take more responsibility for their personal care.

---

enuresis Repeated urination in clothing or in bed.

Checkpoint

Can you . . .

✔ Discuss age differences and cultural variations in sleep patterns?

✔ Identify four common sleep problems and give recommendations for handling them?

Guidepost

3. What are the main motor achievements of early childhood?

gross motor skills Physical skills that involve the large muscles.

fine motor skills Physical skills that involve the small muscles and eye-hand coordination.

Table 7-2   Gross Motor Skills in Early Childhood

3-Year-Olds	4-Year-Olds	5-Year-Olds
Cannot turn or stop suddenly or quickly	Have more effective control of stopping, starting, and turning	Can start, turn, and stop effectively in games
Can jump a distance of 15 to 24 inches	Can jump a distance of 24 to 33 inches	Can make a running jump of 28 to 36 inches
Can ascend a stairway unaided, alternating feet	Can descend a long stairway alternating feet, if supported	Can descend a long stairway unaided, alternating feet
Can hop, using largely an irregular series of jumps with some variations added	Can hop four to six steps on one foot	Can easily hop a distance of 16 feet

Source: Corbin, 1973.

Children make significant advances in motor skills during the preschool years. As they develop physically, they are better able to make their bodies do what they want. Large-muscle development lets them run or ride a tricycle; increasing eye-hand coordination helps them to use scissors or chopsticks. Children with disabilities can do many normal activities with the aid of special devices.

As they develop motor skills, preschoolers continually merge abilities they already have with those they are acquiring, to produce more complex capabilities. Such combinations of skills are known as **systems of action.**

Handedness **Handedness,** the preference for using one hand over the other, is usually evident by age 3. Because the left hemisphere of the brain, which controls the right side of the body, is usually dominant, most people (like Wang Yani) favor their right side. In people whose brains are more functionally symmetrical, the right hemisphere tends to dominate, making them left-handed. Handedness is not always clearcut; not everybody prefers one hand for every task. Boys are more likely to be left-handed than are girls.

Is handedness genetic? One theory proposes the existence of a single gene for right-handedness. According to this theory, people who inherit this gene from either or both parents—about 82 percent of the population—are right-handed. Those who do *not* inherit the gene still have a 50-50 chance of being right-handed; otherwise they will be left-handed or ambidextrous. Random determination of handedness among those who do *not* receive the gene could explain why some monozygotic twins have differing hand preferences as well as why 8 percent of the offspring of two right-handed parents are left-handed. The theory closely predicted the proportion of left-handed offspring in a three-generational sample of families recruited through advertisements (Klar, 1996).

Artistic Development Most preschoolers may not be as accomplished artists as Wang Yani, but with progress in fine motor coordination and growing cognitive powers, they can express themselves through art. Changes in young children's drawings seem to reflect maturation of the brain as well as of the muscles (Kellogg, 1970; see Figure 7-2). Two-year-olds *scribble*—not randomly but in patterns, such as vertical and zigzag lines. By age 3, children draw *shapes*—circles, squares, rectangles, triangles, crosses, and Xs—and then begin combining the shapes into more complex *designs*.

systems of action Increasingly complex combinations of skills, which permit a wider or more precise range of movement and more control of the environment.

handedness Preference for using a particular hand.

Figure 7-2

Artistic development in early childhood. There is a great difference between the very simple shapes shown in (a) and the detailed pictorial drawings in (e). The challenge for adults is to encourage children's creativity while acknowledging their growing facility in drawing. (Source: Kellogg, 1970.)

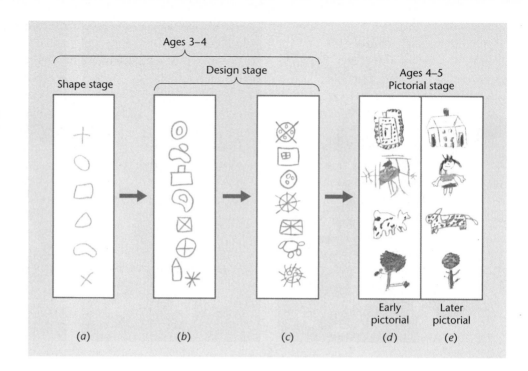

Checkpoint

Can you . . .

✔ List at least three gross motor skills and three fine motor skills that improve during early childhood?

✔ Tell how brain functioning is related to physical skills and handedness?

✔ Identify four stages in young children's drawing?

Guidepost

4. What are the major health and safety risks for young children?

The *pictorial* stage typically begins between ages 4 and 5; Wang Yani reached this stage at age 3.

The switch from abstract form and design to depicting real objects marks a fundamental change in the purpose of children's drawing, reflecting the cognitive development of representational ability. However, greater pictorial accuracy—often encouraged by adults—may come at the cost of the energy and freedom shown in children's early efforts. This was not so in Yani's case. Her father refrained from influencing her artistic style but encouraged her to paint with her whole arm, using large muscles as well as small ones. Her pictorial forms retained a free-flowing, semiabstract quality that gave them the stamp of originality.

Health and Safety

Because of widespread immunization, many of what once were the major diseases of childhood are much less common in Western industrialized countries. In the developing world, however, such vaccine-preventable diseases as measles, pertussis (whooping cough), and tuberculosis still take a large toll. More than 73 percent of deaths of children under age 5 occur in poor, rural regions of sub-Saharan Africa and south Asia, where nutrition is inadequate, water is unsafe, and sanitary facilities are lacking (Black et al., 2003; Bryce, Boschi-Pinto, Shibuya, Black, and the WHO Child Health Epidemiology Reference Group, 2005).

In the United States, deaths in childhood are relatively few compared with deaths in adulthood, and most are caused by injury rather than illness (Hoyert et al., 2005). Still, environmental influences make this a less healthy time for some children than for others.

Accidental Injuries and Deaths

Because young children are naturally venturesome and often unaware of danger, it is hard for caregivers to protect them from harm without *over*protecting them. Although most cuts, bumps, and scrapes are "kissed away" and quickly forgotten, some accidental injuries result in lasting damage or death. Indeed, accidents are the leading cause of death after infancy throughout childhood and adolescence in the United States (NCHS, 2004).

Many kindergartners and first graders walk alone to school, often crossing busy streets without traffic lights, although they do not know how to do this safely (Zeedyk, Wallace, & Spry, 2002). Some children are risk-prone. In one study, 5- and 6-year-olds who tended to take risks in a gambling game were more likely than their peers to say it was safe to cross a busy street between cars without a traffic light or crosswalk (Hoffrage, Weber, Hertwig, & Chase, 2003).

More than one million cases of ingestion of toxic substances by children under 6 were reported to poison control centers in 1998, and the true figure may be more than four million. Medications are responsible for more than half (52 percent) of deaths from poisoning (Litovitz et al., 1999; Shannon, 2000).

U.S. laws requiring "childproof" caps on medicine bottles and other dangerous household products, regulation of product safety, car seats for young children, mandatory helmets for bicycle riders, and safe storage of firearms and of medicines have improved child safety.

Checkpoint
Can you . . .

✔ Compare the health status of young children in developed and developing countries?

✔ Tell where and how young children are most likely to be injured, and list ways in which injuries can be avoided?

Health in Context: Environmental Influences

Why do some children have more illnesses or injuries than others? The genetic heritage contributes: Some children seem predisposed toward some medical conditions. In addition, environmental factors play major roles.

Socioeconomic Status and Race/Ethnicity The lower a family's SES, the greater a child's risks of illness, injury, and death (Chen, Matthews, & Boyce, 2002). Poor children—who represent nearly 1 in 5 U.S. children under 6 (Proctor & Dalaker, 2003) and are disproportionately minority children (NCHS, 2004)—are more likely than other children to have chronic conditions or health-related limitations on activities, to miss school due to illness or injury, to be hospitalized, to have unmet medical and dental needs, to lack health insurance, and to experience delayed medical care (Dey, Schiller, & Tai, 2004; Chen et al., 2002; Flores et al., 2002; Flores, Olson, Tomany-Korman, 2005; NCHS, 2004). Only 4 out of 10 children in poor families, as compared with 6 out of 10 children in nonpoor families, are in excellent health (Dey et al., 2004).

Poor children are more likely than other children to suffer lead poisoning, hearing and vision loss, and iron-deficiency anemia, as well as such stress-related conditions as asthma, headaches, insomnia, and irritable bowel. They also tend to have more behavior problems, psychological disturbances, and learning disabilities (J. L. Brown, 1987; Chen et al., 2002; Egbuono & Starfield, 1982; Santer & Stocking, 1991; Starfield, 1991). Poor children without homes have the greatest health problems of all (see Box 7-1).

Medicaid, a government program that provides medical assistance to eligible low-income persons and families, has been a "safety net" for many poor children since 1965. However, it has not reached millions of children whose families earn too much to qualify but too little to afford private insurance. Furthermore, the safety net for needy families has weakened with the end of national welfare assistance. The federal government in 1997 authorized the State Children's Health Insurance Program (SCHIP) to help states extend health care coverage to uninsured children in poor and near-poor families. By 2003, 5.8 million children had been enrolled (CDF, 2004), and the percentage of eligible children who were uninsured fell by about 25 percent between 1998 and 2003. Still, 16 percent of these children were not covered, and they were three times more likely than average to have unmet medical needs (Cohen & Bloom, 2005).

BOX 7-1

Digging Deeper
Homelessness

Since the 1980s, as affordable rental housing has become scarce and poverty has spread, homelessness has increased dramatically in the United States (National Coalition for the Homeless, 2004). An estimated 1.35 million children experience homelessness each year (National Coalition for the Homeless, 2002, 2004; Urban Institute, 2000). In a survey of 25 cities, 49 percent of the homeless population were African American, 35 percent Caucasian, 13 percent Hispanic, 2 percent Native American, and 1 percent Asian American (U.S. Conference of Mayors, 2003).

Families now comprise about 40 percent of the homeless population, and the proportion is probably higher in rural areas (National Coalition for the Homeless, 2004; U.S. Conference of Mayors, 2003; see figure below).

Many homeless families are headed by single mothers in their 20s (Buckner, Bassuk, Weinreb, & Brooks, 1999). Often these families are fleeing domestic violence (National Coalition for the Homeless, 2004). In New York City alone, the number of families living in shelters has almost doubled since 1998, and a family is likely to stay nearly a year before finding permanent housing (National Coalition for the Homeless, 2004; Santos & Ingrassia, 2002). In 2002 more than half of the city's shelters had to turn away homeless families for lack of resources (CDF, 2004).

Many homeless children spend their crucial early years in unstable, insecure, and often unsanitary environments. They and their parents may be cut off from a supportive community, family ties, and institutional resources and from ready access to medical care and schooling. These children suffer more health problems than poor children who have homes, and they are more likely to die in infancy. They are twice as likely as other children to have respiratory infections, three times more likely to lack immunizations, and two to three times more likely to have iron deficiency anemia. They experience high rates of diarrhea; severe hunger and malnourishment; obesity (from eating excessive carbohydrates and fats); tooth decay; asthma and other chronic diseases; skin, and eye and ear infections; scabies and lice; trauma-related injuries; and elevated levels of lead. Homeless children also tend to suffer severe depression and anxiety and to have neurological and visual deficits, developmental delays, academic and behavior problems, and learning difficulties (AAP Committee on Community Health Services, 1996; Bassuk, 1991; CDF, 2004; Rafferty & Shinn, 1991; Rubin et al., 1996; Weinreb et al., 2002). In large cities that have provided safe housing for poor and homeless families in stable, lower-poverty neighborhoods, the children's behavior and school performance improved greatly (CDF, 2004).

What's Your View?

• What strategies to deal with homelessness do you think would be most effective?

Check It Out

For more information on this topic, go to http://nch.ari.net. This is the Web site for the National Coalition for the Homeless, a national advocacy network.

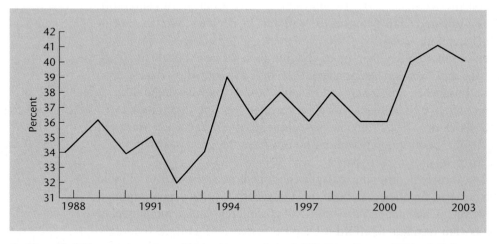

Families with children as a percentage of the homeless population in U.S. cities. (Source: Children's Defense Fund, 2004, p. 19.)

Access to quality health care is a particular problem among black and Latino children, especially those who are poor or near poor (Flores et al., 2005). More than 25 percent of Hispanic American children, especially Mexican American children, lack health insurance, and nearly 18 percent have unmet health care needs due to cost (Scott & Ni, 2004). Nine percent of Hispanic children under 6 years old and 16 percent of those ages 6 to 17 have no usual source of health care (NCHS, 2004). Language and cultural barriers and the need for more Latino care providers may help explain these disparities (Flores et al., 2002). Even Asian American children, who tend to be in better health than non-Hispanic white children, are less likely to access and use health care, perhaps because of similar barriers (Yu, Huang, & Singh, 2004).

What's Your View?

• What can communities do to provide for children's well-being when parents cannot furnish adequate food, clothing, shelter, and health care?

Exposure to Smoking, Air Pollution, and Pesticides Parental smoking is an important preventable cause of childhood illness and death, and the danger of exposure to tobacco is greatest during the early years of life (DiFranza, Aligne, & Weitzman, 2004). This passive exposure increases the risk of contracting a number of medical conditions, including pneumonia, bronchitis, serious infectious illnesses, otitis media (middle ear infection), burns, and asthma. It also may lead to cancer in adulthood (Aligne & Stoddard, 1997; AAP Committee on Environmental Health, 1997; U.S. Environmental Protection Agency, 1994).

Air pollution—particularly from chemical particles and ozone—is associated with increased risks of death and of chronic respiratory disease. A government-funded 8-year study of 10-year-old children in 12 California communities found air pollution levels high enough to have chronic, adverse effects on children's developing lungs (Gauderman et al., 2004). Children tend to spend more time outdoors than adults do and so may have high levels of exposure to airborne traffic and factory exhausts (Schwartz, 2004). Environmental contaminants may play a role in certain childhood cancers, neurological disorders, attention-deficit hyperactivity disorder, and mental retardation (Goldman et al., 2004; Woodruff et al., 2004). Children appear to be more sensitive than adults to some environmental toxins, but more research is needed to determine the risk threshold for each substance and how much exposure is occurring (Brent & Weitzman, 2004).

A total of 4.5 billion pounds of chemical pesticides are used annually in the United States. Pesticide residues are found in food, water, homes, schools, workplaces, lawns, and gardens. More than half of all reported pesticide poisonings—almost 50,000 per year—occur in children younger than 6 (Weiss, Amler, & Amler, 2004).

Children are more vulnerable than adults to chronic pesticide damage (Goldman et al., 2004). In a national survey of human exposure to environmental chemicals, urine levels of dimethylthiophosphate, a chemical produced by metabolism of many organic pesticides, were twice as high in 6- through 11-year-olds as in adults (Centers for Disease Control and Prevention, 2003). There is some, though not definitive, evidence that low-dose pesticide exposure may affect the developing brain (Weiss et al., 2004). In a study of preschool children in two agricultural communities in Mexico, children in the community that used traditional agricultural methods performed better in several measures of neuropsychological development (such as coordination and the ability to draw a person) than children in the other community, which had adopted use of pesticides (Guillette, Meza, Aquilar, Soto, & Garcia, 1998).

Pesticides on a lawn can be dangerous to young children, who may pick up the residue on their fingers and then put them in their mouths. Children are more vulnerable than adults to chronic pesticide damage, which may affect the developing brain.

Young children who live in old, dilapidated buildings with peeling lead paint are at risk for lead poisoning, which can adversely affect the developing brain.

Checkpoint

Can you . . .

✔ Discuss several environmental influences that endanger children's health and development?

Guidepost

1. What are typical cognitive advances and immature aspects of preschool children's thinking?

preoperational stage In Piaget's theory, the second major stage of cognitive development, in which children become more sophisticated in their use of symbolic thought but are not yet able to use logic.

Parents can take precautions against pesticide damage by applying pesticides prudently, storing them in their original containers where children cannot reach them, and washing fresh produce before it is eaten. Insect repellants should be applied only to exposed skin and washed off with soap and water when a child comes indoors (Weiss et al., 2004).

Exposure to Lead Children can get lead in the bloodstream from lead-contaminated food or water, from putting contaminated fingers in their mouths, or from inhaling dust in homes or schools where there is lead-based paint. Lead poisoning can seriously interfere with cognitive development and can bring on a variety of neurological and behavioral problems (AAP Committee on Environmental Health, 1998; Canfield et al., 2003; Needleman, Riess, Tobin, Biesecker, & Greenhouse, 1996; Tesman & Hills, 1994). Its effects in children's still-developing brains are apparently irreversible (Bellinger, 2004). Yet it can be completely prevented by removing sources of lead from children's environment (Tesman & Hills, 1994).

An estimated 8 percent of children in the United States, most of them poor and on Medicaid, have dangerously elevated blood lead levels (Rogan et al., 2001). There is no safe level of exposure to lead (Bellinger, 2004). The degree of toxicity depends on the dose, how long a child is exposed, and the child's developmental and nutritional vulnerability (AAP Committee on Environmental Health, 1998). Even low levels of exposure may have detrimental effects in young children, particularly those who have other risk factors, such as poverty and maternal depression (Canfield et al., 2003).

COGNITIVE DEVELOPMENT

Piagetian Approach: The Preoperational Child

Jean Piaget called early childhood the **preoperational stage** of cognitive development because children this age are not yet ready to engage in logical mental operations, as they will be in the stage of concrete operations in middle childhood (Chapter 9). However, the preoperational stage, which lasts from approximately ages 2 to 7, is characterized by a great expansion in the use of symbolic thought, or representational ability, which first emerges at the end of the sensorimotor stage (refer back to Chapter 5). Let's look at some advances and immature aspects of preoperational thought (see Tables 7-3 and 7-4) and at recent research, some of which challenges Piaget's conclusions.

Advances of Preoperational Thought

Advances in symbolic thought are accompanied by a growing understanding of space, causality, identities, categorization, and number. Some of these understandings have roots in infancy and toddlerhood; others begin to develop in early childhood but are not fully achieved until middle childhood.

The Symbolic Function "I want ice cream!" announces Kerstin, age 4, trudging indoors from the hot, dusty backyard. She has not seen anything that triggered this desire—no open freezer door, no television commercial. She no longer needs this kind of sensory cue to think about something. She remembers ice cream, its coldness and taste, and she purposefully seeks it out. This absence of sensory or

Table 7-3 Cognitive Advances During Early Childhood

Advance	Significance	Example
Use of symbols	Children do not need to be in sensorimotor contact with an object, person, or event in order to think about it.	Simon asks his mother about the elephants they saw on their trip to the circus several months earlier.
	Children can imagine that objects or people have properties other than those they actually have.	Rolf pretends that a slice of apple is a vacuum cleaner "vrooming" across the kitchen table.
Understanding of identities	Children are aware that superficial alterations do not change the nature of things.	Antonio knows that his teacher is dressed up as a pirate but is still his teacher underneath the costume.
Understanding of cause and effect	Children realize that events have causes.	Seeing a ball roll from behind a wall, Aneko looks behind the wall for the person who kicked the ball.
Ability to classify	Children organize objects, people, and events into meaningful categories.	Rosa sorts the pine cones she collected on a nature walk into two piles according to their size: "big" and "little."
Understanding of number	Children can count and deal with quantities.	Lindsay shares some candy with her friends, counting to make sure that each girl gets the same amount.
Empathy	Children become more able to imagine how others might feel.	Emilio tries to comfort his friend when he sees that his friend is upset.
Theory of mind	Children become more aware of mental activity and the functioning of the mind.	Blanca wants to save some cookies for herself, so she hides them from her brother in a pasta box. She knows her cookies will be safe there because her brother will not look in a place where he doesn't expect to find cookies.

Table 7-4 Immature Aspects of Preoperational Thought (According to Piaget)

Limitation	Description	Example
Centration: inability to decenter	Children focus on one aspect of a situation and neglect others.	Timothy teases his younger sister that he has more juice than she does because his juice box has been poured into a tall, skinny glass, but hers has been poured into a short, wide glass.
Irreversibility	Children fail to understand that some operations or actions can be reversed, restoring the original situation.	Timothy does not realize that the juice in each glass can be poured back into the juice box from which it came, contradicting his claim that he has more than his sister.
Focus on states rather than transformations	Children fail to understand the significance of the transformation between states.	In the conservation task, Timothy does not understand that transforming the shape of a liquid (pouring it from one container into another) does not change the amount.
Transductive reasoning	Children do not use deductive or inductive reasoning; instead they jump from one particular to another and see cause where none exists.	Sarah was mean to her brother. Then her brother got sick. Sarah concludes that she made her brother sick.
Egocentrism	Children assume everyone else thinks, perceives, and feels as they do.	Kara doesn't realize that she needs to turn a book around so that her father can see the picture she is asking him to explain to her. Instead, she holds the book directly in front of her, where only she can see it.
Animism	Children attribute life to objects not alive.	Amanda says that spring is trying to come but winter is saying, "I won't go! I won't go!"
Inability to distinguish appearance from reality	Children confuse what is real with outward appearance.	Courtney is confused by a sponge made to look like a rock. She states that it looks like a rock and it really is a rock.

symbolic function Piaget's term for ability to use mental representations (words, numbers, or images) to which a child has attached meaning.

motor cues characterizes the **symbolic function:** the ability to use symbols, or mental representations—words, numbers, or images to which a person has attached meaning. The use of symbols is a universal mark of human culture. Without symbols, people could not communicate verbally, make change, read maps, or treasure photos of distant loved ones. Symbols help children to remember and think about things that are not physically present, as Wang Yani did when she drew or painted from memory.

Preschool children show the symbolic function through the growth of deferred imitation, pretend play, and language. *Deferred imitation,* which becomes more robust after 18 months (refer back to Chapter 5), is based on a mental representation of a previously observed event. In **pretend play,** also called *fantasy play, dramatic play,* or *imaginary play,* children may make an object, such as a doll, represent, or symbolize, something else, such as a person. *Language,* discussed later in this chapter, uses a system of symbols (words) to communicate.

Understanding of Objects in Space As reported in Chapter 5, until at least age 3 most children do not reliably grasp the relationships between pictures, maps, or scale models and the objects or spaces they represent. Older preschoolers can use simple maps, and they can transfer the spatial understanding gained from working with models to maps and vice versa (DeLoache, Miller, & Pierroutsakos, 1998). Scaling ability develops gradually. In a series of experiments, 3- to 5-year-olds were asked to use a simple map to find or place an object at the corresponding location in a similarly shaped but much larger space. About half of the 3-year-olds and all the 4-year-olds could perform scale adjustments along a single dimension (Huttenlocher, Newcombe, & Vasilyeva, 1999). However, only 60 percent of 4-year-olds could do a similar task with regard to a two-dimensional space, such as a rug—a task that 90 percent of 5-year-olds could do (Vasilyeva & Huttenlocher, 2004).

As Anna pretends to take Grover's blood pressure, she is showing a major cognitive achievement: deferred imitation, the ability to act out an action she observed some time before.

pretend play Play involving imaginary people and situations; also called *fantasy play, dramatic play,* or *imaginative play.*

transduction Piaget's term for a preoperational child's tendency to mentally link particular phenomena, whether or not there is logically a causal relationship.

Understanding of Causality Although Piaget recognized that toddlers have some understanding of a connection between actions and reactions, he believed that preoperational children cannot yet reason logically about cause and effect. Instead, he said, they reason by **transduction.** They mentally link two events, especially events close in time, whether or not there is logically a causal relationship. For example, Luis may think that his "bad" thoughts or behavior caused his own or his sister's illness or his parents' divorce.

Yet, when tested on situations they can understand, young children do seem to grasp cause and effect. One research team set up a series of experiments using a device called a "blicket detector," rigged to light up and play music only when certain objects (called "blickets") were placed on it. Even 2-year-olds were able to decide, by observing the device in operation, which objects were blickets (because they activated the blicket detector) and which were not (Gopnik, Sobel, Schulz, & Glymour, 2001). Apparently, then, young children's understanding of familiar events in the physical world enables them to think logically about causation (Wellman & Gelman, 1998).

In naturalistic observations of 2½- to 5-year-olds' everyday conversations with their parents, children showed flexible causal reasoning, appropriate to the subject.

Types of explanations ranged from physical ("The scissors have to be clean so I can cut better") to social-conventional ("I have to stop now because you said to"). Causal statements were more frequent among older children (Hickling & Wellman, 2001). However, preschoolers seem to view all causal relationships as equally and absolutely predictable. In one series of experiments, 3- to 5-year-olds, unlike adults, were just as sure that a person who does not wash his or her hands before eating will get sick as they were that a person who jumps up will come down (Kalish, 1998).

Understanding of Identities and Categorization The world becomes more orderly and predictable as preschool children develop a better understanding of *identities:* the concept that people and many things are basically the same even if they change in form, size, or appearance. This understanding underlies the emerging self-concept (see Chapter 8).

Categorization, or classification, requires a child to identify similarities and differences. By age 4, many children can classify by two criteria, such as color and shape. Children use this ability to order many aspects of their lives, categorizing people as "good," "bad," "nice," "mean," and so forth. Thus, categorization is a cognitive ability with psychosocial implications.

Can preschoolers distinguish living from nonliving things? When Piaget asked young children whether the wind and the clouds were alive, their answers led him to think they were confused about what is alive and what is not. The tendency to attribute life to objects that are not alive is called **animism.** However, when later researchers questioned 3- and 4-year-olds about something more familiar to them—differences between a rock, a person, and a doll—the children showed they understood that people are alive and rocks and dolls are not. They did not attribute thoughts or emotions to rocks, and they cited the fact that dolls cannot move on their own as evidence that dolls are not alive (Gelman, Spelke, & Meck, 1983).

animism Tendency to attribute life to objects that are not alive.

Of course, plants do not move on their own either, nor do they utter sounds, as most animals do. Yet preschoolers know that both plants and animals can grow and decay and, when injured, can heal (Rosengren, Gelman, Kalish, & McCormick, 1991; Wellman & Gelman, 1998). Culture can affect such beliefs. In one study, 5- to 9-year-old Israeli children, whose tradition views plants primarily in terms of their usefulness as food, were less likely than U.S. and Japanese children to attribute to plants the qualities of living things, such as respiration, growth, and death. Japanese children were more likely to attribute such qualities to inanimate objects, such as a stone and a chair, which, in their culture, are sometimes viewed as if they were alive and had feelings (Hatano et al., 1993).

Understanding of Number In early childhood, U.S. children come to recognize five principles of counting (Gelman & Gallistel, 1978; Sophian, 1988):

1. The *1-to-1 principle:* Say only one number-name for each item being counted ("One . . . two . . . three . . .").

2. The *stable-order principle:* Say number-names in a set order ("One, two, three . . ." rather than "Three, one, two . . .").

3. The *order-irrelevance principle:* Start counting with any item, and the total count will be the same.

4. The *cardinality principle:* The last number-name used is the total number of items being counted. (If there are five items, the last number-name will be "5.")

5. The *abstraction principle:* The previous principles apply to any kind of object.

Research findings suggest that children extract these principles from their experience with counting (Ho & Fuson, 1998; Siegler, 1998). By age 5, most children can count to 20 or more and know the relative sizes of the numbers 1 through 10, and some can do single-digit addition and subtraction (Siegler, 1998).

How quickly children learn to count depends in part on the number system of their culture and in part on schooling (Naito & Miura, 2001). Through age 3, when most number learning is focused on counting from 1 through 10, U.S. and Chinese children perform about equally well. At ages 4 and 5, when U.S. children are learning separate names for the numbers between 11 and 20, Chinese youngsters learn their language's more efficient system based on 10s and 1s (10 + 1, 10 + 2, and so forth). It's not surprising, then, that U.S. children's performance begins to lag (Miller, Smith, Zhu, & Zhang, 1995).

Ordinality—the concept of *more* or *less, bigger* or *smaller*—seems to begin around 12 to 18 months and at first is limited to comparisons of very few objects (Siegler, 1998). By age 4 or 5, children can solve ordinality problems ("Megan picked six apples, and Joshua picked four apples; which child picked more?") with up to nine objects (Byrnes & Fox, 1998). Ordinal knowledge appears to be universal but develops at different rates, depending on how important counting is in a particular family or culture (Resnick, 1989; Saxe, Guberman, & Gearhart, 1987; Siegler, 1998).

Immature Aspects of Preoperational Thought

One of the main characteristics of preoperational thought is **centration:** the tendency to focus on one aspect of a situation and neglect others. According to Piaget, preschoolers come to illogical conclusions because they cannot **decenter**—think about several aspects of a situation at one time. Centration can limit young children's thinking about social as well as physical relationships.

Egocentrism **Egocentrism** is an expression of centration. According to Piaget, young children center so much on their own point of view that they cannot take in another's. Three-year-olds are not as egocentric as newborn babies; but, said Piaget, they still think the universe centers on them. Egocentrism may help explain why young children (as we will see) sometimes have trouble separating reality from what goes on inside their own heads and why they may show confusion about what causes what. When Luis believes that his "bad thoughts" have made his sister sick, or that he caused his parents' marital troubles, he is thinking egocentrically.

To study egocentrism, Piaget designed the *three-mountain task* (see Figure 7-3). A child sits facing a table that holds three large mounds. A doll is placed on a chair at the opposite side of the table. The investigator asks the child how the "mountains" would look to the doll. Piaget found that young children usually could not answer

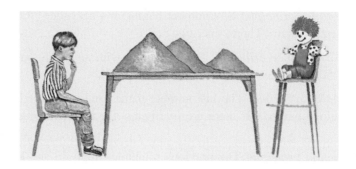

Figure 7-3

Piaget's three-mountain task. A preoperational child is unable to describe the "mountains" from the doll's point of view—an indication of egocentrism, according to Piaget.

Checkpoint

Can you . . .

✔ Summarize findings about preschool children's understanding of symbols, space, causality, identities, categorization, and number?

the question correctly; instead, they described the "mountains" from their own perspective. Piaget saw this as evidence that preoperational children cannot imagine a different point of view (Piaget & Inhelder, 1967).

However, another experimenter who posed a similar problem in a different way got different results (Hughes, 1975). A child sat in front of a square board divided by "walls" into four sections. A toy police officer stood at the edge of the board; a doll was moved from one section to another. After each move the child was asked, "Can the police officer see the doll?" Then another toy police officer was brought into the action, and the child was told to hide the doll from both officers. Thirty children between ages 3½ and 5 were correct 9 out of 10 times.

Why were these children able to take another person's point of view (the police officer's) when those doing the mountain task were not? It may be because the "police officer" task calls for thinking in more familiar, less abstract ways. Most children do not look at mountains and do not think about what other people might see when looking at one, but most 3-year-olds know about dolls and police officers and hiding. Thus, young children may show egocentrism primarily in situations beyond their immediate experience.

Conservation Another classic example of centration is the failure to understand **conservation,** the fact that two things that are equal remain so if their appearance is altered, so long as nothing is added or taken away. Piaget found that children do not fully grasp this principle until the stage of concrete operations and that they develop different kinds of conservation at different ages—a phenomenon called **horizontal décalage.** Table 7-5 shows how various dimensions of

conservation Piaget's term for awareness that two objects that are equal according to a certain measure remain equal in the face of perceptual alteration so long as nothing has been added to or taken away from either object.

horizontal décalage Piaget's term for inability to transfer learning about one type of conservation to other types, which causes a child to master different types of conservation tasks at different ages.

Table 7-5	Tests of Various Kinds of Conservation			
Conservation Task	**What Child Is Shown***	**Transformation**	**Question for Child**	**Preoperational Child's Usual Answers**
Number	Two equal, parallel rows of candies	Space the candies in one row farther apart.	"Are there the same number of candies in each row or does one row have more?"	"The longer one has more."
Length	Two parallel sticks of the same length	Move one stick to the right.	"Are both sticks the same size or is one longer?"	"The one on the right (or left) is longer."
Liquid	Two identical glasses holding equal amounts of liquid	Pour liquid from one glass into a taller, narrower glass.	"Do both glasses have the same amount of liquid or does one have more?"	"The taller one has more."
Matter (mass)	Two balls of clay of the same size	Roll one ball into a sausage shape.	"Do both pieces have the same amount of clay or does one have more?"	"The sausage has more."
Weight	Two balls of clay of the same weight	Roll one ball into a sausage shape.	"Do both weigh the same or does one weigh more?"	"The sausage weighs more."
Area	Two toy rabbits, two pieces of cardboard (representing grassy fields), with blocks or toys (representing barns on the fields); same number of "barns" on each board	Rearrange the blocks on one piece of board.	"Does each rabbit have the same amount of grass to eat or does one have more?"	"The one with the blocks close together has more to eat."
Volume	Two glasses of water with two equal-sized balls of clay in them	Roll one ball into a sausage shape.	"If we put the sausage back in the glass, will the water be the same height in each glass, or will one be higher?"	"The water in the glass with the sausage will be higher."

*Child then acknowledges that both items are equal.

Lifemap CD

Watch the video, "Development of the Concept of Conservation," in Chapter 7 of your CD to observe preschoolers' varying ability to understand the idea of conservation of mass.

irreversibility Piaget's term for a preoperational child's failure to understand that an operation can go in two or more directions.

Checkpoint

Can you . . .

✔ Tell how centration limits preoperational thought?

✔ Discuss research that challenges Piaget's views on egocentrism in early childhood?

✔ Give several reasons preoperational children have difficulty with conservation?

theory of mind Awareness and understanding of mental processes.

conservation have been tested. The ages at which some of them develop are given in Chapter 9.

In one type of conservation task, conservation of liquid, a 5-year-old we'll call Timothy is shown two identical clear glasses, each one short and wide and each holding the same amount of water. Timothy is asked, "Is the amount of water in the two glasses equal?" When he agrees, the researcher pours the water in one glass into a third glass, a tall, thin one. Timothy is now asked, "Do both glasses contain the same amount of water? Or does one contain more? Why?" In early childhood—after watching the water being poured out of one of the short, fat glasses into a tall, thin glass or even after pouring it himself—Timothy will say that either the taller glass or the wider one contains more water. When asked why, he says, "This one is bigger this way," stretching his arms to show the height or width. Preoperational children cannot consider height *and* width at the same time. Since they center on one aspect, they cannot think logically, said Piaget.

The ability to conserve is also limited by **irreversibility:** failure to understand that an operation or action can go two or more ways. Once Timothy can imagine restoring the original state of the water by pouring it back into the other glass, he will realize that the amount of water in both glasses is the same.

Preoperational children commonly think as if they were watching a slide show with a series of static frames: They *focus on successive states,* said Piaget, and do not recognize the transformation from one state to another. In the conservation experiment, they focus on the water as it stands in each glass rather than on the water being poured from one glass to another, and so they fail to realize that the amount of water is the same.

Do Young Children Have Theories of Mind?

Piaget (1929) was the first scholar to investigate children's **theory of mind,** their emerging awareness of their own mental processes and those of other people. He asked children such questions as "Where do dreams come from?" and "What do you think with?" On the basis of the answers, he concluded that children younger than 6 cannot distinguish between thoughts or dreams and real physical entities and have no theory of mind. However, more recent research indicates that between ages 2 and 5, children's knowledge about mental processes—their own and others'—grows dramatically (Astington, 1993; Bower, 1993; Flavell et al., 1995; Wellman, Cross, & Watson, 2001).

Again, methodology seems to have made the difference. Piaget's questions were abstract, and he expected children to be able to put their understanding into words. Contemporary researchers use vocabulary and objects children are familiar with. Instead of talking in generalities, they observe children in everyday activities or give them concrete examples. In this way, we have learned, for example, that 3-year-olds can tell the difference between a boy who has a cookie and a boy who is thinking about a cookie; they know which boy can touch, share, and eat it (Astington, 1993). Let's look at several aspects of theory of mind.

Knowledge about Thinking and Mental States Between ages 3 and 5, children come to understand that thinking goes on inside the mind; that it can deal with either real or imaginary things; that someone can be thinking of one thing while doing or looking at something else; that a person whose eyes and ears are covered can think about objects; that someone who looks pensive is probably thinking; and that thinking is different from seeing, talking, touching, and knowing (Flavell et al., 1995).

However, preschoolers generally believe that mental activity starts and stops. Not until middle childhood do children know that the mind is continuously active

(Flavell, 1993; Flavell et al., 1995). Preschoolers also have little or no awareness that they or other people think in words, or "talk to themselves in their heads," or that they think while they are looking, listening, reading, or talking (Flavell, Green, Flavell, & Grossman, 1997). Preschoolers tend to equate dreams with imagining; they believe they can dream about anything they wish. Five-year-olds recognize that experiences, emotions, knowledge, and thoughts can affect the content of dreams. Not until age 11, however, do children fully realize that they cannot control their dreams (Woolley & Berger, 2002).

Social cognition, the recognition that others have mental states (refer back to Chapter 6), is a distinctly human capacity (Povinelli & Giambrone, 2001) that accompanies the decline of egocentrism and the development of empathy. By age 3, children realize that a person who does not immediately find what she wants will keep looking. They know that if someone gets what he wants he will be happy, and if not, he will be sad (Wellman & Woolley, 1990). Four-year-olds begin to understand that people have differing beliefs about the world—true or mistaken—and that these beliefs affect their actions.

False Beliefs and Deception   A researcher shows 3-year-old Mariella a candy box and asks what is in it. "Candy," she says. But when Mariella opens the box, she finds crayons, not candy. "What will a child who hasn't opened the box think is in it?" the researcher asks. "Crayons," says Mariella, not understanding that another child would be fooled by the box, as she was. And then she says that she herself originally thought crayons would be in the box (Flavell, 1993; Flavell et al., 1995).

The understanding that people can hold false beliefs flows from the realization that people hold mental representations of reality, which can sometimes be wrong. Three-year-olds like Mariella appear to lack such an understanding (Flavell et al., 1995). An analysis of 178 studies in various countries, using a number of variations on, and simplifications of, false belief tasks, found this consistent developmental pattern (Wellman & Cross, 2001; Wellman, Cross & Watson, 2001). When preschoolers were taught to respond to a false-belief task with gestures rather than with words, children near their fourth birthday—but not younger children—did better than on the traditional verbal-response tasks. Thus, gestures may help children on the verge of grasping the idea of false beliefs to make that conceptual leap (Carlson, Wong, Lemke, & Cosser, 2005).

Three-year-olds' failure to recognize false beliefs may stem from egocentric thinking. At that age, children tend to believe that everyone else knows what they know and believes what they do, and, like Mariella, they have trouble understanding that their own beliefs can be false (Lillard & Curenton, 1999). Four-year-olds understand that people who see or hear different versions of the same event may come away with different beliefs. Not until about age 6, however, do children realize that two people who see or hear the *same* thing may interpret it differently (Pillow & Henrichon, 1996).

Deception is an effort to plant a false belief in someone else's mind, and it requires a child to suppress the impulse to be truthful. In other words, lying represents cognitive development! Some studies have found that children become capable of deception as early as age 2 or 3; others, at 4 or 5. The difference may have to do with the means of deception children are expected to use. In a series of experiments, 3-year-olds were asked whether they would like to play a trick on an experimenter by giving a false clue about which of two boxes a ball had been hidden in. The children were better able to carry out the deception when asked to put a picture of the ball on the wrong box, or to point to that box with an arrow, than when they pointed with their fingers, which children this age are accustomed to doing truthfully (Carlson, Moses, & Hix, 1998).

Piaget maintained that young children regard all falsehoods—intentional or not—as lies. However, when 3- to 6-year-olds were told a story about the danger of eating contaminated food and were given a choice between interpreting a character's action as a lie or a mistake, about three-fourths of the children in all age groups characterized it accurately (Siegal & Peterson, 1998). Apparently, then, even 3-year-olds have some understanding of the role of intent in deception.

Is it really the Cookie Monster and Elmo? These young boys don't seem quite sure. The ability to distinguish appearance from reality develops between ages 3 and 6.

Distinguishing Between Appearance and Reality According to Piaget, only at age 5 or 6 do children begin to understand the distinction between what *seems* to be and what *is*. Much research bears him out, though some studies have found this ability beginning to emerge before age 4 (Friend & Davis, 1993; C. Rice, Koinis, Sullivan, Tager-Flusberg, & Winner, 1997).

In one classic series of experiments (Flavell, Green, & Flavell, 1986), 3-year-olds seemed to confuse appearance and reality in a variety of tests. For example, when the children put on special sunglasses that made milk look green, they said the milk *was* green, even though they had just seen white milk. However, 3-year-olds' difficulty in distinguishing appearance from reality may itself be more apparent than real. When children were asked questions about the uses of such objects as a candle wrapped like a crayon, only 3 out of 10 answered correctly. But when asked to respond with actions rather than words ("I want a candle to put on a birthday cake"), 9 out of 10 handed the experimenter the crayonlike candle (Sapp, Lee, & Muir, 2000).

Distinguishing Between Fantasy and Reality Sometime between 18 months and 3 years, children learn to distinguish between real and imagined events. Three-year-olds know the difference between a real dog and a dog in a dream, and between something invisible (such as air) and something imaginary. They can pretend and can tell when someone else is pretending (Flavell et al., 1995). By 3, and, in some cases, by 2 years of age, they know that pretense is intentional; they can tell the difference between trying to do something and pretending to do the same thing (Rakoczy, Tomasello, & Striano, 2004).

Still, the line between fantasy and reality may seem to blur at times, as it did for Yani when she made up stories about her monkey friends. In one study (Harris, Brown, Marriott, Whittall, & Harmer, 1991), 4- to 6-year-olds, left alone in a room, preferred to touch a box holding an imaginary bunny rather than a box holding an imaginary monster, even though most of the children claimed they were just pretending. However, in a partial replication of the study, in which the experimenter stayed in the room and clearly ended the pretense, only about 10 percent of the children touched or looked in either of the boxes, and almost all showed a clear understanding that the creatures were imaginary (Golomb & Galasso, 1995). Thus it is difficult to know, when questioning children about "pretend" objects, whether children are giving serious answers or are keeping up the pretense (M. Taylor, 1997).

Magical or wishful thinking in children age 3 and older does *not* stem from confusion between fantasy and reality, a review of the literature suggests. Often magical thinking is a way to explain events that do not seem to have obvious realistic explanations (usually because children lack knowledge about them), or simply to indulge in the pleasures of pretending (Woolley, 1997).

In What Order Do Theory-of-Mind Abilities Develop? Do some theory-of-mind skills develop earlier than others? One research team (Wellman & Liu, 2004), on the basis of a review of the literature, constructed a developmental scale showing the order in which various theory-of-mind understandings develop. They then tested it on 75 three- to five-year-olds from three preschools serving a largely European American but 25 percent minority population.

The researchers found that understanding of desires precedes understanding of beliefs: Children become aware that two people can have differing desires for the same object before they understand that two people can have different beliefs about the same object. Only after they show an understanding of diverse beliefs can they judge that someone can have a false belief. Even later comes the ability to differentiate between real and apparent emotion. What this means is that no single type of task, such as a false-belief test, can capture the course of children's theory-of-mind development. A scale such as this can make it easier to identify influences on that development and individual differences in it (Wellman & Liu, 2004).

Influences on Individual Differences in Theory-of-Mind Development Some children develop theory-of-mind abilities earlier than others. In part this development reflects brain maturation and general improvements in cognition. What other influences explain these individual differences?

Social competence and language development contribute to an understanding of thoughts and emotions (Cassidy, Werner, Rourke, Zubernis, & Balaraman, 2003). Children whose teachers and peers rate them high on social skills are better able to recognize false beliefs, to distinguish between real and feigned emotion, and to take another person's point of view; and these children also tend to have strong language skills (Cassidy et al., 2003; Watson, Nixon, Wilson, & Capage, 1999).

The kind of talk a young child hears at home may make a difference (Jenkins, Turrell, Kogushi, Lollis, & Ross, 2003). Three-year-olds whose mothers talk with them about others' mental states tend to show better theory-of-mind skills (Ruffman, Slade, & Crowe, 2002).

Families that encourage pretend play stimulate the development of theory-of-mind skills. As children play roles, they try to assume others' perspectives. When children pretend together, they must deal with other children's views of their imaginary world. Talking with children about how the characters in a story feel helps them develop social understanding (Lillard & Curenton, 1999). Empathy usually arises earlier in children whose families talk a lot about feelings and causality (Dunn, Brown, Slomkowski, Tesla, & Youngblade, 1991; Dunn, 1991).

Bilingual children, who speak and hear more than one language at home, do somewhat better than children with only one language on certain theory-of-mind tasks (Bialystok & Senman, 2004; Goetz, 2003). Bilingual children know that an object or idea can be represented linguistically in more than one way, and this knowledge may help them see that different people may have different perspectives. Bilingual children also recognize the need to match their language to that of their partner, and this may make them more aware of others' mental states. Finally, bilingual children tend to have better attentional control, and this may enable them to focus on what is true or real rather than on what only seems to be so (Bialystok & Senman, 2004; Goetz, 2003).

Different cultures have different ways of looking at the mind, and these cultural attitudes influence children (Lillard, 1998). Middle-class northern Europeans and Americans pay much attention to how mental states affect behavior. Asians focus on situations that call for certain behaviors. Japanese parents and teachers frequently talk to children about how their behavior affects other people's feelings

Checkpoint

Can you...

✔ Give examples of research that challenges Piaget's views on young children's cognitive limitations?

✔ Describe changes between the ages of 3 and 6 in children's knowledge about the way their minds work, and identify influences on that development?

(Azuma, 1994). A Japanese child who refuses to finish a meal may be told that the farmer who worked hard to grow the food will be hurt if the child doesn't eat it.

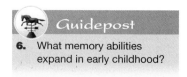

6. What memory abilities expand in early childhood?

Information-Processing Approach: Memory Development

During early childhood, children improve in attention and in the speed and efficiency with which they process information; and they begin to form long-lasting memories. Still, young children do not remember as well as older ones. For one thing, young children tend to focus on exact details of an event, which are easily forgotten, whereas older children and adults generally concentrate on the gist of what happened. Also, young children, because of their lesser knowledge of the world, may fail to notice important aspects of a situation, such as when and where it occurred, which could help jog their memory.

Basic Processes and Capacities

encoding Process by which information is prepared for long-term storage and later retrieval.

storage Retention of information in memory for future use.

retrieval Process by which information is accessed or recalled from memory storage.

Information-processing theorists think of memory as a filing system that has three steps, or processes: *encoding, storage,* and *retrieval.* **Encoding** is like putting information in a folder to be filed in memory; it attaches a "code" or "label" to the information so that it will be easier to find when needed. Events are encoded along with information about the context in which they are encountered. **Storage** is putting the folder away in the filing cabinet. **Retrieval** occurs when the information is needed; the child then searches for the file and takes it out. Difficulties in any of these processes can interfere with efficiency.

The way the brain stores information is believed to be universal, though the efficiency of the system varies (Siegler, 1998). Information-processing models depict the brain as containing three "storehouses": *sensory memory, working memory,* and *long-term memory.*

sensory memory Initial, brief, temporary storage of sensory information.

working memory Short-term storage of information being actively processed.

Sensory memory is a temporary "holding tank" for incoming sensory information. Sensory memory shows little change from infancy on (Siegler, 1998). However, without processing (encoding), sensory memories fade quickly.

Information being encoded or retrieved is kept in **working memory,** a short-term "storehouse" for information a person is actively working on: trying to understand, remember, or think about. Brain imaging studies have found that working memory is located partly in the *prefrontal cortex,* the large portion of the frontal lobe directly behind the forehead (Nelson et al., 2000). This region of the brain develops more slowly than any other (M. H. Johnson, 1998).

The efficiency of working memory is limited by its capacity. Researchers may assess the capacity of working memory by asking children to recall a series of scrambled digits (for example, 2-8-3-7-5-1 if they heard 1-5-7-3-8-2). The capacity of working memory—the number of digits a child can recall—increases rapidly. At age 4, children usually remember only two digits; at 12 they typically remember six (Zelazo, Müller, Frye, & Marcovitch, 2003).

The growth of working memory may permit the development of *executive function,* the planning and carrying out of goal-directed mental activity. The development of executive function in early childhood can be seen in the complexity of the rules children formulate and use in solving problems (Zelazo et al., 2003).

central executive In Baddeley's model, element of working memory that controls the processing of information.

According to a widely used model, a **central executive** controls processing operations in working memory (Baddeley, 1981, 1986, 1992, 1996, 1998). The central executive, which seems to mature between ages 8 and 10 (Cowan et al., 1999), orders information encoded for transfer to **long-term memory,** a "storehouse" of virtually unlimited capacity that holds information for long periods of time. The central executive also retrieves information from long-term memory for further processing. The central executive can temporarily expand the capacity of working memory by moving information into two separate subsidiary systems while the central executive is occupied with other tasks. One of these subsidiary systems holds verbal information (as in the digit task) and the other, visual/spatial images.

Recognition and Recall

Recognition and *recall* are types of retrieval. **Recognition** is the ability to identify something encountered before (for example, to pick out a missing mitten from a lost-and-found box). **Recall** is the ability to reproduce knowledge from memory (for example, to describe the mitten to someone, or to draw letters in the air after seeing them once, as Yani did). Preschool children, like all age groups, do better on recognition than on recall, but both abilities improve with age. The more familiar children are with an item, the better they can recall it (Lange, MacKinnon, & Nida, 1989).

Young children often fail to use strategies for remembering—even strategies they already know—unless reminded (Flavell, 1970). This tendency not to generate efficient strategies may reflect lack of awareness of how a strategy would be useful (Sophian, Wood, & Vong, 1995). Older children tend to become more efficient in the spontaneous use of memory strategies (see Chapter 9).

How well do preschoolers recognize a familiar face? Not as well as older children and adults do, according to an Australian study—perhaps because young children have not yet had enough experience with faces. However, 4- and 5-year-olds do seem to process face-recognition information holistically, as adults do. Both young children and adults can more easily tell which of two noses belongs to a familiar face when the noses are depicted on the face than when the noses alone are shown (Pellicano & Rhodes, 2003).

 Lifemap CD

View the video, "Improvements in Memory," in Chapter 7 of your CD for an illustration of the memory skills of a 3-year-old and 4-year-old.

Checkpoint
Can you . . .

✔ Identify the three basic processes and three storehouses of memory and discuss their development?

✔ Compare preschoolers' recognition and recall ability?

Forming Childhood Memories

Memory of experiences in early childhood is rarely deliberate: Young children simply remember events that made a strong impression. Most of these early conscious memories seem to be short-lived. One investigator has distinguished three types of childhood memory that serve different functions: *generic, episodic,* and *autobiographical* (Nelson, 1993b).

Generic memory, which begins at about age 2, produces a **script,** or general outline of a familiar, repeated event without details of time or place. The script contains routines for situations that come up again and again; it helps a child know what to expect and how to act. For example, Briana may have scripts for riding the bus to preschool or having lunch at Grandma's house.

Episodic memory refers to awareness of having experienced a particular incident that occurred at a specific time and place. Young children remember more clearly events that are new to them. Three-year-olds may recall details about a trip to the circus for a year or longer (Fivush, Hudson, & Nelson, 1983), whereas generic memories of frequent events (such as lunch at Grandma's house) tend to blur together. Given a young child's limited memory capacity, episodic memories are temporary. Unless they recur several times (in which case they are transferred to generic memory), they last for a few weeks or months and then fade. The reliability of children's episodic memory has become an important issue in lawsuits involving charges of child abuse (see Box 7-2).

BOX 7-2

Practically Speaking
How Reliable Is Children's Eyewitness Testimony?

Child abuse is a crime that often can be proved only by the testimony of a young child. If a child's testimony is inaccurate, an innocent adult may be unfairly punished. On the other hand, if a child's testimony is *not* believed, a dangerous adult may be set free.

Young children may not know whether they actually experienced an event or merely imagined it or were told or asked about it (Woolley & Bruell, 1996). Thus, children responding to adults' suggestions have been known to "remember" events that never occurred. In one experiment, researchers had a man called "Sam Stone" drop in at a child care center for a few minutes (Leichtman & Ceci, 1995). The visitor commented on a story that was being read, strolled around the room, and then waved good-bye and left. Some of the children who witnessed the event had repeatedly been told stories about "Sam Stone" before his visit, depicting him as a well-meaning bumbler, and/or were given false suggestions afterward that he had ripped a book and dirtied a teddy bear.

After four weekly interviews, nearly half of the 3- and 4-year-olds and 30 percent of 5- and 6-year-olds who had heard the stories about Sam Stone's bumbling and had been given the false suggestions spontaneously reported the book-ripping and teddy-bear-dirtying to a new interviewer; and when asked probing questions, nearly three-fourths of the younger children said the visitor

had done one or both. By contrast, *none* of the children in a control group, who had *not* been given prejudicial information or false suggestions, made false reports. Thus, young children's testimony *can* be accurate when elicited neutrally.

Preschoolers tend to be more suggestible than older children. This difference may be due to younger children's weaker memory for specific events and their greater vulnerability to bribes, threats, and adult expectations (Bruck, Ceci, & Hembrooke, 1998; Ceci & Bruck, 1993; Leichtman & Ceci, 1995). In one study, 5-year-olds were more likely to "remember" a false event than were 7- or 9-year-olds or adults (Ghetti & Alexander, 2004). However, some children, regardless of age, are more suggestible than others (Bruck & Ceci, 1997).

Reports are likely to be more reliable if children are interviewed only once, soon after the event, by people who do not have an opinion about what took place; if the interviewers do not ask leading questions, ask open-ended rather than yes/no questions, and do not repeatedly ask the same questions; if the interviewers are patient and nonjudgmental; and if they do not selectively reward or reinforce responses or convey veiled threats or accusations (Bruck & Ceci, 1997; Bruck, Ceci, & Hembrooke, 1998; Leichtman & Ceci, 1995; Steward & Steward, 1996).

---

autobiographical memory
Memory of specific events in one's own life.

Autobiographical memory refers to memories that form a person's life history. These memories are specific and long lasting. Autobiographical memory is a type of episodic memory, but not everything in episodic memory becomes part of it—only those memories that have a special, personal meaning to the child. For most people, autobiographical memory goes back to age 3 or 4, but some adults have documented memories from about age 2 (Howe, 2003). On the other hand, some people do not remember much before age 8 (Nelson, 1992).

As we mentioned in Chapter 5, one suggested explanation for the relatively late arrival of autobiographical memory is that children cannot store in memory events pertaining to their own lives until they develop a concept of self around which to organize those memories (Howe, 2003; Howe & Courage, 1993, 1997). The emergence of autobiographical memory also may be linked with the development of language. The ability to talk about an event, as Yani and her father often did, may affect whether and how the memory is carried into later life. Not until children can put memories into words can they hold them in their minds, reflect on them, and compare them with the memories of others (Fivush & Schwarzmueller, 1998).

Why do some early memories last longer than others? One factor is the uniqueness of the event. A second factor is children's active participation, either in the event itself or in its retelling or reenactment—as Yani did in drawing the monkeys she recalled so vividly. Preschoolers tend to remember things they *did* better than things they merely *saw* (Murachver, Pipe, Gordon, Owens, & Fivush, 1996). A third factor is talk with parents about past events. In one study, 2½- to 3-year-olds engaged in pretend play with their mothers about a camping trip, a bird-watching adventure, and the opening of an ice cream shop. Children who jointly handled *and* jointly discussed with their mothers various items connected with these events

—continued

Young children are apt to err in recalling precise details of a frequently repeated event (Powell & Thomson, 1996). They tend to confuse what happened during a particular episode with what happened during other, similar episodes. Thus, a child may have trouble answering questions about a *specific instance* of abuse, even though the child accurately remembers a *pattern* of abuse.

Often young children's testimony is excluded because they cannot demonstrate a clear understanding of the difference between truth and falsehood and of the morality and consequences of telling a lie. Often they do not understand such questions the way they are asked or cannot explain the concepts involved. Furthermore, many abused children have seriously delayed language skills. The Lyon-Saywitz Oath-Taking Competency Picture Task avoids these problems by simply asking a prospective young witness whether a child in a story is telling the truth about a pictured event and what would happen if the child told a lie. Among 192 maltreated 4- to 7-year-olds awaiting court appearances, a majority of 5-year-olds successfully performed this task, and even 4-year-olds did better than chance would predict (Lyon & Saywitz, 1999).

Issues concerning the reliability of young children's testimony are still being sorted out, but it appears that children *can* give reliable testimony if care is taken to avoid biased interviewing techniques. Researchers are trying to develop and validate "model" interview techniques that will expose adults who harm children while protecting those who may be falsely accused (Bruck et al., 1998).

What's Your View?

• What information would you seek and what factors would you consider in deciding whether to believe a preschooler's testimony in a child abuse case?

Check It Out

For more information on this topic, go to http://www.ojp.usdoj.gov/ovc/factshts/monograph.htm. This is a June 1999 monograph from the U.S. Department of Justice Office for Victims of Crime, "Breaking the Cycle of Violence: Recommendations to Improve the Criminal Justice Response to Child Victims and Witnesses." Or go to http://www.aap.org/policy/re9923.html. This is a policy statement from the American Academy of Pediatrics, "The Child in Court: A Subject Review" (RE9923).

recalled them better one to three days later than children who had only handled or only discussed the items (Haden, Ornstein, Eckerman, & Didow, 2001).

The *way* adults talk with a child about a shared experience can influence how well the child will remember it (Haden & Fivush, 1996; McGuigan & Salmon, 2004; Reese & Fivush, 1993). When a child gets stuck, adults with a *repetitive* conversational style tend to repeat their own previous statements or questions. A repetitive-style parent might ask, "Do you remember how we traveled to Florida?" and then, receiving no answer, ask, "How did we get there? We went in the ___." Adults with an *elaborative* style would move on to a different aspect of the event or add more information: "Did we go by car or by plane?" Elaborative parents seem focused on having a mutually rewarding conversation and affirming the child's responses, whereas repetitive parents seem focused on checking the child's memory performance. Children of elaborative-style parents take part in longer, more detailed conversations about events at age 3 and tend to remember the events better at 5 and 6 (Reese, Haden, & Fivush, 1993).

"Remember when we went to the zoo?" Young children remember better events that are unique and new, and they may recall details from a special trip for a year or longer.

What's Your View?

- Since an elaborative conversational style seems most effective in jogging young children's memory, would you favor training mothers to use it? Why or why not?

In a study of 3- and 5-year-olds who participated in a staged event (a visit to a "zoo"), elaborative talk a few days *after* the event had greater influence on correct recall two weeks later than did such talk before or during the event. In fact, for 3-year-olds, elaborative talk before or during an event had no more effect on later recall than "empty" talk—talk that conveyed no specific information (McGuigan & Salmon, 2004).

How does elaborative talk enhance recall? Such talk may help a child encode recently experienced information by providing verbal labels for aspects of the event and by giving it an orderly, comprehensible structure. Elaborative talk also may create "boundaries" around children's mental representations of the event, preventing intrusion by irrelevant or distorted information (McGuigan & Salmon, 2004).

social interaction model   Model, based on Vygotsky's sociocultural theory, which proposes that children construct autobiographical memories through conversation with adults about shared events.

Social Interaction, Culture, and Memory

Social interaction not only helps children remember, it may even be the key to memory formation. Investigators influenced by Vygotsky's sociocultural theory support a **social interaction model,** which holds that children collaboratively construct autobiographical memories with parents or other adults as they talk about shared events (Nelson, 1993a). Adults initiate and guide these conversations, which show children how memories are organized in narrative form in their culture (Welch-Ross, 1997). When parents prompt 2- and 3-year-olds with frequent questions about context ("When did you find the pine cone?" "Where did you find it?" "Who was with you?"), children soon learn to include this information (Peterson & McCabe, 1994). When parents of 3-year-olds comment on subjective reactions ("You *wanted* to go on the slide," "It was a *huge* bowl," "Mommy was *wrong*"), the children at 5½ are more likely to weave such comments into their reminiscences (Haden, Haine, & Fivush, 1997).

This mother's comments and questions as her son tells about something they did or saw may help structure the way he remembers it, according to Vygotsky's social interaction model.

Culture affects what children remember about an experience and the way parents talk with them about it. In one study (Wang, 2004), 180 European American and Chinese preschoolers, kindergartners, and second graders were asked such questions as "How did you spend your last birthday?" and "Tell me about a time when your mom or dad scolded you about something." U.S. children told about particular events; their narratives were longer and more detailed and contained more opinion and emotion than those of the Chinese children. Chinese children's accounts centered on daily routines, group activities, and social interactions and roles. The U.S. children were the chief characters of their stories, whereas the Chinese children shared the "stage" with others. In discussions of shared memories with 3-year-olds, U.S. mothers used elaboration to encourage the child's active participation ("Do you remember when you went swimming at Nana's? What did you do that was really neat?"). Chinese mothers asked leading questions containing most of the content of the memory, leaving little for the child to add ("What did you play at the place of skiing? Sat on the ice ship, right?").

Checkpoint

Can you . . .

- ✔ Identify three types of memories in early childhood?

- ✔ Identify factors that affect how well a preschool child will remember an event?

- ✔ Compare two types of parental styles of discussing shared memories with a child?

- ✔ Give examples of how social interaction and culture influence autobiographical memory?

Intelligence: Psychometric and Vygotskian Approaches

Guidepost

7. How is preschoolers' intelligence measured, and what are some influences on it?

One factor that may affect the strength of early cognitive skills is intelligence. Let's look at two ways intelligence is measured—through traditional psychometric tests and through newer tests of cognitive potential.

Traditional Psychometric Measures

The precise nature of intelligence has been debated for many years, as has the best way to measure it. Beginning in the 19th century, there were attempts to measure intelligence by such characteristics as head size and reaction time, and then by tests that scored strength of hand squeeze, pain sensitivity, weight discrimination, judgment of time, and rote recall. These tests had little predictive value.

At the beginning of the 20th century, school administrators in Paris asked the psychologist Alfred Binet to devise a way to identify children who could not handle academic work and who should be given special training. The test that Binet and his colleague Theodore Simon developed was the forerunner of psychometric tests, now used for children of all levels of ability, that score intelligence by numbers.

Preschool children are easier to test than infants and toddlers, but they still need to be tested individually. Because 3- to 5-year-olds are more proficient with language than younger children, intelligence tests for this age group can include more verbal items; and these tests produce more reliable results than the largely nonverbal tests used in infancy. The two most commonly used individual tests for preschoolers are the Stanford-Binet Intelligence Scale and the Wechsler Preschool and Primary Scale of Intelligence.

The **Stanford-Binet Intelligence Scales,** used for ages 2 and up, is an American version of the traditional Binet-Simon tests. The test takes 45 to 60 minutes. The child is asked to define words, string beads, build with blocks, identify the missing parts of a picture, trace mazes, and show an understanding of numbers. The child's score is supposed to measure fluid reasoning (the ability to solve abstract or novel problems), knowledge, quantitative reasoning, visual-spatial processing, and working memory. The fifth edition, revised in 2003, includes nonverbal methods of testing all five of these dimensions of cognition and permits comparisons of verbal and nonverbal performance. In addition to providing a full-scale IQ, the Stanford-Binet yields separate measures of verbal and nonverbal IQ plus composite scores spanning the five cognitive dimensions.

The **Wechsler Preschool and Primary Scale of Intelligence, Revised (WPPSI-III),** an individual test taking 30 to 60 minutes, has separate levels for ages 2½ to 4 and 4 to 7. It yields separate verbal and performance scores as well as a combined score. The 2002 revision includes new subtests designed to measure both verbal and nonverbal fluid reasoning, receptive versus expressive vocabulary, and processing speed. Both the Stanford-Binet and the WPPSI-III have been restandardized on samples of children representing the population of preschool-age children in the United States. The WPPSI-III also has been validated for special populations, such as children with intellectual disabilities, developmental delays, language disorders, and autistic disorders.

Despite the widespread use of these tests, fierce controversies remain over what intelligence is and how it can be measured—or whether it can be fairly measured at all (see Chapter 9).

Stanford-Binet Intelligence Scale Individual intelligence test for ages 2 and up used to measure fluid reasoning, knowledge, quantitative reasoning, visual-spatial processing, and working memory.

Wechsler Preschool and Primary Scale of Intelligence, Revised (WPPSI-III) Individual intelligence test for children ages 2½ to 7 that yields verbal and performance scores as well as a combined score.

Influences on Measured Intelligence

One common misconception is that IQ scores represent a fixed quantity of inborn intelligence. In reality, an IQ score is simply a measure of how well a child can do certain tasks at a certain time in comparison with others of the same age. Indeed, test scores of children in industrialized countries have risen steadily since testing began, forcing test developers to raise standardized norms (Flynn, 1984, 1987). This trend may in part reflect exposure to educational television, preschools, better-educated parents, and a wider variety of experiences, as well as changes in the tests themselves.

How well a particular child does on IQ tests may be influenced by several factors: temperament, social and emotional maturity, ease in the testing situation, preliteracy or literacy skills, socioeconomic status, ethnicity or culture, and the match between the child's cognitive style and the tasks posed. (We will examine several of these factors in Chapter 9.)

At one time developmental scientists believed that the family environment played a major role in influencing a child's intelligence. Now the extent of that influence is in question. We do not know how much of parents' influence on intelligence comes from their genetic contribution and how much from the fact that they provide a child's earliest environment for learning. Twin and adoption studies suggest that family life has its strongest influence in early childhood, and this influence diminishes greatly by adolescence (McGue, 1997; Neisser et al., 1996). However, these studies have been done largely with white, middle-class samples; their results may not apply to low-income and nonwhite families (Neisser et al., 1996). In a longitudinal study of low-income African American children, the influence of the home environment remained substantial—at least as strong as the influence of the mother's IQ (Burchinal et al., 1997).

The correlation between socioeconomic status and IQ is well documented (Neisser et al., 1996). Family income is associated with cognitive development and achievement in the preschool years and beyond. Family economic circumstances can exert a powerful influence, not so much in themselves as in the way they affect other factors such as health, stress, parenting practices, and the atmosphere in the home (Brooks-Gunn, 2003; Evans, 2004; McLoyd, 1990, 1998; Rouse, Brooks-Gunn, & McLanahan, 2005; see Chapter 10).

Both genetic and environmental factors influence children's vulnerability to economic deprivation and their ability to surmount it. In a study of 1,116 twin pairs born in England and Wales in 1994 and 1995 and assessed at age 5 (Kim-Cohen, Moffitt, Caspi, & Taylor, 2004), children in deprived families tended, as in other studies, to have lower IQs. However, a child's outgoing temperament together with maternal warmth and stimulating activities in the home (which, again, may be influenced by parental IQ) served as protective factors.

Testing and Teaching Based on Vygotsky's Theory

According to Vygotsky, children learn by internalizing the results of interactions with adults. This interactive learning is most effective in helping children cross the **zone of proximal development (ZPD),** the gap between what they are already able to do and what they are not quite ready to accomplish by themselves. (*Proximal* means "nearby.") Children in the ZPD for a particular task can almost, but not quite, perform the task on their own. With the right kind of guidance, however, they can do it successfully. The ZPD can be assessed by *dynamic tests* (see Chapter 9), which, according to Vygotskyan theory, provide a better measure of children's intellectual potential than do traditional psychometric tests that measure what children have already mastered.

zone of proximal development (ZPD) Vygotsky's term for the difference between what a child can do alone and what the child can do with help.

By giving suggestions for solving a puzzle until the child can do it on her own, this mother guides her daughter's cognitive progress.

Some followers of Vygotsky (Wood, 1980; Wood, Bruner, & Ross, 1976) have applied the metaphor of scaffolds—the temporary platforms on which construction workers stand—to this way of teaching. **Scaffolding** is the temporary support that parents, teachers, or others give a child to do a task until the child can do it alone. Scaffolding can help parents and teachers efficiently guide children's cognitive progress. The less able a child is to do a task, the more direction an adult must give. As the child can do more and more, the adult helps less and less. When the child can do the job alone, the adult takes away the "scaffold" that is no longer needed.

By enabling children to become aware of and monitor their own cognitive processes and to recognize when they need help, parents can help children take responsibility for learning. Prekindergarten children who receive this kind of scaffolding are better able to regulate their own learning when they get to kindergarten (Neitzel & Stright, 2003). In a longitudinal study of 289 urban and rural low-SES, largely African American families with infants, the skills children developed during interactions with their mothers at 2 and 3½ enabled them, at 4½, to regulate their own goal-directed problem solving and to initiate social interactions (Landry, Smith, Swank, & Miller-Loncar, 2000).

> **scaffolding** Temporary support to help a child master a task.

Checkpoint

Can you . . .

✔ Describe two commonly used individual intelligence tests for preschoolers?

✔ List and discuss several influences on measured intelligence?

✔ Explain why an intelligence test score using the ZPD might be significantly different from a traditional psychometric test score?

Language Development

Preschoolers are full of questions: "How many sleeps until tomorrow?" "Who filled the river with water?" "Do babies have muscles?" "Do smells come from inside my nose?" Young children's growing facility with language helps them express their unique view of the world. The child who, at 3, describes how Daddy "hatches" wood (chops with a hatchet) or asks Mommy to "piece" her food (cut it into little pieces) may, by the age of 5, tell her mother, "Don't be ridiculous!" or proudly point to her toys and say, "See how I organized everything?"

Guidepost

8. How does language improve, and what happens when its development is delayed?

Vocabulary

At 3 the average child knows and can use 900 to 1,000 words. By age 6, a child typically has an expressive (speaking) vocabulary of 2,600 words and understands more than 20,000 (Owens, 1996).* With the help of formal schooling, a child's passive, or receptive, vocabulary (words she can understand) will quadruple to 80,000 words by the time she enters high school (Owens, 1996).

This rapid expansion of vocabulary may occur through **fast mapping,** which allows a child to pick up the approximate meaning of a new word after hearing it only once or twice in conversation. From the context, children seem to form a quick hypothesis about the meaning of the word, which then is refined with further exposure and usage. Linguists are not sure how fast mapping works, but it seems likely that children draw on what they know about the rules for forming words, about similar words, about the immediate context, and about the subject under discussion. Names of objects (nouns) seem to be easier to fast map than names of actions (verbs), which are less concrete. Yet one experiment showed that children just under 3 years old can fast map a new verb and apply it to another situation in which the same action is being performed (Golinkoff, Jacquet, Hirsh-Pasek, & Nandakumar, 1996).

Theory-of-mind development—the increasing ability to infer another's mental state—seems to play a role in vocabulary learning. In one study, preschoolers learned "nonsense" words better from a speaker who seemed certain what the word meant than from one who seemed unsure (Sabbagh & Baldwin, 2001).

> **fast mapping** Process by which a child absorbs the meaning of a new word after hearing it once or twice in conversation.

*Unless otherwise referenced, this discussion of preschoolers' language development is indebted to Owens (1996).

Many 3- and 4-year-olds seem able to tell when two words refer to the same object or action (Savage & Au, 1996). They know that a single object cannot have two proper names (a dog cannot be both Spot and Fido). They also know that more than one adjective can apply to the same noun ("Fido is spotted and furry") and that an adjective can be combined with a proper name ("smart Fido!") (Hall & Graham, 1999).

Grammar and Syntax

The ways children combine syllables into words, and words into sentences, grow increasingly sophisticated during early childhood. At 3, children typically begin to use plurals, possessives, and past tense and know the difference between *I, you,* and *we.* Their sentences are generally short and simple, often omitting articles, such as *a* and *the,* but including some pronouns, adjectives, and prepositions. Although they most often use declarative sentences ("Kitty wants milk"), they can ask—and answer—*what* and *where* questions. (*Why* and *how* are harder to grasp.)

However, they still overregularize because they have not yet learned or absorbed exceptions to rules (refer back to Chapter 5). Saying "holded" instead of "held" or "eated" instead of "ate" is a normal sign of linguistic progress. When young children discover a rule, such as adding *-ed* to a verb for past tense, they tend to use it even with words that do not conform to the rule. Eventually, they notice that *-ed* is not always used to form the past tense of a verb.

Between ages 4 and 5, sentences average four to five words and may be declarative, negative ("I'm not hungry"), interrogative ("Why can't I go outside?"), or imperative ("Catch the ball!"). Four-year-olds use complex, multiclause sentences ("I'm eating because I'm hungry") more frequently if their parents often use such sentences (Huttenlocher, Vasilyeva, Cymerman, & Levine, 2002). Children this age tend to string sentences together in long run-on narratives (". . . And then . . . And then . . ."). In some respects, comprehension may be immature. For example, 4-year-old Noah can carry out a command that includes more than one step ("Pick up your toys and put them in the cupboard"). However, if his mother tells him "You may watch TV after you pick up your toys," he may process the words in the order in which he hears them and think he can first watch television and then pick up his toys.

By ages 5 to 7, children's speech has become quite adultlike. They speak in longer and more complicated sentences. They use more conjunctions, prepositions, and articles. They use compound and complex sentences and can handle all parts of speech. Still, although children this age speak fluently, comprehensibly, and fairly grammatically, they have yet to master many fine points of language. They rarely use the passive voice ("I was dressed by Grandpa"), conditional sentences ("If I were big, I could drive the bus"), or the auxiliary verb *have* ("I have seen that lady before") (C. S. Chomsky, 1969).

Pragmatics and Social Speech

As children learn vocabulary, grammar, and syntax, they become more competent in **pragmatics**—the practical knowledge of how to use language to communicate. This includes knowing how to ask for things, how to tell a story or joke, how to begin and continue a conversation, and how to adjust comments to the listener's perspective. These are all aspects of **social speech:** speech intended to be understood by a listener.

With improved pronunciation and grammar, it becomes easier for others to understand what children say. Most 3-year-olds are quite talkative, and they pay attention to the effect of their speech on others. If people cannot understand them, they try to explain themselves more clearly. Four-year-olds, especially girls, simplify their language and use a higher register when speaking to 2-year-olds (Owens, 1996; Shatz & Gelman, 1973).

pragmatics The practical knowledge needed to use language for communicative purposes.

social speech Speech intended to be understood by a listener.

Most 5-year-olds can adapt what they say to what the listener knows. They can now use words to resolve disputes, and they use more polite language and fewer direct commands in talking to adults than to other children. Almost half of all 5-year-olds can stick to a conversational topic for about a dozen turns—if they are comfortable with their partner and if the topic is one they know and care about.

Private Speech

Anna, age 4, was alone in her room painting. When she finished, she was overheard saying aloud, "Now I have to put the pictures somewhere to dry. I'll put them by the window. They need to get dry now. I'll paint some more dinosaurs."

Private speech—talking aloud to oneself with no intent to communicate with others—is common in childhood, accounting for 20 to 50 percent of what 4- to 10-year-old children say (Berk, 1986a). Two- to 3-year-olds engage in "crib talk," playing with sounds and words. Four- and 5-year-olds use private speech as a way to express fantasies and emotions (Berk, 1992; Small, 1990). Older children "think out loud" or mutter in barely audible tones.

Piaget (1962/1923) saw private speech as a sign of cognitive immaturity. According to Piaget, because young children are *egocentric*—unable to to recognize others' viewpoints—they cannot communicate meaningfully. Instead, they simply vocalize whatever is on their own minds. Also, young children talk while they do things, said Piaget, because they do not yet distinguish between words and the actions the words symbolize. By the end of the preoperational stage, he said, with cognitive maturation and social experience, children become less egocentric and more capable of symbolic thought and so discard private speech.

Vygotsky (1962/1934) did not look upon private speech as egocentric. He saw it as a special form of communication: conversation with the self. As such, he said, it serves a very important function in the transition between early social speech (often experienced in the form of adult commands) and inner speech (thinking in words)—a transition toward internal control of behavior ("Now I have to put the pictures somewhere to dry"). Vygotsky suggested that private speech follows a bell-shaped curve: It increases during the preschool years and fades away during the early elementary school years as children become more able to guide and master their actions.

Research generally supports Vygotsky as to the functions of private speech. In an observational study of 93 low- to middle-income 3- to 5-year-olds, 86 percent of the children's remarks were *not* egocentric (Berk, 1986a). The most sociable children, and those who engage in the most social speech, tend to use the most private speech as well, apparently supporting Vygotsky's view that private speech is stimulated by social experience (Berk, 1986a, 1986b, 1992; Berk & Garvin, 1984; Kohlberg, Yaeger, & Hjertholm, 1968).

There also is evidence for the role of private speech in self-regulation, a child's efforts to control his or her own behavior (Berk & Garvin, 1984; Furrow, 1984). Private speech tends to increase when children are trying to do difficult tasks, especially without adult supervision (Berk, 1992; Berk & Garvin, 1984).

How much do children engage in private speech? Some studies have reported no age changes in its overall use; others have found variations in the timing of its decline. Whereas Vygotsky considered the need for private speech a universal stage of cognitive development, studies have found a wide range of individual differences, with some children using it very little or not at all (Berk, 1992).

Understanding the significance of private speech has practical implications, especially in school (Berk, 1986a). Talking to oneself or muttering should not be considered misbehavior; a child may be struggling with a problem and may need to think out loud.

private speech Talking aloud to oneself with no intent to communicate.

Checkpoint
Can you . . .

✔ Trace normal progress in 3- to 6-year-olds' vocabulary, grammar, syntax, and conversational abilities?

✔ Give reasons why children of various ages use private speech?

Delayed Language Development

It is unclear why some children speak late. They do not necessarily lack linguistic input at home. These children may have a cognitive limitation that makes it hard for them to learn the rules of language (Scarborough, 1990). Children with delayed language may have problems in fast mapping; they may need to hear a new word more often than other children do before they can incorporate it into their vocabularies (M. L. Rice, 1989; M. Rice, Oetting, Marquis, Bode, & Pae, 1994). Boys are more likely than girls to be late talkers (Dale et al., 1998).

Many children who speak late—especially those whose comprehension is normal—eventually catch up (Dale, Price, Bishop, & Plomin, 2003; Thal, Tobias, & Morrison, 1991). Some late speakers have a history of otitis media (an inflammation of the middle ear) between 12 and 18 months of age; these children improve dramatically in language ability when the infection, with its related hearing loss, clears up (Lonigan, Fischel, Whitehurst, Arnold, & Valdez-Menchaca, 1992). For some children, however, severe early language delays, if left untreated, may signal a persistent language impairment that can have far-reaching cognitive, social, and emotional consequences. In a longitudinal study, 31 children identified at age 2 as late talkers had less sophisticated narrative skills at ages 8 and 9 than a control group who had not been late talkers (Manhardt & Rescorla, 2002). Children who do not speak or understand as well as their peers tend to be judged negatively by adults and other children (M. L. Rice, Hadley, & Alexander, 1993) and to have trouble finding playmates or friends (Gertner, Rice, & Hadley, 1994).

Because heredity seems to play a major role, especially in the most severe and persistent cases of language delay (Dale et al., 1998), family history needs to be considered in recommending a child for treatment (Bishop, Price, Dale, & Plomin, 2003). In a Finnish study, late talkers with a family history of dyslexia had persistent language difficulties, but those without such a history had normal speech by age 3½ (Lyytinen, Poikkeys, Laakso, Eklund, & Lyytinen, 2001).

Speech and language therapy can be effective, especially if begun early. It may include strategies focusing on specific language forms, a specialized preschool program targeting language skills, and follow-up programs either in or out of school during the elementary school years (M. L. Rice, 1989).

Social Interaction and Preparation for Literacy

To understand what is on the printed page, children first need to master certain prereading skills (Lonigan, Burgess, & Anthony, 2000; Muter, Hulme, Snowling, & Stevenson, 2004). **Emergent literacy** refers to the development of these skills, along with the knowledge and attitudes that underlie reading and writing.

Prereading skills include (1) general linguistic skills, such as vocabulary, syntax, narrative structure, and the understanding that language is used to communicate; and (2) specific phonological skills, such as *phonemic awareness*—the realization that words are composed of distinct sounds, or *phonemes*—and *phoneme-grapheme correspondence,* the ability to link sounds with the corresponding letters or combinations of letters (Whitehurst & Lonigan, 1998; Lonigan et al., 2000). In a two-year longitudinal study of 90 British children who entered school at an average age of 4 years and 9 months, the development of word recognition appeared critically dependent on specific phonological skills (letter knowledge and phonemic awareness). On the other hand, general linguistic skills, such as vocabulary and grammatical skills, were more important predictors of reading comprehension (Muter et al., 2004).

Social interaction can promote emergent literacy. Children are more likely to become good readers and writers if, during the preschool years, parents provide

emergent literacy Preschoolers' development of skills, knowledge, and attitudes that underlie reading and writing.

conversational challenges the children are ready for—if they use a rich vocabulary and center dinner-table talk on the day's activities, on mutually remembered past events, or on questions about why people do things and how things work (Reese, 1995; Snow, 1990, 1993). It is likely that Yani's frequent hiking expeditions with her father, when he told her stories about the clouds and they talked about the things they saw around them, contributed to her emergent literacy.

As children learn the skills they will need to translate the written word into speech, they also learn that writing can express ideas, thoughts, and feelings. Preschool children in the United States pretend to write by scribbling, lining up their marks from left to right (Brenneman, Massey, Machado, & Gelman, 1996). Later they begin using letters, numbers, and letterlike shapes to represent words, syllables, or phonemes. Often their spelling is so inventive that they cannot read it themselves (Whitehurst & Lonigan, 1998)!

Reading to children is one of the most effective paths to literacy. According to a U.S. government report, 86 percent of girls and 82 percent of boys are read to at home at least three times a week (Freeman, 2004). Children who are read to from an early age learn that reading and writing in English move from left to right and from top to bottom and that words are separated by spaces. They also are motivated to learn to read (Siegler, 1998; Whitehurst & Lonigan, 1998).

Moderate exposure to educational television can help prepare children for literacy, especially if parents talk with children about what they see. In one study, the more time 3- to 5-year-olds spent watching *Sesame Street*, the more their vocabulary improved (M. L. Rice, Huston, Truglio, & Wright, 1990). In a longitudinal study, the content of television programs viewed at ages 2 and 4 predicted academic skills three years later (Wright et al., 2001).

Toys and games that familiarize children with the alphabet and the sounds the letters make can give them a head start in learning to read.

Checkpoint

Can you . . .

✔ Discuss possible causes, consequences, and treatment of delayed language development?

✔ Explain how social interaction can promote preparation for literacy?

Early Childhood Education

Going to preschool is an important step, widening a child's physical, cognitive, and social environment. The transition to kindergarten, the beginning of "real school," is another momentous step. In 2001, 64 percent of 3- to 5-year-olds were enrolled in preprimary or primary education,* and the rates were higher in many industrial countries (Sen, Partelow, & Miller, 2005).

Guidepost

9. What purposes does early childhood education serve, and how do children make the transition to kindergarten?

Goals and Types of Preschools: A Cross-Cultural View

In some countries, such as China, preschools are expected to provide academic preparation for schooling. In contrast, most preschools in the United States and many other western countries traditionally have followed a "child-centered" philosophy stressing social and emotional growth in line with young children's developmental needs—though some, such as those based on the theories of Piaget or the Italian educator Maria Montessori, have a stronger cognitive emphasis.

As part of a debate over how to improve education, pressures have grown to offer instruction in basic academic skills in U.S. preschools. Defenders of the traditional

What's Your View?

• Should the primary purpose of preschool be to provide a strong academic foundation or to foster social and emotional development?

*Seven percent of 5-year-olds were enrolled in primary schooling.

These preschoolers playing Candyland are improving in physical coordination, counting skills, and the ability to take turns and cooperate in play. A good preschool stimulates all aspects of development through interaction with trained teachers, playmates, and carefully chosen materials.

developmental approach maintain that academically oriented programs neglect young children's need for exploration and free play and that too much teacher-initiated instruction may stifle their interest and interfere with self-initiated learning (Elkind, 1986; Zigler, 1987).

What type of preschool is best for children? Studies in the United States support the child-centered, developmental approach. One field study (Marcon, 1999) compared 721 four- and 5-year-olds from three types of preschool classrooms in Washington, DC: *child-initiated, academically directed,* and *middle-of-the-road* (a blend of the other two approaches). Children from child-initiated programs, in which they actively directed their own learning experiences, excelled in basic academic skills. They also had more advanced motor skills than the other two groups and scored higher than the middle-of-the-road group in behavioral and communicative skills. These findings suggest that a single, coherent philosophy of education may work better than an attempt to blend diverse approaches and that a child-centered approach seems more effective than an academically oriented one.

Compensatory Preschool Programs

The higher the family's socioeconomic status, the more likely a child is to be ready for school (Rouse et al., 2005). According to estimates, more than two-thirds of children in poor urban areas enter school poorly prepared to learn (Zigler, 1998). Since the 1960s, large-scale programs have been developed to help such children compensate for what they have missed and to prepare them for school.

The best-known compensatory preschool program for children of low-income families in the United States is Project Head Start, a federally funded program launched in 1965. Consistent with its "whole child" approach, its goals are not only to enhance cognitive skills, but also to improve physical health and to foster self-confidence, relationships with others, social responsibility, and a sense of dignity and self-worth for the child and the family. The program provides medical, dental, and mental health care, social services, and at least one hot meal a day.

Has Head Start lived up to its name? Data support its effectiveness in improving school readiness (Ripple et al., 1999; USDHHS, 2003b). Similarly, children who attend the newer state-sponsored programs tend to show better cognitive and language skills and do better in school than children who do not attend (USDHHS, 2003a). Yet, even though Head Start children make gains in vocabulary, letter recognition, early writing, and early mathematics, their readiness skills remain far below average (USDHHS, 2003b). And, although they do better on intelligence tests than other children from comparable backgrounds, this advantage disappears after they start school (Ripple et al., 1999; Zigler & Styfco, 1993, 1994).

Still, children from Head Start and other compensatory programs are less likely to be placed in special education or to repeat a grade and are more likely to finish high school than low-income children who did not attend such programs (Neisser et al., 1996). "Graduates" of one such program, the Perry Preschool Project, were also much less likely to become juvenile delinquents or to become pregnant in their teens (Berrueta-Clement, Schweinhart, Barnett, Epstein, & Weikart, 1985; Schweinhart, Barnes, & Weikart, 1993; see Chapter 17).

Outcomes are best with earlier and longer-lasting intervention through high quality, center-based programs (Brooks-Gunn, 2003; Reynolds & Temple, 1998; Zigler & Styfco, 1993, 1994, 2001). The most successful Head Start programs are those with the most parental participation, the best-trained teachers, the lowest staff-to-child ratios, the longest school days and weeks, and the most extensive services (Ramey, 1999).

In 1995, an Early Head Start program began offering child and family development services to pregnant women and to infants and toddlers from birth to age 3. By 2002, the program was operating in 664 communities and serving about 55,000 children (Love et al., 2002). A large-scale, randomized evaluation found modest but consistent positive impacts when the children were 2 and 3 years old. Participants scored higher on standardized developmental and vocabulary tests and were at less risk of slow development than children not in the program. At age 3, they were less aggressive, more attentive to playthings, and more positively engaged with their parents. The impact was greatest on African American families, families who enrolled during pregnancy, and families with moderately (but not very) high demographic risk factors. Programs that offered a mix of center-based and home services showed better results than those that concentrated on one setting or the other (Commissioner's Office of Research and Evaluation and Head Start Bureau, 2001; Love et al., 2002).

The Chicago Child Parent Centers, a large-scale, federally funded compensatory program, extends from preschool through third grade. The added years of academic enrichment have significantly increased participants' reading achievement and decreased grade retention and special education placement through seventh grade, as compared with children who participated for only two or three years (Reynolds, 1994; Reynolds & Temple, 1998). At age 20, among 989 poverty-level children who had begun the program by age 4, nearly half (49.7 percent) had graduated from high school, as compared with 38.5 percent of a control group who had attended less intensive preschools or no preschool; and 16.9 percent had been arrested for juvenile crimes as compared with 25.1 percent of the control group (Reynolds, Temple, Robertson, & Mann, 2001).

The Transition to Kindergarten

Originally a year of transition between the relative freedom of home or preschool and the structure of "real school," kindergarten in the United States has become more like first grade. Children spend less time on self-chosen activities and more time on worksheets and preparing to read.

Although some states do not require kindergarten programs or kindergarten attendance (Vecchiotti, 2003), most 5-year-olds attend kindergarten. Since the late 1970s, an increasing number of kindergarteners (60 percent in 2001) spend a full day in school, rather than the traditional half day (National Center for Education Statistics, 2004a). A practical impetus for this trend is the growing number of single-parent and dual-earner households. In addition, large numbers of children already have experienced preschool, prekindergarten programs, or full-time child care and are ready for a more rigorous, time-intensive kindergarten curriculum (Walston & West, 2004). Poor and minority children, especially black children, are disproportionately likely to spend a full day in kindergarten (National Center for Education Statistics, 2004a; Walston & West, 2004).

Do children learn more in full-day kindergarten? According to longitudinal research on a nationally representative sample of children who started kindergarten in the fall of 1998, public school children in full-day kindergarten are more likely than half-day students to receive daily instruction in prereading skills, math skills, social studies, and science (Walston & West, 2004) and tend to do better by the end of kindergarten and in the primary grades (Vecchiotti, 2003; Walston & West, 2004). However, by the end of third grade, children who went to full-day and half-day kindergarten are substantially equal in reading, math, and science achievement (Rathburn, West, & Germino-Hausken, 2004).

Findings highlight the importance of the preparation a child receives *before* kindergarten. Children who come to kindergarten from advantaged home environments tend to do better in reading and math, and the achievement gap between advantaged and disadvantaged children widens during the first four years of school (Denton, West, & Walston, 2003; Rathbun et al., 2004).

Emotional and social adjustment are important factors in readiness for kindergarten and strongly predict school success. More important than knowing the alphabet or being able to count to 20, kindergarten teachers say, are the abilities to sit still, follow directions, wait one's turn, and regulate one's own learning (Blair, 2002; Brooks-Gunn, 2003; Raver, 2002). How well a child adjusts to kindergarten may depend on the child's age, gender, temperament, cognitive and social competencies, and coping skills as well as the support or stress generated by the home, school, and neighborhood environments (Blair, 2002; Ladd, 1996; Ladd, Birch, & Buhs, 1999). Children with extensive preschool experience tend to adjust to kindergarten more easily than those who spent little or no time in preschool (Ladd, 1996).

Because cutoff birth dates for kindergarten entrance vary among the states, children enter kindergarten at ages ranging from 4 to 6. In addition, as academic and emotional pressures mount, many parents are holding children back for a year, and some states are moving up their cutoff dates in the belief that children whose birthdays are close to the cutoff will be more ready for kindergarten if they wait a year. However, research gives limited support to that idea. Children who are older at kindergarten entry do have a modest initial academic advantage, but by third grade that advantage typically disappears (Stipek, 2002; Stipek & Byler, 2001).

Proposals have been made to lengthen the school year. When an elementary school in a midsized southeastern city added 30 days to its school year, children who completed kindergarten outperformed their counterparts in a traditional 180-day program on tests of math, reading, general knowledge, and cognitive competence (Frazier & Morrison, 1998).

Checkpoint
Can you . . .

✔ Compare goals and effectiveness of varying types of preschool programs?

✔ Assess the benefits of compensatory preschool education?

✔ Discuss factors that affect adjustment to kindergarten?

Refocus

Thinking back to the Focus vignette about Wang Yani at the beginning of this chapter:

- What aspects of Wang Yani's physical and cognitive development in early childhood seem to have been fairly typical, and in what ways was her development advanced?

- Can you give examples of how Yani's physical, cognitive, and psychosocial development interacted?

- What more would you like to know about Yani's early development if you had the chance to interview her or her parents?

The burgeoning physical and cognitive skills of early childhood have psychosocial implications, as we'll see in Chapter 8.

SUMMARY AND KEY TERMS

Physical Development Aspects of Physical Development

Guidepost 1: How do children's bodies change between ages 3 and 6, and what are their nutritional and dental needs?

- Physical growth continues during the years from 3 to 6, but more slowly than during infancy and toddlerhood. Boys are on average slightly taller, heavier, and more muscular than girls. Internal body systems are maturing, and all primary teeth are present.

- The prevalence of overweight among preschoolers has increased.

- Malnutrition can affect all aspects of development.

- Tooth decay has decreased since the 1970s but remains a problem among disadvantaged children.

Guidepost 2: What sleep patterns tend to develop during early childhood, and what sleep problems may occur?

- Sleep patterns change during early childhood, as throughout life, and are affected by cultural expectations.

- It is normal for preschool children to develop bedtime rituals that delay going to sleep. Occasional sleepwalking, sleep terrors, and nightmares are common, but persistent sleep problems may indicate emotional disturbances.

- Bed-wetting is usually outgrown without special help.

  enuresis *(242)*

Motor Development

Guidepost 3: What are the main motor achievements of early childhood?

- Children progress rapidly in gross and fine motor skills, developing more complex systems of action.

- Handedness is usually evident by age 3, reflecting dominance by one hemisphere of the brain.

- Stages of art production, which appear to reflect brain development and fine motor coordination, are the scribbling stage, shape stage, design stage, and pictorial stage.

  gross motor skills *(242)*

  fine motor skills *(242)*

  systems of action *(243)*

  handedness *(243)*

Health and Safety

Guidepost 4: What are the major health and safety risks for young children?

- Although major contagious illnesses are rare today in industrialized countries due to widespread immunization, preventable disease continues to be a major problem in the developing world.

- Accidents, most commonly motor vehicle injuries, are the leading cause of death in childhood in the United States.

- Environmental factors such as exposure to poverty, homelessness, smoking, air pollution, and pesticides increase the risks of illness or injury. Lead poisoning can have serious physical, cognitive, and behavioral effects.

Cognitive Development
Piagetian Approach: The Preoperational Child

Guidepost 5: What are typical cognitive advances and immature aspects of preschool children's thinking?

- Children in the preoperational stage show several important advances, as well as some immature aspects of thought.

- The symbolic function enables children to reflect upon people, objects, and events that are not physically present. It is shown in deferred imitation, pretend play, and language.
- Early symbolic development helps preoperational children make more accurate judgments of spatial relationships. They can understand the concept of identity, link cause and effect with regard to familiar situations, categorize living and nonliving things, and understand principles of counting.
- Preoperational children appear to be less egocentric than Piaget thought.
- Centration keeps preoperational children from understanding principles of conservation. Their logic also is limited by irreversibility and a focus on states rather than transformations.
- The theory of mind, which develops markedly between the ages of 3 and 5, includes awareness of a child's own thought processes, social cognition, understanding that people can hold false beliefs, ability to deceive, ability to distinguish appearance from reality, and ability to distinguish fantasy from reality.
- Understanding of others' desires precedes understanding of their beliefs. The ability to differentiate between real and apparent emotion follows later.
- Maturational and environmental influences affect individual differences in theory-of-mind development.

  preoperational stage *(248)*

  symbolic function *(250)*

  pretend play *(250)*

  transduction *(250)*

  animism *(251)*

  centration *(252)*

  decenter *(252)*

  egocentrism *(252)*

  conservation *(253)*

  horizontal décalage *(253)*

  irreversibility *(253)*

  theory of mind *(254)*

Information-Processing Approach: Memory Development

Guidepost 6: What memory abilities expand in early childhood?

- Information-processing models describe three steps in memory: encoding, storage, and retrieval.
- Although sensory memory shows little change with age, the capacity of working memory increases greatly. The central executive controls the flow of information to and from long-term memory.
- At all ages, recognition is better than recall, but both increase during early childhood.
- Early episodic memory is only temporary; it fades or is transferred to generic memory.
- Autobiographical memory typically begins at about age 3 or 4 but sometimes as early as 2; it may be related to early self-recognition ability and language development.
- According to the social interaction model, children and adults co-construct autobiographical memories by talking about shared experiences.

- Children are more likely to remember unusual activities that they actively participate in. The way adults talk with children about events influences memory formation.

  encoding *(258)*

  storage *(258)*

  retrieval *(258)*

  sensory memory *(258)*

  working memory *(258)*

  central executive *(258)*

  long-term memory *(259)*

  recognition *(259)*

  recall *(259)*

  generic memory *(259)*

  script *(259)*

  episodic memory *(259)*

  autobiographical memory *(260)*

  social interaction model *(262)*

Intelligence: Psychometric and Vygotskian Approaches

Guidepost 7: How is preschoolers' intelligence measured, and what are some influences on it?

- The two most commonly used psychometric intelligence tests for young children are the Stanford-Binet Intelligence Scale and the Wechsler Preschool and Primary Scale of Intelligence, Revised (WPPSI-III).
- Intelligence test scores have been rising in industrialized countries.
- Intelligence test scores may be influenced by a number of factors, including the home environment and SES.
- Newer tests based on Vygotsky's concept of the zone of proximal development (ZPD) indicate immediate potential for achievement. Such tests, when combined with scaffolding, can help parents and teachers guide children's progress.

  Stanford-Binet Intelligence Scales *(263)*

  Wechsler Preschool and Primary Scale of Intelligence, Revised (WPPSI-III) *(263)*

  zone of proximal development (ZPD) *(264)*

  scaffolding *(265)*

Language Development

Guidepost 8: How does language improve in early childhood, and what happens when its development is delayed?

- During early childhood, vocabulary increases greatly, and grammar and syntax become fairly sophisticated. Children become more competent in pragmatics.
- Private speech is normal and common; it may aid in the shift to self-regulation and usually disappears by age 10.
- Causes of delayed language development are unclear. If untreated, language delays may have serious cognitive, social, and emotional consequences.

- Interaction with adults can promote emergent literacy.

  fast mapping *(265)*

  pragmatics *(266)*

  social speech *(266)*

  private speech *(267)*

  emergent literacy *(268)*

Early Childhood Education

Guidepost 9: **What purposes does early childhood education serve, and how do children make the transition to kindergarten?**

- Goals of preschool education vary across cultures.

- The academic content of early childhood education programs in the United States has increased, but studies support a child-centered approach.

- Compensatory preschool programs have had positive outcomes, but participants generally have not equaled the performance of middle-class children. Compensatory programs that start early and extend into the primary grades have better long-term results.

- Many children today attend full-day kindergarten. Success in kindergarten depends largely on emotional and social adjustment and prekindergarten preparation.

CHAPTER 8

Psychosocial Development in Early Childhood

*Children's playings are not sports
and should be deemed as their
most serious actions.*

Montaigne, *Essays*

Focus
Isabel Allende, Militant Writer

Isabel Allende

Isabel Allende* has been called Latin America's foremost woman writer. Her best-selling novels and short stories, which evoke her imaginative inner world, have been translated into thirty languages and have sold an estimated 11 million copies worldwide. Perhaps her most moving work is *Paula* (1995), the memoir she began scribbling on yellow pads as she sat at the bedside of her 27-year-old daughter, Paula Frías, in a Madrid hospital, waiting for her to awaken from a coma that never lifted. The words Allende poured out were as much a reminiscence of her own tempestuous life as a tribute to her dying daughter.

Born August 2, 1942, in Lima, Peru, Isabel Allende was the daughter of a Chilean diplomat, a cousin of the Chilean revolutionary hero Salvador Allende, who was assassinated in a military coup in 1973. Her emotional connection with the cause of her oppressed people became the backdrop for much of her later writing. Her major theme is the role of women in a highly patriarchal society.

When she was almost 3, Isabel's father abandoned her mother, Doña Panchita, in childbirth. Left with no means of support and humiliated by the failure of her marriage, Doña Panchita returned in disgrace with her three young children to her parents' household in Santiago. She got a low-paying job in a bank and supplemented her salary by making hats. Although there was no divorce in Chile, the marriage was annulled. "Those were difficult years for my mother," Allende (1995, p. 32) writes; "she had to contend with poverty, gossip, and the snubs of people who had been her friends."

A second blow to young Isabel was the death of her beloved grandmother. Suddenly the house became dim and cheerless. A small, fearful, isolated child, often left

*Sources of information on Isabel Allende were Agosin (1999), Allende (1995), Perera (1995), Piña (1999), Rodden (1999), and various biographical materials from Allende's Web site, http://www .isabelallende.com.

in the care of a harsh, threatening maid, Isabel found refuge in silent games and in the fanciful stories her mother told at night in the dark. She felt "different," "like an outcast" (Allende, 1995, p. 50), and she had a rebellious streak. Although she loved her mother deeply and wanted to protect her, she did not want to be like her. She wanted to be strong and independent like her grandfather. "I think Tata was always sorry I wasn't a boy," she writes in *Paula* (p. 37); "had I been, he could have taught me to play jai alai, and use his tools, and hunt." He tacitly condoned the "character-building" tactics of the two bachelor uncles who lived in the household and played rough "games" with the children that today would be considered physically or emotionally abusive.

When Isabel was about 5, Ramón Huidobro, the Chilean consul who had helped the family return to Chile, moved in with Doña Panchita and eventually married her, displacing Isabel and her brothers from their mother's bedroom. It was during these pivotal early years that Allende's fervent feminism was born. "When I was a little girl," she says, "I felt anger towards my grandfather, my stepfather, and all the men in the family, who had all the advantages while my mother was the victim. . . . She had to please everyone and everyone told her what to do" (Piña, 1999, pp. 174–175).

It took Isabel years to accept her stepfather. "He raised us with a firm hand and unfailing good humor; he set limits and sent clear messages, without sentimental demonstrations, and without compromise. . . . he put up with my contrariness without trying to buy my esteem or ceding an inch of his authority, until he won me over totally," she writes (Allende, 1995, pp. 48–49).

Through her books, Allende has come to a greater understanding and acceptance of herself and her gender. Many of her characters are extraordinary women who break with tradition despite their place in society. Being a woman, she says, "was like being handicapped in many ways. In that macho culture where I was brought up. . . . I would have liked to be a man." Not until she was forty did she "finally accept that I was always going to . . . be the person I am" (Foster, 1999, p. 107).

---

*T*he years from ages 3 to 6 are pivotal ones in children's psychosocial development, as they were for Isabel Allende. A child's emotional development and sense of self are rooted in the experiences of those years. Yet the story of the self is not completed in early childhood; like Allende, we continue to write it even as adults. Allende's story also highlights the importance of the cultural context. As a girl growing up in a male-dominated culture, she faced attitudes very different from what she might have experienced in a less tightly gender-based society.

In this chapter we discuss preschool children's understanding of themselves and their feelings. We see how their sense of male or female identity arises and how it affects their behavior. We describe the activity on which children, at least in industrialized countries, typically spend most of their time: play. We consider the influence, for good or ill, of what parents do. Finally, we discuss relationships with siblings and other children.

After you have read and studied this chapter, you should be able to answer each of the Guidepost questions that appear at the top of the next page. Look for them again in the margins, where they point to important concepts throughout the chapter. To check your understanding of these Guideposts, review the end-of-chapter summary. Checkpoints located at periodic spots throughout the chapter will help you verify your understanding of what you have read.

1. How does the self-concept develop during early childhood, and how do children develop self-esteem?

2. How do young children advance in understanding and regulating their emotions?

3. How do boys and girls become aware of the meaning of gender, and what explains differences in behavior between the sexes?

4. How do preschoolers play, and how does play contribute to and reflect development?

5. How do parenting practices influence development?

6. Why do young children help or hurt others, and why do they develop fears?

7. How do young children get along with—or without—siblings?

8. How do young children choose playmates and friends, and why are some children better liked than others?

Guideposts for Study

The Developing Self

"Who in the world am I? Ah, *that's* the great puzzle," said Alice in Wonderland, after her size had abruptly changed—again. Solving Alice's "puzzle" is a lifelong process of getting to know one's self.

The Self-Concept and Cognitive Development

The **self-concept** is our total image of ourselves. It is what we believe about who we are—our total picture of our abilities and traits. It is "a *cognitive construction, . . . a system of descriptive and evaluative representations about the self*," which determines how we feel about ourselves and guides our actions (Harter, 1996, p. 207). The sense of self also has a social aspect: Children incorporate into their self-image their growing understanding of how others see them.

The picture of the self comes into focus in toddlerhood, as children develop self-awareness. The self-concept becomes clearer and more compelling as a person gains in cognitive abilities and deals with the developmental tasks of childhood, of adolescence, and then of adulthood.

Changes in Self-Definition: The 5 to 7 Shift Self-concept development takes a jump between about ages 5 and 7, as evidenced by changes in **self-definition**: the cluster of characteristics by which children describe themselves. At age 4, Jason says:

> My name is Jason and I live in a big house with my mother and father and sister, Lisa. I have a kitty that's orange and a television set in my own room. . . . I like pizza and I have

 Guidepost

1. How does the self-concept develop during early childhood, and how do children develop self-esteem?

self-concept Sense of self; descriptive and evaluative mental picture of one's abilities and traits.

self-definition Cluster of characteristics used to describe oneself.

A young child's self-concept is based mainly on external characteristics, such as physical features.

a nice teacher. I can count up to 100, want to hear me? I love my dog, Skipper. I can climb to the top of the jungle gym, I'm not scared! Just happy. You can't be happy *and* scared, no way! I have brown hair, and I go to preschool. I'm really strong. I can lift this chair, watch me! (Harter, 1996, p. 208)

The way Jason describes himself is typical of U.S. children his age. He talks mostly about concrete, observable behaviors; external characteristics, such as physical features; preferences; possessions; and members of his household. He mentions particular skills (climbing) rather than general abilities (being athletic). His self-descriptions are unrealistically positive, and they frequently spill over into demonstrations; what he *thinks* about himself is almost inseparable from what he *does*. Not until middle childhood (around age 7 or 8) will he describe himself in terms of generalized traits, such as *popular, smart,* or *dumb;* recognize that he can have conflicting emotions; and be self-critical while holding a positive overall self-concept. How does this change come about?

What specific changes bring about the "age 5 to 7 shift"? An analysis based on neo-Piagetian theory (Case, 1985, 1992; Fischer, 1980) describes the 5 to 7 shift as occurring in three steps, which actually form a continuous progression.* At 4, Jason is at the first step: his statements about himself are **single representations**—isolated, one-dimensional items. His thinking jumps from particular to particular, without logical connections. At this stage he cannot imagine having two emotions at once ("You can't be happy *and* scared"). In part because of his limited working memory capacity, he cannot *decenter,* that is, consider different aspects of himself at the same time (refer back to Chapter 7). His thinking is all-or-nothing. He cannot acknowledge that his **real self,** the person he actually is, is not the same as his **ideal self,** the person he would like to be; so he describes himself as a paragon of virtue and ability.

At about age 5 or 6, Jason moves up to the second step as he begins to link one aspect of himself to another: "I can run fast, and I can climb high. I'm also strong. I can throw a ball real far, I'm going to be on a team some day!" (Harter, 1996, p. 215). However, these **representational mappings**—logical connections among parts of his image of himself—are still expressed in completely positive, all-or-nothing terms. Since good and bad are opposites, he cannot see how he might be good at some things and not at others.

The third step, *representational systems,* takes place in middle childhood (see Chapter 10), when children begin to integrate specific features of the self into a general, multidimensional concept. As all-or-nothing thinking declines, Jason's self-descriptions will become more balanced ("I'm good at hockey but bad at arithmetic").

Cultural Differences in Self-Description Does culture affect young children's self-concept? Research suggests that it does. Parents subtly transmit, through everyday conversations, cultural ideas and beliefs about how to define the self. For example, Chinese parents tend to encourage *interdependent* aspects of the self: compliance with authority, appropriate conduct, humility, and a sense of belonging to the community. European American parents encourage *independent* aspects of the self: individuality, self-expression, and self-esteem. These differing cultural values influence the way children in each culture perceive themselves (Wang, 2004).

A comparative study of 180 European American and Chinese preschoolers, kindergartners, and second graders (Wang, 2004) found that children absorb differing cultural styles of self-definition as early as age 3 or 4, and these differences increase with age. European American children, like European American adults, tend to

single representations In neo-Piagetian terminology, first stage in development of self-definition, in which children describe themselves in terms of individual, unconnected characteristics and in all-or-nothing terms.

real self The self one actually is.

ideal self The self one would like to be.

representational mappings In neo-Piagetian terminology, second stage in development of self-definition, in which a child makes logical connections between aspects of the self but still sees these characteristics in all-or-nothing terms.

*This discussion of children's developing understanding of themselves from age 4 on is indebted to Susan Harter (1990, 1993, 1996, 1998).

describe themselves in terms of personal attributes and beliefs ("I am big"), whereas Chinese children, like Chinese adults, talk more about social categories and relationships ("I have a sister"). European American children and adults more often describe themselves in terms of personality traits and tendencies ("I'm good at sports"), whereas Chinese children and adults describe specific, overt behaviors ("I play Snowmoon with my neighbor"). European American children and adults tend to put themselves in an unqualifiedly positive light ("I am smart"), whereas Chinese children and adults describe themselves more neutrally ("I sometimes forget my manners").

Self-Esteem

Self-esteem is the self-evaluative part of the self-concept, the judgment children make about their overall worth. From a neo-Piagetian perspective, self-esteem is based on children's growing cognitive ability to describe and define themselves.

self-esteem The judgment a person makes about his or her self-worth.

Developmental Changes in Self-Esteem Children do not generally articulate a concept of self-worth until about age 8, but younger children show by their behavior that they have one. Attempts to measure young children's self-esteem often incorporate teacher and parent reports (Davis-Kean & Sandler, 2001) or puppets and doll play (Measelle, Ablow, Cowan, & Cowan, 1998) in addition to self-reports.

In a study in Belgium (Verschueren, Buyck, & Marcoen, 2001), researchers measured 5-year-olds' self-representations, using two instruments: (1) the Harter (1985b) Self-Perception Profile for Children (SPPC), which covers overall (global) self-worth, as well as specific perceptions about physical appearance, scholastic and athletic competence, social acceptance, and behavioral conduct; and (2) the Puppet Interview (Cassidy, 1988; Verschueren, Marcoen, & Schoefs, 1996), in which puppets are used to reveal a child's perception of what another person thinks of him or her. Children's positive or negative self-perceptions at age 5 tended to predict their self-perceptions and socioemotional functioning, as reported by teachers, at age 8.

Still, before the 5 to 7 shift, young children's self-esteem is not necessarily based on a realistic appraisal. Although they can make judgments about their competence

This mother's approval of her 3-year-old son's artwork is an important contributor to his self-esteem. Not until middle childhood do children develop strong internal standards of self-worth.

What's Your View?

- Can you think of ways in which your parents or other adults helped you develop self-esteem?

at various activities, they are not yet able to rank them in importance. They tend to accept the judgments of adults, who often give positive, uncritical feedback, and thus may overrate their abilities (Harter, 1990, 1993, 1996, 1998).

Like the self-concept itself, self-esteem in early childhood tends to be all-or-none: "I am good" or "I am bad" (Harter, 1996, 1998). Not until middle childhood do personal evaluations of competence and adequacy based on internalization of parental and societal standards normally become critical in shaping and maintaining a sense of self-worth (Harter, 1990, 1996, 1998).

Contingent Self-Esteem: The "Helpless" Pattern When self-esteem is high, a child is motivated to achieve. However, if self-esteem is *contingent* on success, children may view failure or criticism as an indictment of their worth and may feel helpless to do better. About one-third to one-half of preschoolers, kindergartners, and first-graders show elements of this "helpless" pattern: self-denigration or self-blame, negative emotion, lack of persistence, and lowered self-expectations (Burhans & Dweck, 1995; Ruble & Dweck, 1995).

Instead of trying a different way to complete a puzzle, as a child with unconditional self-esteem might do, "helpless" children feel ashamed and give up or go back to an easier puzzle they have already done. They do not expect to succeed, and so they do not try. Whereas older children who fail may conclude that they are "dumb," preschoolers interpret poor performance as a sign of being "bad." Furthermore, they believe that "badness" is permanent. This sense of being a bad person may persist into middle childhood and on into adulthood.

Children who believe their attributes are permanent tend to become demoralized when, say, they fail a test, believing there is nothing they can do to improve. Often these children attribute poor performance or social rejection to their own personality deficiencies, which they believe they are helpless to change. Rather than trying new ways to gain approval, they repeat unsuccessful strategies or just give up. Children with high self-esteem, by contrast, tend to attribute failure or disappointment to factors outside themselves or to the need to try harder. If initially unsuccessful or rejected they persevere, trying new strategies until they find one that works (Erdley, Cain, Loomis, Dumas-Hines, & Dweck, 1997; Harter, 1998; Pomerantz & Saxon, 2001). Children with high self-esteem tend to have parents and teachers who give specific, focused feedback rather than criticize the child as a person ("Look, the tag on your shirt is showing in front," not "Can't you see your shirt is on backwards? When are you going to learn to dress yourself?").

Checkpoint

Can you . . .

✔ Trace early self-concept development and discuss cultural influences on self-definition?

✔ Explain the significance of the 5 to 7 shift?

✔ Tell how young children's self-esteem differs from that of older children?

✔ Describe how the "helpless pattern" arises and how it can affect children's reactions to failure or social rejection?

Guidepost

2. How do young children advance in understanding and regulating their emotions?

Understanding and Regulating Emotions

Understanding and regulating their own emotions contributes to children's social competence, their ability to get along with others (Denham et al., 2003). It helps them guide their behavior and talk about feelings (Laible & Thompson, 1998). Understanding their emotions enables them to control the way they show their feelings and to be sensitive to how others feel (Garner & Power, 1996). As we will discuss in a later section, it even affects the types of play they engage in (Spinrad et al., 2004). Much of this development occurs during the preschool years (Denham et al., 2003).

Because early emotional experience occurs within the family, it should not be surprising that family relationships affect the development of emotional understanding, as they did with Isabel Allende. A study of 41 preschoolers found a relationship between security of attachment to the mother and a child's understanding of others' negative emotions, such as fear, anger, and sadness—both as observed among their peers, and as inferred from stories enacted by puppets (Laible & Thompson, 1998).

Preschoolers can talk about their feelings and often can discern the feelings of others, and they understand that emotions are connected with experiences and desires (Saarni et al., 1998). However, they still lack a full understanding of such self-directed emotions as shame and pride, and they have trouble reconciling conflicting emotions, such as being happy about getting a new bicycle but disappointed because it's the wrong color (Kestenbaum & Gelman, 1995).

Emotions Directed Toward the Self As we mentioned in Chapter 6, emotions directed toward the self, such as guilt, shame, and pride, typically develop by the end of the third year, after children gain self-awareness and accept the standards of behavior their parents have set. But even children a few years older often lack the cognitive sophistication to *recognize* these emotions and what brings them on—a necessary step toward emotional regulation.

In one study (Harter, 1993), 4- to 8-year-olds were told two stories. In the first story, a child takes a few coins from a jar after being told not to do so; in the second story, a child performs a difficult gymnastic feat—a flip on the bars. Each story was presented in two versions: one in which a parent sees the child doing the act, and another in which no one sees the child. The children were asked how they and the parent would feel in each circumstance.

The answers revealed a gradual progression in understanding of feelings about the self (Harter, 1996). At ages 4 to 5, children did not say that either they or their parents would feel pride or shame. Five- to 6-year-olds said their parents would be ashamed or proud of them but did not acknowledge feeling these emotions themselves. At 6 to 7, children said they would feel proud or ashamed, but only if they were observed. Not until ages 7 to 8 did children say that they would feel ashamed or proud of themselves even if no one saw them. By this age, the standards that produce pride and shame appear to be fully internalized and to affect children's opinion of themselves (Harter, 1993, 1996).

Simultaneous Emotions Part of the confusion in younger children's understanding of their feelings is difficulty in recognizing that they can experience different emotional reactions at the same time, as Isabel Allende did toward her grandfather, both resenting and admiring him.

Individual differences in understanding conflicting emotions are evident by age 3. Three-year-olds who could identify whether a face looked happy or sad and could tell how a puppet felt when enacting a situation involving happiness, sadness, anger, or fear were better able at the end of kindergarten to explain a story character's conflicting emotions. These children tended to come from families that often discussed why people behave as they do (J. R. Brown & Dunn, 1996). During middle childhood children acquire a more sophisticated understanding of simultaneous emotions and greater ability to manage them (see Chapter 10).

Erikson: Initiative Versus Guilt

The need to deal with conflicting feelings about the self is at the heart of the third stage of personality development identified by Erik Erikson (1950): **initiative versus guilt.** The conflict arises from the growing sense of purpose, which spurs a child to plan and carry out activities, and the growing pangs of conscience the child may have about such plans.

Preschool children can do—and want to do—more and more. At the same time, they are learning that some of the things they want to do meet social approval,

initiative versus guilt Erikson's third stage in psychosocial development, in which children balance the urge to pursue goals with moral reservations that may prevent carrying them out.

Checkpoint

Can you...

✔ Trace the typical progression in understanding of (1) emotions directed toward the self and (2) simultaneous emotions?

✔ Explain the significance of Erikson's third stage of personality development?

whereas others do not, as when Isabel Allende, at 6, was expelled from a parochial school for organizing her classmates to show their underpants. How do children reconcile their desire to *do* with their desire for approval?

This conflict marks a split between two parts of the personality: the part that remains a child, full of exuberance and a desire to try new things and test new powers, and the part that is becoming an adult, constantly examining the propriety of motives and actions. Children who learn how to regulate these opposing drives develop the "virtue" of *purpose,* the courage to envision and pursue goals without being unduly inhibited by guilt or fear of punishment (Erikson, 1982).

Gender

Gender identity, awareness of one's femaleness or maleness and all it implies in one's society of origin, is an important aspect of the developing self-concept. As we have seen, Isabel Allende's awareness of what it meant to be female in a "man's world" went back to her early years.

How different are young boys and girls? What causes those differences? How do children develop gender identity, and how does it affect their attitudes and behavior?

Gender Differences

Gender differences are psychological or behavioral differences between males and females, as opposed to *sex differences,* the physical differences between them. How pronounced are gender differences?

As we pointed out in Chapter 6, measurable differences—both physical and behavioral—between baby boys and girls are few. Although some gender differences become more pronounced after age 3, boys and girls on average remain more alike than different. The main difference is in boys' more aggressive behavior, discussed later in this chapter. Also, most studies find that girls are more empathic and helpful (Keenan & Shaw, 1997), and some find that girls are more compliant and cooperative with parents and seek adult approval more than boys do (N. Eisenberg, Fabes, Schaller, & Miller, 1989; M. L. Hoffman, 1977; Maccoby, 1980; Turner & Gervai, 1995). In early childhood and again during preadolescence and adolescence, girls tend to use more responsive language, such as praise, agreement, acknowledgment, and elaborating on what someone else has said (Leaper & Smith, 2004).

Overall, intelligence test scores show no gender differences (Keenan & Shaw, 1997); the most widely used tests are designed to eliminate gender bias (Neisser et al., 1996). However, there are differences in specific abilities. Females tend to do better at verbal tasks (but not analogies), at mathematical computation, and at tasks requiring fine motor and perceptual skills. Males tend to excel in most spatial abilities and in abstract mathematical and scientific reasoning (Halpern, 1997). Some of these cognitive differences, which seem to exist across cultures, begin early in life. Girls' superiority in perceptual speed and verbal fluency appears during infancy and toddlerhood, and boys' greater ability to mentally manipulate figures and shapes and solve mazes becomes evident early in the preschool years. Other differences do not become apparent until preadolescence or beyond (Halpern, 1997; Levine, Huttenlocher, Taylor, & Langrock, 1999).

As toddlers, boys and girls are equally likely to hit, bite, and throw temper tantrums, and they are just as likely to show "difficult" temperament. Around age 4, however, problem behavior diminishes in girls, whereas boys tend to get in trouble or "act up." This difference persists into adolescence, when girls become more prone to anxiety and depression (Keenan & Shaw, 1997; see Chapter 11).

Guidepost

3. How do boys and girls become aware of the meaning of gender, and what explains differences in behavior between the sexes?

gender identity Awareness, developed in early childhood, that one is male or female.

We need to remember, of course, that gender differences are valid for large groups of boys and girls but not necessarily for individuals. By knowing a child's sex, we cannot predict whether that *particular* boy or girl will be faster, stronger, smarter, more obedient, or more assertive than another child.

Checkpoint
Can you . . .

✔ Summarize the main behavioral and cognitive differences between boys and girls?

Perspectives on Gender Development

What accounts for gender differences, and why do some of them emerge with age? The most influential explanations, until recently, centered on the differing experiences and social expectations that boys and girls meet almost from birth (Halpern, 1997; Neisser et al., 1996). These experiences and expectations concern three related aspects of gender identity: *gender roles, gender-typing,* and *gender stereotypes.*

Gender roles are the behaviors, interests, attitudes, skills, and personality traits that a culture considers appropriate for males or females. All societies have gender roles. Historically, in most cultures, as in Isabel Allende's Chile, women have been expected to devote most of their time to caring for the household and children, while men were providers and protectors. Women were expected to be compliant and nurturant; men, to be active, aggressive, and competitive. It is these culturally defined roles that Allende rebelled against. Today, gender roles in western cultures have become more diverse and more flexible than before.

Gender-typing, the process by which children acquire a gender role (refer back to Chapter 6), takes place early in childhood, but children vary in the degree to which they become gender-typed. **Gender stereotypes** are preconceived generalizations about male or female behavior, such as, "All females are passive and dependent; all males are aggressive and independent." Gender stereotypes pervade many cultures. They appear to some degree in children as young as 2 or 3, increase during the preschool years, and reach a peak at age 5 (Campbell, Shirley, & Candy, 2004; Ruble & Martin, 1998). Preschoolers—and even older children—often attribute positive qualities to their own sex and negative qualities to the other sex (Egan & Perry, 2001; Ruble & Martin, 1998; Underwood, Schockner, & Hurley, 2001). Still, among preschoolers, *both* boys and girls call boys strong, fast, and cruel, and girls fearful and helpless (Ruble & Martin, 1998).

How do children acquire gender roles, and why do they adopt gender stereotypes? Are these purely social constructs, or do they reflect underlying biological differences between males and females? Do social and cultural influences create gender differences, or merely accentuate them?

The answers to these questions are not either-or. Both nature and nurture probably play important parts in what it means to be male or female. Biological influences are not necessarily universal, inevitable, or unchangeable; nor are social and cultural influences easily overcome.

Let's look, then, at four perspectives on gender development (summarized in Table 8-1): *biological, psychoanalytic, cognitive,* and *socialization-based* approaches. Each of these perspectives can contribute to our understanding, but none fully explains why boys and girls develop differently in some respects and not in others.

Biological Approaches The existence of similar gender roles in many cultures suggests that some gender differences, at least, may be biologically based, and today investigators are uncovering evidence of biological explanations for gender differences: genetic, hormonal, and neurological.

gender roles Behaviors, interests, attitudes, skills, and traits that a culture considers appropriate for each sex; differs for males and females.

gender-typing Socialization process whereby children, at an early age, learn appropriate gender roles.

gender stereotypes Preconceived generalizations about male or female role behavior.

This preschool boy dressed as a gunslinger has developed a strong sense of gender roles. The clearest behavioral difference between young boys and young girls is boys' greater aggressiveness.

Table 8-1 Four Perspectives on Gender Development

Theories	Major Theorists	Key Processes	Basic Beliefs
Biological Approach		Genetic, neurological, and hormonal activity	Many or most behavioral differences between the sexes can be traced to biological differences.
Psychoanalytic Approach			
Psychosexual theory	Sigmund Freud	Resolution of unconscious emotional conflict	Gender identity occurs when child identifies with same-sex parent.
Cognitive Approach			
Cognitive-developmental theory	Lawrence Kohlberg	Self-categorization	Once a child learns she is a girl or he is a boy, child sorts information about behavior by gender and acts accordingly.
Gender-schema theory	Sandra Bem, Carol Lynn Martin, & Charles F. Halverson	Self-categorization based on processing of cultural information	Child organizes information about what is considered appropriate for a boy or a girl on the basis of what a particular culture dictates and behaves accordingly. Child sorts by gender because the culture dictates that gender is an important schema.
Socialization Approach			
Social cognitive theory	Albert Bandura	Modeling, reinforcement, and teaching	Gender-typing is a result of interpretation, evaluation, and internalization of socially transmitted standards.

Hormones in the bloodstream before or about the time of birth may affect the developing brain. The male hormone testosterone along with low levels of the neurotransmitter serotonin may be related to aggressiveness, competitiveness, and dominance, perhaps through action on such brain structures as the hypothalamus and amygdala—though evidence of such a relationship is mixed (Bernhardt, 1997; Book, Starzyk, & Quinsey, 2001; Ramirez, 2003).

By age 5, when the brain reaches approximate adult size, boys' brains are about 10 percent larger than girls' brains, mostly because boys have more gray matter in the cerebral cortex, whereas girls have greater neuronal density. What these findings may tell us about brain organization and functioning is unknown (Reiss, Abrams, Singer, Ross, & Denckla, 1996). We do have evidence that size differences in the *corpus callosum,* the band of tissue joining the right and left hemispheres, are correlated with verbal fluency (Hines, Chiu, McAdams, Bentler, & Lipcamon, 1992). Because girls have a larger corpus callosum, better coordination between the two hemispheres may help explain girls' superior verbal abilities (Halpern, 1997).

Some research focuses on children with unusual hormonal histories. Girls with a disorder called *congenital adrenal hyperplasia (CAH)* have high prenatal levels of androgens (male sex hormones), resulting in ambiguous genitalia (an enlarged clitoris with the urethral opening at the base). As these girls grow older, they tend to develop facial, pubic, and armpit hair and deep voices and may not menstruate at puberty or may have abnormal menstrual periods. They tend to develop into "tomboys," showing preferences for "boys' toys," rough play, and male playmates, as well as strong spatial skills. Estrogens (female hormones) seem to have less influence on boys' gender-typed behavior (Ruble & Martin, 1998). In a study of 3- to 10-year-old children, girls with CAH showed more male-typical toy choices than their unaffected sisters even though their parents encouraged gender-appropriate behavior. Boys with CAH played no differently than their unaffected brothers (Pasterski et al., 2005).

Perhaps the most dramatic examples of biologically based research have to do with infant boys who have been medically assigned to female sex because of missing or ambiguous sexual organs (part male and part female). These studies suggest that gender identity may be rooted in chromosomal structure or prenatal development and cannot easily be changed.

In the classic case of a 7-month-old boy whose penis was accidentally destroyed during circumcision, the decision was made at 17 months to rear the child as a girl, and four months later doctors performed surgical reconstruction (Money & Ehrhardt, 1972). The child later rejected female identity and, at puberty, switched to living as a male (Diamond & Sigmundson, 1997). However, his life as an adult was troubled (Colapinto, 2000), and in 2004 he committed suicide (Colapinto, 2004).

A related study underlines the difficulty of predicting whether sex assignment at birth will "take." Fourteen genetically male children born without normal penises but with testes were legally and surgically assigned to female sex during the first month of life and were raised as girls. Between ages 5 and 16, however, eight of them declared themselves male (though two were living ambiguously). Five declared unwavering female identity but expressed difficulty fitting in with other girls; and one, after learning that she had been born male, refused to discuss the subject with anyone. Meanwhile, two boys whose parents had refused the initial sexual assignment remained male (Reiner & Gearhart, 2004). In another case, 25 of 27 genetically male children born without penises were raised as girls but considered themselves boys and, as children, engaged in rough play (Reiner, 2000).

Psychoanalytic Approaches "Daddy, where will you live when I grow up and marry Mommy?" asks Timmy, age 4. From the psychoanalytic perspective, Timmy's question is part of his acquisition of gender identity. That process, according to Freud, is one of **identification,** the adoption of characteristics, beliefs, attitudes, values, and behaviors of the parent of the same sex. Freud and other classical psychoanalytic theorists considered identification an important personality development of early childhood. Some social learning theorists also have used the term.

According to classical Freudian theory, identification will occur for Timmy when he represses or gives up the wish to possess the parent of the other sex (his mother) and identifies with the parent of the same sex (his father). Although this explanation for gender development has been influential, it has been difficult to test. Despite some evidence that preschoolers tend to act more affectionately toward the opposite-sex parent and more aggressively toward the same-sex parent (Westen, 1998), most developmental psychologists today favor other explanations.

Cognitive Approaches Sarah figures out she is a girl because people call her a girl. She figures out that she will always be a girl. She comes to understand gender the same way she comes to understand everything else: by actively thinking about and constructing her own gender-typing. This is the heart of Lawrence Kohlberg's (1966) cognitive-developmental theory.

According to Kohlberg and other cognitive theorists, children actively search for cues about gender in their social world—who does what, and who can play with whom. As children come to realize which gender they belong to, they adopt behaviors they perceive as consistent with being male or female. Thus, 3-year-old Sarah prefers dolls to trucks because she sees girls playing with dolls and therefore views playing with dolls as consistent with her idea of herself as a girl. And she plays mostly with other girls, whom she assumes will share her interests (Ruble & Martin, 1998; Martin & Ruble, 2004).

The acquisition of gender roles, said Kohlberg, hinges on **gender constancy,** also called *sex-category constancy*—a child's realization that his or her sex will always be the same. Once children realize they are permanently male or female, they adopt what they see as behaviors appropriate to their sex. Gender constancy seems

identification In Freudian theory, the process by which a young child adopts characteristics, beliefs, attitudes, values, and behaviors of the parent of the same sex.

gender constancy Awareness that one will always be male or female. Also called *sex-category constancy.*

In one study, children saw three photos of this little boy: nude, dressed in boys' clothes, and dressed in girls' clothes. Preschoolers who identified the child's sex by genitals rather than by dress were more likely to show gender constancy—to know that they themselves would remain the sex they were.

to develop in three stages: *gender identity, gender stability,* and *gender consistency* (Ruble & Martin, 1998; Szkrybalo & Ruble, 1999). *Gender identity*—awareness of one's own gender and that of others—typically arrives between ages 2 and 3. *Gender stability* comes when a girl realizes that she will grow up to be a woman, and a boy that he will grow up to be a man, in other words, that gender remains the same with age. Children at this stage may base judgments about gender on superficial external appearances and stereotyped behaviors. Finally, sometime between ages 3 and 7 or even later, comes *gender consistency:* the realization that a girl remains a girl even if she has a short haircut and wears pants, and a boy remains a boy even if he has long hair and earrings.

Much research challenges Kohlberg's view that gender-typing depends on gender constancy. Long before children attain the final stage of gender constancy—as early as 12 to 24 months—they show gender-typed preferences in toys and playmates (Bussey & Bandura, 1992; Martin & Ruble, 2004; Ruble & Martin, 1998). They categorize activities and objects by gender, know a lot about what males and females do, and often acquire gender-appropriate behaviors (G. D. Levy & Carter, 1989; Luecke-Aleksa, Anderson, Collins, & Schmitt, 1995). However, gender-typing may be heightened by the more sophisticated understanding that gender constancy brings (Martin & Ruble, 2004).

A second cognitive approach, which combines elements of cognitive-developmental and social learning theory, is **gender-schema theory,** which seeks to describe a cognitive mechanism through which gender learning and gender-typing occur. Among its leading proponents is Sandra Bem (1983, 1985, 1993); others are Carol Lynn Martin and Charles F. Halverson (1981). A *schema* (much like Piaget's *schemes*) is a mentally organized network of information that influences a wide variety of behaviors. According to gender-schema theory, children begin (very likely in infancy) to categorize events and people, organizing their observations around the schema, or category, of gender. They organize information on this basis because they see that their society classifies people that way: Males and females wear different clothes, play with different toys, and use separate bathrooms. Once children know what sex they are, they take on gender roles by developing a concept of what it means to be male or female in their culture. Children then match their own behavior to their culture's gender schema—what boys and girls are "supposed" to be and do.

According to this theory, gender schemas promote gender stereotypes by influencing judgments about behavior. When a new boy his age moves in next door, 4-year-old Brandon knocks on his door, carrying a toy truck—apparently assuming that the new boy will like the same toys he likes. Bem suggests that children who show such stereotypical behavior may be experiencing pressure for gender

gender-schema theory Theory, proposed by Bem, that children socialize themselves in their gender roles by developing a mentally organized network of information about what it means to be male or female in a particular culture.

conformity that inhibits healthy self-exploration. However, there is little evidence that gender schemas are at the root of stereotyped behavior or that children who are highly gender-typed necessarily feel pressure to conform (Yunger, Carver, & Perry, 2004).

Another problem with both gender-schema theory and Kohlberg's theory is that gender-sterotyping does not always become stronger with increased gender knowledge; in fact, the opposite is often true (Bussey & Bandura, 1999). A current view, which has research support, is that gender-stereotyping rises and then falls in a developmental pattern (Ruble & Martin, 1998; Welch-Ross & Schmidt, 1996). Around ages 4 to 6, when, according to gender-schema theory, children are constructing and then consolidating their gender schemas, they notice and remember only information consistent with these schemas and even exaggerate it. In fact, they tend to *mis*-remember information that challenges gender stereotypes, such as photos of a girl sawing wood or a boy cooking, and to insist that the genders in the photos were the other way around. Young children are quick to accept gender labels; when told that an unfamiliar toy is for the other sex, they will drop it like a hot potato, and they expect others to do the same (C. L. Martin, Eisenbud, & Rose, 1995; Martin & Ruble, 2004; Ruble & Martin, 1998).

By ages 5 and 6, children develop a repertoire of rigid sterotypes about gender that they apply to themselves and others. A boy will pay more attention to what he considers "boys' toys" and a girl to "girls' toys." A boy will expect to do better at "boy things" than at "girl things," and if he does try, say, to dress a doll, he will be all thumbs. Then, around age 7 or 8, schemas become more complex as children begin to take in and integrate contradictory information, such as the fact that many girls wear pants. Children develop more complex beliefs about gender and become more flexible in their views about gender roles (Martin & Ruble, 2004; Ruble & Martin, 1998; M. G. Taylor, 1996; Trautner et al., 2003).

Cognitive approaches to gender development have made an important contribution by exploring how children think about gender and what they know about it at various ages. However, these approaches may not fully explain the link between knowledge and conduct. There is disagreement about precisely what mechanism prompts children to act out gender roles and why some children become more strongly gender-typed than others (Bussey & Bandura, 1992, 1999; Martin & Ruble, 2004; Ruble & Martin, 1998). Some investigators point to socialization.

Socialization-Based Approaches In traditional social learning theory, children acquire gender roles by observing models. Children generally choose models they see as powerful or nurturing. Typically, one model is a parent, often of the same sex, but children also pattern their behavior after other adults or after peers. (Isabel Allende, uncomfortable with the subordinate roles of the women she saw, sought to model herself after her grandfather.) Behavioral feedback together with direct teaching by parents, teachers, and other adults reinforces gender-typing. A boy who models his behavior after his father or male peers is commended for acting "like a boy." A girl gets compliments on a pretty dress or hairstyle.

Albert Bandura's (1986; Bussey & Bandura, 1999) **social cognitive theory,** an expanded version of social learning theory, sees gender identity as the outcome of a complex array of interacting influences, personal and social. Socialization—the way a child interprets and internalizes experiences with parents, teachers, peers, and cultural institutions—plays a central part.

Socialization begins in infancy, long before a conscious understanding of gender begins to form. Gradually, as children begin to regulate their own activities, standards of behavior become internalized. A child no longer needs praise, rebukes, or a model's presence to act in socially appropriate ways. Children feel good about

Lifemap CD

Watch the video, "Gender Stereotypes in Early Childhood," in Chapter 8 of your CD, to learn one six-year-old's perspective on how boys and girls should behave.

social cognitive theory Albert Bandura's expansion of social learning theory; holds that children learn gender roles through socialization.

themselves when they live up to their internal standards and feel bad if they do not. A substantial part of the shift from socially guided control to self-regulation of gender-related behavior may take place between ages 3 and 4 (Bussey & Bandura, 1992). How do parents, peers, and the media influence this development?

Family Influences When Louisiana Governor Kathleen Blanco's 4-year-old grandson David was asked what he wanted to be when he grew up, he wasn't sure. He shrugged off all his mother's suggestions—firefighter, soldier, policeman, airplane pilot. Finally, she asked whether he'd like to be governor. "Mom," he replied, "I'm a boy!" (Associated Press, 2004a).

David's response illustrates how strong family influences can be, even in fostering counterstereotypical preferences. Usually, though, experience in the family reinforces gender-typical preferences and attitudes.

Boys tend to be more strongly gender-socialized concerning play preferences than girls. Parents, especially fathers, generally show more discomfort if a boy plays with a doll than if a girl plays with a truck (Lytton & Romney, 1991; Ruble & Martin, 1998; Sandnabba & Ahlberg, 1999). Girls have more freedom than boys in their clothes, games, and choice of playmates (Miedzian, 1991).

In egalitarian households, the father's role in gender socialization seems especially important (Fagot & Leinbach, 1995). In an observational study of 4-year-olds in British and Hungarian cities, boys and girls whose fathers did more housework and child care were less aware of gender stereotypes and engaged in less gender-typed play (Turner & Gervai, 1995).

Do siblings influence each other's gender development? Yes, according to a three-year longitudinal study of 198 first- and secondborn siblings (median ages of 10 and 8) and their parents. Secondborns tended to become more like their older siblings in attitudes, personality, and leisure activities. Firstborns were more influenced by their parents and less by their younger siblings (McHale, Updegraff, Helms-Erikson, & Crouter, 2001).

Peer Influences Anna, at age 5, insisted on dressing in a new way. She wanted to wear leggings with a skirt over them, and boots—indoors and out. When her mother asked her why, Anna replied, "Because Katie dresses like this—and Katie's the king of the girls!"

Even in early childhood, the peer group is a major influence on gender-typing (Turner & Gervai, 1995). Peers begin to reinforce gender-typed behavior by age 3, and their influence increases with age (Ruble & Martin, 1998). Children, like their parents, show more disapproval of boys who act "like girls" than of girls who are tomboys (Ruble & Martin, 1998).

Indeed, play choices at this age may be more strongly influenced by peers and the media than by the models children see at home (Turner & Gervai, 1995). Generally, however, peer and parental attitudes reinforce each other. Social cognitive theory sees peers, not as an independent influence for socialization, but as part of a complex cultural system that encompasses parents and other socializing agents as well (Bussey & Bandura, 1999).

Cultural Influences When a Hindu girl in a village in Nepal touched the plow that her brother was using, she was severely rebuked. In this way she learned that as a female she was restricted from acts her brother was expected to perform (D. Skinner, 1989). Isabel Allende, at 5, received similar instruction when told that she must sit and knit with her legs together when her brothers were out climbing trees.

In the United States, television is a major channel for the transmission of cultural attitudes toward gender. Although women in television programs and commercials

What's Your View?

- Should parents and teachers encourage girls to play with trucks and boys with dolls?

- Where would you place your own views on the continuum between the following extremes? Explain.

  1. Family A thinks girls should wear only ruffly dresses and boys should never wash dishes or cry.

  2. Family Z treats sons and daughters exactly alike, without making any references to the children's sex.

are now more likely to be working outside the home and men are sometimes shown caring for children or cooking, for the most part life as portrayed on television continues to be more stereotyped than life in the real world (Coltrane & Adams, 1997; Ruble & Martin, 1998).

Social learning theory predicts that children who watch a lot of television will become more gender-typed by imitating the models they see on the screen. Dramatic supporting evidence emerged from a natural experiment in several Canadian towns that obtained access to television transmission for the first time. Children who had had relatively unstereotyped attitudes showed marked increases in traditional views two years later (Kimball, 1986). In another study, children who watched a series of nontraditional episodes, such as a father and son cooking together, had less stereotyped views than children who had not seen the series (J. Johnston & Ettema, 1982).

Children's books, especially illustrated ones, have long been a source of gender stereotypes. Today, the proportion of women as main characters has greatly increased, and children are more frequently shown in nongender-typed activities (girls dressing up as pilots or ambulance drivers, boys attending tea parties or helping with laundry). However, even in the finest picture books, women are still shown mostly in traditional domestic roles, whereas men are seldom seen caring for children or doing housework (Gooden, 2001). Fathers, in fact, are largely absent; and when they do appear, they are shown as withdrawn and ineffectual parents (Anderson & Hamilton, 2005).

Major strengths of the socialization approach include the breadth and multiplicity of processes it examines and the scope for individual differences it reveals. But this very complexity makes it difficult to establish clear causal connections between the way children are raised and the way they think and act. Just what aspects of the home environment and the peer culture promote gender-typing? Do parents and peers treat boys and girls differently because they *are* different or because the culture says they *should be* different? Does differential treatment *produce* or *reflect* gender differences? Or, as social cognitive theory suggests, is there a bidirectional relationship? Further research may help show how socializing agents mesh with children's own biological tendencies and cognitive understandings with regard to gender-related attitudes and behavior.

Checkpoint

Can you . . .

✔ Distinguish among four basic approaches to the study of gender development?

✔ Assess evidence for biological explanations of gender differences?

✔ Compare how various theories explain the acquisition of gender roles, and assess the support for each theory?

Play: The Business of Early Childhood

Guidepost

4. How do preschoolers play, and how does play contribute to and reflect development?

Play is the work of the young, and it contributes to all domains of development. Through play, children stimulate the senses, learn how to use their muscles, coordinate sight with movement, gain mastery over their bodies, and acquire new skills. As they sort blocks of different shapes, count how many they can pile on each other, or announce that "my tower is bigger than yours," they lay the foundation for mathematical concepts (Jarrell, 1998). As they play with computers, they learn new ways of thinking (Silvern, 1998). As they cooperate to build sandcastles or tunnels on the beach, they learn social skills.

Preschoolers engage in different types of play at different ages. As gross motor skills improve, preschoolers run, jump, skip, hop, throw, and aim. Toward the end of this period and into middle childhood, *rough-and-tumble play* involving wrestling, kicking, and sometimes chasing becomes more common (Pellegrini, 1998; see Chapter 9). Also, particular children have different styles of play, and they play at different things. Researchers categorize children's play by its *content* (what children do when they play) and its *social dimension* (whether they play alone or with others).

Cognitive Levels of Play

Carol, at 3, "talked for" a doll, using a deeper voice than her own. Miguel, at 4, wore a kitchen towel as a cape and "flew" around as Batman. These children were engaged in pretend play involving make-believe people or situations.

Pretend play is one of four categories of play identified by Piaget and others as showing increasing levels of cognitive complexity (Piaget, 1951; Smilansky, 1968). The simplest form, which begins during infancy, is active **functional play** involving repetitive muscular movements (such as rolling or bouncing a ball). The second level is **constructive play** (using objects or materials to make something, such as a house of blocks or a crayon drawing). Four-year-olds in preschools or day care centers may spend more than half their time in this kind of play, which becomes more elaborate by ages 5 and 6 (J. E. Johnson, 1998).

The third level, **pretend play,** also called *fantasy play, dramatic play,* or *imaginative play,* rests on the symbolic function, which, as we noted in Chapter 7, emerges during the last part of the second year (Piaget, 1962) along with the development of language and representational ability. Pretend play, discussed in a subsequent section, typically increases during the preschool years and then declines as school-age children become more involved in the fourth cognitive level of play, *formal games with rules*—organized games with known procedures and penalties, such as hopscotch and marbles. An estimated 10 to 17 percent of preschoolers' play and 33 percent of kindergartners' is pretend play, often using dolls and real or imaginary props (Bretherton, 1984; Garner, 1998; J. E. Johnson, 1998; K. H. Rubin, Fein, & Vandenberg, 1983). However, the current trend toward more academically oriented and tightly scheduled kindergarten programs (refer back to Chapter 7) may limit the amount of time children can spend in pretend play (Bergen, 2002).

Pretend play involves a combination of cognition, emotion, language, and sensorimotor behavior and thus may strengthen the development of dense connections in the brain and strengthen the later capacity for abstract thought. Children who watch a great deal of television tend to play less imaginatively, perhaps because they are accustomed to passively absorbing images rather than generating their own (Howes & Matheson, 1992).

functional play Play involving repetitive muscular movements.

constructive play Play involving use of objects or materials to make something.

pretend play Play involving imaginary people or situations; also called *fantasy play, dramatic play, or imaginative play.*

This young "veterinarian" examining his toy dog is showing an important cognitive development of early childhood, which underlies imaginative play: the ability to use symbols to stand for people or things in the real world.

The Social Dimension of Play

In a classic study done in the 1920s, Mildred B. Parten (1932) identified six types of early play, ranging from the least to the most social (see Table 8-2). She found that as children grow older, their play tends to become more interactive and more cooperative. At first children play alone, then alongside other children, and finally together. Today, however, many researchers view Parten's characterization of children's play development as too simplistic. Children of all ages engage in all of Parten's categories of play (K. H. Rubin et al., 1998).

Is nonsocial play less mature than social play? Parten seemed to think so. She and some other observers suggested that young children who play alone may be at risk of developing social, psychological, and educational problems. However, other researchers have observed that certain types of nonsocial play, particularly solitary

Table 8-2	Parten's Categories of Social and Nonsocial Play

Category	Description
Unoccupied behavior	The child does not seem to be playing but watches anything of momentary interest.
Onlooker behavior	The child spends most of the time watching other children play. The onlooker talks to them, asking questions or making suggestions, but does not enter into the play. The onlooker is definitely observing particular groups of children rather than anything that happens to be exciting.
Solitary independent play	The child plays alone with toys that are different from those used by nearby children and makes no effort to get close to them.
Parallel play	The child plays independently but among the other children, playing with toys like those used by the other children but not necessarily playing with them in the same way. Playing *beside* rather than *with* the others, the parallel player does not try to influence the other children's play.
Associative play	The child plays with other children. They talk about their play, borrow and lend toys, follow one another, and try to control who may play in the group. All the children play similarly if not identically; there is no division of labor and no organization around any goal. Each child acts as she or he wishes and is interested more in being with the other children than in the activity itself.
Cooperative or organized supplementary play	The child plays in a group organized for some goal—to make something, play a formal game, or dramatize a situation. One or two children control who belongs to the group and direct activities. By a division of labor, children take on different roles and supplement each other's efforts.

Source: Adapted from Parten, 1932, pp. 249–251.

independent play and parallel play, may consist of activities that foster cognitive, physical, and social development and thus may show independence and maturity, not poor social adjustment (Harrist, Zain, Bates, Dodge, & Pettit, 1997; K. H. Rubin et al., 1998). In a study of 567 kindergartners, their teachers and classmates as well as independent observers rated almost 2 out of 3 children who played alone as socially and cognitively competent; they simply preferred to play that way (Harrist et al., 1997). Children who prefer such play may be more object or task oriented than people oriented (Coplan, Prakash, O'Neil, & Armer, 2004). On the other hand, solitary play in *some* children may be a sign of shyness, anxiety, fearfulness, or social rejection (Coplan et al., 2004; Henderson, Marshall, Fox, & Rubin, 2004; Spinrad et al., 2004).

Reticent play, a combination of Parten's onlooker and unoccupied categories, is often a manifestation of shyness (Coplan et al., 2004). However, such reticent behaviors as playing near other children, watching what they do, or wandering aimlessly may sometimes be a prelude to joining in others' play (K. H. Rubin, Bukowski, & Parker, 1998; Spinrad et al., 2004). In a short-term longitudinal study, reticent children, though hesitant to join in other children's play, were well liked and showed few problem behaviors (Spinrad et al., 2004). Nonsocial play, then, seems to be far more complex than Parten imagined and bears further study.

One kind of play that typically becomes more social during the preschool years is imaginative play, which often shifts from solitary pretending to dramatic play involving other children (K. H. Rubin et al., 1998; Singer & Singer, 1990). As imaginative play becomes more collaborative, story lines become more complex and innovative. Dramatic play offers rich opportunities to practice interpersonal skills and to explore social roles and conventions. In pretending, children cope with

 Lifemap CD

To watch parallel play in action, turn to the video "Parallel Play in the Sandbox," in Chapter 8 of your CD.

What's Your View?

• How do you think use of computers might affect preschool children's cognitive and social development?

Checkpoint

Can you . . .

✔ Describe four cognitive levels of play, according to Piaget and others, and six categories of social and nonsocial play, according to Parten?

✔ Explain how cognitive and social dimensions of play may be connected?

uncomfortable emotions, gain understanding of other people's perspectives, and construct an image of the social world (Bergen, 2002; Bodrova & Leong, 1998; Christie, 1991; J. I. F. Davidson, 1998; Furth & Kane, 1992; J. E. Johnson, 1998; Nourot, 1998; Singer & Singer, 1990). They develop joint problem-solving, planning, and goal-seeking skills (Bergen, 2002). Children often follow unspoken rules in organizing dramatic play, staking out territory ("I'm the daddy; you're the mommy"), negotiating ("Okay, I'll be the daddy tomorrow"), or setting the scene ("Watch out—there's a train coming!"). Children who often play imaginatively tend to cooperate more with other children and to be more popular and more joyful than those who do not (Singer & Singer, 1990). Studies have found the quality of pretend play to be associated with social and linguistic competence (Bergen, 2002). By making "tickets" for an imaginary train trip or "reading" eye charts in a "doctor's office," children build emergent literacy skills (Christie, 1991, 1998).

Imaginary Companions

At 3½, Anna had 23 "sisters" with such names as Och, Elmo, Zeni, Aggie, and Ankie. She often talked to them on the telephone, since they lived about 100 miles away, in the town where her family used to live. During the next year, most of the sisters disappeared, but Och continued to visit, especially for birthday parties. Och had a cat and a dog (which Anna had begged for in vain), and whenever Anna was denied something she saw advertised on television, she announced that she already had one at her sister's house. But when a live friend came over and Anna's mother happened to mention one of her imaginary companions, Anna quickly changed the subject.

All 23 sisters—and some "boys" and "girls" who have followed them—lived only in Anna's imagination, as she well knew. Like an estimated 25 to 65 percent of children between ages 3 and 10 (Woolley, 1997), she created imaginary companions, with whom she talked and played. This normal phenomenon of childhood is seen most often in firstborn and only children, who lack the close company of siblings. Like Anna, most children who create imaginary companions have many of them (Gleason, Sebanc, & Hartup, 2000). Girls are more likely than boys to have imaginary "friends," or at least to acknowledge them; boys are more likely to impersonate imaginary characters (Carlson & Taylor, in press).

Children who have imaginary companions can distinguish fantasy from reality, but in free-play sessions they are more likely to engage in pretend play than are children without imaginary companions (M. Taylor, Cartwright, & Carlson, 1993). They play more happily and more imaginatively than other children and are more cooperative with other children and adults (D. G. Singer & Singer, 1990; J. L. Singer & Singer, 1981); and they do not lack for friends at preschool (Gleason et al., 2000). They are more fluent with language, watch less television, and show more curiosity, excitement, and persistence during play. In one study of 152 preschoolers, 4-year-olds who reported having imaginary companions did better on theory-of-mind tasks (such as differentiating appearance and reality and recognizing false beliefs) than children who did not create such companions (M. Taylor & Carlson, 1997), and these children showed greater emotional understanding three years later. Having imaginary companions remains common in the early school years; almost one-third of the children who reported having had imaginary companions (65 percent of the sample in all) were still playing with them at age 7 (Taylor, Carlson, Maring, Gerow, & Charley, 2004).

Children's relationships with imaginary companions are like peer relationships; they are usually sociable and friendly, in contrast with the way children "take care of" personified objects, such as stuffed animals and dolls (Gleason et al., 2000). Imaginary playmates are good company for an only child like Anna. They provide wish-fulfillment mechanisms ("There was a monster in my room, but Elmo scared it off with magic dust"), scapegoats ("I didn't eat those cookies—Och must have done it!"), displacement agents for the child's own fears ("Aggie is afraid she's going to be washed down the drain"), and support in difficult situations. (One 6-year-old "took" her imaginary companion with her to see a scary movie.)

What's Your View?

• How should parents respond to children's talk about imaginary companions?

How Gender Influences Play

A tendency toward sex segregation in play seems to be universal across cultures. From an evolutionary viewpoint, gender differences in children's play provide practice for adult behaviors important for reproduction and survival. Boys' rough-and-tumble play mirrors adult males' competition for dominance and status and for fertile mates. Girls' "playing house" prepares them to care for the young (Geary, 1999). Socialization reinforces those tendencies.

Sex segregation is common among preschoolers and becomes even more prevalent in middle childhood (Fabes, Martin, & Hanish, 2003; Maccoby, 1988, 1990, 1994; Ramsey & Lasquade, 1996; Snyder, West, Stockemer, Gibbons, & Almquist-Parks, 1996). Even when boys and girls play with the same toys, they play more socially with others of the same sex (Neppl & Murray, 1997). Most of the time, though, boys and girls play differently. Most boys like active, forceful play in fairly large groups; girls are inclined to quieter, more harmonious play with one playmate. Boys play spontaneously on sidewalks, streets, or empty lots; girls tend to choose more structured, adult-supervised activities. All these tendencies are more pronounced when children play in groups (Benenson, 1993; Fabes et al., 2003; Maccoby, 1980; Serbin, Moller, Gulko, Powlishta, & Colburne, 1994). In mixed-sex groups, play tends to revolve around traditionally masculine activities, perhaps because boys' play preferences are more stereotyped than girls' (Fabes et al., 2003).

Preschool girls and preschool boys usually do not play together, but when they do, they usually play with "masculine" toys such as cars, trucks, and blocks.

How Culture Influences Play

The frequency of specific forms of play differs across cultures and is influenced by the play environments adults set up for children, which in turn reflect cultural values (Bodrova & Leong, 1998).

One observational study compared 48 middle-class Korean American and 48 middle-class Anglo American children in separate preschools (Farver, Kim, & Lee, 1995). The Anglo American preschools, in keeping with typical American values, encouraged independent thinking, problem solving, and active involvement in learning by letting children select from a wide range of activities. The Korean American preschool, in keeping with traditional Korean values, emphasized development of academic skills and completion of tasks. The Anglo American preschools encouraged social interchange among children and collaborative activities with teachers. In the Korean American preschool, children were allowed to talk and play only during outdoor recess.

Not surprisingly, the Anglo American children engaged in more social play, whereas the Korean Americans engaged in more unoccupied or parallel play. Korean American children played more cooperatively, often offering toys to other children—very likely a reflection of their culture's emphasis on group harmony. Anglo American children were more aggressive and often responded negatively to other children's suggestions, reflecting the competitiveness of their culture.

Checkpoint

Can you . . .

✔ Discuss the significance of imaginary companions?

✔ Tell how gender and culture influence the way children play, and give examples?

An ethnographic study compared pretend play among middle-class 2½- to 4-year-olds in five Irish American families in the United States and nine Chinese families in Taiwan. Play was primarily social in both cultures. Irish American children were more likely to pretend with other children and Chinese children with caregivers, who often used the play as a vehicle to teach proper conduct—a major emphasis in Chinese culture (Haight, Wang, Fung, Williams, & Mintz, 1999). Broadening the study of play to a wider variety of cultures can enhance our knowledge of the meanings and purposes of play.

Parenting

As children gradually become their own persons, their upbringing can be a complex challenge. Parents must deal with small people who have minds and wills of their own, but who still have a lot to learn about what kinds of behavior work well in society. Furthermore, each child is different, and these individual characteristics affect the type of parenting each child receives.

Forms of Discipline

discipline Methods of molding children's character and of teaching them to exercise self-control and engage in acceptable behavior.

Discipline refers to methods of molding character and of teaching self-control and acceptable behavior. It can be a powerful tool for socialization with the goal of developing *self*-discipline. What forms of discipline work best? Researchers have looked at a wide range of techniques.

Reinforcement and Punishment "What are we going to do with that child?" Noel's mother says. "The more we punish him, the more he misbehaves!"

Parents sometimes punish children to stop undesirable behavior, but children usually learn more from being reinforced for good behavior. *External* reinforcements may be tangible (candy, money, toys, or gold stars) or intangible (a smile, a word of praise, a hug, extra attention, or a special privilege). Whatever the reinforcement, the child must see it as rewarding and must receive it fairly consistently after showing the desired behavior. Eventually, the behavior should provide its own *internal* reward: a sense of pleasure or accomplishment. In Noel's case, his parents often ignore him when he behaves well but scold or spank him when he acts up. In other words, they unwittingly reinforce his *mis*behavior by giving him attention when he does what they do *not* want him to do.

Still, at times punishment, such as isolation or denial of privileges, is necessary. Children may have to be prevented from running out into traffic or hitting another child. Sometimes a child is willfully defiant. In such situations, punishment, if consistent, immediate, and clearly tied to the offense, may be effective. It should be administered calmly, in private, and aimed at eliciting compliance, not guilt. It is most effective when accompanied by a short, simple explanation (AAP Committee on Psychosocial Aspects of Child and Family Health, 1998; Baumrind, 1996a, 1996b).

corporal punishment Use of physical force with the intention of causing pain but not injury so as to correct or control behavior.

Corporal punishment has been defined as "the use of physical force with the intention of causing a child to experience pain, but not injury, for the purpose of correction or control of the child's behavior" (Straus, 1994a, p. 4). It can include spanking, hitting, slapping, pinching, shaking (which can be fatal to infants—refer back to Box 4-2 in Chapter 4), and other physical acts. Unlike child abuse, which bears little or no relationship to the child's personality or behavior, corporal punishment is more frequently used with children who are aggressive and hard to manage, characteristics that may be genetically based (Jaffee et al., 2004). Corporal punishment is popularly believed to be more effective than other remedies and to be harmless if done in moderation by loving parents (McLoyd & Smith, 2002); but a growing body of evidence suggests that corporal punishment can have serious negative consequences and should not be used (Straus, 1999; Straus & Stewart, 1999; see Box 8-1).

Harsh punishment can be counterproductive. Children who are punished harshly and frequently may have trouble interpreting other people's actions and words; they may attribute hostile intentions where none exist (B. Weiss, Dodge, Bates, & Pettit, 1992). Young children who have been punished harshly may later act aggressively, even though the punishment is intended to stop what a parent sees as purposely aggressive behavior (Nix et al., 1999). Or such children may become passive because they feel helpless. Children may become frightened if parents lose control and may eventually try to avoid a punitive parent, undermining the parent's ability to influence behavior (Grusec & Goodnow, 1994).

Some studies suggest that African American families approve and use harsher discipline than European American families. However, in a survey of 175 African American parents with children under age 4, harsh spanking was unusual, and parents tended to favor other methods, such as explanations and time-outs. Lower-SES parents were more likely to endorse spanking in response to unsafe behavior (Horn, Cheng, & Joseph, 2004).

Characteristics of the parents and their marriage may influence their use of physical punishment. In a longitudinal study of couples expecting their first child, those who had hostile personalities (as measured by self-report scales) or were observed to have high levels of marital conflict tended to use more frequent and severe physical punishment when their children were 2 and 5 years old (Kanoy, Ulku-Steiner, Cox, & Burchinal, 2003).

Power Assertion, Induction, and Withdrawal of Love Looking at reinforcement and punishment alone may be an oversimplification of how parents influence behavior. Contemporary research has focused on three broader categories of discipline: *power assertion, induction,* and *temporary withdrawal of love.*

Power assertion is intended to stop or discourage undesirable behavior through physical or verbal enforcement of parental control; it includes demands, threats, withdrawal of privileges, spanking, and other punishments. These were the kinds of techniques used by the feared maid who took care of Isabel Allende and her brothers. **Inductive techniques** are designed to encourage desirable behavior (or discourage undesirable behavior) by reasoning with a child; they include setting limits, demonstrating logical consequences of an action, explaining, discussing, and getting ideas from the child about what is fair. **Withdrawal of love** may include ignoring, isolating, or showing dislike for a child. The choice and effectiveness of a disciplinary strategy may depend on the parent's personality, the child's personality and age, and the quality of their relationship, as well as on culturally based customs and expectations (Grusec & Goodnow, 1994).

Most parents call upon more than one strategy, depending on the situation. Parents tend to use reasoning to get a child to show concern for others. They use power assertion to stop play that gets too rough, and they use both power assertion and reasoning to deal with lying and stealing (Grusec & Goodnow, 1994). The strategy parents choose may depend not only on their belief in its effectiveness, but also on their confidence that they can carry it out (Perozynski & Kramer, 1999).

Induction is usually the most effective method and power assertion the least effective method of getting children to accept parental standards (M. L. Hoffman, 1970a, 1970b; Jagers, Bingham, & Hans, 1996; McCord, 1996). Inductive reasoning tends to arouse empathy for the victim of wrongdoing as well as guilt on the part of the wrongdoer (Krevans & Gibbs, 1996). Kindergartners whose mothers

power assertion Disciplinary strategy designed to discourage undesirable behavior through physical or verbal enforcement of parental control.

inductive techniques Disciplinary techniques designed to induce desirable behavior by appealing to a child's sense of reason and fairness.

withdrawal of love Disciplinary strategy that involves ignoring, isolating, or showing dislike for a child.

BOX 8-1

Practically Speaking
The Case Against Corporal Punishment

"Spare the rod and spoil the child" may sound old-fashioned, but corporal punishment has become a hot issue. Many people continue to believe that spanking instills respect for authority, motivates good behavior, and is a necessary part of responsible parenting (Kazdin & Benjet, 2003). On the other hand, some professionals view any corporal punishment as verging on child abuse (Straus, 1994b); they consider it wrong to inflict pain on children and warn that "violence begets violence" (Kazdin & Benjet, 2003). Other professionals find no harm in corporal punishment in moderation when prudently administered by loving parents (Baumrind, 1996a, 1996b; Baumrind et al., 2002).

Corporal punishment is now banned in Austria, Croatia, Cyprus, Denmark, Finland, Germany, Iceland, Israel, Latvia, Norway, Romania, Sweden, and Ukraine. In the United States, corporal punishment in schools has been outlawed in 28 states (Randall, 2005). All states except Minnesota allow parents to administer it, though some insist that it be reasonable, appropriate, moderate, or necessary, and some recognize that excessive corporal punishment can be abusive (Gershoff, 2002). The Supreme Court of Canada in January 2004 ruled out corporal punishment in schools and also forbade it for infants or teenagers (Center for Effective Discipline, 2005). The United Nations Convention on the Rights of Children opposes all forms of physical violence against children.

Some form of corporal punishment is widely used on U.S. infants and is near-universal among parents of toddlers. In interviews with a nationally representative sample of 991 parents in 1995, 35 percent reported using corporal punishment—usually hand slapping—on infants during the previous year, and fully 94 percent on 3- and 4-year-olds. About half of the parents continued to use corporal punishment by the time their children were 12, one-third at age 14, and 13 percent at age 17 (Straus & Stewart, 1999).

Why do so many parents hit their children? No doubt because it gets children to comply (Gershoff, 2002). However, a large body of research has found negative short-term and long-term associations with its use. Apart from the risk of injury or abuse, these outcomes may include, in childhood, lack of moral internalization, poor parent-child relationships, increased physical aggressiveness,

antisocial behavior, and delinquency, and diminished mental health. Outcomes in adulthood can include aggression, criminal or antisocial behavior, anxiety disorders, depression, alcohol problems, and partner or child abuse (Gershoff, 2002; MacMillan et al., 1999; Strassberg, Dodge, Pettit, & Bates, 1994).

Most of this research was cross-sectional or retrospective or did not consider that the spanked children may have been aggressive in the first place and that their aggressive behavior or some other factor might have led their parents to spank them (Gershoff, 2002). Since 1997, several large, nationally representative landmark studies (Brezina, 1999; Gunnoe & Mariner, 1997; Simons, Lin, & Gordon, 1998; Strauss & Paschall, 1999; Straus, Sugarman, & Giles-Sims, 1997) sought to control for the child's own behavior at the time of first measurement. These studies, which included children ranging from age 3 through adolescence, found that the more physical punishment a child receives, the more aggressive the child becomes and the more likely that child is to be antisocial or aggressive as an adult (Straus & Stewart, 1999).

Why the link between spanking and aggressive behavior? As social learning theory would predict, children may imitate the punisher and may come to consider infliction of pain an acceptable response to problems. Corporal punishment also may arouse anger and resentment, causing children to focus on their own hurts rather than on the wrong they have done to others and thus make them less receptive to parental teachings. Furthermore, as with any punishment, the effectiveness of spanking diminishes with repeated use; children may feel free to misbehave if they are willing to take the consequences. Reliance on physical punishment may weaken parents' authority when children become teenagers, too big and strong to spank, even if spanking were appropriate (AAP Committee on Psychosocial Aspects of Child and Family Health, 1998; Gershoff, 2002; McCord, 1996). Frequent spanking may even inhibit cognitive development (Straus & Paschall, 1999).

Critics of this research point out that corporal punishment does not occur in isolation; we cannot be sure that the observed outcomes were attributable to it and not to other parental behaviors

reported using reasoning were more likely to see the moral wrongness of behavior that hurts other people (as opposed to merely breaking rules) than children whose mothers took away privileges (Jagers et al., 1996).

The child's cognitive level, temperament, and emotionality may affect the child's response (Grusec et al., 2000). Gentle guidance seems particularly suited to temperamentally fearful or anxious children, who tend to become upset when they misbehave. Such a child will readily internalize parental messages with a minimum of prodding; displays of power would merely make the child more anxious (Kochanska, 1995, 1997a). Shame tends to arise when parents are angry or rejecting and do not use appropriate discipline of any kind (Eisenberg, 2000). Children in such situations may feel unworthy of their parents' attention.

The effectiveness of parental discipline may hinge on how well the child understands and accepts the parent's message, both cognitively and emotionally (Grusec & Goodnow, 1994). For the child to accept the message, the child has to recognize

What's Your View?

• As a parent, what forms of discipline would you favor in what situations? Give specific examples, and tell why.

—continued

or family circumstances, such as stressful events, marital discord, lack of parental warmth, or substance abuse (Kazdin & Benjet, 2003). A 6-year study of 1,990 European American, African American, and Hispanic children found that spanking does *not* predict

A child who is spanked is likely to imitate that behavior. Studies show that children who are spanked tend to become aggressive.

an increase in problem behavior *if* it is done in the context of a mother's strong emotional support (McLoyd & Smith, 2002).

Still, the research strongly suggests that frequent or severe corporal punishment is potentially harmful to children. Furthermore, there is no clear line between mild and harsh spanking, and one often leads to the other (Kazdin & Benjet, 2003). Thus, even though no harm from very mild spanking has been established (Larzalere, 2000), it seems prudent to choose other, less risky means of discipline that have *no* adverse effects (Kazdin & Benjet, 2003).

The American Academy of Pediatrics Committee on Psychosocial Aspects of Child and Family Health (1998) urges parents to avoid spanking. Instead, the committee suggests such inductive methods as teaching children to use words to express feelings, giving them choices and helping them evaluate the consequences, and modeling orderly behavior and cooperative conflict resolution. The committee recommends positive reinforcement to encourage desired behaviors, and verbal reprimands, "time-outs" (brief isolation to give the child a chance to cool down), or removal of privileges to discourage undesired behaviors—all within a positive, supportive, loving parent-child relationship.

What's Your View?

Did your parents ever spank you? If so, how often and in what kinds of situations? Would you spank, or have you ever spanked, your own child? Why or why not?

Check It Out

For more information on this topic, go to the World Wide Web: http://www.aap.org/policy/re9740.html. This is a policy statement from the American Academy of Pediatrics, "Guidance for Effective Discipline (RE9740). Or go to http://www.stophitting.com, the Web site of the Center for Effective Discipline. This site offers research-based information about corporal punishment in the home and in schools as well as up-to-date information on related legislation and court decisions.

---

it as appropriate; so parents need to be fair and accurate as well as clear and consistent about their expectations. They need to fit the discipline to the misdeed and to the child's temperament and cognitive and emotional level. A child may be more motivated to accept the message if the parents are normally warm and responsive and if they arouse the child's empathy for someone the child has harmed (Grusec & Goodnow, 1994).

The line between some forms of discipline and physical or emotional maltreatment (refer back to Chapter 6) is not always easy to draw. "Discipline" clearly becomes abusive when it results in injury to a child. **Psychological aggression** refers to verbal attacks that may result in psychological harm, such as yelling and screaming (the most frequent form), swearing, calling names, threatening to spank, or threatening to kick a child out of the house. Psychological aggression occurs at least once or twice a year in nearly 9 out of 10 households, and some psychologists consider it equivalent to emotional abuse. According to self-reports, about 10 to

psychological aggression
Verbal attacks on a child by a parent that may result in psychological harm.

Checkpoint
Can you . . .

✔ Compare various forms of
discipline, and identify
factors that influence their
effectiveness?

20 percent of parents of toddlers engage in *severe* psychological aggression, and the prevalence rises to about 50 percent among parents of teenagers. Psychological aggression generally backfires, resulting in *more* behavior problems, not less, and may even lead to mental illness (Straus & Field, 2003).

One point on which experts agree is that a child interprets and responds to discipline in the context of an ongoing relationship with a parent (McLoyd & Smith, 2002). Some researchers therefore look beyond specific parental practices to overall styles, or patterns, of parenting.

Parenting Styles

Why does Stacy hit and bite the nearest person when she cannot finish a jigsaw puzzle? What makes David sit and sulk when he cannot finish the puzzle, even though his teacher offers to help him? Why does Consuelo work on the puzzle for 20 minutes and then shrug and try another? Why are children so different in their responses to the same situation? Temperament is a major factor, of course, but some research suggests that styles of parenting may affect children's competence in dealing with their world.

Baumrind's Model Are some ways of socializing children more effective than others? In pioneering research, Diana Baumrind (1971, 1996b; Baumrind & Black, 1967) studied 103 preschool children from 95 families. Through interviews, testing, and home studies, she measured how the children were functioning, identified three parenting styles, and described typical behavior patterns of children raised according to each. Baumrind's findings were correlational and did not consider innate factors, such as temperament. However, Baumrind's work and the large body of research it inspired have established strong associations between each parenting style and a particular set of child behaviors (Baumrind, 1989; Darling & Steinberg, 1993; Pettit, Bates, & Dodge, 1997).

Authoritarian parents, according to Baumrind, value control and unquestioning obedience. They try to make children conform to a set standard of conduct and punish them arbitrarily and forcefully for violating it. They are more detached and less warm than other parents. Their children tend to be more discontented, withdrawn, and distrustful.

Permissive parents value self-expression and self-regulation. They make few demands and allow children to monitor their own activities as much as possible. When they do have to make rules, they explain the reasons for them. They consult with children about policy decisions and rarely punish. They are warm, noncontrolling, and undemanding. Their preschool children tend to be immature—the least self-controlled and the least exploratory.

Authoritative parents value a child's individuality but also stress social constraints. They have confidence in their ability to guide children, but they also respect children's independent decisions, interests, opinions, and personalities. They are loving and accepting but also demand good behavior, are firm in maintaining standards, and are willing to impose limited, judicious punishment when necessary, within the context of a warm, supportive relationship. They explain the reasoning behind their stands and encourage verbal give-and-take. Their children apparently feel secure in knowing that they are both loved and firmly guided. Preschoolers with authoritative parents tend to be the most self-reliant, self-controlled, self-assertive, exploratory, and content. (Isabel Allende's description of how her stepfather, Tió Ramón, took charge and raised her and her brothers fits this description perfectly; his parenting style was more effective than those of their authoritarian grandfather and permissive mother.)

Eleanor Maccoby and John Martin (1983) added a fourth parenting style—*neglectful,* or *uninvolved*—to describe parents who, sometimes because of stress or depression, focus on their own needs rather than on those of the child. Neglectful

authoritarian In Baumrind's terminology, parenting style emphasizing control and obedience.

permissive In Baumrind's terminology, parenting style emphasizing self-expression and self-regulation.

authoritative In Baumrind's terminology, parenting style blending respect for a child's individuality with an effort to instill social values.

parenting has been linked with a variety of behavioral disorders in childhood and adolescence (Baumrind, 1991; Parke & Buriel, 1998; R. A. Thompson, 1998).

Why does authoritative parenting seem to enhance children's social competence? It may be because authoritative parents like Ramón set sensible expectations and realistic standards. By making clear, consistent rules, they let children know what is expected of them. In authoritarian homes, children are so strictly controlled that often they cannot make independent choices about their own behavior. In permissive homes, children receive so little guidance that they may become uncertain and anxious about whether they are doing the right thing. In authoritative homes, children know when they are meeting expectations and can decide whether it is worth risking parental displeasure to pursue a goal. These children are expected to perform well, fulfill commitments, and participate actively in family duties as well as family fun. They know the satisfaction of accepting responsibilities and achieving success. Parents who make reasonable demands show that they believe their children can meet them—and that the parents care enough to insist that they do.

When conflict arises, an authoritative parent can teach the child positive ways to communicate his or her own point of view and negotiate acceptable alternatives. ("If you don't want to throw away those rocks you found, where do you think we should keep them?") Internalization of this broader set of skills, not just of specific behavioral demands, may well be a key to the success of authoritative parenting (Grusec & Goodnow, 1994).

What's Your View?

• If you have or were to have children, to what extent would you want them to adopt your values and behavioral standards? Give examples.

Support and Criticisms of Baumrind's Model In research based on Baumrind's work, the superiority of authoritative parenting (or similar conceptions of parenting style) has repeatedly been supported (Baumrind, 1989; Darling & Steinberg, 1993). For example, a longitudinal study of 585 ethnically and socioeconomically diverse families in Tennessee and Indiana with children from prekindergarten through grade 6 found that four aspects of early supportive parenting—warmth, use of inductive discipline, interest and involvement in children's contacts with peers, and proactive teaching of social skills—predicted children's later behavioral, social, and academic outcomes (Pettit, Bates, & Dodge, 1997).

Still, because Baumrind's model seems to suggest that there is one "right" way to raise children well, it has provoked controversy. Because Baumrind's findings are correlational, they merely establish associations between each parenting style and a particular set of child behaviors. They do not show that different styles of child rearing *cause* children to be more or less competent. It is also impossible to know whether the children Baumrind studied were, in fact, raised in a particular style. It may be that some of the better-adjusted children were raised inconsistently, but by the time of the study their parents had adopted the authoritative pattern (Holden & Miller, 1999). In addition, Baumrind did not consider innate factors, such as temperament, that might have affected children's competence and exerted an influence on the parents.

Cultural Differences in Parenting Styles Another concern is that Baumrind's categories reflect the dominant North American view of child development and may be misleading when applied to some cultures or socioeconomic groups. Among Asian Americans, obedience and strictness, rather than being associated with harshness and domination, have more to do with caring, concern, and involvement and with maintaining family harmony. Traditional Chinese culture, with its emphasis on respect for elders, stresses adults' responsibility to maintain the social order by teaching children socially proper behavior. This obligation is carried out through firm and just control and governance of the child and even by physical punishment if necessary (Zhao, 2002). Although Asian American parenting is frequently described as authoritarian, the warmth and supportiveness that characterize Chinese American

Checkpoint

Can you . . .

✔ Describe and evaluate Baumrind's model of parenting styles?

✔ Discuss how parents' way of resolving conflicts with young children can contribute to the success of authoritative child rearing?

✔ Discuss criticisms of Baumrind's model and cultural variations in parenting styles?

Guidepost

6. Why do young children help or hurt others, and why do they develop fears?

altruism Behavior intended to help others out of inner concern and without expectation of external reward; may involve self-denial or self-sacrifice.

prosocial behavior Any voluntary behavior intended to help others.

What's Your View?

• In a society in which "good Samaritans" are sometimes reviled for "butting into other people's business" and sometimes attacked by the very persons they try to help, is it wise to encourage children to offer help to strangers?

family relationships may more closely resemble Baumrind's authoritative parenting but without the emphasis on the American values of individuality, choice, and freedom (Chao, 1994) and with stricter parental control (Chao, 2001).

Furthermore, the idea of a dichotomy between the individualistic values of western parenting and the collectivist values of Asian parenting may be overly simplistic. In interviews with 64 Japanese mothers of 3- to 6-year-olds (Yamada, 2004), the mothers' descriptions of their parenting practices reflected the search for a balance between granting appropriate autonomy and exercising disciplinary control. The mothers let children make their own decisions within what they saw as the child's personal domain, such as play activities, playmates, and clothing, and this domain enlarged with the child's age; but the mothers also encouraged their children to take responsibility for their decisions and not change their minds. When health or safety, moral issues, or conventional social rules were involved, the mothers set limits or exercised control. When conflicts arose, the mothers used reasoning rather than power-assertive methods or sometimes gave in to the child, apparently on the theory that the issue wasn't worth struggling over—or that the child might be right after all.

Promoting Altruism and Dealing with Aggression and Fearfulness

Three specific issues of special concern to parents, caregivers, and teachers of preschool children are how to promote altruism, curb aggression, and deal with fears that often arise at this age.

Prosocial Behavior   Alex, at 3½, responded to two fellow preschoolers' complaints that they did not have enough modeling clay, his favorite plaything, by giving them half of his. By acting out of concern for others with no expectation of reward, Alex was showing **altruism.** Altruistic acts like Alex's often entail cost, self-sacrifice, or risk. Altruism is the heart of **prosocial behavior,** voluntary activity intended to benefit another.

Even before the second birthday, children often help others, share belongings and food, and offer comfort. Such behaviors may reflect a growing ability to imagine how another person might feel (Zahn-Waxler, Radke-Yarrow, Wagner, & Chapman, 1992). An analysis of 179 studies found increasing evidence of concern for others from infancy throughout childhood and adolescence (Fabes & Eisenberg, 1996). Although girls tend to be more prosocial than boys, the differences are small (Eisenberg & Fabes, 1998).

Is there a prosocial personality or disposition? A longitudinal study that followed 32 four- and 5-year-olds into early adulthood suggests that there is and that it emerges early and remains somewhat consistent throughout life. Preschoolers who were sympathetic and spontaneously shared with classmates tended to show prosocial understanding and empathic behavior as much as 17 years later. A prosocial disposition may be partly temperamental or genetic, as it involves *inhibitory control* (self-control or self-denial). Preschoolers who are shy or withdrawn tend to be less prosocial, perhaps because they hesitate to reach out to others (Coplan et al., 2004).

The family is important as a model and as a source and reinforcer of explicit standards of behavior (Eisenberg & Fabes, 1998; Eisenberg, Guthrie et al., 1999). Parents of prosocial children typically are prosocial themselves. They point out models of prosocial behavior and steer children toward stories, films, and television programs that depict cooperation, sharing, and empathy and encourage sympathy, generosity, and helpfulness (Singer & Singer, 1998). Parents encourage prosocial behavior when they use inductive disciplinary methods (Eisenberg & Fabes, 1998). When Mara took candy from a store, her father did not lecture her on honesty, spank her, or tell her what a bad girl she had been. Instead, he explained how the owner of the store would be harmed by her failure to pay for the candy, asked her how she thought the store owner might feel, and then took her back to the store to return the candy. Relationships with siblings (discussed later in this chapter) provide an important "laboratory" for trying out caring behavior and learning to see another person's point of view. Peers and teachers also can model and reinforce prosocial behavior (Eisenberg, 1992; Eisenberg & Fabes, 1998).

Motives for prosocial behavior may change as children grow older and develop more mature moral reasoning (see Chapters 9 and 11). Preschoolers tend to have egocentric motives; they want to earn praise and avoid disapproval. They weigh costs and benefits and consider how they would like others to act toward them. As children grow older, their motives become less self-centered. They adopt societal standards of "being good," which eventually become internalized as principles and values (Eisenberg & Fabes, 1998).

Cultures vary in the degree to which they foster prosocial behavior. Traditional cultures in which people live in extended family groups and share work seem to foster prosocial values more than cultures that stress individual achievement (Eisenberg & Fabes, 1998).

Children given responsibilities at home tend to develop prosocial qualities, such as cooperation and helpfulness. This 3-year-old girl, who is learning to care for plants, is likely to have caring relationships with people as well.

Aggression When Peter roughly snatches a ball away from Tommy, he is interested only in getting the ball, not in hurting or dominating Tommy. This is **instrumental aggression,** or aggression used as an instrument to reach a goal—the most common type of aggression in early childhood. Between ages 2½ and 5, children frequently struggle over toys and control of space. Aggression surfaces mostly during social play; children who fight the most also tend to be the most sociable and competent. In fact, the ability to show some instrumental aggression may be a necessary step in social development.

instrumental aggression
Aggressive behavior used as a means of achieving a goal.

hostile aggression Aggressive behavior intended to hurt another person.

Between ages 2 and 4, as children develop more self-control and become better able to express themselves verbally, they typically shift from showing aggression with blows to doing it with words (Coie & Dodge, 1998). Individual differences remain; children who more frequently hit or grab toys from other children at age 2 are likely to be more physically aggressive at age 5 (Cummings, Iannotti, & Zahn-Waxler, 1989); and children who, as preschoolers, often engaged in violent fantasy play may, at age 6, be prone to displays of anger (Dunn & Hughes, 2001). After age 6 or 7, most children become less aggressive as they grow more cooperative, less egocentric, more empathic, and better able to communicate. They can now put themselves in someone else's place, can understand why the other person may be acting in a certain way, and can develop more positive ways of asserting themselves. However, as aggression declines overall, **hostile aggression**—action intended to hurt another person—proportionately increases (Coie & Dodge, 1998; see Chapter 10).

Are boys more aggressive than girls? Much research says yes. Indeed, as we have mentioned, some studies suggest that the male hormone testosterone may underlie aggressive behavior. From infancy, boys are more likely to grab things

The kind of aggression involved in fighting over a toy, without intention to hurt or dominate the other child, is known as instrumental aggression. It surfaces mostly during social play and normally declines as children learn to ask for what they want.

from others. As children learn to talk, girls are more likely to rely on words to protest and to work out conflicts (Coie & Dodge, 1998).

However, girls may be more aggressive than they seem; they just show aggressiveness differently (McNeilly-Choque, Hart, Robinson, Nelson, & Olsen, 1996; Putallaz & Bierman, 2004). Boys engage in more **overt aggression,** either instrumental or hostile. Overt aggression, either physical or verbal, is openly directed against its target. Girls tend to practice **relational aggression** (also called *covert* or *indirect aggression*). This more subtle kind of aggression consists of damaging or interfering with relationships, reputation, or psychological well-being, often through teasing, manipulation, or bids for control. It may take such forms as spreading rumors, name-calling, put-downs, or excluding someone from a group or a team. Among preschoolers, it tends to be direct and face-to-face ("You can't come to my party if you don't give me that toy"). In middle childhood and adolescence, relational aggression becomes more sophisticated and indirect (Crick, Casas, & Nelson, 2002). Relational aggression may be no more frequent among girls than among boys, but its consequences may be more serious for girls, who tend to be more preoccupied with relationships than boys are (Cillessen & Mayeux, 2004; Crick et al., 2002).

Sources of Aggression Why are some children more aggressive than others? Biology may play a part. So may temperament: Children who are intensely emotional and low in self-control tend to express anger aggressively (Eisenberg, Fabes, Nyman, Bernzweig, & Pinuelas, 1994). Aggressive behavior also tends to be bred from early childhood by a combination of a stressful and unstimulating home atmosphere, harsh discipline, lack of maternal warmth and social support, exposure to aggressive adults and neighborhood violence, and transient peer groups, which prevent stable friendships. Through such negative socializing experiences, children growing up in high-risk surroundings may absorb antisocial attitudes despite their parents' best efforts (Dodge, Pettit, & Bates, 1994; Grusec & Goodnow, 1994).

In longitudinal studies, insecure attachment and lack of maternal warmth and affection in infancy predicted aggressiveness in early childhood (Coie & Dodge, 1998; MacKinnon-Lewis, Starnes, Volling, & Johnson, 1997). Negative parent-child relationships may set the stage for prolonged, destructive sibling conflicts, in which children imitate their parents' hostile behavior. These coercive family processes may foster aggressive tendencies that are carried over to peer relations (MacKinnon-Lewis et al., 1997) and to conduct at home and at school (Garcia, Shaw, Winslow, & Yaggi, 2000).

Triggers of Aggression Exposure to violence can trigger aggression. In a classic social learning experiment (Bandura, Ross, & Ross, 1961), 3- to 6-year-olds individually watched adult models play with toys. Children in one experimental group saw the adult play quietly. The model for a second experimental group began to assemble Tinker Toys but then spent the rest of the 10-minute session punching, throwing, and kicking a life-size inflated doll. A control group did not see any model. After the sessions, the children, who were mildly frustrated by seeing toys they were not allowed to play with, went into another playroom. The children who had seen the aggressive model acted much more aggressively than those in the other groups, imitating many of the same things they had seen the model say and do. The children who had been with the quiet model were less aggressive than the control group. This finding suggests that parents may be able to moderate the effects of frustration by modeling nonaggressive behavior.

Television has enormous power for modeling either prosocial behavior or aggression. In Chapter 10 we discuss the influence of televised violence on aggressive behavior.

Influence of Culture How much influence does culture have on aggressive behavior? One research team asked closely matched samples of 30 Japanese and 30 U.S.

middle- to upper-middle-class preschoolers to choose pictured solutions to hypothetical conflicts or stressful situations (such as having to stop playing and go to bed, hearing parents argue, or fighting on a jungle gym). The children also were asked to act out and complete such situations using dolls and props. The U.S. children showed more anger, more aggressive behavior and language, and less control of emotions than the Japanese children (Zahn-Waxler, Friedman, Cole, Mizuta, & Hiruma, 1996).

These results are consistent with childrearing values in the two cultures. In Japan, anger and aggression are seen as clashing with the emphasis on harmonious relationships. Japanese mothers are more likely than U.S. mothers to use reasoning and induce guilt, pointing out how aggressive behavior hurts others. Japanese mothers also strongly show their disappointment when children fail to meet their behavioral standards. However, the cross-cultural difference in children's anger and aggressiveness was significant even apart from mothers' behavior, suggesting that temperamental differences also may be at work (Zahn-Waxler et al., 1996).

Fearfulness "My childhood was a time of unvoiced fears," writes Isabel Allende (1995, p. 50): fear of her family's tyrannical maid; fear that her mother would die and her father would come back to claim her; fear of the devil; fear of her sadistic uncles; fear of gypsies; and fear of what "bad men can do to little girls."

Passing fears are common in early childhood. Many 2- to 4-year-olds are afraid of animals, especially dogs. By 6 years, children are more likely to be afraid of the dark. Other common fears are of thunderstorms, doctors, and imaginary creatures (DuPont, 1983; Stevenson-Hinde & Shouldice, 1996). Most of these disappear as children grow older and lose their sense of powerlessness.

Young children's fears stem largely from their intense fantasy life and their tendency to confuse appearance with reality. Sometimes their imaginations get carried away, making them worry about being attacked by a lion or being abandoned. Young children are more likely to be frightened by something that looks scary, such as a cartoon monster, than by something capable of doing great harm, such as a nuclear explosion (Cantor, 1994). For the most part, older children's fears are more realistic and self-evaluative (for example, fear of failing a test), since they know they are being evaluated by others (Stevenson-Hinde & Shouldice, 1996; see Table 8-3).

Fears may come from personal experience or from hearing about other people's experiences (Muris, Merckelbach, & Collaris, 1997). A preschooler whose mother is sick in bed may become upset by a story about a mother's death, even if it is an animal mother. Often fears come from appraisals of danger, such as the likelihood of being bitten by a dog, or are triggered by events, as when a child who was hit by a car becomes afraid to cross the street. Children who have lived through an earthquake, a kidnapping, or some other frightening event may fear that it will happen again (Kolbert, 1994).

Parents can help prevent children's fears by instilling a sense of trust and normal caution without being too protective, and also by overcoming their own unrealistic fears. They can help a fearful child by reassurance and by encouraging open expression of feelings. Ridicule ("Don't be such a baby!"), coercion ("Pat the nice doggie—it won't hurt you"), and logical persuasion ("The closest bear is 20 miles away, locked in a zoo!") are not helpful. Not until elementary school can children tell themselves that what they fear is not real (Cantor, 1994).

Children can be helped to overcome fears by *systematic desensitization,* a therapeutic technique involving gradual exposure to a feared object or situation. This technique has been used successfully to help children overcome fears ranging from snakes to elevators (Murphy & Bootzin, 1973; Sturges & Sturges, 1998).

What's Your View?

• Are there situations in which a child should be encouraged to be aggressive?

A young girl (right) gets up the courage to touch a tarantula in a petting zoo as her cousin watches with interest. Systematic desensitization, *gradual exposure to a feared animal or object, can help children overcome fears.*

Checkpoint

Can you . . .

✔ Discuss influences that contribute to altruism, aggression, and fearfulness?

Table 8-3	Childhood Fears
Age	**Fears**
0–6 months	Loss of support, loud noises
7–12 months	Strangers; heights; sudden, unexpected, and looming objects
1 year	Separation from parent; toilet; injury; strangers
2 years	Many stimuli, including loud noises (vacuum cleaners, sirens and alarms, trucks, and thunder), animals, dark rooms, separation from parent, large objects or machines, changes in personal environment, unfamiliar peers
3 years	Masks; dark; animals; separation from parent
4 years	Separation from parent; animals; dark; noises (including noises at night)
5 years	Animals; "bad" people; dark; separation from parent; bodily harm
6 years	Supernatural beings (e.g., ghost, witches); bodily injury; thunder and lightning; dark; sleeping or staying alone; separation from parent
7–8 years	Supernatural beings; dark; media events (e.g., news reports on the threat of nuclear war or child kidnapping); staying alone; bodily injury
9–12 years	Tests and examinations in school; school performances; bodily injury; physical appearance; thunder and lightning; death; dark

Source: From Morris, R. J. & Kratochwill, T. R. *Treating Children's Fears and Phobias: A Behavioral Approach,* Allyn and Bacon, Boston, MA. Copyright © 1983 by Pearson Education. Reprinted by permission of the publisher.

Relationships with Other Children

Although the most important people in young children's world are the adults who take care of them, relationships with siblings and playmates become more important in early childhood. Virtually every characteristic activity and personality issue of this age, from gender development to prosocial or aggressive behavior, involves other children. Sibling and peer relationships provide a measuring stick for *self-efficacy,* children's growing sense of capability to master challenges and achieve their goals. By competing with and comparing themselves with other children, they can gauge their physical, social, cognitive, and linguistic competencies and gain a more realistic sense of self (Bandura, 1994).

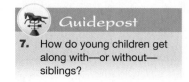

Guidepost

7. How do young children get along with—or without—siblings?

Siblings—or Their Absence

Ties between brothers and sisters often set the stage for later relationships. Let's look at sibling relationships, and then at children who grow up with no siblings.

Brothers and Sisters

"It's mine!"

"No, it's mine!"

"Well, I was playing with it first!"

The earliest, most frequent, and most intense disputes among siblings are over property rights—who owns a toy or who is entitled to play with it. Although exasperated adults may not always see it that way, sibling disputes and their settlement can be viewed as socialization opportunities, in which children learn to stand up for moral principles (Ross, 1996).

Despite the frequency of conflict, sibling rivalry is *not* the main pattern between brothers and sisters early in life. Although some rivalry exists, so do affection, interest, companionship, and influence, as was true of Isabel Allende and her younger brothers. Observations spanning three-and-a-half years, which began when younger siblings were about 1½ years old and the older ones ranged from 3 to 4½, found prosocial and play-oriented behaviors to be more common than rivalry, hostility, and competition (Abramovitch, Corter, & Lando, 1979; Abramovitch, Corter, Pepler, & Stanhope, 1986; Abramovitch, Pepler, & Corter, 1982). Older siblings initiated more behavior, both friendly and unfriendly; younger siblings tended to imitate the older ones. As the younger children reached their fifth birthday, the siblings became less physical and more verbal, both in showing aggression and in showing care and affection. At least one finding of this research has been replicated in many studies: same-sex siblings, particularly girls, are closer and play together more peaceably than boy-girl pairs (Kier & Lewis, 1998).

The quality of relationships with brothers and sisters often carries over to relationships with other children; a child who is aggressive with siblings is likely to be aggressive with friends as well (Abramovitch et al., 1986). Children with siblings get along better with kindergarten classmates than do only children (Downey & Condron, 2004).

The Only Child Are only children spoiled, selfish, lonely, or maladjusted? Research does not bear out this stereotype. According to an analysis of 115 studies, "onlies" do comparatively well. In occupational and educational achievement and intelligence, they surpass children with siblings. Only children also tend to be more mature and motivated to achieve and to have higher self-esteem. They do not differ, however, in overall adjustment or sociability. Perhaps these children do better because their parents spend more time and focus more attention on them, talk to them more, do more with them, and expect more of them (Falbo & Polit, 1986; Polit & Falbo, 1987).

Research in China, which mandates one-child families, also has produced encouraging findings about only children (see Box 8-2).

Playmates and Friends

Friendships develop as people develop. Toddlers play alongside or near each other, but not until about age 3 do children begin to have friends. Through friendships and interactions with casual playmates, young children learn how to get along with others. They learn that being a friend is the way to have a friend. They learn how to solve problems in relationships and how to put themselves in another person's place, and they see models of various kinds of behavior. They learn moral values and gender-role norms, and they practice adult roles.

Preschoolers usually like to play with children of their own age and sex. In preschool, they tend to spend most of their time with a few other children with whom they have had positive experiences and whose behavior is like their own. Children who have frequent positive experiences with each other are most likely to become friends (Rubin et al., 1998; Snyder et al., 1996). About 3 out of 4 preschoolers have such mutual friendships (Hartup & Stevens, 1999).

The traits that young children look for in a playmate are similar to the traits they look for in a friend (C. H. Hart, DeWolf, Wozniak, & Burts, 1992). In one study, 4- to 7-year-olds rated the most important features of friendships as: doing things together, liking and caring for each other, sharing and helping one another, and to a lesser degree, living nearby or going to the same school. Younger children rated physical traits, such as

Checkpoint
Can you . . .

✔ Explain how the resolution of sibling disputes contributes to socialization?

✔ Tell how birth order and gender affect typical patterns of sibling interaction?

✔ Compare development of only children with that of children with siblings?

Guidepost

8. How do young children choose playmates and friends, and why are some children better liked than others?

Young children learn the importance of being a friend in order to have a friend. One way of being a friend is for a sighted child to help a blind playmate enjoy the feel of the sand and the sound of the surf.

BOX 8-2

Window on the World

A Nation of Only Children

In 1979, to control an exploding population, the People's Republic of China established an official policy of limiting families to one child each. In addition to propaganda campaigns and incentives to induce voluntary compliance—money, child care, health care, housing, and preference in school placement—thousands of involuntary abortions have taken place. People who have had children without first getting a permit have faced fines, loss of jobs, or forced sterilization (Abrams, 2004). By 1985, at least 8 out of 10 young urban couples and half of those in rural areas had only one child (Yang, Ollendick, Dong, Xia, & Lin, 1995), and by 1997, the country's estimated population growth was holding steady at a little more than 1 percent.

Today the one-child policy is no longer as rigorously or uniformly enforced (Faison, 1997), especially in rural areas and among dwindling minority populations (Yardley, 2005). The State Family Planning Commission has prohibited forced sterilizations and abortions and instead has begun to stress education and contraceptive choice, while imposing extra taxes on families with more than one child. In a small but growing number of counties, fixed quotas and permit requirements have even been eliminated (Rosenthal, 1998).

Still, in many Chinese cities, kindergartens and primary classrooms are almost completely filled with children who have no brothers or sisters. This situation marks a great change in Chinese society, where newlyweds were traditionally congratulated with the wish, "May you have a hundred sons and a thousand grandsons." It offers researchers a natural experiment: an opportunity to study the adjustment of large numbers of only children.

Among 4,000 third and sixth graders, personality differences between only children and those with siblings—as rated by parents, teachers, peers, and the children themselves—were few. Only children's academic achievement and physical growth were about the same as, or better than, those with siblings (Falbo & Poston, 1993). In a randomized study in Beijing first-grade classrooms (Jiao, Ji, & Jing, 1996), only children outperformed classmates with siblings in memory, language, and mathematics skills. This finding may reflect the greater attention, stimulation, hopes, and expectations that parents shower on a baby they know will be their first and last. Fifth-grade only children, who were born before the one-child policy was strongly enforced—and whose parents may have originally planned on a larger family—did not show a pronounced cognitive edge.

A review of the literature found no significant differences in behavioral problems. The small number of severe problems that did appear in only children could be attributed to parental overindulgence and overprotection (Tao, 1998). Indeed, only children seem to be at a distinct psychological advantage in a society that favors and rewards such a child. Among 731 urban children and adolescents, those with siblings reported higher levels of fear, anxiety, and depression than only children, regardless of sex or age (Yang et al., 1995).

Both of these studies used urban samples. Further research may reveal whether the findings hold up in rural areas and small towns, where children with siblings are more numerous, and whether only children maintain their cognitive superiority as they move through school.

China's population policy has wider implications. If it succeeds, most Chinese will eventually lack aunts, uncles, nephews, nieces, and cousins, as well as siblings. How this will affect individuals, families, and the social fabric is incalculable.

A more sinister question is this: What happened to the girls? About 119 boys are born in China for every 100 girls, and in some agricultural regions, where sons are needed for farm work, the ratio is as high as 134 to 100. In part, the explanation is selective abortion of female fetuses, which is officially banned but often can be bought by bribing a physician (Yardley, 2005). Since the adoption of the one-child policy, many parents have reportedly abandoned or killed baby girls so as to try to bear more culturally valued sons. A more benign explanation is that these girls were hidden and raised secretly to evade the one-child policy (Carmichael, 2004; Kristof, 1991, 1993). An increasing number are being sold or given up for adoption by foreigners; in 2000, the U.S. government issued 5,053 visas for orphans from China, as compared with only 61 visas in 1991 (Kreider, 2003; Rosenthal, 2003). These trends are producing a growing surplus of young men who cannot find mates and may threaten social stability (Hudson & den Boer, 2004; Lee, 2004). Concern about these unforeseen effects of China's one-child policy may be one factor in the recent relaxation of enforcement. The government also is testing a program of pensions to rural elderly people who have two daughters so as to reduce the incentive to abort them (Yardley, 2005).

What's Your View?

Governmental control of reproduction may seem like the ultimate in totalitarianism, but what course of action would you propose for a country that cannot support an exploding population?

Check It Out

For more information on this topic, go to http://www.pbs.org/sixbillion/china/ch-repro.html. This is the Web site of the Public Broadcasting Corporation, featuring a story on China and reproductive issues.

appearance and size, higher than did older ones and rated affection and support lower (Furman & Bierman, 1983). Preschool children prefer prosocial playmates (C. H. Hart et al., 1992). They reject disruptive, demanding, intrusive, or aggressive children and ignore those who are shy or withdrawn (Ramsey & Lasquade, 1996; Roopnarine & Honig, 1985). Shy boys, especially, may be excluded by peers (Coplan et al., 2004).

Well-liked preschoolers and kindergartners and those who are rated by parents and teachers as socially competent generally cope well with anger. They avoid insults and threats. Instead, they respond directly, in ways that minimize further conflict and keep relationships going. Unpopular children tend to hit back or tattle (Fabes & Eisenberg, 1992).

Checkpoint
Can you . . .

✔ Explain how preschoolers choose playmates and friends, how they behave with friends, and how they benefit from friendships?

✔ Discuss how relationships at home can influence relationships with peers?

Refocus

Thinking back to the Focus vignette about Isabel Allende at the beginning of this chapter:

- From what you have read, would you guess that Isabel Allende had high or low self-esteem as a young child? Why?

- Which of the theories of gender formation seems to best describe Allende's development? Which do you think she would agree with most?

- Isabel Allende describes herself as a solitary child, who lived and played largely in the world of her own imagination. Would Parten have considered her immature? Would you?

- Allende and her mother shared an unconditional love, yet she seemed to have greater respect for her stepfather. Why?

- Allende says little about relationships with other children besides her younger brothers. Thinking about her personality, would you expect her to have been popular or unpopular with peers?

Peer relationships become even more important during middle childhood, which we examine in Chapters 9 and 10.

SUMMARY AND KEY TERMS

The Developing Self

Guidepost 1: How does the self-concept develop during early childhood, and how do children develop self-esteem?

- The self-concept undergoes major change in early childhood. According to neo-Piagetians, self-definition shifts from single representations to representational mappings. Young children do not see the difference between the real self and the ideal self.
- Culture affects the self-definition.
- Self-esteem in early childhood tends to be global and unrealistic, reflecting adult approval.

  self-concept *(279)*

  self-definition *(279)*

  single representations *(280)*

  real self *(280)*

  ideal self *(280)*

  representational mappings *(280)*

  self-esteem *(281)*

Guidepost 2: How do young children advance in understanding and regulating their emotions?

- Understanding of emotions directed toward the self and of simultaneous emotions develops gradually.
- According to Erikson, the developmental conflict of early childhood is initiative versus guilt. Successful resolution of this conflict results in the "virtue" of *purpose.*

  initiative versus guilt *(283)*

Gender

Guidepost 3: How do boys and girls become aware of the meaning of gender, and what explains differences in behavior between the sexes?

- Gender identity is an aspect of the developing self-concept.
- The main gender difference in early childhood is boys' greater aggressiveness. Girls tend to be more empathic and prosocial and less prone to problem behavior. Some cognitive differences appear early, others not until preadolescence or later.
- Children learn gender roles at an early age through gender-typing. Gender stereotypes peak during the preschool years.
- Four major perspectives on gender development are biological, psychoanalytic, cognitive, and socialization-based.
- Evidence suggests that some gender differences may be biologically based.
- In Freudian theory, a child identifies with the same-sex parent after giving up the wish to possess the other parent.
- Cognitive-developmental theory maintains that gender identity develops from thinking about one's gender. According to Kohlberg, gender constancy leads to acquisition of gender roles. Gender-schema theory holds that children categorize gender-related information by observing what males and females do in their culture.
- According to social cognitive theory, children learn gender roles through socialization. Parents, peers, the media, and culture influence gender-typing.

gender identity *(284)*

gender roles *(285)*

gender-typing *(285)*

gender stereotypes *(285)*

identification *(287)*

gender constancy *(287)*

gender-schema theory *(288)*

social cognitive theory *(289)*

Play: The Business of Early Childhood

Guidepost 4: How do preschoolers play, and how does play contribute to and reflect development?

- Play has physical, cognitive, and psychosocial benefits. Changes in the types of play children engage in reflect cognitive and social development.
- According to Piaget and Smilansky, children progress cognitively from functional play to constructive play, pretend play, and then formal games with rules. Pretend play becomes increasingly common during early childhood and helps children develop social and cognitive skills. Rough-and-tumble play also begins during early childhood.
- According to Parten, play becomes more social during early childhood. However, later research has found that nonsocial play is not necessarily immature.

- Children prefer to play with (and play more socially with) others of their sex.
- Cognitive and social aspects of play are influenced by the culturally approved environments adults create for children.

functional play *(292)*

constructive play *(292)*

pretend play *(292)*

Parenting

Guidepost 5: How do parenting practices influence development?

- Discipline can be a powerful tool for socialization.
- Both positive reinforcement and prudently administered punishment can be appropriate tools of discipline within the context of a positive parent-child relationship.
- Power assertion, inductive techniques, and withdrawal of love each can be effective in certain situations. Reasoning is generally the most effective and power assertion the least effective in promoting internalization of parental standards. Spanking and other forms of corporal punishment can have negative consequences.
- Baumrind identified three childrearing styles: authoritarian, permissive, and authoritative. A fourth style, neglectful or uninvolved, was identified later. Authoritative parents tend to raise more competent children. However, Baumrind's findings may be misleading when applied to some cultures or socioeconomic groups.

discipline *(296)*

corporal punishment *(296)*

power assertion *(297)*

inductive techniques *(297)*

withdrawal of love *(297)*

psychological aggression *(299)*

authoritarian *(300)*

permissive *(300)*

authoritative *(300)*

Guidepost 6: Why do young children help or hurt others, and why do they develop fears?

- The roots of altruism and prosocial behavior appear early. This may be an inborn disposition, which can be cultivated by parental modeling and encouragement.
- Instrumental aggression—first physical, then verbal—is most common in early childhood.
- Most children become less aggressive after age 6 or 7, but hostile aggression proportionately increases. Boys tend to practice overt aggression, whereas girls often engage in relational aggression.
- Preschool children show temporary fears of real and imaginary objects and events; older children's fears tend to be more realistic.

altruism *(302)*

prosocial behavior *(302)*

instrumental aggression *(303)*

hostile aggression *(303)*

overt aggression *(304)*

relational aggression *(304)*

Relationships with Other Children

Guidepost 7: **How do young children get along with (or without) siblings?**

- Sibling and peer relationships contribute to self-efficacy.
- Most sibling interactions are positive. Older siblings tend to initiate activities, and younger ones to imitate. Same-sex siblings, especially girls, get along best.
- Siblings tend to resolve disputes on the basis of moral principles.

- The kind of relationship children have with siblings often carries over into other peer relationships.
- Only children seem to develop at least as well as children with siblings in most respects.

Guidepost 8: **How do young children choose playmates and friends, and why are some children better liked than others?**

- Preschoolers choose playmates and friends who are like them and with whom they have positive experiences.
- Aggressive children are less popular than prosocial children.

PART 4

- Malnutrition can hamper cognitive and psychosocial development.

- Physical appearance plays a large part in self-esteem.

- Moral development may be linked to cognitive growth.

- IQ can be affected by nutrition, socioeconomic status, culture, rapport with the examiner, and familiarity with the surroundings.

- Parenting styles can affect school achievement.

- A decline in egocentric thinking permits deeper, more intimate friendships.

- Children who are good learners and problem solvers tend to be resilient in coping with stress.

The middle years of childhood, from about age 6 to about age 11, are often called the school years. School is the central experience during this time—a focal point for physical, cognitive, and psychosocial development. As we see in Chapter 9, children grow taller, heavier, and stronger and acquire the motor skills needed to participate in organized games and sports. They also make major advances in thinking, in moral judgment, in memory, and in literacy. Individual differences become more evident and special needs more important, as competencies affect success in school.

Competencies also affect self-esteem and popularity, as we see in Chapter 10. Although parents continue to be important, the peer group is more influential than before. Children develop physically, cognitively, and emotionally, as well as socially, through contacts with other youngsters.

Middle Childhood

PREVIEW

CHAPTER 9
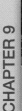

Physical and Cognitive Development in Middle Childhood

CHAPTER 10

Psychosocial Development in Middle Childhood

Growth slows.

Strength and athletic skills improve.

Respiratory illnesses are common, but health is generally better than at any other time in the life span.

Egocentrism diminishes.

Children begin to think logically but concretely.

Memory and language skills increase.

Cognitive gains permit children to benefit from formal schooling.

Some children show special educational needs and strengths.

Self-concept becomes more complex, affecting self-esteem.

Coregulation reflects gradual shift in control from parents to child.

Peers assume central importance.

Physical and Cognitive Development in Middle Childhood

CHAPTER 9

> What we must remember above all in the
> education of our children is that their
> love of life should never weaken.

Natalia Ginzburg, *The Little Virtues*, 1985

Focus
Ann Bancroft, Polar Explorer

Ann Bancroft

Ann Bancroft* is the first woman in history to reach both the North and South Poles by nonmotorized means. In 1986, she dogsledded 1,000 miles from the Northwest Territories in Canada to the North Pole as the only female member of an international expedition. After surviving eight months of grueling training and enduring temperatures as low as −70 degrees for 56 days, Bancroft stood on top of the world. Seven years later she led three other women in a 67-day, 660-mile ski trek to the South Pole, reaching it on January 14, 1993. For these exploits, she was inducted into the National Women's Hall of Fame. In 2000, she and Liv Arneson of Norway became the first team of women to ski across the landmass of Antarctica; and in 2002 the two women reunited for a kayaking voyage from the north shore of Lake Superior to the St. Lawrence Seaway.

How did this five-foot-three-inch, 125-pound woman achieve these remarkable feats? The answers go back to her childhood in then-rural Mendota Heights, Minnesota.

Born September 29, 1955, into what she calls a family of risk takers, Ann showed her climbing instincts as soon as she could walk. As a toddler, she would climb her grandmother's bookcase to reach things on top. Instead of trying to stop her from climbing, her parents said, "Go ahead and try; you might just get what you want."

Ann was an outdoor girl. She and her two brothers and two sisters spent hours roaming the fields surrounding their farmhouse. Ann would "pretend she was a pirate building rafts to float down the creek, or an adventurer canoeing in the far north. During the winter she would build snow forts, sleeping shacks, and tunnels" (Wenzel, 1990, p. 15).

Her father often took the family on camping and canoe trips in the wilds of northern Minnesota. When she was 8, Ann started camping out in her backyard in winter with her cousins and the family dog. When she was 10, her parents went to Africa as missionaries. Ann's two years in Kenya kindled her thirst to see other parts of the world.

*Biographical information about Ann Bancroft came primarily from Noone (2000), Wenzel (1990), and Bancroft's Web site, http://www.yourexpedition.com. Other sources were "Ann Bancroft, 1955– " (1998), "Ann Bancroft, 1955– " (1999), "Ann Bancroft, Explorer" (undated), "First Woman to Both Poles" (1997), and "Minnesota Explorer Ann Bancroft" (2002).

In school Ann was a poor student and had to be tutored to keep up. A natural athlete, her favorite class was gym. Not until seventh grade did she learn that she had dyslexia, a reading disability. Around that time Ann came across a book about Sir Ernest Shackleton's unsuccessful effort to reach the South Pole in 1914. She was drawn to the photographs. "I was so fascinated by the images that I no longer was intimidated by the words and thickness of the book," Ann recalls. "I wanted to know about this adventure at the bottom of the world. This began my curiosity with Antarctica and the dream of one day crossing it."

Ann became a physical education teacher and athletic director in St. Paul. In 1983, she and a friend climbed Alaska's Mount McKinley (now Denali), the highest peak in North America—an expedition that could have ended in disaster for her partner, who developed hypothermia, had it not been for Ann's training in first aid and emergency medicine. Two years later, Ann was invited to join the Steger International Polar Expedition to the North Pole as a medic and trip photographer.

"The goal was not so much reaching the pole itself," Bancroft recalls. "It was . . . more universal. Why do we all take on struggles? Why run a marathon? I think we're all striving to push ourselves. And in the process of overcoming struggle and challenges, we get to know ourselves better."

Today Bancroft is an instructor for Wilderness Inquiry, a program for both able-bodied people and those with disabilities. During her first South Pole expedition, she lugged a 30-pound radio set across the ice so she could send progress reports to students around the world. On her last expedition to Antarctica with Arneson, children in more than 40 countries followed the journey with the help of an interactive Web site. She has coauthored a book about her adventures (Loewen & Bancroft, 2001)—for her, perhaps the greatest challenge of all. Her goal is to "inspire children around the globe to pursue their dreams" as she has (Noone, 2000, p. 1). "It is totally energizing," she says, "to step out each day living a dream."

As a schoolgirl, Ann Bancroft may not have seemed extraordinary except that her dyslexia marked her as a child with special needs. Her childhood struggle with dyslexia helps explain the determination that helped her succeed as a polar explorer. "I get stubborn and dig in when people tell me I can't do something and I think I can," she explains. "I never wanted to be perceived as handicapped or limited in any way." Bancroft's story illustrates how a dream formed in childhood can inspire later accomplishments. She is a living example of the power of attitudes and desires to shape physical and cognitive development.

Although motor abilities improve less dramatically in middle childhood than before, these years are an important time for the development of strength, stamina, endurance, and motor proficiency. In this chapter we look at these and other physical developments. Cognitively, we see how attainment of Piaget's stage of concrete operations enables children to think logically and to make more mature judgments. We see how children improve in memory and problem solving, how their intelligence is tested, and how the abilities to read and write open the door to participation in a wider world. We look at factors affecting school achievement, and we examine the controversies over IQ testing, methods of teaching reading, and second-language education. Finally, we see how schools educate children with exceptional needs, like Ann Bancroft.

After you have read and studied this chapter, you should be able to answer each of the Guidepost questions that appear at the top of the next page. Look for them again in the margins, where they point to important concepts throughout the chapter. To check your understanding of these Guideposts, review the end-of-chapter summary. Checkpoints located at periodic spots throughout the chapter will help you verify your understanding of what you have read.

**Guideposts
for Study**

1. What gains in growth and motor development occur in school-age children, and what are their nutritional needs?

2. What are the principal health and fitness concerns for school-age children, and what can be done to make these years healthier and safer?

3. How do school-age children's thinking and moral reasoning differ from those of younger children?

4. What advances in memory and other information-processing skills occur during middle childhood?

5. How accurately can schoolchildren's intelligence be measured?

6. How do communicative abilities and literacy expand during middle childhood?

7. What influences school achievement?

8. How do schools meet the needs of non-English-speaking children and those with learning problems?

9. How is giftedness assessed and nurtured?

PHYSICAL DEVELOPMENT

Aspects of Physical Development

If we were to walk by a typical elementary school just after the three o'clock bell, we would see a virtual explosion of children of all shapes and sizes. Tall ones, short ones, husky ones, and slender ones would be bursting out of the school doors into the open air. We would see that school-age children look very different from children a few years younger. They are taller, and most are fairly wiry; but more are likely to be overweight than in past decades.

Guidepost

1. What gains in growth and motor development occur in school-age children, and what are their nutritional needs?

Growth

Growth during middle childhood slows considerably. Still, although day-by-day changes may not be obvious, they add up to a startling difference between 6-year-olds, who are still small children, and 11-year-olds, many of whom are now beginning to resemble adults.

Children grow about 2 to 3 inches each year between ages 6 and 11 and approximately double their weight during that period (Ogden, Fryar, Carroll, & Flegal, 2004). Girls retain somewhat more fatty tissue than boys, a characteristic that will persist through adulthood. The average 10-year-old weighs about 11 pounds more than 40 years ago—nearly 85 pounds for a boy and 88 pounds for a girl (Ogden et al., 2004). African American boys and girls tend to grow faster than white children. By about age 6, African American girls have more muscle and bone mass than European American (white) or Mexican American girls, and Mexican American girls have a higher percentage of body fat than white girls the same size (Ellis, Abrams, & Wong, 1997).

Nutrition and Sleep

To support their steady growth and constant exertion, schoolchildren need, on average, 2,400 calories every day—more for older children and less for younger ones. Nutritionists recommend a varied diet including plenty of grains, fruits, and vegetables and high levels of complex carbohydrates, found in potatoes, pasta, bread, and cereals.

To avoid overweight and prevent cardiac problems, children (like adults) should get only about 30 percent of their total calories from fat and less than 10 percent of the total from saturated fat (AAP Committee on Nutrition, 1992a; U.S. Department of Agriculture & USDHHS, 2000). Studies have found no negative effects on height, weight, body mass, or neurological development from a moderately low-fat diet at this age (Rask-Nissilä et al., 2000; Shea et al., 1993).

Sleep needs decline from about 11 hours a day at age 5 to a little more than 10 hours at age 9 and about 9 hours at age 13. Healthy school-age children should be highly alert in the daytime. However, sleep problems, such as resistance to going to bed, insomnia, and daytime sleepiness are common during these years, in part because many children, as they grow older, are allowed to set their own bedtimes (Hoban, 2004).

Motor Development

Motor skills continue to improve in middle childhood (see Table 9-1). By this age, however, children in most nonliterate and transitional societies go to work, and this plus more household labor, especially for girls, leaves them little time and freedom for physical play (Larson & Verma, 1999). In the United States, children's lives today

Checkpoint

Can you . . .

✔ Summarize typical growth patterns of boys and girls in middle childhood and give reasons for variations?

✔ Summarize the nutritional needs of school-age children?

Table 9-1	Motor Development in Middle Childhood

Age	Selected Behaviors
6	Girls are superior in movement accuracy; boys are superior in forceful, less complex acts. Skipping is possible.
	Children can throw with proper weight shift and step.
7	One-footed balancing without looking becomes possible.
	Children can walk 2-inch-wide balance beams.
	Children can hop and jump accurately into small squares.
	Children can execute accurate jumping-jack exercise.
8	Children have 12-pound pressure on grip strength.
	The number of games participated in by both sexes is greatest at this age.
	Children can engage in alternate rhythmic hopping in a 2-2, 2-3, or 3-3 pattern.
	Girls can throw a small ball 40 feet.
9	Boys can run 16½ feet per second.
	Boys can throw a small ball 70 feet.
10	Children can judge and intercept pathways of small balls thrown from a distance.
	Girls can run 17 feet per second.
11	A standing broad jump of 5 feet is possible for boys and of 6 inches less for girls.

Source: From Bryant J. Cratty, *Perceptual and Motor Development in Infants and Children*, 3rd ed. Copyright © 1986 by Allyn & Bacon. Adapted by permission of the publisher.

are more sedentary than they were when Ann Bancroft was camping out in her back-yard. A nationally representative survey based on time-use diaries found that school-age children spend less time each week on sports and other outdoor activities than in the early 1980s and more hours on schooling and homework, in addition to time spent on television—an average of 12 to 14 hours a week—and on computer activities, which scarcely existed 20 years ago (Juster, Ono, & Stafford, 2004).

Recess-Time Play The games children play at recess tend to be informal and spontaneously organized. One child may play alone while nearby a group of class-mates are chasing each other around the schoolyard. Boys play more physically active games, whereas girls favor games that include verbal expression or counting aloud, such as hopscotch and jumprope. Such recess-time activities promote growth in agility and social competence and foster adjustment to school (Pellegrini, Kato, Blatchford, & Baines, 2002).

About 10 percent of schoolchildren's free play at recess in the early grades con-sists of **rough-and-tumble play,** vigorous play that involves wrestling, kicking, tum-bling, grappling, and chasing, often accompanied by laughing and screaming. This kind of play peaks in middle childhood; the proportion typically drops to about 5 per-cent at age 11, about the same as in early childhood (Pellegrini, 1998; Pellegrini & Smith, 1998). Rough-and-tumble play seems to be universal; it takes place in such diverse places as India, Mexico, Okinawa, the Kalahari in Africa, the Philippines, Great Britain, and the United States (Humphreys & Smith, 1984). Rough-and-tumble play helps children jockey for dominance by assessing their own and each other's strength. Boys around the world participate in rough-and-tumble play more than girls do, a fact generally attributed to a combina-tion of hormonal differences and socializa-tion (Pellegrini, 1998; Pellegrini et al., 2002; Pellegrini & Smith, 1998).

> **rough-and-tumble play** Vigorous play involving wrestling, hitting, and chasing, often accompanied by laughing and screaming.

Organized Sports After children outgrow rough-and-tumble play and begin playing games with rules, some join organized, adult-led sports. In a nationally representative sur-vey of U.S. 9- to 13-year-olds and their par-ents, 38.5 percent reported participation in organized athletics outside of school hours during the previous week—most often in baseball, softball, soccer, or basketball. About twice as many children (77.4 percent) partic-ipated in unorganized physical activity, such as bicycling and shooting baskets (Duke et

According to a nationally representative survey, 38.5 percent of 9- to 13-year-olds participate in organized after-school sports, such as soccer. To help children improve motor skills, such programs should emphasize skill-building rather than competition and should include as many children as possible regardless of ability.

al., 2003). Girls spend less time than boys on sports and more time on household work, studying, and personal care (Juster et al., 2004).

To help children improve their motor skills, organized athletic programs should offer the chance to try a variety of sports, should gear coaching to building skills rather than winning games, and should include as many children as possible rather than concentrating on a few natural athletes like Ann Bancroft. Programs should include a variety of sports that can be part of a lifetime fitness regimen, such as tennis, bowling, running, swimming, golf, and skating (AAP Committee on Sports Medicine & Fitness, 1997).

Checkpoint

Can you . . .

✔ Cite differences in boys' and girls' recess-time activities?

✔ Explain the significance of rough-and-tumble play?

✔ Tell what types of physical play children engage in as they grow older?

Guidepost

2. What are the principal health and fitness concerns for school-age children, and what can be done to make these years healthier and safer?

Health, Fitness, and Safety

The development of vaccines for major childhood illnesses has made middle childhood a relatively safe time of life, especially in developed countries. The death rate in these years is the lowest in the life span. Still, an increasing proportion of children are overweight, and some suffer from chronic medical conditions or accidental injuries or from lack of access to health care.

Obesity/Overweight

Childhood overweight has become a major health issue in the United States; its prevalence has doubled in school-age children and more than tripled in adolescents since the early 1980s (NCHS, 2004). About 16 percent of 6- to 11-year-olds are overweight, and an additional 15 percent are near-overweight. Boys are more likely to be overweight than girls (Hedley et al., 2004).

Causes of Overweight   As we reported in Chapters 3 and 7, overweight or obesity often results from an inherited tendency aggravated by too little exercise and too much or the wrong kinds of food (AAP Committee on Nutrition, 2003; Chen et al., 2004). On a typical day, more than 30 percent of a nationally representative sample of 6,212 children and adolescents reported eating fast foods high in fat, carbohydrates, and sugar additives (Bowman, Gortmaker, Ebbeling, Pereira, & Ludwig, 2004).

As we have mentioned, school-age children today spend less time than the children of 20 years ago on outdoor play and sports (Juster et al., 2004). In many communities, physical education has been cut back (AAP Committee on Nutrition, 2003). Most U.S. schoolchildren *do* get enough exercise to meet national goals, but many children are not as active as they should be. In one national survey, 22.6 percent of 9- to 13-year-olds engaged in *no* free-time physical activity (Duke, Huhman, & Heitzler, 2003).

Why Is Childhood Overweight a Serious Concern?   Being overweight is a decided disadvantage for school-age children. In a longitudinal study of 1,456 primary students in Victoria, Australia, children classified as overweight or obese fell behind their classmates in physical and social functioning by age 10 (Williams, Wake, Hesketh, Maher, & Waters, 2005). When 106 severely obese children and adolescents were asked to rate their health-related quality of life (for example, their ability to walk more than one block, to sleep well, to get along with others, and to keep up in school), they reported significant impairment as compared with healthy peers (Schwimmer, Burwinkle, & Varni, 2003).

Overweight children often suffer emotionally and may compensate by indulging themselves with treats, making their physical and social problems even worse. These children are at risk for behavior problems, depression, and low self-esteem (AAP Committee on Nutrition, 2003; Datar & Sturm, 2004a; Mustillo et al., 2003). They commonly have medical problems, including high blood pressure (discussed in the next section), high cholesterol, and high insulin levels (AAP Committee on Nutrition, 2003; NCHS, 2004).

Overweight children tend to become obese adults, at risk for high blood pressure, heart disease, orthopedic problems, and diabetes. Indeed, childhood overweight may be a stronger predictor of some diseases than adult overweight (AAP Committee on Nutrition, 2003; AAP, 2004; Li et al., 2004; Center for Weight and Health, 2001; Must, Jacques, Dallal, Bajema, & Dietz, 1992). Even children in the upper half of the *normal* weight range are more likely than their peers to become overweight or obese as young adults (Field, Cook, & Gillman, 2005).

Prevention and Treatment of Overweight Prevention of weight gain is easier, less costly, and more effective than treating overweight (Center for Weight and Health, 2001). Less time in front of television and computers, changes in food labeling and advertising, healthier school meals, education to help children make better food choices, and more physical education programs would help (AAP, 2004). Regular physical activity has immediate and long-term health benefits in addition to weight control: lower blood pressure, improved cardiorespiratory functioning, and enhanced well-being. Parents can make exercise a family activity by hiking or playing ball together, building strength on playground equipment, walking whenever possible, using stairs instead of elevators, and limiting television.

Parents should watch children's eating and activity patterns and address excessive weight gain *before* a child becomes severely overweight (AAP Committee on Nutrition, 2003). Treatment should begin early, involve the family, and promote permanent changes in lifestyle, not weight loss alone (Barlow & Dietz, 1998; Miller-Kovach, 2003). During a 12-week experiment with 10 obese 8- to 12-year-olds, those whose television viewing was limited to the amount of time they spent pedaling an exercise bicycle watched much less television and showed significantly greater reductions in body fat than a control group (Faith et al., 2001).

Overweight and Childhood Hypertension **Hypertension** (high blood pressure) once was relatively rare in childhood, but it has been termed an "evolving epidemic" of cardiovascular risk, especially among ethnic minorities (Sorof, Lai, Turner, Poffenbarger, & Portman, 2004, p. 481).

In nationally representative samples of U.S. children and adolescents ages 8 to 17, average blood pressure rose between 1988 and 2000, in part due to increases in overweight (Muntner, He, Cutler, Wildman, & Whelton, 2004). A series of screenings of 5,102 children ages 10 to 19 in eight Houston public schools found an estimated 4.5 percent prevalence of hypertension, with overweight the major contributing factor (Sorof et al., 2004).

Weight reduction through dietary modification and regular physical activity is the primary treatment for overweight-related hypertension. If blood pressure does not come down, drug treatment can be considered. However, care must be taken in prescribing such drugs, as their long-term effects on children are unknown—as are the long-term consequences of untreated hypertension in children (National High Blood Pressure Education Program Working Group on High Blood Pressure in Children and Adolescents, 2004).

hypertension Chronically high blood pressure.

Checkpoint
Can you . . .

✔ Discuss why childhood overweight has increased, how it can affect health, and how it can be treated?

✔ Explain why some children are not as physically fit as they should be?

Other Medical Problems

Illness in middle childhood tends to be brief. **Acute medical conditions**—occasional, short-term conditions, such as infections, allergies, and warts—are common. Six or seven bouts a year with colds, flu, or viruses are typical at this age, as germs pass among children at school or at play (Behrman, 1992). As children's experience with illness increases, so does their cognitive understanding of the causes of health and illness and of how people can promote their own health (see Box 9-1).

According to a nationwide survey of 30,032 families, an estimated 18 percent of children under age 18 in 1994 had **chronic medical conditions:** physical,

acute medical conditions Illnesses that last a short time.

chronic medical conditions Illnesses or impairments that persist for at least 3 months.

BOX 9-1

Digging Deeper
Children's Understanding of Illness

From a Piagetian perspective, children's understanding of health and illness is tied to cognitive development. As they mature, their explanations for disease change. Before middle childhood, children are egocentric; they tend to believe that illness is magically produced by human actions, often their own ("I was a bad boy, so now I feel bad"). Later they explain all diseases—only a little less magically—as the doing of all-powerful germs; the only "protection" is a variety of superstitious behaviors to ward them off. "Watch out for germs," a child may say. As children approach adolescence, they see that there can be multiple causes of disease, that contact with germs does not automatically lead to illness, and that people can do much to keep healthy.

Children's understanding of AIDS increases with age, like their understanding of colds and of cancer, but they understand the cause of colds earlier than they do the causes of the other two illnesses, probably because they are more familiar with colds (Kistner et al., 1997; Schonfeld, Johnson, Perrin, O'Hare, & Cicchetti, 1993). Although most 6- and 7-year-olds have heard of HIV/AIDS, misconceptions about its causes and symptoms persist. These misconceptions can be harmful, because children who harbor them are likely to unnecessarily avoid contact with classmates with AIDS (Kistner et al., 1997).

Interviews with 361 children in kindergarten through sixth grade (Schonfeld et al., 1993) found that children often give superficially correct explanations but lack real understanding of the processes involved in AIDS. For example, although 96 children mentioned drug use as a cause, most did not seem to realize that the disease is spread through blood adhering to a needle shared by drug users. One second-grader gave this version of how someone gets AIDS: "Well, by doing drugs and something like that . . . by going by a drug dealer who has AIDS. . . . Well, you go by a person who's a drug dealer and you might catch the AIDS from 'em by standing near 'em" (Schonfeld et al., 1993, p. 393).

From a young child's point of view, such a statement may be a logical extension of the belief that germs cause disease. The child may wrongly assume that AIDS can be caught, as colds are, from sharing cups and utensils, from being near someone who is coughing or sneezing, or from hugging and kissing. One AIDS education program (Sigelman et al., 1996) sought to replace such intuitive "theories" with scientifically grounded ones and to test Piaget's idea that if children have not mastered a concept, they are probably not yet ready to do so. The developers of the program hypothesized that what young children lack is knowledge about the disease, not the ability to think about it.

A carefully scripted program was tried on 306 third-, fifth-, and seventh-graders in Tucson. Trained health instructors conducted two 50-minute sessions consisting of lectures, video clips, drawings, and discussion, and using vocabulary appropriate for third-graders. The curriculum emphasized that there are only a few ways to get AIDS and that normal contact with infected people is *not* one of them.

Experimental and control groups were tested before the program began and again about two weeks afterward. Students who had received instruction knew more about AIDS and its causes than those who had not, were no more (and no less) worried about it than before, and were more willing to be with people with AIDS. Almost a year later, the gains generally were retained. The success of this program shows that, contrary to Piaget, even relatively young children can grasp complex scientific concepts about disease if teaching is geared to their level of understanding.

What's Your View?

How old do you think children should be before being taught about AIDS?

Check It Out

For more information on this topic, go to http://wwwtest .library.ucla.edu/libraries/biomed/ref/doctor/doctor1/lu_chiun .htm [a University of California library site with information about how to search databases such as MEDLINE and PSYCINFO for sources about children's understanding of illness] or http://www.aegis.com/pubs/aidsline/1992/jan/M9210769.html [a link to an article in *Dissertation Abstracts:* "An Examination of the Relation Between Children's Understanding of Illness and Their Acceptance of Medically Ill Peers"].

---

developmental, behavioral, and/or emotional conditions requiring special health services (Newacheck et al., 1998). Let's look at a few chronic conditions.

Vision and Hearing Problems   Most school-age children have keener vision than when they were younger. Children under 6 years old tend to be farsighted. By age 6, vision typically is more acute; and because the two eyes are better coordinated, they can focus better.

Almost 13 percent of children under 18 are estimated to be blind or to have impaired vision. Vision problems are reported more often for white and Latino children than for African Americans (Newacheck, Stoddard, & McManus, 1993). About 15 percent of 6- to 19-year-olds, mostly boys, have some hearing loss. Current screening guidelines may miss many children with very high-frequency impairments.

This is of concern, since even slight hearing loss can affect communication, behavior, and social relationships (Niskar et al., 1998).

Asthma   **Asthma,** a chronic respiratory disease characterized by sudden attacks of coughing, wheezing, and difficulty in breathing, is a major cause of childhood disability. About 12 percent of U.S. children and adolescents have been diagnosed with asthma at some time. Apparently allergy based, it is 30 percent more common in boys than in girls (Dey, Schiller, & Tai, 2004; NCHS, 2004). Asthma's prevalence nearly doubled between 1980 and 1995 but seems to have leveled off (Goldman et al., 2004; Moss, 2003; Woodruff et al., 2004).

The cause of the asthma explosion is uncertain. Some experts point to tightly insulated houses that intensify exposure to indoor environmental toxins and allergens (Nugent, 1999; Sly, 2000; Stapleton, 1998), such as tobacco smoke, dust mites, molds, and cockroach droppings. Use of a gas stove for heat and allergies to household pets also may be risk factors (Bollinger, 2003; Etzel, 2003; Lanphear, Aligne, Auinger, Weitzman, & Byrd, 2001). In a randomized, controlled study, a one-year program to reduce indoor allergens and tobacco smoke in the homes of children with asthma in seven major cities reduced asthma symptoms and asthma-related illnesses (Morgan et al., 2004).

Children with asthma miss an average of 10 days of school each year and experience 20 days of limited activity—almost twice the amount for children with other chronic ailments (Newacheck & Halfon, 2000). Attacks tend to follow severely stressful events, such as illness, parental separation or divorce, the death of a grandparent, a close friend moving away, or becoming a victim of bullying (Sandberg, Järvenpää, Penttinen, Paton, & McCann, 2004). Black children are three times more likely than white children to be hospitalized with asthma and four times more likely to die from it (Moss, 2003).

Many children get inadequate treatment (Halterman, Aligne, Auinger, McBride, & Szilagyi, 2000; Shields, Comstock, & Weiss, 2004). In a randomized, controlled study of 134 asthmatic inner-city children ages 8 to 16, use of the Internet to educate patients and their families in symptom monitoring and medication led to improved compliance and reduced symptoms (Dorsey & Schneider, 2003).

HIV and AIDS   Worldwide, an estimated 2.2 million children under age 15 are living with the human immunodeficiency virus (HIV) (UNAIDS/WHO, 2004). These children are at high risk of developing AIDS (acquired immune deficiency syndrome), if they have not done so already. Many of these children acquired the AIDS virus from their mothers, usually in the womb (AAP Committee on Pediatric AIDS and Committee on Infectious Diseases, 1999; refer back to Chapter 3). Others are victims of sexual abuse. In 2004, 510,000 children under 15 died of AIDS (UNAIDS/WHO, 2004).

Prospects for children born with HIV infection have improved. Although some develop full-blown AIDS by their first or second birthday, others live for years without apparently being affected much, if at all (European Collaborative Study, 1994; Grubman et al., 1995; Nielsen et al., 1997; Nozyce et al., 1994). Those with symptoms of AIDS may develop central nervous system dysfunction that can interfere with their ability to learn, but antiretroviral therapy can improve their functioning (AAP Committee on Pediatric AIDS, 2000). A combination therapy including protease inhibitors has markedly reduced mortality among HIV-infected children and adolescents (Gortmaker et al., 2001). Genetic factors may affect the immune system's response to the virus, causing symptoms to develop more slowly in some children than in others (Singh et al., 2003).

Although most school-age children have excellent vision, some, like this boy, need corrective lenses.

asthma   A chronic respiratory disease characterized by sudden attacks of coughing, wheezing, and difficulty in breathing.

What's Your View?

- Medical evidence shows virtually no evidence that children with HIV infection who are symptom-free can transmit the virus to others except through bodily fluids. Yet many parents are afraid to have their children go to school with a child who is HIV-positive. Can you suggest ways to deal with parents who have this concern?

Safety-approved helmets protect children of all ages from disabling or fatal head injuries.

Most children infected with HIV who reach school age function normally. Because there is virtually no risk of infecting classmates (refer back to Box 9-1), children who carry the AIDS virus do not need to be isolated. They should be encouraged to participate in all school activities, including athletics, to the extent they are able (AAP Committee on Sports Medicine and Fitness, 1999; AAP Committee on Pediatric AIDS, 2000).

Accidental Injuries

As in early childhood, accidental injuries are the leading cause of death among school-age U.S. children (Anderson & Smith, 2003; Kochanek et al., 2004). In a 9-year study of 96,359 children born in Alberta, Canada, 21 percent suffered at least one injury each year, and 73 percent had repeat injuries during the study period. Boys were more likely to be injured than girls and to have repeat injuries (Spady, Saunders, Schopflocher, & Svenson, 2004). Firearm injuries are a growing public health concern affecting children age 14 and younger (see Chapter 10).

An estimated 23,000 children each year suffer serious brain injuries from bicycle accidents, and as many as 88 percent of these injuries could be prevented by using helmets (AAP Committee on Injury and Poison Prevention, 2001a). Protective headgear also is vital for baseball and softball, football, roller skating, rollerblading, skateboarding, scooter riding, horseback riding, hockey, speed sledding, snowmobiling, and tobogganing. For soccer, protective goggles and mouth guards may help reduce head and facial injuries. "Heading" the ball should be minimized because of the danger of brain injury (AAP Committee on Sports Medicine and Fitness, 2000, 2001). The AAP Committee on Accident and Poison Prevention (1988) recommends that children under 16 *not* use snowmobiles, and that older riders be required by law to be licensed. Because of the need for stringent safety precautions and constant supervision for trampoline use, the AAP Committee on Injury and Poison Prevention and Committee on Sports Medicine and Fitness (1999) recommend that parents not buy trampolines and that children not use them on playgrounds or at school.

Checkpoint

Can you . . .

✔ Distinguish between acute and chronic medical conditions, and discuss how chronic conditions can affect everyday life?

✔ Identify factors that increase the risks of accidental injury?

COGNITIVE DEVELOPMENT

Guidepost

3. How do school-age children's thinking and moral reasoning differ from those of younger children?

concrete operations Third stage of Piagetian cognitive development (approximately from ages 7 to 12), during which children develop logical but not abstract thinking.

Piagetian Approach: The Concrete Operational Child

At about age 7, according to Piaget, children enter the stage of **concrete operations** when they can use mental operations, such as reasoning, to solve concrete (actual) problems, such as where to find a missing mitten. Children this age can think logically because they are less egocentric than before and can take multiple aspects of a situation into account. However, their thinking is still limited to real situations in the here and now.

Cognitive Advances

In the stage of concrete operations, children have a better understanding than preoperational children of spatial concepts, causality, categorization, inductive and deductive reasoning, conservation, and number (see Table 9-2).

Table 9-2	Advances in Selected Cognitive Abilities During Middle Childhood
Ability	**Example**
Spatial thinking	Danielle can use a map or model to help her search for a hidden object and can give someone else directions for finding the object. She can find her way to and from school, can estimate distances, and can judge how long it will take her to go from one place to another.
Cause and effect	Douglas knows which physical attributes of objects on each side of a balance scale will affect the result (i.e., number of objects matters but color does not). He does not yet know which spatial factors, such as position and placement of the objects, make a difference.
Categorization	Elena can sort objects into categories, such as shape, color or both. She knows that a subclass (roses) has fewer members than the class of which it is a part (flowers).
Seriation and transitive inference	Catherine can arrange a group of sticks in order, from the shortest to the longest, and can insert an intermediate-size stick into the proper place. She knows that if one stick is longer than a second stick, and the second stick is longer than a third, then the first stick is longer than the third.
Inductive and deductive reasoning	Dominic can solve both inductive and deductive problems and knows that inductive conclusions (based on particular premises) are less certain than deductive ones (based on general premises).
Conservation	Felipe, at age 7, knows that if a clay ball is rolled into a sausage, it still contains the same amount of clay (conservation of substance). At age 9, he knows that the ball and the sausage weigh the same. Not until early adolescence will he understand that they displace the same amount of liquid if dropped in a glass of water.
Number and mathematics	Kevin can count in his head, can add by counting up from the smaller number, and can do simple story problems.

Spatial Relationships and Causality With a better understanding of spatial relationships, children in the stage of concrete operations have a clearer idea of how far it is from one place to another and how long it will take to get there, and they can more easily remember the route and the landmarks along the way. Experience plays a role in this development: a child who walks to school becomes more familiar with the neighborhood outside the home.

Both the ability to use maps and models and the ability to communicate spatial information improve with age (Gauvain, 1993). Judgments about cause and effect also improve. When 5- to 12-year-olds were asked to predict how levers and balance scales would perform under varying conditions, the older children gave more correct answers. Children understood the influence of physical attributes (the number of objects on each side of a scale) earlier than they recognized the influence of spatial factors (the distance of objects from the center of the scale) (Amsel, Goodman, Savoie, & Clark, 1996).

Categorization The ability to categorize helps children think logically. Categorization includes such relatively sophisticated abilities as *seriation, transitive inference,* and *class inclusion*, which improve gradually between early and middle childhood. Children show that they understand **seriation** when they can arrange objects in a series according to one or more dimensions, such as weight (lightest to heaviest) or color (lightest to darkest). By 7 or 8, children can grasp the relationships among a group of sticks on sight and arrange them in order of size (Piaget, 1952).

Transitive inference is the ability to infer a relationship between two objects from the relationship between each of them and a third object. Catherine is shown three sticks: a yellow one, a green one, and a blue one. She is shown that the yellow stick is longer than the green one, and the green one is longer than the blue.

seriation Ability to order items along a dimension.

transitive inference Understanding of the relationship between two objects by knowing the relationship of each to a third object.

Without physically comparing the yellow and blue sticks, she immediately says that the yellow one is longer than the blue one (Chapman & Lindenberger, 1988; Piaget & Inhelder, 1967). However, we do not know whether Catherine arrives at this conclusion through conceptual reasoning, as Piaget suggested, or through perceptual comparison (Flavell, Miller, & Miller, 2002).

Class inclusion is the ability to see the relationship between a whole and its parts. Piaget (1964) found that when preoperational children are shown a bunch of 10 flowers—7 roses and 3 carnations—and are asked whether there are more roses or more flowers, they are likely to say there are more roses, because they are comparing the roses with the carnations rather than with the whole bunch. Not until age 7 or 8, and sometimes not even then, do children consistently reason that roses are a subclass of flowers and that, therefore, there cannot be more roses than flowers (Flavell, 1963; Flavell et al., 2002). However, even 3-year-olds show a rudimentary awareness of inclusion, depending on the type of task, the practical cues they receive, and their familiarity with the categories of objects they are tested on (Johnson, Scott, & Mervis, 1997). Understanding of class inclusion is closely related to *inductive* and *deductive reasoning*.

Inductive and Deductive Reasoning   According to Piaget, children in the stage of concrete operations use only **inductive reasoning.** Starting with observations about particular members of a class of people, animals, objects, or events, they then draw general conclusions about the class as a whole. ("My dog barks. So does Terry's dog and Melissa's dog. So it looks as if all dogs bark.") Inductive conclusions must be tentative because it is always possible to come across new information (a dog that does not bark) that does not support the conclusion.

Deductive reasoning, which Piaget believed does not develop until adolescence, starts with a general statement (premise) about a class and applies it to particular members of the class. If the premise is true of the whole class and the reasoning is sound, then the conclusion must be true: "All dogs bark. Spot is a dog. Spot barks."

Researchers gave 16 inductive and deductive problems to 16 kindergartners, 17 second-graders, 16 fourth-graders, and 17 sixth-graders. The problems were designed so as *not* to call upon knowledge of the real world. For example, one deductive problem was "All poggops wear blue boots. Tombor is a poggop. Does Tombor wear blue boots?" The corresponding inductive problem was "Tombor is a poggop. Tombor wears blue boots. Do all poggops wear blue boots?" Contrary to Piagetian theory, second-graders (but not kindergartners) were able to answer both kinds of problems correctly, to see the difference between them, and to explain their responses, and they (appropriately) expressed more confidence in their deductive answers than in their inductive ones (Galotti, Komatsu, & Voelz, 1997).

Conservation   In solving various types of conservation problems, children in the stage of concrete operations can work out the answers in their heads; they do not have to measure or weigh the objects.

If one of two identical clay balls is rolled or kneaded into a different shape, say, a long, thin "sausage," Felipe, who is in the stage of concrete operations, will say that the ball and the "sausage" still contain the same amount of clay. Stacy, who is in the preoperational stage, is deceived by appearances. She says the long, thin roll contains more clay because it looks longer.

Felipe, unlike Stacy, understands the principle of *identity:* He knows the clay is still the same clay, even though it has a different shape. He also understands the principle of *reversibility:* He knows he can change the sausage back into a ball. And he can *decenter:* He can focus on both length and width. He recognizes that although

class inclusion   Understanding of the relationship between a whole and its parts.

inductive reasoning   Type of logical reasoning that moves from particular observations about members of a class to a general conclusion about that class.

deductive reasoning   Type of logical reasoning that moves from a general premise about a class to a conclusion about a particular member or members of the class.

What's Your View?

• How can parents and teachers help children improve their reasoning ability?

the ball is shorter than the "sausage," it is also thicker. Stacy centers on one dimension (length) while excluding the other (thickness).

Typically, children can solve problems involving conservation of substance, like this one, by about age 7 or 8. However, in tasks involving conservation of weight—in which they are asked, for example, whether the ball and the "sausage" weigh the same—children typically do not give correct answers until about age 9 or 10. In tasks involving conservation of volume—in which children must judge whether the "sausage" and the ball displace an equal amount of liquid when placed in a glass of water—correct answers are rare before age 12.

Piaget's term for this inconsistency in the development of different types of conservation is *horizontal décalage* (refer back to Chapter 7). Children's thinking at this stage is so concrete, so closely tied to a particular situation, that they cannot readily transfer what they have learned about one type of conservation to another type, even though the underlying principles are the same.

Does one ball of clay displace more water than the other? A child who has achieved conservation of volume knows that the answer does not depend on the ball's shape.

Abilities such as conservation may depend in part on familiarity with the materials being manipulated; children can think more logically about things they know something about. Mexican children, who make pottery from an early age, understand that a clay ball that has been rolled into a coil still has the same amount of clay sooner than they understand other types of conservation (Broude, 1995). Thus, understanding of conservation may come not only from new patterns of mental organization, but also from culturally defined experience with the physical world.

Number and Mathematics   By age 6 or 7, many children can count in their heads. They also learn to *count on:* to add 5 and 3, they start counting at 5 and then go on to 6, 7, and 8 to add the 3. It may take two or three more years for them to perform a comparable operation for subtraction, but by age 9 most children can either count up from the smaller number or down from the larger number to get the answer (Resnick, 1989).

Children also become more adept at solving simple story problems, such as "Pedro went to the store with $5 and spent $2 on candy. How much did he have left?" When the original amount is unknown ("Pedro went to the store, spent $2 and had $3 left. How much did he start out with?"), the problem is harder because the operation needed to solve it (addition) is not as clearly indicated. Few children can solve this kind of problem before age 8 or 9 (Resnick, 1989).

Research with minimally schooled people in developing countries suggests that the ability to add develops nearly universally and often intuitively, through concrete experience in a cultural context (Guberman, 1996; Resnick, 1989). These intuitive procedures are different from those taught in school. In a study of Brazilian street vendors ages 9 to 15, a researcher acting as a customer said, "I'll take two coconuts." Each one cost 40 cruzeiros; she paid with a 500-cruzeiros bill and asked, "What do I get back?" The child counted up from 80: "Eighty, 90, 100 . . ." and gave the customer 420 cruzeiros. However, when this same child was given a similar problem in the classroom ("What is 500 minus 80?"), he arrived at the wrong answer by incorrectly using a series of steps learned in school (Carraher, Schliemann, & Carraher, 1988). This suggests that teaching math through concrete applications, not only through abstract rules, may be more effective.

Some intuitive understanding of fractions seems to exist by age 4 (Mix, Levine, & Huttenlocher, 1999), as children show when they deal a deck of cards or distribute portions of pizza (Frydman & Bryant, 1988; Sophian, Garyantes, & Chang, 1997). However, children tend not to think about the quantity a fraction represents; instead, they focus on the numerals that make it up. Thus, they may say that 1/2 plus 1/3 equals 2/5. Also difficult for many children to grasp at first is the fact that 1/2 is bigger than 1/4—that the smaller fraction (1/4) has the larger denominator (Siegler, 1998; Sophian & Wood, 1997).

The ability to estimate is important in many areas of daily life. How much time will I need to walk to school? How long will tonight's homework take? A study of 85 middle- and low-income schoolchildren found that estimating abilities progress with age (Siegler & Booth, 2004). When asked to place 24 numbers along a line from 0 to 100, almost all kindergartners exaggerated the differences between low numbers and minimized the distances between high numbers. Most second graders produced number lines that were more evenly spaced.

This developmental progression may result in part from the experience children gain in dealing with larger numbers in first and second grades as well as with board games in which they move a token in accordance with a number shown on a spinner or on dice. A study in which second-, fourth-, and sixth-graders placed numbers on a line from 0 to 1,000 found a similar progression, indicating that experience with this larger range of numbers increases accuracy of estimation (Siegler & Opfer, 2003).

Influences of Neurological Development and Processing Skills

Piaget maintained that the shift from the rigid, illogical thinking of younger children to the flexible, logical thinking of older ones depends on both neurological development and experience in adapting to the environment. Cross-cultural studies support the progression from preoperational to operational thought (Broude, 1995; Gardiner & Kosmitzki, 2005), lending support to a neurological influence. Additional support comes from scalp measurements of brain activity during a conservation task. Children who had achieved conservation of volume had different brain wave patterns from those who had not yet achieved it, suggesting that they may have been using different brain regions for the task (Stauder, Molenaar, & Van der Molen, 1993).

Improvements in information processing may help explain the advances Piaget described. For example, 9-year-olds may be better able than 5-year-olds to find their way to and from school because they can scan a scene, take in its important features, and remember objects in context in the order in which they were encountered (Allen & Ondracek, 1995).

Improvements in memory may contribute to the mastery of conservation tasks. Young children's working memory is so limited that they may not be able to remember all the relevant information (Siegler & Richards, 1982). They may forget, for example, that two differently shaped pieces of clay were originally identical. Gains in working memory may enable older children to solve such problems.

Robbie Case (1985, 1992), a neo-Piagetian theorist (refer back to Chapter 2), suggested that as a child's application of a concept or scheme becomes more automatic, it frees space in working memory to deal with new information. This may help explain horizontal décalage: Children may need to be able to use one type of conservation without conscious thought before they can extend that scheme to other types of conservation.

Checkpoint

Can you . . .

✔ Identify six types of cognitive abilities that emerge or strengthen during middle childhood, and explain how?

✔ Name three principles that help school-aged children understand conservation, and explain why children master different kinds of conservation at different ages?

✔ Give examples of how neurological development and improved processing skills can affect improvements in Piagetian tasks?

Moral Reasoning

To draw out children's moral thinking, Piaget (1932) would tell them a story about two little boys: "One day Augustus noticed that his father's inkpot was empty and decided to help his father by filling it. While he was opening the bottle, he spilled a lot of ink on the tablecloth. The other boy, Julian, played with his father's inkpot, even though he knew he shouldn't, and spilled a little ink on the cloth." Then Piaget would ask, "Which boy was naughtier, and why?"

Children younger than 7 usually considered Augustus naughtier, since he made the bigger stain. Older children recognized that Augustus meant well and made the large stain by accident, whereas Julian made a small stain while doing something he should not have been doing. Immature moral judgments, Piaget concluded, center only on the degree of offense; more mature judgments consider intent.

Piaget (1932; Piaget & Inhelder, 1969) proposed that moral reasoning develops in three stages. Children move gradually from one stage to another, at varying ages.

The first stage (approximately ages 2–7, corresponding with the preoperational stage) is based on obedience to authority. Young children think rigidly about moral concepts. Because they are egocentric, they cannot imagine more than one way of looking at a moral issue. They believe that rules come from adult authorities and cannot be bent or changed, that behavior is either right or wrong, and that any offense (like Augustus's) deserves punishment, regardless of intent.

The second stage (ages 7 or 8 to 10 or 11, corresponding with the stage of concrete operations) is characterized by increasing flexibility and some degree of autonomy based on mutual respect and cooperation. As children interact with more people and come into contact with a wider range of viewpoints, they begin to discard the idea that there is a single, absolute standard of right and wrong and to develop their own sense of justice based on fairness, or equal treatment for all. Because they can consider more than one aspect of a situation, they can make more subtle moral judgments, such as taking into consideration the intent behind Augustus's and Julian's behavior.

Around age 11 or 12, when children may become capable of formal reasoning (see Chapter 11), the third stage of moral development arrives. Now "equality" takes on a different meaning for the child. The belief that everyone should be treated alike gradually gives way to the idea of *equity*, of taking specific circumstances into account. Thus, a child of this age might say that a 2-year-old who spilled ink on the tablecloth should be held to a less demanding moral standard than a 10-year-old who did the same thing.

One aspect of moral reasoning is the ability to understand reciprocal obligations and to anticipate how a person might feel when a promise has been violated. In a pair of studies, 122 three- to 10-year-old Berliners responded to stories involving hypothetical violations of agreements ("If Maxi keeps his room tidy for two weeks, his mother will give him a bike for Christmas"). Children of all age levels understood that the victim of a broken promise would feel bad, but preschoolers and kindergartners were less likely than older children to recognize that the person breaking the promise might feel bad as well (Keller, Gummerum, Wang, & Lindsey, 2004).

Lawrence Kohlberg's theory of moral reasoning, which builds on Piaget's, is discussed in Chapter 11; Carol Gilligan's gender-based theory is discussed in Chapter 13.

Information Processing Approach: Memory and Other Processing Skills

As children move through the school years, they make steady progress in their abilities to process and retain information. Reaction time improves, and processing speed for such tasks as matching pictures, adding numbers in one's head,

What's Your View?

- Do you think intent is an important factor in morality? In what ways does the criminal justice system reflect or contradict this view?

Checkpoint
Can you . . .

✔ Summarize Piaget's three stages of moral development and explain their links to cognitive maturation?

Guidepost

4. What advances in memory and other information-processing skills occur during middle childhood?

Checkpoint

Can you . . .

✔ Identify four ways in which information processing improves during middle childhood?

and recalling spatial information increases rapidly as unneeded synapses in the brain are pruned away (Hale et al., 1997; Janowsky & Carper, 1996; Kail, 1991, 1997; Kail & Park, 1994). Faster, more efficient processing increases the amount of information a child can keep in working memory, making possible better recall and more complex, higher-level thinking (Flavell et al., 2002). School-age children also understand more about how memory works and can use strategies, or deliberate techniques, to help them remember. As their knowledge expands, they become more aware of what kinds of information are important to pay attention to and remember.

Metamemory: Understanding Memory

Between ages 5 and 7, the brain's frontal lobes undergo significant development and reorganization. These changes make improved recall and **metamemory,** knowledge about the processes of memory, possible (Janowsky & Carper, 1996). A related ability is **metacognition,** awareness of one's own thinking processes.

From kindergarten through fifth grade, children advance steadily in understanding memory (Flavell et al., 2002; Kreutzer, Leonard, & Flavell, 1975). Kindergartners and first-graders know that people remember better if they study longer, that people forget things with time, and that relearning something is easier than learning it for the first time. By third grade, children know that some people remember better than others and that some things are easier to remember than others.

One pair of experiments looked at preschoolers', first-graders', and third-graders' beliefs about what influences remembering and forgetting. Most children in all three age groups believed that important events in a story about a birthday party (such as a guest falling into the cake) were more likely to be retained than minor details (such as a guest bringing a ball as a present). Most first- and third-graders but not most preschoolers believed that a later experience (playing with a friend who was not at the party) might color a child's recollection of who was at the party. Not until third grade did most children recognize that memory can be distorted by suggestions from others—say, a parent who suggests that the friend was at the party (O'Sullivan, Howe, & Marche, 1996).

Mnemonics: Strategies for Remembering

Devices to aid memory are called **mnemonic strategies.** The most common mnemonic strategy among both children and adults is use of *external memory aids.* Other common mnemonic strategies are *rehearsal, organization,* and *elaboration.*

Writing down a telephone number, making a list, setting a timer, and putting a library book by the front door are examples of **external memory aids:** prompts by something outside the person. Saying a telephone number over and over after looking it up, so as not to forget it before dialing, is a form of **rehearsal,** or conscious repetition. **Organization** is mentally placing information into categories (such as animals, furniture, vehicles, and clothing) to make it easier to recall. In **elaboration,** children associate items with something else, such as an imagined scene or story. To remember to buy lemons, ketchup, and napkins, for example, a child might imagine a ketchup bottle balanced on a lemon, with a pile of napkins handy to wipe up spilled ketchup.

As children get older, they develop better strategies, use them more effectively, and tailor them to meet specific needs (Bjorklund, 1997; see Table 9-3). When taught to use a strategy, older children are more likely to apply it to other situations (Flavell et al., 2002). Children often use more than one strategy for a task and choose different kinds of strategies for different problems (Coyle & Bjorklund, 1997).

metamemory Understanding of processes of memory.

metacognition Awareness of a person's own mental processes.

mnemonic strategies Techniques to aid memory.

external memory aids Mnemonic strategies using something outside the person.

rehearsal Mnemonic strategy to keep an item in working memory through conscious repetition.

organization Mnemonic strategy of categorizing material to be remembered.

elaboration Mnemonic strategy of making mental associations involving items to be remembered.

Contestants in a spelling bee can make good use of mnemonic strategies—devices to aid memory—such as rehearsal (repetition), organization, and elaboration.

Selective Attention

School-age children can concentrate longer than younger children and can focus on the information they need and want while screening out irrelevant information. For example, they can summon up the appropriate meaning of a word they read and suppress other meanings that do not fit the context. Fifth-graders are better able than

Table 9-3	Four Common Memory Strategies		
Strategy	**Definition**	**Development in Middle Childhood**	**Example**
External memory aids	Prompting by something outside the person	5- and 6-year-olds can do this, but 8-year-olds are more likely to think of it.	Dana makes a list of the things she has to do today.
Rehearsal	Conscious repetition	6-year-olds can be taught to do this; 7-year-olds do it spontaneously.	Ian says the letters in his spelling words over and over until he knows them.
Organization	Grouping by categories	Most children do not do this until at least age 10, but younger children can be taught to do it.	Luis recalls the animals he saw in the zoo by thinking first of the mammals, then the reptiles, then the amphibians, then the fish, and then the birds.
Elaboration	Associating items to be remembered with something else, such as a phrase, scene, or story	Older children are more likely to do this spontaneously and remember better if they make up their own elaboration; younger children remember better if someone else makes it up.	Yolanda remembers the lines of the musical staff (E, G, B, D, F) by associating them with the phrase "*Every good boy does fine.*"

Checkpoint

Can you . . .

✔ Name four common mnemonic aids and discuss developmental differences in their use?

✔ Explain the importance of metamemory and selective attention?

Otis-Lennon School Ability Test Group intelligence test for kindergarten through twelfth grade.

Wechsler Intelligence Scale for Children (WISC-III) Individual intelligence test for school-age children, which yields verbal and performance scores as well as a combined score.

first-graders to keep discarded information from reentering working memory and vying with other material for attention (Harnishfeger & Pope, 1996).

This growing capacity for selective attention is believed to be due to neurological maturation and is one of the reasons memory improves during middle childhood (Bjorklund & Harnishfeger, 1990; Harnishfeger & Bjorklund, 1993). Older children may make fewer mistakes in recall than younger ones because they are better able to select what they want to remember and what they can forget (Lorsbach & Reimer, 1997).

Psychometric Approach: Assessment of Intelligence

Psychometric intelligence tests for school-age children can be administered to groups, such as a whole class, or individually. One popular group test, the **Otis-Lennon School Ability Test,** has levels for kindergarten through twelfth grade. Children are asked to classify items, to show an understanding of verbal and numerical concepts, to display general information, and to follow directions. Separate scores for verbal comprehension, verbal reasoning, pictorial reasoning, figural reasoning, and quantitative reasoning can identify strengths and weaknesses.

The most widely used individual test is the **Wechsler Intelligence Scale for Children (WISC-III).** This test for ages 6 through 16 measures verbal and performance abilities, yielding separate scores for each, as well as a total score. Another commonly used individual test is the Stanford-Binet Intelligence Scale, described in Chapter 7. A child's score on any of these tests is compared with *standardized norms*—standards obtained from the scores of a large, representative sample of children of the same age.

The IQ Controversy

The use of psychometric intelligence tests is controversial. On the positive side, because IQ tests have been standardized and widely used, there is extensive information about their validity and reliability (refer back to Chapter 2). IQ scores taken during middle childhood are fairly good predictors of school achievement, especially for highly verbal children, and scores are more reliable than during the preschool years. IQ at age 11 even has been found to predict length of life and the presence or absence of functional independence and dementia in late adulthood (Starr, Deary, Lemmon, & Whalley, 2000; Whalley & Deary, 2001; Whalley et al., 2000).

But are IQ tests really valid? Critics claim that the tests underestimate the intelligence of children who are in ill health (Sternberg, 2004) or, for one reason or another, do not do well on tests (Anastasi, 1988; Ceci, 1991). Because the tests are timed, they equate intelligence with speed and penalize a child who works slowly and deliberately. Their appropriateness for diagnosing learning disabilities has been questioned (Benson, 2003).

A more fundamental criticism is that IQ tests do not directly measure native ability; instead, they infer intelligence from what children already know. As we'll see, it is virtually impossible to design a test that requires no prior knowledge (Sternberg, 2004). Further, the tests are validated against measures of achievement, such as school performance, which are affected by such factors as schooling and culture. There is also controversy over whether intelligence is a single, general ability or whether there are types of intelligence not captured by IQ tests. For these and other reasons, there is strong disagreement over how accurately these tests assess children's intelligence.

Influence of Schooling Schooling does seem to increase tested intelligence (Ceci & Williams, 1997; Neisser et al., 1996). Children whose school entrance was significantly delayed (as happened, for example, in South Africa due to a teacher shortage and in the Netherlands during the Nazi occupation) lost as many as 5 IQ points each year, and some of these losses were never recovered (Ceci & Williams, 1997). IQ scores also drop during summer vacation (Ceci & Williams, 1997). Among a national sample of 1,500 children, language, spatial, and conceptual scores improved much more between October and April, the bulk of the school year, than between April and October, which includes summer vacation and the beginning and end of the school year (Huttenlocher, Levine, & Vevea, 1998).

Influences of Race/Ethnicity and Culture   Average test scores vary among racial or ethnic groups, inspiring claims that the tests are unfair to minorities. Although some African Americans score higher than most whites, black children, on average, score about 15 points lower than white children and show a comparable lag on school achievement tests. Average IQ scores of Hispanic children fall between those of black and white children, and their scores, too, tend to predict school achievement. Yet Asian Americans, whose scholastic achievements consistently outstrip those of other ethnic groups, do not seem to have a significant edge in IQ—a reminder of the limited predictive power of intelligence testing (Neisser et al., 1996). Instead, as we'll see later in this chapter, Asian American children's strong scholastic achievement seems to be best explained by cultural factors.

What accounts for ethnic differences in IQ? Although there is strong evidence of a genetic influence on individual differences in intelligence within a population, there is *no* direct evidence that average differences among ethnic, cultural, or racial groups are hereditary (Neisser et al., 1996; Sternberg et al., 2005). Many studies attribute ethnic differences in IQ to inequalities in environment (Nisbett, 1998)—in income, nutrition, living conditions, health, parenting practices, early child care, intellectual stimulation, schooling, culture, or other circumstances such as the effects of oppression and discrimination that can affect self-esteem, motivation, and academic performance. Environmental differences affect readiness for school (Rouse et al., 2005), which, in turn, affects measured intelligence as well as achievement.

The strength of genetic influence itself appears to vary with socioeconomic status. In a longitudinal study of 319 pairs of twins followed from birth, the genetic influence on IQ scores at age 7 among children from impoverished families was close to zero and the influence of environment was strong, whereas among children in affluent families the opposite was true. In other words, the genetic influence was accentuated in more favorable environments (Turkheimer, Haley, Waldron, D'Onofrio, & Gottesman, 2003). The IQ and achievement test gaps between white and black Americans appear to be narrowing as the life circumstances and educational opportunities of many African American children improve. However, although socioeconomic status and IQ are strongly correlated, SES does not seem to explain the entire intergroup variance in IQ (Neisser et al., 1996; Suzuki & Valencia, 1997).

Some critics attribute ethnic differences in IQ to **cultural bias:** a tendency to include questions that use vocabulary or call for information or skills more familiar or meaningful to some cultural groups than to others (Sternberg, 1985a, 1987). These critics argue that intelligence tests are built around the dominant thinking style and language of white people of European ancestry, putting minority children at a disadvantage (Heath, 1989; Helms, 1992). Cultural bias also may affect the testing situation. For example, a child from a culture that stresses sociability and cooperation may be handicapped taking a test alone (Kottak, 1994). Still, although cultural bias may play a part in some children's performance, controlled studies have failed to show that it contributes substantially to overall group differences in IQ (Neisser et al., 1996).

Test developers have tried to design **culture-free** tests—tests with no culture-linked content—by posing tasks that do not require language, such as tracing mazes,

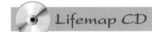

Lifemap CD

The video, "Parental Influence on Children's IQ," in Chapter 9 of your CD explores one researcher's findings on this controversial topic.

cultural bias   Tendency of intelligence tests to include items calling for knowledge or skills more familiar or meaningful to some cultural groups than to others.

culture-free   Describing an intelligence test that, if it were possible to design, would have no culturally linked content.

culture-fair Describing an intelligence test that deals with experiences common to various cultures, in an attempt to avoid cultural bias.

culture-relevant Describing an intelligence test that would draw on and adjust for culturally related content.

Checkpoint

Can you . . .

✔ Name and describe two traditional intelligence tests for schoolchildren?

✔ Give arguments for and against IQ tests?

✔ Assess explanations that have been given for differences in the performance of children of various ethnic and cultural groups on intelligence tests?

putting the right shapes in the right holes, and completing pictures; but they have been unable to eliminate all cultural influences. Test designers also have found it virtually impossible to produce **culture-fair** tests consisting only of experiences common to people in various cultures.

Robert Sternberg (2004) maintains that intelligence and culture are inextricably linked. Behavior seen as intelligent in one culture may be viewed as foolish in another. For example, when given a sorting task, North Americans would be likely to place a robin under the category of birds, whereas the Kpelle people in North Africa would consider it more intelligent to place the robin in a functional category (flying things) (Cole, 1998). Thus a test of intelligence developed in one culture may not be equally valid in another. Furthermore, the schooling offered in a culture may prepare a child to do well in certain tasks and not others; and the competencies taught and tested in school are not necessarily the same as the practical skills needed to succeed in everyday life (Sternberg, 2004).

Sternberg (2004) defines *successful intelligence* as the skills and knowledge needed for success within a particular social and cultural context. The mental processes that underlie intelligence may be the same across cultures, says Sternberg, but their products may be different—and so should the means of assessing performance. Sternberg proposes **culture-relevant** tests that take into account the adaptive tasks that confront children in various cultures.

Is There More Than One Intelligence?

A serious criticism of IQ tests is that they focus almost entirely on abilities that are useful in school. They do *not* assess other important aspects of intelligent behavior, such as common sense, social skills, creative insight, and self-knowledge. Yet these abilities, in which some children with modest academic skills excel, may become equally or more important in later life (Gardner, 1993; Sternberg, 1985a, 1987, 2004) and may even be considered separate forms of intelligence. Two of the chief advocates of this position are Robert Sternberg and Howard Gardner.

triarchic theory of intelligence Sternberg's theory describing three types of intelligence: componential, experiential, and contextual.

componential element Sternberg's term for the analytic aspect of intelligence.

experiential element Sternberg's term for the insightful or creative aspect of intelligence.

contextual element Sternberg's term for the practical aspect of intelligence.

Sternberg's Triarchic Theory of Intelligence Sternberg's (1985a, 2004) **triarchic theory of intelligence** embraces three elements, or aspects, of intelligence: *componential, experiential,* and *contextual.*

- The **componential element** is the *analytic* aspect of intelligence; it determines how efficiently people process information. It tells people how to solve problems, how to monitor solutions, and how to evaluate the results.

- The **experiential element** is *insightful* or *creative;* it determines how people approach novel or familiar tasks. It allows people to compare new information with what they already know and to come up with new ways of putting facts together—in other words, to think originally.

- The **contextual element** is *practical;* it determines how people deal with their environment. It is the ability to size up a situation and decide what to do: adapt to it, change it, or get out of it.

According to Sternberg, everyone has these three kinds of abilities to a greater or lesser extent. A person may be strong in one, two, or all three. Conventional IQ tests measure mainly componential ability; and since this ability is the kind most school tasks require in western societies, it's not surprising that the tests are fairly good predictors of school performance. Their failure to measure experiential (insightful or creative) and contextual (practical) intelligence, says Sternberg, may explain why they are less useful in predicting success in the outside world. In studies in Usenge, Kenya and among Yup'ik Eskimo children in southwestern Alaska, children's

tacit knowledge of such practical matters as medicinal herbs, hunting, fishing, and preserving plants—information gleaned informally, not explicitly taught—showed no correlation with conventional measures of intelligence (Grigorenko et al., in press; Sternberg, 2004; Sternberg et al., 2001).

The **Sternberg Triarchic Abilities Test (STAT)** (Sternberg, 1993) seeks to measure each of the three aspects of intelligence—analytic, creative, and practical—through multiple-choice and essay questions in three domains: *verbal, quantitative,* and *figural* (or spatial). For example, a test of practical-quantitative intelligence might be to solve an everyday math problem having to do with buying tickets to a ball game or following a recipe for making cookies. A creative-verbal item might ask children to solve deductive reasoning problems that start with factually false premises (such as, "Money falls off trees"). An analytical-figural item might ask children to identify the missing piece of a figure.

Preliminary validation has found correlations with several other tests of critical thinking, creativity, and practical problem solving. As predicted, the three kinds of abilities are only weakly correlated with each other (Sternberg, 1997; Sternberg & Clinkenbeard, 1995).

Gardner's Theory of Multiple Intelligences Is a child who is good at analyzing paragraphs and making analogies more intelligent than someone who can play a difficult violin solo, or someone who can organize a closet or design a group project, or someone who can pitch a curve ball at the right time? The answer is no, according to Gardner's (1993) **theory of multiple intelligences.**

Gardner, a neuropsychologist and educational researcher at Harvard University, originally identified seven distinct types of intelligence. According to Gardner, conventional intelligence tests tap only three "intelligences": linguistic, logical-mathematical, and, to some extent, spatial. The other four, which are not reflected in IQ scores, are musical, bodily-kinesthetic, interpersonal, and intrapersonal. Gardner (1998) recently added an eighth type, naturalist intelligence. (Table 9-4 gives definitions of each intelligence and examples of fields in which it most useful.)

According to Howard Gardner, musical ability—which includes the ability to perceive and create patterns of pitch and rhythm—is one of several separate kinds of intelligence.

High intelligence in one area does not necessarily accompany high intelligence in any of the others. A person may be extremely gifted in art (a spatial ability), precision of movement (bodily-kinesthetic), social relations (interpersonal), or self-understanding (intrapersonal), but not have a high IQ. Thus Albert Einstein, the poet Gwendolyn Brooks, and the cellist Pablo Casals may have been equally intelligent, each in a different area.

Gardner (1995) would assess each intelligence directly by observing its products—how well a child can tell a story, remember a melody, or get around in a strange area—and not by standardized tests. To monitor spatial ability, for example, the examiner might hide an object from a 1-year-old, ask a 6-year-old to do a jigsaw puzzle, and give a Rubik's cube to a preadolescent. The purpose would be, not to compare individuals, but to reveal strengths and weaknesses so as to help children realize their potential. Of course, such assessments would be far more time-consuming and more open to observer bias than paper-and-pencil tests.

Other New Directions in Intelligence Testing

Some new diagnostic and predictive tools are based on neurological research and information-processing theory. The second edition of the **Kaufman Assessment**

tacit knowledge Sternberg's term for information that is not formally taught, or openly expressed but is necessary to function successfully.

Sternberg Triarchic Abilities Test (STAT) Test that seeks to measure componential, experiential, and contextual intelligence.

theory of multiple intelligences Gardner's theory that each person has several distinct forms of intelligence.

What's Your View?

- Which of Sternberg's and Gardner's types of intelligence are you strongest in?

- Did your education include a focus on any of these aspects?

Table 9-4 Eight Intelligences, According to Gardner

Intelligence	Definition	Fields or Occupations Where Used
Linguistic	Ability to use and understand words and nuances of meaning	Writing, editing, translating
Logical-mathematical	Ability to manipulate numbers and solve logical problems	Science, business, medicine
Spatial	Ability to find one's way around in an environment and judge relationships between objects in space	Architecture, carpentry, city planning
Musical	Ability to perceive and create patterns of pitch and rhythm	Musical composition, conducting
Bodily-kinesthetic	Ability to move with precision	Dancing, athletics, surgery
Interpersonal	Ability to understand and communicate with others	Teaching, acting, politics
Intrapersonal	Ability to understand the self	Counseling, psychiatry, spiritual leadership
Naturalist	Ability to distinguish species and their characteristics	Hunting, fishing, farming, gardening, cooking

Source: Based on Gardner, 1993, 1998.

Kaufman Assessment Battery for Children (K-ABC) Nontraditional individual intelligence test designed to provide fair assessments of minority children and children with disabilities.

Battery for Children (K-ABC-II) (Kaufman & Kaufman, 1983, 2003), an individual test for ages 3 to 18, is designed to evaluate cognitive abilities in children with diverse needs (such as autism, hearing impairments, and language disorders) and from varying cultural and linguistic backgrounds. It has subtests designed to minimize verbal instructions and responses as well as items with limited cultural content. The norm sample closely matches 2001 census data with respect to race/ethnicity, gender, SES, region, and special education status. The KABC-II offers a choice of interpretive scales based on two different theoretical models: one that focuses solely on mental processing abilities and a second that includes memory, visual processing, reasoning, and acquired knowledge. There is also a nonverbal index for children whose language skills are severely limited.

Dynamic tests based on Vygotsky's theories emphasize potential rather than present achievement. In contrast with traditional "static" tests that measure a child's current abilities, these tests seek to capture the dynamic nature of intelligence by measuring learning processes directly rather than through the products of past learning (Sternberg, 2004). Dynamic tests contain items up to two years above a child's current level of competence. Examiners help the child when necessary by asking leading questions, giving examples or demonstrations, and offering feedback; thus, the test itself is a learning situation. The difference between the items a child can answer alone and the items the child can answer with help is the child's zone of proximal development (ZPD).

Vygotsky (1956) gives an example of two children, each with a mental age of 7 years (based on ability to do various cognitive tasks). With the sort of help just described, Natasha can easily solve problems geared to a mental age of 9, two years beyond her current mental age, but Ivan, with the same kind of help, can reach only a 7½-year-old level. If we measure these children by what they can do on their own (as traditional IQ tests do), their intelligence seems about the same; but if we measure them by their immediate potential development (their ZPD), we can see that their aptitude is quite different.

By pointing to what a child is ready to learn, dynamic testing may give teachers more useful information than does a psychometric test and can aid in designing interventions to help children progress. It can be particularly effective with disadvantaged

What's Your View?

• If you were a teacher in the primary grades, would you rather know a pupil's IQ or ZPD?

Checkpoint

Can you . . .

✔ Compare Sternberg's and Gardner's theories of intelligence and the specific abilities proposed by each?

✔ Identify several new directions in intelligence testing?

✔ Explain the difference between dynamic testing and traditional psychometric testing?

children (Grigorinko & Sternberg, 1998; Rutland & Campbell, 1996). However, the ZPD is quite labor-intensive and may be difficult to measure precisely.

Language and Literacy

Language abilities continue to grow during middle childhood. School-age children are better able to understand and interpret oral and written communication and to make themselves understood.

Guidepost

6. How do communicative abilities and literacy expand during middle childhood?

Vocabulary, Grammar, and Syntax

As vocabulary grows, children use increasingly precise verbs to describe an action (*hitting, slapping, striking, pounding*). They learn that a word like *run* can have more than one meaning, and they can tell from the context which meaning is intended. They can use many more words and can select the right word for a particular use. *Simile* and *metaphor*, figures of speech in which a word or phrase that usually designates one thing is compared or applied to another, become increasingly common (Owens, 1996; Vosniadou, 1987). Although grammar is quite complex by age 6, children during the early school years rarely use the passive voice (as in "The sidewalk is being shoveled"), verb tenses that include the auxiliary *have* ("I have already shoveled the sidewalk"), and conditional sentences ("If Barbara were home, she would help shovel the sidewalk") (C. S. Chomsky, 1969).

Up to and possibly after age 9, children's understanding of rules of *syntax* (how words are organized into phrases and sentences) becomes more sophisticated, and sentence structure becomes more elaborate. Older children use more subordinate clauses ("The boy *who delivers the newspapers* rang the doorbell"), and they look at the semantic effect of a sentence as a whole, rather than focus on word order as a signal of meaning. Still, some constructions, such as clauses beginning with *however* and *although,* are not common until early adolescence (Owens, 1996).

Pragmatics: Knowledge about Communication

The major area of linguistic growth during the school years is in **pragmatics:** the practical use of language to communicate.* Pragmatics includes both conversational and narrative skills.

pragmatics Set of linguistic rules that govern the use of language for communication.

Good conversationalists probe by asking questions before introducing a topic with which the other person may not be familiar. They quickly recognize a breakdown in communication and do something to repair it. There are wide individual differences in such skills; some 7-year-olds are better conversationalists than some adults (Anderson, Clark, & Mullin, 1994). There are also gender differences. In one study, 120 middle-class London fourth-graders were paired up to solve a mathematical problem. When boys and girls worked together, boys tended to use more controlling statements and to utter more negative interruptions, whereas girls phrased their remarks in a more tentative, conciliatory way. Children's communication was more collaborative when working with a partner of their own sex (Leman, Ahmed, & Ozarow, 2005).

When first-graders tell stories, they usually do not make them up; they are more likely to relate a personal experience. Most 6-year-olds can retell the plot of a short book, movie, or television show. They are beginning to describe motives and causal links. By second grade, children's stories become longer and more complex. Fictional tales often have conventional beginnings and endings ("Once upon a time . . ." and "They lived happily ever after," or simply "The end"). Word use is more varied than before, but characters do not show growth or change, and plots are not fully developed.

*This section is largely indebted to Owens (1996).

Older children usually "set the stage" with introductory information about the setting and characters, and they clearly indicate changes of time and place during the story. They construct more complex episodes than younger children do, but with less unnecessary detail. They focus more on the characters' motives and thoughts, and they think through how to resolve problems in the plot.

Literacy

Learning to read and write frees children from the constraints of face-to-face communication, giving them access to the ideas and imagination of people in faraway lands and long-ago times. Once children can translate the marks on a page into patterns of sound and meaning, they can develop increasingly sophisticated strategies to understand what they read; and they can use written words to express ideas, thoughts, and feelings.

decoding Process of phonetic analysis by which a printed word is converted to spoken form before retrieval from long-term memory.

visually based retrieval Process of retrieving the sound of a printed word upon seeing the word as a whole.

phonetic, or code-emphasis approach Approach to teaching reading that emphasizes decoding of unfamiliar words.

whole-language approach Approach to teaching reading that emphasizes visual retrieval and use of contextual clues.

Reading   Children can identify a printed word in two ways. One is called **decoding:** The child "sounds out" the word, translating it from print to speech before retrieving it from long-term memory. To do this, the child must master the phonetic code that matches the printed alphabet to spoken sounds. The second method is **visually based retrieval:** The child simply looks at the word and then retrieves it. These two methods form the core of two contrasting approaches to reading instruction. The traditional approach, which emphasizes decoding, is called the **phonetic, or code emphasis approach.** The more recent **whole-language approach** emphasizes visual retrieval and the use of contextual cues.

The whole-language approach is based on the belief that children can learn to read and write naturally, much as they learn to understand and use speech. Whole-language proponents assert that children learn to read with better comprehension (understanding) and more enjoyment if they experience written language from the outset as a way to gain information and express ideas and feelings, not as a system of isolated sounds and syllables to be learned by memorization and drill. In contrast with the rigorous, teacher-directed tasks involved in phonics instruction, whole-language programs feature real literature and open-ended, student-initiated activities.

Although the whole-language approach is widely used, research has found little support for its claims. Critics say that whole-language teaching encourages children to skim through a text, guessing at words and their meaning, without trying to correct reading or spelling errors. Many experts recommend a blend of both approaches: teaching children phonetic skills along with strategies to help them understand what they read (National Reading Panel, 2000). Children who can summon both visually based and phonetic strategies, using visual retrieval for familiar words and phonetic decoding for unfamiliar words, become better, more versatile readers (Siegler, 1998). The developmental processes that improve comprehension are similar to those that improve memory. As word identification becomes more automatic and the capacity of working memory increases, children can focus on the meaning of what they read and can adjust their speed and attentiveness to the importance and difficulty of the material. As children's store of knowledge increases, they can more readily check new information against what they already know (Siegler, 1998). Metacognition helps children monitor their comprehension and develop strategies to clear up any problems—such strategies as reading slowly, rereading difficult passages, trying to visualize information, and thinking of examples. Having students recall, summarize, and ask questions about what they read can enhance comprehension (National Reading Panel, 2000).

Writing   The acquisition of writing skills goes hand in hand with the development of reading. Older preschoolers begin using letters, numbers, and letterlike shapes as symbols to represent words or parts of words—syllables or phonemes. Often their spelling is quite inventive—so much so that they may not be able to read it themselves (Whitehurst & Lonigan, 1998).

Writing is difficult for young children, and early compositions usually are quite short. Unlike conversation, which offers constant feedback, writing requires the child to judge independently whether the goal has been met. The child also must keep in mind a variety of other constraints: spelling, punctuation, grammar, and capitalization, as well as the physical task of forming letters (Siegler, 1998).

In the typical classroom, children are discouraged from discussing their work with other children in the belief that they will distract one another. Research based on Vygotsky's social interaction model of language development suggests that this is not so. In one study, fourth-graders working in pairs wrote stories with more solutions to problems, more explanations and goals, and fewer errors in syntax and word use than did children working alone (Daiute, Hartup, Sholl, & Zajac, 1993).

Efforts to improve the teaching of reading and writing seem to be paying off. The National Assessment of Educational Progress in 2002 and 2003 found significant improvements in the proportions of fourth- and eighth-graders who read and write proficiently. Still, fewer than one-third of students in both grades read and write at that level (NCES, 2004a). In national and international assessments, girls tend to outperform boys in reading and writing (Freeman, 2004).

What's Your View?

- Why might social interaction improve children's writing?

Checkpoint

Can you . . .

✔ Summarize improvements in language skills during middle childhood?

✔ Compare the phonetic and whole-language methods of teaching reading, and discuss how comprehension improves?

✔ Explain why writing is hard for young children?

The Child in School

School is a major formative experience, affecting every aspect of development. In school, children gain knowledge, skills, and social competence, stretch their bodies and minds, and prepare for adult life. Worldwide, more children are going to school than ever before. In highly developed countries such as the United States, Canada, France, Germany, Italy, Japan, and the United Kingdom, participation in elementary education is almost universal (Sen, Partelow, & Miller, 2005). Worldwide, however, 103.5 million primary-age children—57 percent of them girls—are *not* in school, and in nearly one-third of 91 countries reporting, less than 75 percent of students reach fifth grade (UNESCO, 2004).

 Guidepost

7. What influences school achievement?

The earliest school experiences are critical in setting the stage for future success or failure. Let's look at the first-grade experience and at influences on school achievement. Then we'll consider how schools educate children who are not native English speakers, children with learning problems, and those who are identified as gifted.

Entering First Grade

Even today, when nearly 3 out of 4 U.S. children go to kindergarten (NCES, 2004a), children often approach the start of first grade with a mixture of eagerness and anxiety. The first day of "regular" school is a milestone—a sign of the developmental advances that make this new status possible.

To make the most academic progress, a child needs to be involved in what is going on in class. The better first-graders feel about their academic skills, the more engaged they tend to be; and the harder children work in school, the more self-confidence they develop (Valeski & Stipek, 2001). Interest, attention, and active participation are positively associated with achievement test scores and, even more so, with teachers' marks from first grade through at least fourth grade (K. L. Alexander, Entwisle, & Dauber, 1993).

Extracurricular activities are important too. In a large-scale prospective longitudinal study, children who, during kindergarten and first grade,

Children who participate actively tend to do well in school.

consistently participated in organized sports, music and dance lessons, or clubs scored better on standardized tests of prereading and math skills near the end of first grade (NICHD Early Childhood Research Network, 2004a).

Influences on School Achievement

As Bronfenbrenner's bioecological theory would predict, in addition to children's own characteristics, each level of the context of their lives—from the immediate family to what goes on in the classroom to the messages children receive from peers and from the larger culture (such as "It's not cool to be smart")—influences how well they do in school. Let's look at this web of influences.

The Child: Self-Efficacy Beliefs and Gender   According to Albert Bandura's social cognitive theory (Bandura, Barbaranelli, Caprara, & Pastorelli, 1996; Zimmerman, Bandura, & Martinez-Pons, 1992), students high in *self-efficacy*—who believe that they can master schoolwork and regulate their own learning—are more likely to try to achieve and more likely to succeed than students who do not believe in their own abilities. It was Ann Bancroft's self-efficacy that helped her get through school despite her learning disability.

Girls tend to do better in school than boys; they are less likely to repeat grades, have fewer school problems, and, as we have noted, outperform boys in national reading and writing assessments. Girls do about as well as boys in math and science, but boys tend to like those subjects better (Freeman, 2004).

Parenting Practices   Parents of achieving children create an environment for learning. They provide a place to study and to keep books and supplies; they set times for meals, sleep, and homework; they monitor how much television their children watch and what their children do after school; and they show interest in their children's lives by talking with them about school and being involved in school activities. Children whose parents are involved in their schools do better in school (Hill & Taylor, 2004).

How do parents motivate children to do well? Some use *extrinsic* (external) means—giving children money or treats for good grades or punishing them for bad ones. Others encourage children to develop *intrinsic* (internal) motivation by praising them for ability and hard work. Intrinsic motivation seems more effective. In a study of 77 third- and fourth-graders, those who were interested in the work itself did better in school than those who mainly sought grades or parents' approval (Miserandino, 1996).

Parenting styles may affect motivation. In one study, the highest-achieving fifth-graders had *authoritative* parents. These children were curious and interested in learning; they liked challenging tasks and enjoyed solving problems by themselves. *Authoritarian* parents, who kept after children to do their homework, supervised closely, and relied on extrinsic motivation, tended to have lower-achieving children. So did children of *permissive* parents,

A parent's attitude about the importance of homework tends to "rub off" on a child. A parent whose child is motivated to achieve does not need to bribe or threaten to make sure that homework gets done.

who were uninvolved and did not seem to care how the children did in school (G. S. Ginsburg & Bronstein, 1993).

Socioeconomic Status Socioeconomic status can be a powerful factor in educational achievement—not in and of itself, but through its influence on such factors as family atmosphere, choice of neighborhood, and parenting practices (Evans, 2004; National Research Council [NRC], 1993a; Rouse et al., 2005). Children of poor parents are more likely to experience negative home and school atmospheres, stressful events, and unstable, chaotic households (Evans, 2004; Felner et al., 1995). They tend to live in deteriorating, dangerous neighborhoods and to go to low-quality schools (Evans, 2004; Pong, 1997). SES can affect parents' ability to provide an environment that enhances learning (G. H. Brody, Stoneman, & Flor, 1995; G. H. Brody, Flor, & Gibson, 1999; Rouse et al., 2005). In a nationally representative study of children who entered kindergarten in 1998 (refer back to Chapter 7), achievement gaps between advantaged and disadvantaged students widened during the first four years of schooling (Rathbun, West, & Germino-Hausken, 2004).

However, SES is not the only factor in achievement. In a longitudinal study, children whose home environment at age 8 was cognitively stimulating showed higher intrinsic motivation for academic learning at ages 9, 10, and 13 than children who lived in less stimulating homes. This was true over and above effects of SES (Gottfried, Fleming, & Gottfried, 1998).

Why do some young people from disadvantaged homes and neighborhoods do well in school and improve their condition in life? What may make the difference is **social capital**: the networks of community resources children and families can draw upon (J. S. Coleman, 1988). In a three-year experimental intervention in which working poor parents received wage supplements and subsidies for child care and health insurance, their school-age sons' academic achievement and behavior improved (Huston et al., 2001). Both boys and girls in low-income families seem to benefit academically from the more favorable environment a working mother's income can provide (Chase-Lansdale et al., 2003; Goldberg, Greenberger, & Nagel, 1996; Vandell & Ramanan, 1992).

social capital Family and community resources on which a person can draw.

Checkpoint
Can you . . .

✔ Tell how self-efficacy beliefs and parenting practices can influence school success?

✔ Discuss the impact of socioeconomic status on school achievement?

The Educational System How can school best enhance children's development? Throughout the 20th century, conflicting educational philosophies, along with historical events, brought great swings in educational theory and practice—from the "three R's" (reading, 'riting, and 'rithmetic) to "child-centered" methods that focused on children's interests and then, when competition from Russia and, later, from Japan loomed and standardized test scores plummeted, back to the "basics." In the 1980s, a series of governmental and educational commissions proposed plans for improvement, ranging from more homework (see Box 9-2) to a longer school day and school year to a total reorganization of schools and curricula.

In 2001, Congress adopted the No Child Left Behind (NCLB) Act, a sweeping educational reform emphasizing accountability, parental options, and expanded local control and flexibility. The intent is to funnel federal funding to research-based programs and practices, with special emphasis on reading and mathematics. Students in grades 3 through 8 are tested annually to see if they are meeting statewide progress objectives. Children in schools that fail to meet state standards can transfer to another school. Critics, such as the National Education Association (NEA), a national teachers' organization, claim that NCLB emphasizes punishment rather than assistance for failing schools; rigid, largely unfunded mandates rather than support for proven practices; and standardized testing rather than teacher-led, classroom-focused solutions. More than 50 national education, civil rights, children's, and citizens

BOX 9-2

Practically Speaking
The Homework Debate

Historical swings in homework use have reflected shifts in educational philosophy in the United States (Cooper, 1989; Gill & Schlossman, 1996). During the 19th century, the mind was considered a muscle, and homework a means of exercising it. But antihomework crusaders argued that assignments lasting far into the evening endangered children's physical and emotional health and interfered with family life. By the 1940s, "progressive," child-centered education had become popular and homework had lost favor. A number of states and school districts banned it (Gill & Schlossman, 1996). In the 1950s, when the Soviet Union's Sputnik launch brought calls for more rigorous science and math education, and again in the early 1980s, amid worries about the United States' competitive position toward Japan, "More homework!" became a battle cry in campaigns to upgrade U.S. educational standards (Cooper, 1989).

Homework advocates claim that it disciplines the mind, develops good work habits, improves retention, and enables students to cover more ground than they could in the classroom alone. Homework is a bridge between home and school, increasing parental involvement. Opponents claim that too much homework leads to boredom, anxiety, or frustration; puts unnecessary pressure on children; discourages intrinsic motivation; and usurps time from other worthwhile activities. They say that parental "help" can be counterproductive if parents become overly intrusive or use teaching methods that conflict with those used at school (Cooper, 1989). Once again, some critics (Kralovec & Buell, 2000) want to ban homework, at least for young children.

Research supports a balanced view, recognizing that homework can improve achievement but also has costs (Larson & Verma, 1999). A comprehensive review of nearly 120 studies found that, although homework has strong benefits for high school students, it has only moderate benefits for junior high school students (and then only if limited to two hours a night), and virtually no benefits for elementary school students as compared with in-class study. Homework seems to work best when assignments are not overly complicated or completely unfamiliar, when material is spread out over several assignments, and when the need for parental involvement is kept to a minimum (Cooper, 1989).

Junior high and high school students who spend more time on homework tend to get better grades (Cooper et al., 1998; Cooper, Valentine, Nye, & Lindsay, 1999), but this is less true at the elementary level. In a survey of 709 second- through twelfth-graders, about one-third of lower-grade students said they typically did not finish their homework. Even in the upper grades, students who received lengthy assignments tended not to complete them (Cooper et al., 1998).

Research-based homework recommendations range from one to three 15-minute assignments a week in the primary grades to four or five assignments a week, each lasting 75 to 120 minutes, in grades 10 to 12. Instead of grading homework, teachers should use it to diagnose learning problems (Cooper, 1989).

Homework, then, has value—but only in moderation and when geared to students' developmental levels. For young children, it can develop good study habits and an understanding that learning can take place at home as well as in school. In junior high, a mix of mandatory and voluntary homework can promote academic goals and motivate children to pursue studies that interest them. In high school, homework can provide opportunities for practice, review, and integration of what is being learned at school (Cooper, 1989).

What's Your View?

How much homework do you think is appropriate for children of various ages?

Check It Out

For more information on this topic, go to http://nces.ed.gov. This is the site of the National Center for Education Statistics.

What's Your View?

- Which approach to education do you favor for children in the primary grades: instruction in the "basics," a more flexible, child-centered curriculum, or a combination of the two?

groups have called for substantial changes in NCLB, and the NEA has sued the Bush administration for failure to pay for programs mandated under the act.

Meanwhile, in 2003, U.S. fourth- and eighth-graders scored well above average in an international math and science assessment. The eighth-graders did better than their counterparts in the 1990s, but the fourth-grade scores showed no improvement. However, achievement gaps between white and black students at both grade levels narrowed (Gonzales et al., 2004). Also, U.S. fourth-graders scored higher than their counterparts in any of eight other industrialized countries except England on an international literacy test (Sen, Partelow, & Miller, 2005).*

The School Environment Children learn better and teachers teach better in a comfortable, healthful environment. Adequate air quality, temperature, humidity, lighting, and acoustics improve student performance. Yet such facilities are substandard in many aging U.S. schools. The size of a school matters, too; students generally do

*The other countries were Canada, France, Germany, Italy, Japan, and the Russian Federation.

best in elementary schools of about 300 to 400 students and high schools of no more than 1,000 (Schneider, 2002).

Most educators consider small class size a key factor, especially in the early grades, though findings on this point are mixed (Schneider, 2002). A longitudinal study involving 11,600 kindergarten and primary students in Tennessee public elementary schools found lasting academic benefits for students randomly assigned to very small classes (15 students as compared with 22 in regular classes) (Krueger, 2003; Krueger & Whitmore, 2000). However, in most places "small" classes are larger than that. In classroom observations of 890 first-graders, classes with 25 students or less tended to be more social and interactive (with a bit more disruptive behavior) and to enable higher quality instruction and emotional support. Students in these classes tended to score higher on standardized achievements tests and beginning reading skills. In larger classes, students spent more time on structured, teacher-directed group activities but received less instructional support and were rated by their teachers as less well adjusted (NICHD Early Childhood Research Network, 2004b).

Current Educational Innovations   When the Chicago public schools in 1996 ended **social promotion,** the practice of promoting children to keep them with their age-mates even when they do not meet academic standards, many observers hailed the change. Others warned that, although retention in some cases can be a "wake-up call," more often it is the first step on a remedial track that leads to lowered expectations, poor performance, and dropping out of school (J. M. Fields & Smith, 1998; Lugaila, 2003; McCoy & Reynolds, 1999; McLeskey, Lancaster, & Grizzle, 1995; Temple, Reynolds, & Miedel, 2000). Indeed, studies by University of Chicago researchers found that Chicago's retention policy (which has since been modified) did *not* improve third-graders' test scores, hurt sixth-graders' scores, and greatly increased eighth grade and high school dropout rates for retained students (Nagaoka & Roderick, 2004; Roderick et al., 2003).

social promotion Policy of automatically promoting children even if they do not meet academic standards.

Many educators say the only real solution to a high failure rate is to identify at-risk students early and intervene *before* they fail (Bronner, 1999). In 2000–2001, 39 percent of U.S. public school districts provided alternative schools or programs for at-risk students, offering smaller classes, remedial instruction, counseling, and crisis intervention (NCES, 2003). Summer school may be effective as an early intervention. In one study, first-graders who attended summer instruction in reading and writing at least 75 percent of the time outscored 64 percent of their peers who did not participate (Borman, Boulay, Kaplan, Rachuba, & Hewes, 1999).

Some parents, unhappy with their public schools or seeking a particular style of education, are choosing charter schools or homeschooling. Charter schools tend to be smaller than regular public schools and have a unique philosophy, curriculum, structure, or organizational style. Although parents are generally satisfied with their charter schools, their effect on student outcomes is in dispute (Bulkley & Fisler, 2002; Center for Education Reform, 2004; Detrich, Phillips, & Durett, 2002; National Assessment of Educational Progress, 2004; Schemo, 2004).

Homeschooling is legal in all 50 states. In 2003 some 1.1 million U.S. students representing 2.2 percent of the school-age population were homeschooled, 4 out of 5 of them full time—a 29 percent increase from 1999. In a nationally representative government survey, the main reasons parents gave for choosing to homeschool their children were concern about a poor learning environment in the schools and the desire to provide religious or moral instruction (Princiotta, Bielick, & Chapman, 2004).

Computer and Internet Use   Children's computer and Internet use has greatly increased in the past decade. About three-quarters of U.S. children and adolescents have home computers and Internet access (Juster et al., 2004). By 2002, 99 percent of U.S. public schools had Internet access, 92 percent in instructional rooms (Kleiner & Lewis, 2003). Nine out of ten 8- to 10-year-olds use computers, and more than half use the Internet for school assignments, e-mail, or computer games. However, fewer black and Hispanic children than white children and fewer poor children than nonpoor children use these technologies (DeBell & Chapman, 2003).

Computer literacy and the ability to navigate the World Wide Web are opening new possibilities for individualized instruction, global communication, and early training in independent research skills. However, this tool poses dangers. First is the risk of exposure to harmful or inappropriate material. Second, students need to learn to evaluate critically information they find in cyberspace and to separate facts from opinion and advertising (J. Lee, 1998). Finally, a focus on "visual literacy" could divert financial resources from other areas of the curriculum.

The Culture In the United States, minorities constitute an increasing proportion of public school students—39 percent in 2000, a 17 percent increase since 1972 (Llagas & Snyder, 2003). Some minority children, particularly those of East Asian extraction, tend to do especially well in school. Cultural influences in their countries of origin may hold the key.

East Asian cultures share values that foster educational success (Chao, 1994). Chinese and Japanese mothers view academic achievement as a child's most important pursuit (H. W. Stevenson, 1995; H. W. Stevenson, Chen, & Lee, 1993; H. W. Stevenson, Lee, Chen, & Lummis, 1990; H. W. Stevenson, Lee, Chen, Stigler, et al., 1990). Whereas U.S. students socialize after school and engage in sports and other activities, Asian students devote themselves almost entirely to study (Fuligni & Stevenson, 1995; H. W. Stevenson, 1995; H. W. Stevenson et al., 1993).

Many Asian American families see education as the best route to upward mobility (Chao, 1996; Sue & Okazaki, 1990). The child's school success is a prime goal of parenting (Chao, 1994, 1996; Huntsinger & Jose, 1995). Of course, as Asian American children grow up in U.S. culture and absorb its values, their attitudes toward learning may change (C. Chen & Stevenson, 1995; Huntsinger et al., 1998).

Checkpoint
Can you . . .

✔ Evaluate the effects of the school environment on children's achievement?

✔ Discuss changes and innovations in educational philosophy and practice?

Children of East Asian extraction often do better in school than other U.S. youngsters. The reasons seem to be cultural, not genetic.

Unlike Asian Americans, some minority children whose cultural values differ markedly from those of the dominant culture are at a disadvantage in school (Helms, 1992; Tharp, 1989). The Kamehameha Early Education Program (KEEP) has produced dramatic improvements in primary-grade Hawaiian children's cognitive performance by designing educational programs to fit cultural patterns—for example, having children work in small, collaborative groups and training teachers to adjust to cultural speaking and learning styles (Tharp, 1989).

Second-Language Education

In 2000, 18 percent of the U.S. population spoke a language other than English at home, and 3 million children were defined as English Language Learners, representing 7 percent of the public school population (National Center for Education Statistics, 2004b). Increasingly, the primary language these children speak is Spanish.

Some schools use an **English-immersion** approach, in which minority children are immersed in English from the beginning, in special classes. Other schools have adopted programs of **bilingual education,** in which children are taught in two languages, first learning in their native language with others who also speak it and then switching to regular classes in English when they become more proficient in it. These programs can encourage children to become **bilingual** (fluent in two languages) and to feel pride in their cultural identity.

Advocates of early *English immersion* claim that the sooner children are exposed to English and the more time they spend speaking it, the better they learn it. Support for this view comes from findings that the effectiveness of second-language learning declines from early childhood through late adolescence (Newport, 1991). Proponents of *bilingual* programs claim that children progress faster academically in their native language and later make a smoother transition to all-English classrooms (Padilla et al., 1991). Because foreign-speaking children can understand only simple English at first, the curriculum must be watered down, and children are less prepared to handle complex material later (Collier, 1995).

A study of 70,000 non–English-speaking students in high-quality second-language programs in five districts across the United States offers strong support for a bilingual

Checkpoint
Can you . . .

✔ Give reasons why children of East Asian extraction tend to do well in school?

✔ Identify some ways of addressing cultural differences in the classroom?

Guidepost

8. How do schools meet the needs of non–English-speaking children and those with learning problems?

English-immersion Approach to teaching English as a second language in which instruction is presented only in English.

bilingual education System of teaching non–English-speaking children in their native language while they learn English, and later switching to all-English instruction.

bilingual Fluent in two languages.

Advocates of bilingual instruction claim that children who learn in their native language as well as in English, like these fourth-graders, make faster academic progress than in English alone.

two-way (dual-language) learning Approach to second-language education in which English speakers and non-English speakers learn together in their own and each other's languages.

Checkpoint

Can you . . .

✔ Describe and evaluate various types of second-language education?

mental retardation Significantly subnormal cognitive functioning.

dyslexia Developmental disorder in which reading achievement is substantially lower than predicted by IQ or age.

approach (Collier, 1995; W. P. Thomas & Collier, 1997). The study compared not only English proficiency but also long-term academic achievement. In the primary grades, the type of language teaching made little difference; but from seventh grade on, children who had remained in bilingual programs at least through sixth grade caught up with or even surpassed their native English-speaking peers. At the same time, the relative performance of children who had been in traditional immersion programs began to decline. By the end of high school, those in part-time immersion programs trailed 80 percent of native English speakers their age. Most successful was a third, less common approach: **two-way,** or **dual-language learning,** in which English-speaking and foreign-speaking children learn together in their own and each other's languages (Collier, 1995; W. P. Thomas & Collier, 1997, 1998).

Despite such findings, many critics claim that bilingual education has produced millions of children who do not know enough English to hold a job. California, Arizona, and Massachusetts, which together account for one-half of students who speak languages other than English at home, have outlawed bilingual education by referendum and required English immersion. Initial results in California, the first state to ban bilingual education in 1998, were positive. In 2002, Colorado became the first state to vote down such an initiative (ProEnglish, 2002).

Children with Learning Problems

Just as educators have become more sensitive to teaching children from varied cultural backgrounds, they also have sought to meet the needs of children like Ann Bancroft with special educational needs.

Mental Retardation **Mental retardation** is significantly subnormal cognitive functioning. It is indicated by an IQ of about 70 or less, coupled with a deficiency in age-appropriate adaptive behavior (such as communication, social skills, and self-care), appearing before age 18 (Kanaya, Scullin, & Ceci, 2003). Fewer than 1 percent of U.S. children are mentally retarded (NCHS, 2004; Woodruff et al., 2004).

A problem in identification of the mentally retarded arises because of the rising historical trend in IQ scores (refer back to Chapter 7). To adjust for this trend, intelligence tests are periodically renormed (made harder). Thus, whether a child with borderline intelligence is classified as mentally retarded may depend on whether the child was tested before or after the introduction of stiffer norms (Kanaya et al., 2003).

In 30 to 50 percent of cases the cause of mental retardation is unknown. Known causes include genetic disorders, traumatic accidents, prenatal exposure to infection or alcohol, and environmental exposure to lead or high levels of mercury (Woodruff et al., 2004). Many cases of retardation may be preventable through genetic counseling, prenatal care, amniocentesis, routine screening and health care for newborns, and nutritional services for pregnant women and infants.

Most retarded children can benefit from schooling. Intervention programs have helped many mildly or moderately retarded adults and those considered "borderline" (with IQs ranging from 70 up to about 85) to hold jobs, live in the community, and function fairly well in society. The profoundly retarded need constant care and supervision, usually in institutions. For some, day care centers, hostels for retarded adults, and homemaking services for caregivers can be less costly and more humane alternatives.

Learning Disabilities Ann Bancroft is far from the only eminent person who has struggled with learning problems. Nelson Rockefeller, former vice president of the United States, is one of many eminent persons who have suffered from **dyslexia,**

Children with dyslexia have trouble reading and writing, and often doing arithmetic, because they may confuse up and down and left and right. Dyslexia may be part of a more general language impairment.

a developmental reading disability in which reading achievement is substantially below the level predicted by IQ or age. Others include the singer Harry Belafonte; the actors Tom Cruise, Whoopi Goldberg, and Cher; the fairy tale author Hans Christian Anderson; baseball Hall-of-Famer Nolan Ryan; television host Jay Leno; Alexander Graham Bell, inventor of the telephone; Albert Einstein, father of nuclear energy; and the novelist John Irving.

Dyslexia is the most commonly diagnosed of a large number of **learning disabilities (LDs).** These are disorders that interfere with specific aspects of school achievement, such as listening, speaking, reading, writing, or mathematics, resulting in performance substantially lower than would be expected given a child's age, intelligence, and amount of schooling (APA, 1994). Mathematical disabilities, as an example, include difficulty in counting, comparing numbers, calculating, and remembering basic arithmetic facts. Each of these may involve distinct disabilities. A growing number of children—8 percent of the U.S. school population in 2002—have LDs, and 5 percent are served by federally supported programs (National Center for Learning Disabilities, 2004b).

Children with learning disabilities often have near-average to higher-than-average intelligence and normal vision and hearing, but they seem to have trouble processing sensory information. Although causes are uncertain, they may include genetic factors, complications of pregnancy or birth, or injuries after birth, such as head trauma, nutritional deprivation, and exposure to lead (National Center for Learning Disabilities, 2004b).

Children with LDs tend to be less task oriented and more easily distracted than other children; they are less well organized as learners and less likely to use memory strategies. Of course, not all children who have trouble with reading, arithmetic, or other specific school subjects have LDs. Some haven't been taught properly, are anxious, have trouble reading or hearing directions, lack motivation or interest in the subject, or have a developmental delay, which may eventually disappear (Geary, 1993; Ginsburg, 1997; Roush, 1995).

learning disabilities (LDs)
Disorders that interfere with specific aspects of learning and school achievement.

About 4 out of 5 children with LDs have been identified as dyslexic. Dyslexia is generally considered to be a chronic, persistent medical condition and tends to run in families (S. E. Shaywitz, 1998, 2003). It hinders the development of oral as well as written language skills and may cause problems with writing, spelling, grammar, and understanding speech as well as with reading (National Center for Learning Disabilities, 2004a). Reading disability is more frequent in boys than in girls (Rutter et al., 2004).

Dyslexia in English-speaking children is believed to result from a neurological defect in processing speech sounds: an inability to recognize that words consist of smaller units of sound, which are represented by printed letters. This defect in *phonological processing* makes it harder to decode words (Morris et al., 1998; S. E. Shaywitz, 1998, 2003). Brain imaging has revealed differences or underactivity in the regions of the brain activated during the processing of spoken language in dyslexic as compared with normal readers (Breier et al., 2003; Eden et al., 2004; Horwitz, Rumsey, & Donohue, 1998; T. L. Richards et al., 1999; Shaywitz, 2003; Shaywitz et al., 1998) and significantly reduced volumes of gray matter in persons with familial dyslexia (Brambati et al., 2004). Many children—and even adults—with dyslexia can be taught to read through systematic phonological training, but the process does not become automatic, as it does with most readers (Eden et al., 2004; S. E. Shaywitz, 1998, 2003).

The biology of dyslexia may vary by culture. In brain imaging studies, Chinese children used different parts of the brain in reading than English speakers do, and different parts were affected by dyslexia. This is not surprising, since the Chinese language is not phonological but instead relies on memory for visual symbols. About 2 to 7 percent of Chinese children are dyslexic (Sick, Perfetti, Jin, & Tan, 2004).

Attention-Deficit/Hyperactivity Disorder Attention-deficit/hyperactivity dis-order (ADHD) is a chronic condition usually marked by persistent inattention, distractibility, impulsivity, low tolerance for frustration, and a great deal of activity at the wrong time and the wrong place, such as the classroom (APA, 1994; Woodruff et al., 2004). Among the well-known people who reportedly have had ADHD are the singer and composer John Lennon, U.S. Senator Robert Kennedy, and the actors Robin Williams and Sylvester Stallone. It may affect an estimated 2 to 11 percent or more of school-age children worldwide (Zametkin & Ernst, 1999) and 3 to 7 per-cent in the United States (Dey et al., 2004; NCHS, 2004). Boys are more than twice as likely to be diagnosed as girls (Dey et al., 2004; NCHS, 2004). The prevalence of ADHD is in dispute, however; some research suggests that it may be underesti-mated (Rowland et al., 2002), but some physicians warn that the disorder may be overdiagnosed, resulting in unnecessary overmedication of children whose parents or teachers do not know how to control them (Elliott, 2000).

The disorder has two different but sometimes overlapping sets of symptoms, making diagnosis imprecise. Some children are inattentive but not hyperactive; oth-ers show the reverse pattern (USDHHS, 1999b). However, in 85 percent of cases, the two types of symptoms go together (Barkley, 1998a). These characteristics appear to some degree in most children; there is cause for concern when they are unusu-ally frequent and so severe as to interfere with the child's functioning in school and in daily life (AAP Committee on Children with Disabilities and Committee on Drugs, 1996; Barkley, 1998b; USDHHS, 1999b).

ADHD has a substantial genetic basis, with heritability approaching 80 percent (Acosta, Arcos-Burgos, & Muenke, 2004; APA, 1994; Barkley, 1998b; Elia, Ambrosini, & Rapoport, 1999; USDHHS, 1999b; Zametkin, 1995; Zametkin & Ernst, 1999). Parents of children with ADHD are 24 times more likely to have had

attention-deficit/hyperactivity disorder (ADHD) Syndrome characterized by persistent inattention and distractibility, impulsivity, low tolerance for frustration, and inappropriate overactivity.

Lifemap CD

The "Attention Deficit Disorder" video in Chapter 9 of your CD illustrates how one boy deals with the challenges posed by this disorder.

the disorder themselves than parents of children without the disorder (Chronis et al., 2003). One gene linked strongly with ADHD is related to novelty seeking, a behavior that may once have helped humans adapt to rapidly changing environments. This evolutionary advantage may explain why the disorder has become relatively common (Ding et al., 2002). Birth complications that may play a part include prematurity, a prospective mother's alcohol or tobacco use, exposure to high levels of lead or PCBs, and oxygen deprivation (Barkley, 1998b; Thapar et al., 2003; USDHHS, 1999b; Woodruff et al., 2004).

Children with ADHD have unusually small brain structures in the cortical regions that regulate attention and impulse control (Sowell et al., 2003). They tend to forget responsibilities, to speak aloud rather than giving themselves silent directions, to be frustrated or angered easily, and to give up when they don't see how to solve a problem. Parents and teachers may be able to help these children by giving them a structured environment: breaking down tasks into small "chunks," providing frequent prompts about rules and time, and giving frequent, immediate rewards for small accomplishments (Barkley, 1998b).

Problems with impulse control and overactivity often decline with age, but inattention persists into adolescence (Whalen, Jamner, Henker, Delfino, & Lozano, 2002) and can lead to excessive injuries, academic problems, antisocial behavior, risky driving, substance abuse or dependence, and anxiety or depression (Barkley, 1998b; Barkley, Murphy, & Kwasnik, 1996; Elia et al., 1999; McGee, Partridge, Williams, & Silva, 1991; Molina & Pelham, 2003; USDHHS, 1999b; Wender, 1995; Whalen et al., 2002; Zametkin, 1995). ADHD sometimes continues into adulthood; it is estimated to affect 4 percent of adults worldwide (Wilens, Faraone, & Biederman, 2004).

ADHD is often managed with drugs, sometimes combined with behavioral therapy, counseling, training in social skills, and special classroom placement. A 14-month randomized study of 579 children with ADHD found a carefully monitored program of Ritalin treatment, alone or in combination with behavior modification, more effective than the behavioral therapy alone or standard community care (MTA Cooperative Group, 1999). However, the superior benefits of the program diminished over the following 10 months (MTA Cooperative Group, 2004a). A side effect of the combined treatment was slower growth in height and weight (MTA Cooperative Group, 2004b). Also, long-term effects of Ritalin are unknown.

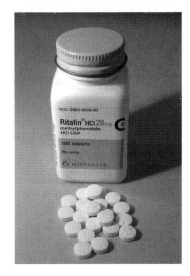

The drug known as Ritalin can be effective in treating attention-deficit/hyperactivity disorder (ADHD), but its long-term effects are unknown. Some physicians warn that Ritalin may be overprescribed, resulting in overmedication of children.

What's Your View?

- Long-term effects of drug treatment for ADHD are unknown, but leaving the condition untreated also carries risks. If you had a child with ADHD, what would you do?

Educating Children with Disabilities In 2000–2001, 13.3 percent of public school students in the United States were receiving special educational services under the Individuals with Disabilities Education Act, which ensures a free, appropriate public education for all children with disabilities. About 45 percent of these children had learning disabilities, 17 percent had speech or language impairments, and 9.5 percent had mental retardation (Snyder & Hoffman, 2003). An individualized program must be designed for each child, with parental involvement. Children must be educated in the "least restrictive environment" appropriate to their needs; which means, whenever possible, the regular classroom.

Many of these students can be served by "inclusion" programs, in which they are integrated with nondisabled

This deaf girl learns in a class with hearing children through the aid of a special teacher who communicates with her in sign language.

Checkpoint
Can you . . .

✔ Describe the causes and prognoses for three common types of conditions that interfere with learning?

✔ Discuss the impact of federal requirements for the education of children with disabilities?

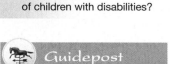

children for all or part of the day. About half of all students with disabilities spend at least 80 percent of their day in regular classrooms (NCES, 2005b). Inclusion can help children with disabilities learn to get along in society and can help nondisabled children know and understand people with disabilities (Kleiner & Farris, 2002). A potential problem with inclusion is that children with learning disabilities may be evaluated by unrealistic standards, resulting in their being held back and made to repeat grades. This has already happened on a large scale in some schools, despite evidence that retention is ineffective even with children of normal abilities (McLeskey et al., 1995).

Gifted Children

Giftedness is hard to define and measure. Educators disagree on who qualifies as gifted, on what basis, and what kinds of educational programs these children need. Another source of confusion is that creativity and artistic talent are sometimes viewed as aspects or types of giftedness and sometimes as independent of it.

Identifying Gifted Children The traditional criterion of giftedness is high general intelligence, as shown by an IQ score of 130 or higher. This definition tends to exclude highly creative children (whose unusual answers often lower their test scores), children from minority groups (whose abilities may not be well developed, though the potential is there), and children with specific aptitudes (who may be only average or even show learning problems in other areas). Most states and school districts have therefore adopted a broader definition, which includes children who have shown high *potential* or *achievement* in one or more of the following: general intellect, specific aptitude (such as in mathematics or science), creative or productive thinking, leadership, talent in the arts (such as painting, writing, music, or acting), and psychomotor ability (Cassidy & Hossler, 1992). Many school districts now use multiple criteria for admission to programs for the gifted, including achievement test scores, grades, classroom performance, creative production, parent and teacher nominations, and student interviews; but IQ remains an important and sometimes the determining factor.

creativity Ability to see situations in a new way, to produce innovations, or to discern previously unidentified problems and find novel solutions.

Defining and Measuring Creativity One definition of **creativity** is the ability to see things in a new light—to produce something never seen before or to discern problems others fail to recognize and find new and unusual solutions. High creativity and high academic intelligence (IQ) do not necessarily go hand in hand (Anastasi & Schaefer, 1971; Getzels, 1964, 1984; Getzels & Jackson, 1962, 1963).

J. P. Guilford (1956, 1959, 1960, 1967, 1986) distinguished between two kinds of thinking: *convergent* and *divergent*. **Convergent thinking**—the kind IQ tests measure—seeks a single correct answer; **divergent thinking** comes up with a wide array of fresh possibilities. Tests of creativity call for divergent thinking. The Torrance Tests of Creative Thinking (Torrance, 1966, 1974; Torrance & Ball, 1984), among the most widely known tests of creativity, include such tasks as listing unusual uses for a paper clip, completing a figure, and writing down what a sound brings to mind.

convergent thinking Thinking aimed at finding the one right answer to a problem.

divergent thinking Thinking that produces a variety of fresh, diverse possibilities.

One problem with many of these tests is that the score depends partly on speed, which is not a hallmark of creativity. Moreover, although the tests yield fairly reliable results, there is dispute over whether they are valid—whether they identify children who are creative in everyday life (Simonton, 1990). As Guilford recognized, divergent thinking may not be the only, or even the most important, factor in creative performance.

Educating Gifted Children About 68 percent of public elementary and secondary schools have special programs for the gifted (Snyder & Hoffman, 2003), and according to a national survey of 10,445 U.S. parents, 13 percent of children ages 6 to 11 are enrolled in such programs (Lugaila, 2003). These programs generally follow one of two approaches: *enrichment* or *acceleration.* **Enrichment** broadens and deepens knowledge and skills through extra classroom activities, research projects, field trips, or coaching by experts. **Acceleration,** often recommended for highly gifted children, speeds up their education through early school entrance, grade skipping, placement in fast-paced classes, or advanced courses in specific subjects. Moderate acceleration does not seem to harm social adjustment, at least in the long run (Winner, 1997).

Children in programs for the gifted not only make academic gains, but also tend to improve in self-concept and social adjustment (Ford & Harris, 1996). However, competition for funding and opposition to "elitism" threatens the continuation of these programs (Purcell, 1995; Winner, 1997). Some educators advocate moving away from an all-or-nothing definition of giftedness and including a wider range of students in more flexible programs (J. Cox, Daniel, & Boston, 1985; Feldhusen, 1992). Some say that if the level of education were significantly improved for all children, only the most exceptional would need special classes (Winner, 1997).

enrichment Approach to educating the gifted, which broadens and deepens knowledge and skills through extra activities, projects, field trips, or mentoring.

acceleration Approach to educating the gifted that moves them through the curriculum at an unusually rapid pace.

Checkpoint

Can you . . .

✔ Tell how gifted children are identified?

✔ Discuss the relationship between IQ and creativity?

✔ Describe two approaches to the education of gifted children?

Ref⊕cus

Thinking back to the Focus vignette about Ann Bancroft at the beginning of this chapter:

- How much impact do you think psychosocial factors such as motivation, determination, and self-confidence had in Bancroft's physical and cognitive development?

- How did Bancroft's childhood experiences with her parents and siblings influence her later achievements?

- What can we learn from Bancroft's experience about the diagnosis and treament of a child who is not doing well in reading? About the kinds of activities that can lead to lifetime fitness?

There is no firm dividing line between being gifted and not being gifted, creative and not creative. All children benefit from being encouraged in their areas of interest and ability. What we learn about fostering intelligence and creativity in the most able youngsters may help all children make the most of their potential. The degree to which they do this will affect their self-concept and other aspects of personality, as we discuss in Chapter 10.

SUMMARY AND KEY TERMS

PHYSICAL DEVELOPMENT

Aspects of Physical Development

Guidepost 1: **What gains in growth and motor development occur in school-age children, and what are their nutritional needs?**

- Physical development is less rapid in middle childhood than in earlier years. Wide differences in height and weight exist.

- Proper nutrition and sleep are essential for normal growth and health.

- Because of improved motor development, boys and girls in middle childhood can engage in a wide range of motor activities.

- Informal recess-time activities help develop physical and social skills. Boys' games tend to be more physical and girls' games more verbal.

- About 10 percent of schoolchildren's play, especially among boys, is rough-and-tumble play.

- Many children, mostly boys, engage in organized, competitive sports. A sound physical education program should aim at skill development and fitness for all children.

rough-and-tumble play *(319)*

Health and Safety

Guidepost 2: What are the principal health and fitness concerns for school-age children, and what can be done to make these years healthier and safer?

- Middle childhood is a relatively healthy period; most children are immunized against major illnesses, and the death rate is the lowest in the life span.
- Overweight, which is increasingly common among U.S. children, entails multiple risks. It is influenced by genetic and environmental factors and is more easily prevented than treated. Many children do not get enough physical activity.
- Hypertension is becoming more common along with the rise in overweight.
- Respiratory infections and other acute medical conditions are common at this age. Chronic conditions such as asthma are most prevalent among poor and minority children.
- Vision becomes keener during middle childhood, but some children have defective vision or hearing.
- Prospects for children born with HIV have improved. Most children who are HIV-positive function normally in school and should not be excluded from any activities of which they are capable.
- Accidents are the leading cause of death in middle childhood. Use of helmets and other protective devices and avoidance of trampolines, snowmobiling, and other dangerous sports can greatly reduce injuries.

hypertension (321)

acute medical conditions (321)

chronic medical conditions (321)

asthma (323)

COGNITIVE DEVELOPMENT

Piagetian Approach: The Concrete Operational Child

Guidepost 3: How do school-age children's thinking and moral reasoning differ from those of younger children?

- A child from about age 7 to age 12 is in the stage of concrete operations. Children are less egocentric than before and are more proficient at tasks requiring logical reasoning, such as spatial thinking, understanding of causality, categorization, inductive and deductive reasoning, and conservation. However, their reasoning is largely limited to the here and now.
- Neurological development and improvements in processing and memory seem to contribute to the rate of development of Piagetian skills.
- According to Piaget, moral development is linked with cognitive maturation and occurs in three stages as children move from rigid to more flexible thinking.

concrete operations (324)

seriation (325)

transitive inference (325)

class inclusion (326)

inductive reasoning (326)

deductive reasoning (326)

Information Processing Approach: Memory and Other Processing Skills

Guidepost 4: What advances in memory and other information-processing skills occur during middle childhood?

- Reaction time, processing speed, metamemory, metacognition, selective attention, and use of mnemonic strategies improve during the school years.

metamemory (330)

metacognition (330)

mnemonic strategies (330)

external memory aids (330)

rehearsal (330)

organization (330)

elaboration (330)

Psychometric Approach: Assessment of Intelligence

Guidepost 5: How accurately can schoolchildren's intelligence be measured?

- IQ tests are fairly good predictors of school success but may be unfair to some children.
- Differences in IQ among ethnic groups appear to result to a considerable degree from socioeconomic and other environmental differences.
- Schooling seems to increase measured intelligence.
- Attempts to devise culture-free or culture-fair tests have been unsuccessful. Indeed, intelligence seems inextricably linked with culture.
- According to Robert Sternberg's triarchic theory, IQ tests measure mainly the componential element of intelligence, not the experiential and contextual elements.
- IQ tests tap only three of the "intelligences" in Howard Gardner's theory of multiple intelligences.
- New directions in intelligence testing include the Sternberg Triarchic Abilities Tests (STAT), Kaufman Assessment Battery for Children (K-ABC), and dynamic tests based on Vygotsky's theory.

Otis-Lennon School Ability Test (332)

Wechsler Intelligence Scale for Children (WISC-III) (332)

cultural bias (333)

culture-free (333)

culture-fair (334)

culture-relevant (334)

triarchic theory of intelligence (334)

componential element (334)

experiential element (334)

contextual element (334)

tacit knowledge (335)

Sternberg Triarchic Abilities Test (STAT) (335)

theory of multiple intelligences (335)

Kaufman Assessment Battery for Children (K-ABC) (336)

Language and Literacy

Guidepost 6: How do communicative abilities and literacy expand during middle childhood?

- Use of vocabulary, grammar, and syntax become increasingly sophisticated, but the major area of linguistic growth is in pragmatics.
- Despite the popularity of whole-language programs, early phonics training is a key to reading proficiency.
- Interaction with peers fosters development of writing skills.

pragmatics (337)

decoding (338)

visually based retrieval (338)

phonetic, or code emphasis approach (338)

whole-language approach (338)

The Child in School

Guidepost 7: What influences school achievement?

- Because schooling is cumulative, the foundation laid in first grade is very important.
- Children's self-efficacy beliefs affect school achievement.
- Girls tend to do better in school than boys.
- Parents influence children's learning by becoming involved in their schooling, motivating them to achieve, and transmitting attitudes about learning. Socioeconomic status can influence parental beliefs and practices that, in turn, influence achievement.
- The school environment and class size affect learning.
- Current educational issues and innovations include the amount of homework assigned, social promotion, charter schools, homeschooling, and computer literacy.
- The superior achievement of children of East Asian extraction seems to stem from cultural factors. Some minority children may benefit from educational programs adapted to their cultural styles.

social capital (341)

social promotion (343)

Guidepost 8: How do schools meet the needs of non–English-speaking children and those with learning problems?

- Methods of second-language education are controversial. Issues include speed and facility with English, long-term achievement in academic subjects, and pride in cultural identity.
- Three frequent sources of learning problems are mental retardation, learning disabilities (LDs), and attention-deficit/hyperactivity disorder (ADHD). Dyslexia is the most common learning disability.
- In the United States, all children with disabilities are entitled to a free, appropriate education. Children must be educated in the least restrictive environment possible, often in the regular classroom.

English-immersion (345)

bilingual education (345)

bilingual (345)

two-way (dual-language) learning (346)

mental retardation (346)

dyslexia (346)

learning disabilities (LDs) (347)

attention-deficit/hyperactivity disorder (ADHD) (348)

Guidepost 9: How is giftedness assessed and nurtured?

- An IQ of 130 or higher is a common standard for identifying gifted children. Broader definitions include creativity, artistic talent, and other attributes and rely on multiple criteria for identification.
- Creativity and IQ are *not* closely linked. Tests of creativity seek to measure divergent thinking, but their validity has been questioned.
- Special educational programs for gifted children stress enrichment or acceleration.

creativity (350)

convergent thinking (350)

divergent thinking (350)

enrichment (351)

acceleration (351)

Psychosocial Development in Middle Childhood

Have you ever felt like nobody?
Just a tiny speck of air.
When everyone's around you,
And you are just not there.

Karen Crawford, age 9

Focus
Marian Anderson, Operatic Trailblazer

Marian Anderson

The African American contralto Marian Anderson (1897–1993)* had—in the words of the great Italian conductor Arturo Toscanini—a voice heard "once in a hundred years." She was also a pioneer in breaking racial barriers. Turned away by a music school in her hometown of Philadelphia, she studied voice privately and in 1925 won a national competition to sing with the New York Philharmonic. When she was refused the use of a concert hall in Washington, D.C., First Lady Eleanor Roosevelt arranged for her to sing on the steps of the Lincoln Memorial. The unprecedented performance on Easter Sunday, 1939, drew 75,000 people and was broadcast to millions. Several weeks later, Marian Anderson became the first black singer to perform at the White House. But not until 1955 did Anderson, at age 57, become the first person of her race to sing with New York's Metropolitan Opera.

A remarkable story lies behind this woman's "journey from a single rented room in South Philadelphia" (McKay, 1992, p. xxx). It is a story of nurturing family ties—bonds of mutual support, care, and concern that extended from generation to generation.

Marian Anderson was the eldest of three children of John and Annie Anderson. Two years after her birth, the family left their one-room apartment to move in with her father's parents and then into a small rented house nearby.

At the age of 6, Marian joined the junior choir at church. There she made a friend, Viola Johnson, who lived across the street from the Andersons. Within a year or two, they sang a duet together—Marian's first public performance.

*The chief source of biographical material about Marian Anderson and her family is Anderson (1992). Some details come from Freedman (2004), Jones (2004), Kernan (1993), Women in History (2004), and from obituaries published in *Time* (April 19, 1993), *People Weekly, The New Yorker,* and *Jet* (April 26, 1993).

Although Anderson always gave her birthdate as 1902, her birth certificate, released after her death, showed it as 1897.

When Marian was in eighth grade, her beloved father died, and the family again moved in with his parents, his sister, and her two daughters. Marian's grandfather had a steady job. Her grandmother took care of all the children, her aunt ran the house, and her mother contributed by cooking dinners, working as a cleaning woman, and taking in laundry, which Marian and her sister Alyce delivered.

The most important influence in Marian Anderson's life was the counsel, example, and spiritual guidance of her hardworking, unfailingly supportive mother. Annie Anderson placed great importance on her children's schooling and saw to it that they didn't skimp on homework. Even when she was working full-time, she cooked their dinner every night, and she taught Marian to sew her own clothes. "Not once can I recall . . . hearing Mother lift her voice to us in anger . . . ," Marian wrote. "She could be firm, and we learned to respect her wishes" (Anderson, 1992, p. 92).

When Marian Anderson became a world-renowned concert artist, she often returned to her old neighborhood in Philadelphia. Her mother and sister Alyce shared a modest house, and the other sister, Ethel, lived next door with her son, James.

"It is the pleasantest thing in the world to go into that home and feel its happiness, . . ." the singer wrote. "They are all comfortable, and they cherish and protect one another. . . . I know that it warms [Mother] to have her grandson near her as he grows up, just as I think that when he gets to be a man, making his own life, he will have pleasant memories of his home and family" (1992, p. 93). Anderson herself married but had no children. In 1992, widowed and frail at age 95, she went to live with her nephew, James DePriest, then music director of the Oregon Symphony. She died of a stroke at his home the following year.

Marian Anderson "lived through momentous changes in America and the world" and in African American life (McKay, 1992, p. xxiv), but one thing that never changed in her life was the strong, supportive network of relationships that sustained her and her family. The kind of household a child lives in and the relationships within the household can have profound effects on psychosocial development in middle childhood, when children are developing a stronger sense of what it means to be responsible, contributing members, first of a family and then of society. The family is part of a web of contextual influences, including the peer group, the school, and the neighborhood in which the family lives. Marian Anderson's first friend, her church choir, and the neighbors for whom she did odd jobs to earn the price of a violin all played parts in her development. Above and beyond these influences were the overarching cultural patterns of time and place, which presented special challenges to African American families and communities and called forth mutually supportive responses.

In this chapter, we see how children develop a more realistic self-concept and become more self-reliant and in control of their emotions. Through being with peers they make discoveries about their own attitudes, values, and skills. Still, the family remains a vital influence. Children's lives are affected not only by the way parents approach the task of child raising but also by whether and how they are employed, by the family's economic circumstances, and by the makeup of the household. Although most children are emotionally healthy, some have mental health problems; we look at several of these. We also describe resilient children, who are able to surmount difficult obstacles and maintain a healthy level of functioning.

After you have read and studied this chapter, you should be able to answer each of the Guidepost questions that appear at the top of the next page. Look for them again in the margins, where they point to important concepts throughout the chapter. To check your understanding of these Guideposts, review the end-of-chapter summary. Checkpoints located at periodic spots throughout the chapter will help you verify your understanding of what you have read.

**Guideposts
for Study**

1. How do school-age children develop a realistic self-concept, and what contributes to self-esteem?

2. How do school-age children show emotional growth?

3. How do parent-child relationships change in middle childhood?

4. What are the effects of parents' work and of poverty on children's well-being?

5. What impact does family structure have on children's development?

6. How do siblings influence and get along with one another, and what part do pets play in children's development?

7. How do relationships with peers change in middle childhood, and what influences popularity and choice of friends?

8. What are the most common forms of aggressive behavior in middle childhood, and what influences contribute to it?

9. What emotional disorders may develop in childhood, and how are they treated?

10. How do the stresses of modern life affect children, and why are some children more resilient than others?

The Developing Self

The cognitive growth that takes place during middle childhood enables children to develop more complex concepts of themselves and to gain in emotional understanding and control.

Guidepost

1. How do school-age children develop a realistic self-concept, and what contributes to self-esteem?

Self-Concept Development: Representational Systems

Around age 7 or 8, children reach the third of the neo-Piagetian stages of self-concept development described in Chapter 8. Judgments about the self become more conscious, realistic, balanced, and comprehensive as children form **representational systems:** broad, inclusive self-concepts that integrate various aspects of the self (Harter, 1993, 1996, 1998).

"At school I'm feeling pretty smart in certain subjects, Language Arts and Social Studies," says 8-year-old Lisa. "I got A's in these subjects on my last report card and was really proud of myself. But I'm feeling really dumb in Arithmetic and Science, particularly when I see how well the other kids are doing. . . . I still like myself as a person, because Arithmetic and Science just aren't that important to me. How I look and how popular I am are more important" (Harter, 1996, p. 208).

Lisa's self-description shows that she can focus on more than one dimension of herself. She has outgrown an all-or-nothing, black-or-white self-definition; she recognizes that she can be "smart" in certain subjects and "dumb" in others. Her self-descriptions are more balanced; she can verbalize her self-concept better, and she can weigh different aspects of it ("How I look and how popular I am are more important."). She can compare her *real self* with her *ideal self* and can judge how well she measures up to social standards in comparison with others. All of these

representational systems In neo-Piagetian terminology, the third stage in development of self-definition, characterized by breadth, balance, and the integration and assessment of various aspects of the self.

changes contribute to the development of self-esteem, her assessment of her *global self-worth* ("I like myself as a person").

Self-Esteem

According to Erikson (1982), a major determinant of self-esteem is children's view of their capacity for productive work. The issue to be resolved in middle childhood is **industry versus inferiority.** Children need to learn skills valued in their society. Arapesh boys in New Guinea learn to make bows and arrows and to lay traps for rats; Arapesh girls learn to plant, weed, and harvest. Inuit children of Alaska learn to hunt and fish. Children in industrialized countries learn to read, write, count, and use computers. Like Marian Anderson, many children learn household skills and help out with odd jobs.

The "virtue" that develops with successful resolution of this stage of psychosocial development is *competence,* a view of the self as able to master skills and complete tasks. Children compare their abilities with those of their peers; if they feel inadequate, they may retreat to the protective embrace of the family. If, on the other hand, they become too industrious, they may neglect social relationships and turn into "workaholics."

Parents strongly influence beliefs about competence. In a longitudinal study of 514 middle-class U.S. suburban children, parents' beliefs about their children's competence in math and sports were strongly associated with the children's beliefs. This was especially true of fathers' beliefs about sports competence (Fredricks & Eccles, 2002).

In contrast to the importance Erikson placed on mastery of skills, Susan Harter (1985a) found that 8- to 12-year-olds, at least in North America, judge themselves more by good looks and popularity. A major contributor to self-esteem, according to Harter, is social support from parents, peers, and teachers; but this generally will not

Middle childhood, according to Erikson, is a time for learning the skills one's culture considers important. In driving geese to market, this Vietnamese girl is developing a sense of competence and gaining self-esteem. In addition, by taking on responsibilities to match her growing capabilities, she learns about how her society works, her role in it, and what it means to do a job well.

compensate for a low self-evaluation. If Juanita thinks good looks are important but that she is not pretty, she will lose self-esteem no matter how much praise she gets from others.

Children with low self-esteem may be overly concerned about their performance in social situations. They may attribute social rejection to their own personality deficiencies, which they believe they are helpless to change. Rather than trying new ways to gain approval, they repeat unsuccessful strategies or just give up. (This is similar to the "helpless pattern" in younger children, described in Chapter 8.) Children with high self-esteem tend to attribute failure to factors outside themselves or to the need to try harder. If initially unsuccessful, they persevere, trying new strategies until they find one that works (Erdley, Cain, Loomis, Dumas-Hines, & Dweck, 1997). Children with high self-esteem tend to be more willing to volunteer to help those who are less fortunate than they are, and volunteering, in turn, helps build self-esteem. The reason may have to do with a belief that others, like oneself, can change and improve (Karafantis & Levy, 2004).

Emotional Growth and Prosocial Behavior

As children grow older, they are more aware of their own and other people's feelings. They can better regulate their emotions and can respond to others' emotional distress (Saarni et al., 1998).

By age 7 or 8, children typically are aware of feeling shame and pride, and they have a clearer idea of the difference between guilt and shame (Harris, Olthof, Meerum Terwogt, & Hardman, 1987; Olthof, Schouten, Kuiper, Stegge, & Jennekens-Schinkel, 2000). These emotions affect their opinion of themselves (Harter, 1993, 1996). Children also can verbalize conflicting emotions. As Lisa says, "Most of the boys at school are pretty yukky. I don't feel that way about my little brother Jason, although he does get on my nerves. I love him but at the same time, he also does things that make me mad. But I control my temper; I'd be ashamed of myself if I didn't" (Harter, 1996, p. 208).

By middle childhood, children are aware of their culture's "rules" for emotional expression (Cole, Bruschi, & Tamang, 2002), which parents communicate through reactions to children's displays of feelings (Eisenberg et al., 1996). Children learn the difference between having an emotion and expressing it. They learn what makes them angry, fearful, or sad and how other people react to a display of these emotions, and they learn to adapt their behavior accordingly. Kindergartners believe that a parent can make a child less sad by telling the child to stop crying or can make a child less afraid of a dog by telling the child there is nothing to be afraid of. Sixth-graders know that an emotion may be suppressed, but it still exists (Rotenberg & Eisenberg, 1997).

Emotional self-regulation involves effortful (voluntary) control of emotions, attention, and behavior (Eisenberg et al., 2004). Children low in effortful control tend to become visibly angry or frustrated when interrupted or prevented from doing something they want to do. Children with high effortful control can stifle the impulse to show negative emotion at inappropriate times. Effortful control may be temperamentally based but generally increases with age; low effortful control may predict later behavior problems (Eisenberg et al., 2004). Effortful control affects children's adjustment to school. Among 4½- to 8-year-olds in a southwestern U.S. city and 7- to 10-year-olds in Beijing, China, children with high effortful control tended to be well adjusted (Eisenberg et al., 2004; Zhou, Eisenberg, Wang, & Reiser, 2004).

Children tend to become more empathic and more inclined to prosocial behavior in middle childhood, and such behavior is a sign of positive emotional adjustment. Prosocial children tend to act appropriately in social situations, to be relatively

Checkpoint

Can you . . .

✔ From a neo-Piagetian perspective, tell how the self-concept develops in middle childhood?

✔ Compare Erikson's and Harter's views about sources of self-esteem?

✔ Describe how the "helpless pattern" can affect children's reactions to social rejection?

✔ Explain the relationship between self-esteem and volunteer activity?

 Guidepost

2. How do school-age children show emotional growth?

Checkpoint
Can you . . .

✔ Identify some aspects of
emotional growth in middle
childhood, and tell how
parental treatment may affect
children's handling of negative
emotions?

Guidepost

3. How do parent-child relationships change in middle
childhood?

free from negative emotion, and to cope with problems constructively (Eisenberg, Fabes, & Murphy, 1996). Parents who acknowledge children's feelings of distress and help them focus on solving the root problem foster empathy, prosocial development, and social skills (Bryant, 1987; Eisenberg et al., 1996). When parents respond with disapproval or punishment, emotions such as anger and fear may become more intense and may impair children's social adjustment (Fabes, Leonard, Kupanoff, & Martin, 2001). Or the children may become secretive and anxious about negative feelings. As children approach early adolescence, parental intolerance of negative emotion may heighten parent-child conflict (Eisenberg, Fabes et al., 1999).

The Child in the Family

School-age children spend more of their free time away from home than when they were younger, visiting and socializing with peers. They also spend more time at school and on studies and less time at family meals than 20 years ago (Juster et al., 2004). Still, home and the people who live there remain an important part of most children's lives. According to a national survey of 10,445 U.S. parents, 65 percent of children ages 6 to 17 have dinner each night with at least one parent, and about 75 percent talk to or play with a parent at least once a day (Lugaila, 2003).

To understand the child in the family we need to look at the family environment—its atmosphere and structure. These in turn are affected by what goes on beyond the walls of the home. As Bronfenbrenner's theory predicts, additional layers of influence—including parents' work and socioeconomic status and societal trends such as urbanization, changes in family size, divorce, and remarriage—help shape the family environment and, thus, children's development. Culture, too, defines rhythms of family life and roles of family members. African American families like Marian Anderson's, for example, carry on extended-family traditions that include living near or with kin, a strong sense of family obligation, ethnic pride, and mutual aid (Parke

Although school-age children spend less time at home than before, parents continue to be very important in children's lives. Parents who enjoy being with their children tend to raise children who feel good about themselves—and about their parents.

& Buriel, 1998). As we look at the child in the family, then, we need to be aware of outside forces that affect the family.

Family Atmosphere

The most important influences of the family environment on children's development come from the atmosphere within the home. Is it supportive and loving or conflict ridden? One contributing factor is how well parents handle school-age children's growing need—and ability—to make their own decisions. Another factor is the family's economic situation. How does parents' work affect children's well-being? Does the family have enough money to provide for basic needs?

Parenting Issues: Coregulation and Discipline During the course of childhood, control of behavior gradually shifts from parents to child. Middle childhood brings a transitional stage of **coregulation,** in which parent and child share power. Parents exercise oversight, but children enjoy moment-to-moment self-regulation (Maccoby, 1984). With regard to problems among peers, for example, parents now rely less on direct management and more on discussion with their own child (Parke & Buriel, 1998). Children are more apt to follow their parents' wishes when they recognize that the parents are fair and are concerned about the child's welfare and that they may "know better" because of experience. It helps if parents try to defer to children's maturing judgment and take strong stands only on important issues (Maccoby, 1984).

> **coregulation** Transitional stage in the control of behavior in which parents exercise general supervision and children exercise moment-to-moment self-regulation.

The shift to coregulation affects the way parents handle discipline (Maccoby, 1984; Roberts, Block, & Block, 1984). Parents of school-age children are more likely to use inductive techniques. For example, 8-year-old Jared's father points out how his actions affect others: "Hitting Jermaine hurts him and makes him feel bad." In other situations, Jared's parents may appeal to his self-esteem ("What happened to the helpful boy who was here yesterday?"), sense of humor ("If you go one more day without a bath, we'll know when you're coming without looking!"), moral values ("A big, strong boy like you shouldn't sit on the train and let an old person stand"), or appreciation ("Aren't you glad that your father cares enough to remind you to wear boots so that you won't catch a cold?"). Above all, Jared's parents let him know that he must bear the consequences of his behavior ("No wonder you missed the school bus today—you stayed up too late last night! Now you'll have to walk to school").

The way parents and children resolve conflicts may be more important than the specific outcomes. If family conflict is constructive, it can help children see the need for rules and standards. They also learn what kinds of issues are worth arguing about and what strategies can be effective (A. R. Eisenberg, 1996). However, as children become preadolescents and their striving for autonomy becomes more insistent, the quality of family problem solving often deteriorates (Vuchinich, Angelelli, & Gatherum, 1996).

Checkpoint

Can you . . .

✔ Describe how coregulation works and how discipline and the handling of family conflict change during middle childhood?

Effects of Parents' Work In 2002, nearly 4 out of 5 U.S. mothers with children ages 6 to 17 were in the workforce (Bureau of Labor Statistics, 2002a). With more than half of all new mothers in the United States going to work within a year of giving birth (Bureau of Labor Statistics, 2002b), many children have never known a time when their mothers were *not* working outside the home.

Guidepost

4. What are the effects of parents' work and of poverty on children's well-being?

Most studies of the impact of parents' work on children's well-being have focused on employed mothers. In general, the more satisfied a mother is with her employment status, the more effective she is likely to be as a parent (Parke & Buriel, 1998). However, the impact of a mother's work depends on many other factors, including the child's age, sex, temperament, and personality; whether the mother works full- or part-time; why she is working; whether she has a supportive or unsupportive partner, or none; the family's socioeconomic status; and the kind of care the child receives before and/or after school (Parke & Buriel, 1998). Often a single mother like Marian Anderson's must work to stave off economic disaster. How her working affects her children may hinge on how much time and energy she has left over to spend with them and what sort of role model she is (B. L. Barber & Eccles, 1992)—clearly, a positive one in Annie Anderson's case.

How well parents keep track of their children may be more important than whether the mother works outside the home (Crouter, MacDermid, McHale, & Perry-Jenkins, 1990). Some children of employed mothers are supervised before and after school by their fathers, other relatives, or baby-sitters. Some, especially if their mothers are single or employed full-time, go to structured child care programs or enrichment activities. Many children experience several types of out-of-school care (NICHD Early Child Care Research Network, 2004).

Like good child care for preschoolers, good after-school programs have relatively low enrollment, low child-staff ratios, and well-educated staff (Rosenthal & Vandell, 1996). Children, especially boys, in organized after-school programs with flexible programming and a positive emotional climate tend to adjust better and do better in school (Pierce, Hamm, & Vandell, 1999; Posner & Vandell, 1999).

About 9 percent of school-aged children and 23 percent of early adolescents are reported to be in *self-care,* regularly caring for themselves at home without adult supervision (Hofferth & Jankuniene, 2000; NICHD Early Childhood Research Network, 2004). This arrangement is advisable only for older children who are mature, responsible, and resourceful and know how to get help in an emergency—and, even then, only if a parent stays in touch by telephone.

Poverty and Parenting Close to 17 percent of all U.S. children under 18—about 12.1 million in all—lived in poverty in 2002 (Children's Defense Fund, 2004; Proctor & Dalaker, 2003), and about 60 percent of black and Hispanic children were poor or near-poor (NCHS, 2004). Poverty can inspire people like Marian Anderson's mother to work hard and make a better life for their children—or it can crush their spirits.

Poor children are more likely than other children to have emotional or behavioral problems, and their cognitive potential and school performance suffer even more (Brooks-Gunn, Britto, & Brady, 1998; Brooks-Gunn & Duncan, 1997; Duncan & Brooks-Gunn, 1997; McLoyd, 1998). Poverty can harm children's development through its impact on parents' emotional state and parenting practices and on the home environment they create (Brooks-Gunn & Duncan, 1997; Brooks-Gunn et al., 1998; Evans, 2004). Vonnie McLoyd's (1990, 1998; Mistry, Vandewater, Huston, & McLoyd, 2002) ecological analysis of the effects of poverty traces a route that leads to adult psychological distress, to effects on child rearing, and finally to emotional, behavioral, and academic problems in children. Parents who live in poverty are likely to become anxious, depressed, and irritable. They may become less affectionate with and less responsive to their children. They may discipline inconsistently, harshly, and arbitrarily. The children, in turn, tend to become depressed themselves, to have trouble getting along with peers, to lack self-confidence, to develop behavioral and academic problems, and to engage in antisocial acts (Brooks-Gunn et al., 1998; Evans, 2004; Evans & English, 2002; J. M. Fields & Smith, 1998; McLoyd, 1990, 1998; Mistry et al., 2002). Families under economic stress are less likely to monitor their children's activities, and lack of monitoring is associated with poorer school performance and social adjustment (Bolger, Patterson, Thompson, & Kupersmidt, 1995).

The effects of *persistent* poverty can be complex. In a six-year longitudinal study of children who had been in Head Start, those who had been continuously poor since

What's Your View?

• If finances permit, should one parent stay home to take care of the children?

age 5 showed no worse academic and behavioral outcomes in fifth grade than children who had been poor for only the last four of those six years or children who had been poor only intermittently. What seemed to be more damaging to children were family characteristics that may accompany poverty—unstable adult relationships, psychiatric problems, and violent or criminal behavior (Ackerman, Brown, & Izard, 2004).

The findings just discussed come largely from studies of African American and European American families but may apply as well to Latino families. In a study of 111 European American and 167 Mexican American urban families, all with children in fifth grade, parents under economic pressure—regardless of ethnicity—tended to show symptoms of depression, which, in turn, were associated with marital problems and negative parenting (rejection, hostile control, or withdrawal) (Parke et al., 2004).

Parents who can turn to relatives (as Annie Anderson did) or to community representatives for emotional support, help with child care, and child-rearing information often can parent their children more effectively. A four-year longitudinal study of 152 single mother-headed African American families in four economically depressed counties of Georgia found an ecological pattern opposite to the one McLoyd described. Mothers who, despite economic stress, were emotionally healthy and had relatively high self-esteem tended to have academically and socially competent children who reinforced the mothers' positive parenting; and this, in turn, supported the children's continued academic success and socially desirable behavior (Brody, Kim, Murry, & Brown, 2004).

Family Structure

Family structure in the United States has changed dramatically. In earlier generations, the vast majority of children grew up in families with two married biological or adoptive parents. Today, although 7 in 10 children under 18 live with two parents (not necessarily married), that proportion represents a dramatic decline (Fields, 2003; see Figure 10-1). Between 1970 and 2003, the proportion of family groups with children that contained two parents fell from 87 percent to 68 percent, while the

Checkpoint

Can you . . .

✔ Identify ways in which parents' work can affect children?

✔ Discuss effects of poverty on child raising?

Guidepost

5. What impact does family structure have on children's development?

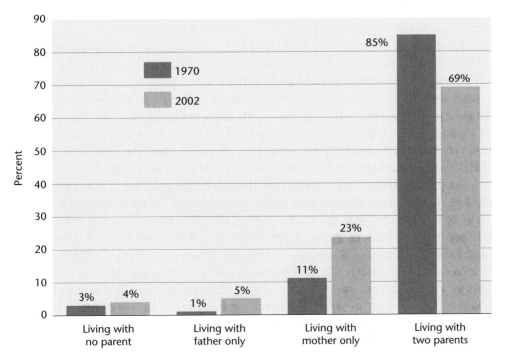

Figure 10-1

Living arrangements of children younger than 18, 1970–2002. Most children under 18 in the United States live with two parents, but this proportion dropped during the past quarter-century. Many of these two-parent families are stepfamilies. Note: Percentages do not add up to 100 percent because fractional amounts have been dropped. (Source: Data from U.S. Department of Commerce, 1996; Lugaila, 1998, Table A; Fields, 2003.)

proportion of single-mother families grew from 12 percent to 26 percent, and that of single-father families grew from 1 percent to 6 percent (Fields, 2004). Furthermore, many two-parent families are stepfamilies resulting from divorce and remarriage. Another increasingly common family type is the gay or lesbian family. (Grandparent-headed families are discussed in Chapter 16.)

Other things being equal, children tend to do better in traditional two-parent families than in cohabiting, divorced, single-parent, or stepfamilies (Brown, 2004). Data from a national survey of 35,938 U.S. families show worse emotional, behavioral, and academic outcomes for 6- to 11-year-old children living with cohabiting biological parents than for those living with married biological parents. However, the difference in outcomes can be explained largely by differences in economic resources, parental well-being, and parenting effectiveness (Brown, 2004). Thus, structure in itself is not necessarily the key; the parents' relationship with each other and their ability to create a favorable atmosphere may affect children's adjustment more than does marital status (Bray & Hetherington, 1993; Bronstein et al., 1993; D.A. Dawson, 1991).

Adoptive Families   Adoption is found in all cultures throughout history. It is not only for infertile people; single people, older people, gays and lesbians, and people who already have biological children have become adoptive parents. (Adoption by gays and lesbians is discussed later in this chapter.) In 2000, about 1.6 million U.S. children under 18—2.5 percent—were adopted (Kreider, 2003). An estimated 60 percent of legal adoptions are by stepparents or relatives, usually grandparents (Goodman, Emery, & Haugaard, 1998; Haugaard, 1998; Kreider, 2003).

Adoptions usually take place through public or private agencies. Agency adoptions are supposed to be confidential, with no contact between the birth mother and the adoptive parents, and the identity of the birth mother is kept secret. However, in recent years independent adoptions, made by direct agreement between birth parents and adoptive parents, have become more common (Brodzinsky, 1997; Goodman et al., 1998). Often these are **open adoptions,** in which the parties share information or have direct contact. Studies suggest that the presumed risks of open adoption, such as fear that a birth mother who knows her child's whereabouts will try to reclaim the child, are overstated (Grotevant, McRoy, Elde, & Fravel, 1994). In a survey of 1,059 California adoptive families, whether an adoption was open bore no relation to the children's adjustment or to the parents' satisfaction with the adoption, both of which were very high (Berry, Dylla, Barth, & Needell, 1998).

Adoptions of foreign-born children by U.S. families nearly quadrupled between 1978 and 2001, from 5,315 to an estimated 20,000 (Bosch et al., 2003), and 13 percent of adopted children in 2000 were foreign born. Because of the cultural preference for boys in Asian countries, more girls are available for adoption there. About 17 percent of adoptions are transracial, most often involving white parents adopting an Asian or Latin American child (Kreider, 2003). Rules governing interracial adoption vary from state to state; some states give priority to same-race adoption, whereas others require that race *not* be a factor in approval of an adoption.

Adopting a child carries special challenges: integrating the adopted child into the family, explaining the adoption to the child, helping the child develop a healthy sense of self, and perhaps eventually helping the child find and contact the biological parents. A review of the literature found few significant differences in adjustment between adopted and nonadopted children (Haugaard, 1998). Children adopted in infancy are least likely to have adjustment problems (Sharma, McGue, & Benson, 1996b). Any problems that do occur may surface during middle childhood, when children become more aware of differences in the way families are formed (Freeark et al., 2005), or in adolescence (Goodman et al., 1998; Sharma, McGue, & Benson, 1996a), particularly for boys (Freeark et al., 2005).

open adoption   Adoption in which the birth parents and the adoptive parents know each other's identities and share infomation or have direct contact.

This Caucasian woman reading to her African American and Hispanic adopted daughters is part of a trend toward transracial adoptions. Adoptive parents face special challenges, such as the need to explain the adoption to the child. But most adoptive children view their adoption positively and see it as playing only a minor role in their identity.

Perhaps because females tend to be more verbal and more concerned about emotional matters, adoptive mothers are more likely than adoptive fathers to bring up the topic of a child's adoption and to discuss its implications. By the same token, adopted girls are more receptive to such conversations than adopted boys and may become more comfortable with their adoptive status (Freeark et al., 2005).

Does foreign adoption entail special problems? Aside from the possibility of malnourishment or other serious medical conditions in children from developing countries (Bosch et al., 2003), a number of studies say no. In fact, children adopted from abroad tend to have even fewer behavior and mental health problems than other adoptees (Juffer & van IJzendoorn, 2005). One study looked at 100 Israeli families with 7- to 13-year-olds adopted soon after birth—half from South America and half from within Israel. The researchers found no significant differences in the children's psychological adjustment, school adjustment and performance, or observed behavior at home or in the way they coped with being adopted (Levy-Shiff, Zoran, & Shulman, 1997). However, not all international adoptions proceed so smoothly, especially when (as with some of the Romanian children adopted from orphanages) the children have experienced substandard care or are older at the time of adoption (refer back to Chapter 4).

When Parents Divorce   The United States has one of the highest divorce rates in the world. The annual number of divorces has tripled since 1960 (Harvey & Pauwels, 1999), but the divorce rate has remained stable or declined slightly since 2001 (Munson & Sutton, 2004). More than 1 million children are involved in divorces each year (Harvey & Pauwels, 1999).

Adjusting to Divorce   Divorce is stressful for children. First there is the stress of marital conflict and then of parental separation and the abrupt departure of one parent, usually the father. Children may not fully understand what is happening and why. Divorce is, of course, stressful for the parents as well and may negatively affect

What's Your View?

- If you were infertile, do you think you would try to adopt?

- If so, would you want the adoption to be open? Why or why not?

Checkpoint
Can you . . .

✔ Discuss trends in adoption and the adjustment of adopted children?

their parenting. The family's standard of living is likely to drop; and, if a parent moves away, a child's relationship with the noncustodial parent may suffer (Kelly & Emery, 2003). A parent's remarriage or second divorce after remarriage can increase the stress on children, renewing feelings of loss (Ahrons & Tanner, 2003; Amato, 2003).

Children's emotional or behavioral problems may reflect the level of parental conflict *before* the divorce. If predivorce discord was chronic, overt, or destructive, children may be as well, or better, off after a divorce (Amato, 2003; Amato & Booth, 1997). However, in as many as 1 in 5 divorced families, parental conflict continues or escalates. Two years after a divorce, children suffer more from dissension in a divorced family than do children in a nondivorced family. Thus, if conflict is going to *continue*, children may be better off in an acrimonious two-parent household than if the parents divorce (Hetherington & Stanley-Hagan, 1999).

A child's adjustment to divorce may depend in part on the child's age or maturity, gender, temperament, and psychosocial adjustment before the divorce. Younger children tend to be more anxious about divorce, have less realistic perceptions of what caused it, and are more likely to blame themselves; but they may adapt more quickly than older children, who better understand what is going on. School-age children are sensitive to parental pressures and loyalty conflicts and, like younger children, may fear abandonment and rejection. Boys generally find it harder to adjust than girls do (Bray, 1991; Hetherington, Stanley-Hagan, & Anderson, 1989; Hetherington et al., 1998; Hines, 1997; Masten, Best, & Garmezy, 1990; Parke & Buriel, 1998).

Lifemap CD

How can parents best help their children adjust to a divorce? For one expert's suggestions, watch the "Children and Divorce" video in Chapter 10 of your CD.

Children of divorce tend to be better adjusted if they have reliable, frequent contact with the noncustodial parent, usually the father.

The way parents handle such issues as custody and visitation arrangements, finances, reorganization of household duties, household relocation, contact with the noncustodial parent, remarriage, and the child's relationship with a stepparent makes a difference. Children do better after divorce if the custodial parent is warm, supportive, and authoritative, monitors the child's activities, and holds age-appropriate expectations; if parental conflict subsides; and if the nonresident parent maintains close contact and involvement (Ahrons & Tanner, 2003; Kelly & Emery, 2003).

Parent education programs that teach separated or divorced couples how to prevent or deal with conflict, keep lines of communication open, develop an effective coparenting relationship, and help children adjust to divorce have been introduced in many courts, with measurable success. One such program dramatically reduced the children's likelihood of showing mental health problems six years later as compared with a control group who merely received books on adjusting to divorce (Wolchik et al., 2002).

Custody and Visitation Issues In most divorce cases, the mother gets custody, though paternal custody is a growing trend. Children living with divorced mothers do better when the father pays child support, which may be a barometer of the tie between father and child and also of cooperation between the ex-spouses. Frequency of contact with the father is not as important as the quality of the father-child relationship and the level of parental conflict. Children who are close to their nonresident fathers, and whose fathers are authoritative parents, tend to do better in school and are less likely to have behavior problems (Amato & Gilbreth, 1999; Kelly & Emery, 2003).

Joint custody, custody shared by both parents, can be advantageous in some cases, if the parents can cooperate, since both parents can continue to be closely involved with the child. When parents have joint *legal* custody, they share the right and responsibility to make decisions regarding the child's welfare. When parents have joint *physical* custody (which is less common), the child is supposed to live part-time with each of them. An analysis of 33 studies found that children in either legal or physical joint custody were better adjusted and had higher self-esteem and better family relationships than children in sole custody. In fact, the joint custody children were as well-adjusted as children in nondivorced families (Bauserman, 2002). It is likely, though, that couples who choose joint custody are those that have less conflict.

Long-term Effects Most children of divorce adjust reasonably well, but divorce increases the risk of problems in adolescence or adulthood, such as antisocial behavior, difficulties with authority figures (Amato, 2003; Kelly & Emery, 2003), and dropping out of school (McLanahan & Sandefur, 1994). According to some research, 25 percent of children of divorce reach adulthood with serious social, emotional, or psychological problems, as compared with 10 percent of children whose parents stay together (Hetherington & Kelly, 2002). Furthermore, divorce may have consequences for generations unborn at the time of the breakup. In a 20-year longitudinal study of a random sample of 2,033 married persons in the United States, the children of those who divorced tended to have lower educational levels, more instability in their own marriages, and increased tension with their own children than those whose parents had remained married. The children of these "children of divorce" (the grandchildren of the original respondents), in turn, also tended to have lower educational levels and more marital discord as well as weak bonds with their parents (Amato & Cheadle, 2005).

The anxiety connected with parental divorce may surface as children enter adulthood and try to form intimate relationships of their own (Amato, 2003; Wallerstein, Lewis, & Blakeslee, 2000). Having experienced their parents' divorce, some young adults are afraid of making commitments that might end in disappointment and are intent on protecting their independence (Glenn & Marquardt, 2001; Wallerstein & Corbin, 1999). Even when adult children of divorce have no serious problems, they may have lingering feelings of sadness, worry, or regret or even pain and distress, often related to a sense of lack of control over their lives (Kelly & Emery, 2003). Much depends on how young people resolve and interpret the experience of parental divorce. Some, who saw a high degree of conflict between their parents, are able to learn from that negative example and to form highly intimate relationships themselves (Shulman, Scharf, Lumer, & Maurer, 2001).

Living in a One-Parent Family One-parent families result from divorce or separation, unwed parenthood, or death. The number of single-parent families in the United States has more than tripled since 1970 (Fields, 2004) with rising rates of divorce and of parenthood outside of marriage. Today 28 percent of U.S. children live with only one parent (Fields, 2003; refer back to Figure 10-1). Many of these "single-parent" households are actually cohabiting households that include the mother's or, more typically, the father's unwed partner (Fields, 2003; see Figure 10-2).

Children are more than four times more likely to live with a single mother than with a single father, but 1 in 6 single-parent U.S. families are headed by the father (Fields, 2004; refer to Figures 10-1 and 10-2). The number of father-only families has more than quadrupled since 1970, apparently due largely to the increase in paternal custody after divorce (Fields, 2004).

Although children in single-parent families do well overall, some studies have found that these children tend to lag socially and educationally behind peers in

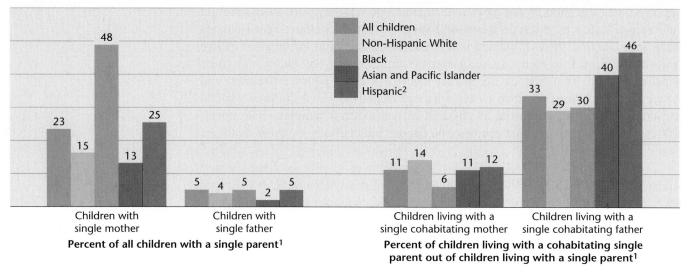

¹The parent is the householder or partner in an unmarried-partner household.
Single means the parent has no spouse in the household.
²People of Hispanic origin may be of any race.

Figure 10-2

Children living with single parents or single cohabiting parents, March 2002. (Source: Fields, 2003. Data from U.S. Census Bureau, Annual Demographic Supplement in the March 2002 Current Population Survey.)

two-parent families. Children living with married parents tend to have more daily interaction with their parents, are read to more often, progress more steadily in school, and participate more in extracurricular activities than children living with a single parent (Lugaila, 2003). However, negative outcomes for children living with a single parent are far from inevitable. The child's age and level of development, the family's financial circumstances, whether there are frequent moves, and other aspects of the family situation make a difference (Seltzer, 2000). In a longitudinal study of 1,500 white, black, and Hispanic families with 6- and 7-year-old children, the mother's educational and ability level and, to a lesser extent, family income and the quality of the home environment accounted for any negative effects of single parenting on academic performance and behavior. The same remained true when the children reached adolescence (Ricciuti, 1999, 2004; see Chapter 12).

Because single parents often lack the resources needed for good parenting, potential risks to children in these families might be reduced or eliminated through increased access to economic, social, educational, and parenting support. In international math and science tests in 11 industrialized countries,* the achievement gap between third- and fourth-graders living in single-parent households and those living with two biological parents was greater for U.S. children than for any other country except New Zealand. Children of single parents did better in countries with supportive family policies such as child and family allowances, tax benefits to single parents, maternity leave, and released time from work (Pong et al., 2003).

Living in a Stepfamily   The stepfamily is different from the "natural" family. It has a larger cast, which may include the relatives of up to four adults (the remarried pair plus one or two former spouses). A child's loyalties to an absent or dead parent may interfere with forming ties to a stepparent. Adjustment is harder when there are many children, including those from both partners' previous marriages, or

*Australia, Austria, Canada, England, Ireland, Iceland, Netherlands, New Zealand, Norway, Scotland, and the United States.

when a new child is born (Hetherington et al., 1989). Many children maintain ties with their noncustodial parents. Noncustodial mothers tend to keep in touch more than do noncustodial fathers and offer more social support (Gunnoe & Hetherington, 2004).

Findings on the impact of remarriage on children are mixed (Parke & Buriel, 1998). Some studies have found that boys—who often have more trouble than girls in adjusting to divorce and single-parent living, usually with the mother—benefit from a stepfather. A girl, on the other hand, may find the new man in the house a threat to her independence and to her close relationship with her mother and may be less likely to accept him (Bray & Hetherington, 1993; Hetherington, 1987; Hetherington et al., 1989; Hetherington et al., 1998; Hines, 1997). In a longitudinal study of a nationally representative sample of U.S. adults, mothers who remarried or formed new cohabiting relationships used less harsh discipline than mothers who remained single, and their children reported better relationships with them. On the other hand, supervision was greatest in stable single-mother families (Thomson, Mosley, Hanson, & McLanahan, 2001).

In a study of 173 college students of mixed ethnicity in a large midwestern U.S. city, those raised in stepfamilies tended to report lower well-being than those raised in intact families, and they also were less likely to recall having been securely attached. Thus, attachment quality may help explain why people from stepfamilies tend not to fare as well emotionally, socially, and psychologically as those from intact families (Love & Murdock, 2004).

Living with Gay or Lesbian Parents An estimated 1 to 9 million U.S. children and adolescents have at least one gay or lesbian parent. Some gays and lesbians are raising children born of previous heterosexual relationships. Others conceive by artificial means, use surrogate mothers, or adopt children (Perrin and AAP Committee on Psychosocial Aspects of Child and Family Health, 2002).

A considerable body of research has examined the development of children of gays and lesbians, including physical and emotional health, intelligence, adjustment, sense of self, moral judgment, and social and sexual functioning, and has indicated no special concerns (AAP Committee on Psychosocial Aspects of Child and Family Health, 2002; Mooney-Somers & Golombok, 2000; C. J. Patterson, 1992, 1995a, 1995b, 1997; Perrin and AAP Committee on Psychosocial Aspects of Child and Family Health, 2002; Wainwright, Russell, & Patterson, 2004). There is *no* consistent difference between homosexual and heterosexual parents in emotional health or parenting

This girl has two fathers—and both obviously dote on the child. Contrary to popular stereotypes, children living with homosexual parents are no more likely than other children to have social or psychological problems or to turn out to be homosexual themselves.

skills and attitudes (Perrin and AAP Committee on Psychosocial Aspects of Child and Family Health, 2002). Openly gay or lesbian parents usually have positive relationships with their children, and the children are no more likely than children raised by heterosexual parents to have social or psychological problems (Chan, Raboy, & Patterson, 1998; Mooney-Somers & Golombok, 2000; C. J. Patterson, 1992, 1995a, 1997; Wainwright et al., 2004). Furthermore, children of gays and lesbians are no more likely to be homosexual themselves or to be confused about their gender than are children of heterosexuals (Anderssen, Amlie, & Ytteroy, 2002;

Checkpoint

Can you . . .

✔ Discuss the impact of parental divorce on children and how living in a single-parent household can affect children's well-being?

✔ Identify some special issues and challenges of a stepfamily?

✔ Summarize findings on outcomes of child raising by gay and lesbian parents?

Guidepost

6. How do siblings influence and get along with one another, and what part do pets play in children's development?

B. M. King, 1996; Mooney-Somers & Golombok, 2000; C. J. Patterson, 1997; Wainwright et al., 2004).

Such findings have social policy implications for legal decisions on custody and visitation disputes, foster care, and adoptions. In the face of controversy over gay and lesbian marriage or civil unions, with its implications for the security of children, several states have considered or adopted legislation sanctioning second-parent adoption by same-sex partners. The American Academy of Pediatrics supports legislative and legal efforts to permit a partner in a same-sex couple to adopt the other partner's child so that the child may enjoy a right to a continuing relationship with both (AAP Committee on Psychosocial Aspects of Child and Family Health, 2002).

Sibling Relationships

In remote rural areas or villages of Asia, Africa, Oceania, and Central and South America, it is common to see older girls caring for three or four younger siblings: feeding, comforting, and toilet training them; disciplining them; assigning chores; and generally keeping an eye on them. In such a community, older siblings have an important, culturally defined role. Parents train children early to teach younger sisters and brothers how to gather firewood, carry water, tend animals, and grow

This boy in Surinam has an important responsibility: taking care of his younger brother. Siblings in nonindustrialized societies have clear, culturally defined roles throughout life.

food. Younger siblings absorb intangible values, such as respecting elders and placing the welfare of the group above that of the individual (Cicirelli, 1994). Often this culturally important learning arises spontaneously as older siblings care for the younger (Maynard, 2002). In industrialized societies such as the United States, parents generally try not to "burden" older children with the regular care of siblings (Weisner, 1993). Older siblings do teach younger ones, but this usually happens informally and not as an established part of the social system (Cicirelli, 1994).

The number of siblings in a family and their spacing, birth order, and gender often determine roles and relationships. The larger number of siblings in nonindustrialized societies helps the family carry on its work and provide for aging members. In industrialized societies, siblings tend to be fewer and farther apart in age, enabling parents to focus more resources and attention on each child (Cicirelli, 1994).

Two longitudinal studies in England and in Pennsylvania, based on naturalistic observation of siblings and mothers and interviews with the mothers, found that changes in sibling relationships were most likely to occur when one sibling was between ages 7 and 9. Both mothers and children often attributed these changes to outside friendships, which led to jealousy and competitiveness or loss of interest in and intimacy with the sibling. Sometimes the younger sibling's growing assertiveness played a part (Dunn, 1996).

Sibling relations are a laboratory for conflict resolution. Siblings are motivated to make up after quarrels, since they know they will see each other every day. They learn that expressing anger does not end a relationship. Children are more apt to squabble with same-sex siblings; two brothers quarrel more than any other combination (Cicirelli, 1976, 1995).

Siblings influence each other's gender development. In a 3-year longitudinal study of 198 siblings (median ages 10 and 8), secondborns tended to become more like their older siblings in gender-related attitudes, personality, and leisure activities. Firstborns were more influenced by parents and less by younger siblings (McHale, Updegraff, Helms-Erikson, & Crouter, 2001).

Siblings influence each other, not only *directly,* through their own interactions, but also *indirectly* through their impact on each other's relationship with the parents. Specifically, parents' experience with an older sibling influences their expectations and treatment of a younger one (Brody, 2004). Also, behavior patterns established with parents tend to "spill over" into a child's behavior with siblings (Brody, Stoneman, & Gauger, 1996).

Companion Animals

When the older daughter of one of the authors of this book brought home a collection of poetry her fifth-grade class had "published," more of the compositions dealt with pets than with sisters and brothers. The children wrote about bathing and training a dog, about the way a fish moves, about having to release a baby frog into a pond, about going to a store in winter to buy food for a hungry cat, and about the anger a pet dog showed after having been left with the veterinarian while the family went away for a weekend.

Animal companions play an important and often overlooked role in children's personality development. Families with school-age children are most likely to have pets, and many families have more than one. In studies in California, the midwestern United States, and Hesse, Germany, 70 to 90 percent of families with children in this age group owned or recently had owned pets (Melson, 1998).

Companion animals may contribute to what Erikson called *basic trust* and help children meet the challenges of autonomy and industry (Melson, 1998). Even very young children form trustful attachments to animals and turn to them for emotional support. Having a pet may teach an older child about empathy, responsibility, and caring for others. When 22 seven- and 8-year-olds in a small English town were asked to list the people and animals most important to them, 17 of the 18 children who had pets ranked them among their 10 most important relationships. When asked to whom they would turn in various hypothetical situations (such as being ill, scared, or embarrassed; after having a bad day; or when having a problem or special secret), children often chose pets (McNicholas & Collis, 2001).

What's Your View?

• Did you have one or more pets as a child? If so, in what ways did they contribute to your development?

Checkpoint

Can you . . .

✔ Compare the roles and responsibilities of siblings in industrialized and nonindustrialized countries?

✔ Give examples of ways in which siblings affect each other's development?

✔ Tell how pets affect children's personality development?

The Child in the Peer Group

In middle childhood the peer group comes into its own. Groups form naturally among children who live near one another or go to school together; thus, peer groups often consist of children of the same racial or ethnic origin (Pellegrini et al., 2002) and similar socioeconomic status. Children who play together are usually close in age and of the same sex (Hartup, 1992). Groups of boys more consistently pursue gender-typed activities, but girls are more likely to engage in "cross-gender" activities, such as team sports, which are valued by both boys and girls (McHale, Kim, Whiteman, & Crouter, 2004).

How does the peer group influence children? What determines their acceptance by peers and their ability to make friends?

Guidepost

7. How do relationships with peers change in middle childhood, and what influences popularity and choice of friends?

Positive and Negative Effects of Peer Relations

Children benefit from doing things with peers. They develop skills needed for sociability and intimacy, they enhance relationships, and they gain a sense of belonging. They are motivated to achieve, and they attain a sense of identity. They learn

Among their peers, children get a sense of how smart, how athletic, and how likable they are. Both competition and shared confidences build the self-concept, helping children develop social skills and a sense of belonging. Peer groups tend to be of the same sex, enabling boys and girls to learn gender-appropriate behaviors.

leadership and communication skills, cooperation, roles, and rules (Pellegrini, Kato, Blatchford, & Baines, 2002; Zarbatany, Hartmann, & Rankin, 1990).

As children begin to move away from parental influence, the peer group opens new perspectives and frees them to make independent judgments. Testing values they previously accepted unquestioningly against those of their peers helps them decide which to keep and which to discard. In comparing themselves with others their age, children can gauge their abilities more realistically and gain a clearer sense of self-efficacy (Bandura, 1994). The peer group helps children learn how to get along in society—how to adjust their needs and desires to those of others, when to yield, and when to stand firm. The peer group offers emotional security. It is reassuring for children to find out that they are not alone in harboring thoughts that might offend an adult.

Same-sex peer groups may help children learn gender-appropriate behaviors and incorporate gender roles into their self-concept. In a two-year study of 106 ethnically diverse but mostly middle-class third- through seventh-graders, a sense of being typical of one's gender and being content with that gender contributed to self-esteem and well-being, whereas feeling pressure—from parents, peers, or oneself—to conform to gender stereotypes lessened well-being (Yunger, Carver, & Perry, 2004).

On the negative side, peer groups can be cliques, intent on exclusion as well as inclusion. They may reinforce **prejudice:** unfavorable attitudes toward "outsiders," especially members of certain racial or ethnic groups. A study in Montreal, Canada, where tensions exist between French-speaking and English-speaking citizens, found signs of prejudice among 254 English-speaking children in kindergarten through sixth grade (Powlishta, Serbin, Doyle, & White, 1994). The researchers asked boys and girls whether each of two cartoon children—one English speaking and the other French speaking—would be likely to be, for example, *helpful, smart, mean,* and *naughty* and which of the two pictured children they would like to play with. A similar procedure was followed using male and female figures (with regard to such gender stereotypes as *ambitious* and *gentle*) and figures of overweight and normal-weight children. Children tended to apply positive adjectives to children like themselves, but these biases, except for a preference for children of the same sex,

prejudice Unfavorable attitude toward members of certain groups outside one's own, especially racial or ethnic groups.

What's
Your View?

• How can parents and schools reduce racial, religious, and ethnic prejudice?

diminished with age and cognitive development. Children with flexible beliefs about people's ability to change are less likely to hold such stereotyped ideas (Karafantis & Levy, 2004).

The peer group also can foster antisocial tendencies. Preadolescent children are especially susceptible to pressure to conform. To be part of a peer group, a child is expected to accept its values and behavioral norms, and even though these may be socially undesirable, children may not have the strength to resist. It is usually in the company of peers that some children shoplift and begin to use drugs (Hartup, 1992). Of course, some degree of conformity to group standards is healthy. It is unhealthy when it becomes destructive or prompts people to act against their own better judgment.

Checkpoint

Can you . . .

✔ Tell some ways in which members of a peer group tend to be alike?

✔ Identify positive and negative effects of the peer group?

Popularity

Popularity becomes more important in middle childhood. Schoolchildren whose peers like them are likely to be well adjusted as adolescents. Those who are not accepted by peers or who are overly aggressive are more likely to develop psychological problems, drop out of school, or become delinquent (Hartup, 1992; Kupersmidt & Coie, 1990; Morison & Masten, 1991; Newcomb, Bukowski, & Pattee, 1993; Parker & Asher, 1987).

Popularity can be measured in two ways, and the results may differ. Researchers measure *sociometric popularity* by asking children which peers they like most and least. Such studies have identified five *peer status groups: popular* (youngsters who receive many positive nominations), *rejected* (those who receive many negative nominations), *neglected* (those who receive few nominations of either kind), *controversial* (those who receive many positive and many negative nominations), and *average* (those who do not receive an unusual number of nominations of either kind). *Perceived popularity* is measured by asking children which children are best liked by their peers.

Sociometrically popular children typically have good cognitive abilities, are high achievers, are good at solving social problems, help other children, and are assertive without being disruptive or aggressive. They are kind, trustworthy, cooperative, loyal, and self-disclosing and provide emotional support. Their superior social skills make others enjoy being with them (Cillessen & Mayeux, 2004; LaFontana & Cillessen, 2002; Masten & Coatsworth, 1998; Newcomb et al., 1993). On the other hand, as we will discuss in a subsequent section, some school-aged children with *perceived* popularity, that is, high status, may be dominant, arrogant, and aggressive. Children with perceived popularity tend to be physically attractive and to have athletic and, to a lesser extent, academic ability (Cillessen & Mayeux, 2004; LaFontana & Cillessen, 2002).

Children can be *un*popular (either rejected or neglected) for many reasons. Although some unpopular children are aggressive, others are hyperactive, inattentive, or withdrawn (Dodge, Coie, Pettit, & Price, 1990; Masten & Coatsworth, 1998; Newcomb et al., 1993; A. W. Pope, Bierman, & Mumma, 1991). Still others act silly and immature or anxious and uncertain. Unpopular children are often insensitive to other children's feelings and do not adapt well to new situations (Bierman, Smoot, & Aumiller, 1993). Some show undue interest in being with groups of the other sex (Sroufe, Bennett, Englund, Urban, & Shulman, 1993). Some unpopular children *expect* not to be liked, and this becomes a self-fulfilling prophecy (Rabiner & Coie, 1989).

It is often in the family that children acquire behaviors that affect popularity (Masten & Coatsworth, 1998). Authoritative parents tend to have more popular children than authoritarian parents (Dekovic & Janssens, 1992). Children of authoritarian

BOX 10-1

Window on the World

Popularity: A Cross-Cultural View

How does culture affect popularity? Would a child who is popular in one culture be equally popular in another? Researchers compared 480 second- and fourth-graders in Shanghai, China, with 296 children the same ages in Ontario, Canada (X. Chen, Rubin, & Sun, 1992). Although the two samples were quite different—for example, none of the Canadian children came from peasant families, but many of the Chinese children did—both samples were representative of school-age children in the two countries.

The researchers assessed the children's popularity by two kinds of peer perceptions. The children filled out a sociometric rating telling which three classmates they most and least liked to be with and which three classmates were their best friends. The results showed that certain traits were valued similarly in both cultures. A sociable, cooperative child was likely to be popular in both China and Canada, and an aggressive child was likely to be rejected in both countries. However, one important difference emerged: shy, sensitive children were well liked in China, but not in Canada. This was not surprising. Chinese children traditionally were encouraged to be cautious, to restrain themselves, and to inhibit their urges; thus a quiet, shy youngster was considered well behaved. In a western

During middle childhood, shy, sensitive children are better liked in China than in western cultures, because they are considered well behaved. Children this age tend to accept adult standards of behavior.

Checkpoint

Can you . . .

✔ Describe characteristics of popular and unpopular children, and tell how they may vary?

✔ Identify family and cultural influences on popularity?

parents who punish and threaten are likely to threaten or act mean with other children; they are less popular than children whose authoritative parents reason with them and try to help them understand how another person might feel (C. H. Hart, Ladd, & Burleson, 1990).

In both western and Chinese cultures, sociability and cooperativeness are associated with social and school adjustment, whereas aggression is generally associated with peer rejection and adjustment problems. In both cultures boys tend to be more aggressive and to have more problems in school than girls (Chen, Cen, Li, & He, 2005). One cultural difference is in the social acceptance of shy, sensitive children (see Box 10-1).

Friendship

Children may spend much of their free time in groups, but only as individuals do they form friendships. Popularity is the peer group's opinion of a child, but friendship is a two-way street.

Children look for friends who are like them in age, sex, ethnicity, and interests. A friend is someone a child feels affection for, is comfortable with, likes to do things with, and can share feelings and secrets with. Friends know each other well, trust each other, feel a sense of commitment to one another, and treat each other as equals. The strongest friendships involve equal commitment and mutual give-and-take. Even unpopular children can make friends; but they have fewer culture, by contrast, such a child is likely to be seen as socially immature, fearful, and lacking in self-confidence.

A follow-up study at ages 8 and 10 (X. Chen, Rubin, & Li, 1995) again found that shy, sensitive Chinese children were popular with peers. They also were rated by teachers as socially competent, as leaders, and as academic achievers. However, by age 12, an interesting twist had occurred: shy, sensitive Chinese children were no longer popular. They tended to be rejected by their peers, just as in western cultures.

The researchers suggested that shyness and sensitivity might take on different social meanings in China as children enter adolescence, when peer relationships become more important and adult approval becomes less so, and that even in China, with its strong tradition of obedience to authority, the influence of adult social standards may wane as children's urge to make their own independent judgments of their peers asserts itself.

A more recently published study concerning younger children, however, points to effects of social change resulting from the radical restructuring of China's economic system, particularly since the late 1990s. During that time China has shifted from a completely collectivist system toward a more competitive, technologically advanced market economy with its associated individualistic values.

In the current study (Chen, Cen, Li, & He, 2005), researchers administered sociometric measures and peer assessments of social functioning to three cohorts of third- and fourth-graders in Shanghai schools in 1990, 1998, and 2002. They examined the children's school records and teacher ratings. As in the earlier studies, prosocial behavior was associated with social status and school achievement,

whereas aggression was generally associated with peer rejection and adjustment problems. However, a striking change emerged with regard to shyness/sensitivity. In the 1990 cohort, shy children were accepted by peers and were high in academic achievement, leadership, and teacher-rated competence. By 2002, the results were just the reverse: Shy children tended to be rejected by peers, to be depressed, and to be rated by teachers as low in competence. The results for the 1998 cohort were mixed, likely reflecting the attitudes of a society in transition. These findings suggest that the social acceptability of shy children is closely related to cultural norms. In the quasicapitalistic society that China has become, social assertiveness and initiative may be more highly appreciated and encouraged than in the past, and shyness and sensitivity may lead to social and psychological difficulties for children.

What's Your View?

How would you advise parents of a shy, sensitive child who complains of being rejected by other children?

Check It Out

For more information on this topic, go to http://www.pbs.org/kcts/preciouschildren/resources/index.html, where you will find links about China from the PBS documentary, "Precious Children," and http://www.pbs.org/inthemix, the Web site for the PBS program "In The Mix." Search available transcripts for the show called "Cliques: Behind the Labels."

---

friends than popular children and tend to find friends among younger children, other unpopular children, or children in a different class or a different school (George & Hartmann, 1996; Hartup, 1992, 1996a, 1996b; Newcomb & Bagwell, 1995).

With their friends, children learn to communicate and cooperate. They learn about themselves and others. They help each other weather stressful transitions, such as starting at a new school or adjusting to parents' divorce. The inevitable quarrels help children learn to resolve conflicts (Furman, 1982; Hartup, 1992, 1996a, 1996b; Hartup & Stevens, 1999; Newcomb & Bagwell, 1995). Children who avoid or blame a friend who needs help or support (for example, after being teased or laughed at by classmates) tend to have few and low-quality friendships. Those who shun a friend's attempts to help also tend to have few friends (Rose & Asher, 2004).

Friendship seems to help children feel good about themselves, though it's also likely that children who feel good about themselves have an easier time making friends. Peer rejection and friendlessness in middle childhood

School-age friends often share secrets—and laughs—as Anna and her friend Christina are doing. Friendship becomes deeper and more stable in middle childhood, reflecting cognitive and emotional growth. Girls tend to have fewer friends, but more intimate ones, than boys do.

Chapter 10 Psychosocial Development in Middle Childhood   375

Lifemap CD

How do children's ideas about friendship evolve during middle childhood? Consider this question as you watch the video, "Development of Friendships in Middle Childhood," in Chapter 10 of your CD.

Checkpoint

Can you . . .

✔ Distinguish between popularity and friendship?

✔ Compare two measures of popularity and discuss reasons for unpopularity?

✔ List characteristics children look for in friends?

✔ Tell how age and gender affect friendships?

may have long-term effects. In one longitudinal study, fifth-graders who had no friends were more likely than their classmates to have low self-esteem in young adulthood and even to show symptoms of depression (Bagwell, Newcomb, & Bukowski, 1998).

Children's concepts of friendship and the ways they act with their friends change with age, reflecting cognitive and emotional growth. Preschool friends play together, but friendship among school-age children is deeper and more stable. Children cannot be or have true friends until they achieve the cognitive maturity to consider other people's views and needs as well as their own (Hartup, 1992; Hartup & Stevens, 1999; Newcomb & Bagwell, 1995). On the basis of interviews with more than 250 people between ages 3 and 45, Robert Selman (1980; Selman & Selman, 1979) traced changing conceptions of friendship through five overlapping stages (see Table 10-1). He found that most school-age children are in stage 2 (reciprocal friendship based on self-interest), but some older children, ages 9 and up, may be in stage 3 (intimate, mutually shared relationships).

School-age children distinguish among "best friends," "good friends," and "casual friends" on the basis of intimacy and time spent together (Hartup & Stevens, 1999). Children this age typically have three to five "best" friends but usually play with only one or two at a time (Hartup, 1992; Hartup & Stevens, 1999). School-age girls care less about having many friends than about having a few close friends they can rely on. Boys have more friendships, but they tend to be less intimate and affectionate (Furman, 1982; Furman & Buhrmester, 1985; Hartup & Stevens, 1999).

Table 10-1 Selman's Stages of Friendship

Stage	Description	Example
Stage 0: Momentary playmateship (ages 3 to 7)	On this *undifferentiated* level of friendship, children are egocentric and have trouble considering another person's point of view; they tend to think only about what they want from a relationship. Most very young children define their friends in terms of physical closeness and value them for material or physical attributes.	"She lives on my street" or "He has the Power Rangers."
Stage 1: One-way assistance (ages 4 to 9)	On this *unilateral* level, a "good friend" does what the child wants the friend to do.	"She's not my friend anymore, because she wouldn't go with me when I wanted her to" or "He's my friend because he always says yes when I want to borrow his eraser."
Stage 2: Two-way fair-weather cooperation (ages 6 to 12)	This *reciprocal* level overlaps stage 1. It involves give-and-take but still serves many separate self-interests, rather than the common interests of the two friends.	"We are friends; we do things for each other" or "A friend is someone who plays with you when you don't have anybody else to play with."
Stage 3: Intimate, mutually shared relationships (ages 9 to 15)	On this *mutual* level, children view a friendship as having a life of its own. It is an ongoing, systematic, committed relationship that incorporates more than doing things for each other. Friends become possessive and demand exclusivity.	"It takes a long time to make a close friend, so you really feel bad if you find out that your friend is trying to make other friends too."
Stage 4: Autonomous interdependence (beginning at age 12)	In this *interdependent* stage, children respect friends' needs for both dependency and autonomy.	"A good friendship is a real commitment, a risk you have to take; you have to support and trust and give, but you have to be able to let go too."

Source: Selman, 1980; Selman & Selman, 1979.

Aggression and Bullying

During the early school years, as discussed in Chapter 8, aggression generally declines or changes in form. **Instrumental aggression** (aggression aimed at achieving an objective), the hallmark of the preschool period, becomes much less common (Coie & Dodge, 1998). **Hostile aggression** (aggression aimed at hurting its target) often takes *relational* (social) rather than *overt* (physical) form. Nine-year-olds recognize such behavior as teasing and spreading rumors as "mean"; they realize that it stems from anger and is aimed at hurting others (Crick, Bigbee, & Howes, 1996; Crick et al., 2002; Galen & Underwood, 1997).

A small minority of children do not learn to control physical aggression (Coie & Dodge, 1998), and these children tend to remain physically aggressive throughout childhood. They tend to have social and psychological problems, but it is not clear whether aggression causes these problems or is a reaction to them, or both (Crick & Grotpeter, 1995). Highly aggressive children tend to egg each other on to antisocial acts. Thus, school-age boys who are physically aggressive are candidates for juvenile delinquency in adolescence (Broidy et al., 2003).

As we've already mentioned, aggressors tend to be disliked, but physically aggressive boys and some relationally aggressive girls are perceived as among the most popular in the classroom (Cillessen & Mayeux, 2004; Rodkin, Farmer, Pearl, & Van Acker, 2000). In a study of "rejected" fourth-graders, aggressive boys tended to gain in social status by the end of fifth grade, suggesting that behavior shunned by younger children may be seen as "cool" or glamorous by preadolescents (Sandstrom & Coie, 1999). In a longitudinal study of a multiethnic group of 905 fifth- through ninth-graders in a northeastern U.S. city (Cillessen & Mayeux, 2004), physical aggression became less disapproved as children moved into adolescence, and relational aggression was increasingly reinforced by high status among peers.

Types of Aggression and Social Information Processing What makes children act aggressively? One answer may lie in the way they process social information: what features of the social environment they pay attention to and how they interpret what they perceive (Crick & Dodge, 1994, 1996).

Instrumental (or *proactive*) aggressors view force and coercion as effective ways to get what they want. They act deliberately, not out of anger. In social learning terms, they are aggressive because they expect to be rewarded for it; and when they *are* rewarded, their belief in the effectiveness of aggression is reinforced (Crick & Dodge, 1996). By contrast, a child who is accidentally bumped in line may push back angrily, assuming that the other child bumped her on purpose. This is hostile, or *reactive,* aggression. Such children often have a *hostile attribution bias;* they see other children as trying to hurt them, and they strike out in retaliation or self-defense (Crick & Dodge, 1996; de Castro, Veerman, Koops, Bosch, & Monshouwer, 2002; Waldman, 1996).

Children who seek dominance and control may react aggressively to threats to their status, which they may attribute to hostility (de Castro et al., 2002; Erdley et al., 1997). Rejected children and those exposed to harsh parenting also tend to have a hostile attribution bias (Coie & Dodge, 1998; Masten & Coatsworth, 1998; Weiss, Dodge, Bates, & Pettit, 1992). Since people often *do* become hostile toward someone who acts aggressively toward them, a hostile bias may become a self-fulfilling prophecy, setting in motion a cycle of aggression (de Castro et al., 2002).

Psychological differences between aggressive children and their peers become increasingly marked during middle childhood. Among a representative sample of 11,160 New York public school children who were questioned about their fantasies, their behavior, and their reactions to hypothetical situations, hostile attribution bias and aggressive fantasies became more common between ages 6 and 12, but so did

Guidepost

8. What are the most common forms of aggressive behavior in middle childhood, and what influences contribute to such behavior?

Instrumental aggression Aggressive behavior used as a means of achieving a goal.

hostile aggression Aggressive behavior intended to hurt another person.

more constructive responses to conflict. Although girls were less aggressive than boys at age 6, by age 11 girls were almost as likely to show hostile attribution bias and to give aggressive responses to hypothetical conflicts (Aber, Brown, & Jones, 2003).

Both instrumental and hostile aggressors need help in altering the way they process social information so that they do not interpret aggression as either justified or useful. Adults can help children curb *hostile* aggression by teaching them how to recognize when they are getting angry and how to control their anger. *Instrumental* aggression tends to stop if it is not rewarded (Crick & Dodge, 1996). In a New York City school study, children exposed to a conflict resolution curriculum that involved discussions and group role playing showed less hostile attribution bias, less aggression, fewer behavior problems, and more effective responses to social situations than children who did not participate in the program (Aber et al., 2003).

Does Media Violence Stimulate Aggression? Children between ages 2 and 18 spend an average of 6 1/2 hours a day consuming entertainment media—television, videos, video games, print, radio, recorded music, computer games, and the Internet—more time than in any other activity besides sleeping (AAP Committee on Public Education, 2001b).

About 6 out of 10 U.S. television programs portray violence, usually glamorized, glorified, or trivialized. The highest proportion of violence is in children's shows (National Television Violence Study, 1995, 1996). All G-rated animated feature films produced in the United States between 1937 and 1999, many of which are periodically replayed on television, portray violence, and the violent content has increased through the years (Yokota & Thompson. 2000). In addition, there is constant, repetitive news coverage of natural disasters and violent acts. As much as 30 percent of broadcast time is devoted to detailed crime reporting (American Academy of Child & Adolescent Psychiatry, 2002). In a study of 50 major televised sporting events, such as the Superbowl, 49 percent of commercial breaks contained at least one commercial showing unsafe behavior or violence (Tamburro, Gordon, D'Apolito, & Howard, 2004). Music videos disproportionately feature violence against women and blacks. The motion picture, music, and video game industries aggressively market violent, adult-rated products to children. The ratings themselves are confusing and inconsistent, and surveys find that most parents do not use them (AAP Committee on Public Education, 2001b).

Because of the high proportion of their time that children spend with media, the images they see can become primary role models and sources of information about how people behave in the world. The vast preponderance of experimental, longitudinal, epidemiological, and cross-cultural studies supports a causal relationship between media violence and aggressive behavior in childhood, adolescence, and adulthood. In fact, the strongest single correlate of violent behavior is previous exposure to violence (AAP Committee on Public Education, 2001b; Anderson, Huston et al., 2001; Anderson, Berkowitz, et al., 2003; Huesmann, Moise-Titus, Podolski, & Eron, 2003).

How does media violence lead to long-term aggressiveness? Research has found that viewing media violence lowers inhibitions. Because media violence is usually glamorized—calculated to evoke visceral thrills without showing the human cost—children may come to view aggression as acceptable. Television, movies, and music videos depict the carrying and use of weapons as a source of personal power. Children who see both heroes and villains achieving their aims through violence are likely to conclude that violence is an effective way to resolve conflicts. They may become less sensitive to the pain it causes. They may learn to take violence for granted and may be less likely to intervene when they see it. The more realistically violence is portrayed, the more likely it is to be tolerated and learned (AAP Committee on Public Education, 2001b; Anderson, Berkowitz, et al., 2003).

Children are more vulnerable than adults to the influence of televised violence (AAP Committee on Public Education, 2001b; Coie & Dodge, 1998). Classic social learning research suggests that children imitate filmed models even more than live ones (Bandura, Ross, & Ross, 1963). The influence is stronger if the child believes the violence on the screen is real, identifies with the violent character, finds that character attractive, and watches without parental supervision or intervention (Anderson, Berkowitz, et al., 2003; Coie & Dodge, 1998). Exposure to extensive media violence may lead young people to view the world as a dangerous place, in which weapon-carrying and aggressive behavior are necessary for self-protection (AAP Committee on Public Education, 2001b). Highly aggressive children are more strongly affected by media violence than are less aggressive children (Anderson, Berkowitz, et al., 2003).

The long-term influence of televised violence is greater in middle childhood than at earlier ages (Eron & Huesmann, 1986). Among 427 children whose viewing habits were studied at age 8, the best predictor of aggressiveness at age 19 was the degree of violence in the shows they had watched as children (Eron, 1980, 1982). In a follow-up study, the amount of television viewed at age 8 and the preference among boys for violent shows predicted the severity of criminal offenses at age 30 (Huesmann, 1986; Huesmann & Eron, 1984).

What's Your View?
- What can and should be done about children's exposure to media violence?

Less research has been done on effects of newer, interactive media, such as video games and the Internet, but initial studies suggest that "effects of child-initiated virtual violence may be more profound than those of passive media, such as television." Rather than merely let a child observe rewards for violent behavior, video games "place the child in the role of the aggressor and reward him or her for successful violent behavior" (AAP Committee on Public Education, 2001b, pp. 1223–1224). One study found that fourth- through eighth-graders prefer video games that give points for violence against others (Funk & Buchman, 1996). Video games are addictive as children seek to improve their scores and advance to higher levels (Griffiths & Hunt, 1998). In experimental studies, young people after playing video games have shown decreases in prosocial behavior and increases in aggressive thoughts and violent retaliation to provocation (Anderson, 2000).

Research shows that children who see televised violence tend to act aggressively. When the violence is child-initiated, as in video games, the effect may be even stronger.

Media-induced aggressiveness can be minimized by cutting down on television use and by parental monitoring and guidance of the shows children watch (Anderson, Berkowitz, et al., 2003). The American Academy of Pediatrics Committee on Public Education (2001b) recommends that parents limits children's media exposure to one to two hours a day. Third- and fourth-graders who participated in a six-month curriculum aimed at motivating them to monitor and reduce the time they spent on television, videotapes, and video games showed significant decreases in peer-rated aggression, as compared with a control group (Robinson, Wilde, Navracruz, Haydel, & Varady, 2001).

Bullies and Victims Aggression becomes **bullying** when it is deliberately, persistently directed against a particular target: a victim who typically is weak, vulnerable, and defenseless. More than 2 million U.S. schoolchildren—about

Checkpoint
Can you . . .

✔ Tell how aggression changes during middle childhood and how social information processing and media violence can contribute to it?

bullying Aggression deliberately and persistently directed against a particular target, or victim, typically one who is weak, vulnerable, and defenseless.

Bullying tends to peak in the middle grades. Boys are more likely to use overt aggression; girls, relational aggression.

30 percent of those in grades 6 through 10—are either bullies or victims, according to a survey of nearly 16,000 students (Nansel et al., 2001). Bullying also is a problem in other industrialized countries, such as England and Japan (Hara, 2002; Kanetsuna & Smith, 2002; Ruiz & Tanaka, 2001). In Japan and Korea, school bullying has been associated with a growing wave of student suicide and suicidal thoughts and behavior (Kim, Koh, & Leventhal, 2005; Rios-Ellis, Bellamy, & Shoji, 2000).

Patterns of bullying and victimization may become established as early as kindergarten. As tentative peer groups form, aggressors soon get to know which children make the easiest "marks." Bullying and aggression increase through the transition to middle school and then decline. This temporary rise in bullying may reflect the difficulty children have forming social networks at a new school. During this transition, boys, particularly, use bullying as a way to establish dominance in the peer group. Boys tend to victimize other boys, and female bullies tend to target other girls (Pellegrini & Long, 2002). Male bullies tend to use overt, physical aggression; female bullies may use relational aggression (Boulton, 1995; Nansel et al., 2001).

Unlike the pattern for bullying, the likelihood of *being* bullied decreases steadily. As children get older, most of them may learn how to discourage bullying, leaving a smaller "pool" of available victims (Pellegrini & Long, 2002; P. K. Smith & Levan, 1995). Risk factors for victimization seem to be similar across cultures (Schwartz, Chang, & Farver, 2001). Victims tend to be anxious and submissive and to cry easily, or to be argumentative and provocative (Hodges, Boivin, Vitaro, & Bukowski, 1999; Olweus, 1995). They tend to have few friends and to live in harsh, punitive family environments that leave them vulnerable to further punishment or rejection (Nansel et al., 2001; Schwartz, Dodge, Pettit, & Bates and the Conduct Problems Prevention Research Group, 2000). They are apt to have low self-esteem—though it is not clear whether low self-esteem leads to or follows from victimization. Male victims tend to be physically weak (Boulton & Smith, 1994; Olweus, 1995). Among 5,749 Canadian children, those who were overweight were most likely to become victims or bullies (Janssen, Craig, Boyce, & Pickett, 2004).

Victims of bullying may develop behavior problems, such as hyperactivity, and may become more aggressive themselves (Schwartz, McFadyen-Ketchum, Dodge, Pettit, & Bates, 1998). In the wave of school shootings since 1994, the perpetrators often had been victims of bullying (Anderson, Kaufman et al., 2001).

Schools that do not effectively counteract aggressive behavior, such as bullying and intimidation, may contribute to the escalation of the problem by permitting an atmosphere in which such behavior is deemed acceptable. Such a climate can lead to more severe violence (Wilson, Lipsey, & Derzon, 2003). An intervention program in grades four through seven in Norwegian schools cut bullying in half and also reduced other antisocial behavior. This was accomplished by creating an authoritative atmosphere, better supervision at recess and lunch time, rules against bullying, and serious talks with bullies, victims, and parents (Olweus, 1995). A growing number of U.S. schools are adopting such programs (Guerrero, 2001). In 2004 the U.S. Department of Health and Human Services announced a campaign to educate the public about how to prevent bullying and youth violence. An analysis of 221 studies of such programs, mostly in the United States, found significant reductions in aggressive behavior in groups that received the interventions but not in control groups. Unfortunately, most of these studies were done on demonstration programs; the few studies of programs in normal, routine use showed much smaller effects (Wilson et al., 2003).

Checkpoint
Can you . . .

✔ Describe how patterns of bullying and victimization become established and change?

Mental Health

The term *mental health* is somewhat of a misnomer because it usually refers to emotional health. Although most children are fairly well adjusted, approximately 5 percent of children ages 4 through 17 have emotional or behavioral difficulties, according to parental reports, and 80 percent of these are severe enough to interfere with the child's everyday functioning (Simpson, Bloom, Cohen, Blumberg, & Bourdon, 2005). Diagnosis of mental disorders in children is important because they often lead to psychiatric disorders in adulthood (Kim-Cohen et al., 2003). In fact, half of all cases of mental disorders begin by age 14 (Kessler et al., 2005). Let's look at several common emotional disturbances and then at types of treatment.

Guidepost

9. What emotional disorders may develop in childhood and adolescence, and how are they treated?

Common Emotional Disturbances

The most commonly diagnosed emotional disorders in childhood are *disruptive conduct disorders* (showing aggression, defiance, or antisocial behavior) and *anxiety* or *mood disorders* (feeling sad, depressed, unloved, nervous, fearful, or lonely). Some problems seem to be associated with a particular phase of a child's life and go away on their own, but others need to be treated to prevent future trouble (Achenbach & Howell, 1993; USDHHS, 1999b).

Disruptive Behavior Disorders   Temper tantrums and defiant, argumentative, hostile, or deliberately annoying behavior—common among 4- and 5-year-olds—typically are outgrown by middle childhood. When such a pattern of behavior persists until age 8, children (usually boys) may be diagnosed with **oppositional defiant disorder (ODD),** a pattern of defiance, disobedience, and hostility toward adult authority figures lasting at least 6 months and going beyond the bounds of normal childhood behavior. Onset is typically by age 8. Children with ODD constantly fight, argue, lose their temper, snatch things, blame others, are angry and resentful, have few friends, are in constant trouble in school, and test the limits of adults' patience (APA, 2000; National Library of Medicine, 2004).

oppositional defiant disorder (ODD)   Pattern of behavior, persisting into middle childhood, marked by negativity, hostility, and defiance.

Some children with ODD also have **conduct disorder (CD),** a persistent, repetitive pattern, beginning at an early age, of aggressive, antisocial acts, such as truancy, setting fires, habitual lying, fighting, bullying, theft, vandalism, assaults, and drug and alcohol use (APA, 2000; National Library of Medicine, 2003b). About 1 to 4 percent of noninstitutionalized 9- to 17-year-olds in the United States have CD (USDHHS, 1999b). Many children with conduct disorder also have attention-deficit hyperactivity disorder (ADHD; refer back to Chapter 9). Some 11- to 13-year-olds progress from conduct disorder to criminal violence—mugging, rape, and break-ins—and by age 17 may be frequent, serious offenders (Coie & Dodge, 1998. (In Chapter 12, we discuss roots of antisocial behavior and juvenile delinquency.) Between 25 and 50 percent of these highly antisocial children become antisocial adults (USDHHS, 1999b). *Antisocial personality disorder* is a chronic psychiatric condition characterized by behavior, often criminal, that manipulates, exploits, or violates the rights of others. Genetic factors or child abuse may contribute to the development of this condition. It is difficult to treat, but it may peak in the late teens

conduct disorder (CD)   Repetitive, persistent pattern of aggressive, antisocial behavior violating societal norms or the rights of others.

or early twenties and improve on its own by the early forties (National Library of Medicine, 2003a).

School Phobia and Other Anxiety Disorders   Children with **school phobia** have an unrealistic fear of going to school. Some children have realistic reasons to fear going to school: a sarcastic teacher, overly demanding work, or a bully in the school yard. In such cases, the environment may need changing, not the child (Kochenderfer & Ladd, 1996). True school phobia may be a type of **separation anxiety disorder,** a condition involving excessive anxiety for at least four weeks concerning separation from home or from people to whom the child is attached. Although separation anxiety is normal in infancy, when it persists in older children it is cause for concern. Separation anxiety disorder affects some 4 percent of children and young adolescents and may persist through the college years. These children often come from close-knit, caring families. They may develop the disorder spontaneously or after a stressful event, such as the death of a pet, an illness, or a move to a new school (APA, 2000; Harvard Medical School, 2004a). Many children with separation anxiety also show symptoms of depression (USDHHS, 1999b).

Sometimes school phobia may be a form of **social phobia,** or *social anxiety:* extreme fear and/or avoidance of social situations. Social-phobic children are painfully shy and tend to cling to their parents (Harvard Medical School, 2004a). They may be so afraid of embarrassment that they break into blushes, sweats, or palpitations when asked to speak in class or when meeting an acquaintance on the street (USDHHS, 1999b). Social phobia affects about 5 percent of children and 8 percent of adults. Social phobias run in families, so there may be a genetic component. Often these phobias are triggered by traumatic experiences, such as a child's mind going blank when the child is called on in class (Beidel & Turner, 1998). Social anxiety tends to increase with age, whereas separation anxiety decreases (Costello et al., 2003).

Some children have a **generalized anxiety disorder,** not focused on any specific part of their lives. These children worry about just about everything: school grades, storms, earthquakes, hurting themselves on the playground, or the amount of gas in the tank. They tend to be self-conscious, self-doubting, and excessively concerned with meeting the expectations of others. They seek approval and need constant reassurance, but their worry seems independent of performance or of how they are regarded by others (APA, 1994; Harvard Medical School, 2004a; USDHHS, 1999b). Far less common is **obsessive-compulsive disorder (OCD).** Sufferers from this disorder may be obsessed by repetitive, intrusive thoughts, images, or impulses (often involving irrational fears) or may show compulsive behaviors, such as constant hand-washing, or both (APA, 2000; Harvard Medical School, 2004a; USDHHS, 1999b).

Anxiety disorders tend to run in families (Harvard Medical School, 2004a) and are twice as common among girls as among boys. The heightened female vulnerability to anxiety begins as early as age 6. Females also are more susceptible to depression, which is similar to anxiety and often goes hand in hand with it (Lewinsohn, Gotlib, Lewinsohn, Seeley, & Allen, 1998). Both anxiety and depression may be neurologically based or may stem from insecure attachment, exposure to an anxious or depressed parent, or other early experiences that make children feel a lack of control over what happens around them (Chorpita & Barlow, 1998; Harvard Medical School, 2004a). Parents who reward an anxious child with attention to the anxiety may unwittingly perpetuate it through operant conditioning (Harvard Medical School, 2004a).

Childhood Depression   **Childhood depression** is a disorder of mood that goes beyond normal, temporary sadness. Depression is estimated to occur in 2 percent of elementary

school phobia   Unrealistic fear of going to school; may be a form of *separation anxiety disorder* or *social phobia.*

separation anxiety disorder   Condition involving excessive, prolonged anxiety concerning separation from home or from people to whom a person is attached.

social phobia   Extreme fear and/or avoidance of social situations.

generalized anxiety disorder   Anxiety not focused on any single target.

obsessive-compulsive disorder (OCD)   Anxiety aroused by repetitive, intrusive thoughts, images, or impulses, often leading to compulsive ritual behaviors.

childhood depression   Mood disorder characterized by such symptoms as a prolonged sense of friendlessness, inability to have fun or concentrate, fatigue, extreme activity or apathy, feelings of worthlessness, weight change, physical complaints, and thoughts of death or suicide.

school children (NCHS, 2004), but at any given time between 10 and 15 percent of children and adolescents may have symptoms of the disorder (USDHHS, 1999b), such as inability to have fun or concentrate, fatigue, extreme activity or apathy, crying, sleep problems, weight change, physical complaints, feelings of worthlessness, a prolonged sense of friendlessness, or frequent thoughts about death or suicide. Any five of these symptoms, lasting at least two weeks, may point to depression (APA, 2000). Childhood depression may signal the beginning of a recurrent problem that is likely to persist into adulthood (Birmaher, 1998; Birmaher et al., 1996; Cicchetti & Toth, 1998; Kye & Ryan, 1995; USDHHS, 1999b; Weissman et al., 1999).

The exact causes of childhood depression are not known. Twin studies have found its heritability to be modest, though 20 to 50 percent of depressed children and adolescents have a family history of it. Depressed children tend to come from families with high levels of parental depression, anxiety, substance abuse, or anti-social behavior; and the atmosphere in such families may increase children's risk of depression (Cicchetti & Toth, 1998; USDHHS, 1999b).

Children as young as 5 or 6 can accurately report depressed moods and feelings that forecast later trouble, from academic problems to major depression and ideas of suicide (Ialongo, Edelsohn, & Kellam, 2001). Depression often emerges during the transition to middle school and may be related to stiffer academic pressures (Cicchetti & Toth, 1998), weak self-efficacy beliefs, and lack of personal investment in academic success (Rudolph, Lambert, Clark, & Kurlakowsky, 2001). Depression becomes more prevalent during adolescence (Costello et al., 2003; see Chapter 11).

Treatment Techniques

Psychological treatment for emotional disturbances can take several forms. In **individual psychotherapy,** a therapist sees a child one-on-one, to help the child gain insights into his or her personality and relationships and to interpret feelings and behavior. Such treatment may be helpful at a time of stress, such as the death of a parent or parental divorce, even when a child has not shown signs of disturbance. Child psychotherapy is usually more effective when combined with counseling for the parents.

In **family therapy,** the therapist sees the family together, observes how members interact, and points out both growth-producing and growth-inhibiting or destructive patterns of family functioning. Therapy can help parents confront their own conflicts and begin to resolve them. This is often the first step toward resolving the child's problems as well.

Behavior therapy, or *behavior modification* (refer back to Chapter 2), is a form of psychotherapy that uses principles of learning theory to eliminate undesirable behaviors or to develop desirable ones. A statistical analysis of many studies found that psychotherapy is generally effective with children and adolescents, but behavior therapy is more effective than nonbehavioral methods. Results are best when treatment is targeted to specific problems and desired outcomes (Weisz, Weiss, Han, Granger, & Morton, 1995). *Cognitive behavioral therapy,* which seeks to change negative thoughts through gradual exposure, modeling, rewards, or "talking" to oneself has proven the most effective treatment for anxiety disorders in children and adolescents (Harvard Medical School, 2004a).

When children have limited verbal and conceptual skills or have suffered emotional trauma, **art therapy** can help them describe what is troubling them without the need to put their feelings into words. The child may express deep emotions through choice of colors and subjects to depict (Kozlowska & Hanney, 1999).

individual psychotherapy Psychological treatment in which a therapist sees a troubled person one-on-one.

family therapy Psychological treatment in which a therapist sees the whole family together to analyze patterns of family functioning.

behavior therapy Therapeutic approach using principles of learning theory to encourage desired behaviors or eliminate undesired ones; also called *behavior modification.*

art therapy Therapeutic approach that allows a person to express troubled feelings without words, using a variety of art materials and media.

In play therapy, the therapist observes as a child acts out troubled feelings, using developmentally appropriate materials.

Observing how a family plans, carries out, and discusses an art project can reveal patterns of family interactions (Kozlowska & Hanney, 1999).

Play therapy, in which a child plays freely while a therapist occasionally comments, asks questions, or makes suggestions, has proven effective with a variety of emotional, cognitive, and social problems, especially when consultation with parents or other close family members is part of the process (Athansiou, 2001; Bratton & Ray, 2002; Leblanc & Ritchie, 2001; Ryan & Needham, 2001; Wilson & Ryan, 2001).

The use of **drug therapy**—antidepressants, stimulants, tranquilizers, and antipsychotic medications—to treat childhood and adolescent emotional disorders has greatly increased in the United States and some European and South American countries, with the most dramatic increases in the United Kingdom (a 68 percent rise between 2000 and 2002). However, sufficient research on the effectiveness and safety of these drugs for children, especially, is generally lacking (Murray, de Vries, & Wong, 2004; USDHHS, 1999b; Wong, Murray, Camilleri-Novak, & Stephens, 2004; Zito et al., 2003). A possible exception is the use of Ritalin to treat attention-deficit hyperactivity disorder (refer back to Chapter 9). The use of *selective serotonin reuptake inhibitors (SSRIs)* to treat obsessive-compulsive, depressive, and anxiety disorders is increasingly common (Murray et al., 2004; NCHS, 2004; Research Unit on Pediatric Psychopharmacology Anxiety Study Group, 2001), but the United Kingdom's drug regulatory agency has recommended withdrawing SSRIs from use with children pending further research (Wong et al., 2004). (Use of SSRIs for adolescent depression is discussed in Chapter 11.)

Stress and Resilience: Protective Factors

Stressful events are part of childhood, and most young people learn to cope. Stress that becomes overwhelming, however, can lead to psychological problems. Severe stressors, such as kidnapping or child abuse, may have long-term effects on physical and psychological well-being. Yet some individuals show remarkable resilience in surmounting such ordeals.

Stresses of Modern Life   The child psychologist David Elkind (1981, 1986, 1997, 1998) has called today's child the "hurried child." He warns that the pressures of modern life are forcing children to grow up too soon and are making their childhood too stressful. Today's children are expected to succeed in school, to compete in sports, and to meet parents' emotional needs. Children are exposed to many adult problems on television and in real life before they have mastered the problems of childhood. They know about sex and violence, and they often must shoulder adult responsibilities. Many children move frequently and have to change schools and leave old friends (Fowler, Simpson, & Schoendorf, 1993; G. A. Simpson & Fowler, 1994). The tightly scheduled pace of life also can be stressful (Hofferth & Sandberg, 1998). Yet children are not small adults. They feel and think like children, and they need the years of childhood for healthy development.

Given how much stress children are exposed to, it should not be surprising that anxiety in childhood has increased greatly (Twenge, 2000). Fears of danger and death are the most consistent fears of children at all ages (Gullone, 2000; Silverman, La Greca, & Wasserstein, 1995). This intense anxiety about safety may reflect the high rates of crime and violence in the larger society—including rare but highly publicized killings

Checkpoint

Can you . . .

✔ Identify causes and symptoms of disruptive behavior disorders, anxiety disorders, and childhood depression?

✔ Describe and evaluate six common types of therapy for emotional disorders?

Guidepost

10. How do the stresses of modern life affect children, and why are some children more resilient than others?

play therapy   Therapeutic approach in which a child plays freely while a therapist observes and occasionally comments, asks questions, or makes suggestions.

drug therapy   Administration of drugs to treat emotional or psychological disorders.

in schools (Anderson, Kaufman et al., 2001; DeVoe et al., 2004; Garbarino, Dubrow, Kostelny, & Pardo, 1992, 1998; see Box 12-2 in Chapter 12). Between 1993 and 2000, an estimated 5,542 U.S. children 14 years old or younger died from firearm injuries, and more than half of these were homicides (Eber, Annest, Mercy, & Ryan, 2004).

The findings about children's fears have been corroborated in a wide range of developed and developing societies, including Australia, China, the United Kingdom, Israel, Italy, Nigeria, and Northern Ireland, in addition to the United States. Poor children—who may see their environment as threatening—tend to be more fearful than children of higher socioeconomic status (Gullone, 2000; Ollendick, Yang, King, Dong, & Akande, 1996). Children who grow up constantly surrounded by violence often have trouble concentrating and sleeping. Some become aggressive, and some come to take brutality for granted. Many do not allow themselves to become attached to other people for fear of more hurt and loss (Garbarino et al., 1992, 1998).

Exposure to violence on news programs can feed anxiety, depression, nightmares, and sleep disturbances (AAP Committee on Public Education, 2001b). Most children who watched news coverage of the September 11, 2001, terrorist attacks on New York and Washington, DC, experienced profound stress, even if they were not directly affected (Walma & van der Molen, 2004). An estimated 10.5 percent of New York City schoolchildren suffered from post-traumatic stress disorder after the attacks (Hoven, Mandell, & Duarte, 2003).

Children's reactions to such a traumatic event vary with age (see Table 10-2). For some, the effects may remain for years. Children may lose trust in adults' ability

Table 10-2	Children's Age-Related Reactions to Trauma
Age	**Typical Reactions**
5 years or less	Fear of separation from parent
	Crying, whimpering, screaming, trembling
	Immobility or aimless motion
	Frightened facial expressions
	Excessive clinging
	Regressive behaviors (thumbsucking, bed-wetting, fear of dark)
6 to 11 years	Extreme withdrawal
	Disruptive behavior
	Inability to pay attention
	Stomachaches or other symptoms with no physical basis
	Declining school performance, refusal to go to school
	Depression, anxiety, guilt, irritability, or emotional numbing
	Regressive behavior (nightmares, sleep problems, irrational fears, outbursts of anger or fighting)
12 to 17 years	Flashbacks, nightmares
	Emotional numbing, confusion
	Avoidance of reminders of the traumatic event
	Revenge fantasies
	Withdrawal, isolation
	Substance abuse
	Problems with peers, antisocial behavior
	Physical complaints
	School avoidance, academic decline
	Sleep disturbances
	Depression, suicidal thoughts

Source: NIMH, 2001a.

Practically Speaking
Talking to Children about Terrorism and War

In today's world, parents are faced with the challenge of explaining violence, terrorism and war to children. Although difficult, these conversations are extremely important. They give parents an opportunity to help their children feel more secure and understand the world in which they live. The following information can be helpful to parents when discussing these issues.

Listen to Children

1. Create a time and place for children to ask their questions. Don't force children to talk about things until they're ready.

2. Remember that children tend to personalize situations. For example, they may worry about friends or relatives who live in a city or state associated with incidents or events.

3. Help children find ways to express themselves. Some children may not be able to talk about their thoughts, feelings, or fears. They may be more comfortable drawing pictures, playing with toys, or writing stories or poems directly or indirectly related to current events.

Answer Children's Questions

1. Use words and concepts your child can understand. Make your explanation appropriate to your child's age and level of understanding. Don't overload a child with too much information.

2. Give children honest answers and information. Children will usually know if you're not being honest.

3. Be prepared to repeat explanations or have several conversations. Some information may be hard to accept or understand.

Asking the same question over and over may be your child's way of asking for reassurance.

4. Acknowledge and support your child's thoughts, feelings, and reactions. Let your child know that you think their questions and concerns are important.

5. Be consistent and reassuring, but don't make unrealistic promises.

6. Avoid stereotyping groups of people by race, nationality, or religion. Use the opportunity to teach tolerance and explain prejudice.

7. Remember that children learn from watching their parents and teachers. They are very interested in how you respond to events. They learn from listening to your conversations with other adults.

8. Let children know how you are feeling. It's OK for them to know if you are anxious or worried about events. However, don't burden them with your concerns.

9. Don't confront your child's way of handling events. If a child feels reassured by saying that things are happening "very far away," it's usually best not to disagree. The child may need to think about events this way to feel safe.

Provide Support

1. Don't let children watch lots of violent or upsetting images on TV. Repetitive frightening images or scenes can be very disturbing, especially to young children.

---

to protect them and may fear that the event will happen again. Children who have previously experienced trauma, such as family or community violence, are most likely to be deeply scarred (NIMH, 2001a). Parents' responses to a violent event or disaster and the way they talk with a child about it strongly influence the child's ability to recover (NIMH, 2001a). Box 10-2 gives suggestions for talking with children about terrorism and war.

resilient children Children who weather adverse circumstances, function well despite challenges or threats, or bounce back from traumatic events.

Coping with Stress: The Resilient Child Resilient children are those who weather circumstances that might blight others, who maintain their composure and competence under challenge or threat, or who bounce back from traumatic events. These children do not possess extraordinary qualities. They simply manage, despite adverse circumstances, to derive strength from the basic systems and resources that promote positive development in normal children (Masten, 2001; see Table 10-3).

protective factors Influences that reduce the impact of early stress and tend to predict positive outcomes.

The two most important **protective factors** that seem to help children and adolescents overcome stress and contribute to resilience are good *family relationships* and *cognitive functioning* (Masten & Coatsworth, 1998). Resilient children are likely to have good relationships and strong bonds with at least one supportive parent (Pettit et al., 1997) or caregiver or other caring, competent adult (Masten & Coatsworth, 1998).

—continued

2. Help children establish a predictable routine and schedule. Children are reassured by structure and familiarity. School, sports, birthdays, holidays, and group activities take on added importance during stressful times.

3. Coordinate information between home and school. Parents should know about activities and discussions at school. Teachers should know about the child's specific fears or concerns.

4. Children who have experienced trauma or losses may show more intense reactions to tragedies or news of war or terrorist incidents. These children may need extra support and attention.

5. Watch for physical symptoms related to stress. Many children show anxiety and stress through complaints of physical aches and pains.

6. Watch for possible preoccupation with violent movies or war theme video/computer games.

7. Children who seem preoccupied or very stressed about war, fighting, or terrorism should be evaluated by a qualified mental health professional. Other signs that a child may need professional help include ongoing trouble sleeping, persistent upsetting thoughts, fearful images, intense fears about death, and trouble leaving their parents or going to school. The child's physician can assist with appropriate referrals.

8. Help children communicate with others and express themselves at home. Some children may want to write letters to the President, Governor, local newspaper, or grieving families.

9. Let children be children. They may not want to think or talk a lot about these events. It is OK if they'd rather play ball, climb trees, or ride their bike, etc.

War and terrorism are not easy for anyone to comprehend or accept. Understandably, many young children feel confused, upset, and anxious. Parents, teachers, and caring adults can help by listening and responding in an honest, consistent, and supportive manner. Most children, even those exposed to trauma, are quite resilient. Like most adults, they can and do get through difficult times and go on with their lives. By creating an open environment where they feel free to ask questions, parents can help them cope and reduce the likelihood of emotional difficulties.

Source: American Academy of Child & Adolescent Psychiatry, 2003.

What's Your View?

Which of the suggestions in this box do you think would be most helpful in talking with a child about a war or terrorist attack? Why?

Check It Out

For more information on this topic, go to http://www.nccev .org/violence/events.html. This is a page on the Web site of the National Center for Children Exposed to Violence, which deals specifically with catastrophic events. It has summaries of research and statistics, recommended reading, and links to relevant Web sites.

Table 10-3	Characteristics of Resilient Children and Adolescents
Source	**Characteristic**
Individual	Good Intellectual functioning
	Appealing, sociable, easygoing disposition
	Self-efficacy, self-confidence, high self-esteem
	Talents
	Faith
Family	Close relationship to caring parent figure
	Authoritative parenting: warmth, structure, high expectations
	Socioeconomic advantages
	Connections to extended supportive family networks
Extrafamilial context	Bonds to prosocial adults outside the family
	Connections to prosocial organizations
	Attending effective schools

Source: Masten & Coatsworth, 1998, p. 212.

What's
Your View?

- Do you recall an experience with a caring adult that helped you deal with adversity?

Resilient children also tend to have high IQs and to be good problem solvers. Their superior information-processing skills may help them cope with adversity, protect themselves, regulate their behavior, and learn from experience. They may attract the interest of teachers, who can act as guides, confidants, or mentors (Masten & Coatsworth, 1998). They may even have protective genes (Caspi et al., 2002; Kim-Cohen, Moffitt, Caspi, & Taylor, 2004).

Other frequently cited protective factors (Ackerman, Kogos, Youngstrom, Schoff, & Izard, 1999; Eisenberg et al., 2004; Eisenberg et al., 1997; Masten et al., 1990; Masten & Coatsworth, 1998; E. E. Werner, 1993) include the following:

- *The child's temperament or personality:* Resilient children are adaptable, friendly, well liked, independent, and sensitive to others. They are competent and have high self-esteem. They are creative, resourceful, independent, and pleasant to be with. When under stress, they can regulate their emotions by shifting attention to something else.

- *Compensating experiences:* A supportive school environment or successful experiences in studies, sports, or music or with other children or adults can help make up for a destructive home life.

- *Reduced risk:* Children who have been exposed to only one of a number of factors for psychiatric disorder (such as parental discord, low social status, a disturbed mother, a criminal father, and experience in foster care or an institution) are often better able to overcome stress than children who have been exposed to more than one risk factor.

All this does not mean that bad things that happen in a child's life do not matter. In general, children with unfavorable backgrounds have more adjustment problems than children with more favorable backgrounds. Even some outwardly resilient children may suffer internal distress that may have long-term consequences (Masten & Coatsworth, 1998). Still, what is heartening about these findings is that negative childhood experiences do not necessarily determine the outcome of a person's life and that many children have the strength to rise above the most difficult circumstances.

Checkpoint
Can you . . .

✔ Explain Elkind's concept of the "hurried child"?

✔ Name the most common sources of fear, stress, and anxiety in children?

✔ Identify protective factors that contribute to resilience?

Refocus

Thinking back to the Focus vignette about Marian Anderson at the beginning of this chapter:

- What do you think were major sources of self-esteem for Marian Anderson as a child? Would you estimate her self-esteem as high or low?

- How would you describe the family atmosphere in Anderson's home? Was her upbringing authoritarian, authoritative, or permissive?

- How did poverty, and the need for her mother to work outside the home, affect Anderson?

- How did Anderson's experience living in an extended-family household affect her?

- Was Anderson's choice of her first friend consistent with what you have learned in this chapter about children's choice of friends?

- Can you point to examples of resilience in Marian Anderson's childhood and adult life? What do you think accounted for her resilience?

Adolescence, too, is a stressful, risk-filled time—more so than middle childhood. Yet most adolescents develop the skills and competence to deal with the challenges they face, as we'll see in Chapters 11 and 12.

SUMMARY AND KEY TERMS

The Developing Self

Guidepost 1: How do school-age children develop a realistic self-concept, and what contributes to self-esteem?

- The self-concept becomes more realistic during middle childhood, when, according to neo-Piagetian theory, children form representational systems.
- According to Erikson, the chief source of self-esteem is children's view of their productive competence. This "virtue" develops through resolution of the conflict of industry versus inferiority. According to Susan Harter's research, however, self-esteem arises primarily from self-evaluation and social support.

  representational systems *(357)*

  industry versus inferiority *(358)*

Guidepost 2: How do school-age children show emotional growth?

- School-age children have internalized shame and pride and can better understand and regulate negative emotions.
- Empathy and prosocial behavior increase.
- Emotional growth is affected by parents' reactions to displays of negative emotions.
- Emotional regulation involves effortful control.

The Child in the Family

Guidepost 3: How do parent-child relationships change in middle childhood?

- School-age children spend less time with parents and are less close to them than before, but relationships with parents continue to be important. Culture influences family relationships and roles.
- The family environment has two major components: family structure and family atmosphere.
- The emotional tone of the home, the way parents handle disciplinary issues and conflict, the effects of parents' work, and the adequacy of financial resources all contribute to family atmosphere.
- Development of coregulation may affect the way a family handles conflicts and discipline.

  coregulation *(361)*

Guidepost 4: What are the effects of parents' work and of poverty on children's well-being?

- The impact of mothers' employment depends on many factors concerning the child, the mother's work and her feelings about it; whether she has a supportive partner; the family's socioeconomic status; and the type of care and degree of monitoring the child receives.

- Poverty can harm children's development indirectly through its effects on parents' well-being and parenting practices. Persistent poverty may be especially damaging.

Guidepost 5: What impact does family structure have on children's development?

- Many children today grow up in nontraditional family structures. Other things being equal, children tend to do better in traditional two-parent families than in cohabiting, divorced, single-parent, or stepfamilies. The structure of the family, however, is less important than its effects on family atmosphere.
- Adopted children are generally well adjusted, though they face special challenges.

  open adoption *(364)*

- Children's adjustment to divorce depends on factors concerning the child, the parents' handling of the situation, custody and visitation arrangements, financial circumstances, contact with the noncustodial parent (usually the father), and a parent's remarriage.
- The amount of conflict in a marriage and the likelihood of its continuing after divorce may influence whether children are better off if the parents stay together.
- In most divorces the mother gets custody, though paternal custody is a growing trend. Quality of contact with a noncustodial father is more important than frequency of contact.
- Joint custody can be beneficial to children when the parents can cooperate. Joint legal custody is more common than joint physical custody.
- Although parental divorce increases the risk of long-term problems for children, most adjust reasonably well.
- Children living with only one parent are at heightened risk of behavioral and academic problems, largely related to socioeconomic status.
- Boys tend to have more trouble than girls in adjusting to divorce and single-parent living but tend to adjust better to the mother's remarriage.
- Studies have found no ill effects on children living with gay or lesbian parents.

Guidepost 6: How do siblings influence and get along with one another, and what part do pets play in children's development?

- The roles and responsibilities of siblings in nonindustrialized societies are more structured than in industrialized societies.
- Siblings learn about conflict resolution from their relationships with each other. Relationships with parents affect sibling relationships.
- Pets help children develop basic trust, autonomy, and industry.

The Child in the Peer Group

Guidepost 7: How do relationships with peers change in middle childhood, and what influences popularity and choice of friends?

- The peer group becomes more important in middle childhood. Peer groups generally consist of children who are similar in age, sex, ethnicity, and socioeconomic status and who live near one another or go to school together.

- The peer group helps children develop social skills, allows them to test and adopt values independent of parents, gives them a sense of belonging, and helps develop the self-concept and gender identity. It also may encourage conformity and prejudice.

- Popularity in middle childhood tends to influence future adjustment. It can be measured sociometrically or by perceived social status, and the results may differ. Popular children tend to have good cognitive abilities and social skills. Behaviors that affect popularity may be derived from family relationships and cultural values.

- Intimacy and stability of friendships increase during middle childhood. Boys tend to have more friends, whereas girls have closer friends.

prejudice *(372)*

Guidepost 8: What are the most common forms of aggressive behavior in middle childhood, and what influences contribute to such behavior?

- During middle childhood, aggression typically declines. Relational aggression becomes more common than overt aggression. Instrumental aggression generally gives way to hostile aggression, often with a hostile bias. Highly aggressive children tend to be unpopular, but this may change as children move into adolescence.

instrumental aggression *(377)*

hostile aggression *(377)*

- Aggressiveness is promoted by exposure to media violence and can extend into adult life.

- Middle childhood is a prime time for bullying, but patterns of bullying and victimization may be established much earlier. Victims tend to be weak and submissive or argumentative and provocative and to have low self-esteem.

- School interventions are needed to stop or prevent bullying.

bullying *(379)*

Mental Health

Guidepost 9: What are some common emotional disturbances, and how are they treated?

- Common emotional and behavioral disorders among school-age children include disruptive behavioral disorders, anxiety disorders, and childhood depression.

- Treatment techniques include individual psychotherapy, family therapy, behavior therapy, art therapy, play therapy, and drug therapy. Often therapies are used in combination.

oppositional defiant disorder (ODD) *(381)*

conduct disorder (CD) *(381)*

school phobia *(382)*

separation anxiety disorder *(382)*

social phobia *(382)*

generalized anxiety disorder *(382)*

obsessive-compulsive disorder (OCD) *(382)*

childhood depression *(382)*

individual psychotherapy *(383)*

family therapy *(383)*

behavior therapy *(383)*

art therapy *(383)*

play therapy *(384)*

drug therapy *(384)*

Guidepost 10: How do the stresses of modern life affect children, and what enables "resilient" children to withstand them?

- As a result of the pressures of modern life, many children experience stress. Children tend to worry about school, health, and personal safety and may be traumatized by exposure to terrorism or war.

- Resilient children are better able than others to withstand stress. Protective factors involve family relationships, cognitive ability, personality, degree of risk, and compensating experiences.

resilient children *(386)*

protective factors *(386)*

PART 5

- Both hormonal and social influences may contribute to heightened emotion and moodiness in adolescence.

- Early or late physical maturation can affect emotional and social adjustment.

- Conflict between adolescents and their parents may sometimes stem from immature aspects of adolescent thinking.

- Parental involvement and parenting styles influence academic achievement.

- The ability of low-income children to do well in school may depend on the availability of family and community resources.

- Physical characteristics play an important part in molding adolescents' self-concept.

- Girls who are knowledgeable about sex are most likely to postpone sexual activity.

- The intensity and intimacy of adolescent friendships is in part due to cognitive development.

In adolescence, young people's appearance changes; as a result of the hormonal events of puberty, they take on the bodies of adults. Their thinking changes, too; they are better able to think abstractly and hypothetically. Their feelings change about almost everything. All areas of development converge as adolescents confront their major task: establishing an identity—including a sexual identity—that will carry over to adulthood.

In Chapters 11 and 12, we see how adolescents incorporate their drastically changed appearance, their puzzling physical yearnings, and their new cognitive abilities into their sense of self. We see how the peer group serves as the testing ground for teenagers' ideas about life and about themselves. We look at risks and problems that arise during the teenage years, as well as at characteristic strengths of adolescents.

Adolescence

CHAPTER 11

Physical and Cognitive Development in Adolescence

What I like in my adolescents is that they have not yet hardened. We all confuse hardening and strength. Strength we must achieve, but not callousness.

Anaïs Nin, *The Diaries of Anaïs Nin*, Vol. IV

Focus
Anne Frank, Diarist of the Holocaust*

Anne Frank

For her thirteenth birthday on June 12, 1942, Anne Frank's parents gave her a diary. This small, cloth-covered volume was the first of several notebooks in which Anne recorded her experiences and reflections during the next two years. Little did she dream that her jottings would become one of the most famous published accounts by victims of the Holocaust during World War II.

Anne Frank (1929–1945), her parents, Otto and Edith Frank, and her older sister, Margot, were German Jews who fled to Amsterdam after Hitler came to power in 1933, only to see the Netherlands fall to Nazi conquest seven years later. In the summer of 1942, when the Nazis began rounding up Dutch Jews for deportation to concentration camps, the family went into hiding on the upper floors of the building occupied by Otto Frank's pharmaceutical firm. Behind a door concealed by a movable cupboard, a steep stairway led to the four rooms Anne called the "Secret Annexe." For two years, the Franks stayed in those confined quarters with a couple named "Van Daan,"** their 15-year-old son, "Peter,"** and a middle-aged dentist, "Albert Dussel,"** who shared Anne's room. Then, on August 4, 1944, German and Dutch security police raided the "Secret Annexe" and sent its occupants to concentration camps, where all but Anne's father died.

Anne's writings, published by Otto Frank after the war, describe the life the fugitives led. During the day they had to be completely quiet so as not to alert people in the offices below. They saw no one except a few trusted Christian helpers who risked their lives to bring food, books, newspapers, and essential supplies. To venture

*Sources of biographical information about Anne Frank were Bloom (1999), Frank (1958, 1995), Lindwer (1991), Müller (1998), and Netherlands State Institute for War Documentation (1989). Page references are to the 1958 paperback version of the diary.

**Fictional names Anne invented for use in her diary.

outside—which would have been necessary to replace Anne's quickly outgrown clothes or to correct her worsening nearsightedness—was unthinkable.

The diary reveals the thoughts, feelings, daydreams, and mood swings of a high-spirited, introspective adolescent coming to maturity under traumatic conditions. Anne wrote of her concern about her "ugly" appearance, of her wish for "a real mother who understands me," and of her adoration for her father (Frank, 1958, pp. 36, 110). She expressed despair at the adults' constant criticism of her failings and at her parents' apparent favoritism toward her sister. She wrote about her fears, her urge for independence, her hopes for a return to her old life, and her aspirations for a writing career.

As tensions rose in the "Secret Annexe," Anne lost her appetite and began taking antidepressant medication. But as time went on, she became less self-pitying and more serious-minded. When she thought back to her previous carefree existence, she felt like a different person from the Anne who had "grown wise within these walls" (p. 149).

She was deeply conscious of her sexual awakening: "I think what is happening to me is so wonderful, and not only what can be seen on my body, but all that is taking place inside. . . . Each time I have a period . . . I have the feeling that . . . I have a sweet secret, and . . . I always long for the time that I shall feel that secret within me again" (pp. 115–116).

Anne originally had regarded Peter as shy and gawky—not a very promising companion; but eventually she began visiting his attic room for long, intimate talks and finally, her first kiss. Her diary records the conflict between her stirring sexual passion and her strict moral upbringing.

One of the last diary entries is dated July 15, 1944, less than three weeks before the raid and eight months before Anne's death in the concentration camp at Bergen-Belsen: ". . . in spite of everything, I still believe that people are really good at heart. . . . I hear the ever approaching thunder, which will destroy us too, I can feel the suffering of millions and yet, if I look up into the heavens, I think that it will all come right, that this cruelty too will end, and that peace and tranquillity will return again" (p. 233).

The moving story of Anne Frank's tragically abbreviated adolescence points up the insistent role of biology and its interrelationships with inner and outer experience. Anne's "coming of age" occurred under highly unusual conditions. Yet her normal physical maturation went on, along with a host of cognitive and psychosocial changes heightened by her stressful circumstances.

In this chapter, we describe the physical transformations of adolescence and how they affect young people's feelings. We look at the not-yet-mature adolescent brain, and we discuss health issues associated with this time of life. Turning to cognitive development, we examine the Piagetian stage of formal operations, which makes it possible for a young person like Anne Frank to visualize an ideal world. We also look at some immature aspects of adolescents' thought and at their information-processing skills and linguistic and moral development. Finally, we explore issues of education and vocational choice, which continued to concern Anne Frank no matter how narrowly circumscribed her life became.

After you have read and studied this chapter, you should be able to answer each of the Guidepost questions that follow. Look for them again in the margins, where they point to important concepts throughout the chapter. To check your understanding of these Guideposts, review the end-of-chapter summary. Checkpoints located at periodic spots throughout the chapter will help you verify your understanding of what you have read.

1. What is adolescence, when does it begin and end, and what opportunities and risks does it entail?

2. What physical changes do adolescents experience, and how do these changes affect them psychologically?

3. What brain developments occur during adolescence, and how do they affect adolescent behavior?

4. What are some common health problems in adolescence, and how can they be prevented?

5. How do adolescents' thinking and use of language differ from younger children's?

6. On what basis do adolescents make moral judgments?

7. What influences affect school success, and why do some students drop out?

8. What factors affect educational and vocational planning and aspirations?

Adolescence: A Developmental Transition

Rituals to mark a child's "coming of age" are common in many societies For example, Apache tribes celebrate a girl's first menstruation with a four-day ritual of sunrise-to-sunset chanting. In modern industrial societies, the passage from childhood to adulthood is marked, not by a single event, but by a long period known as **adolescence**—a developmental transition that lasts from about age 10 or 11 or even earlier until the late teens or early twenties and entails major, interrelated physical, cognitive, and psychosocial changes. Adolescence is generally considered to begin with the onset of **puberty,** the process that leads to sexual maturity, or fertility—the ability to reproduce.*

Adolescence is a social construction (refer back to Chapter 1). Before the twentieth century, there was no such concept; children in western cultures entered the adult world when they matured physically or when they began a vocational apprenticeship. Today entry into adulthood takes longer and is less clear-cut. Puberty begins earlier than it used to; and entrance into a vocation tends to occur later in complex societies, which require longer periods of education or vocational training to prepare for adult responsibilities.

Early adolescence (approximately ages 10 or 11 to 14), the transition out of childhood, offers opportunities for growth, not only in physical dimensions, but also in cognitive and social competence, autonomy, self-esteem, and intimacy. This period also carries risks. Some young people have trouble handling so many changes at once and may need help in overcoming dangers along the way. Adolescence is a time of increasing divergence between the majority of young people, who are headed for a fulfilling and productive adulthood, and a sizable minority who will be dealing

Guidepost

1. What is adolescence, when does it begin and end, and what opportunities and risks does it entail?

adolescence Developmental transition between childhood and adulthood entailing major physical, cognitive, and psychosocial changes.

puberty Process by which a person attains sexual maturity and the ability to reproduce.

---

*Some people use the term *puberty* to mean the end point of sexual maturation and refer to the process as *pubescence,* but our usage conforms to that of most psychologists today.

In many cultures, special celebrations herald entrance to puberty. These 9-year-old schoolgirls in Tehran celebrate the ceremony of Taqlif, which marks their readiness to begin the religious duties of Islam.

with major problems (Offer, 1987; Offer, Kaiz, Ostrov, & Albert, 2002; Offer, Offer, & Ostrov, 2004; Offer & Schonert-Reichl, 1992).

U.S. adolescents today face a number of hazards to their physical and mental well-being, including high death rates from accidents, homicide, and suicide (National Center for Health Statistics [NCHS], 2004). Across ethnic and social-class lines, use of drugs, driving while intoxicated, and sexual activity increase throughout the teenage years (see Figure 11-1). As we will see, such risky behaviors may reflect immaturity of the adolescent brain.

However, a government survey shows encouraging trends. High school students are becoming less likely to engage in marijuana use, risky sexual behavior, carrying of weapons, and riding in cars without seat belts or with drivers who have been drinking (Grunberg et al., 2002). Avoidance of such risky behaviors increases the

Checkpoint

Can you . . .

✔ Explain why adolescence is a social construction?

✔ Identify risky behavior patterns common during adolescence?

Figure 11-1

Prevalence of high-risk behaviors by age. (Source: Adapted from Elliott, 1993.)

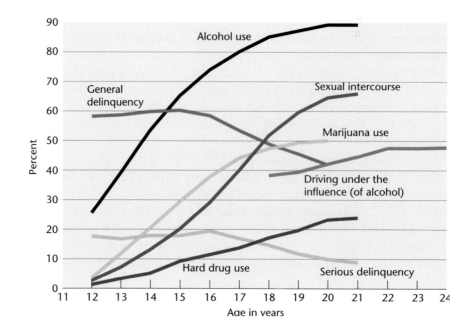

chances that young people will come through the teenage years in good physical and mental health.

PHYSICAL DEVELOPMENT

Puberty: The End of Childhood

The biological changes of puberty, which signal the end of childhood, include rapid growth in height and weight, changes in body proportions and form, and attainment of sexual maturity. These dramatic physical changes are part of a long, complex process of maturation that begins even before birth, and their psychological ramifications continue into adulthood.

Guidepost

2. What physical changes do adolescents experience, and how do these changes affect them psychologically?

How Puberty Begins: Hormonal Changes

Puberty begins with a sharp increase in production of sex-related hormones and takes place in two stages: *adrenarche,* the maturing of the adrenal glands, followed a few years later by *gonadarche,* the maturing of the sex organs and the appearance of more obvious pubertal changes.

First, sometime between ages 6 and 9 (Susman, Dorn, & Schiefelbein, 2003), the adrenal glands, located above the kidneys, secrete gradually increasing levels of androgens, principally *dehydroepiandrosterone* (DHEA). DHEA plays a part in the growth of pubic, axillary (armpit), and facial hair, as well as in faster body growth, oilier skin, and the development of body odor. By age 10, levels of DHEA are 10 times what they were between ages 1 and 4. In several studies, adolescent boys and girls—whether homosexual or heterosexual—recalled their earliest sexual attraction as having taken place at that age (McClintock & Herdt, 1996).

The maturing of the sex organs two to four years later triggers a second burst of DHEA production, which then rises to adult levels. In this second stage, gonadarche, a girl's ovaries step up their output of estrogen, which stimulates growth of female genitals and development of breasts. In boys, the testes increase the manufacture of androgens, particularly testosterone, which stimulate growth of male genitals, muscle mass, and body hair. Boys and girls have both types of hormones, but girls have higher levels of estrogen, and boys have higher levels of androgens. In girls, testosterone influences growth of the clitoris as well as of the bones and of pubic and axillary hair.

The precise time when this rush of hormonal activity begins seems to depend on reaching a critical weight level. Studies of mice and humans have found that leptin, a brain protein secreted by fatty tissue and identified as having a role in overweight, is needed to trigger the onset of puberty. An accumulation of leptin in the bloodstream may stimulate the hypothalamus to signal the pituitary gland, which in turn, may signal the sex glands to increase their secretion of hormones (Chehab, Mounzih, Lu, & Lim, 1997; Clément et al., 1998; O'Rahilly, 1998; Strobel, Camoin, Ozata, & Strosberg, 1998). Scientists have identified a gene, *GPR54,* on chromosome 19 that is essential for this development to occur (Seminara et al., 2003). Girls with a higher percentage of body fat in early childhood and those who experience unusual weight gain between ages 5 and 9 tend to show more advanced pubertal development (Davison, Susman, & Birch, 2003).

Some research attributes the heightened emotionality and moodiness of early adolescence—so apparent in Anne Frank's diary—to these hormonal developments. However, other influences, such as sex, age, temperament, and the timing of puberty, may moderate or even override hormonal ones (Buchanan, Eccles, & Becker, 1992).

Timing, Sequence, and Signs of Puberty and Sexual Maturity

There is about a seven-year range for the onset of puberty in boys and an eight-year range in girls. The process typically takes about four years for both sexes and begins up to three years earlier in girls than in boys. In the United States, the average age for boys' entry into puberty is 10 to 11 (Susman et al., 2003), but boys may begin to show changes any time between 9 and 16. Most girls begin to show pubertal changes at 9 or 10 years of age, but some do so as early as 6 or as late as 13 or 14.

Physical changes in both boys and girls during puberty include the development of pubic hair, deepening of the voice, the adolescent growth spurt, and muscular growth. The maturation of reproductive organs brings the beginning of menstruation in girls and the production of sperm in boys. These changes unfold in a sequence that is much more consistent than their timing (see Table 11-1), though it does vary somewhat. One girl may develop breasts and body hair at about the same rate; in another girl, body hair may reach adultlike growth a year or so before breasts develop. Similar variations occur among boys. Let's look more closely at these changes.

primary sex characteristics
Organs directly related to reproduction, which enlarge and mature during adolescence.

Primary and Secondary Sex Characteristics   The **primary sex characteristics** are biological changes that directly involve the organs necessary for reproduction. In the female, these organs are the ovaries, fallopian tubes, uterus, and vagina; in the male, they are the testes, penis, scrotum, seminal vesicles, and prostate gland. During puberty, these organs enlarge and mature. In boys, the first sign of puberty is the growth of the testes and scrotum. In girls, the growth of the primary sex characteristics is not readily apparent because these organs are internal.

secondary sex characteristics
Physiological signs of sexual maturation (such as breast development and growth of body hair) that do not involve the sex organs.

The **secondary sex characteristics** (see Table 11-2) are physiological signs of sexual maturation that do not directly involve the sex organs: for example, the breasts of females and the broad shoulders of males. Other secondary sex characteristics are changes in the voice and skin texture, muscular development, and the growth of pubic, facial, axillary, and body hair.

Table 11-1   Usual Sequence of Physiological Changes in Adolescence

Female Characteristics	Age of First Appearance
Growth of breasts	6–13
Growth of pubic hair	6–14
Body growth	9.5–14.5
Menarche	10–16.5
Appearance of underarm hair	About 2 years after appearance of pubic hair
Increased output of oil- and sweat-producing glands (which may lead to acne)	About the same time as appearance of underarm hair

Male Characteristics	Age of First Appearance
Growth of testes, scrotal sac	9–13.5
Growth of pubic hair	12–16
Body growth	10.5–16
Growth of penis, prostate gland, seminal vesicles	11–14.5
Change in voice	About the same time as growth of penis
First ejaculation of semen	About 1 year after beginning of growth of penis
Appearance of facial and underarm hair	About 2 years after appearance of pubic hair
Increased output of oil- and sweat-producing glands (which may lead to acne)	About the same time as appearance of underarm hair

Table 11-2 Secondary Sex Characteristics

Girls	Boys
Breasts	Pubic hair
Pubic hair	Axillary (underarm) hair
Axillary (underarm) hair	Muscular development
Changes in voice	Facial hair
Changes in skin	Changes in voice
Increased width and depth of pelvis	Changes in skin
Muscular development	Broadening of shoulders

The first reliable sign of puberty in girls is the growth of the breasts. The nipples enlarge and protrude, the *areolae* (the pigmented areas surrounding the nipples) enlarge, and the breasts assume first a conical and then a rounded shape. Some adolescent boys experience temporary breast enlargement, much to their distress; this is normal and may last up to 18 months.

The voice deepens, especially in boys, partly in response to the growth of the larynx and partly in response to the production of male hormones. The skin becomes coarser and oilier. Increased activity of the sebaceous glands may give rise to pimples and blackheads. Acne is more common in boys than in girls and seems related to increased levels of testosterone.

Pubic hair, at first straight and silky, eventually becomes coarse, dark, and curly. Adolescent boys are usually happy to see hair on the face and chest; but girls are usually dismayed at the appearance of even a slight amount of hair on the face or around the nipples, though this is normal.

Influences on Onset of Puberty On the basis of historical sources, developmental scientists have found a **secular trend**—a trend that spans several generations—in the onset of puberty: a drop in the age when puberty begins and when young people reach adult height and sexual maturity. The trend began about 100 years ago and has occurred in the United States, western Europe, and Japan, continuing at least in the United States (Anderson, Dallal, & Must, 2003). A possible explanation is a higher standard of living. Children who are healthier, better nourished, and better cared for might be expected to mature earlier and grow bigger. Thus, the average age of sexual maturity is earlier in developed countries than in developing ones. A large contributor to the secular trend in the United States during the last part of the 20th century appears to be the increase in overweight among young girls (Anderson et al., 2003).

African American and Mexican American girls generally enter puberty earlier than white girls. Black girls typically begin to show breast budding and pubic hair at age 9½, as compared with about 10 for Mexican American girls and close to 10½ for white girls (Wu, Mendola, & Buck, 2002). However, some African American girls experience these changes as early as age 6, and some white girls do so as early as age 7 (Kaplowitz et al., 1999).

A longitudinal study suggests that the relationship with the father may be a key to pubertal timing. Girls who, as preschoolers, had close, supportive relationships with their parents—especially with an affectionate, involved father—entered puberty later than girls whose parental relationships had been cold or distant or those who were raised by single mothers (Ellis, McFadyen-Ketchum, Dodge, Pettit, & Bates, 1999).

secular trend Trend that can be seen only by observing several generations, such as the trend toward earlier attainment of adult height and sexual maturity, which began a century ago.

How might family relationships affect pubertal development? One suggestion is that this occurs through *pheromones,* odorous chemicals given off by men and women, which attract mates. The existence of pheromones is supported by brain imaging studies in which the odors of male sweat and women's urine activated the hypothalamus, a brain structure that controls sexual behavior, in the other sex (Savic, Berglund, Gulyas, & Roland, 2001). As a natural incest-prevention mechanism, sexual development may be inhibited in girls who are heavily exposed to their fathers' pheromones, as would happen in a close father-daughter relationship. On the other hand, frequent exposure to the pheromones of unrelated adult males, such as a stepfather or a single mother's boyfriend, may speed up pubertal development (Ellis & Garber, 2000). Both a father's absence and early pubertal timing have been identified as risk factors for sexual promiscuity and teenage pregnancy; thus, a father's early presence and active involvement may be important to girls' healthy sexual development (Ellis et al., 1999).

The Adolescent Growth Spurt In Anne Frank's diary, she made rueful references to her physical growth—to shoes she could no longer get into and vests "so small that they don't even reach my tummy" (Frank, 1958, p. 71). Anne obviously was in the **adolescent growth spurt**—a rapid increase in height and weight that generally begins in girls between ages 9½ and 14½ (usually at about 10) and in boys, between 10½ and 16 (usually at 12 or 13). The growth spurt typically lasts about two years; soon after it ends, the young person reaches sexual maturity. Since girls' growth spurt usually occurs earlier than that of boys, girls between ages 11 and 13 tend to be taller, heavier, and stronger than boys the same age. After their growth spurt, boys are again larger, as before. Both boys and girls reach nearly their full height by age 18.

Boys and girls grow differently, of course. A boy becomes larger overall: his shoulders wider, his legs longer relative to his trunk, and his forearms longer relative to his upper arms and his height. A girl's pelvis widens to make childbearing easier, and layers of fat accumulate under her skin, giving her a more rounded appearance.

The adolescent growth spurt affects practically all skeletal and muscular dimensions. Muscular growth peaks at age 12½ for girls and 14½ for boys. Even the eye grows faster, causing (as in Anne Frank) an increase in nearsightedness, a problem that affects about one-fourth of 12- to 17-year-olds (Gans, 1990). The lower jaw becomes longer and thicker, and the jaw and nose project more. Because each of these changes follows its own timetable, parts of the body may be out of proportion for a while. The result is the familiar teenage gawkiness Anne noticed in Peter Van Daan, which accompanies unbalanced, accelerated growth.

These dramatic physical changes have psychological ramifications. Most young teenagers are more concerned about their appearance than about any other aspect of themselves, and many do not like what they see in the mirror. Girls tend to be unhappier about their looks than boys are, reflecting the greater cultural emphasis on women's physical attributes (Rosenblum & Lewis, 1999). As we will discuss in a subsequent section, these attitudes may lead to eating problems.

Signs of Sexual Maturity: Sperm Production and Menstruation The principal sign of sexual maturity in boys is the production of sperm. The first ejaculation, or **spermarche,** occurs at an average age of 13. A boy may wake up to find a wet spot or a hardened, dried spot on the sheets—the result of a *nocturnal emission,* an involuntary ejaculation of semen (commonly referred to as a *wet dream*).

adolescent growth spurt Sharp increase in height and weight that precedes sexual maturity.

Many girls of junior high school age tower above their male classmates. At ages 11 to 13, girls are, on average, taller, heavier, and stronger than boys, who reach their adolescent growth spurt later than girls do.

spermarche Boy's first ejaculation.

Most adolescent boys have these emissions, sometimes in connection with an erotic dream.

The principal sign of sexual maturity in girls is *menstruation,* a monthly shedding of tissue from the lining of the womb—what Anne Frank called her "sweet secret." The first menstruation, **menarche,** occurs fairly late in the sequence of female development; its normal timing can vary from ages 10 to 16½ (refer back to Table 11-1). Consistent with the secular trend mentioned previously, the average age of menarche in U.S. girls fell from more than 14 years before 1900 to 12½ years in the 1990s. On average, a black girl first menstruates shortly after her 12th birthday and a white girl about six months later (Anderson et al., 2003).

A combination of genetic, physical, emotional, and environmental influences may affect the timing of menarche. The age of a girl's first menstruation tends to be similar to that of her mother. Bigger girls and those whose breasts are more developed tend to menstruate earlier. Nutrition is a factor. Strenuous exercise, as in competitive athletics, can delay menarche (Ellis & Garber, 2000; Graber, Brooks-Gunn, & Warren, 1995; Moffitt, Caspi, Belsky, & Silva, 1992; Steinberg, 1988). In a study of Akewsasne Mohawk girls, exposure to lead was associated with delayed menarche, whereas PCB exposure was related to early menarche (Denham et al., 2005).

Psychological effects of the timing of puberty and sexual maturation depend on how the adolescent and other people in his or her world interpret the accompanying changes. Effects of early or late maturation are most likely to be negative when adolescents are much more or less developed than their peers; when they do not see the changes as advantageous; and when several stressful events occur at about the same time (Petersen, 1993; Simmons, Blyth, & McKinney, 1983).

The Adolescent Brain

The adolescent brain is a work in progress. Dramatic changes in brain structures involved in emotions, judgment, organization of behavior, and self-control take place between puberty and young adulthood and may help explain teenagers' penchant for emotional outbursts and risky or even violent behavior (ACT for Youth, 2002; Steinberg & Scott, 2003; see Box 11-1).

Two major changes in the adolescent brain parallel processes that occur before birth and during infancy: the growth and pruning of gray matter. A second spurt in production of gray matter—neurons, axons, and dendrites—begins just before puberty and may be related to the surge of sex hormones at this time. The growth spurt takes place chiefly in the frontal lobes, which handle planning, reasoning, judgment, emotional regulation, and impulse control. After the growth spurt, unused connections are pruned, and those that remain are strengthened. Like the pruning that occurs early in life, this process makes the brain more efficient (ACT for Youth, 2002; NIMH, 2001b).

The pattern of gray matter growth contrasts with the pattern for white matter, the nerve fibers that connect distant regions of the brain. These connections thicken and myelinate earlier in childhood, beginning with the frontal lobes and moving toward the rear of the brain. Between ages 6 and 13, striking growth takes place in connections between the temporal and parietal lobes, which deal with sensory functions, language, and spatial understanding. White matter growth then drops off precipitously at about the end of the critical period for language learning. Whereas white matter growth proceeds from front to back, gray matter growth proceeds in the opposite direction, the frontal lobes not fully maturing until young adulthood. Continuing myelination of gray matter in the frontal lobes facilitates the maturation of cognitive processing (NIMH, 2001b).

menarche Girl's first menstruation.

What's Your View?

- Did you mature early, late, or "on time"? How did the timing of your maturation affect you psychologically?

Checkpoint

Can you . . .

✔ Tell how puberty begins and how its timing and length vary?

✔ Describe typical pubertal changes in boys and girls, and identify factors that affect psychological reactions to these changes?

Guidepost

3. What brain developments occur during adolescence, and how do they affect adolescent behavior?

Lifemap CD

To learn why teens' brains have yet to fully mature, view the video, "The Adolescent Brain," in Chapter 11 of your CD.

BOX 11-1

Practically Speaking
Should Adolescents Be Exempt from the Death Penalty?

On March 1, 2005, the U.S. Supreme Court, in a controversial 5-4 decision, ruled the death penalty unconstitutional for a convicted murderer who was 17 years old when he committed the crime (Mears, 2005). The Court had previously permitted the death penalty for 16- and 17-year-olds but not for younger minors. The new decision invalidates laws of 19 states that permit execution of offenders who were 16 or 17 years old at the time of their crimes and brings U.S. juvenile criminal policy in line with that of almost all other countries in the world. In addition execution of juveniles is expressly forbidden in the International Covenant on Civil and Political Rights, the American Convention on Human Rights, the Geneva Convention relating to protection of civilians in times of war, and the United Nations Convention on the Rights of the Child (Montaldo, 2005).

Opponents of exempting adolescent offenders from the death penalty argue that the decision should be made on a case-by-case basis, depending on the nature of the crime and the maturity of the offender. However, the Supreme Court majority gave weight to published research suggesting that adolescents *as a group* should not be held to the same criminal standard as adults because they are developmentally less mature.

Laurence Steinberg, a Temple University psychologist specializing in adolescent behavior, and Elizabeth S. Scott, a professor at the University of Virginia School of Law, in an article published in 2003, offered three reasons that adolescence should be a mitigating factor, whether in a capital case or a trial for a lesser offense: (1) Adolescents are deficient in decision-making capacity; (2) they are especially vulnerable to coercive circumstances, such as peer pressure; and (3) their character, or personality, is not yet fully formed.

Deficiencies in Decision-Making Capacity As we discuss later in this chapter, even if adolescents are capable of logical reasoning (and many are not), they do not always use it in decision making. This is especially true in highly emotional situations. Adolescents are prone to risky behavior; whether because of cognitive limitations or limited life experience, they think less about hypothetical future consequences and more about immediate rewards. Also, adolescents are more impulsive than adults and have more difficulty regulating their moods and behavior.

Some of these well-known differences between adolescent and adult decision making seem to have a neurological basis. The regions of the brain involved in long-term planning, regulation of emotion, impulse control, and evaluation of risk and reward are still developing during adolescence. Changes in the limbic system around puberty may lead adolescents to seek novelty and take risks and may contribute to heightened emotionality and vulnerability to

stress. The prefrontal cortex, which is involved in long-term planning, judgment, and decision making, may be immature until late adolescence or adulthood. Steinberg and Scott argue that adolescents, because of their immature judgment, should no more be held fully responsible for their actions than should adults who are mentally retarded.

Vulnerability to Peer Influence Because of their immaturity, adolescents may give in to pressures that adults would be able to resist. As we discuss in Chapter 12, peer influence increases in adolescence as young people seek independence from parental control. Young people's desire for peer approval and fear of social rejection affect their decisions, even in the absence of overt coercion. Popular peers serve as models for an adolescent's own behavior.

Unformed Character Courts typically allow mitigation of the penalty based on evidence, provided by character witnesses, of a defendant's good character or citizenship. Steinberg and Scott argue that adolescents' character, identity, and values are not yet fully formed. Juvenile crime often represents a temporary phase of experimentation and risk taking, not a deep-seated, lasting moral deficiency. As we discuss in Chapter 12, most adolescent offenders grow up to be law-abiding citizens.

Steinberg and Scott call for more research that would (a) link developmental changes in decision making to changes in brain structure and (b) examine age differences in decision making in real-life circumstances. Until more definitive knowledge is available, they urge that courts err, if anything, on the side of life for juvenile offenders, as the Supreme Court has now done.

Source: Steinberg and Scott (2003).

What's Your View?

Are there circumstances under which you think an adolescent should be eligible for the death penalty? If so, at what age? What other factors, if any, should enter into such a decision?

Check It Out
For more information on Laurence Steinberg's work, go to http://astro.temple.edu/~lds. This site contains links to several of Steinberg's books on adolescent psychology and parenting.

Adolescents process information about emotions differently than adults do. In one line of research, researchers scanned adolescents' brain activity while they identified emotions on pictures of faces on a computer screen. Early adolescents (ages 11 to 13) tended to use the amygdala, a small, almond-shaped structure deep in the temporal lobe that is heavily involved in emotional and instinctual reactions. Older adolescents, like adults, were more likely to use the frontal lobe, which permits more accurate, reasoned judgments. Thus, in early adolescence, immature brain development may permit feelings to override reason—a possible reason for some young people's unwise choices, such as abuse of alcohol or drugs and sexual risk taking (Baird et al., 1999; Yurgelon-Todd, 2002). In addition, underdevelopment of frontal cortical systems associated with motivation, impulsivity, and addiction may help explain adolescents' thrill and novelty seeking and also may explain why many adolescents find it hard to focus on long-term goals (Bjork et al., 2004; Chambers, Taylor, & Potenza, 2003). The immaturity of their brains may keep some adolescents from heeding warnings that seem logical and persuasive to an adult.

Because the adolescent brain is still developing, teenagers can exert some control over that development. Adolescents who "'exercise' their brains by learning to order their thoughts, understand abstract concepts, and control their impulses are laying the neural foundations that will serve them for the rest of their lives" (ACT for Youth, 2002, p. 1).

Checkpoint
Can you . . .

✔ Describe two major changes in the adolescent brain?

✔ Identify immature features of the adolescent brain, and explain how this immaturity can affect behavior?

Physical and Mental Health

Nine out of 10 early and midadolescents consider themselves healthy, according to an international school-based survey of more than 120,000 eleven-, thirteen-, and fifteen-year-olds in the United States and 27 other western industrialized countries* under the auspices of the World Health Organization (WHO) (Scheidt, Overpeck, Wyatt, & Aszmann, 2000). However, many younger adolescents, especially girls, report frequent health problems, such as headache, stomachache, backache, nervousness, and feeling tired, lonely, or "low." Such reports are most common in the United States and Israel, where life tends to be fast paced and stressful (Scheidt et al., 2000).

Many health problems are preventable, stemming from lifestyle or poverty. In industrialized countries, according to the WHO survey, adolescents from less affluent families tend to report poorer health and more frequent symptoms. More affluent adolescents, who are likely to be better educated, tend to have healthier diets and to be more physically active (Mullan & Currie, 2000).

Let's look at several specific health concerns: physical fitness, sleep needs, eating disorders, drug abuse, sexually transmitted diseases, depression, and causes of death in adolescence.

Guidepost

4. What are some common health problems in adolescence, and how can they be prevented?

Physical Activity

Exercise—or lack of it—affects both physical and mental health. It improves strength and endurance, helps build healthy bones and muscles, helps control weight, reduces anxiety and stress, and increases self-confidence and well-being. Even moderate physical activity has health benefits if done regularly for at least 30 minutes almost every day. A sedentary lifestyle that carries over into adulthood may result in increased risk of overweight, heart disease, cancer, and type 2 diabetes—a growing problem among children and adolescents (Centers for Disease Control and Prevention, 2000a; Hickman, Roberts, & de Matos, 2000; NCHS, 2004; Troiano, 2002).

---

*The other countries were Belgium, Canada, Czech Republic, Denmark, England, Estonia, Finland, France, Germany, Greece, Greenland, Hungary, Republic of Ireland, Israel, Latvia, Lithuania, Northern Ireland, Norway, Poland, Portugal, Russian Federation, Scotland, Slovak Republic, Spain, Sweden, Switzerland, and Wales

Figure 11-2
High school students who do not
engage in recommended amounts
of physical activity (moderate or
vigorous) by grade and sex, United
States, 2003. (Source: NCHS, 2004,
Figure 14, p. 34.)

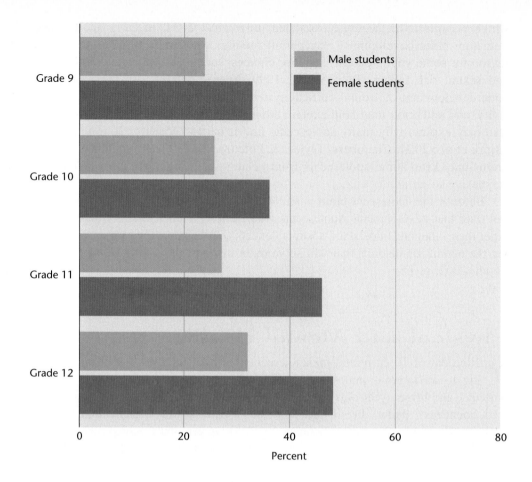

Checkpoint

Can you . . .

✓ Summarize the status of adolescents' health and discuss
prevalent health problems?

✓ Explain why physical activity is
important in adolescence, and
discuss risks and benefits of
athletic activity for adolescent
girls?

Unfortunately, one-third of U.S. high school students do *not* engage in the recommended amounts of physical activity, and the proportion of young people who are inactive increases throughout the high school years (NCHS, 2004; see Figure 11-2). U.S.
adolescents exercise less often than in past years and less frequently than adolescents
in most other industrialized countries (CDC, 2000a; Hickman et al., 2000). Three-
fourths of sixth- through eighth-graders participate in extracurricular team sports
(Kleiner, Nolin, & Chapman, 2004), but barely half (55 percent) of high school senior
boys and less than one-third (30 percent) of senior girls do (Snyder & Hoffman, 2002).

Sleep Needs

Many adolescents do not get enough sleep. Average nighttime sleep declines from
more than ten hours at age 9 to slightly less than eight hours at age 16 (Hoban,
2004). Adolescents tend to be sleepy during the daytime even when they sleep a full
nine hours, suggesting that they need as much as or more sleep than before (Hoban,
2004; Iglowstein, Jenni, Molinari, & Largo, 2003). "Sleeping in" on weekends does
not make up for the loss (Hoban, 2004; Sadeh, Raviv, & Gruber, 2000). In the WHO
study, an average of 40 percent of adolescents (mostly boys) in 28 industrialized
countries reported morning sleepiness at least once a week, and 22 percent said they
are sleepy most days (Scheidt et al., 2000).

A pattern of late bedtimes and oversleeping in the mornings can contribute to
insomnia, a problem that often begins in late childhood or adolescence. Daytime
naps worsen the problem (Hoban, 2004). In a longitudinal study of 2,259 middle
school students, sixth-graders who slept less than their peers were more likely to
show depressive symptoms and to have low self-esteem (Fredriksen, Rhodes, Reddy,
& Way, 2004).

Why do adolescents stay up late? In part it may be because they need to do homework, want to talk on the phone with friends or surf the Web, or wish to act "grown up." However, physiological changes also may be involved (Sadeh et al., 2000). Adolescents undergo a shift in the brain's natural sleep cycle, or *circadian timing system*. The timing of secretion of the hormone *melatonin* is a gauge of when the brain is ready for sleep. After puberty, this secretion takes place later at night (Carskadon, Acebo, Richardson, Tate, & Seifer, 1997). Thus, adolescents need to go to bed later and get up later than younger children; yet most secondary schools start earlier than elementary schools. Their schedules are out of sync with students' biological rhythms (Hoban, 2004). Teenagers tend to be least alert and most stressed early in the morning. Starting school later, or at least offering difficult courses later in the day, would help improve students' concentration (Crouter & Larson, 1998).

Nutrition and Eating Disorders

U.S. adolescents have less healthy diets than those in most other western industrialized countries. They eat fewer fruits and vegetables and more sweets, chocolate, soft drinks, and other "junk" foods, which are high in cholesterol, fat, and calories and low in nutrients (Vereecken & Maes, 2000). Deficiencies of calcium, zinc, and iron are common at this age (Lloyd et al., 1993; Bruner, Joffe, Duggan, Casella, & Brandt, 1996); iron deficiency has been linked to lower standardized math scores (Halterman, Kaczorowski, Aligne, Auinger, & Szilagyi, 2001).

Adolescents who engage in sports tend to feel better than those who do not. Those who take safety precautions, such as wearing helmets while batting, are less likely to be injured in organized sports.

Although poor nutrition is most common in economically depressed or isolated populations, it also may result from concern with body image and weight control (Vereecken & Maes, 2000). Eating disorders, including obesity or overweight, are most prevalent in industrialized societies, where food is abundant and attractiveness is equated with slimness (APA, 1994; Becker, Grinspoon, Klibanski, & Herzog, 1999; Makino, Tsuboi, & Dennerstein, 2004). However, eating disorders appear to be gradually increasing in nonwestern countries as well (Makino et al., 2004).

Obesity/Overweight The average teenage girl needs about 2,200 calories per day; the average teenage boy needs about 2,800. Many adolescents eat more calories than they expend and thus accumulate excess body fat.

Between 1960 and 2002, the mean weight of 12- to 17-year-old boys increased from 125 to 141 pounds, and the mean weight of girls increased from 118 to 130 pounds, with only negligible gains in height (Ogden, Fryar, Carroll, & Flegal, 2004). The percentage of U.S. adolescents who are overweight more than tripled between 1980 and 2002, from 5 to 16 percent. Mexican American and non-Hispanic black adolescents are 1½ times more likely to be overweight than non-Hispanic white adolescents (23 and 21 percent, respectively, compared with 14 percent) (NCHS, 2004).

U.S. teens are more likely to be overweight than their age-mates in 14 other industrialized countries,* according to self-reports of height and weight from 29,242

Checkpoint

Can you . . .

✔ Explain why adolescents often get too little sleep and how sleep deprivation can affect them?

✔ Summarize the normal nutritional needs and typical dietary deficiencies of adolescent boys and girls?

*Austria, Czech Republic, Denmark, Flemish Belgium, Finland, France, Germany, Greece, Ireland, Israel, Lithuania, Portugal, Slovakia, and Sweden.

boys and girls ages 13 and 15. Twenty-six to 31 percent of U.S. teens had a body mass index (BMI) at or above the 85th or 95th percentiles for age and sex, compared with an average of 15 percent for all 15 countries (Lissau et al., 2004). Similarly, a nationally representative U.S. study found nearly 31 percent of 12- to 19-year-olds overweight or at risk of overweight in 1999–2002 (Hedley et al., 2004).

Overweight or obese teenagers tend to be in poorer health than their peers and are more likely to have functional limitations, such as difficulty attending school, performing household chores, or engaging in strenuous activity or personal care (Swallen, Reither, Haas, & Meier, 2005). They are at heightened risk of high cholesterol, hypertension, and diabetes (NCHS, 2004). They tend to become obese adults, subject to a variety of physical, social, and psychological risks (Gortmaker, Must, Perrin, Sobol, & Dietz, 1993).

Genetic and other factors having nothing to do with willpower or lifestyle choices seem to make some people susceptible to overweight or obesity (refer back to Chapters 3 and 9). Among these factors are faulty regulation of metabolism, inability to recognize body cues about hunger and satiation, and development of an abnormally large number of fat cells. However, in a study of 878 California 11- to 15-year-olds, lack of exercise was the main risk factor for overweight in boys and girls (Patrick et al., 2004).

Weight-loss programs that use behavioral modification techniques to help adolescents make changes in diet and exercise have had some success. For many preadolescents and adolescents, however, dieting may be counterproductive. In a prospective three-year study of 8,203 girls and 6,769 boys ages 9 to 14, those who dieted gained more weight than those who did not diet (Field et al., 2003). Use of sibutramine, a weight-loss medication usually used with adults, in conjunction with behavioral modification may improve results, but more study is needed on the drug's safety and efficacy with this age group (Berkowitz, Wadden, Tershakovec, & Cronquist, 2003).

Body Image and Eating Disorders Sometimes a determination *not* to become overweight can result in graver problems than overweight itself. A concern with **body image**—how one believes one looks—often begins in middle childhood or earlier, intensifies in adolescence, and may lead to obsessive efforts at weight control (Davison & Birch, 2001; Schreiber et al., 1996; Vereecken & Maes, 2000). This pattern is more common among girls than among boys and is less likely to be related to actual weight problems.

Because of the normal increase in girls' body fat during puberty, many girls, especially if they are advanced in pubertal development, become unhappy about their appearance, reflecting the cultural emphasis on female physical attributes (Richards, Boxer, Petersen, & Albrecht, 1990; Rosenblum & Lewis, 1999; Swarr & Richards, 1996). Girls' dissatisfaction with their bodies increases during early to midadolescence, whereas boys, who are becoming more muscular, become more satisfied with their bodies (Feingold & Mazella, 1998; Rosenblum & Lewis, 1999; Swarr & Richards, 1996). By age 15, more than half the girls sampled in 16 countries were dieting or thought they should be. The United States was at the top of the list, with 47 percent of 11-year-old girls and 62 percent of 15-year-olds concerned about overweight (Vereecken & Maes, 2000). African American girls are generally more satisfied with their bodies and less concerned about weight and dieting than are white girls (Kelly, Wall, Eisenberg, Story, & Neumark-Sztainer, 2004; Wardle et al., 2004). According to a large prospective cohort study, parental attitudes and media images play a greater part than peer influences in encouraging weight concerns (Field et al., 2001).

Excessive concern with weight control and body image may be signs of *anorexia nervosa* or *bulimia nervosa,* both of which involve abnormal patterns of food intake

body image Descriptive and evaluative beliefs about one's appearance.

(Harvard Medical School, 2002b). These chronic disorders affect an estimated 5 million Americans each year in all major ethnic groups and social classes (Becker et al., 1999), mostly adolescent girls and young women (Andersen, 1995). These disorders are especially common among girls driven to excel in ballet, competitive swimming, long-distance running, figure skating, and gymnastics ("Eating Disorders—Part II," 1997; Skolnick, 1993); girls with single or divorced parents; and girls who frequently eat alone (Martínez-González et al., 2003).

Anorexia Nervosa **Anorexia nervosa,** or self-starvation, is potentially life threatening. People with anorexia have a distorted body image; though they are constantly dieting and eat next to nothing, they think they are too fat. Anorexia may be accompanied by irregularity or cessation of menstruation and growth of soft, fuzzy body hair. An estimated 0.5 percent of adolescent girls and young women and a smaller but growing percentage of boys and men in western countries are affected. They often are good students, described by their parents as "model" children. They may be withdrawn or depressed and may engage in repetitive, perfectionist behavior (AAP Committee on Adolescence, 2003; Martínez-González et al., 2003). Early warning signs include determined, secret dieting; dissatisfaction after losing weight; setting new, lower weight goals after reaching an initial desired weight; excessive exercising; and interruption of regular menstruation.

> **anorexia nervosa** Eating disorder characterized by self-starvation.

Anorexia has been attributed to a variety of genetic and environmental factors. A variant of a gene that may lead to decreased feeding signals has been found in anorexic patients (Vink et al., 2001). Some authorities point to a deficiency of a crucial chemical in the brain, a disturbance of the hypothalamus, or high levels of opiatelike substances in the spinal fluid ("Eating Disorders—Part I," 1997). Researchers in London, Sweden, and Germany have found reduced blood flow to certain parts of the brain in patients with anorexia, including an area thought to control visual self-perception and appetite (Gordon, Lask, Bryantwaugh, Christie, & Timini, 1997). Others see anorexia as a psychological disturbance related to fear of growing up or fear of sexuality or to a malfunctioning family ("Eating Disorders—Part I," 1997; Garner, 1993).

Anorexics, like this adolescent girl, have a distorted body image. They are so afraid of obesity that they see themselves as fat even when they are emaciated.

Anorexia is, paradoxically, both deliberate and nonvolitional: An affected person deliberately refuses food needed for sustenance, yet cannot stop doing so even when rewarded or punished. This pattern of behavior seems to have existed in all parts of the world and dates back at least to medieval times. Thus, anorexia in the Western world today may be in part a reaction to societal pressure to be slender, but this does not seem to be a sufficient or even a necessary factor (Keel & Klump, 2003). A related disorder in nonwestern cultures involves self-starvation without an abnormal focus on weight and appearance and is rooted in religious traditions of fasting and self-mortification (Keel et al., 2003).

Bulimia Nervosa In **bulimia nervosa,** a person regularly goes on huge eating binges within a short time, usually two hours or less, and then may try to undo the high caloric intake with self-induced vomiting, strict dieting or fasting, excessively

> **bulimia nervosa** Eating disorder in which a person regularly eats huge quantities of food and then purges the body by laxatives, induced vomiting, fasting, or excessive exercise.

vigorous exercise, or laxatives, enemas, or diuretics to purge the body. These episodes occur at least twice a week for at least three months (APA, 2000). People with bulimia are obsessed with their weight and shape. They become overwhelmed with shame, self-contempt, and depression over their eating habits. They have low self-esteem and a history of wide weight fluctuation, dieting, or frequent exercise (Kendler et al. 1991).

A related *binge eating disorder* involves frequent bingeing but without subsequent fasting, exercise, or vomiting. Bulimia and binge eating disorder are much more common than anorexia. About 3 percent of women and 0.3 percent of men have become regular binge eaters at some time in their lives, and much larger numbers have an occasional episode (Harvard Medical School, 2002b). There is some overlap between anorexia and bulimia; some victims of anorexia have bulimic episodes, and some people with bulimia lose large amounts of weight ("Eating Disorders—Part I," 1997; Edwards, 1993; Kendler et al., 1991). Nevertheless, the two are separate disorders. Unlike anorexia, there is little evidence of bulimia either historically or in cultures not subject to Western influence. The reasons may be that binge eating, unlike anorexia, requires an abundance of food and purging would be difficult to hide without modern plumbing (Keel & Klump, 2003).

Bulimia seems to be related to low levels of the brain chemical serotonin ("Eating Disorders—Part I," 1997; K. A. Smith, Fairburn, & Cowen, 1999), but no causative connection has been shown. It may share genetic roots with major depression or with phobias and panic disorder (Keel et al., 2003). There also may be a psychoanalytic explanation: People with bulimia are thought to crave food to satisfy their hunger for love and attention ("Eating Disorders—Part I," 1997; Humphrey, 1986).

Treatment and Outcomes of Anorexia and Bulimia The immediate goal of treatment for anorexia is to get patients to eat and gain weight. Patients who show signs of severe malnutrition, are resistant to treatment, or do not make progress on an outpatient basis may be admitted to a hospital, where they can be given 24-hour nursing. Once their weight is stabilized, patients may enter less intensive daytime care (McCallum & Bruton, 2003). They may be given drugs to encourage eating and inhibit vomiting. Behavior therapy, which rewards eating with such privileges as being allowed to get out of bed and leave the room, may be part of the treatment (Beumont et al., 1993), as well as cognitive therapy to change a distorted body image. Once the weight goal is reached, patients can be taught to eat a balanced, moderate diet and to manage stress (McCallum & Bruton, 2003).

Bulimia, too, may be treated with behavior therapy in 24-hour or daytime settings. Patients keep daily diaries of their eating patterns and are taught ways to avoid the temptation to binge. Individual, group, or family psychotherapy can help both anorexics and bulimics, usually after initial behavior therapy has brought symptoms under control. Since these patients are at risk for depression and suicide, antidepressant drugs may be combined with psychotherapy (Becker et al., 1999; Edwards, 1993; Fluoxetine-Bulimia Collaborative Study Group, 1992; Harvard Medical School, 2002b; Hudson & Pope, 1990; Kaye, Weltzin, Hsu, & Bulik, 1991; McCallum & Bruton, 2003).

Adolescents, with their need for autonomy, may reject family intervention and may need the structure of an institutional setting. Still, any treatment program for adolescents must involve the family. It also must provide for adolescents' developmental needs, which may be different from the needs of adult patients, and must offer the opportunity to keep up with schooling (McCallum & Bruton, 2003).

As many as one-third of patients with anorexia drop out of treatment before achieving an appropriate weight (McCallum & Bruton, 2003). The outlook for people with bulimia is better because bulimic patients generally want treatment ("Eating Disorders—

What's Your View?

- Can you suggest ways to reduce the prevalence of eating disorders?

Part II," 1997; Herzog et al., 1999; Keel & Mitchell, 1997). Recovery rates from bulimia average 50 percent after six months to five years (Harvard Medical School, 2002b). People with anorexia often have long-term psychological and health problems even after they have stopped starving themselves (Beaumont, Russell, & Touyz, 1993; "Eating Disorders—Part I," 1997; Sullivan, Bulik, Fear, & Pickering, 1998).

Checkpoint
Can you . . .

✔ Discuss risk factors for, effects of, treatment of, and prognoses for overweight, anorexia, and bulimia?

Use and Abuse of Drugs

Although the great majority of adolescents do not abuse drugs, a significant minority do. **Substance abuse** is harmful use of alcohol or other drugs. It is a poorly adaptive behavior pattern lasting more than one month, in which a person continues to use a substance after knowingly being harmed by it or uses it repeatedly in a hazardous situation, such as while driving (APA, 1994). Abuse can lead to **substance dependence** (addiction), which may be physiological, psychological, or both and is likely to continue into adulthood. Addictive drugs are especially dangerous for adolescents because they stimulate parts of the brain that are changing in adolescence (Chambers et al., 2003).

substance abuse Repeated, harmful use of a substance, usually alcohol or other drugs.

substance dependence Addiction (physical or psychological, or both) to a harmful substance.

Trends in Drug Use Use of illicit drugs has been declining steadily since 1996 among U.S. eighth-graders and since 2001 among tenth- and twelfth-graders and is well below its peaks during the late 1970s and early 1980s (see Figure 11-3). In 2004, 15.2 percent of eighth-graders, 31.1 percent of tenth-graders, and 38.8 percent of twelfth-graders reported using illicit drugs during the previous year (L. D. Johnston, O'Malley, Bachman, & Schulenberg, 2004b, 2005).

These findings come from the latest in a series of annual government surveys of a nationally representative sample of 49,474 students in 406 schools across the United States. These surveys probably underestimate adolescent drug use because they do not reach high school dropouts, who are likely to have higher rates.

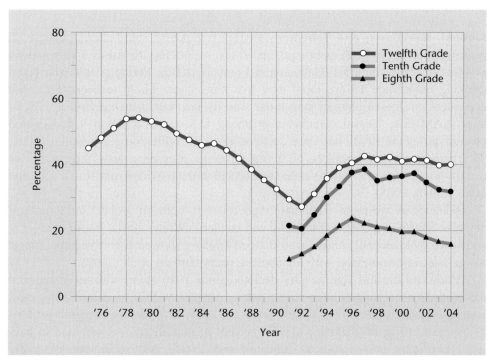

Figure 11-3

Trends in past-year use of illicit drugs by U.S. 8th-, 10th-, and 12th- graders. Only 12th- graders were surveyed before 1991. (Source: Johnston, O'Malley, Bachman, & Schulenberg, 2005.)

One exception to the general trend is a resurgence in 2004 in the use of inhalants, especially by eighth-graders. Inhalants are chemical vapors, often from common household products such as glues, solvents, gasoline, butane, and aerosols, that adolescents sniff to get high. Because inhalants are inexpensive and easy to obtain, they are most often used by younger adolescents. Sniffing can damage hearing, brain, bone marrow, liver, and kidneys and also can cause oxygen depletion, heart failure, and death. Inhalant use had been on the decline since 1995, along with growing peer disapproval of its use, but it appears that this trend may be shifting (L. D. Johnston et al., 2004b, 2005).

Risk Factors for Drug Abuse What is the likelihood that a particular young person will abuse drugs? Risk factors include (1) "difficult" temperament; (2) poor impulse control and a tendency to seek out sensation (which may have a biochemical basis); (3) family influences (such as a genetic predisposition to alcoholism, parental use or acceptance of drugs, poor or inconsistent parenting practices, family conflict, and troubled or distant family relationships); (4) early and persistent behavior problems, particularly aggression; (5) academic failure and lack of commitment to education; (6) peer rejection; (7) associating with drug users; (8) alienation and rebelliousness; (9) favorable attitudes toward drug use; and (10) early initiation into drug use. The earlier young people start using a drug, the more frequently they are likely to use it and the greater their tendency to abuse it (Hawkins, Catalano, & Miller, 1992; Johnson, Hoffmann, & Gerstein, 1996; Masse & Tremblay, 1997; USDHHS, 1996b). The more risk factors that are present, the greater the chance that an adolescent or young adult will abuse drugs.

Drug use often begins when children enter middle school, where they make new friends and become more vulnerable to peer pressure. Fourth- to sixth-graders may start using cigarettes, beer, and inhalants and, as they get older, move on to marijuana or harder drugs (National Parents' Resource Institute for Drug Education, 1999). Let's look more closely at alcohol, marijuana, and tobacco, the three drugs most popular with adolescents. They are sometimes called **gateway drugs** because their use tends to lead to use of "hard" (more addictive) drugs.

gateway drugs Drugs such as alcohol, tobacco, and marijuana, the use of which tends to lead to use of more addictive drugs.

Marijuana is the most widely used illicit drug in the United States. Aside from its own ill effects, marijuana use may lead to addiction to hard drugs.

Alcohol, Marijuana, and Tobacco Alcohol is a potent, mind-altering drug with major effects on physical, emotional, and social well-being. Its use is a very serious problem in many countries (Gabhainn & François, 2000). Young people who begin drinking before age 15 are more than five times more likely to become alcohol dependent or alcohol abusers than those who do not start drinking until age 21 or later (SAMHSA, 2004a). Alcohol use among U.S. teenagers, which had drifted upward during the 1990s, has since declined along with illicit drug use. Still, in 2004, 36.7 percent of eighth-graders, 58.2 percent of tenth-graders, and 70.6 percent of twelfth-graders reported having used alcohol within the previous year (L. D. Johnston et al., 2004b, 2005).

Adolescents are more vulnerable than adults to both immediate and long-term negative effects of alcohol on learning and memory (White, 2001). In one study, 15- and 16-year-old alcohol abusers who stopped drinking showed cognitive impairments weeks later in comparison with nonabusing peers (Brown et al., 2000).

Marijuana use has significantly declined since 1996 along with an increase in the proportion of students who see its use as dangerous. Still, it is by far the most widely used illicit drug in the United States. In 2004, 11.8 percent of eighth-graders, 27.5 percent of tenth-graders, and 34.3 percent of twelfth-graders admitted to having used it in the past year (L. D. Johnston et al., 2004b, 2005). Girls are less likely than boys to be current users of either alcohol or marijuana (Freeman, 2004). Contrary to common belief, marijuana use may be addictive (Tanda, Pontieri, & DiChiara, 1997) and tends to lead to hard drug use (Lynskey et al., 2003).

Adolescent tobacco use is a less widespread problem in the United States than in most other industrialized countries (Gabhainn & François, 2000). Smoking rates have declined by one-half among U.S. eighth- and tenth-graders and by one-third among twelfth-graders since the mid-1990s. The change was due in part to adverse publicity about the tobacco industry and its practices and in part to an antismoking campaign initiated under the terms of settlement of a lawsuit by several states against the tobacco companies. Still, 9.2 percent of eighth-graders, 16 percent of tenth-graders, and 25 percent of twelfth-graders were current (past-month) smokers in 2004 (L. D. Johnston et al., 2004a, 2005).

Adolescents who begin smoking by age 11 are twice as likely as other young people to engage in risky behaviors, such as riding in a car with a drinking driver; carrying knives or guns to school; using inhalants, marijuana, or cocaine; and making suicide plans. Early use of alcohol and marijuana also are associated with multiple risk behaviors (DuRant, Smith, Kreiter, & Krowchuk, 1999).

Peer influence on smoking and drinking has been documented extensively (Center on Addiction and Substance Abuse at Columbia University [CASA], 1996; Cleveland & Wiebe, 2003). Among 6,529 California and Oregon students, African American and Hispanic American youths were more likely than white and Asian American students to start smoking by age 13. However, by age 15, fewer black adolescents were regular smokers than adolescents in the other three ethnic groups (Ellickson, Orlando, Tucker, & Klein, 2004).

An important early influence may be the omnipresence of substance use in the media. A random sample of major motion pictures found a decline in depiction of smoking from 10.7 incidents per hour in 1950 to 4.9 in 1980–1982, but by 2002 portrayals of smoking had reverted to 1950 levels (Glantz, Kacirk, & McCulloch, 2004). In the National Longitudinal Survey of Youth, 10- to 15-year-olds who watched at least four or five hours of television each day were 5 to 6 times more likely to start smoking within the next two years than those who watched less than two hours a day (Gidwani, Sobol, DeJong, Perrin, & Gortmaker, 2002).

In a randomized, controlled trial, nicotine replacement therapy plus behavioral skills training was effective in helping teenagers stop smoking. After 10 weeks of treatment, 28 percent of teens who got a nicotine patch had quit completely. After six months, only 7 percent were completely smoke-free, but most cut down to a few cigarettes a day or less (Killen et al., 2004).

Depression

In view of the desperate situation in which Anne Frank found herself, it is not surprising that she took an antidepressant. Even in normal surroundings, the prevalence of depression increases during adolescence, occurring in an estimated 4 to 8 percent of young people (NCHS, 2004). Depression in young people does not necessarily appear as sadness but as irritability, boredom, or inability to experience pleasure. It needs to be taken seriously because of the danger of suicide (Brent & Birmaher, 2002).

Adolescent girls, especially early maturing girls, and adult women are more subject to depression than males (Birmaher et al., 1996; Brent & Birmaher, 2002; Cicchetti & Toth, 1998; Ge, Conger, & Elder, 2001; Stice et al., 2001). This gender difference may be related to biological changes connected with puberty or to the way girls are socialized (Birmaher et al., 1996) and their greater vulnerability to stress in social relationships (Ge et al., 2001; USDHHS, 1999b). Besides female gender, risk factors for depression include anxiety, fear of social contact, stressful life events, chronic illnesses such as diabetes or epilepsy, parent-child conflict, abuse or neglect, and having a parent with a history of depression (Brent & Birmaher, 2002).

What's Your View?

- Should marijuana be legal, like alcohol? Why or why not?
- Should there be tighter restrictions on cigarette advertising? If so, what kinds of restrictions?
- How can adolescents be helped to avoid or change risky behaviors?

Checkpoint

Can you . . .

✔ Summarize recent trends in drug use among adolescents?

✔ Discuss risk factors and influences connected with use of drugs, specifically alcohol, marijuana, and tobacco?

This teenage boy may be worried about his grades on a test or about a rejection by a girlfriend. Such worries are not unusual in adolescence; but if sadness persists, accompanied by such symptoms as inability to concentrate, fatigue, apathy, and feelings of worthlessness, the young person may be depressed. As many as one in five adolescents experience at least one episode of depression.

Body-image and eating disturbances can aggravate depressive symptoms (Stice & Bearman, 2001).

Depressed adolescents who do not respond to outpatient treatment or who have substance dependence or psychosis or seem suicidal may need to be hospitalized. At least 1 in 5 people who experience bouts of depression in childhood or adolescence are at risk for bipolar disorder, in which depressive episodes ("low" periods) alternate with "high" periods characterized by increased energy, euphoria, grandiosity, and risk taking (Brent & Birmaher, 2002). Even adolescents with depressive symptoms not severe enough for a diagnosis of depression are at elevated risk of depression and suicidal behavior by age 25, according to a 25-year longitudinal study of 1,265 New Zealand children (Fergusson, Horwood, Ridder, & Beautrais, 2005).

SSRIs, a type of antidepressant medication (refer back to Chapter 10), are the most common treatment for adolescent depression, and their rapidly increasing use since the mid-1990s (NCHS, 2004) has been accompanied by a modest reduction in suicide rates (Olfson, Shaffer, Marcus, & Greenberg, 2003). Short-term cognitive behavioral therapy also can be effective. In this type of therapy, patients learn to choose pleasurable activities, improve social skills, and modify self-defeating ways of thinking that can lead to depression (Brent & Birmaher, 2002). A randomized, controlled trial of 439 adolescents with major depressive disorder found Prozac, the most popular of the SSRIs, more effective than cognitive behavioral therapy. A combination of the two therapies was most effective of all (Emslie, 2004; Glass, 2004; Treatment for Adolescents with Depression Study [TADS] Team, 2004). However, as with the use of SSRIs for children, there is concern about the long-term safety of these medications (NCHS, 2004).

Death in Adolescence

Not every death in adolescence is as widely remembered as Anne Frank's. Still, death this early in life is always tragic and (unlike Anne's) usually accidental (Anderson & Smith, 2003)—but not entirely so. The frequency of car crashes, handgun deaths, and suicide in this age group reflects a violent culture as well as adolescents' inexperience and immaturity, which often lead to risk taking and carelessness.

Deaths from Vehicle Accidents and Firearms   Motor vehicle collisions are the leading cause of death among U.S. teenagers, accounting for 2 out of 5 deaths in adolescence. The risk of collision is greater for 16- to 19-year-olds than for any other age group and especially so among young people who recently have started to drive (McCartt, 2001; National Center for Injury Prevention and Control [NCIPC], 2004). Collisions are more likely to be fatal when teenage passengers are in the vehicle; apparently, adolescents tend to drive more recklessly in the presence of peers (Chen, Baker, Braver, & Li, 2000). In 2002, 29 percent of drivers ages 15 to 20 who died in motor crashes had been drinking alcohol, and 77 percent of those were not wearing seat belts (National Highway Traffic Safety Administration, 2003).

Firearm-related deaths of 15- to 19-year-olds (including homicide, suicide, and accidental deaths) are far more common in the United States than in other industrialized countries. They comprise about one-third of all injury deaths and more than 85 percent of all homicides in that age group. The chief reason for these grim statistics seems to be the relative ease of obtaining a gun in the United States (AAP Committee on Injury and Poison Prevention, 2000). For many adolescents, the easiest place to get a gun is at home. Guns in the home are 43 times more likely to kill a family member or acquaintance than to be used in self-defense (AAP Committee on Injury and Poison Prevention, 2000).

Suicide   Ready availability of guns also is a major factor in teenage suicide, the third leading cause of death among U.S. 15- to 19-year-olds in 2002 (Anderson & Smith, 2005). Firearms were used in 52 percent of completed suicides in 2001 (NCIPC, 2001). Restrictions on children's access to firearms may help explain the dramatic drop in gun suicides included in a 25 percent reduction in overall suicide rates among 10- to 19-year-olds between 1992 and 2001 (Lubell, Swahn, Crosby, & Kegler, 2004).

Almost one-fourth of U.S. high school students have reported seriously considering suicide during the past year (AAP Committee on Adolescence, 2000), and close to 9 percent report actually attempting suicide (NCHS, 2004). Although most young people who *attempt* suicide do it by taking pills or ingesting other substances, those who succeed are most likely to use firearms (Borowsky, Ireland, & Resnick, 2001). For this reason, adolescent boys, who are more apt to use guns, are five times more likely than adolescent girls to succeed in taking their lives, even though girls are more likely to consider or attempt suicide (NCHS, 2004). Girls are more likely to have suicidal thoughts if they feel isolated and friendless or if they know someone who has committed suicide (Bearman & Moody, 2004).

Although suicide occurs in all ethnic groups, Native American boys have the highest rates and African American girls the lowest. Gay, lesbian, and bisexual youths, who have high rates of depression, also have unusually high rates of suicide and attempted suicide (AAP Committee on Adolescence, 2000; Remafedi, French, Story, Resnick, & Blum, 1998).

Young people who consider or attempt suicide tend to have histories of emotional illness. They tend to be either perpetrators or victims of violence and to have school problems, academic or behavioral. Many have suffered from maltreatment in childhood, leading to severe problems with relationships in adolescence. They tend to think poorly of themselves, to feel hopeless, and to have poor impulse control and low tolerance for frustration and stress. These young people are often alienated from their parents and have no one outside the family to turn to. They also tend to have attempted suicide before or to have friends or family members who did (Borowsky et al., 2001; Deykin, Alpert, & McNamara, 1985; Garland & Zigler, 1993; Johnson et al., 2002; National Committee for Citizens in Education, 1986; NIMH, 1999a; Slap, Vorters, Chaudhuri, & Centor, 1989; "Suicide—Part I," 1996; Swedo et al., 1991). Alcohol plays a part in half of all teenage suicides (AAP Committee on Adolescence, 2000). Protective factors that reduce the risk of suicide include a sense of connectedness to family and school, emotional well-being, and academic achievement (Borowsky et al., 2001).

Telephone hotlines are the most prevalent type of suicide intervention for adolescents, but their effectiveness appears to be minimal (Borowsky et al., 2001; Garland & Zigler, 1993). School-based screening programs have proliferated in recent years. Although some observers worry that such programs may "put ideas in young people's heads," a randomized controlled trial of 2,342 high school students in New York state found *no* basis for that concern (Gould et al., 2005).

However, the American Academy of Child and Adolescent Psychiatry questions the effectiveness of such programs; as with hotlines, there is little evidence that they reduce the risk of suicide or motivate adolescents who are contemplating suicide to seek help (Harvard Mental Health Letter, 2003). In fact, some of these programs may do harm by exaggerating the extent of teenage suicide and painting it as a reaction to normal stresses of adolescence rather than a pathological act. Instead, some experts suggest, programs should identify and treat young people at particular risk of suicide, including those who have already attempted it. Equally important is to attack the risk factors through programs to reduce substance abuse, violence, and access to guns and to strengthen families and improve parenting skills (Borowsky et al., 2001; Garland & Zigler, 1993).

Checkpoint

Can you . . .

✔ Discuss factors affecting gender differences in adolescent depression?

✔ Name the three leading causes of death among adolescents, and discuss the dangers of firearm injury?

✔ Assess risk factors and prevention programs for teenage suicide?

COGNITIVE DEVELOPMENT

Guidepost

4. How do adolescents' thinking and use of language differ from younger children's?

Aspects of Cognitive Maturation

Despite the perils of adolescence, most young people emerge from the teenage years with mature, healthy bodies and a zest for life. Their cognitive development has continued, too. Adolescents not only look different from younger children; they also think differently. Although their thinking may remain immature in some ways, many are capable of abstract reasoning and sophisticated moral judgments and can plan more realistically for the future.

Piaget's Stage of Formal Operations

formal operations Piaget's final stage of cognitive development, characterized by the ability to think abstractly.

According to Piaget, adolescents enter the highest level of cognitive development—**formal operations**—when they develop the capacity for abstract thought. This development, usually around age 11, gives them a new, more flexible way to manipulate information. No longer limited to the here and now, they can understand historical time and extraterrestrial space. They can use symbols for symbols (for example, letting the letter X stand for an unknown numeral) and thus can learn algebra and calculus. They can better appreciate metaphor and allegory and thus can find richer meanings in literature. They can think in terms of what *might* be, not just what *is*. They can imagine possibilities and can form and test hypotheses.

The ability to think abstractly has emotional implications, too. Earlier, a child could love a parent or hate a classmate. Now "the adolescent can love freedom or hate exploitation. . . . The possible and the ideal captivate both mind and feeling" (H. Ginsburg & Opper, 1979, p. 201). Thus could Anne Frank, in her attic hideout, express her ideals and her hopes for the future.

Hypothetical-Deductive Reasoning   To appreciate the difference formal reasoning makes, let's follow the progress of a typical child in dealing with a classic Piagetian problem, the pendulum problem.* The child, Adam, is shown the pendulum—an object hanging from a string. He is then shown how he can change any of four factors: the length of the string, the weight of the object, the height from which the object is released, and the amount of force he may use to push the object. He is asked to figure out which factor or combination of factors determines how fast the pendulum swings. (Figure 11-4 depicts this and other Piagetian tasks for assessing the achievement of formal operations.)

When Adam first sees the pendulum, he is not yet 7 years old and is in the preoperational stage. Unable to formulate a plan for attacking the problem, he tries one thing after another in a hit-or-miss manner. First he puts a light weight on a long string and pushes it; then he tries swinging a heavy weight on a short string; then he removes the weight entirely. Not only is his method random, he also cannot understand or report what has happened.

Adam next encounters the pendulum at age 10, when he is in the stage of concrete operations. This time, he discovers that varying the length of the string and the weight of the object affects the speed of the swing. However, because he varies both factors at the same time, he cannot tell which is critical or whether both are.

Adam is confronted with the pendulum for a third time at age 15, and this time he goes at the problem systematically. He designs an experiment to test all the possible hypotheses, varying one factor at a time—first, the length of the string; next,

*This description of age-related differences in the approach to the pendulum problem is adapted from H. Ginsburg and Opper (1979).

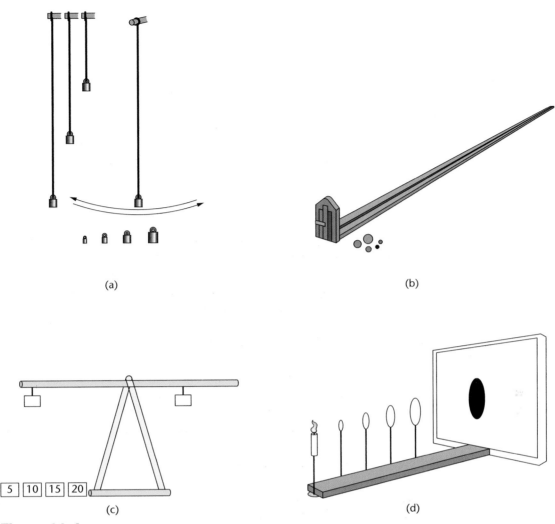

Figure 11-4

Piagetian tasks for measuring attainment of formal operations.

(a) Pendulum. The pendulum's string can be shortened or lengthened, and weights of varying sizes can be attached to it. The student must determine what variables affect the speed of the pendulum's swing.

(b) Motion in a horizontal plane. A spring device launches balls of varying sizes, which roll in a horizontal plane. The student must predict their stopping points.

(c) Balance beam. A balance scale comes with weights of varying sizes, which can be hung at different points along the crossbar. The student must determine what factors affect whether or not the scale will balance.

(d) Shadows. A board containing a row of peg holes is attached perpendicular to the base of a screen. A light source and rings of varying diameters can be placed in the holes, at varying distances from the screen. The student must produce two shadows of the same size, using different-sized rings. (Source: Adapted from Small, 1990, Figure 8-12.)

the weight of the object; then the height from which it is released; and finally, the amount of force used—each time holding the other three factors constant. In this way, he is able to determine that only one factor—the length of the string—determines how fast the pendulum swings.

Adam's solution of the pendulum problem shows that he has arrived at the stage of formal operations. He is now capable of **hypothetical-deductive reasoning.** He can develop a hypothesis and can design an experiment to test it. He considers all the relationships he can imagine and tests them systematically, one by one, to eliminate the false and arrive at the true. Hypothetical-deductive reasoning gives him a tool to solve problems, from fixing the family car to constructing a political theory.

Studies of problem-solving behavior support Piaget's analysis of how concrete operations differ from formal operations. In one such study (Schauble, 1996),

hypothetical-deductive reasoning Ability, believed by Piaget to accompany the stage of formal operations, to develop, consider, and test hypotheses.

fifth- and sixth-graders and noncollege-educated adults were asked to design experiments to understand physical phenomena, such as factors affecting the speed of a vessel through a canal. Preadolescents were less systematic than adults in exploring such problems, typically varying more than one factor at the same time, as Adam did with the pendulum at that age.

What brings about the shift to formal reasoning? Piaget attributed it to a combination of brain maturation and expanding environmental opportunities. Both are essential: Even if young people's neurological development has advanced enough to permit formal reasoning, they can attain it only with appropriate stimulation. One way this can happen is through cooperative effort (Johnson, Johnson, & Tjosvold, 2000). When college students (average age, 18½) were told to set up their own experiments to solve a chemistry problem, students randomly assigned to work in pairs solved more problems than those who worked alone. The more the partners challenged each other's reasoning, the greater were their advances in thinking (Dimant & Bearison, 1991).

As with the development of concrete operations, culture and schooling seem to play a role—as Piaget (1972) ultimately recognized. When adolescents in New Guinea and Rwanda were tested on the pendulum problem, none were able to solve it. On the other hand, Chinese children in Hong Kong, who had been to British schools, did at least as well as U.S. or European children. Schoolchildren in Central Java and New South Wales also showed some formal operational abilities (Gardiner & Kosmitzki, 2005). Apparently, this kind of thinking is a learned ability that is not equally necessary or equally valued in all cultures.

Evaluating Piaget's Theory   Although adolescents *do* tend to think more abstractly than younger children, there is debate about the precise age at which this advance emerges (Eccles, Wigfield, & Byrnes, 2003). Piaget's own writings provide many examples of children displaying aspects of scientific thinking well before adolescence. At the same time, Piaget seems to have *over*estimated some older children's abilities. Many late adolescents and adults—perhaps one-third to one-half—seem incapable of abstract thought as Piaget defined it (Gardiner & Kosmitzki, 2005; Kohlberg & Gilligan, 1971; Papalia, 1972), and even those who are capable of this kind of thinking do not always use it.

Piaget, in most of his early writings, paid little attention to individual differences, to variations in the same child's performance on different kinds of tasks, or to social and cultural influences. In his later years, Piaget himself "came to view his earlier model of the development of children's thinking, particularly formal operations, as flawed because it failed to capture the essential *role of the situation* in influencing and constraining . . . children's thinking" (Brown, Metz, & Campione, 1996, pp. 152–153). Neo-Piagetian research suggests that children's cognitive processes are closely tied to specific content (what a child is thinking *about*) as well as to the context of a problem and the kinds of information and thought a culture considers important (Case & Okamoto, 1996).

Finally, Piaget's theory does not adequately consider such cognitive advances as gains in information-processing capacity, accumulation of knowledge and expertise in specific fields, and the role of *metacognition,* the awareness and monitoring of one's own mental processes and strategies (Flavell et al., 2002).

Elkind: Immature Characteristics of Adolescent Thought

We have seen how children develop from egocentric beings whose interest extends not much beyond the nipple to persons able to solve abstract problems and imagine ideal societies. Yet in some ways adolescents' thinking seems

What's Your View?

• How can parents and teachers help adolescents improve their reasoning ability?

Checkpoint

Can you . . .

✔ Explain the difference between formal operational and concrete operational thinking, as exemplified by the pendulum problem?

✔ Cite factors influencing adolescents' development of formal reasoning?

✔ Evaluate strengths and weaknesses of Piaget's theory of formal operations?

strangely immature. They may be rude to adults, they have trouble making up their minds what to wear each day, and they often act as if the whole world revolved around them.

According to the psychologist David Elkind (1984, 1998), such behavior stems from adolescents' inexperienced ventures into formal operational thought. This new way of thinking, which fundamentally transforms the way they look at themselves and their world, is as unfamiliar to them as their reshaped bodies, and they sometimes feel just as awkward in its use. As they try out their new powers, they may sometimes stumble, like an infant learning to walk.

This immaturity of thinking manifests itself in at least six characteristic ways, according to Elkind:

1. *Idealism and criticalness:* As adolescents envision an ideal world, they realize how far the real world, for which they hold adults responsible, falls short. They become super-conscious of hypocrisy; with their sharpened verbal reasoning, they relish magazines and entertainers that attack public figures with satire and parody. Convinced that they know better than adults how to run the world, they frequently find fault with their parents.

2. *Argumentativeness:* Adolescents are constantly looking for opportunities to try out and show off their reasoning abilities. They often become argumentative as they marshal facts and logic to build a case for, say, staying out later than their parents think they should.

3. *Indecisiveness:* Adolescents can keep many alternatives in mind at the same time yet may lack effective strategies for choosing among them. They may have trouble making up their minds even about such simple things as whether to go to the mall with a friend or to the computer to work on a school assignment.

Argumentativeness—usually with parents—is a typical characteristic of adolescent thought, according to David Elkind.

4. *Apparent hypocrisy:* Young adolescents often do not recognize the difference between expressing an ideal, such as conserving energy, and making the sacrifices necessary to live up to it, such as driving less often.

5. *Self-consciousness:* Adolescents in the stage of formal operations can think about thinking—their own and other people's. However, in their preoccupation with their own mental state, adolescents often assume that everyone else is thinking about the same thing they are thinking about: themselves. A teenage girl may be mortified if she wears "the wrong thing" to a party, thinking that everyone else must be looking askance at her. Elkind refers to this self-consciousness as the **imaginary audience,** a conceptualized "observer" who is as concerned with a young person's thoughts and behavior as he or she is. The imaginary audience fantasy is especially strong in the early teens but persists to a lesser degree into adult life.

6. *Specialness and invulnerability:* Elkind uses the term **personal fable** to denote a belief by adolescents that they are special, that their experience is unique, and that they are not subject to the rules that govern the rest of the world ("Other people get hooked from taking drugs but not me," or, "No one has ever been as deeply in love as I am"). According to Elkind, this special form of egocentrism underlies much risky, self-destructive behavior. Like the

imaginary audience Elkind's term for observer who exists only in an adolescent's mind and is as concerned with the adolescent's thoughts and actions as the adolescent is.

personal fable Elkind's term for conviction that one is special, unique, and not subject to the rules that govern the rest of the world.

imaginary audience, the personal fable continues in adulthood. It is the personal fable, says Elkind, that persuades people to take such everyday risks as driving a car despite statistics on highway deaths.

The concepts of the imaginary audience and the personal fable have been widely accepted, but their validity as distinct earmarks of adolescence has little independent research support. In some studies of the personal fable, adolescents were *more* likely than college students or adults to see themselves as vulnerable to certain risks, such as alcohol and other drug problems, not *less* likely, as the personal fable would predict (Quadrel, Fischoff, & Davis, 1993). Rather than constituting universal features of adolescents' cognitive development, the imaginary audience and personal fable may be related to specific social experiences. Because these concepts grew out of Elkind's clinical observations, they may be more characteristic of young people who are experiencing difficulties in adjustment (Vartanian & Powlishta, 1996).

Changes in Information Processing in Adolescence

Information-processing researchers have identified two broad categories of measurable change in adolescent cognition: *structural change* and *functional change* (Eccles et al., 2003).* Let's look at each.

Structural Change *Structural* changes in adolescence include (1) changes in information-processing capacity and (2) the increasing amount of knowledge stored in long-term memory.

The capacity of working memory, which enlarges rapidly in middle childhood, continues to increase during adolescence. The expansion of working memory may enable older adolescents to deal with complex problems or decisions involving multiple pieces of information.

Information stored in long-term memory can be declarative, procedural, or conceptual. **Declarative knowledge** ("knowing that . . .") consists of all the factual knowledge a person has acquired (for example, knowing that 2 + 2 = 4 and that George Washington was the first U.S. president). **Procedural knowledge** (knowing how to . . .") consists of all the skills a person has acquired, such as being able to multiply and divide and drive a car. **Conceptual knowledge** ("knowing why") is an understanding of, for example, why an algebraic equation remains true if the same amount is added or subtracted from both sides.

In the United States, the National Assessment of Educational Progress (NAEP) has found that children gain in all three areas of subject-matter knowledge between fourth and eighth grades and between eighth and twelfth grades. Still, these gains are often modest, depending on the particular domain and on the quality of education.

Functional Change Processes for obtaining, handling, and retaining information are *functional* aspects of cognition. Among these are learning, remembering, reasoning, and decision making. Mathematical, spatial, and scientific reasoning are a few of the functional processes that typically improve during adolescence.

Adolescents gradually become more proficient in drawing conclusions, explaining their reasoning, and testing hypotheses, particularly if the premises are familiar and true. When experimental premises are contrary to common knowledge ("All elephants are small. This is an elephant. Is it small?"), fewer than half of older adolescents or adults can make the appropriate logical deduction.

*Unless otherwise referenced, the discussion in this section is indebted to Eccles et al., 2003.

✓ **Checkpoint**
Can you . . .

✔ Describe Elkind's six proposed aspects of immature adolescent thought, and explain how they may grow out of the transition to formal operational thought?

declarative knowledge Acquired factual knowledge stored in long-term memory.

procedural knowledge Acquired skills stored in long-term memory.

conceptual knowledge Acquired interpretive understandings stored in long-term memory.

Improvements observed in laboratory situations do not necessarily carry over to real life, where behavior depends in part on motivation and emotion regulation. Many older adolescents make poorer real-world decisions than younger adolescents do. In the game Twenty Questions, the object is to ask as few yes or no questions as necessary to discover the identity of a person, place, or thing by systematically narrowing down the categories within which the answer might fall. The efficiency with which young people can do this generally improves between middle childhood and late adolescence. However, in one study (Drumm & Jackson, 1996), high school students, especially boys, showed a greater tendency than either early adolescents or college students to jump to guessing the answer. This pattern of guesswork may reflect a penchant for impulsive, risky behavior. As we discussed earlier in this chapter, adolescents' rash judgments may be related to immature brain development, which may permit feelings to override reason.

Language Development

Although individual differences are great, by ages 16 to 18 the average young person knows about 80,000 words (Owens, 1996). With the advent of formal thought, adolescents can define and discuss such abstractions as *love, justice,* and *freedom.* They more frequently use such terms as *however, otherwise, anyway, therefore, really,* and *probably* to express logical relations between clauses or sentences. They become more conscious of words as symbols that can have multiple meanings; they enjoy using irony, puns, and metaphors (Owens, 1996).

Adolescents also become more skilled in *social perspective-taking,* the ability to understand another person's point of view and level of knowledge and to speak accordingly. This ability is essential in order to persuade or just to engage in conversation. Conscious of their audience, adolescents speak a different language with peers than with adults (Owens, 1996; see Box 11-2). Teenage slang is part of the process of developing an independent identity separate from parents and the adult world. In creating such expressions as "awesome" and "geek," young people use their newfound ability to play with words "to define their generation's unique take on values, tastes, and preferences" (Elkind, 1998, p. 29).

Checkpoint
Can you . . .

✔ Name two major kinds of changes in adolescents' information-processing capabilities, and give examples of each?

✔ Identify several characteristics of adolescents' language development that reflect cognitive advances?

Moral Reasoning: Kohlberg's Theory

A woman is near death from cancer. A druggist has discovered a drug that doctors believe might save her. The druggist is charging $2,000 for a small dose—ten times what the drug costs him to make. The sick woman's husband, Heinz, borrows from everyone he knows but can scrape together only $1,000. He begs the druggist to sell him the drug for $1,000 or let him pay the rest later. The druggist refuses, saying "I discovered the drug and I'm going to make money from it." Heinz, desperate, breaks into the man's store and steals the drug. Should Heinz have done that? Why or why not? (Kohlberg, 1969).

Heinz's problem is the most famous example of Lawrence Kohlberg's approach to studying moral development. Starting in the 1950s, Kohlberg and his colleagues posed hypothetical dilemmas like this one to 75 boys ages 10, 13, and 16 and continued to question them periodically for more than 30 years. At the heart of each dilemma was the concept of justice. By asking respondents how they arrived at their answers, Kohlberg concluded that the way people look at moral issues reflects cognitive development.

Guidepost
6. On what basis do adolescents make moral judgments?

Kohlberg's Levels and Stages Moral development in Kohlberg's theory bears some resemblance to Piaget's (refer back to Chapter 9), but his model is more complex. On the basis of thought processes shown by responses to his dilemmas,

BOX 11-2

Window on the World

"Pubilect": The Dialect of Adolescence

"What a hottie!"
"We're tight!"
"Filthy!"
"Let's bounce!"

Adolescents' conversation is mainly about the people and events in their everyday world (Labov, 1992). They use slang (nonstandard speech) to label people ("player" or "slacker"), to pronounce positive or negative judgments ("That's my fave" or "She's a babe."), and to describe alcohol or drug-related activity ("She's wasted" or "He's faded").

The Canadian linguist Marcel Danesi (1994)* argues that adolescent speech is more than just slang (which, of course, adults can use, too). Instead, it constitutes a dialect of its own: *pubilect,* "the social dialect of puberty" (p. 97).

Pubilect is more than an occasional colorful expression. It is the primary mode of verbal communication among teenagers, by which they differentiate themselves from adults. As they approach puberty, youngsters absorb this dialect from slightly older peers. Like any other linguistic code, pubilect serves to strengthen group identity and to shut outsiders (adults) out. Teenage vocabulary is characterized by rapid change. Although some of its terms have entered common discourse, adolescents keep inventing new ones all the time.

Analysis of recorded samples of adolescent conversation reveals several key features of pubilect. First, it is an *emotive* code. Through exaggerated tone, slow and deliberate delivery, prolonged stress, accompanying gestures, and vulgar interjections, it draws attention to feelings and attitudes ("Yeah, riiight!" "Well, duuuh!"). Such emotive utterances seem to constitute about 65 percent of adolescent speech. The use of fillers, such as the word *like,* as well as the typical pattern of narrative intonation, in which each phrase or sentence seems to end with a question mark, reflects unconscious uncertainty and serves to draw the listener into the speaker's state of mind.

A second feature of pubilect is its *connotative* function. Teenagers coin descriptive words (or extend the meaning of existing words) to convey their view of their world and the people in it—often, in highly metaphorical ways. A person does not need a dictionary to figure out the meanings of such expressions as

*Unless otherwise referenced, the source of this discussion is Danesi, 1994.

"floss" and "butterface." Such terms provide a ready lexicon for quick, automatic value judgments about others.

In the United States, there is not just a single youth culture, but many subcultures. Vocabulary may differ by gender, ethnicity, age, geographical region, neighborhood (city, suburban, or rural) and type of school (public or private) (Labov, 1992). Also, pubilect is *clique-coded:* It varies from one clique to another. "Druggies" and "jocks" engage in different kinds of activities, which form the main subjects of their conversation. This talk, in turn, cements bonds within the clique. Males use verbal dueling to assert power. Contenders for leadership trade insults and clever retorts in an effort to symbolically gain the upper hand in front of the group.

A study of teenage speech patterns in Naples, Italy, suggests that similar features may emerge "in any culture where teenagerhood constitutes a distinct social category" (Danesi, 1994, p. 123). Neapolitan teenagers use "mmmm" much as U.S. teenagers use "like": "Devo, mmmm, dire che, mmmm, non capisco, mmmm, . . ." ("I have, mmmm, to say that, mmmm, I don't understand, mmmm, . . ."). Exaggerated tone and rising intonation at the ends of phrases are also common. The Italian young people have terms roughly equivalent to the English "cool" (*togo*), "loser" (*grasta*), and "dork" or "nerd" (*secchione*). Other investigators report that adolescents in Milan, Bologna, and other northern Italian cities speak "the language of rock and roll." This cultural borrowing—the result of wide dissemination of English-language television channels, such as MTV—may well be creating a "symbolic universe" for teenagers around the world (Danesi, 1994, p. 123).

What's Your View?

Can you remember "pubilect" expressions from your own adolescence? When and why did you use such expressions? What was their effect on others your age? On adults?

Check It Out

For more information on this topic, go to http://www.slanguage.com [a Web site called American Slanguages].

---

preconventional morality First level of Kohlberg's theory of moral reasoning in which control is external and rules are obeyed in order to gain rewards or avoid punishment or out of self-interest.

conventional morality (or morality of conventional role conformity) Second level in Kohlberg's theory of moral reasoning in which standards of authority figures are internalized.

Kohlberg (1969) described three levels of moral reasoning, each divided into two stages (see Table 11-3):

- *Level I:* **Preconventional morality.** People act under external controls. They obey rules to avoid punishment or reap rewards, or act out of self-interest. This level is typical of children ages 4 to 10.

- *Level II:* **Conventional morality (or morality of conventional role conformity).** People have internalized the standards of authority figures. They are concerned about being "good," pleasing others, and maintaining the social order. This level is typically reached after age 10; many people never move beyond it, even in adulthood.

Table 11-3 Kohlberg's Six Stages of Moral Reasoning

Levels	Stages of Reasoning	Typical Answers to Heinz's Dilemma
Level I: Preconventional morality (ages 4 to 10)	*Stage 1: Orientation toward punishment and obedience.* "What will happen to me?" Children obey rules to avoid punishment. They ignore the motives of an act and focus on its physical form (such as the size of a lie) or its consequences (for example, the amount of physical damage).	*Pro:* "He should steal the drug. It isn't really bad to take it. It isn't as if he hadn't asked to pay for it first. The drug he'd take is worth only $200; he's not really taking a $2,000 drug." *Con:* "He shouldn't steal the drug. It's a big crime. He didn't get permission; he used force and broke and entered. He did a lot of damage and stole a very expensive drug."
	Stage 2: Instrumental purpose and exchange. "You scratch my back, I'll scratch yours." Children conform to rules out of self-interest and consideration for what others can do for them. They look at an act in terms of the human needs it meets and differentiate this value from the act's physical form and consequences.	*Pro:* "It's all right to steal the drug, because his wife needs it and he wants her to live. It isn't that he wants to steal, but that's what he has to do to save her." *Con:* "He shouldn't steal it. The druggist isn't wrong or bad; he just wants to make a profit. That's what you're in business for—to make money."
Level II: Conventional morality (ages 10 to 13 or beyond)	*Stage 3: Maintaining mutual relations, approval of others, the golden rule.* "Am I a good boy or girl?" Children want to please and help others, can judge the intentions of others, and develop their own ideas of what a good person is. They evaluate an act according to the motive behind it or the person performing it, and they take circumstances into account.	*Pro:* "He should steal the drug. He is only doing something that is natural for a good husband to do. You can't blame him for doing something out of love for his wife. You'd blame him if he didn't love his wife enough to save her." *Con:* "He shouldn't steal. If his wife dies, he can't be blamed. It isn't because he's heartless or that he doesn't love her enough to do everything that he legally can. The druggist is the selfish or heartless one."
	Stage 4: Social concern and conscience. "What if everybody did it?" People are concerned with doing their duty, showing respect for higher authority, and maintaining the social order. They consider an act always wrong, regardless of motive or circumstances, if it violates a rule and harms others.	*Pro:* "You should steal it. If you did nothing, you'd be letting your wife die. It's your responsibility if she dies. You have to take it with the idea of paying the druggist." *Con:* "It is a natural thing for Heinz to want to save his wife, but it's still always wrong to steal. He knows he's taking a valuable drug from the man who made it."
Level III: Postconventional morality (early adolescence, or not until young adulthood, or never)	*Stage 5: Morality of contract, of individual rights, and of democratically accepted law.* People think in rational terms, valuing the will of the majority and the welfare of society. They generally see these values as best supported by adherence to the law. While they recognize that there are times when human need and the law conflict, they believe it is better for society in the long run if they obey the law.	*Pro:* "The law wasn't set up for these circumstances. Taking the drug in this situation isn't really right, but it's justified." *Con:* "You can't completely blame someone for stealing, but extreme circumstances don't really justify taking the law into your own hands. You can't have people stealing whenever they are desperate. The end may be good, but the ends don't justify the means."
	Stage 6: Morality of universal ethical principles. People do what they as individuals think is right, regardless of legal restrictions or the opinions of others. They act in accordance with internalized standards, knowing that they would condemn themselves if they did not.	*Pro:* "This is a situation that forces him to choose between stealing and letting his wife die. In a situation where the choice must be made, it is morally right to steal. He has to act in terms of the principle of preserving and respecting life." *Con:* "Heinz is faced with the decision of whether to consider the other people who need the drug just as badly as his wife. Heinz ought to act not according to his feelings for his wife, but considering the value of all the lives involved."

Source: Adapted from Kohlberg, 1969; Lickona, 1976.

- *Level III:* **Postconventional morality (or morality of autonomous moral principles).** People recognize conflicts between moral standards and make their own judgments on the basis of principles of right, fairness, and justice. People generally do not reach this level of moral reasoning until at least early adolescence, or more commonly in young adulthood, if ever.

Kohlberg later added a transitional level between levels II and III, when people no longer feel bound by society's moral standards but have not yet reasoned out their own principles of justice. Instead, they base their moral decisions on personal feelings.

In Kohlberg's theory, it is the reasoning underlying a person's response to a moral dilemma, not the answer itself, that indicates the stage of moral development. As illustrated in Table 11-2, two people who give opposite answers may be at the same stage if their reasoning is based on similar factors.

Some adolescents and even some adults remain at Kohlberg's level I. Like young children, they seek to avoid punishment or satisfy their own needs. Most adolescents and most adults seem to be at level II. They conform to social conventions, support the status quo, and do the "right" thing to please others or to obey the law. (Toward the end of Anne Frank's diary, we can see her begin to emerge from this stage as she argues with her father and herself about the morality of a more physically intimate relationship with Peter.)

Before people can develop a fully principled (level III) morality, Kohlberg held, they must recognize the relativity of moral standards. Many young people question their earlier moral views when they enter high school or college or the world of work and encounter people whose values, culture, and ethnic background are different from their own. Still, very few people reach a level where they can choose among differing moral standards. In fact, at one point Kohlberg questioned the validity of Stage 6, morality based on universal ethical principles, because so few people seem to attain it. Later, he proposed a seventh, "cosmic" stage, in which people consider the effect of their actions not only on other people but on the universe as a whole (Kohlberg, 1981; Kohlberg & Ryncarz, 1990).

Evaluating Kohlberg's Theory Kohlberg, building on Piaget, brought about a profound shift in the way we look at moral development. Instead of viewing morality solely as the attainment of control over self-gratifying impulses, investigators now study how children and adults base moral judgments on their growing understanding of the social world.

Initial research supported Kohlberg's theory. The American boys whom Kohlberg and his colleagues followed through adulthood progressed through Kohlberg's stages in sequence, and none skipped a stage. Their moral judgments correlated positively with age, education, IQ, and socioeconomic status (Colby, Kohlberg, Gibbs, & Lieberman, 1983). However, a more recent study of children's judgments about laws and lawbreaking suggests that children can reason flexibly about such issues at an earlier age than either Piaget or Kohlberg proposed—even as early as age 6 (Helwig & Jasiobedzka, 2001).

Furthermore, research has noted the lack of a clear relationship between moral reasoning and moral behavior. People at postconventional levels of reasoning do not necessarily act more morally than those at lower levels. Other factors, such as specific situations, conceptions of virtue, and concern for others contribute to moral behavior (Colby & Damon, 1992; Fischer & Pruyne, 2003).

One reason the ages attached to Kohlberg's levels are so variable is that people who have achieved a high level of cognitive development do not always reach a comparably high level of moral development. A certain level of cognitive development is *necessary* but not *sufficient* for a comparable level of moral development. Thus, other processes besides cognition must be at work. Some critics claim that moral activity is motivated not only by abstract considerations of justice, but also by such emotions as empathy, guilt, and distress and the internalization of prosocial norms (Gibbs, 1991, 1995; Gibbs & Schnell, 1985). It also has been argued that Kohlberg's Stages 5 and 6 cannot fairly be called the most mature stages of moral development because they restrict "maturity" to a select group of people given to philosophical reflection (J. C. Gibbs, 1995).

A practical problem in using Kohlberg's system is its time-consuming testing procedures. The standard dilemmas need to be presented to each person individually and then scored by trained judges. One alternative is the Defining Issues Test (DIT), in which students rate and rank a list of statements rather than being asked to articulate the issues and arguments involved (Rest, 1975; Rest, Deemer, Barnett, & Spickelm, 1986). The DIT can be given quickly to a group and scored objectively. However, the DIT may tend to overestimate the degree of moral development (Rest et al., 1999).

Family Influences Neither Piaget nor Kohlberg considered parents important to children's moral development. More recent research, however, emphasizes parents' contribution in both the cognitive and the emotional realms. In one study, parents of 63 students in grades 1, 4, 7, and 10 were asked to talk with their children about two dilemmas: a hypothetical one and an actual one that the child described (L. J. Walker & Taylor, 1991). The young people who, during the next two years, showed the greatest progress through Kohlberg's stages were those whose parents had used humor and praise, listened to them, and asked their opinions. These parents had asked clarifying questions, reworded answers, and checked to be sure the children understood the issues. They reasoned with their children at a slightly higher level than the children were currently at, much as in the method of scaffolding. The children who advanced the least were those whose parents had lectured them or challenged or contradicted their opinions.

Validity for Women and Girls On the basis of research on women, Carol Gilligan (1982) asserted that Kohlberg's theory is oriented toward values more important to men than to women. Gilligan claimed that women see morality, not so much in terms of justice and fairness, as of responsibility to show care and avoid harm. Research has not supported Gilligan's claim of a male bias in Kohlberg's stages, and she has since modified her position. Moreover, in some research on gender differences in moral judgments in early adolescence, girls scored *higher* than boys (Garmon, Basinger, Gregg, & Gibbs, 1996; Skoe & Gooden, 1993). This may be because girls generally mature earlier and have more intimate social relationships (Garmon et al., 1996; Skoe & Diessner, 1994). Early adolescent girls do tend to emphasize care-related concerns more than boys do, especially when tested with open-ended questions ("How important is it to keep promises to a friend?") or self-chosen moral dilemmas related to their own experience (Garmon et al., 1996).

Cross-Cultural Validity Cross-cultural studies support Kohlberg's sequence of stages—up to a point. Older people from countries other than the United States do tend to score at higher stages than younger people. However, people in nonwestern cultures rarely score above Stage 4 (Edwards, 1981; Nisan & Kohlberg, 1982; Snarey, 1985), suggesting that some aspects of Kohlberg's model may not fit the cultural values of these societies. When Kohlberg's dilemmas were tested in India, Buddhist monks scored lower than laypeople. Apparently Kohlberg's model was inadequate to capture postconventional Buddhist principles of cooperation and nonviolence (Gielen & Kelly, 1983).

What's Your View?

• Kohlberg's method of assessing moral development by evaluating participants' reactions to moral dilemmas is widely used. Does this seem like the most appropriate method? Why or why not? Can you suggest an alternative measure?

• Can you think of a time when you or someone you know acted contrary to personal moral judgment? Why do you think this happened?

Checkpoint
Can you . . .

✔ List Kohlberg's levels and stages, and discuss factors that influence how rapidly children and adolescents progress through them?

✔ Evaluate Kohlberg's theory with regard to the role of emotion and socialization, family influences, gender, and cultural validity?

Educational and Vocational Preparation

Guidepost

7. What influences affect adolescents' school success, and why do some students drop out?

School is a central organizing experience in most adolescents' lives. It offers opportunities to learn information, master new skills, and sharpen old ones; to participate in sports, the arts, and other activities; to explore vocational choices; and to be with friends. It widens intellectual and social horizons. Some adolescents, however, experience school not as an opportunity but as one more hindrance on the road to adulthood.

In the United States, as in all other industrialized countries and in some developing countries as well, more students finish high school than ever before, and many enroll in higher education (Eccles et al., 2003; OECD, 2004). In 2002, 90 percent of U.S. 16- to 24-year-olds not enrolled in elementary or secondary schools had finished high school (NCES, 2005b). Among the 30 member countries of the Organisation for Economic Cooperation and Development* (OECD, 2004), average levels of educational attainment range from only 7.4 years of schooling in Mexico to 13.8 years in Norway. The United States, with an average of 12.7 years of schooling, is on the high end of this international comparison. However, U.S. adolescents, on average, do less well on academic achievement tests than adolescents in many other countries (Lemke et al., 2004; Snyder & Hoffman, 2001). Furthermore, although fourth- and eighth-grade student achievement, as measured by the National Assessment of Educational Progress, has improved in several areas, twelfth-grade achievement generally has not (NCES, 2003, 2005b).

Let's look at influences on school achievement and then at young people who drop out. Finally, we'll consider planning for higher education and vocations.

Influences on Motivation and Achievement

Students who do well in school are likely to remain in school. As in the elementary grades, such factors as parenting practices, socioeconomic status, and the quality of the home environment influence the course of school achievement in adolescence (Jimerson, Egeland, & Teo, 1999). Other factors include gender, ethnicity, peer influence, quality of schooling, and—first and foremost—students' belief in themselves.

Self-Efficacy Beliefs As discussed in Chapter 9, students high in *self-efficacy*—who believe that they can master tasks and regulate their own learning—are most likely to do well in school. In one study, 116 ninth- and tenth-graders of various ethnic backgrounds in two eastern high schools were asked such questions as "How well can you finish homework assignments by deadlines? Concentrate on school subjects? Plan and organize your schoolwork?" The students' perceived self-efficacy predicted the social studies grades they hoped for, expected, and achieved. Students' goals were influenced by their parents' goals for them, but stu-

Adolescents who take responsibility for their own learning, like this boy doing library research, are most likely to get good grades.

*Australia, Austria, Belgium, Canada, Czech Republic, Denmark, Finland, France, Germany, Greece, Hungary, Iceland, Ireland, Italy, Japan, Korea, Luxembourg, Mexico, Netherlands, New Zealand, Norway, Poland, Portugal, Slovak Republic, Spain, Sweden, Switzerland, Turkey, United Kingdom, and United States.

Even though adolescents are more independent than younger children, the home atmosphere continues to influence school achievement. Parents help not only by monitoring homework but also by taking an active interest in other aspects of teenagers' lives. Children of authoritative parents, who discuss issues openly and offer praise and encouragement, tend to do best in school.

dents' beliefs about their own abilities were more influential (Zimmerman et al., 1992). The message is clear: If parents want their children to do well in school, they must see that children have learning experiences that build a belief in their ability to succeed.

Parenting Styles, Ethnicity, and Peer Influence   The benefits of *authoritative parenting* continue in adolescence (Baumrind, 1991), affecting school achievement. Authoritative parents urge adolescents to look at both sides of issues, welcome their participation in family decisions, and admit that children sometimes know more than parents. These parents strike a balance between making demands and being responsive. Their children receive praise and privileges for good grades; poor grades bring encouragement to try harder and offers of help.

Authoritarian parents, by contrast, tell adolescents not to argue with or question adults and tell them they will "know better when they are grown up." Good grades bring admonitions to do even better; poor grades may be punished by reduced allowances or "grounding." *Permissive parents* seem indifferent to grades, make no rules about watching television, do not attend school functions, and neither help with nor check their children's homework. These parents may not be neglectful or uncaring; they may, in fact, be nurturant. They may simply believe that teenagers should be responsible for their own lives.

What accounts for the academic success of authoritatively raised adolescents? Authoritative parents' greater involvement in schooling may be a factor as well as their encouragement of positive attitudes toward work. A more subtle mechanism, consistent with findings on self-efficacy, may be parents' influence on how children explain success or failure. In a study of 2,353 high school students in California and Wisconsin, students who saw their parents as nonauthoritative were more likely than their peers to attribute poor grades to external causes or to low ability—forces beyond their control—rather than to their own efforts. A year later, such students tended to pay less attention in class and to spend less time on homework (Glasgow et al.,

Asian American students tend to do well in school because both they and their parents and friends seriously value learning and achievement.

1997). Thus, a sense of helplessness associated with nonauthoritative parenting may become a self-fulfilling prophecy, discouraging students from trying to succeed.

Among some ethnic groups, parenting styles may be less important than other factors, such as peer influence, that affect motivation. In one study, Latino and African American adolescents, even those with authoritative parents, did less well in school than European American students, apparently because of lack of peer support for academic achievement (Steinberg, Dornbusch, & Brown, 1992). On the other hand, Asian American students, whose parents are sometimes described as authoritarian, get high grades and score better than European American students on math achievement tests, apparently because they like math and because both parents *and* peers prize achievement (C. Chen & Stevenson, 1995). The strong school achievement of many young people from a variety of immigrant backgrounds reflects their families' and friends' strong emphasis on and support of educational success (Fuligni, 1997).

Peer influence may help explain the downward trend in academic motivation and achievement that begins for many students in early adolescence. In a longitudinal study of students entering an urban middle school after sixth grade, motivation and grades declined, on average, during the seventh-grade year. However, students whose peer group were high achievers showed less decline in achievement and enjoyment of school, while those who associated with low achievers showed greater declines (Ryan, 2001).

Gender Adolescent boys and girls score about the same on standardized tests in most subject-matter areas, but girls tend to have more confidence in their academic abilities. They like school a little better, earn better grades, and are more likely to graduate from high school and to plan to attend and finish college and graduate or professional schools. Boys are more likely to be underachievers, to be assigned to special or remedial education, and to be expelled from or drop out of school (Eccles et al., 2003; Freeman, 2004).

Boys have had a slight edge on standardized tests of math and science, perhaps because they like these courses better than girls do, but this gender gap appears to be shrinking as girls take equally challenging math and science courses and do well in them. Girls do better than boys on assessments of reading and writing (Freeman, 2004; Sen et al., 2005). Internationally, in 2000, girls were better readers than boys in all of 43 participating countries; boys were ahead in mathematical literacy in about half of the countries, though these gender differences were smaller (OECD, 2004).

Teachers tend to discipline boys more harshly than girls. On the other hand, they tend to give more favorable attention to high-achieving boys than to high-achieving girls. Boys are more likely than girls to be encouraged to take honors courses, to apply to top colleges, and to aim for challenging careers (Eccles et al., 2003).

The Educational System The quality of a school strongly influences student achievement. A good high school has an orderly, unoppressive atmosphere; an active, energetic principal; and teachers who take part in making decisions. Principal and

Checkpoint

Can you . . .

✔ Explain how self-efficacy beliefs can contribute to adolescents' motivation to learn?

✔ Assess the influences of parents and peers on academic achievement?

✔ Identify ethnic and gender differences in achievement and attitudes toward school?

teachers have high expectations for students, emphasize academics more than extracurricular activities, and closely monitor student performance.

Students who like school do better academically. Adolescents are more satisfied with school if they are allowed to participate in making rules and feel support from teachers and other students (Samdal & Dür, 2000).

Schools that tailor teaching to students' abilities get better results than schools that try to teach all students in the same way. Research on Sternberg's triarchic theory of intelligence (refer back to Chapter 9) has found that students high in practical or creative intelligence do better when taught in a way that allows them to capitalize on those strengths (Sternberg, 1997; Sternberg, Torff, & Grigorenko, 1998).

Some big-city school systems, such as New York's, Philadelphia's, and Chicago's, are experimenting with small schools, in which students, teachers, and parents form a learning community united by a common vision of good education. The curriculum may have a special focus, such as ethnic studies. Teaching is flexible, innovative, and personalized; teachers work together closely and get to know students well (Meier, 1995; Rossi, 1996). However, some small schools that originally showed promise have closed or declined in quality due to funding problems, increased enrollment, or staff turnover (Gootman & Herszenhorn, 2005).

The transition to college, with its higher educational standards and expectations for self-direction, can be a shock for some students. Early College High Schools—small, personalized, high-quality schools operated in cooperation with nearby colleges—are intended primarily for low-income and minority students and first-generation English language learners, groups statistically underrepresented in higher education. By combining a nurturing atmosphere with clear, rigorous standards, these schools enable students to complete high school requirements plus the first two years of college ("The Early College High School Initiative," undated).

Dropping Out of High School

Although more U.S. youths are completing high school than ever before, 5 percent of high school students dropped out during the 2000–2001 school year (Kaufman Alt, & Chapman, 2004), and 10.7 percent of 16- to 24-year-olds in 2001 were out of high school without a diploma or equivalent—this at a time when high school graduation is, for most purposes, a minimum requirement for labor force entry (Kaufman et al., 2001, 2004; NCES, 2003).

Dropout rates are higher among boys than among girls (Freeman, 2004). Hispanic students are more likely to drop out than African Americans, who are more likely to drop out than non-Hispanic whites (NCES, 2003); and low-income students are much more likely to drop out than middle- or high-income students (NCES, 2004a). The higher dropout rates among minority groups living in poverty may stem in part from the poor quality of their schools as compared with those attended by more advantaged children. Among other possible reasons for the high Latino dropout rates are language difficulties, financial pressures, and a culture that puts family first; these students often leave school to help support their families (U.S. Department of Education, 1992).

Society suffers when young people do not finish school. Dropouts are more likely to be unemployed or to have low incomes, to end up on welfare, and to become involved with drugs, crime, and delinquency. In addition, the loss of taxable income burdens the public treasury (NCES, 1999, 2001, 2003, 2004a).

Perhaps the most important factor in keeping adolescents in school is **active engagement:** the extent to which the student is personally involved in schooling. On the most basic level, active engagement means coming to class on time, being

What's Your View?

● How can parents, educators, and societal institutions encourage young people to finish high school?

active engagement Personal involvement in schooling, work, family life, or other activity.

Checkpoint

Can you . . .

✔ Give examples of educational practices that can help high school students succeed?

✔ Discuss trends in high school completion, and cite risk factors and protective factors?

Guidepost

8. What factors affect educational and vocational planning and aspirations?

prepared, listening and responding to the teacher, and obeying school rules. A second level of engagement consists of getting involved with the coursework—asking questions, taking the initiative to seek help when needed, or doing extra projects. Both levels of active engagement tend to pay off in positive school performance (Finn & Rock, 1997). Students who participate in extracurricular activities also are less likely to drop out (Mahoney, 2000; Shanahan & Flaherty, 2001); those who have full-time jobs are more likely to do so (Shanahan & Flaherty, 2001).

What factors promote active engagement? Family encouragement is one. Others may include small class size and a warm, supportive school environment. Preschool experience—or the lack of it—may set the stage for high school success or failure. In a Chicago longitudinal study, young people who had been in a high-quality early childhood education program were less likely to be held back or to drop out of high school (Temple, Reynolds, & Miedel, 2000).

Educational and Vocational Aspirations

How do young people develop career goals? How do they decide whether to go to college and, if not, how to enter the world of work? Many factors enter in, including individual ability and personality, education, socioeconomic and ethnic background, the advice of school counselors, life experiences, and societal values. Let's look at some influences on educational and vocational aspirations. Then we'll examine provisions for young people who are not college-bound.

Influences on Students' Aspirations Students' self-efficacy beliefs—often influenced by parents' beliefs and aspirations—shape the occupational options the students consider and the way they prepare for careers (Bandura, Barbaranelli, Caprara, & Pastorelli, 2001; Bandura et al., 1996). Parents' values with regard to academic achievement influence adolescents' values and occupational goals (Jodl, Michael, Malanchuk, Eccles, & Sameroff, 2001). This is especially apparent among children of East Asian immigrant families, who strongly value education. Although high school graduates from immigrant families in general are as likely to go on to college as peers from American-born families, the proportion of children of East Asian families who do so (96 percent) is much higher than among some other immigrant groups (Fuligni & Witkow, 2004).

Despite the greater flexibility in career goals today, gender—and gender-stereotyping—may influence vocational choice (Eccles et al., 2003). Girls and boys in the United States are now equally likely to take challenging math and science courses in high school (Freeman, 2004) and to plan careers in those fields, but boys are much more likely to earn college degrees in engineering, physics, and computer science (NCES, 2001), whereas girls are still more likely to go into nursing, social welfare professions, and teaching (Eccles et al., 2003). Much the same is true in other industrialized countries (OECD, 2004).

The educational system itself may act as a brake on vocational aspirations. Students who can memorize and analyze tend to do well on intelligence tests and in classrooms where teaching is geared to those abilities. Thus, as predicted by the tests, these students are achievers in a system that stresses the abilities in which they happen to excel. Students whose strength is in creative or practical thinking—areas critical to success in certain fields—never get a chance to show what they can do (Sternberg, 1997). Recognition of a broader range of "intelligences" (refer back to Chapter 9), combined with more flexible teaching and career counseling, could allow more students to get the education and enter the occupations they desire and to make the contributions of which they are capable.

Guiding Students *Not* Bound for College Most industrialized countries offer guidance to noncollege-bound students. Germany, for example, has an apprenticeship system in which high school students go to school part-time and spend the rest of the week in paid on-the-job training supervised by an employer-mentor. About 60 percent of German high school students take advantage of this program each year, and 85 percent of those who complete it find jobs (Hopfensperger, 1996).

Lifemap CD

What challenges face high-school students who do not plan to attend college? To find out, view the video, "Non-College Bound Adolescents," in Chapter 11 of your CD.

In the United States, vocational counseling is generally oriented toward college-bound youth. Whatever vocational training programs do exist for the approximately 38 percent of high school graduates who do *not* immediately go on to college (NCES, 2003) tend to be less comprehensive than the German model and less closely tied to the needs of businesses and industries. Most of these young people must get training on the job or in community college courses. Many, ignorant about the job market, do not obtain the skills they need. Others take jobs beneath their abilities. Some do not find work at all (NRC, 1993a).

In some communities, demonstration programs help in the school-to-work transition. The most successful ones offer instruction in basic skills, counseling, peer support,

This young man—one of approximately 38 percent of U.S. high school graduates who do not immediately go on to college—is learning electronics servicing and repair. Vocational training, to be effective, must be tied to the current needs of the job market.

mentoring, apprenticeship, and job placement (NRC, 1993a). In 1994, Congress passed the School to Work Opportunities Act, which allocated $1.1 billion to help states and local governments develop vocational training programs. In 2000–2001 nearly half of public alternative schools and programs for at-risk youth offered vocational training (NCES, 2003).

Checkpoint

Can you . . .

✔ Discuss influences on educational and vocational planning?

Ref⊕cus

Thinking back to the Focus vignette about Anne Frank at the beginning of this chapter:

- What typical pubertal changes did Anne Frank's diary describe? How did these changes affect Anne psychologically?

- What evidence did Anne show of cognitive maturation, linguistic and moral development, and vocational aspirations?

- In what ways might Anne's development have been similar, and in what ways different, under normal circumstances?

Vocational planning is one aspect of an adolescent's search for identity. The question "What shall I do?" is very close to "Who shall I be?" People who feel they are doing something worthwhile, and doing it well, feel good about themselves. Those who feel that their work does not matter—or that they are not good at it—may wonder about the meaning of their lives. A prime personality issue in adolescence, which we discuss in Chapter 12, is the effort to define the self.

SUMMARY AND KEY TERMS

Adolescence: A Developmental Transition

Guidepost 1: **What is adolescence, when does it begin and end, and what opportunities and risks does it entail?**

- Adolescence, in modern industrial societies, is the transition from childhood to adulthood. It lasts from age 10 or 11 until the late teens or early twenties.
- Early adolescence is full of opportunities for physical, cognitive, and psychosocial growth, but also of risks to healthy development. Risky behavior patterns, such as drinking alcohol, drug abuse, sexual and gang activity, and use of firearms, tend to increase throughout the teenage years, but most young people experience no major problems.

    adolescence *(397)*

    puberty *(397)*

PHYSICAL DEVELOPMENT

Puberty: The End of Childhood

Guidepost 2: **What physical changes do adolescents experience, and how do these changes affect them psychologically?**

- Puberty is triggered by hormonal changes. Puberty takes about four years, typically begins earlier in girls than in boys, and ends when a person can reproduce; but the timing of these events varies considerably.
- Sexual attraction seems to begin at about age 10, when the adrenal glands increase their hormonal output.
- During puberty, both boys and girls undergo an adolescent growth spurt. The reproductive organs enlarge and mature, and secondary sex characteristics appear.
- A secular trend toward earlier attainment of adult height and sexual maturity began about 100 years ago, probably because of improvements in living standards.
- The principal signs of sexual maturity are production of sperm (for males) and menstruation (for females).

    primary sex characteristics *(400)*

    secondary sex characteristics *(400)*

    secular trend *(401)*

    adolescent growth spurt *(402)*

    spermarche *(402)*

    menarche *(403)*

The Adolescent Brain

Guidepost 3: **What brain developments occur during adolescence, and how do they affect adolescent behavior?**

- The adolescent brain is not yet fully mature. It undergoes a second wave of overproduction of gray matter, especially in the frontal lobes, followed by pruning of excess nerve cells. Continuing myelination of the frontal lobes facilitates the maturation of cognitive processing.
- Adolescents process information about emotions with the amygdala, whereas adults use the frontal lobe. Thus adolescents tend to make less accurate, less reasoned judgments.
- Underdevelopment of frontal cortical systems connected with motivation, impulsivity, and addiction may help explain adolescents' tendency toward risk taking.

Physical and Mental Health

Guidepost 4: **What are some common health problems in adolescence, and how can they be prevented?**

- For the most part, the adolescent years are relatively healthy. Health problems often are associated with poverty or lifestyle.
- Many adolescents do not engage in regular vigorous physical activity.
- Many adolescents do not get enough sleep because the high school schedule is out of sync with their natural body rhythms.
- Concern with body image, especially among girls, may lead to eating disorders.
- Three common eating disorders in adolescence are obesity/overweight, anorexia nervosa, and bulimia nervosa. All can have serious long-term effects. Anorexia and bulimia affect mostly girls. Outcomes for bulimia tend to be better than for anorexia.
- Adolescent substance use has lessened in recent years; still, drug use often begins as children move into middle school.
- Marijuana, alcohol, and tobacco are the most popular drugs with adolescents. All involve serious risks. Marijuana use can lead to the use of hard drugs.
- The prevalence of depression increases in adolescence, especially among girls.
- Leading causes of death among adolescents include motor vehicle accidents, firearm use, and suicide.

    body image *(408)*

    anorexia nervosa *(409)*

    bulimia nervosa *(409)*

    substance abuse *(411)*

    substance dependence *(411)*

    gateway drugs *(412)*

COGNITIVE DEVELOPMENT

Aspects of Cognitive Maturation

Guidepost 5: **How do adolescents' thinking and use of language differ from younger children's?**

- People in Piaget's stage of formal operations can engage in hypothetical-deductive reasoning. They can think in terms of possibilities, deal flexibly with problems, and test hypotheses.

- Because environmental stimulation plays an important part in attaining this stage, not all people become capable of formal operations; and those who are capable do not always use them.

- Piaget's proposed stage of formal operations does not take into account such developments as accumulation of knowledge and expertise, gains in information processing, and the growth of metacognition. Piaget also paid little attention to individual differences, between-task variations, and the role of the situation.

- According to Elkind, immature thought patterns can result from adolescents' inexperience with formal thinking. These thought patterns include idealism and criticalness, argumentativeness, indecisiveness, apparent hypocrisy, self-consciousness, and an assumption of specialness and invulnerability. Research has cast doubt on the special prevalence of the latter two patterns during adolescence.

- Research has found both structural and functional changes in adolescents' information processing. Structural changes include increases in declarative, procedural, and conceptual knowledge and expansion of the capacity of working memory. Functional changes include progress in deductive reasoning. However, emotional immaturity may lead older adolescents to make poorer decisions than younger ones.

- Vocabulary and other aspects of language development, especially those related to abstract thought, such as social perspective-taking, improve in adolescence. Adolescents enjoy wordplay and create their own "dialect."

formal operations *(416)*

hypothetical-deductive reasoning *(417)*

imaginary audience *(419)*

personal fable *(419)*

declarative knowledge *(420)*

procedural knowledge *(420)*

conceptual knowledge *(420)*

Guidepost 6: **On what basis do adolescents make moral judgments?**

- According to Kohlberg, moral reasoning is based on a developing sense of justice and growing cognitive abilities. Kohlberg proposed that moral development progresses from external control to internalized societal standards to personal, principled moral codes.

- Kohlberg's theory has been criticized on several grounds, including failure to credit the roles of emotion, socialization, and parental guidance. The applicability of Kohlberg's system to women and girls and to people in nonwestern cultures has been questioned.

preconventional morality *(422)*

conventional morality (or morality of conventional role conformity) *(422)*

postconventional morality (or morality of autonomous moral principles) *(424)*

Educational and Vocational Preparation

Guidepost 7: **What influences affect school success, and why do some students drop out?**

- Self-efficacy beliefs, parental practices, cultural and peer influences, gender, and quality of schooling affect adolescents' educational achievement.

- Although most Americans graduate from high school, the dropout rate is higher among poor, Hispanic, and African American students. Active engagement in studies is an important factor in keeping adolescents in school.

active engagement *(429)*

Guidepost 8: **What factors affect educational and vocational planning and aspirations?**

- Educational and vocational aspirations are influenced by several factors, including self-efficacy and parental values. Gender stereotypes have less influence than in the past.

- High school graduates who do not immediately go on to college can benefit from vocational training.

CHAPTER 12

Psychosocial Development in Adolescence

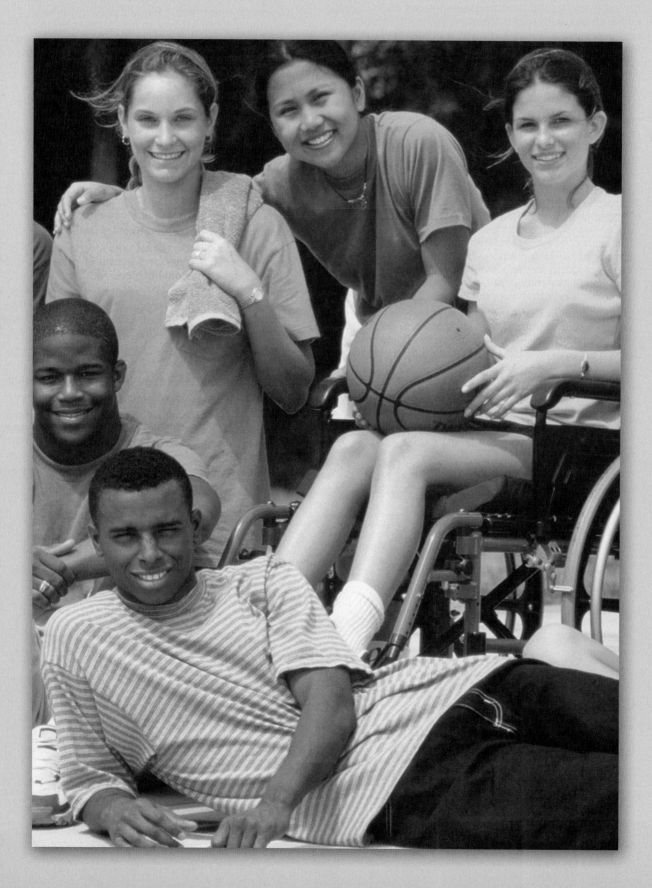

This face in the mirror
stares at me
demanding *Who are you? What will you become?*
And taunting, *You don't even know.*
Chastened, *I* cringe and agree
and then
because *I'm* still young,
I stick out my tongue.

Eve Merriam, "Conversation with Myself," 1964

Focus
Jackie Robinson, Baseball Legend*

Jackie Robinson

On April 15, 1947, when 28-year-old Jack Roosevelt ("Jackie") Robinson (1919–1972) put on a Brooklyn Dodgers uniform and strode onto Ebbets Field, he became the first African American in the twentieth century to play major league baseball. By the end of a spectacular first season in which he was named Rookie of the Year, Robinson's name had become a household word. Two years later, he was voted baseball's Most Valuable Player. During his ten years with the Dodgers, the team won six pennants, and Robinson played in six consecutive All-Star games. After his retirement, he won first-ballot election to the Hall of Fame.

His triumph did not come easily. When the Dodgers' manager, Branch Rickey, decided to bring Robinson up from the Negro Leagues, several players petitioned to keep him off the team. But Robinson's athletic prowess and dignified demeanor in the face of racist jibes, threats, hate mail, and attempts at bodily harm won the respect of the baseball world. Within the next decade, most major league teams signed African American players. Baseball had become "one of the first institutions in modern society to accept blacks on a relatively equal basis" (Tygiel, 1983).

Behind the Jackie Robinson legend is the story of a prodigiously talented boy growing up in a nation in which opportunities for black youth were extremely limited. His grandfather had been a slave. Jackie's father, a Georgia sharecropper, abandoned his wife and five children when the boy was 6 months old. His mother, Mallie Robinson, was a determined, deeply religious woman, who imbued her children with moral strength and pride. Intent on providing them with a good education, she moved her family to Pasadena, California. But Pasadena turned out to be almost as rigidly segregated as the Deep South.

*Sources of biographical information about Jackie Robinson were Falkner (1995), Rampersad (1997), J. Robinson (1995), S. Robinson (1996), and Tygiel (1983, 1997).

435

Jackie Robinson lived for sports. He idolized his older brother Mack, who won a silver medal in the 1936 Olympics. By the time Jackie was in junior high school, he was a star in his own right. He also did odd jobs after school.

Still, he had time on his hands. He joined a street gang of poor black, Mexican, and Japanese boys who seethed with "a growing resentment at being deprived of some of the advantages the white kids had" (J. Robinson, 1995, p. 6). The gang's activities were serious enough to get them in trouble—throwing rocks at cars and street lamps, smashing windows, and swiping apples from fruit stands. But once they were taken to jail at gunpoint merely for swimming in the reservoir when they were not allowed entrance to the whites-only municipal pool.

Robinson later reflected that he "might have become a full-fledged juvenile delinquent" had it not been for the influence of two men. One was an auto mechanic, Carl Anderson, who pointed out that "it didn't take guts to follow the crowd, that courage and intelligence lay in being willing to be different" (J. Robinson, 1995, pp. 6–7). The other was a young African American minister, Karl Downs, who lured Robinson and his friends into church-sponsored athletics, listened to their worries, helped them find jobs, and got them to help build a youth center—"an alternative to hanging out on street corners" (J. Robinson, 1995, p. 8). Later, while in college, Robinson served as a volunteer Sunday school teacher at the church.

A dolescence is a time of both opportunities and risks. Teenagers are on the threshold of love, of life's work, and of participation in adult society. Yet adolescence is also a time when some young people engage in behavior that closes off their options and limits their possibilities. Today, research is increasingly focusing on how to help young people whose environments are not optimal to avoid hazards that can keep them from fulfilling their potential. What saved Jackie Robinson—in addition to the influence of his indomitable, hardworking mother, his older brothers, and his adult mentors—were his talent and his passion for athletics, which ultimately enabled him to channel his drive, energy, audacity, and rebellion against racism in a positive direction.

In Chapter 11 we looked at some physical and cognitive factors that contribute to an adolescent's sense of self, such as appearance and school achievement. In this chapter, we turn to psychosocial aspects of the quest for identity. We discuss how adolescents come to terms with their sexuality. We consider how teenagers' burgeoning individuality expresses itself in relationships with parents, siblings, and peers. We examine sources of antisocial behavior and ways of reducing the risks of adolescence so as to make it a time of positive growth and expanding possibilities.

After you have read and studied this chapter, you should be able to answer each of the Guidepost questions that follow. Look for them again in the margins, where they point to important concepts throughout the chapter. To check your understanding of these Guideposts, review the end-of-chapter summary. Checkpoints located at periodic spots throughout the chapter will help you verify your understanding of what you have read.

1. How do adolescents form an identity?

2. What determines sexual orientation, and how do people become aware of their sexual identity?

3. What sexual practices are common among adolescents, and what leads some teenagers to engage in risky sexual behavior?

4. How common are sexually transmitted diseases and teenage pregnancy, and what are the usual outcomes?

5. How typical is "adolescent rebellion"?

6. How do adolescents relate to parents, siblings, and peers?

7. What are the root causes of antisocial behavior and juvenile delinquency, and what can be done to reduce these and other risks of adolescence?

Guideposts for Study

The Search for Identity

The search for **identity**—which Erikson defined as a coherent conception of the self, made up of goals, values, and beliefs to which the person is solidly committed—comes into focus during the teenage years. Adolescents' cognitive development now enables them to construct a "theory of the self" (Elkind, 1998). As Erikson (1950) emphasized, a teenager's effort to make sense of the self is not "a kind of maturational malaise." It is part of a healthy, vital process that builds on the achievements of earlier stages—on trust, autonomy, initiative, and industry—and lays the groundwork for coping with the challenges of adult life.

Erikson: Identity versus Identity Confusion

The chief task of adolescence, said Erikson (1968), is to confront the "crisis" of **identity versus identity confusion** (or *identity versus role confusion*) so as to become a unique adult with a coherent sense of self and a valued role in society. The concept of the "identity crisis" was based in part on Erikson's life experience. Growing up in Germany as the out-of-wedlock son of a Jewish woman from Denmark who had separated from her first husband, Erikson never knew his biological father. Though adopted at age 9 by his mother's second husband, a German Jewish pediatrician, he felt confusion about who he was. He floundered for some time before settling on his vocation. When he came to the United States, he needed to redefine his identity as an immigrant. All these issues found echoes in the identity crises he observed among disturbed adolescents, soldiers in combat, and members of minority groups (Erikson, 1968, 1973; L. J. Friedman, 1999).

According to Erikson, adolescents form their identity by synthesizing earlier identifications into "a new psychological structure, greater than the sum of its parts" (Kroger, 1993, p. 3). Identity forms as young people resolve three major issues: the choice of an *occupation,* the adoption of *values* to live by, and the development of a satisfying *sexual identity.* The "identity crisis" is seldom fully resolved in adolescence; issues concerning identity crop up again and again throughout adult life.

Guidepost

1. How do adolescents form an identity?

identity According to Erikson, a coherent conception of the self, made up of goals, values, and beliefs to which a person is solidly committed.

identity versus identity confusion Erikson's fifth stage of psychosocial development, in which an adolescent seeks to develop a coherent sense of self, including the role she or he is to play in society. Also called *identity versus role confusion.*

Mastering the challenge of rock climbing may help this adolescent boy assess his abilities, interests, and desires. According to Erikson, this process of self-assessment helps adolescents resolve the crisis of identity versus identity confusion.

During middle childhood, children acquire skills needed for success in their culture. As adolescents, they need to find ways to use these skills. When young people have trouble settling on an occupational identity—or when their opportunities are artificially limited, as they were for Jackie Robinson and his friends—they are at risk of behavior with serious negative consequences, such as criminal activity or early pregnancy.

According to Erikson, the *psychosocial moratorium,* the "time out" period that adolescence provides, allows young people to search for commitments to which they can be faithful. These youthful commitments may shape a person's life for years to come. Jackie Robinson's commitments were to develop his athletic potential and to help improve the position of African Americans in society. By remaining faithful to their commitments, as Robinson did, young people are better able to resolve the identity crisis. Adolescents who resolve that crisis satisfactorily develop the "virtue" of *fidelity:* sustained loyalty, faith, or a sense of belonging to a loved one or to friends and companions. Fidelity also can mean identification with a set of values, an ideology, a religion, a political movement, a creative pursuit, or an ethnic group (Erikson, 1982).

Fidelity is an extension of trust. In infancy, it is important for trust of others to outweigh mistrust; in adolescence, it becomes important to be trustworthy oneself. Adolescents extend their trust to mentors or loved ones. In sharing thoughts and feelings, an adolescent clarifies a tentative identity by seeing it reflected in the eyes of the beloved. However, these adolescent "intimacies" differ from mature intimacy, which involves greater commitment, sacrifice, and compromise.

Erikson saw the prime danger of this stage as identity or role confusion, which can greatly delay reaching psychological adulthood. (He himself did not resolve his own identity crisis until his mid-20s.) Some degree of identity confusion is normal. According to Erikson, it accounts for the seemingly chaotic nature of much adolescent behavior and for teenagers' painful self-consciousness. Cliquishness and intolerance of differences, both hallmarks of the adolescent social scene, are defenses against identity confusion. Adolescents also may show confusion by regressing into childishness to avoid resolving conflicts or by committing themselves impulsively to poorly thought-out courses of action.

Erikson's theory describes male identity development as the norm. According to Erikson, a man is not capable of real intimacy until after he has achieved a stable identity, whereas women define themselves through marriage and motherhood (something that may have been truer when Erikson developed his theory than it is today). Thus, said Erikson, women (unlike men) develop identity *through* intimacy, not before it. As we'll see, this male orientation of Erikson's theory has prompted criticism. Still, Erikson's concept of the identity crisis has inspired much valuable research.

Marcia: Identity Status—Crisis and Commitment

Four hypothetical young people are about to graduate from high school. Caterina has considered her interests and her talents and plans to become an engineer. She has narrowed her college choices to three schools that offer good programs in this field.

Andrea knows exactly what she is going to do with her life. Her mother, a union leader at a plastics factory, has arranged for Andrea to enter an apprenticeship program there. Andrea has never considered doing anything else.

Table 12-1 Identity-Status Interview

Sample Questions	Typical Answers for the Four Statuses
About occupational commitment: "How willing do you think you'd be to give up going into _____ if something better came along?"	*Identity achievement.* "Well, I might, but I doubt it. I can't see what 'something better' would be for me." *Foreclosure.* "Not very willing. It's what I've always wanted to do. The folks are happy with it and so am I." *Moratorium.* "I guess if I knew for sure, I could answer that better. It would have to be something in the general area—something related . . ." *Identity diffusion.* "Oh, sure. If something better came along, I'd change just like that."
About ideological commitment: "Have you ever had any doubts about your religious beliefs?"	*Identity achievement.* "Yes, I started wondering whether there is a God. I've pretty much resolved that now. The way it seems to me is . . ." *Foreclosure.* "No, not really; our family is pretty much in agreement on these things." *Moratorium.* "Yes, I guess I'm going through that now. I just don't see how there can be a God and still so much evil in the world. . . ." *Identity diffusion.* "Oh, I don't know. I guess so. Everyone goes through some sort of stage like that. But it really doesn't bother me much. I figure that one religion is about as good as another!"

Source: Adapted from Marcia, 1966.

Nick, on the other hand, is agonizing over his future. Should he attend a community college or join the army? He cannot decide what to do now or what he wants to do eventually.

Mark still has no idea what he wants to do, but he is not worried. He figures he can get some sort of a job and make up his mind about the future when he is ready.

These four young people are involved in identity formation. What accounts for the differences in the way they go about it, and how will these differences affect the outcome? According to research by the psychologist James E. Marcia (1966, 1980), these students are in four different **identity statuses,** states of ego (self) development.

Through 30-minute, semistructured identity-status interviews (see Table 12-1), Marcia distinguished four types of identity status: **identity achievement, foreclosure, moratorium,** and **identity diffusion.** The four categories differ according to the presence or absence of **crisis** and **commitment,** the two elements Erikson saw as crucial to forming identity. Marcia defined *crisis* as a period of conscious decision making and *commitment* as a personal investment in an occupation or system of beliefs (ideology). He found relationships between identity status and such characteristics as anxiety, self-esteem, moral reasoning, and patterns of behavior. Building on Marcia's theory, other researchers have identified additional personality and family variables related to identity status (Kroger, 2003; see Table 12-2). Here is a more detailed sketch of young people in each identity status:

1. **Identity achievement** (*crisis leading to commitment*). Caterina has resolved her identity crisis. During the crisis period, she devoted much thought and some emotional struggle to major issues in her life. She has made choices and expresses strong commitment to them. Her parents have encouraged her to make her own decisions; they have listened to her ideas and given their opinions without pressuring her to adopt them. Research in a number of cultures has found people in this category to be more mature and more socially competent than people in the other three (Kroger, 2003; Marcia, 1993).

identity statuses Marcia's term for states of ego development that depend on the presence or absence of crisis and commitment.

identity achievement Identity status, described by Marcia, that is characterized by commitment to choices made following a crisis, a period spent in exploring alternatives.

foreclosure Identity status, described by Marcia, in which a person who has not spent time considering alternatives (that is, has not been in crisis) is committed to other people's plans for his or her life.

moratorium Identity status, described by Marcia, in which a person is currently considering alternatives (in crisis) and seems headed for commitment.

identity diffusion Identity status, described by Marcia, that is characterized by absence of commitment and lack of serious consideration of alternatives.

crisis Marcia's term for period of conscious decision making related to identity formation.

commitment Marcia's term for personal investment in an occupation or system of beliefs.

Table 12-2 Family and Personality Factors Associated with Adolescents in Four Identity Statuses*

Factor	Identity Achievement	Foreclosure	Moratorium	Identity Diffusion
Family	Parents encourage autonomy and connection with teachers; differences are explored within a context of mutuality.	Parents are overly involved with their children; families avoid expressing differences.	Adolescents are often involved in an ambivalent struggle with parental authority.	Parents are laissez-faire in childrearing attitudes; are rejecting or not available to children.
Personality	High levels of ego development, moral reasoning, self-certainty, self-esteem, performance under stress, and intimacy.	Highest levels of authoritarianism and stereotypical thinking, obedience to authority, dependent relationships, low level of anxiety.	Most anxious and fearful of success; high levels of ego development, moral reasoning, and self-esteem.	Mixed results, with low levels of ego development, moral reasoning, cognitive complexity, and self-certainty; poor cooperative abilities.

*These associations have emerged from a number of separate studies. Because the studies have all been correlational, rather than longitudinal, it is impossible to say that any factor caused placement in any identity status.

Source: Kroger, 1993.

2. **Foreclosure** (*commitment without crisis*). Andrea has made commitments, not as a result of exploring possible choices, but by accepting someone else's plans for her life. She is happy and self-assured, but she becomes dogmatic when her opinions are questioned. She has close family ties, is obedient, and tends to follow a powerful leader, like her mother, who accepts no disagreement.

3. **Moratorium** (*crisis with no commitment yet*). Nick is in crisis, struggling with decisions. He is lively, talkative, self-confident, and scrupulous but also anxious and fearful. He is close to his mother but resists her authority. He wants to have a girlfriend but has not yet developed a close relationship. He will probably come out of his crisis eventually with the ability to make commitments and achieve identity.

4. **Identity diffusion** (*no commitment, no crisis*). Mark has not seriously considered options and has avoided commitments. He is unsure of himself and tends to be uncooperative. His parents do not discuss his future with him; they say it's up to him. People in this category tend to be unhappy and often lonely.

These categorizations are likely to change as these young people continue to develop (Marcia, 1979). When middle-aged people look back on their lives, they most commonly trace a path from foreclosure to moratorium to identity achievement (Kroger & Haslett, 1991). From late adolescence on, as Marcia proposed, more and more people are in moratorium or achievement: seeking or finding their own identity. About half of late adolescents remain in foreclosure or diffusion, but when development does occur, it is typically in the direction Marcia described (Kroger, 2003). Furthermore, although people in foreclosure seem to have made final decisions, that is often not so.

Gender Differences in Identity Formation

Much research supports Erikson's view that, for women, identity and intimacy develop together. Rather than view this pattern as a departure from a male norm, however, some researchers see it as pointing to a weakness in Erikson's theory, which, they claim, is based on male-centered western concepts of individuality, autonomy, and competitiveness. According to Carol Gilligan (1982, 1987a, 1987b; L. M. Brown & Gilligan, 1990), the female sense of self develops not so much through achieving a separate identity as through establishing relationships. Girls and women, says Gilligan, judge themselves on their handling of their responsibilities and on their ability to care for others as well as for themselves.

Some developmental scientists question how different the male and female paths to identity really are—especially today—and suggest that individual differences may be more important than gender differences (Archer, 1993; Marcia, 1993). Indeed, Marcia (1993) argues that an ongoing tension between independence and connectedness is at the heart of all of Erikson's psychosocial stages for *both* men and women. In research on Marcia's identity statuses, few gender differences have appeared (Kroger, 2003).

However, the development of self-esteem during adolescence, largely in the context of relationships with same-sex peers, seems to support Gilligan's view. Male self-esteem is linked with striving for individual achievement, whereas female self-esteem depends more on connections with others (Thorne & Michaelieu, 1996).

Some research suggests that adolescent girls have lower self-esteem than adolescent boys (Chubb, Fertman, & Ross, 1997). Highly publicized studies during the early 1990s found that girls' self-confidence and self-esteem stay fairly high until age 11 or 12 and then tend to falter (American Association of University Women [AAUW] Educational Foundation, 1992; L. M. Brown & Gilligan, 1990). However, an analysis of hundreds of studies involving nearly 150,000 respondents concluded that, although boys and men do have higher self-esteem than girls and women, especially in late adolescence, the difference is small. Contrary to the earlier finding, both males and females seemed to gain self-esteem with age (Kling, Hyde, Showers, & Buswell, 1999).

Ethnic Factors in Identity Formation

How is young people's identity affected when the values of their racial or ethnic community conflict with those of the larger society—for example, when American Indians are expected to participate in a tribal ceremony on a day when they are also supposed to be in school? Or when discrimination limits their occupational choices, as it did for Jackie Robinson's brother Mack, who, after his Olympic glory, came home to a succession of menial jobs? All these situations can lead to identity confusion.

Identity development can be especially complicated for young people from minority groups. Ethnicity—and the conflicts with the dominant culture it entails—may play a central part in their identity formation.

For young people in minority groups, race/ethnicity may be central to identity formation (Kroger, 2003). Research has identified four stages of ethnic identity based on Marcia's identity statuses (Phinney, 1998):

1. *Diffuse:* Juanita has done little or no exploration of her ethnicity and does not clearly understand the issues involved.

2. *Foreclosed:* Kwame has done little or no exploration of his ethnicity but has clear feelings about it. These feelings may be positive or negative, depending on the attitudes he absorbed at home.

3. *Moratorium:* Cho-san has begun to explore her ethnicity but is confused about what it means to her.

4. *Achieved:* Diego has explored his identity and understands and accepts his ethnicity.

On the basis of interviews and questionnaires of 64 U.S.-born African American, Asian American, and Hispanic tenth-graders in two Los Angeles high schools (Phinney, 1998), researchers assigned the respondents to three identity statuses (see Table 12-3). About half of the sample (33) were *diffuse/foreclosed*. (The researchers combined these two categories—both involving lack of exploration of

Table 12-3	Representative Quotations from Each Stage of Ethnic Identity Development

Diffusion

"Why do I need to learn about who was the first black woman to do this or that? I'm just not too interested." (Black female)

Foreclosure

"I don't go looking for my culture. I just go by what my parents say and do, and what they tell me to do, the way they are." (Mexican American male)

Moratorium

"There are a lot of non-Japanese people around and it gets pretty confusing to try and decide who I am." (Asian American male)

Achieved

"People put me down because I'm Mexican, but I don't care anymore. I can accept myself more." (Mexican American female)

Source: Phinney, 1998, Table 2, p. 277.

Lifemap CD

To appreciate the struggles of two 16-year-old girls to define their racial and ethnic identities, view the video, "Ethnic and Racial Identity," in Chapter 12 of your CD.

Checkpoint

Can you . . .

✔ List the three major issues involved in identity formation, according to Erikson?

✔ Describe four types of identity status found by Marcia?

✔ Discuss how gender and ethnicity can affect identity formation?

ethnicity—because they could not clearly distinguish between them on the basis of the young people's responses.) The other half were either in *moratorium* (14) or had apparently *achieved* identity (13).

Members of various ethnic groups found differing issues critical. Hispanic Americans were highly conscious of prejudice against their group. Asian Americans struggled with pressures for academic achievement. African American girls were keenly aware that they did not meet white standards of beauty; African American boys were more concerned about job discrimination and the negative societal image of black males. About one-fifth of the participants (some at each stage) had negative attitudes toward their own ethnic group. However, those in the achieved stage showed better overall adjustment than those in the other groups. They thought more highly of themselves, had a greater sense of mastery, and reported more positive family relationships and social and peer interactions.

Contrary to a common belief, minority adolescents—both boys and girls—gain in self-esteem with age, according to an analysis of questionnaires filled out by urban black, Latino, and Asian American high school students from lower- and working-class families. High levels of support and a positive school climate were related to higher levels of self-esteem, but family experiences were the strongest factor (Greene & Way, 2005).

Sexuality

Seeing oneself as a sexual being, recognizing one's sexual orientation, coming to terms with sexual stirrings, and forming romantic or sexual attachments all are parts of achieving *sexual identity*. Awareness of sexuality is an important aspect of identity formation, profoundly affecting self-image and relationships. Although this process is biologically driven, its expression is in part culturally defined.

It is difficult to do research on sexual expression. People willing to answer questions about sex tend to be sexually active and liberal in their attitudes toward sex and thus are not representative of the population. Also, there is often a discrepancy between what people say about sex and what they do, and there is no way to corroborate what people say. Problems multiply in surveying young people. For one thing, parental consent is often required, and parents who grant permission may not be typical. Methodology can make a difference: in one study, adolescent boys were more open in reporting certain types of sexual activity when surveys were self-administered by computer (C. F. Turner et al., 1998). Still, even if we cannot

Attitudes toward sexuality have liberalized in the United States during the past 50 years. This "sexual evolution" includes more open acceptance of sexual activity and a decline in the double standard by which males are freer sexually than females.

generalize findings to the population as a whole, within the groups that take part in surveys we can see trends in sexual mores.

During the 20th century the United States and other industrialized countries underwent a major change in sexual attitudes and behavior, bringing more widespread acceptance of premarital sex, homosexuality, and other previously disapproved forms of sexual activity. With the advent of the Internet, casual sex with fleeting cyber-acquaintances who "hook up" through online chat rooms or singles' meeting sites has become commonplace. Cell phones, e-mail, and instant messaging make it easy for lone adolescents to arrange these hookups with disembodied strangers, insulated from adult scrutiny. All of these changes have brought increased concerns about sexual risk taking. On the other hand, the AIDS epidemic has led many young people to abstain from sexual activity outside of committed relationships or to engage in "safer" sexual practices.

Sexual Orientation and Identity

Although present in younger children, it is in adolescence that a person's **sexual orientation** generally becomes a pressing issue: whether that person will consistently be sexually attracted to persons of the other sex (*heterosexual*), of the same sex (*homosexual*), or of both sexes (*bisexual*).

Heterosexuality predominates in nearly every known culture throughout the world. Homosexuality is common in some cultures, such as the Melanesian islands in the South Pacific (King, 1996), but not in the United States and other western countries. In one study of 38,000 U.S. seventh- through twelfth-graders, about 88 percent described themselves as predominantly heterosexual and only 1 percent as predominantly homosexual or bisexual. About 11 percent, mostly younger students, were unsure of their sexual orientation (Remafedi, Resnick, Blum, & Harris, 1992).

 Guidepost

2. What determines sexual orientation, and how do people become aware of their sexual identity?

sexual orientation Focus of consistent sexual, romantic, and affectionate interest, either heterosexual, homosexual, or bisexual.

However, social stigma may bias such self-reports, underestimating the prevalence of homosexuality and bisexuality.

Causes and Signs of Sexual Orientation Most research has focused on efforts to explain homosexuality. Although it once was considered a mental illness, several decades of research have found no association between homosexual orientation and emotional or social problems—apart from those apparently caused by societal treatment of homosexuals, such as a tendency to depression (American Psychological Association, undated; C. J. Patterson, 1992, 1995a, 1995b). These findings led the psychiatric profession in 1973 to stop classifying homosexuality as a mental disorder.

Many young people have one or more homosexual experiences as they are growing up, usually before age 15; but isolated experiences or even homosexual attractions or fantasies do not determine sexual orientation. Sexual orientation seems to be partly genetic (Diamond & Savin-Williams, 2003). In U.S. and Australian twin studies, both male and female sexual orientation have been found to be moderately heritable (Bailey, Dunne, & Martin, 2000; Kendler et al., 2000). The first full genome-wide scan for male sexual orientation has identified three stretches of DNA on chromosomes 7, 8, and 10 that appear to be involved in whether a man is heterosexual or gay (Mustanski et al., 2005). However, because research has not found perfect concordance in identical twins, nongenetic factors must be involved. Furthermore, different combinations of causes may operate in different individuals, and this may account for individual differences in the age at which same-sex attraction first appears (Diamond & Savin-Williams, 2003).

Children whose behavior is not gender-typical, especially boys who show strongly feminine interests, tend to grow up to be homosexual adults, according to a review of both prospective and retrospective studies (Bailey & Zucker, 1995). For boys, sexual arousal is likely to be the main way in which they learn their sexual orientation. This is probably less true of girls. In a study of men's and women's sexual arousal, heterosexual men were more aroused, both subjectively and genitally, by films showing female-to-female sexual activity, whereas homosexual men were more aroused by films of male-to-male sexual activity. By contrast, both heterosexual and homosexual women tended to be strongly aroused by viewing *either* male-to-male or female-to-female sexual activity. This suggests that the relationship between sexual orientation and sexual arousal is different in women than in men (Chivers, Rieger, Latty, & Bailey, 2004).

One researcher has reported a difference in the size of the hypothalamus, a brain structure that governs sexual activity, in heterosexual and gay men. However, it is not known whether this difference arises before birth or later (LeVay, 1991). In a brain-imaging study on the effects of pheromones, odors that attract mates (refer back to Chapter 11), the odor of male sweat activated the hypothalamus in both women and gay men, whereas both heterosexual and gay men's hypothalamus was affected by the odor of female urine (Savic, Berglund, & Lindström, 2005). Again, we do not know whether this difference in the brains of gay men is a cause of homosexuality or an effect of it.

Homosexual and Bisexual Identity and Behavior Although there is more acceptance of homosexuality than in the past, adolescents who openly identify as gay, lesbian, or bisexual often feel isolated in a hostile environment. They may be subject to discrimination and even violence. They may be reluctant to disclose their sexual orientation, even to their parents, for fear of strong disapproval or a rupture in the family (Hillier, 2002; C. J. Patterson, 1995b). They may find it difficult to meet and identify potential same-sex partners. As a result, for sexual minorities the recognition and expression of sexual identity is more complex and follows a less defined timetable than for heterosexuals (Diamond & Savin-Williams, 2003).

There is no single route to the development of gay, lesbian, or bisexual identity and behavior. Gender, ethnicity, personal characteristics, SES, and place of residence (urban or rural) may make a difference (Diamond & Savin-Williams, 2003). Because of the lack of socially sanctioned ways to explore their sexuality, many gay and lesbian adolescents experience identity confusion (Sieving, Oliphant, & Blum, 2002). Some adolescents, regardless of sexual orientation, experiment with diverse sexual partners, perhaps out of curiosity or in response to social pressure. And many gay and bisexual youth have serious romantic relationships with persons of the other sex (Diamond & Savin-Williams, 2003).

One model for the development of gay or lesbian sexual identity proposes the following sequence: (1) awareness of same-sex attraction (beginning at ages 8 to 11); (2) same-sex sexual behaviors (ages 12 to 15); (3) identification as gay or lesbian (ages 15 to 18); (4) disclosure to others (ages 17 to 19); and (5) development of same-sex romantic relationships (ages 18 to 20). However, this model may not accurately reflect the experience of younger gay men, many of whom feel freer than in the past to openly declare their sexual orientation; of lesbian and bisexual women, whose sexual identity development may be slower, more flexible, and more tied to emotional and situational factors than that of homosexual men; and of ethnic minorities, whose traditional communities and cultures may espouse strong religious beliefs or sterotypical gender roles, leading to internal and family conflict (Diamond, 1998, 2000; Diamond & Savin-Williams, 2003; Dubé & Savin-Williams, 1999). Gay males may pursue exclusively sexual same-sex liaisons, whereas lesbians, especially in early adolescence, engage in passionate but nonsexual friendships with same-sex partners. Some minority youths show same-sex behavior only with strangers and relate romantically to people of the other sex. Or they may postpone same-sex behavior until recognition of their sexual orientation becomes pressing (Diamond & Savin-Williams, 2003).

In interviews and questionnaires, 139 young males ages 16 to 26—white, African American, Latino, and Asian American—explored what it meant to them to grow up gay or bisexual. About half felt that they had fully accepted their sexual identities, and most had become sexually and romantically involved with other men. Latino youths reported earlier awareness of same-sex attractions than the other groups, perhaps because, in a culture with rigid gender roles, boys who do not fit the male norm become aware of their "differentness" early (Dubé & Savin-Williams, 1999).

Sexual Behavior

Internationally, there are wide variations in timing of heterosexual initiation. The percentage of women who report having first intercourse by age 17 is 10 times greater in Mali (72 percent) than in Thailand (7 percent) or the Philippines (6 percent). Similar differences exist for men. Although earlier male initiation is the norm in most cultures, in Mali and Ghana more women than men become sexually active at an early age (Singh, Wulf, Samara, & Cuca, 2000).

Sexual initiation generally occurs earlier in the United States than it did a generation ago (Sieving, Oliphant, & Blum, 2002). The average girl in the United States has her first sexual intercourse at 17, only one year later than the average boy (Singh et al., 2000). The percentage of students who have had intercourse increases with age: from 34.4 percent of ninth-graders to 60.5 percent of twelfth-graders (Brener et al., 2002). African Americans and Latinos tend to begin sexual activity earlier than white youth (Kaiser Family Foundation, Hoff, Greene, & Davis, 2003). Whereas

Checkpoint

Can you . . .

✔ Discuss theories and research regarding origins of sexual orientation?

✔ Discuss homosexual identity and relationship formation?

Guidepost

3. What sexual practices are common among adolescents, and what leads some to engage in risky sexual behavior?

teenage boys in previous years were more likely to be sexually experienced than teenage girls, that is no longer true: In 2002, 46 percent of 15- to 19-year-old boys and 47 percent of girls in that age group reported ever having had sex. The main reasons teenagers give for *not* yet having had sex are that it is against their religion or morals, followed by not wanting to get (or get a girl) pregnant (Abma, Martinez, Mosher, & Dawson, 2004).

In the study of gay and bisexual males mentioned in the previous section, the first reported male-to-male sexual encounters among Asian American youths took place about three years later than for other young men. This pattern of delayed sexual activity, which also has been found among Asian American heterosexuals, may reflect strong cultural pressures to save sex for marriage or adulthood and then to have children who will carry on the family name (Dubé & Savin-Williams, 1999).

Sexual Risk Taking Two major concerns about adolescent sexual activity are the risks of contracting sexually transmitted diseases (STDs) and, for heterosexuals, of pregnancy. Nearly nine out of ten 15- to 17-year-olds in a nationally representative survey sponsored by the Kaiser Family Foundation said they were "very" or "somewhat" concerned about these risks (Kaiser Family Foundation, Hoff, Green, & Davis, 2003).

Most at risk are young people who start sexual activity early, have multiple partners, do not use contraceptives regularly, and have inadequate information—or misinformation—about sex (Abma et al., 1997). The proportion of high school students who have had four or more sex partners decreased 24 percent between 1991 and 2001, but 14.2 percent of students still fall in that category (Brener et al., 2002). Other risk factors are living in a socioeconomically disadvantaged community, substance use, antisocial behavior, and association with deviant peers. Parental monitoring can help reduce these risks (Baumer & South, 2001; Capaldi, Stoolmiller, Clark, & Owen, 2002). Adolescents who can regulate their emotions and behavior are less likely to engage in risky sexual activity (Raffaelli & Crockett, 2003).

Why do some adolescents become sexually active at an early age? Various factors, including early entrance into puberty, poverty, poor school performance, lack of academic and career goals, a history of sexual abuse or parental neglect, and cultural or family patterns of early sexual experience, may play a part (AAP Committee on Adolescence, 1999). The absence of a father, especially early in life, is a strong risk factor (Ellis et al., 2003). Teenagers who have close, warm relationships with their mothers are more likely to delay sexual activity than their peers. So are those who perceive that their mothers disapprove of sexual activity (Jaccard & Dittus, 2000; Sieving, McNeely, & Blum, 2000).

One of the most powerful influences is perception of peer group norms. Young people often feel under pressure to engage in activities they do not feel ready for. In the Kaiser report, nearly one-third of 15- to 17-year-olds, especially boys, said they had experienced pressure to have sex. Sixty-three percent of 15- to 17-year-olds and 53 percent of 13- and 14-year-olds agreed that "waiting to have sex is a nice idea but nobody really does" (Kaiser Family Foundation et al., 2003).

As U.S. adolescents have become more aware of the risks of sexual activity, the percentage who have ever had intercourse has declined, especially among boys (from 55 percent in 1995 to 46 percent in 2002) and girls ages 15 to 17 (from 38 percent in 1995 to 30 percent in 2002) (Abma et al., 2004). However, noncoital forms of genital sexual activity, such as oral and anal sex and mutual masturbation, are common. Many heterosexual teens do not regard these activities as "sex" but as substitutes for, or precursors of, sex, or even as abstinence (Remez, 2000). In the Kaiser survey, more than one-third of 15- to 17-year-olds reported having had oral sex (Kaiser Family Foundation et al., 2003). These statistics are disturbing because,

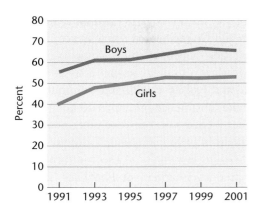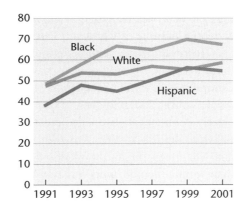

Figure 12-1

Percentage of U.S. high school students who report using a condom the last time they had sexual intercourse, by gender and race/ethnicity. (Source: Graphic from *The New York Times,* March 17, 2004, page 36. Copyright © 2004 The New York Times Graphics. Reprinted with permission.)

contrary to what many adolescents believe, oral and anal sex involve risks of sexually transmitted disease (Remez, 2000).

A special risk for girls is sexual violence or abuse. One in 10 teenage girls report that their first intercourse was not voluntary (Abma et al., 2004). In a nationally representative sample of high school girls, nearly 1 in 10 reported having been victims of dating violence (Wang, 2003).

Use of Contraceptives The use of contraceptives among teenagers has increased since 1990 (Abma et al., 2004), but teens who use contraceptives do not necessarily do so all of the time (Kaiser Family Foundation et al., 2003). About 75 percent of teenage girls and 82 percent of boys in one survey said they used some form of contraception at their first intercourse, and about 83 percent of girls and 91 percent of boys said they did so the most recent time they had sex. The older a girl is at her first intercourse, the more likely she is to use contraceptive protection (Abma et al., 2004). Teens who, in their first relationship, delay intercourse, discuss contraception before having sex, or use more than one method of contraception are more likely to use contraceptives consistently throughout that relationship (Manlove, Ryan, & Franzetta, 2003).

The best safeguard for sexually active teens is regular use of condoms, which gives some protection against STDs as well as against pregnancy. Condom use has increased in recent years (see Figure 12-1), as has use of the pill and new hormonal and injectable methods or combinations of methods (Abma et al., 2004). Still, in one survey, only 57.9 percent of high school students reported having used condoms the last time they had intercourse (Brener et al., 2002). There is *no* evidence that education about condom use and availability contributes to increased sexual activity (AAP Committee on Adolescence, 2001; Blake et al., 2003).

Most minor adolescent girls who seek contraceptives at federally funded family planning clinics report that their parents are aware they are doing so, according to a national survey. However, if parental notification were mandated by law, 1 in 5 of these girls said they would use no contraception or rely on the risky withdrawal method (Jones, Purcell, Singh, & Finer, 2005).

Where Do Teenagers Get Information About Sex? Adolescents get their information about sex primarily from friends, parents, sex education in school, and the media (Kaiser Family Foundation et al., 2003). Adolescents who can talk about sex with older siblings as well as with parents are more likely to have positive attitudes toward safe sexual practices (Kowal & Pike, 2004).

Since 1998, federally and state-funded sex education programs stressing abstinence from sex until marriage as the best or only option have become common (Devaney, Johnson, Maynard, & Trenholm, 2002). Programs that encourage abstinence but also discuss STD prevention and safer sexual practices for the sexually active have been

What's Your View?

- How can adolescents be helped to avoid or change risky sexual behavior?

found to delay sexual initiation and increase contraceptive use (AAP Committee on Psychosocial Aspects of Child and Family Health and Committee on Adolescence, 2001).

However, some school districts promote abstinence as the *only* option, even though abstinence-only courses have *not* been shown to delay sexual activity (AAP Committee on Psychosocial Aspects of Child and Family Health and Committee on Adolescence, 2001; Satcher, 2001). Furthermore, abstinence programs do not always clearly define what abstinence means—whether it covers oral sex and other noncoital activity (Remez, 2000). Likewise, virginity pledges have only limited effectiveness, and when teens break the pledge they are one-third less likely to use contraceptives than young people who did not take the pledge (Bearman & Bruckner, 2001). Although more than 4 out of 5 teenagers report receiving formal instruction in how to say no to sex, only 2 out of 3 have been taught about birth control. Only half of girls and one-third of boys ages 18 and 19 say they talked with a parent about birth control before their 18th birthday (Abma et al., 2004).

Unfortunately, many teenagers get much of their "sex education" from the media, which present a distorted view of sexual activity, associating it with fun, excitement, competition, danger, or violence and rarely showing the risks of unprotected sex. Some studies suggest a link between media influence and early sexual activity (Peterson, Moore, & Furstenberg, 1991; Strasburger & Donnerstein, 1999). However, much more extensive research needs to be done on the impact of all forms of mass media on adolescents' sexual attitudes and behaviors (Escobar-Chavez et al., 2005.)

Sexually Transmitted Diseases (STDs)

Sexually transmitted diseases (STDs) are diseases spread by sexual contact. Table 12-4 summarizes some common STDs: their causes, most frequent symptoms, treatment, and consequences.

About 1 in 4 new cases of STDs in the United States occurs in 15- to 19-year-olds (CDC, 2000c). The chief reasons for the prevalence of STDs among teenagers are early sexual activity, which increases the likelihood of having multiple high-risk partners, failure to use condoms or to use them regularly and correctly, and, for women, the tendency to have sex with older partners. STDs are most likely to develop undetected in adolescent girls (AGI, 1999a).

The most prevalent STD, according to some estimates, is human papilloma virus (HPV), which sometimes produces warts on the genitals. Also common among young people is trichomoniasis, a parasitic infection (Weinstock et al., 2004).

Genital herpes simplex is a chronic, recurring, often painful, and highly contagious disease caused by a virus. This condition can be fatal to a person with a deficiency of the immune system or to the newborn infant of a mother who has an outbreak at the time of delivery. There is no cure, but the antiviral drug acyclovir can prevent active outbreaks. The incidence of genital herpes has increased dramatically during the past three decades. Hepatitis B remains a prominent STD despite the availability of a preventive vaccine for more than 20 years (Weinstock et al., 2004).

The most common *curable* STDs are chlamydia and gonorrhea. These diseases, if undetected and untreated, can lead to severe health problems, including, in women, pelvic inflammatory disease (PID), a serious abdominal infection. Forty percent of chlamydia cases are reported among 15- to 19-year-olds; more than 1 in 10 teenage girls and 1 in 5 boys are affected (CDC, 2000c).

The human immunodeficiency virus (HIV), which causes AIDS, is transmitted through bodily fluids (mainly blood and semen), usually by sharing of intravenous drug needles or by sexual contact with an infected partner. The virus attacks the body's immune system, leaving a person vulnerable to a variety of fatal diseases. Symptoms of AIDS, which include extreme fatigue, fever, swollen lymph nodes, weight loss,

Checkpoint

Can you...

✔ Cite trends in sexual activity among adolescents?

✔ Identify factors that increase or decrease the risks of sexual activity?

Guidepost

4. How common are sexually transmitted diseases and teenage pregnancy, and what are their usual outcomes?

sexually transmitted diseases (STDs) Diseases spread by sexual contact.

Table 12-4 Common Sexually Transmitted Diseases

Disease	Cause	Symptoms: Male	Symptoms: Female	Treatment	Consequences If Untreated
Chlamydia	Bacterial infection	Pain during urination, discharge from penis	Vaginal discharge, abdominal discomfort[†]	Tetracycline or erythromycin	Can cause pelvic inflammatory disease or eventual sterility
Trichomoniasis	Parasitic infection, sometimes passed on in moist objects such as towels and bathing suits	Often absent	Absent or may include vaginal discharge, discomfort during intercourse, odor, painful urination	Oral antibiotic	May lead to abnormal growth of cervical cells
Gonorrhea	Bacterial infection	Discharge from penis, pain during urination[*]	Discomfort when urinating, vaginal discharge, abnormal menses[†]	Penicillin or other antibiotics	Can cause pelvic inflammatory disease or eventual sterility; can also cause arthritis, dermatitis, and meningitis
HPV (genital warts)	Human papilloma virus	Painless growths that usually appear on penis but may also appear on urethra or in rectal area[*]	Small, painless growths on genitals and anus; may also occur inside the vagina without external symptoms[*]	Removal of warts; but infection often reappears	May be associated with cervical cancer; in pregnancy, warts enlarge and may obstruct birth canal
Herpes	Herpes simplex virus	Painful blisters anywhere on the genitalia, usually on the penis[*]	Painful blisters on the genitalia, sometimes with fever and aching muscles; women with sores on cervix may be unaware of outbreaks[*]	No known cure but controlled with antiviral drug acyclovir	Possible increased risk of cervical cancer
Hepatitis B	Hepatitis B virus	Skin and eyes become yellow	Same as in men	No specific treatment; no alcohol	Can cause liver damage, chronic hepatitis
Syphilis	Bacterial infection	In first stage, reddish-brown sores on the mouth or genitalia or both, which may disappear, though the bacteria remain; in the second, more infectious stage, a widespread skin rash[*]	Same as in men	Penicillin or other antibiotics	Paralysis, convulsions, brain damage, and sometimes death
AIDS (acquired immune deficiency syndrome)	Human immunodeficiency virus (HIV)	Extreme fatigue, fever, swollen lymph nodes, weight loss, diarrhea, night sweats, susceptibility to other diseases[*]	Same as in men	No known cure; protease inhibitors and other drugs appear to extend life	Death, usually due to other diseases, such as cancer

[*]May be asymptomatic.

[†]Is often asymptomatic.

diarrhea, and night sweats, may not appear until six months to 10 or more years after initial HIV infection. In the United States, more than 1 out of 4 persons living with HIV or AIDS were infected in their teens (Kaiser Family Foundation et al., 2003).

As of now, AIDS is incurable, but increasingly the related infections that kill people are being stopped with antiviral therapy, including protease inhibitors (Palella et al., 1998; Weinstock et al., 2004). Many HIV-infected people lead active lives for years. Because symptoms may not appear until a disease has progressed to the point of causing serious long-term complications, early detection is important. Regular,

BOX 12-1

Window on the World

Preventing Teenage Pregnancy

Although teenage pregnancy and birthrates in the United States dropped dramatically during the 1990s, they remain many times higher than in other industrialized countries, where adolescents begin sexual activity just as early or earlier (Darroch, Singh, Frost, & the Study Team, 2001). Teenage birthrates in recent years have been nearly five times as high in the United States as in Denmark, Finland, France, Germany, Italy, the Netherlands, Spain, Sweden, and Switzerland and twelve times as high as in Japan (Ventura, Mathews, & Hamilton, 2001). Twenty-two percent of American girls have had children before age 20, as compared with 15 percent of British girls, 11 percent of Canadian girls, 6 percent of French girls, and 4 percent of Swedish girls (Darroch, Singh, Frost, and the Study Team, 2001).

Why are the U.S. rates so high? Experts disagree. Some observers point to such factors as the reduced stigma on unwed motherhood, media glorification of sex, the lack of a clear message that sex and parenthood are for adults, the influence of childhood sexual abuse, and failure of parents to communicate with children.

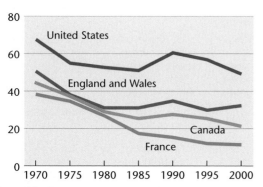

Figure 12-2

Trends in teenage birthrates per 1,000 girls ages 15 to 19 in selected western countries. The U.S. teenage birthrate has fallen since 1990, but it remains significantly higher than in England and Wales, Canada, and France. (Source: Graphic from *The New York Times,* March 17, 2004, page 36. Copyright © 2004 The New York Times Graphics. Reprinted with permission.)

Comparisons with the European experience suggest the importance of other factors: U.S. girls are more likely to have multiple sex partners and less likely to use contraceptives (Darroch et al., 2001).

Europe's industrialized countries have provided universal, comprehensive sex education for a much longer time than the United States. Comprehensive programs encourage young teenagers to delay intercourse but also aim to improve contraceptive use among sexually active adolescents. Such programs include education about sexuality and acquisition of skills for making responsible sexual decisions and communicating with partners. They provide information about risks and consequences of teenage pregnancy, about birth control methods, and about where to get medical and contraceptive help (AAP Committee on Psychosocial Aspects of Child and Family Health and Committee on Adolescence, 2001; AGI, 1994; Kirby, 1997; I. C. Stewart, 1994). Programs aimed at adolescent boys emphasize the wisdom of delaying fatherhood and the need to take responsibility when it occurs (Children's Defense Fund, 1998).

In the United States the provision and content of sex education programs is a political issue. Some critics claim that community- and school-based sex education leads to more or earlier sexual activity, even though evidence shows otherwise (AAP Committee on Adolescence, 2001; Children's Defense Fund, 1998; Eisen & Zellman, 1987; Satcher, 2001).

An important component of pregnancy prevention in European countries is access to reproductive services. Contraceptives are provided free to adolescents in Britain, France, Sweden, and, in many cases, the Netherlands. Sweden showed a fivefold reduction in the teenage birthrate following introduction of birth control education, free access to contraceptives, and free abortion on demand (Bracher & Santow, 1999). Indeed, U.S. teens who use contraception in their first sexual experience are much less likely to bear a child by age 20 (Abma et al., 2004).

The problem of teenage pregnancy requires a multifaceted solution. It must include programs and policies to encourage postponing or refraining from sexual activity, but it also must recognize that many young people do become sexually active

Checkpoint

Can you . . .

✔ ~~Identify the most common~~ sexually transmitted diseases, and list risk factors for developing an STD during adolescence?

school-based screening and treatment, together with programs that promote abstention from or postponement of sexual activity, responsible decision making, and ready availability of condoms for those who are sexually active may have some effect in controlling the spread of STDs (AAP Committee on Adolescence, 1994; AGI, 1994; Cohen, Nsuami, Martin, & Farley, 1999; Rotheram-Borus & Futterman, 2000).

Teenage Pregnancy and Childbearing

A dramatic drop in teenage pregnancy and birthrates has accompanied the steady decreases in early intercourse and in sex with multiple partners and the increases in contraceptive use. Birthrates for U.S. 15- to 19-year-old girls fell by one-third between 1991 and 2003 to 41.7 births per 1,000 girls in that age group, the lowest rate in more than 60 years. Teen pregnancy rates fell almost as rapidly—27 percent between 1990 and 2000, to 84.5 pregnancies per 1,000 girls, the lowest reported rate since 1976 (Martin et al., 2005). Birthrates for *unmarried* teenagers, who bear about 81 percent of all babies born to adolescent mothers, also have declined since and need education and information to prevent pregnancy and infection (AGI, 1999b). Ultimately, it requires attention to under-lying factors that put teenagers and families at risk: reducing poverty, school failure, behavioral and family problems, and expanding employment, skills training, and family life education (AGI, 1994; Children's Defense Fund, 1998; Kirby, 1997). Comprehensive early intervention programs for preschoolers and elementary school students have reduced teenage pregnancy (Lonczak et al., 2002; Hawkins et al., 1999; Schweinhart, Barnes, & Weikart, 1993).

Because adolescents with high aspirations are less likely to become pregnant, programs that motivate young people to achieve and raise their self-esteem have had some success. Teen Outreach Program (TOP), which began in 1978, helps teenagers make decisions, handle emotions, and deal with peers and adults. The program also includes community service. By encouraging students to select a volunteer activity, the program helps them see themselves as autonomous and competent. Among 1,600 students in TOP and 1,600 in a control group, TOP participants had about half the risk of pregnancy or school suspension and 60 percent of the risk of failure of nonparticipants (Allen & Philliber, 2001). This is evidence that teenage pregnancy and school failure are not isolated problems but are part of a larger developmental picture.

Having a baby when you're a teenager can do more than just take away your freedom, it can take away your dreams.

THE CHILDREN'S DEFENSE FUND

To many teenagers, one of the most persuasive arguments against sexual risk taking is the danger that pregnancy will ruin their lives. Teenage girls respond better when the advice comes from other girls close to their own age.

What's Your View?

If you were designing a school-based or community-based sexuality education program, what would you include? Do you favor or oppose programs that provide contraceptives to teenagers?

Check It Out

For more information on this topic, go to http://www.plannedparenthood.org/TEENISSUES/BCCHOICES/BCCHOICES.HTML. This site, called Birth Control Choices for Teens, is located on the Planned Parenthood Web site. Or visit http://www.teenpregnancy.org, the Web site of the National Campaign to Prevent Teen Pregnancy.

1994, especially among younger teens (Hamilton, Martin, & Sutton, 2004; Martin et al., 2003). The vast majority (88 percent) of births to teenagers ages 17 and younger result from unintended pregnancies (Abma et al., 2004).

More than half (an estimated 56 percent) of pregnant teenagers have their babies, and most of these girls plan to raise them themselves. Some miscarry (15 percent) or choose to abort (29 percent). A small proportion place their infants for adoption (AAP Committee on Adolescence, 1999; Adler, Ozer, & Tschann, 2003; AGI, 1994, 1999a; Children's Defense Fund, 1998; Martin et al., 2005; Ventura, Abma, Mosher, & Henshaw, 2004).

Although declines in teenage childbearing have occurred among all population groups, birthrates have fallen most sharply among black teenagers. Still, black and Hispanic girls are more likely to have babies than white, American Indian, or Asian American girls. And U.S. teens are more likely to become pregnant and give birth than teenagers in most other industrialized countries (Martin et al., 2005; see Figure 12-2 and Box 12-1).

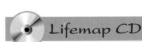

Lifemap CD

Why do some teenagers choose to become parents? For the perspective of a couple who decided to have a baby at age 15, view the video, "Thoughts on Becoming Teen Parents," in Chapter 12 of your CD.

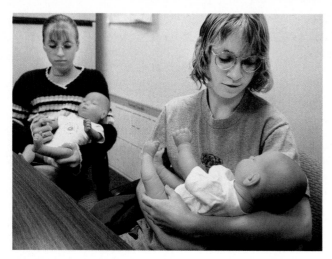

At the Child Support Agency in Appleton, Wisconsin, teenage girls try to comfort computerized dolls that cry and fuss like real babies. The program is designed to dramatize what it means to become mothers at an early age.

Many of these girls are sexually inexperienced (AGI, 1994; Children's Defense Fund, 1998; Ventura, Mathews, & Curtin, 1999). Many grew up without a father (Ellis et al., 2003). Among 9,159 women at a California primary care clinic, those who had become pregnant in adolescence were likely, as children, to have been physically, emotionally, or sexually abused and/or exposed to parental divorce or separation, domestic violence, substance abuse, or a household member who was mentally ill or engaged in criminal behavior (Hillis et al., 2004).

Teenage pregnancies often have poor outcomes. Many of the mothers are impoverished and poorly educated, and some are drug users. Many do not eat properly, do not gain enough weight, and get inadequate prenatal care or none at all. Their babies are likely to be premature or dangerously small and are at heightened risk of late fetal, neonatal, or infant death; health and academic problems; abuse and neglect; and developmental disabilities that may continue into adolescence (AAP Committee on Adolescence, 1999; AAP Committee on Adolescence and Committee on Early Childhood, Adoption, and Dependent Care, 2001; AGI, 1999a; Children's Defense Fund, 1998, 2004; Menacker et al., 2004).

Babies of more affluent teenage mothers also may be at risk. Among more than 134,000 white, largely middle-class girls and women, 13- to 19-year-olds were more likely than 20- to 24-year-olds to have low-birth-weight babies, even when the mothers were married and well educated and had adequate prenatal care. Prenatal care apparently cannot always overcome the biological disadvantage inherent in being born to a still-growing girl whose own body may be competing for vital nutrients with the developing fetus (Fraser et al., 1995).

Teenage unwed mothers and their families are likely to suffer financial hardship. Child support laws are spottily enforced, court-ordered payments are often inadequate, and many young fathers cannot afford them (AAP Committee on Adolescence, 1999). In the past, many teenage mothers went on public assistance, but under the 1996 federal welfare reform law such assistance is severely limited. Unmarried parents under age 18 are now eligible only if they live with their parents and go to school.

Teenage mothers are likely to drop out of school and to have repeated pregnancies. They and their partners may lack the maturity, skills, and social support to be good parents. Their children, in turn, are likely to drop out of school, to be depressed, to get in trouble with the law, and to become adolescent parents themselves (AAP Committee on Adolescence and Committee on Early Childhood, Adoption, and Dependent Care, 2001; CDF, 2004). However, these outcomes are far from inevitable. In a 20-year study of more than 400 teenage mothers in Baltimore, two-thirds of the daughters did *not* become teenage mothers themselves, and most graduated from high school (Furstenberg, Levine, & Brooks-Gunn, 1990).

Checkpoint

Can you . . .

✔ Summarize trends in teenage pregnancy and birthrates?

✔ Cite ways to prevent teenage pregnancy?

✔ Discuss risk factors, problems, and outcomes connected with teenage pregnancy?

Guidepost

5. How typical is "adolescent rebellion"?

Relationships with Family, Peers, and Adult Society

Age becomes a powerful bonding agent in adolescence. Adolescents spend more time with peers and less with family. However, most teenagers' fundamental values (like Jackie Robinson's) remain closer to their parents' than is generally realized (Offer & Church, 1991). Even as adolescents turn to peers for role models, companionship, and intimacy, they—much like toddlers beginning to explore a wider world—look to parents for a "secure base" from which they can try their wings. The most secure adolescents have strong, supportive relationships with parents who are attuned to the way the young people see themselves, permit and encourage their strivings for independence, and provide a safe haven in times of emotional stress (Allen et al., 2003; Laursen, 1996).

Is Adolescent Rebellion a Myth?

The teenage years have been called a time of **adolescent rebellion,** involving emotional turmoil, conflict within the family, alienation from adult society, reckless behavior, and rejection of adult values. Yet school-based research on adolescents the world over suggests that only about 1 in 5 teenagers fits this pattern (Offer & Schonert-Reichl, 1992).

The idea of adolescent rebellion may have been born in the first formal theory of adolescence, that of the psychologist G. Stanley Hall. Hall (1904/1916) believed that young people's efforts to adjust to their changing bodies and to the imminent demands of adulthood usher in a period of "storm and stress" that produces conflict between the generations. Sigmund Freud (1935/1953) and his daughter Anna Freud (1946) described "storm and stress" as universal and inevitable, growing out of a resurgence of early sexual drives toward the parents.

However, the anthropologist Margaret Mead (1928, 1935; see Chapter 2 Focus), who studied growing up in Samoa and other South Pacific islands, concluded that when a culture provides a gradual, serene transition from childhood to adulthood, "storm and stress" is not typical. Although her research in Samoa was later challenged (Freeman, 1983), her observation was eventually supported by research in 186 preindustrial societies (Schlegel & Barry, 1991).

Full-fledged rebellion now appears to be relatively uncommon even in western societies, at least among middle-class adolescents who are in school. Most young people feel close to and positive about their parents, share similar opinions on major issues, and value their parents' approval (Offer et al., 1989; Offer & Church, 1991; Offer, Ostrov, Howard, & Atkinson, 1988).

Furthermore, contrary to a popular belief, apparently well-adjusted adolescents are not "ticking time bombs" set to "explode" later in life. In a 34-year longitudinal study of 67 fourteen-year-old suburban boys, the vast majority adapted well to their life experiences (Offer, Offer, & Ostrov, 2004). The relatively few deeply troubled adolescents tended to come from disrupted families and, as adults, continued to have unstable family lives and to reject cultural norms. Those raised in intact two-parent homes with a positive family atmosphere tended to sail through adolescence with no serious problems and, as adults, to have solid marriages and lead well-adjusted lives (Offer, Kaiz, Ostrov, & Albert, 2002).

Still, adolescence can be a tough time for young people and their parents. Family conflict, depression, and risky behavior are more common than during other parts of the life span (Arnett, 1999; Petersen et al., 1993). Negative emotionality and mood swings are most intense during early adolescence, perhaps due to the stress connected with puberty. By late adolescence, emotionality tends to become more stable (Larson, Moneta, Richards, & Wilson, 2002).

Recognizing that adolescence may be a difficult time can help parents and teachers put trying behavior in perspective. But adults who assume that adolescent turmoil is normal and necessary may fail to heed the signals of the relatively few young persons who need special help.

Changing Time Use and Changing Relationships

One way to measure changes in adolescents' relationships with the important people in their lives is to see how they spend their discretionary time. The amount of time U.S. adolescents spend with their families declines dramatically between ages 10 and 18, from 35 percent to 14 percent of waking hours (Larson, Richards, Moneta,

adolescent rebellion Pattern of emotional turmoil, characteristic of a minority of adolescents, which may involve conflict with family, alienation from adult society, reckless behavior, and rejection of adult values.

What's Your View?

- Are your values mainly similar to or different from those of your parents? If different, how did you develop these values?

Checkpoint

Can you . . .

✔ Assess the extent of "storm and stress" during the teenage years?

Guidepost

6. How do adolescents relate to parents, siblings, and peers?

In contrast with young people in developing countries, U.S. adolescents have a great deal of free, discretionary time, and they spend much of it "hanging out" with peers.

Checkpoint

Can you . . .

✔ Identify and discuss age and cultural differences in how young people spend their time?

Holmbeck, & Duckett, 1996). Disengagement is not a rejection of the family, but a response to developmental needs. Early adolescents often retreat to their rooms; they seem to need time alone to step back from the demands of social relationships, regain emotional stability, and reflect on identity issues (Larson, 1997).

Cultural variations in time use reflect varying cultural needs, values, and practices (Verma & Larson, 2003). Young people in tribal or peasant societies spend most of their time producing bare necessities of life and have much less time for socializing than adolescents in technologically advanced societies (Larson & Verma, 1999). In some postindustrial societies such as Korea and Japan, where the pressures of schoolwork and family obligations are strong, adolescents have relatively little free time. To relieve their stress, they spend it mainly in passive pursuits, such as watching television and "doing nothing" (Verma & Larson, 2003).

By comparison, U.S. adolescents have a good deal of discretionary time, most of which they spend with peers, increasingly of the other sex (Juster et al., 2004; Larson & Seepersad, 2003; Verma & Larson, 2003). Weekend partying, sometimes in friends' homes without direct adult supervision, is frequent among older adolescents. Without appropriate parental monitoring, such activities can lead to substance use and deviant behavior (Larson & Seepersad, 2003).

African American teenagers, who may look upon their families as havens in a hostile world, tend to maintain more intimate family relationships and less intense peer relations than white teenagers (Giordano, Cernkovich, & DeMaris, 1993). Mexican American boys, but not girls, tend to become closer to their parents during puberty. This may reflect the unusually close-knit nature of Mexican American families as well as the importance these families place on the traditional male role (Molina & Chassin, 1996). For Chinese American youth from immigrant families, the need to adapt to U.S. society often conflicts with the pull of traditional family obligations (Fuligni, Yip, & Tseng, 2002).

With such cultural variations in mind, let's look more closely at relationships with parents, and then with siblings and peers.

Adolescents and Parents

Just as adolescents feel tension between dependency on their parents and the need to break away, parents often have mixed feelings. They want their children to be independent, yet they find it hard to let go. Parents have to walk a fine line between giving adolescents enough independence and protecting them from immature lapses in judgment. These tensions often lead to family conflict, and parenting styles can influence its shape and outcome. Also, as with younger children, teenagers' relationships with their parents are affected by the parents' life situation—their work and marital and socioeconomic status.

Family Conflict Family conflict may arise over the pace of adolescents' growth toward independence (Arnett, 1999). Most arguments concern day-to-day matters—chores, schoolwork, dress, money, curfews, dating, and friends—rather than fundamental values (Adams & Laursen, 2001; B. K. Barber, 1994). However, some of these minor issues may be proxies for more serious ones, such as substance use, safe driving, and sex. An accumulation of frequent "hassles" can add up to a stressful family atmosphere (Arnett, 1999).

The level of family discord seems to hinge primarily on adolescents' personalities and on parents' treatment of them. In a study of 335 two-parent rural midwestern families with teenagers, conflict declined during early to middle adolescence in warm, supportive families but worsened in a hostile, coercive, or critical family atmosphere (Rueter & Conger, 1995).

Family conflict is most frequent during early adolescence but most intense in midadolescence (Laursen, Coy, & Collins, 1998). The frequency of strife in early adolescence may be related to the strains of puberty and the need to assert autonomy. The more highly charged arguments in midadolescence and, to a lesser extent, in late adolescence may reflect the emotional stress that occurs as adolescents try their wings. The reduced frequency of conflict in late adolescence may signify adjustment to the momentous changes of the teenage years and a renegotiation of the balance of power between parent and child (Fuligni & Eccles, 1993; Laursen et al., 1998; Molina & Chassin, 1996; Steinberg, 1988).

Some research suggests that late adolescents (ages 18 and 19) who are still living at home tend to be less close to their parents and to have more negative interactions with them than late adolescents who have left home for college or work. However, this research was almost entirely done on European American middle-class families. A 5-year longitudinal study of 76 middle-class African American adolescents found a similar pattern for girls in late adolescence but not for boys, possibly because African American boys living at home tend to be given more freedom than girls are. Young people who had been closest to their parents in early adolescence remained the closest throughout (Smetana, Metzger, & Campione-Barr, 2004).

Parenting Styles As with cognitive development, authoritative parenting seems to foster adolescents' character development (Baumrind, 1991). Overly strict, authoritarian parenting may lead adolescents to reject parental influence and seek peer support and approval at all costs (Fuligni & Eccles, 1993).

Authoritative parents insist on important rules, norms, and values but are willing to listen, explain, and negotiate (Lamborn, Mounts, Steinberg, & Dornbusch, 1991). They exercise appropriate control over a child's conduct but not over the child's sense of self (Steinberg & Darling, 1994). Parents who show disappointment in teenagers' misbehavior are more effective in motivating them to behave responsibly than parents who punish them harshly (Krevans & Gibbs, 1996).

Authoritative parenting may bolster an adolescent's self-image. A questionnaire survey of 8,700 U.S. high school students concluded that "the more involvement, autonomy granting, and structure that adolescents perceive from their parents, the more positively teens evaluate their own general conduct, psychosocial development, and mental health" (Gray & Steinberg, 1999, p. 584). When adolescents thought their parents were trying to dominate their psychological experience, their emotional health suffered more than when parents tried to control their behavior. Teens whose parents were firm in enforcing behavioral rules had more self-discipline and fewer behavior problems than those with more permissive parents. Those whose parents gave them psychological autonomy tended to become self-confident and competent in both the academic and social realms. They wanted to achieve and believed they could do what they set out to do.

Family Structure, Mothers' Employment, and Economic Stress Many adolescents today live in families that are very different from families a few decades

What's Your View?

- What kinds of issues caused the most conflict in your family when you were a teenager, and how were they resolved?

- If you lived with both parents, were your conflicts more with one parent than with the other? Did your mother and father handle such issues similarly or differently?

Communication between parents and adolescents may flow more naturally when they are engaged in a shared pursuit. Grinding corn in the traditional manner strengthens the bond between this Navajo mother and daughter. Most adolescents feel close to and positive about their parents, appreciate their approval, and have similar values on major issues.

ago. Many households, like Jackie Robinson's, are fatherless, many parents are cohabiting, and many mothers, like his, work outside the home. How do these family situations affect adolescents?

A multiethnic study of 12- and 13-year-old children of single mothers—first assessed when the children were 6 and 7 years old—found no negative effects of single parenting on school performance and no greater risk of problem behavior. What mattered most, as other studies have found, were the mother's educational level and ability, family income, and the quality of the home environment (Ricciuti, 2004). In another longitudinal study, adolescent boys and girls whose parents later divorced showed more academic, psychological, and behavioral problems *before* the breakup than peers whose parents did not divorce (Sun, 2001).

A large national survey reported in Chapter 10 found that adolescents in cohabiting families tend to have greater behavioral and emotional problems than adolescents in married families; and, when one of the cohabiting parents is not the biological parent, school engagement suffers as well. For adolescents, unlike younger children, these effects are independent of economic resources, parental well-being, or effectiveness of parenting, suggesting that parental cohabitation itself may be more troublesome for adolescents than for younger children (Brown, 2004).

The impact of a mother's work outside the home may depend on whether there are two parents or only one in the household. Often a single mother like Mallie Robinson must work to stave off economic disaster; how her working affects her teenage children may hinge on how much time and energy she has left over to spend with them, how well she keeps track of their whereabouts, and what kind of role model she provides (B. L. Barber & Eccles, 1992). A longitudinal study of 819 ten- to 14-year-olds from low-income urban families points up the importance of the type of care and supervisions adolescents receive after school. Those who are on their own after school, away from home, tend to become involved in alcohol and drug use and in misconduct in school, especially if they have an early history of problem behavior. However, this is less likely to happen when parents monitor their children's activities and neighbors are actively involved (Coley, Morris, & Hernandez, 2004).

As we have discussed earlier, a major problem in many single-parent families is lack of money. One study looked at single African American mothers of seventh- and eighth-graders in a midwestern city that was experiencing widespread manufacturing layoffs. Unemployed mothers, especially those without outside help and support, tended to become depressed; and depressed mothers tended to perceive their maternal role negatively and punish their children harshly. Young people who saw their relationships with their mothers deteriorate tended to become depressed themselves and to have trouble in school (McLoyd, Jayaratne, Ceballo, & Borquez, 1994). A similar pattern occurred in 378 white two-parent families in an economically declining area of rural Iowa. Parental depression and marital conflict worsened financial conflicts between parents and adolescents, increasing the risk of teenage behavior problems (R. C. Conger et al., 1994).

On the other hand, many adolescents in economically distressed families benefit from accumulated social capital—the support of kin and community. In 51 poor, urban African American families in which teenagers were living with their mothers, grandmothers, or aunts, women who had strong kinship networks exercised firmer control and closer monitoring while granting appropriate autonomy, and their teenage charges were more self-reliant and had fewer behavior problems (R. D. Taylor & Roberts, 1995).

Checkpoint
Can you . . .

✔ Identify factors that affect conflict with parents?

✔ Discuss the impact on adolescents of parenting styles and of marital status, mothers' employment, and economic stress?

Adolescents and Siblings

Adolescents are less close to siblings than to either parents or friends, are less influenced by them, and become even more distant as they move through adolescence (Laursen, 1996). Changes in sibling relationships may well precede similar changes in the relationship between adolescents and parents: more independence on the part of the younger person and less authority exerted by the older person. As children approach high school, their relationships with their siblings become progressively more equal. Older siblings exercise less power over younger ones, and younger siblings no longer need as much supervision. As relative age differences shrink, so do differences in competence and independence (Buhrmester & Furman, 1990).

Older and younger siblings tend to have different feelings about their changing relationship. As the younger sibling grows up, the older one may look on a newly assertive younger brother or sister as a pesky annoyance. Younger siblings still tend to look up to older ones—as Jackie Robinson did to his brother Mack—and try to feel more "grown up" by identifying with and emulating them (Buhrmester & Furman, 1990).

Sibling relationships become more equal as the younger sibling approaches or reaches adolescence and the relative difference in age diminishes. Even so, this younger sister still looks up to her "big sister" and may try to emulate her.

Adolescents and Peers

As Jackie Robinson found, an important source of emotional support during the complex transition of adolescence, as well as a source of pressure for behavior that parents may deplore, is a young person's growing involvement with peers. The peer group is a source of affection, sympathy, understanding, and moral guidance; a place for experimentation; and a setting for achieving autonomy and independence from parents. It is a place to form intimate relationships that serve as "rehearsals" for adult intimacy (Buhrmester, 1996; Gecas & Seff, 1990; Laursen, 1996).

What's Your View?

• If you have one or more brothers or sisters, did your relationships with them change during adolescence?

The peer group is an important source of emotional support during adolescence. Young people going through rapid physical changes feel more comfortable with peers who are experiencing similar changes.

The influence of peers is strongest in early adolescence; it normally peaks at ages 12 to 13 and declines during middle and late adolescence, as relationships with parents are renegotiated. Attachment to peers in early adolescence does not forecast trouble unless the attachment is so strong that the young person is willing to give up obeying household rules, doing schoolwork, and developing his or her own talents in order to win peer approval and popularity (Fuligni et al., 2001).

In childhood, most peer interactions are *dyadic,* or one-to-one, though somewhat larger groupings do begin to form in middle childhood (refer back to Chapter 10). As children move into adolescence, the peer social system becomes more elaborate and diverse. Although adolescents continue to have one-to-one friendships, *cliques*—structured groups of friends who do things together—become more important. A third, and larger, type of grouping, *crowds,* which does not normally exist before adolescence, is based not on personal interactions but on reputation, image, or identity. Crowd membership is a social construction, a set of labels by which young people divide the social map based on neighborhood, ethnicity, socioeconomic status, or other factors. All three of these levels of peer groupings may exist simultaneously, and some may overlap in membership, which may change over time (Brown & Klute, 2003).

Friendships Friendships have been more extensively studied than other peer relationships. The intensity and importance of friendships and the amount of time spent with friends are probably greater in adolescence than at any other time in the life span. Friendships, on the whole, tend to become more reciprocal, more equal, and more stable; those that are less satisfying in these respects may lose importance or be abandoned. Adolescents tend to choose friends who are like them in gender, race/ethnicity, and other respects. Friends also influence each other, particularly toward risky or problem behavior; a young person is more likely to start smoking if a friend is already doing it (Brown & Klute. 2003). Friends tend to have similar academic attitudes and performance and, especially, similar levels of drug use (Hamm, 2000). However, such correlations may overestimate the influence of friends on risky behavior; the qualities that lead friends to choose each other may propel their development in independent but parallel ways. By controlling for these selection effects, a one-year longitudinal study of 1,700 adolescent friendship pairs found that peer influence on binge drinking and sexual activity was fairly weak (Jaccard, Blanton, & Dodge, 2005).

A stress on intimacy, loyalty, and sharing marks a transition toward adultlike friendships. Adolescents begin to rely more on friends than on parents for intimacy and support, and they share confidences more than younger friends do (Berndt & Perry, 1990; Buhrmester, 1990, 1996; Hartup & Stevens, 1999; Laursen, 1996). Girls' friendships tend to be more intimate than boys', with frequent sharing of confidences (Brown & Klute, 2003). Intimacy with same-sex friends increases during early to midadolescence, after which it typically declines as intimacy with the other sex grows (Laursen, 1996).

The increased intimacy of adolescent friendship reflects cognitive as well as emotional development. Adolescents are now better able to express their private thoughts and feelings. They can more readily consider another person's point of view, and so it is easier for them to understand a friend's thoughts and feelings. Increased intimacy reflects early adolescents' concern with getting to know themselves. Confiding in a friend helps young people explore their own feelings, define their identity, and validate their self-worth. Friendship provides a safe place to venture opinions, admit weaknesses, and get help with problems (Buhrmester, 1996).

The capacity for intimacy is related to psychological adjustment and social competence. Adolescents who have close, stable, supportive friendships generally have a high opinion of themselves, do well in school, are sociable, and are unlikely to be hostile, anxious, or depressed (Berndt & Perry, 1990; Buhrmester, 1990; Hartup & Stevens, 1999). They also tend to have established strong bonds with parents (Brown & Klute, 2003). A bidirectional process seems to be at work: Good relationships foster adjustment, which in turn fosters good friendships.

The transitions from elementary to junior high school and from junior high to high school seem to be particularly hard for young people identified in sociometric studies as *rejected* or *neglected* (Hatzichristou & Hopf, 1996; refer back to Chapter 10). Close, supportive friendships can be especially important in insulating such young people from social rejection (Brown & Klute, 2003).

Cliques Cliques may exist among preadolescent children but are a more prominent feature of early adolescence. As expanded circles of friends, they usually consist of young people of the same age, gender, and ethnicity. However, membership in cliques tends to be based not only on personal affinity but also on popularity, or social status. A person may belong to more than one clique or to no clique, and the membership of a clique may be stable or shifting. At any given time, an adolescent can be a *member* of a clique, whose ties are almost entirely within that group; a *liaison,* who has ties to more than one clique and serves to link them, or an *isolate,* who is not connected with any recognized clique. Isolates may have friends, but they do not have enough ties to any one clique to be a part of it. As young people move through adolescence, the number of isolates and liaisons increases, creating a more fluid, loosely knit structure (Brown & Klute, 2003).

The dynamics of clique membership in preadolescence are highly status-based, especially among girls. The members with highest status are acknowledged leaders, with the ultimate say over who is in and who is out. Cliques themselves form a hierarchy; higher-status cliques are most desirable to outsiders but maintain the tightest control of membership (Adler & Adler, 1995). In early adolescence this social control may become somewhat less rigid (Brown & Klute, 2003).

The clique structure can seem harsh to outsiders, but it effectively serves the purpose of "redirecting young people's priorities from childhood to adolescent social norms. It sends a blunt message as to who is in charge of the peer social system (peers, rather than adults) and provides unequivocal information about how to proceed within that system" (Brown & Klute, 2003, p. 341). It also can create emotional distress among those who are less than successful in negotiating the system (Brown & Klute, 2003).

Crowds Leonard Bernstein's musical *West Side Story* vividly illustrates the power of adolescent crowds. Crowd labels are cognitive designations for a feature that members of the crowd have in common, such as neighborhood (west siders or south siders), ethnic background (Puerto Ricans or Italians), peer status (snobs or nobodies), or abilities, interests, or lifestyle (brains, jocks, druggies). The specific categories by which adolescents describe their social landscape may vary from one community to another.

Crowds serve several purposes. They help adolescents establish their identity and reinforce allegiance to the behavioral norms of ethnic or socioeconomic groups. As *West Side Story* dramatizes, being part of a crowd makes it easier to establish relationships with peers in the same crowd and harder with outsiders. As with cliques, crowd affiliation tends to become looser as adolescence progresses (Brown & Klute, 2003).

Romantic Relationships Romantic relationships are a central part of most adolescents' social worlds. These relationships arouse strong emotions, both positive and negative. They contribute to the development of both intimacy and identity. Unfortunately, because they are likely to involve sexual contact, they also entail risks of pregnancy, STDs, and sometimes of sexual victimization. Breakups with romantic partners are among the strongest predictors of depression and suicide (Bouchey & Furman, 2003).

With the onset of puberty, most heterosexual boys and girls begin to think about and interact more with members of the other sex. Typically they move from mixed groups or group dates to one-on-one romantic relationships that, unlike other-sex friendships, they describe as involving passion and a sense of commitment. Gay, lesbian, and bisexual youth who are unable to establish groups that share their sexual orientation may struggle with the recognition of which sex they are attracted to (Bouchey & Furman, 2003; Furman & Wehner, 1997).

Romantic relationships tend to become more intense and more intimate across adolescence (Bouchey & Furman, 2003). This development can be described on the basis of the changing roles a partner may play. Romantic partners can be attachment figures, to be sought out in times of distress; companions and friends who engage in intimacy, affection, mutual cooperation, help, care, and nurturance; and sources of sexual fulfillment. A romantic partner may fill one or more of these roles, and the relative importance of particular roles may change with age or as a relationship develops (Furman & Wehner, 1997).

Early adolescents think primarily about how a romantic relationship may affect their status in the peer group (Bouchey & Furman, 2003). Early adolescents generally pay little or no attention to attachment or support needs, and their attention to sexual needs is limited to how to engage in sexual activity and which activities to engage in (Bouchey & Furman, 2003; Furman & Wehner, 1997).

In midadolescence, most young people have at least one exclusive partner lasting for several months to about a year, and the effect of the choice of partner on peer status tends to become less important (Furman & Wehner, 1997). By age 16, adolescents interact with and think about romantic partners more than parents, friends, or siblings (Bouchey & Furman, 2003). Not until late adolescence or early adulthood, though, do romantic relationships begin to serve the full gamut of

What's Your View?

• As an adolescent, were you part of a clique or crowd? If so, how did it affect your social relationships and attitudes?

emotional needs that such relationships can serve and then only in relatively long-term relationships (Furman & Wehner, 1997).

Relationships with parents and peers may affect the quality of romantic relationships (Bouchey & Furman, 2003). Adolescents tend to view their romantic attachments as secure or insecure, depending on their experience in previous close relationships (Furman & Wehner, 1997). Parents' own marriage or romantic relationship may serve as a model for their adolescent child. The peer group forms the context for most romantic relationships and may affect an adolescent's choice of a partner and the way the relationship develops. Adolescents may behave toward romantic partners much as they do toward friends, especially those of the other sex (Bouchey & Furman, 2003).

Adolescents in Trouble: Antisocial Behavior and Juvenile Delinquency

What influences young people to engage in—or refrain from—violence (see Box 12-2) or other antisocial acts? How do "problem behaviors" escalate into chronic delinquency—an outcome Jackie Robinson managed to avoid? What determines whether a juvenile delinquent will grow up to be a hardened criminal? By what processes do antisocial tendencies develop? What interventions are most effective, and why? The answers are varied, complex, multilayered, and not yet fully understood (Rutter, 2003). The interaction between environmental and genetic or biological risk factors is one of several relevant topics that need more study.

Becoming a Delinquent: How Parental, Peer, and Community Influences Interact As Bronfenbrenner's theory would suggest, antisocial behavior seems to be influenced by multileveled, interacting factors ranging from microsystem influences, such as parenting practices and peer deviance, to macrosystem influences, such as community structure and neighborhood social support (Tolan, Gorman-Smith, & Henry, 2003). This network of interacting influences begins to be woven early in childhood.

Parents begin to shape prosocial or antisocial behavior through their responses to children's basic emotional needs (Krevans & Gibbs, 1996; Staub, 1996). Parents of children who become antisocial often failed to reinforce good behavior in early childhood and were harsh or inconsistent—or both—in punishing misbehavior (Coie & Dodge, 1998; Snyder, Cramer, Afrank, & Patterson, 2005). They tended to believe that their children purposely misbehaved (Snyder et al., 2005). Through the years these parents may not have been closely and positively involved in their children's lives (G. R. Patterson, DeBaryshe, & Ramsey, 1989). The children may get payoffs for antisocial behavior: When they act up, they may gain attention or get their own way. These early negative patterns pave the way for negative peer influences that promote and reinforce antisocial behavior (Collins et al., 2000; B. B. Brown, Mounts, Lamborn, & Steinberg, 1993).

Genetic studies have found that choice of antisocial peers is affected mainly by environmental factors (Iervolino et al., 2002). Young people gravitate to others brought up like themselves who are similar in school achievement, adjustment, and prosocial or antisocial tendencies (Collins et al., 2000; B. B. Brown, Mounts, Lamborn, & Steinberg, 1993). Children with behavior problems tend to do poorly in school and do not get along with well-behaved classmates. Unpopular, low-achieving, and highly aggressive children gravitate toward each other and egg each other on to further misconduct (G. R. Patterson, Reid, & Dishion, 1992; Hartup, 1989, 1992, 1996a; Hartup & Stevens, 1999; Masten & Coatsworth, 1998; G. R. Patterson, Reid, & Dishion, 1992). As in childhood, antisocial adolescents tend to have antisocial

Guidepost

7. What are the root causes of antisocial behavior and juvenile delinquency, and what can be done to reduce these and other risks of adolescence?

BOX 12-2

Digging Deeper
The Youth Violence Epidemic

On April 20, 1999, 18-year-old Eric Harris and 17-year-old Dylan Klebold entered Columbine High School in Littleton, Colorado, wearing black trench coats and carrying a rifle, a semiautomatic pistol, two sawed-off shotguns, and more than 30 homemade bombs. Laughing and taunting, they began spraying bullets at fellow students, killing 12 classmates and one teacher before fatally shooting themselves.

The massacre in Littleton was not an isolated event, but school violence is not as common as is generally believed. Between 1993 and 2003, about 7 to 9 percent of high school students each year reported being threatened or injured by a weapon (gun, knife, or club) on school property (DeVoe et al., 2004); and between July 1, 1999 and June 30, 2000, 24 people, 16 of them children, were killed at school. Although the occasional youth killing may make the headlines, such crimes as forcible rape, robbery, and assault are much more prevalent (Snyder, 2000). Between 1992 and 2002, the rate of violent crimes at school against students ages 12 to 18 dropped by about half, as did the proportion of students who admitted carrying a weapon to school (DeVoe et al., 2004).

School violence is not a peculiarly U.S. phenomenon. In a Japanese elementary school in June 2004, an 11-year-old girl stabbed her 12–year-old classmate to death after an argument over messages sent to each other over the Internet—one of several such incidents in recent years ("Japan in shock at school murder," 2004). A survey by the World Health Organization found young adolescents in the United States no more likely to engage in violence than youth in four other industrialized countries: Ireland, Israel, Portugal, and Sweden. Forty percent of adolescents in all five countries had engaged in occasional fights during the previous year, about 11 percent carried weapons, and about 15 percent were injured in fights (Smith-Khuri et al., 2004).

In the United States, gun violence is a leading killer of children and adolescents. Each year 3,500 adolescents are murdered and more than 150,000 arrested for violent crimes. Black males are disproportionately both offenders and victims (AAP Committee on Public Education, 2001a).

Why do some young people engage in such destructive behavior? One answer lies in the immaturity of the adolescent brain, particularly the prefrontal cortex, which is critical to judgment and impulse suppression (refer back to Chapter 11). Another answer is ready access to guns in a culture that "romanticizes gunplay" (Weinberger, 2001, p. 2).

Youth violence is strongly related to the presence of gangs at school (NCES, 2003; "Youth Violence," 2001). For many adolescents, gangs satisfy unfulfilled needs for identity, connection, and a sense of power and control. For young people who lack positive family relationships, a gang can become a substitute family. Gangs promote a sense of "us-versus-them." Violence against outsiders strengthens bonds of loyalty and support within the gang (Staub, 1996).

Teenage violence and antisocial behavior have roots in childhood. Children, especially boys, who are aggressive in elementary school tend to be violently antisocial in adolescence (Broidy et al.,

These sixteen-year-old girls console each other at a vigil service for victims of a shooting spree by teenage gunmen at Columbine High School in Littleton, Colorado, on April 20, 1999. This and other school shootings are part of what has been called an epidemic of youth violence.

—continued

2003). Children raised in a rejecting or coercive atmosphere or in an overly permissive or chaotic one tend to behave aggressively, and the hostility they evoke in others increases their own aggression. Their negative self-image prevents them from succeeding at school or developing other constructive interests, and they generally associate with peers who reinforce their antisocial attitudes and behavior (Staub, 1996). Boys in poor, unstable inner-city neighborhoods with high crime rates and low community involvement and neighborhood support are most likely to become involved in violence (Tolan et al., 2003), but the shootings at Columbine show that even middle-class students in a suburban school are not immune.

Adolescents are more likely to develop conduct problems, such as fighting and vandalism, if they have witnessed or have been victims of neighborhood violence or have been exposed to media violence (Pearce, Jones, Schwab-Stone, & Ruchkin, 2003; Strasburger & Donnerstein, 1999). As we discussed in Chapter 10, a steady diet of media violence can breed aggression, and adolescents are no exception (Johnson, Cohen, Smailes, Kasen, & Brook, 2002). Religiosity and parental involvement tend to buffer the negative effects of exposure to violence (Pearce et al., 2003).

Psychologists point to potential warning signs. Adolescents likely to commit violence often refuse to listen to parents and teachers; ignore the feelings and rights of others; mistreat people; rely on violence or threats to solve problems; and believe that life has treated them unfairly. They tend to do poorly in school; to cut classes or play truant; to be held back or suspended or to drop out; to be victims of bullying; to use alcohol, inhalants, and/or drugs; to engage in early sexual activity; to join gangs; and to fight, steal, or destroy property (American Psychological Association and American Academy of Pediatrics [AAP], 1996; Resnick et al., 1997; Smith-Khuri et al., 2004; "Youth Violence," 2001). Harris and Klebold showed several of these characteristics.

A report by the Surgeon General of the United States challenges some myths, or stereotypes, about youth violence ("Youth violence," 2001; see table below). One of the worst is the myth that nothing can be done to prevent or treat violent behavior. School-based programs designed to prevent violent behavior by promoting social competence and emotional awareness and control have been modestly successful (Henrich, Brown, & Aber, 1999). Unfortunately, about half of the hundreds of programs being used in schools and communities fall short when rigorously evaluated. A program in Galveston, Texas, that addressed specific risk factors led to a drop in arrests for juvenile crime (Thomas, Holzer, & Wall, 2002).

What's Your View?

What methods for controlling youth violence seem to you most likely to work?

Check It Out

For more information on this topic, go to http://www .searchinstitute.org. The Search Institute is an organization dedicated to "raising caring and responsible children and teenagers" by providing "developmental assets" and creating healthy communities.

Five Myths About Youth Violence

Myth	Fact
Most future offenders can be identified in early childhood.	Children with conduct disorders or uncontrolled behavior do not necessarily turn out to be violent adolescents.
African American and Hispanic youth are more likely than other ethnic youth to become involved in violence.	Although arrest rates differ, self-reports suggest that race and ethnicity have little effect on the overall proportion of nonfatal violent behavior.
A new breed of "super-predators," who grew to adolescence in the 1990s, threatens to make the United States an even more violent place than it is.	There is no evidence that young people involved in violence during the peak 1990s were more violent or more vicious than youths in earlier years.
Trying young offenders in tough adult criminal courts makes them less likely to commit more violent crimes.	Juveniles handled in adult courts have significantly higher rates of repeat offenses and of later felonies than young offenders handled in juvenile courts.
Most violent youths will end up being arrested for violent crimes.	Most youths involved in violent behavior will never be arrested for a violent crime.

Source: Based on data from "Youth Violence," 2001.

friends, and their antisocial behavior increases when they associate with each other (Dishion, McCord, & Poulin, 1999; Hartup & Stevens, 1999; Vitaro, Tremblay, Kerr, Pagani, & Bukowski, 1997). The way antisocial teenagers talk, laugh, or smirk about rule breaking and nod knowingly among themselves constitutes a sort of "deviancy training" (Dishion et al., 1999). These "problem children" continue to elicit ineffective parenting, which predicts delinquent behavior and association with deviant peer groups or gangs (Simons, Chao, Conger, & Elder, 2001; Tolan et al., 2003).

Authoritative parenting can help young people internalize standards that may insulate them against negative peer influences and open them to positive ones (Collins et al., 2000; Mounts & Steinberg, 1995). Improved parenting during adolescence can reduce delinquency by discouraging association with deviant peers (Simons et al., 2001). As we have discussed, adolescents whose parents know where they are and what they are doing are less likely to engage in delinquent acts (Laird, Pettit, Bates, & Dodge, 2003) or to associate with deviant peers (Lloyd & Anthony, 2003).

Family circumstances may influence the development of antisocial behavior. Persistent economic deprivation can undermine sound parenting by depriving the family of social capital. Poor children are more likely than other children to commit antisocial acts, and those whose families are continuously poor tend to become more antisocial with time. When families rise from poverty while a child is still young, the child is no more likely to develop behavior problems than a child whose family was never poor (Macmillan, McMorris, & Kruttschnitt, 2004).

Collective efficacy—the strength of social connections within a neighborhood and the extent to which residents monitor or supervise each other's children—can make a difference (Sampson, 1997). A combination of nurturant, involved parenting and collective efficacy can discourage adolescents from association with deviant peers (Brody et al., 2001).

Long-Term Prospects Many, if not most, adolescents, like Jackie Robinson and his friends, at some point engage in antisocial behavior or even in violence. The vast majority of these young people do not become adult criminals but rather tame their urges to sow "wild oats" (Kosterman, Graham, Hawkins, Catalano, & Herrenkohl, 2001; Moffitt, 1993).

Delinquency peaks at about age 15 and then declines as most adolescents and their families come to terms with young people's need to assert independence. However, teenagers who do not see positive alternatives are more likely to adopt a permanently antisocial lifestyle (Elliott, 1993). Those most likely to persist in violence are boys who had early antisocial influences. Least likely to persist are boys and girls who were early school achievers and girls who showed early prosocial development (Kosterman et al., 2001). Because adolescents' character is still in flux, many developmental psychologists deplore the current trend toward transferring juvenile offenders from the juvenile court system, which is aimed at rehabiliation, to criminal courts where they are tried and sentenced as adults (Steinberg, 2000; Steinberg & Scott, 2003).

Preventing and Treating Delinquency Because juvenile delinquency has roots early in childhood, so should preventive efforts that attack the multiple factors that can lead to delinquency. Adolescents who have taken part in certain early childhood intervention programs are less likely to get in trouble than their equally underprivileged peers (Yoshikawa, 1994; Zigler, Taussig, & Black, 1992). Effective programs are those that targeted high-risk urban children and lasted at least two years during the child's first five years of life. They influenced children directly, through high-quality day care or education, and at the same time indirectly, by offering families assistance and support geared to their needs (Berrueta-Clement et al., 1985;

What's Your View?

• How should society deal with youthful offenders?

Will this street gang member, who has served time in prison, become a hardened criminal? Teenagers who do not see positive alternatives are more likely to adopt a permanently antisocial lifestyle. Those most likely to persist in antisocial behavior are boys who had early antisocial influences. Harsh or inconsistent parenting, association with deviant peers, a troubled neighborhood—all these interwoven factors may contribute.

Berrueta-Clement, Schweinhart, Barnett, & Weikart, 1987; Schweinhart et al., 1993; Seitz, 1990; Yoshikawa, 1994; Zigler et al., 1992).

These programs operated on Bronfenbrenner's mesosystem by affecting interactions between the home and the school or child care center. The programs also went one step further to the exosystem by creating supportive parent networks and linking parents with such community services as prenatal and postnatal care and educational and vocational counseling (Yoshikawa, 1994; Zigler et al., 1992). Through their multipronged approach, these interventions had an impact on several early risk factors for delinquency.

The Chicago Child-Parent Centers, a preschool program for disadvantaged children in the Chicago Public Schools, offers follow-up services through age 9. Participants studied at age 20 had better educational and social outcomes and fewer juvenile arrests than a comparison group who had received less extensive early interventions (Reynolds et al., 2001).

Once children reach adolescence, especially in poor, crime-ridden neighborhoods, interventions need to focus on spotting troubled adolescents and preventing gang recruitment by bolstering parenting skills and neighborhood social support (Tolan et al., 2003). Adult-monitored activities after school, on weekend evenings, and in summer, when adolescents are most likely to be idle and to get in trouble, can reduce their exposure to high-risk settings that encourage antisocial behavior. As Jackie Robinson's experience shows, getting teenagers involved in constructive activities during their free time can pay long-range dividends (Larson, 1998). Participation in extracurricular school activities tends to cut down on dropout and criminal arrest rates among high-risk boys and girls (Mahoney, 2000).

One multifaceted intervention, Equipping Youth to Help One Another (EQUIP), uses daily, adult-guided peer support groups. Peers help teach each other how to manage anger, make moral decisions, and learn social skills (Gibbs, Potter, Barriga, & Liau, 1996; Gibbs, Potter, Goldstein, & Brendtro, 1998). Among 57 male juvenile offenders in a medium-security correctional facility, EQUIP participants improved significantly in conduct within the institution and had lower repeat offense rates during the first year after release than control groups that did not have the training (Leeman, Gibbs, & Fuller, 1993).

Fortunately, the great majority of adolescents do not get into serious trouble. Those who do show disturbed behavior can—and should—be helped. With love, guidance, and support, adolescents can avoid risks, build on their strengths, and explore their possibilities as they approach adult life.

Checkpoint

Can you . . .

✔ Explain how parental, peer, and neighborhood influences may interact to promote antisocial behavior and delinquency?

✔ Give examples of programs that have been successful in preventing or stopping delinquency and other risky behavior?

Refocus

Thinking back to the Focus vignette about Jackie Robinson at the beginning of this chapter:

• What evidence suggests that Jackie Robinson may have gone through Erikson's stage of identity versus identity confusion?

• Which of Marcia's identity statuses did Robinson seem to fall into at that time, both with regard to his identity in general and his ethnicity in particular?

• Did Robinson's relationships with his mother and his peers seem consistent with the findings reported in this chapter?

• Would you say that Robinson showed adolescent rebellion?

• Based on the material in this chapter, why do you think Robinson did not become a full-fledged juvenile delinquent?

The normal developmental changes in the early years of life are obvious and dramatic signs of growth. The infant lying in the crib becomes an active, exploring toddler. The young child enters and embraces the worlds of school and society. The adolescent, with a new body and new awareness, prepares to step into adulthood.

Growth and development do not screech to a stop after adolescence. People change in many ways throughout early, middle, and late adulthood, as we will see in the remaining chapters of this book.

SUMMARY AND KEY TERMS

The Search for Identity

Guidepost 1: How do adolescents form an identity?

- A central concern during adolescence is the search for identity, which has occupational, sexual, and values components. Erik Erikson described the psychosocial conflict of adolescence as *identity versus identity confusion*. The "virtue" that should arise from this conflict is *fidelity*.

- James Marcia, in research based on Erikson's theory, described four identity statuses: identity achievement, foreclosure, moratorium, and identity diffusion.

- Researchers differ on whether girls and boys take different paths to identity formation. Although some research suggests that girls' self-esteem tends to fall in adolescence, later research does not support that finding.

- Ethnicity is an important part of identity. Minority adolescents seem to go through stages of ethnic identity development much like Marcia's identity statuses.

  identity *(437)*

  identity versus identity confusion *(437)*

  identity statuses *(439)*

  identity achievement *(439)*

  foreclosure *(439)*

  moratorium *(439)*

  identity diffusion *(439)*

  crisis *(439)*

  commitment *(439)*

Sexuality

Guidepost 2: What determines sexual orientation, and how do people become aware of their sexual identity?

- Sexual orientation appears to be influenced by an interaction of biological and environmental factors and to be at least partly genetic.

- The course of homosexual identity and relationship development may vary with cohort, gender, and ethnicity.

  sexual orientation *(443)*

Guidepost 3: What sexual practices are common among adolescents, and what leads some teenagers to engage in risky sexual behavior?

- Teenage sexual activity is more prevalent than in the past but involves risks of pregnancy and sexually transmitted disease. Adolescents at greatest risk are those who begin sexual activity early, have multiple partners, do not use contraceptives, and are ill-informed about sex.

- Regular condom use is the best safeguard for sexually active teens.

- Comprehensive sex education programs delay sexual initiation and encourage contraceptive use. Abstinence-only programs have not been as effective.

Guidepost 4: How common are sexually transmitted diseases and teenage pregnancy, and what are their usual outcomes?

- Rates of sexually transmitted diseases (STDs) in the United States are among the highest in the industrialized world. STDs can be transmitted by oral sex as well as intercourse. They are more likely to develop undetected in girls than in boys.

- Teenage pregnancy and birthrates in the United States have declined. Most of the births are to unmarried mothers.

- Teenage childbearing often has negative outcomes. Teenage mothers and their families tend to suffer ill health and financial hardship, and the children often suffer from ineffective parenting.

  sexually transmitted diseases (STDs) *(448)*

Relationships with Family, Peers, and Adult Society

Guidepost 5: How typical is "adolescent rebellion"?

- Although relationships between adolescents and their parents are not always smooth, full-scale adolescent rebellion is unusual. For the majority of teens, adolescence is a fairly smooth transition. For the minority who seem more deeply troubled, it can predict a troubled adulthood.

  adolescent rebellion *(453)*

Guidepost 6: How do adolescents relate to parents, siblings, and peers?

- Adolescents spend an increasing amount of time with peers, but relationships with parents continue to be influential.
- Conflict with parents tends to be most frequent during early adolescence and most intense during middle adolescence. Authoritative parenting is associated with the most positive outcomes.
- Effects of divorce, single parenting, and maternal employment on adolescents' development depend on such factors as economic resources, the quality of the home environment, and how closely parents monitor adolescents' whereabouts. Parental cohabitation seems to have more negative effects on teenagers than on younger children.
- Relationships with siblings tend to become more distant during adolescence, and the balance of power between older and younger siblings becomes more equal.

- The influence of the peer group is strongest in early adolescence. The structure of the peer group becomes more elaborate, involving cliques and crowds as well as friendships.
- Friendships, especially among girls, become more intimate, stable, and supportive in adolescence.
- Romantic relationships meet a variety of needs and develop with age and experience.

Guidepost 7: What are the root causes of antisocial behavior and juvenile delinquency, and what can be done to reduce the risks of adolescence?

- Chronic delinquency is associated with multiple interacting risk factors, including ineffective parenting, school failure, peer influence, and low socioeconomic status. Programs that attack such risk factors from an early age have had success.

PART 6

Linkups
to look for

- Income, education, and marital status influence health.

- Cognitive and moral development reflect life experience.

- Emotions may play a part in intelligence.

- Gender-typing may affect women's choice of careers and use of their talents.

- The gender revolution has diminished differences in men's and women's life course and health patterns.

- Infertility can lead to marital problems.

- Pressures at work can affect family relationships.

- People without friends or family are more likely to become ill and die.

At one time, developmental scientists considered the years from the end of adolescence to the onset of old age a relatively uneventful plateau, but research tells us that this is not so. Growth and decline go on throughout life, in a balance that differs for each individual. Choices and events during young adulthood (which we define approximately as the span between ages 20 and 40) have much to do with how that balance is struck.

During these two decades, as we see in Chapters 13 and 14, human beings build a foundation for much of their later development. This is when people typically leave their parents' homes, start jobs or careers, get married or establish other intimate relationships, have and raise children, and begin to contribute significantly to their communities. They make decisions that will affect the rest of their lives—their health, their happiness, and their success. However, the transition from adolescence to the responsibilities of adulthood is not necessarily immediate and clearcut. As we discuss in Chapters 13 and 14, developmental scientists have now identified this transition as a period of *emerging adulthood*.

Young Adulthood

Physical and Cognitive Development in Young Adulthood

If . . . happiness is the absence of fever then I will never know happiness. For I am possessed by a fever for knowledge, experience, and creation.

Diary of Anaïs Nin (1931–1934),
written when she was between 28 and 31

Focus
Arthur Ashe, Tennis Champion*

Arthur Ashe

The tennis champion Arthur Ashe (1943–1993) was one of the most respected athletes of all time. "Slim, bookish and bespectacled" (Finn, 1993, p. B1), he was known for his quiet, dignified manner on and off the court; he did not dispute calls, indulge in temper tantrums, or disparage opponents.

The first African American to win the Wimbledon tournament and the United States and Australian Opens, Ashe grew up in Richmond, Virginia, where he began playing on segregated public courts and was barred from a city tennis tournament because of his race. As a young adult, the only black star in a white-dominated game, Ashe was a target for bigotry; but he maintained his composure and channeled his aggressive impulses into the game.

Ashe used his natural physical gifts and stellar reputation to combat racism and increase opportunity for disadvantaged youth. He conducted tennis clinics and helped establish tennis programs for inner-city youngsters. Twice refused a visa to play in the South African Open, he was finally allowed to compete in 1973 and again in 1974 and 1975. Despite South Africa's rigid apartheid system of racial separation, he insisted on nonsegregated seating at his matches.

Ashe continued to work against apartheid, for the most part quietly, behind the scenes. Accused of being an "Uncle Tom" by angry militants who shouted him down while he was giving a speech, he politely rebuked them: "What do you expect to achieve when you give in to passion and invective and surrender the high moral ground that alone can bring you to victory?" (Ashe & Rampersad, 1993, pp. 117, 118). Several years later, he was arrested in a protest outside the South African embassy in Washington, D.C. He felt tremendous pride when he saw Nelson Mandela, the symbol of opposition to apartheid, released from prison in 1990, riding in a ticker-tape

*Sources of biographical information about Arthur Ashe were Ashe and Rampersad (1993), Finn (1993), and Witteman (1993).

471

parade in New York City. But Ashe would not live to see Mandela become president of South Africa.

In 1979, at age 36, at the height of a brilliant career, Ashe suffered the first of several heart attacks and underwent quadruple bypass surgery. Forced to retire from competitive play, he served for five years as captain of the U.S. Davis Cup team. In 1985, barely past young adulthood, he was inducted into the Tennis Hall of Fame.

One summer morning in 1988, Ashe woke up and could not move his right arm. He was given two options: immediate brain surgery, or wait and see. He opted for action. Preparatory blood tests showed that he had AIDS, probably from a blood transfusion during his heart surgery five years earlier. Ashe refused to panic or to give up. Relying on the best medical knowledge, he chose to do all he could to fight his illness. He also chose to keep quiet about it—in part to protect his family's privacy and in part because, as he insisted, "I am not sick." He played golf, appeared on the lecture circuit, wrote columns for the *Washington Post,* was a television commentator for HBO and ABC Sports, and composed a three-volume history of African American athletes.

In 1992, warned that *USA Today* planned to reveal his secret, Ashe called a press conference and announced that he had AIDS. He became a tireless leader in the movement for AIDS research, establishing a foundation and launching a $5 million fund-raising campaign.

Ashe died of AIDS-related pneumonia in 1993, at age 49. Shortly before, he had summed up his situation in his usual style: "I am a fortunate, blessed man. Aside from AIDS and heart disease, I have no problems" (Ashe & Rampersad, 1993, p. 328).

Arthur Ashe's characteristic way of coping with trouble or bigotry was to meet it as he did an opponent on the tennis court: with grace, determination, moral conviction, and coolness under fire. Again and again, he turned adversity into opportunity. Arthur Ashe was a "can-do" person.

Even for people who lack Ashe's outstanding athletic skills, young adulthood typically is a "can-do" period. Most people at this age are on their own for the first time, setting up and running households and proving themselves in their chosen pursuits. Every day, they test and expand their physical and cognitive abilities. They encounter the "real world" and find their way through or around problems of everyday living. They make decisions that help determine their health, their careers, and the kinds of people they wish to be.

In this chapter, we look at young adults' physical functioning, which is usually at its height; and we note factors that can affect health in young adulthood and in later life. We discuss aspects of cognition that come to the fore in adulthood, and how education can stimulate cognitive growth. We examine how culture and gender affect moral development. Finally, we discuss one of the most important tasks during this period: entering the world of work.

After you have read and studied this chapter, you should be able to answer each of the Guidepost questions that follow. Look for them again in the margins, where they point to important concepts throughout the chapter. To check your understanding of these Guideposts, review the end-of-chapter summary. Checkpoints located at periodic spots throughout the chapter will help you verify your understanding of what you have read.

1. What does it mean to be an adult, and what factors affect the timing of entrance to adulthood?

2. In what physical condition is the typical young adult, and what factors affect health and well-being?

3. What are some sexual and reproductive issues at this time of life?

4. What is distinctive about adult thought and intelligence?

5. How does moral reasoning develop?

6. How do emerging adults make the transitions to higher education and work, and how do these experiences affect cognitive development?

7. How can young people be helped to make the transition to the workplace?

Emerging Adulthood

When does a person become an adult? Contemporary U.S. society has a variety of markers. *Sexual maturation,* as we discussed in Chapter 11, arrives during adolescence; *cognitive* maturity, which Piaget defined as the capacity for abstract thought, may take longer. There are *legal* definitions of adulthood: At 17, young people may enlist in the armed forces; at 18, they can vote, and, in most states, they may marry without their parents' permission; at 18 to 21 (depending on the state), they may enter into binding contracts. Using *sociological* definitions, people may be considered adults when they are self-supporting or have chosen a career, have married or formed a significant romantic partnership, or have started a family.

Psychological maturity may depend on such achievements as discovering one's identity, becoming independent of parents, developing a system of values, and forming relationships. Some psychologists suggest that the onset of adulthood is marked, not by external criteria, but by such internal indicators as a sense of autonomy, self-control, and personal responsibility—that it is more a state of mind than a discrete event (Shanahan, Porfeli, & Mortimer, 2005). From this point of view, some people never become adults, no matter what their chronological age.

In modern industrialized countries, entrance into adulthood takes longer and follows more varied routes than in the past. Before the mid-twentieth century, a young man just out of high school could, in short order, obtain a stable job, marry, and start a family. For a young woman, the chief route to adulthood was marriage, which occurred as soon as she could find a suitable mate. Since the 1950s, the technological revolution has made higher education or specialized training increasingly essential. The gender revolution has brought more women into the workforce and broadened accepted female roles (Furstenberg, Rumbaut, & Settersten, Jr., 2005; Fussell & Furstenberg, 2005). Today the road to adulthood may be marked by multiple milestones—entering college (full or part time), working (full or part time), moving away from home, getting married, and having children—and the order and timing of these transitions vary (Schulenberg, O'Malley, Bachman, & Johnston, 2005). Thus, some developmental scientists suggest that the period from the late teens through the mid- to late twenties has become a distinct period of the life

Guidepost

1. What does it mean to be an adult, and what factors affect the timing of entrance to adulthood?

What's Your View?

• What criteria for adulthood do you consider most relevant?

• Do you think those criteria are influenced by the culture in which you live or grew up?

Checkpoint

Can you . . .

✔ Compare varying conceptions of what it means to be an adult?

✔ Explain how the process of entrance to adulthood has changed in the United States and other technologically advanced societies, and tell what is meant by emerging adulthood?

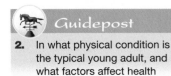

emerging adulthood Proposed transitional period between adolescence and adulthood, usually extending from the late teens through the midtwenties.

course, **emerging adulthood**—a time when young people are no longer adolescents but have not yet become fully adult (Arnett, 2000, 2004; Furstenberg et al., 2005). We will look more closely at the varied paths of emerging adulthood later in this chapter and in Chapter 14.

PHYSICAL DEVELOPMENT

Health and Physical Condition

Guidepost

2. In what physical condition is the typical young adult, and what factors affect health and well-being?

Your favorite spectator sport may be tennis, basketball, figure skating, or football. Whatever it is, most of the athletes you root for (like Arthur Ashe in his time) are young adults, people in prime physical condition. Most young adults are at their peak of health, strength, energy, endurance, and sensory and motor functioning. Visual acuity is keenest from about age 20 to age 40; taste, smell, and sensitivity to pain and temperature generally remain undiminished until at least 45. However, a gradual hearing loss, especially for higher-pitched sounds, typically begins during adolescence and becomes more apparent after age 25.

Health Status

Most young adults in the United States are in good to excellent health; only 5.5 percent of 18- to 44-year-olds call their health fair or poor. The most common sources of activity limitations are arthritis and other muscular and skeletal disorders. Accidents are the leading cause of death for young Americans up to age 44 (NCHS, 2004). Death rates for young adults have been nearly cut in half during the past 50 years, and mortality rates for other age groups have dropped as well (Kochanek, Murphy, Anderson, & Scott, 2004; Pastor, Makuc, Reuben, & Xia, 2002). On the other hand, too many adults—even young ones—are overweight, get too little exercise, and engage in other health-threatening behaviors.

In young adulthood, the foundation for lifelong physical functioning is laid. Health may in part be influenced by the genes, but behavioral factors—what young adults eat, whether they get enough sleep, how physically active they are, and whether they smoke, drink, or use drugs—contribute greatly to present and future health and well-being. Poverty and racial discrimination also contribute to disparities in health (Sankar et al., 2004).

Playing volleyball takes strength, energy, endurance, and muscular coordination. Young adults like these typically are in prime physical condition.

Genetic Influences on Health

The mapping of the human genome is enabling scientists to discover genetic roots of many disorders, from obesity to certain cancers (notably lung, prostate, and breast cancer) to mental health conditions, such as alcoholism (discussed later in this chapter) and depression. For example, researchers have identified 19 different chromosomal regions linked with familial early-onset depression (Zubenko et al., 2003). Scientists also have discovered a genetic component in HIV/AIDS, one of the top six killers in young adults (Anderson & Smith, 2005). People with more copies of a gene that helps fight HIV are less likely to become infected with the virus or to develop AIDS than people of the same regional ancestry who have fewer copies of the gene (Gonzalez et al., 2005).

Atherosclerosis, or narrowing of the arteries, may begin in childhood and can become a threat by the forties or fifties. One risk factor for atherosclerosis is cholesterol levels in the blood. (Other risk factors are high blood pressure and smoking.) Cholesterol, in combination with proteins and triglycerides (fatty acids), circulates through the bloodstream, carried by low-density lipoprotein (LDL), commonly called "bad" cholesterol. High-density lipoprotein (HDL), or "good" cholesterol, flushes cholesterol out of the system. An estimated 80 percent of the variation in HDL levels within the population is due to genetic factors ("How to Raise HDL," 2001). However, as we discuss in the next section, behavioral factors also influence cholesterol levels. Indeed, most diseases involve both genetic and environmental influences.

Behavioral Influences on Health and Fitness

The link between behavior and health illustrates the interrelationship among physical, cognitive, and emotional aspects of development. What people know about health affects what they do, and what they do affects how they feel.

Preventive measures can pay dividends. Regular screening tests, such as pap smears to detect cervical cancer and testicular or breast self-examinations to detect lumps, can prevent diseases or catch them in early, treatable stages. Many musculoskeletal disorders are work related and preventable. Back injuries often result from overexertion in lifting, pushing, pulling, or carrying objects. Repetitive motion injuries, such as carpal tunnel syndrome, can be controlled by such measures as proper placement of computer keyboards and good posture (Bernard, 1997; National Research Council, 1998, 2001).

Knowing about good health habits is not enough, however. Personality, emotions, and social surroundings often outweigh what people know they should do and lead them into unhealthful behavior. In a national random telephone survey of more than 153,000 adults, only 3 percent said they followed all four of the following healthy lifestyle indicators: not smoking, maintaining a healthy weight; eating five fruits and vegetables each day, and regular physical activity (Reeves & Rafferty, 2005).

Let's look at several lifestyle factors that are strongly and directly linked with health and fitness: diet and weight control, physical activity, sleep, and alcohol and drug use. Stress, which can activate hormonal and nervous system reactions and induce such detrimental behaviors as sleep loss, smoking, drinking, and drug use, is discussed in detail in Chapter 15. In the next section of this chapter we consider indirect influences on health: socioeconomic status, race/ethnicity, gender, and relationships.

Diet and Nutrition The saying "You are what you eat" sums up the importance of nutrition for physical and mental health. What people eat affects how they look, how they feel, and how likely they are to get sick or even die. In 2000 an estimated 365,000 U.S. adults died from causes related to poor diet and lack of physical activity (Mokdad, Marks, Stroup, & Gerberding, 2005).

Eating habits play an important part in heart disease—which, as Arthur Ashe's story shows, is not necessarily limited to later life. People who eat a variety of fruits and vegetables, especially those rich in carotenoids (such as carrots, sweet potatoes, broccoli, spinach, and cantaloupe) may lessen their chances of heart disease (Liu, Manson, Lee, et al., 2000; Rimm et al., 1996), and stroke (Gillman et al., 1995) but apparently not of breast cancer (van Gils, 2005).

National nutritional guidelines suggest that adults consume no more than 20 to 35 percent of calories from fats (including no more than 10 percent of calories from saturated fat and as little transfat as possible) and less than 300 milligrams of cholesterol each day (U.S. Department of Agriculture & USDHHS, 2005). The average American of all ages greatly exceeds those levels (Ervin, Wright, Wang, & Kennedy-Stephenson, 2004).

What's Your View?

- What specific things could you do to have a healthier lifestyle?

This juicy hamburger is dripping with calories and also is high in animal fat, which has been linked with heart disease and some cancers.

Excess fat consumption, especially of saturated fats, increases cardiovascular risks, particularly cholesterol levels (Ervin et al., 2004), which are directly related to the risk of death from coronary heart disease (Verschuren et al., 1995). Controlling cholesterol through diet and, if necessary, medication can significantly lower this risk (Scandinavian Simvastatin Survival Study Group, 1994; Shepherd et al., 1995). A diet high in animal fat or in red or processed meat has been linked with colorectal cancer (Chao et al., 2005; Willett, Stampfer, Colditz, Rosner, & Speizer, 1990) and prostate cancer (Giovannucci et al., 1993; Hebert et al., 1998; Willett, 1994; Willett et al., 1992).

Obesity/Overweight   As we mentioned in Chapter 3, *obesity* in adulthood is generally defined as having a body mass index (BMI), or weight-height comparison, of 30 or more; *overweight* is sometimes defined as having a BMI of 25 to 29.

The World Health Organization (WHO) has called obesity a worldwide epidemic (WHO, 1998). Obesity more than doubled in the United Kingdom between 1980 and 1994, and similar increases have been reported in Brazil, Canada, and several countries in Europe, the Western Pacific, Southeast Asia, and Africa (Taubes, 1998).

In the United States, the average man or woman is more than 24 pounds heavier than in the early 1960s but is only about 1 inch taller. More than 65 percent of the adult population ages 20 to 74 were overweight in 1999–2002, including 31 percent who were obese—up from 45 percent and 13 percent, respectively, in 1960–1962. Young adults are less likely to be overweight than older ones, but more than half of 20- to 34-year-old men and women were overweight in 1999–2002, and the proportion who were overweight increased dramatically after age 34 (Ogden et al., 2004).

Obesity is especially prevalent among black and Mexican American women; 50 percent of non-Hispanic black women ages 20 to 74 are obese, as compared with 39 percent of Mexican American women and 31 percent of non-Hispanic white women. Obesity has increased 60 percent among black women since 1976–1980 (NCHS, 2004). Immigrants to the United States are more likely to become overweight the longer they stay there (Goel, McCarthy, Phillips, & Wee, 2004).

What explains the obesity epidemic? Experts point to an increase in snacking (Zizza, Siega-Riz, & Popkin, 2001), availability of inexpensive "fast foods," "supersized" portions, high-fat diets, labor-saving technologies, and sedentary recreational pursuits, such as watching television and using computers (Harvard Medical School, 2004a; Pereira et al., 2005; Young & Nestle, 2002). An inherited tendency toward obesity may interact with these environmental and behavioral factors (Comuzzie & Allison, 1998; NCBI, 2002). Researchers have identified a genetic mutation in mice that may disrupt the appetite control center in the brain by inhibiting production of *leptin,* a hormone that tells the brain when the body has consumed enough (Campfield, Smith, Guisez, Devos, & Burns, 1995; Halaas et al., 1995; Pelleymounter et al., 1995; Zhang et al., 1994). In humans, overeating may result from the brain's failure to respond to this protein's signals (Campfield et al., 1998; Travis, 1996). Other weight-regulating hormones may be involved. Nearly two dozen genes are known to control the production of these hormones (Harvard Medical School, 2004a).

In a society that values slenderness, obesity can lead to emotional problems. It also carries risks of high blood pressure, heart disease, stroke, diabetes, gallstones, arthritis and other muscular and skeletal disorders, and some cancers and diminishes quality and length of life (Gregg et al., 2005; Harvard Medical School, 2004a; Hu et al., 2001, 2004; Mokdad, Bowman, et al., 2001; Mokdad, Ford, et al., 2003; NCHS, 2004; Pereira et al., 2005; Peeters et al., 2003; Sturm, 2002). Cardiovascular and mortality risks have declined in the past four decades, probably due to improved medical care, but obese adults remain at greater risk than their lean counterparts, though adults who are merely overweight apparently do not (Flegal, Graubard, Williamson, & Gail, 2005; Gregg et al., 2005). Underweight adults (those with a BMI of less than 18.5) are at greater risk than those of normal weight (BMI of 18.5 to less than 25) (Flegal et al., 2005).

Because obesity becomes more prevalent with age, prevention of weight gain during young adulthood through healthy diet and regular physical activity is the most prudent approach (Wickelgren, 1998). In a 15-year longitudinal study of more than 5,000 young men and women, those who maintained their weight—even if they were overweight—had lower risks of heart disease in middle age (Lloyd-Jones et al., 2004).

Checkpoint
Can you . . .

✔ Summarize the typical health status of young adults in the United States, and identify the leading cause of death in young adulthood?

✔ Tell how diet can affect the likelihood of cancer and heart disease?

✔ Give reasons for the "obesity epidemic"?

Physical Activity   Adults who are physically active reap many benefits. Aside from helping to maintain desirable body weight, physical activity builds muscles; strengthens heart and lungs; lowers blood pressure; protects against heart disease, stroke, diabetes, colon cancer, endometrial cancer, and osteoporosis (a thinning of the bones that is most prevalent in middle-aged and older women, causing fractures); relieves anxiety and depression; and lengthens life (Barnes & Schoenborn, 2003; Boulé, Haddad, Kenny, Wells, & Sigal, 2001; NCHS, 2004; Pratt, 1999; WHO, 2002a). Inactivity is a global public health problem. A sedentary lifestyle is one of the world's ten leading causes of death and disability (WHO, 2002a).

Even moderate exercise has health benefits (NCHS, 2004; WHO, 2002a). Incorporating more physical activity into daily life—for example, by walking instead of driving short distances, and climbing stairs instead of taking elevators—can be as effective as structured exercise (Andersen et al., 1999; Dunn et al., 1999; Pratt, 1999). Yet, despite all the advantages of exercise, about one-third of U.S. 18- to 44-year-olds—nearly 30 percent of men and 35 percent of women—engage in *no* regular leisure-time physical activity, and the percentages rise with age (NCHS, 2004). In a randomized trial of 201 sedentary women in a university-based weight control program, a combination of diet and exercise (primarily walking) for 12 months produced significant weight loss and improved cardiorespiratory fitness (Jakicic, Marcus, Gallagher, Napolitano, & Lang, 2003).

Young adults like these, who engage in regular physical activity, are likely to be healthier, happier, and live longer than if they rarely exercised.

Sleep   Many young adults, especially those who work abnormal hours, such as medical interns, go without adequate sleep (Monk, 2000). Sleep deprivation affects not only health, but also cognitive, emotional, and social functioning.

In a large-scale poll by the National Sleep Foundation (2001), respondents said they were more likely to make mistakes, become impatient or aggravated when waiting, or to get upset with their children or others when they had not had enough sleep the night before. Sleep deprivation can be lethal on the road; drowsy drivers cause an estimated 3.6 percent of all fatal crashes (Peters et al., 1994). Sleep deprivation may even lead to premature aging. In one study, 36 hours of sleep deprivation in young adults produced effects on the prefrontal cortex—a part of the brain heavily involved in working memory and verbal fluency—similar to those found in nonsleep-deprived 60-year-olds (Harrison, Horne, & Rothwell, 2000).

Adequate sleep improves learning of complex motor skills (Walker, Brakefield, Morgan, Hobson, & Stickgold, 2002) and consolidates previous learning. Even a short nap can prevent burnout—oversaturation of the brain's perceptual processing systems (Mednick et al., 2002). Sleep deprivation tends to impair verbal learning (Horne, 2000), some aspects of memory (Harrison & Horne, 2000b) and speech articulation (Harrison & Horne, 1997), and to increase distractibility (Blagrove,

Alexander, & Horne, 1995). Impairment seems to be selective, mainly affecting dull, monotonous tasks (Horne, 2000). However, high-level decision making can be impaired, especially in emergency situations that require innovation, flexibility, avoidance of distraction, realistic risk assessment, metamemory, and communication skills (Harrison & Horne, 2000a).

Compensatory changes in the brain can help maintain initial cognitive performance after short-term loss of sleep (Drummond et al., 2000). However, chronic sleep deprivation (less than six hours' sleep each night for three or more nights) can seriously worsen cognitive performance even when a person is not aware of it (Van Dongen, Maislin, Mullington, & Dinges, 2003).

Because smoking is addictive, it is hard for some smokers to quit despite knowledge of the health risks. Smoking is especially harmful to African Americans, who metabolize more nicotine in their blood and are more subject to lung cancer than white Americans.

Smoking Smoking has become less common in the United States since 1964, when the U.S. Surgeon General reported a link between cigarette smoking and lung cancer, but the decline has slowed since 1990. Smoking is still the leading preventable cause of death among U.S. adults, linked not only to lung cancer, but also to increased risks of heart disease, stroke, and chronic lung disease (NCHS, 2004). Smoking is also associated with cancer of the stomach, liver, larynx, mouth, esophagus, bladder, kidney, pancreas, and cervix; gastrointestinal problems, such as ulcers; respiratory illnesses, such as bronchitis and emphysema; and osteoporosis (Hopper & Seeman, 1994; International Agency for Cancer Research, 2002; National Institute on Aging [NIA], 1993; Slemenda, 1994; Trimble et al., 2005).

Secondhand, or passive, smoke exposes nonsmokers to the same carcinogens that active smokers inhale (International Agency for Cancer Research, 2002). Exposure to passive smoke—even for only 30 minutes—has been shown to cause circulatory dysfunction and increase the risk of cardiovascular disease (Otsuka et al., 2001). Passive smoke also may increase the risk of cervical cancer (Trimble et al., 2005).

Despite these risks, about 1 in 4 men and 1 in 5 women over 18 in the United States are current smokers (NCHS, 2004). Emerging adults ages 18 to 25 are more likely to smoke than any other age group (see Figure 13-1); nearly 45 percent report using tobacco products, mostly cigarettes (Substance Abuse and Mental Health Services Adminstration (SAMHSA), 2004b). American Indians are most likely and Asian Americans least likely to smoke (Lethbridge-Cejku et al., 2004; SAMHSA, 2004b).

Figure 13-1

Current (past month) cigarette use and nicotine dependence by age: U.S., 2003. Cigarette use peaks in emerging adulthood, but the proportion of users who are nicotine-dependent generally increases with age. (Source: SAMHSA, 2004b, Figure 4.7.)

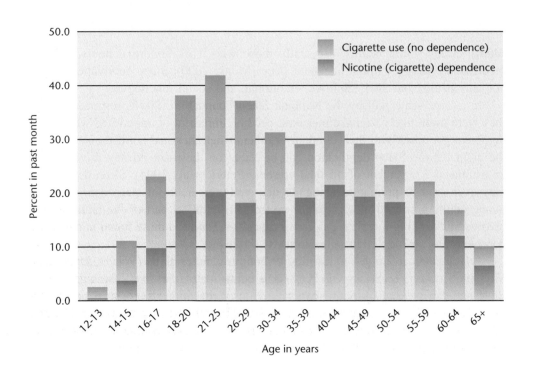

In 2000, smoking killed almost 5 million people worldwide, about half in developing countries and half in industrialized countries. More than half of these deaths were of smokers ages 30 to 69. Men were three times as likely as women to die prematurely from smoking (Ezzati & Lopez, 2004). By 2020, if current trends continue, tobacco will account for one-third of all adult deaths in the world (International Agency for Cancer Research, 2002; WHO, 2002b).

In view of the known risks of smoking, why do many people do it? One reason is that smoking is addictive. A tendency to addiction may be genetic, and certain genes may affect the ability to quit (Lerman et al., 1999; Pianezza et al., 1998; Sabol et al., 1999). The omnipresence of smoking in the media (refer back to Chapter 11) can be another powerful influence.

Giving up smoking reduces the risks of heart disease and stroke (Kawachi et al., 1993; NIA, 1993; Wannamethee, Shaper, Whincup, & Walker, 1995). Nicotine chewing gum, nicotine patches, and nicotine nasal sprays and inhalers, especially when combined with counseling, can help addicted persons taper off gradually and safely. Long-term, however, nicotine therapy does not work as well for women as for men unless it is part of a more comprehensive smoking cessation program (Cepeda-Benito, Reynoso, & Erath, 2004).

Alcohol The United States is a drinking society. Advertising equates liquor, beer, and wine with the good life and with being "grown up." Alcohol use peaks in emerging adulthood; about 70 percent of 21- to 25-year-olds report using alcohol in the past month, and nearly 48 percent of 21-year-olds are binge drinkers, downing five or more drinks in one session (SAMHSA, 2004b).

College is a prime time and place for drinking. Although frequent drinking is common at this age, college students tend to drink more frequently and more heavily than their noncollegiate peers (SAMHSA, 2004b). Alcohol use is associated with other risks characteristic of young adulthood, such as traffic accidents, crime, and HIV infection (Leigh, 1999) and illicit drug and tobacco use. More than 31 percent of 18- to 24-year-old college students admit to driving under the influence of alcohol. Each year more than 1,700 college students die from alcohol-related injuries (Hingson, Heeren, Winter, & Wechsler, 2005), and drinking contributes to 70,000 cases of date rape or sexual assault (SAMHSA, 2001; NIAAA, 2002).

Light-to-moderate alcohol consumption seems to reduce the risk of fatal heart disease and stroke, and also of dementia later in life (Ruitenberg et al., 2002). However, heavy drinking over the years may lead to cirrhosis of the liver, other gastrointestinal disorders (including ulcers), pancreatic disease, certain cancers, heart failure, stroke, damage to the nervous system, psychoses, and other medical problems (AHA, 1995; Fuchs et al., 1995). The risks of cancer of the mouth, throat, and esophagus are greater for excessive drinkers who smoke (NIAAA, 1998). Regular, long-term drinking increases the risk of breast cancer (Singletary & Gapstur, 2001; Smith-Warner et al., 1998).

Illicit Drug Use Use of illicit drugs peaks at ages 18 to 20; more than 23 percent of this age group report indulging during the past month. As emerging adults settle down and take responsibility for their future, they tend to cut down on drug use. Nearly half (46.1 percent) of adults ages 26 and older have tried illicit drugs, most commonly marijuana, but only 5.6 percent are current users. Usage rates drop sharply during the twenties, plateau at 8 to 9 percent in the thirties and early forties, and then decline again into old age (SAMHSA, 2004b; see Figure 13-2) Illicit drug use is highest among American Indians or Alaska Natives and lowest among Asian Americans (SAMHSA, 2004b).

Figure 13-2

Current (past month) illicit drug use by age: 2003. (Source: SAMHSA, 2004b, Figure 2.5.)

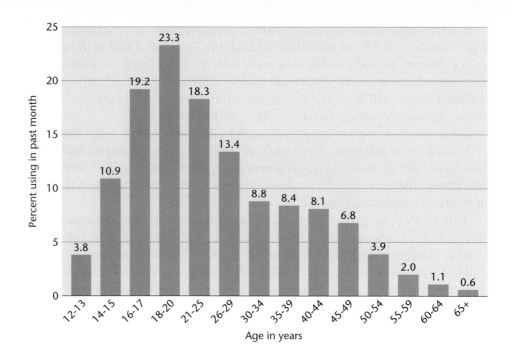

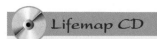

Is marijuana really harmful? Watch the video, "Marijuana Use Among Young Adults," in Chapter 13 of your CD for one expert's perspective.

As in adolescence, marijuana is by far the most popular illicit drug among young adults. In 2003, 17 percent of 18- to 25-year-olds had used marijuana within the previous month as compared with 2.2 percent who had used cocaine and less than 1 percent who had used inhalants (SAMHSA, 2004b).

Long-term marijuana use is associated with significant losses in memory and attention (Solowij et al., 2002). Chronic, heavy cocaine use also can impair cognitive functioning (Bolla, Cadet, & London, 1998; Bolla, Rothman, & Cadet, 1999). Although the prevalence of overall marijuana use among the adult population remained stable between 1991 and 2002, the prevalence of marijuana abuse and dependence increased, particularly among young black and Hispanic men (Compton, Grant, Colliver, Glantz, & Stinson, 2004). In 2003, adults who had used illicit drugs were more than twice as likely to have serious mental illness (18.1 percent) as adults who had never used illicit drugs (7.8 percent) (SAMHSA, 2004b).

Substance Use Disorders An estimated 1 in 10 U.S. adults meet clinical criteria for a substance use disorder involving alcohol, drugs, or both. Most prevalent are alcohol abuse and dependence, reported by 17.6 million Americans, 8.5 percent of the adult population (Grant et al., 2004).

alcoholism Chronic disease involving dependence on use of alcohol, causing interference with normal functioning and fulfillment of obligations.

Alcohol abusers repeatedly drink in hazardous situations, get in trouble because of drinking, or drink to the point of interference with social relationships or inability to fulfill normal obligations. Alcohol dependence, or **alcoholism,** is a physical condition characterized by compulsive drinking, which a person is unable to control (Grant et al., 2004). The heritability of alcoholism is 50 to 60 percent (Bouchard, 2004). The disorder runs in families; close relatives of people who are addicted to alcohol are three to four times more likely to become dependent on it than people whose relatives are not addicted (APA, 2000; McGue, 1993).

Alcoholism, like other addictions, seems to result from long-lasting changes in patterns of neural signal transmission in the brain. Exposure to a substance that creates a euphoric mental state brings about neurological adaptations that produce feelings of discomfort and craving when it is no longer present. Six to 48 hours after the last drink, alcoholics experience strong physical withdrawal symptoms (anxiety, agitation, tremors, elevated blood pressure, and sometimes seizures). Alcoholics, like drug addicts, develop a tolerance for the substance and need more and more to get the desired high (NIAAA, 1996b).

Treatment for alcoholism may include detoxification (removing all alcohol from the body), hospitalization, medication, individual and group psychotherapy, and referral to a support organization, such as Alcoholics Anonymous. Although not a cure, treatment can give alcoholics new tools for coping with their addiction and leading a productive life (Friedmann, Saitz, & Samet, 1998). Studies of adult rats have found that brain damage caused by alcohol dependency can be stopped and even reversed by abstinence, as brain cells begin to regenerate and cognitive function returns (Nixon & Crews, 2004).

About 20 percent of persons with substance use disorders also have mood (depression) or anxiety disorders, and vice versa. Thus people who show symptoms of substance use disorders should also be assessed for other mental health problems (Grant et al., 2004).

Checkpoint
Can you . . .

✔ Cite benefits of exercise?

✔ Explain why sleep deprivation is harmful?

✔ Discuss trends and risks involved in smoking and alcohol and drug use?

Indirect Influences on Health and Fitness

Apart from the things people do, or refrain from doing, which affect their health directly, there are indirect influences on health. Among these are income, education, race/ethnicity, and gender. Relationships also seem to make a difference, as do the paths young people take into adulthood. Binge drinking, for example, is most common among college students living away from home; and substance use declines most rapidly among young adults who are married (Schulenberg et al., 2005).

Socioeconomic Status and Race/Ethnicity The connection between socioeconomic status and health has been widely documented. Higher-income people rate their health as better and live longer than lower-income people (NCHS, 2004). Education is important, too. The less schooling people have had, the greater the chance that they will develop and die from communicable diseases, injuries, or chronic ailments (such as heart disease), or that they will become victims of homicide or suicide (NCHS, 2004; Pamuk, Makuc, Heck, Reuben, & Lochner, 1998).

This does not mean that income and education *cause* good health; instead, they are related to environmental and lifestyle factors that tend to be causative. Poverty is associated with poor nutrition, substandard housing, unhealthy lifestyles, exposure to pollutants and violent behavior, and limited access to health care (Adler & Newman, 2002; Lethbridge-Cejku et al., 2004; NCHS, 2004). Better-educated and more affluent people have healthier diets and better preventive health care and medical treatment. They exercise more, are less likely to be overweight, smoke less, and are less likely to use illicit drugs. They are more likely to use alcohol but to use it in moderation (NCHS, 2004; Pamuk et al., 1998; SAMHSA, 2004b). They tend to have better vision and dental health (Lethbridge-Cejku et al., 2004).

Living in poverty, like this mother and daughter sharing a single room in a shelter dormitory, can affect health through poor nutrition, substandard housing, and inadequate health care.

The association between SES and health sheds light on the relatively poor state of health in some minority populations (Kiefe et al., 2000). Young black adults are 20 times more likely to have high blood pressure than young white adults (Agoda, 1995). African Americans are about twice as likely as white people to die in young adulthood, in part because young black men are about 7 times as likely to be victims of homicide (NCHS, 2004).

However, factors associated with SES do not tell the whole story. For example, although African Americans smoke less than white Americans, they metabolize more nicotine in the blood, are more subject to lung cancer, and have more trouble breaking the habit. Possible reasons may be genetic, biological, or behavioral (Caraballo et al., 1998; Pérez-Stable, Herrera, Jacob III, & Benowitz, 1998; Sellers, 1998). A congressionally mandated review of more than 100 studies found that racial/ethnic minorities tend to receive lower-quality health care than whites do, even when insurance status, income, age, and severity of conditions are similar (Smedley, Stith, & Nelson, 2002).

Disparities in most indicators of health lessened during the 1990s for most racial/ethnic groups, but not for American Indians and Alaska Natives. Racial/ethnic disparities *widened* in deaths from work-related injuries, motor vehicle crashes, and suicide (Keppel, Pearcy, & Wagener, 2002). We further discuss the relationship between ethnicity and health in Chapter 15.

Gender Which sex is healthier: women or men? We know that women have a higher life expectancy than men and lower death rates throughout life (Kochanek et al., 2004; see Figure 13-3 and Chapter 17). Women's greater longevity has been attributed to genetic protection given by the second X chromosome (which men do not have) and, before menopause, to beneficial effects of the female hormone estrogen, particularly on cardiovascular health (Rodin & Ickovics, 1990; USDHHS, 1992). However, psychosocial and cultural factors, such as men's greater propensity for risk taking and their preference for meat and potatoes rather than fruits and vegetables, also may play a part (Liebman, 1995a; Schardt, 1995).

Figure 13-3

Life expectancy by sex and race: United States, 1970–2002. (Source: Kochanek, Murphy, & Anderson, 2004.)

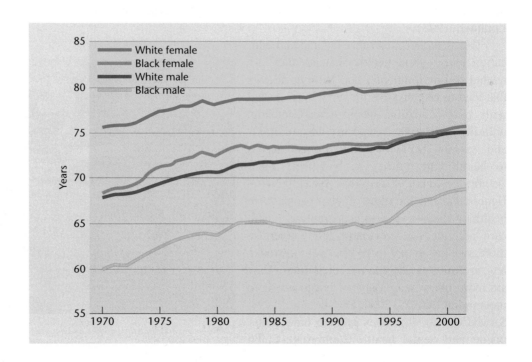

Despite their longer life, women are more likely than men to report being in fair or poor health, go to doctors or seek outpatient or emergency room care more often, are more likely to seek treatment for minor illnesses, and report more unexplained symptoms. Men are *less* likely to seek professional help for health problems, but they have longer hospital stays, and their health problems are more likely to be chronic and life-threatening (Addis & Mahalik, 2003; Kroenke & Spitzer, 1998; NCHS, 2004; Rodin & Ickovics, 1990).

Women's greater tendency to seek medical care does not necessarily mean that they are in worse health than men, nor that they are imagining ailments or are preoccupied with illness (Kroenke & Spitzer, 1998). They may simply be more health-conscious. Men may feel that illness is not "masculine," and seeking help means a loss of control. Research suggests that a man is least likely to seek help when he perceives a health problem as nonnormative or as a threat to his self-esteem or if he believes his male peers would look down on him (Addis & Mahalik, 2003). It may well be that the better care women take of themselves helps them live longer than men.

Public awareness of men's health issues has increased. The availability of impotence treatment and of screening tests for prostate cancer is bringing more men into doctor's offices. Meanwhile, as women's lifestyles have become more like men's, so—in some ways—have their health patterns. Women now account for 39 percent of all smoking-related deaths in the United States (Satcher, 2001). Whereas fewer men are dying of lung cancer, more women are. In fact, lung cancer is now the leading cause of cancer death among white, black, and Asian/Pacific Islander women, and among Hispanic women it is second only to breast cancer (U.S. Cancer Statistics Working Group, 2004). The gender gap in deaths from heart disease has actually reversed, perhaps in part because of the sharper decline in men's smoking and women's greater tendency to overweight and sedentary lifestyles. Such trends help explain why the difference between women's and men's life expectancy shrank from 7.6 years in 1970 to 5.4 years in 2002 (Kochanek et al., 2004; NCHS, 2004).

Relationships and Health Social relationships seem to be vital to health and well-being (Cohen, 2004). Research has identified at least two important aspects of the social environment that can promote health: *social integration* and *social support* (Cohen, 2004).

Social integration is active engagement in a broad range of social relationships, activities, and roles (spouse, parent, neighbor, friend, colleague, and the like). Social networks can influence emotional well-being as well as participation in healthful behaviors, such as exercising, eating nutritiously, and refraining from substance use (Cohen, 2004). Social integration has repeatedly been associated with lower mortality rates (Berkman & Glass, 2000; Rutledge et al., 2004). People with wide social networks and multiple social roles are more likely to survive heart attacks, less likely to experience a recurrence of cancer, and less likely to be anxious or depressed (Cohen, Gottlieb, & Underwood, 2000). They even are less susceptible to colds (Cohen, Doyle, Skoner, Rabin, & Gwaltney, 1997).

Social support refers to material, informational, and psychological resources derived from the social network, on which a person can rely for help in coping with stress. In highly stressful situations, people who are in touch with others may be more likely to eat and sleep sensibly, get enough exercise, and avoid substance abuse and less likely to be distressed, anxious, or depressed or even to die (Cohen, 2004).

Because marriage offers a readily available system for both social integration and social support, it is not surprising that marriage tends to benefit health, especially

This happy couple are the picture of good health. Although there is a clear association between relationships and health, it isn't clear which is the cause and which the effect.

Checkpoint
Can you . . .

✔ Point out some differences in health and mortality that reflect income, education, race or ethnicity, and gender?

✔ Discuss how relationships, particularly marriage, may affect physical and mental health?

for men (Wu & Hart, 2002). An interview survey of 127,545 U.S. adults found that married people, particularly in young adulthood, tend to be healthier physically and psychologically than those who are never-married, cohabiting, widowed, separated, or divorced. The sole exception is that married people, especially husbands, are more likely to be overweight or obese (Schoenborn, 2004). Dissolving a marriage (or a cohabitation) tends to have negative effects on physical or mental health or both—but so, apparently, does remaining in a bad relationship (Wu & Hart, 2002).

Married people also tend to be better off financially, a factor associated, as we have seen, with physical and mental health (Ross et al., 1990). People with high incomes, whether married or single, are more likely to survive than are married people with low incomes; and the highest mortality rate is among low-income singles (Rogers, 1995).

Guidepost

3. What are some sexual and reproductive issues at this time of life?

Sexual and Reproductive Issues

Sexual and reproductive activity can bring pleasure and sometimes parenthood. These natural and important functions also may involve physical concerns. Three such concerns are disorders related to menstruation, sexually transmitted diseases (STDs), and infertility.

Menstrual Disorders

premenstrual syndrome (PMS) Disorder producing symptoms of physical discomfort and emotional tension during the one to two weeks before a menstrual period.

Premenstrual syndrome (PMS) is a disorder that produces physical discomfort and emotional tension during the two weeks before a menstrual period. Symptoms may include fatigue, headaches, swelling and tenderness of the breasts, swollen hands or feet, abdominal bloating, nausea, cramps, constipation, food cravings, weight gain, anxiety, depression, irritability, mood swings, tearfulness, and difficulty concentrating or remembering (American College of Obstetricians & Gynecologists [ACOG], 2000b; Moline & Zendell, 2000). Up to 85 percent of menstruating women may have some symptoms, but only in 5 to 10 percent do they warrant a diagnosis of PMS (ACOG, 2000b).

The cause of PMS is not fully understood, but it appears to be an abnormal response to normal monthly surges of the female hormones estrogen and progesterone (Schmidt, Nieman, Danaceau, Adams, & Rubinow, 1998) as well as to levels of the male hormone testosterone and of serotonin, a brain chemical (ACOG, 2000b). Because it is linked to ovulation, it is not present during pregnancy or after menopause.

Managing PMS can include patient education, aerobic exercise, eating frequent small meals, a diet high in complex carbohydrates and low in salt and caffeine, and regular sleep routines. Calcium, magnesium, and vitamin E supplements may help. Medications may relieve specific symptoms—for example, a diuretic for bloating and weight gain (ACOG, 2000b; Moline & Zendell, 2000). Oral contraceptives and alternative treatments such as natural progesterone, primrose oil, and vitamin B6 have limited effectiveness, if any (ACOG, 2000b).

PMS sometimes is confused with *dysmenorrhea,* painful menstruation (commonly called "cramps") with no apparent organic cause. Cramps tend to afflict adolescents and young women, whereas PMS is more typical in women in their thirties or older. Between 40 and 90 percent of women are believed to suffer from dysmenorrhea, and in 10 to 15 percent of cases the pain is so severe as to be disabling (Newswise, 2004). Dysmenorrhea is caused by contractions of the uterus, which are set in motion by prostaglandin, a hormone-like substance; it can be treated with prostaglandin inhibitors, such as ibuprofen. Unusual stress during a previous menstrual cycle can lead to dysmenorrhea in the next cycle (Wang et al., 2004).

Sexually Transmitted Diseases (STDs)

About 15 million people in the United States become infected with one or more STDs each year, and about half contract lifelong infections. Not surprisingly, the highest rates for most STDs are among adolescents and young adults, the age groups most likely to engage in risky sexual activity (refer back to Chapter 12). Although some STDs—notably syphilis—have become less prevalent, others, such as gonorrhea and genital herpes, are on the rise. STDs are found in all racial/ethnic groups but are more common among African Americans than among white Americans, in part due to poverty, drug use, and sexual networks in which STDs are widespread (CDC, 2000c).

In December 2004, an estimated 39.4 million people worldwide, ages 15 to 49—a record number—were living with HIV; 4.3 million contracted the infection that year, and 2.6 million died of AIDS. The number of people living with HIV has risen in every region of the world since 2002, with the steepest increases in East and Central Asia and Eastern Europe (see Figure 13-4). Still, sub-Saharan Africa remains by far the worst affected. Worldwide, nearly half of all infected people are female. A growing proportion of new infections occur in women, especially in places where heterosexual transmission is predominant, such as sub-Saharan Africa and the Caribbean. In the United States, most infections occur through drug abusers who share contaminated hypodermic needles, unprotected sex among gay or bisexual men (who may then pass on the infection to female partners), or commercial sex with prostitutes (UNAIDS/WHO, 2004). Only about 1 percent of cases are in people who (like Arthur Ashe) have received transfusions of infected blood or blood products (CDC, 2001b).

Lifemap CD

Watch the video, "The Surprisingly Fast Spread of a 'New' STD," in Chapter 13 of your CD to consider the factors involved in transmission of a disease from one part of the world to another.

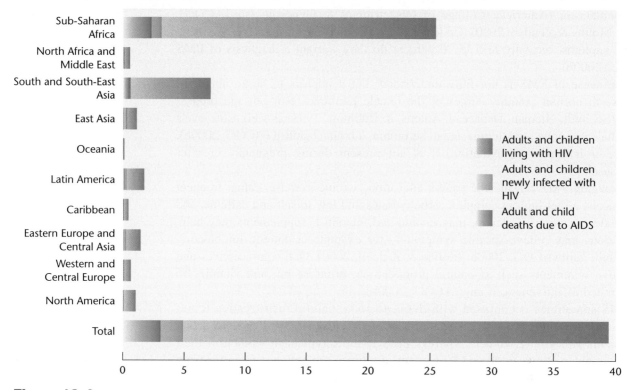

Figure 13-4

Global and regional prevalence of HIV and AIDS, 2004. (Source: UNAIDS/WHO, 2004).

The AIDS epidemic in the United States has begun to come under control. In 1995 AIDS became the leading cause of death for 25- to 44-year-olds. In 2002, it was sixth (Hoyert et al., 1999; NCHS, 2004). Getting men to use condoms, the most effective means of preventing STDs, is key. A three-session intervention among U.S. Marine security guards resulted in increased perception of social support for condom use and stronger intentions to practice safe sex (Booth-Kewley, Minagawa, Shaffer, & Brodine, 2002). Global funding for AIDS prevention and care has nearly tripled since 2001, and access to services has improved, but much more needs to be done (UNAIDS, 2004).

Infertility

An estimated 7 percent of U.S. couples experience **infertility:** inability to conceive a baby after 12 to 18 months of trying (Centers for Disease Control & Prevention, 2001a). Women's fertility begins to decline in the late twenties, with substantial decreases during the thirties. Men's fertility is less affected by age but declines significantly by the late thirties (Dunson, Colombo, & Baird, 2002). Infertility can burden a marriage emotionally, but only when infertility leads to permanent, involuntary childlessness is it associated with long-term psychological distress (McQuillan, Greil, White, & Jacob, 2003).

The most common cause of infertility in men is production of too few sperm. Although only one sperm is needed to fertilize an ovum, the enzymes released by millions of sperm are necessary to break down the ovum's protective layers; thus, a sperm count lower than 60 to 200 million per ejaculation makes conception unlikely. In some instances an ejaculatory duct may be blocked, preventing the exit of sperm, or sperm may be low in motility—unable to "swim" well enough to reach the cervix. Some cases of male infertility seem to have a genetic basis (King, 1996; Reijo, Alagappan, Patrizio, & Page, 1996; Phillips, 1998).

Checkpoint

Can you . . .

✔ Discuss ways to control the spread of STDs?

infertility Inability to conceive after 12 months of trying.

In a woman, the cause of infertility may be the failure to produce ova or to produce normal ova; mucus in the cervix, which might prevent sperm from penetrating it; or endometriosis, a disease of the uterine lining, which might prevent implantation of the fertilized ovum. A major cause of declining fertility in women after age 30 is deterioration in the quality of ova (van Noord-Zaadstra et al., 1991). However, the most common cause is blockage of the fallopian tubes, preventing ova from reaching the uterus. In about half of these cases, the tubes are blocked by scar tissue from sexually transmitted diseases (King, 1996).

Sometimes hormone treatment, drug therapy, or surgery may correct the problem. However, fertility drugs increase the likelihood of multiple, high-risk births. Men undergoing fertility treatment are at increased risk of producing sperm with chromosomal abnormalities (Levron et al., 1998). Daily supplements of coenzyme Q10, an antioxidant, may help increase sperm motility (Balercia et al., 2004).

Couples who have been unable to bear children after one year should not necessarily rush into fertility treatments. Unless there is a known cause for failure to conceive, the chances of success after 18 months to two years are high (Dunson, 2002). For couples who give up on the natural way, science today offers several alternative ways to parenthood (see Box 13-1).

The birth of quadruplets is a frequent occurrence in recent years. Delayed childbearing, use of fertility drugs, and assisted reproduction techniques such as in vitro fertilization increase the likelihood of multiple, usually premature, births.

Checkpoint

Can you . . .

✔ Identify several causes of and treatments for male and female infertility?

COGNITIVE DEVELOPMENT

Perspectives on Adult Cognition

Developmental theorists and researchers have studied adult cognition from a variety of perspectives. Some investigators seek to identify distinctive cognitive capacities that emerge in adulthood or distinctive ways in which adults use their cognitive abilities at successive stages of life. Other investigators focus on aspects of intelligence that exist throughout life but tend to come to the fore in adulthood. One current theory, which may apply to children as well as adults, highlights the role of emotion in intelligent behavior.

Guidepost

4. What is distinctive about adult thought and intelligence?

Beyond Piaget: New Ways of Thinking in Adulthood

Although Piaget described the stage of formal operations as the pinnacle of cognitive achievement, some developmental scientists maintain that changes in cognition extend beyond that stage. One line of neo-Piagetian theory and research concerns higher levels of abstract reasoning, or *reflective thinking.* Another line of investigation deals with *postformal thought,* which combines logic with emotion and practical experience in the resolution of ambiguous problems.

BOX 13-1

Practically Speaking

Assisted Reproduction Technology

Assisted reproduction technology (ART) began in 1978 with the birth of Louise Brown of England by means of *in vitro fertilization (IVF)*, fertilization outside the mother's body. In 2000, more than 25,000 U.S. women, with technological help, gave birth to more than 35,000 babies (Wright, Schieve, Reynolds, & Jeng, 2003), nearly 1 percent of all U.S. births in that year (Martin, Hamilton et al., 2002).

Techniques and Outcomes   In IVF, the most common assisted reproduction procedure, fertility drugs are given to increase production of ova. Then one or more mature ova are surgically removed, fertilized in a laboratory dish, and implanted in the woman's uterus. Usually several embryos are transferred to the uterus to increase the chances of pregnancy. This also increases the likelihood of multiple, usually premature, births (Wennerholm & Bergh, 2000). However, since 1999, the proportion of procedures involving implantation of three or more embryos has declined (Reynolds, Schieve, Martin, Jeng, & Macaluso, 2003).

A newer technique, *in vitro maturation (IVM)* is performed earlier in the monthly cycle, when as many as 30 to 50 ovum follicles are developing. Normally, only one of these will mature. Harvesting a large number of follicles before ovulation is complete and then allowing them to mature in the laboratory can make hormone injections unnecessary and diminish the likelihood of multiple births (Duenwald, 2003).

Many women, like Louise Brown's mother, turned to IVF because their fallopian tubes were blocked or scarred beyond surgical repair. This method also can address severe male infertility; a single sperm can be injected into the ovum—a technique called *intracytoplasmic sperm injection (ICSI)*.

Artificial insemination—injection of sperm into a woman's vagina, cervix, or uterus—is commonly used when a man has a low sperm count. Sperm from several ejaculations can be combined for one injection. If the man is infertile, a couple may choose *artificial insemination by a donor (AID)*.

A woman who is producing poor-quality ova or who has had her ovaries removed may try *ovum transfer*. In this procedure, an ovum, or *donor egg*—provided, usually anonymously, by a fertile young woman—is fertilized in the laboratory and implanted in the prospective mother's uterus. In *blastocyst transfer*, the fertilized ovum is kept in the culture until it grows to the blastocyst stage; but this method has been linked to an increase in identical twin births (Duenwald, 2003). Alternatively, the ovum can be fertilized in the donor's body by artificial insemination. The donor's uterus is flushed out a few days later, and the embryo is retrieved and inserted into the recipient's uterus.

Although success rates have improved since 1978 (Duenwald, 2003), only 30.8 percent of the 99,629 U.S. women who attempted assisted reproduction in 2000 had live births, and 53 percent of these were multiple births. Chances of success are highest for women under age 35 (Wright et al., 2003). Two relatively new techniques with higher success rates are *gamete intrafallopian transfer (GIFT)* and *zygote intrafallopian transfer (ZIFT)*, in which either the egg and sperm or the fertilized egg is inserted in the fallopian tube (CDC, 2002b; Schieve et al., 2002; Society for Assisted Reproductive Technology, 1993, 2002).

How do children conceived by artificial means turn out? In a longitudinal study of 1,523 British, Belgian, Danish, Swedish, and Greek infants, there were no major differences in physical development, health, or other aspects of development at age 5 between those born through IVF or ICSI and those conceived normally. However, children born through ICSI did have a higher rate of congenital urological and kidney abnormalities (Barnes et al., 2003; Sutcliffe, Loft, Wennerholm, Tarlatzis, & Bonduelle, 2003).

---

reflective thinking   Type of logical thinking that may emerge in adulthood, involving continuous, active evaluation of information and beliefs in the light of evidence and implications.

Reflective Thinking   **Reflective thinking** is a complex form of cognition, first defined by the American philosopher and educator John Dewey (1910/1991) as "active, persistent, and careful consideration" of information or beliefs in the light of the evidence that supports them and the conclusions to which they lead. Reflective thinkers continually question supposed facts, draw inferences, and make connections. Building on Piaget's stage of formal operations, reflective thinkers can create complex intellectual systems that reconcile apparently conflicting ideas or considerations—for example, by putting together various theories of modern physics or of human development into a single overarching theory that explains many different kinds of behavior (Fischer & Pruyne, 2003).

The capacity for reflective thinking is thought to emerge between ages 20 and 25. Not until then are the cortical regions of the brain that handle higher-level thinking fully myelinated (refer back to Chapter 4). At the same time the brain is forming new neurons and synapses and dendritic connections. Environmental support can stimulate the development of thicker, denser cortical connections. Thus, though almost all adults develop the *capacity* for becoming reflective thinkers, few attain optimal proficiency in this skill, and even fewer can apply it consistently to various kinds of problems. For example, a young adult may understand the concept of

—continued

In interviews with 100 sets of parents of 9- to 12-month-olds, parents who had used artificial means were rated as having more positive relationships and more emotional involvement with their babies than parents who had conceived naturally (Golombok, Lycett, et al., 2004). Longitudinal studies found little or no difference in socioemotional development at age 12 between children conceived by IVF or donor insemination and children who had been conceived naturally or adopted (Golombok, MacCallum, & Goodman, 2001; Golombok, MacCallum, Goodman, & Rutter, 2002).

Surrogate Pregnancy In *surrogate motherhood,* a fertile woman is impregnated by the prospective father, usually by artificial insemination. She carries the baby to term and gives the child to the father and his mate. A newer method, *gestational surrogacy,* utilizes IVF, with the prospective parents contributing both the ovum and sperm; thus the surrogate is not the biological mother. In one unusual case, 55-year-old Tina Cade gave birth to her own three grandchildren. The embryos were implanted in Cade after her daughter had tried for four years to become pregnant (Gelineau, 2004).

In a study of 42 families with infants born through surrogacy, the parents reported lower stress, showed more warmth to their babies, and enjoyed parenthood more than parents who had conceived and borne children naturally or through ovum donation—perhaps because these were highly committed parents raising extremely wanted children (Golombok, Murray, Jadva, MacCallum, & Lycett, 2004).

Issues Concerning Assisted Reproduction Assisted reproduction has created a tangled web of legal, ethical, and psychological dilemmas (ISLAT Working Group, 1998; Schwartz, 2003). Should single people and cohabiting and homosexual couples have access to these methods? What about older people? Should the children know about their parentage? Should genetic tests be performed on prospective donors and surrogates? When IVF results in multiple fertilized ova, should some be discarded so as to improve the chances of health for the survivors? What should be done with any unused embryos? Should fertility clinics be required to disclose risks, options, and success rates?

The issues multiply when a surrogate is involved (Schwartz, 2003). Who is the "real" parent—the surrogate or the woman whose baby she bears? What if a surrogate wants to keep the baby, as has happened in a few highly publicized cases? What if the intended parents refuse to go through with the contract? Another controversial aspect of surrogacy is the payment of money. The creation of a "breeder class" of poor and disadvantaged women who carry the babies of the well-to-do strikes many people as wrong. Similar concerns have been raised about payment for donor eggs (Gabriel, 1996).

One thing seems certain: As long as there are people who want children but are unable to conceive or bear them, human ingenuity and technology will come up with ways to satisfy their need.

What's Your View?

If you or your partner were infertile, would you seriously consider or undertake one of the methods of assisted reproduction described here? Why or why not?

Check It Out

For more information on this topic, go to http://www.nichd .nih.gov/publications/pubs/counrs/sub3.htm. This Web site features research highlights about assisted reproduction technology.

---

justice but may have difficulty weighing it in relation to other concepts such as social welfare, law, ethics, and responsibility. This may help explain why, as we discuss later in this chapter, few adults—not to speak of adolescents—reach Kohlberg's highest levels of moral reasoning. For many adults, as we also discuss later in this chapter, college education stimulates progress toward reflective thinking (Fischer & Pruyne, 2003).

Postformal Thought Research and theoretical work since the 1970s suggest that mature thinking may be richer and more complex than Piaget described (Arlin, 1984; Labouvie-Vief, 1985, 1990a; Labouvie-Vief & Hakim-Larson, 1989; Sinnott, 1984, 1989a, 1989b, 1991, 1998, 2003). It is characterized by the ability to deal with uncertainty, inconsistency, contradiction, imperfection, and compromise (as Arthur Ashe did when faced with physical limitations on his ability to continue his tennis career). This higher stage of adult cognition is sometimes called **postformal thought.**

Postformal thought is flexible, open, adaptive, and individualistic. It draws on intuition and emotion as well as on logic to help people cope with a seemingly chaotic world. It applies the fruits of experience to ambiguous situations.

postformal thought Mature type of thinking that relies on subjective experience and intuition as well as logic and is useful in dealing with ambiguity, uncertainty, inconsistency, contradiction, imperfection, and compromise.

Postformal thought is relativistic. Like reflective thinking, it enables adults to transcend a single logical system (such as Euclidean geometry or a particular theory of human development or an established political system) and reconcile or choose among conflicting ideas or demands (such as those of the Israelis and Palestinians or those of two romantic partners), each of which, from its own perspective, may have a valid claim to truth (Labouvie-Vief, 1990a, 1990b; Sinnott, 1996, 1998, 2003). Immature thinking sees black and white (right versus wrong, intellect versus feelings, mind versus body); postformal thinking sees shades of gray. Like reflective thinking, it often develops in response to events and interactions that open up unaccustomed ways of looking at things and challenge a simple, polarized view of the world.

One prominent researcher, Jan Sinnott (1984, 1998, 2003), has proposed several criteria of postformal thought:

- *Shifting gears.* Ability to think within at least two different logical systems and to shift back and forth between abstract reasoning and practical, real-world considerations. ("This might work on paper but not in real life.")

- *Problem definition.* Ability to define a problem as falling within a class or category of logical problems and to define its parameters. ("This is an ethical problem, not a legal one, so judicial precedents don't really help solve it.")

- *Process-product shift.* Ability to see that a problem can be solved either through a *process* with general application to similar problems or through a *product,* a concrete solution to the particular problem. ("I've come up against this type of problem before, and this is how I solved it" or "In this case, the best available solution would be . . .")

- *Pragmatism.* Ability to choose the best of several possible logical solutions and to recognize criteria for choosing. ("If you want the cheapest solution, do this; if you want the quickest solution, do that.")

- *Multiple solutions.* Awareness that most problems have more than one cause, that people may have differing goals, and that a variety of methods can be used to arrive at more than one solution. ("Let's try it your way; if that doesn't work, we can try my way.")

- *Awareness of paradox.* Recognition that a problem or solution involves inherent conflict. ("Doing this will give him what he wants, but it will only make him unhappy in the end.")

- *Self-referential thought.* A person's awareness that he or she must be the judge of which logic to use; in other words, that he or she is using postformal thought.

Postformal thinking often operates in a social and emotional context. Unlike the problems Piaget studied, which involve physical phenomena and require dispassionate, objective observation and analysis, social dilemmas are less clearly structured and often fraught with emotion. It is in these kinds of situations that mature adults tend to call on postformal thought (Berg & Klaczynski, 1996; Sinnott, 1996, 1998, 2003).

In an intimate union, a couple must deal with three different logical realities: those of each partner and of the relationship itself, which comes to take on a life of its own. Instead of allowing one partner's way of thinking to dominate and expecting the other partner to capitulate, postformal thought may permit a synthesis, a win-win situation for both partners, leading to cognitive and emotional growth. For example, if a dual-career couple disagree about who should do what around the house, postformal thought can help them get beyond attitudes and beliefs about gender roles that have been shaped by family history and societal dictates (Sinnott, 2003).

Some research has found a progression toward postformal thought throughout young and middle adulthood, especially when emotions are involved. In one study, participants were asked to judge what caused the outcomes of a series of hypothetical situations, such as a marital conflict. Adolescents and young adults tended to blame individuals, whereas middle-aged people were more likely to attribute behavior to the interplay among persons and environment. The more ambiguous the situation, the greater were the age differences in interpretation (Blanchard-Fields & Norris, 1994).

Empirical evidence of the value of postformal thought emerged from a longitudinal study of 130 freshman medical students. Their degree of tolerance for ambiguity together with their empathy as juniors and seniors (a combination of emotion and cognition), predicted their clinical performance as rated by patients (Morton et al., 2000). We further discuss postformal thought in Chapter 15.

Schaie: A Life-Span Model of Cognitive Development

K. Warner Schaie's life-span model of cognitive development (1977–1978; Schaie & Willis, 2000) looks at the developing *uses* of intellect within a social context. His seven stages revolve around objectives that come to the fore at various stages of life. These objectives shift from acquisition of information and skills *(what I need to know)* to practical integration of knowledge and skills *(how to use what I know)* to a search for meaning and purpose *(why I should know)*. The seven stages are as follows:

1. **Acquisitive stage** (childhood and adolescence). Children and adolescents acquire information and skills mainly for their own sake or as preparation for participation in society.

2. **Achieving stage** (late teens or early twenties to early thirties). Young adults no longer acquire knowledge merely for its own sake; they use what they know to pursue goals, such as career and family.

3. **Responsible stage** (late thirties to early sixties). Middle-aged people use their minds to solve practical problems associated with responsibilities to others, such as family members or employees.

4. **Executive stage** (thirties or forties through middle age). People in the executive stage, which may overlap with the achieving and responsible stages, are responsible for societal systems (such as governmental or business organizations) or social movements. They deal with complex relationships on multiple levels.

5. **Reorganizational stage** (end of middle age, beginning of late adulthood). People who enter retirement reorganize their lives and intellectual energies around meaningful pursuits that take the place of paid work.

6. **Reintegrative stage** (late adulthood). Older adults, who may have let go of some social involvement and whose cognitive functioning may be limited by biological changes, are often more selective about what tasks they expend effort on. They focus on the purpose of what they do and concentrate on tasks that have the most meaning for them.

7. **Legacy-creating stage** (advanced old age). Near the end of life, once reintegration has been completed (or along with it), older people may create instructions for the disposition of prized possessions, make funeral arrangements, provide oral histories, or write their life stories as a legacy for their loved ones. All of these tasks involve the exercise of cognitive competencies within a social and emotional context.

acquisitive stage First of Schaie's seven cognitive stages, in which children and adolescents learn information and skills largely for their own sake or as preparation for participation in society.

achieving stage Second of Schaie's seven cognitive stages, in which young adults use knowledge to gain competence and independence.

responsible stage Third of Schaie's seven cognitive stages, in which middle-aged people are concerned with long-range goals and practical problems related to their responsibility for others.

executive stage Fourth of Schaie's seven cognitive stages, in which middle-aged people responsible for societal systems deal with complex relationships on several levels.

reorganizational stage Fifth of Schaie's seven cognitive stages, in which adults entering retirement reorganize their lives around nonwork-related activities.

reintegrative stage Sixth of Schaie's seven cognitive stages, in which older adults choose to focus limited energy on tasks that have meaning to them.

legacy-creating stage Seventh of Schaie's seven cognitive stages, in which very old people prepare for death by recording their life stories, distributing possessions, and the like.

Not everyone goes through these stages within the suggested time frames. Indeed, Arthur Ashe, by the time of his premature death, had moved through all of them. As a boy in the *acquisitive stage,* Ashe gained the knowledge and skills needed to become a top tennis player. While still in high school and college, he was already entering the *achieving stage,* refining his knowledge and skills as he used them to win amateur tournaments and lay the groundwork for a professional tennis career. In his thirties he moved into the *responsible stage,* helping to found a tennis players' union, serving as its president, and then becoming captain of the U.S. Davis Cup team. He also became more keenly aware of his responsibility to use his position to promote racial justice and equal opportunity. Shifting into the *executive stage,* he served as chairman of the National Heart Association and on the boards of directors of corporations, and established tennis programs for inner-city youths in several cities. Meanwhile, his early retirement from tennis and then his struggle with AIDS led him into the *reorganizational stage,* lecturing, writing, playing golf, and acting as a television sports commentator. His ultimate decision to "go public" with the news of his illness pushed him into the *reintegrative* and *legacy-creating stages:* spearheading a nationwide movement for AIDS research and education and writing books on African American history—projects that would have a lasting impact.

If adults do go through stages such as these, then traditional psychometric tests, which use the same kinds of tasks to measure intelligence at all periods of life, may be inappropriate for them. Tests developed to measure knowledge and skills in children may not be suitable for measuring cognitive competence in adults, who use knowledge and skills to solve practical problems and achieve self-chosen goals. Thus we may need measures that show competence in dealing with real-life challenges, such as balancing a checkbook, reading a railroad timetable, and making informed decisions about medical problems. Robert Sternberg's work has taken this direction.

Sternberg: Insight and Know-How

Alix, Barbara, and Courtney applied to graduate programs at Yale University. Alix had earned almost straight A's in college, scored high on the Graduate Record Examination (GRE), and had excellent recommendations. Barbara's grades were only fair, and her GRE scores were low by Yale's standards, but her letters of recommendation enthusiastically praised her exceptional research and creative ideas. Courtney's grades, GRE scores, and recommendations were good but not among the best.

Alix and Courtney were admitted to the graduate program. Barbara was not admitted but was hired as a research associate and took graduate classes on the side. Alix did very well for the first year or so, but less well after that. Barbara confounded the admissions committee by doing outstanding work. Courtney's performance in graduate school was only fair, but she had the easiest time getting a good job afterward (Trotter, 1986).

According to Sternberg's (1985a, 1987) triarchic theory of intelligence (introduced in Chapter 9), Barbara and Courtney were strong in two aspects of intelligence that psychometric tests miss: creative insight (what Sternberg calls the **experiential element**) and practical intelligence (the **contextual element**). Because insight and practical intelligence are very important in adult life, psychometric tests are much less useful in gauging adults' intelligence and predicting their life success than in measuring children's intelligence and predicting their school success. As an undergraduate, Alix's **componential** (analytical) ability helped her sail through examinations. However, in graduate school, where original thinking is expected, Barbara's superior experiential intelligence—her fresh insights and innovative ideas—began to shine. So did Courtney's practical, contextual

Checkpoint

Can you . . .

✔ Explain the differences between reflective and postformal thinking, and tell how and when these advanced types of thinking seem to develop?

✔ Tell why postformal thought may be especially suited to solving social problems?

✔ Describe Schaie's seven stages of cognitive development?

experiential element Sternberg's term for the insightful or creative aspect of intelligence.

contextual element Sternberg's term for the practical aspect of intelligence.

componential element Sternberg's term for the analytic aspect of intelligence.

intelligence—her "street smarts." She knew her way around. She chose "hot" research topics, submitted papers to the "right" journals, and knew where and how to apply for jobs.

Age-Related Changes in Intelligence   Creative production and the ability to solve practical problems seem to grow or at least remain stable until midlife (see Chapter 15), whereas the ability to solve academic problems generally declines (Sternberg, Wagner, Williams, & Horvath, 1995). Practical problems emerge from personal experience, as does the information needed to solve them. Being more relevant to the solver, they evoke more careful thinking and provide a better gauge of cognitive ability than academic problems disconnected from everyday life. Academic problems generally have a definite answer and one right way to find it. Practical problems are often ill-defined and have a variety of possible solutions and ways of reaching them, each with its advantages and disadvantages (Neisser, 1976; Sternberg & Wagner, 1989; Wagner & Sternberg, 1985). Life experience helps adults solve such problems. In a study of Russian adults' adjustment to the changeover from communism to capitalism, all three of Sternberg's aspects of intelligence were adaptive, but practical intelligence was the best predictor of mental and physical health (Grigorenko & Sternberg, 2001).

Tacit Knowledge   An important aspect of practical intelligence is **tacit knowledge** (refer back to Chapter 9): "inside information," "know-how," or "savvy" that is not formally taught or openly expressed (Sternberg, Grigorenko, & Oh, 2001; Sternberg & Wagner, 1993; Sternberg et al., 1995; Wagner & Sternberg, 1986). Tacit knowledge, acquired largely on one's own, is "commonsense" knowledge of how to get ahead—how to win a promotion or cut through red tape. It is not well correlated with measures of general cognitive ability, but it may be a better predictor of managerial success (Sternberg, Grigorenko, & Oh, 2001).

Tacit knowledge may include *self-management* (knowing how to motivate oneself and organize time and energy), *management of tasks* (knowing, for example, how to write a term paper or grant proposal), and *management of others* (knowing when and how to reward or criticize subordinates) (E. A. Smith, 2001). Sternberg's method of testing tacit knowledge is to compare a test-taker's chosen course of action in hypothetical, work-related situations (such as how best to angle for a promotion) with the choices of experts in the field and with accepted "rules of thumb." Tacit knowledge, measured in this way, seems to be unrelated to IQ and predicts job performance better than do psychometric tests (Sternberg et al., 1995).

One study posed simulated critical situations to 16 registered nurses who averaged almost 15 years' experience. One task called for dressing a slightly infected wound on the forearm of a patient who had fallen from a motor bike, and who showed signs of hypoglycemia (weakness, perspiring, trembling, and hunger) and possible head trauma. The nurses who dealt most successfully with the situation showed no greater explicit (consciously learned) knowledge than those who did poorly; the difference was in their

tacit knowledge   Sternberg's term for information that is not formally taught or openly expressed but is necessary to function successfully.

These U.S. soldiers patrolling the outskirts of Fallujah need all the tacit knowledge they have acquired through experience as well as training in order to get their job done and to survive the daily challenge of flushing out insurgents in Iraq.

application of tacit knowledge: their willingness to use their feelings and intuitions in deciding how to act and their organization of knowledge in a holistic, interactive way (Herbig, Büssing, & Ewert, 2001).

Of course, tacit knowledge is not all that is needed to succeed; other aspects of intelligence count, too. However, in studies of business managers, tests of tacit knowledge together with IQ and personality tests predicted virtually *all* of the variance in performance, as measured by such criteria as salary, years of management experience, and the company's success (Sternberg et al., 1995). In one study, tacit knowledge was related to the salaries managers earned at a given age and to how high their positions were, independent of family background and education. The most knowledgeable managers were not those who had spent many years with a company or many years as managers, but those who had worked for the most companies, perhaps gaining a greater breadth of experience (Sternberg et al., 2000).

Emotional Intelligence

In 1990, two psychologists, Peter Salovey and John Mayer, coined the term **emotional intelligence** (sometimes called *EI*). It refers to the ability to recognize and deal with one's own feelings and the feelings of others. Daniel Goleman (1995, 1998, 2001), the psychologist and science writer who popularized the concept, expanded it to include such qualities as optimism, conscientiousness, motivation, empathy, and social competence. According to Goleman, these qualities may be more important to success, on the job and elsewhere, than is IQ.

The idea that emotions influence success is not new; neither does it apply only to adults. However, it is in adult life, with its "make-or-break" challenges, that we can perhaps see most clearly the role of the emotions in influencing how effectively people use their minds—as Arthur Ashe demonstrated again and again.

Goleman cites studies of nearly 500 corporations in which people who scored highest on EI rose to the top. EI seems to underlie competencies that contribute to effective performance at work. These competencies, according to Goleman (1998, 2001) fall under the heads of *self-awareness* (emotional self-awareness, accurate self-assessment, and self-confidence), *self-management* (self-control, trustworthiness, conscientiousness, adaptability, achievement drive, and initiative), *social awareness* (empathy, service orientation, and organizational awareness), and *relationship management* (developing others, exerting influence, communication, conflict management, leadership, being a catalyst for change, building bonds, and teamwork and collaboration. Excelling in at least one competency in each of these four areas seems to be a key to success in almost any job (Cherniss, 2002; Cherniss & Adler, 2000; Goleman, 1998).

Emotional intelligence may play a part in the ability to acquire and use tacit knowledge, as in the nurses' study discussed in the previous section. In nursing, as in other fields, EI may be vital to the abilities to work effectively in teams, to recognize and respond appropriately to one's own and another's feelings, and to motivate oneself and others (Cadman & Brewer, 2001). It also may affect how well people navigate intimate relationships and how healthy they remain under stress (Cherniss, 2002).

Emotional intelligence is not the opposite of cognitive intelligence, says Goleman; some people are high in both, whereas others have little of either. Emotional intelligence is reminiscent of Gardner's proposed intrapersonal and interpersonal intelligences (refer back to Chapter 9). It also resembles postformal thought in its connection between emotion and cognition.

Although research supports the role of emotions in intelligent behavior, the concept of EI is controversial. Hard as it is to assess cognitive intelligence, EI may be even harder to measure. For one thing, lumping the emotions together can be misleading. How do we assess someone who can handle fear but not guilt, or who can face stress better than boredom? Then too, the usefulness of a certain emotion may depend on the circumstances. Anger, for example, can lead to either destructive or constructive behavior. Anxiety may alert a person to danger but also may block effective action (Goleman, 1995). Furthermore, most of the alleged components of EI are usually considered personality traits. One investigation found that objective measures of EI, as currently defined, are unreliable, and those that depend on self-ratings are almost indistinguishable from personality tests (Davies, Stankov, & Roberts, 1998).

Ultimately, acting on emotions often comes down to a value judgment. Is it smarter to obey or disobey authority? To inspire others or exploit them? "Emotional skills, like intellectual ones, are morally neutral. . . . Without a moral compass to guide people in how to employ their gifts, emotional intelligence can be used for good or evil" (Gibbs, 1995, p. 68). Let's look next at the development of that "moral compass" in adulthood.

Checkpoint

Can you . . .

✔ Compare several theoretical views on adult cognition?

✔ Cite support for, and criticisms of, the concept of emotional intelligence?

Moral Reasoning

In Kohlberg's theory, introduced in Chapter 11, moral development of children and adolescents accompanies cognitive maturation. Young people advance in moral judgment as they shed egocentrism and become capable of abstract thought. In adulthood, however, moral judgments often become more complex.

Guidepost

5. How does moral reasoning develop?

According to Kohlberg, advancement to the third level of moral reasoning—fully principled, postconventional morality—is chiefly a function of experience. Most people do not reach this level until their twenties, if ever (Kohlberg, 1973). Two experiences that spur moral reasoning in young adults are encountering conflicting values away from home (as happens in college or the armed services or sometimes in foreign travel) and being responsible for the welfare of others (as in parenthood).

Experience may lead adults to reevaluate their criteria for what is right and fair. Some adults spontaneously offer personal experiences as reasons for their answers to moral dilemmas. For example, people who have had cancer, or whose relatives or friends have had cancer, are more likely to condone a man's stealing an expensive drug to save his dying wife, and to explain this view in terms of their own experience (Bielby & Papalia, 1975). Arthur Ashe's experiences in a highly competitive environment may have led him to be more activist and outspoken in his advocacy of an end to apartheid in South Africa. Such experiences, strongly colored by emotion, trigger rethinking in a way that hypothetical, impersonal discussions cannot and are more likely to help people see other points of view.

With regard to moral judgments, then, cognitive stages do not tell the whole story. Of course, someone whose thinking is still egocentric is unlikely to make moral decisions at a postconventional level; but even someone who can think abstractly may not reach the highest level of moral development unless experience catches up with cognition. Many adults who are capable of thinking for themselves do not break out of a conventional mold unless their experiences have prepared them for the shift.

Shortly before his death in 1987, Kohlberg proposed a seventh stage of moral reasoning, which moves beyond considerations of justice. In the seventh stage, adults reflect on the question "*Why* be moral?" (Kohlberg & Ryncarz, 1990, p. 192; emphasis added). The answer, said Kohlberg, lies in achieving a cosmic perspective: "a sense of unity with the cosmos, nature, or God," which enables a person to see moral

BOX 13-2

Digging Deeper
Development of Faith Across the Life Span

Can faith be studied from a developmental perspective? Yes, according to James Fowler (1981, 1989). Fowler defined faith as a way of seeing or knowing the world. To find out how people arrive at this knowledge, Fowler and his students at Harvard Divinity School interviewed more than 400 people of all ages with various ethnic, educational, and socioeconomic backgrounds and various religious or secular identifications and affiliations.

Fowler's theory focuses on the *form* of faith, not its content or object; it is not limited to any particular belief system. Faith can be religious or nonreligious: People may have faith in a god, in science, in humanity, or in a cause to which they attach ultimate worth and which gives meaning to their lives.

According to Fowler, faith develops—as do other aspects of cognition—through interaction between the maturing person and the environment. As in other stage theories, Fowler's stages of faith progress in an unvarying sequence, each building on those that went before. New experiences—crises, problems, or revelations—that challenge or upset a person's equilibrium may prompt a leap from one stage to the next. The ages at which these transitions occur are variable, and some people never leave a particular stage.

Fowler's stages correspond roughly to those described by Piaget, Kohlberg, and Erikson. The beginnings of faith, says Fowler, come at about 18 to 24 months of age, after children become self-aware, begin to use language and symbolic thought, and have developed what Erikson called *basic trust:* the sense that their needs will be met by powerful others.

- *Stage 1: Intuitive-projective faith* (ages 18–24 months to 7 years). As young children struggle to understand the forces that control their world, they form powerful, imaginative, often terrifying, and sometimes lasting images of God, heaven, and hell, drawn from the stories adults read to them. These images are often irrational, since preoper-

ational children tend to be confused about cause and effect and may have trouble distinguishing between reality and fantasy. Still egocentric, they have difficulty distinguishing God's point of view from their own or their parents'. They think of God mainly in terms of obedience and punishment.

- *Stage 2: Mythic-literal faith* (ages 7 to 12 years). Children are now more logical and begin to develop a more coherent view of the universe. Not yet capable of abstract thought, they tend to take religious stories and symbols literally, as they adopt their family's and community's beliefs and observances. They can now see God as having a perspective beyond their own, which takes into account people's effort and intent. They believe that God is fair and that people get what they deserve.

- *Stage 3: Synthetic-conventional faith* (adolescence or beyond). Adolescents, now capable of abstract thought, begin to form ideologies (belief systems) and commitments to ideals. As they search for identity, they seek a more personal relationship with God. However, their identity is not on firm ground; they look to others (usually peers) for moral authority. Their faith is unquestioning and conforms to community standards. This stage is typical of followers of organized religion; about 50 percent of adults may never move beyond it.

- *Stage 4: Individuative-reflective faith* (early to middle twenties or beyond). Adults who reach this postconventional stage examine their faith critically and think out their own beliefs, independent of external authority and group norms. Because young adults are deeply concerned with intimacy, movement into this stage is often triggered by divorce, the death of a friend, or some other stressful event.

issues "from the standpoint of the universe as a whole" (Kohlberg & Ryncarz, 1990, pp. 191, 207). The achievement of such a perspective is so rare that Kohlberg himself had questions about calling it a stage of development. Kohlberg did note that it parallels the most mature stage of faith that the theologian James Fowler (1981) identified (see Box 13-2), in which "one experiences a oneness with the ultimate conditions of one's life and being" (Kohlberg & Ryncarz, 1990, p. 202).

Culture and Moral Reasoning

Kohlberg proposed that his stages of moral development are universal. To test that proposition, researchers have tested Kohlberg's moral dilemmas in several nonwestern cultures. In India, Buddhist monks scored lower than laypeople, apparently because Kohlberg's model was inadequate for rating postconventional Buddhist principles of cooperation and nonviolence (Gielen & Kelly, 1983).

Heinz's dilemma was revised for use in Taiwan. In the revision, a shopkeeper will not give a man *food* for his sick wife. This version would seem unbelievable to Chinese villagers, who are more accustomed to hearing a shopkeeper in such a

—continued

- *Stage 5: Conjunctive faith* (midlife or beyond). Middle-aged people become more aware of the limits of reason. They recognize life's paradoxes and contradictions, and they often struggle with conflicts between fulfilling their own needs and sacrificing for others. As they begin to anticipate death, they may achieve a deeper understanding and acceptance by integrating into their faith aspects of their earlier beliefs.

- *Stage 6: Universalizing faith* (late life). In this rare, ultimate category Fowler placed such moral and spiritual leaders as Mahatma Gandhi, Martin Luther King, and Mother Teresa, whose breadth of vision and commitment to the well-being of all humanity profoundly inspire others. Consumed with a sense of "participation in a power that unifies and transforms the world," they seem "more lucid, more simple, and yet somehow more fully human than the rest of us" (Fowler, 1981, p. 201). Because they threaten the established order, they often become martyrs; and though they love life, they do not cling to it. This stage parallels Kohlberg's proposed seventh stage of moral development.

As one of the first researchers to systematically study how faith develops, Fowler has had great impact; his work has become required reading in many divinity schools. It also has been criticized on several counts (Koenig, 1994). Critics say Fowler's concept of faith is at odds with conventional definitions, which involve acceptance, not introspection. They challenge his emphasis on cognitive knowledge and claim that he underestimates the maturity of a simple, solid, unquestioning faith (Koenig, 1994). Critics also question whether faith develops in universal stages—at least in those Fowler identified. Fowler himself has cautioned that his advanced stages should not be seen as better or truer than others, though he does portray people at his highest stage as moral and spiritual exemplars.

Fowler's sample was not randomly selected; it consisted of paid volunteers who lived in or near North American cities with major colleges or universities. Thus the findings may be more representative of people with above average intelligence and education (Koenig, 1994). Neither are the findings representative of nonwestern cultures. Also, the initial sample included few people over age 60. To remedy this weakness, Richard N. Shulik (1988) interviewed 40 older adults and found a strong relationship between their stages of faith and their Kohlbergian levels of moral development. However, he also found that older people at intermediate levels of faith development were less likely to be depressed than older people at higher or lower stages. Thus Fowler's theory may overlook the adaptive value of conventional religious belief for many older adults (Koenig, 1994; see Box 18-1 in Chapter 18).

Some of these criticisms resemble those made against other models of life-span development. Piaget's, Kohlberg's, and Erikson's initial samples were not randomly selected either. More research is needed to confirm, modify, or extend Fowler's theory, especially in nonwestern cultures.

What's Your View?

- Is faith in God necessary to be a religious person?

- Do you fit into one of the stages of faith that Fowler described?

Check It Out

For more information on this topic, go to http://www.psywww.com/psyrelig (a Web site intended as an introduction to psychology of religion, which describes "what psychologists have learned about how religion influences people's lives").

---

situation say, "You have to let people have things whether they have money or not" (Wolf, 1968, p. 21).

Whereas Kohlberg's system is based on justice, the Chinese ethos leans toward conciliation and harmony. In Kohlberg's format, respondents make an either-or decision based on their own value systems. In Chinese society, people faced with moral dilemmas are expected to discuss it openly, be guided by community standards, and try to find a way of resolving the problem to please as many parties as possible. In the west, even good people may be harshly punished if, under the force of circumstances, they break a law. The Chinese are unaccustomed to universally applied laws; they are taught to abide by the decisions of a wise judge (Dien, 1982).

However, we need to be careful to avoid making broad-brush generalizations about cultural attitudes. Concepts of rights, welfare, and justice exist in all cultures, though they may be differently applied. To say that western cultures are individualistic and eastern cultures are collectivist ignores individual differences and even diametrically opposed attitudes within each culture, and the specific contextual situations in which moral judgments are applied (Turiel, 1998). For example, the outpouring of relief funds from the United States for survivors of the tsunami in

What's Your View?

- Have you ever observed or had an experience with a person from another culture that revealed cultural differences in moral principles?

Carol Gilligan (center) studied moral development in women and, later, in men and concluded that concern for others is at the highest level of moral thought.

Southeast Asia and of Hurricane Katrina in New Orleans showed that compassion may be as strong a part of the American ethos as competition.

Gender and Moral Reasoning

Because Kohlberg's original studies were done on boys and men, Carol Gilligan (1982, 1987a, 1987b) argued that his system gives a higher place to "masculine" values of justice and fairness than to "feminine" values of compassion, responsibility, and caring. Gilligan suggested that a woman's central moral dilemma is the conflict between her own needs and those of others. While most societies typically expect assertiveness and independent judgment from men, they expect from women self-sacrifice and concern for others.

To find out how women make moral choices, Gilligan (1982) interviewed 29 pregnant women about their decisions to continue or end their pregnancies. These women saw morality in terms of selfishness versus responsibility, defined as an obligation to exercise care and to avoid hurting others. Gilligan concluded that women think less about abstract justice and fairness than men do and more about their responsibilities to specific people. (Table 13-1 lists Gilligan's proposed levels of moral development in women.)

Table 13-1	Gilligan's Levels of Moral Development in Women
Stage	**Description**
Level 1: Orientation of individual survival	The woman concentrates on herself—on what is practical and what is best for her.
Transition 1: From selfishness to responsibility	The woman realizes her connection to others and thinks about what the responsible choice would be in terms of other people (including her unborn baby), as well as herself.
Level 2: Goodness as self-sacrifice	This conventional feminine wisdom dictates sacrificing the woman's own wishes to what other people want—and will think of her. She considers herself responsible for the actions of others, while holding others responsible for her own choices. She is in a dependent position, one in which her indirect efforts to exert control often turn into manipulation, sometimes through the use of guilt.
Transition 2: From goodness to truth	The woman assesses her decisions not on the basis of how others will react to them but on her intentions and the consequences of her actions. She develops a new judgment that takes into account her own needs, along with those of others. She wants to be "good" by being responsible to others, but also wants to be "honest" by being responsible to herself. Survival returns as a major concern.
Level 3: Morality of nonviolence	By elevating the injunction against hurting anyone (including herself) to a principle that governs all moral judgment and action, the woman establishes a "moral equality" between herself and others and is then able to assume the responsibility for choice in moral dilemmas.

Source: Reprinted and adapted by permission of the publisher from *In a Different Voice: Psychological Theory and Women's Development* by Carol Gilligan, Cambridge, Mass.: Harvard University Press. Copyright © 1982, 1993 by Carol Gilligan.

However, other research has not, on the whole, found significant gender differences in moral reasoning (Brabeck & Shore, 2003). One large-scale analysis comparing results from 66 studies found no significant differences in men's and women's responses to Kohlberg's dilemmas across the life span (L. J. Walker, 1984). In the few studies in which men scored slightly higher, the findings were not clearly gender-related, since the men generally were better educated and had better jobs than the women. A more recent analysis of 113 studies reached a slightly more nuanced conclusion. Although women were more likely to think in terms of care, and men were more oriented to justice, these differences were small, especially among university students. Ages of repondents and the types of dilemmas or questions presented were more significant factors than gender (Jaffee & Hyde, 2000). Thus the weight of evidence does not appear to back up either of Gilligan's original contentions: a male bias in Kohlberg's theory or a distinct female perspective on morality (L. Walker, 1995).

In her own later research, Gilligan has described moral development in *both* men and women as evolving beyond abstract reasoning. In studies using real-life moral dilemmas (such as whether a woman's lover should confess their affair to her husband), rather than hypothetical dilemmas like the ones Kohlberg used, Gilligan and her colleagues found that many people in their twenties become dissatisfied with a narrow moral logic and become more able to live with moral contradictions (Gilligan, Murphy, & Tappan, 1990). It seems, then, that if Gilligan's earlier research reflected an alternative value system, it was not gender-based. At the same time, with the inclusion of his seventh stage, Kohlberg's thinking evolved to a point of greater agreement with Gilligan's. Both theories now place responsibility to others at the highest level of moral thought. Both recognize the importance for both sexes of connections with other people and of compassion and care.

What's Your View?

- Which, if either, do you consider to be higher moral priorities: justice and rights, or compassion and responsibility?

Checkpoint

Can you...

✔ Give examples of the roles of experience and culture in adult moral development?

✔ State Gilligan's original position on gender differences in moral development, and summarize research findings on the subject?

Education and Work

Unlike young people in past generations, who typically could expect to move directly from school to work and financial independence, many emerging adults today do not have a clear picture of what they will be doing in the next 10 years. Some alternate between education and work; some pursue both at the same time (Furstenberg et al., 2005; NCES, 2005b). Most of those who do not enroll in postsecondary education, or do not finish, enter the job market, but many return later for more schooling (NCES, 2005b). Many emerging adults who are in school or living in their parents' home remain financially dependent (Schoeni & Ross, 2005). Emerging adults who are neither in school nor working—13 percent of 16- to 24-year-olds in 2003—are more likely to be poor than others in that age group; they are also more likely to be American Indian, black, or Hispanic (NCES, 2004a).

In a nationally representative longitudinal study of 5,464 young adults, 77 percent of the men and 82 percent of the women had completed their education by age 22, but 15 percent of the men and 22 percent of the women later went back to school. By their late twenties, 75 percent of both men and women were on their own and working full time, but 16 percent returned to live in their childhood home at some point before age 35 (Mouw, 2005).

Educational and vocational choices after high school may present opportunities for cognitive growth. Exposure to a new educational or work environment offers the opportunity to hone abilities, question long-held assumptions, and try out new ways

Guidepost

6. How do emerging adults make the transitions to higher education and work, and how do these experiences affect cognitive development?

of looking at the world. For the increasing number of students of nontraditional age (ages 25 and up), college or workplace education can rekindle intellectual curiosity, improve employment opportunities, and enhance work skills.

The College Transition

College is an important path to adulthood, though it is only one such route and, until recently, not the most common one (Montgomery & Côté, 2003). Between 1972 and 2001, the proportion of U.S. high school graduates who went right on to a two- or four-year college grew from less than half (49 percent) to nearly two-thirds (64 percent) (NCES, 2003, 2005b). A majority of undergraduate students attend four-year, degree-granting institutions, but an increasing proportion attend college part time or go to two-year, vocationally oriented community colleges (NCES, 2004a; Seftor & Turner, 2002). Rates of postsecondary enrollment have risen in other industrialized countries as well (NCES, 2004a).

U.S. college enrollment is at a record high—38 percent of all 18- to 24-year-olds in 2003—thanks in large part to a faster growing number of female students (Fox, Connolly, & Snyder, 2005). In 1970, women were less likely than men to go to college and less likely to finish. Today, although more young men are going to college than ever before, young women's participation has outstripped men's (NCES, 2005c), so that women make up 56 percent of undergraduate students (Freeman, 2004). Women also have higher enrollment rates than men in Canada, France, Italy, Japan, the Russian Federation, and the United Kingdom (Sen et al., 2005). In the United States, women earn more than half of all bachelor's degrees (57 percent) and master's degrees (59 percent), and nearly half (46 percent) of doctor's degrees (NCES, 2004a). Women still are more likely than men to major in traditionally "feminine" fields, such as education, nursing, English literature, and psychology; and, although more women than in the past are now earning engineering and computer science degrees, more than 70 percent of degrees in those fields still go to men. However, the gender gap has reversed in the biological and health sciences and is closing in mathematics and physical sciences, especially chemistry (NCES, 2004a; NCES Digest, 2001; see Table 13-2). The percentage of professional degrees (law, medicine, and so forth) awarded to women also has risen dramatically (see Figure 13-5).

Socioeconomic status and race/ethnicity affect access to postsecondary education. In 2001, 80 percent of high school graduates from high-income families, as compared with only 44 percent from low-income families, enrolled in college immediately after high school (NCES, 2003). In 2002, 29 percent of all students enrolled in degree-granting institutions were minorities (NCES, 2005b). The gap in immediate college enrollment between white and black students has narrowed since 1983, but the gap between white and Hispanic students has widened (NCES, 2003). In fact, the college participation rate of young Hispanic men actually declined between 1974 and 2003 (NCES, 2005c). In 2004, only 11 percent of Hispanics and 17 percent of blacks ages 25 to 29 had completed bachelor's degrees, compared with 34 percent of whites (Fox, Connolly, & Snyder, 2005). Young adults from immigrant families tend to have greater academic motivation than youth from U.S.-born families, but the cost of higher education can be a barrier, and the obligation to support and assist their families can interfere with academic aspirations (Tseng, 2004).

Increasingly, college courses and even complete degree or certificate programs are available by *distance learning,* in which courses are delivered via mail, e-mail, the Internet, telephone, video (either live and interactive or prerecorded), or other technological means (Mariani, 2001). More than half (56 percent) of postsecondary

Table 13-2	Percentages of Degrees Awarded to Women, U.S., 1970–2002.	
Bachelor's	**1970–71**	**2001–02**
Engineering	0.8	18.9%
Physics	6.7	22.6%
Geology	11.0	44.7%
Computer Science	13.6	27.6%
Chemistry	18.4	48.4%
Biological Sciences	29.1	60.8%
Mathematics	37.8	46.7%
Health Sciences	77.1	85.5%
Master's	**1970–71**	**2001–02**
Engineering	1.1	21.4%
Physics	6.9	20.9%
Geology	9.7	39.7%
Computer Science	10.3	33.2%
Chemistry	21.4	45.6%
Biological Sciences	33.6	57.8%
Mathematics	27.1	42.4%
Health Sciences	55.4	77.5%
Doctorates	**1970–71**	**2001–02**
Engineering	0.6	17.3%
Physics	2.9	15.5%
Geology	3.4	28.5%
Computer Science	2.3	22.8%
Chemistry	8.0	33.9%
Biological Sciences	16.3	44.3%
Mathematics	7.6	29.0%
Health Sciences	16.5	63.3%

Source: Cox & Alm, 2005.

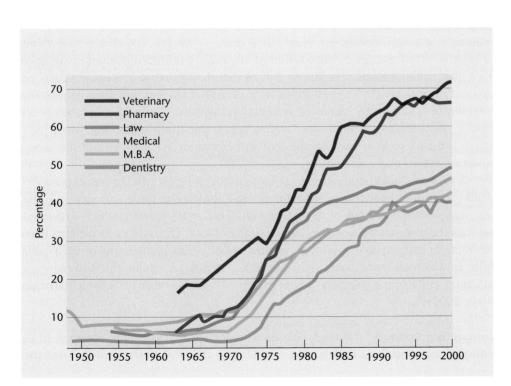

Figure 13-5

Percentage of professional degrees awarded to women: United States, 1950 to 2000. (Source: Cox & Alm, 2005; data from U.S. Department of Education.)

institutions offered distance education in 2000–2001, up from one-third (34 percent) three years earlier (NCES, 2004).

Adjusting to College Many freshmen feel overwhelmed by the demands of college. Family support, both financial and emotional, seems to be a key factor in adjustment, both for students commuting from home and those living on campus. Students who are adaptable, have high aptitude and good problem-solving skills, become actively engaged in their studies and in the academic environment, and enjoy close but autonomous relationships with their parents tend to adjust best and get the most out of college. Students who are independent and achievement-oriented tend to do best in classes that stress self-directed learning, whereas students who are more dependent and conforming learn better in structured environments. Also important is being able to build a strong social and academic network among peers and instructors (Montgomery & Côté, 2003).

Cognitive Growth in College College can be a time of intellectual discovery and personal growth, especially in verbal and quantitative skills, critical thinking, and moral reasoning (Montgomery & Côté, 2003). Students change in response to (1) the curriculum, which offers new insights and new ways of thinking; (2) other students who challenge long-held views and values; (3) the student culture, which is different from the culture of society at large; and (4) faculty members, who provide new role models. In terms of both immediate and long-term benefits, going to college— any college—is more important than which college a person attends (Montgomery & Côté, 2003).

The college experience may lead to fundamental change in the way students think (Fischer & Pruyne, 2003). In a classic study that foreshadowed current research on reflective and postformal thought, William Perry (1970) interviewed 67 Harvard and Radcliffe students throughout their undergraduate years and found that their thinking progressed from *rigidity* to *flexibility* and ultimately to *freely chosen commitments*. Many students come to college with rigid ideas about truth; they cannot conceive of any answer but the "right" one. As students begin to encounter a wide range of ideas and viewpoints, said Perry, they are assailed by uncertainty. They consider this stage temporary, however, and expect to learn the "one right answer" eventually. Next, they come to see all knowledge and values as relative. They recognize that different societies and different individuals have their own value systems. They now realize that their opinions on many issues are as valid as anyone else's, even those of a parent or teacher, but they cannot find meaning or value in this maze of systems and beliefs. Chaos has replaced order. Finally, they achieve *commitment within relativism:* they make their own judgments and choose their own beliefs and values despite uncertainty and the recognition of other valid possibilities.

A diverse student body can contribute to cognitive growth. In one experiment, small-group discussions were held among 357 students at three selective universities. Each group consisted of three white students and a fourth student, collaborating with the researchers, who was either white or black. Discussions in which a black collaborator participated produced greater novelty and complexity of ideas than those in which all participants were white. So, to a lesser extent, did discussions in which the collaborator (black or white) disagreed with the other participants (Antonio et al., 2004).

Completing College Although college entrance has become more common in the United States, *finishing* college has not. Only 1 out of 4 young people who start

What's Your View?

- From your observation, does college students' thinking typically seem to follow the stages Perry outlined?

- Have you found that ethnic diversity increases the intellectual level of a discussion?

college (1 out of 2 at four-year institutions) have received a degree after five years (Horn & Berger, 2004; NCES, 2004a). This does not mean that the rest drop out. A growing number of students, especially men, remain in college more than five years or switch from two-year to four-year institutions, showing persistence in their efforts to earn a degree (Horn & Berger, 2004; Peter & Horn, 2005).

Whether a person completes college may depend, not only on motivation, academic aptitude and preparation, and ability to work independently, but also on social integration and social support: employment opportunities, financial support, suitability of living arrangements, quality of social and academic interactions, and the fit between what the college offers and what the student wants and needs. Intervention programs for at-risk students have improved college attendance rates by creating meaningful bonds between students and teachers, finding opportunities for students to work while in college, providing academic assistance, and helping students see how college can move them toward a better future (Montgomery & Côté, 2003).

Checkpoint
Can you . . .

✔ Discuss factors affecting who goes to college and who finishes?

✔ Tell how college can affect cognitive development?

Entering the World of Work

The nature of work is changing. By 2000, there were almost four times as many Americans in service and retail jobs (61 million workers) as in manufacturing (18.4 million) (Bureau of Labor Statistics, 2001). Work arrangements are becoming more varied and less stable. More and more adults are self-employed, working at home, telecommuting, on flexible work schedules, or acting as independent contractors (Clay, 1998; McGuire, 1998; Bureau of Labor Statistics, 1998). These changes, together with a more competitive job market and the demand for a highly skilled workforce, make education and training more vital (Corcoran & Matsudaira, 2005). Higher education expands employment opportunities and earning power and enhances long-term quality of life for adults worldwide (Centre for Educational Research and Innovation, 2004; Montgomery & Côté, 2003).

Although income differentials between male and female workers exist at all levels of educational attainment, these gaps have narrowed considerably. In 1971, the average young man earned 56 percent more than the average young woman; in 2002 the difference was only 18 percent (NCES, 2004a). Female college graduates still earn less than men in several fields (Peter & Horn, 2005).

The future looks bright for this young woman graduating from the University of California at Berkeley. Today more women than men enter college and earn degrees. A college education is often the key to a good job or career and a healthy, satisfying lifestyle. Many colleges and universities provide special services and accommodations for students with disabilities.

Cognitive Growth at Work Do people change as a result of the kind of work they do? Some research says yes: People seem to grow in challenging jobs, the kind that are becoming increasingly prevalent today. Research has revealed a reciprocal relationship between the **substantive complexity** of work—the degree of thought and independent judgment it requires—and a person's flexibility in coping with cognitive demands (Kohn, 1980).

Brain research casts light on how people deal with complex work. Full development of the frontal lobes during young adulthood may equip people to handle several tasks at the same time. Magnetic resonance imaging shows that the most frontward part of the frontal lobes has a special function in problem solving and planning. This portion of the brain springs into action when a person needs to put an unfinished task "on hold" and shift attention to another task. It permits a worker to keep the first task in working memory while attending to the second—for example,

substantive complexity Degree to which a person's work requires thought and independent judgment.

to resume reading a report after being interrupted by the telephone (Koechlin, Basso, Pietrini, Panzer, & Grafman, 1999).

Cognitive growth need not stop at the end of the work day. According to the **spillover hypothesis,** cognitive gains from work carry over to nonworking hours. Studies support this hypothesis: Substantive complexity of work strongly influences the intellectual level of leisure activities (Kohn, 1980; K. Miller & Kohn, 1983).

Combining Work and Schooling According to time use diaries kept by young adults ages 18 to 34 in 11 countries, students spent more time working in the 1990s than in the previous decade (Gauthier & Furstenberg, 2005). How does juggling work and study affect cognitive development and career preparation? One longitudinal study followed a random sample of incoming freshmen at 23 two- and four-year colleges and universities in 16 states through their first 3 years of college. During the first 2 years, on- or off-campus work had little or no effect on reading comprehension, mathematical reasoning, or critical thinking skills. By the third year, part-time work had a positive effect, perhaps because employment forces students to organize their time efficiently and learn better work habits. However, working more than 15 to 20 hours a week tended to have a negative impact (Pascarella, Edison, Nora, Hagedorn, & Terenzini, 1998).

Eighty percent of graduate and professional students in the United States are employed, 63 percent full time and year-round. About 70 percent of these employed students say their jobs help them prepare for careers. However, they also report drawbacks, such as limitations on course scheduling and number and choice of classes (Snyder & Hoffman, 2002).

Adult Education and Work Skills About 47 percent of Americans ages 16 and up who are not enrolled in full-time schooling leading to a diploma or degree participate in adult educational activities, most of them work-related (NCES, 2003).

About 75 percent of work-related education for 25- to 64-year-olds is employer-supported (NCES, 2003)—and for good reason. Most occupations, especially high-paying ones, that do not require a college degree do require on-the-job training (Bureau of Labor Standards, 2000–2001). Employers see benefits of workplace education in improved morale, increased quality of work, better teamwork and problem solving, and greater ability to cope with new technology and other changes in the workplace (Conference Board, 1999).

Technological skills are increasingly necessary for success in the modern world and are a major component of work-related adult education. The increase in Internet use is a global phenomenon. More than half of all Americans use the Internet, and more than two million people go online for the first time each month. In a single year, between August 2000 and September 2001, Internet use at work among employed adults ages 25 and over increased from 26.1 percent to 41.7 percent. Young and middle-aged adults are more likely to use the Internet and e-mail at work than employed older adults (Department of Commerce, 2002).

Literacy Training **Literacy** is a fundamental requisite for participation not only in the workplace but in all facets of a modern, information-driven society. Literate adults are those who can use printed and written information to function in society, achieve their goals, and develop their knowledge and potential. At the turn of the century, a person with a fourth-grade education was considered literate; today, a high school diploma is barely adequate.

According to national and international literacy surveys conducted during the 1990s, nearly half of U.S. adults cannot understand written material, manipulate

spillover hypothesis Hypothesis that there is a positive correlation between intellectuality of work and of leisure activities because of a carryover of cognitive gains from work to leisure.

Checkpoint

Can you . . .

✔ Summarize current changes in the workplace?

✔ Explain the relationship between substantive complexity of work and cognitive development?

✔ Discuss advantages and drawbacks of combining work and schooling?

literacy In an adult, ability to use printed and written information to function in society, achieve goals, and develop knowledge and potential.

numbers, and use documents well enough to succeed in today's economy (Sum, Kirsch, & Taggart, 2002). In 2003, U.S. adults performed worse on an international literacy test than adults in Bermuda, Norway, and Switzerland but better than those in Italy (Lemke et al., 2005).

Globally, about 800 million adults were illiterate in 2002, mostly in sub-Saharan Africa and East and South Asia (UNESCO, 2004). Illiteracy is especially common among women in developing countries, where education typically is considered unimportant for females. In 1990, the United Nations launched literacy programs in such developing countries as Bangladesh, Nepal, and Somalia (Linder, 1990). In the United States, the National Literacy Act requires the states to establish literacy training centers with federal funding assistance.

Smoothing the Transition to the Workplace

Although some emerging adults successfully navigate the worlds of education and work, others flounder or sink. What can be done to ease the transition to adult responsibilities?

Some developmental scientists (Furstenberg et al., 2005; Settersten, 2005) suggest measures to strengthen the links between work and educational institutions, especially community colleges:

- Improve dialogue between educators and employers.

- Modify school and work schedules to adapt to the needs of working students.

- Let employers help design work-study programs.

- Increase availability of temporary and part-time work.

- Relate better what students learn at work and in school.

- Improve training of vocational guidance counselors.

- Make better use of study and support groups and tutoring and mentoring programs.

- Provide scholarships, financial aid, and health insurance to part-time as well as full-time students and employees.

Guidepost

7. How can young people be helped to make the transition to the workplace?

Checkpoint

Can you . . .

✔ Explain the need for work-related education?

✔ Discuss trends in adult literacy?

✔ List proposals for easing the transition to the workplace?

Refocus

Thinking back to the Focus vignette about Arthur Ashe at the beginning of this chapter:

- What direct and indirect influences on health and fitness does Ashe's story illustrate?

- Do you see evidence of reflective thinking, postformal thought, tacit knowledge, emotional intelligence, or moral reasoning in the way Ashe handled the opportunities and challenges of his career and personal life?

Work affects day-to-day life, not only on the job but also at home, and it brings both satisfaction and stress. In Chapter 14, we explore the effects of work on relationships as we look at psychosocial development in young adulthood.

SUMMARY AND KEY TERMS

Emerging Adulthood

Guidepost 1: What does it mean to be an adult, and what factors affect the timing of entrance to adulthood?

- In advanced technological societies, entrance into adulthood is not clearly marked; it takes longer and follows more varied routes than in the past. Thus, some developmental scientists suggest that the period from the late teens through the midtwenties has become a distinct transitional period called *emerging adulthood.*

- Emerging adulthood consists of multiple milestones or transitions, and their order and timing vary. Passage of these milestones, or other culture-specific criteria, may determine when a young person feels like an adult.

   emerging adulthood *(474)*

PHYSICAL DEVELOPMENT

Health and Physical Condition

Guidepost 2: In what physical condition is the typical young adult, and what factors affect health and well-being?

- The typical young adult is in good condition; physical and sensory abilities are usually excellent.

- Accidents are the leading cause of death in young adulthood.

- The mapping of the human genome is enabling the discovery of genetic bases for certain disorders.

- Lifestyle factors such as diet, obesity, exercise, sleep, smoking, and substance use or abuse can affect health and survival.

- Good health is related to higher income and education. African Americans and some other minorities tend to be less healthy than other Americans, in part due to SES.

- Women tend to live longer than men, in part for biological reasons, but perhaps also because they are more health-conscious.

- Social relationships, especially marriage, tend to be associated with physical and mental health.

   alcoholism *(480)*

Sexual and Reproductive Issues

Guidepost 3: What are some sexual and reproductive issues at this time of life?

- Menstrual disorders, sexually transmitted diseases, and infertility can be concerns during young adulthood.

- Although some STDs have become less prevalent, others are on the rise.

- The AIDS epidemic is coming under control in the United States, but heterosexual transmission has increased, particularly among young women.

- The most common cause of infertility in men is a low sperm count; the most common cause in women is blockage of the fallopian tubes.

- Infertile couples now have several options for assisted reproduction, but these techniques may involve ethical and practical issues.

   premenstrual syndrome (PMS) *(484)*

   infertility *(486)*

COGNITIVE DEVELOPMENT

Perspectives on Adult Cognition

Guidepost 4: What is distinctive about adult thought and intelligence?

- Some investigators propose distinctively adult forms of cognition beyond formal operations. Reflective thinking emphasizes complex logic; postformal thought involves intuition and emotion as well.

- Schaie proposed seven stages of age-related cognitive development: acquisitive (childhood and adolescence), achieving (young adulthood), responsible and executive (middle adulthood), and reorganizational, reintegrative, and legacy-creating (late adulthood).

- According to Sternberg's triarchic theory of intelligence, the experiential and contextual elements become particularly important during adulthood. Tests that measure tacit knowledge are useful complements to traditional intelligence tests.

- Emotional intelligence may play an important part in life success. However, emotional intelligence is controversial and hard to measure.

   reflective thinking *(488)*

   postformal thought *(489)*

   acquisitive stage *(491)*

   achieving stage *(491)*

   responsible stage *(491)*

   executive stage *(491)*

   reorganizational stage *(491)*

   reintegrative stage *(491)*

   legacy-creating stage *(491)*

   experiential element *(492)*

   contextual element *(492)*

   componential element *(492)*

   tacit knowledge *(493)*

   emotional intelligence *(494)*

Moral Reasoning

Guidepost 5: How does moral reasoning develop?

- According to Lawrence Kohlberg, moral development in adulthood depends primarily on experience, though it cannot exceed the limits set by cognitive development. Experience may be interpreted differently in various cultural contexts.

- Kohlberg, shortly before his death, proposed a seventh stage of moral development, which involves seeing moral issues from a cosmic perspective. This is similar to the highest stage of faith proposed by James Fowler.
- Carol Gilligan initially proposed that women have an ethic of care, whereas Kohlberg's theory emphasizes justice. However, later research, including her own, has not supported a distinction between men's and women's moral outlook.

Education and Work

Guidepost 6: **How do emerging adults make the transitions to higher education and work, and how do these experiences affect cognitive development?**

- A majority of emerging adults now go to college, either to two-year or four-year institutions. More women than men now go to college, and an increasing number pursue traditionally male-dominated fields.
- Depending on their major field, college students often show specific kinds of improvement in reasoning abilities.

- According to Perry, college students' thinking tends to progress from rigidity to flexibility to freely chosen commitments.
- Research has found a relationship between substantive complexity of work and cognitive growth, as well as between complex work and intellectually demanding leisure activities.
- Changes in the workplace call for higher education or training. Work-related continuing education can help adults improve their workplace skills.
- Both in the United States and internationally, programs are being developed to help adults with low literacy skills. In developing countries, illiteracy is more common among women than among men.

substantive complexity *(503)*

spillover hypothesis *(504)*

literacy *(504)*

Guidepost 7: **How can young people be helped to make the transition to the workplace?**

- The transition to the workplace could be eased through measures to strengthen vocational education and its links with work.

Psychosocial Development in Young Adulthood

*Every adult is in need of help,
of warmth, of protection . . .
in many ways differing [from]
and yet in many ways similar
to the needs of the child.*

Erich Fromm, *The Sane Society*, 1955

Focus
Ingrid Bergman, "Notorious" Actress*

Ingrid Bergman

Ingrid Bergman (1915–1982) was one of the world's most distinguished stage and screen actresses. Perhaps best remembered for her starring role in *Casablanca,* she won Academy Awards for *Gaslight, Anastasia,* and *Murder on the Orient Express;* the New York Film Critics' Award for *Autumn Sonata;* and an Emmy for *The Turn of the Screw.* In 1981, a year before her death, she came out of retirement to play the Israeli prime minister Golda Meir in the Emmy-winning *A Woman Called Golda.*

Bergman's personal life was as dramatic as any movie plot. One of her film titles, *Notorious,* sums up the abrupt change in her public image in 1949, when Bergman—known as a paragon of wholesomeness and purity—shocked the world by leaving her husband and 10-year-old daughter for the Italian film director Roberto Rossellini. Compounding the scandal was the news that Bergman was pregnant by Rossellini, a married man.

Bergman had been obsessed with acting since she had seen her first play at the age of 11 in her native Sweden. Tall, awkward, and shy, she came alive onstage. Plucked out of Stockholm's Royal Dramatic School at 18 to make her first film, she braved the wrath of the school's director, who warned that movies would destroy her talent.

At 22, she married Dr. Petter Lindstrom, a handsome, successful dentist eight years her senior, who later became a prominent brain surgeon. It was he who urged her to accept the producer David Selznick's invitation to go to Hollywood to make *Intermezzo.* At 23, she arrived, to be joined later by her husband and infant daughter, Pia.

Her filmmaking was punctuated by periodic spells of domesticity. "I have plenty to do as usual, and having a home, husband and child ought to be enough for any woman's life," she wrote during one such interlude. "But still I think every day is a lost day. As if only half of me is alive" (Bergman & Burgess, 1980, p. 110).

*Sources of biographical information about Ingrid Bergman are Bergman and Burgess (1980) and Spoto (1997).

509

Bergman began to see her husband—whom she had always leaned on for help and decisions—as overprotective, controlling, jealous, and critical. The couple spent long hours, days, and weeks apart—she at the studio or on tour, he at the hospital.

Meanwhile, Bergman was becoming dissatisfied with filming on studio lots. When she saw Rossellini's award-winning *Open City,* she was stunned by its power and realism and by Rossellini's artistic freedom and courage. She wrote to him, offering to come to Italy and work with him. The result was *Stromboli*—and the end of what she now saw as a constrictive, unfulfilling marriage. "It was not my intention to fall in love and go to Italy forever," she wrote to Lindstrom apologetically. "But how can I help it or change it?"

At 33, Bergman, who had been number one at the box office, became a Hollywood outcast. Her affair with Rosselini made headlines worldwide. So did the illegitimate birth of Robertino in 1950, Bergman's hurried Mexican divorce and proxy marriage there to Rossellini (who had had his own marriage annulled), the birth of twin daughters in 1952, and the struggle over visitation rights with Pia, who took her father's side and did not see her guilt-ridden mother for six years.

The tempestuous Bergman-Rossellini love match did not last. Every picture they made together failed, and finally, so did the marriage. But their mutual bond with their children, to whom Bergman gave Rossellini custody to avoid another bitter battle, made these ex-spouses a continuing part of each other's lives. In 1958, at the age of 43, Ingrid Bergman—her career, by this time, rehabilitated and peace made with her eldest daughter—began her third marriage, to Lars Schmidt, a Swedish-born theatrical producer. It lasted sixteen years, despite constant work-related separations, and ended in an amicable divorce. Schmidt and Bergman remained close friends for the rest of her life.

Ingrid Bergman's story is a dramatic reminder of the impact of cultural change on personal attitudes and behavior. The furor over her affair with Rossellini may seem strange today, when cohabitation, extramarital sex, divorce, and out-of-wedlock birth have become more common. Yet, now as then, personal choices made in young adulthood establish a framework for the rest of life. Bergman's marriages and divorces, the children she bore and loved, her passionate pursuit of her vocation, and her agonizing over the conflicting demands of work and family were akin to the life events and issues that confront many young women today.

Did Bergman change with maturity and experience? On the surface, she seemed to keep repeating the same cycle again and again. Yet, in her handling of her second and third divorces, she seemed calmer, more pragmatic, and more in command. Still, her basic approach to life remained the same: She did what she felt she must, come what may.

Does personality stop growing when the body does, or does it keep developing throughout life? How have paths to adulthood and intimate relationships changed in recent decades? In this chapter, we explore questions such as these. We examine the choices that frame personal and social life: adopting a sexual lifestyle; marrying, cohabiting, or remaining single; having children or not; and establishing and maintaining friendships.

After you have read and studied this chapter, you should be able to answer each of the Guidepost questions that follow. Look for them again in the margins, where they point to important concepts throughout the chapter. To check your understanding of these Guideposts, review the end-of-chapter summary. Checkpoints located at periodic spots throughout the chapter will help you verify your understanding of what you have read.

1. Does personality change during adulthood, and if so, how?

2. How have paths to adulthood changed in recent decades, and what influences those transitions?

3. How is intimacy expressed in friendship, love, and sexuality?

4. Why do some people remain single?

5. What is the nature of gay and lesbian relationships?

6. What explains the rise in cohabitation, and what forms does it take?

7. What do adults gain from marriage, what cultural patterns surround it, and why do some marriages succeed while others fail?

8. When do most adults become parents, and how does parenthood affect a marriage?

9. How do dual-earner couples divide responsibilities and deal with role conflicts?

10. Why have divorce rates risen, and how do adults adjust to divorce, remarriage, and stepparenthood?

Personality Development: Four Views

Whether personality primarily shows stability or change depends in part on how we study and measure it. Four classic approaches to adult psychosocial development are represented by *normative-stage models,* the *timing-of-events model, trait models,* and *typological models.*

Normative-stage models portray age-related development that continues throughout the adult life span, much as in childhood and adolescence. Normative-stage research has found major, predictable changes in adult personality. The **timing-of-events model** holds that change is related not so much to age as to the expected or unexpected occurrence and timing of important life events.

Trait models focus on mental, emotional, temperamental, and behavioral traits, such as cheerfulness and irritability. Most trait-based studies find that adult personality typically changes noticeably through emerging adulthood and more slowly, if at all, after that. **Typological models** identify broader personality types, or styles, that represent how personality traits are organized within the individual. These models tend to find considerable stability in personality.

These four approaches to personality development (see Table 14-1) ask different questions about adult development, look at different aspects of development, and often use different methods. For example, normative-stage models were built on in-depth interviews and biographical materials, whereas trait researchers rely heavily on personality inventories and questionnaires. It is not surprising, then, that researchers within each of these traditions often come out with results that are difficult to reconcile or even to compare.

 Guidepost

1. Does personality change during adulthood, and if so, how?

normative-stage models
Theoretical models that describe psychosocial development in terms of a definite sequence of age-related changes.

timing-of-events model
Theoretical model that describes adult psychosocial development as a response to the expected or unexpected occurrence and timing of important life events.

trait models Theoretical models of personality development that focus on mental, emotional, temperamental, and behavioral traits, or attributes.

typological models Theoretical models of personality development that identify broad personality types, or styles.

Table 14-1 Four Views of Personality Development

Models	Questions Asked	Methods Used	Change or Stability
Normative-stage models	Does personality change in typical ways at certain periods throughout the life course?	In-depth interviews, biographical materials	Normative personality changes, having to do with personal goals, work, and relationships, occur in stages.
Timing-of-events model	When do important life events typically occur? What if they occur earlier or later than usual?	Statistical studies, interviews, questionnaires	Nonnormative timing of life events can cause stress and affect personality development.
Trait models	Do personality traits fall into groups, or clusters? Do these clusters of traits change with age?	Personality inventories, questionnaires, factor analysis	Personality changes substantially until age 30, more slowly thereafter.
Typological models	Can basic personality types be identified, and how well do they predict the life course?	Interviews, clinical judgments, Q-sorts, behavior ratings, self-reports	Personality types tend to show continuity from childhood through adulthood; but certain events can change the life course.

Normative-Stage Models

Normative-stage models hold that adults follow the same basic sequence of age-related psychosocial changes. The changes are *normative* in that they seem to be common to most members of a population; and they emerge in successive periods, or *stages*, sometimes marked by emotional crises that pave the way for further development.

Erikson: Intimacy versus Isolation Erikson's sixth stage of psychosocial development, **intimacy versus isolation,** turns on the major issue of young adulthood. If young adults cannot make deep personal commitments to others, said Erikson, they risk becoming overly isolated and self-absorbed. However, they do need some isolation to reflect on their lives. As they work to resolve conflicting demands of intimacy, competitiveness, and distance, they develop an ethical sense, which Erikson considered the mark of the adult. Intimate relationships demand sacrifice and compromise. Young adults who have developed a strong sense of self during adolescence are ready to fuse their identity with that of another person.

Resolution of this stage results in the "virtue" of *love:* mutual devotion between partners who have chosen to share their lives, have children, and help those children achieve their own healthy development. A decision not to fulfill the natural procreative urge has serious consequences for development, according to Erikson. His theory has been criticized for excluding single, celibate, homosexual, and childless people from his blueprint for healthy development, as well as for taking the male pattern of developing intimacy after identity as the norm (refer back to Chapter 12). However, we need to remember that Erikson developed his theory in the mid-twentieth century, in a different societal context from the one in which we now live.

Erikson's Heirs: Vaillant and Levinson Erik Erikson's belief that personality changes throughout life inspired classic studies by George Vaillant and Daniel Levinson. In 1938, 268 eighteen-year-old self-reliant and emotionally and physically healthy Harvard undergraduates were selected for the Grant Study. By the time they reached midlife, Vaillant (1977) saw a typical developmental pattern. At age 20, many men were still dominated by their parents. During their twenties, and sometimes their thirties, they achieved autonomy, married, had children, and deepened friendships. They worked hard at their careers and devoted themselves to their families, rarely questioning whether they had chosen the right woman or the right occupation.

intimacy versus isolation
Erikson's sixth stage of psychosocial development, in which young adults either make commitments to others or face a possible sense of isolation and self-absorption.

Intimacy, the major achievement of young adulthood in Erikson's theory of personality development, comes about through commitment to a relationship that may demand sacrifice and compromise. According to Erikson, intimacy is possible for a man only after he has achieved his own identity, but women achieve identity through intimacy. Gilligan and other researchers propose a different sequence for women, who, they say, often achieve intimacy first and then go on to find identity later, sometimes years later.

Levinson (1978, 1980, 1986) and his colleagues at Yale University, through in-depth interviews and personality tests of 40 men ages 35 to 45, formed a theory of personality development based on an evolving **life structure:** "the underlying pattern or design of a person's life at a given time" (1986, p. 6). Adults, according to Levinson, shape their life structures during overlapping eras of about 20 to 25 years, each divided into entry and culminating phases. Each phase has its own tasks, whose accomplishment becomes the foundation for the next life structure. The eras and phases are linked by transitional periods, when people reappraise, and think about restructuring, their lives. Indeed, according to Levinson, people spend nearly half their adult lives in transitions, which may involve crises.

In the entry phase of young adulthood (ages 17 to 33), according to Levinson, a man builds his first provisional life structure. He leaves his parents' home, perhaps to go to college or into the armed services, and becomes financially and emotionally independent. He chooses an occupation, perhaps a wife, and forms a *dream* about what he hopes to achieve in the future. In the age-30 transition, he reevaluates his entry life structure. Then, in the culminating phase of early adulthood, he settles down and sets goals (a professorship, for instance, or a certain level of income) and a time for achieving them (say, by age 40). He anchors his life in family, occupation, and community. How he deals with the issues of this phase will affect the midlife transition (see Chapter 16).

Normative Studies of Women In a companion study of 45 women, Levinson (1996) found that women go through similar eras, phases, and transitions as those he had found for men; but because of traditional cultural divisions between masculine and feminine roles, women may face different psychological and environmental constraints in forming their life structures, and their transitions tend to take longer.

In a longitudinal study of 140 women from the classes of 1958 and 1960 at Mills College in Oakland, California, researchers found evidence of normative personality change. One such change in young adulthood was an increase and then a decline in traits associated with femininity (sympathy and compassion combined with a sense of vulnerability, self-criticism, and lack of confidence and initiative). Between ages 27 and 43, the women developed more self-discipline and commitment, independence, confidence, and coping skills (Helson & Moane, 1987).

Evaluating Normative-Stage Models Both the Grant Study and Levinson's early work were based on small groups of all or mostly white middle-class to upper-middle-class men born in the 1920s or 1930s. Likewise, Levinson's small sample of women born between about 1935 and 1945 and Helson's Mills College graduates were not representative. These men's and women's development was affected by societal events that did not affect earlier or later cohorts, as well as by their socioeconomic status, ethnicity, and gender.

Many of the men in Vaillant's and Levinson's studies grew up during the economic depression of the 1930s and, as they moved into the world of work, benefited from an expanding economy after World War II. Levinson's and Helson's women lived through a time of great change in women's roles brought about by the women's movement, economic trends, and changing patterns in family life and in the workplace. Today, when young adults follow much more diverse developmental paths, and choices in women's roles are widely accepted, young adults may develop differently than did the men and women in these studies. In addition, the findings of normative-stage research may not apply to other cultures, some of which have very different patterns of life course development (see Box 16-1 in Chapter 16 for a discussion of life stages among the Gusii people of southwestern Kenya).

life structure In Levinson's theory, the underlying pattern of a person's life at a given time, built on whatever aspects of life the person finds most important.

developmental tasks In normative-stage theories, typical challenges that need to be mastered for successful adaptation to each stage of life.

Nevertheless, normative-stage research has had a continuing impact. Psychologists, drawing especially upon the work of Erikson, have identified **developmental tasks** that need to be accomplished for successful adaptation to each stage of life (Roisman, Masten, Coatsworth, & Tellegen, 2004). Among the developmental tasks of young adulthood are leaving the childhood home for advanced schooling, work, or military service; developing new and more intimate friendships and romantic relationships; and developing a sense of efficacy and *individuation*—a sense of the self as independent and self-reliant (Arnett, 2000, 2004; Scharf, Mayseless, & Kivenson-Baron, 2004). Other developmental tasks of this period, discussed in Chapter 13, include completing education, entering the world of work, and becoming financially independent.

Perhaps the most important message of normative-stage models is that adults continue to develop. Whether or not people develop in the particular ways suggested by these models, they have challenged the notion that hardly anything important happens to personality after adolescence.

Timing-of-Events Model

Instead of looking at adult personality development as a function of age, the *timing-of-events model,* supported by Bernice Neugarten and others (Neugarten, Moore, & Lowe, 1965; Neugarten & Neugarten, 1987), holds that the course of development depends on when certain events occur in people's lives.

normative life events In the timing-of-events model, commonly expected life experiences that occur at customary times.

As we discussed in Chapter 1, **normative life events** (also called *normative age-graded events*) are those that typically happen at certain times of life—such events as marriage, parenthood, grandparenthood, and retirement. Events that occur when expected are *on time;* events that occur earlier or later than usual are *off time.* Events that are normative when they are "on time" become nonnormative when they are "off time." According to this model, people usually are keenly aware of their own timing and of the **social clock,** their society's norms or expectations for the appropriate timing of life events.

social clock Set of cultural norms or expectations for the times of life when certain important events, such as marriage, parenthood, entry into work, and retirement, should occur.

If events occur on time, development proceeds smoothly. If not, stress can result. Stress may come from an unexpected event (such as losing a job), an event that happens off time (being widowed at age 35 or being forced to retire at 50), or the failure of an expected event to occur at all (never being married, or being unable to have a child). Personality differences influence the way people respond to life events and may even influence their timing. For example, a resilient person is likely to experience an easier transition to adulthood and the tasks and events that lie ahead than an overly anxious person, who may put off relationship or career decisions.

The typical timing of events varies from culture to culture and from generation to generation. One illustration is the rise since 1970 in the average age when adults first marry in the United States (Fields, 2004); another is the trend toward delayed first childbirth (Martin et al., 2005). A timetable that seems right to people in one cohort may not seem so to the next.

Architect Harold Fisher, who at age 100 was named America's oldest worker, is living proof that there is no longer a single "right time" for retirement in U.S. society.

Since the mid-twentieth century western societies have become less age-conscious. Today people are more accepting of 40-year-old first-time parents and 40-year-old grandparents, 50-year-old retirees and 75-year-old workers, 60-year-olds in jeans and 30-year-old college presidents. This widened range of age norms undermines the predictability on which the timing-of-events model is based.

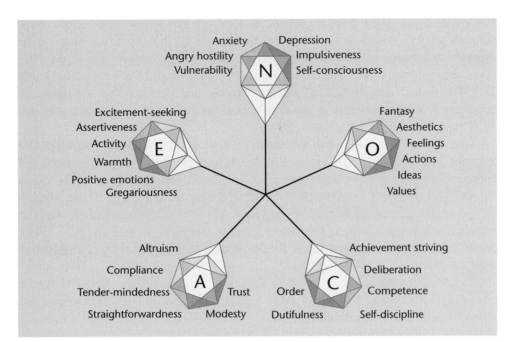

Figure 14-1

Costa and McCrae's five-factor model. Each factor, or domain of personality, represents a cluster of related traits or facets. N = neuroticism, E = extraversion, O = openness to experience, A = agreeableness, C = conscientiousness. (Source: Adapted from Costa & McCrae, 1980.)

The timing-of-events model has made an important contribution to our understanding of adult personality by emphasizing the individual life course and challenging the idea of universal, age-related change. However, its usefulness may well be limited to cultures and historical periods in which norms of behavior are stable and widespread.

Trait Models: Costa and McCrae's Five Factors

Trait models look for stability or change in personality traits. Paul T. Costa and Robert R. McCrae have developed and tested a **five-factor model** (see Figure 14-1) consisting of factors or dimensions that seem to underlie five groups of associated traits, known as the "Big Five." They are (1) *neuroticism (N)*, (2) *extraversion (E)*, (3) *openness to experience (O)*, (4) *conscientiousness (C)*, and (5) *agreeableness (A)*. Studies in more than 30 cultures, from Zimbabwe to Peru, have found the same five factors, which appear, therefore, to be universal. However, they may not be equally important in every culture, and additional factors may exist in some cultures (McCrae, 2002).

Neuroticism is a cluster of six traits indicating emotional instability: anxiety, hostility, depression, self-consciousness, impulsiveness, and vulnerability. *Extraversion* also has six facets: warmth, gregariousness, assertiveness, activity, excitement-seeking, and positive emotions. We can speculate that Ingrid Bergman would have had fairly high scores on some facets of neuroticism and extraversion and low scores on others.

People who are *open to experience* are willing to try new things and embrace new ideas. Ingrid Bergman probably would have scored high in this area.

Conscientious people are achievers: They are competent, orderly, dutiful, deliberate, and disciplined. *Agreeable* people are trusting, straightforward, altruistic, compliant, modest, and easily swayed. Some of these characteristics could be identified with Ingrid Bergman in her youth but less so as she got older.

Continuity and Change in the Five-Factor Model By analyzing cross-sectional, longitudinal, and sequential data from several large samples of U.S. men and women of all ages, Costa and McCrae (1980, 1988, 1994a, 1994b; Costa et al., 1986;

five-factor model Theoretical model of personality, developed and tested by Costa and McCrae, based on the "Big Five" factors underlying clusters of related traits: neuroticism, extraversion, openness to experience, conscientiousness, and agreeableness.

McCrae & Costa, 1984; McCrae, Costa, & Busch, 1986) found considerable continuity in all five domains. Furthermore, heritability of the Big Five seems to be somewhere between 40 and 66 percent (Bouchard, 1994). At least one of the "Big Five," agreeableness, seems to be identifiable in childhood. In a longitudinal study of 194 boys and girls in Central Finland, teacher and peer reports of aggression, compliance, and self-control at age 8 predicted the degree of agreeableness at age 36 (Laursen, Pulkkinen, & Adams, 2002).

The U.S. studies did reveal noticeable changes in all five factors between adolescence and age 30, with much slower change thereafter. Agreeableness and conscientiousness generally increase during adulthood, whereas neuroticism, extraversion, and openness to experience decline (McCrae et al., 2000). These patterns of age-related change appear to be universal and thus, these researchers suggest, maturational. Similar patterns have been found in Germany, Italy, Portugal, Croatia, South Korea, Estonia, Russia, Japan, Spain, Britain, Turkey, and the Czech Republic (McCrae, 2002).

Gender differences also seem to be universal, suggesting that they may have a biological basis. Women typically score higher than men on both neuroticism and agreeableness and on certain facets of extraversion and openness to experience, namely, warmth and openness to aesthetic experience. Men usually score higher on two other facets of E and O, assertiveness and openness to ideas. There are few gender differences in conscientiousness (McCrae, 2002).

In a study of representative samples of adults ages 25 to 65 in the United States and Germany, the "Big Five" (especially neuroticism) were associated with subjective feelings of health and well-being (Staudinger, Fleeson, & Baltes, 1999). Conscientiousness has been linked with health-related behaviors that contribute to long life (Bogg & Roberts, 2004; see Box 18-1 in Chapter 18). Various "Big Five" traits also have been associated with marital satisfaction (Gattis, Berus, Simpson, & Christensen, 2004), parent-infant relationships (Kochanska, Friesenborg, Lange, & Martel, 2004), and personality disorders. People high in neuroticism tend to be subject to anxiety and depression; people low in extraversion are prone to social phobia and agoraphobia (fear of open spaces) (Bienvenu, Nestadt, Samuels, Costa, & Eaton, 2001).

Evaluating the Five-Factor Model This body of work has made a powerful case for continuity of personality, especially after age 30. Still, the five-factor model has critics. Contextualist theories point to experiential factors, such as social roles, life events, and social environments, as influences on personality. Baltes's lifespan developmental approach (refer back to Chapter 1) proposes that personality shows considerable plasticity throughout life.

A study of 132,515 mostly white, middle-class volunteers, ages 21 to 60, in the United States and Canada, who filled out personality measures on the Internet, sought to test both the five-factor model and the contextualist approach (Srivastava, John, Gosling, & Potter, 2003). Although the *direction* of change for each of the Big Five traits was similar to what Costa and McCrae have found, there was no marked slowdown in change after age 30. Instead, this research found gradual, systematic change through early and middle adulthood. Also, the course of development was different for different traits. Conscientiousness showed the greatest change during emerging adulthood, when many adults are entering and advancing in the world of work and are forming committed partnerships, but agreeableness showed the greatest change from the late twenties through the thirties, when adults typically are raising children.

However, the direction of causation needs further study. Do maturational changes impel people to seek out social roles that fit their maturing personalities, or do adults change to meet the demands of their new roles? Or is change bidirectional? In a longitudinal study of 980 people born in Dunedin, New Zealand, in a single year, personality traits at age 18 affected work experiences in emerging adulthood, and work experiences, in turn, effected modest changes in personality as measured at age 26. For example, adolescents who were sociable and affable tended to rise faster in their early careers; and in turn, those who were in higher status, more satisfying jobs tended to become more sociable and affable (Roberts, Caspi, & Moffitt, 2003). This research suggests that personality in adulthood may be more malleable and more complex than previous trait research suggests.

Other criticisms of the five-factor model are methodological. Jack Block (1995a, 1995b) argues that, because the five-factor model is based largely on subjective ratings, it may lack validity unless supplemented by other measures. The selection of factors and their associated facets is arbitrary and perhaps not all-inclusive; other researchers have chosen different factors and have divided up the associated traits differently. (For example, is warmth a facet of extraversion, as in the Big Five model, or is it better classified as an aspect of agreeableness?) Finally, personality is more than a collection of traits. A model that looks only at individual differences in trait groupings offers no theoretical framework for understanding how personality works within the person.

Typological Models

Block (1971) was a pioneer in the *typological approach*. Typological research seeks to complement and expand trait research by looking at personality as a functioning whole.

Using a variety of techniques, researchers working independently have identified several basic personality types: *ego-resilient, overcontrolled,* and *undercontrolled*. People of these three types differ in **ego-resiliency**, or adaptability under stress, and **ego-control**, or self-control. *Ego-resilient* people are well adjusted: self-confident, independent, articulate, attentive, helpful, cooperative, and task-focused. *Overcontrolled* people are shy, quiet, anxious, and dependable; they tend to keep their thoughts to themselves and to withdraw from conflict, and they are the most subject to depression. *Undercontrolled* people are active, energetic, impulsive, stubborn, and easily distracted. These or similar personality types seem to exist in both sexes, across cultures and ethnic groups, and in children, adolescents, and adults (Caspi, 1998; Hart, Hofmann, Edelstein, & Keller, 1997; Pulkkinen, 1996; Robins, John, Caspi, Moffitt, & Stouthamer-Loeber, 1996; van Lieshout, Haselager, Riksen-Walraven, & van Aken, 1995).

In a longitudinal study of 1,024 three-year-olds in New Zealand, observer-rated personality types similar to the three categories just described showed predictable relationships to personality characteristics at age 19 (Caspi & Silva, 1995). Of course, the finding of a tendency toward continuity of attitudes and behavior does not mean that personalities never change, or that certain people are condemned to a life of maladjustment. Undercontrolled children may get along better in early adulthood if they find niches in which their energy and spontaneity are considered a plus. Overcontrolled youngsters, like Ingrid Bergman in her youth, may come out of their shell if they find that their quiet dependability is valued.

Although personality types established in childhood may predict *trajectories,* or long-term patterns of behavior, certain events may change the life course (Caspi, 1998). For some young adults, military service offers a "time-out" period and an opportunity to redirect their lives. For young people with adjustment problems, marriage to a supportive spouse can be a turning point, leading to more positive outcomes.

ego-resiliency Adaptability under potential sources of stress.

ego-control Self-control.

A bicycle messenger's job requires energy, spontaneity, and risk taking—qualities that adults who were undercontrolled in childhood are likely to show.

What's Your View?

• Which of the models presented here seems to you to most accurately describe psychosocial development in adulthood?

Checkpoint

Can you . . .

✔ Compare four theoretical approaches to adult psychosocial development and discuss attempts to synthesize them?

Guidepost

2. How have paths to adulthood changed in recent decades, and what influences those transitions?

Integrating Approaches to Personality Development

Advocates of personality stability and advocates of change often defend their positions zealously, but personality development clearly entails some of both. In an effort to integrate diverse approaches to personality development, Costa and McCrae have mapped six interrelated elements that "make up the raw material of most personality theories" (1994a, p. 23). These elements are *basic tendencies, external influences, characteristic adaptations, self-concept, objective biography,* and *dynamic processes.*

Basic tendencies include not only personality traits, but also physical health, appearance, gender, sexual orientation, intelligence, and artistic abilities. These tendencies, which may be either inherited or acquired, interact with *external* (environmental) *influences* to produce certain *characteristic adaptations:* social roles, attitudes, interests, skills, activities, habits, and beliefs. For example, it takes a combination of musical inclination (a basic tendency) and exposure to an instrument (an external influence) to produce musical skill (a characteristic adaptation). Adaptations may occur in response to new responsibilities and demands, traumatic events, or major cultural transformations (such as the feminist movement), but basic tendencies remain unchanged and influence the way a person adapts (Caspi, 1998; Clausen, 1993; Costa & McCrae, 1994a).

Basic tendencies and characteristic adaptations help shape the *self-concept,* which bears only a partial resemblance to the *objective biography,* the actual events of a person's life. Thus a woman may think of herself as having more musical ability than she has objectively demonstrated, and her behavior may be influenced by that self-image. *Dynamic processes* link the other five elements; one such process is learning, which enables people to adapt to external influences (for example, to become accomplished in playing a musical instrument) (Costa & McCrae, 1994a).

Various theorists emphasize one or another of these elements. Trait models focus on basic tendencies, which are the least likely to change. Typological models seek to identify certain characteristic adaptations, such as resiliency. Normative-crisis models and the timing-of-events model highlight dynamic processes that reflect universal or particular aspects of the objective biography (Costa & McCrae, 1994a).

Changing Paths to Adulthood

If some of the classic theories of adult psychosocial development, particularly normative-stage and timing-of-events models, seem out of date, it is largely because paths to adulthood are far more varied than they used to be. Before the 1960s, young people in the United States typically finished school, left home, got a job, got married, and had children, in that order. By the 1990s, only 1 in 4 young adults followed that sequence (Mouw, 2005).

For many young people today, emerging adulthood, the period from about age 18 to the mid- or even late twenties, is a time of experimentation before assuming adult roles and responsibilities. A young man or woman may get a job and an apartment and revel in the single life. A young married couple may move in with parents while they "get on their feet" or finish school or after a job loss. Such traditional developmental tasks as finding stable work and developing long-term romantic relationships may be postponed until the thirties or even later (Roisman, Masten, Coatsworth, & Tellegen, 2004). What influences affect these varied paths to adulthood?

Influences on Paths to Adulthood

Individual paths to adulthood are influenced by such factors as gender, academic ability, early attitudes toward education, expectations in late adolescence, and social class (Mouw, 2005; Osgood et al., 2005). Young men tend to leave home earlier than young women and to get married later. Young women tend to finish their education earlier but are more likely to return to school (Mouw, 2005).

Increasingly, however, emerging adults of both sexes extend education and delay parenthood (Osgood et al., 2005), and these are usually keys to future success (Sandefur, Eggerling-Boeck, & Park, 2005) as well as to current well-being. In a longitudinal study that followed a nationally representative sample of high school seniors each year since 1975, emerging adults with the highest well-being were those who were not yet married, had no children, attended college, and lived away from home (Schulenberg et al., 2005).

One research team (Sanderfur et al., 2005) looked at longitudinal studies of two cohorts of young adults: one group of 28-year-olds born in 1964 and another group of 26-year-olds born in 1974. Young people who were white, had highly educated parents, and had attended private or parochial high schools were more likely than their peers to have earned college degrees and postponed starting families. Women from two-parent families or whose parents had had some college education were less likely to be single mothers.

Among U.S. immigrant and minority groups, the paths of emerging adults tend to parallel their parents' educational patterns—except among Chinese American families. In interviews with 3,424 young people ages 18 to 32 in New York City from a variety of ethnic and immigrant groups, 46 percent of Chinese American young people whose parents had no more than a high school education went on to college, as compared with only 8 to 19 percent of those in other ethnic groups. Chinese youth tended to live with their parents longer, get support from more adults, and have fewer siblings to divide parents' time. They concentrated on education and put off full-time work and family responsibilities. By contrast, youth who were downwardly mobile tended to leave home earlier, get less support from parents, forgo higher education, and have children earlier. Early parenthood particularly limited future prospects (Mollenkopf, Waters, Holdaway, & Kasinitz, 2005).

Do Relationships with Parents Affect Adjustment to Adulthood?

A measure of how successfully emerging adults handle the developmental task of leaving the childhood home is their ability to maintain close but autonomous relationships with their parents (Scharf et al., 2004). As young people leave home, they must complete the negotiation of autonomy begun in adolescence and redefine their relationships with their parents (Lambeth & Hallett, 2002; Mitchell, Wister, & Burch, 1989). Unless emerging adults can resolve conflicts with parents in a wholesome way, they may find themselves reenacting similar conflicts in relationships with friends, colleagues, and partners (Lambeth & Hallett, 2002).

In a longitudinal study of more than 900 New Zealand families, positive parent-child relationships during early adolescence predicted warmer and less conflicted relationships with both mothers and fathers when the children reached age 26 (Belsky, Jaffee, Hsieh, & Silva, 2001). However, when researchers controlled for the quality of parent-child relationships during early adolescence, these relationships were better at age 26 when the young adult was married but childless, engaging in productive activity (either school, employment, or homemaking), and not living in the childhood home. This suggests that parents and young adult children get along best when the young adult is following a normative life course but has deferred the responsiblity of parenthood until other adult roles are well established (Belsky, Jaffee, Caspi, Moffitt, & Silva, 2003).

Experiences with parents going back to infancy may affect adaptation to adulthood. In Israel, the normative transition upon leaving home after high school is into

Checkpoint

Can you . . .

✔ Give examples of various paths to adulthood?

✔ Discuss influences on paths young people take to adulthood?

✔ Explain how relationships with parents from infancy on affect adjustment to adulthood?

Guidepost

3. What is intimacy, and how is it expressed in friendship, love, and sexuality?

universal military service. In one study (Scharf et al., 2004), researchers interviewed 88 Israeli boys during their senior year in high school, again a year later during military training, and then three years later when their military service was over. At the initial assessment the researchers administered the Adult Attachment Interview (AAI) (George, Kaplan, & Main, 1985; Main, 1995; Main, Kaplan, & Cassidy, 1985; refer back to Chapter 6), a semistructured interview in which adults are asked to recall and interpret feelings and experiences related to their childhood attachments.

Men who, on the basis of the AAI, were rated as *secure-autonomous*—who could coherently discuss and evaluate their early attachment experiences—coped better with military training and, three years later, functioned better in relationships with friends, romantic partners, and parents than men who dismissed the importance of early attachment experiences or had trouble recalling them. Autonomous young men, by their own reports and those of their parents, tended to make better use of military service as a stepping stone to maturity. Thus early relationships with parents may lay the groundwork for adjustment to the tasks of adulthood (Scharf et al., 2004).

Foundations of Intimate Relationships

Erikson saw the development of intimate relationships as the crucial task of young adulthood. The need to form strong, stable, close, caring relationships is a powerful motivator of human behavior. An important element of intimacy is *self-disclosure:* "revealing important information about oneself to another" (Collins & Miller, 1994, p. 457). People become intimate—and remain intimate—through shared disclosures, responsiveness to one another's needs, and mutual acceptance and respect (Harvey & Omarzu, 1997; Reis & Patrick, 1996).

Intimate relationships require such skills as self-awareness, empathy, the ability to communicate emotions, conflict resolution, the ability to sustain commitments, and, if the relationship is potentially a sexual one, sexual decision making. Such skills are pivotal as young adults decide whether to marry or form unwed or homosexual partnerships and to have or not to have children (Lambeth & Hallett, 2002).

Let's look more closely at three expressions of intimacy in young adulthood: friendship, love, and sexuality.

Friendship

Friendships during young (and middle) adulthood tend to center on work and parenting activities and the sharing of confidences and advice (Hartup & Stevens, 1999). Some friendships are extremely intimate and supportive; others are marked by frequent conflict. Some friends have many interests in common; others are based on a single shared interest. Some friendships are lifelong; others are fleeting (Hartup & Stevens, 1999). Some "best friendships" are more stable than ties to a lover or spouse.

Young singles rely more on friendships to fulfill their social needs than young marrieds or young parents do (Carbery & Buhrmester, 1998). The number of friends and the amount of time spent with them generally decrease by middle age. Still, friendships are important to young adults. People with friends tend to have a sense of well-being; either having friends makes people feel good about themselves, or people who feel good about themselves have an easier time making friends (Hartup & Stevens, 1999; Myers, 2000).

Women typically have more intimate friendships than men and find friendships with other women more satisfying than those with men. Men are more likely to share information and activities, not confidences, with friends (Rosenbluth & Steil, 1995). Women are more likely than men to talk with their friends about marital problems and to receive advice and support (Helms, Crouter, & McHale, 2003).

Love

Most people like love stories, including their own. According to a subtheory of Robert J. Sternberg's (1995; 1998b; in press) duplex theory of love, the way love develops *is* a story. The lovers are its authors, and the kind of story they create reflects their personalities and their conceptions of love.

Love, to some people, is an addiction—a strong, anxious, clinging attachment. For others it is a fantasy, in which one person (usually the woman) expects to be saved by a "knight in shining armor" (usually the man). Still others think of love as a game or a war with a winner and loser. Love can be a horror story, with abuser and victim, a mystery, or a detective story, in which one partner constantly tries to keep tabs on the other. Or it can be the story of a journey, or a democracy (an equal partnership), or a garden that needs to be tended and nurtured. People who have similar stories tend to be attracted to each other and to be more satisfied with their relationships, though some stories (including several of those just listed) in themselves can lead to dissatisfaction (Sternberg, Hojjat, & Barnes, 2001).

Couples in love tend to have similar interests and temperament. These rollerbladers may have been drawn together by their sense of adventure and enjoyment of risk taking.

Stories, once begun, are hard to change because that would involve reinterpreting and reorganizing everything the couple have understood about their relationship (Sternberg, 1995). When something occurs that conflicts with that understanding, such as an extramarital affair, people resist changing their story. Instead they try to interpret the new information to fit it ("She's been under stress; I'm sure she'll come to her senses"). In Piaget's terms, people prefer to *assimilate* the new information into the existing story line rather than *accommodate* the story to it.

Thinking of love as a story may help us see how people select and mix the elements of the "plot." According to the other subtheory of Sternberg's theory, his **triangular subtheory of love** (1986; 1998a; in press), the three elements, or components, of love are intimacy, passion, and commitment. *Intimacy,* the emotional element, involves self-disclosure, which leads to connection, warmth, and trust. *Passion,* the motivational element, is based on inner drives that translate physiological arousal into sexual desire. *Commitment,* the cognitive element, is the decision to love and to stay with the beloved. The degree to which each of the three elements is present determines what kind of love people feel (see Table 14-2). Triangles differ in size (how much people love each other) and balance (what proportion of each of the three components is present). According to Sternberg, couples tend to be happiest when their triangles match fairly closely (Sternberg, in press).

During the past two centuries, in western societies and in some nonwestern ones as well (Goleman, 1992), marriage has come to be built on love. Romantic love is more commonly accepted in individualistic societies than in collectivist ones. In Communist China, for example, such love is frowned upon. Chinese see themselves in terms of social roles and relationships and view self-indulgent emotional displays as weakening the social fabric (Beall & Sternberg, 1995).

The saying "Opposites attract" is not borne out by research, but neither do adults necessarily choose partners like themselves. In one study, 180 couples were tested on the Big Five personality traits and on *positive expressivity* (warmth, emotionality, devotion to others, and prosocial behavior). Happily married couples matched up only weakly on agreeableness and not on other personality dimensions. Unhappy couples showed even weaker correlations, both positive and negative. These findings suggest that similarities or differences in personality have little to

triangular subtheory of love
Sternberg's theory that patterns of love hinge on the balance among three elements: intimacy, passion, and commitment.

What's Your View?

- Other than sexual relations, what difference, if any, do you see between a friend and a lover?

- If you have ever been in love, do any of the theories and hypotheses presented in this section ring true, in your experience?

Table 14-2 Patterns of Loving

Type	Description
Nonlove	All three components of love—intimacy, passion, and commitment—are absent. This describes most interpersonal relationships, which are simply casual interactions.
Liking	Intimacy is the only component present. There is closeness, understanding, emotional support, affection, bondedness, and warmth. Neither passion nor commitment is present.
Infatuation	Passion is the only component present. This is "love at first sight," a strong physical attraction and sexual arousal, without intimacy or commitment. Infatuation can flare up suddenly and die just as fast—or, given certain circumstances, can sometimes last for a long time.
Empty love	Commitment is the only component present. Empty love is often found in long-term relationships that have lost both intimacy and passion, or in arranged marriages.
Romantic love	Intimacy and passion are both present. Romantic lovers are drawn to each other physically and bonded emotionally. They are not, however, committed to each other.
Companionate love	Intimacy and commitment are both present. This is a long-term, committed friendship, often occurring in marriages in which physical attraction has died down but in which the partners feel close to each other and have made the decision to stay together.
Fatuous love	Passion and commitment are present without intimacy. This is the kind of love that leads to a whirlwind courtship, in which a couple make a commitment on the basis of passion without allowing themselves the time to develop intimacy. This kind of love usually does not last, despite the initial intent to commit.
Consummate love	All three components are present in this "complete" love, which many people strive for, especially in romantic relationships. It is easier to achieve it than to hold onto it. Either partner may change what he or she wants from the relationship. If the other partner changes, too, the relationship may endure in a different form. If the other partner does not change, the relationship may dissolve.

Source: Based on Sternberg, 1986.

Lifemap CD

For one couple's insights on how they decided they were right for each other, watch the "Falling in Love" video in Chapter 14 of your CD.

do with the choice of a partner or with the likelihood of marital happiness (Gattis et al., 2004). On the other hand, the Seattle Longitudinal Study, a major study of adult intelligence, found remarkably similar intellectual functioning in married couples (Schaie, 2005).

Sexuality

Common sense suggests that women and men differ in their sexuality, and, though there are individual differences, a large body of research supports that view. A review of many studies (Peplau, 2003), mostly of white, middle-class U.S. samples, found four major differences between men's and women's sexual appetites, regardless of sexual orientation. First, men tend to show greater sexual desire than women do. Men tend to want sex more frequently, and they are more likely to masturbate, early and often. Second, men seek primarily physical pleasure, whereas women tend to want sex within intimate, committed relationships. Third, aggression is more strongly linked to sexuality for men than for women. Finally, women's sexuality tends to show more plasticity than men's. Women's beliefs and attitudes about sexuality are more influenced by cultural, social, and situational factors, such as going to college. The frequency of women's sexual activity varies more than men's, and their sexual identification is more responsive to outside influences (Peplau, 2003).

Views about sexual activity fall into three main categories, according to a major national survey of sexual attitudes and behavior. About 30 percent of Americans have traditional, or *reproductive* attitudes about sex—that sex is permissible only for reproductive purposes within marriage. Another 25 percent (more men than women) have a *recreational* view of sex: that whatever feels good and doesn't hurt anyone is fine. Roughly 45 percent take a *relational* view: that sex should be accompanied by love or affection, but not necessarily marriage (Laumann & Michael, 2000). These three views structure the national debate in the United States about what is right and wrong when it comes to sexual behavior.

Although men tend to have more permissive attitudes than women toward casual premarital sex (Peplau, 2003), neither men nor women appear to be as promiscuous as is sometimes thought. The median number of sex partners after age 18 is two for women and six for men. About 30 percent of adults, because of the threat of AIDS, say they have modified their sexual behavior by having fewer partners, choosing them more carefully, using condoms, or abstaining from sex (Feinleib & Michael, 2000; Laumann, Gagnon, Michael, & Michaels, 1994; Michael, Gagnon, Laumann, & Kolata, 1994).

Acquaintance rape is a problem on many college campuses (Lambeth & Hallett, 2002). College women are approximately three times more likely to become rape victims than women in the population as a whole (Gidycz, Hanson, & Layman, 1995). Rape-prevention programs have had some success. In one study, college men who participated in an hour-long session designed to provide accurate information about rape and debunk myths about it became more empathic toward rape victims than a control group and also became more aware of what constitutes rape (Pinzone-Glover, Gidycz, & Jacobs, 1998).

Negative attitudes toward homosexuality are slowly diminishing in the United States, especially among young adults (Smith, 2003). Still, according to a Newsweek poll (2000), nearly half of the population consider homosexuality a sin, and one-third of respondents in another survey (Americans on Values, 1999) believe that it is an illness—contrary to the stated position of the American Psychological Association (1997, 2000). The social stigma against homosexuality may significantly affect gays' and lesbians' mental health. Studies have found a higher risk of anxiety, depression, and other psychiatric disorders among homosexuals than among heterosexuals (Cochran, 2001).

Young adults of both sexes have become less permissive in their attitudes toward extramarital sex (Smith, 2005). In fact, disapproval of extramarital sex, though perhaps not as intense or as publicly expressed as in Ingrid Bergman's time, is even greater in U.S. society today (94 percent) than disapproval of homosexuality. The pattern of strong disapproval of homosexuality, even stronger disapproval of extramarital sex, and far weaker disapproval of premarital sex also holds true in such European countries as Britain, Ireland, Germany, Sweden, and Poland, though degrees of disapproval differ from one country to another. The United States has more restrictive attitudes than any of these countries except Ireland, where the influence of the Catholic Church is strong (Scott, 1998). In the Netherlands, much as in the United States, attitudes toward extramarital sex liberalized between 1965 and 1975 and then became more restrictive (Kraaykamp, 2002). In China, sexual attitudes and both premarital and extramarital sexual activity have liberalized dramatically despite official prohibition of sex outside marriage (Gardiner & Kosmitzki, 2005).

Nonmarital and Marital Lifestyles

In many western countries, today's rules for socially acceptable lifestyles are more elastic than they were during the first half of the twentieth century. People marry later nowadays, if at all; more have children outside of marriage, if at all; and more break up their marriages. People may stay single, live with a partner of either sex, divorce, remarry, be single parents, or remain childless; and a person's choices may change during the course of adulthood.

In the United States, the proportion of households consisting of married couples with their own children dropped from 40 percent in 1970 to 23 percent in 2003, while the proportion of households in which one person lives alone increased from 17 percent to 26 percent. Still, 72 percent of men and women have been married by the time they reach their early thirties, and 96 percent have been married at some time before age 65 (Fields, 2004). Some married couples with separate careers have

Checkpoint

Can you . . .

✔ Identify factors that promote and maintain intimacy?

✔ Describe characteristic features of friendship in young adulthood?

✔ Discuss theories and research about the nature of love and how men and women choose mates?

✔ Summarize differences between men's and women's sexuality and trends in sexual attitudes and behavior?

"commuter marriages," sometimes called "living apart together." Such dual-resident marriages exist in other countries, such as Thailand, as well (Adams, 2004).

Using national surveys in the United States, Canada, the former West Germany, Italy, and Sweden, one research team (Fussell & Gauthier, 2005) compared two cohorts of women: one group who had reached their twenties in the 1970s and another group who had reached their twenties in the 1980s. Except in the United States, the study found an increase between the two cohorts in the proportion of women who, by age 25 or older, had left home and were living on their own but had not yet married or started families. By age 35, however, all but 3 to 10 percent of the women in the second cohort had formed families with children.

Strong national differences appeared. In highly conservative Italy, where there is little state support for families, more than 60 percent of young women in both cohorts were still living at home at age 20, when most women in other countries had left. In Sweden, where cohabitation is as acceptable as marriage and welfare benefits are available to families regardless of marital status, cohabitation was very common; but the percentage of Swedish mothers who cohabited before marriage declined between cohorts, and more women in the second cohort chose not to marry at all. Canadian, German, and U.S. women were more likely than women in Italy and Sweden to be single mothers, and the proportion of single mothers increased between cohorts in the United States and Canada. Still, more than half of the young women in those three countries continued to follow traditional routes to marriage and motherhood (Fussell & Gauthier, 2005).

In this section, we look more closely at marital and nonmarital lifestyles. In the next section we examine parenthood.

These African American women seem to enjoy their single status, which is not unusual in their ethnic group.

Guidepost

4. Why do some people remain single?

Single Life

As we just mentioned, the proportion of young adults in the United States who have not yet married has increased dramatically. In 2003, about 75 percent of 20- to 24-year-old women and 86 percent of men that age had never married as compared with 36 percent and 55 percent, respectively, in 1970. Even among 30- to 34-year-olds, 23 percent of women and 33 percent of men had not married by 2003 (Fields, 2004).

The trend is particularly pronounced among African American women, 35 percent of whom are still single in their late thirties (Teachman, Tedrow, & Crowder, 2000). In a study of 300 black, white, and Latina single women in the Los Angeles area (Tucker & Mitchell-Kernan, 1998), members of all three groups had difficulty finding eligible men with similar educational and social backgrounds; but unlike the other two groups, African American women, whose average age was 40, seemed relatively untroubled by the situation. Perhaps, as the timing-of-events model might predict, this is because they saw singlehood as normative in their ethnic group.

Interviews with 1,062 U.S. college women found that 83 percent want to get married, and 63 percent hope to meet their future husbands in college. However, the old social norms of dating and courtship have largely disappeared, and there is little opportunity for young people to explore a variety of relationships before settling on one. The college social scene today tends to be characterized either by casual "hookups" (purely physical encounters), "hanging out" in groups, or fast-moving committed relationships that include eating, sleeping, and studying together (Glenn & Marquardt, 2001).

Although some young adults stay single because they have not found the right mates, others are single by choice. More women today are self-supporting, and there is less social pressure to marry. Some people want to be free to take risks, experiment, and make changes—move across the country or across the world, pursue careers, further their education, or do creative work without worrying about how their quest for self-fulfillment affects another person. Some enjoy sexual freedom. Some find the lifestyle exciting. Some just like being alone. And some postpone or avoid marriage because of fear that it will end in divorce. Postponement makes sense because, as we'll see, the younger people are when they first marry, the likelier they are to split up.

Gay and Lesbian Relationships

Fewer than 3 percent of U.S. men and 1½ percent of women call themselves homosexual or bisexual. Slightly more—5 percent of men and 4 percent of women—report at least one homosexual encounter in adulthood. Gay or lesbian identification is more common in big cities—9 percent for men and 3 percent for women (Laumann et al., 1994; Laumann & Michael, 2000; Michael et al., 1994). Identification, however, is not necessarily equivalent to orientation. In one study of 80 predominantly white, well-educated young women, more than one-fourth reported giving up lesbian or bisexual identity and reducing same-sex behavior over a five-year period, but their attractions did not significantly change (Diamond, 2003).

Long-term gay and lesbian relationships are more common in societies that tolerate, accept, or support them (Gardiner & Kosmitzki, 2005). But even in the United States, surveys suggest that 40 to 60 percent of gay men and 45 to 80 percent of lesbians are in romantic relationships, and 8 to 28 percent of these couples have lived together for at least 10 years (Kurdek, 2004). The ingredients of long-term satisfaction are very similar in homosexual and heterosexual relationships (Patterson, 1995b).

In longitudinal studies of 80 gay and 53 lesbian cohabiting couples, all childless, and 80 married heterosexual couples with children, the homosexual relationships were at least as healthy as the heterosexual ones (Kurdek, 2004). (The investigator chose to compare childless homosexual couples with heterosexual couples with children because this is the most common family form for each type of relationship.) The factors that predicted the quality and stability of a relationship— psychological adjustment, personality traits, perceptions of equality between the partners, ways of resolving conflicts, and satisfaction with social support—also were the same for both heterosexual and homosexual couples. The gay and lesbian couples fared as well or better than the heterosexual couples in all these areas except social

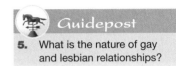

Guidepost

5. What is the nature of gay and lesbian relationships?

Most gays and lesbians, like most heterosexuals, seek love, companionship, and sexual fulfillment in a committed relationship.

support. However, gay and lesbian couples dissolved their relationships more frequently than heterosexual couples, perhaps in part because of the lack of legal barriers or of children to hold the partners together.

The Netherlands was the first country to legalize same-sex marriage in 2001; Belgium followed suit in 2003 and Spain and Canada in 2005. By February 2005, 16 European countries* had recognized civil unions or partnerships (Associated Press, 2005; Knox, 2004). Under civil unions, partners generally are entitled to coverage under each other's health insurance and pension plans, can file joint tax returns, and can receive bereavement leave and other customary benefits of marriage.

Gays and lesbians in the United States are struggling to obtain legal recognition of their unions and the right to adopt children or raise their own. Gays and lesbians also are pressing for an end to discrimination in employment, housing, and military service.

According to a USA TODAY/CNN/Gallup Poll in March 2004, about half of U.S. 18- to 20-year-olds but only 19 percent of U.S. adults older than 65 favor same-sex marriage (Knox, 2004). Vermont in 2000 was the first state to recognize civil unions for gays and lesbians; California, Hawaii, Maine, Maryland, and New Jersey followed with domestic partnership laws that give limited marital rights to same-sex couples. However, civil unions or domestic partnerships do not provide any of the federal benefits conferred by marriage.

In November 2003 the Massachusetts Supreme Court held that same-sex marriage was permitted under the state constitution (Peterson, 2005). By May 2005, nearly 5,400 gay and lesbian couples had married in that state (Bellafante, 2005). It is unclear what will be the status of those marriages if a proposed state constitutional amendment banning same-sex marriage is adopted. Meanwhile, lower court rulings in California, New York, and Washington that would allow same-sex marriage are pending appeal (Peterson, 2005).

Opponents of same-sex marriage have failed so far to pass a federal constitutional amendment banning it, but Congress and 38 states have adopted laws defining marriage as solely heterosexual. In addition, voters in 18 states have approved state constitutional bans on same-sex marriage, and at least eight of these also banned same-sex civil unions (Kranish, 2004; Peterson, 2005). Similar referenda have been scheduled or are pending in at least 17 other states. In May 2005, a federal district court in Nebraska struck down a Nebraska state constitutional amendment that banned legal recognition for any form of same-sex relationship (Citizens for Equal Protection et al. v. Bruning & Johanns, 2005).

According to a study of same-sex couples with and without civil unions, lesbians in civil unions are more open about their sexual orientation than lesbians who are not in civil unions, and gay men in civil unions are closer to their family of origin than gay men not in civil unions. With or without civil unions, gay and lesbian couples tend to have a less traditional division of labor than married heterosexual couples (Solomon, Rothblum, & Balsam, 2004).

Cohabitation

Cohabitation is an increasingly common lifestyle in which an unmarried couple involved in a sexual relationship live together. Its rise in recent decades reflects the exploratory nature of emerging adulthood and the trend toward postponing marriage.

Types of Cohabitation: International Comparisons Surveys in 14 European countries, Canada, New Zealand, and the United States found wide variations in the

Guidepost

6. What explains the rise in cohabitation, and what forms does it take?

cohabitation Status of an unmarried couple who live together and maintain a sexual relationship.

*Denmark, Norway, Sweden, Luxembourg, Iceland, Hungary, Spain, France, Germany, Portugal, Switzerland, Finland, Croatia, Poland, Britain, and Scotland. At this writing, the Czech Republic was considering recognition of civil unions.

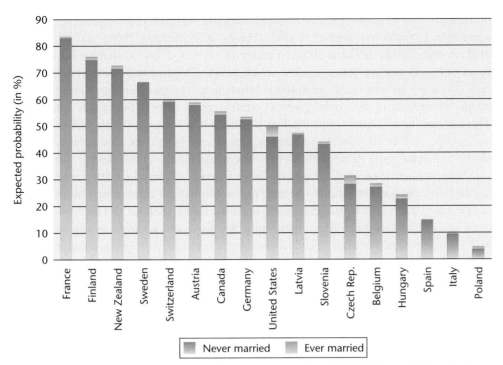

Figure 14-2

Expected probability (%) of a woman's experiencing at least one adult cohabitation by age 45,* by previous marital status, selected western countries. (Source: Heuveline & Timberlake, 2004. Data come from Family and Fertility Surveys in member countries of the United Nations Economic Commission for Europe and were collected during the early to mid-1990s.)

Note: Countries sorted in descending order by total percentage expected to cohabit. Estimates derived from single decrement life tables.

probability that a woman will cohabit at least once before age 45,* ranging from more than 83 percent in France down to less than 5 percent in Poland. In all countries the overwhelming majority of cohabiting women have never been married (Heuveline & Timberlake, 2004; see Figure 14-2).

A British demographer (Kiernan, 2002) suggests that the various types or functions of cohabitation reflect successive stages in its acceptance. In stage 1, as in Italy, Spain, and Greece, cohabitation is a fringe or avant garde phenomenon. In stage 2, as in most European countries, it is a testing ground for marriage. In stage 3, as in France, it becomes an alternative to marriage; and in stage 4, as in Sweden and Denmark, it is indistinguishable from marriage. Cohabitors who do not marry tend to stay together longer in countries where cohabitation is an alternative or tantamount to marriage than in countries where it usually leads to marriage (Heuveline & Timberlake, 2004).

Consensual or *informal unions,* almost indistinguishable from marriage (as in stage 4), have become the norm in a few European countries, notably Sweden and Denmark, where cohabiting couples have practically the same legal rights as married ones (Popenoe & Whitehead, 1999; Seltzer, 2000). Consensual unions have long been accepted instead of marriage in many Latin American countries (Seltzer, 2000). Canada, where cohabitors have, since 2000, gained legal benefits and obligations close to those of married couples, seems to have entered stage 3 (Cherlin, 2004; Le Bourdais & Lapierre-Adamcyk, 2004). In most western countries, unmarried couples who cohabit typically intend to, and do, marry (stage 2), and these cohabitations tend to be relatively short (Heuveline & Timberlake, 2004). Premarital cohabitation in Great Britain and the United States has accompanied a trend toward delayed marriage (Ford, 2002).

Cohabitation in the United States The United States, according to one analysis, appears to be in transition from stage 2 to stage 3, as cohabitation becomes a lifestyle in itself rather than a transition to marriage (Cherlin, 2004). The widespread acceptance of cohabitation in the United States is remarkable. In 2003, 4.6 million U.S.

*Age 36 in Germany, 37 in Belgium and Hungary, 38 in Sweden, 40 in the Czech Republic and the United States, 41 in Slovenia, and 43 in Italy and Switzerland.

households—more than 4 percent of all households—consisted of cohabiting couples, more than 10 times the number in 1960 (Fields, 2004; Seltzer, 2004), and 41 percent of these households included children under 18 (Fields, 2004). Cohabitation is much more common among young adults; an estimated 25 percent of unmarried women ages 25 to 39 are currently cohabiting. Much larger proportions have *ever* cohabitated—45 percent of 20- to 44-year-old women as of 1995 (Bumpass & Lu, 2000). The increase in cohabitation in the United States has occurred among all racial/ethnic groups and at all educational levels, but people with less education are more likely to cohabit than those with higher education (Fields, 2004; Seltzer, 2004).

More than half of all U.S. couples who marry have lived together first, as did Ingrid Bergman and Roberto Rossellini; and about half of cohabiting couples eventually marry, though that proportion has been declining (Seltzer, 2000, 2004). However, as cohabitation becomes increasingly accepted, cohabiting couples are under less social pressure to marry; and, although U.S. family law gives cohabitors few of the legal rights and benefits of marriage, this is changing, particularly with regard to protection for children of cohabiting couples (Cherlin, 2004; Seltzer, 2004).

Cohabiting relationships tend to be less satisfying and less stable than marriages (Binstock & Thornton, 2003; Bramlett & Mosher, 2002; Heuveline & Timberlake, 2004; Seltzer, 2000, 2004). About half of U.S. cohabitations end within the first year—often in marriage—and only 1 in 10 lasts five years (Seltzer, 2004).

Some research suggests that cohabiting couples who marry tend to have unhappier marriages and greater likelihood of divorce than those who wait to live together until marriage (Bramlett & Mosher, 2002; Dush, Cohan, & Amato, 2003; Popenoe & Whitehead, 1999; Seltzer, 2000). However, in a nationally representative cross-sectional survey of 6,577 women ages 15 to 45, women who cohabited or had premarital sex *only with their future husbands* had no special risk of marital dissolution (Teachman, 2003b). Also, according to a longitudinal study of 136 couples, partners who cohabit after engagement are less likely to have troubled relationships, before and after marriage, than couples who cohabit before becoming engaged (Kline et al., 2004). Couples who conceive a child during cohabitation are more likely to marry and less likely to split; but those who *bear* a child during cohabitation are *more* likely to break up after marriage (Manning, 2004).

The higher divorce rates among people who have cohabited before marriage may reflect the kinds of people who choose cohabitation and not the experience of cohabitation itself. Cohabitants tend to have unconventional attitudes about family life, and they are less likely than most other people to select partners like themselves in age, race or ethnicity, and previous marital status. They are more likely to have divorced parents and stepchildren, to have experienced unconventional family arrangements or frequent transitions in living arrangements as children, and to have liberal attitudes toward divorce. All these factors tend to predict unstable marriages (Cohan & Kleinbaum, 2002; Fields & Casper, 2001; D. R. Hall & Zhao, 1995; Popenoe & Whitehead, 1999; Seltzer, 2000; Teachman, 2003a). However, this may have been more true in earlier decades, when cohabitation was less accepted.

Marriage

Marriage customs vary widely, but the universality of some form of marriage throughout history and around the world suggests that it meets fundamental needs. *Monogamy*—marriage to one mate—is the norm in most developed societies. *Polygyny*—a man's marriage to more than one woman at a time—is common in Islamic countries, African societies, and parts of Asia. In *polyandrous* societies, where women generally wield more economic power, a woman may take several husbands (Gardiner & Kosmitzki, 2005; Kottak, 1994).

What's Your View?

- From your experience or observation, is it a good idea to cohabit before marriage? Why or why not? Does it make a difference whether children are involved?

Checkpoint

Can you . . .

✔ State reasons why people remain single?

✔ Discuss issues that may arise in gay and lesbian relationships?

✔ Give reasons for the rise in cohabitation, compare several types of cohabitation, and cite factors in its outcome?

Guidepost

7. What do adults gain from marriage, what cultural patterns surround it, and why do some marriages succeed while others fail?

Benefits of Marriage In most societies, the institution of marriage is considered the best way to ensure orderly raising of children. It allows for a division of labor within a consuming and working unit. Ideally, it offers intimacy, commitment, friendship, affection, sexual fulfillment, companionship, and an opportunity for emotional growth, as well as new sources of identity and self-esteem (Gardiner & Kosmitzki, 2005; Myers, 2000). In certain Eastern philosophical traditions, the harmonious union of male and female is considered essential to spiritual fulfillment and the survival of the species (Gardiner & Kosmitzki, 2005).

Today, in many parts of the industrialized world, important benefits of marriage, such as sexual expression, intimacy, and economic security, are not confined to matrimony. Indeed, with the changing division of household labor between men and women, the rise of cohabitation, divorce, remarriage, and childbearing outside marriage, and the movement to legitimize same-sex marriage, one researcher (Cherlin, 2004) sees a trend toward deinstitutionalization of marriage—a weakening of the social norms that once made marriage almost universal and its meaning universally understood (see Box 14-1).

Entering Matrimony Historically and across cultures, the most common way of selecting a mate has been through arrangement, either by the parents or by professional matchmakers. Sometimes betrothal takes place in childhood. The bride and groom may not even meet until their wedding day. Only in modern times has free choice of mates on the basis of love become the norm in the western world (Broude, 1994; Ingoldsby, 1995).

The mass wedding in India is an example of the variety of marriage customs around the world.

The typical "marrying age" has increased in industrialized countries. Thirty to 50 years ago, most people married in or before their early twenties, as Ingrid Bergman did. Today such nations as her native Sweden are seeing a trend toward later marriage as young adults take time to pursue educational and career goals or to explore relationships. In the United States, in 2003, the median age of first-time bridegrooms was about 27 and of first-time brides, 25—a rise of about four years since the 1970s (Fields, 2004; Kreider, 2005; see Figure 14-3). In England, France, Germany, and Italy the average marrying age is even higher: 29 or 30 for men and 27 for women (van Dyk, 2005). In Canada, the average age of first marriage for women has risen since 1961 from about 23 to 26, and for men from about 26 to 28 (van Dyk, 2005; Wu, 1999).

The transition to married life brings major changes in sexual functioning, living arrangements, rights and responsibilities, attachments, and loyalties. Among other tasks, marriage partners need to redefine the connection with their original families, balance intimacy with autonomy, and establish a fulfilling sexual relationship.

Sexual Activity after Marriage Americans apparently have sex less often than media images suggest, and married people do so more often than singles, though not

BOX 14-1

Digging Deeper
Is Marriage a Dying Institution?

Marriage is a basic—some would say *the* basic—social institution, though its meaning varies among cultures. Today, in the United States and, to a lesser extent, in Canada and some European countries, the meaning and importance of marriage have changed radically, according to Andrew J. Cherlin (2004), a sociologist at Johns Hopkins University. Some observers call this phenomenon a "retreat from marriage" (Oropesa & Landale, 2004).

Fifty years ago, when Ingrid Bergman's extramarital behavior raised eyebrows, marriage was *the* socially acknowledged setting for bearing and raising children and for family economic and social activity. Since the 1970s, the connection between "marriage as a couple relationship and marriage as a parental partnership" has weakened, as the focus of marriage has shifted from children to adults (Whitehead & Popenoe, 2003). As Cherlin puts it, marriage has become deinstitutionalized: The social norms or expectations that defined the behavior of married persons have weakened. In a time of social instability and shifting social roles, couples can no longer take for granted a shared understanding of how they are to act toward each other, their children (if any), and the outside world.

At least four factors—all discussed in this chapter—have contributed to undermining the institution of marriage: (1) the changing division of labor within the home due to the influx of women into the workforce, (2) the increase in childbearing outside marriage, (3) the growing acceptance of cohabitation, and (4) the emergence of same-sex marriage.

Two major transitions in the institution of marriage occurred during the 20th century, Cherlin suggests. The first great transition was the rise of *companionate marriage,* emphasizing romantic love. More than in the past, the satisfaction of the partners became the most important measure of a marriage's success. However, basic marital roles remained largely unchanged. Marriage was still, as Ingrid Bergman found out, the only socially acceptable way to have a sexual relationship and raise children. Men and women achieved gratification from being good providers or homemakers and responsible parents.

The second great shift, which accompanied rising standards of living and the movement of married women into the workforce in the last few decades of the 20th century, was from companionate marriage to *individualized marriage,* emphasizing individual self-expression and gratification. Three themes typified this transition: self-development (rather than self-sacrifice); flexible, negotiable gender roles; and open communication. The quality of a marriage began to be judged by personal satisfaction, not by the satisfactory fulfillment of marital roles.

As choices multiplied and paths to adulthood diverged, marriage "lost ground . . . as a cultural ideal" (Cherlin, 2004, p. 852). People now marry later than before and divorce more readily when marriage no longer seems to meet their needs. Many couples cohabit before marriage. Increasing numbers of women postpone childbearing. Childbirth outside of marriage is far more acceptable than in Bergman's time; indeed, many young adults see marriage and parenting as separate pursuits. Same-sex marriage is controversial but no longer unthinkable.

A central focus of personal development became the quest for intimacy—a pure, free-floating intimacy detached from any institutional framework. In a survey of young adults ages 20 to 29, 94 percent of singles agreed that "when you marry, you want your spouse to be your soul mate, first and foremost," and 79 percent disagreed with the statement that the main purpose of marriage is to have children (Whitehead & Popenoe, 2003).

Now that marriage has become a lifestyle choice, why do so many people still marry? The major benefit may be what Cherlin calls *enforceable trust.* Marriage is a public commitment, and partners who make such a commitment can place more reliance on it. However, the difference in enforceable trust between marriage and cohabitation is diminishing as divorce becomes more acceptable and cohabitants obtain legal rights previously reserved for marital partners.

Today marriage has more symbolic than practical significance, says Cherlin: "It has evolved from a marker of conformity to a marker of prestige"—the capstone of adult personal life (2004, p. 855). The wedding is often a highly individualized event centered on and run by the couple themselves, not their families, and representing recognition of this new stage in their self-development.

Some observers see pitfalls in the pursuit of a soul-mate marriage. Unrealistic expectations of marital intimacy may lead to discontent and conflict, especially when demands of work and children interfere. Divorce and the beginning of a search for a new soul mate may offer an apparently easy out but no permanent solution. Children's needs take a back seat to the needs of adults (Whitehead & Popenoe, 2003).

As we discussed in Chapter 10, most research now agrees that stable, healthy marriages are good for children. Some observers argue that such marriages are best for adults as well (Whitehead & Popenoe, 2003). If that is so, perhaps the institution of marriage will again evolve into a new form fulfilling both personal and social needs.

Source: Unless otherwise attributed, the source for material in this box is Cherlin (2004).

What's Your View?

How do you imagine that marriage will change in the future?

Check It Out

For more information on this topic, go to http://marriage.rutgers.edu. This is the home page of the National Marriage Project, codirected by David Popenoe, professor of sociology at Rutgers University, and Barbara Dafoe Whitehead, a distinguished writer on family issues. The National Marriage Project seeks to educate the public on the social, economic, and cultural conditions affecting marital success and children's well-being.

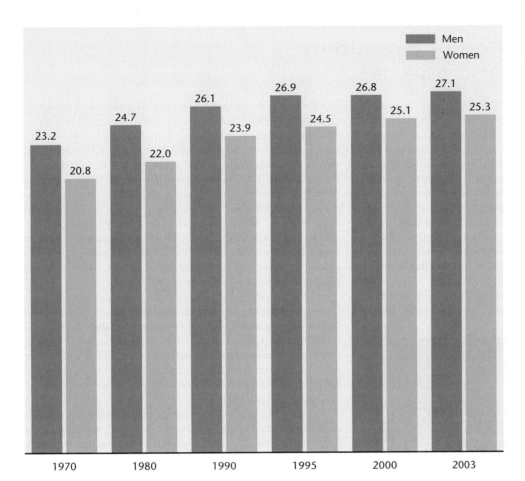

Figure 14-3

Median age at first marriage for men and women ages 15 years and over: United States, 1970 to 2003.

(Source: Fields, 2004, Figure 5.)

as often as cohabitors. Face-to-face interviews with a random sample of 3,432 men and women ages 18 to 59 found that only about one-third, including 40 percent of married couples, have intercourse at least twice a week (Laumann et al., 1994; Laumann & Michael, 2000; Michael et al., 1994). However, married couples report more emotional satisfaction from sex than single or cohabiting couples (Waite & Joyner, 2000).

It is hard to know just how common extramarital sex is, because there is no way to tell how truthful people are about their sexual practices, but surveys suggest that it is much less common than is generally assumed. An estimated 3 percent of married people reported having a sexual partner other than their spouses in 2002, and about 18 percent reported having had extramarital relations at some time during their married lives. Current extramarital activity is most prevalent among younger adults and about twice as common among husbands as among wives (4.3 percent versus 1.9 percent) (T. W. Smith, 2003).

Marital Satisfaction Married people tend to be happier than unmarried people, though those in *unhappy* marriages are less happy than those who are unmarried or divorced (Myers, 2000). People who marry and stay married, especially women, tend to become more affluent than those who do not marry or who divorce (Hirschl, Altobelli, & Rank, 2003; Wilmoth & Koso, 2002). However, we do not know that marriage *causes* wealth; it may be that people who seek wealth and who have characteristics favorable to obtaining it are more likely to marry and to stay married (Hirschl et al., 2003). Neither is it certain that marriage causes happiness; the greater happiness of married people may reflect a greater tendency of happy people to marry (Lucas, Clark, Georgellis, & Diener, 2003).

Marriages, by and large, are just about as happy as they were 20 years ago, and partners are no more or less likely to divorce; but husbands and wives spend less

BOX 14-2

Practically Speaking
Partner Violence

Partner violence, or *domestic violence,* is the physical, sexual, or psychological maltreatment of a spouse, a former spouse, or an intimate partner. Nearly 9 out of 10 victims of partner violence in the United States are women, typically young, poor, uneducated and single, divorced, or separated. According to one estimate, about 1 woman in 5 has been physically assaulted by a partner or mate at some time in her life; about 40 percent of domestic assaults cause injury, and 10 percent are serious enough to require medical care. However, the true extent of domestic violence is hard to ascertain, in large part because the victims are often too ashamed or afraid to report what has happened. In one survey, only 8 percent of abused women had told a doctor about the abuse, and less than half had told anyone (Harvard Medical School, 2004b).

Two distinct types of partner violence have been identified. One type is *situational couple violence*—physical confrontations

Most victims of domestic violence are women, and they are more likely to be seriously hurt. Men who abuse their partners often seek to control or dominate. Many were brought up in violent homes themselves.

that develop in the heat of an argument. This type of violence may be initiated by either partner and is unlikely to escalate in severity. The other, and more serious, type is *intimate terrorism*—a man's systematic use of emotional abuse, coercion, and, sometimes, threats and violence to gain or enforce power or control over a female partner. This type of partner abuse tends to become more frequent and severe as time goes on, but its most important distinguishing characteristic is its underlying control-seeking motivation (DeMaris, Benson, Fox, Hill, & Van Wyk, 2003; Leone, Johnson, Cohan, & Lloyd, 2004). Victims of intimate terrorism are more likely than those involved in situational couple violence to experience physical injuries, time lost from work, poor health, and psychological distress (Leone et al., 2004).

Intimate terrorism may be a way to assert masculine identity. Interviews and diaries of 22 men with a history of violence found that such men tend to have difficulty expressing feelings. If a relationship becomes tense or they feel psychologically threatened, they may lose control and take out their repressed feelings on their partners or wives. Some men rationalize their violent acts as having been provoked by their wives or partners (Umberson, Anderson, Williams, & Chen, 2003).

Couples are at greater risk for either type of partner violence if they have been together a relatively short time, are both in their first union, formed it at an early age, or have frequent or hostile disagreements. Anything that places strains on a relationship—for example, one or both partners being substance abusers or only one of the two being employed (especially if it is the woman)—can heighten the risk (DeMaris et al., 2003).

Emotional abuse may occur either with or without physical violence. A survey of 25,876 Canadian men and women found that about 12 percent of married or cohabiting couples experience partner violence or emotional abuse, or both. About 8 percent of the women who had *not* been physically victimized (as well as more than half of those who had) experienced tactics of emotional control, such as

time doing things together. Those conclusions come from two national surveys of married individuals, one in 1980 and the other in 2000. Marital happiness was positively affected by increased economic resources, equal decision making, nontraditional gender attitudes, and support for the norm of lifelong marriage but was negatively affected by premarital cohabitation, extramarital affairs, wives' job demands, and wives' longer working hours. Increases in husbands' share of housework appeared to lower marital satisfaction among husbands but improve it among wives (Amato, Johnson, Booth, & Rogers, 2003). In a study of 197 Israeli couples, a tendency toward emotional instability and negativity in either spouse was a strong predictor of marital unhappiness (Lavee & Ben-Ari, 2004).

Factors in Marital Success or Failure Can the outcome of a marriage be predicted before the couple tie the knot? In one study, researchers followed 100 mostly European American couples for 13 years, starting when they were not yet married. Such factors as premarital income and education levels, whether a couple cohabited before marriage or had premarital sex, and how long they had known each other or dated before marriage had no effect on marital success. What did matter were the

—continued

social isolation, putdowns, and control of family finances. Emotional abuse tended to occur when a woman's education, occupational status, and income were higher than her partner's; such behavior may be a man's way of asserting dominance (Kaukinen, 2004).

Why do women stay with men who abuse them? Some blame themselves. Constant ridicule, criticism, threats, punishment, and psychological manipulation destroy their self-confidence and overwhelm them with self-doubt. Some are more concerned about preserving the family than about protecting themselves. Often women feel trapped in an abusive relationship. Their partners isolate them from family and friends. They may be financially dependent and lack outside social support. Some are afraid to leave—a realistic fear, since some abusive husbands track down, harass, and beat or even kill their estranged wives (Fawcett, Heise, Isita-Espejel, & Pick, 1999; Harvard Medical School, 2004b; Walker, 1999). If they are on welfare, as many of these women are, and have used up their eligibility time, they are likely to be denied further benefits. To ameliorate this problem, some states screen and identify victims of partner violence, with the option to waive the time limit requirement (Leone et al., 2004).

The effects of domestic violence may extend beyond the couple. An estimated 2 to 3 million U.S. children witness domestic violence each year (Harvard Medical School, 2004b). An analysis of 118 studies found that nearly two-thirds of children who witness parental violence have adjustment problems greater than those of children who do not witness domestic violence (Kitzmann, Gaylord, Holt, & Kenny, 2003). Children who witness parental fights tend to become involved in partner violence as adults (Ehrensaft et al., 2003) or to abuse their own children. However, a cycle of violence is not inevitable; most children exposed to family violence or abuse do *not* grow up to be violent or abusive (Heyman & Slep, 2002).

The U.S. Violence Against Women Act, adopted in 1994, provides for tougher law enforcement, funding for shelters, a national domestic violence hotline, and educating judges and court personnel, as well as young people, about domestic violence. Canada has similar programs to help battered women. Efforts to protect women and eliminate gender-based violence also are under way in various European and Latin American countries. In England and Brazil, police are being trained to understand gender-based violence and to help women feel comfortable in reporting it (Walker, 1999). Shelters need to offer expanded employment and educational opportunities for abused women who are economically dependent on their partners, and health providers need to question women about suspicious injuries and tell them about the physical and mental health risks of staying with abusive partners (Kaukinen, 2004).

In the long run, the best hope for eliminating partner abuse is to "change men's socialization patterns so that power over women will no longer be a necessary part of the definition of what it means to be a man" and to "renegotiat[e] the balance of power between women and men at all levels of society" (Walker, 1999, pp. 25, 26). Community standards also can make a difference. In communities with high *collective efficacy*—where neighborhood cohesion and informal social control are strong—rates of intimate partner violence and homicide tend to be low, and women are more likely to disclose their problems and seek social support (Browning, 2002).

What's Your View?

What do you think can or should be done about partner abuse?

Check It Out

For more information on this topic, go to http://www.ncadv.org [the Web site of the National Coalition Against Domestic Violence, with links to information about the problem, community response, getting help, public policy, and other resources].

---

partners' happiness with the relationship, their sensitivity to each other, their validation of each other's feelings, and their communication and conflict management skills (Clements, Stanley, & Markman, 2004).

Age at marriage is another major predictor of whether a union will last. Teenagers have high divorce rates; people who wait until their twenties to marry have a better chance of success. College graduates and couples with high family income are less likely to end their marriages than those with lower education and income levels (Bramlett & Mosher, 2001, 2002). People who attach high importance to religion are less likely to experience marital dissolution than those to whom religion is relatively unimportant (Bramlett & Mosher, 2002).

Looking back on their marriages, 130 divorced women who had been married an average of eight years showed remarkable agreement on the reasons for the failure of their marriages. The most frequently cited reasons were incompatibility and lack of emotional support; for more recently divorced, presumably younger women, this included lack of career support. Spousal abuse was third, suggesting that partner violence may be more frequent than is generally realized (Dolan & Hoffman, 1998; see Box 14-2).

The way people describe their marriage can tell much about the likelihood of success. In a nationally representative longitudinal study, 2,034 married people ages 55 or less were asked what held their marriages together. Those who perceived the cohesiveness of their marriage as based on *rewards,* such as love, respect, trust, communication, compatibility, and commitment to the partner, were more likely to be happy in marriage and to remain married after 14 years than people who referred to *barriers* to leaving the marriage, such as children, religious beliefs, financial interdependence, and commitment to the institution of marriage (Previti & Amato, 2003).

A subtle factor underlying marital conflict and marital failure may be a difference in what the man and woman expect from marriage. Women tend to place more importance on emotional expressiveness in marriage—their own and their husbands'—than men do (Lavee & Ben-Air, 2004). Wives also tend to prolong discussion of an issue and resent it if their husbands seek to retaliate or avoid responsibility for their role in the quarrel. Husbands, on the other hand, tend to be satisfied if their wives simply want to "make up" (Fincham, Beach, & Davila, 2004).

Checkpoint

Can you . . .

✔ Identify several benefits of marriage?

✔ Note cultural differences in methods of mate selection and historical changes in marrying age?

✔ Discuss sexual relations after marriage?

✔ Identify factors in marital success or failure?

Guidepost

8. When do most adults become parents, and how does parenthood affect their development?

Parenthood

Families today are not as big as they used to be. In preindustrial farming societies, large families were a necessity: Children helped with the family's work and would eventually care for aging parents. The death rate in childhood was high, and having many children made it more likely that some would reach maturity. Today, infant and child mortality rates have improved greatly. In developing countries, where overpopulation and hunger are major problems, the need to limit family size and to space children further apart is now recognized. In industrial societies, where large families are no longer an economic asset, not only family size but also the family's composition, structure, and division of labor have changed dramatically. Most mothers now work for pay, in or outside the home, and a small but growing number of fathers are primary caregivers. More single and cohabiting women, typically those with lower educational levels (Musick, 2002), are having or adopting children and raising them (Teachman et al., 2000). Millions of children live with gay or lesbian parents or with stepparents (refer back to Chapter 10).

Sharing in the celebration of a child's birthday is one of the joys of parenthood. Today most families are smaller than in preindustrial times, and many adults start having children later in life.

Not only do people typically have fewer children today, but they also start having them later in life, often because they spend their emerging adult years getting an education and establishing a career. (Ingrid Bergman, like most women of her generation, had her first child at 23.) Today the average age of first-time mothers in the United States is 25.1, an all-time high (Martin et al., 2003). The percentage of women who give birth in their late thirties and even in their forties and fifties has increased dramatically with the help of fertility treatments. Meanwhile, since 1990, birth rates for women under age 30 have declined slightly (Martin et al., 2003; Martin et al., 2005).

Age of first childbirth varies significantly by race/ethnicity; Japanese American mothers, on average, have their first baby at age 31, whereas American Indian mothers

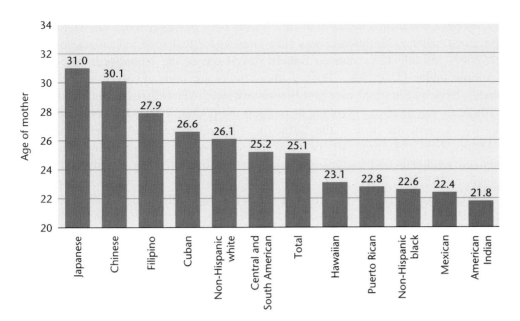

Figure 14-4

Mean age of mother at first birth by race and Hispanic origin of mother: United States, 2002. (Source: Martin et al., 2003, Figure 5.)

first give birth at an average age of 21.8 (Martin et al., 2003; see Figure 14-4). The U.S. fertility rate is higher than in several other developed countries, such as Japan and the United Kingdom (Martin, Hamilton, Ventura, Menacker, & Park, 2002), where average age of first birth is about 29 (van Dyk, 2005).

Ironically, at a time when 34 percent of all U.S. births (and similar or higher percentages in Canada, Great Britain, and the Nordic countries) are to unmarried women (Cherlin, 2004; Martin et al., 2003; Kiernan, 2002), an increasing proportion of couples remain childless. The percentage of U.S. households with children has fallen from 45 percent of all households in 1970 to less than one-third (32 percent) today (Fields, 2004). The aging of the population as well as delays in marriage and childbearing may help explain these data, but some couples undoubtedly remain childless by choice. Many couples see marriage primarily as a way to enhance their intimacy, not as an institution dedicated to the bearing and raising of children (Popenoe & Whitehead, 2003; refer back to Box 14-1). Some couples may be discouraged by the financial burdens of parenthood and the difficulty of combining parenthood with employment. In 2000 the estimated expenditures to raise a child to age 18 in a middle-income two-parent, two-child family were $165,630 (Lino, 2001). Better child care and other support services might help couples make truly voluntary decisions.

Parenthood as a Developmental Experience

A first baby marks a major transition in parents' lives. This totally dependent new person changes individuals and changes relationships. As children develop, parents do, too.

Men's and Women's Involvement in Parenthood Both women and men often have mixed feelings about becoming parents. Along with excitement, they may feel anxiety about the responsibility of caring for a child and the commitment of time and energy it entails.

In a nationally representative longitudinal study of 1,933 childless U.S. adults, becoming a parent had a much stronger impact on the lives of married women than of married men. Married mothers complained of more housework and more marital conflict than did childless women but were less likely to be depressed. Unmarried parents reported lower self-efficacy and more depression than did unmarried adults without children (Nomaguchi & Milkie, 2003).

Petter Lindstrom's decision to care for his baby daughter when his wife, Ingrid Bergman, went to Hollywood was very unusual for that time but is less so today. In 2003, 157,000 U.S. married fathers stayed out of the labor force to care for children under 15 (Fields, 2004). Fathers today are more involved in their children's lives and in child care and housework than ever before. Nonetheless, most fathers are not nearly as involved as mothers are (Coley, 2001; Olmsted & Weikart, 1994). Around the world, the home is still considered the woman's domain (Adams, 2004). The time fathers spend with children is more nearly equal to mothers' on weekends and increases as children get older (Yeung, Sandberg, Davis-Kean, & Hofferth, 2001).

Nearly half of parents report feeling they have too little time with their children, according to two national surveys of 2,817 adults ages 18 and over. Fathers with long working hours, especially, expressed this feeling (Milkie, Mattingly, Nomaguchi, Bianchi, & Robinson, 2004).

Besides time spent in direct child care, fatherhood may change other aspects of men's lives. Among 5,226 men ages 19 to 65, fathers living with their dependent children were less involved in outside social activities than those who had no children but were *more* likely to be engaged in school-related activities, church groups, and community service organizations. The most involved fathers were more satisfied with their lives (Eggebeen & Knoester, 2001).

How Parenthood Affects Marital Satisfaction Marital satisfaction typically declines during the childraising years. An analysis of 146 studies including nearly 48,000 men and women found that parents report lower marital satisfaction than nonparents do, and the more children, the less satisfied parents are with their marriage. The difference is most striking among mothers of infants; 38 percent report high marital satisfaction compared with 62 percent of childless wives, probably due to restriction on mothers' freedom and the need to adjust to a new role (Twenge, Campbell, & Foster, 2003).

Among young Israeli first-time parents, fathers who saw themselves as caring, nurturing, and protecting experienced less decline in marital satisfaction than other fathers and felt better about parenthood. Men who were less involved with their babies, and whose wives were more involved, tended to be more dissatisfied. The mothers who became most dissatisfied with their marriages were those who saw themselves as disorganized and unable to cope with the demands of motherhood (Levy-Shiff, 1994).

How Dual-Earner Families Cope

Most families with children in the United States today are dual-earner families. In 2003, 71 percent of married mothers and 96 percent of married fathers were in the labor force for at least part of the previous year (Fields, 2004).

Dual-earner families take diverse forms (Barnett & Hyde, 2001). In most of these families, traditional gender roles prevail, with the man as the main provider and the woman as secondary provider, but this is changing (Gauthier & Furstenberg, 2005). In 2003, wives' earnings accounted for an average of 35 percent of their families' incomes as compared with only 26 percent in 1973, and 25 percent of working wives earned more than their husbands (Bureau of Labor Statistics, 2005). In some families, both earners have high-powered careers and high earnings. In other families, one or both partners "scale back": cut back on working hours or refuse overtime or turn down jobs that require excessive travel, so as to increase family time and reduce stress (Barnett & Hyde, 2001; Becker & Moen, 1999; Crouter & Manke, 1994). Or a couple may make trade-offs: trading

Checkpoint
Can you . . .

✔ Describe trends in family size and age of parenthood?

✔ Compare men's and women's attitudes toward and exercise of parental responsibilities?

✔ Discuss how parenthood affects marital satisfaction?

Guidepost

9. How do dual-earner couples divide responsibilities and deal with role conflicts?

a career for a job, or trading off whose work takes precedence, depending on shifts in career opportunities and family responsibilities. Wives are more likely to do the scaling back, which usually occurs during the early years of child rearing (Becker & Moen, 1999; Gauthier & Furstenberg, 2005). African American couples tend to be more egalitarian than European American couples (Dillaway & Broman, 2001).

Lifemap CD

Watch the "Dividing the Household Tasks" video in Chapter 14 of your CD for one working mother's views on this subject.

Benefits and Drawbacks of a Dual-Earner Lifestyle Combining work and family roles is generally beneficial to both men and women in terms of mental and physical health and the strength of their relationship (Barnett & Hyde, 2001). Contributing to family income makes women more independent and gives them a greater share of economic power, and it reduces the pressure on men to be providers. Less tangible benefits may include a more equal relationship between husband and wife, greater self-esteem for the woman, and a closer relationship between a father and his children (Gilbert, 1994).

However, the benefits of multiple roles depend on how many roles each partner carries, the time demands of each role, the success or satisfaction the partners derive from their roles, and the extent to which couples hold traditional or non-traditional attitudes about gender roles (Barnett & Hyde, 2001; Voydanoff, 2004). Working couples may face extra demands on time and energy, conflicts between work and family, possible rivalry between spouses, and anxiety and guilt about meeting children's needs. The family is most demanding, especially for women who are employed full time, when there are young children (Milkie & Peltola, 1999; Warren & Johnson, 1995). Careers are especially demanding when a worker is getting established or being promoted. Both kinds of demands frequently occur in young adulthood.

In one study, for three days, 82 husbands and wives with an oldest child in kindergarten each completed questionnaires at the end of their workday and at bedtime. Daily fluctuations in men's and women's work-day pace and in their mood at the end of the workday were reflected in their behavior with their spouses after work, suggesting that the emotions aroused by tension at work spill over to marital relations (Schulz, Cowan, Cowan, & Brennan, 2004).

Division of Domestic Work and Effects on a Marriage In almost all known societies, women—even if they work full time—have primary responsibility for housework and child raising (Gardiner & Kosmitzki, 2005). However, the ways dual-income couples divide household work and the psychological effects of those decisions vary.

In Sweden, the less economically dependent a woman is on her husband, the less of the housework she does—though still the larger share. In the United States, it is less common for a woman to be the main breadwinner, and women, on average, spend 10 to 13 more hours per week on housework than men (Evertsson & Nermo, 2004). Still, the man tends to do more housework and child care than the husband of a full-time home-maker (Almeida, Maggs, & Galambos, 1993; Demo, 1991; Parke & Buriel, 1998) and to do more monitoring of older children's activities, especially when school is not in session (Crouter, Helms-Erikson, Updegraff, & McHale, 1999; Crouter & McHale, 1993). Both men and women sacrifice leisure time for housework and child care (Gauthier & Furstenberg, 2005).

The effects of a dual-earner lifestyle on a marriage may depend largely on how husband and wife view their roles. Unequal roles are not

What's Your View?

• What advice would you give a dual-earner couple on how to handle family responsibilities?

Men in dual-earner marriages tend to do more of the laundry, housework, and child care than men who are the sole breadwinner of the household. Both men and women in dual-earner households tend to give up leisure time to take care of domestic responsibilities.

Checkpoint

Can you . . .

✔ Identify benefits and drawbacks of a dual-earner household, and discuss how division of labor can affect a marriage?

Guidepost

10. Why have divorce rates risen, and how do adults adjust to divorce, remarriage, and stepparenthood?

necessarily seen as inequitable; it may be a *perception* of unfairness that contributes most to marital instability (Grote, Clark, & Moore, 2004). What spouses perceive as fair may depend on the size of the wife's financial contribution, whether she thinks of herself as a coprovider or merely as supplementing her husband's income, and the meaning and importance she and her husband place on her work (Gilbert, 1994). Whatever the actual division of labor, couples who agree on their assessment of it and who enjoy a harmonious, caring, involved family life are more satisfied than those who do not (Gilbert, 1994).

When Marriage Ends

A popular play in the 1950s was *The Seven-Year Itch* by George Axelrod. The title still reflects reality: In the United States, the average marriage that ends in divorce does so after seven to eight years (Kreider, 2005). Divorce, more often than not, leads to remarriage with a new partner and the formation of a stepfamily, which includes children born to or adopted by one or both partners before the current marriage. The high divorce rate shows how hard it is to attain the goals for which people marry, but the high remarriage rate shows that people keep trying, as Ingrid Bergman did.

Divorce

In 2002, the divorce rate in the United States was about 18 divorces per 1,000 married women ages 15 and older. This rate is about twice what it was in 1960, though it has fallen gradually since its peak in the early 1980s. The recent downturn in divorce may reflect higher educational levels and the later age of first marriages, both of which are associated with marital stability (Popenoe & Whitehead, 2004). Still, 1 out of 5 U.S. adults has been divorced (Kreider, 2005). Teenagers, high school dropouts, and nonreligious persons have higher divorce rates (Popenoe & Whitehead, 2004). The rates of marital disruption for black women remain higher than for white women (Sweeney & Phillips, 2004). Divorce has skyrocketed in many other countries; by 800 percent in Argentina between 1960 and 2000, 500 percent in China since 1978, and 300 pecent in Australia since 1970 (Adams, 2004).

Why Are Divorce Rates So High? The increase in divorce in the United States and many other countries since the 1960s accompanied the passage of more liberal divorce laws that eliminate the need to find one partner at fault. No-fault laws were a response to societal developments that prompted a greater demand for divorce (Nakonezny, Shull, & Rodgers, 1995). These developments include the decline in the perception of marriage as a sacred union; the loss of the family's traditional function as a producing unit; sexual infidelity; the spread of values of autonomy, free choice, and romantic love; increased social and economic mobility; and women's widespread entrance into paid employment (Adams, 2004).

In the United States, the higher a woman's income, the less likely she is to remain in a bad marriage; and women today are more likely than men to initiate divorce. According to a randomized telephone survey of 1,704 married persons, the greatest likelihood of *either* spouse's bringing up divorce exists when the couple's economic resources are about equal and their financial obligations to each other are relatively small (Rogers, 2004). Instead of staying together "for the sake of the children," many embattled spouses conclude that exposing children to continued parental conflict does greater damage. And, for the increasing number of childless couples, it's easier to return to a single state (Eisenberg, 1995).

Divorce breeds more divorce. Adults with divorced parents are more likely to expect that their marriages will not last (Glenn & Marquardt, 2001) and to become divorced themselves than those whose parents remained together (Shulman, Scharf, Lumer, & Maurer, 2001). So expectable has divorce become that some sociologists refer to "starter marriages"—first marriages without children, from which a person moves on as from a first house (Amato & Booth, 1997).

Adjusting to Divorce Divorce is not a single event. It is a *process*—"a sequence of potentially stressful experiences that begin before physical separation and continue after it" (Morrison & Cherlin, 1995, p. 801). Ending even an unhappy marriage can be painful, especially when there are children. (Issues concerning children's adjustment to divorce are discussed in Chapter 10.)

Divorce tends to reduce long-term well-being, especially for the partner who did not initiate the divorce or does not remarry. Reasons may include disruption of parent-child relationships, discord with a former spouse, economic hardship, loss of emotional support, and having to move out of the family home (Amato, 2000). Especially for men, divorce can have negative effects on physical or mental health or both (Wu & Hart, 2002). Women are more likely than men to live in poverty after separation or divorce (Kreider & Fields, 2002). Many have to deal with continued struggles with an ex-spouse who may default on child support (Kitson & Morgan, 1990). People who were—or thought they were—happily married tend to react more negatively and adapt more slowly to divorce (Lucas et al., 2003). On the other hand, when a marriage was highly conflicted, its ending can improve well-being (Amato, 2000).

An important factor in adjustment is emotional detachment from the former spouse. People who argue with their ex-mates or have not found a new partner or spouse experience more distress. An active social life, both at the time of divorce and afterward, helps (Amato, 2000; Thabes, 1997; Tschann, Johnston, & Wallerstein, 1989).

What's Your View?

- Has divorce become too easy to obtain in the United States?

Remarriage and Stepparenthood

Remarriage, said the essayist Samuel Johnson, "is the triumph of hope over experience." The high divorce rate is not a sign that people do not want to be married. Instead, it often reflects a desire to be *happily* married and a belief that divorce is like surgery—painful and traumatic, but necessary for a better life.

Internationally, rates of remarriage are high and rising (Adams, 2004). In the United States, more than 1 out of 3 marriages are remarriages for both bride and groom. In 2001, 55 percent of U.S. men ages 25 and older and 44 percent of U.S. women in that age group who had been divorced were remarried (Kreider, 2005). Half of those who remarry after divorce from a first marriage do so within three to four years (Kreider & Fields, 2002; Kreider, 2005). Remarriages are more likely than first marriages to end in divorce (Adams, 2004; Parke & Buriel, 1998).

Stepfamilies are formed not only by remarriage but also, increasingly, by cohabitation. About one-fourth of stepfamilies in the United States and one-half in Canada are formed by cohabitation (Cherlin, 2004). The adjustment to living in a stepfamily can be stressful for both adults and children (Adams, 2004; refer back to Chapter 10). Because the increase in stepfamilies is fairly recent, social

The fairy tale image of the wicked stepmother may have held a grain of truth: Women, particularly, tend to have more trouble raising stepchildren than biological children. Still, with the passage of time and the strengthening of new relationships, the stepfamily can provide a warm, nurturing atmosphere for all its members.

expectations for such families have not caught up. In combining two family units, each with its own web of customs and relationships, remarried families must invent their own ways of functioning (Hines, 1997).

The more recent the current marriage and the older the stepchildren, the harder stepparenting seems to be. Women, especially, seem to have more difficulties in raising stepchildren than in raising biological children, perhaps because women generally spend more time with the children than men do (MacDonald & DeMaris, 1996).

Still, the stepfamily has the potential to provide a warm, nurturing atmosphere, as does any family that cares about all its members. One researcher (Papernow, 1993) identified several stages of adjustment. At first adults expect a smooth, rapid adjustment, while children fantasize that the stepparent will go away and the original parent will return. As conflicts develop, each parent may side with his or her own biological children. Eventually the adults form a strong alliance to meet the needs of all the children. The stepparent gains the role of a significant adult figure, and the family becomes an integrated unit with its own identity.

Checkpoint

Can you . . .

✔ Give reasons for the increase in divorce since 1960?

✔ Discuss factors in adjustment to divorce?

✔ Discuss factors in adjustment to remarriage and stepparenthood?

Refocus

Thinking back to the Focus vignette about Ingrid Bergman at the beginning of this chapter:

- How would a normative-stage theorist, a timing-of-events theorist, a trait theorist, and a typological theorist describe Bergman's personality development?

- Which of Sternberg's patterns of love did Bergman's three marriages seem to illustrate?

- How have attitudes toward extramarital sex, cohabitation, and having a baby out of wedlock changed since Ingrid Bergman's day?

- What factors in marital success or failure do or do not seem to apply to Bergman's marriages?

- Why did Bergman have difficulty balancing her career with marriage and parenthood?

- Does Bergman's story argue for more liberal or less liberal divorce laws?

The bonds forged in young adulthood with friends, lovers, spouses, and children often endure throughout life and influence development in middle and late adulthood. The changes people experience in their more mature years also affect their relationships, as we'll see in Parts 7 and 8.

SUMMARY AND KEY TERMS

Personality Development: Four Views

Guidepost 1: Does personality change during adulthood, and if so, how?

- Four perspectives on adult personality development are offered by normative-stage models, the timing-of-events model, trait models, and typological models.

- Normative-stage models hold that age-related social and emotional change emerges in successive periods sometimes marked by crises. In Erikson's theory, the major issue of young adulthood is intimacy versus isolation.

- The timing-of-events model, advocated by Neugarten, proposes that adult psychosocial development is influenced by the occurrence and timing of normative life events. As society becomes less age-conscious, however, the social clock has less meaning.

- The five-factor model of Costa and McCrae is organized around five groupings of related traits: neuroticism, extraversion, openness to experience, conscientiousness, and agreeableness. Many studies find that people change relatively little in these respects after age 30.

- Typological research, pioneered by Jack Block, has identified personality types that differ in ego-resiliency and ego-control. These types seem to persist from childhood through adulthood.
- Recently there have been attempts to synthesize various approaches to adult personality development.

normative-stage models *(511)*

timing-of-events model *(511)*

trait models *(511)*

typological models *(511)*

intimacy versus isolation *(512)*

life structure *(513)*

developmental tasks *(514)*

normative life events *(514)*

social clock *(514)*

five-factor model *(515)*

ego-resiliency *(517)*

ego-control *(517)*

Changing Paths to Adulthood

Guidepost 2: How have paths to adulthood changed in recent decades, and what influences those transitions?

- Emerging adulthood, the period from about age 18 to the mid- or even late twenties, is often a time of experimentation before assuming stable adult roles and responsibilities. Such traditional developmental tasks as finding stable work and developing long-term romantic relationships may now be postponed until the thirties or even later.
- Individual paths to adulthood may be influenced by gender, academic ability, early attitudes toward education, expectations in late adolescence, and social class.
- Increasingly, emerging adults extend education and delay parenthood.
- A measure of how successfully emerging adults handle the developmental task of leaving the childhood home is their ability to maintain close but autonomous relationships with their parents.
- Attachment experiences going back to infancy may affect adaptation to adulthood.

Foundations of Intimate Relationships

Guidepost 3: What is intimacy, and how is it expressed in friendship, love, and sexuality?

- Young adults seek emotional and physical intimacy in relationships with peers and romantic partners. Self-disclosure and a sense of belonging are important aspects of intimacy.
- Intimate relationships are associated with physical and mental health.
- Most young adults have friends but have increasingly limited time to spend with them. Women's friendships tend to be more intimate than men's.

- According to Sternberg's triangular theory of love, love has three aspects: intimacy, passion, and commitment. These combine into eight types of love relationships.
- Men and women have differing sexual needs and desires.
- Attitudes toward premarital sex have liberalized in the United States, but men and women are less promiscuous than is sometimes believed. Disapproval of homosexuality has declined but remains strong. Disapproval of extramarital sex is stronger.

triangular subtheory of love *(521)*

Nonmarital and Marital Lifestyles

Guidepost 4: Why do some people remain single?

- Today more adults than in the past postpone marriage or never marry. The trend is particularly pronounced among African American women.
- Reasons for staying single include career opportunities, travel, sexual and lifestyle freedom, a desire for self-fulfillment, women's greater self-sufficiency, reduced social pressure to marry, fear of divorce, difficulty in finding a suitable mate, and lack of dating opportunities or of available mates.

Guidepost 5: What is the nature of gay and lesbian relationships?

- Both gay men and lesbians form enduring sexual and romantic relationships.
- The ingredients of long-term satisfaction are similar in homosexual and heterosexual relationships. However, lacking socially endorsed norms, same-sex couples may find it hard to define their relationship.
- Gays and lesbians in the United States are fighting for rights married people enjoy.

Guidepost 6: What explains the rise in cohabitation, and what forms does it take?

- With the new stage of emerging adulthood and the delay in age of marriage, cohabitation has increased and has become the norm in some countries.
- Cohabitation can be a "trial marriage," an alternative to marriage, or, in some places, almost indistinguishable from marriage.
- Cohabiting relationships in the United States tend to be less stable than marriages.

cohabitation *(526)*

Guidepost 7: What do adults gain from marriage, what cultural patterns surround it, and why do some marriages succeed while others fail?

- Marriage (in a variety of forms) is universal and meets basic economic, emotional, sexual, social, and childraising needs.
- Mate selection and marrying age vary across cultures. People in industrialized nations have been marrying later than in past generations.
- Frequency of sexual relations in marriage declines with age and loss of novelty. Fewer people appear to be having extramarital sexual relationships than in the past.

- Success in marriage may depend on partners' happiness with the relationship, their sensitivity to each other, their validation of each other's feelings, and their communication and conflict management skills. Age at marriage is a major predictor of whether a marriage will last. Resilience, compatibility, emotional support, and men's and women's differing expectations may be important factors.

Parenthood

Guidepost 8: When do most adults become parents, and how does parenthood affect a marriage?

- Family patterns vary across cultures and have changed greatly in western societies. Today women are having fewer children and having them later in life, and an increasing number choose to remain childless.
- Fathers are usually less involved in child raising than mothers, but some share parenting equally and some are primary caregivers.
- Marital satisfaction typically declines during the child-bearing years. Expectations and division of tasks can contribute to a marriage's deterioration or improvement.

Guidepost 9: How do dual-earner couples divide responsibilities and deal with role conflicts?

- Dual-earner families show several patterns of handling work and household demands. These lifestyles offer both benefits and drawbacks.

- In most cases, the burdens of a dual-earner lifestyle fall most heavily on the woman. Whether an unequal division of labor contributes to marital distress may depend on how the spouses perceive their roles.
- Family-friendly workplace policies may help alleviate stress.

When Marriage Ends

Guidepost 10: Why have divorce rates risen, and how do adults adjust to divorce, remarriage, and stepparenthood?

- Among the reasons for the rise in divorce are women's greater financial independence, parents' reluctance to expose children to parental conflict, and the greater "expectability" of divorce.
- Adjusting to divorce is a long-term process. Adjustment may depend on the way the divorce is handled, people's feelings about themselves and their ex-partners, emotional detachment from the former spouse, social support, and personal resources.
- Most divorced people remarry within a few years, but remarriages tend to be less stable than first marriages.
- Stepfamilies may go through several stages of adjustment. Women tend to have more difficulty being stepparents than men do.

- Some physical skills improve with age, due to practice, experience, and judgment.

- Physical symptoms associated with menopause seem to be affected by cultural attitudes toward aging.

- Stressful experiences often lead to illness.

- Postformal thinking is especially useful with regard to social problems.

- Personality characteristics play an important role in creative performance.

- Modifications in men's and women's personalities at midlife have been attributed both to hormonal changes and to cultural shifts in gender roles.

- Responsibility for aging parents can affect physical and mental health.

When does middle age begin? Is it at the birthday party when you see your cake ablaze with forty candles? Is it the day your "baby" leaves home? Is it the day when you notice that police officers seem to be getting younger? When does middle age end? Is it at your retirement party? Is it the day you get your Medicare card? Is it the first time someone younger gets up to give you a seat on the bus?

Middle adulthood has many markers, and they are not the same for everyone. The middle years are the central years of the adult life span, but their content varies greatly. At 40, some people become parents for the first time, while others become grandparents. At 50, some people are starting new careers, while others are taking early retirement.

As in earlier years, all aspects of development are interrelated. In Chapters 15 and 16, we note, for example, the psychological impact of menopause (and debunk some myths about it!), and we see how mature thinkers combine logic and emotion.

Middle Adulthood

545

CHAPTER 15

Physical and Cognitive Development in Middle Adulthood

The primitive, physical, functional pattern of the morning of life, the active years before forty or fifty, is outlived. But there is still the afternoon opening up, which one can spend not in the feverish pace of the morning but in having time at last for those intellectual, cultural, and spiritual activities that were pushed aside in the heat of the race.

Anne Morrow Lindbergh, *Gift from the Sea,* **1955**

Focus
Mahatma Gandhi, Father of a Nation

Mahatma Gandhi

Mohandas Karamchand Gandhi (1869–1948)* was called *Mahatma* (Great Soul) by the people of his native India, whom he led to freedom from British colonial rule through a decades-long campaign of nonviolent resistance. His revolutionary ideas and practices profoundly influenced other world leaders, notably Nelson Mandela and Martin Luther King, Jr. He is considered one of the greatest moral exemplars of all time.

The son of an uneducated merchant, Gandhi admitted to less than average intellectual ability, but his linguistic and interpersonal skills were strong. He had a keen moral sense and was a lifelong seeker of truth. He had the courage to challenge authority and take risks for what he saw as a worthy goal.

As a lawyer in South Africa, another British colony, he saw and experienced the discrimination the Indian minority suffered. It was in South Africa that Gandhi began to develop his philosophy of *satyagraha,* nonviolent social action. He organized civil disobedience campaigns and peaceful marches. Time and again, he invited arrest; in 1908, approaching his fortieth year, he was jailed for the first time. Eventually he would spend a total of seven years in prison.

Gandhi "felt he could not proceed as an ethical agent, seeking a better life for his people, unless he had himself attained and come to embody moral authority. He had to purify himself before he could make demands of others" (Gardner, 1997, p. 115). He moved with his wife and four sons from the South African capital, Johannesburg, to a farm outside Durban. He did daily exercises, prepared his own food, and gave up western dress for simple Indian garb. In 1910, he founded a collective farm based

*Sources of biographical information about Gandhi included J. M. Brown (1989), Gandhi (1948), Gardner (1997), and Kumar and Puri (1983).

547

on ascetic and cooperative principles. Returning to India in 1915, Gandhi became the acknowledged leader of a nationalist movement. He taught his people to show forbearance. When a street mob in a small town rioted and killed police, he called off political actions throughout India. When mill owners were unbending and strikers became restive, he put his own physical well-being on the line by fasting until a satisfactory settlement was reached.

In 1930, to protest a tax on manufactured salt, Gandhi, then 60, led a 200-mile march to the sea, where hundreds of followers illegally extracted salt from seawater. The event, reminiscent of the Boston Tea Party, triggered protests all over India. When British police attacked and beat a line of peaceful marchers, their brutality made headlines around the world. It was the beginning of the end for British domination.

Gandhi's influence was the product of a seamless web of body, mind, and spirit. By living out his ideals, he was effective in solving real, almost intractable problems that affected millions of people. In his efforts to defuse conflict and inspire cooperation, he showed wisdom grounded in moral vision.

Few of us reach the moral and spiritual heights Gandhi did, and few of us have such influential careers. But caring and concern for others, including the generations to follow, are important in any adult, as is the work to which one chooses to devote one's life. As with Gandhi, these features tend to intensify or come to fruition in middle age.

In this chapter, we examine physical changes common in middle adulthood. We discuss how health problems may be worsened by poverty, racial discrimination, and other stresses. We consider how intelligence changes, how thought processes mature, what underlies creative performance and moral leadership such as Gandhi's, and how careers develop.

After you have read and studied this chapter, you should be able to answer each of the Guidepost questions that follow. Look for them again in the margins, where they point to important concepts throughout the chapter. To check your understanding of these Guideposts, review the end-of-chapter summary. Checkpoints located at periodic spots throughout the chapter will help you verify your understanding of what you have read.

1. What are the distinguishing features of middle age?

2. What physical changes generally occur during the middle years, and what is their psychological impact?

3. What factors affect health at midlife?

4. What cognitive gains and losses occur during middle age?

5. Do mature adults think differently than younger people do?

6. What accounts for creative achievement, and how does it change with age?

7. How are patterns of work and education changing, and how does work contribute to cognitive development?

Guideposts for Study

Middle Age: A Social Construct

Guidepost

1. What are the distinguishing features of middle age?

The term "midlife" first came into the dictionary in 1895 (Lachman, 2004), as life expectancy began to lengthen. Today, in industrial societies, middle adulthood is considered to be a distinct stage of life with its own societal norms, roles, opportunities, and challenges. Thus, some scholars describe middle age as a social construct (Gullette, 1998; Menon, 2001; Moen & Wethington, 1999). Some traditional societies, such as upper-caste Hindus in rural India (Menon, 2001) and the Gusii in Kenya (see Box 16-1 in Chapter 16), do not recognize a middle stage of adulthood between youth and old age at all. In other parts of India and in Japan, maturation and aging are thought of primarily as social processes involving relationships and roles, rather than in terms of chronological years and biological changes (Menon, 2001).

In the United States, in 2000, more than 80 million baby boomers, born between 1946 and 1964, were between ages 35 and 54 and constituted about 30 percent of the total population (U.S. Census Bureau, 2000). Although the baby boomers are a diverse group, they have shared certain normative historical experiences, such as the Vietnam war, the assassinations of Martin Luther King and John F. Kennedy, and the rise of dual-earner families (Lachman, 2004). On the whole, this is the best educated and most affluent cohort ever to reach middle age anywhere, and it is changing our perspective on that time of life (Willis & Reid, 1999).

Until recently, middle adulthood was the least studied part of the life span. The middle years were considered a relatively uneventful hiatus between the more dramatic changes of young adulthood and old age. Now that the baby-boom generation is moving into and through middle age, research on that period has greatly expanded (Lachman, 2001, 2004). Findings from the Midlife in the United States (MIDUS) study (Brim, Ryff, & Kessler, 2004), a comprehensive survey sponsored by the MacArthur Foundation's Research Network on Successful Midlife Development and conducted by telephone and mail with a national sample of 7,189 noninstitutionalized adults ages 25 to 75, have enabled researchers to study factors that influence health, well-being, and productivity in midlife and how individuals navigate the transition to old age.

Ironically, as medical and nutritional advances have opened up an unprecedented second half of life in developed societies, anxiety about physical and other losses of aging has become a major theme in popular descriptions of middle age. A life-span developmental perspective (refer back to Chapter 1) presents a more balanced, more complex picture. Middle age can be a time, not only or even primarily of decline and loss, but—as with Gandhi—of mastery, competence, and growth. The concept of plasticity suggests that what people do and how they live has much to do with how they age (Heckhausen, 2001; Lachman, 2001, 2004; Staudinger & Bluck, 2001).

When Is Middle Age?

There is no consensus on when middle age begins and ends or on specific biological or social events that mark its boundaries (Lachman, 2004; Staudinger & Bluck, 2001). With improvements in health and length of life, the subjective upper limits of middle age are rising (Lachman, 2001, 2004). One-third of Americans in their seventies, and half of those between 65 and 69, think of themselves as middle aged (National Council on Aging, 2000). On the other hand, people with low socioeconomic status tend to report earlier beginning and endpoints for midlife, perhaps because of poorer health or earlier transitions to retirement and grandparenthood (Lachman, 2004). Middle age in U.S. society is increasingly a state of mind (Menon, 2001).

In this book, we define *middle adulthood* in chronological terms as the years between ages 40 and 65, but, as we have just suggested, this definition is arbitrary. Middle age also can be defined contextually. One context is the family: a middle-aged person is sometimes described as one with grown children and/or elderly parents. Yet today some people in their forties and beyond are still raising young children; and some adults at any age have no children at all. Those with grown children may find the nest emptying—or filling up again. Age also has a biological aspect: A 50-year-old who has exercised regularly is likely to be biologically younger than a 40-year-old whose most strenuous exercise is clicking the remote control.

The Experience of Middle Age

The experience of middle age varies with health, gender, race/ethnicity, socioeconomic status, cohort, and culture, as well as with personality, marital and parental status, and employment (Lachman, 2004). According to the MIDUS data, most middle-aged people in the United States are in good physical, cognitive, and emotional shape and feel good about the quality of their lives (Fleeson, 2004; see Figure 15-1).

What's Your View?

- When would you say middle age begins and ends?

- Think of people you know who call themselves middle-aged. How old are they? Do they seem to be in good health? How involved are they in work or other activities?

Figure 15-1

How U.S. adults of various ages rate aspects of their quality of life and overall quality of life. (Source: Fleeson, 2004; data from MacArthur Foundation Research Network on Successful Midlife Development [The MIDUS National Survey].)

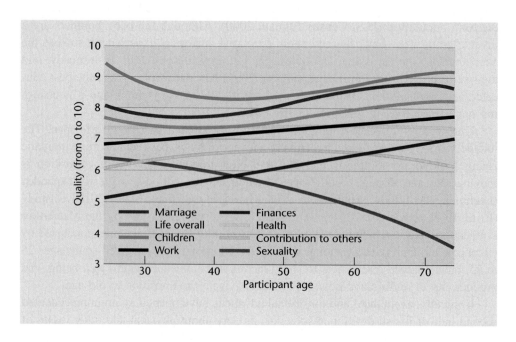

Likewise, in another national sampling, health was the only area in which respondents expected more problems with age (Lachman, 2004).

Typically, however, the experiences, roles, and issues of early middle age differ from those of late middle age (Lachman, 2004; Staudinger & Bluck, 2001). In a representative telephone survey of 3,850 adults ages 18 and older, baby boomers ages 40 to 58 were more like younger adults than like those ages 59 and up in their assessments of their lives. When asked about their satisfaction with physical and mental health, relationships with family and friends, work, leisure, finances, and religious or spiritual life, late middle-aged and older adults tended to be more satisfied than either the boomers or younger adults, who were still looking forward to improvement (Keegan, Gross, Fisher, & Remez, 2004; see Table 15-1).

Many middle-aged people, like Senator Hillary Clinton, are at the peak of their careers, enjoying a sense of freedom, responsibility, and control over their lives.

Table 15-1 Satisfaction with Life Areas by Generation

Overall, how satisfied are you with your _____? Are you very satisfied, somewhat satisfied, not too satisfied or not at all satisfied?

% who say very satisfied with . . .

	Younger Adults	Boomers	Older Adults
Relations with family and friends			
2004	64	62	77
2003	59	64	75
2002	57	63	74
Mental health			
2004	62	59	70
2003	64	59	67
2002	61	61	63
Religious or spiritual life			
2004	44	48	66
2003	39	50	64
2002	34	47	60
Work or career*			
2004	36	40	63
2003	34	37	60
2002	34	39	50
Physical health			
2004	36	32	39
2003	33	32	35
2002	35	31	38
Leisure activities			
2004	33	30	51
2003	30	29	45
2002	33	29	47
Personal finances			
2004	18	22	37
2003	18	21	35
2002	19	20	35

2004: Younger Adults (18–39) N=760; Boomers (40–58) N=2266; Older Adults (59+) N=824
2003: Younger Adults (18–38) N=736; Boomers (39–57) N=2016; Older Adults (58+) N=748
2002: Younger Adults (18–37) N=781; Boomers (38–56) N=2127; Older Adults (57+) N=758

*Asked only of those employed either full-or part-time
2004: Younger Adults N=564; Boomers N=1615; Older Adults N=185
2003: Younger Adults N=555; Boomers N=1485; Older Adults N=197
2002: Younger Adults N=572; Boomers N=1646; Older Adults N=202

Source: Keegan et. al., 2004, Table 1.

According to the MIDUS research, "aging, at least up until the midseventies, appears to be a positive phenomenon" (Fleeson, 2004, p. 269). At the same time, the middle years are marked by growing individual differences and a multiplicity of life paths (Lachman, 2004). Some middle-aged people can run a marathon; others get winded climbing a steep stairway. Some have a sharper memory than ever; others feel their memory beginning to slip. Some are at the height of creativity or careers; others have gotten a slow start or have reached dead ends. Still others dust off mothballed dreams or, like Gandhi, pursue new and more challenging goals.

For many people, middle age is filled with weighty responsibilities and multiple, demanding roles: running households, departments, or enterprises; launching children; and perhaps caring for aging parents or starting new careers. By and large, these are responsibilities and roles that most adults in midlife feel competent to handle, but leisure time often suffers (Lachman, 2001, 2004). At the same time, many middle-aged adults, having made their mark and raised their children, have an increased feeling of freedom and independence (Lachman, 2001). Many experience a heightened sense of success and control in work and social relationships, along with a more realistic awareness of their limitations and of outside forces they cannot control (Clark-Plaskie & Lachman, 1999; Lachman, 2004). The middle years can be a time of reevaluating goals and aspirations and deciding how best to use the remaining part of the life span (Lachman, 2004).

Checkpoint
Can you . . .

✔ Explain why middle age is considered a social construct?

✔ Compare chronological, contextual, and biological definitions of middle age?

✔ Distinguish between early and late middle age?

✔ Cite individual differences in the experience of middle age?

PHYSICAL DEVELOPMENT

Physical Changes

Guidepost

2. What physical changes generally occur during the middle years, and what is their psychological impact?

"Use it or lose it!" Research bears out the wisdom of that popular creed. Although some physiological changes are direct results of biological aging and genetic makeup, behavioral and lifestyle factors dating from youth can affect the likelihood, timing, and extent of physical change. By the same token, health and lifestyle habits in the middle years influence what happens in the years beyond (Lachman, 2004; Whitbourne, 2001).

The more people do, the more they *can* do. People who become active early in life reap the benefits of more stamina and more resilience after age 60 (Spirduso & MacRae, 1990). People who lead sedentary lives lose muscle tone and energy and become even less inclined to exert themselves physically. Still, as Gandhi realized, it is never too late to adopt a healthier lifestyle (Merrill & Verbrugge, 1999).

The mind and the body have ways of compensating for changes that do occur (Lachman, 2004). Most middle-aged people take in stride gradual changes in appearance, in sensory, motor, and systemic functioning, and in reproductive and sexual capacities.

Sensory and Psychomotor Functioning

From young adulthood through the middle years, sensory and motor changes are almost imperceptible (Merrill & Verbrugge, 1999)—until one day a 45-year-old man realizes that he cannot read the telephone directory without eyeglasses, or a 60-year-old woman has to admit that she is not as quick on her feet as she was.

Age-related visual problems occur mainly in five areas: *near vision, dynamic vision* (reading moving signs), *sensitivity to light, visual search* (for example, locating a sign), and *speed of processing* visual information (Kline et al., 1992; Kline & Scialfa, 1996; Kosnik, Winslow, Kline, Rasinski, & Sekuler, 1988). Also common is a slight loss in *visual acuity,* or sharpness of vision. Because of changes in the pupil of the eye, middle-aged people may need about one-third more brightness to compensate for the loss of light reaching the retina (Belbin, 1967; Troll, 1985).

Because the lens of the eye becomes progressively less flexible, its ability to shift focus diminishes. This change usually becomes noticeable in early middle age and is practically complete by age 60 (Kline & Scialfa, 1996). Many people age 40 and older need reading glasses for **presbyopia,** a lessened ability to focus on near objects—a condition associated with aging. (The prefix *presby-* means "with age.") The incidence of **myopia** (nearsightedness) also increases through middle age (Merrill & Verbrugge, 1999). Bifocals and trifocals—corrective eyewear in which lenses for reading are combined with lenses for distant vision—aid the eye in adjusting between near and far objects.

A gradual hearing loss, rarely noticed earlier in life, speeds up in the fifties (Merrill & Verbrugge, 1999). This condition, **presbycusis,** normally is limited to higher-pitched sounds than those used in speech (Kline & Scialfa, 1996). By the end of middle age, 1 person in 4 has significant hearing loss (Horvath & Davis, 1990). Hearing loss proceeds twice as quickly in men as in women (Pearson et al., 1995). Today, a preventable increase in hearing loss is occurring among 45- to 64-year-olds due to continuous or sudden exposure to noise at work, at loud concerts, through earphones, and elsewhere (Wallhagen, Strawbridge, Cohen, & Kaplan, 1997). Hearing losses due to environmental noise can be avoided by wearing hearing protectors, such as earplugs or special earmuffs.

Sensitivity to taste and smell generally begins to decline in midlife (Cain, Reid, & Stevens, 1990; Stevens, Cain, Demarque, & Ruthruff, 1991). As the taste buds become less sensitive and the number of olfactory cells diminishes, foods may seem more bland (Merrill & Verbrugge, 1999; Troll, 1985). Women tend to retain these senses longer than men. There are individual differences, however. A woman might lose her sweet tooth; her husband might find his martinis not sour enough. One person could become less sensitive to salty foods, another to sweet, bitter, or sour foods. And the same person may remain more sensitive to some of these tastes than to others (Stevens, Cruz, Hoffman, & Patterson, 1995; Whitbourne, 1999).

Adults begin to lose sensitivity to touch after age 45, and to pain after age 50. However, pain's protective function remains: Although people feel pain less, they become less able to tolerate it (Katchadourian, 1987).

Strength and coordination decline gradually from their peak during the twenties. Some loss of muscle strength is usually noticeable by age 45; 10 to 15 percent of maximum strength may be gone by 60. The reason is a loss of muscle fiber, which is replaced by fat. Strength training can prevent muscle loss and even regain strength (Whitbourne, 2001).

Endurance often holds up much better than strength (Spirduso & MacRae, 1990). Loss of endurance results from a gradual decrease in the rate of **basal metabolism** (use of energy to maintain vital functions) after age 40 (Merrill & Verbrugge, 1999). "Overpracticed" skills are more resistant to effects of age than those that are used less; thus athletes show a smaller-than-average loss in endurance (Stones & Kozma, 1996).

Manual dexterity generally becomes less efficient after the mid-thirties (Vercruyssen, 1997)—though some pianists, such as Vladimir Horowitz, have continued to perform brilliantly in their eighties. Simple reaction time, which involves a single response to a single stimulus (such as pressing a button when a light flashes) slows by about 20 percent, on average, between ages 20 and 60 (Birren, Woods,

presbyopia Age-related, progressive loss of the eyes' ability to focus on nearby objects due to loss of elasticity in the lens.

myopia Nearsightedness.

presbycusis Age-related, gradual loss of hearing, which accelerates after age 55, especially with regard to sounds at higher frequencies.

basal metabolism Use of energy to maintain vital functions.

Many middle-aged people find that their improved ability to use strategies in a sport as a result of experience and better judgment outweighs changes in strength, coordination, and reaction time. A consistent exercise program beginning in young adulthood, such as playing tennis regularly, can help build muscles and maintain stamina and resilience in middle and old age.

& Williams, 1980). When a vocal rather than a manual response is called for, age differences in simple reaction time are substantially less (S. J. Johnson & Rybash, 1993).

Tasks that involve a choice of responses (such as hitting one button when a light flashes and another button when a tone is heard) and complex motor skills involving many stimuli, responses, and decisions (as in driving a car) decline more; but the decline does not necessarily result in poorer performance. Typically, middle-aged adults are better drivers than younger ones (McFarland, Tune, & Welford, 1964), and 60-year-old typists are as efficient as 20-year-olds (Spirduso & MacRae, 1990; Salthouse, 1984).

In these and other activities, knowledge based on experience may more than make up for physical changes. Skilled industrial workers in their forties and fifties are often more productive than ever, partly because they tend to be more conscientious and careful. Middle-aged workers are less likely than younger workers to suffer disabling injuries on the job (Salthouse & Maurer, 1996)—a likely result of experience and good judgment, which compensate for any lessening of coordination and motor skills.

Structural and Systemic Changes

Changes in appearance, often reflecting changes in body structure and systems, may become noticeable during the middle years. By the fifth or sixth decade, the skin may become less taut and smooth as the layer of fat below the surface becomes thinner, collagen molecules become more rigid, and elastin fibers more brittle. Hair may become thinner, due to a slowed replacement rate, and grayer as production of melanin, the pigmenting agent, declines. People perspire less as the number of sweat glands decreases. They tend to gain weight as a result of accumulation of body fat and lose height due to shrinkage of the intervertebral disks (Merrill & Verbrugge, 1999; Whitbourne, 2001).

Bone density normally peaks in the twenties or thirties. From then on, people typically experience some net loss of bone as more calcium is absorbed than replaced, causing bones to become thinner and more brittle. Bone loss accelerates in the fifties and sixties; it occurs twice as rapidly in women as in men, sometimes leading to osteoporosis (discussed later in this chapter) (Merrill & Verbrugge, 1999; Whitbourne, 2001). Smoking, alcohol use, and a poor diet earlier in adulthood tend to speed bone loss; it can be slowed by aerobic exercise, resistance training with weights, increased calcium intake, and vitamin C. Joints may become stiffer as a result of accumulated stress. Exercises that expand range of motion and strengthen the muscles supporting a joint can improve functioning (Whitbourne, 2001).

Large proportions of middle-aged and even older adults show little or no decline in organ functioning (Gallagher, 1993). In some, however, the heart begins to pump more slowly and irregularly in the midfifties; by 65, it may lose up to 40 percent of its aerobic power. Arterial walls may become thicker and more rigid. Heart disease becomes more common beginning in the late forties or early fifties. **Vital capacity**— the maximum volume of air the lungs can draw in and expel—may begin to diminish at about age 40 and may drop by as much as 40 percent by age 70. Temperature regulation and immune response may begin to weaken, and sleep may become less deep (Merrill & Verbrugge, 1999; Whitbourne, 2001).

vital capacity Amount of air that can be drawn in with a deep breath and expelled.

Checkpoint
Can you . . .

✔ Summarize changes in sensory and motor functioning and body structure and systems that may begin during middle age?

✔ Identify factors that contribute to individual differences in physical condition?

Sexuality and Reproductive Functioning

Sexuality is not only a hallmark of youth. Although both sexes experience losses in reproductive capacity sometime during middle adulthood—women become unable to bear children and men's fertility begins to decline—sexual enjoyment can continue throughout adult life. (Changes in the male and female reproductive systems are summarized in Table 15-2.) Still, many middle-aged people have concerns related to sexuality and reproductive functioning. Let's look at these.

Menopause and Its Meanings **Menopause** takes place when a woman permanently stops ovulating and menstruating and can no longer conceive a child; it is generally considered to have occurred one year after the last menstrual period. This happens, on average, at about age 50 or 51 (Finch, 2001; Whitbourne, 2001).

Menopause is not a single event but a process (Rossi, 2004). Beginning in her midthirties to midforties, a woman's production of mature ova begins to decline, and the ovaries produce less of the female hormone estrogen. The period of three to five years during which this slowing of hormone production and ovulation prior to menopause occurs is called **perimenopause,** also known as the *climacteric,* or "change of life." (Small amounts of estrogen continue to be secreted, in amounts that vary among

menopause Cessation of menstruation and of ability to bear children, typically around age 50.

perimenopause Period of several years during which a woman experiences physiological changes that bring on menopause; also called *climacteric.*

Table 15-2	Changes in Human Reproductive Systems During Middle Age	
	Female	**Male**
Hormonal change	Drop in estrogen and progesterone	Drop in testosterone
Symptoms	Hot flashes, vaginal dryness, urinary dysfunction	Undetermined
Sexual changes	Less intense arousal, less frequent and quicker orgasms	Loss of psychological arousal, less frequent erections, slower orgasms, longer recovery between ejaculations, increased risk of erectile dysfunction
Reproductive capacity	Ends	Continues; some decrease in fertility may occur

individuals, by the adrenal and other glands.) During perimenopause, menstruation becomes irregular, with less flow than before and a longer time between menstrual periods, before it ceases altogether (Finch, 2001; Whitbourne, 2001). The timing of menopause varies greatly; 1 in 4 women in the thirties is already perimenopausal, and 1 in 4 women in the early forties is already postmenopausal (Rossi, 2004).

Attitudes Toward Menopause   During the early nineteenth century in western cultures, the term *climacteric* came to mean the "period of life . . . at which the vital forces begin to decline" (Lock, 1998, p. 48). Menopause was seen as a disease, a failure of the ovaries to perform their natural function.

"Menopause the Musical," a hilarious celebration of women going through "The change," epitomizes the change in attitudes toward this natural biological event. It also satirizes the wide variety of roles (Power Woman, Earth Mother, Housewife, Soap Star) that middle-aged women play in contemporary society.

By contrast, in some cultures, such as that of the southwestern Papago Indians, menopause seems to be virtually ignored. In other cultures, such as those found in India and South Asia, it is a welcome event; women's status and freedom of movement increase once they are free of taboos connected with menstruation and fertility (Avis, 1999; Lock, 1994).

In the United States today, most women who have gone through menopause view it positively. The overwhelming majority of postmenopausal women in the MIDUS study expressed only relief (Rossi, 2004). For many women, menopause is a sign of a transition into the second half of adult life—a time of role changes, greater independence, and personal growth.

How a woman views menopause may depend on the value she places on being young and attractive, her attitudes toward women's roles, and her own circumstances. A childless woman may see menopause as closing off the possibility of motherhood; a woman who has had and raised children may see it as an opportunity for greater sexual freedom and enjoyment (Avis, 1999).

Symptoms and Myths   Most women experience little or no physical discomfort during perimenopause. Most common are "hot flashes," sudden sensations of heat that flash through the body due to erratic changes in hormone secretion that affect the temperature control centers in the brain. However, more than half of perimenopausal and postmenopausal women never have them, whereas only 5 percent of perimenopausal and 12 percent of postmenopausal women have them almost every day (Rossi, 2004). Short-term administration of artificial estrogen, discussed later in this chapter, can alleviate symptoms such as hot flashes but carries risks ("Risk of Hormone Use," 2004).

Other possible physical symptoms include vaginal dryness, burning, and itching; vaginal and urinary infections; and urinary dysfunction caused by tissue shrinkage (Whitbourne, 2001). Because the hormones most directly linked to sexual desire in both men and women are the androgens (such as testosterone), declining estrogen levels in midlife do not seem to affect sexual desire in most women, as long as sexual activity remains comfortable and there are no health-related problems that interfere with a healthy sex life (American Medical Association, 1998). Still, some women do not become sexually aroused as readily as before, and some find intercourse painful because of thinning vaginal tissues and inadequate lubrication. Small doses of testosterone may solve the first problem, and use of water-soluble gels can prevent or relieve the second (Katchadourian, 1987; King, 1996; M. E. Spence, 1989; Williams, 1995).

Such psychological problems as irritability, nervousness, anxiety, depression, memory loss, and even insanity have been blamed on the climacteric, but research shows no reason to attribute mental disturbances to this normal biological change (Lachman, 2004; Whitbourne, 2001). Hot flashes and such associated symptoms as sweating, insomnia, irritability, and painful intercourse are reported by many younger and older women and some men as well (Rossi, 2004). The idea that menopause produces depression may derive from the fact that many women at this time are undergoing changes in roles, relationships, and responsibilities. These changes may be stressful, and the way a woman perceives them—as well as her attitudes toward menopause—may affect her symptoms during menopause (Avis, 1999; Lachman, 2004; Rossi, 2004).

Women who have discomfort during menopause tend to have a history of pain during menstruation, high sensitivity to internal and environmental factors such as temperature changes, and a high degree of stress at home or on the job (Rossi, 2004). Taken together, the research suggests that "so-called menopausal syndrome may be related more to personal characteristics or past experiences than to menopause per se" (Avis, 1999, p. 129). It also may reflect societal views of women and of aging (see Box 15-1). In cultures in which women view menopause positively or in which older women acquire social, religious, or political power after menopause, few problems are associated with this natural event (Aldwin & Levenson, 2001; Avis, 1999; Dan & Bernhard, 1989). However, physical changes in bone density and heart functioning after menopause can affect women's health, as we discuss later in this chapter.

Changes in Male Sexuality Men have no experience comparable to menopause. They do not undergo a sudden drop in hormone production at midlife, as women do. Instead, testosterone levels tend to decrease slowly after the thirties—about 1 percent a year, with wide individual variations. Thus there is little evidence to support the concept of "andropause," or "male menopause" (Asthana et al., 2004; Finch, 2001; Whitbourne, 2001).

The decline in testosterone has been associated with reductions in bone density and muscle mass (Asthana et al., 2004) as well as depression, anxiety, irritability, insomnia, fatigue, weakness, lower sexual drive, erectile failure, and memory loss (Henker, 1981; Sternbach, 1998; Weg, 1989), but it is not clear that these complaints are related to testosterone levels. Men's psychological adjustments, like women's, may stem from such events as illness, worries about work, children leaving home, or the death of parents, as well as from negative cultural attitudes toward aging (King, 1996).

There is no strong relationship between testosterone levels and sexual performance (Finch, 2001). However, men often do experience some changes in sexual functioning related to changes in the circulatory and endocrine systems, as well as to stress, smoking, obesity, health problems such as diabetes, and social factors such as those just mentioned (Finch, 2001; Whitbourne, 2001). Although a man can continue to reproduce until quite late in life, his sperm count begins to decline in the late forties or fifties, making it less likely that he will father a child (Merrill & Verbrugge, 1999). Erections tend to become slower and less firm, orgasms less frequent, and ejaculations less forceful; and it takes longer to recover and ejaculate again (Bremner, Vitiello, & Prinz, 1983; Katchadourian, 1987; King, 1996; Masters & Johnson, 1966). Still, sexual excitation and sexual activity can remain a normal, vital part of life.

Testosterone supplementation therapy is sometimes touted as a boost to sexual desire and a cure for other problems of aging. Preliminary findings suggest that it does improve sexual desire and increases muscle mass but has no effect on bone density except in men whose testosterone levels were particularly low. It may enhance certain specific cognitive functions—working memory, spatial memory, and verbal fluency—and does *not* appear to increase the risk of prostate enlargement or

BOX 15-1

Window on the World

Japanese Women's Experience of Menopause

Many women accept hot flashes and night sweats as normal accompaniments of menopause. However, not all women experience these symptoms.

Margaret Lock (1994) surveyed 1,316 Japanese women ages 45 to 55 and compared the results with data on 9,376 women in Massachusetts and Manitoba, Canada. Japanese women's experience of menopause turned out to be quite different from the experience of western women.

Fewer than 10 percent of Japanese women whose menstruation was becoming irregular reported having had hot flashes during the previous two weeks, compared with about 40 percent of the Canadian sample and 35 percent of the U.S. sample. In fact, fewer than 20 percent of Japanese women had *ever* experienced hot flashes, compared with 65 percent of Canadian women, and most of the Japanese women who had experienced hot flashes reported little or no physical or psychological discomfort. (Indeed, so little importance is given in Japan to what in western cultures is considered the chief symptom of menopause that there is no specific Japanese term for "hot flash," even though the Japanese language makes many subtle distinctions about body states.) Furthermore, only about 3 percent of the Japanese women said they experienced night sweats, and Japanese women were far less likely than western women to suffer from insomnia, depression, irritability, or lack of energy (Lock, 1994).

The Japanese women were more likely to report stiffness in the shoulders, headaches, lower back pain, constipation, and other complaints that, in western eyes, do not appear directly related to the hormonal changes of menopause (Lock, 1994). Japanese physicians link such symptoms with the decline of the female reproductive cycle, which they believe is associated with changes in the autonomic nervous system (Lock, 1998).

The symptoms physicians noted were quite similar to those the women reported. Hot flashes were not at the top of the doctors' lists and in some cases did not appear at all. However, very few Japanese women consult doctors about menopause or its

This middle-aged Japanese woman working in her garden seems the picture of health. Japanese women rarely experience hot flashes, discomfort, or other physical symptoms that some western women associate with menopause.

prostate cancer. However, its long-term risks and benefits have not been sufficiently studied; and results of research now under way will not be available for at least a decade (Asthana et al., 2004). Meanwhile, testosterone therapy is medically advisable only for men with clear hormonal deficiencies (Whitbourne, 2001).

What's Your View?

- How often, and in what ways, do you imagine your parents express their sexuality? When you are their age, do you expect to be more or less sexually active than they seem to be?

Sexual Activity Frequency of sexual activity and satisfaction with sex life tend to diminish gradually during the forties and fifties. In the MIDUS study, 61 percent of married or cohabiting premenopausal women but only 41 percent of postmenopausal women reported having sex once a week or more. This decline was related, not to menopause per se, but to age and physical condition (Rossi, 2004). Possible physical causes include chronic disease, surgery, medications, and too much food or alcohol. Often, however, a decline in frequency has nonphysiological causes: monotony in a relationship, preoccupation with business or financial worries, mental or physical fatigue, depression, failure to make sex a high priority, fear of failure to attain an symptoms, and few physicians prescribe hormone therapy (Lock, 1994).

In Japan, menopause is regarded as a normal event in women's lives, not as a medical condition requiring treatment. The end of menstruation has far less significance than it does for western women; the closest term for it, *kônenki,* refers not specifically to what westerners call menopause, but to a considerably longer period comparable to the perimenopause or climacteric (Lock, 1994, 1998).

Aging in Japan is less feared than in the West. Not until old age can women and men alike escape the daily round of duty and do as they please. Aging brings not only respect for wisdom, but also newfound freedom—as does menopause (Lock, 1998).

Cultural attitudes, then, may affect how women interpret their physical sensations, and these interpretations may be linked to their feelings about menopause. Hot flashes have been found to be rare or infrequent among Mayan women, North African women in Israel, Navajo women, and some Indonesian women (Beyene, 1986, 1989; Flint & Samil, 1990; Walfish, Antonovsky, & Maoz, 1984; Wright, 1983). For example, Mayan women, who are frequently pregnant or nursing babies, tend to regard childbearing as a burden and to look forward to its end (Beyene, 1986, 1989).

Do nutritional practices influence the experience of menopause? Some plants, such as soybeans—a staple of Far Eastern diets—contain relatively high amounts of estrogen-like compounds known as *phytoestrogens.* A diet high in foods made with these plants, such as tofu and soy flour, may influence hormone levels in the blood. This, it has been suggested, might help explain why middle-aged Japanese women do not experience the dramatic effects of a precipitous decline in estrogen levels, as many western women do. It also might explain Japanese women's low incidence of osteoporosis and of deaths from coronary heart disease, conditions that become more common in women after menopause (Margo N. Woods, M.D., Department of Family Medicine and Community Health, Tufts University School of Medicine, personal communication, November, 1996).

In a placebo-controlled, double-blind study in Brazil, daily doses of soy isoflavene decreased hot flashes and other menopausal symptoms while decreasing total cholesterol and LDL, thus offering possible protection against heart disease (Han, Soares, Haidar, de Lima, & Baracat, 2002). However, in a randomized, double-blind, placebo-controlled study of 246 menopausal women ages 45 to 60 who were experiencing at least 35 hot flashes a week, dietary supplements containing isoflavines derived from red clover were clinically no more effective than a placebo in reducing hot flashes or other symptoms of menopause, though one such product, Promensil, reduced them faster (Tice et al., 2003). Also, a double-blind, randomized trial in the Netherlands found no improvement in bone mineral density, cognitive function, or cholesterol levels from the use of supplements containing soy isoflavenes after age 60 (Kreijkamp-Kaspers et al., 2004).

Further conclusions about the influence of diet on women's health during and after menopause must await the completion of additional controlled longitudinal studies. Meanwhile, the findings about Japanese women's experience of menopause show that even this universal biological event has major cultural variations, once again affirming the importance of cross-cultural research.

What's Your View?

What do you think might explain the differences between Japanese and western women's experience of menopause?

Check It Out

For more information on menopause in Japan, and additional data on Japanese women's health and aging, go to http://www.gfmer.ch/Books/bookmp/185.htm [a Web site maintained by members of the Department of Obstetrics and Gynaecology, Kyoto Prefectural University of Medicine in Kyoto, Japan].

---

erection, or lack of a partner (King, 1996; Masters & Johnson, 1966; Weg, 1989). Treating these causes may bring renewed vitality to a person's sex life.

Myths about sexuality in midlife—for example, the idea that satisfying sex ends at menopause—have sometimes become self-fulfilling prophecies. Now advances in health care and more liberal attitudes toward sex are making people more aware that sex can be a vital part of life during these and even later years.

Sexual Dysfunction   For a surprising proportion of adults, sex is not easy or enjoyable. **Sexual dysfunction** is a persistent disturbance in sexual desire or sexual response. It can take the form of lack of interest in or pleasure from sex, painful intercourse, difficulty in arousal, premature orgasm or ejaculation, inability to reach climax, or anxiety about sexual performance.

In interviews with a nationally representative sample of 1,749 women and 1,410 men ages 18 to 59, 43 percent of the women and 31 percent of the men

sexual dysfunction Persistent disturbance in sexual desire or sexual response.

Wrinkles and graying hair often imply that a woman is "over the hill" but that a man is "in the prime of life." This double standard of aging, which downgrades the attractiveness of middle-aged women but not of their partners, can affect a couple's sexual adjustment.

erectile dysfunction Inability of a man to achieve or maintain an erect penis sufficient for satisfactory sexual performance.

reported some form of sexual dysfunction (Laumann et al., 1999). Among women, sexual dysfunction decreases with age; for men, it is just the opposite. Women in their fifties are about half as likely as the youngest women to report nonpleasurable sex or sexual anxiety, and only one-third as likely to report pain during sex. On the contrary, men in their fifties are more than three times as likely to report erection problems and low desire as 18- to 29-year-old men (Laumann, Paik, & Rosen, 1999, 2000).

The most severe form of sexual dysfunction in men is **erectile dysfunction** (popularly called *impotence*): persistent inability to achieve or maintain an erect enough penis for satisfactory sexual performance. An estimated 39 percent of 40-year-old men and 67 percent of 70-year-old men experience erectile dysfunction at least sometimes (Feldman, Goldstein, Hatzichristou, Krane, & McKinlay, 1994; Goldstein et al., 1998). According to the Massachusetts Male Aging Study, about 5 percent of 40-year-old and 15 percent of 70-year-old men are completely impotent (Feldman et al., 1994). Diabetes, hypertension, high cholesterol, kidney failure, depression, neurological disorders, and many chronic diseases are associated with erectile dysfunction (Utiger, 1998). Alcohol, drugs, smoking, poor sexual techniques, lack of knowledge, unsatisfying relationships, anxiety, and stress can be contributing factors.

Some men suffering erectile dysfunction can be helped by treating the underlying causes or by adjusting medications ("Effective Solutions for Impotence," 1994; NIH, 1992). Sildenafil (known as Viagra) and other drugs such as Vardenafil (Levitra) and Taclalafil (Cialis) have been found generally safe and effective (Goldstein et al., 1998; Nurnberg et al., 2003; Utiger, 1998), though there are reports of several dozen men developing a rare eye disease while taking these drugs (Silberner, 2005). Other treatments, each of which has both benefits and drawbacks, include a wraparound vacuum constrictive device, which draws blood into the penis; injections of prostaglandin E1 (a drug found in semen, which widens the arteries); and penile implant surgery. If there is no apparent physical problem, psychotherapy or sex therapy (with the support and involvement of the partner) may help (NIH, 1992).

Checkpoint

Can you . . .

✔ Tell the chief difference between men's and women's reproductive changes at midlife?

✔ Identify factors that can affect women's experience of menopause?

✔ Describe changes in sexual activity during middle age?

✔ Discuss the prevalence of sexual dysfunction among men and women in relation to age?

Health

Guidepost

3. What factors affect health at midlife?

Most middle-aged Americans, like middle-aged people in other industrialized countries, are quite healthy (Lachman, 2004). All but 15 percent of 45- to 64-year-olds consider themselves in good to excellent health. Only 17 percent of this age group—13 percent of 45- to 54-year-olds and 20 percent of 55- to 64-year-olds—are limited in activities because of chronic conditions (chiefly arthritis and circulatory conditions), which increase with age (NCHS, 2004; Schiller & Bernadel, 2004).

Despite their generally good health, many people in midlife, especially those with low socioeconomic status, experience increasing health problems (Lachman, 2004) or are concerned about signs of potential decline. They may have less energy than in their youth and are likely to experience occasional or chronic pains and fatigue. They can no longer "burn the midnight oil" with ease, they are more likely to contract certain diseases, such as hypertension and diabetes, and they take longer to recover from illness or extreme exertion (Merrill & Verbrugge, 1999; Siegler, 1997).

Health Trends at Midlife

Hypertension (chronically high blood pressure) is an increasingly important concern from midlife on as a risk factor for cardiovascular disease and kidney disease. The prevalence of hypertension in the United States has increased 30 percent in the past decade to an all-time high (Fields et al., 2004) and now affects 28.6 percent of adults. Its prevalence increases with age. It is now more common among women than among men, but women are more likely to be aware of the condition and to be treated for it (Glover, Greenlund, Ayala, & Croft, 2005). Certain personality factors, namely, impatience and hostility, increase the long-term risk of developing hypertension (Yan et al., 2003).

hypertension Chronically high blood pressure.

Hypertension can be controlled through blood pressure screening, low-salt diets, and medication; but only 73.5 percent of middle-aged adults with hypertension are aware of having the condition, only 61 percent are under treatment, and in only 40.5 percent is the condition under control (Glover et al., 2005).

Hypertension is 60 percent more prevalent in Europe than in the United States and Canada (Wolf-Maier et al., 2003). The proportion of the world's population with high blood pressure is expected to increase from one-quarter to one-third by 2025, leading to a predicted "epidemic" of cardiovascular disease, which already is responsible for 30 percent of all deaths worldwide (Kearney et al., 2005).

In the United States, cancer (discussed in Chapter 17) has now replaced heart disease as the leading cause of death between ages 45 and 64 (NCHS, 2004). Overall, death rates have declined sharply since the 1970s for people in this age bracket (Hoyert, Arias, Smith, Murphy, & Kochanek, 2001), in large part because of improvements in treatment of heart attack patients (Rosamond et al., 1998). Chest pain is the most common symptom of a heart attack in both men and women, but women may experience other symptoms, such as back and jaw pain, nausea and vomiting, indigestion, difficult breathing, or palpitations (Patel, Rosengren, & Ekman, 2004).

The prevalence of diabetes doubled in the 1990s (Weinstein et al., 2004), making it the fifth leading cause of death in middle age (NCHS, 2004). The most common type, mature-onset (Type II) diabetes, typically develops after age 30 and becomes more prevalent with age (American Diabetes Association, 1992). Unlike juvenile-onset, or insulin-dependent, diabetes, in which the level of blood sugar rises because the body does not produce enough insulin, in mature-onset diabetes glucose levels rise because the cells lose their ability to use the insulin the body produces. As a result, the body may try to compensate by producing too much insulin. People with mature-onset diabetes often do not realize it until they develop such serious complications as heart disease, stroke, blindness, kidney disease, or loss of limbs (American Diabetes Association, 1992).

Behavioral Influences on Health

As in young adulthood, nutrition, smoking, alcohol and drug use, and physical activity continue to affect health in middle age (Lachman, 2004) and beyond. People who do not smoke, are not overweight, and exercise regularly at midlife not only live longer but have shorter periods of disability at the end of life (Vita, Terry, Hubert, & Fries, 1998). Middle-aged men and women who stop smoking lessen their risk of heart disease and stroke (AHA, 1995; Kawachi et al., 1993; Stamler et al., 1993; Wannamethee, Shaper, Whincup, & Walker, 1995). Obesity, lack of exercise, and sedentary behavior such as watching television are associated with heightened risk of diabetes (Hu, Li, Colditz, Willett, & Manson, 2003; Weinstein et al., 2004).

Among a nationally representative sample of 9,824 U.S. adults ages 51 to 61 in 1992, those who engaged in regular moderate or vigorous exercise were about 35 percent less likely to die in the next eight years than those with sedentary lifestyles. Those with cardiovascular risk factors, such as smoking, diabetes, high blood pressure, and a history of coronary artery disease, benefited most from being physically active (Richardson, Kriska, Lantz, & Hayward, 2004). A multicenter study of 936 women with suspected heart disease suggests that physical fitness may be more important than weight as a factor in coronary risk (Wessel et al., 2004).

Indirect influences, such as socioeconomic status, race/ethnicity, and gender, also continue to affect health. So do social relationships (Ryff, Singer, & Palmersheim, 2004). Another important influence is stress, whose cumulative effects on both physical and mental health often begin to appear in middle age (Aldwin & Levenson, 2001).

Socioeconomic Status and Health

Social inequalities continue to affect health in middle age (Marmot & Fuhrer, 2004). People with low socioeconomic status tend to have poorer health, lower life expectancy, more activity limitations due to chronic disease, lower well-being, and more restricted access to health care than people with higher SES (Spiro, 2001). In the MIDUS study, low SES was linked with self-reported health status, overweight, and psychological well-being (Marmot & Fuhrer, 2004). In a follow-up study of 2,606 stroke patients, SES affected the likelihood of death, independent of the severity of the stroke (Arrich, Lalouscheck, & Müllner, 2005).

In part, the reasons for the connection between SES and health may be psychosocial. People with low SES tend to have more negative emotions and thoughts and live in more stressful environments (Gallo & Matthews, 2003). People with higher SES tend to have a greater sense of control over what happens to them as they age; they tend to choose healthier lifestyles and seek medical attention and social support when they need it (Lachman & Firth, 2004; Marmot & Fuhrer, 2004; Whitbourne, 2001). However, there are wide individual differences in health among low-SES adults. Protective influences include the quality of social relationships and the level of religious engagement from childhood on (Ryff, Singer, & Palmersheim, 2004).

As we mentioned in Chapter 13, many poor people lack health insurance. In a prospective national study of 7,577 adults who were 51 to 61 years old in 1992, those without health insurance were 63 percent more likely to show a decline in health during the next four years and 23 percent more likely to develop problems in walking or climbing stairs (Baker, Sudano, Albert, Borawski, & Dor, 2001). However, insurance is not the whole story. In a longitudinal study of 8,355 British civil servants ages 39 to 63, those in the lower ranks had poorer health than those in higher classifications, despite equal access to Britain's national health care system (Hemingway, Nicholson, Stafford, Roberts, & Marmot, 1997).

Race/Ethnicity and Health

Racial/ethnic disparities in health have decreased in the United States since 1990, but substantial differences persist (Keppel, Pearcy, & Wagener, 2002). Although death rates from cancer have generally declined, this is not so among blacks, who continue to have high death rates from lung, colorectal, prostate, and breast cancer (CDC, 2002a; Office of Minority Health, Centers for Disease Control, 2005), mostly attributable to differential treatment (Bach et al., 2002).

As in young adulthood, overall death rates in middle age are higher for African Americans than for white, Hispanic, Asian, and Native Americans (Kochanek et al., 2004). In 2002, non-Hispanic blacks who died from HIV-related conditions lost about 11 times as many years of potential life before age 75 as non-Hispanic whites, 9 times as many years for homicide, and 3 times as many years for diabetes and strokes (Office of Minority Health, Centers for Disease Control, 2005). Blacks who survive stroke are more likely than whites to report activity limitations (McGruder, Greenlund, Croft, & Zheng, 2005).

Hypertension is 50 percent more prevalent among African Americans than among Caucasian Americans. A hormone that promotes salt retention by the kidneys may contribute to that disparity, according to a comparative study of blood chemistry in African Americans and French Canadians (Grim et al., 2005). During 1999–2002, 40.5 percent of U.S. non-Hispanic blacks had hypertension, as compared with 27.4 percent of non-Hispanic whites and 25.1 percent of Mexican Americans. On the other hand, Mexican Americans are less likely to have their blood pressure under control: 17.3 percent as compared with 29.8 percent of non-Hispanic blacks and whites (Glover et al., 2005). Non-Hispanic blacks are more likely than non-Hispanic whites to be obese and to have poor cardiovascular fitness and are less likely to participate in regular, moderate physical activity (Lavie, Kurubanka, Milani, Prasad, & Ventura, 2004; Office of Minority Health, Centers for Disease Control, 2005).

Some observers attribute the health gap between black and white Americans in part to stress and frustration caused by prejudice and discrimination (Whitbourne, 2001). In parts of the Caribbean, where race relations may be smoother than in the United States, blacks' average blood pressure is about the same as that of other ethnic groups (Cooper et al., 1999).

Probably the largest single underlying factor in African Americans' health problems is poverty, which is related to poor nutrition, substandard housing, and poor access to health care (Otten, Teutsch, Williamson, & Marks, 1990; Smedley & Smedley, 2005). Still, poverty cannot be the sole explanation because the death rate for middle-aged Hispanic Americans, who also are disproportionately poor, is lower than that of white Americans (Kochanek et al., 2004).

Hispanic Americans, like African Americans, do have a disproportionate incidence of stroke, liver disease, diabetes, HIV infection, homicide, and cancers of the cervix and stomach (Office of Minority Health, Centers for Disease Control, 2004). They have high rates of eye disease and visual impairment (Globe, Wu, Azen, Varma, & Los Angeles Latino Eye Study Group, 2004; Varma, Torres, & Los Angeles Latino Eye Study Group, 2004; Varma, Fraser-Bell, et al., 2004; Varma, Paz et al., 2004; Varma, Torres et al., 2004; Varma, Ying-Lai, Francis et al., 2004; Varma, Ying-Lai, Klein et al., 2004). They are less likely than non-Hispanic whites to have health insurance and a regular source of health care. They are also less likely to be screened for cholesterol and for breast, cervical, and colorectal cancers or to receive influenza and pneumonia vaccines (Balluz, Okoro, & Strine, 2004).

Hispanic Americans are not a single homogeneous group, and there are significant differences among various subgroups. For example, about 21 percent of Puerto Ricans report activity limitations, as compared with about 15 percent of persons of Mexican, Cuban, or other Hispanic origin. Puerto Ricans also are more likely to

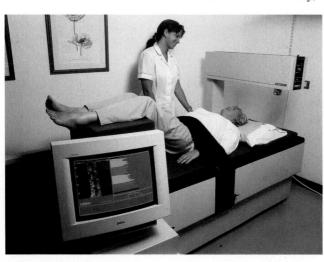

Checkpoint

Can you . . .

✔ Describe the typical health status in middle age, and identify health concerns that become more prevalent at this age?

✔ Discuss socioeconomic and racial/ethnic factors in health and mortality at middle age?

report being in fair or poor health, to spend more days sick in bed, and to see physicians or go to a hospital (Hajat, Lucas, & Kington, 2000). Mexican Americans are more likely to be overweight or obese (Office of Minority Health, Centers for Disease Control, 2004). On the other hand, their culture and family networks may protect their *mental* health. Both Mexican Americans and non-Hispanic whites born in the United States have higher risks of psychiatric disorders than their foreign-born counterparts, but U.S.-born Mexican Americans have lower risks of these disorders than U.S.-born whites (Grant et al., 2004).

Research on the human genome has found distinctive variations in the DNA code among people with European, African, and Chinese ancestry (Hinds et al., 2005). These variations are linked to predispositions to certain diseases, from cancer to obesity. This research may ultimately open the way to targeted treatments or preventive measures.

Gender and Health: Women's Health after Menopause

Differences between men's and women's health, discussed in Chapter 13, continue in midlife. According to the MIDUS survey, women tend to report worse health with more specific symptoms and chronic conditions, except that men are more likely to report alcohol or drug problems. On the other hand, women devote more effort to maintaining their health. They live longer than men (Cleary, Zaborski, & Ayanian, 2004) and have lower death rates in middle age (Kochanek et al., 2004).

Women are at increased risk after menopause, particularly for heart disease and osteoporosis. With longer life spans, women in many developed countries now can expect to live half their adult lives after menopause. As a result, increasing attention is being paid to women's health issues at this time of life (Barrett-Connor et al., 2002).

osteoporosis Condition in which the bones become thin and brittle as a result of rapid calcium depletion.

Bone Loss and Osteoporosis   In women, bone loss rapidly accelerates in the first five to ten years after menopause (Avis, 1999; Barrett-Connor et al., 2002; Levinson & Altkorn, 1998) as levels of estrogen, which helps in calcium absorption, fall. Extreme bone loss may lead to **osteoporosis** ("porous bones"), a condition in which the bones become thin and brittle as a result of calcium depletion. Frequent signs of osteoporosis are marked loss in height and a "hunchbacked" posture that results from compression and collapse of a weakened spinal column. In a national observational study of 200,160 postmenopausal women, almost half had previously undetected low bone mineral density, and 7 percent of these women had osteoporosis (Siris et al., 2001). Osteoporosis is a major cause of broken bones in old age and can greatly affect quality of life and even survival (NIH Consensus Development Panel on Osteoporosis Prevention, Diagnosis, and Therapy, 2001; Siris et al., 2001).

Almost 3 out of 4 cases of osteoporosis occur in white women, most often in those with fair skin, small frame, low weight and BMI, and a family history of the condition, and those whose ovaries were surgically removed before menopause (NIA, 1993; NIH Consensus Development Panel, 2001; "Should You Take," 1994; Siris et al., 2001). African American women, who have greater bone density, are less likely than white women to develop osteoporosis, whereas Hispanic and Asian women are more likely. Other risk factors, besides age, include smoking and lack of exercise (Siris et al., 2001). Since a predisposition to osteoporosis seems to have a genetic basis, measurement of bone density is an especially wise precaution for women with affected family members (Prockop, 1998; Uitterlinden et al., 1998).

A bone density scan is a simple, painless X-ray procedure to measure bone density so as to determine whether osteoporosis is present. Osteoporosis, or thinning of the bones, is most common in women after menopause. The procedure is especially advisable for women with a family history of osteoporosis. Here, the monitor shows an image of this woman's spinal column.

Good lifestyle habits make a significant difference, especially if started early in life (NIH Consensus Development Panel, 2001). Even if bone loss has started, it can be slowed or even reversed with proper nutrition, weight-bearing exercise, and avoidance of smoking (Barrett-Connor et al., 2002; Eastell, 1998). High-intensity strength training and resistance training have proven particularly effective (Layne & Nelson, 1999; Nelson et al., 1994). Women over age 40 should get 1,000 to 1,500 milligrams of dietary calcium a day, along with recommended daily amounts of vitamin D, which helps the body absorb calcium (NIA, 1993). Studies have found value in calcium and vitamin D supplements (Dawson-Hughes, Harris, Krall, & Dallal, 1997; Eastell, 1998; NIH Consensus Development Panel, 2001) and in a daily dose of alendronate (Fosamax) ("Boosting Brittle Bones," 2004). Raloxifene, one of a new group of "designer estrogens," seems to favorably affect bone density and possibly cholesterol levels and reduce the risk of genetic breast cancer without negative side effects (Barrett-Connor et al., 2002). However, the long-term effects of this drug have yet to be documented.

Breast Cancer and Mammography   One in 8 American women and 1 in 9 British women develop breast cancer at some point in their lives (American Cancer Society, 2001; Pearson, 2002). As with other cancers, the chance of developing breast cancer increases with age (Barrett-Connor et al., 2002). Overweight women, those who drink alcohol, those who experienced early menarche and late menopause, those with a family history of breast cancer, and those who bore children late and had fewer children have greater risk of breast cancer, whereas those who are moderately physically active and eat low-fat, high-fiber diets are at less risk (Barrett-Connor et al., 2002; Clavel-Chapelton et al., 2002; McTiernan et al., 2003; U.S. Preventive Services Task Force, 2002).

Scientists have identified two genes, BRCA1 and BRCA2, that may be involved in a small percentage of breast cancers. Because women with the flawed genes have an estimated 85 percent chance of developing breast cancer someday, they may choose to have more frequent examinations and possibly even preventive mastectomy ("The Breast Cancer Genes," 1994).

Advances in diagnosis and treatment have dramatically improved prospects for breast cancer patients. More than 95 percent of women with breast cancer can survive at least five years if the cancer is caught before it spreads, and 50 percent can expect to survive at least fifteen years (American Cancer Society, 2001). Although benefits of **mammography,** diagnostic x-ray examination of the breasts, appear to be strongest for women over 50, a U.S. Preventive Services Task Force (2002) recommends screening every one or two years for all women beginning at age 40, especially those with a family history of breast cancer before menopause.

mammography   Diagnostic X-ray examination of the breasts.

Hysterectomy   Nearly one in three U.S. women has a **hysterectomy,** or surgical removal of the uterus, by age 60 (Farquhar & Steiner, 2002). The surgery is generally done to remove uterine fibroids (benign tumors) or because of abnormal uterine bleeding or endometriosis (Kjerulff, Langenberg, & Rhodes, 2000). Hysterectomy rates are second only to rates for cesarean section in surgery performed on U.S. women (Broder, Kanouse, Mittman, & Bernstein, 2000) and are three to four times higher than in Australia, New Zealand, and most European countries (Farquhar & Steiner, 2002).

hysterectomy   Surgical removal of the uterus.

Many experts believe that hysterectomy is overused. In a study of nine managed care organizations in Southern California, 76 percent of the recommended hysterectomies did not meet established criteria of the American College of Obstetricians and Gynecologists for this type of surgery, usually because of failure to first rule out other conditions or try alternative medical or surgical treatments (Broder et al., 2000).

Hormone Replacement Therapy Because the most troublesome physical effects of menopause are linked to reduced levels of estrogen, **hormone replacement therapy (HRT)** in the form of artificial estrogen has been prescribed to relieve hot flashes, night sweats, and other symptoms. Estrogen taken alone increases the risk of uterine cancer, so women whose uterus had not been surgically removed were usually given estrogen in combination with progestin, a form of the female hormone progesterone. Now, however, medical evidence challenges some of HRT's presumed benefits and bears out its suspected risks.

Contrary to early correlational research, which suggested that HRT cut the risk of heart disease (Davidson, 1995; Ettinger, Friedman, Bush, & Quesenberry, 1996; Grodstein, 1996), a large-scale randomized, controlled study found that hormone treatments either provide no benefit to high-risk women (those who already have heart disease or related conditions) or actually *increase* the risks (Grady et al., 2002; Hulley et al, 2002; Petitti, 2002). Subsequently, a large-scale randomized, controlled trial of estrogen plus progestin in *healthy* women was stopped after five years because the risks of breast cancer, heart attack, stroke, and blood clots exceeded the benefits (Wassertheil-Smoller et al., 2003; Writing Group for the Women's Health Initiative Investigators, 2002).

Additional studies of a portion of the same sample found, contrary to earlier research (Zandhi et al., 2002), that estrogen—either alone or with progestin—does *not* improve cognition or prevent cognitive impairment after age 65; instead, it increases the risk of dementia or cognitive decline (Espeland et al., 2004; Rapp et al., 2003; Shumaker et al., 2003, 2004). Long-term estrogen use also may be associated with increased risk of ovarian cancer (Lacey Jr. et al., 2002; Rodriguez, Patel, Calle, Jacob, & Thun, 2001) and gallbladder disease (Cirillo et al., 2005). Furthermore, in a randomized 3-year study of 16,608 postmenopausal women, HRT had no significant effects on quality of life (Hays et al., 2003).

On the positive side, HRT, when started at menopause and continued for at least five years, can prevent or stop bone loss after menopause (Barrett-Connor et al., 2002; Lindsay, Gallagher, Kleerekoper, & Pickar, 2002) and prevent hip and other bone fractures (Writing Group for the Women's Health Initiative Investigators, 2002). However, bone loss resumes if and when HRT is stopped (Barrett-Connor et al., 2002) and, as we have discussed, can be treated in other, safer ways.

The effect of estrogen on breast cancer is still under study. One large-scale study found the risk of estrogen alone less than when combined with progestin (Schairer et al., 2000). Heightened risk of breast cancer seems to occur mainly among current or recent estrogen users, and the risk increases with length of use (Chen, Weiss, Newcomb, Barlow, & White, 2002; Willett, Colditz, & Stampfer, 2000).

The American Heart Association now advises *against* HRT, though the decision should, of course be made in consultation with a physician (Mosca et al., 2001). Lifestyle changes such as losing weight and stopping smoking, and, if necessary, drugs to lower cholesterol and blood pressure are probably wiser courses for heart disease prevention in most women (Manson & Martin, 2001).

Lifestyle changes, such as getting more exercise and losing weight, are now recommended over hormone replacement therapy (HRT) for postmenopausal women. Recent studies have challenged the health benefits of HRT.

Checkpoint

Can you . . .

✔ Discuss changes in women's health risks after menopause, and weigh the risks and benefits of hormone replacement therapy?

Psychosocial Influences on Health

The ancient proverb of Solomon, "A merry heart doeth good like medicine" (Proverbs 17:22), is being borne out by contemporary research. Negative emotion, such as anxiety or despair is often associated with poor physical and mental health, and positive emotions such as hope with good health and longer life (Ray, 2004; Salovey,

Rothman, Detweiler, & Steward, 2000; Spiro, 2001). Because the nervous system (especially the brain) interacts with all of the body's biological systems, feelings and beliefs affect bodily functions, including the functioning of the immune system (Ray, 2004). Negative moods seem to suppress immune functioning, increasing susceptibility to illness, whereas positive moods seem to enhance it (Salovey et al., 2000).

The health consequences of negative emotionality depend on how well individuals are able to manage and repair their moods, and this may be a function of disposition (Salovey et al., 2000). It should not be surprising, then, that personality is related to health (Ray, 2004; Spiro, 2001). People rated as extraverted, agreeable, or conscientious are more likely to report excellent health than people high in the personality dimension called *neuroticism* (Siegler, 1997; refer back to Chapter 14).

An important aspect of the relationship between personality and health is the way a person handles stress.

Stress and Health

Stress, sometimes called *allostatic load,* is the damage that occurs when coping abilities are inadequate to meet perceived environmental demands, or **stressors** (Ray, 2004). As Hans Selye, a pioneer in the study of stress, said, "It's not what happens that counts; it is how you take it" (quoted in Justice, 1994, p. 258). The body's capacity to adapt to stress, called *allostasis,* involves the brain, which perceives danger (either real or imagined), the adrenal glands, which mobilize the body to fight it, and the immune system, which provides the defenses.

Middle-aged people tend to experience different kinds of stressors than do younger adults (Aldwin & Levenson, 2001). Stress may come from role changes: career transitions, grown children leaving home, and the renegotiation of family relationships (Almeida & Horn, 2004). In the MIDUS study, both young and middle-aged adults reported more frequent, multiple, and severe stressors than did older adults and a greater degree of overload and disruption in their daily lives (Almeida & Horn, 2004). The frequency of interpersonal tensions, such as arguments with spouses, decreased from young to older adulthood, but stressors involving, for example, a sick friend or relative rose. Unique to midlife was a significant increase in stressors posing financial risk or involving children. However, middle-aged people also reported fewer stressors over which they had little or no control (Almeida & Horn, 2004).

Middle-aged people may be better equipped to cope with stress than people in other age groups (Lachman, 2004). They have a better sense of what they can do to change stressful circumstances and may be better able to accept what cannot be changed. They also have learned more effective strategies for avoiding or minimizing stress. For example, instead of having to worry about running out of gas on a long trip, they are likely to check to make sure the gas tank is full before starting out (Aldwin & Levenson, 2001). In a study of 5,823 adults being treated at a university-based pain center, those over age 50 were better able to cope with pain and avoid depression than younger sufferers (Green, Tait, & Gallagher, 2005). (We further discuss coping skills in Chapter 18.)

How Stress Affects Health The more stressful the changes that take place in a person's life, the greater the likelihood of serious illness within the next year or two. That was the finding of a classic study in which two psychiatrists, on the basis of interviews with 5,000 hospital patients, ranked the stressfulness of life events that had preceded their illness (Holmes & Rahe, 1976; see Table 15-3). About half the people with between 150 and 300 "life change units" (LCUs) in a single year, and about 70 percent of those with 300 or more LCUs, became ill.

stressors Perceived environmental demands that may produce stress.

What's Your View?

• What are the main sources of stress in your life? How do you handle stress? What methods have you found most successful?

Table 15-3 Life Events in Order of Diminishing Stressfulness

Life Event	Value	Life Event	Value
Death of spouse	100	Son or daughter leaving home	29
Divorce	73	Trouble with in-laws	29
Marital separation	65	Outstanding personal achievement	28
Jail term	63		
Death of close family member	63	Wife beginning or stopping work	26
Personal injury or illness	53	Beginning or ending school	26
Marriage	50	Revision of habits	24
Being fired at work	47	Trouble with boss	23
Marital reconciliation	45	Change in work hours	20
Retirement	45	Change in residence	20
Change in health of family	44	Change in schools	20
Pregnancy	40	Change in recreation	19
Sex difficulties	39	Change in social activity	18
Gain of new family member	39	Change in sleeping habits	16
Change in financial state	38	Change in number of family get-togethers	15
Death of close friend	37	Change in eating habits	15
Change of work	36	Vacation	13
Change in number of arguments with spouse	35	Minor violations of law	11
Foreclosure of mortgage	30		
Change of responsibility at work	29		

Source: Adapted from Holmes & Rahe, 1976, p. 213.

Change—even positive change—can be stressful, and some people react to stress by getting sick. Stress is under increasing scrutiny as a factor in such age-related diseases as hypertension, heart ailments, stroke, diabetes, osteoporosis, peptic ulcers, and cancer (Baum, Cacioppo, Melamed, Gallant, & Travis, 1995; Levenstein, Ackerman, Kiecolt-Glaser, & Dubois, 1999; Light et al., 1999; Sapolsky, 1992; Wittstein et al., 2005).

The connection between stress and illness has long been observed, but only recently have we begun to understand more about how stress produces illness and why some people handle stress better than others. Many studies have shown that only a small percentage of persons infected with a pathogen, such as a bacterium or fungus, develop symptoms of illness. Illness occurs only when the strength of the infection exceeds the body's ability to adapt to it and maintain allostasis. Genetic factors may be involved. In a longitudinal study of 847 New Zealanders followed from birth, nearly 43 percent of those who experienced multiple stressful events between ages 21 and 26 and who had a stress-sensitive version of the serotonin transponder gene developed depression, compared with only 17 percent of those with a stress-protective version of the gene (Caspi et al., 2003).

Distinct types of stressors affect the immune system differently, according to an analysis of 293 studies involving 18,941 participants. Acute, or short-term, stress, such as the challenge of taking a test or speaking before an audience, "revs up" the immune system; but intense or prolonged stress, such as results from poverty or disability, can weaken or break down the immune system, increasing susceptibility to illness. People who are older or already ill are more prone to stress-related change (Segerstrom & Miller, 2004). Research has found suppressed immune function in breast cancer patients (Compas & Luecken, 2002), abused women, hurricane sur-

Months after the September 11, 2001, terrorist attacks, many Manhattan residents—especially those who lived near the World Trade Center site—experienced post-traumatic stress syndrome or depression.

vivors, and men with a history of post-traumatic stress disorder (PTSD) (Harvard Medical School, 2002a). As we will discuss in Chapter 17, severe long-term stress can cause genetic aging (Epel et al., 2004).

Stress may harm health indirectly, through other lifestyle factors. People under stress may sleep less, smoke and drink more, eat poorly, and pay too little attention to their health. Conversely, regular exercise, good nutrition, at least seven hours of sleep a night, and frequent socializing are associated with lower stress (Baum et al., 1995). Thus educated people, who know more about health and illness, tend to be healthier and live longer (Ray, 2004).

Stress may be related to illness through lack of a sense of mastery or control. People who believe they have control over their lives tend to engage in healthier behaviors. In the MIDUS study, those who had a sense of control, regardless of SES, had fewer illnesses and better physical functioning (Lachman & Firth, 2004). This finding may help explain effects of job-related stress.

Occupational Stress and Burnout A combination of high job demands with low autonomy or control and little pride in the product is a typical stress-producing pattern (Galinsky, Kim, & Bond, 2001; Johnson, Stewart, Hall, Fredlund, & Theorell, 1996; United Nations International Labor Organization [UNILO], 1993; G. Williams, 1991), which increases the risk of high blood pressure and heart disease (Schnall et al., 1990; Siegrist, 1996). Among 10,308 British civil servants ages 35 to 55, low job control and an imbalance between effort and reward were strongly associated with increased coronary risk during the next five years (Bosma, Peter, Siegrist, & Marmot, 1998). On the other hand, employees with a high degree of responsibility on the job who lack confidence in their ability to carry out their responsibilities are also under stress and tend to be vulnerable to respiratory infections (Schaubroeck,

Checkpoint
Can you . . .

✔ Tell how emotions and personality can affect health?

✔ Discuss causes and effects of stress, sources of coping skills, and sources of stress in middle age?

✔ Explain how stress affects health?

What's Your View?

• What would you do if you were told that the job you had been doing for ten years was obsolete or that you were being let go because of downsizing?

Jones, & Xie, 2001). The ability to leave job-related stresses behind at the end of the day may be as important to maintaining good health as the level of perceived stress on the job (Johansson, Evans, Rydstedt, & Carrere, 1998).

Many women, in addition to juggling work and family, are under special pressure in the workplace, especially in corporations, where their superiors often are men. Some women complain that an invisible but inflexible "glass ceiling" inhibits their advancement to the highest ranks (Federal Glass Ceiling Commission, 1995). Another frequent source of stress is *sexual harassment:* psychological pressure created by unwelcome sexual overtures, particularly from a superior, which create a hostile or abusive environment.

Burnout is a prolonged response to chronic stressors in the workplace that result from a misfit between the worker and the job. Either the demands of the job may exceed the worker's coping abilities, or the worker's efforts may not be sufficiently rewarded. Burnout is especially common among people in the helping professions (such as teaching, medicine, therapy, social work, and police work) who feel frustrated by their inability to help people as much as they would like to (Maslach, 2003). Burnout typically involves three dimensions: overwhelming emotional exhaustion, feelings of cynicism and detachment from one's work, and a sense of ineffectiveness and lack of accomplishment (Maslach, 2003).

A common misconception is that burnout is a personal problem—that a person who burns out is trying too hard and doing too much or is simply weak and incompetent. Research has found some modest links to the personality category of neuroticism (specifically, anxiety and emotional instability). However, there is much stronger evidence for the impact of stress-producing characteristics of the work situation: high job demands combined with low resources and the presence of conflict—either between people, between job demands, or between important values (Maslach, 2003).

The most effective way to relieve stress and burnout may be to change the conditions that cause it by seeing that employees have opportunities to do work that is meaningful to them, uses their skills and knowledge, and gives them a sense of achievement and self-esteem (Knoop, 1994). Interventions may be more effective if they focus on building *job engagement,* a persistent, positive feeling of motivation and fulfillment in one's job, rather than on directly reducing burnout (Maslach, 2003).

Unemployment Stress Perhaps the greatest work-related stressor is the loss of a job. In 2004, 5.5 percent of the U.S. labor force was unemployed, that is, actively seeking but unable to find a job (Bureau of Labor Statistics, 2005a).

Research on unemployment has linked it to headaches, stomach trouble, and high blood pressure; to physical and mental illness, including heart attack, stroke, anxiety, and depression; to marital and family problems; to health, psychological, and behavior problems in offspring; and to suicide, homicide, and other crimes (Brenner, 1991; Kessler et al., 2004; Merva & Fowles, 1992; Perrucci, Perrucci, & Targ, 1988; Voydanoff, 1990).

Stress comes not only from loss of income and the resulting financial hardship, but also from declines in psychological well-being following job loss (Murphy & Athanasou, 1999; Winefield, 1995). Among 248 unemployed men and women in Queensland, Australia, the most important psychological factor in diminution of well-being was loss of status, followed by the loss of a sense of collective purpose and of a way to structure time (Creed & Macintyre, 2001). Men who define manhood as supporting a family, and workers of both sexes who derive their identity

burnout Syndrome of emotional exhaustion and a sense that one can no longer accomplish anything on the job.

Corporate downsizing and outsourcing of jobs to lower-paid workers in developing countries have forced many people in industrial societies out of work. People cope better with unemployment when they can draw on financial, psychological, and social resources and can see this forced change as in opportunity to do something new or as a challenge for growth.

from their work and define their worth in terms of its dollar value, lose more than their paychecks when they lose their jobs. They lose a piece of themselves and their self-esteem and feel less in control of their lives (Forteza & Prieto, 1994; Perrucci et al., 1988; Voydanoff, 1987, 1990)—and loss of control is, as we have noted, an important factor in stress (Lachman & Firth, 2004).

The psychological impact of unemployment is generally temporary; finding a new job can restore well-being. Motivation and a sense of mastery are key factors in finding work. However, older workers, women, and nonwhites tend to experience greater problems in job-hunting than younger, male, and white workers (Vinokur, Schul, Vuori, & Price, 2000).

Checkpoint

Can you . . .

✔ Identify sources of occupational stress?

✔ Summarize physical and psychological effects of losing a job?

COGNITIVE DEVELOPMENT

What happens to cognitive abilities in middle age? Do they improve or decline, or both? Do people develop distinctive ways of thinking at this time of life? How does age affect the ability to solve problems, to learn, to create, and to perform on the job?

Measuring Cognitive Abilities in Middle Age

Guidepost

4. What cognitive gains and losses occur during middle age?

The status of cognitive abilities in middle age has been a subject of debate. Studies using different methodologies and measuring different characteristics have had somewhat different findings. Largely cross-sectional studies based on the Wechsler Adult Intelligence Scale, a psychometric instrument (see Chapter 17), show declines in both verbal and performance abilities beginning in young adulthood. However, two other lines of research, K. Warner Schaie's Seattle Longitudinal Study and Horn and Cattell's studies of fluid and crystallized intelligence, have produced more encouraging findings.

K. Warner Schaie: The Seattle Longitudinal Study

Cognitively speaking, in many respects middle-aged people are in their prime. The life of Gandhi amply demonstrates this. So does the Seattle Longitudinal Study of Adult Intelligence, conducted by K. Warner Schaie and his colleagues (Schaie, 1990, 1994, 1996a, 1996b, 2005; Willis & Schaie, 1999).

Although this ongoing study is called longitudinal, it uses sequential methods (refer back to Chapter 2). The study began in 1956 with 500 randomly chosen participants: 25 men and 25 women in each five-year age bracket from 22 to 67. Participants took timed tests of six primary mental abilities based on those identified by Thurstone (1938). (Table 15-4 gives definitions and sample tasks for each ability.) Every seven years, the original participants were retested and new participants were added. By 1994, about 5,000 people, forming a broadly diverse socioeconomic sample from young adulthood to old age, had been tested.

The researchers found no uniform patterns of developmental change, either among individuals or across cognitive abilities (Schaie, 1994, 2005). Although perceptual speed tends to peak in the twenties and numerical ability and verbal fluency in the late thirties, peak performance in three of the six abilities—inductive reasoning, spatial orientation, and vocabulary—occurs during middle adulthood (see Figure 15-2). In all three of these abilities, middle-aged people, especially women, score higher on average than they did at 25.

Table 15-4 Tests of Primary Mental Abilities Given in Seattle Longitudinal Study of Adult Intelligence

Test	Ability Measured	Task	Type of Intelligence*
Vocabulary	Recognition and understanding of words	Find synonym by matching stimulus word with another word from multiple-choice list	Crystallized
Verbal fluency	Retrieving words from long-term memory	Think of as many words as possible beginning with a given letter, in a set time period	Part crystallized, part fluid
Number	Performing computations	Do simple addition problems	Crystallized
Spatial orientation	Manipulating objects mentally in two-dimensional space	Select rotated examples of figure to match stimulus figure	Fluid
Inductive reasoning	Identifying patterns and inferring principles and rules for solving logical problems	Complete a letter series	Fluid
Perceptual speed	Making quick, accurate discriminations between visual stimuli	Identify matching and nonmatching images flashed on a computer screen	Fluid

*Fluid and crystallized intelligence are defined in the next section.

Sources: Schaie, 1989; Willis & Schaie, 1999.

Figure 15-2

Longitudinal change in six basic mental abilities, ages 25 to 67.

(Source: Shaie, 1994; reprinted in Willis & Schaie, 1999, p. 237.)

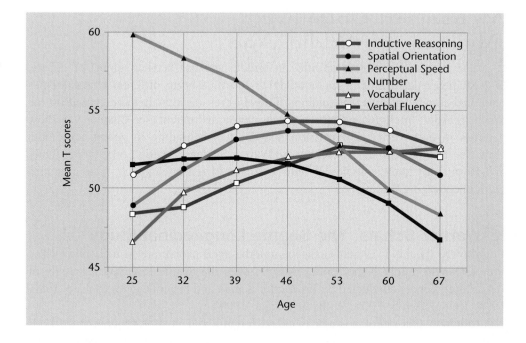

Despite wide individual differences, most participants in the Seattle study showed *no* significant reduction in most abilities until after age 60, and then not in most areas. Virtually no one declined on all fronts, and many people improved in some areas (Schaie, 1994, 2005). Furthermore, possibly because of improvements in education, healthy lifestyles, and other positive environmental influences, successive generations scored progressively higher at the same ages on reasoning, spatial orientation, and vocabulary. However, numerical ability has declined since the cohort born in 1924. Verbal fluency dipped for the 1931 cohort and then returned to its baseline level (Schaie, 2005; Willis & Schaie, 1999; see Figure 15-3).

Individuals who scored highest tended to have high socioeconomic status, to have flexible personalities, to be in intact families, to pursue occupations and other activities that are cognitively complex, to be married to someone more cognitively advanced, and to be satisfied with their accomplishments (Schaie, 1994, 2005).

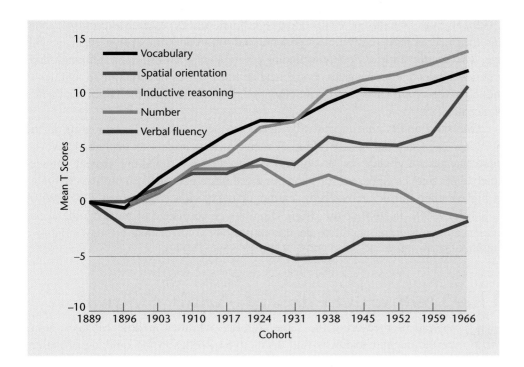

Figure 15-3
Cohort differences in scores on tests of basic mental abilities. In a group with mean birth years from 1889 to 1966, more recent cohorts scored higher on inductive reasoning, verbal meaning, and spatial orientation. Ability with numbers showed a decline. (Source: Schaie, 1994.)

In another longitudinal study of 384 Baltimore adults ages 50 and above, those with larger social networks better maintained their cognitive functioning 12 years later. This association was independent of effects of emotional support. It is not clear, however, whether more social contacts produce or merely reflect better cognitive functioning. If the former, the benefit may result from the wider variety of informational and interactional opportunities that a wide circle of friends and families provides (Holtzman et al., 2004).

Our growing knowledge about the brain's genetic aging may shed light on patterns of cognitive decline. Researchers who examined postmortem brain tissue from 30 people ages 26 to 106 identified two groups of genes that tend to become damaged with age. Among these were genes involved in learning and memory. Middle-aged brains showed the greatest variability, some exhibiting gene patterns much like those of young adults and others showing gene patterns more like older adults (Lu et al., 2004). This finding may help account for the wide range of individual differences in cognitive functioning in midlife. However, it is not clear what causes these variations.

Horn and Cattell: Fluid and Crystallized Intelligence

Another line of research (Cattell, 1965; Horn, 1967, 1968, 1970, 1982a, 1982b; Horn & Hofer, 1992) has distinguished between two aspects of intelligence: *fluid* and *crystallized*. **Fluid intelligence** is the ability to solve novel problems that require little or no previous knowledge, such as discovering the pattern in a sequence of figures. It involves perceiving relations, forming concepts, and drawing inferences. These abilities, which are largely determined by neurological status, tend to decline with age. **Crystallized intelligence** is the ability to remember and use information acquired over a lifetime, for example, in finding a synonym for a word. It is measured by tests of vocabulary, general information, and responses to social situations and dilemmas. These abilities, which depend largely on education and cultural experience, hold their own or even improve with age.

These two kinds of intelligence follow different paths. Typically, fluid intelligence has been found to peak in young adulthood, whereas crystallized intelligence improves through middle age and often until near the end of life (Horn, 1982a,

fluid intelligence Type of intelligence, proposed by Horn and Cattell, which is applied to novel problems and is relatively independent of educational and cultural influences.

crystallized intelligence Type of intelligence, proposed by Horn and Cattell, involving the ability to remember and use learned information; it is largely dependent on education and cultural background.

However, much of this research is cross-sectional and thus may at least partly reflect generational differences rather than changes with age. The Seattle study's sequential findings were somewhat different. Although fluid abilities did decline earlier than crystallized abilities, losses in certain fluid abilities—inductive reasoning and spatial orientation—did not set in until the midfifties (Willis & Schaie, 1999).

One fluid ability that is generally agreed to peak quite early, beginning in the twenties, is perceptual speed. Working memory also begins to decline. However, these changes are gradual and do not necessarily cause functional impairment. Middle-aged adults may compensate for losses in these basic neurological abilities by gains in higher-order abilities affected by learning and experience (Lachman, 2004; Willis & Schaie, 1999). In light of the strong cognitive performance of most middle-agers, evidence of substantial cognitive decline in persons younger than 60 may indicate a neurological problem (Schaie, 2005; Willis & Shaie, 1999).

Checkpoint

Can you . . .

✔ Summarize results of the Seattle Longitudinal Study concerning changes in basic mental abilities in middle age?

✔ Distinguish between fluid and crystallized intelligence and how they are affected by age?

✔ Compare the findings of the Seattle study with those of Horn and Cattell?

Guidepost

5. Do mature adults think differently than younger people do?

The Distinctiveness of Adult Cognition

Instead of measuring the same cognitive abilities at different ages, some developmental scientists find distinctive qualities in the thinking of mature adults. Some, working within the psychometric tradition, claim that accumulated knowledge changes the way fluid intelligence operates. Others, as we noted in Chapter 13, maintain that mature thought represents a new stage of cognitive development—a "special form of intelligence" (Sinnott, 1996, p. 361), which may underlie mature interpersonal skills and contribute to practical problem solving.

The Role of Expertise

encapsulation In Hoyer's terminology, progressive dedication of information processing and fluid thinking to specific knowledge systems, making knowledge more readily accessible.

Two young resident physicians in a hospital radiology laboratory examine a chest X ray. They study an unusual white blotch on the left side. "Looks like a large tumor," one of them says finally. The other nods. Just then, a longtime staff radiologist walks by and looks over their shoulders at the X ray. "That patient has a collapsed lung and needs immediate surgery," he declares (Lesgold, 1983; Lesgold et al., 1988).

Why do mature adults show increasing competence in solving problems in their chosen fields? One answer seems to lie in specialized knowledge, or expertise—a form of crystallized intelligence.

Advances in expertise continue at least through middle adulthood and are relatively independent of general intelligence and of any declines in the brain's information-processing machinery. With experience, it has been suggested, information processing and fluid abilities become *encapsulated*, or dedicated to specific kinds of knowledge, making that knowledge easier to access, add to, and use. In other words, **encapsulation** "captures" fluid abilities for expert problem solving. Thus, although middle-aged people may take somewhat longer than younger people to process new information, in solving problems in their own fields they more than compensate

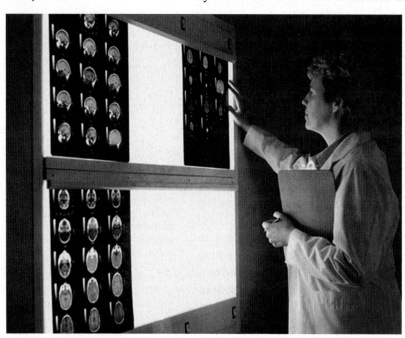

Expertise in interpreting X rays, as in many other fields, depends on accumulated, specialized knowledge, which continues to increase with age. Experts often appear to be guided by intuition and cannot explain how they arrive at conclusions.

with judgment developed from experience (Hoyer & Rybash, 1994; Rybash, Hoyer, & Roodin, 1986).

In one classic study (Ceci & Liker, 1986), researchers identified 30 middle-aged and older men who were avid horse racing fans. On the basis of skill in picking winners, the investigators divided the men into two groups: "expert" and "nonexpert." The experts used a more sophisticated method of reasoning, incorporating interpretations of much interrelated information, whereas nonexperts used simpler, less successful methods. Superior reasoning was not related to IQ; there was no significant difference in average measured intelligence between the two groups, and experts with low IQs used more complex reasoning than nonexperts with higher IQs. Similarly, on a much weightier plane, Gandhi, a man who claimed to have less than average intelligence, worked out an expert solution to the seemingly insoluble problem of empowering a powerless people to achieve independence.

Studies of such diverse occupations as chess players, street vendors, abacus counters, physics experts, hospitality workers, airline counter workers, and airplane pilots illustrate how specific knowledge contributes to superior performance in a particular domain (Billet, 2001) and can help buffer age-related declines in cognitive resources when solving problems in that domain (Morrow, Menard, Stine-Morrow, Teller, & Bryant, 2001).

Experts notice different aspects of a situation than novices do, and they process information and solve problems differently. Their thinking is often more flexible and adaptable. They assimilate and interpret new knowledge more efficiently by referring to a rich, highly organized storehouse of mental representations of what they already know. They sort information on the basis of basic principles, rather than surface similarities and differences. And they are more aware of what they do *not* know (Charness & Schultetus, 1999; Goldman, Petrosino, & Cognition and Technology Group at Vanderbilt, 1999).

Cognitive performance is not the only ingredient of expertise. Problem solving occurs in a social context. Ability to make expert judgments depends on familiarity with the way things are done—with the expectations and demands of the job and the culture of the community or enterprise. (This is somewhat akin to Sternberg's concept of *tacit knowledge,* discussed in Chapter 13.) Even concert pianists, who spend hours practicing in isolation, must adapt to various concert halls with different acoustics, to the musical conventions of the time and place, and to the musical tastes of their audiences (Billet, 2001).

Expert thinking often seems automatic and intuitive. Experts generally are not fully aware of the thought processes that lie behind their decisions (Charness & Schultetus, 1999; Dreyfus, 1993–1994; Rybash et al., 1986). They cannot readily explain how they arrive at a conclusion or where a nonexpert has gone wrong: The experienced radiologist could not see why the residents would even consider diagnosing a collapsed lung as a tumor. Such intuitive, experience-based thinking is also characteristic of what has been called postformal thought.

Integrative Thought

Although not limited to any particular period of adulthood, postformal thought (introduced in Chapter 13) seems well suited to the complex tasks, multiple roles, and perplexing choices and challenges of midlife, such as the need to synthesize and balance work and family demands (Sinnott, 1998, 2003). An important feature of postformal thought is its *integrative* nature. Mature adults integrate logic with intuition and emotion; they integrate conflicting facts and ideas; and they integrate new information with what they already know. They interpret what they read, see, or hear in

Lifemap CD

For a lighthearted view of some "Cognitive Advantages of Middle Age," watch the video of this title in Chapter 15 of your CD.

What's Your View?

- If you needed surgery, would you rather go to a middle-aged doctor or one who is considerably older or younger? Why?

BOX 15-2

Digging Deeper
Moral Leadership in Middle and Late Adulthood

What makes a single mother of four young children, with no money and a tenth-grade education, dedicate her life to religious missionary work on behalf of her equally poor neighbors? What leads a pediatrician to devote much of his practice to the care of poor children instead of to patients whose parents could provide him with a lucrative income?

In the mid-1980s, two psychologists, Anne Colby and William Damon, sought answers to questions like these. They embarked on a two-year search for people who showed unusual moral excellence in their day-to-day lives. The researchers eventually identified 23 "moral exemplars," interviewed them in depth, and studied how they had become moral leaders (Colby & Damon, 1992).

To find moral exemplars, Colby and Damon worked with a panel of 22 "expert nominators," people who in their professional lives regularly think about moral ideas: philosophers, historians, religious thinkers, and so forth. The researchers drew up five criteria: sustained commitment to principles that show respect for humanity; behavior consistent with one's ideals; willingness to risk self-interest; inspiring others to moral action; and humility, or lack of concern for one's ego.

The chosen exemplars varied widely in age, education, occupation, and ethnicity. There were 10 men and 13 women, ages 35 to 86, of white, African American, and Hispanic back-grounds. Education ranged from eighth grade up through M.D.s, Ph.D.s, and law degrees; and occupations included religious callings, business, teaching, and social leadership. Areas of concern involved poverty, civil rights, education, ethics, the environment, peace, and religious freedom.

The research yielded a number of surprises, not least of which was this group's showing on Kohlberg's classic measure of moral judgment. Each exemplar was asked about "Heinz's dilemma" (refer back to Chapter 11) and about a follow-up question: how the man should be punished if he steals the drug. Of 22 exemplars (one response was not scorable), only half scored at the postconventional level; the other half scored at the conventional level. The major difference between the two groups was level of education: Those with college and advanced degrees were much more likely to score at the higher level, and no one with only a high school diploma scored above the conventional level. Clearly, it is not necessary to score at Kohlberg's highest stages to live an exemplary moral life.

How does a person become morally committed? The 23 moral exemplars did not develop in isolation, but responded to social influences. Some of these influences, such as those of parents, were important from childhood on. Many other influences became significant in later years, helping these people evaluate their capacities, form moral goals, and develop strategies to achieve them.

---

terms of its meaning for them. Instead of accepting something at face value, they filter it through their life experience and previous learning.

In one study (C. Adams, 1991), early and late adolescents and middle-aged and older adults were asked to summarize a Sufi teaching tale. In the story, a stream was unable to cross a desert until a voice told it to let the wind carry it; the stream was dubious but finally agreed and was blown across. Adolescents recalled more details of the story than adults did, but their summaries were largely limited to repeating the story line. Adults, especially women, gave summaries that were rich in interpretation, integrating what was in the text with its psychological and metaphorical meaning for them, as in this response of a 39-year-old:

> I believe what this story was trying to say was that there are times when everyone needs help and must sometimes make changes to reach their goals. Some people may resist change for a long time until they realize that certain things are beyond their control and they need assistance. When this is finally achieved and they can accept help and trust from someone, they can master things even as large as a desert. (p. 333)

Society benefits from this integrative feature of adult thought. Generally it is mature adults who, like Gandhi, become moral and spiritual leaders (see Box 15-2) and who translate their knowledge about the human condition into inspirational stories to which younger generations can turn for guidance.

Checkpoint

Can you . . .

✔ Discuss the relationship between expertise, knowledge, and intelligence?

✔ Give an example of integrative thinking?

Guidepost

6. What accounts for creative achievement, and how does it change with age?

Creativity

At about age 40, Frank Lloyd Wright designed Robie House in Chicago, Agnes deMille choreographed the Broadway musical *Carousel,* and Louis Pasteur developed the germ theory of disease. Charles Darwin was 50 when he presented his theory of evolution. Toni Morrison won the Pulitzer Prize for *Beloved,*

—continued

These moral exemplars had a lifelong commitment to change: They focused their energy on changing society and people's lives for the better. But they remained stable in their moral commitments. At the same time, they kept growing throughout life, remained open to new ideas, and continued to learn from others.

The processes responsible for stability in moral commitments were gradual, taking many years to build up. They were also collaborative: Leaders took advice from supporters, and people noted for independent judgment drew heavily on feedback from those close to them—both those people who shared their goals and those who had different perspectives.

Along with their enduring moral commitments, certain personality characteristics seemed to remain with the moral exemplars throughout middle and late adulthood: enjoyment of life, ability to make the best of a bad situation, solidarity with others, absorption in work, a sense of humor, and humility. They tended to believe that change was possible, and this optimism helped them battle what often seemed like overwhelming odds and to persist in the face of defeat.

While their actions often meant risk and hardship, these people did not see themselves as courageous. Nor did they agonize over decisions. Since their personal and moral goals coincided, they just did what they believed needed to be done, not calculating personal consequences to themselves or their families and not feeling that they were sacrificing or martyring themselves.

Of course, there is no "blueprint" for creating a moral giant, just as it does not seem possible to write directions to produce a genius in any field. What studying the lives of such people can bring is the knowledge that ordinary people can rise to greatness and that openness to change and new ideas can persist throughout adulthood.

What's Your View?

Think of someone you would consider a moral exemplar. How do that person's qualities compare to those found in this study?

Check It Out

For more information on this topic, go to http://kenan.ethics .duke.edu/ethic_moral.asp [the Web site of the Kenan Institute for Ethics at Duke University].

---

a novel she wrote at about 55. But creativity is not limited to the Darwins and deMilles; we can see it in an inventor who comes up with a better mousetrap, or a promoter who finds an innovative way to sell it.

Characteristics of Creative Achievers

Creativity begins with talent, but talent is not enough. Children may show *creative potential;* but in adults, what counts is *creative performance:* what, and how much, a creative mind produces (Sternberg & Lubart, 1995). Creative performance is the product of a web of biological, personal, social, and cultural forces. It emerges from the dynamic interaction among the creator, the rules and techniques of the domain, and the colleagues who work in that domain (Gardner, 1986, 1988; Simonton, 2000b).

Exceptional talents are less born than made—they require systematic training and practice (Simonton, 2000b). Extraordinary creative achievement, according to one analysis (Keegan, 1996), results from deep, highly organized knowledge of a subject; intrinsic motivation to work hard for the sake of the work, not for external rewards; and a strong emotional attachment to the work, which spurs the creator to persevere in the face of obstacles. What carries an Einstein "over the threshold from competent but ordinary thinker to extraordinary and creative thinker," says Keegan (p. 63), is the acquisition of expert knowledge. A person must first be thoroughly grounded in a field before she or he can see its limitations, envision radical departures, and develop a new and unique point of view.

Creativity begins with talent, but talent is not enough. The author Toni Morrison, 1993 winner of the Nobel Prize in Literature, worked long, hard hours throughout her prolific career. Her achievements are examples of the creative productivity possible in middle age.

What's
Your View?

- Think of an adult you know
  who is a creative achiever. To
  what combination of personal
  qualities and environmental
  forces would you attribute her
  or his creative performance?

However, the relationship between creativity and expertise is complex. In a study of the careers of 59 classical composers, creativity did not follow a straight upward course. Later compositions often were less aesthetically successful than earlier ones, and the amount of time spent in general musical training and composition was more predictive of aesthetic success in a particular genre, such as composing operas, than was the amount of time spent working in that genre. These findings suggest that overtraining in a particular genre may hamper creativity, and that versatility, not just expertise, may count (Simonton, 2000a).

General intelligence, as measured by standard IQ tests, has little relationship to creative performance (Simonton, 2000b). Highly creative people are self-starters (Torrance, 1988) and risk takers; they tend to be independent, nonconformist, unconventional, and flexible, and they are open to new ideas and experiences (Simonton, 2000b). Their thinking processes are often unconscious, leading to sudden moments of illumination (Torrance, 1988). Like Gandhi, they look at a problem more deeply than other people do and come up with solutions that do not occur to others (Sternberg & Horvath, 1998).

Creativity develops over a lifetime in a social context, and not necessarily in nurturing environments. Instead, as in Gandhi's case, it seems to emerge from diverse experiences that weaken conventional constraints and from challenging experiences that strengthen the ability to persevere and overcome obstacles (Simonton, 2000b).

Creativity and Age

Is there a relationship between creative performance and age? On psychometric tests of divergent thinking (refer back to Chapter 9), age differences consistently appear. Whether data are cross-sectional or longitudinal, scores peak, on average, around the late thirties. A similar age curve emerges when creativity is measured by variations in output (number of publications, paintings, or compositions). A person in the last decade of a creative career typically produces only about half as much as during the late thirties or early forties, though somewhat more than in the twenties (Simonton, 1990).

However, the age curve varies depending on the field. Poets, mathematicians, and theoretical physicists tend to be most prolific in their late twenties or early thirties. Research psychologists reach a peak around age 40, followed by a moderate decline. Novelists, historians, and philosophers become increasingly productive through their late forties or fifties and then level off. These patterns hold true across cultures and historical periods (Dixon & Hultsch, 1999; Simonton, 1990).

Of course, not everything a creator produces is equally notable; even a Picasso is bound to produce some minor material. The *quality ratio*—the proportion of major works to total output—bears no relationship to age. The periods in which a person creates the largest number of memorable works also tend to be the ones in which that same person produces the largest number of forgettable ones (Simonton, 1998). Thus the likelihood that a *particular* work will be a masterpiece has nothing to do with age.

Sometimes losses in productivity are offset by gains in quality. A study of the "swan songs" of 172 composers found that their last works—usually fairly short and melodically simple—were among their richest, most important, and most successful (Simonton, 1989).

Checkpoint
Can you . . .

✔ Discuss prerequisites for
  creative achievement?

✔ Summarize the relationship
  between creative performance
  and age?

Guidepost

7. How are patterns of work
   and education changing,
   and how does work con-
   tribute to cognitive
   development?

Work and Education: Are Age-Based Roles Obsolete?

Traditionally, in industrialized societies, occupational roles are based on age (as in the left side of Figure 15-4). Young people are students; young and middle-aged adults are workers; older adults organize their lives around retirement

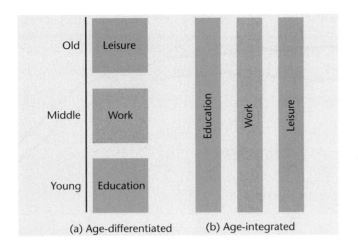

and leisure. Such a life structure is **age-differentiated.** Yet, as the gerontologist Matilda White Riley (1994) has observed:

> . . . these structures fail to accommodate many of the changes in people's lives. After all, does it make sense to spend nearly one-third of adult lifetime in retirement? Or to crowd most work into the harried middle years? Or to label as "too old" those as young as 55 who want to work? Does it make sense to assume that . . . physically capable older people—an estimated 40 million of them in the next century—should expect greater support from society than they contribute to society? . . . Surely, something will have to change! (p. 445)

According to Riley, age-differentiated roles are a holdover from a time when life was shorter and social institutions less diverse. By devoting themselves to one aspect of life at a time, people do not enjoy each period as much as they might and may not prepare adequately for the next phase. By concentrating on work, adults may forget how to play; then, when they retire, they may not know what to do with a sudden abundance of leisure time. Increasing numbers of older adults (like Gandhi in his later years) are able to contribute to society, but opportunities to use and reward their abilities are inadequate.

In an **age-integrated** society (as in the right side of Figure 15-4), all kinds of roles—learning, working, and playing—would be open to adults of all ages (Riley, 1994). They could intersperse periods of education, work, and leisure throughout the life span. Things seem to be moving in that direction. College students take work-study programs or "stop out" for a while before resuming their education. Emerging adults explore various avenues before settling into careers. In a society undergoing dramatic change, career decisions are often open-ended. Mature adults take evening classes or take time off work to pursue a special interest. A person may have several careers in succession, each requiring additional education or training. People retire earlier or later than in the past, or not at all. Retirees devote time to study or to a new line of work.

Much of the existing research on education, work, leisure, and retirement reflects the old, age-differentiated model of social roles and the cohorts whose lives it describes. As age integration becomes more prevalent, future cohorts may have very different experiences and attitudes.

age-differentiated Describing a life structure in which primary roles—learning, working, and leisure—are based on age; typical in industrialized societies. Compare *age-integrated*.

age-integrated Describing a life structure in which primary roles—learning, working, and leisure—are open to adults of all ages and can be interspersed throughout the life span. Compare *age-differentiated*.

Checkpoint
Can you . . .

✔ Explain how an age-integrated society would differ from an age-differentiated society, and give examples?

Work versus Early Retirement

During the economic growth period of the 1990s, public and private pension programs and individual savings contributed to a trend toward early retirement in the United States, as in many industrialized countries, but that trend appears to have leveled off as companies withdraw retiree medical benefits and switch to less generous retirement plans (Porter & Walsh, 2005).

Figure 15-5

Labor force participation rates of men and women by age, United States, 2004. (*Source: Congressional Budget Office, 2004a, Figure 1.*)

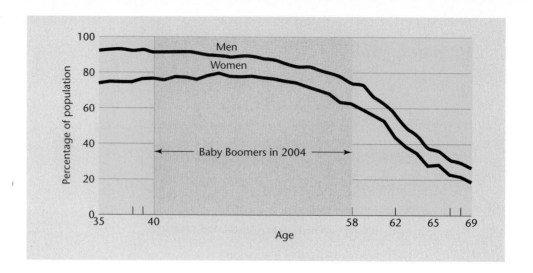

According to the U. S. Congressional Budget Office (CBO) (2004a), 14 percent of men and 24 percent of women ages 50 to 61 were out of the labor force in 2001 (see Figure 15-5). Almost 2 out of 3 of these men and 2 out of 5 of the women cited disability as the reason. Most of the others were retired or, in the case of the women, caring for others or not interested in working.

The main predictors of retirement age are health, pension eligibility, and financial circumstances. Marital status also can make a difference, as decisions about timing of each spouse's retirement have to be negotiated by the couple (Moen, Kim, & Hofmeister, 2001).

People who plan to retire early need to save more to finance a comfortable retirement (CBO, 2004b). Among the baby boom generation now reaching or approaching retirement age, at least half have saved enough to be able to maintain their present standard of living during retirement if current federal benefits do not change. One-fourth are likely to experience moderate declines in living standards during retirement, and one-fourth, who have failed to accumulate significant savings, will be dependent on government benefits (CBO, 2004c).

Many of today's middle-aged and older workers who have inadequate savings or pensions, need continued health insurance, or do not want to give up the stimulation of work are choosing *not* to retire or to try a new line of work. Thus retirement is "increasingly a transition *within,* rather than *from* midlife" (Kim & Moen, 2001, p. 488). That transition has become fuzzier, "involving multiple transitions out of and into paid and unpaid 'work'" (p. 489). Whereas 50-year-olds tend to work primarily for financial reasons, at 60 intrinsic values such as enjoyment of work, wanting to remain productive, and feeling valued and respected become more important determinants of whether a person will continue to work (Sterns & Huyck, 2001).

Work and Cognitive Development

"Use it or lose it" applies to the mind as well as the body. Work can influence future cognitive functioning.

As we mentioned in Chapter 13, some research suggests that flexible thinkers tend to obtain substantively complex work—work requiring thought and independent judgment. This kind of work, in turn, stimulates more flexible thinking; and flexible thinking increases the ability to do complex work (Kohn, 1980). Thus, people who are deeply engaged in complex work tend to show stronger cognitive performance in comparison to their peers as they age (Avolio & Sosik, 1999; Kohn & Schooler, 1983; Schaie, 1984; Schooler, 1984, 1990). Indeed, it has been estimated that as much as one-third of the individual variance in changes in cognitive ability with age may be attributable to such factors as education, occupation, and socioeconomic status (Schaie, 1990). If work could be made more meaningful and challenging, more adults might retain or improve their cognitive abilities (Avolio & Sosik, 1999).

This seems to be happening already. The gains in most cognitive abilities found in recent middle-aged and older cohorts in the Seattle Longitudinal Study may well reflect workplace changes that emphasize self-managed, multifunctional teams and put a premium on adaptability, initiative, and decentralized decision making (Avolio & Sosik, 1999). Unfortunately, older workers are less likely than younger workers to be offered, or to volunteer for, training, education, and challenging job assignments, in the mistaken belief that older people cannot handle such opportunities. Yet the Seattle study found that declines in cognitive ability generally do not occur until very late in life, well after the working years. Indeed, work performance shows greater variability *within* age groups than between them (Avolio & Sosik, 1999).

Adults can actively affect their future cognitive development by the occupational choices they make. Those who constantly seek more stimulating opportunities are likely to remain mentally sharp (Avolio & Sosik, 1999). A study in Frankfurt, Germany, compared 195 patients with dementia, ages 55 and up, with 229 nondemented adults ages 60 and up. Those who had worked in intellectually demanding jobs that called for a high degree of control and involved wide circles of communication were less likely to have dementia (Seidler et al., 2004; Wilson, 2005).

These women improving their computer skills are among the 39 percent of middle-aged people in the United States who participate in work-related adult education. Adult learners need instructional methods geared toward their motives, goals, and experiences. Self-generated projects are particularly effective for mature adults.

The Mature Learner

Changes in the workplace often entail a need for more training or education. Expanding technology and shifting job markets require a life-span approach to learning. For many adults, formal learning is a way to develop their cognitive potential and to keep up with the changing world of work. Some women who have devoted their young adult years to homemaking and parenting are taking the first steps toward reentering the job market. People close to retirement often want to expand their minds and skills to make more productive and interesting use of leisure. Some adults simply enjoy learning and want to keep doing it throughout life.

In 1999–2000, nearly 12 percent of U.S. college undergraduates were 40 or older (NCES, 2003). Some colleges accommodate the practical needs of students of nontraditional age by granting credit for life experience and previous learning. Many offer part-time matriculation, Saturday and night classes, independent study, child care, financial aid, free or reduced-tuition courses, and distance learning via computers or closed-circuit broadcasts (refer back to Chapter 13).

Not all adults who participate in formal education are in colleges or universities. In 2002-2003, 39 percent of U.S. 45- to 64-year-olds participated in work-related adult education, and all but 2 percent were in seminars or courses not leading to diplomas or degrees (NCES, 2004a). Some adults seek specialized training to update their knowledge and skills. Some train for new occupations. Some want to move up the career ladder or to go into business for themselves.

Unfortunately, some learning institutions are not structured to meet mature adults' educational and psychological needs or to take advantage of their cognitive strengths. Adult learners have their own motives, goals, developmental tasks, and experiences. They need knowledge they can apply to specific problems. Cooperative study built around self-generated problems or projects is most appropriate to a mature adult (Sinnott, 1998).

What's Your View?

• From what you have seen, do students of nontraditional age seem to do better or worse in college than younger students? How would you explain your observation?

Checkpoint
Can you . . .

✔ Discuss trends in work and early retirement in middle age?

✔ Explain how work can affect cognitive functioning?

✔ Give reasons why mature adults return to the classroom, and tell some ways in which educational institutions attempt to meet their needs?

Refocus

Thinking back to the Focus vignette about Mahatma Gandhi at the beginning of this chapter:

- How does Gandhi's story exemplify the significance of middle adulthood?

- Why do you think Gandhi undertook such major changes in middle age?

- How would you expect the regimen Gandhi adopted when he moved to the farm outside Durban to have influenced his health?

- In what ways do Gandhi's decisions and actions seem to show fluid or crystallized intelligence? Postformal thought? Practical problem solving? Creativity?

- Does Gandhi seem to fit the profile of the moral exemplars described in Box 15-2?

Research about education and work—as well as about problem solving, creativity, and moral choices—shows that the mind continues to develop during adulthood. Such research illustrates the links between the cognitive side of development and its social and emotional aspects, to which we turn again in Chapter 16.

SUMMARY AND KEY TERMS

Middle Age: A Social Construct

Guidepost 1: What are the distinguishing features of middle age?

- The concept of middle age is a social construct. It came into use as an increasing life span led to new roles at midlife.
- The span of middle adulthood can be defined chronologically, contextually, or biologically.
- Middle adulthood is a time of both gains and losses.
- Most middle-aged people are in good physical, cognitive, and emotional condition. They have heavy responsibilities and multiple roles and feel competent to handle them.
- Middle age is a time for taking stock and making decisions about the remaining years.

PHYSICAL DEVELOPMENT

Physical Changes

Guidepost 2: What physical changes generally occur during the middle years, and what is their psychological impact?

- Although some physiological changes result from aging and genetic makeup, behavior and lifestyle can affect their timing and extent.
- Most middle-aged adults compensate well for gradual, minor declines in sensory and psychomotor abilities. Losses in bone density and vital capacity are common.

- Menopause occurs, on average, at about age 50 or 51, following the physiological changes of perimenopause. Symptoms of menopause and attitudes toward it may depend on personal characteristics, past experiences, and cultural factors.
- Although men can continue to father children until late in life, many middle-aged men experience a decline in fertility and in frequency of orgasm.
- Sexual activity generally diminishes slightly and gradually, and the quality of sexual relations may improve.
- Among women, sexual dysfunction decreases with age; in men, it is just the opposite. A large proportion of middle-aged men experience erectile dysfunction. Sexual dysfunction can have physical causes but also may be related to health, lifestyle, and emotional well-being.

presbyopia *(553)*
myopia *(553)*
presbycusis *(553)*
basal metabolism *(553)*
vital capacity *(555)*
menopause *(555)*
perimenopause *(555)*
sexual dysfunction *(559)*
erectile dysfunction *(560)*

Health

Guidepost 3: What factors affect health at midlife?

- Most middle-aged people are healthy and have no functional limitations.

- Hypertension is a major health problem beginning in midlife. Cancer has passed heart disease as the number one killer in midlife. The prevalence of diabetes has doubled, and it is now the fifth leading cause of death in this age group.
- Diet, exercise, alcohol use, and smoking affect present and future health. Preventive care is important.
- Low income is associated with poorer health, in part because of lack of insurance.
- Racial and ethnic disparities in health and health care have decreased but still persist.
- Postmenopausal women become more susceptible to heart disease and bone loss leading to osteoporosis. Chances of developing breast cancer also increase with age, and routine mammography is recommended for women beginning at age 40.
- Nearly one in three U.S. women has a hysterectomy by age 60. Many experts believe this procedure is overused.
- There is mounting evidence that the risks of hormone replacement therapy may outweigh its benefits.
- Personality and negative emotionality can affect health.
- Stress occurs when the body's ability to cope is not equal to the demands on it. Stress is related to a variety of age-related physical and psychological problems. Prolonged, severe stress can affect immune functioning.
- Role and career changes and other experiences typical of middle age can be stressful.
- Causes of occupational stress include a combination of high pressure and low control and inability to "unwind."
- Burnout may occur when there is a misfit between person and job. It is usually accompanied by overwhelming emotional fatigue, cynicism, and a sense of inability to accomplish goals.
- Unemployment creates psychological as well as financial stress. Physical and psychological effects may depend on coping resources.

hypertension *(561)*

osteoporosis *(564)*

mammography *(565)*

hysterectomy *(565)*

hormone replacement therapy (HRT) *(566)*

stressors *(567)*

burnout *(570)*

COGNITIVE DEVELOPMENT

Measuring Cognitive Abilities in Middle Age

Guidepost 4: What cognitive gains and losses occur during middle age?

- The Seattle Longitudinal Study found that three of six basic mental abilities peak during middle age, but there is great individual variability in cognitive performance in midlife.
- Fluid intelligence declines earlier than crystallized intelligence.

fluid intelligence *(573)*

crystallized intelligence *(573)*

The Distinctiveness of Adult Cognition

Guidepost 5: Do mature adults think differently than younger people do?

- Some theorists propose that cognition takes distinctive forms at midlife. Advances in expertise, or specialized knowledge, have been attributed to encapsulation of fluid abilities within a person's chosen field.
- Postformal thought seems especially useful in situations calling for integrative thinking.

encapsulation *(574)*

Creativity

Guidepost 6: What accounts for creative achievement, and how does it change with age?

- Creative performance depends on personal attributes and environmental forces, as well as cognitive abilities.
- Creativity is not strongly related to intelligence.
- An age-related decline appears in both psychometric tests of divergent thinking and actual creative output, but peak ages for output vary by occupation. Losses in productivity with age may be offset by gains in quality.

Work and Education: Are Age-Based Roles Obsolete?

Guidepost 7: How are patterns of work and education changing, and how does work contribute to cognitive development?

- A shift from age-differentiated to age-integrated roles appears to be occurring in response to longer life and social change.
- Most Americans who stop working in late midlife do so because of disability, but a substantial proportion who can afford to do so choose early retirement.
- Complex work may improve cognitive flexibility. Changes in the workplace may make work more meaningful and cognitively challenging for many people.
- Many adults go to college at a nontraditional age or participate in continuing education. Adults go to school chiefly to improve work-related skills and knowledge or to prepare for a change of career.
- Mature adults have special educational needs and strengths.

age-differentiated *(579)*

age-integrated *(579)*

CHAPTER 16

Psychosocial Development in Middle Adulthood

> To accept all experience as raw material
> out of which the human spirits distill
> meanings and values is a part of
> the meaning of maturity.
>
> ――――――
>
> Howard Thurman, *Meditations of the Heart*, 1953

Focus
Madeleine Albright, Diplomat

Madeleine Albright

On January 23, 1997, four months before her sixtieth birthday, Madeleine Korbel Albright* (b. 1937) was sworn in as U.S. secretary of state, the first woman to achieve such a high rank. It was a heady moment for a woman who had arrived at age 11 with her family as refugees from Communist Czechoslovakia.

Albright's life is the story of "someone who has again and again reinvented herself" (Heilbrunn, 1998, p. 12). First there was the journey from her childhood as the daughter of a diplomat in war-torn Europe to her adolescence as a scholarship student at a private school in Denver. Then came a scholarship to Wellesley College; and, three days after commencement, her "Cinderella marriage" to Joseph Medill Patterson Albright, heir to a prominent publishing family, followed by the birth of twin girls. Thirteen years and a third daughter later, she obtained a Ph.D. in political science at Columbia University.

As the women's movement gathered steam, President Jimmy Carter's national security adviser, Zbigniew Brzezinski, tapped Albright, his former student at Columbia, as congressional liaison for the National Security Council. Less than a year after the Carter presidency and Albright's White House stint ended, her husband of twenty-three years announced that he was in love with a younger woman. The divorce in 1982 was a turning point in her life. At 45, she was a single mother of three (one still in high school), "aching to chart a new path" (Blackman, 1998, p. 187). She joined the faculty of Georgetown University's School of Foreign Service and became a "regular" on public television talk shows. The woman whom colleagues had seen as shy and self-effacing, whose self-esteem had been shattered by divorce, developed confidence and self-assurance as she honed her crisp, succinct speaking style.

*Sources of biographical material about Madeleine Albright were Albright (2003), Blackman (1998), and Blood (1997).

585

Albright broke into the national limelight as foreign policy adviser to vice-presidential candidate Geraldine Ferraro in 1984 and to presidential candidate Michael Dukakis in 1988. It was in the Dukakis campaign that Albright, then over 50, met Bill Clinton, who, in 1992—just ten years after her divorce—appointed her ambassador to the United Nations for his incoming presidential administration and four years later chose her to head the State Department, a portfolio she held until Clinton left the presidency in 2001. "I didn't want it to end," she wrote in her memoir (Albright, 2003, p. 3).

As her middle years came to an end, Albright's life was full and fulfilling. Her bonds with her married daughters, her grandchildren, and the many friends who had supported her throughout her career were strong.

One more twist in the "reinvention" of Madeleine Albright had come as she began her tenure at the State Department. Press reports revealed that Albright, who was raised Catholic, had been born Jewish and that several close relatives had perished in the Holocaust.

Her now-deceased parents had never told her of her Jewish heritage. At 59, she had to come to a new understanding of her identity and her family history—an understanding brought home when she walked through the old Jewish cemetery in Prague and came face-to-face with the synagogue wall on which the names of her grandparents were inscribed along with nearly eighty thousand other victims of Nazism. As she stood there, silent, she thought about her parents and the "excruciating decision" they had made to cut off their roots by converting to Catholicism in order to save their children from "certain death" (Blackman, 1998, p. 293).

"I'm very proud of what my parents did for me and my brother and sister," Albright told the press. "I was very close to them. . . . I have always been very proud of my heritage. And as I find out more about it, I am even more proud" (Blood, 1997, p. 226).

Although the specifics of Madeleine Albright's story are unusual, its main thrust is similar to the adult experience of many other women her age: marriage and motherhood, followed by a midlife career, sometimes a midlife divorce, and a blossoming of possibilities that comes with the emptying of the nest.

One of Albright's greatest assets is adaptability. Again and again, she has adjusted to new environments, learned new languages, mastered new challenges, and reshaped her identity. As she did, she grew in personal strength. Much of that mastery and growth occurred during middle age. Her divorce represented a sharp break with her past: a trauma that forced her to rethink who she was and what she wanted to do.

Midlife is a special time. Middle-aged people are not only in the middle of the adult life span, in a position to look back and ahead in their own lives; they also bridge older and younger generations. Very often, they are the ones who hold families together and, like Madeleine Albright, make societal institutions and enterprises work. Much can happen during the twenty-five-year span we call *middle adulthood;* and these experiences affect the way people look, feel, and act as they enter old age.

In this chapter we look at theoretical perspectives and research on psychosocial issues and themes at midlife. We then focus on intimate relationships, which shape the occurrence and timing of life events. As we examine marriage and divorce, gay and lesbian relationships, and friendship, as well as relationships with maturing children, aging parents, siblings, and grandchildren, we see how richly textured are these middle years.

After you have read and studied this chapter, you should be able to answer each of the Guidepost questions that follow. Look for them again in the margins, where they point to important concepts throughout the chapter. To check your understanding of these Guideposts, review the end-of-chapter summary. Checkpoints located at periodic spots throughout the chapter will help you verify your understanding of what you have read.

Guideposts
for Study

1. How do developmental scientists approach the study of psychosocial development in middle adulthood?

2. What do classic theorists have to say about psychosocial change in middle age?

3. What issues concerning the self come to the fore during middle adulthood?

4. What role do social relationships play in the lives of middle-aged people?

5. Do marriages typically become happier or unhappier during the middle years, and does cohabitation at this stage of life provide benefits similar to those of marriage?

6. How common is divorce at this time of life?

7. How do midlife gay and lesbian relationships compare with heterosexual ones?

8. How do friendships fare during middle age?

9. How do parent-child relationships change as children approach and reach adulthood?

10. How do middle-aged people get along with parents and siblings?

11. How has grandparenthood changed, and what roles do grandparents play?

Looking at the Life Course in Middle Age

 Guidepost

1. How do developmental scientists approach the study of psychosocial development in middle adulthood?

Developmental scientists view the course of midlife psychosocial development in several ways. *Objectively,* they look at trajectories or pathways, such as Madeleine Albright's evolution from a wife and mother with a passion for politics to the highest-ranking woman in the U.S. government. But continuities and changes in roles and relationships also have a *subjective* side: People actively construct their sense of self and the structure of their lives. Thus it is important to consider how a person like Albright defines herself and how satisfied she is with her life (Moen & Wethington, 1999).

Change and continuity in middle age must be seen in the perspective of the entire life span. Albright's midlife career built on her childhood experiences and youthful strivings. But early patterns are not necessarily blueprints for later ones (Lachman & James, 1997); neither are the concerns of early middle age the same as those of late middle age (Lachman, 2004). Just think of the difference between Albright's life at 40 and her life at 60!

Furthermore, lives do not progress in isolation. Individual pathways intersect or collide with those of family members, friends and acquaintances, and strangers. Work and personal roles are interdependent, as exemplified by Albright's career change after her divorce; and those roles are affected by trends in the larger society, as Albright's opportunities were enhanced by the changing status of women.

Cohort, gender, ethnicity, culture, and socioeconomic status can profoundly affect the life course. Madeleine Albright's path has been very different from that of her mother, who made her family her total life's work. Her course also was different

Checkpoint

Can you...

✔ Distinguish between objective and subjective views of the life course?

✔ Identify several factors that affect the life course at middle age?

Guidepost

2. What do classic theorists have to say about psychosocial change in middle age?

from that of most educated young women today, who embark on careers before marriage and motherhood. We can speculate on what Albright's expectations and trajectory would have been had she been a man, rather than a woman seeking to use her capabilities in a society based on male dominance. Albright's path also would have been different had she not married into a wealthy family, affording her the means to hire housekeepers while her children were young and she was working on her doctorate. All these factors, and more, enter into the study of psychosocial development in middle adulthood.

Change at Midlife: Classic Theoretical Approaches

In psychosocial terms, middle adulthood once was considered a relatively settled period. Freud (1906/1942) saw no point in psychotherapy for people over 50 because he believed personality is permanently formed by that age. Costa and McCrae (1994a), whose trait model we introduced in Chapter 14, also describe middle age as a time of essential stability in personality.

By contrast, humanistic theorists such as Abraham Maslow and Carl Rogers looked on middle age as an opportunity for positive change. According to Maslow (1968), *self-actualization* (full realization of human potential) can come only with maturity. Rogers (1961) held that full human functioning requires a constant, lifelong process of bringing the self in harmony with experience.

As we noted in Chapter 14, developmental research today has moved beyond the debate over stability versus change. A number of longitudinal studies show that psychosocial development involves both (Franz, 1997; Helson, 1997). The question is, what *kinds* of changes occur and what brings them about?

Normative-Stage Models

Two early normative-stage theorists whose work continues to provide a frame of reference for much developmental theory and research on middle adulthood are Carl G. Jung and Erik Erikson.

Carl G. Jung: Individuation and Transcendence Swiss psychologist Carl Jung (1933, 1953, 1969, 1971), the first major theorist about adult development, held that healthy midlife development calls for **individuation,** the emergence of the true self through balancing or integrating conflicting parts of the personality, including those parts that previously have been neglected. Until about age 40, said Jung, adults concentrate on obligations to family and society and develop those aspects of personality that will help them reach external goals. Women emphasize expressiveness and nurturance; men are primarily oriented toward achievement. At midlife, people shift their preoccupation to their inner, spiritual selves. Both men and women seek a "union of opposites" by expressing their previously "disowned" aspects.

Two necessary but difficult tasks of midlife are giving up the image of youth and acknowledging mortality. According to Jung (1966), the need to acknowledge mortality requires a search for meaning within the self. This inward turn may be unsettling; as people question their commitments, they may temporarily lose their moorings. But people who avoid this transition and do not reorient their lives appropriately miss the chance for psychological growth.

Erik Erikson: Generativity versus Stagnation In contrast to Jung, who saw midlife as a time of turning inward, Erikson described an outward turn. Erikson saw the years around age 40 as the time when people enter their seventh normative stage,

individuation Jung's term for emergence of the true self through balancing or integration of conflicting parts of the personality.

generativity versus stagnation. Generativity, as Erikson defined it, is the concern of mature adults for establishing and guiding the next generation, perpetuating oneself through one's influence on those to follow. People who do not find an outlet for generativity become self-absorbed, self-indulgent, or stagnant (inactive or lifeless). The "virtue" of this period is *care:* "a widening commitment to *take care of* the persons, the products, and the ideas one has learned *to care for*" (Erikson, 1985, p. 67).

How does generativity arise? According to one model (McAdams, 2001), inner desires for symbolic immortality or a need to be needed combine with external demands (in the form of increased expectations and responsibilities) to produce a conscious concern for the next generation. This, together with what Erikson called "belief in the species," leads to generative commitments and actions.

Erikson believed that generativity is not limited to middle age. It can be expressed not only through parenting and grandparenting, but through teaching or mentorship, productivity or creativity, and "self-generation," or self-development. It can extend to the world of work, to politics, to hobbies, to art, music, and other spheres—or as Erikson called it, "maintenance of the world." In *Gandhi's Truth,* Erikson (1969) pointed out how Gandhi—who was not a good father—emerged as "father of his country" at age 49, expressing generativity in his concern for the well-being of an entire nation.

A later theorist (Kotre, 1984) distinguished four specific forms of generativity: *biological* (conceiving and bearing children), *parental* (nurturing and raising children), *technical* (teaching skills to apprentices), and *cultural* (transmitting cultural values and institutions). Regardless of the form, Kotre said, generativity can be expressed in two different ways, or styles: *communal* (involving care and nurturance of others) or *agentic* (personal contributions to society—creative, scientific, or entrepreneurial).

Jung's and Erikson's Legacy: Vaillant and Levinson
Jung's and Erikson's ideas and observations inspired George Vaillant's (1977) and Daniel Levinson's (1978) longitudinal studies of men (introduced in Chapter 14). Both described major midlife shifts—from occupational striving in the thirties to reevaluation and often drastic restructuring of lives in the forties to mellowing and relative stability in the fifties.*

Vaillant, like Jung, reported a lessening of gender differentiation at midlife and a tendency for men to become more nurturant and expressive. Likewise, Levinson's men at midlife became less obsessed with personal achievement and more concerned with relationships; and they showed generativity by becoming mentors to younger people. As we discuss later in this chapter, Vaillant has studied the relationship between generativity and mental health.

Vaillant also echoed Jung's concept of turning inward. In the forties, many of his sample of Harvard graduates abandoned the "compulsive, unreflective busywork of their occupational apprenticeships and once more [became] explorers of the world within" (1977, p. 220). Bernice Neugarten (1977) noted a similar introspective

*Levinson's description of the fifties was only projected.

generativity versus stagnation Erikson's seventh stage of psychosocial development, in which the middle-aged adult develops a concern with establishing, guiding, and influencing the next generation or else experiences stagnation (a sense of inactivity or lifelessness).

generativity Erikson's term for concern of mature adults for establishing, guiding, and influencing the next generation.

What Erikson called generativity—*a concern for guiding the younger generation—can be expressed through coaching or mentoring. Generativity may be a key to well-being at midlife.*

BOX 16-1

Window on the World

A Society Without Middle Age

The universality of the midlife crisis is questionable even in the United States. What, then, happens in nonwestern cultures, some of which do not even have a clear concept of middle age? One such culture is that of the Gusii, a rural society of more than 1 million people in southwestern Kenya (Levine, 1980; LeVine & LeVine, 1998). The Gusii have a "life plan" with well-defined expectations for each stage, but this plan is very different from that in western societies. It is a hierarchy of stages based largely on the anticipation and achievement of reproductive capacity and its extension through the next generation.

The Gusii have no words for "adolescent," "young adult," or "middle-aged." A boy or girl is circumcised sometime between ages 9 and 11 and becomes an elder when his or her first child marries. Between these two events, a man is in the stage of *omomura*, or "warrior." The *omomura* stage may last anywhere from twenty-five to forty years, or even longer. Because of the greater importance of marriage in a woman's life, women have an additional stage: *omosubaati*, or "young married woman."

Childbearing is not confined to early adulthood. As in other preindustrial societies where many hands are needed to raise crops and death in infancy or early childhood is common, fertility is highly valued. Today, even though babies are much more likely to survive than in the past, people continue to reproduce as long as

Many Gusii in western Kenya become ritual practitioners after their children are grown, seeking spiritual powers to compensate for their waning physical strength. For women like the diviner shown here, ritual practice may be a way to wield power in a male-dominated society.

they are physiologically able. The average woman bears ten children. When a woman reaches menopause, her husband may take a younger wife and breed another family.

---

interiority Neugarten's term for a concern with inner life (introversion or introspection), which usually appears in middle age.

tendency at midlife, which she called **interiority.** For Levinson's men, the transition to middle adulthood was stressful enough to be called a "crisis."

As we pointed out in Chapter 14, these classic studies, insightful as they may have been, had serious weaknesses of sampling and methodology. Despite Levinson's (1996) posthumous publication of a small study of women, his model and that of Vaillant were built on research on mostly middle-class or upper-middle-class men, whose experiences were taken as norms. Furthermore, their findings reflected the experiences of particular members of a particular cohort in a particular culture. They may not apply in a society in which masculinity and femininity no longer have such distinct meanings, and in which career development and life choices for both men and women have become more varied and more flexible. These findings also may not apply to people for whom economic survival is a pressing issue, or to cultures that have very different patterns of life course development (see Box 16-1). Finally, these studies dealt exclusively with heterosexuals and may not apply to gays and lesbians. More recent research on midlife psychosocial development is more broadly based, uses more diverse samples and research designs, and covers more dimensions of personality and experience.

Timing of Events: The Social Clock

According to the timing-of-events model introduced in Chapter 14, adult personality development hinges less on age than on important life events. Middle age often brings a restructuring of social roles: launching children, becoming grandparents, changing jobs or careers, and eventually, retirement. For the cohorts represented by the early normative-stage studies, the occurrence and timing of such major events were fairly predictable. Today lifestyles are more diverse, and a "fluid life cycle"

What's Your View?

• On the basis of your observations, do you believe that adults' personalities change significantly during middle age? If so, do such changes seem related to maturation, or do they accompany important events, such as divorce, occupational change, or grandparenthood?

—continued

In Gusii society, then, transitions depend on life events. Status is linked to circumcision, marriage (for women), having children, and finally, becoming a parent of a married child and thus a prospective grandparent and respected elder. The Gusii have a "social clock," a set of expectations for the ages at which these events should normally occur. People who marry late or do not marry at all, men who become impotent or sterile, and women who fail to conceive, have their first child late, bear no sons, or have few children are ridiculed and ostracized and may undergo rituals to correct the situation.

Although the Gusii have no recognized midlife transition, some of them do reassess their lives around the time they are old enough to be grandparents. Awareness of mortality and of waning physical powers, especially among women, may lead to a career as a ritual healer. The quest for spiritual powers has a generative purpose, too: Elders are responsible for ritually protecting their children and grandchildren from death or illness. Many older women who become ritual practitioners or witches seek power either to help people or to harm them, perhaps to compensate for their lack of personal and economic power in a male-dominated society.

Gusii society has undergone change, particularly since the 1970s, as a result of British colonial rule and its aftermath. With infant mortality curtailed, rapid population growth is straining the supply of food and other resources, and a life plan organized around maximizing reproduction is no longer adaptive. Growing acceptance of birth limitation among younger Gusii suggests that "conceptions of adult maturity less centered on fertility will eventually become dominant in the Gusii culture" (LeVine & LeVine, 1998, p. 207).

What's Your View?

Given the current dramatic changes in Gusii society, would you expect shifts in the way the Gusii define life's stages? If so, in what direction?

Check It Out

For more information about the Gusii, go to the Web site for the Kenya Project, http://www.cam.ac.uk/societies/kenyap/gusii/html.

---

has blurred the boundaries of middle adulthood (Neugarten & Neugarten, 1987) and "erased the old definitions of the 'social clock'" (Josselson, 2003, p. 431).

When occupational patterns were more stable and retirement at age 65 was almost universal, the meaning of work at midlife for both men and women may have been different from its current meaning in a period of frequent job changes, downsizing, and early or delayed retirement. When women's lives revolved around bearing and rearing children, the end of the reproductive years meant something different from what it means now, when so many middle-aged women (like Madeleine Albright) have entered the workforce. When people died earlier, middle-aged survivors felt old, realizing that they too were nearing the end of their lives. Many middle-aged people now find themselves busier and more involved than ever—some still raising young children while others redefine their roles as parents to adolescents and young adults and often as caregivers to aging parents. Yet despite the multiple challenges and variable events of midlife, most middle-aged adults seem well able to handle them (Lachman, 2001, 2004).

The Self at Midlife: Issues and Themes

"I'm a completely different person now from the one I was twenty years ago," said a 47-year-old architect as six friends, all in their forties and fifties, nodded vigorously in agreement. Many people feel and observe personality change occurring at midlife. Whether we look at middle-aged people objectively, in terms of their outward behavior, or subjectively, in terms of how they describe themselves, certain issues and themes emerge. Is there such a thing as a "midlife crisis"? How does identity

Checkpoint

Can you . . .

✔ Identify three types of change that researchers study, and give an example of each?

✔ Summarize important changes that occur at midlife, according to Jung and Erikson, and tell how their ideas have influenced other research?

✔ Tell how historical and cultural changes have affected the social clock for middle age?

Guidepost

3. What issues concerning the self come to the fore during middle adulthood?

develop in middle age? Do men and women change in different ways? What contributes to psychological well-being? All of these questions revolve around the self.

Is There a Midlife Crisis?

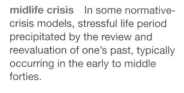

midlife crisis In some normative-crisis models, stressful life period precipitated by the review and reevaluation of one's past, typically occurring in the early to middle forties.

What's Your View?

- As far as you know, did one or both of your parents go through what appeared to be a midlife crisis? If you are middle-aged or older, did you go through such a crisis? If so, what issues made it a crisis? Did it seem more serious than transitions at other times of life?

Changes in personality and lifestyle during the early to middle forties are often attributed to the **midlife crisis,** a supposedly stressful period triggered by review and reevaluation of one's life. The midlife crisis was conceptualized as a crisis of identity; indeed, it has been called a second adolescence. What brings it on, said Elliott Jacques (1967), the psychoanalyst who coined the term, is awareness of mortality. Many people now realize that they will not be able to fulfill the dreams of their youth, or that fulfillment of their dreams has not brought the satisfaction they expected. They know that if they want to change direction, they must act quickly. Levinson (1978, 1980, 1986, 1996) maintained that midlife turmoil is inevitable as people struggle with the need to restructure their lives.

However, the term *midlife crisis* is now considered an inaccurate representation of what most people experience in midlife (Lachman, 2004). In fact, its occurrence seems to be fairly unusual (Aldwin & Levenson, 2001; Heckhausen, 2001; Lachman, 2004; Lachman & Bertrand, 2001). Some middle-aged people may experience crisis or turmoil, but others feel at the peak of their powers. Still others may fall somewhere in the middle—with neither a peak nor a crisis—or may experience both crisis and competence at different times or in different domains of life (Lachman, 2004).

The onset of middle age may be stressful, but no more so than some events of young adulthood (Chiriboga, 1997; Wethington et al., 2004). Indeed, some researchers have proposed the occurrence of a "quarterlife crisis" in the mid-twenties to early thirties, as emerging adults seek to settle into satisfying work and relationships (Lachman, 2004; Robbins & Wilner, 2001).

Apparently, midlife is just one of life's *turning points*—psychological transitions that involve significant change or transformation in the perceived meaning, purpose, or direction of a person's life. Turning points may be triggered by major life events, normative changes, or a new understanding of past experience, either positive or negative, and they may be stressful. However, in the MIDUS survey and a follow-up study of Psychological Turning Points (PTP), many respondents reported positive growth from successful resolution of stressful situations (Wethington et al., 2004; see Figure 16-1).

Figure 16-1

Turning points reported in the past five years by 25- to 74-year-olds.
(Source: Wethington et al., 2004, Figure 3.)

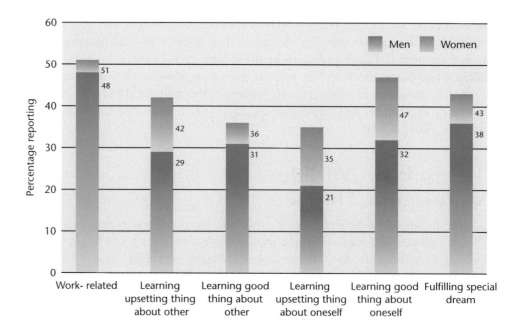

Turning points often involve an introspective review and reappraisal of values and priorities (Helson, 1997; Reid & Willis, 1999; Robinson, Rosenberg, & Farrell, 1999). The **midlife review** can be a time of stocktaking, yielding new insights into the self and spurring midcourse corrections in the design and trajectory of one's life. Along with recognition of the finitude of life, a midlife review may bring regret over failure to achieve a dream or keener awareness of *developmental deadlines*—time constraints on, say, the ability to have a child or to make up with an estranged friend or family member (Heckhausen, 2001; Heckhausen, Wrosch, & Fleeson, 2001; Wrosch & Heckhausen, 1999).

midlife review Introspective examination that often occurs in middle age, leading to reappraisal and revision of values and priorities.

Whether a turning point becomes a crisis may depend less on age than on individual circumstances and personal resources. According to Susan Krauss Whitbourne (see p. 594), a midlife crisis may be "an extreme accommodative reaction to a set of experiences that no longer can be processed through identity assimilation" (Whitbourne & Connolly, 1999, p. 30). People high in neuroticism are more likely to experience midlife crises (Lachman, 2004). People with *ego-resiliency*—the ability to adapt flexibly and resourcefully to potential sources of stress—and those who have a sense of mastery and control are more likely to navigate the midlife crossing successfully (Heckhausen, 2001; Klohnen et al., 1996; Lachman, 2004; Lachman & Firth, 2004). (Table 16-1 outlines qualities considered most and least characteristic of ego-resilient adults.) For people with resilient personalities, like Madeleine Albright, even negative events, such as an unwanted divorce, can become springboards for positive growth (Klohnen et al., 1996; Moen & Wethington, 1999).

Identity Development: Current Theoretical Approaches

Although Erikson defined identity formation as the main concern of adolescence, he noted that identity continues to develop. Indeed, some developmental scientists view the process of identity formation as the central issue of adulthood (McAdams & de St. Aubin, 1992). Most middle-aged adults have a well-developed sense of self and

Checkpoint
Can you . . .

✔ Explain and compare the concepts of the midlife crisis and of turning points and discuss their prevalence?

✔ State typical concerns of the midlife transition and factors that affect how successfully people come through it?

Table 16-1 Characteristics of Ego-Resilient Adults

Most Characteristic	Most Uncharacteristic
Has insight into own motives and behavior	Has brittle ego-defense; maladaptive under stress
Has warmth; capacity for close relationships	Is self-defeating
Has social poise and presence	Is uncomfortable with uncertainty and complexities
Is productive; gets things done	Overreacts to minor frustrations; is irritable
Is calm, relaxed in manner	Denies unpleasant thoughts and experiences
Is skilled in social techniques of imaginary play	Does not vary roles; relates to all in same way
Is socially perceptive of interpersonal cues	Is basically anxious
Can see to the heart of important problems	Gives up and withdraws from frustration or adversity
Is genuinely dependable and responsible	Is emotionally bland
Responds to humor	Is vulnerable to real or fancied threat; fearful
Values own independence and autonomy	Tends to ruminate and have preoccupying thoughts
Tends to arouse liking and acceptance	Feels cheated and victimized by life
Initiates humor	Feels a lack of personal meaning in life

Note: These items are used as criteria for rating ego-resiliency, using the California Adult Q-Set.

Source: Adapted from Block, 1991, as reprinted in Klohnen, 1996.

can cope well with change (Lachman, 2004). Let's look at current theories and research on identity development, particularly in middle age.

identity process model
Whitbourne's model of identity development based on processes of assimilation and accommodation.

identity assimilation
Whitbourne's term for effort to fit new experience into an existing self-concept.

identity accommodation
Whitbourne's term for adjusting the self-concept to fit new experience.

identity style Whitbourne's term for a characteristic way of confronting, interpreting, and responding to experience.

Susan Krauss Whitbourne: Identity as a Process The **identity process model** of Susan Krauss Whitbourne (1987, 1996; Whitbourne & Connolly, 1999), which draws on Erikson, Marcia, and Piaget, views identity as "an organizing schema through which the individual's experiences are interpreted" (Whitbourne & Connolly, 1999, p. 28). Identity is made up of accumulated perceptions of the self, both conscious and unconscious. Perceived personality traits ("I am sensitive" or "I am stubborn"), physical characteristics, and cognitive abilities are incorporated into the identity schema. These self-perceptions are continually confirmed or revised in response to incoming information, which can come from intimate relationships, work-related situations, community activities, and other experiences.

People interpret their interactions with the environment by means of two ongoing processes, similar to those Piaget described for children's cognitive development (refer back to Chapter 2): *identity assimilation* and *identity accommodation.* **Identity assimilation** is an attempt to fit new experience into an existing schema; **identity accommodation** is adjustment of the schema to fit the new experience. Identity assimilation tends to maintain continuity of the self; identity accommodation tends to bring about needed change. Most people use both processes to some extent. Madeleine Albright, when confronted with proof of her Jewish birth, accommodated her identity schema to include her Jewishness but also assimilated her new knowledge to her image of herself as the daughter of loving parents who had done their utmost to protect her. People often resist accommodation (as Albright apparently did for a while) until events (in this case, the imminence of press reports) force them to recognize the need.

The equilibrium a person customarily reaches between assimilation and accommodation determines his or her **identity style.** A person who uses assimilation more than accommodation has an *assimilative identity style.* A person who uses accommodation more has an *accommodative identity style.* Overuse of either assimilation or accommodation is unhealthy, says Whitbourne. People who constantly *assimilate* are inflexible and do not learn from experience; they see only what they are looking for. They may go to great lengths to avoid recognizing their inadequacies. People who constantly *accommodate* are weak, easily swayed, and highly vulnerable to criticism; their identity is easily undermined. Most healthy is a *balanced identity style,* in which "identity is flexible enough to change when warranted but not unstructured to the point that every new experience causes the person to question fundamental assumptions about the self" (Whitbourne & Connolly, 1999, p. 29). Whitbourne sees identity styles as related to Marcia's identity statuses (refer back to Chapter 12); for example, a person who has achieved identity in Marcia's terms would be expected to have a balanced identity style, whereas a person in foreclosure would most likely have an assimilative style.

According to Whitbourne, people deal with physical, mental, and emotional changes associated with the onset of aging much as they deal with other experiences that challenge the identity schema. Assimilative people seek to maintain a youthful self-image at all costs. Accommodative people may see themselves—

The increasing popularity of Botox injections to temporarily smoothe lines and wrinkles may express what Susan Krauss Whitbourne calls an accommodative identity style. *Accommodative people tend to be preoccupied with signs of aging.*

perhaps prematurely—as old and may become preoccupied with symptoms of aging and disease. People with a balanced style realistically recognize changes that are occurring and seek to control what can be controlled and accept what cannot. Identity styles can shift in the face of highly unsettling events, such as loss of a long-time job to a younger person.

Whitbourne's model is a comprehensive attempt to account for both stability and change in the self. However, it is in need of longitudinal research support (Lachman & Bertrand, 2001).

Generativity, Identity, and Age Erikson saw generativity as an aspect of identity formation. As he wrote, "I am what survives me" (1968, p. 141). Research supports this connection. In a study of 40 middle-class female bank employees in their early forties, who were mothers of school-age children, women who had achieved identity by Marcia's criteria were the most psychologically healthy. They also expressed the greatest degree of generativity, bearing out Erikson's view that successful achievement of identity paves the way for other tasks (DeHaan & MacDermid, 1994). In a cross-sectional study of 333 female, mostly white University of Michigan graduates, for those in their sixties "increased certainty about one's identity, high levels of generativity, and a sense of confident power" went hand in hand (Zucker, Ostrove, & Stewart, 2002).

Instruments—behavioral checklists, Q-sorts, and self-reports (see Table 16-2)—have been devised to measure generativity. Using such techniques, researchers have found that although the age at which individuals achieve generativity varies, middle-aged people tend to score higher on generativity than younger and older ones (McAdams, de St. Aubin, & Logan, 1993; Keyes & Ryff, 1998; Stewart & Vandewater, 1998) and women generally report higher levels of generativity than men. In old age, men's and women's generative concerns tend to be equal (Keyes & Ryff, 1998).

Checkpoint
Can you . . .

✔ Summarize Whitbourne's model of identity, and describe how people with each of the three identity styles might deal with signs of aging?

Table 16-2   A Self-Report Test for Generativity

- I try to pass along the knowledge I have gained through my experiences.
- I do not feel that other people need me.
- I think I would like the work of a teacher.
- I feel as though I have made a difference to many people.
- I do not volunteer to work for a charity.
- I have made and created things that have had an impact on other people.
- I try to be creative in most things that I do.
- I think that I will be remembered for a long time after I die.
- I believe that society cannot be responsible for providing food and shelter for all homeless people.
- Others would say that I have made unique contributions to society.
- If I were unable to have children of my own, I would like to adopt children.
- I have important skills that I try to teach others.
- I feel that I have done nothing that will survive after I die.
- In general, my actions do not have a positive effect on others.
- I feel as though I have done nothing of worth to contribute to others.
- I have made many commitments to many different kinds of people, groups, and activities in my life.
- Other people say that I am a very productive person.
- I have a responsibility to improve the neighborhood in which I live.
- People come to me for advice.
- I feel as though my contributions will exist after I die.

Source: Loyola Generativity Scale. Reprinted from McAdams & de St. Aubin, 1992.

Volunteering for community service or a political cause is an expression of communal generativity. As Erikson's theory predicts, the MIDUS study found that volunteering increases between very early and middle adulthood. It then declines slightly after age 55 and rises again after 65 (Hart, Southerland, & Atkins, 2003). A decline in primary family and work responsibilities may free middle-aged and older adults to express generativity on a broader scale (Keyes & Ryff, 1998). Adults who have high educational attainment and are connected with religious communities are more likely than others to do volunteer work, as are people high in empathy and prosocial attitudes (Hart et al., 2003).

These studies were cross-sectional and so cannot with certainty trace a connection between generativity and age. However, the few longitudinal studies of generativity also support this connection (Stewart & Vandewater, 1998). As the men in Vaillant's (1993) Grant Study approached and moved through middle age, an increasing proportion were rated as having achieved generativity: 50 percent at age 40 and 83 percent at 60. An analysis of two longitudinal studies of women from the 1964 class of Radcliffe College and the 1967 class of the University of Michigan suggests that, although the *desire* for generativity tends to arise in young adulthood, its accomplishment—and the sense of capacity for generativity—tends to come in middle age (Stewart & Vandewater, 1998). However, these findings may be class- and cohort-biased and may disguise individual differences.

Instead of defining generativity as a midlife stage in development, some investigators argue for a *life-course perspective on generativity.* Generativity at any point in time may be affected by social expectations, social roles (work, marital, parenting, civic, and the like) and their timing and sequence, as well as by gender, education, race/ethnicity, and cohort (McAdams, 2001; Cohler, Hostetler, & Boxer, 1998). Generativity may express itself differently or with different timing in gays and lesbians, who may develop intimate relationships or become parents later than heterosexuals typically do or may never have these experiences. Many gays and lesbians express generativity through social activism (Cohler et al., 1998).

Narrative Psychology: Identity as a Life Story   The relatively new field of *narrative psychology* views the development of the self as a continuous process of constructing one's own life story—a dramatic narrative to help make sense of one's life. Indeed, some narrative psychologists view identity itself as this internalized story or "script." People follow the script they have created as they act out their identity (McAdams, Diamond, de St. Aubin, & Mansfield, 1997). Midlife often is a time for revision of the life story (McAdams, 1993) or a break in the continuity and coherence of the story line (Rosenberg et al., 1999).

Narrative psychologists are interested in intentional self-development guided by long-term goals that foster personal growth. These *life span growth goals* may be either *exploratory* (aimed at a mature, complex understanding of self and others) or *intrinsic* (aimed at well-being or happiness) or both. Studies based on narrative techniques have found that mature and happy people tend to plan their future through relevant growth goals (Bauer & McAdams, 2004) and to frame their autobiographical memories in those terms. Older adults tend to be more mature and more satisfied with their lives than younger adults, in part because they are more likely to interpret their memories in terms of personal growth (Bauer, McAdams, & Sakaeda, 2005).

As young people grow older, generativity may become an important theme of the life story. A *generativity script* can give the life story a happy ending. It is built on the conviction that generative acts make a difference and that the results of one's life can outlive the self (McAdams, 2001; McAdams & de St. Aubin, 1992).

Highly generative adults often tell a *commitment story* (McAdams et al., 1997). Typically, such people have enjoyed privileged lives and want to alleviate the suffering of others. They dedicate their lives to social improvement and do not swerve from that mission despite grievous obstacles, which eventually have positive outcomes. Moral exemplars organize their lives around such commitment stories (Colby & Damon, 1992; refer back to Box 15-2 in Chapter 15).

Gender Identity   As Erikson observed, identity is closely tied to social roles and commitments ("I am a parent," "I am a teacher," "I am a citizen"). Changing roles and relationships at midlife may affect gender identity, but the most profound midlife revisions may be internal, in the way a person understands and thinks about himself or herself (Josselson, 2003).

In many studies during the 1960s, 1970s, and 1980s, middle-aged men were more open about feelings, more interested in intimate relationships, and more nurturing—characteristics traditionally labeled as feminine—than at earlier ages, whereas middle-aged women (like Madeleine Albright) became more assertive, self-confident, and achievement-oriented, characteristics traditionally labeled as masculine (Cooper & Gutmann, 1987; Cytrynbaum et al., 1980; Helson & Moane, 1987; Huyck, 1990, 1999; Neugarten, 1968). Jung saw these changes as part of the process of individuation, or balancing the personality. The psychologist David Gutmann (1975, 1977, 1985, 1987) offers an explanation that goes further than Jung's.

Traditional gender roles, according to Gutmann, evolved to ensure the well-being of growing children. The mother must be the caregiver, the father the provider. Once active parenting is over, there is not just a balancing but a reversal of roles—a **gender crossover.** Men, now free to explore their previously repressed "feminine" side, become more passive; women become more dominant and independent.

These changes may have been normative in the preliterate agricultural societies Gutmann studied, which had very distinct gender roles, but they are not necessarily universal (Franz, 1997). In U.S. society today, men's and women's roles are becoming less distinct. In an era in which most young women combine employment with child rearing, when many men take an active part in parenting, and when childbearing may not even begin until midlife, gender crossover in middle age seems less likely (Antonucci & Akiyama, 1997; Barnett, 1997; James & Lewkowicz, 1997).

A sequential analysis of data from two longitudinal studies that together followed 20-, 30-, and 40-year-old, mostly well-educated men and women for more than two decades found age-related change in personality, but *no* gender crossover. *Both* men and women became increasingly "masculine" (or decreasingly "feminine") during their twenties, but this trend leveled off by the forties. And, regardless of age or cohort, men remained more "masculine" than women.

In the Mills longitudinal study (introduced in Chapter 14), between the beginning and the end of active parenting the women increased more than their male partners in competence, confidence, and independence, and the men increased more in affiliative traits (Helson, 1997). Again, however, these changes did *not* amount to a gender crossover (Helson, 1993). Whereas most of the Mills graduates had found their early forties a time of turmoil, by the early fifties they rated their quality of life as high (Helson & Wink, 1992). Similarly, among a cross-sectional sample of nearly 700 Mills College alumnae ages 26 to 80, women in their early fifties most often described their lives as "first-rate" (Mitchell &

What's Your View?

• From what you have observed, do men seem to become less masculine and women less feminine at midlife?

gender crossover   Gutmann's term for reversal of gender roles after the end of active parenting.

Women in their early fifties are in what Ravenna Helson and her colleagues call "the prime of life"—young enough to be healthy and active but old enough to have launched their children and to have the time and resources for enjoying friends and fun. Women this age tend to be comfortable with themselves and no longer concerned about meeting social expectations.

Checkpoint

Can you . . .

✔ Explain the connection
between generativity and
identity and discuss research
on generativity and age?

✔ Explain the concept of identity
as a life story, and how it
applies to the midlife transition
and to generativity?

✔ Compare Jung's and
Gutmann's concepts of
changes in gender identity
at midlife, and assess their
research support?

✔ Discuss the value of a midlife
review or revision?

Helson, 1990). In line with Jung's view, the highest quality of life at this age was associated with a balance between autonomy and involvement in an intimate relationship (Helson, 1993).

Enhanced well-being may be the outcome of a midlife review or revision—a search for balance through the pursuit of previously submerged desires and aspirations (Josselson, 2003). In the Radcliffe longitudinal study, about two-thirds of the women made major life changes between ages 37 and 43. Women who had midlife regrets—many, about educational or work options they had put aside to assume traditional family roles—and changed their lives accordingly had greater well-being and better psychological adjustment in the late forties than those who had regrets but did *not* make desired changes (Stewart & Ostrove, 1998; Stewart & Vandewater, 1999).

Of course, these findings may be limited by class, cohort, and culture. They may not apply to more recent cohorts who have started careers earlier and put off motherhood longer, or to women of other socioeconomic groups (Stewart & Ostrove, 1998; Stewart & Vandewater, 1999). For contemporary women whose young adult lives have been strongly career-focused, midlife may bring a desire to deepen neglected relationships or awareness of one's own emotional needs (Josselson, 2003).

Psychological Well-Being and Positive Mental Health

Mental health is not just the absence of mental illness. *Positive* mental health involves a sense of psychological well-being, which goes hand in hand with a healthy sense of self (Keyes & Shapiro, 2004; Ryff & Singer, 1998). This subjective sense of well-being, or happiness, is a person's evaluation of his or her own life (Diener, 2000), and it tends to increase in middle age (Lachman, 2004). How do developmental scientists measure well-being, and what factors affect well-being at midlife?

Emotionality Many studies, including the MIDUS survey, have found a gradual average decline in such negative emotions as anger, fear, and anxiety through midlife and beyond. Women in the MIDUS study reported slightly more negative emotionality at all ages than men (Mroczek, 2004). According to the MIDUS findings, positive emotionality (such as cheerfulness) increases, on average, among men but falls among women in middle age and then rises sharply for both sexes, but especially men, in late adulthood. The general trends in positive and negative emotionality may suggest that as people age, they tend to have learned to accept what comes (Carstensen, Pasupathi, Mayr, & Nesselroade, 2000) and to regulate their emotions effectively (Lachman, 2004).

Middle-aged adults in the MIDUS study, like younger adults, had greater individual variation in emotionality than older adults. What was unique about middle-aged respondents were the factors that affected emotionality. Only physical health had a consistent impact on emotionality in adults of all ages, but two other factors—marital status and education—had significant impacts only in middle age. Married people at midlife tended to report more positive emotion and less negative emotion than unmarried people. The picture regarding education was more complicated. People with higher education had more positive and less negative emotionality—but only when stress was controlled. Apparently work and relationship stress, both of which tend to be high at midlife (refer back to Chapter 15), take their greatest emotional toll in this age group (Mroczek, 2004).

Life Satisfaction In numerous surveys worldwide using various techniques for assessing subjective well-being, most people of all ages, both sexes, and all races report being satisfied with their lives (Myers, 2000; Myers & Diener, 1995, 1996;

Walker, Skowronski, & Thompson, 2003). One reason for this general finding of life satisfaction is that the positive emotions associated with pleasant memories tend to persist, whereas the negative feelings associated with unpleasant memories fade. Most people have good coping skills (Walker et al., 2003). After either especially happy or distressing events, such as marriage or divorce, they generally adapt, and subjective well-being returns to, or close to, its previous level (Lucas et al., 2003; Diener, 2000).

Social support—friends and spouses—and religiosity are important contributors to happiness (Csikszenmihalyi, 1999; Diener, 2000; Myers, 2000; see Chapter 18). So are certain personality dimensions—extraversion and conscientiousness (Mroczek & Spiro, 2005; Siegler & Brummett, 2000)—and the quality of work and leisure (Csikszenmihalyi, 1999; Diener, 2000; Myers, 2000).

Even people with severe illnesses and disabilities report being in good moods most of the time (Riis et al., 2005). "Counting one's blessings" can help improve life satisfaction; in a study of 65 women and men ages 22 to 77 with neuromuscular disease, those who were asked to write down each day for three weeks up to five things they felt grateful or thankful for reported more satisfaction with their lives, more optimism about the coming week, and a greater sense of connection to others than a control group who did not fill out the "gratitude" forms (Emmons & McCullough, 2003).

Does life satisfaction change with age? In a 22-year longitudinal study of 1,927 men, most of whom served in the military during World War II or the Korean war, life satisfaction gradually rose, peaked at age 65, and then gradually declined. Again, however, there were significant individual differences (Mroczek & Spiro, 2005). In a 17-year longitudinal study of a nationally representative sample of 3,608 Germans ages 16 to 40 at first measurement, about 1 in 4 people experienced significant change (Fujita & Diener, 2005).

What does it mean to have a good life? Among a subsample of middle-aged MIDUS respondents, well-being was strongly affected by physical health, a capacity for enjoying life, and positive feelings about the self, as well as a certain serenity in looking at life events. Educational level made a striking difference. With respect to financial resources, health status, health habits, divorce rates, and length of life, college-educated adults enjoyed more favorable circumstances than the high school-educated. Yet both the highly educated and less educated were reasonably satisfied with their lives (Markus, Ryff, Curhan, & Palmersheim, 2004).

Carol Ryff: Multiple Dimensions of Well-Being   Carol Ryff and her colleagues (Keyes & Ryff, 1999; Ryff, 1995; Ryff & Singer, 1998), drawing on a range of theorists from Erikson to Maslow, have developed a model that includes six dimensions of well-being and a self-report scale, the Ryff Well-Being Inventory (Ryff & Keyes, 1995), to measure them. The six dimensions are *self-acceptance, positive relations with others, autonomy, environmental mastery, purpose in life,* and *personal growth* (see Table 16-3).

According to Ryff, psychologically healthy people have positive attitudes toward themselves and others. They make their own decisions and regulate their own behavior, and they choose or shape environments compatible with their needs. They have goals that make their lives meaningful, and they strive to explore and develop themselves as fully as possible.

A series of cross-sectional studies using Ryff's scale have shown midlife to be a period of generally positive mental health (Ryff & Singer, 1998). Middle-aged people expressed greater well-being than older and younger adults in some areas but not in others. They were more autonomous than younger adults but somewhat less purposeful and less focused on personal growth—future-oriented dimensions that

Table 16-3   Dimensions of Well-Being Used in Ryff's Scale

Self-Acceptance

High scorer: possesses a positive attitude toward the self, acknowledges and accepts multiple aspects of self including good and bad qualities; feels positive about past life.

Low scorer: feels dissatisfied with self; is disappointed with what has occurred in past life; is troubled about certain personal qualities; wishes to be different [from] what he or she is.

Positive Relations with Others

High scorer: has warm, satisfying, trusting relationships with others; is concerned about the welfare of others; [is] capable of strong empathy, affection, and intimacy; understands give and take of human relationships.

Low scorer: has few close, trusting relationships with others; finds it difficult to be warm, open, and concerned about others; is isolated and frustrated in interpersonal relationships; [is] not willing to make compromises to sustain important ties with others.

Autonomy

High scorer: is self-determining and independent; [is] able to resist social pressures to think and act in certain ways; regulates behavior from within; evaluates self by personal standards.

Low scorer: is concerned about the expectations and evaluations of others; relies on judgments of others to make important decisions; conforms to social pressures to think and act in certain ways.

Environmental Mastery

High scorer: has a sense of mastery and competence in managing the environment; controls complex array of external activities; makes effective use of surrounding opportunities; [is] able to choose or create contexts suitable to personal needs and values.

Low scorer: has difficulty managing everyday affairs; feels unable to change or improve surrounding context; is unaware of surrounding opportunities; lacks sense of control over external world.

Purpose in Life

High scorer: has goals in life and a sense of directedness; feels there is meaning to present and past life; holds beliefs that give life purpose; has aims and objectives for living.

Low scorer: lacks a sense of meaning in life; has few goals or aims, lacks sense of direction; does not see purpose in past life; has no outlooks or beliefs that give life meaning.

Personal Growth

High scorer: has a feeling of continued development; sees self as growing and expanding; is open to new experiences; has sense of realizing his or her potential; sees improvement in self and behavior over time; is changing in ways that reflect more self-knowledge and effectiveness.

Low scorer: has a sense of personal stagnation; lacks sense of improvement or expansion over time; feels bored [with] and uninterested [in] life; feels unable to develop new attitudes or behaviors.

Source: Adapted from Keyes & Ryff, 1999, Table 1, p. 163.

declined even more sharply in late adulthood. Environmental mastery, on the other hand, increased between middle and late adulthood. Self-acceptance was relatively stable for all age groups. Of course, since this research was cross-sectional, we do not know whether the differences were due to maturation, aging, or cohort factors. Overall, men's and women's well-being were quite similar, but women had more positive social relationships (Ryff & Singer, 1998).

Ryff's scale was used to measure the psychological well-being of various subgroups in the MIDUS study as well as additional samples of African Americans from New York City and Mexican Americans from Chicago, with a resulting total sample of 1,493 men and 1,862 women. This collective portrait replicated the age-related patterns just reported. However, black and Hispanic women scored lower than black and Hispanic men in several areas, revealing "a wider expanse of compromised well-being among ethnic/minority women of differing ages" (Ryff, Keyes, & Hughes, 2004, p. 417).

Surprisingly, when employment and marital status were controlled, minority status predicted *positive* well-being in several areas, even when education and perceived discrimination were accounted for. It may be that such factors as self-regard, mastery, and personal growth are strengthened by meeting the challenges of minority life (Ryff et al., 2004).

Research has found that Hispanic and Asian immigrants to the United States are more physically and mentally healthy than those who have been here for two or more generations. Why? One study, in which Ryff's Well-Being Inventory was used to assess 312 first-generation Mexican American and Puerto Rican immigrants and 242 second-generation Puerto Ricans from the Chicago and New York City areas, found that resistance to assimilation promotes well-being in the immigrant generation, especially in the domains of autonomy, quality of relationships, and purpose in life. The researchers propose the term *ethnic conservatism* for this tendency to resist assimilation and cling to familiar values and practices that give meaning to life. Ethnic conservatism was less effective in promoting well-being among the second generation in these Hispanic communities, who may find it harder or more psychologically conflicting to resist the pull of assimilation (Horton & Schweder, 2004).

Social Well-Being *Social well-being*—the quality of a person's self-reported relationships with other people, the neighborhood, and the community—is a relatively unstudied aspect of mental health. One research team (Keyes & Shapiro, 2004) looked at five dimensions of social well-being in the MIDUS sample: (1) *social actualization,* belief in society's potential to evolve in a positive direction; (2) *social coherence,* seeing the world as intelligible, logical, and predictable; (3) *social integration,* feeling part of a supportive community; (4) *social acceptance,* having positive, accepting attitudes toward other people; and (5) *social contribution,* believing that one has something valuable to give to society.

The survey responses suggest that a majority of U.S. adults have moderate to high levels of social well-being, but a substantial minority have very low levels. Nearly 40 percent of adults ages 25 to 74 scored in the top one-third on at least three of the five dimensions, but as many as 16 percent did not score in the upper third on *any* of them, and 10 percent scored in the *lower* third on three or more dimensions. Overall, social well-being is highest among men, people with high occupational status, and married or never-married people. Social well-being is lowest among women, those with low occupational status, and those who are previously married, who tend to have low occupational status.

Generativity as a Factor in Psychosocial Adjustment and Well-Being Generativity, according to Erikson, is "a sign of both psychological maturity and psychological health" (McAdams, 2001, p. 425). Generativity emerges as the defining feature of psychosocial adjustment at midlife, according to Erikson, because the roles and challenges of this period—the demands of work and family—call for generative responses. Research has generally supported and expanded on Erikson's view.

In their fifties, the best-adjusted men in Vaillant's (1989) sample of Harvard alumni were the most generative, as measured by their responsibility for other people at work, their gifts to charity, and the accomplishments of their children (Soldz & Vaillant, 1998). In an ongoing longitudinal study of Radcliffe College's class of 1964, women who had attained generativity at age 43, as measured by a Q-sort instrument, reported greater investment ten years later in their cross-generational roles as daughter and mother and felt less burdened by the care of aging parents (Peterson, 2002).

Generativity, then, may derive from involvement in multiple roles—as heads of families and leaders in organizations and communities (Staudinger & Bluck, 2001). Such involvement has been linked to well-being and satisfaction both in midlife

Checkpoint

Can you . . .

✔ Explain the concept of positive mental health?

✔ Discuss trends in life satisfaction and emotionality, especially at midlife?

✔ Explain the importance of a multifaceted measure of well-being, and name and describe the six dimensions in Ryff's model?

✔ Identify five dimensions of social well-being and tell how they appear to change with age?

✔ Explain and cite support for the relationship between generativity, mental health, and well-being?

(McAdams, 2001) and in later life (Sheldon & Kasser, 2001; Vandewater, Ostrove, & Stewart, 1997), perhaps through the sense of having contributed meaningfully to society. However, because these findings are correlational, we cannot be sure that generativity causes well-being; it may be that people who are happy with their lives are more likely to be generative (McAdams, 2001).

Relationships at Midlife

It is hard to generalize about the meaning of relationships in middle age today. Not only does that period cover a quarter-century of development; it also embraces a greater multiplicity of life paths than ever before (Brown, Bulanda, & Lee, 2005). One 45-year-old may be happily married and raising children; another may be contemplating marriage, cohabiting, or, like Madeleine Albright, on the brink of divorce. One 60-year-old may have a large network of friends, relatives, and colleagues; another may have no known living relatives and only a few intimate friendships. For most middle-aged people, however, relationships with others are very important—perhaps in a different way than earlier in life.

Theories of Social Contact

According to **social convoy theory,** people move through life surrounded by *social convoys:* circles of close friends and family members of varying degrees of closeness, on whom they can rely for assistance, well-being, and social support, and to whom they in turn also offer care, concern, and support (Antonucci & Akiyama, 1997; Kahn & Antonucci, 1980). Characteristics of the person (gender, race, religion, age, education, and marital status) together with characteristics of that person's situation (role expectations, life events, financial stress, daily hassles, demands, and resources) influence the size and composition of the convoy, or support network; the amount and kinds of social support a person receives; and the satisfaction derived from this support. All of these factors contribute to health and well-being (Antonucci, Akiyama, & Merline, 2001).

Although convoys usually show long-term stability, their composition can change. At one time, bonds with siblings may be more significant; at another time, ties with friends (Paul, 1997). Middle-aged people in industrialized countries tend to have the largest convoys because they are likely to be married, to have children, to have living parents, and to be in the workforce unless they have retired early (Antonucci et al., 2001). Women's convoys, particularly the inner circle, tend to be larger than men's (Antonucci & Akiyama, 1997).

Laura Carstensen's (1991, 1995, 1996; Carstensen, Isaacowitz, & Charles, 1999) **socioemotional selectivity theory** offers a life-span perspective on how people choose with whom to spend their time. According to Carstensen, social interaction has three main goals: (1) it is a source of information; (2) it helps people develop and maintain a sense of self; and (3) it is a source of pleasure and comfort, or emotional well-being. In infancy, the third goal, the need for emotional support, is paramount. From childhood through young adulthood, information-seeking comes to the fore. As young people strive to learn about their society and their place in it, strangers may well be the best sources of knowledge. By middle age, although information-seeking remains important (Fung, Carstensen, & Lang, 2001), the original, emotion-regulating function of social contacts begins to reassert itself. In other words, middle-aged people increasingly seek out others who make them feel good (see Figure 16-2). In research testing the theory, middle-aged and older adults placed greater emphasis than young adults on emotional affinity in choosing hypothetical social partners (Carstensen et al., 1999).

Guidepost

4. What role do social relationships play in the lives of middle-aged people?

social convoy theory Theory, proposed by Kahn and Antonucci, that people move through life surrounded by concentric circles of intimate relationships on which they rely for assistance, well-being, and social support.

What's Your View?

• Does either the social convoy model or the socioemotional selectivity theory fit your own experience and observations?

socioemotional selectivity theory Theory, proposed by Carstensen, that people select social contacts on the basis of the changing relative importance of social interaction as a source of information, as an aid in developing and maintaining a self-concept, and as a source of emotional well-being.

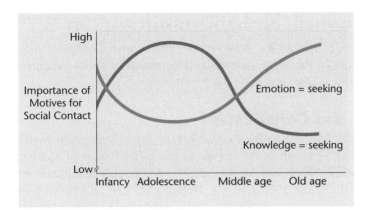

Figure 16-2

How motives for social contact change across the life span. According to socioemotional selectivity theory, infants seek social contact primarily for emotional comfort. In adolescence and young adulthood, people tend to be most interested in seeking information from others. From middle age on, emotional needs increasingly predominate. (Source: Adapted from Carstensen, Gross, & Fung, 1997.)

Relationships, Gender, and Quality of Life

For most middle-aged adults, relationships are the most important key to well-being (Markus et al., 2004). They can be a major source of health and satisfaction but also can present stressful demands (Lachman, 2004). These demands tend to fall most heavily on women. A sense of responsibility and concern for others may impair a woman's well-being when problems or misfortunes beset her mate, children, parents, friends, or coworkers. This "vicarious stress" may help explain why middle-aged women are especially susceptible to depression and other mental health problems and why, as we will see, they tend to be unhappier with their marriages than are men (Antonucci & Akiyama, 1997; Thomas, 1997).

In studying midlife social relationships, then, we need to keep in mind that their effects can be both positive and negative. In the remaining sections of this chapter, we examine how intimate relationships develop during the middle years. We look first at relationships with spouses, cohabiting partners, homosexual partners, and friends; next at bonds with maturing children; and then at ties with aging parents, siblings, and grandchildren.

Checkpoint

Can you . . .

✔ Summarize two theoretical models of the selection of social contacts?

✔ Discuss how relationships can affect quality of life in middle adulthood?

These middle-aged friends snacking and drinking around a kitchen table seem to be having the time of their lives. For most middle-aged adults, relationships are the most important ingredient of well-being—a source of health and satisfaction.

Consensual Relationships

Marriages, cohabitations, homosexual unions, and friendships typically involve two people of the same generation who mutually choose each other. How do these relationships fare in middle age?

Marriage and Cohabitation

Despite popular concern about the stability of the institution of marriage, by ages 40 to 59 all but 5 percent of Americans in the MIDUS sample had been married at least once (Marks, Bumpass, & Jun, 2004). Although cohabitation in midlife has increased greatly since 1960 (Brown, Bulanda, & Lee, 2005), with about 1 in 20 men and women engaging in this lifestyle, it is only half as common as in young adulthood (Marks et al., 2004). However, with the aging of the baby boom generation, it is becoming more so (Brown et al., 2005).

Marital State and Well-Being   As in young adulthood, marriage offers major benefits: social support, encouragement of health-promoting behaviors, greater socioeconomic resources (Gallo, Troxel, Matthews, & Kuller, 2003) and wealth accumulation (Wilmoth & Koso, 2002), and better physical and mental health (Brown, Bulanda, & Lee, 2005). In the MIDUS sample, men's and women's well-being benefited equally from marriage; but the single state seemed emotionally hardest on midlife men, who tended to be more anxious, sad, or restless and less generative than their younger counterparts. Formerly married, noncohabiting women and men reported more negative emotionality than those still in a first marriage. Still, midlife women in nontraditional roles (divorced, remarried, or cohabiting) experienced more well-being than did their younger counterparts—suggesting that life experience is an asset for women in such roles (Marks et al., 2004).

Among 494 mostly white women ages 42 to 50 followed for 13 years, those in highly satisfying marital *or* cohabiting relationships had lower risk factors for cardiovascular disease than women who were not currently in such relationships. However, this was not true of women who were less satisfied with their relationships. Thus, the stress of a bad relationship may cancel out the potential benefits (Gallo et al., 2003).

Marital Satisfaction   Midlife marriage today is very different from what it used to be. When life expectancies were shorter, couples who remained together for 25, 30, or 40 years were rare. The most common pattern was for marriages to be broken by death and for survivors to remarry. People had many children and expected them to live at home until they married. It was unusual for a middle-aged husband and wife to be alone together. Today, more marriages end in divorce, but couples who stay together can often look forward to twenty or more years of married life after the last child leaves home.

What happens to the quality of a longtime marriage? An analysis of data from two surveys of a total of 8,929 men and women in first marriages, conducted in 1986 and 1987–88 (Orbuch et al., 1996), sought to ascertain patterns in marital satisfaction. The researchers found a U-shaped pattern. During the first 20 to 24 years of marriage, the longer a couple have been married, the less satisfied they tend to be. Then the association between marital satisfaction and length of marriage begins to turn positive. At 35 to 44 years of marriage, a couple tend to be even more satisfied than during the first 4 years.

The U-shaped curve generally hits bottom early in middle age, when many couples have teenage children and are heavily involved in careers. Satisfaction usually reaches a height when children are grown; many people are entering or are in

Guidepost

5. Do marriages become happier or unhappier during the middle years, and does cohabitation at this stage of life provide benefits similar to those of marriage?

What's Your View?

- How many longtime happily married couples do you know? Are the qualities that seem to characterize these marriages similar to those mentioned in the text?

retirement, and a lifetime accumulation of assets helps ease financial worries (Orbuch et al., 1996). On the other hand, these changes may produce new pressures and challenges (Antonucci et al., 2001).

Marital satisfaction is affected by each partner's mental state. In a study of 774 married couples, a partner's level of anxiety and, especially, depression predicted that partner's level of marital satisfaction; and one partner's depression negatively affected the other partner's marital satisfaction as well. These findings point to the importance of examining the mental health of both partners in a troubled marriage before the relationship deteriorates too far. Promptly treating each partner's psychological needs may prevent a marital breakup (Whisman, Uebelacker, & Weinstock, 2004.)

Cohabitation and Mental Health Do cohabitants reap the same rewards as married people? Although there is little research on cohabitation among middle-aged and older people, one study suggests that the answer, at least for men, is no. Among 18,598 Americans over age 50, cohabiting men (but not cohabiting women) are more likely to be depressed than their married counterparts, even when such variables as physical health, social support, and economic resources are controlled. Indeed, cohabiting men are about as likely to be depressed as men without partners—widowed, divorced, separated, or never-married. It may be that men and women view their relationships differently. Women, like men, may want an intimate companion but may be able to enjoy that companionship without the commitment of formal marriage—a commitment that, in middle age, may come to mean the possibility of having to care for an infirm husband. Aging men, by the same token, may need or anticipate needing the kind of care that wives traditionally provide and may worry about not getting it (Brown et al., 2005).

The launching of a son or daughter may give a midlife marriage a new lease on life. Marital satisfaction generally improves when children are grown.

Midlife Divorce

Divorce in midlife is relatively uncommon, though it is becoming less so (Aldwin & Levenson, 2001). Most divorces occur during the first ten years of marriage (Clarke, 1995; Bramlett & Mosher, 2002). Thus, for people who, like Madeleine Albright, go through a divorce at midlife when they may have assumed their lives were settled, the breakup can be traumatic. In an American Association of Retired Persons (AARP) survey of 581 men and 566 women ages 40 to 79 who had been divorced at least once in their forties, fifties, or sixties, most respondents described the experience as more emotionally devastating than losing a job and about as devastating as a major illness, though less devastating than a spouse's death. Midlife divorce seems especially hard for women, like Albright (Montenegro, 2004), who are more negatively affected by divorce at any age than men are (Marks & Lambert, 1998).

Long-standing marriages may be less likely to break up than more recent ones because as couples stay together they build **marital capital,** financial and emotional benefits of marriage that become difficult to give up (Becker, 1991; Jones, Tepperman, & Wilson, 1995). College education decreases the risk of separation or divorce after the first decade of marriage, perhaps because educated couples tend to have accumulated marital assets and may have too much to lose financially from divorce (Hiedemann et al., 1998). Middle-aged divorcees, especially women, who do not remarry tend to be less financially secure than those who remain married (Wilmoth & Koso, 2002) and may have to go to work, perhaps for the first time (Huyck, 1999). According to the AARP survey, loss of financial security is a major concern of people in their forties (as Albright was) who need to show they can get on with their lives.

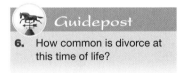

Guidepost

6. How common is divorce at this time of life?

marital capital Financial and emotional benefits built up during a long-standing marriage, which tend to hold a couple together.

Figure 16-3

Self-reported reasons for divorce at midlife or later. (Source: Montenegro, 2004, Figure 4.)

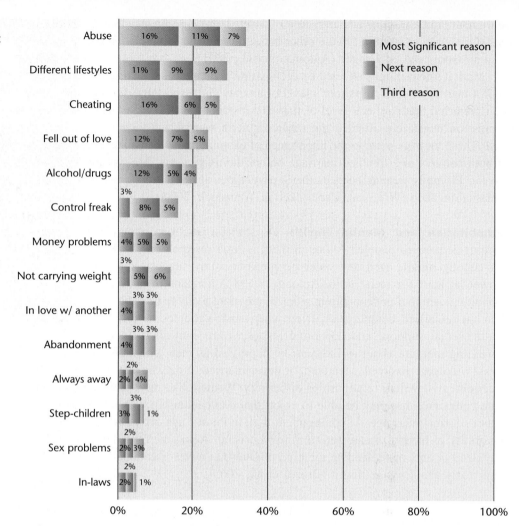

However, people in their fifties had the most difficulty with midlife divorce, perhaps because they worried more about their chances of remarriage and, unlike older divorcees, were more concerned about their future (Montenegro, 2004).

Why do middle-aged people divorce? The number one reason given by the AARP respondents was partner abuse—verbal, physical, or emotional. Other frequent reasons were differing values or lifestyles, infidelity, alcohol or drug abuse, and simply falling out of love (see Figure 16-3).

Most middle-aged divorced people bounce back eventually, as Albright did. On average, the AARP respondents rated their outlook on life as highly as does the general over-45 population and higher than that of singles in their age group. Three out of 4 said that ending their marriage was the right decision. About one-third (32 percent) had remarried—6 percent to their former spouses—and their outlook was better than that of those who had not remarried (Montenegro, 2004).

Still, stress often remains, for whatever reason. Nearly half (49 percent) of the AARP respondents—especially women—said they suffered highly from stress and 28 percent from depression. These proportions are similar to the rates among singles the same age (Montenegro, 2004). On the positive side, as with Albright, the stress of divorce may lead to personal growth (Aldwin & Levenson, 2001; Helson & Roberts, 1994).

The sense of violated expectations that Albright felt may be diminishing as midlife divorce becomes more common (Marks & Lambert, 1998; Norton & Moorman, 1987). This change appears to be due largely to women's growing economic independence (Hiedemann et al., 1998). Divorce rates among aging baby boomers now in their fifties, many of whom married later and had fewer children than in previous generations, are projected to continue to rise (Hiedemann et al., 1998; Uhlenberg, Cooney, & Boyd, 1990). Even in long marriages, the increasing number of years that people can expect to live in good health after child rearing ends may make the dissolution of a marginal marriage and the prospect of possible remarriage a more practical and attractive option (Hiedemann et al., 1998).

Indeed, divorce today may be *less* a threat to well-being in middle age than in young adulthood. That conclusion comes from a 5-year longitudinal study that compared the reactions of 6,948 young and middle-aged adults taken from a nationally representative sample. The researchers used Ryff's six-dimensional measure of psychological well-being, as well as other criteria. In almost all respects, middle-aged people showed more adaptability than younger people in the face of separation or divorce, despite their more limited prospects for remarriage (Marks & Lambert, 1998).

Gay and Lesbian Relationships

Gays and lesbians now in middle age grew up at a time when homosexuality was considered a mental illness, and homosexuals tended to be isolated not only from the larger community but from each other. Today this pioneer generation is just beginning to explore the opportunities inherent in the growing acceptance of homosexuality.*

Because many homosexuals still do not come out until well into adulthood, the timing of this crucial event can affect other aspects of development. Some middle-aged gays and lesbians may be associating openly for the first time and establishing relationships. Many are still working out conflicts with parents and other family members (sometimes including spouses) or hiding their homosexuality from them.

Due to the secrecy and stigma that have surrounded homosexuality, studies of gays and lesbians tend to have sampling problems. What little research exists on gay men has focused mostly on urban white men with above-average income and education. Lesbians studied so far also tend to be mostly white, professional, and middle or upper class. In one study, more than 25 percent of middle-aged lesbians lived alone, even if they were in intimate relationships (Bradford & Ryan, 1991). This may in part be a cohort effect; lesbians who grew up in the 1950s may be uncomfortable about living openly with a partner, as many younger lesbians do now.

Gay men who do not come out until midlife often go through a prolonged search for identity, marked by guilt, secrecy, heterosexual marriage, and conflicted relationships with both sexes. By contrast, those who recognize and accept their sexual orientation early in life often cross racial, socioeconomic, and age barriers within the gay community. Some move to cities with large gay populations where they can more easily seek out and form relationships.

This lesbian couple, proudly displaying the certificate of civil union they obtained from the town hall in Williston, Vermont, exemplify the growing acceptance of homosexuality in parts of the United States and other western industrialized countries. Many gays and lesbians still do not "come out" until well into adulthood and develop intimate relationships later in life than most heterosexuals do.

*Unless otherwise referenced, this discussion is based on Kimmel & Sang (1995).

Checkpoint

Can you . . .

✔ Describe the U-shaped curve of marital satisfaction, and cite factors that may help explain it?

✔ Compare the mental health of married and cohabiting men and women?

✔ Give reasons for the tendency for divorce to occur early in a marriage, and cite factors that may increase the risk of divorce in midlife?

Guidepost

7. How do midlife gay and lesbian relationships compare with heterosexual ones?

For the most part, the principles that apply to sustaining a heterosexual marriage also apply to maintaining gay and lesbian partnerships. Gay and lesbian relationships tend to be stronger if known as such to family and friends, and if the couple seek out supportive gay and lesbian environments (Haas & Stafford, 1998). Coming out to parents is often difficult but need not necessarily have an adverse impact on the couple's relationship (LaSala, 1998). When family and friends are supportive and validate the relationship, its quality tends to be higher (R. B. Smith & Brown, 1997).

Gay and lesbian couples tend to be more egalitarian than heterosexual couples, but, as with many heterosexual couples, balancing commitments to careers and relationship can be difficult. Gay couples in which one partner is less career-oriented than the other have an easier time, but couples in which both partners are relationship-centered tend to be happiest.

Friendships

Guidepost

8. How do friendships fare during middle age?

As Carstensen's theory predicts, social networks tend to become smaller and more intimate at midlife. Still, friendships persist and, as with Madeleine Albright, are a strong source of emotional support and well-being, especially for women (Adams & Allan, 1998; Antonucci et al., 2001). Friendships often revolve around work and parenting; others are based on neighborhood contacts or on association in volunteer organizations (Antonucci et al., 2001; Hartup & Stevens, 1999).

The quality of midlife friendships often makes up for what they lack in quantity of time spent. Especially during a crisis, such as a divorce or a problem with an aging parent, adults turn to friends for emotional support, practical guidance, comfort, companionship, and talk (Antonucci & Akiyama, 1997; Hartup & Stevens, 1999; Suitor & Pillemer, 1993). Conflicts with friends often center on differences in values, beliefs, and lifestyles; friends usually can "talk out" these conflicts while maintaining mutual dignity and respect (Hartup & Stevens, 1999).

The importance of friendships can vary from time to time. In a longitudinal study of 155 mostly white men and women from middle- and lower-class backgrounds, friends were more important to women's well-being in early middle age, but to men's well-being in late middle age (Paul, 1997).

Friendships often have a special importance for homosexuals. Lesbians are more likely to get emotional support from lesbian friends, lovers, and even ex-lovers than from relatives. Gay men, too, rely on friendship networks, which they actively create and maintain. Friendship networks provide solidarity and contact with younger people, which middle-aged heterosexuals normally get through family. Loss of friends to the scourge of AIDS has been traumatic for many in the gay community (Kimmel & Sang, 1995).

Checkpoint

Can you . . .

✔ Compare the formation and maintenance of homosexual relationships and heterosexual ones?

✔ Discuss the quantity, quality, and importance of friendships at midlife?

Relationships with Maturing Children

Guidepost

9. How do parent-child relationships change as children approach and reach adulthood?

Parenthood is a process of letting go. This process usually approaches or reaches its climax during the parents' middle age (Marks et al., 2004). It is true that, with contemporary trends toward delaying marriage and parenthood, some middle-aged people (about 3 percent of men and 7 percent of women in the MIDUS study—Marks et al., 2004) now face such issues as finding a good day care or preschool program and screening the content of Saturday morning cartoons. Still, most parents in the early part of middle age must cope with a different set of issues, which arise from living with children who will soon be leaving the nest. Once children become adults and have their own children, the intergenerational family multiplies in number and in connections. It is middle-aged parents, usually women, who tend to be the family "kinkeepers," maintaining ties among the various branches of the extended family (Putney & Bengtson, 2001).

Families today are diverse and complex. Increasingly, middle-aged parents have to deal with an adult child's continuing to live in the family home or leaving it only to return. But one thing has not changed: parents' well-being tends to hinge on how their children turn out (Allen, Blieszner, & Roberto, 2000).

Adolescent Children: Issues for Parents

Ironically, the people at the two times of life popularly linked with emotional crises—adolescence and midlife—often live in the same household. It is usually middle-aged adults who are the parents of adolescent children. While dealing with their own special concerns, parents have to cope daily with young people who are undergoing great physical, emotional, and social changes.

Although research contradicts the stereotype of adolescence as a time of inevitable turmoil and rebellion (refer back to Chapter 12), some rejection of parental authority is necessary. An important task for parents is to accept maturing children as they are, not as what the parents had hoped they would be.

Theorists from a variety of perspectives have described this period as one of questioning, reappraisal, or diminished well-being for parents. However, this too is not inevitable. In the MIDUS study, being a parent was associated with more psychological distress than being child-free but also brought greater psychological wellness and generativity, especially to men (Marks et al., 2004).

A questionnaire survey of 129 two-parent, intact, mostly white, socioeconomically diverse families with a firstborn son or daughter between ages 10 and 15 found more complex gender differences. For some parents, especially white-collar and professional men with sons, a child's adolescence brought increased satisfaction, well-being, and even pride. For most parents, the normative changes of adolescence elicited a mixture of positive and negative emotions. This was particularly true of mothers with early adolescent daughters, whose relationships generally tend to be both close and conflict-filled. Most vulnerable were mothers who were not heavily invested in paid work (Silverberg, 1996). In a longitudinal study of 191 families with adolescent children, parents tended to compensate for lack of acceptance and warmth in mother-son and father-daughter relationships by increasing their emotional involvement with work and, in the case of fathers, spending more time there (Fortner, Crouter, & McHale. 2004).

Lifemap CD

The "Tips for Parenting Adolescents" video in Chapter 16 of your CD offers practical advice from an expert who has studied adolescents for decades.

When Children Leave: The Empty Nest

Research is also challenging popular ideas about the **empty nest**—a supposedly difficult transition, especially for women, that occurs when the youngest child leaves home. Although some women, heavily invested in mothering, do have problems in adjusting to the empty nest, they are far outnumbered by those who, like Madeleine Albright, find the departure liberating (Antonucci et al., 2001; Antonucci & Akiyama, 1997; Barnett, 1985; Chiriboga, 1997; Helson, 1997; Mitchell & Helson, 1990). Today, the refilling of the nest by grown children returning home (discussed in an upcoming section) may be far more stressful (Thomas, 1997).

The effects of the empty nest on a marriage depend on its quality and length. In a good marriage, the departure of grown children may usher in a second honeymoon (Robinson & Blanton, 1993). In a shaky marriage, if a couple have stayed together for the sake of the children, they may now see no reason to prolong the bond.

For some women, the empty nest may bring relief from what Gutmann called the "chronic emergency of parenthood" (Cooper & Gutmann, 1987, p. 347). Like

empty nest Transitional phase of parenting following the last child's leaving the parents' home.

Madeleine Albeight, they can pursue their own interests as they bask in their grown children's accomplishments. The empty nest may be harder on couples whose identity is dependent on the parental role, or who now must face marital problems they had previously pushed aside under the press of parental responsibilities (Antonucci et al., 2001).

The empty nest does not signal the end of parenthood. It is a transition to a new stage: the relationship between parents and adult children.

Parenting Grown Children

Elliott Roosevelt, a son of President Franklin Delano Roosevelt, used to tell this story about his mother, Eleanor Roosevelt: At a state dinner, Eleanor, who was seated next to him, leaned over and whispered in his ear. A friend later asked Elliott, then in his forties, what she had said. "She told me to eat my peas," he answered.

Even after the years of active parenting are over and children have left home for good, parents are still parents. The midlife role of parent to young adults raises new issues and calls for new attitudes and behaviors on the part of both generations. More than half (54 percent) of the middle-aged women in the MIDUS survey and about 38 percent of the men were in this stage (Marks et al., 2004).

In middle-class families, at least, middle-aged parents generally give their children more support than they get from them as the young adults establish careers and families (Antonucci et al., 2001). Some parents have difficulty treating their offspring as adults, and many young adults have difficulty accepting their parents' continuing concern about them. In a warm, supportive family environment, such conflicts can be managed by an open airing of feelings (Putney & Bengtson, 2001).

Most young adults and their middle-aged parents enjoy each other's company and get along well. However, intergenerational families do not all fit one mold. An estimated 25 percent of intergenerational families are *tight-knit,* both geographically and emotionally; they have frequent contact with mutual help and support. Another 25 percent are *sociable,* but with less emotional affinity or commitment. About 16 percent have *obligatory* relationships, with much interaction but little emotional attachment; and 17 percent are *detached,* both emotionally and geographically. An in-between category consists of those who are *intimate but distant* (16 percent), spending little time together but retaining warm feelings that might lead to a renewal of contact and exchange. Adult children tend to be closer to their mothers than to their fathers (Bengtson, 2001; Silverstein & Bengtson, 1997).

Prolonged Parenting: The "Cluttered Nest"

What happens if the nest does not empty when it normally should, or unexpectedly refills? Since the 1980s, in most Western nations, more and more adult children have delayed leaving home until the late twenties or beyond (Mouw, 2005). Furthermore, the **revolving door syndrome** (sometimes called the *boomerang phenomenon*) has become more common, as increasing numbers of young adults, especially men, return to their parents' home, sometimes more than once, and sometimes with their own families (Aquilino, 1996; Putney & Bengtson, 2001).

In the United States, in 2000, 10.5 percent of 25- to 34-year-olds were living in the family home (Greider, 2001). Most likely to come home are single, divorced, or separated children and those who end a cohabiting relationship. The family home can be a convenient, supportive, and affordable haven while young adults are getting on their feet or regaining their balance in times of financial, marital, or other trouble (Aquilino, 1996; Putney & Bengtson, 2001).

Prolonged parenting may lead to intergenerational tension when it contradicts normative expectations (Putney & Bengtson, 2001). As children move from

revolving door syndrome Tendency for young adults who have left home to return to their parents' household in times of financial, marital, or other trouble.

What's Your View?

- Do you think it is a good idea for adult children to live with their parents? If so, under what circumstances? What "house rules" do you think should apply?

adolescence to young adulthood, parents typically expect them to become independent, and they themselves expect to do so. An adult child's autonomy is a sign of parental success. As the timing-of-events model would predict, then, a grown child's delayed departure from the nest or return to it may produce stress (Antonucci et al., 2001; Aquilino, 1996). Thus, as we mentioned in Chapter 14, parents and adult children tend to get along best when the young adults are employed and living away from the parental home (Belsky, Jaffee, Caspi, Moffitt, & Silva, 2003). When adult children live with parents, relations tend to be smoother when the parents see the adult child moving toward autonomy—for example, by enrolling in college (Antonucci et al., 2001; Aquilino, 1996).

However, the "nonnormative" experience of parent-child coresidence is becoming less so, especially for parents with more than one child. Rather than an abrupt leave-taking, the empty nest transition is coming to be seen as a more prolonged process of separation, often lasting several years (Aquilino, 1996; Putney & Bengtson, 2001). A nationally representative longitudinal survey of 1,365 mostly white, middle-aged, married householders with grown children, up to 28 percent of whom had one or more adult children living at home, suggests that prolonged parenting need not be a disruptive experience. The presence of adult children seemed to have no effect on the parents' marital happiness, on the amount of marital conflict, or on the amount of time couples had with each other. Coresidence with adult children may be seen as an expression of family solidarity, an extension of the normative expectation of assistance from parents to young adult children (Ward & Spitze, 2004).

Checkpoint
Can you . . .

✔ Discuss the changes parents of adolescent children tend to go through?

✔ Tell how most women and men respond to the empty nest?

✔ Describe typical features of relationships between parents and grown children?

✔ Give reasons for the prolonged parenting phenomenon, and discuss its effects on family relations?

Other Kinship Ties

Except in times of need, ties with the family of origin—parents and siblings—tend to recede in importance during young adulthood, when work, spouses or partners, and children take precedence. At midlife, these earliest kinship ties may reassert themselves in a new way, as the responsibility for care and support of aging parents may begin to shift to their middle-aged children. In addition, a new relationship typically begins at this time of life: grandparenthood.

Guidepost

10. How do middle-aged people get along with parents and siblings?

Relationships with Aging Parents

The middle years may bring dramatic, though gradual, changes in filial relationships. Many middle-aged people look at their parents more objectively than before, seeing them as individuals with both strengths and weaknesses. Something else may happen during these years: One day a middle-aged adult may look at a mother or father and see an old person, who may need a daughter's or son's care (Troll & Fingerman, 1996).

Contact and Mutual Help Most middle-aged adults and their parents have warm, affectionate relationships based on frequent contact and mutual help (Antonucci & Akiyama, 1997; Bengtson, 2001). Relations between daughters and older mothers tend to be especially close (Bengtson, 2001; Willson, Shuey, & Elder, 2003).

Mostly, help and assistance continue to flow from parents to child, especially in times of crisis (Bengtson, 2001). But while most older adults are physically fit, vigorous, and independent, some seek their children's assistance in making decisions and may depend on them for daily tasks and financial help. There may even be a role reversal; a parent, especially after the death of her or his spouse, now becomes the one who needs help

Most middle-aged adults and their aging parents have warm, affectionate relationships—as do this mother and daughter.

from the child (Antonucci et al., 2001). In the MIDUS study, 1 in 5 adults ages 40 to 59 had a sole surviving parent in poor health, usually the mother (Marks et al., 2004).

With the lengthening of the life span, some developmental scientists have proposed a new life stage called **filial maturity,** when middle-aged children "learn to accept and to meet their parents' dependency needs" (Marcoen, 1995, p. 125). This normative development is seen as the healthy outcome of a **filial crisis,** in which adults learn to balance love and duty to their parents with autonomy within a two-way relationship. Most middle-aged people willingly accept their obligations to their parents (Antonucci et al., 2001).

However, family relations in middle and late adulthood can be complex. With increasing longevity, couples with limited emotional and financial resources may need to allocate them among two sets of aging parents as well as provide for their own (and possibly their own adult children's) needs. In a continuation of the Elder study of Iowa farm families, begun in 1989 (refer back to Box 1-1 in Chapter 1), researchers interviewed 738 middle-aged sons and daughters from 420 mostly two-parent close-knit households. More than 25 percent of the relationships between adult children and their aging parents or in-laws were characterized by ambivalence—nearly 8 percent by a high degree of ambivalence. This was particularly true in relationships with in-laws, relationships between a woman and her mother or mother-in-law, relationships with parents or in-laws in poor health, relationships in which a daughter was providing assistance, and families in which adult children did not get along with their parents in early life (Willson et al., 2003).

Ambivalence may surface in trying to juggle competing needs. In a national longitudinal survey of 3,622 married couples with at least one surviving parent, the allocation of assistance to aging parents involved trade-offs and often depended on family lineage. Most couples contributed time or money, but not both, and few assisted both sets of parents. Couples tended to respond more readily to the needs of the wife's parents, presumably because of her greater closeness to them. African American and Hispanic couples were more likely than white couples to provide consistent assistance of all types to parents on each side of the family (Shuey & Hardy, 2003).

Becoming a Caregiver for Aging Parents The generations typically get along best while parents are healthy and vigorous. When older people become infirm—especially if they undergo mental deterioration or personality changes—the burden of caring for them may strain the relationship (Antonucci et al., 2001; Marcoen, 1995). Longer life, especially in developed countries, means more risk of chronic diseases and disabilities; and families are smaller than in the past, with fewer siblings to share in a parent's care (Kinsella & Velkoff, 2001). Given the high cost of nursing homes and most older people's reluctance to enter and stay in them (see Chapter 18),

This middle-aged daughter is beginning to realize that her mother is no longer a tower of strength but instead is beginning to lean on her. With filial maturity, *middle-aged children learn to accept and meet their parents' dependency needs with a combination of love and a sense of duty, while letting the parents retain as much autonomy as possible.*

many dependent elders receive long-term care in their own home or that of a care-giver (Sarkisian & Gerstel, 2004).

The world over, caregiving is typically a female function (Kinsella & Velkoff, 2001). When an ailing mother is widowed or a divorced woman can no longer manage alone, it is most likely that a daughter will take on the caregiving role (Antonucci et al., 2001; Schulz & Martire, 2004). Perhaps because of the intimate nature of the contact and the strength of the mother-daughter bond, mothers may prefer a daughter's care (Lee et al., 1993), and women tend to be more responsive to parental needs. Another reason for the gender gap in caregiving may be the reverse gender gap in employment—in the amounts women and men earn and the types of jobs they hold—though, as we have pointed out, this gap is closing. A woman who earns less than her spouse or has a career that can be put on hold may find it more feasible to take time away from work than a man does. Sons do contribute to caregiving, especially if they are not employed (Sarkisian & Gerstel, 2004), but they are less likely to provide primary, personal care (Marks, 1996; Matthews, 1995).

Strains of Caregiving Caregiving can be stressful (Schulz & Martire, 2004). Many caregivers find the task a physical, emotional, and financial burden, especially if they work full time, have limited financial resources, or lack support and assistance (Lund, 1993a; Schulz & Martire, 2004). It is hard for women who work outside the home to assume an added caregiving role (Marks, 1996), but reducing work hours or quitting a job to meet caregiving obligations can increase financial stress (Schulz & Martire, 2004). (Flexible work schedules and family and medical leave can help alleviate this problem.) On the other hand, the need to care for aging parents may come at a time when a middle-aged child is preparing to retire and can ill afford the additional costs of caring for a frail older person or may have health problems of his or her own (Kinsella & Velkoff, 2001).

Caring for a person with physical impairments is hard. It can be even more difficult to care for someone with dementia, who, in addition to being unable to carry on basic functions of daily living, may be incontinent, suspicious, agitated or depressed, subject to hallucinations, likely to wander about at night, dangerous to self and others, and in need of constant supervision (Biegel, 1995; Schultz & Martire, 2003). Spending hours on end with an elderly, demented parent who may not even recognize her caregiver can be agonizingly isolating (Climo & Stewart, 2003), and the relationship between the two may deteriorate. Sometimes the caregiver becomes physically or mentally ill under the strain (Schultz & Martire, 2004; Vitaliano, Zhang, & Scanlan, 2003). Because women are more likely than men to give personal care, their well-being is more likely to suffer (Climo & Stewart, 2003). Sometimes the stress created by the incessant, heavy demands of caregiving is so great as to lead to abuse, neglect, or even abandonment of the dependent elderly person (see Chapter 18).

A result of these and other strains may be **caregiver burnout,** a physical, mental, and emotional exhaustion that can affect adults who care for aged relatives (Barnhart, 1992). (Box 16-2 discusses sources of assistance to help prevent caregiver burnout.) Sometimes other arrangements must be made, such as institutionalization, assisted living, or a division of responsibilities among siblings (Shuey & Hardy, 2003).

Emotional strain may come not only from caregiving itself but from the need to balance it with the many other responsibilities of midlife (Antonucci et al., 2001; Climo & Stewart, 2003). Elderly parents may become dependent at a time when middle-aged adults are trying to launch their own children or, if parenthood was delayed, to raise them. Members of this "generation in the middle," sometimes called the **sandwich generation,** may be caught in a squeeze between these competing needs and their limited resources of time, money, and energy.

caregiver burnout Condition of physical, mental, and emotional exhaustion affecting adults who provide continuous care for sick or aged persons.

sandwich generation Middle-aged adults squeezed by competing needs to raise or launch children and to care for elderly parents.

BOX 16-2

Practically Speaking
Preventing Caregiver Burnout

Even the most patient, loving caregiver may become frustrated, anxious, or resentful under the constant strain of meeting an older person's seemingly endless needs. Often families and friends fail to recognize that caregivers have a right to feel discouraged, frustrated, and put upon. Caregivers need a life of their own, beyond the loved one's disability or disease (J. Evans, 1994).

Community support programs can reduce the strains and burdens of caregiving, prevent burnout, and postpone the need for institutionalization of the dependent person. Support services may include meals and housekeeping; transportation and escort services; and adult day care centers, which provide supervised activities and care while caregivers work or attend to personal needs. *Respite care* (substitute supervised care by visiting nurses or home health aides) gives regular caregivers some time off, whether for a few hours, a day, a weekend, or a week. Temporary admission to a nursing home is another alternative. Through counseling, support, and self-help groups, caregivers can share problems, gain information about community resources, and improve skills.

Although there is some dispute about their effectiveness, some research suggests that such programs do improve caregivers' morale and reduce stress (Gallagher-Thompson, 1995). In one longitudinal study, caregivers with adequate community support reported many dimensions of personal growth. Some had become more empathic, caring, understanding, patient, and compassionate, closer to the person they were caring for, and more appreciative of their own good health. Others felt good about having fulfilled their responsibilities. Some had "learned to value life more and to take one day at a time," and a few had learned to "laugh at situations and events" (Lund, 1993a).

More recently, randomized controlled trials have focused on more broadly based interventions targeting both the caregiver and the patient and offering individual or family counseling, case management, skills training, environmental modification, and behavior management strategies. Evidence from these studies has found that a combination of diverse services and supports such as these can significantly reduce caregivers' burdens and improve their skills, satisfaction, and well-being—and even, sometimes, improve the patient's symptoms (Schulz & Martire, 2004).

Behavioral training and psychotherapy can help caregivers deal with a patient's difficult behavior and their own tendency toward depression (Gallagher-Thompson, 1995). One behavioral training program at the University of Chicago had considerable success in getting patients to handle some self-care and to be more sociable and less verbally abusive. Caregivers learned such techniques as contingency contracting ("If you do this, the consequence will be . . .), modeling desired behaviors, rehearsal, and giving feedback (Gallagher-Thompson, 1995).

A "Caregiver's Bill of Rights" (Home, 1985) can help caregivers keep a positive perspective and remind them that their needs count too:

A Caregiver's Bill of Rights
I have the right

- to take care of myself. This is not an act of selfishness. It will give me the capability of taking better care of my relative.

- to seek help from others even though my relative may object. I recognize the limits of my own endurance and strength.

- to maintain facets of my own life that do not include the person I care for, just as I would if he or she were healthy. I know that I do everything that I reasonably can for this person, and I have the right to do some things just for myself.

- to get angry, be depressed, and express other difficult feelings occasionally.

- to reject any attempt by my relative (either conscious or unconscious) to manipulate me through guilt, anger, or depression.

- to receive consideration, affection, forgiveness, and acceptance for what I do from my loved ones for as long as I offer these qualities in return.

- to take pride in what I am accomplishing and to applaud the courage it has sometimes taken to meet the needs of my relative.

- to protect my individuality and my right to make a life for myself that will sustain me in the time when my relative no longer needs my full-time help.

- to expect and demand that as new strides are made in finding resources to aid physically and mentally impaired older persons in our country, similar strides will be made toward aiding and supporting caregivers.

- to (*add your own statements of rights to this list. Read this list to yourself every day*).

What's Your View?

What more could be done to ease caregivers' burdens?

Check It Out

For more information on caregiver respite and support, go to http://www.helpguide.org/elder/respite.htm. Or go to http://www.acponline.org/public/h_care/6-respit.htm. This is an article from the American College of Physicians and the American Society of Internal Medicine entitled "Getting 'Respite' Care or Extra Help at Home."

Some research challenges the extent of the "sandwich" problem (Kinsella & Velkoff, 2001; Putney & Bengtson, 2001; Staudinger & Bluck, 2001). Studies in the United States, Europe, and Canada have found relatively few middle-aged adults sandwiched between caregiving, work, and dependent children (Hagestad, 2000; Marks, 1998; Penning, 1998; Rosenthal, Martin-Andrews, & Matthews, 1996). Children generally have left the nest before the need for caregiving arises.

Some family caregivers, looking back, regard the experience as uniquely rewarding (Climo & Stewart, 2003). Although role conflicts can seem overwhelming, some middle-aged adults flourish in multiple roles. Circumstances and contexts make a difference, as do the attitudes a person brings to the task (Bengtson, 2001). In the Radcliffe women's study, women who had attained generativity early in middle age felt less burdened when called upon to care for aging parents (Peterson, 2002). If a caregiver deeply loves an infirm parent, cares about family continuity, looks at caregiving as a challenge, and has adequate personal, family, and community resources to meet that challenge, caregiving can be an opportunity for personal growth in competence, compassion, self-knowledge, and self-transcendence (Bengtson, 2001; Climo & Stewart, 2003; Bengtson, Rosenthal, & Burton, 1996; Biegel, 1995; Lund, 1993a).

What's Your View?

- What would you do if one or both of your parents required long-term care? To what extent should children or other relatives be responsible for such care? To what extent, and in what ways, should society help?

Relationships with Siblings

In some cross-sectional research, sibling relationships over the life span appear to take the form of an hourglass, with the most contact at the two ends—childhood and middle to late adulthood—and the least contact during the childraising years. After establishing careers and families, siblings may renew ties (Bedford, 1995; Cicirelli, 1995; Putney & Bengtson, 2001). Other studies indicate a decline in frequency of contact throughout adulthood. Sibling conflict tends to diminish with age—perhaps because siblings who do *not* get along see each other less (Putney & Bengtson, 2001).

Relationships with siblings who remain in contact are important to psychological well-being in midlife (Antonucci et al., 2001), though their importance relative to other relationships, such as friendships, may rise and fall from time to time. Sibling relationships seem to serve somewhat different purposes for men and women. For women, positive feelings toward siblings are linked with a favorable self-concept; for men, with high morale. The more contact both men and women have with their siblings, the less likely they are to show symptoms of psychological problems (Paul, 1997).

Dealing with the care of aging parents brings some siblings closer together but can cause resentment and conflict (Antonucci et al., 2001; Bedford, 1995; Bengtson et al., 1996). Disagreements may arise over the division of care (Lerner, Somers, Reid, Chiriboga, & Tierney, 1991; Strawbridge & Wallhagen, 1991) or over an inheritance, especially if the sibling relationship has not been good.

The issue of sharing of care with siblings arose in 16 out of 17 small-group discussion groups involving 63 middle-aged adults in dual-earner couples who were caring for elderly parents. Some participants, distressed by what they saw as an inequitable division of care, had asked their siblings to do more; but if refused, they felt even more upset. Others used cognitive strategies to make the situation *seem* more equitable. Overinvolved sisters might minimize their brothers' underinvolvement by telling themselves that caregiving is women's work. Some participants tried to justify why a particular sibling did the most by pointing to such factors as who lived closer to the parent, who had shorter working hours or fewer family responsibilities, and whose personality was more fitted to the task (Ingersoll-Dayton, Neal, Ha, & Hammer, 2003).

Checkpoint

Can you . . .

✔ Describe the change in the balance of filial relationships that often occurs between middle-aged children and elderly parents?

✔ Cite sources of potential strain in caregiving for elderly parents?

✔ Discuss the nature and importance of sibling relationships in middle age as compared with other parts of the life span?

11. How has grandparenthood changed, and what roles do grandparents play?

Grandparenthood

Often grandparenthood begins before the end of active parenting. Adults in the United States become grandparents at an average age of 48, according to a telephone survey of 1,500 grandparents belonging to the American Association of Retired Persons (AARP) (Davies & Williams, 2002). With today's lengthening life spans, many adults spend several decades as grandparents and live to see grandchildren become adults (Reitzes & Mutran, 2004).

Grandparenthood today is different in other ways from grandparenthood in the past. The average U.S. grandparent has 6 grandchildren (Davies & Williams, 2002), compared with 12 to 15 around the turn of the century (Szinovacz, 1998; Uhlenberg, 1988). With the rising incidence of midlife divorce, about one in five grandparents is divorced, widowed, or separated (Davies & Williams, 2002), and many children have stepgrandparents. Grandmothers of younger children are more likely to be in the workforce (and thus less available to help out). On the other hand, trends toward early retirement free some grandparents to spend more time with grandchildren. Many grandparents still have living parents, whose care they must balance with grandchildren's needs. And many grandparents in both developed and developing countries provide part-time or primary care for grandchildren (Kinsella & Velkoff, 2001; Szinovacz, 1998).

The Grandparent's Role In many developing societies, such as those in Latin America and Asia, extended-family households predominate, and grandparents play an integral role in child raising and family decisions. In such Asian countries as Thailand and Taiwan, about 40 percent of the population ages 50 and over live in the same household with a minor grandchild, and half of those with grandchildren ages 10 or younger—usually grandmothers—provide care for the child (Kinsella & Velkoff, 2001).

In the United States, the extended family household is common in some minority communities, but the dominant household pattern is the nuclear family. When

In Japan, grandmothers like this one traditionally wear red as a sign of their noble status. Grandparenthood is an important milestone in western societies as well.

Grandparents, like this grandmother teaching her granddaughter to make a quilt, can have an important influence on their grandchildren's development. Grandmothers tend to have closer, warmer relationships with their grandchildren than grandfathers.

children grow up, they typically leave home and establish new, autonomous nuclear families wherever their inclinations, aspirations, and job-hunts take them. Although 68 percent of the grandparents in the AARP survey see at least one grandchild every one or two weeks, 45 percent live too far away to see their grandchildren regularly (Davies & Williams, 2002). However, distance does not necessarily affect the quality of relationships with grandchildren (Kivett, 1991, 1993, 1996). Many middle-aged and older men and women consider grandparenthood among their most central roles (Reitzes & Mutran, 2002).

Grandmothers tend to be kinkeepers; they are the ones who keep in touch with the grandchildren. In general, grandmothers have closer, warmer, more affectionate relationships with their grandchildren (especially granddaughters) than grandfathers do, and see them more (Putney & Bengtson, 2001). Grandparents who have frequent contact with their grandchildren, feel positively about grandparenthood, attribute importance to the role, and have high self-esteem tend to be more satisfied with being grandparents (Reitzes & Mutran, 2004).

The most frequent activities grandparents in the AARP sample do with their grandchildren are having dinner together, watching television, going shopping, and reading to them; more than half exercise or play sports with their grandchildren. More than half spend money on their grandchildren's educational needs, and about 45 percent say they help pay grandchildren's living expenses. About 15 percent provide child care while the parents work (Davies & Williams, 2002). Indeed, grandparents are now the nation's number one child care providers; 21 percent of all preschoolers and 15 percent of grade-school-age children stay with grandparents while their mothers work (Smith, 2002). A similar trend exists in some other developed countries (Kinsella & Velkoff, 2001).

As grandchildren grow older, contact tends to diminish, but affection grows. The decline in contact is more rapid among younger cohorts of grandparents, who tend to have better health, more money, and busier lives (Silverstein & Long, 1998).

Grandparenting after Divorce and Remarriage   One result of the rise in divorce and remarriage is a growing number of grandparents and grandchildren whose relationships are endangered or severed. After a divorce, because the mother usually has

What's Your View?

• Have you had a close relationship with a grandmother or grandfather? If so, in what specific ways did that relationship influence your development?

Checkpoint
Can you . . .

✔ Tell how grandparenthood has changed in recent generations?

✔ Describe the roles grandparents play in family life?

custody, her parents tend to have more contact and stronger relationships with their grandchildren, and the paternal grandparents tend to have less (Cherlin & Furstenberg, 1986; Myers & Perrin, 1993). A divorced mother's remarriage typically reduces her need for support from her parents, but not their contact with their grandchildren. For paternal grandparents, however, the new marriage increases the likelihood that they will be displaced or that the family will move away, making contact more difficult (Cherlin & Furstenberg, 1986).

Because ties with grandparents are important to children's development, every state in the Union has given grandparents (and in some states, great-grandparents, siblings, and others) the right to visitation after a divorce or the death of a parent, if a judge finds it in the best interests of the child. However, a few state courts have struck down such laws, and some legislatures have restricted grandparents' visitation rights. The Supreme Court in June 2000 invalidated Washington state's "grandparents' rights" law as too broad an intrusion on parental rights (Greenhouse, 2000a).

The remarriage of either parent often brings a new set of grandparents into the picture, and often stepgrandchildren as well. Stepgrandparents may find it hard to become close to their new stepgrandchildren, especially older children and those who do not live with the grandparent's adult child (Cherlin & Furstenberg, 1986; Longino & Earle, 1996; Myers & Perrin, 1993).

With the increase in midlife divorce, more families are dealing with the impact of grandparents' divorce. Research based on the ongoing longitudinal Elder study of rural Iowa families finds that divorced grandparents' relations with their grandchildren tend to suffer, often because divorced grandparents tend to live farther away from their grandchildren and have weaker bonds with their adult children. This is especially true of grandfathers and paternal grandparents. However, a good grandparent-parent relationship can compensate for such potentially negative effects (King, 2003).

Raising Grandchildren Many grandparents are their grandchildren's sole or primary caregivers. One reason, in developing countries, is the migration of rural parents to urban areas to find work. These "skip-generation" families exist in all regions of the world, particularly in Afro-Caribbean countries. In sub-Saharan Africa, the AIDS epidemic has left many orphans whose grandparents step into the parents' place (Kinsella & Velkoff, 2001).

In the United States, an increasing number of grandparents (and even great-grandparents) are serving as "parents by default" for children whose parents are unable to care for them—often as a result of teenage pregnancy, substance abuse, illness, divorce, or death (Allen et al., 2000). In 2001, about 2.4 million grandparents were raising grandchildren (U.S. Census Bureau, 2002). Nine percent of African American children were living in grandparent-headed households compared with 6 percent of Hispanic children and 4 percent of non-Hispanic white children (Fields, 2003). Many of these caregiver-grandparents are divorced or widowed and live on fixed incomes (Hudnall, 2001), and many are in dire financial straits (Casper & Bryson, 1998). In 2000, 4 out of 5 African American grandmother caregivers who were below the poverty line were not receiving public assistance (Minkler & Fuller-Thomson, 2005).

Unplanned surrogate parenthood can be a physical, emotional, and financial drain on middle-aged or older adults. They may have to quit their jobs, shelve their retirement plans, drastically reduce their leisure pursuits and social life, and endanger their health. Most grandparents do not have as much energy, patience, or stamina as they once had, and may not be up on current educational and social trends (Hudnall, 2001).

Most grandparents who take on the responsibility to raise their grandchildren do it because they love the children and do not want them placed in a stranger's foster home. However, the age difference can become a barrier, and both generations may feel cheated out of their traditional roles. At the same time, grandparents often have to deal not only with a sense of guilt because the adult children they raised have failed their own children, but with the rancor they feel toward this adult child. For some caregiver couples, the strains produce tension in their own relationship. If one or both parents later resume their normal roles, it may be emotionally wrenching to return the child (Crowley, 1993; Larsen, 1990–1991).

Grandparents providing **kinship care** who do not become foster parents or gain custody have no legal status and no more rights than unpaid baby-sitters. They may face many practical problems, from enrolling the child in school and gaining access to academic records to obtaining medical insurance for the child. Grandchildren are usually not eligible for coverage under employer-provided health insurance even if the grandparent has custody. Like working parents, working grandparents need good, affordable child care and family-friendly workplace policies, such as time off to care for a sick child. The federal Family and Medical Leave Act of 1993 does cover grandparents who are raising grandchildren, but many do not realize it.

kinship care Care of children living without parents in the home of grandparents or other relatives, with or without a change of legal custody.

Checkpoint
Can you . . .

✔ Tell how parents' divorce and remarriage can affect grandparents' relationships with grandchildren?

✔ Discuss the challenges involved in raising grandchildren?

Refocus

Thinking back to the Focus vignette about Madeleine Albright at the beginning of this chapter:

- In what ways did Albright's life course in middle age reflect the points discussed in this chapter?

- How would each of the theories discussed in this chapter describe and explain the changes Albright went through in her middle years?

- Did Albright show the changes in gender identity described by either Jung or Gutmann or in the Mills Longitudinal Study?

- How do you think Albright would score herself on Ryff's six dimensions of well-being?

- What aspects of the discussions on changing relationships at midlife seem to apply to Albright?

Grandparents can be sources of guidance, companions in play, links to the past, and symbols of family continuity. They express generativity, a longing to transcend mortality by investing themselves in the lives of future generations. Men and women who do not become grandparents may fulfill generative needs by becoming foster grandparents or volunteering in schools or hospitals. By finding ways to develop what Erikson called the "virtue" of care, adults prepare themselves to enter the culminating period of adult development, which we discuss in Part 8.

SUMMARY AND KEY TERMS

Looking at the Life Course in Middle Age

Guidepost 1: How do developmental scientists approach the study of psychosocial development in middle adulthood?

- Developmental scientists view midlife psychosocial development both objectively, in terms of trajectories or pathways, and subjectively, in terms of people's sense of self and the way they actively construct their lives.
- Change and continuity must be seen in context and in terms of the whole life span.

Change at Midlife: Classic Theoretical Approaches

Guidepost 2: What do classic theorists have to say about psychosocial change in middle age?

- Although some theorists hold that personality is essentially formed by midlife, there is a growing consensus that midlife development shows change as well as stability. Change can be maturational (normative) or nonnormative.
- Humanistic theorists such as Maslow and Rogers saw middle age as an opportunity for positive change.

- Carl Jung held that men and women at midlife express previously suppressed aspects of personality. Two necessary tasks are giving up the image of youth and acknowledging mortality.
- Erikson's seventh psychosocial stage is generativity versus stagnation. Generativity can be expressed through parenting and grandparenting, teaching or mentorship, productivity or creativity, self-development, and "maintenance of the world." The "virtue" of this period is *care.*
- Vaillant and Levinson found major midlife shifts, or crises, in lifestyle or personality.
- The greater fluidity of the life cycle today has partly undermined the assumption of a "social clock."

individuation (588)

generativity versus stagnation (589)

generativity (589)

interiority (590)

The Self at Midlife: Issues and Themes

Guidepost 3: What issues concerning the self come to the fore during middle adulthood?

- Key psychosocial issues and themes during middle adulthood concern the existence of a midlife crisis, identity development (including gender identity), and psychological well-being.
- Research does not support a normative midlife crisis. It is more accurate to refer to a transition that often involves a midlife review, which may be a psychological turning point.
- According to Whitbourne's model, identity development is a process in which people continually confirm or revise their self-perceptions based on experience and feedback from others. Identity style can predict adaptation to the onset of aging.
- Generativity is an aspect of identity development. Current research on generativity finds it most prevalent at middle age but not universally so. Generativity may be affected by social roles and expectations and by individual characteristics.
- Narrative psychology describes identity development as a continuous process of constructing a life story.
- Research has found increasing "masculinization" of women and "feminization" of men at midlife, but this may be largely a cohort effect and may reflect the types of measures used. Research generally does *not* support Gutmann's proposed gender crossover.
- Research based on Ryff's six-dimensional scale has found that midlife is generally a period of positive mental health and well-being, though socioeconomic status is a factor.
- Limited research on social well-being suggests that it tends to be high in midlife but very low among a substantial minority. Marriage and SES are important factors.
- Generativity is related to psychological well-being in middle age. It may derive from involvement in multiple roles, but not necessarily in all roles equally.
- Much research suggests that for women the fifties—and even the sixties—may be a "prime time" of life.

midlife crisis (592)

midlife review (593)

identity process model (594)

identity assimilation (594)

identity accommodation (594)

identity style (594)

gender crossover (597)

Relationships at Midlife

Guidepost 4: What role do social relationships play in the lives of middle-aged people?

- Two theories of the changing importance of relationships are Kahn and Antonucci's social convoy theory and Laura Carstensen's socioemotional selectivity theory. According to both theories, social-emotional support is an important element in social interaction at midlife and beyond.
- Relationships at midlife are important to physical and mental health but also can present stressful demands.

social convoy theory (602)

socioemotional selectivity theory (602)

Consensual Relationships

Guidepost 5: Do marriages become happier or unhappier during the middle years, and does cohabitation at this stage of life provide benefits similar to those of marriage?

- Research on the quality of marriage suggests a dip in marital satisfaction during the years of child rearing, followed by an improved relationship after the children leave home.
- Cohabitation in midlife may negatively affect men's but not women's well-being.

Guidepost 6: How common is divorce at this time of life?

- Divorce at midlife is relatively uncommon but is increasing and can be stressful but life-changing. Marital capital tends to dissuade midlife divorce.
- Divorce today may be less threatening to well-being in middle age than in young adulthood.

marital capital (605)

Guidepost 7: How do midlife gay and lesbian relationships compare with heterosexual ones?

- Because many homosexuals delay coming out, at midlife they are often just establishing intimate relationships.
- Gay and lesbian couples tend to be more egalitarian than heterosexual couples but experience similar problems in balancing family and career commitments.

Guidepost 8: How do friendships fare during middle age?

- Middle-aged people tend to invest less time and energy in friendships than younger adults do but depend on friends for emotional support and practical guidance.
- Friendships may have special importance for homosexuals.

Relationships with Maturing Children

Guidepost 9: How do parent-child relationships change as children approach and reach adulthood?

- Parents of adolescents have to come to terms with a loss of control over their children's lives, and some parents do this more easily than others.
- The "emptying of the nest" is liberating for most women but may be stressful for couples whose identity is dependent on the parental role or those who now must face previously submerged marital problems.
- Middle-aged parents tend to remain involved with their adult children, and most are generally happy with the way their children turned out. Conflict may arise over grown children's need to be treated as adults and parents' continuing concern about them.
- Today, more young adults are delaying departure from their childhood home or are returning to it, sometimes with their own families. Adjustment tends to be smoother if the parents see the adult child as moving toward autonomy.

empty nest *(609)*

revolving door syndrome *(610)*

Other Kinship Ties

Guidepost 10: How do middle-aged people get along with parents and siblings?

- Relationships between middle-aged adults and their parents are usually characterized by a strong bond of affection. The two generations generally maintain frequent contact and offer and receive assistance. Aid usually flows from parents to children.
- As life lengthens, more and more aging parents become dependent for care on their middle-aged children. Acceptance of these dependency needs is the mark of filial maturity and may be the outcome of a filial crisis.
- The chances of becoming a caregiver to an aging parent increase in middle age, especially for women.
- Caregiving can be a source of considerable stress but also of satisfaction. Community support programs can help prevent caregiver burnout.
- Although siblings tend to have less contact at midlife than before and after, most middle-aged siblings remain in touch, and their relationships are important to well-being.

Guidepost 11: How has grandparenthood changed, and what roles do grandparents play?

- Most U.S. adults become grandparents in middle age and have an average of six grandchildren.
- Although most American grandparents today are less intimately involved in grandchildren's lives than in the past (often because of geographic separation), they can play an important role.
- Grandmothers tend to be more involved in "kinkeeping" than grandfathers.
- Divorce and remarriage of an adult child or of the grandparents themselves can affect grandparent-grandchild relationships.
- An increasing number of grandparents are raising grandchildren whose parents are unable to care for them. Raising grandchildren can create physical, emotional, and financial strains.

filial maturity *(612)*

filial crisis *(612)*

caregiver burnout *(613)*

sandwich generation *(613)*

kinship care *(619)*

PART 8

Linkups to look for

- Comprehension of health-related information can affect access to appropriate care.

- Exercise may improve mental alertness and morale.

- Blood flow to the brain can affect cognitive performance.

- Confidence, interest, and motivation can influence performance on intelligence tests.

- Conscientiousness and marital stability tend to predict long life.

- Cognitive appraisal of emotion-laden problems may help people develop coping strategies.

- Men who continue to work after age 65 tend to be in better health and better educated than those who retire, and they are more likely to view paid work as necessary to self-fulfillment.

- Physical limitations and cultural patterns affect older people's choice of living arrangements.

- People who can confide in friends tend to live longer.

Age 65 is the traditional entrance point for late adulthood, the last phase of life. Yet many adults at 65—or even 75 or 85—do not feel or act "old."

Individual differences become more pronounced in the later years, and "use it or lose it" becomes an urgent mandate. Most older adults enjoy good physical and mental health; people who keep physically and intellectually active can hold their own in most respects and even grow in competence. Physical and cognitive functioning in turn have psychosocial effects, often determining an older person's emotional state and whether she or he can live independently.

Late Adulthood

PREVIEW

CHAPTER 17

Physical and Cognitive Development in Late Adulthood

Most people are healthy and active, although health and physical abilities decline somewhat.

Slowing of processing time affects some aspects of functioning.

Most people are mentally alert.

Although intelligence and memory may deteriorate in some areas, most people find ways to compensate.

CHAPTER 18

Psychosocial Development in Late Adulthood

Retirement may offer new options for exploration of interests and activities.

People need to cope with personal losses and impending death as they seek to understand the meaning and purpose of their lives.

Relationships with family and close friends can provide emotional support.

Search for meaning in life assumes central importance.

CHAPTER 17

Physical and Cognitive Development in Late Adulthood

Why not look at these new years of life in terms of continued or new roles in society, another stage in personal or even spiritual growth and development?

Betty Friedan, *The Fountain of Age*, 1993

Focus
John Glenn, Space Pioneer

John Glenn

When John H. Glenn, Jr.* (b. 1921) blasted off from the Kennedy Space Center at Cape Canaveral on October 29, 1998, as a payload specialist on the shuttle *Discovery*, he became a space pioneer for the second time. In 1962, at the age of 40, Glenn had been the first American to orbit the earth. What made him a pioneer in 1998, when he next donned the orange jumpsuit, was that he was 77 years old—the oldest person ever to go into outer space.

Throughout his adult life, Glenn has won medals and set records. As a fighter pilot during the Korean War, he earned five Distinguished Flying Crosses. In 1957 he made the first cross-country supersonic jet flight. In 1962, when his Friendship 7 one-man space capsule circled the globe three times in less than five hours, he instantly became a national hero.

Glenn was elected a U.S. senator from Ohio in 1974 and served four terms. As a member of the Senate Special Committee on Aging, his interest in the subject of aging prompted him to offer himself as a human guinea pig on the nine-day *Discovery* mission.

As Glenn discovered while browsing through a medical textbook, the zero gravity conditions of space flight mimic at accelerated speed what normally happens to the body as it ages. Thus, Glenn reasoned, sending an older man into space might give scientists a thumbnail glimpse of processes of aging. By studying how weightlessness affected Glenn's bones, muscles, blood pressure, heart rates, balance, immune system, and sleep cycles, as well as his ability to bounce back after the flight as compared with younger astronauts, medical researchers could obtain information that might ultimately have broader applications. The data would not, of course, provide

*Sources of information about John Glenn were Cutler (1998), Eastman (1965), and articles from the *New York Times* and other newspapers.

conclusive findings but, as in any good case study, could generate hypotheses to be tested by further research with larger groups of participants. The flight also would have an important side effect: to demolish common stereotypes about aging.

Space travel is a challenge even for the youngest and most physically fit adults. Not everyone can be an astronaut; candidates have to pass stringent physical and mental tests. Because of his age, Glenn was held to even tougher physical standards. An avid weight-lifter and power-walker, he was in superb physical condition. He passed the examinations with flying colors and then spent nearly 500 hours in training.

It was a clear, cloudless October day when, after two suspenseful delays, the shuttle *Discovery* lifted off with what the countdown commentator called "a crew of six astronaut heroes and one American legend." Three hours and ten minutes later, 342 miles above Hawaii, a beaming Glenn repeated his own historic words broadcast thirty-six years before: "Zero G, and I feel fine." On November 7, *Discovery* touched down at Cape Canaveral, and John Glenn, though weak and wobbly, walked out of the shuttle on his own two feet. Within four days he had fully recovered his balance and was completely back to normal.

Glenn's achievement proved that, at 77, he still had "the right stuff." His heroic exploit captured public imagination around the world. As Stephen J. Cutler, president of the Gerontological Society of America, put it, ". . . it's hard to imagine a better demonstration of the capabilities of older persons and of the productive contributions they can make" (1998, p. 1).

John Glenn epitomizes a new view of aging, challenging the formerly pervasive picture of old age as a time of inevitable physical and mental decline. On the whole, people today are living longer and better than at any time in history. In the United States, older adults as a group are healthier, more numerous, and younger at heart than ever before. With improved health habits and medical care, it is becoming harder to draw the line between the end of middle adulthood and the beginning of late adulthood. Many 70-year-olds act, think, and feel much as 50-year-olds did a decade or two ago.

In this chapter we begin by sketching demographic trends among today's older population. We look at the increasing length and quality of life in late adulthood and at theories and research on causes of biological aging. We examine physical changes and health. We then turn to cognitive development: changes in intelligence and memory, the emergence of wisdom, and the prevalence of continuing education in late life. In Chapter 18, we look at adjustment to aging and at changes in lifestyles and relationships. What emerges is a picture not of "the elderly" but of individual human beings—some needy and frail, but most of them independent, healthy, and involved.

After you have read and studied this chapter, you should be able to answer each of the Guidepost questions that follow. Look for them again in the margins, where they point to important concepts throughout the chapter. To check your understanding of these Guideposts, review the end-of-chapter summary. Checkpoints located at periodic spots throughout the chapter will help you verify your understanding of what you have read.

1. How is today's older population changing?

2. How has life expectancy changed, and how does it vary?

3. What theories have been advanced for causes of aging, and what does research suggest about possibilities for extending the life span?

4. What physical changes occur during old age, and how do these changes vary among individuals?

5. What health problems are common in late adulthood, and what factors influence health at that time?

6. What mental and behavioral disorders do some older people experience?

7. What gains and losses in cognitive abilities tend to occur in late adulthood, and are there ways to improve older people's cognitive performance?

8. What educational opportunities can older adults pursue?

Guideposts for Study

Old Age Today

In Japan, old age is a mark of status. There, for example, travelers checking into hotels are often asked their age to ensure that they will receive proper deference.

In the United States, by contrast, aging is generally seen as undesirable. Unconscious stereotypes about aging, internalized in youth and reinforced for decades by societal attitudes, may become self-stereotypes, unconsciously affecting older people's own expectations about their behavior and often acting as self-fulfilling prophecies (Levy, 2003).

Today, efforts to combat **ageism**—prejudice or discrimination based on age—are making headway, thanks to the growing visibility of active, healthy older adults such as John Glenn. Reports about aging achievers appear frequently in the media. On television, older people are less often portrayed as doddering, cranky, and helpless and more often as level-headed, respected, and wise.

We need to look beyond distorted images of age to its true, multifaceted reality. What does today's older population look like?

The Graying of the Population

The global population is aging. In 2000, the number of persons age 60 or older was estimated at 605 million. By 2050, the percentage of older adults worldwide is expected, for the first time in history, to surpass the population of children ages 14 and under. Most of this rapid growth of the older population will be in less developed countries (Administration on Aging, 2003b; see Figure 17-1). Longer life spans result from economic growth, better nutrition, healthier lifestyles, improved control of infectious disease, safer water and sanitation facilities, and advances in science, technology, and medicine (Administration on Aging, 2003b; Kinsella & Velkoff, 2001).

In the United States, the graying of the population has several specific causes, among them high birthrates and high immigration rates during the early to mid-twentieth century and a trend toward smaller families, which has reduced the relative

What's Your View?

• What stereotypes about aging have you heard in the media and in everyday life?

ageism Prejudice or discrimination against a person (most commonly an older person) based on age.

Guidepost

1. How is today's older population changing?

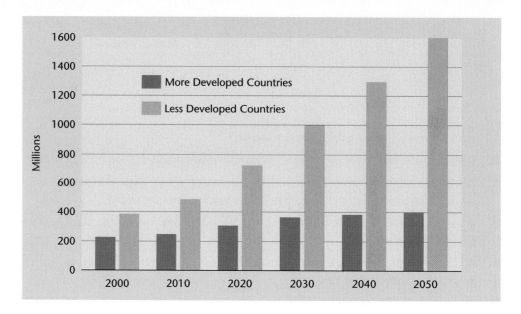

size of younger age groups. Since 1900, the proportion of Americans who are 65 and over has more than tripled, from 4.1 to 12.4 percent, still relatively low compared with most developed countries. The older population will swell after 2010, as the baby boom generation begin to turn 65. By 2030, nearly 20 percent of Americans—71.5 million—are likely to be 65 and over, twice as many as in 2000. The growth rate of the older population is projected to slow after 2030, when the last baby boomers reach 65 (Federal Interagency Forum on Aging-Related Statistics, 2004; see Figure 17-2).

The aged population itself is aging. Its fastest-growing segment consists of people in their eighties and older. In 2000, this age group constituted 17 percent of the world's elderly (Administration on Aging, 2001; Kinsella & Velkoff, 2001; U.S. Census Bureau, 2001) and 12 percent of the U.S. older adult population (Gist & Hetzel, 2004). In the United States, the proportion of people 85 years and older is almost 38 times larger than in 1900 and is projected to rise more rapidly after 2030 when baby boomers begin to move into this age group (Federal Interagency Forum on Aging-Related Statistics, 2004; refer to Figure 17-2).

Ethnic diversity among older adults is increasing. In 2003, more than 17 percent of older Americans were members of minority groups; by 2050, nearly 39 percent

Figure 17-2
United States population age 65 and over, 1900–2000 and 2010–2050, projected. (Source: Federal Interagency Forum on Aging-Related Statistics, 2004, p. 2.)

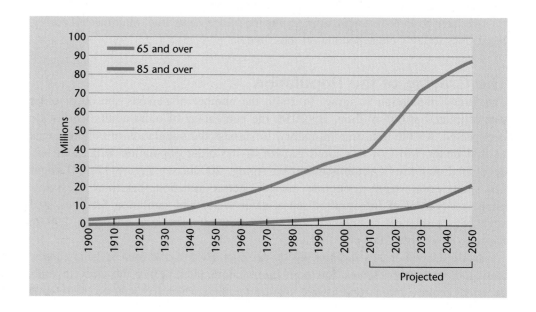

will be. The older Hispanic population is projected to grow most rapidly, from about 2 million in 2003 to 15 million in 2050 and will become the largest older minority population by 2028 (Federal Interagency Forum on Aging-Related Statistics, 2004).

Young Old to Oldest Old

The economic impact of a graying population depends on the proportion of that population which is healthy and able-bodied. In this regard, the trend is encouraging. Many problems that used to be considered an unavoidable part of old age are now understood to be due, not to aging itself, but to lifestyle factors or diseases.

Primary aging is a gradual, inevitable process of bodily deterioration that begins early in life and continues through the years, irrespective of what people do to stave it off. **Secondary aging** results from disease, abuse, and disuse—factors that are often within a person's control (Busse, 1987; J. C. Horn & Meer, 1987).

Health and longevity are closely linked to education and other aspects of socioeconomic status (Kinsella & Velkoff, 2001). In George Vaillant's 60-year longitudinal study of 237 Harvard students and 332 disadvantaged urban youth, the disadvantaged men's health deteriorated faster—unless they had finished college. Certain predictors of health and length of life were beyond the individual's control: parents' social class, cohesion of the childhood family, ancestral longevity, and childhood temperament. Other predictors, besides higher education, were at least partly controllable: alcohol abuse, smoking, body mass index, exercise, marital stability, and coping techniques (Vaillant & Mukamal, 2001).

Today, social scientists who specialize in the study of aging refer to three groups of older adults: the "young old," "old old," and "oldest old." Chronologically, *young old* generally refers to people ages 65 to 74, who are usually active, vital, and vigorous. The *old old,* ages 75 to 84, and the *oldest old,* ages 85 and above, are more likely to be frail and infirm and to have difficulty managing activities of daily living.

A more meaningful classification is by **functional age:** how well a person functions in a physical and social environment in comparison with others of the same chronological age. A person of 90 who is still in good health may be functionally younger than a person of 65 who is not. Thus we can use the term *young old* for the healthy, active majority of older adults (such as John Glenn), and *old old* for the frail, infirm minority, regardless of chronological age (Neugarten & Neugarten, 1987). Functional age may be related to *subjective age*—the age people feel themselves to be. In a nationally representative telephone survey, more than half of people ages 65 to 74 and one-third of those 75 and older said they considered themselves to be middle-aged or young (National Council on the Aging, 2002). Research in **gerontology,** the study of the aged and aging processes, and **geriatrics,** the branch of medicine concerned with aging, has underlined the need for support services, especially for the oldest old, many of whom have outlived their savings and cannot pay for their own care.

primary aging   Gradual, inevitable process of bodily deterioration throughout the life span.

secondary aging   Aging processes that result from disease and bodily abuse and disuse and are often preventable.

functional age   Measure of a person's ability to function effectively in his or her physical and social environment in comparison with others of the same chronological age.

gerontology   Study of the aged and the process of aging.

geriatrics   Branch of medicine concerned with processes of aging and medical conditions associated with old age.

Checkpoint
Can you . . .

✔ Discuss the causes and impact of the aging population?

✔ State two criteria for differentiating among the young old, old old, and oldest old?

PHYSICAL DEVELOPMENT

Longevity and Aging

How long will you live? Why do you have to grow old? Would you want to live forever? Human beings have been wondering about these questions for thousands of years.

The first question involves several related concepts. **Life expectancy** is the age to which a person born at a certain time and place is statistically likely to live, given

life expectancy   Age to which a person in a particular cohort is statistically likely to live (given his or her current age and health status), on the basis of average longevity of a population.

longevity Length of an individual's life.

life span The longest period that members of a species can live.

his or her current age and health status. Life expectancy is based on the average **longevity,** or actual length of life, of members of a population. Gains in life expectancy reflect declines in *mortality rates,* or death rates (the proportions of a total population or of certain age groups who die in a given year). The human **life span** is the longest period that members of our species can live.

The second question expresses an age-old theme: a yearning for a fountain or potion of youth. Behind this yearning is a fear, not so much of chronological age as of biological aging: loss of health and physical powers. The third question expresses a concern not just with length but with quality of life.

Trends and Factors in Life Expectancy

Guidepost

2. How has life expectancy changed, and how does it vary?

The graying of the population reflects a rapid rise in life expectancy. A baby born in the United States in 2003 could expect to live 77.6 years, according to preliminary data, about 30 years longer than a baby born in 1900 (Hoyert, Kung, & Smith, 2005) and three times as long as at the dawn of human history (Wilmoth, 2000). Worldwide, average life expectancy in 2002 was 65.2 years as compared with 46.5 years in 1950–1955 (WHO, 2003b). Such long life is unprecedented in the history of humankind (see Figure 17-3). Several noted gerontologists predict that, in the absence of major lifestyle changes, life expectancy in the United States may halt its upward trend and even decline during coming decades as a rise in obesity-related and infectious diseases offsets gains from medical advances (Olshansky et al., 2005; Preston, 2005).

Gender Differences Nearly all over the world, women typically live longer than men (Kinsella & Velkoff, 2001). Women's longer life has been attributed to their greater tendency to take care of themselves and to seek medical care, the higher level of social support they enjoy, and the greater biological vulnerability of males throughout life.

Women in the United States benefited more than men from the gains in life expectancy during the twentieth century. In 1900, women's life expectancy was only two years longer than men's. The gender gap widened to 7.8 years in 1979, mainly due to men's increased deaths from smoking-related illnesses (heart disease and lung cancer) and the reduction in women's deaths from childbirth. Since then it has narrowed to 5.3 years (Hoyert et al., 2005), largely because of proportionately larger increases in women's deaths from cancer, heart disease, and chronic lower respiratory disease (NCHS, 2004).

Because of the difference in life expectancy, older women in the United States outnumber older men by nearly 3 to 2 (Administration on Aging, 2003a), and this disparity increases with advancing age. By age 85, the ratio of women to men is more than 2 to 1 (Gist & Hetzel, 2004). Similar gender ratios exist internationally (Kinsella & Velkoff, 2001).

Regional and Ethnic Differences There is a vast gap in life expectancies between developed and developing countries. More than 6 out of 10 people in developed countries, but only 3 out of 10 in developing countries, live to their 70th birthdays. In the African nation of Sierra Leone, a woman born in 2002 could expect to live less than 36 years, as compared to 85 years for a woman in Japan (WHO, 2003b).

With increased longevity, multigenerational families—like these four generations of Arapaho women on a reservation in Wyoming—are becoming increasingly common, and it is not unusual for a great-grandmother to watch her great-grandchild grow up. Women, on average, have greater life expectancy than men. Today many older adults are healthy and able-bodied.

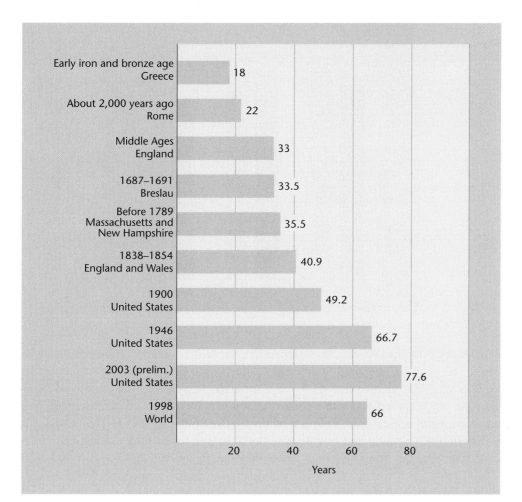

Figure 17-3
Changes in life expectancy from ancient to modern times. (Source: Adapted from Katchadourian, 1987; 1998 world data from WHO, 1998; preliminary 2003 U.S. data from Hoyert et al., 2005.)

The most dramatic improvements in developing regions have occurred in East Asia, where life expectancy grew from less than 45 years in 1950 to more than 72 years in 2000. In some places, though, life expectancy has *decreased*. Between 1987 and 1994 life expectancy for Russian men dropped by 7.3 years (Kinsella & Verloff, 2001), due largely to economic and social instability, high rates of alcohol and tobacco use, poor nutrition, depression, and deterioration of the health care system (Notzon et al., 1998). In parts of Africa hard hit by the scourge of AIDS, life expectancy may be at least 30 years lower by 2010 than otherwise expected (Kinsella & Velkoff, 2001).

Wide disparities also exist within the United States. On average, white Americans live about five years longer than African Americans, though this difference has narrowed with increasing life expectancies for both groups (Hoyert et al., 2005; NCHS, 2004; see Figure 17-4). As discussed in previous chapters, African Americans, especially men, are more vulnerable than white Americans to illness and death from infancy through middle adulthood. However, the gap begins to close in older adulthood, and by age 85 African Americans can expect slightly more remaining years than whites (Federal Interagency Forum on Aging-Related Statistics, 2004).

A new way to look at life expectancy is in terms of the number of years a person can expect to live in good health, free of

This elderly Japanese woman doing tai chi is a picture of health and serenity. Japan has the longest life expectancy among industrialized countries.

Figure 17-4

Life expectancy at birth in years, by sex and race: United States, 2003.

(Source: Hoyert et al., 2005. Note: Data are preliminary.)

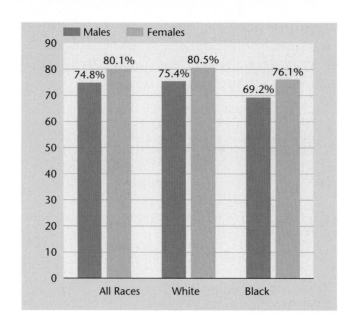

Checkpoint

✔ Summarize trends in life expectancy, including gender, regional, and ethnic differences?

Guidepost

3. What theories have been advanced for causes of aging, and what does research suggest about possibilities for extending the life span?

---

senescence Period of the life span marked by declines in physical functioning usually associated with aging; begins at different ages for different people.

disabilities. Among 191 countries, Japan has the longest *healthy* life expectancy at birth, 74.5 years. The United States ranks 24th, with a healthy life expectancy of 70 to 72.6 years for women and 67.5 years for men. Reasons for this relatively poor showing as compared with other industrialized nations include ill health among the urban poor and some ethnic groups; a relatively large proportion of HIV-related death and disability in young and middle adulthood; high rates of lung disease and coronary heart disease; and fairly high levels of violence (WHO, 2000).

Why People Age

Hope of further extending healthy life expectancy depends on our growing knowledge of what happens to the human body with the passage of time. What causes **senescence,** a period marked by obvious declines in body functioning associated with aging, and why does its onset vary from one person to another? For that matter, why do people age at all?

Most theories about biological aging fall into two categories (summarized in Table 17-1): *genetic-programming theories* and *variable-rate theories.*

Table 17-1 Theories of Biological Aging	
Genetic-Programming Theories	**Variable-Rate Theories**
Programmed senescence theory. Aging is the result of the sequential switching on and off of certain genes. Senescence is the time when the resulting age-associated deficits become evident.	*Wear-and-tear theory.* Cells and tissues have vital parts that wear out.
Endocrine theory. Biological clocks act through hormones to control the pace of aging.	*Free-radical theory.* Accumulated damage from oxygen radicals causes cells and eventually organs to stop functioning.
Immunological theory. A programmed decline in immune system functions leads to increased vulnerability to infectious disease and thus to aging and death.	*Rate-of-living theory.* The greater an organism's rate of metabolism, the shorter its life span.
Evolutionary theory. Aging is an evolved trait enabling members of a species to live only long enough to reproduce.	*Autoimmune theory.* Immune system becomes confused and attacks its own body cells.

Source: Adapted from NIH/NIA, 1993, p. 2.

Genetic-Programming Theories Genetic-programming theories hold that bodies age according to a normal developmental timetable built into the genes. Failure might come through *programmed senescence*: specific genes "switching off" before age-related losses (for example, in vision, hearing, and motor control) become evident. A study of worms found that fragmentation of *mitochondria,* minute organisms that generate energy for cell processes, prompts cells to self-destruct (Jagasia, Grote, Westermann, & Conradt, 2005), and such defects may be a major cause of aging (Holliday, 2004). Or the biological clock might act through genes that control *hormonal changes* or cause problems in the *immune system,* leaving the body vulnerable to infectious disease. Some physical changes, such as loss of muscle strength, accumulation of fat, and atrophy of organs, may be related to declines in hormonal activity (Lamberts, van den Beld, & van der Lely, 1997; Rudman et al., 1990). The efficiency of the immune system also declines with age (Holliday, 2004; Kiecolt-Glaser & Glaser, 2001).

One line of research suggests that the biological clock is regulated by a gradual shrinking of the *telomeres,* the protective tips of chromosomes, which shorten each time cells divide. This programmed erosion may eventually progress to the point where cell division stops (de Lange, 1998). A study of 143 normal, unrelated adults ages 60 and up found a link between shorter telomeres in blood DNA and early death, particularly from heart disease and infectious disease (Cawthon, Smith, O'Brien, Sivatchenko, & Kerber, 2003). A study of a family-based cohort in Belgium suggests that telomere length may be inherited via the X chromosome, which a son receives only from the mother (Nawrot, Staessen, Gardner, & Aviv, 2004). However, analysis of blood samples from 58 young and middle-aged mothers found that those caring for children with chronic disorders had shorter telomeres and lower levels of *telomerase,* an enzyme that enables sex chromosomes to repair their telomeres— changes typical of older women. These findings suggest that stress can affect telomere change (Epel et al., 2004).

A variant of genetic-programming theory is the *evolutionary theory of aging.* According to this theory, reproductive fitness is the primary aim of natural selection, and no reproductive purpose is served by putting genetic resources into life beyond reproductive age (Baltes, 1997). Thus, aging is an evolved trait enabling members of a species to live only long enough to reproduce. What, then, explains human beings' lengthening life span? One hypothesis is that life span lengthens when adults do not have to compete with their young for available resources (Travis, 2004). Another proposal is that humans continue to serve a reproductive purpose through continuing care of their young (Lee, 2003; Rogers, 2003).

Variable-Rate Theories Variable-rate theories, sometimes called *error theories,* view aging as a result of random processes that vary from person to person. In most variable-rate theories, aging involves damage due to chance errors in, or environmental assaults on, biological systems. Other variable-rate theories focus on internal processes such as **metabolism** (the process by which the body turns food and oxygen into energy), which may directly and continuously influence the rate of aging (NIA, 1993; Schneider, 1992).

Wear-and-tear theory holds that the body ages as a result of accumulated damage to the system at the molecular level (Hayflick, 2004; Holliday, 2004). As we mentioned in Chapter 3, the body's cells are constantly multiplying through cell division; this process is essential to balance the programmed death of useless or potentially dangerous cells and to keep organs and systems functioning properly. As people age, they are less able to repair or replace damaged parts. Internal and external stressors (including the accumulation of harmful materials, such as chemical by-products of metabolism) may aggravate the wearing-down process.

genetic-programming theories Theories that explain biological aging as resulting from a genetically determined developmental timetable.

variable-rate theories Theories explaining biological aging as a result of processes that vary from person to person and are influenced by both the internal and the external environment; sometimes called *error theories.*

metabolism Conversion of food and oxygen into energy.

free radicals Unstable, highly reactive atoms or molecules, formed during metabolism, which can cause internal bodily damage.

Free-radical theory focuses on harmful effects of **free radicals:** highly unstable oxygen atoms or molecules formed during metabolism, which react with and can damage cell membranes, cell proteins, fats, carbohydrates, and even DNA. Damage from free radicals accumulates with age; it has been associated with arthritis, muscular dystrophy, cataracts, cancer, late-onset diabetes, and neurological disorders such as Parkinson's disease (Stadtman, 1992; Wallace, 1992). Support for free-radical theory comes from research in which fruit flies, given extra copies of genes that eliminate free radicals, lived as much as one-third longer than usual (Orr & Sohal, 1994). Conversely, a strain of mice bred without a gene called *MsrA* that normally protects against free radicals had shorter-than-normal life spans (Moskovitz et al., 2001).

Rate-of-living theory suggests that the body can do just so much work, and that's all; the faster it works, the more energy it uses, and the faster it wears out. Thus, speed of metabolism, or energy use, determines length of life. Fish whose metabolism is lowered by putting them in cooler water live longer than they would in warm water (Schneider, 1992). (We present additional evidence for rate-of-living theory in the next section.)

Autoimmune theory suggests that an aging immune system can become "confused" and release antibodies that attack the body's own cells. This malfunction, called **autoimmunity,** is thought to be responsible for some aging-related diseases and disorders (Holliday, 2004). A part of the picture seems to be how cell death is regulated. Normally this process is genetically programmed. However, when mechanisms for destruction of unneeded cells malfunction, a breakdown in cell clean-out can lead to stroke damage, Alzheimer's disease, cancer, or autoimmune disease. Problems also may be caused by the death of *needed* cells (Aggarwal, Gollapudi, & Gupta, 1999).

Genetic-programming and variable-rate theories have practical implications. If human beings are programmed to age at a certain rate, they can do little to retard

autoimmunity Tendency of an aging body to mistake its own tissues for foreign invaders and to attack and destroy them.

Can regular exercise and other healthful habits stave off harmful effects of aging, or are people genetically programmed to age at a certain pace? Theorists differ, but it seems likely that both genetic and lifestyle factors play a part.

Practically Speaking

BOX 17-1

Do "Anti-Aging" Remedies Work?

Throughout much of human history people have sought elixirs or other means to stop or reverse the aging process (Binstock, 2004; Haber, 2004). In the 13th century, the British scientist Sir Roger Bacon suggested that "inhaling the breath of young virgins would rejuvenate very old men" (Hayflick, 1994). In 1889 Charles Edouard Brown-Sequard claimed that old men could regain strength and vigor by drinking an extract of dog's testicles. The explorer Ponce de León's search for the legendary Fountain of Youth ended in failure. Today, as the Baby Boom generation grows older, hucksters on the Internet and elsewhere tout anti-aging products and therapies—from yogurt cures to glandular extracts and hormone injections—that claim to have proven results (Perls, 2004).

Such claims have no scientific basis, according to a position paper issued by 51 top scientists in the field of aging (Olshansky, Hayflick, & Carnes, 2002b). As three major researchers in the field of aging concluded, "there is no empirical evidence to support the claim that aging in humans can be modified by any means, nor is there evidence that . . . anti-aging products extend the duration of life" (Olshansky, Hayflick, & Perls, 2004, p. 513).

The gerontologists warned that anti-aging products not only delude or defraud consumers, but may actually do physical harm. Dietary supplements carry "no guarantees of purity or potency, no established guidelines on dosage, and often no warnings" of possible interaction effects with other medications (Olshansky et al., 2002a, p. 94). Significant benefits for growth hormone treatments have not been demonstrated, and there can be negative side effects, such as excessive bone growth, carpal tunnel syndrome, joint pain and swelling, and possibly added cancer risk (Harman & Blackman, 2004; Olshansky et al., 2002a).

Although, as reported in this chapter, antioxidants such as vitamins C and E in the diet may help combat certain diseases, research on the reputed effects of antioxidant *supplements* in counteracting free radical activity is generally inconclusive (International Longevity Center, 2002; Olshansky et al., 2002a), and there can be adverse side effects. Large, randomized, controlled studies do not support their use by well-nourished older adults (Dangour, Sibson, & Fletcher, 2004).

The herbal extract ginkgo biloba, vitamin E, and other nonprescription supplements have been promoted as having positive effects on memory and cognition. Preliminary controlled studies on some of these substances have been mildly promising, but more rigorous research needs to be done on healthy older adults before sound conclusions can be reached (McDaniel, Maier, & Einstein, 2002). With regard to ginkgo biloba in particular, a review of the research found no basis for either conclusively supporting or refuting its reputed effects (Gold, Cahill, & Wenk, 2002). A six-week randomized placebo-controlled trial of more than 200 men and women ages 60 and up found no measurable benefits to memory or cognitive functioning in healthy adults (Solomon, Adams, Silver, Zimmer, & DeVeaux, 2002).

One reason it is difficult to test the efficacy of anti-aging products is that scientists have as yet found no clear biomarkers of aging—measurable biological changes that would apply to everyone at a given age. Thus there is no objective way to assess claims that a particular remedy can set back the biological clock (Butler et al., 2004; International Longevity Center, 2002; Olshansky et al., 2002a; Warner, 2004).

The fundamental assumption of the quest for anti-aging remedies is that something is wrong with aging—indeed, that aging is a disease. Actually, it is a natural part of life. Instead of looking for anti-aging remedies, gerontologists urge that more resources be devoted to research on "longevity medicine"—ways to combat specific diseases and thus prolong life (International Longevity Center, 2002; Olshansky et al., 2002a).

What's Your View?

Have you, or has someone you know, ever taken a remedy claimed to improve memory or combat other effects of aging? If so, what, if any, were the effects? How do you know?

Check It Out

For futher information on this topic, go to http://www.ilcusa .org. This is the Web site of the International Longevity Center at Mount Sinai School of Medicine, a nonprofit organization that coordinates research, policy, and education to help societies address issues of population aging and longevity. The center has collaborating partners in Japan, the United Kingdom, France, and the Dominican Republic.

the process except to try to alter the appropriate genes. If, on the other hand, aging is variable, then sound lifestyle and health practices (like John Glenn's exercise regimen) may influence it. However, there is *no* evidence to support the profusion of commercial "anti-aging" remedies now on the market (International Longevity Center, 2002; Olshansky, Hayflick, & Carnes, 2002a, 2002b; Olshansky, Hayflick, & Perls, 2004; see Box 17-1).

It seems likely that several of these theoretical perspectives offer parts of the truth (Holliday, 2004). Controllable environmental and lifestyle factors may interact with genetic factors to determine how long a person lives and in what condition. In a study of 1,402 adults of various ages, genetic factors explained 57 percent of the variance in biological age of bone tissue. The remaining variance was presumably environmentally influenced (Karasik, Hannan, Cupples, Felson, & Kiel, 2004).

A current theory incorporating both evolutionary and variable-rate theories (Hayflick, 2004) is that natural selection has resulted in energy resources sufficient only to maintain the body until reproduction. After reproduction, there is insufficient energy left to continue to maintain the molecular integrity of body cells and systems. As time goes on, these deteriorate randomly, beyond the body's capacity to repair them, resulting in increased vulnerability to disease and death. Although everyone goes through the same aging process, its rate varies from cell to cell, tissue to tissue, and organ to organ.

How Far Can the Life Span Be Extended?

The concept of *prolongevity*—that people can control the length and quality of their lives—goes back to Luigi Cornaro, a nobleman of the 16th century Italian Renaissance (Haber, 2004). Cornaro practiced moderation in all things, and he lived to be 98—close to what scientists once considered the upper limit of the human life span. Today that limit has been greatly exceeded. On February 28, 2005, when Maria Olivia da Silva of Astorga, Brazil, celebrated her 125th birthday, she became the world's oldest known living person as well as the record-holder for the longest documented human life span (Lehman, 2005). That record previously was held by Jeanne Calment of France, who died in 1997 at the age of 122. Is it possible for human beings to live even longer?

Until recently, **survival curves**—percentages of people or animals who live to various ages—supported the idea of a biological limit to the life span, with more and more members of a species dying each year as they approach it. Although many people were living longer than in the past, the curves still ended around age 100; this suggested that, regardless of health and fitness, the maximum life span is not much higher.

Leonard Hayflick (1974) found that human cells will divide in the laboratory no more than fifty times; this is called the **Hayflick limit,** and it has been shown to be genetically controlled (Schneider, 1992). If, as Hayflick (1981) suggested, cells go through the same process in the body as in a laboratory culture, there might be a biological limit to the life span of human cells, and therefore of human life—a limit Hayflick estimated at 110 years.

However, the pattern appears to change at very old ages. In Sweden, for example, the maximum life span increased from about 101 years in the 1860s to 108 years in the 1990s, mainly due to reductions in death rates after age 70 (Wilmoth, Deegan, Lundstrom, & Horiuchi, 2000). Furthermore, death rates actually *decrease* after 100 (Coles, 2004). People at 110 are no more likely to die in a given year than people in their eighties (Vaupel et al., 1998). In other words, people hardy enough to reach a certain age are likely to go on living a while longer. This is why life expectancy at 65, for example, is greater than life expectancy at birth (Administration on Aging, 2003a; NCHS, 2004). From this and other demographic evidence, at least one researcher suggests that there is no fixed limit on the human life span (Wilmoth, 2000).

Others believe that genetics plays at least a partial role in human longevity (Coles, 2004) and that the idea of an exponential increase in the human life span is

Maria Olivia da Silva of Astorga, Brazil, is the world's oldest known living person. Born in 1880, she celebrated her 125th birthday on February 28, 2005.

survival curves Curves, plotted on a graph, showing percentages of a population that survive at each age level.

Hayflick limit Genetically controlled limit, proposed by Hayflick, on the number of times cells can divide in members of a species.

unrealistic (Holliday, 2004). Gains in life expectancy since the 1970s have come from reductions in age-related diseases, such as heart disease, cancer, and stroke, and further gains will be far more difficult to achieve unless scientists find ways to modify the basic processes of aging (Hayflick, 2004; International Longevity Center, 2002; Olshansky, Carnes, & Desesquelles, 2001; Olshansky, Hayflick, & Carnes, 2002a)—a feat some gerontologists consider impossible (Hayflick, 2004; Holliday, 2004).

Animal research, however, is challenging the idea of an unalterable biological limit for each species. Scientists have extended the healthy life spans of worms, fruit flies, and mice through slight genetic mutations (Ishii et al., 1998; T. E. Johnson, 1990; Kolata, 1999; Lin, Seroude, & Benzer, 1998; Parkes et al., 1998; Pennisi, 1998). Such research suggests the possibility of delayed senescence and a significant increase in the average and maximum life span (Arking, Novoseltsev, & Novoseltseva, 2004). In human beings, of course, genetic control of a biological process may be far more complex. Because no single gene or process seems responsible for senescence and the end of life, we are less likely to find genetic "quick fixes" for human aging (Holliday, 2004; Olshansky et al., 2002a).

One promising line of research—inspired by rate-of-living theories that view the speed of metabolism, or energy use, as the crucial determinant of aging—is on dietary restriction (International Longevity Center, 2002). Drastic caloric reduction (but still including all necessary nutrients) has been found to greatly extend life in worms and fish—in fact, in nearly all species on which it has been tried (Heilbronn & Ravussin, 2003; Weindruch & Walford, 1988). A modest caloric reduction—as little as 10 percent—has increased rodent survival by about 24 percent (Duffy et al., 2001). In a longitudinal laboratory experiment with 117 rhesus monkeys, 8 were fed only enough to maintain a normal lean weight while the others fed at will. After 25 years, the calorically restricted monkeys had a median survival age 7 years longer than their peers and showed less evidence of age-related disease (Bodkin, Alexander, Ortmeyer, Johnson, & Hansen, 2003).

Systematic dietary restriction experiments on human beings are probably impractical because of their long life span, but a prospective epidemiological study of 1,915 healthy, nonsmoking middle-aged to older Japanese American men on the island of Oahu, Hawaii provides intriguing results. The men recorded what they ate each day for 36 years. Men who consumed at least 15 percent less than the group average had the lowest risk of death, but a caloric intake below 50 percent of the average increased the risk of death (Willcox et al., 2004).

Is it caloric reduction that causes long life, or some related factor? Among 700 healthy men with normal diets, those who lived longest showed three physiological markers associated with long-term caloric restriction in monkeys: low body temperature, low blood insulin levels, and high blood levels of dehydroepiandrosterone sulfate (DHEAS), a steroid hormone that diminishes during normal aging. This suggests that life might be lengthened without caloric restriction through treatments that would affect these markers directly (Roth et al., 2002).

If human beings someday realize the age-old dream of a fountain of youth, some gerontologists fear a rise in age-related diseases and disabling infirmities (Banks & Fossel, 1997; Cassel, 1992; Stock & Callahan, 2004; Treas, 1995). However, life-extension studies in animals and research on human centenarians suggest that such fears may be unwarranted and that fatal diseases would come very near the end of a longer life (International Longevity Center, 2002; see Box 17-2).

What's Your View?

- If you could live as long as you wanted to, how long would you choose to live? What factors would affect your answer?

- Which would you rather do: live a long life, or live a shorter time with a higher quality of life?

Checkpoint
Can you . . .

✔ Compare two kinds of theories of biological aging, their implications and supporting evidence?

✔ Describe two lines of research on extension of life and discuss the import of their findings?

BOX 17-2

Digging Deeper
Centenarians

At 98, Ella May Stumpe of Frederick, Maryland, taught herself to use Microsoft software. Five years later, by 103, she had written several books on her computer, one of them entitled *My Life at 100.* Stumpe credited her longevity to a moderate way of life, including the nonacidic diet she adopted after having an ulcer at 30 (Ho, 1999).

At the turn of the twentieth century in the United States only about one person in 100,000 was 100 years or older. Today about 10 times as many have reached that age (Terry, Wilcox, McCormick, & Perls, 2004). In 2002, the U.S. population included 50,364 centenarians—a 35 percent increase since 1990 (Administration on Aging, 2003a). The centenarian population also has increased dramatically in Europe (Kinsella & Velkoff, 2001), particularly in Switzerland, where the likelihood of reaching 100 rose from 1.5 per 10,000 people born in 1860 to 38.5 per 10,000 born in 1900 (Benloucif, Zee et al., 2005).

Research on the exploding centenarian population is challenging long-established beliefs about health and aging and about the limits of human life, once thought to be about 100 years. As mentioned in this chapter, mortality rates have been shown to decline after age 100 (Coles, 2004; Vaupel et al., 1998). However, very few people live beyond 110 (Coles, 2004). Studies of these "supercentenarians"—of whom there were reliably known to be only 45 worldwide in 2003, all of them extremely frail—suggest that without some unforeseen medical breakthrough the limit on human life will not go much higher than 125 years (Coles, 2004).

Leading gerontologists have warned that a longer lifespan will mean an increasing number of people with chronic disease. Instead, growing evidence supports the *compression-of-morbidity model*—the hypothesis that, in persons who approach the limits of the human life span, serious illness occurs only in a brief period near the end of life. An Okinawa woman who died at age 100 of

At 104, Anna Grupe of Sherburn, Minnesota, continued to write stories about her life and her family. The United States may have the largest proportion of centenarians among developed countries. Most are women, and a surprising number are healthy and active.

bronchial pneumonia typifies this model. She was remarkably healthy until age 97. Only in the three years before her death did she experience a series of falls and fractures, show apparent cognitive impairment, become fully dependent on caregiving, and develop repeated respiratory infections (Bernstein et al., 2004).

A study of 424 centenarians in the United States and Canada found three alternative patterns in their health histories. Nearly 1 in 5 (32 percent of the men and 15 percent of the women) were *escapers*—they were disease-free. *Survivors* (24 percent of the men and 43 percent of the women) had been diagnosed with an age-associated illness (stroke, heart disease, cancer, hypertension, osteoporosis, thyroid disorder, Parkinson's disease, diabetes,

Guidepost

4. What physical changes occur during old age, and how do these changes vary among individuals?

Watch the video on "Physical Changes in Later Adulthood" in Chapter 17 of your CD to hear one woman describe how she is experiencing these changes.

Physical Changes

Some physical changes typically associated with aging are obvious to a casual observer. Older skin tends to become paler, splotchier, and less elastic; and, as fat and muscle shrink, the skin may wrinkle. Varicose veins of the legs become more common. The hair on the head turns white and becomes thinner, and body hair becomes sparser.

Older adults become shorter as the disks between their spinal vertebrae atrophy. Thinning of the bones may cause a "dowager's hump" at the back of the neck, especially in women with osteoporosis. In addition, the chemical composition of the bones changes, creating a greater risk of fractures. Less visible changes affect internal organs and body systems; the brain; and sensory, motor, and sexual functioning.

Organic and Systemic Changes

Changes in organic and systemic functioning are highly variable, both among and within individuals. Some body systems decline rapidly, others hardly at all (see Figure 17-5). Aging, together with chronic stress, can depress immune function, making older people more susceptible to respiratory infections (Kiecolt-Glaser &

—continued

chronic obstructive pulmonary disease, or cataracts) before age 80 but had survived it. The largest category, *delayers* (44 percent of the men and 42 percent of the women), had managed to delay the onset of age-related disease until age 80 or later. Remarkably, about one-half of both male and female centenarians in this study were free of heart disease, stroke, and cancer (other than skin cancer), the three most common causes of mortality in old age. Altogether, 87 percent of the men and 83 percent of the women had escaped or delayed these diseases (Evert, Lawler, Bogan, & Perls, 2003).

What might explain this picture? One possibility is exceptional genes, which may offer protection against dread diseases of old age, such as cancer and Alzheimer's (Silver et al., 2001). Centenarians tend to be relatively free of genes linked to age-related fatal diseases and premature death. A region on chromosome 4, shared by many of the centenarians studied, has been linked to exceptionally long life (Perls, Kunkel & Puca, 2002a, 2002b; Puca et al., 2001) and also to healthy aging (Reed, Dick, Uniacke, Foroud, & Nichols, 2004). Centenarians—and supercentenarians—tend to come from long-lived families (Coles, 2004). Also, sons and daughters of centenarians tend to show marked delays in the age of onset of cardiovascular disease, diabetes, hypertension, and stroke, though not of other age-related diseases (Terry, Wilcox, McCormick, & Perls, 2004).

Genetic factors emerged strongly in a study of 41 living centenarians in eight New England towns. Siblings of centenarians tended to be centenarians as well (Perls, Wilmoth et al., 2002). Nine out of 10 of the Massachusetts centenarians had been cognitively and physically independent up to an average age of 92, and 3 out of 4 at an average age of 95 (Hitt, Young-Xu, & Perls, 1999). One out of 3 had no diagnosable dementia (Silver, Jilinskaia, & Perls, 2001). These centenarians varied widely in educational level, socioeconomic status, religion, ethnicity, and diet patterns;

some were vegetarians, while others ate a lot of saturated fats. Some were athletes and some did no strenuous activity. However, few were obese, and heavy smoking was rare among them. A disproportionate number were never-married women; and among those who were mothers, a disproportionate number had had children after age 40. The only shared personality trait was the ability to manage stress (Perls, Alpert, & Fretts, 1997; Perls, Hutter-Silver, & Lauerman, 1999; Silver, Bubrick, Jilinskaia, & Perls, 1998).

Perhaps this quality is exemplified by Anna Morgan of Rehoboth, Massachusetts. Before her death at 101, she made her own funeral arrangements. "I don't want my children to be burdened with all this," she explained to the researchers. "They're old, you know" (Hilts, 1999, p. D7).

What's Your View?

Have you ever known someone who lived past 100? If so, to what did that person attribute his or her longevity? Did he or she have family members who also were long-lived?

Check It Out

For more information on this topic, go to http://www.bumc.bu .edu/Dept/Content.aspx?DepartmentID=361&PageID=5749. This is a page on the Web site of Boston University School of Medicine, which gives background information on centenarians and links to information about the New England Centenarians Study. Or visit http://www.grg.org/calment.html. This Web site contains lists of supercentenarians currently alive, as well as information on past supercentenarians recorded throughout history.

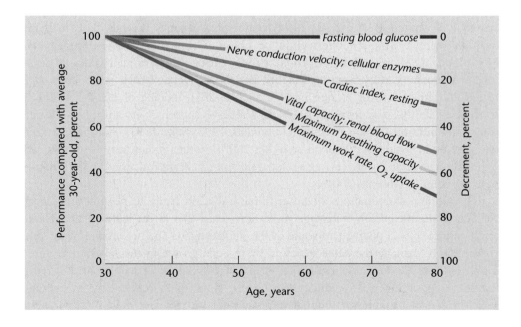

Figure 17-5

Declines in organ functioning. Differences in functional efficiency of various internal body systems are typically very slight in young adulthood but widen by old age.

(Source: Katchadourian, 1987.)

Glaser, 2001) and less likely to ward them off (Koivula, Sten, & Makela, 1999). The digestive system, on the other hand, remains relatively efficient. The rhythm of the heart tends to become slower and more irregular. Deposits of fat accumulate around the heart and may interfere with functioning, and blood pressure often rises.

reserve capacity Ability of body organs and systems to put forth four to ten times as much effort as usual under acute stress; also called *organ reserve.*

Another important change that may affect health is a decline in **reserve capacity** (or *organ reserve*), a backup capacity that helps body systems function to their utmost limits in times of stress. With age, reserve levels tend to drop, and many older people cannot respond to extra physical demands as well as before. A person who used to be able to shovel snow and then go skiing afterward may now exhaust the heart's capacity just by shoveling or may have to stop shoveling and rest periodically.

Still, many normal, healthy older adults like John Glenn barely notice changes in systemic functioning. Many activities do not require peak performance to be enjoyable and productive. By pacing themselves, most older adults can do almost anything they need and want to do.

The Aging Brain

In normal, healthy older people, changes in the brain are generally modest; they make little difference in functioning (Kemper, 1994) and vary considerably from one person to another (Deary et al., 2003; Selkoe, 1991, 1992). After age 30, the brain typically loses weight, at first slightly, then more rapidly, until, by age 90, it may have lost up to 10 percent of its weight. This weight loss has been attributed to a loss of *neurons* (nerve cells) in the *cerebral cortex,* the part of the brain that handles most cognitive tasks. Newer research suggests that the cause is not a widespread reduction in the *number* of neurons, but rather a shrinkage in neuronal *size* due to loss of connective tissue: axons, dendrites, and synapses (refer back to Chapter 4). This shrinkage seems to begin earliest and to advance most rapidly in the frontal cortex, which is important to memory and high-level cognitive functioning (West, 1996; Wickelgren, 1996). Along with loss of brain matter may come a gradual slowing of the central nervous system, which may affect both physical coordination and cognition.

Formation of lesions in the white matter of the axons, perhaps due in part to hypertension, can reduce cognitive performance. In a longitudinal study of 83 Scotch men and women born in 1921, white matter abnormalities contributed about 14 percent to variances in cognitive function at age 78, independent of mental functioning in early life (Deary, Leaper, Murray, Staff, & Whalley, 2003).

Certain brain structures, including the cerebral cortex, shrink more rapidly in men than in women (Coffey et al., 1998). but cerebral atrophy is more likely to occur early in women who are overweight or obese (Gustafson, Lissner, Bengtsson, Björkelund, & Skoog, 2004). Cortical atrophy also occurs more rapidly in less-educated people (Coffey, Saxton, Ratcliff, Bryan, & Lucke, 1999). It has been suggested that education (or related factors, such as high income or decreased likelihood of disability) may increase the brain's reserve capacity—its ability to tolerate potentially injurious effects of aging (Friedland, 1993; Satz, 1993). Aerobic exercise can slow brain tissue loss (Colcombe et al., 2003). In rats, a diet heavy in fruits and vegetables can retard or reverse age-related declines in brain function (Galli, Shukitt-Hale, Youdim, & Joseph, 2002).

Postmortem examinations of brain tissue collected from 30 people ages 26 to 106 found significant DNA damage in certain genes that affect learning and memory in most very old people and some of the middle-aged. The researchers were able to selectively damage the same genes in brain cells grown in the laboratory, mimicking changes in the aging brain (Lu et al., 2004). An experiment with 48 aging beagles suggests that such changes can be prevented or minimized by an antioxidant-fortified diet combined with regular physical activity and mental stimulation.

Dogs that received either the dietary or environmental intervention performed better on cognitive tests than a control group, but dogs that received both interventions did best (Milgram et al., 2005).

Not all changes in the brain are destructive. Researchers have discovered that older brains can grow new nerve cells—something once thought impossible. Evidence has been found of cell division in a section of the hippocampus, a portion of the brain involved in learning and memory (Eriksson et al., 1998). In adult mice, such newly generated hippocampal cells matured into functional neurons (Van Praag et al., 2002). These discoveries raise hope that scientists may eventually find ways to use the brain's own restorative potential to cure such disorders as Alzheimer's disease.

Sensory and Psychomotor Functioning

Individual differences in sensory and motor functioning increase with age. Some older people experience sharp declines; others find their abilities virtually unchanged. One 80-year-old man can hear every word of a whispered conversation; another cannot hear the doorbell. One 70-year-old woman runs five miles a day; another cannot walk around the block. Impairments tend to be more severe among the old old. Visual and hearing problems may deprive them of social relationships and independence (Desai, Pratt, Lentzner, & Robinson, 2001; O'Neill, Summer, & Shirey, 1999), and motor impairments may limit everyday activities.

New technologies to improve vision and hearing can help many older adults avoid sensory limitations. Table 17-2 lists ways in which inventors are redesigning the physical environment to meet the needs of an aging population.

Checkpoint
Can you . . .

✔ Summarize common changes and variations in systemic functioning during late life?

✔ Identify a likely source of loss of brain weight, and explain the importance of regenerative changes in the brain?

Table 17-2 Coming Environmental Changes for an Aging Population*

Aids to Vision
- Brighter reading lights
- Larger-print books
- Carpeted or textured (not shiny) floors
- Spoken as well as visual signals: "talking" exit signs, appliances that speak up when they get hot, cameras that announce when the light is too low, automobiles that warn of an impending collision

Aids to Hearing
- Public address systems and recordings engineered to an older adult's auditory range
- Park benches and couches angled or clustered so older adults can communicate face-to-face

Aids to Manual Dexterity
- Comb and brush extenders
- Stretchable shoelaces
- Velcro tabs instead of buttons
- Lightweight motorized pot-and-pan scrubbers and garden tools
- Tap turners on faucets
- Foot mops that eliminate bending
- Voice-activated telephone dialers
- Long-handled easy-grip zippers
- Contoured eating utensils

Aids to Mobility and Safety in the Home
- Ramps instead of stairs
- Levers instead of knobs
- Lower closet shelves
- Lower windows for people who sit a lot
- Regulators to keep tap water from scalding
- "Soft tubs" to prevent slips, add comfort, and keep bath water from cooling too fast
- Sensors to monitor the movements of an older person living alone and alert friends or relatives to any unusual pattern

Aids to Pedestrian Safety
- Street lights that change more slowly
- Traffic islands to let slow walkers pause and rest
- Lower bus platforms and steps

Aids to Safe Driving
- Clearer road signs and pavement markings
- Automobiles programmed to operate windows, radio, heater, lights, wipers, and even the ignition by verbal commands
- Windshields that automatically adjust their tint to weather and light conditions and are equipped with large, liquid-crystal displays of speed and other information, so that older drivers need not take their eyes off the road and readjust their focus

Temperature Adjustments
- Homes and hotels with heated furniture
- Thermostats in each room
- Heated clothing
- Heat-producing foods

*Many of these innovations are already in place; others are likely to occur in the near future.

Sources: Dychtwald & Flower, 1990; Eisenberg, 2001; Staplin, Lococo, Byington, & Harkey, 2001a, 2001b.

Vision and Hearing   Eighteen percent of older people in the United States say they have trouble seeing (Federal Interagency Forum on Aging-Related Statistics, 2004). They may have difficulty with depth or color perception or with such daily activities as reading, sewing, shopping, and cooking (Desai et al., 2001). Losses in visual contrast sensitivity can cause difficulty reading very small or very light print (Akutsu, Legge, Ross, & Schuebel, 1991; Kline & Scialfa, 1996). Vision problems can cause accidents and falls. Approximately 1.8 million community-dwelling older adults report difficulty with bathing, dressing, and walking around the house, in part because they are visually impaired (Desai et al., 2001).

Older eyes need more light to see, are more sensitive to glare, and may have trouble locating and reading signs; thus driving may become hazardous, especially at night (D. W. Kline et al., 1992; D. W. Kline & Scialfa, 1996). Among 2,085 men and women ages 55 and older in Sonoma, California, nearly 47 percent reported that they limit or avoid driving. The most frequently cited reason, especially for women, was vision problems (Ragland, Satariano, & MacLeod, 2004; Satariano, MacLeod, Cohn, & Ragland, 2004).

Moderate visual problems often can be helped by corrective lenses, medical or surgical treatment, or changes in the environment, such as those listed in Table 17-3. However, nearly 1 in 5 adults age 70 or older has visual losses that cannot be corrected by prescription eyewear (Desai et al., 2001).

Most visual impairments (including blindness) are caused by cataracts, age-related macular degeneration, glaucoma, or diabetic retinopathy (a complication of diabetes not related to age). More than half of people over 65 develop **cataracts,** cloudy or opaque areas in the lens of the eye that eventually cause blurred vision (Schaumberg et al., 2004). Surgery to remove cataracts is usually successful and is one of the most common operations among older Americans. **Age-related macular degeneration,** in which the center of the retina gradually loses the ability to sharply distinguish fine details, is the leading cause of visual impairment in older adults. In some cases, treatments such as laser surgery, photodynamic therapy, and antioxidant and zinc supplements can prevent further vision loss (Foundation Fighting Blindness, 2005).

Glaucoma is irreversible damage to the optic nerve caused by increased pressure in the eye; if left untreated it can cause blindness. In 1995, 8 percent of the elderly population reported having glaucoma, but many more may be unaware they have it. African Americans are twice as likely to develop glaucoma as white people (Desai et al., 2001). Early treatment can lower elevated pressure in the eye and delay the onset of the condition (Heijl et al., 2002).

cataracts   Cloudy or opaque areas in the lens of the eye, which cause blurred vision.

age-related macular degeneration   Condition in which the center of the retina gradually loses its ability to discern fine details; leading cause of irreversible visual impairment in older adults.

glaucoma   Irreversible damage to the optic nerve caused by increased pressure in the eye.

In age-related macular degeneration, the leading cause of visual impairment in older adults, the center of the regina gradually loses the ability to distinguish details. (Left) An image as seen by a person with normal vision. (Right) The same image as seen by a person with macular degeneration.

The hearing aid in this man's ear makes it easier for him to understand his young granddaughter's high-pitched speech. About one-third of 65- to 74-year-olds and one-half of those 85 and older have some degree of hearing loss that interferes with everyday activities.

Nearly 47 percent of older men and 30 percent of older women in the United States report having trouble hearing. Hearing impairments increase with age (Federal Interagency Forum on Aging-Related Statistics, 2004), affecting 60 percent of people ages 85 and over (Federal Interagency Forum on Aging-Related Statistics, 2004), whites more than blacks (Lee, Gómez-Marín, Lam, & Zheng, 2004). About 17 percent of persons 85 and older are totally deaf (Desai et al., 2001). Hearing loss may contribute to a false perception of older people as distractible, absentminded, and irritable and tends to have a negative impact on the well-being, not only of the impaired person, but also of his or her spouse or partner (Wallhagen, Strawbridge, Shema, & Kaplan, 2004). It also may contribute to difficulty in remembering what others say (Wingfield, Tun, & McCoy, 2005).

Hearing aids can help but can be hard to adjust to, since they tend to magnify background noises as well as the sounds a person wants to hear. Only 10 percent of older women and 19 percent of older men report having worn a hearing aid (Federal Interagency Forum on Aging-Related Statistics, 2004). Another device for assisting hearing is a built-in telephone amplifier (Desai et al., 2001).

Strength, Endurance, Balance, and Reaction Time Adults generally lose about 10 to 20 percent of their strength up to age 70 and more after that. Walking endurance declines more consistently with age, especially among women, than some other aspects of fitness, such as flexibility (Van Heuvelen, Kempen, Ormel, & Rispens, 1998). Declines in muscle strength and power may result from a combination of natural aging, decreased activity, and disease (Barry & Carson, 2004).

These losses seem to be partly reversible. In controlled studies with people in their sixties to nineties, weight training, power training, or resistance training programs lasting eight weeks to two years increased muscle strength, size, and mobility; speed, endurance, and leg muscle power; and spontaneous physical activity (Ades, Ballor, Ashikaga, Utton, & Nair, 1996; Fiatarone et al., 1990, 1994; Fiatarone, O'Neill, & Ryan, 1994; Foldvari et al., 2000; McCartney, Hicks, Martin, & Webber, 1996). Even low-impact, moderate-intensity aerobic dance and exercise training can increase peak oxygen uptake, leg muscle strength, and vigor (Engels, Drouin, Zhu, & Kazmierski, 1998). Although these gains may result to some extent from improvements in muscle mass, the primary factor in older adults is likely to be a

Table 17-3	Safety Checklist for Preventing Falls in the Home
Stairways, hallways, and pathways	Free of clutter
	Good lighting, especially at top of stairs
	Light switches at top and bottom of stairs
	Tightly fastened handrails on both sides and full length of stairs
	Carpets firmly attached and not frayed; rough-textured or abrasive strips to secure footing
Bathrooms	Grab bars conveniently located inside and outside of tubs and showers and near toilets
	Nonskid mats, abrasive strips, or carpet on all surfaces that may get wet
	Night lights
Bedrooms	Telephones and night lights or light switches within easy reach of beds
All living areas	Electrical cords and telephone wires out of walking paths
	Rugs and carpets well secured to floor
	Inspect for hazards, such as exposed nails and loose threshold trim
	Furniture and other objects in familiar places and not in the way; rounded or padded table edges
	Couches and chairs proper height to get into and out of easily

Source: Adapted from NIA, 1993.

training-induced adaptation in the brain's ability to activate and coordinate muscular activity (Barry & Carson, 2004).

This evidence of *plasticity* in older adults is especially important because people whose muscles have atrophied are more likely to suffer falls and fractures and to need help with tasks of day-to-day living. One reason for older adults' susceptibility to falls is reduced sensitivity of the receptor cells that give the brain information about the body's position in space—information needed to maintain balance. Slower reflexes and impaired depth perception also contribute to loss of balance (Agency for Healthcare Research and Quality and CDC, 2002; Neporent, 1999).

Many falls and fractures are preventable by boosting muscle strength, balance, and gait speed (Agency for Healthcare Research and Quality and CDC, 2002) and by eliminating hazards commonly found in the home (Gill, Williams, Robison, & Tinetti, 1999; NIH Consensus Development Panel, 2001; see Table 17-3). Exercises designed to improve balance can restore body control and postural stability. The traditional Chinese practice of *tai chi* is especially effective in maintaining balance, strength, and aerobic capacity (Li, Harmer, Fisher, & McAuley, 2004).

Sleep

Older people tend to sleep less and dream less than before. Their hours of deep sleep are more restricted, and they may awaken more easily because of physical problems or exposure to light (Czeisler et al., 1999; Lamberg, 1997). However, the assumption that sleep problems are normal in old age can be dangerous; chronic *insomnia*, or sleeplessness, can be a symptom or, if untreated, a forerunner of depression.

Cognitive-behavioral therapy (staying in bed only when asleep, getting up at the same time each morning, and learning about false beliefs pertaining to sleep needs) has produced long-term improvement with or without drug treatment (Morin, Colecchi, Stone, Sood, & Brink, 1999; Reynolds, Buysse, & Kupfer, 1999). In a 2-week study of 12 older men and women, 90 minutes daily of mild to moderate physical activity interspersed with socializing improved cognitive functioning and self-perceived sleep quality (Benloucif, Orbeta et al., 2004).

Sexual Functioning

The most important factor in maintaining sexual functioning is consistent sexual activity over the years. A healthy man who has been sexually active generally can continue some form of active sexual expression into his seventies or eighties. Women are physiologically able to be sexually active as long as they live; their main barrier to a fulfilling sexual life is likely to be lack of a partner (Masters & Johnson, 1966, 1981; NIA, 1994; NFO Research Inc., 1999).

Sex is different in late adulthood from what it was earlier. Men typically take longer to develop an erection and to ejaculate, may need more manual stimulation, and may experience longer intervals between erections. Erectile dysfunction may increase, but it is often treatable (Bremner, Vitiello, & Prinz, 1983; NIA, 1994; refer back to Chapter 15). Women's breast engorgement and other signs of sexual arousal are less intense than before. The vagina may become less flexible and may need artificial lubrication.

Still, most older men and women can enjoy sexual expression (Bortz, Wallace, & Wiley, 1999). Sexual activity can be more satisfying for older people if both young and old recognize it as normal and healthy. Housing arrangements and care providers should consider the sexual needs of elderly people. Physicians should avoid prescribing drugs that interfere with sexual functioning if alternatives are available and, when such a drug must be taken, should alert the patient to its effects.

Physical and Mental Health

Increasing life expectancy is raising pressing questions about the relationship between longevity and health, both physical and mental. How healthy are older adults today, and how can they stave off declines in health?

Health Status

Poor health is not an inevitable consequence of aging (Moore, Moir, & Patrick, 2004). Most older adults in the United States are in good general health, though not as good, on average, as younger and middle-aged adults. About 73 percent of Americans ages 65 and older consider themselves in good to excellent health, though whites rate their health higher than do African Americans and Hispanics. At age 85 and over, 67 percent of non-Hispanic whites, but only 52 and 53 percent of blacks and Hispanics, respectively, say they are in good to excellent health (Federal Interagency Forum on Aging-Related Statistics, 2004). As earlier in life, poverty is strongly related to poor health and to limited access to, and use of, health care (NCHS, 2004).

Chronic Conditions and Disabilities

At least 80 percent of older Americans have at least one chronic condition, and 50 percent have at least two (Moore, Moir, & Patrick, 2004). A much smaller proportion—but about half of those over 85—are *frail*: weak and vulnerable to stress, disease, disability and death. Frailty is not simply a function of physical change; in a 7-year longitudinal study of 1,558 older Mexican Americans, those who had a positive outlook, had high self-esteem, and enjoyed life were less likely to become frail (Ostir, Ottenbacher, & Markides, 2004).

Common Chronic Conditions The four leading causes of death in old age in the United States are chronic conditions—heart disease, cancer, stroke, and chronic lower respiratory disease (NCHS, 2004). In fact, heart disease, cancer, and stroke

Checkpoint
Can you . . .

✔ Describe typical changes in sensory and motor functioning and in sleep needs, and tell how they can affect everyday living?

✔ Discuss changes in sexual functioning and possibilities for sexual activity in late life?

Guidepost

5. What health problems are common in late adulthood, and what factors influence health at that time?

Table 17-4	Warning Signs of Stroke

- Sudden numbness or weakness of the face, arm, or leg, especially on one side of the body.
- Sudden confusion, trouble speaking or understanding.
- Sudden trouble seeing in one or both eyes.
- Sudden trouble walking, dizziness, loss of balance or coordination.
- Sudden, severe headache with no known cause.

Source: American Stroke Association, 2005.

account for 60 percent of all deaths among older Americans (Moore, Moir, & Patrick, 2004). Almost 95 percent of health care costs for older Americans are for chronic diseases (Moore, Moir, & Patrick, 2004). Worldwide, the leading causes of death at age 60 and above are heart disease, stroke, chronic pulmonary disease, lower respiratory infections, and lung cancer (WHO, 2003a). As we will discuss, many of these deaths could be prevented through healthier lifestyles.

Hypertension and diabetes are increasing in prevalence, affecting about 50 percent and 16 percent of the older population, respectively. Hypertension, which can affect blood flow to the brain, is a risk factor for stroke. (Table 17-4 lists warning signs for stroke.) Hypertension also is related to cognitive declines in attention, learning, memory, executive functions, psychomotor abilities, and visual, perceptual, and spatial skills (Waldstein, 2003). Other common chronic conditions include arthritis (36 percent), heart disease (31 percent), and cancer (21 percent). Women are more likely to report hypertension, asthma, chronic bronchitis, and arthritic symptoms, whereas men are more likely to have heart disease, cancer, diabetes, and emphysema (Federal Interagency Forum on Aging-Related Statistics, 2004). Chronic conditions also vary by race/ethnicity. In 2000–2001, 65 percent of older African Americans had hypertension, compared with fewer than half of older whites and Hispanics. Both blacks and Hispanics were almost twice as likely as whites to have diabetes—25 percent and 23 percent, respectively, as compared with 14 percent. On the other hand, 22 percent of whites had cancer, compared with 10 percent of blacks and Hispanics (Moore, Moir, & Patrick, 2004).

Disabilities and Activity Limitations   The proportion of older adults with chronic physical disabilities or activity limitations has declined since the mid-1980s in the United States (Federal Interagency Forum on Aging-Related Statistics, 2004) and in France, perhaps due in part to the increasing number of educated older adults knowledgeable about preventive measures. Trends are more mixed in other industrialized countries (Robine & Michel, 2004).

Fewer than 10 percent of older Americans have difficulty carrying out such essential **activities of daily living (ADLs)** as dressing, bathing, and getting around the house; more than 20 percent have difficulty with more complex **instrumental activities of daily living (IADLs),** such as going shopping or to a doctor's office alone, which are indicators of the ability to function independently. About 22 percent of 65- to 74-year-olds, 33 percent of 75- to 84-year-olds, and 53 percent of those 85 and older limit their *functional activities* (such as walking, climbing stairs, reaching, lifting, or carrying) because of chronic conditions (Gist & Hetzel, 2004).

When a condition is not severe, it can usually be managed so that it does not interfere with daily life. A person who is arthritic or short of breath may take fewer steps or move items to lower shelves within easy reach. However, in the presence of chronic conditions and loss of reserve capacity, even a minor illness or injury can have serious repercussions. In a longitudinal study of 754 older adults in New Haven,

activities of daily living (ADLs) Essential activities that support survival, such as eating, dressing, bathing, and getting around the house.

instrumental activities of daily living (IADLs) Indicators of functional well-being and of the ability to live independently.

Connecticut, those who had to be hospitalized or had at least one period of restricted activity (for example, due to a fall) were more likely to develop permanent disabilities (Gill, Allore, Holford, & Guo, 2004).

Lifestyle Influences on Health and Longevity

The chances of remaining healthy and fit in late life often depend on lifestyle, especially exercise and diet (de Groot et al., 2004).

Physical Activity A lifelong program of exercise, such as John Glenn followed, may prevent many physical changes once associated with normal aging. Regular exercise can strengthen the heart and lungs and decrease stress. It can protect against hypertension, hardening of the arteries, heart disease, osteoporosis, and diabetes. It helps maintain speed, stamina, strength, and endurance, and such basic functions as circulation and breathing. It reduces the chance of injuries by making joints and muscles stronger and more flexible, and it helps prevent or relieve lower-back pain and symptoms of arthritis. It may improve mental alertness and cognitive performance, may help relieve anxiety and mild depression, and often improves morale. It can enable people with such conditions as lung disease and arthritis to remain independent and can help prevent the development of limitations on mobility (Agency for Healthcare Research and Quality and CDC, 2002; Blumenthal et al., 1991; Butler, Davis, Lewis, Nelson, & Strauss, 1998a, 1998b; Kramer et al., 1999; Kritchevsky et al., 2005; Mazzeo et al., 1998; NIA, 1995; NIH Consensus Development Panel, 2001; Rall, Meydani, Kehayias, Dawson-Hughes, & Roubenoff, 1996).

*In*activity contributes to heart disease, diabetes, colon cancer, and high blood pressure. It may lead to obesity, which affects the circulatory system, the kidneys, and sugar metabolism; contributes to degenerative disorders; and tends to shorten life (Agency for Healthcare Research and Quality and CDC, 2002). In a Canadian epidemiological study of 9,008 community-dwelling older adults, those who did little or no exercise were more likely to die or become institutionalized within the next five years (Rockwood et al., 2004). In a longitudinal study of 7,553 white older women, those who increased their activity levels over a 6-year period had lower

What's Your View?

- Do you engage regularly in physical exercise? How many of the older people you know do so? What kinds of physical activity do you think you will be able to maintain as you get older?

These enthusiastic cross-country skiiers are deriving the benefits of regular physical exercise in old age, along with having fun. Exercise may well help them extend their lives and avoid some of the physical changes commonly—and apparently mistakenly—associated with "normal aging."

death rates during the folowing 6½ years (Gregg et al., 2003). Even among the very old and frail, moderate exercise seems to increase chances of survival (Landi et al., 2004). In a 12-month randomized, controlled study of 201 adults ages 70 and older at a senior center in Washington state, a combination of exercise, training in self-management of chronic disease, and peer support improved the ability of those with mild to moderate disabilities to carry out activities of daily living (Phelan, Williams, Penninx, LoGerfo, & Leveille, 2004).

Nutrition According to a national nutritional survey, 81 percent of older Americans report diets that are considered poor or in need of improvement. The main dietary deficiencies are in daily servings of fruit and dairy products (Federal Interagency Forum on Aging-Related Statistics, 2004).

Nutrition plays a large part in susceptibility to such chronic illnesses as atherosclerosis, heart disease, and diabetes as well as functional or activity limitations (Houston, Stevens, Cai, & Haines, 2005). A healthy diet can reduce risks of obesity as well as of high blood pressure and high cholesterol (Federal Interagency Forum for Aging-Related Statistics, 2004). A Mediterranean diet (high in olive oil, whole grains, vegetables, and nuts) has been found to reduce cardiovascular risk (Esposito et al., 2004) and—in combination with physical activity, moderate alcohol use, and refraining from smoking—cut 10-year mortality from all causes in healthy 70- to 90-year-old Europeans by nearly two-thirds (Knoops et al., 2004; Rimm & Stampfer, 2004). Eating fruits and vegetables—especially those rich in vitamin C, citrus fruits and juices, green leafy vegetables, broccoli, cabbage, cauliflower, and brussels sprouts—lowers the risk of stroke (Joshipura et al., 1999).

Loss of teeth due to decay or *periodontitis* (gum disease), often attributable to infrequent dental care (NCHS, 1998), can have serious implications for nutrition. Although more older Americans are keeping their natural teeth than ever before, in 2002 almost 1 in 4, mostly poor and minorities, had lost all of their teeth (Moore, Moir, & Patrick, 2004; Vargas, Kramarow, & Yellowitz, 2001).

Checkpoint

Can you . . .

✔ Summarize the health status of older adults, and identify several chronic conditions common in late life?

✔ Give evidence of the influences of exercise and nutrition on health and longevity?

Guidepost

6. What mental and behavioral disorders do some older people experience?

Symptoms of depression are common in older adults but are often overlooked because they are wrongly thought to be a natural accompaniment of aging. Some older people become depressed as a result of physical and emotional losses, and some apparent "brain disorders" are actually due to depression. Depression often can be relieved if older people seek help.

Mental and Behavioral Problems

Contrary to common belief, mental health tends to improve with age. Only 6 percent of older Americans report frequent mental distress (Moore, Moir, & Patrick, 2004). However, mental and behavioral disturbances that do occur in older adults can result in functional impairment in major life activities as well as in cognitive decline (van Hooren et al., 2005).

Many older people and their families mistakenly believe that they can do nothing about mental and behavioral problems, even though close to 100 such conditions can be prevented, cured, or alleviated. Among these are drug intoxication, delirium, metabolic or infectious disorders, malnutrition, anemia, low thyroid functioning, minor head injuries, alcoholism, and depression (NIA, 1980, 1993; Wykle & Musil, 1993).

Depression In 2002, 11 percent of older men and 18 percent of older women in the United States reported symptoms of clinical depression (Federal Interagency Forum on Aging-Related Statistics, 2004). Brain imaging shows that depression is associated with a neurochemical imbalance and malfunctioning of neural circuits that regulate moods, thinking, sleep, appetite, and behavior (NIMH, 1999b).

Heredity may account for 40 to 50 percent of the risk for major depression (Bouchard, 2004; Harvard Medical School, 2004d). Vulnerability seems to result from the influence of multiple genes interacting with environmental factors (NIMH, 1999b), such as stressful events, loneliness, and substance abuse. Special risk factors in late adulthood include chronic illness or disability, cognitive decline, and divorce, separation, or widowhood (Harvard Medical School, 2003d; Mueller et al., 2004).

Roots of depression may be found early in life. In the MIDUS survey (introduced in Chapters 15 and 16), a reported lack of parental emotional support during childhood was associated with depressive symptoms and chronic health conditions in adulthood and old age (Shaw, Krause, Chatters, Connell, & Ingersoll-Dayton, 2004).

Depression is often coupled with other medical conditions. Some physicians, when treating multiple illnesses, may give depression lower priority than a physical ailment, such as diabetes or arthritis. Yet, in a study of 1,801 older adults with clinically severe depression—each of whom had, on average, four chronic medical illnesses—depression played a more pervasive role in mental functional status, disability, and quality of life than did any of the other conditions (Noël et al., 2004).

Because depression can speed physical declines of aging, accurate diagnosis, prevention, and treatment could help many older people live longer and remain more active (Penninx et al., 1998). Depression can be treated by antidepressant drugs, psychotherapy, or both (Harvard Medical School, 2005). Regular aerobic exercise can reduce symptoms of mild to moderate depression (Dunn, Trivedi, Kampert, Clark, & Chambliss, 2005).

Dementia **Dementia** is the general term for physiologically caused cognitive and behavioral decline sufficient to interfere with daily activities (American Psychiatric Association [APA], 1994). Although some degree of cognitive decline is common with advanced age, cognitive impairment severe enough to be diagnosed as dementia is far from inevitable.

dementia Deterioration in cognitive and behavioral functioning due to physiological causes.

Education and large head size seem to be protective against dementia (Mortimer, Snowdon, & Markesbery, 2002), as is having a challenging job (Seidler et al., 2004). Cognitive impairment is more likely in people in poor physical health, especially those who have had strokes or diabetes (Tilvis et al., 2004). The risk of cognitive impairment may be lessened by walking or by other long-term, regular physical activity (Abbott et al., 2004; van Gelder et al., 2004; Weuve et al., 2004) and possibly by nutritional supplements (Manders et al., 2004). In one study, older women who drank moderate amounts of alcohol each day had a 40 percent lower risk of cognitive impairment or dementia (Espeland et al., 2005). A longitudinal study of 354 adults ages 50 and older found that people who had large social networks or had frequent social contact or could rely on emotional support from family or friends were less likely to show cognitive decline 12 years later (Holtzman et al., 2004).

Most forms of dementia are irreversible, but about 10 percent of cases can be reversed with early diagnosis and treatment (NIA, 1980, 1993; Wykle & Musil, 1993). About two-thirds of cases of dementia may be caused by **Alzheimer's disease (AD),** a progressive, degenerative brain disorder (Small et al., 1997). **Parkinson's disease,** the second most common disorder involving progressive neurological degeneration, is characterized by tremor, stiffness, slowed movement, and unstable posture (Nussbaum, 1998). These two diseases, together with *multi-infarct dementia (MD),* which is caused by a series of small strokes, account for at least 8 out of 10 cases of dementia, all irreversible.

Alzheimer's disease Progressive, irreversible, degenerative brain disorder characterized by cognitive deterioration and loss of control of bodily functions, leading to death.

Parkinson's disease Progressive, irreversible degenerative neurological disorder, characterized by tremor, stiffness, slowed movement, and unstable posture.

Alzheimer's Disease Early in the 1990s, Ronald Reagan's longtime golf buddies began to realize something was wrong when the former U.S. president, a noted wit, would start to tell a joke and then be unable to finish it. Several years later, Reagan had to discontinue his weekly golf outings because he didn't know where he was.

Artwork by Esther Lipman Rosenthal shows progressive deterioration in her depiction of the same subject, her husband golfing, before and after the onset of Alzheimer's disease. (a) Picture done at age 55 before Alzheimer's disease. (b) Picture done at age 75 during the early middle stage of Alzheimer's disease. Photos courtesy of Linda Goldman.

At the time of his death in 2004 at age 93, he hadn't recognized his children in years (Blood & Rogers, 2004).

Alzheimer's disease (AD) is one of the most common and most feared terminal illnesses among aging persons; it affects at least 15 million people throughout the world (Reisberg et al., 2003) and is the sixth leading cause of death among older Americans (NCHS, 2004). It gradually robs patients of intelligence, awareness, and even the ability to control their bodily functions—and finally kills them. An estimated 4.5 million people in the United States have AD, and by 2050 the incidence is projected to be 13.2 million. The risk rises dramatically with age; thus, increases in longevity mean that more people will survive to an age when the risk of AD is greatest (Hebert, Scherr, Bienias, Bennett, & Evans, 2003).

Symptoms The classic symptoms of Alzheimer's disease are memory impairment, deterioration of language, and deficits in visual and spatial processing (Cummings, 2004). The most prominent early symptom is inability to recall recent events or take in new information. A person may repeat questions that were just answered or leave an everyday task unfinished. These early signs may be overlooked because they look like ordinary forgetfulness or may be interpreted as signs of normal aging. (Table 17-5 compares early warning signs of Alzheimer's disease with normal mental lapses.)

Personality changes—most often, rigidity, apathy, egocentricity, and impaired emotional control—tend to occur early in the disease's development and may aid in early detection and diagnosis (Balsis, Carpenter, & Storandt, 2005). More symptoms follow: irritability, anxiety, depression, and, later, delusions, delirium, and wandering. Long-term memory, judgment, concentration, orientation, and speech all become impaired, and patients have trouble handling basic activities of daily life. By the end, the patient cannot understand or use language, does not recognize family members, cannot eat without help, cannot control the bowels and bladder, and loses the ability to walk, sit up, and swallow solid food. Death usually comes within eight to ten years after symptoms appear ("Alzheimer's Disease, Part I," 1998; Cummings, 2004; Hoyert & Rosenberg, 1999; Small et al., 1997).

Table 17-5 Alzheimer's Disease versus Normal Behavior

Normal Behavior	Symptoms of Disease
Temporarily forgetting things	Permanently forgetting recent events; asking the same questions repeatedly
Inability to do some challenging tasks	Inability to do routine tasks with many steps, such as making and serving a meal
Forgetting unusual or complex words	Forgetting simple words
Getting lost in a strange city	Getting lost on one's own block
Becoming momentarily distracted and failing to watch a child	Forgetting that a child is in one's care and leaving the house
Making mistakes in balancing a checkbook	Forgetting what the numbers in a checkbook mean and what to do with them
Misplacing everyday items	Putting things in inappropriate places where one cannot usefully retrieve them (e.g., a wristwatch in a fishbowl)
Occasional mood changes	Rapid, dramatic mood swings and personality changes; loss of initiative

Source: Adapted from Alzheimer's Association (undated).

Causes and Risk Factors Accumulation of an abnormal protein called *beta amyloid peptide* appears to be the main culprit contributing to the development of Alzheimer's disease (Bird, 2005; Cummings, 2004). The brain of a person with AD contains excessive amounts of **neurofibrillary tangles** (twisted masses of dead neurons) and large waxy clumps of **amyloid plaque** (nonfunctioning tissue formed by beta amyloid in the spaces between neurons). Because these plaques are insoluble, the brain cannot clear them away. They may become dense, spread, and destroy surrounding neurons (Harvard Medical School, 2003a).

Alzheimer's disease, or at least its age of onset, is strongly heritable (Bird, 2005; Harvard Medical School, 2003a). However, education and cognitively stimulating activities have consistently been associated with reduced risk of AD (Crowe, Andel, Pedersen, Johansson, & Gatz, 2003; Wilson & Bennett, 2003). A 4-year longitudinal study of older residents of a biracial community suggests that the protective effect is due, not to education itself, but to the fact that educated people tend to be cognitively active (Wilson & Bennett, 2003). In a study of 10,079 Swedish twins, complexity of work—especially of work with people—reduced the risk of AD (Andel et al., 2005).

How might cognitive activity protect against AD? One hypothesis is based on the concept of **cognitive reserve,** which—much like organ reserve—may enable a deteriorating brain to continue to function under stress, up to a point, without showing signs of impairment. Ongoing cognitive activity may build cognitive reserve and thus delay the onset of dementia (Crowe et al., 2003).

Diet, exercise, and other lifestyle factors also may play a part. Foods rich in vitamin E, n-3 fatty acids, and unhydrogenated unsaturated fats—such as oil-based salad dressings, nuts, seeds, fish, mayonnaise, and eggs—may be protective against AD, whereas foods high in saturated and transunsaturated fats, such as red meats, butter, and ice cream, may be harmful (Morris, 2004). Smoking is associated with increased risk of AD (Launer et al., 1999; Ott et al., 1998). Other possible risk factors under investigation include sleep apnea and head injuries earlier in life ("Alzheimer's Disease, Part III," 2001).

neurofibrillary tangles Twisted masses of protein fibers found in brains of persons with Alzheimer's disease.

amyloid plaque Waxy chunks of insoluble tissue found in brains of persons with Alzheimer's disease.

cognitive reserve Hypothesized fund of energy that may enable a deteriorating brain to continue to function normally.

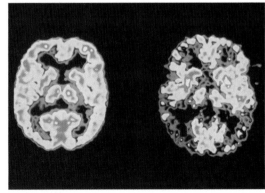

These PET (positron emission tomography) scans show dramatic deterioration in the brain of an Alzheimer's patient (right) as compared with a normal brain (left). The red and yellow areas represent high brain activity; the blue and black areas, low activity. The scan on the right shows reduction of both function and blood flow in both sides of the brain, a change often seen in Alzheimer's disease. To obtain the PET scans, a radioactive tracer is injected into the blood to reveal metabolic activity in the brain.

Diagnosis and Prediction AD can be diagnosed definitively only by postmortem examination of brain tissue, but scientists are rapidly developing tools to enable fairly reliable diagnosis in a living person. Neuroimaging is one such tool, particularly useful in excluding alternative causes of dementia (Cummings, 2004) and in allowing researchers to actually see brain lesions indicative of AD in a living patient (Shoghi-Jadid et al., 2002). A longitudinal study using brain scanning found that reduced metabolic activity in the hippocampus of healthy middle-aged and older adults can accurately predict who will get Alzheimer's or a related memory impairment within the next nine years (Mosconi et al., 2005). In what could lead to a definitive test for early AD, researchers at Northwestern University used a new bio-barcode amplification (BCA) technology to detect minuscule amounts of proteins called amyloid beta-derived diffusible ligands (ADDLs) in cerebrospinal fluid (Georganopoulou et al., 2005). Blood tests that measure levels of the amino acid homocysteine (Seshadri et al., 2002) and of amyloid precursor proteins (Padovani et al., 2002) may predict or diagnose AD or other forms of dementia in the early stages.

Neurocognitive screening tests can make initial distinctions between patients experiencing cognitive changes related to normal aging and those in early stages of dementia ("Early Detection," 2002; Solomon et al., 1998). In a study at the University of California in San Diego, performance on paper-and-pencil cognitive tests predicted which participants would develop AD within a year or two (Jacobson, Delis, Bondi, & Salmon, 2002). In the Seattle Longitudinal Study of Adult Intelligence (introduced in Chapter 15), results of psychometric tests were predictive of dementia as much as 14 years prior to diagnosis (Schaie, 2005).

Despite the identification of several genes associated with AD (Bertram et al., 2005; Bird, 2005), particularly an early-onset form that appers in middle age, genetic testing so far has a limited role in prediction and diagnosis. Still, it may be useful in combination with cognitive tests, brain scans, and clinical evidence of symptoms ("Alzheimer's Disease, Part I," 2001). Healthy, middle-aged people without apparent symptoms who have the APOE-e4 gene associated with early-onset AD have shown deficits in spatial attention and working memory (Parasuraman, Greenwood, & Sunderland, 2002) and in *prospective memory,* the ability to remember what to do at a future time, such as take medicine or keep an appointment (Driscoll, McDaniel, & Guynn, 2005). Such deficits may be indicative of early AD.

In the Nun Study, a longitudinal study of Alzheimer's disease and aging in 678 Roman Catholic nuns, a research team examined autobiographies the nuns had written in their early twenties. The women whose autobiographies were densely packed with ideas were least likely to become cognitively impaired or to develop Alzheimer's disease later in life (Riley, Snowdon, Desrosiers, & Markesbery, 2005).

Treatment and Prevention Although no cure has yet been found, early diagnosis and treatment can slow the progress of Alzheimer's disease and improve quality of life. One medication approved by the U.S. Food and Drug Administration is memantine (commercially known as Namenda). Memantine inhibits the action of glutamate, a brain chemical that can overstimulate brain cells, resulting in cell damage or death. In a double-blind, placebo-controlled trial, daily doses of memantine taken for 28 weeks reduced deterioration in patients with moderate to severe AD without significant adverse effects (Reisberg et al., 2003).

Cholinesterase inhibitors, such as donepezil (commercially known as Aricept), have become standard treatment for slowing or stabilizing the progress of mild to moderate AD (Cummings, 2004). However, hopes for long-term effectiveness were shattered when a 5-year trial of Aricept found no significant difference after the first two years between patients taking Aricept and those given a placebo (AD2000 Collaborative Group, 2004). Similarly, in a 3-year double-blind study, donepezil therapy had no effect after the first year and none at all over the entire three-year period (Petersen et al., 2005).

Cholinesterase inhibitors are often given in combination with memantine and high-dose vitamin E. However, studies are mixed as to the effectiveness of vitamin E (Cummings, 2004); a recent three-year study found no benefit (Petersen et al., 2005). Also being tested are anti-inflammatory drugs and the herbal remedy gingko biloba, but there is insufficient evidence of their effectiveness (Cummings, 2004; Foley & White, 2002; Harvard Medical School, 2003a; Morris et al., 2002). A promising experimental approach is immunotherapy. In one study, Alzheimer's patients vaccinated with beta amyloid performed better on memory tests up to a year later than patients injected with a placebo (Fox et al., 2005; Gilman et al., 2005).

In the absence of a cure, management of the disease is critical (Cummings, 2004). In the early stages, memory training and memory aids may improve cognitive functioning (Camp et al., 1993; Camp & McKitrick, 1992; McKitrick, Camp, & Black, 1992). Behavioral therapies can slow deterioration, improve communication, and reduce disruptive behavior (Barinaga, 1998). Drugs can relieve agitation, lighten depression, and help patients sleep. Proper nourishment and fluid intake, together with exercise, physical therapy, and control of other medical conditions, are important, and cooperation between the physician and the caregiver is essential (Cummings, 2004).

Checkpoint

Can you...

✔ Tell why late-life depression may be more common than is generally realized?

✔ Name the three main causes of dementia in older adults?

✔ Summarize what is known about the prevalence, symptoms, diagnosis, causes, risk factors, treatment, and prevention of Alzheimer's disease?

COGNITIVE DEVELOPMENT

Aspects of Cognitive Development

Old age "adds as it takes away," wrote the poet William Carlos Williams in one of three books of verse he produced between his first stroke at the age of 68 and his death at 79. This comment seems to sum up current findings about cognitive functioning in late adulthood. As Baltes's life-span developmental approach suggests, age brings gains as well as losses. Let's look first at intelligence and general processing abilities, then at memory, and then at wisdom, which is popularly associated with the later years.

Guidepost

7. What gains and losses in cognitive abilities tend to occur in late adulthood, and are there ways to improve older people's cognitive performance?

Intelligence and Processing Abilities

Does intelligence diminish in late adulthood? The answer depends on what abilities are being measured, and how. Some abilities, such as speed of mental processes and abstract reasoning, may decline in later years, but other abilities tend to improve throughout most of adult life. And, although changes in processing abilities may reflect neurological deterioration, there is much individual variation, suggesting that declines in functioning are not inevitable and may be preventable.

Several physical and psychological factors may lead to underestimation of older adults' intelligence. Vision and hearing losses may make understanding test instructions difficult. The time limits on most intelligence tests are particularly hard on older people; they do better when allowed as much time as they need (Hertzog, 1989; Schaie & Hertzog, 1983). Older adults may expect to do poorly, and this may become a self-fulfilling prophecy (Schaie, 1996b). They may lack motivation unless they are taking the test to qualify for a job or for some other important purpose.

Measuring Older Adults' Intelligence To measure the intelligence of older adults, researchers often use the **Wechsler Adult Intelligence Scale (WAIS).** Scores on the WAIS subtests yield a verbal IQ, a performance IQ, and a total IQ. Older adults tend not to perform as well as younger adults on the WAIS, but the difference is primarily in nonverbal performance. On the five subtests in the performance scale (such as

Wechsler Adult Intelligence Scale (WAIS) Intelligence test for adults, which yields verbal and performance scores as well as a combined score.

Figure 17-6

Classic aging pattern on the revised version of the Wechsler Adult Intelligence Scale (WAIS-R). Scores on the performance subtests decline far more rapidly with age than scores on the verbal subtests. (Source: Botwinick, 1984.)

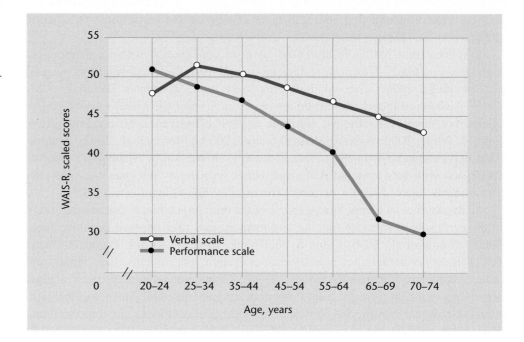

identifying the missing part of a picture, copying a design, and mastering a maze), scores drop with age; but on the six tests making up the verbal scale—particularly tests of vocabulary, information, and comprehension—scores fall only slightly and very gradually (see Figure 17-6). This is called the *classic aging pattern* (Botwinick, 1984).

What might account for this pattern? For one thing, the verbal items that hold up with age are based on knowledge; they do not require the test taker to figure out or do anything new. The performance tasks involve the processing of new information; they require perceptual speed and motor skills, which can reflect muscular and neurological slowing. The variance in retention of different types of cognitive skills in old age has generated several lines of theory and research.

Two Kinds of Intelligence One line of research, introduced in Chapter 15, has distinguished between *fluid* and *crystallized* abilities, the former depending largely on neurological status and the latter on accumulated knowledge. As in the classic aging pattern on the WAIS, these two kinds of intelligence follow different paths. In the classic aging pattern, however, the trend in both verbal and performance scores is downward throughout most of adulthood; the difference, though substantial, is one of degree. Far more encouraging is the pattern of crystallized intelligence, which improves until fairly late in life, even though fluid intelligence declines earlier (see Figure 17-7). Indeed, it has been argued that the importance of crystallized intelligence increases in later life and may even outweigh declines in fluid abilities (Sternberg et al., 2001).

Such instrumental activities of daily living (IADLs) as filling out a Medicare form, looking up an emergency telephone number, and reading a medicine label are more highly related to fluid intelligence than to crystallized intelligence and show age-related decline (Diehl, Willis, & Schaie, 1994; Schaie, 1996a; Schaie & Willis, 1996; Willis & Schaie, 1986a). Declines may occur sooner in people with especially slow perceptual speed (Willis & Schaie, 1999; Willis et al., 1998).

Paul Baltes (1997) and his colleagues have proposed a **dual-process model,** which seeks to measure aspects of intelligence that may continue to advance as well as aspects that are more likely to deteriorate. In this model, **mechanics of intelligence** are the brain's neurophysiological "hardware": information-processing and problem-solving functions independent of any particular content. This dimension, like fluid intelligence, often declines with age. **Pragmatics of intelligence** are the culture-based "software":

dual-process model Model of cognitive functioning, proposed by Baltes, which identifies and seeks to measure two dimensions of intelligence: mechanics and pragmatics.

mechanics of intelligence In Baltes's dual-process model, the abilities to process information and solve problems, irrespective of content; the area of cognition in which there is often an age-related decline.

pragmatics of intelligence In Baltes's dual-process model, the dimension of intelligence that tends to grow with age and includes practical thinking, application of accumulated knowledge and skills, specialized expertise, professional productivity, and wisdom.

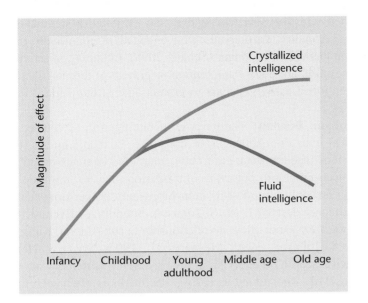

Figure 17-7

Changes in fluid intelligence and crystallized intelligence across the life span. According to classic studies by Horn and Cattell, fluid abilities (largely biologically determined) decline after young adulthood, but crystallized abilities (largely culturally influenced) increase until late adulthood. More recently, the Seattle Longitudinal Study found a more complex pattern, with some fluid abilities holding their own until late middle age (refer back to Figure 15-2 in Chapter 15). (Source: J. L. Horn & Donaldson, 1980.)

practical thinking, application of accumulated knowledge and skills, specialized expertise, professional productivity, and wisdom. This domain, which may continue to develop until very late adulthood, is similar to, but broader than, crystallized intelligence and includes information and know-how garnered from education, work, and life experience.

The Berlin Aging Study, a 6-year longitudinal study of 132 Berliners ranging from 70 to 100 years of age, found changes consistent with the dual-process model. Mechanical or fluid abilities—episodic memory, fluency (the ability to come up with words beginning with a certain letter), and perceptual speed—tended to decline with age, whereas vocabulary knowledge (pragmatic-crystallized) remained fairly stable until age 90 (Singer, Verhaeghen et al., 2003).

An important part of the dual-process model is the concept of **selective optimization with compensation (SOC).** Older people may use their pragmatic strengths and other physical, cognitive, and psychosocial resources to compensate for weakened mechanical abilities (Baltes, 1993; Baltes, Lindenberger, & Staudinger, 1998; Lang, Rieckmann, & Baltes, 2002; Marsiske, Lang, Baltes, & Baltes, 1995). For example, a typist may compensate for losses in reaction time by reading further along in the text (Salthouse, 1991). However, at some point compensation becomes less efficient and pragmatics decline as well. (SOC will be discussed further in Chapter 18.)

selective optimization with compensation (SOC) In Baltes's dual-process model, enhancing overall cognitive functioning by using stronger abilities to compensate for those that have weakened.

The Seattle Longitudinal Study: Use It or Lose It In the Seattle Longitudinal Study of Adult Intelligence, researchers measured six primary mental abilities: vocabulary, verbal fluency, number (computational ability), spatial orientation, inductive reasoning, and perceptual speed. Consistent with other studies, perceptual speed tended to decline earliest and most rapidly (refer back to Figure 15-2 in Chapter 15). Cognitive decline in other respects was slow and not across-the-board. If they live long enough, it seems, most people's functioning will flag at some point; but very few weaken in all or even most abilities, and many improve in some areas. Most fairly healthy older adults show only small losses until the late sixties or seventies. Not until the eighties do they fall below the average performance of younger adults. And even then, declines in verbal abilities and reasoning are modest (Schaie, 2005).

The most striking feature of the Seattle findings is the tremendous variation among individuals. Some participants showed declines during their forties, but a few maintained full functioning very late in life. Even in their late eighties, virtually all participants retained their competence in one or more of the abilities tested (Schaie, 2005). Those most likely to show declines were men who had low educational levels, were dissatisfied with their success in life, and exhibited a significant decrease in flexibility of personality. Participants who engaged in cognitively complex work tended to retain their abilities longer (Schaie, 2005). Engaging in activities that challenge cognitive skills promotes the retention or growth of those skills (Schaie, 1983) and, as we mentioned earlier, appears to protect against dementia.

Everyday Problem Solving   The purpose of intelligence, of course, is not to take tests but to deal with the challenges of daily life. In many studies, the quality of practical decisions (such as what car to buy, what kind of treatment to get for breast cancer, how much money to put away in a pension plan, or how to compare insurance policies) bore only a modest relationship, if any, to performance on tasks like those on intelligence tests (M. M. S. Johnson, Schmitt, & Everard, 1994; Meyer, Russo, & Talbot, 1995) and, often, no relationship to age (Capon, Kuhn, & Carretero, 1989; M. M. S. Johnson, 1990; Meyer et al., 1995; Walsh & Hershey, 1993). Similarly, much research on everyday problem solving (such as what to do about a flooded basement) has *not* found as early a decline as is often seen in measures of fluid intelligence, and some research has found marked improvement at least through middle age (Berg & Klaczynski, 1996; Cornelius & Caspi, 1987; Perlmutter, Kaplan, & Nyquist, 1990; Sternberg, Grigorenko, & Oh, 2001).

In a classic study (Denney & Palmer, 1981), 84 adults ages 20 to 79 were given hypothetical problems such as the following: *You are stranded in a car during a blizzard* or *Your 8-year-old child is 1½ hours late coming home from school.* High scores were given for generating the largest number of practical solutions. According to this criterion, the best practical problem solvers were people in their forties and fifties, suggesting that this ability peaks in middle age. A follow-up study posed problems with which elderly people would be especially familiar (concerning retirement, widowhood, and ill health), yet people in their forties still came up with more solutions (Denney & Pearce, 1989). However, in other studies in which problems were real rather than hypothetical and were brought up by the participants themselves and in which solutions were rated by quality rather than quantity, practical problem-solving ability did *not* seem to decline after middle age (Camp, Doherty, Moody-Thomas, & Denney, 1989; Cornelius & Caspi, 1987).

What explains these inconsistencies? As we have just seen, there are differences in the kinds of problems various researchers study, in the relevance of these problems to real life, and in the criteria used to rate the solutions. Also, individual differences—for example, in educational level—may affect how people perceive and solve problems (Berg & Klaczynski, 1996; Blanchard-Fields, Chen, & Norris, 1997; Thornton & Dumke, 2005).

A review and analysis of the literature, while taking note of such variables, concluded that the effectiveness of everyday problem solving does *not* peak in middle age. Instead, it remains stable from young adulthood until late life and then declines. However, because most studies of everyday problem solving have been cross-sectional, we cannot be sure that the findings actually show changes with age. Age differences are reduced in studies that focus on interpersonal problems rather than on instrumental problems, such as how to return defective merchandise (Thornton & Dumke, 2005). Older adults may be more effective problem solvers when a problem has emotional relevance for them; for this type of problem they have more extensive and varied repertoires of strategies to apply to different situations (Berg & Klaczynski, 1996; Blanchard-Fields, Chen, & Norris, 1997).

However, thinking based on personal experience may not necessarily produce the best results. When 172 young, middle-aged, and older adults were presented with hypothetical research findings about effects of religion and social class on such behaviors as drug use, creative performance, parenting skills, and conformity to authority, middle-aged and older adults were more likely than younger adults to uncritically accept evidence that supported their preconceptions and to dismiss evidence to the contrary. One possible explanation offered by the researchers was that the use of personal experience in solving everyday problems, as middle-aged and older adults tend to do, may interfere with analytical thinking (Klaczynski & Robinson, 2000).

Changes in Processing Abilities What explains the varying course of cognitive abilities in late adulthood? A general slowdown in central nervous system functioning, as measured by reaction time, is widely believed to contribute to changes in cognitive abilities and efficiency of information processing. Still, losses in processing speed do not tell the whole story. Older adults tend to decline in processing abilities needed for acquiring complex new skills but do better on tasks that depend on ingrained habits and knowledge (Bialystok, Craik, Klein, & Viswanathan, 2004; Craik & Salthouse, 2000).

Until recently the evidence for the role of processing speed in cognitive performance—like the evidence for cognitive decline itself—came almost entirely from cross-sectional studies, which may confound cohort with age. Longitudinal studies do *not* show such marked declines in performance. However, the longitudinal design may favor an older sample because of attrition and practice effects (Singer, Verhaeghen et al., 2003). For example, in a 17-year longitudinal study of 5,899 middle-aged and older English adults (ages 49 to 92), practice effects were found to mask declines in fluid intelligence (Rabbitt et al., 2004).

One study measured links between age, speed, and cognition longitudinally as well as cross-sectionally among 302 adults ages 66 to 92. Speed of processing accounted for most of the cross-sectional age differences in cognitive abilities, but these effects were reduced or eliminated by controlling for individual differences in longitudinal decline. Thus "changes in speed are not nearly as strong a determinant of within-person, age-related decline as cross-sectional analyses would suggest" (Sliwinski & Buschke, 1999, p. 32).

Cognitive neuroscientists, by observing the complex steps in stimulus-and-response processing that enter into reaction time, have challenged the long-held view that all components of processing slow equally. In one study, researchers measured the electrical activity of the brain in young and older adults in a reaction-time task. Participants were to press a button when they located a particular word amid a jumbled mass of characters. The older adults were slower only in the final step of processing, the pressing of the button. This finding suggests that the brain's slowing is *not* global, but specific to certain tasks and operations (Bashore, Ridderinkhof, & van der Molen, 1998).

One ability that appears to slow with age is ease in switching attention from one task or function to another (Salthouse, Fristoe, McGuthry, & Hambrick, 1998). This may help explain, for example, why older adults tend to have difficulty driving a car, which requires rapid attentional shifts. However, this is less true of bilingual adults, who, in juggling two languages, need to continually maintain attentional control so as to shut out information that is irrelevant at the moment. Thus, in a study that measured reaction time, bilingual middle-aged and older adults did better than adults their age who used only one language (Bialystok et al., 2004).

Cognitive Abilities and Mortality Intelligence may be an important predictor of how long and in what condition adults will live. That was the conclusion of an epidemiological study of 2,230 Scottish adults who, at age 11, had taken a psychometric intelligence test that has a high correlation with the Stanford Binet. On average, someone who had a childhood IQ 15 points lower than another participant was only 79 percent as likely to live to age 76 (Gottfredson & Deary, 2004). The same IQ differential was associated with a 27 percent increase in cancer deaths among men and a 40 percent increase among women (Deary, Whalley, & Starr, 2003). Similarly,

Checkpoint

Can you . . .

✔ Give several reasons why older adults' intelligence tends to be underestimated?

✔ Compare the classic aging pattern on the WAIS with the trajectories of fluid and crystallized intelligence and with Baltes's dual-process model?

✔ Summarize findings of the Seattle Longitudinal Study with regard to cognitive changes in old age?

✔ Discuss the relationship between practical problem solving and age?

✔ Discuss findings on the slowdown in neural processing and its relationship to cognitive decline?

in the Berlin Aging Study, older adults with higher initial levels and smaller declines in cognitive functioning were more likely to survive at the end of a 6-year period (Singer, Verhaeghen et al., 2003).

However, in another study, reaction time at age 56 more strongly predicted mortality by age 70 than did IQ, suggesting that efficiency of information processing may explain the link between intelligence and timing of death (Deary & Der, 2005). Another possible explanation is that intelligent people learn information and problem-solving skills that help them prevent chronic disease and accidental injury and cooperate in their treatment when they do get sick or hurt (Deary & Der, 2005; Gottfredson & Deary, 2004).

Memory: How Does It Change?

Failing memory is often considered a sign of aging. The man who always kept his schedule in his head now has to write it in a calendar; the woman who takes several medicines now measures out each day's dosages and puts them where she is sure to see them. Loss of memory is the chief worry reported by older Americans (National Council on the Aging, 2002). Yet in memory, as in other cognitive abilities, older people's functioning declines slowly and varies greatly. In 2002, 32 percent of Americans ages 85 and over had moderate or severe memory impairment, as compared with only 5 percent of adults ages 65 to 69 (Federal Interagency Forum for Aging-Related Statistics, 2004).

To understand age-related memory decline, we need to review the various memory systems, introduced in Chapters 7 and 9, which enable the brain to process information for use at a later time (Budson & Price, 2005). These systems are traditionally classified as "short-term" or "long-term."

sensory memory Initial, brief, temporary storage of sensory information.

working memory Short-term storage of information being actively processed.

Short-Term Memory Researchers assess short-term memory by asking a person to repeat a sequence of numbers, either in the order in which they were presented (*digit span forward*) or in reverse order (*digit span backward*). Digit span forward ability holds up well with advancing age (Craik & Jennings, 1992; Poon, 1985; Wingfield & Stine, 1989), but digit span backward performance does not (Craik & Jennings, 1992; Lovelace, 1990). Why? A widely accepted explanation is that immediate forward repetition requires only **sensory memory,** which retains efficiency throughout life, whereas backward repetition requires the manipulation of information in **working memory,** which gradually shrinks in capacity after about age 45 (Swanson, 1999), making it harder to handle more than one task at a time (Smith et al., 2001).

A key factor is the complexity of the task (Kausler, 1990; Wingfield & Stine, 1989). Tasks that require only *rehearsal,* or repetition, show very little decline. Tasks that require *reorganization* or *elaboration* show greater falloff (Craik & Jennings, 1992). If you are asked to verbally rearrange a series of items (such as "Band-Aid, elephant, newspaper") in order of increasing size ("Band-Aid, newspaper, elephant"), you must call to mind your previous knowledge of Band-Aids, newspapers, and elephants (Cherry & Park, 1993). More mental effort is needed to keep this additional information in mind, using more of the limited capacity of working memory.

episodic memory Long-term memory of specific experiences or events, linked to time and place.

Long-Term Memory Information-processing researchers divide long-term memory into three main systems: *episodic memory, semantic memory,* and *procedural memory.*

Do you remember what you had for breakfast this morning? Did you lock your car when you parked it? Such information is stored in **episodic memory,** the long-term memory system most likely to deteriorate with age. The ability to recall newly encountered information, especially, seems to drop off (Poon, 1985; A. D. Smith & Earles, 1996).

Because episodic memory is linked to specific events, you retrieve an item from this mental "diary" by reconstructing the original experience in your mind. Older adults are less able than younger people to do this, perhaps because they focus less on context (where something happened, who was there) and so have fewer connections to jog their memory (Kausler, 1990; Lovelace, 1990). Also, older people have had many similar experiences that tend to run together. When older people perceive an event as distinctive, they can remember it as well as younger ones (Camp, 1989; Cavanaugh, Kramer, Sinnott, Camp, & Markley, 1985; Kausler, 1990).

Semantic memory is like a mental encyclopedia; it holds stored knowledge of historical facts, geographic locations, social customs, meanings of words, and the like. Semantic memory does *not* depend on remembering when and where something was learned, and it shows little decline with age (Camp, 1989; Horn, 1982b; Lachman & Lachman, 1980). In fact, vocabulary and knowledge of rules of language may even increase (Camp, 1989; Horn, 1982b). In a large-scale, representative sequential study of 829 adults ages 35 to 80, semantic memory showed substantially less decline after age 60 than episodic memory (Rönnlund, Nyberg, Bäckman, & Nilsson, 2005).

Remembering how to ride a bicycle or use a typewriter is an example of **procedural memory** (Squire, 1992, 1994). This includes motor skills, habits, and processes that, once learned, can be activated without conscious effort. Procedural memory is relatively unaffected by age, though older adults may need to compensate for an age-related slowing in responses (Kauster, 1990, Salthouse, 1985).

A special type of unconscious memory that holds up with age is **priming,** an increased ability to solve a problem, answer a question, or do a task that a person has previously encountered (A. D. Smith & Earles, 1996). Much as priming a surface prepares it for paint, priming the memory prepares a person to answer a test question by first seeing it on a list for review or to do a math problem involving the same process as one done in class. Priming can improve all three types of long-term memory. It explains why older adults are about as likely as younger ones to identify a familiar picture or recall a familiar word association (for example, *dragon* and *fire,* but not *dragon* and *fudge*).

Speech and Memory: Effects of Aging Have you ever been unable to come up with a word you knew perfectly well? This experience occurs among people of all ages but becomes increasingly common—and increasingly frustrating—in late adulthood (Burke & Shafto, 2004). On a test that calls for definitions of words, older adults often do better than younger ones, but they have more trouble coming up with a word when given its meaning (A. D. Smith & Earles, 1996). Such "tip-of-the-tongue" experiences may relate to problems in working memory (Heller & Dobbs, 1993; Light, 1990; Schonfield, 1974; Schonfield & Robertson, 1960, cited in Horn, 1982b). Older adults also make more errors in naming pictures of objects aloud, make more ambiguous references and slips of the tongue in everyday speech, and more frequently fill in pauses with "um" or "er." Older adults also show an increasing tendency to misspell words (such as *indict*) that are spelled differently than they sound (Burke & Shafto, 2004). These problems reflect not a failure of vocabulary *knowledge*—which, as we have seen, usually remains strong—but a failure of verbal *retrieval*.

What other aspects of speech decline with age? In a longitudinal study, researchers asked 30 healthy older adults, ages 65 to 75, such questions as "Describe the person who most influenced your life" and "Describe an unexpected event that happened to you." Participants' oral answers showed a decline between ages 65 and 80—most rapid in the mid-seventies—in both grammatical complexity and propositional content (density of concepts and conceptual relationships). In a comparative

semantic memory Long-term memory of general factual knowledge, social customs, and language.

procedural memory Long-term memory of motor skills, habits, and ways of doing things, which often can be recalled without conscious effort; sometimes called *implicit memory.*

Knowing how to ride a bicycle is an example of procedural memory. *Once learned, procedural skills can be activated without conscious effort. Even an older person riding a bike for the first time in years remembers how to do it.*

priming Increase in ease of doing a task or remembering information as a result of a previous encounter with the task or information.

study of older adults diagnosed with probable Alzheimer's disease, the corresponding declines were more rapid regardless of age (Kemper, Thompson, & Marquis, 2001).

Why Do Some Memory Systems Decline? What explains older adults' memory losses? Investigators have offered several hypotheses. One approach focuses on problems with the three steps required to process information in memory: *encoding, storage,* and *retrieval.* Another approach focuses on the biological structures that make memory work.

Problems in Encoding, Storage, and Retrieval Older adults tend to be less efficient and precise than younger adults in *encoding* new information to make it easier to remember—for example, by arranging material alphabetically or creating mental associations (Craik & Byrd, 1982). Most studies have found that older and younger adults are about equally knowledgeable as to effective encoding strategies (Salthouse, 1991). Yet in laboratory experiments, older adults are less likely to *use* such strategies unless trained—or at least prompted or reminded—to do so (Craik & Jennings, 1992; Salthouse, 1991). When younger and older adults were briefly instructed in an effective memory strategy (visual imagery) for recalling associated word pairs (such as *king* and *crown*), age differences in frequency of use of the strategy were fairly small and did not adequately account for age differences in recall. Thus, even when older adults use the same strategy as younger adults, they may use it less effectively (Dunlosky & Hertzog, 1998).

Another hypothesis is that material in *storage* may deteriorate to the point where retrieval becomes difficult or impossible. Some research suggests that a small increase in "storage failure" may occur with age (Camp & McKitrick, 1989; Giambra & Arenberg, 1993). However, since traces of decayed memories are likely to remain, it may be possible to reconstruct them, or at least to relearn the material speedily (Camp & McKitrick, 1989; Chafetz, 1992).

Older adults have more trouble with recall than younger adults but do about as well with recognition, which puts fewer demands on the *retrieval* system (Hultsch, 1971; Lovelace, 1990). Even in recognition tasks, however, it takes older people longer than younger ones to search their memories (Lovelace, 1990).

We must keep in mind that most research on encoding, storage, and retrieval has been done in the laboratory. Those functions may operate somewhat differently in the real world.

Neurological Change The decline in processing speed (described earlier in this chapter), which reflects a general slowdown in central nervous system functioning, seems to be a fundamental contributor to age-related memory loss (Luszcz & Bryan, 1999; Hartley, Speer, Jonides, Reuter-Lorenz, & Smith, 2001). In a number of studies, controlling for perceptual speed eliminated virtually the entire age-related drop in memory performance (A. D. Smith & Earles, 1996).

As discussed in Chapter 5, different memory systems depend on different brain structures. Thus a disorder that damages a particular brain structure may impair the type of memory associated with it. For example, Alzheimer's disease disrupts working memory (located in the prefrontal cortex) as well as semantic and episodic memory (located in the frontal and temporal lobes), whereas Parkinson's disease affects procedural memory, located in the cerebellum, basal ganglia, and other areas (Budson & Price, 2005; refer back to Figure 4-6 in Chapter 4).

The *hippocampus,* a small, centrally located structure that seems critical to the ability to store new information in episodic memory (Budson & Price, 2005; Squire, 1992), loses an estimated 20 percent of its nerve cells with advancing age (Ivy, MacLeod, Petit, & Markus, 1992). Unconscious learning—apparently independent of the hippocampus—is less affected (Moscovitch & Winocur, 1992). So is recall of prior learning, which may even improve as a result of the growing complexity of neural connections in the cortex (Squire, 1992). In the Nun Study, a comparison of postmortem brain imaging studies with word recall tests taken a year before death underlined the role of hippocampal atrophy in cognitive decline in both demented and nondemented persons (Mortimer, Gosche, Riley, Markesbery, & Snowdon, 2004). Lesions in the hippocampus or other brain structures involved in episodic memory may result in loss of recent memories (Budson & Price, 2005).

The *frontal lobes* are involved in both encoding and retrieval of episodic memories. Dysfunction of the frontal lobes may cause "false" memories—"remembering" events that never occurred (Budson & Price, 2005). Early decline in the *prefrontal cortex,* which is essential to working memory, may underlie such common problems as inability to concentrate or pay attention and difficulty in performing a task with several steps (Budson & Price, 2005).

The brain often compensates for age-related declines in specialized regions by tapping other regions to help. In one study, researchers compared brain activity of college students with that of older adults during two memory tasks. When asked to remember sets of letters on a computer screen, the students used only the left hemisphere; when asked to remember the location of points on the screen, they used only the right hemisphere. The older adults, who did just as well as the students, used *both* the right and left frontal lobes for both tasks (Reuter-Lorenz, Stanczak, & Miller, 1999; Reuter-Lorenz et al., 2000). In another study, educated younger and older adults activated different brain regions in performing memory tasks: younger adults relied more on the medial temporal lobes, whereas older adults relied more on the frontal lobes (Springer, McIntosh, Winocur, & Grady, 2005). The brain's ability to shift functions in this way may help explain why symptoms of Alzheimer's disease often do not appear until the disease is well advanced, and previously unaffected regions of the brain, which have taken over for impaired regions, also lose working capacity ("Alzheimer's Disease, Part I," 1998).

Checkpoint
Can you . . .

✔ Identify two aspects of memory that tend to decline with age, and give reasons for this decline?

✔ Explain how problems in encoding, storage, and retrieval may affect memory in late adulthood?

✔ Point out several neurological changes related to memory?

Metamemory: The View from Within

"I'm less efficient at remembering things now than I used to be."
"I have little control over my memory."
"I am just as good at remembering as I ever was."

These items come from **Metamemory in Adulthood (MIA),** a questionnaire designed to measure *metamemory,* beliefs or knowledge about how memory works.

Older adults taking the MIA report more perceived change in memory, less memory capacity, and less control over their memory than young adults do (Dixon, Hultsch, & Hertzog, 1988). However, these perceptions may, at least in part, reflect personality characteristics (Pearman & Storandt, 2004) or stereotyped expectations of memory loss in old age (Hertzog, Dixon, & Hultsch, 1990; Poon, 1985) and not actual memory performance. In a study of 283 community-dwelling adults ages 45 to 94, personality traits (conscientiousness and neuroticism) and self-esteem accounted for about one-third of the variance in memory complaints (Pearman & Storandt, 2004).

Older people's performance may itself may be affected by internalized social attitudes. Older adults in cultures, such as China, that have positive views of aging tend to do better on memory tests than older adults in the United States. (Levy & Langer, 1994). In a pair of experiments, before taking memory tests, younger and older adults were "primed" with either positive or negative stereotypes about aging. Older adults showed greater recall when exposed to positive priming than when exposed to negative priming. The priming did *not* affect test results of younger adults, suggesting that the effects were specific to the age group at which the stereotypes were aimed (Hess, Hinson, & Statham, 2004). In another comparative study of older and younger

Metamemory in Adulthood (MIA) Questionnaire designed to measure various aspects of adults' metamemory, including beliefs about their own memory and the selection and use of strategies for remembering.

adults, beliefs about control of memory significantly affected performance. Older adults were more likely to believe they had low control, and their performance was lower. Both older and younger adults were able to do better by setting goals, but older adults tended to set lower goals and to improve less (West & Yassuda, 2004).

Can Older People Improve Their Cognitive Performance?

Plasticity is a key feature of Baltes's life-span developmental approach, and he and his colleagues have been in the forefront of research in training older adults to improve their cognitive performance. Several of these studies have been based on the Adult Development and Enrichment Project (ADEPT), originated at Pennsylvania State University (Baltes & Willis, 1982; Blieszner, Willis, & Baltes, 1981; Plemons, Willis, & Baltes, 1978; Willis, Blieszner, & Baltes, 1981).

In one study based on ADEPT, adults with an average age of 70 who received training in figural relations (rules for determining the next figure in a series), a measure of fluid intelligence, improved more than a control group who received no training. A third group who worked with the same training materials and problems without formal instruction also did better than the control group, and this self-taught group maintained their gains better after one month (Blackburn, Papalia-Finlay, Foye, & Serlin, 1988). Apparently the opportunity to work out their own solutions fostered more lasting learning.

In training connected with the Seattle Longitudinal Study (Schaie, 1990, 1994, 1996b; Schaie & Willis, 1986; Willis & Schaie, 1986b), older people who already had shown declines in intelligence gained significantly in two fluid abilities: spatial orientation and, especially, inductive reasoning. In fact, about 4 out of 10 participants regained levels of proficiency they had shown 14 years earlier. Gains measured in the laboratory showed substantial correlations with objective measures of everyday functioning (Schaie, 1994, 2005; Willis, Jay, Diehl, & Marsiske, 1992).

Longitudinal findings suggest that training may enable older adults not only to recover lost competence but even to surpass their previous attainments (Schaie &

Young people are not the only ones becoming computer-literate these days. Many older people are joining the computer age and learning useful new skills. Research has found that older adults can improve their cognitive performance with training and practice.

Willis, 1996). In both the ADEPT and Seattle studies, trained participants retained an edge over an untrained control group, even after seven years (Schaie, 1994, 1996a, 1996b; Willis, 1990; Willis & Nesselroade, 1990).

Cognitive deterioration, then, often may be related to disuse (Schaie, 1994, 1996b, 2005). Much as many aging athletes can call on physical reserves, older people who get training, practice, and social support seem to be able to draw on mental reserves. Adults may be able to maintain or expand this reserve capacity and avoid cognitive decline by engaging in a lifelong program of mental exercise (Dixon & Baltes, 1986).

Some investigators have offered training programs in *mnemonics* (refer back to Chapter 9): techniques designed to help people remember, such as visualizing a list of items, making associations between a face and a name, or transforming the elements in a story into mental images. An analysis of thirty-three studies found that older people benefit from mnemonic training. The particular type of mnemonic made little difference (Verhaeghen, Marcoen, & Goossens, 1992). However, the effectiveness of memory training in very old age appears to be limited. In a study of 96 participants in the Berlin Aging Study, ages 75 to 101, gains after mnemonic instruction were modest, and subsequent practice made very little difference (Singer, Lindenberger, & Baltes, 2003).

An experiment with mice has raised hopes that genetic manipulation might be able to counteract memory loss. The gene involved controls a unit of a neural signal receptor that becomes less active with age. A strain of mice bred with extra copies of this gene performed better than normal mice on memory tests (Tang et al., 1999). In another experiment with rats, diets high in antioxidant fruits and vegetables, such as blueberries and spinach, retarded or even reversed age-related declines in brain function and in cognitive and motor performance (Galli, Shukitt-Hale, Youdim, & Joseph, 2002). On the other hand, there is little evidence that highly touted memory-enhancing drugs such as ginkgo biloba have much, if any, effect (refer back to Box 17-1).

Lifemap CD

The "Cognitive Functioning in Centenarians" video in Chapter 17 of your CD provides an inspiring example of the "use it or lose it" principle in action.

Checkpoint

Can you . . .

✔ Discuss how well older adults judge their memory capacities, and cite ways in which their memory can be improved?

✔ Cite evidence of the plasticity of cognitive abilities, and its limits, in late adulthood?

Wisdom

With the graying of the planet, wisdom—long the subject of philosophical speculation—has become an important topic of psychological research. Psychological approaches to the study of wisdom focus on either *social judgments, personality,* or *cognitive expertise.* Each of these approaches can yield valuable information about what it means to be wise (Shedlock & Cornelius, 2003).

The *social judgments* approach explores people's conceptions of the prototypical "wise person" and looks for commonalities among them (Sternberg, 1990). *Personality* theorists, such as Jung and Erikson (see Chapter 18), view wisdom as the culmination of a lifetime of personal growth and ego development.

As a *cognitive* ability, wisdom may be defined as "exceptional breadth and depth of knowledge about the conditions of life and human affairs and reflective judgment about the application of this knowledge" (Kramer, 2003, p. 132). It may involve insight and awareness of the uncertain, paradoxical nature of reality and may lead to *transcendence,* detachment from preoccupation with the self (Kramer, 2003). Some theorists define wisdom as an extension of postformal thought, a synthesis of reason and emotion (Labouvie-Vief, 1990a, 1990b).

Robert Sternberg (1998) sees wisdom as a special form of practical intelligence with a moral aspect. It involves value judgments about what ends are good and tacit knowledge of how best to reach them. It aims to achieve a common good through the balancing of multiple, often conflicting interests. An example might be John Glenn's decision to return to space, which balanced the potential benefits to medical science and his own sense of fulfillment against the risks involved and his family's anxiety.

The most extensive research on wisdom as a cognitive ability has been done by Paul Baltes and his colleagues (Baltes, 1993; Baltes & Staudinger, 2000; Pasupathi,

The average age of members of the United States Supreme Court in 2005 (before the retirement of Justice Sandra Day O'Connor, front, 2nd from right, and the death of Chief Justice William Rehnquist, front, center) was 65. Are older people wiser than younger people? Not necessarily, according to research.

What's Your View?

- In what ways do your observations of older adults' cognitive functioning agree or differ with the research reported in this chapter?

- What are some ways to sustain a high level of intellectual activity in late life? Do you think you need to develop new or broader interests that you will want to pursue as you age?

- Think of the wisest person you know. Which, if any, of the criteria for wisdom mentioned in this chapter seem to describe this person? If none do, how would you define and measure wisdom?

Checkpoint

Can you . . .

✔ Compare several approaches to the study of wisdom?

✔ Summarize findings from Baltes's studies of wisdom?

Staudinger, & Baltes, 2001). Baltes's dual-process model includes wisdom in the pragmatics of intelligence—a crystallized form that resists neurological decline.

In a series of studies, Baltes and his associates at the Max Planck Institute in Berlin asked adults of various ages and occupations to think aloud about hypothetical dilemmas. Responses were rated according to whether they showed rich factual and procedural knowledge about the human condition and about dealing with life's problems. Other criteria were awareness that contextual circumstances can influence problems, that problems tend to lend themselves to multiple interpretations and solutions, and that choices of solutions depend on individual values, goals, and priorities (Baltes & Staudinger, 2000; Pasupathi et al., 2001).

In one of these studies (J. Smith & Baltes, 1990), 60 well-educated German professionals ages 25 to 81 were given four dilemmas involving such issues as weighing career against family needs and deciding whether to accept early retirement. Of 240 solutions, only 5 percent were rated wise, and these responses were distributed nearly evenly among young, middle-aged, and older adults. Participants showed more wisdom about decisions applicable to their own stage of life. For example, the oldest group gave its best answers to the problem of a 60-year-old widow who, having just started her own business, learns that her son has been left with two young children and wants her to help care for them.

In another study, the researchers assembled 14 middle-aged and older adults (average age, 67) who were named by others as wise. When presented with two dilemmas—the one about the 60-year-old widow and another about a phone call from a friend who intends to commit suicide—these "wisdom nominees" equaled the performance of clinical psychologists about the same age (the best performers in other studies), who were trained to deal with the kinds of problems presented. Both of these "expert" groups gave wiser answers than control groups of older and younger adults with similar education and professional standing (Baltes, Staudinger, Maercker, & Smith, 1995).

Apparently, then, wisdom is not necessarily a property of old age—or of any age. Instead, it appears to be a relatively rare and complex phenomenon that shows relative stability or slight growth in certain individuals (Staudinger & Baltes, 1996; Staudinger, Smith, & Baltes, 1992). A variety of factors, including personality and life experience—either direct or vicarious, may contribute to it (Shedlock & Cornelius, 2003), and guidance from mentors may help prepare the way (Baltes & Staudinger, 2000; Pasupathi et al., 2001).

Lifelong Learning

 **Guidepost**

8. What educational opportunities can older adults pursue?

Qian Likun, a star student who walks to his classes on health care and ancient Chinese poetry, took part in a 2.3-mile footrace. This might not seem unusual until you learn that Qian is 102 years old, one of thousands of students in China's vast network of "universities for the aged." China's program exemplifies a trend toward **lifelong learning:** organized, sustained study by adults of all ages.

lifelong learning Organized, sustained study by adults of all ages.

Many older people in rural areas of developing countries have low literacy levels, having grown up when education was not widespread there. By contrast, in many developed countries older adults are better educated than their predecessors, and this trend will continue as younger cohorts age. In 1950, about 17 percent of older Americans had finished high school, and only 3 percent had bachelor's degrees. By 2003, 72 percent were high school graduates, and 17 percent held at least a bachelor's degree (Federal Interagency Forum for Aging-Related Statistics, 2004).

In today's complex society, the need for education is never over. Educational programs specifically designed for mature adults are booming. In one category are free or low-cost classes, taught by professionals or volunteers, at neighborhood senior centers, community centers, religious institutions, or storefronts. These classes generally have a practical or social focus (Moskow-McKenzie & Manheimer, 1994). In Japan, for example, *kominkans* (community educational centers) offer classes in child care, health, traditional arts and crafts, hobbies, exercise, and sports (Nojima, 1994). A second category consists of college- and university-based programs with education as the primary goal (Moskow-McKenzie & Manheimer, 1994). Elderhostel is an international not-for-profit network of educational and cultural institutions, which offers low-cost, noncredit residential courses and outdoor learning adventures for adults ages 55 and over. Each year nearly 200,000 adults take part in more than 10,000 Elderhostel programs in 90 countries ("What is Elderhostel?" 2005).

In the United States, continuing education courses for older people have mushroomed since the mid-1970s (Moskow-McKenzie & Manheimer, 1994). Many regional community colleges and state universities, as well as some private universities, offer special programs for older adults.

Older people learn best when the materials and methods take into account physiological, psychological, and cognitive changes they may be experiencing (Fisk & Rogers, 2002). For example, in learning to calibrate a blood glucose meter, older adults performed more poorly than younger ones when using a manual but did just as well as the younger learners and retained their learning when taught by a user-friendly video demonstration (Mykityshyn, Fisk, & Rogers, in press).

Checkpoint
Can you . . .

✔ Differentiate between two types of educational programs for older adults?

✔ Identify conditions conducive to older adults' learning?

Refocus

Thinking back to the Focus vignette about John Glenn at the beginning of this chapter:

• How did Glenn's *Discovery* voyage help shatter ageist stereotypes?

• How does Glenn exemplify the distinction between "young old" and "old old"?

• Which of the theories and research findings presented in this chapter seem to best explain Glenn's physical and cognitive condition in late adulthood?

The trend toward continuing education in late life illustrates how each stage of life could be made more satisfying by restructuring the course of life (refer back to Chapter 15). If people wove work, leisure, and study into their lives at all ages, young adults would feel less pressure to establish themselves early, middle-aged people would feel less burdened, and older people would be more stimulated and would feel—and be—more useful. Such a pattern might make an important contribution to emotional well-being in late adulthood, as we discuss in Chapter 18.

SUMMARY AND KEY TERMS

Old Age Today

Guidepost 1: **How is today's older population changing?**

- Efforts to combat ageism are making headway, thanks to the visibility of a growing number of active, healthy older adults.
- The proportion of older people in the United States and world populations is greater than ever before and is expected to continue to grow. People over 80 are the fastest-growing age group.
- Today, many older people are healthy, vigorous, and active. Although effects of primary aging may be beyond people's control, they often can avoid effects of secondary aging.
- Specialists in the study of aging sometimes refer to people between ages 65 and 74 as the *young old,* those over 75 as the *old old,* and those over 85 as the *oldest old.* However, these terms may be more useful when used to refer to functional age.

ageism *(627)*

primary aging *(629)*

secondary aging *(629)*

functional age *(629)*

gerontology *(629)*

geriatrics *(629)*

PHYSICAL DEVELOPMENT

Longevity and Aging

Guidepost 2: **How has life expectancy changed, and how does it vary?**

- Life expectancy has increased dramatically. The longer people live, the longer they are likely to live.
- In general, life expectancy is greater in developed countries than in developing countries, among white Americans than among African Americans, and among women as compared to men.
- Recent gains in life expectancy come largely from progress toward reducing death rates from diseases affecting older people. Further large improvements in life expectancy may depend on whether scientists can learn to modify basic processes of aging.

life expectancy *(629)*

longevity *(630)*

life span *(630)*

Guidepost 3: **What theories have been advanced for causes of aging, and what does research suggest about possibilities for extending the life span?**

- Theories of biological aging fall into two categories: genetic-programming theories and variable-rate, or error theories.
- Research on extension of the life span through genetic manipulation or caloric restriction has challenged the idea of a biological limit to the life span.

senescence *(632)*

genetic-programming theories *(633)*

variable-rate theories *(633)*

metabolism *(633)*

free radicals *(634)*

autoimmunity *(634)*

survival curves *(636)*

Hayflick limit *(636)*

Physical Changes

Guidepost 4: **What physical changes occur during old age, and how do these changes vary among individuals?**

- Changes in body systems and organs are highly variable and may be results of disease, which in turn may be affected by lifestyle.
- Most body systems generally continue to function fairly well, but the heart becomes more susceptible to disease. Reserve capacity declines.
- Although the brain changes with age, the changes are usually modest. They include loss or shrinkage of nerve cells and a general slowing of responses. However, the brain also seems able to grow new neurons and build new connections late in life.
- Older people tend to sleep less and dream less than before, but chronic insomnia can be an indication of depression.
- Visual and hearing problems may interfere with daily life but often can be corrected. Irreversible damage may result from age-related macular degeneration or glaucoma. Losses in taste and smell may lead to poor nutrition. Training can improve muscular strength, balance, and reaction time. Older adults tend to be susceptible to accidents and falls.
- Many older people are sexually active, though the frequency and intensity of sexual experience are generally lower than for younger adults.
- Intelligence tends to predict longevity.

reserve capacity *(640)*

cataracts *(642)*

age-related macular degeneration *(642)*

glaucoma *(642)*

Physical and Mental Health

Guidepost 5: What health problems are common in late adulthood, and what factors influence health at that time?

- Most older people are reasonably healthy, especially if they follow a healthy lifestyle. Most do have chronic conditions, but these usually do not greatly limit activities or interfere with daily life.
- Exercise and diet are important influences on health. Loss of teeth can seriously affect nutrition.

  activities of daily living (ADLs) *(646)*

  instrumental activities of daily living (IADLs) *(646)*

Guidepost 6: What mental and behavioral disorders do some older people experience?

- Most older people are in good mental health. Depression, alcoholism, and many other conditions can be reversed with treatment; a few, such as Alzheimer's disease, are irreversible.
- Alzheimer's disease becomes more prevalent with age. It is highly heritable, but diet, exercise, and other lifestyle factors may play a part. Cognitive activity may be protective by building up a cognitive reserve that enables the brain to function under stress. Behavioral and drug therapies can slow deterioration. Mild cognitive impairment can be an early sign of the disease, and researchers are attempting to develop tools for early diagnosis.

  dementia *(649)*

  Alzheimer's disease *(649)*

  Parkinson's disease *(649)*

  neurofibrillary tangles *(651)*

  amyloid plaque *(651)*

  cognitive reserve *(651)*

COGNITIVE DEVELOPMENT

Aspects of Cognitive Development

Guidepost 7: What gains and losses in cognitive abilities tend to occur in late adulthood, and are there ways to improve older people's cognitive performance?

- Physical and psychological factors that influence older people's performance on intelligence tests may lead to underestimation of their intelligence. Cross-sectional research showing declines in intelligence may reflect cohort differences.
- Measures of fluid and crystallized intelligence show a more encouraging pattern, with crystallized abilities increasing into old age.
- In Baltes' dual-process model, the mechanics of intelligence often decline, but the pragmatics of intelligence may continue to grow.

- The Seattle Longitudinal Study found that cognitive functioning in late adulthood is highly variable. Few people decline in all or most areas, and many people improve in some. The engagement hypothesis seeks to explain these differences.
- Although findings are mixed, it appears that practical problem solving tends to decline in late adulthood. Older adults do better on problems that have emotional relevance for them.
- A general slowdown in central nervous system functioning may affect the speed of information processing. However, this slowdown may be limited to certain processing tasks and may vary among individuals.
- Intelligence may be a predictor of longevity.
- Sensory memory, semantic and procedural memory, and priming appear nearly as efficient in older adults as in younger people. The capacity of working memory and the ability to recall specific events or recently learned information are often less efficient.
- Older adults have more problems with oral word retrieval and spelling than younger adults. Grammatical complexity and propositional content of speech decline, but vocabulary remains strong.
- Neurological changes, as well as declines in perceptual speed, may account for much of the decline in memory functioning in older adults. However, the brain can compensate for some age-related declines.
- According to studies of metamemory, some older adults may overestimate their memory loss, perhaps because of stereotypes about aging.
- Older people show considerable plasticity in cognitive performance and can benefit from training.
- According to Baltes's studies, wisdom is not age-related, but people of all ages give wiser responses to problems affecting their own age group.

  Wechsler Adult Intelligence Scale (WAIS) *(653)*

  dual-process model *(654)*

  mechanics of intelligence *(654)*

  pragmatics of intelligence *(654)*

  selective optimization with compensation (SOC) *(655)*

  sensory memory *(658)*

  working memory *(658)*

  episodic memory *(658)*

  semantic memory *(659)*

  procedural memory *(659)*

  priming *(659)*

  Metamemory in Adulthood (MIA) *(661)*

Lifelong Learning

Guidepost 8: What educational opportunities can older adults pursue?

- Lifelong learning can keep older people mentally alert.
- Educational programs for older adults are proliferating. Most of these programs have either a practical-social focus or a more serious educational one.
- Older adults learn better when material and methods are geared to the needs of this age group.

  lifelong learning *(665)*

CHAPTER 18

Psychosocial Development in Late Adulthood

There is still today
And tomorrow fresh with dreams:
Life never grows old

Rita Duskin, "Haiku," *Sound and Light,* 1987

Focus
Jimmy Carter, "Retired" President

Jimmy Carter

James Earl ("Jimmy") Carter, Jr. (b. 1924)* was one of the most unpopular presidents of the United States in the twentieth century. Yet, a quarter century after having been turned out of office, he is one of the most active and admired ex-presidents in American history, "pursuing lost and neglected causes with a missionary's zeal"—and amazing success (Nelson, 1994).

In 1976, in the wake of the Watergate scandal, Carter, a peanut farmer who had completed a term as governor of Georgia, became the first southerner in the twentieth century to be elected president. His appeal was as an outsider who would clean up government and restore a moral tone. But despite such historic achievements as peace between Israel and Egypt, he became bogged down in the interminable Iranian hostage crisis and was blamed for high fuel prices and a sagging economy. After a devastating defeat in 1980, he retired from political life at the age of 56.

Carter and his wife and longtime helpmate, Rosalynn, faced a devastating crisis. His farm and warehouse business were deeply in debt, and he had no immediate prospects for work. "We thought the best of our life was over," he recalls. "And we went through a very difficult time with each other" (Beyette, 1998, p. 6A). Finally, determined to take charge of the remaining part of their lives, they asked themselves what experiences they could build on, what interests they had had too little time to pursue, and what talents they had not been able to fully develop.

What has Carter done since then? He is a professor at Emory University and teaches in a Baptist Sunday school. He helps build houses for low-income families through Habitat for Humanity. He established the Carter Center, which sponsors international

*Sources of biographical information on Jimmy Carter were Beyette (1998), Bird (1990), Carter (1975, 1998), Carter Center (1995), J. Nelson (1994), Spalding (1977), Wooten (1995), and various news articles.

programs in human rights, education, preventive health care, agricultural techniques, and conflict resolution and has secured the release of hundreds of political prisoners. As a roving peacemaker and guardian of freedom, Carter oversaw the Nicaraguan elections that ousted the Sandanistas. He brokered a cease-fire between Bosnian Muslims and Serbs. He has observed or helped set up fair elections in Indonesia, China, Nigeria, Mozambique, and several other developing countries. He was the first former U.S. president to visit Communist Cuba. For these acts of courage, idealism, and service, he received the Presidential Medal of Freedom and the first United Nations Human Rights Prize. In 2002, at 78, he won the Nobel Peace Prize.

It has been said that Carter "used his presidency as a stepping stone to higher things" (Bird, 1990, p. 564). Freed from the pressures of politics, he has risen to the role of elder statesman.

Carter has written fourteen books, most recently *The Virtues of Aging*. In it, he talks about how he and Rosalynn have learned to "give each other some space"; how becoming grandparents deepened their relationship; how the active lives of close friends and acquaintances have served as examples and inspiration; how he handled the loss of his mother, brother, and two sisters; and how his religious faith helps him face the prospect of his own death without fear.

What does Carter see as the virtues of aging? "We have an unprecedented degree of freedom to choose what we want to do. . . . We have a chance to heal wounds. . . . We have an opportunity to expand the ties of understanding with the people we love most." And there are still new worlds to conquer. "Our primary purpose" says Carter, "is not just to stay alive . . . but to savor every opportunity for pleasure, excitement, adventure and fulfillment" (Beyette, 1998, pp. 6A–7A).

A lthough few adults have the resources and opportunities of an ex-president, Jimmy Carter is far from unique in using his retirement years productively. He is one of many older adults whose activism is creating a new view of life in old age.

In the early 1980s, shortly after Carter left office, the writer Betty Friedan was asked to organize a seminar at Harvard University on "Growth in Aging." The distinguished behaviorist B. F. Skinner declined to participate. Age and growth, he said, were "a contradiction in terms" (Friedan, 1993, p. 23). Skinner was far from alone in that belief. Yet two decades later, late adulthood is increasingly recognized as a time of potential growth.

Today, such terms as *successful aging* and *optimal aging* appear frequently in the theoretical and research literature. These terms are controversial because they seem to imply that there is a "right" or "best" way to age. Still, some older adults, like the Carters, do seem to get more out of life than others. "Growth in aging" *is* possible; and many older adults who feel healthy, competent, and in control of their lives experience this last stage of life as a positive one.

In this chapter, we look at theory and research on psychosocial development in late adulthood. We discuss such late-life options as work, retirement, and living arrangements and their impact on society's ability to support an aging population and to care for the frail and infirm. Finally, we look at relationships with families and friends, which greatly affect the quality of these last years.

After you have read and studied this chapter, you should be able to answer each of the Guidepost questions that follow. Look for them again in the margins, where they point to important concepts throughout the chapter. To check your understanding of these Guideposts, review the end-of-chapter summary. Checkpoints located at periodic spots throughout the chapter will help you verify your understanding of what you have read.

1. Does personality change in old age, and what special issues or tasks do older people need to deal with?

2. How do older adults cope?

3. What is successful aging and how can it be measured?

4. What are some issues regarding work and retirement in late life, and how do older adults handle time and money?

5. What options for living arrangements do older adults have?

6. How do personal relationships change in old age, and what is their effect on well-being?

7. What are the characteristics of long-term marriages in late life, and what impact do divorce, remarriage, and widowhood have at this time?

8. How do unmarried older people and those in gay and lesbian relationships fare?

9. How does friendship change in old age?

10. How do older adults get along with—or without—grown children and with siblings, and how do they adjust to great-grandparenthood?

Theory and Research on Psychosocial Development

The examples of such people as Jimmy Carter lead some theorists to view late adulthood as a developmental stage with its own special issues and tasks—a time when people reexamine their lives, complete unfinished business, and decide how best to channel their energies and spend their remaining days, months, or years. Some wish to leave a legacy to their grandchildren or to the world, pass on the fruits of their experience, or validate the meaning of their lives. Others simply want to enjoy favorite pastimes or to do things they never had enough time for when they were younger. Some, like Sanny Sue Holland-Hoffman—who, shortly before her 70th birthday, became a flight attendant and remarried after being a widow for 20 years—embark on major new directions in life (Thomas, 2005).

Let's see what theory and research on psychosocial development can tell us about this final phase of the life span: about the stability of personality and emotionality, about how older people cope with stress and loss, and about what constitutes "successful" aging.

Personality in Late Life

Does personality change in late life? The answer may depend in part on the way stability and change are measured.

Measuring Stability and Change in Personality Traits Stability and change in personality traits can be measured in several ways. The type of long-term stability reported by Costa and McCrae (refer back to Chapters 14 and 16) is in *average levels*

Guidepost

1. Does personality change in old age, and what special issues or tasks do older people need to deal with?

BOX 18-1

Digging Deeper
Does Personality Predict Health and Longevity?

In the Terman study of gifted children, childhood personality characteristics and family environment played an important part in adult success. Now it appears that such factors may influence how long people live.

Most of the approximately 1,500 California schoolchildren chosen for the study at about age 11 on the basis of high IQ have been followed periodically since 1921. Between 1986 and 1991, when the survivors were approaching age 80, a group of researchers (Friedman et al., 1993; Friedman, Tucker, Schwartz, Martin et al., 1995; Friedman, Tucker, Schwartz, Tomlinson-Keasey et al., 1995; Tucker & Friedman, 1996)* decided to find out how many had died and at what ages, so as to spot predictors of longevity. Because the "Termites" as a group were bright and well educated, the results were not likely to be confounded by poor nutrition, poverty, or inadequate medical care. Although these highly intelligent people, on the whole, have lived longer than average, their individual longevity was affected by such factors as health-related behaviors, psychological adjustment, personality, and social relationships, which influence mortality risk of people in general (Friedman & Markey, 2003).

Surprisingly, neither childhood self-confidence, energy, nor sociability turned out to be related to longevity. Nor was optimism in childhood associated with long life. In fact, the reverse was true: cheerful children were more likely to die young. What *did* strongly predict longevity was the personality dimension called *conscientiousness,* or dependability—sometimes described as orderliness, prudence, or self-control.

This older couple seem comfortable with, and supportive of, each other. According to the Terman study, *conscientiousness (dependability) and marital stability are related to long life.*

This research suggests that cheerful children may grow up to be more careless about their health than conscientious children. Although a carefree, optimistic approach to life may be helpful in coping with short-term situations, such as recovery from illness, in the long run it may be unhealthy if it leads a person to ignore warnings and engage in risky behaviors (Martin et al., 2002). In contrast, an analysis of many studies found that conscientious people

of various traits within a population. According to the five-factor model and its supporting research, hostile people, on average, are unlikely to mellow much with age unless they get psychotherapeutic treatment, and optimistic people are likely to remain their hopeful selves. Certain persistent trait patterns may contribute to adaptation to aging and may even predict health and longevity (Baltes, Lindenberger, & Staudinger, 1998; see Box 18-1).

Another way to assess stability or change is *within individuals.* A 6-year randomized study of 2,117 55- to 85-year olds in the Netherlands found little individual change in neuroticism, and what changes did occur were independent of deterioration in physical health or cognitive function (Steunenberg, Twisk, Beekman, Deeg, & Kerkhof, 2005).

A third way to measure stability or change is in *rank-order comparisons* of different people on a given trait. A review of 152 longitudinal studies found that relative differences among individuals become increasingly stable until sometime between ages 50 and 70 and then plateau (Roberts & DelVecchio, 2000). Thus, if Elsa is more conscientious than Manuel as a young adult, she is likely to remain the more conscientious of the two in late adulthood. A study of 484 middle-aged and older adults in Victoria, B.C., supported this type of stability with regard to the five-factor model (Small et al., 2003). Thus, all three types of trait measurements point to stability of personality in late adulthood.

Early cross-sectional research suggested that personality becomes more rigid in old age. However, McCrae and Costa (1994), in large longitudinal studies using a variety of samples and measures, have shown that this is *not* true for most people.

—continued

tend to engage in behaviors beneficial to health. They are unlikely to smoke, to drink excessively, to use drugs, to adopt sedentary lifestyles, and to choose unhealthful diets. They are also unlikely to engage in violence, risky sexual behavior, risky driving, and suicide (Bogg & Roberts, 2004).

Similarly, in a longitudinal study of 883 aging members of Catholic clergy, highly conscientious people had half the risk of death during a 5-year period as people low in conscientiousness, whereas people high in neuroticism had nearly double the risk compared with those low in neuroticism (Wilson, Mendes de Leon, Bienias, Evans, & Bennett, 2004).

In the Terman study, conscientiousness was related to a variety of variables that have positive influences on longevity. By midlife, conscientious children tended to have finished more years of education than less conscientious children and were less likely to have shown mental problems. They also were less likely to have been divorced or to have experienced parental divorce in their childhood.

Apparently it is not marriage itself but marital *stability* that can lead to long life. Termites who, at age 40, were in their first marriages tended to live significantly longer than those who had been divorced, whether or not the latter had remarried. By contrast, Termites who had *never* married had only slightly increased risk of early death.

Marital instability in the childhood home also was a threat to longevity. People who, before the age of 21, had experienced the divorce of their parents—13 percent of the sample—lived, on average, four years less than those whose parents had stayed together. Early death of a parent, on the other hand, made little difference.

The findings about marital stability and personality are interrelated. Children rated as impulsive were more likely to grow into adults with unstable marital histories and were more likely to die young. Also, children of divorce were more likely to go through divorce themselves—explaining part of the influence of parental divorce on longevity.

It seems, then, that people who are dependable, trustworthy, and diligent both in taking good care of themselves and in preserving their marriages—and who are fortunate enough to have had parents who stayed married—may be rewarded with more years of life.

*Unless otherwise referenced, the aforementioned studies are the sources for this box.

What's Your View?

Think of someone you know who lived a very long life. Did that person have a conscientious personality? A stable marriage?

Check It Out

For more information on this topic, go to http://www.cpc.unc .edu/projects/lifecourse/terman. This is the site for the Lewis Terman Study at Stanford University.

Likewise, personality tests of 3,442 participants in the Seattle Longitudinal Study found no age-related trends in inflexibility (Schaie, 2005). Indeed, people in more recent cohorts seem to be more flexible (that is, less rigid) than previous cohorts. These findings suggest that "increases" in rigidity found in the early studies may actually have been tied, not to age, but to the life experience that a particular cohort carried throughout adulthood (Schaie & Willis, 1991).

Personality, Emotionality, and Well-Being Personality is a strong predictor of emotionality and subjective well-being—stronger in most respects than social relationships and health (Isaacowitz & Smith, 2003). In a longitudinal study that followed four generations for 23 years, self-reported *negative* emotions such as restlessness, boredom, loneliness, unhappiness, and depression decreased with age (though the *rate* of decrease slowed after 60). At the same time, *positive* emotionality—excitement, interest, pride, and a sense of accomplishment—tended to remain stable until late life and then declined only slightly and gradually (Charles, Reynolds, & Gatz, 2001).

A possible explanation for this generally positive picture comes from socioemotional selectivity theory (introduced in Chapter 16): as people get older, they tend to seek out activities and people that give them emotional gratification. In addition, older adults' greater ability to regulate their emotions may help explain why they tend to be happier and more cheerful than younger adults and to experience negative emotions less often and more fleetingly (Blanchard-Fields, Stein, & Watson, 2004; Carstensen, 1999; Mroczek & Kolarz, 1998)).

Two of the Big Five personality traits—extraversion and neuroticism—tend to modify the pattern just described. As Costa and McCrae (1980) predicted, people with *extraverted* personalities (outgoing and socially oriented) tend to report especially high levels of positive emotion initially and are more likely than others to retain their positivity throughout life (Charles et al., 2001; Isaacowitz & Smith, 2003). Similarly, in a 22-year longitudinal study of 1,927 men, most of them ages 40 to 85, those highest in extraversion were more likely than their peers to maintain a high level of life satisfaction in old age (Mroczek & Spiro, 2005).

People with *neurotic* personalities (moody, touchy, anxious, and restless) tend to report negative and not positive emotions, and they tend to become no less negative and less positive as they age (Charles et al., 2001; Isaacowitz & Smith, 2003). Neuroticism is a far more powerful predictor of moods and mood disorders than age, race, gender, income, education, and marital status (Costa & McCrae, 1996).

Erik Erikson: Normative Issues and Tasks Whereas trait models emphasize the fundamental stability of personality, other models look at factors that may contribute to personal growth. According to normative-stage theorists, growth depends on carrying out the psychological tasks of each stage of life in an emotionally healthy way.

For Erikson, the crowning achievement of late adulthood is a sense of *ego integrity*, or integrity of the self, an achievement based on reflection about one's life. In the eighth and final stage of the life span, **ego integrity versus despair,** older adults need to evaluate and accept their lives so as to accept death. Building on the outcomes of the seven previous stages, they struggle to achieve a sense of coherence and wholeness, rather than give way to despair over their inability to relive the past differently (Erikson, Erikson, & Kivnick, 1986). People who succeed in this final, integrative task gain a sense of the meaning of their lives within the larger social order. The "virtue" that may develop during this stage is *wisdom,* an "informed and detached concern with life itself in the face of death itself" (Erikson, 1985, p. 61).

Wisdom, said Erikson, means accepting the life one has lived, without major regrets: without dwelling on "should-have-dones" or "might-have-beens." It means accepting imperfection in the self, in parents, in children, and in life. (This definition of *wisdom* as an important psychological resource differs from the largely cognitive definitions explored in Chapter 17.)

Although integrity must outweigh despair if this stage is to be resolved successfully, Erikson maintained that some despair is inevitable. People need to mourn—not only for their own misfortunes and lost chances but for the vulnerability and transience of the human condition.

Yet, Erikson believed, even as the body's functions weaken, people must maintain a "vital involvement" in society. On the basis of studies of life histories of people in their eighties, he concluded that ego integrity comes not just from reflecting on the past but, as with Jimmy Carter, from continued stimulation and challenge—whether through political activity, fitness programs, creative work, or relationships with grandchildren (Erikson et al., 1986). Research inspired by Erikson's theory supports the importance men and women place on striving for ego integrity in late adulthood (Sheldon & Kasser, 2001).

ego integrity versus despair According to Erikson, the eighth and final stage of psychosocial development, in which people in late adulthood either achieve a sense of integrity of the self by accepting the lives they have lived, and thus accept death, or yield to despair that their lives cannot be relived.

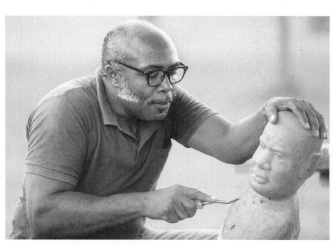

According to Erikson, ego integrity in late adulthood requires continuing stimulation and challenge, which, for this elderly sculptor, come from creative work. Sources of ego integrity vary widely, from political activity to fitness programs to building relationships with grandchildren.

Checkpoint

Can you . . .

✔ Summarize what is known about stability of personality traits and emotionality in old age?

✔ Describe Erikson's crisis of ego integrity versus despair, and tell what Erikson meant by *wisdom*?

Models of Coping

Their health may not be what it was, they've lost old friends and family members—often spouses—and they probably don't earn the money they once did. Their lives keep changing in countless stressful ways. Yet in general, older adults have fewer mental disorders and are more satisfied with life than younger ones (Mroczek & Kolarz, 1998; Wykle & Musil, 1993). What accounts for this remarkable ability to cope?

Coping is adaptive thinking or behavior aimed at reducing or relieving stress that arises from harmful, threatening, or challenging conditions. It is an important aspect of mental health. Let's look at two theoretical approaches to the study of coping: adaptive defenses and the cognitive-appraisal model. Then we'll look at a support system to which many older adults turn: religion.

George Vaillant: Adaptive Defenses What makes for positive mental health in old age? According to three 50-year prospective studies, an important predictive factor is the use of mature *adaptive defenses* in coping with problems earlier in life.

Vaillant (2000) looked at the survivors of his own Grant Study of Harvard men born around 1920 (refer back to Chapter 14), as well as his study of inner-city men born around 1930 and a subsample of women from Terman's study of gifted California schoolchildren born about 1910 (refer back to Box 18-1). In all three groups, those who, in old age, showed the best psychosocial adjustment, had the highest incomes and the strongest social supports, and reported the greatest marital satisfaction and joy in living were those who, earlier in adulthood, had used such mature adaptive defenses as altruism, humor, suppression (keeping a stiff upper lip), anticipation (planning for the future), and sublimation (redirecting negative emotions into productive pursuits). Use of adaptive defenses was relatively independent of IQ, education, and parents' social class.

How do adaptive defenses work? According to Vaillant (2000), they can change people's perceptions of realities they are powerless to change. For example, in the three studies just mentioned, the use of adaptive defenses predicted *subjective* physical functioning even though it did *not* predict objective physical health as measured by physicians.

Adaptive defenses may be unconscious or intuitive. By contrast, the cognitive-appraisal model, to which we turn now, emphasizes consciously chosen coping strategies.

Cognitive-Appraisal Model In the **cognitive-appraisal model** (Lazarus & Folkman, 1984), people consciously choose coping strategies on the basis of the way they perceive and analyze a situation. Coping occurs when a person perceives a situation as taxing or exceeding his or her resources and thus demanding unusual effort. Coping includes anything an individual thinks or does in trying to adapt to stress, regardless of how well it works. Choosing the most appropriate strategy requires continuous reappraisal of the relationship between person and environment (see Figure 18-1).

Coping Strategies: Problem-focused versus Emotion-focused Coping strategies may be either *problem-focused* or *emotion-focused*. **Problem-focused coping** involves the use of *instrumental*, or action-oriented, strategies to eliminate, manage, or improve a stressful condition. This type of coping generally predominates when a person sees a realistic chance of changing the situation, as Jimmy Carter and his wife did in looking at their options after his defeat for reelection. **Emotion-focused coping**, sometimes called *palliative coping*, is directed toward "feeling better": managing the emotional response to a stressful situation to relieve its physical or psychological impact. This type of coping is likely to predominate when a person concludes that

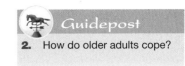

Guidepost

2. How do older adults cope?

coping Adaptive thinking or behavior aimed at reducing or relieving stress that arises from harmful, threatening, or challenging conditions.

cognitive-appraisal model Model of coping, proposed by Lazarus and Folkman, which holds that, on the basis of continuous appraisal of their relationship with the environment, people choose appropriate coping strategies to deal with situations that tax their normal resources.

problem-focused coping In the cognitive-appraisal model, coping strategy directed toward eliminating, managing, or improving a stressful situation.

emotion-focused coping In the cognitive-appraisal model, coping strategy directed toward managing the emotional response to a stressful situation so as to lessen its physical or psychological impact; sometimes called *palliative coping*.

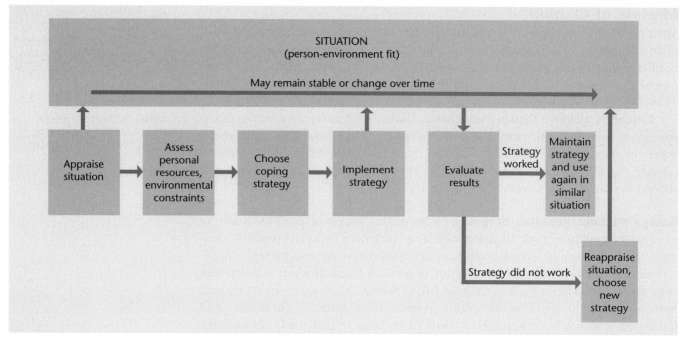

Figure 18-1

Cognitive-appraisal model of coping. (Source: Based on Lazarus & Folkman, 1984.)

little or nothing can be done about the situation itself. One emotion-focused strategy is to divert attention away from a problem; another is to give in; still another is to deny that the problem exists. Problem-focused responses to a series of harsh reprimands from an employer might be to work harder, seek ways to improve one's work skills, or look for another job. Emotion-focused responses might be to refuse to think about the reprimands or to convince oneself that the boss didn't really mean to be so critical.

Age Differences in Choice of Coping Styles Older adults tend to do more emotion-focused coping than younger people (Folkman, Lazarus, Pimley, & Novacek, 1987; Prohaska, Leventhal, Leventhal, & Keller, 1985). Is that because they are less able to focus on problems, or because they are better able to control their emotions? Research suggests that the latter is the answer (Blanchard-Fields, Stein, & Watson, 2004).

In studies in which young, middle-aged, and older adults were asked how they would deal with various kinds of problems, participants, regardless of age, most often picked problem-focused strategies (either direct action or analyzing the problem so as to understand it better). The largest age differences appeared in problems with highly emotional or stressful implications, such as that of a divorced man who is allowed to see his child only on weekends but wants to see the child more often. Adults of all ages were more likely to use emotion-focused coping in such situations, but older adults chose emotion-focused strategies (such as doing nothing, waiting until the child is older, or trying not to worry about it) more often than younger adults did (Blanchard-Fields, Jahnke, & Camp, 1995; Blanchard-Fields et al., 2004).

Apparently, with age, people develop a more flexible repertoire of coping strategies (Blanchard-Fields, Stein, & Watson, 2004). Older adults *can* employ problem-focused strategies but may be more able than younger adults to use emotion regulation when a situation seems to call for it—when problem-focused action might be futile or counterproductive (Blanchard-Fields & Camp, 1990; Blanchard-Fields, Chen, & Norris, 1997; Blanchard-Fields & Irion, 1987; Folkman & Lazarus, 1980; Labouvie-Vief, Hakim-Larson, & Hobart, 1987).

More recent research has distinguished between two types of emotion-focused coping: *proactive* (confronting or expressing one's emotions or seeking social support) and *passive* (avoidance, denial, or suppression of emotions or acceptance of the situation as it is). In one study (Blanchard-Fields et al., 2004), adults of all ages were, as in previous research, equally likely to use problem-focused strategies in solving social problems. When it came to emotionally charged interpersonal problems, such as losing a loved one, middle-aged adults were more likely to use proactive emotion-regulation strategies, whereas both young and older adults tended to use passive strategies. Why might this be? Young adults may not have enough experience in dealing with interpersonal conflict to use proactive strategies; older adults may have less energy for emotional exploration than middle-aged adults and may instead use their available resources to maintain a positive outlook. On the other hand, older adults' tendency toward emotional passivity may be a cohort effect, as today's older adults grew up during the Great Depression, when "it was quite adaptive to suppress feelings and keep a stiff upper lip" (p. P267). (Table 18-1 gives examples of instrumental (problem-focused), passive emotional, and proactive emotional strategies.)

What's Your View?

- Which type of coping do you tend to use more: problem-focused, proactive emotion-focused, or passive emotion-focused? Which type do your parents use more? Your grandparents? In what kinds of situations does each type of coping seem most effective?

Table 18-1 Types of Coping Strategies

Coping Strategy	Description	Example
Instrumental strategies		
Cognitive analysis	Intrapsychic or cognitive efforts to understand the problem better, or to solve it through logical analysis	"One of the ways that I handle situations is that I get out my yellow pad, and I put down 'plus' and I put down 'minus' And then I add them up and see what I did, because this helps me to analyze what I did."
Planful problem solving	Self-initiated, overt behaviors that deal directly with the problem and its effects	"I knew what the problem was and just tackled it."
Regulation/inclusion of others	Attempts to shape another's opinions or behaviors to conform to that of problem solver	"I just gave him some suggestions about different things . . . just offered some advice."
Passive emotional regulation		
Avoidance/denial/escape	Intentionally redirecting thoughts and behaviors away from the situation	"Look for something else to do that day to . . . channel my energies into another outlet."
Managing reactions through suppression of emotions	Attempts not to feel or show emotional reactions	"I tried to stay calm and . . . not be frustrated with my father, so I tried to be calm with him, and not be so snippy."
Passive-dependant	Accepting the situation as is; heavy dependence on someone else for a solution	"I'm just going day by day, and seeing how our life works out."
Proactive emotional regulation		
Managing reactions through confrontive emotion coping	Expressing the emotions to other person(s) seen as the cause of the problem	"I told them how I felt about everything."
Reflection of emotions	Consciously dealing with the emotions of self or others; looking at another's viewpoint	"Trying to understand what he was going through . . . and so, to try to solve it was to understand those feelings. I'm glad that I had the open mind to at least try to see his feelings, and not just mine."
Acceptance of responsibility	Acknowledging one's obligations; accepting duties	"I thought how selfish I was, to think that she, my own sister, was invading my privacy, she was just wondering what I had done that day."
Seek social support	Seek assistance in dealing with the emotions	"I've gone to a support group for single parents. And I've gone to a priest and talked about my problems."

Source: Adapted from Blanchard-Fields et al., 2004, Table 1.

ambiguous loss A loss that is not clearly defined or does not bring closure.

Emotion-focused coping can be especially useful in coping with what the family therapist Pauline Boss (1999, 2004) calls **ambiguous loss** (see Box 19-1 in Chapter 19). Boss applies that term to losses that are not clearly defined or do not bring closure, such as the loss of a still-living loved one to Alzheimer's disease or the loss of a homeland, which elderly immigrants may feel as long as they live. In such situations, experience may teach people to accept what they cannot change—a lesson often reinforced by religion.

Does Religion or Spirituality Affect Health and Well-Being? Religion seems to play a supportive role for many elderly people, such as Jimmy Carter. Some possible explanations include social support, encouragement of healthy lifestyles, the perception of a measure of control over life through prayer, fostering of positive emotional states, reduction of stress, and faith in God as a way of interpreting misfortunes (Seybold & Hill, 2001). But does religion actually improve health and well-being?

Substantial evidence points to a positive link between religion or spirituality and health, but much of this research is not methodologically sound (Miller & Thoresen, 2003; Seeman, Dubin, & Seeman, 2003; Sloan & Bagiella, 2002), and definitions of these terms are often imprecise (Hill & Pargament, 2003; Miller & Thoresen, 2003; Wink & Dillon, 2003). A review of studies with relatively sound methodology found a 25 percent reduction in risk of mortality among healthy adults who attended religious services weekly. Religion or spirituality tended to protect against cardiovascular disease, mainly through the healthy lifestyle it encourages, but there was no evidence that either slows the progression of cancer, improves recovery from acute illness, or protects against disability (Powell, Shahabi, & Thoresen, 2003).

Another research review found positive associations between religiosity or spirituality and measures of health, well-being, marital satisfaction, and psychological functioning and negative associations with suicide, delinquency, criminality, and drug and alcohol use (Seybold & Hill, 2001). Still another review found evidence supporting the physiological benefits of meditation (Seeman et al., 2003). In a study of 223 British older adults, spiritual or religious beliefs significantly predicted well-being and moderated the negative impact of frailty on well-being (Kirby, Coleman, & Daley, 2004).

This elderly woman seems to find sustenance in prayer. Religious activity helps many people cope with the stresses and losses of late life.

Checkpoint

Can you . . .

✔ Identify five mature adaptive mechanisms identified by Vaillant and discuss how they work?

✔ Describe the cognitive-appraisal model of coping, and discuss the relationship between age and choice of coping strategies?

✔ Discuss how religiosity and spirituality relate to mortality risk, health, and well-being in late life?

Relatively little of the research on religion and spirituality has been done with racial/ethnic minorities. Among 3,050 older Mexican Americans, those who attended church once a week had 32 percent lower mortality risk than those who never attended. This was true even when sociodemographic characteristics, cardiovascular health, activities of daily living, cognitive functioning, physical functioning, social support, health behaviors, mental health, and perceived health were controlled (Hill, Angel, Ellison, & Angel, 2005).

Older African Americans tend to be more involved in religious activity than elderly white people, and black women tend to be more involved than black men (Coke & Twaite, 1995; Levin & Taylor, 1993; Levin, Taylor, & Chatters, 1994). For elderly black people, religion is closely related to life satisfaction and well-being (Coke, 1992; Coke & Twaite, 1995; Krause, 2004a; Walls & Zarit, 1991). A special factor is the belief held by many black people that the church helps sustain them in confronting racial injustice (Krause, 2004a).

Models of "Successful" or "Optimal" Aging

 *Guidepost*

3. What is successful aging and how can it be measured?

The concept of *successful,* or *optimal aging*—in contrast to the older idea that aging results from inevitable, intrinsic processes of loss and decline—represents a major change in focus in gerontology in response to the growing number of active, healthy older adults. Given that modifiable factors play a part in rates of aging (refer back to Chapter 17), it follows, according to the "new" gerontology, that some people may age more successfully than others (Rowe & Kahn, 1997).

A considerable body of work supported by the MacArthur Foundation Research Network on Successful Aging (Rowe & Kahn, 1997) has identified three main components of successful aging: (1) avoidance of disease or disease-related disability, (2) maintenance of high physical and cognitive functioning, and (3) sustained, active engagement in social and productive activities (activities, paid or unpaid, that create social value). Successful agers tend to have social support, both emotional and material, which aids mental health; and as long as they remain active and productive, they do not think of themselves as old.

Another approach is to examine subjective experience: to what degree individuals attain their goals and how satisfied they are with their lives. One model, for example, emphasizes the amount of control people retain over various aspects of their lives (Schulz & Heckhausen, 1996). In one study, people reported greater feelings of control over their work, finances, and marriages as they aged, but less control over their sex lives and relationships with children (Lachman & Weaver, 1998). Another study found that people tend to live longer if they have a sense of control over the role (such as spouse, parent, provider, or friend) that is most important to them (Krause & Shaw, 2000).

All definitions of *successful,* or *optimal, aging* are value-laden—unavoidably so. These terms, critics say, may burden, rather than liberate, older people by putting pressure on them to meet standards they cannot or do not wish to meet (Holstein & Minkler, 2003). The concept of successful aging, according to these critics, does not pay enough attention to the constraints that may limit lifestyle choices. Not all adults have the good genes, education, and favorable circumstances to "construct the kind of life they choose" (p. 792), and the "already marginalized" are most likely to "come up on the wrong side of . . . "the either-or divide" (p. 791). An unintended result of labeling older adults as successful or unsuccessful may be to "blame the victims" and drive them to self-defeating "anti-aging" strategies (refer back to Box 17-1 in Chapter 17). It also tends to demean old age itself and to deny the importance of accepting, or adapting to, what cannot be changed.

Keeping these concerns in mind, let's look at some classic and current theories and research about aging well.

Disengagement Theory versus Activity Theory Who is making a healthier adjustment to old age: a person who tranquilly watches the world go by from a rocking chair or one who keeps busy from morning till night? According to **disengagement theory,** aging normally brings a gradual reduction in social involvement and greater preoccupation with the self. According to **activity theory,** the more active older people remain, the better they age.

Disengagement theory was one of the first influential theories in gerontology. Its proponents (Cumming & Henry, 1961) saw disengagement as a universal condition of aging. They maintained that declines in physical functioning and awareness of the approach of death result in a gradual, inevitable withdrawal from social roles (worker, spouse, parent); and,

disengagement theory Theory of aging, proposed by Cumming and Henry, which holds that successful aging is characterized by mutual withdrawal between the older person and society.

activity theory Theory of aging, proposed by Neugarten and others, which holds that in order to age successfully a person must remain as active as possible.

The author Betty Friedan, whose 1963 book, The Feminine Mystique, *is credited with launching the women's movement in the United States, exemplifies successful aging as described by activity theory. At age 60, she went on the first Outward Bound survival expedition for people over 55. In her seventies she was teaching at universities in California and New York and, in 1993, published another best-seller,* The Fountain of Age.

because society stops providing useful roles for the older adult, the disengagement is mutual. Disengagement is thought to be accompanied (as Jung suggested) by introspection and a quieting of the emotions. However, after nearly four decades, disengagement theory has received little independent research support and has "largely disappeared from the empirical literature" (Achenbaum & Bengtson, 1994, p. 756).

Activity theory, in contrast to disengagement theory, links activity with life satisfaction. Because activities tend to be tied in with social roles, the greater the loss of roles—through retirement, widowhood, distance from children, or infirmity—the less satisfied a person will be. People who are aging well keep up as many activities as possible and find substitutes for lost roles (Neugarten, Havighurst, & Tobin, 1968). Indeed, research has found that the loss of major role identities is a risk factor for declines in well-being and mental health (Greenfield & Marks, 2004).

Nevertheless, activity theory, as originally framed, is now regarded as oversimplistic. In early research (Neugarten et al., 1968), activity generally was associated with satisfaction. However, some disengaged people also were well adjusted. This finding suggests that although activity may work best for most people, disengagement may be appropriate for some, and that generalizations about a particular pattern of successful aging may be risky (Moen, Dempster-McClain, & Williams, 1992; Musick, Herzog, & House, 1999). Furthermore, much research has found that healthy older people *do* tend to cut down on social contacts and that activity *in and of itself* bears little relationship to psychological well-being or satisfaction with life (Carstensen, 1995, 1996; Lemon, Bengtson, & Peterson, 1972).

A more specific version of activity theory proposes that it is the *frequency* and social *intimacy* of activities that are important to life satisfaction (Lemon, Bengtson, & Peterson, 1972). In several studies, either the number of activities older people engage in or the frequency with which they engage in them was positively related to well-being and also predicted physical health, functional and cognitive status, incidence of Alzheimer's disease, and survival. However, inconsistencies in defining *activities* make it difficult to compare studies (Menec, 2003). Furthermore, most of the research on activity theory has been correlational. If a relationship between activity levels and successful aging was found, it would not reveal whether people age well because they are active or whether people remain active because they are aging well (Musick et al., 1999).

continuity theory   Theory of aging, described by Atchley, which holds that in order to age successfully people must maintain a balance of continuity and change in both the internal and external structures of their lives.

Continuity Theory   Continuity theory, proposed by the gerontologist Robert Atchley (1989), emphasizes people's need to maintain a connection between past and present. In this view, activity is important not for its own sake, but to the extent that it represents the continuation of a lifestyle. For older adults who always have been active and involved, it may be important to continue a high level of activity. Many retired people are happiest pursuing work or leisure activities similar to those they have enjoyed in the past (J. R. Kelly, 1994). Women who have been involved in multiple roles (such as wife, mother, worker, and volunteer) tend to continue those involvements—and to reap the benefits—as they age (Moen et al., 1992). On the other hand, people who have been less active may do better in the proverbial rocking chair.

When aging brings marked physical or cognitive changes, a person may become dependent on caregivers or may have to make new living arrangements. Support from family, friends, or community services can help minimize discontinuity. Continuity theory, then, offers a reason to keep older adults out of institutions and in the community and to help them live as independently as possible.

The Role of Productivity   Some researchers focus on productive activity, either paid or unpaid, as a key to aging well. (We discuss volunteer activity later in this chapter.) People who are high in physical and cognitive functioning, are well educated, and have a strong sense of self-efficacy, mastery, and control—and who are resilient enough to bounce back from temporary stress or disability—are most likely to engage in sustained productive activity in old age (Rowe & Kahn, 1997).

Research supports the idea that productive activity plays an important part in successful aging. Older people not only can continue to be productive but can become even more so (Glass et al., 1995). A six-year longitudinal study of 3,218 older adults in Manitoba, Canada, found that social and productive activities (such as visiting family or housework and gardening) were related to self-rated happiness, better physical functioning, and less chance of having died six years later. Solitary activities, such as reading and handiwork, did not have physical benefits but *were* related to happiness, perhaps by promoting a sense of engagement with life (Menec, 2003).

However, some research suggests that frequent participation in *leisure* activities can be as beneficial to health and well-being as frequent participation in productive ones. It may be that *any* regular activity that expresses and enhances some aspect of the self can contribute to successful aging (Herzog et al., 1998).

Selective Optimization with Compensation According to Baltes and his colleagues (Baltes, 1997; Baltes & Baltes, 1990; Riediger, Freund, & Baltes, 2005), development occurs through a process of allocating personal resources—sensorimotor, cognitive, personality, and social—to the achievement of goals. Development throughout life brings both gains and losses, but in late adulthood the balance tends to shift to the negative side. Thus there is a necessary deflection of resources from growth and maintenance toward dealing with loss (Baltes, 1997).

According to this model, introduced in Chapter 17, successful aging involves *selective optimization with compensation (SOC)*. SOC can enable older adults to conserve resources by *selecting* fewer and more meaningful activities on which to focus their efforts; *optimizing,* or making the most of, abilities that remain strong; and *compensating* for losses by mobilizing resources in other areas (Baltes, 1997; Lang, Rieckmann, & Baltes, 2002). The celebrated concert pianist Arthur Rubinstein, who gave his farewell concert at 89, compensated for memory and motor losses by maintaining a smaller repertoire, practicing longer each day, and playing more slowly before fast movements (which he could no longer play at top speed) to heighten the contrast (Baltes & Baltes, 1990).

The same principles apply to psychosocial development. In the face of stress, older adults may select emotion-focusing strategies and seek to optimize their effectiveness to compensate for loss of control over certain areas of their lives. Also, according to Carstensen's (1991, 1995, 1996) socioemotional selectivity theory, older adults become more selective about social contacts, keeping up with friends and relatives who can best meet their current needs for emotional satisfaction. Such meaningful contacts may help older adults compensate for the narrowing of possibilities in their lives. A 6-year longitudinal study of 516 men and women between ages 70 and 103 found that older adults may cut down on some activities in order to focus on others they consider more important and may compensate for energy depletion by taking naps during the day (Lang, Rieckmann, & Baltes, 2002).

As in cognitive-appraisal theory, assessment of available resources is important (Baltes et al., 1998). In the study just mentioned, older people who were rich in resources were more likely to survive, more active, and more likely to use SOC strategies to adapt to aging losses than participants poorer in resources (Lang et al., 2002). Sticking to one's goals is also important—and, according to a study of adults of various ages, older adults are more likely to do so (Riediger, Freund, & Baltes, 2005).

What's Your View?

- Are you satisfied with any of the definitions of successful (or optimal) aging presented in this section? Why or why not?

BOX 18-2

Window on the World

Aging in Asia

Since the 1940s Asia has been the most successful region of the world in reducing fertility. At the same time, higher standards of living, better sanitation, and immunization programs have extended the adult life span (Kinsella & Velkoff, 2001; Martin, 1988). The result: fewer young people to care for the old.

In Japan, nearly 1 person in 6 is now older than 65 (Kinsella & Velkoff, 2001), accounting for close to half of the nation's total government-sponsored health care spending. By 2025 Japan is projected to have twice as many older adults as children, nearly 40 percent of them at least 80 years old. Pension reserves will likely be exhausted, and the social welfare burden—largely for retirement and health care costs for the elderly—may consume nearly three-fourths of the national income (Kinsella & Velkoff, 2001; WuDunn, 1997).

The Japanese pension sysem is a pay-as-you-go plan like social security in the United States, and it has similar problems. Everyone is required to join and to pay a basic minimum into the fund. However, many self-employed people do not make their required contributions because they no longer trust the system. Many people also belong to supplementary corporate plans, but with the stock market collapse in the early 1990s, many of those plans went bankrupt or were underfunded.

Today's retirees, many of whom joined pension plans late in their working lives but collect full benefits, are doing well. The crunch will come when younger workers, who now are subsidizing the elderly, are ready to retire. As in the United States, the Japanese government plans to gradually raise the retirement age (now 60 in Japan). There also is talk of cutting benefits by one-fifth. Middle-aged workers worry that they cannot count on adequate pensions when they retire (WuDunn, 1997).

Multigenerational households like this one are becoming less common in Japan. There, as in the west, migration to cities and the movement of women into the workforce make home care of elderly relatives more difficult than in the past.

Throughout Asia, a large proportion of older people live with their children, but as financial and health status improve, this

---

Checkpoint

Can you . . .

✔ Tell what is meant by *successful aging,* and why the concept is controversial?

✔ Compare disengagement theory, activity theory, continuity theory, and productive aging?

✔ Give examples of how selective optimization with compensation applies to the psychosocial domain?

Eventually, however, older people may reach the limit of their available resources or may exhaust reserve capacities, and compensatory effort may no longer seem worthwhile. In a 4-year longitudinal study of 762 late middle-aged and older adults, compensatory efforts increased up to age 70 but then declined. Among young-old and middle-old participants, compensatory activities sufficed to maintain previous levels of performance, but this was no longer true of the old-old. Thus, adjusting one's own standards to changes in what is possible to achieve may be essential to maintaining a positive outlook on life (Rothermund & Brandstädter, 2003).

The argument about what constitutes successful or optimal aging is far from settled, and may never be. One thing is clear: People differ greatly in the ways they can and do live—and want to live—the later years of life.

Guidepost

4. What are some issues affecting work and retirement in late life, and how do older adults handle time and money?

Lifestyle and Social Issues Related to Aging

"I—will—never—retire!" wrote the comedian George Burns (1983, p. 138) at age 87. Burns, who continued performing until two years before his death at the age of 100, was one of many late-life achievers who have kept their minds and bodies active doing the work they love.

—continued

pattern is less common than it used to be. In Japan, only about 55 percent of the aged lived with relatives in 1995 as compared with more than 80 percent in 1960. At the same time, the proportions who live alone or only with spouses have increased (Kinsella & Velkoff, 2001). Along with the shifting balance between old and young, such trends as urbanization, migration, and a larger proportion of women in the workforce make home care of elderly relatives less feasible. To halt the erosion in family care, Japan has made it a legal obligation to care for elderly relatives and has provided tax relief to those who give older relatives financial help (Martin, 1988; Oshima, 1996).

Although institutionalization is seen as a last resort for those who are destitute or without families, eventually Japan's exploding older population will outgrow family-based care. Six percent of the elderly were in institutional care in the early to mid-1990s; such facilities were virtually nonexistent in 1960 (Kinsella & Velkoff, 2001).

China, too, is an aging nation. The portion of the population over age 60 was nearly 10 percent in 2002 and is expected to reach 20 percent by 2030. In its rapid transition to a market economy, China has not established a functioning system of social security and old-age insurance. Also, housing is scarce and transportation minimal. Thus the tradition of coresidence of older parents and adult children—and also of younger adult couples with parents—remains strong in urban areas. This is less true of the new entrepreneurial class, which can better afford socially provided care.

Widowed parents who move in with adult children typically follow the traditional patriarchal pattern in which sons were expected to support their parents in old age. However, the decision may depend on particular situations and family resources. For example, an older woman is less likely to move in with a child if she has at least one brother (Pimentel & Liu, 2004; Zhang, 2004).

In Taiwan, another newly industrialized society that has experienced a rapid rise in life expectancy, aging parents live with adult children, especially married sons. Placing parents in a nursing home is seen as a violation of traditional filial obligations, and, as in China, the government provides minimal economic protection. Here too, because of the patriarchal structure of the society, in which a woman's filial obligations are transferred to her husband's parents after marriage, sons generally assume the major responsibility for care of aging parents (Lin et al., 2003).

Thus, although the challenges of an aging population are common to eastern and western societies, differing cultural traditions and economic systems affect the way various societies deal with these challenges.

What's Your View?

In what ways is aging in Asia becoming similar to what happens in the United States? In what ways is it different?

Check It Out

For more information on aging in Japan, go to http://www.indiana.edu/~japan/#. This is the Web site of the National Clearinghouse for U.S.-Japan Studies and contains a set of Web links to discussions of Japan's aging population.

Whether and when to retire are among the most crucial lifestyle decisions people make as they approach late adulthood. These decisions affect their financial situation and emotional state, as well as the ways they spend their waking hours and the ways they relate to family and friends. The need to provide financial support for large numbers of retired older people also has serious implications for society, especially as the baby-boom generation nears old age. Another social issue is the need for appropriate living arrangements and care for older people who can no longer manage on their own. (Box 18-2 reports on issues related to support of the aging in Asia.)

Work and Retirement

Retirement is a relatively new idea; it took hold in many industrialized countries during the late nineteenth and early twentieth centuries as life expectancy increased. In the United States, the economic depression of the 1930s was the impetus for the Social Security system, which, together with company-sponsored pension plans negotiated by labor unions, made it possible for many older workers to retire with financial security. Eventually, mandatory retirement at age 65 became almost universal.

Since the 1950s compulsory retirement has been virtually outlawed in the United States as a form of age discrimination (except for certain occupations, such as airline pilots), and the line between work and retirement is not as clear as it used to be. There are no longer norms concerning the timing of retirement, how to plan for it, and what to do afterward. Adults have many choices, among them early retirement (refer back to Chapter 15), retiring from one career or job to start another, working part time to keep busy or to supplement income, going back to school, doing volunteer work, pursuing other leisure interests—or not retiring at all. The biggest factors in the decision usually are health and financial considerations (Kim & Moen, 2001).

Trends in Late-Life Work and Retirement   Most adults who *can* retire *do* retire; and, with increasing longevity, they spend more time in retirement than in the past (Kim & Moen, 2001; Kinsella & Velkoff, 2001; see Figure 18-2).

Proportions of older adults in the labor force generally depend on whether a country is poor or rich. In most of the developing world, it is common for older people to continue to work, mostly on farms. In industrialized countries, work force participation rates for men ages 65 and over range from less than 3 percent in Belgium to more than 15 percent in Japan, but most countries have participation rates less than 10 percent. Older women in developed countries are more likely than older men to work part time (Kinsella & Velkoff, 2001).

In the United States, older men's participation in the labor force declined during the past four decades, but the participation of older women—many of whom did not work outside the home when they were younger—rose. In 2003 about 33 percent of men ages 65 to 69 and 23 percent of women in that age group were

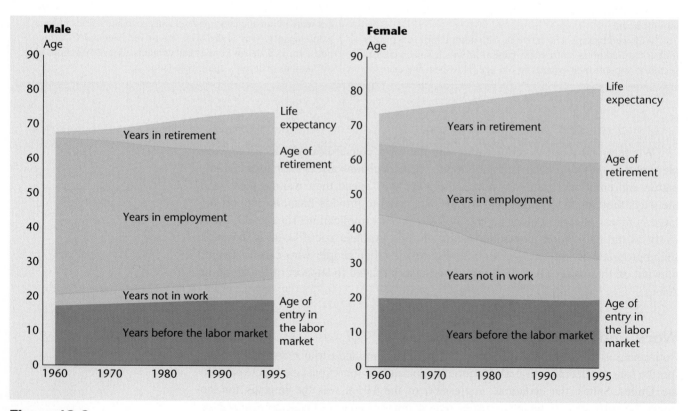

Figure 18-2

Changes in average number of years spent in and out of the work force in 15 industrialized countries, 1960–1995. With increasing life expectancy, the number of years spent in retirement has increased, especially for women. Although women (unlike men) spend more years in employment than in the past, they also tend to retire earlier than before. (Source: Kinsella & Velkoff, 2001, Figure 10-13, p. 111, from Organization for Economic Co-Operation and Development, 1998.)

in the workforce, but the rates decreased rapidly with age to 12 percent and 6 percent, respectively, from age 70 on (Federal Interagency Forum for Aging-Related Statistics, 2004). Older black men are less likely to remain in the workforce than older white men, often because of health problems that force them to stop working before normal retirement age. Those who do remain healthy tend to continue working longer than white men (Gendell & Siegel, 1996; Hayward, Friedman, & Chen, 1996).

For many Americans, retirement is a "phased phenomenon, involving multiple transitions out of and into paid and unpaid 'work'" (Kim & Moen, 2001, p. 489). Some retire into "bridge jobs," new part-time or full-time jobs that may serve as bridges to eventual complete retirement. Some are semiretired; they keep doing what they were doing before but cut down on their hours and responsibilities. A survey by the National Council on the Aging (2002) found that 58 percent of older Americans are completely retired (not working), 23 percent are both retired and working, and 19 percent are not retired at all. Because homemaking was identified as a form of work, more women than men (26 percent as compared with 20 percent) considered themselves to be both retired and working.

How Does Age Affect Attitudes Toward Work and Job Performance? People who continue to work after age 65 or 70 usually like their work and do not find it unduly stressful. They tend to be better educated than those who retire and in better health (Kiefer, Summer, & Shirey, 2001; Kiefer et al., 2001; Kim & Moen, 2001; Parnes & Sommers, 1994).

Contrary to ageist stereotypes, older workers are often more productive than younger workers. Although they may work more slowly than younger people, they are more accurate (Czaja & Sharit, 1998; Salthouse & Maurer, 1996; Treas, 1995). Older workers tend to be more dependable, careful, responsible, and frugal with time and materials than younger workers; and their suggestions are more likely to be accepted. Although younger workers tend to be better at tasks requiring quick responses, older workers tend to be more capable of work that depends on precision, a steady pace, and mature judgment (Forteza & Prieto, 1994; Warr, 1994). A key factor may be experience rather than age: When older people perform better, it may be because they have been on a job, or have done similar work, longer (Warr, 1994).

In the United States, the Age Discrimination in Employment Act (ADEA), which applies to firms with twenty or more employees, protects workers ages 40 and older from being denied a job, fired, paid less, or forced to retire because of age. A task force commissioned by Congress found that (1) physical fitness and mental abilities vary increasingly with age and differ more within age groups than between age groups, and (2) tests of specific psychological, physical, and perceptual-motor abilities can predict job performance far better than age can (Landy, 1992, 1994). Still, many employers exert subtle pressures on older employees (Landy, 1994), and age discrimination cases can be difficult to prove (Carpenter, 2004).

Life After Retirement Retirement is not a single event but an ongoing process. Personal resources (health, SES, and personality), economic resources, and social-relational resources, such as support from a partner and friends, can affect how well retirees weather this transition (Kim & Moen, 2001, 2002). So can a person's attachment to work. In a study of 559 older Dutch couples who experienced the retirement of one of the partners, those who had held full-time jobs for many years tended to have more difficulty adjusting, as did those whose retirement had been involuntary, those who had had negative expectations before retirement, and those who were low in self-efficacy (van Solinge & Henkens, 2005).

What's Your View?

- At what age, if ever, do you expect to retire? Why? How would you like to spend your time if and when you retire?

In a two-year longitudinal study of 458 relatively healthy married men and women ages 50 to 72, men whose morale at work had been low tended to enjoy a boost during the "honeymoon period" immediately following retirement, but *continuous* retirement was associated with an increase in depressive symptoms. Women's well-being was less influenced by retirement—their own or their husbands'; their morale was more affected by marital quality. A sense of personal control was a key predictor of morale in both men and women (Kim & Moen, 2002). In still another longitudinal study, the most powerful predictor of satisfaction with retirement was the size of a retiree's social support network (Tarnowski & Antonucci, 1998).

Continuity theory suggests that people who maintain their earlier activities and lifestyles adjust most successfully. Socioeconomic status may affect the way retired people use their time. One common pattern, the **family-focused lifestyle,** consists largely of accessible, low-cost activities that revolve around family, home, and companions: conversation, watching television, visiting with family and friends, informal entertaining, playing cards, or just doing "what comes along." A second pattern, **balanced investment,** is typical of more educated people, who allocate their time more equally among family, work, and leisure (J. R. Kelly, 1987, 1994). These patterns may change with age. In one study, younger retirees who were most satisfied with their quality of life were those who traveled regularly and went to cultural events; but after age 75, family- and home-based activity yielded the most satisfaction (J. R. Kelly, Steinkamp, & Kelly, 1986).

Sunday painters, amateur carpenters, and others who have made the effort to master a craft or pursue an intense interest often make that passion central to their lives during retirement (Mannell, 1993). This third lifestyle pattern, **serious leisure,** is dominated by activity that "demands skill, attention, and commitment" (J. R. Kelly, 1994, p. 502). Retirees who engage in this pattern tend to be extraordinarily satisfied with their lives.

Since the late 1960s the proportion of U.S. older adults doing volunteer work (like Jimmy and Rosalynn Carter) has increased greatly (Chambre, 1993). In one poll, 57 percent of retirees said they had done volunteer or community service work during the past year (Peter D. Hart Research Associates, 1999). Volunteer work is closely tied to well-being during retirement; it may "help replace the social capital lost when an individual exits the world of work" (Kim & Moen, 2001, p. 510). In a subsample of 373 adults ages 65 to 74 from the MIDUS study, volunteering predicted positive emotionality. It also tended to protect against declines in well-being associated with major role-identity losses (Greenfield & Marks, 2004). In Japan, older adults who are healthy and active are encouraged to be volunteers. In a longitudinal study of 784 older Japanese adults, those who rated themselves as useful to others and to society were more likely to survive six years later, even after adjustment for self-rated health (Okamoto & Tanaka, 2004).

The many paths to a meaningful, enjoyable retirement have two things in common: doing satisfying things and having satisfying relationships. For most older people, both "are an extension of histories that have developed throughout the life course" (J. R. Kelly, 1994, p. 501).

family-focused lifestyle Pattern of retirement activity that revolves around family, home, and companions.

balanced investment Pattern of retirement activity allocated among family, work, and leisure.

serious leisure Leisure activity requiring skill, attention, and commitment.

By using his leisure time to work as a volunteer tutoring a community college student, this retiree is helping not only the young man and the community but also himself. The self-esteem gained from using hard-won skills and from continuing to be a useful, contributing member of society is a valuable byproduct of volunteer service.

How Do Older Adults Fare Financially?

Even Jimmy and Rosalynn Carter had to face financial issues after retirement. So do most older adults.

Since the 1960s, Social Security has provided the largest share of older Americans' income. Nine out of 10 older Americans report income from this source (Administration on Aging, 2003a). In 2002, Social Security accounted for 39 percent of older Americans' aggregate income, followed by earnings (25 percent), pensions (19 percent), and asset income (14 percent). Dependence on Social Security and asset income rises with age. The proportion of income represented by Social Security rises dramatically from 20 percent for the highest-income portion of the population to 83 percent for the lowest (Federal Interagency Forum on Aging-Related Statistics, 2004; see Figure 18-3). For Americans born after 1937, the age of eligibility for full social security benefits increases incrementally from 65 to 67 (for those born in 1960 or later).

Social security and other government programs, such as Medicare, which covers basic health insurance for U.S. residents who are 65 or older or are disabled, have enabled today's older Americans, as a group, to live fairly comfortably. Since 1959 the proportion of older adults living in poverty fell from 35 percent to 10 percent in 2002 (Federal Interagency Forum for Aging-Related Statistics, 2004), and the poverty rate for older adults was lower than that of the total population (Gist & Hetzel, 2004).

Women—especially if they are single, widowed, separated, or divorced or if they were previously poor or worked only part time in middle age—are more likely than men to live in poverty in old age (Administration on Aging, 2003a; Vartanian & McNamara, 2002). Older African Americans and Hispanic Americans are about two-and-a-half times more likely to do so than older white Americans. The highest poverty rates are among older Hispanic women who live alone (Administration on Aging, 2003a).

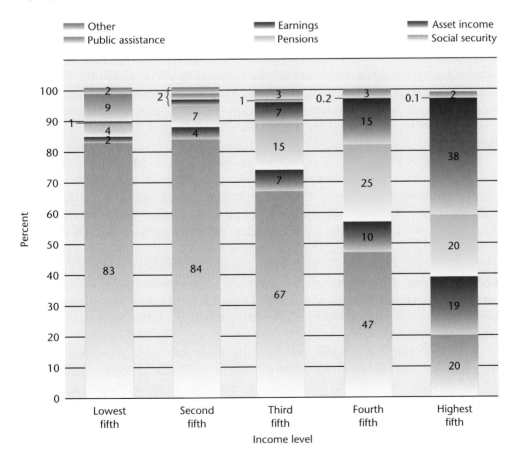

Figure 18-3

Sources of income of Americans ages 65 and older by income quintile, 2002. (Source: Federal Interagency Forum for Aging-Related Statistics, 2004, p. 15.)

How will today's middle-aged adults fare financially during retirement? Recent defaults on pension plans, such as that of United Airlines, together with a shift from defined benefit plans that guarantee a fixed retirement income to riskier defined contribution plans, in which benefits depend on returns from invested funds, make the financial future less certain for many workers (Towers Perrin, 2004). With a graying population and proportionately fewer workers to contribute to the Social Security system, it seems likely that, unless changes are made, benefits will eventually decline, though the timing and severity of the problem are in dispute (Sawicki, 2005).

One controversial proposal is to partially privatize Social Security by giving workers the option to place part of their contributions in personal accounts (President's Commission to Strengthen Social Security, 2001). Proponents of privatization argue that it would enable retirees to earn better returns on their contributions (Tanner, 2001). Opponents fear that if the money placed in personal accounts is taken from payroll taxes currently used to fund basic benefits, it will undermine the purpose of Social Security—a guaranteed floor on income in old age—and that the cost of state and local support for retirees with drastically reduced benefits could be astronomical (Diamond & Orszag, 2002; Weller, 2005). Other options include raising the income cap on payroll taxes, indexing benefits to prices instead of wages, further raising the retirement age, adjusting the cost of living adjustment, and offering personal accounts *in addition to* the present system (Bethell, 2005).

Living Arrangements

In developing countries, older adults typically live with adult children and grandchildren in multigenerational households. In developed countries, the main person many older people depend on for care and support is a spouse (Kinsella & Velkoff, 2001).

In the United States, in 2003, 95.5 percent of persons ages 65 and older lived in the community, 5 percent of them in special housing facilities with supportive services available (Administration on Aging, 2003a). Because of women's greater life expectancy, 73 percent of noninstitutionalized men but only 50 percent of noninstitutionalized women lived with a spouse. About 5 percent of the men and 9 percent of the women lived with other relatives, including children, and the rest lived alone. Minority elders, especially Asian and Hispanic Americans, in keeping with their traditions, were more likely than white elders to live in extended-family households (Federal Interagency Forum for Aging-Related Statistics, 2004; see Figure 18-4).

Living arrangements alone do not tell us much about older adults' well-being. For example, living alone does not necessarily imply lack of family cohesion and support; instead, it may reflect an older person's good health, economic self-sufficiency, and desire for independence. By the same token, living with adult children tells us nothing about the quality of relationships in the household (Kinsella & Velkoff, 2001).

Aging in Place About 8 out of 10 older heads of households in the United States own their homes, nearly 3 out of 4 free and clear (Administration on Aging, 2003a). Most prefer to stay there, many even after being widowed (Administration on Aging, 2001; Treas, 1995).

"Aging in place" may make sense for those who can manage on their own or with minimal help, have an adequate income or a paid-up mortgage, can handle the upkeep, are happy in the neighborhood, and want to be independent, to have privacy, and to be near friends, adult children, or grandchildren (Gonyea, Hudson, & Seltzer, 1990). For older people with impairments that make it hard to get along entirely on their own, minor support—such as meals, transportation, and home health

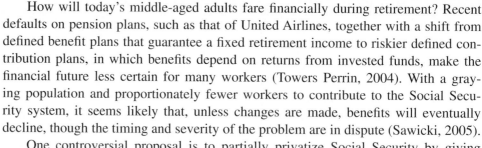

Checkpoint

Can you . . .

✔ Describe current trends in late-life work and retirement?

✔ Cite findings on the relationship between aging and work attitudes and skills?

✔ Discuss how retirement can affect well-being, and describe three common lifestyle patterns after retirement?

✔ Discuss the economic status of older adults and issues concerning Social Security and pension plans?

Guidepost

5. What options for living arrangements do older adults have?

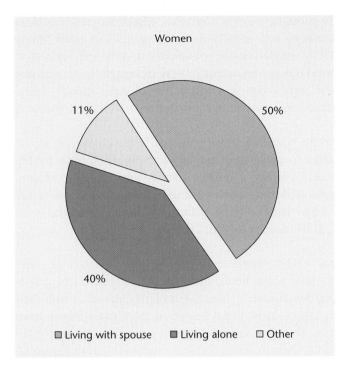

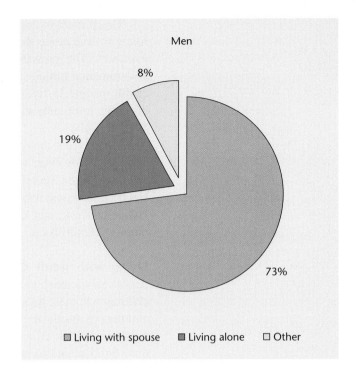

Figure 18-4

Living arrangements of noninstitutionalized men and women ages 65 and over, United States, 2003. In part because of women's longer life expectancy, women are more likely to live alone (especially as they get older), while men are more likely to live with a spouse. The "Other" category includes those living with relatives and with nonrelatives. Note: Totals may not equal 100 percent because of rounding. (Source: Data from Federal Interagency Forum on Aging-Related Statistics, 2004.)

aides—often can help them stay put. So can ramps, grab bars, and other modifications within the home. In a nationally representative study of 60,000 households, approximately 14 percent of respondents had a housing-related disability. Of those, 49 percent had made at least one modification to their homes, and 23 percent had an unmet need for modifications (Newman, 2003).

Most older people do not need much help; and those who do can often remain in the community if they have at least one person to depend on. The single most important factor keeping people out of institutions is being married. As long as a couple are in relatively good health, they can usually live fairly independently and care for each other. The issue of living arrangements becomes more pressing when one or both become frail, infirm, or disabled, or when one spouse dies (Chappell, 1991).

Let's look more closely at the two most common living arrangements for older adults without spouses—living alone and living with adult children—and then at living in institutions and alternative forms of group housing. Finally, we'll discuss a serious problem for frail or demented older adults: maltreatment by those on whose care they depend.

Living Alone The number of older adults living alone has increased greatly since the 1960s, though they are still in the minority (Kinsella & Velkoff, 2001). In 2000, 28 percent of older Americans lived alone (Gist & Hetzel, 2004). Because women live longer than men and are more likely to be widowed, older women in the United States are more than twice as likely as older men to live alone, and the likelihood increases with age. Among women ages 75 and over, almost 50 percent live alone, as compared with 23 percent of men in that age group. Older people living alone are more likely than older people with spouses to be in poverty (Federal Interagency Forum for Aging-Related Statistics, 2004) and to end up in institutions (McFall & Miller, 1992; Steinbach, 1992).

The picture is similar in most developed countries: Older women are more likely to live alone than older men, who usually live with spouses or other family members. The growth of elderly single-person households may be due in part to governmental policies: increased old age benefits, "reverse mortgage" programs that enable people to live off their homes' equity, construction of elder-friendly housing, and long-term care policies that discourage institutional living (Kinsella & Velkoff, 2001).

It may seem that older people who live alone, particularly the oldest old, would be lonely. However, such factors as personality, cognitive abilities, physical health, and a depleted social network may play a greater role in loneliness (P. Martin, Hagberg, & Poon, 1997). Social activities, such as going to a senior center or doing volunteer work, can help an older person living alone stay connected to the community (Hendricks & Cutler, 2004; Kim & Moen, 2001).

Living with Adult Children Older people in many African, Asian, and Latin American societies can expect to live and be cared for in their children's or grandchildren's homes; in Singapore, for example, about 9 out of 10 elders live with their children (Kinsella & Velkoff, 2001). Most older people in the United States, even those in difficult circumstances, do not wish to do so. They are reluctant to burden their families and to give up their own freedom. It can be inconvenient to absorb an extra person into a household, and everyone's privacy—and relationships—may suffer. The parent may feel useless, bored, and isolated from friends. If the adult child is married and the spouse and parent do not get along well, or caregiving duties become too burdensome, the marriage may be threatened (Lund, 1993a; Shapiro, 1994). (Caregiving for elderly parents is discussed in Chapter 16 and later in this chapter.)

The success of such an arrangement depends largely on the quality of the relationship that has existed in the past and on the ability of both generations to communicate fully and frankly. The decision to move a parent into an adult child's home should be mutual and needs to be thought through carefully and thoroughly. Parents and children need to respect each other's dignity and autonomy and accept their differences (Shapiro, 1994).

Living in Institutions The use of nonfamily institutions for care of the frail elderly varies greatly around the world. Institutionalization is very rare in developing regions but is becoming less so in Southeast Asia, where declines in fertility have resulted in a rapidly aging population and a shortage of family caregivers. In developed countries the percentage of elderly people in institutional care in the 1990s ranged from 2 percent in Portugal to nearly 9 percent in the Netherlands and Sweden (Kinsella & Velkoff, 2001). Comprehensive geriatric home visitation programs in some countries, such as the United Kingdom, Denmark, and Australia have been effective in preventing functional decline and holding down nursing home admissions (Stuck, Egger, Hammer, Minder, & Beck, 2002).

In all countries, the likelihood of living in a nursing home increases with age (Kinsella & Velkoff, 2001)—in the United States, from about 1 percent at ages 65 to 74 to 18 percent at ages 85 and over (Administration on Aging, 2003a). Most older nursing-home residents worldwide and almost 3 out of 4 in the United States are women (Federal Interagency Forum for Aging-Related Statistics, 2004; Kinsella & Velkoff, 2001). At highest risk of institutionalization are those living alone, those who do not take part in social activities, those whose daily activities are limited by poor health or disability, and those whose informal caregivers are overburdened (McFall & Miller, 1992; Steinbach, 1992). A large minority of nursing home residents are incontinent. Many have visual and hearing problems. A little over half are cognitively impaired. On average, they need help with four to five of six basic ADLs: bathing, eating, dressing, getting into a chair, toileting, and walking (Sahyoun, Pratt, Lentzner, Dey, & Robinson, 2001).

The number of U.S. nursing home residents has increased considerably since the late 1970s due to growth of the older population, but their proportion of the older population has declined from 5.1 percent in 1990 to 4.5 percent in 2000 (Administration on Aging, 2003a; U.S. Census Bureau, 2001). This decline may be attributed in part to a reduction in the proportion of the older population with disabilities. In addition, liberalization of Medicare long-term care coverage and the emergence of widespread private long-term care insurance have spurred a shift from institutionalization to less expensive alternate living options (discussed in the next section) and home health care (Ness, Ahmed, & Aronow, 2004). However, as the baby-boom generation ages and if current nursing home usage rates continue, the number of residents is projected to double by 2030 (Sahyoun, Pratt et al., 2001). Such growth would greatly burden Medicaid, the major source of payments for nursing home usage (Ness et al., 2004).

Federal law (the Omnibus Budget Reconciliation Act of 1987 and 1990) sets strict requirements for nursing homes and gives residents the right to choose their own doctors, to be fully informed about their care and treatment, and to be free from physical or mental abuse, corporal punishment, involuntary seclusion, and physical or chemical restraints. Some states train volunteer ombudsmen to act as advocates for nursing home residents, to explain their rights, and to resolve their complaints about such matters as privacy, treatment, food, and financial issues.

An essential element of good care is the opportunity for residents to make decisions and exert some control over their lives. Among 129 intermediate-care nursing home residents, those who had higher self-esteem, less depression, and a greater sense of satisfaction and meaning in life were less likely to die within four years—perhaps because their psychological adjustment motivated them to want to live and to take better care of themselves (O'Connor & Vallerand, 1998).

Watch the video, "A Day in the Life of a Nursing Home Resident," in Chapter 18 of your CD for some insights into the needs of nursing home residents and the care they receive.

Alternative Housing Options Some older adults who cannot or do not want to maintain a house, do not need special care, do not have family nearby, prefer a different locale or climate, or want to travel move into low-maintenance or

Pennsylvania University officials break ground for a retirement community, "The Village at Penn State." Such projects, which offer units for rent or for sale—often along with support services and recreational facilities—are becoming popular for independent older adults who want to live in a self-contained community.

Table 18-2 Group Living Arrangements for Older Adults

Facility	Description
Retirement hotel	Hotel or apartment building remodeled to meet the needs of independent older adults. Typical hotel services (switchboard, maid service, message center) are provided.
Retirement community	Large, self-contained development with owned or rental units or both. Support services and recreational facilities are often available.
Shared housing	Housing can be shared informally by adult parents and children or by friends. Sometimes social agencies match people who need a place to live with people who have houses or apartments with extra rooms. The older person usually has a private room but shares living, eating, and cooking areas and may exchange services such as light housekeeping for rent.
Accessory apartment or ECHO (elder cottage housing opportunity) housing	An independent unit created so that an older person can live in a remodeled single-family home or in a portable unit on the grounds of a single-family home—often, but not necessarily, that of an adult child. Units offer privacy, proximity to caregivers, and security.
Congregate housing	Private or government-subsidized rental apartment complexes or mobile home parks designed for older adults provide meals, housekeeping, transportation, social and recreational activities, and sometimes health care. One type of congregate housing is called a group home. A social agency that owns or rents a house brings together a small number of elderly residents and hires helpers to shop, cook, do heavy cleaning, drive, and give counseling. Residents take care of their own personal needs and take some responsibility for day-to-day tasks.
Assisted-living facility	Semi-independent living in one's own room or apartment. Similar to congregate housing, but residents receive personal care (bathing, dressing, and grooming) and protective supervision according to their needs and desires. Board-and-care homes are similar but smaller and offer more personal care and supervision.
Foster-care home	Owners of a single-family residence take in an unrelated older adult and provide meals, housekeeping, and personal care.
Continuing care retirement community	Long-term housing planned to provide a full range of accommodations and services for affluent elderly people as their needs change. A resident may start out in an independent apartment; then move into congregate housing with such services as cleaning, laundry, and meals: then into an assisted-living facility; and finally into a nursing home. Life-care communities are similar but guarantee housing and medical or nursing care for a specified period or for life; they require a substantial entry fee in addition to monthly payments.

Source: Laquatra & Chi, 1998; Porcino, 1993.

maintenance-free townhouses, condominiums, cooperative or rental apartments, or mobile homes. For those who cannot or prefer not to live completely independently, a wide array of group housing options have emerged (Kinsella & Velkoff, 2001; see Table 18-2), enabling older people with health problems or disabilities to receive needed services or care without sacrificing autonomy, privacy, and dignity (Laquatra & Chi, 1998; Porcino, 1993; Sahyoun, Pratt, et al., 2001).

In 2000, nearly 6 percent of older adults lived in group housing (Gist & Hetzel, 2004), as compared with only 1 percent in the mid-1990s. If more such residences were available, as many as 50 percent of people who would otherwise go into nursing homes might be able to stay in the community at lower cost (Laquatra & Chi, 1998).

One popular option is *assisted living,* the fastest-growing form of housing specifically for older adults in the United States (Hawes, Phillips, Rose, Holan, & Sherman, 2003). Assisted-living facilities enable tenants to have their own homelike space while giving them easy 24-hour access to needed personal and health care services (Citro & Hermanson, 1999; Hawes et al., 2003). In most of these facilities a person can "age in place," moving, when and if necessary, from relative independence (with housekeeping and meals provided) to help with bathing, dressing, managing medications, and using a wheelchair to get around. However, assisted-living facilities vary widely in accommodations, operation, philosophy, and rates, and those offering adequate privacy and services are generally not affordable for moderate- and low-income persons 75 and older unless they dispose of or spend down their assets to supplement their income (Hawes et al., 2003).

What's Your View?

- As you become older and possibly incapacitated, what type of living arrangement would you prefer?

Assisted living in a homelike facility with easy access to medical and personal care is an increasingly popular alternative to nursing homes. These residents in an assisted-living facility can maintain a large degree of autonomy, as well as dignity, privacy, and companionship.

Mistreatment of the Elderly

A middle-aged woman drives up to a hospital emergency room in a middle-sized American city. She lifts a frail, elderly woman (who appears somewhat confused) out of the car and into a wheelchair, wheels her into the emergency room, and quietly walks out and drives away, leaving no identification (Barnhart, 1992).

"Granny dumping" is an example of **elder abuse:** maltreatment or neglect of dependent older persons or violation of their personal rights. Mistreatment of the elderly may fall into any of six categories: (1) *physical abuse*—physical force that may cause bodily injury, physical pain, or impairment; (2) *sexual abuse*—nonconsensual sexual contact with an elderly person; (3) *emotional or psychological abuse*—infliction of anguish, pain, or distress (such as the threat of abandonment or institutionalization); (4) *financial or material exploitation*—illegal or improper use of an elder's funds, property, or assets; (5) *neglect*—refusal or failure to fulfill any part of one's obligations or duties to an elder; and (6) *self-neglect*—behaviors of a depressed, frail, or mentally incompetent elderly person that threaten his or her own health or safety, such as failure to eat or drink adequately or take prescribed medications (National Center on Elder Abuse & Westat, Inc., 1998). The American Medical Association (1992) has added a seventh category: *violating personal rights*—for example, the older person's right to privacy and to make her or his own personal and health decisions.

In almost 90 percent of cases with a known perpetrator, that person is a family member; and 2 out of 3 of these perpetrators are spouses or adult children (National Center on Elder Abuse & Westat, Inc., 1998). Neglect by family caregivers is usually unintentional. Many do not know how to give proper care or are in poor health themselves. The states of mind of caregivers and the older persons under their care may reinforce each other. When older women receiving informal long-term care feel respected and valued by their caregivers, they are less likely to be depressed (Wolff & Agree, 2004).

Other types of elder abuse should be recognized as forms of domestic violence. Abusers need counseling or treatment to recognize what they are doing and assistance to reduce the stress of caregiving (AARP, 1993). Self-help groups may help victims acknowledge what is happening, recognize that they do not have to put up with mistreatment, and find out how to stop it or get away from it.

elder abuse Maltreatment or neglect of dependent older persons, or violation of their personal rights.

Table 18-3 United Nations Principles for Older Persons

Independence	Participation
Older persons should have access to adequate food, water, shelter, clothing, and health care through the provision of income, family and community support, and self-help.	Older persons should remain integrated in society, participate actively in the formulation and implementation of policies that directly affect their well-being, and share their knowledge and skills with younger generations.
Older persons should have the opportunity to work or to have access to other income-generating opportunities.	Older persons should be able to seek and develop opportunities for service to the community and to serve as volunteers in positions appropriate to their interests and capabilities.
Older persons should be able to participate in determining when and at what pace withdrawal from the labor force takes place.	Older persons should be able to form movements or associations of older persons.
Older persons should have access to appropriate educational and training programs.	
Older persons should be able to live in environments that are safe and adaptable to personal preferences and changing capacities.	
Older persons should be able to reside at home for as long as possible.	

Care	Self-fulfilment
Older persons should benefit from family and community care and protection in accordance with each society's system of cultural values.	Older persons should be able to pursue opportunities for the full development of their potential.
Older persons should have access to health care to help them to maintain or regain the optimum level of physical, mental, and emotional well-being and to prevent or delay the onset of illness.	Older persons should have access to the educational, cultural, spiritual, and recreational resources of society.
Older persons should have access to social and legal services to enhance their autonomy, protection, and care.	**Dignity**
Older persons should be able to utilize appropriate levels of institutional care providing protection, rehabilitation, and social and mental stimulation in a humane and secure environment.	Older persons should be able to live in dignity and security and be free of exploitation and physical or mental abuse.
Older persons should be able to enjoy human rights and fundamental freedoms when residing in any shelter, care, or treatment facility, including full respect for their dignity, beliefs, needs, and privacy and for the right to make decisions about their care and the quality of their lives.	Older persons should be treated fairly regardless of age, gender, racial or ethnic background, disability or other status, and be valued independently of their economic contribution.

Checkpoint
Can you . . .

✔ Compare various kinds of living arrangements for older adults, their relative prevalence, and their advantages and disadvantages?

✔ Identify five types of elder abuse, give examples of each, and tell where and by whom abuse is most likely to occur?

✔ List several internationally adopted principles regarding the rights and needs of older adults?

Guidepost

6. How do personal relationships change in old age, and what is their effect on well-being?

Because the needs and human rights of older adults have become an international concern, the United Nations General Assembly in 1991 adopted a set of Principles for Older Persons. They cover rights to independence, participation in society, care, and opportunities for self-fulfillment (see Table 18-3).

Personal Relationships in Late Life

As people age, they tend to spend less time with others (Carstensen, 1996). Work is often a convenient source of social contact; thus, longtime retirees have fewer social contacts than more recent retirees or those who continue to work. For some older adults, infirmities make it harder to get out and see people. Yet the relationships older adults *do* maintain are more important to their well-being than ever (Antonucci & Akiyama, 1995; Carstensen, 1995; Lansford, Sherman, & Antonucci, 1998). In a National Council on the Aging (2002) survey, only about 1 out of 5 U.S.

older adults reported loneliness as a serious problem, and nearly 9 out of 10 placed the highest importance on family and friends for a meaningful, vital life.

Theories of Social Contact and Social Support

According to *social convoy theory* (introduced in Chapter 16), aging adults maintain their level of social support by identifying members of their social network who can help them and avoiding those who are not supportive. As former coworkers and casual friends drop away, most older adults retain a stable inner circle of social convoys: close friends and family members on whom they can rely and who strongly affect their well-being (Antonucci, 1991; Antonucci & Akiyama, 1995; Kahn & Antonucci, 1980).

A slightly different explanation of changes in social contact comes from *socio-emotional selectivity theory* (Carstensen, 1991, 1995, 1996). As remaining time becomes short, older adults choose to spend time with people and activities that meet immediate emotional needs. A college student may put up with a disliked teacher for the sake of gaining needed knowledge; an older adult may be less willing to spend precious time with a friend who gets on her nerves. Young adults with a free half hour may spend it with someone they would like to get to know better; older adults tend to choose someone they know well.

Thus, even though older adults may have smaller social networks than younger adults do, they tend to have as many very close relationships (Lang & Carstensen, 1994, 1998) and to be more satisfied with those they have (Antonucci & Akiyama, 1995). Although the size of the social network may shrink and the frequency of contacts decline, neither the quality nor the quantity of social support normally suffers (Bosse, Aldwin, Levenson, Spiro, & Mroczek, 1993) except in older adults who are depressed or cognitively impaired.

The Importance of Social Relationships

As earlier in life, social relationships and health go hand in hand (Bosworth & Schaie, 1997; Vaillant, Meyer, Mukamal, & Soldz, 1998). In fact, social contact seems to prolong life. In a 10-year longitudinal study of 28,369 men, the most socially isolated men were 53 percent more likely than the most socially connected men to die from cardiovascular disease and more than twice as likely to die from accidents or suicide (Eng, Rimm, Fitzmaurice, & Kawachi, 2002). Also, as reported in Chapter 17, older adults with large social networks and frequent social contacts are less likely to experience cognitive decline (Holtzman et al., 2004).

Emotional support helps older people—especially the oldest old—maintain life satisfaction in the face of stress and trauma, such as the loss of a spouse or child or a life-threatening illness or accident (Krause, 2004b), and positive ties tend to improve health and well-being. However, conflicted relationships may play an even larger negative role. A longitudinal survey of 515 older adults found that difficult or unpleasant relationships marred by criticism, rejection, competition, violation of privacy, or lack of reciprocity can themselves be chronic stressors. Older people who encounter problems in one relationship (for example, with children) tend to have problems in others as well (for example, with friends) and thus may themselves be at least part of the source of the problems. On the other hand, some negative relationships may reflect, not poor social skills, but a reaction to shared stress, such as financial and disabling health problems (Krause & Rook, 2003).

The Multigenerational Family

The late-life family has special characteristics. Historically, even when and where the multigenerational family was prevalent, the family rarely spanned more than three generations. Today, many families in developed countries include four or even

What's Your View?

- Have you ever lived in a multi-generational household? Do you think you ever might? What aspects of this lifestyle do or do not appeal to you?

Checkpoint

Can you . . .

✔ Tell how social contact changes in late life, and discuss theoretical explanations of this change?

✔ Discuss the importance of positive social contact and social support, and cite evidence for a relationship between social interaction and health?

✔ Discuss characteristics of the new multigenerational family?

Guidepost

7. What are the characteristics of long-term marriages in late life, and what impact do divorce, remarriage, and widowhood have at this time?

Lifemap CD

In the "Marriage in Later Adulthood" video in Chapter 18 of your CD, a wife describes how she and her husband manage household tasks now that they are retired.

five generations, making it possible for a person to be both a grandparent and a grandchild at the same time (Kinsella & Velkoff, 2001).

The presence of so many family members can be enriching but also can create special pressures. Increasing numbers of families are likely to have at least one member who has lived long enough to have several chronic illnesses and whose care may be physically and emotionally draining (C. L. Johnson, 1995). Now that the fastest-growing group in the population is age 85 and over, many people in their late sixties or beyond, whose own health and energy may be faltering, find themselves serving as caregivers. Indeed, many women spend more of their lives caring for parents than for children (Abel, 1991).

The ways families deal with these issues often have cultural roots. The nuclear family and the desire of older adults to live apart from their children reflect dominant American values of individualism, autonomy, and self-reliance. Hispanic and Asian American cultures traditionally emphasize *lineal,* or intergenerational, obligations with power and authority lodged in the older generation. However, this pattern is being modified through assimilation into the dominant U.S. culture. African Americans and Irish Americans, whose cultures have been heavily impacted by poverty, stress *collateral,* egalitarian relationships. Household structures may be highly flexible, often taking in siblings, aunts, uncles, cousins, or friends who need a place to stay. These varied cultural patterns affect family relationships and responsibilities toward the older generation (C. L. Johnson, 1995).

In the remainder of this chapter we'll look more closely at older people's relationships with family and friends. We'll also examine the lives of older adults who are divorced, remarried, or widowed, those who have never married, and those who are childless. Finally we'll consider the importance of a new role: that of great-grandparent.

Consensual Relationships

Unlike other family relationships, marriage—at least in contemporary western cultures—is generally formed by mutual consent. Thus, in its effect on well-being, it has characteristics of both friendship and kinship ties (Antonucci & Akiyama, 1995). It can provide both the highest emotional highs and the lowest lows a person experiences (Carstensen et al., 1996). What happens to marital satisfaction in late life?

Long-Term Marriage

The long-term marriage is a relatively new phenomenon. Most marriages, like most people, used to have a shorter life span. Today, about 1 marriage in 5, like Jimmy and Rosalynn Carter's, lasts fifty or more years (Brubaker, 1983, 1993). Because women usually marry older men and outlive them and because men are more likely to remarry after divorce or widowhood, in most countries many more men than women are married in late life (Administration on Aging, 2001; Kinsella & Velkoff, 2001). Almost all (96 percent) of older men and women in the United States have been married (Fields, 2004), but in late adulthood less than 57 percent—a far greater proportion of men than of women—are still married (Federal Interagency Forum for Aging-Related Statistics; see Figure 18-5).

Married couples who are still together in late adulthood are more likely than middle-aged couples to report their marriage as satisfying, and many say it has improved (Carstensen et al., 1996; Gilford, 1986). Because divorce has been easier to obtain for some years, spouses who remain together are likely to have worked out their differences and to have arrived at mutually satisfying accommodations (Huyck, 1995). With the end of child rearing, children tend to become a source of

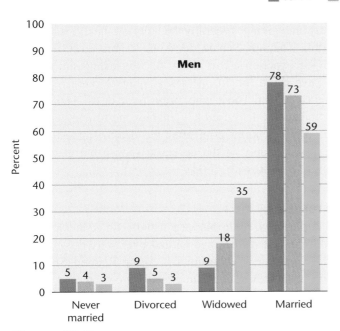
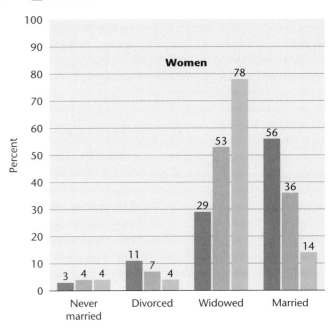

Figure 18-5

Marital status of the U.S. population ages 65 and over by age group and sex, 2003. (Source: Federal Interagency Forum on Aging-Related Statistics, 2004, p. 5.)

shared pleasure and pride instead of a source of conflict (Carstensen et al., 1996). Still, according to the MacArthur Successful Aging Study, men receive social support primarily from their wives, whereas women rely more heavily on friends, relatives, and children (Gurung, Taylor, & Seeman, 2003).

The way couples resolve conflicts is a key to marital satisfaction throughout adulthood. Patterns of conflict resolution tend to remain fairly constant throughout a marriage, but older couples' greater ability to regulate their emotions may make their conflicts less severe (Carstensen et al., 1996).

Throughout the developed world, married people are healthier and live longer than unmarried people (Kinsella & Velkoff, 2001), but the relationship between marriage and health may be different for husbands than for wives. Whereas being married *itself* seems to have health benefits for older men, older women's health seems to be linked to the *quality* of the marriage (Carstensen, Graff, Levenson, & Gottman, 1996).

Late-life marriage can be severely tested by advancing age and physical ills. Spouses who must care for disabled partners may feel isolated, angry, and frustrated, especially when they are in poor health themselves. Such couples may be caught in a "vicious cycle": the illness puts strains on the marriage, and these strains may aggravate the illness, stretching coping capacity to the breaking point (Karney & Bradbury, 1995) and putting the caregiver's life at heightened risk (Kiecolt-Glaser & Glaser, 1999; Schulz & Beach, 1999).

A longitudinal study of 818 late-life couples captured the fluid character of spousal caregiving in late life. Only about one-fourth of the 317 persons who had been caring for spouses at the outset were still doing so five years later; the rest either had died, or their spouses had died or been

Many couples who are still together late in life, especially in the middle to late sixties, say that they are happier in marriage now than they were in their younger years. Important benefits of marriage, which may help older couples face the ups and downs of late life, include intimacy, sharing, and a sense of belonging to one another. Romance, fun, and sensuality have their place, too, as this couple in a hot tub demonstrate.

placed in long-term care. Meanwhile, only about half of the 501 persons *not* caring for spouses at the outset remained noncaregivers five years later. Those in both groups who moved into heavy caregiving generally had poorer health and more symptoms of depression (Burton, Zdaniuk, Schulz, Jackson, & Hirsch, 2003).

The quality of the caregiving experience can affect the way caregivers react to the death of the person they have cared for. In one study, spousal caregivers were interviewed before and after bereavement. Those who, prior to the death, had emphasized benefits of caregiving ("makes me feel useful," "enables me to appreciate life more") more than its burdens reported more grief after the death, suggesting that grief was accentuated by the loss not only of the deceased spouse but also of the caregiving role (Boerner, Schulz, & Horowitz, 2004).

Divorce and Remarriage

Divorce in late life is rare; couples who take this step usually do it much earlier. Only 9 percent of women and 7 percent of men age 65 and over were divorced and not remarried in 2003 (Federal Interagency Forum for Aging-Related Statistics, 2004; refer back to Figure 18-5). However, these numbers have increased significantly since 1980 (Administration on Aging, 2003a) and probably will continue to increase as younger cohorts with larger proportions of divorced people reach late adulthood (Administration on Aging, 2001; Kinsella & Velkoff, 2001).

Remarriage in late life may have a special character. Among 125 well-educated, fairly affluent men and women, those in late-life remarriages seemed more trusting and accepting and less in need of deep sharing of personal feelings. Men, but not women, tended to be more satisfied in late-life remarriages than in midlife ones (Bograd & Spilka, 1996).

Remarriage has societal benefits. Older married people are less likely than those living alone to need help from the community. Remarriage could be encouraged by letting people keep pension and Social Security benefits derived from a previous marriage and by greater availability of group housing and other shared living quarters.

Widowhood

In the United States, more than 900,000 people are widowed each year. Almost 3 out of 4 are over 65 (Boerner, Wortman, & Bonanno, 2005), and most of them are women. U.S. women ages 65 and over are three times more likely than men of the same age to be widowed—44 percent as compared with 14 percent (Federal Interagency Forum for Aging-Related Statistics, 2004; refer back to Figure 18-5). In most countries, more than half of older women are widows (Kinsella & Velkoff, 2001).

Just as older men are more likely than women to be married, older women are more likely than men to be widowed, and for similar reasons. Women tend to outlive their husbands and are less likely than men to marry again. As the gender gap in life expectancy narrows, as it has done in the United States since 1990, an increasing proportion of older men will outlive their wives (Hetzel & Smith, 2001). Issues concerning adjustment to widowhood are discussed in Chapter 19.

Single Life

In more than half of the world, 5 percent or less of elderly men and 10 percent or less of elderly women have never married. In Europe, this gender difference may reflect the toll on marriageable men taken by World War II, when the current elderly cohort were of marrying age. In some Latin American and Caribbean countries, proportions of never-marrieds are higher, probably due to the prevalence of consensual unions (Kinsella & Velkoff, 2001). In the United States, only about 4 percent of men and women 65 years and older have never married (Federal Interagency

Checkpoint

Can you . . .

✔ Explain the difference in marital satisfaction between middle and late adulthood?

✔ Tell how remarriage may differ in earlier and late adulthood?

✔ Summarize gender differences in the prevalence of widowhood?

Guidepost

8. How do unmarried older people and those in gay and lesbian relationships fare?

Forum on Aging-Related Statistics, 2004; refer back to Figure 18-5). This percentage is likely to increase as today's middle-aged adults grow old because larger proportions of that cohort, especially African Americans, have remained single (U.S. Bureau of the Census, 1991a, 1991b, 1992, 1993).

Older never-married people are more likely than older divorced or widowed people to prefer single life and less likely to be lonely (Dykstra, 1995). Never-married, childless women in one study rated three kinds of roles or relationships as important: bonds with blood relatives, such as siblings and aunts; parent-surrogate ties with younger people; and same-generation, same-sex friendships (Rubinstein, Alexander, Goodman, & Luborsky, 1991).

Previously married older men are much more likely to date than older women, probably because of the greater availability of women in this age group. Most elderly daters are sexually active but do not expect to marry. Among both whites and African Americans, men are more interested in romantic involvement than women, who may fear getting "locked into" traditional gender roles (K. Bulcroft & O'Conner, 1986; R. A. Bulcroft & Bulcroft, 1991; Tucker, Taylor, & Mitchell-Kernan, 1993).

Gay and Lesbian Relationships

There is little research on homosexual relationships in old age, largely because the current cohort of older adults grew up at a time when living openly as a homosexual was rare (Huyck, 1995). For aging gays and lesbians who recognized their homosexuality before the rise of the gay liberation movement in the late 1960s, their self-concept tended to be shaped by the then-prevailing stigma against homosexuality. Those who came of age after the liberation movement (and the shift in public discourse it brought about) was in full swing are more likely to view their homosexuality simply as a *status:* a characteristic of the self like any other (Rosenfeld, 1999).

Gay and lesbian relationships in late life tend to be strong, supportive, and diverse. Many homosexuals have children from earlier marriages; others have adopted children. Friendship networks or support groups may substitute for the traditional family (Reid, 1995). Those who have maintained close relationships and strong involvement in the homosexual community tend to adapt to aging with relative ease (Friend, 1991; Reid, 1995).

Intimacy is important to older lesbians and gays, as it is to older heterosexual adults. Contrary to stereotype, homosexual relationships in late life are generally strong and supportive.

The main problems of many older gays and lesbians grow out of societal attitudes: strained relationships with the family of origin, discrimination in nursing homes and elsewhere, lack of medical or social services and social support, insensitive policies of social agencies, and, when a partner falls ill or dies, dealing with health care providers, bereavement and inheritance issues, and lack of access to a partner's Social Security benefits (Berger & Kelly, 1986; Kimmel, 1990; Reid, 1995).

Friendships

Most older people have close friends, and, as in early and middle adulthood, those with an active circle of friends tend to be healthier and happier (Antonucci & Akiyama, 1995; Babchuk, 1978–1979; Lemon et al., 1972; Steinbach, 1992). People who can confide their feelings and thoughts and can talk about their worries and pain with friends tend to deal better with the changes and crises of aging (Genevay, 1986; Lowenthal & Haven, 1968) and to live longer (Steinbach, 1992). The element of choice in friendship may be especially important to older people, who may feel their control over their lives slipping away (R. G. Adams, 1986). Intimacy is another important benefit of friendship for older adults who need to know that they are still valued and wanted despite physical and other losses (Essex & Nam, 1987).

Older people enjoy time spent with their friends more than time spent with their families. As earlier in life, friendships revolve around pleasure and leisure, whereas

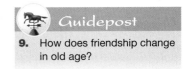

Guidepost

9. How does friendship change in old age?

Older people often enjoy the time they spend with friends more than the time they spend with family members. The openness and excitement of relationships between friends help them rise above worries and problems. Intimate friendships give older people a sense of being valued and wanted and help them deal with the changes and crises of aging.

Checkpoint

Can you . . .

✔ Discuss differences between never-married and previously married singles in late life?

✔ Give reasons for the diversity of gay and lesbian relationships in late life and identify factors that influence homosexuals' adaption to aging?

✔ Cite special benefits of friendship in old age and tell in what ways friendships tend to change?

Guidepost

10. How do older adults get along with—or without—grown children and with siblings, and how do they adjust to great-grandparenthood?

family relationships tend to involve everyday needs and tasks (Antonucci & Akiyama, 1995; Larson, Mannell, & Zuzanek, 1986). Friends are a powerful source of *immediate* enjoyment; the family provides greater emotional security and support. Thus friendships have the greatest positive effect on older people's well-being; but when family relationships are poor or absent, the negative effects can be profound (Antonucci & Akiyama, 1995).

People usually rely on neighbors in emergencies and on relatives for long-term commitments, such as caregiving; but friends may, on occasion, fulfill both these functions. Although friends cannot replace a spouse or partner, they can help compensate for the lack of one (Hartup & Stevens, 1999). Among 131 older adults in the Netherlands who were never married or were divorced or widowed, those who received high levels of emotional and practical support from friends were less likely to be lonely (Dykstra, 1995).

In line with social convoy and socioemotional selectivity theories, longtime friendships often persist into very old age (Hartup & Stevens, 1999). Sometimes, however, relocation, illness, or disability make it hard to keep up with old friends. Although many older people do make new friends, even after age 85 (C. L. Johnson & Troll, 1994), older adults are more likely than younger ones to attribute the benefits of friendship (such as affection and loyalty) to specific individuals, who cannot easily be replaced if they die, go into a nursing home, or move away (de Vries, 1996).

Nonmarital Kinship Ties

Some of the most lasting and important relationships in late life come, not from mutual choice (as marriages, homosexual partnerships, and friendships do), but from kinship bonds. Let's look at these.

Relationships with Adult Children—or Their Absence

Four out of 5 older adults have living children, 6 out of 10 see their children at least once a week, and 3 out of 4 talk on the phone that often (AARP, 1995). Children provide a link with other family members, especially with grandchildren. Parents who have good relationships with their adult children are less likely to be lonely or depressed than those whose parent-child relationships are not so good (Koropeckyj-Cox, 2002).

The mother-daughter relationship tends to be especially close and influences other family relations. In one study, researchers audiotaped conversations between 48 mostly European American, well-educated mother-daughter pairs. The mothers were over age 70 and in good health. Each pair was asked to construct a story about a picture of an older and a younger woman—first separately and then together. These conversations were characterized by warmth and mutual affection, encouragement, and support, with little criticism, hostility, or judgmentalism. The daughters tended to take the lead, spoke more than the mothers did, and were more likely to direct their mothers. Both mothers and daughters held their relationship in high regard, reporting that they had many positive feelings and few negative ones toward each other (Lefkowitz & Fingerman, 2003).

The balance of mutual aid between parents and their adult children tends to shift as parents age, with children providing a greater share of support (Bengtson et al., 1990; 1996). This is especially true in developing countries. Even there, however, older adults make important contributions to family well-being, largely through housekeeping and child care (Kinsella & Velkoff, 2001). In the United States and other developed countries, institutional supports such as social security and Medicare have lifted some responsibilities for older adults from family members; but many adult children do provide significant assistance and care to aged parents (refer back to Chapter 16). Still, the parents, at least in North America, are more likely to provide financial support than to receive it (Kinsella & Velkoff, 2001). An exception is the relatively small category of immigrants who arrived as older adults; they are more likely to live with adult children and to be dependent on them (Glick & Van Hook, 2002).

Older adults tend to be depressed if they need help from their children. Parents do not want to be a burden on their children or to deplete their children's resources. Yet parents also may be depressed if they fear that their children will *not* take care of them (G. R. Lee, Netzer, & Coward, 1995).

Older parents continue to show strong concern about their children (Bengtson et al., 1996). They tend to be distressed or become depressed if their children have serious problems and may consider such problems a sign of their own failure (G. R. Lee et al., 1995; Pillemer & Suitor, 1991; Suitor, Pillemer, Keeton, & Robison, 1995; Troll & Fingerman, 1996). Many older people whose adult children are mentally ill, retarded, physically disabled, or stricken with serious illnesses serve as primary caregivers for as long as both parent and child live (Brabant, 1994; Greenberg & Becker, 1988; Ryff & Seltzer, 1995).

In addition, a growing number of older adults, particularly African Americans, raise or help raise grandchildren or great-grandchildren. As we discussed in Chapter 16, these nonnormative caregivers, pressed into active parenting at a time when such a role is unexpected, frequently feel strain. Often ill-prepared physically, emotionally, and financially for the task, they may not know where to turn for help and support (Abramson, 1995).

What about the increasing number of older adults *without* living children, including 1 out of 5 older women in the United States in 1998 (Kinsella & Velkoff, 2001)? According to interviews and questionnaires with a nationally representative sample of late middle-aged and older adults, the impact of childlessness on well-being is influenced by gender and by a person's feelings about being childless. Childless women who said it would be better to have a child were more likely to be lonely and depressed than women who did not agree with that statement. That was *not* true of men, probably because of the greater importance of motherhood to women's identity. However, mothers *and* fathers who had poor relationships with their children

Bessie and Sadie Delany, daughters of a freed slave, were best friends all their lives—more than 100 years—and wrote two books together about the values they grew up with and the story of their long, active lives. Elderly siblings are an important part of each other's support network, and sisters are especially vital in maintaining family relationships.

were more likely to be lonely or depressed. Thus, parenthood does not guarantee well-being in old age, nor does childlessness necessarily harm it. Attitudes and the quality of relationships are what count (Koropeckyj-Cox, 2002).

Relationships with Siblings

When Elizabeth ("Bessie") Delany was 102 and her sister Sarah ("Sadie") was 104, they published a best-selling book, *Having Our Say: The Delany Sisters' First 100 Years* (Delany, Delany, & Hearth, 1993). The daughters of a freed slave, they overcame racial and gender discrimination—Bessie to become a dentist and Sadie a high school teacher. The sisters never married; for three decades they lived together in Mount Vernon, New York. Although their personalities were as different as sugar and spice, the two women were best friends, sharing a sense of fun and the values their parents had instilled in them.

More than 3 out of 4 Americans age 60 and older have at least one living sibling, and those in the "young-old" bracket average 2 or 3 (Cicirelli, 1995). Brothers and sisters play important roles in older people's support networks. Siblings, more than other family members, provide companionship, as friends do; but siblings, more than friends, also provide emotional support (Bedford, 1995). Conflict and overt rivalry generally decrease by old age, and some siblings try to resolve earlier conflicts; but underlying feelings of rivalry may remain, especially between brothers (Cicirelli, 1995).

Most older adult siblings say they stand ready to provide tangible help and would turn to a sibling for such help if needed, but relatively few actually do so except in emergencies such as illness (when they may become caregivers) or the death of a spouse (Cicirelli, 1995). Siblings in developing countries are more likely to furnish economic aid (Bedford, 1995). Regardless of how much help they actually give, siblings' *readiness* to help is a source of comfort and security in late life (Cicirelli, 1995).

The nearer older people live to their siblings and the more siblings they have, the more likely they are to confide in them (Connidis & Davies, 1992). Reminiscing about shared early experiences becomes more frequent in old age; it may help in reviewing a life and putting the significance of family relationships into perspective (Cicirelli, 1995).

Sisters are especially vital in maintaining family relationships and well-being, perhaps because of women's emotional expressiveness and traditional role as nurturers (Bedford, 1995; Cicirelli, 1989, 1995). Older people who are close to their sisters feel better about life and worry less about aging than those without sisters, or without close ties to them (Cicirelli, 1977, 1989).

Although the death of a sibling in old age may be understood as a normative part of that stage of life, survivors may grieve intensely and become lonely or depressed. The loss of a sibling represents not only a loss of someone to lean on and a shift in the family constellation, but perhaps even a partial loss of identity. To mourn for a sibling is to mourn for the lost completeness of the original family within which one came to know oneself. It also can bring home one's own nearness to death (Cicirelli, 1995).

Becoming Great-Grandparents

As grandchildren grow up, grandparents generally see them less often (see the discussion of grandparenthood in Chapter 16). Then, when grandchildren become parents, grandparents move into a new role: great-grandparenthood.

Grandparents and great-grandparents are an important source of wisdom and companionship, a link to the past, and a symbol of the continuity of family life. This African American great-grandfather points out to his great-granddaughter where her ancestors came from.

What's Your View?

• Which theories of psychosocial development in late life seem best supported by the information in this chapter on work, retirement, living arrangements, and relationships? Why?

Checkpoint

Can you . . .

✔ Tell how contact and mutual aid between parents and grown children changes during late adulthood, and how childlessness can affect older people?

✔ Discuss the importance of sibling relationships in late life?

✔ Identify several values great-grandparents find in their role?

Because of age, declining health, and the scattering of families, great-grandparents tend to be less involved than grandparents in a child's life; and, because four- or five-generation families are relatively new, there are few generally accepted guidelines for what great-grandparents are supposed to do (Cherlin & Furstenberg, 1986). Still, most great-grandparents find the role fulfilling (Pruchno & Johnson, 1996). Great-grandparenthood offers a sense of personal and family renewal, a source of diversion, and a mark of longevity. When 40 great-grandfathers and great-grandmothers, ages 71 to 90, were interviewed, 93 percent made such comments as "Life is starting again in my family," "Seeing them grow keeps me young," and "I never thought I'd live to see it" (Doka & Mertz, 1988, pp. 193–194). More than one-third of the sample (mostly women) were close to their great-grandchildren. The ones with the most intimate connections were likely to live nearby and to be close to the children's parents and grandparents as well, often helping out with loans, gifts, and baby-sitting.

Refocus

Thinking back to the Focus vignette about Jimmy Carter at the beginning of this chapter:

• How did Carter and his wife, Rosalynn, resolve Erikson's stage of ego integrity versus despair?

• What techniques of coping did they use?

• Which model of successful aging does Carter best illustrate?

• Which pattern of use of time after retirement does he exemplify?

• Does the Carters' pattern of late-life relationships seem to illustrate either social convoy theory or socioemotional selectivity theory?

• What do you think might account for the success of their long-term marriage?

Grandparents and great-grandparents are important to their families. They are sources of wisdom, companions in play, links to the past, and symbols of the continuity of family life. They are engaged in the ultimate generative function: expressing the human longing to transcend mortality by investing themselves in the lives of future generations.

SUMMARY AND KEY TERMS

Theory and Research on Psychosocial Development

Guidepost 1: Does personality change in old age, and what special issues or tasks do older people need to deal with?

- Personality traits tend to remain stable in late adulthood, though there are individual differences.
- Emotional resilience and life satisfaction tend to increase with age, but not for people high in neuroticism.
- Older adults in recent cohorts seem to be less rigid in personality than in previous cohorts.
- Emotionality tends to become more positive and less negative in old age, but personality traits can modify this pattern.
- Erik Erikson's final stage, ego integrity versus despair, culminates in the "virtue" of *wisdom,* or acceptance of one's life and impending death.
- Erikson maintained that people must maintain a vital involvement in society.

  ego integrity versus despair (674)

Guidepost 2: How do older adults cope?

- George Vaillant found that the use of mature adaptive mechanisms earlier in adulthood predicts psychosocial adjustment in late life.
- In the cognitive-appraisal model, adults of all ages generally prefer problem-focused coping, but older adults do more emotion-focused coping than younger adults when the situation calls for it and are more likely to use passive than proactive strategies.
- Religion is an important source of emotion-focused coping for many older adults. The link between religion or spirituality and health, longevity, or well-being is an important new area of study, but many studies have had weak methodology or inconclusive findings.

  coping (675)

  cognitive-appraisal model (675)

  problem-focused coping (675)

  emotion-focused coping (675)

  ambiguous loss (678)

Guidepost 3: What is successful aging and how can it be measured?

- The concept of successful or optimal aging reflects the growing number of healthy, vital older adults, but there is dispute over how to define and measure it and over the validity of the concept.

- Two contrasting early models of "successful" or "optimal" aging are disengagement theory and activity theory. Disengagement theory has little support, and findings on activity theory are mixed. Newer refinements of activity theory include continuity theory and a distinction between productive and leisure activity.
- Baltes and his colleagues suggest that successful aging, in the psychosocial as well as the cognitive realm, may depend on selective optimization with compensation.

  disengagement theory (679)

  activity theory (679)

  continuity theory (680)

Lifestyle and Social Issues Related to Aging

Guidepost 4: What are some issues regarding work and retirement in late life, and how do older adults handle time and money?

- Some older people continue to work for pay, but most are retired. However, many retired people start new careers or do part-time paid or volunteer work. Often retirement is a phased phenomenon.
- Older adults tend to be more satisfied with their work and more committed to it than younger ones. Age has both positive and negative effects on job performance, and individual differences are more significant than age differences.
- Retirement is an ongoing process, and its emotional impact must be assessed in context. Personal, economic, and social resources, as well as the length of time a person has been retired, may affect morale.
- Common lifestyle patterns after retirement include a family-focused lifestyle, balanced investment, and serious leisure.

  family-focused lifestyle (686)

  balanced investment (686)

  serious leisure (686)

- The financial situation of older Americans has improved, and fewer live in poverty. Women, Hispanic Americans, and African Americans are most likely to be poor in old age. For many of today's middle-aged adults, retirement funding is shaky.

Guidepost 5: What options for living arrangements do older adults have?

- In developing countries, the elderly often live with children or grandchildren. In developed countries, most older people live with a spouse, and a growing minority live alone. Minority elders are more likely than white elders to live with extended family members.

- Most older Americans prefer to "age in place." Most can remain in the community if they can depend on a spouse or child for help.
- Older women are more likely than older men to live alone. Most Americans who live alone are widowed.
- Older Americans, unlike older adults in more traditional cultures, typically do not expect to live with adult children and do not wish to do so.
- Institutionalization is rare in developing countries. Its extent varies in developed countries. In the United States, only about 4.5 percent of the older population are institutionalized, but their numbers have increased with the growth of the older population, and the proportion increases greatly with age. Most likely to be institutionalized are older women, older adults who live alone or do not take part in social activities, those who have poor health or disabilities, and those whose informal caregivers are overburdened.
- Fast-growing alternatives to institutionalization include assisted-living facilities and other kinds of group housing.
- Elder abuse is most often suffered by a frail or demented older person living with a spouse or child.

elder abuse (693)

Personal Relationships in Late Life

Guidepost 6: How do personal relationships change in old age, and what is their effect on well-being?

- Relationships are very important to older people, even though frequency of social contact declines in old age.
- Social interaction associated with good health, and isolation is a risk factor for mortality.
- According to social convoy theory, reductions or changes in social contact in late life do not impair well-being because a stable inner circle of social support is maintained. According to socioemotional selectivity theory, older people choose to spend time with people who enhance their emotional well-being.
- The way multigenerational late-life families function often has cultural roots.

Consensual Relationships

Guidepost 7: What are the characteristics of long-term marriages in late life, and what impact do divorce, remarriage, and widowhood have at this time?

- As life expectancy increases, so does the potential longevity of marriage. More men than women are married in late life. Marriages that last into late adulthood tend to be relatively satisfying.
- Divorce is relatively uncommon among older people, and most older adults who have been divorced are remarried. Divorce can be especially difficult for older people. Remarriages may be more relaxed in late life.
- Although a growing proportion of men are widowed, women tend to outlive their husbands and are less likely to marry again.

Guidepost 8: How do unmarried older people and those in gay and lesbian relationships fare?

- A small but increasing percentage of adults reach old age without marrying. Never-married adults are less likely to be lonely than divorced or widowed ones.
- Older homosexuals, like heterosexuals, have needs for intimacy, social contact, and generativity. Many gays and lesbians adapt to aging with relative ease. Adjustment may be influenced by coming-out status.

Guidepost 9: How does friendship change in old age?

- Friendships in old age focus on companionship and support, not on work and parenting. Most older adults have close friends, and those who do are healthier and happier.
- Older people enjoy time spent with friends more than with family, but the family is the main source of emotional support.

Nonmarital Kinship Ties

Guidepost 10: How do older adults get along with—or without—grown children and with siblings, and how do they adjust to great-grandparenthood?

- Elderly parents and their adult children frequently see or contact each other, are concerned about each other, and offer each other assistance. An increasing number of elderly parents are caregivers for adult children, grandchildren, or great-grandchildren.
- In some respects, childlessness does not seem to be an important disadvantage in old age, but providing care for infirm elderly people without children can be a problem.
- Often siblings offer each other emotional support, and sometimes more tangible support as well. Sisters in particular maintain sibling ties.
- Great-grandparents are less involved in children's lives than grandparents, but most find the role fulfilling.

PART 9

- Death has biological, psychological, social, and cultural aspects.

- People approaching death often suffer cognitive declines.

- Mourning customs reflect a society's understanding of what death is and what happens afterward.

- Immediately following a death, survivors often experience intense physical as well as emotional reactions.

- Children and adolescents at different ages show grief in special ways, depending on cognitive and emotional development.

- It is not unusual for a widowed person to die soon after the spouse.

- The issue of aid in dying involves deep-seated emotions, moral and ethical rights and principles, societal attitudes, and medical techniques for relief of pain.

Human beings are individuals; they undergo different experiences and react to them in different ways. Yet one unavoidable part of everyone's life is its end. Death is an integral element of the life span. The better we understand this inevitable event and the more wisely we approach it, the more fully we can live until it comes.

In facing death and bereavement, as in all other aspects of life, physical, cognitive, and psychosocial elements intertwine. The psychological experience surrounding the biological fact of death depends on our understanding of its meaning. That understanding reflects the way a society defines death and the customs that have evolved around it.

The End of Life

PREVIEW

Dealing with Death and Bereavement

Cultures have varying customs related to death.

Individuals differ in their ways of facing death and patterns of grieving.

Attitudes toward death and bereavement change across the life span.

Current issues concerning the "right to die" include euthanasia and assisted suicide.

Facing death honestly can help give meaning and purpose to life.

Dealing with Death and Bereavement

The key to the question of death unlocks the door of life.

Elisabeth Kübler-Ross, *Death: The Final Stage of Growth,* 1975

All the while I thought I was learning how to live, I have been learning how to die.

Notebooks of Leonardo da Vinci

Focus
Louisa May Alcott, Devoted Sister

Louisa May Alcott

One of the most moving parts of the classic nineteenth-century novel *Little Women* by Louisa May Alcott (1832–1888) is the chapter recounting the last year in the life of gentle, home-loving Beth, the third of the March sisters (the others being Meg, Jo, and Amy). Beth's life and her death at age 18 are based on those of Alcott's own sister Elizabeth (Lizzie), who wasted away and died at 23.* Alcott's fictionalized account of her family's growing intimacy in the face of tragedy has struck an empathic chord in generations of readers and in viewers of the four film versions of the book, many of whom have never actually seen a person die.

In the novel, realizing that Beth's illness was terminal, "the family accepted the inevitable, and tried to bear it cheerfully. . . . They put away their grief, and each did his or her part toward making that last year a happy one.

"The pleasantest room in the house was set apart for Beth, and in it was gathered everything that she most loved. . . . Father's best books found their way there, mother's easy chair, Jo's desk, Amy's finest sketches; and every day Meg brought her babies on a loving pilgrimage, to make sunshine for Aunty Beth. . . .

"Here, cherished like a household saint in its shrine, sat Beth, tranquil and busy as ever. . . . The feeble fingers were never idle, and one of her pleasures was to make little things for the school-children daily passing to and fro . . ." (Alcott, 1929, pp. 533–534).

As Beth's illness progressed, the increasingly frail invalid put down the sewing needle that had become "so heavy." Now "talking wearied her, faces troubled her, pain claimed her for its own, and her tranquil spirit was sorrowfully perturbed by the

---

*This comparison of the real and fictional accounts of Louisa May Alcott's sister Elizabeth's death is based on Alcott (1929); Elbert (1984); MacDonald (1983); Myerson, Shealy, and Stern (1987); and Stern (1950).

709

ills that vexed her feeble flesh." But with "the wreck of her frail body, Beth's soul grew strong." Jo stayed with Beth constantly (as Alcott herself stayed with her sister Lizzie), sleeping on a couch by her side and "waking often to renew the fire, to feed, lift, or wait upon the patient creature" (pp. 534–535). Beth finally drew her last quiet breath "on the bosom where she had drawn her first"; and "mother and sisters made her ready for the long sleep that pain would never mar again" (p. 540).

The sequence of events described in *Little Women* is strikingly close to reality, as outlined by one of Alcott's biographers: "In February, Lizzie began to fail rapidly from what Dr. Geist labeled consumption. With aching heart Louisa watched while her sister sewed or read or lay looking at the fire. . . . Anna [Alcott's older sister] did the housekeeping so that Mother and Louisa could devote themselves to Lizzie. The sad, quiet days stretched on in her room, and during endless nights Louisa kindled the fire and watched her sister" (Stern, 1950, pp. 85–86).

Alcott herself wrote after her sister's death, "Our Lizzie is well at last, not in this world but another where I hope she will find nothing but rest from her long suffering. . . . Last Friday night after suffering much all day, she asked to lie in Father's arms & called us all about her holding our hands & smiling at us as she silently seemed to bid us good bye. . . . At midnight she said 'Now I'm comfortable & so happy,' & soon after became unconscious. We sat beside her while she quietly breathed her life away, opening her eyes to give us one beautiful look before they closed forever" (Myerson, Shealy, & Stern, 1987, pp. 32–33).

J n Louisa May Alcott's time, death was a frequent, normal, expected event, sometimes welcomed as a peaceful end to suffering. Caring for a dying loved one at home, as the Alcott family did, was a common experience, as it still is in many contemporary rural communities. In western urban societies, by contrast, most deaths now take place late in life in more impersonal settings such as hospitals or nursing homes with less opportunity for close, informal family connection.

Looking death in the eye, bit by bit, day by day, Alcott and her family absorbed an important truth: that dying is part of living. It is also an important chapter in human development. People change in response to death and dying, whether their own or that of a loved one. The ways people face death, as well as its meaning and impact, are profoundly influenced by what people feel and do, and people's feelings and behavior are shaped by the time and place in which they live.

In this chapter, we look at the many interwoven aspects of death (the state) and dying (the process), including societal views and customs surrounding death and mourning. We examine how people of different ages think and feel about dying. We describe various forms grief can take and how people deal with the loss of a spouse, parent, or child. We discuss suicide and controversial issues that revolve around a "right to die." Finally, we see how confronting death can give deeper meaning and purpose to life.

After you have read and studied this chapter, you should be able to answer each of the Guidepost questions that follow. Look for them again in the margins, where they point to important concepts throughout the chapter. To check your understanding of these Guideposts, review the end-of-chapter summary. Checkpoints located at periodic spots throughout the chapter will help you verify your understanding of what you have read.

**Guideposts
for Study**

1. How do attitudes and customs concerning death differ across cultures?

2. What are the implications of the "mortality revolution" in developed countries, and how does it affect care of the dying?

3. How do people change as they approach death?

4. Is there a normal pattern of grieving?

5. How do attitudes and understandings about death and bereavement differ across the life span?

6. What special challenges are involved in surviving a spouse, a parent, or a child, or in mourning a miscarriage?

7. How common is suicide?

8. Why are attitudes toward hastening death changing, and what concerns do such practices raise?

9. How can people overcome fear of dying and come to terms with death?

The Many Faces of Death

Death is a *biological* fact; but it also has *social, cultural, historical, religious, legal, psychological, developmental, medical,* and *ethical* aspects, and often these are closely intertwined.

Although death and loss are universal experiences, they have a cultural context. Cultural and religious attitudes toward death and dying affect psychological and developmental aspects of death: how people of various ages face their own death and the deaths of those close to them. Death may mean one thing to an elderly Japanese Buddhist, imbued with teachings of accepting the inevitable, and another to a third-generation Japanese American youth who has grown up with a belief in directing one's own destiny.

Death is generally considered to be the cessation of bodily processes. However, criteria for death have become more complex with the development of medical apparatus that can prolong basic signs of life. These medical developments have raised questions about whether or when life supports may be withheld or removed and whose judgment should prevail. In some places, the claim of a "right to die" has led to laws either permitting or forbidding physicians to help a person who is terminally ill end a life that has become a burden.

We explore all these issues in this chapter. First let's look at death and mourning in their cultural and historical context.

The Cultural Context

Customs concerning disposal and remembrance of the dead, transfer of possessions, and even expression of grief vary greatly from culture to culture and often are governed by religious or legal prescriptions that reflect a society's view of what death is and what happens afterward. Cultural aspects of death include care of and behavior toward the dying and the dead, the setting where death usually takes place, and

Guidepost

1. How do attitudes and customs concerning death differ across cultures?

Flying the flag at half-mast is a way that Americans officially show grief over the death of an important public figure. Customary expressions of grief vary from one culture to another.

mourning customs and rituals—from the all-night Irish wake, at which friends and family toast the memory of the dead person, to the week-long Jewish *shiva,* at which mourners vent their feelings and share memories of the deceased. Some cultural conventions, such as flying a flag at half-mast after the death of a public figure, are codified in law.

In Malayan society, as in many other preliterate societies, death was seen as a gradual transition. A body was at first given only provisional burial. Survivors continued to perform mourning rites until the body decayed to the point where the soul was believed to have left it and to have been admitted into the spiritual realm. In ancient Romania, warriors went laughing to their graves in the expectation of meeting Zalmoxis, their supreme god.

In ancient Greece, bodies of heroes were publicly burned as a sign of honor. Cremation still is widely practiced by Hindus in India and Nepal. By contrast, cremation is prohibited under Orthodox Jewish law in the belief that the dead will rise again for a Last Judgment and the chance for eternal life (Ausubel, 1964).

In Japan, religious rituals encourage survivors to maintain contact with the deceased. Families keep an altar in the home dedicated to their ancestors; they talk to their dead loved ones and offer them food or cigars. In Gambia the dead are considered part of the community; among Native Americans, the Hopi fear the spirits of the dead and try to forget a deceased person as quickly as possible. Muslims in Egypt show grief through expressions of deep sorrow; Muslims in Bali are encouraged to suppress sadness, to laugh, and to be joyful (Stroebe, Gergen, Gergen, & Stroebe, 1992). All these varied customs and practices help people deal with death and bereavement through well-understood cultural meanings that provide a stable anchor amid the turbulence of loss.

Some modern social customs have evolved from ancient ones. Embalming goes back to a practice common in ancient Egypt and China: *mummification,* preserving a body so the soul can return to it. A traditional Jewish custom is never to leave a dying person alone. Anthropologists suggest that the original reason for this may have been a belief that evil spirits hover around, trying to enter the dying body (Ausubel, 1964). Such rituals give people facing a loss something predictable and important to do at a time when they otherwise might feel confused and helpless.

The Mortality Revolution

Guidepost

2. What are the implications of the "mortality revolution" in developed countries, and how does it affect care of the dying?

Reading *Little Women* is a vivid reminder of the great historical changes regarding death and dying that have taken place since the late nineteenth century, especially in developed countries. Advances in medicine and sanitation, new treatments for many once-fatal illnesses, and a better-educated, more health-conscious population have brought about a "mortality revolution." Women today are less likely to die in childbirth, infants are more likely to survive their first year, children are more likely to grow to adulthood, young adults like Alcott's sister Lizzie are more likely to reach old age, and older people often can overcome illnesses they grew up regarding as fatal.

The top causes of death in the United States in the 1900s were diseases that most often affected children and young people: pneumonia and influenza, tuberculosis, diarrhea, and enteritis. Today nearly three-quarters of all deaths in the United States occur among people ages 65 and over, and about half of all deaths are from heart disease, cancer, and stroke, the three leading causes of death in late adulthood (NCHS, 2004).

As death increasingly became a phenomenon of late adulthood, it became "invisible and abstract" (Fulton & Owen, 1987–1988, p. 380). Many older people lived and died in retirement communities. Care of the dying and the dead became largely a task for professionals. Such social conventions as placing the dying person in a hospital or nursing home and refusing to openly discuss his or her condition reflected and perpetuated attitudes of avoidance and denial of death. Death—even of the very old—came to be regarded as a failure of medical treatment rather than as a natural end to life (McCue, 1995).

Today, this picture is changing. Violence, drug abuse, poverty, natural disasters, and the spread of AIDS make it harder to deny the reality of death. **Thanatology,** the study of death and dying, is arousing interest, and educational programs have been established to help people deal with death. Because of the prohibitive cost of extended hospital care that cannot save the terminally ill, many more deaths are occurring at home (Techner, 1994).

thanatology Study of death and dying.

hospice care Warm, personal patient- and family-centered care for a person with a terminal illness.

palliative care Care aimed at relieving pain and suffering and allowing the terminally ill to die in peace, comfort, and dignity.

Care of the Dying

Along with a growing tendency to face death more honestly, movements have arisen to make dying more humane. These include hospice care and self-help support groups for dying people and their families.

Hospice care is personal, patient- and family-centered care for the terminally ill. Its focus is on **palliative care:** relief of pain and suffering, control of symptoms, maintaining a satisfactory quality of life, and allowing the patient to die in peace and dignity. Hospice care usually takes place at home; but such care can be given in a hospital or another institution, at a hospice center, or through a combination of home and institutional care. Family members often take an active part. In 2001 about 3,200 hospice programs in the United States provided care to an estimated 775,000 patients (National Hospice and Palliative Care Organization, 2002).

Many terminally ill people are able to remain in their own homes, with family members involved in their care, under the guidance and support of hospice workers. Hospice care seeks to ease patients' pain and treat their symptoms, to keep them as comfortable and alert as possible, to show interest and kindness to them and their families, and to help families deal with illness and death.

What does it mean to preserve the dignity of a patient who is dying? One research team decided to ask patients themselves. From interviews with fifty Canadian patients with advanced terminal cancer, the researchers developed a list of dignity-related questions, concerns, and treatment guidelines (Chochinov, Hack, McClement, Harlos, & Kristjanson, 2002; see Table 19-1). Above all, the researchers concluded, dignity-conserving care depends not only on how patients are treated, but on how they are regarded: "When dying patients are seen, and know that they are seen, as being worthy of honor and esteem by those who care for them, dignity is more likely to be maintained" (Chochinov, 2002, p. 2259).

Checkpoint
Can you . . .

✔ Give examples of cross-cultural differences in customs and attitudes related to death?

✔ Explain how death became increasingly "invisible and abstract" in developed countries and how attitudes are changing today?

✔ Tell the chief goals of hospice care?

Facing Death and Loss: Psychological Issues

What changes do people undergo shortly before death? How do they come to terms with its imminence? How do people deal with grief?

Confronting One's Own Death

In the absence of any identifiable illness, people around the age of 100—close to the present limit of the human life span—tend to suffer functional declines, lose interest in eating and drinking, and die a natural death (Johansson et al., 2004;

Guidepost
3. How do people change as they approach death?

Table 19-1 Dignity-Conserving Interventions for Patients Nearing Death

Factors/Subthemes	Dignity-Related Questions	Therapeutic Interventions
Illness-Related Concerns		
Symptom distress		
Physical distress	"How comfortable are you?" "Is there anything we can do to make you more comfortable?"	Exercise vigilance in symptom management. Do frequent assessments. Apply comfort care.
Psychological distress	"How are you coping with what is happening to you?"	Assume a supportive stance. Be an empathetic listener. Consider referral to counseling.
Medical uncertainty	"Is there anything further about your illness that you would like to know?" "Are you getting all the information you feel you need?"	Upon request, provide accurate, understandable information and strategies to deal with possible future crises.
Death anxiety	"Are there things about the later stages of your illness that you would like to discuss?"	
Level of independence		
Independence	"Has your illness made you more dependent on others?"	Have patients participate in decision making, regarding both medical and personal issues.
Cognitive acuity	"Are you having any difficulty with your thinking?"	Treat delirium. When possible, avoid sedating medication.
Functional capacity	"How much are you able to do for yourself?"	Use orthotics, physiotherapy, and occupational therapy.
Dignity-Conserving Repertoire		
Dignity-conserving perspectives		
Continuity of self	"Are there things about you that this disease does not affect?"	Acknowledge and take interest in those aspects of the patient's life that he/she most values.
Role preservation	"What things did you do before you were sick that were most important to you?"	See the patient as worthy of honor, respect, and esteem.
Maintenance of pride	"What about yourself or your life are you most proud of?"	Encourage and enable the patient to participate in meaningful or purposeful activities.
Hopefulness	"What is still possible?"	

Source: Adapted from Chochinov, 2002, p. 2255.

McCue, 1995; Rabbitt et al., 2003; Singer et al., 2003; Small et al., 2003). Such changes also have been noted in younger people whose death is near. In a 22-year longitudinal study of 1,927 men, life satisfaction showed steep declines within one year before death, regardless of self-rated health (Mroczek & Spiro, 2005).

Terminal drop, or *terminal decline,* refers specifically to a widely observed decline in cognitive abilities shortly before death. This effect has been found in longitudinal studies in various countries—not only of the very old (Johansson et al., 2004; Singer, Verhaeghen, Ghisletta, Lindenberger, & Baltes, 2003; Small, Fratiglioni, von Strauss, & Bäckman, 2003), but also of adults of a wide range of ages—and it operates regardless of apparent health status, gender, SES, or cause of death (Rabbitt et al., 2002; Small et al., 2003). Terminal declines have been found to predict death as much as 11 years later. A decline in verbal ability, which is normally least affected by increasing age, may be an especially important marker of terminal drop (Rabbitt et al., 2002). An English study of 3,572 active adults ages 49 to 93 in England suggests that depression, which can have negative effects on brain function, may help explain terminal drop (Rabbitt et al., 2002).

Some people who have come close to death have had "near-death" experiences, often involving a sense of being out of the body and visions of bright lights or mystical encounters. These are sometimes interpreted as resulting from physiological

terminal drop A frequently observed decline in cognitive abilities near the end of life. Also called *terminal decline.*

Factors/Subthemes	Dignity-Related Questions	Therapeutic Interventions
Autonomy/control	"How in control do you feel?"	Involve patient in treatment and care decisions.
Generativity/legacy	"How do you want to be remembered?"	Suggest life projects (e.g., making audio/videotapes, writing letters, journaling). Provide dignity psychotherapy.
Acceptance	"How at peace are you with what is happening to you?"	Support the patient in his/her outlook. Encourage doing things that enhance his/her sense of well-being (e.g., meditation, light exercise, listening to music, prayer).
Resilience/fighting spirit	"What part of you is strongest right now?"	
Dignity-conserving practices		
Living in the moment	"Are there things that take your mind away from illness, and offer you comfort?"	Allow the patient to participate in normal routines, or take comfort in momentary distractions (e.g., daily outings, light exercise, listening to music).
Maintaining normalcy	"Are there things you still enjoy doing on a regular basis?"	
Finding spiritual comfort	"Is there a religious or spiritual community that you are, or would like to be, connected with?"	Make referrals to chaplain or spiritual leader. Enable the patient to participate in particular spiritual and/or culturally based practices.
Social Dignity Inventory		
Privacy boundaries	"What about your privacy or your body is important to you?"	Ask permission to examine patient. Ensure proper draping to safeguard and respect privacy.
Social support	"Who are the people that are most important to you?" "Who is your closest confidante?"	Adopt liberal policies about visitation, rooming in. Enlist involvement of a wide support network.
Care tenor	"Is there anything in the way you are treated that is undermining your sense of dignity?"	Treat the patient as worthy of honor, esteem, and respect; adopt a stance conveying this.
Burden to others	"Do you worry about being a burden to others?" "If so, to whom and in what ways?"	Encourage explicit discussion about these concerns with those they fear they are burdening.
Aftermath concerns	"What are your biggest concerns for the people you will leave behind?"	Encourage the settling of affairs, preparation of an advanced directive, making a will, funeral planning.

changes that accompany the process of dying or psychological responses to the perceived threat of death.

The psychiatrist Elisabeth Kübler-Ross, in her pioneering work with dying people, found that most of them welcomed an opportunity to speak openly about their condition and were aware of being close to death, even when they had not been told. After speaking with some 500 terminally ill patients, Kübler-Ross (1969, 1970) outlined five stages in coming to terms with death: (1) *denial* ("This can't be happening to me!"); (2) *anger* ("Why me?"); (3) *bargaining for extra time* ("If I can only live to see my daughter married, I won't ask for anything more"); (4) *depression;* and ultimately (5) *acceptance.* She also proposed a similar progression in the feelings of people facing imminent bereavement (Kübler-Ross, 1975).

Kübler-Ross's model has been criticized and modified by other professionals who work with dying patients. Although the emotions she described are common, not everyone goes through all five stages and not necessarily in the same sequence. A person may go back and forth between anger and depression, for example, or may feel both at once. Unfortunately, some health professionals assume that these stages are inevitable and universal, and others feel that they have failed if they cannot bring a patient to the final stage of acceptance.

Dying, like living, is an individual experience. For some people, denial or anger may be a healthier way to face death than the calm acceptance exemplified by Beth in *Little Women*. Kübler-Ross's findings, valuable as they are in helping us understand the feelings of those who are facing the end of life, should not be considered a model or a criterion for a "good death."

Patterns of Grieving

Bereavement—the loss of someone to whom a person feels close and the process of adjusting to it—can affect practically all aspects of a survivor's life. Bereavement often brings a change in status and role (for example, from a wife to a widow or from a son or daughter to an orphan). It may have social and economic consequences—a loss of friends and sometimes of income. But first there is **grief**—the emotional response experienced in the early phases of bereavement.

Grief, like dying, is a highly personal experience. Today research has challenged earlier notions of a single, "normal" pattern of grieving and a "normal" timetable for recovery. A widow talking to her late husband might once have been considered emotionally disturbed; now this is recognized as a common and helpful behavior (Lund, 1993b). Some people recover fairly quickly after bereavement; others never do.

The Classic Grief Work Model   A classic pattern of grief is a three-stage one, in which the bereaved person accepts the painful reality of the loss, gradually lets go of the bond with the dead person, and readjusts to life by developing new interests and relationships. This process of **grief work,** the working out of psychological issues connected with grief, generally takes the following path—though, as with Kübler-Ross's stages, it may vary (J. T. Brown & Stoudemire, 1983; R. Schulz, 1978).

1. *Shock and disbelief.* Immediately following a death, survivors often feel lost and confused. As awareness of the loss sinks in, the initial numbness gives way to overwhelming feelings of sadness and frequent crying. This first stage may last several weeks, especially after a sudden or unexpected death.

2. *Preoccupation with the memory of the dead person.* In the second stage, which may last 6 months to 2 years or so, the survivor tries to come to terms with the death but cannot yet accept it. A widow may relive her husband's death and their entire relationship. From time to time, she may be seized by a feeling that her dead husband is present. These experiences diminish with time, though they may recur—perhaps for years—on such occasions as the anniversary of the marriage or of the death.

3. *Resolution.* The final stage has arrived when the bereaved person renews interest in everyday activities. Memories of the dead person bring fond feelings mingled with sadness, rather than sharp pain and longing.

Grieving: Multiple Variations   Although the pattern of grief work just described is common, grieving does not necessarily follow a straight line from shock to resolution. One team of psychologists (Wortman & Silver, 1989) reviewed studies of reactions to major losses: the death of a loved one or the loss of mobility due to spinal injury. Rather than a single three-stage pattern, this research found three main patterns of grieving. In the *commonly expected* pattern, the mourner goes from high to low distress. In a second pattern (sometimes called *absent grief*), the mourner does not experience intense distress immediately or later. In a third pattern, the mourner remains distressed for a long time (*chronic grief*) (Wortman & Silver, 1989).

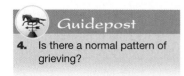

4. Is there a normal pattern of grieving?

bereavement   Loss, due to death, of someone to whom one feels close and the process of adjustment to the loss.

grief   Emotional response experienced in the early phases of bereavement.

grief work   Working out of psychological issues connected with grief.

Specifically, these researchers found some common assumptions to be more myth than fact.

First, depression is far from universal. From 3 weeks to 2 years after their loss, only 15 to 35 percent of widows, widowers, and victims of spinal cord injury showed signs of depression. *Second,* high distress at the outset does not necessarily avert long-term problems; the people who were most upset immediately after a loss or injury were likely to be most troubled up to two years later. *Third,* not everyone needs to "work through" a loss or will benefit from doing so; some of the people who did the most intense grief work had more problems later. *Fourth,* not everyone returns to normal quickly. More than 40 percent of widows and widowers show moderate to severe anxiety up to four years after the spouse's death, especially if it was sudden. *Fifth,* people cannot always resolve their grief and accept their loss. Parents and spouses of people who die in car accidents often have painful memories of the loved one even after many years (Wortman & Silver, 1989). Acceptance may be particularly difficult when a loss is *ambiguous,* as when a loved one is missing and presumed dead (see Box 19-1).

In the Changing Lives of Older Couples (CLOC) study, researchers interviewed 1,532 married older adults and then did follow-up interviews on 185 (161 women

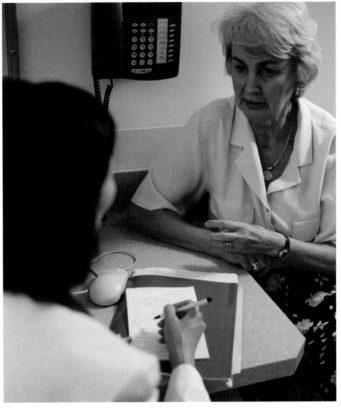

Grief therapy can help a bereaved person express her feelings, review her relationship with the deceased, and go on with her life.

and 24 men) whose spouses had died. The interviews took place six months and again up to four years after the loss (Boerner, Wortman, & Bonanno, 2005; Bonanno, Wortman, & Nesse, 2004; Bonanno et al., 2002).

Common grief—depression that sets in immediately after bereavement and subsides over time, as in the classic three-stage grief work pattern, was surprisingly *un*common (11 percent of the sample). Also, there was no clear evidence of either *absent* or *delayed grief*—lack of overt grieving immediately after the death, which, in the delayed pattern, is thought to result in a later unhealthy eruption of distress. Instead, by far the most prevalent pattern (shown by 46 percent of the sample) was *resilience:* a low and gradually diminishing level of distress. The resilient mourners expressed acceptance of death as a natural process. After their loss, they spent relatively little time thinking and talking about it or searching for meaning in it, though the majority did report some yearning and emotional pangs during the first six months. These findings challenge the assumption that something is wrong if a bereaved person shows only mild distress and demonstrates that "'doing well' after a loss is not necessarily a cause for concern but rather a normal response for many older adults" (Boerner et al., 2005, p. P72).

Among those widowed persons who showed high long-term distress, the researchers distinguished between *chronic grievers* (16 percent), who became depressed following their loss, and the *chronically depressed* (8 percent), who had been depressed beforehand and became more so afterward. Chronic grievers tended to have been excessively dependent, both on their spouses and in general. They were most likely to keep thinking about, talking about, and searching for meaning in their loss, but they did "get over it" by the 48-month mark, whereas the chronically depressed did not. Thus, chronically depressed widows and widowers may be the most likely candidates for treatment. On the other hand, some mourners (10 percent) who had shown high levels of depression before their loss *improved during*

BOX 19-1

Digging Deeper
Ambiguous Loss

A woman whose husband was in the World Trade Center at the time of the terrorist attack on September 11, 2001, did not truly believe he was dead until months later, when clean-up workers turned up a shard of his bone. Survivors of the December 2004 tsunami in Southeast Asia grieve for partners, children, and parents swept away without a trace by the massive waves. Middle-aged women and men fly to Southeast Asia to search for the remains of husbands and fathers whose planes were shot down decades ago. A woman whose father committed suicide and who did not have an opportunity to view his body before burial has recurring dreams that he is still alive.

Dealing with the death of a loved one is difficult enough under normal circumstances. But when there is no body—no clear evidence of death—it can be harder to face the finality of loss. This is especially true in U.S. culture, with its tendency to deny the reality of death. "People yearn for a body," says the family therapist Pauline Boss (2002, p. 15), "because, paradoxically, *having* the body enables them to let go of it." Viewing the body overcomes confusion, "provides cognitive certainty of death," and thus enables the bereaved to begin mourning. Without a body, survivors feel cheated out of the chance to say goodbye and to honor the loved one properly. Boss tells of a woman whose husband was missing in the World Trade Center, who wished for just a part of him to bury—even a fingernail.

Boss (1999, 2002, 2004; Boss, Beaulieu, Wieling, Turner, & LaCruz, 2003) applies the term *ambiguous loss* (introduced in Chapter 18) to situations in which loss is not clearly defined and therefore is confusing and difficult to resolve. Ambiguous loss is not a psychological disorder but a relational disorder in which grief remains frozen and resolution cannot occur. It is not an illness but a source of debilitating stress. When loss lacks tangible confirmation, people are denied ritual and emotional closure and may be immobilized—unable to go on with the necessary task of reorganizing family roles and relationships. The loss goes on and on, creating physical and emotional exhaustion, and the support of friends and family may drop away.

In New York, after the September 11th attack, thousands of families had to cope with this kind of loss. Giving the situation a name seems to alleviate the anguish of the bereaved, who otherwise may blame themselves for feeling confused, helpless, anxious, and unable to grieve normally. Boss also has applied the concept of ambiguous loss to situations in which the loved one is physically present but psychologically absent, as in Alzheimer's disease, drug addiction, and other chronic mental illnesses.

People who can best tolerate ambiguous loss tend to have certain characteristics: (1) They are deeply spiritual and do not expect to understand what happens in the world—they have faith and trust in the unknown. (2) They are optimistic by nature. (3) They can hold two opposite ideas at one time ("I need to reorganize my life but keep hope alive") and thus can live with uncertainty. (4) Often they grew up in a family or culture where mastery, control, and finding answers to questions were less important than learning to live with what is.

Some Native American cultures provide rituals, ceremonies, and symbols to mark ambiguous loss. An Anishinabe woman in northern Minnesota, who was taking care of her demented mother, held a "funeral" for her "because the woman that I knew was just not there anymore" (Boss, 1999, p. 17). In New York, Mayor Rudolph Giuliani offered official certificates of presumed death and an urn of ashes from Ground Zero. Some people accepted these tokens as evidence of death, allowing themselves to begin the grieving process, but others chose to wait for more solid proof. Different families, different cultures, and different people within a family may have different ways of coping.

Therapy can help people to "understand, cope, and move on after the loss, even if it remains unclear" (Boss, 1999, p. 7). Telling and hearing stories about the missing person may begin the healing process. Reconstructing family rituals can affirm that family life goes on.

Therapists working with people suffering from ambiguous loss need to be able to tolerate ambiguity themselves. They must recognize that the classic stages of grief work (described in this chapter) do not apply. Pressing for closure will bring resistance. Families can learn to manage the stress of ambiguous loss at their own pace and in their own way.

Source: Boss (1999, 2002, 2004); Boss et al. (2003).

What's Your View?

Have you ever experienced an ambiguous loss, or do you know someone who has? If so, what coping strategies seemed most effective?

Check It Out

For more information related to this topic, go to http://www.nytimes.com to see "Portraits of Grief," a way of remembering the missing and dead from the World Trade Center attack.

bereavement. For this group, the death appeared to represent the end of a chronic stressor. They tended to have been negative or ambivalent about their marriages, and many of their spouses had been seriously ill before death.

The finding that grief takes varied forms and patterns has important implications for helping people deal with loss (Boerner et al., 2004, 2005; Bonanno et al., 2002). It may be unnecessary and even harmful to urge or lead mourners to "work through" a loss, or to expect them to follow a set pattern of emotional reactions—just as it may be unnecessary and harmful to expect all dying patients to experience Kübler-Ross's stages. Respect for different ways of showing grief can help the bereaved deal with loss without making them feel that their reactions are abnormal.

Grief Therapy

Most bereaved people eventually are able to come to terms with their loss and resume normal lives, often with the help of family and friends. For some, however, **grief therapy**—treatment to help the bereaved cope with their loss—is indicated. Professional grief therapists help survivors express sorrow, guilt, hostility, and anger. They encourage clients to review the relationship with the deceased and to integrate the fact of the death into their lives. In helping people handle grief, counselors need to take into account ethnic and family traditions and individual differences.

Often, unfortunately, studies find that grief therapy is ineffectual or, in a disturbing proportion of cases (38 percent, according to one study), even harmful (Fortner, Neimeyer, Anderson, & Berman, reported in Neimeyer 2000). The findings reported in the previous section (Boerner et al., 2005; Bonanno et al., 2002) suggest that many bereaved persons are unlikely to need or benefit from counseling. Typical assumptions of grief therapy—that "absent grief" represents unacknowledged problems related to the loss and that bereavement is one of the most stressful life events most people ever encounter—need to be reevaluated.

Chronic grievers are most likely to benefit from treatment that acknowledges the centrality of their loss and helps them to process it, build self-esteem, and restructure their lives. The chronically depressed might be helped more by interventions that focus on their ongoing emotional problems and assist them in dealing with the everyday strains of widowhood. If that approach is unsuccessful, some may need to be treated with antidepressant drugs (Boerner et al., 2005).

Death and Bereavement Across the Life Span

There is no single way of viewing death at any age; people's attitudes toward it reflect their personality and experience, as well as how close they believe they are to dying. Still, broad developmental differences apply. As the timing-of-events model suggests, death probably does not mean the same thing to an 85-year-old man with excruciatingly painful arthritis, a 56-year-old woman at the height of a brilliant legal career who discovers she has breast cancer, and a 15-year-old who dies of an overdose of drugs. Typical changes in attitudes toward death across the life span depend both on cognitive development and on the normative or nonnormative timing of the event.

Childhood and Adolescence

According to early neo-Piagetian research (Speece & Brent, 1984), sometime between ages 5 and 7 most children come to understand that death is *irreversible*—that a dead person, animal, or flower cannot come to life again. At about the same age, children realize two other important concepts about death: first, that it is *universal* (all living things die) and therefore *inevitable*; and second, that a dead person is *nonfunctional* (all life functions end at death). Before then, children may believe that certain groups of people (say, teachers, parents, and children) do not die, that a person who is smart enough or lucky enough can avoid death, and that they themselves will be able to live forever. They also may believe that a dead person still can think and feel. The concepts of irreversibility, universality, and cessation of functions, these studies suggest, usually develop during the shift from preoperational to concrete operational thinking, when concepts of causation become more mature.

grief therapy Treatment to help the bereaved cope with loss.

Checkpoint

Can you...

✔ Summarize changes that may occur in a person close to death?

✔ Name Kübler-Ross's five stages of confronting death and tell why her work is controversial?

✔ Identify the three stages of common *grief work*, and discuss newer findings of variations in the grieving process?

✔ Tell how grief therapy is conducted and in what situations it can be most effective?

Guidepost

5. How do attitudes and understandings about death and bereavement differ across the life span?

Table 19-2 Statements About Dying at Various Stages of Development and Strategies to Help Children Cope

Examples of Questions and Statements About Dying at Approximate Age	Thoughts That Guide Behavior	Developmental Understanding of Dying	Strategies and Responses to Questions and Statements About Dying
1–3 years "Mommy, after I die, how long will it be before I'm alive again?" "Daddy, will you still tickle me while I'm dead?"	Limited understanding of accidental events, of future and past time, and of the difference between living and nonliving.	Death is often viewed as continuous with life. Life and death are often considered alternate states, like being awake and being asleep, or coming and going.	Maximize physical comfort, familiar persons, and favorite toys. Be consistent. Use simple physical contact and communication to satisfy child's need for sense of self-worth and love. "I will always love you." "You are my wonderful child and I will always find a way to tickle you."
3–5 years "I've been a bad boy, so I have to die." "I hope the food is good in heaven."	Concepts are crude and irreversible. The child may not distinguish between reality and fantasy. Perceptions dominate judgment.	The child sees death as temporary and reversible and not necessarily universal (only old people die). Because of their egocentricity, the child often believes that he or she somehow caused the death, or views it as a punishment. Death is like an external force that can get you and may be personified (e.g., the bogeyman).	Correct the child's perception of illness as a punishment. Maximize the child's presence with his or her parents. Children at this age may be concerned about how the family will function without them. Help parents accept and appreciate the openness of these discussions. Reassure the child and help parents lessen the guilt that the child may feel about leaving by using honest and precise language. "When you die, we will always miss you, but we will know you are with us and that you are in a safe wonderful place [perhaps with another loved one who has died]."
5–10 years "How will I die? Will it hurt? Is dying scary?"	The child begins to demonstrate organized, logical thought. Thinking becomes less egocentric. The child begins to problem-solve concretely, reason logically, and organize thoughts coherently. However, he or she has limited abstract reasoning.	The child begins to understand death as real and permanent. Death means that your heart stops, your blood does not circulate, and you do not breathe. It may be viewed as a violent event. The child may not accept that death could happen to himself or herself or anyone he or she knows but starts to realize that people he or she knows will die.	Be honest and provide specific details if they are requested. Help and support the child's need for control. Permit and encourage the child's participation in decision making. "We will work together to help you feel comfortable. It is very important that you let us know how you are feeling and what you need. We will always be with you so that you do not need to feel afraid."

Source: Hurwitz, Duncan, & Wolfe, 2004.

More recent research suggests that children may acquire a partial understanding of what happens after death as early as age 4, but that understanding may not be complete until well into the school years. In a series of studies at two suburban university-affiliated schools, most preschoolers and kindergartners expressed knowledge that a dead mouse will never be alive again or grow up to be an old mouse, but 54 percent said the mouse might still need to eat. By age 7, 91 percent of the children were consistent in their knowledge that such biological processes as eating and drinking cease at death. Yet, when similar questions were put in psychological terms ("Is he still hungry?"), children this age and younger were less consistent. Only 21 percent of kindergartners and 55 percent of early elementary students knew, for example, that a dead mouse would no longer feel sick, as compared with 75 percent

Examples of Questions and Statements About Dying at Approximate Age	Thoughts That Guide Behavior	Developmental Understanding of Dying	Strategies and Responses to Questions and Statements About Dying
Adolescents			
10–13 years			
I'm afraid if I die my mom will just break down. I'm worried that when I die, I'll miss my family, or forget them or something."	Thinking becomes more abstract, incorporating the principles of formal logic. The ability to generate abstract propositions, multiple hypotheses, and their possible outcomes becomes apparent.	The child begins to understand death as real, final, and universal. It could happen to him or her or family members. The biological aspects of illness and death and details of the funeral may begin to interest the child. The child may see death as a punishment for poor behavior. The child may worry about who will care for him or her if a parent or caregiver dies. He or she needs reassurance that he or she will continue to be cared for and loved.	Help reinforce the adolescent's self-esteem, sense of worth, and self-respect. Allow and respect the adolescent's need for privacy, but maintain his or her access to friends and peers. Tolerate the teenager's need to express strong emotions and feelings. Support the need for independence, and permit and encourage participation in decision making. "Though I will miss you, you will always be with me and I will rely on your presence in me to give me strength."
14–18 years			
"This is so unfair! I can't believe how awful this cancer made me look." "I just need to be alone!" "I can't believe I'm dying. . . . What did I do wrong?"	Thinking becomes more abstract. Adolescence is marked by risk-taking behavior that seems to deny the teenager's own mortality. At this age, the teenager needs someone to use as a sounding board for his or her emotions.	A more mature and adult understanding of death develops. Death may be viewed as an enemy that can be fought against. Thus, dying may be viewed by the teenager as a failure, as giving up.	"I can't imagine how you must be feeling. You need to know that despite it all, you are doing an incredible job handling all of this. I'd like to hear more about what you are hoping for and what you are worrying about."

of late elementary students (ages 11 to 12). The understanding that cognitive states cease at death lagged even further; only 30 percent of the late elementary group consistently answered questions about whether thoughts, feelings, and desires persist after death (Bering & Bjorklund, 2004).

Table 19-2 summarizes the developmental sequence in understanding of death. It gives examples of questions dying children of various ages typically ask and how caregivers can respond.

Children can be helped to understand death if they are introduced to the concept at an early age and are encouraged to talk about it. The death of a pet may provide a natural opportunity. If another child dies, teachers and parents need to try to allay the surviving children's anxieties. For children with cancer or other terminal

Table 19-3	Manifestations of Grief in Children		
Under 3 years	**3 to 5 years**	**School-Age Children**	**Adolescents**
Regression	Increased activity	Deterioration of school performance caused by loss of concentration, lack of interest, lack of motivation, failure to complete assignments, and daydreaming in class	Depression
Sadness	Constipation		Somatic complaints
Fearfulness	Soiling		Delinquent behavior
Loss of appetite	Bed-wetting		Promiscuity
Failure to thrive	Anger and temper tantrums		Suicide attempts
Sleep disturbance			Dropping out of school
Social withdrawal	"Out-of-control" behavior	Resistance to attending school	
Developmental delay	Nightmares	Crying spells	
Irritability	Crying spells	Lying	
Excessive crying		Stealing	
Increased dependency		Nervousness	
Loss of speech		Abdominal pain	
		Headaches	
		Listlessness	
		Fatigue	

Source: Adapted from AAP Committee on Psychosocial Aspects of Child and Family Health, 1992.

illness, the need to understand death may be more pressing and more concrete. Yet parents may avoid bringing up the subject, whether because of their own difficulty in accepting the prospect of loss or because they are trying to protect their child. In so doing, they may miss an opportunity for the child and family to prepare emotionally for what is to come (Wolfe, 2004).

Like their understanding of death, the way children show grief depends on cognitive and emotional development (see Table 19-3). Children sometimes express grief through anger, acting out, or refusal to acknowledge a death, as if the pretense that a person is still alive will make it so. They may be confused by adults' euphemisms: that someone "expired" or that the family "lost" someone or that someone is "asleep" and will never awaken. A loss is more difficult if the child had a troubled relationship with the person who died; if a troubled surviving parent depends too much on the child; if the death was unexpected, especially if it was a murder or suicide; if the child has had previous behavioral or emotional problems; or if family and community support are lacking (AAP Committee on Psychosocial Aspects of Child and Family Health, 1992).

Parents and other adult caregivers can help children deal with bereavement by helping them understand that death is final and inevitable and that they did not cause the death by their misbehavior or thoughts. Children need reassurance that they will continue to receive care from loving adults. It is usually advisable to make as few changes as possible in a child's environment, relationships, and daily activities; to answer questions simply and honestly; and to encourage the child to talk about his or her feelings and about the person who died (AAP Committee on Psychosocial Aspects of Child & Family Health, 2000).

Death is not something adolescents normally think much about unless they are directly faced with it, as the March sisters were in *Little Women*. As we have discussed in earlier chapters, in many communities in which adolescents (and even younger children) live, violence and the threat of death are inescapable facts of daily life. Many other adolescents take heedless risks. They hitchhike, drive recklessly, and experiment with drugs and sex—often with tragic results. In their urge to discover and express their identity, they may be more concerned with *how* they live than with how *long* they will live.

Adulthood

Young adults who have finished their education and have embarked on careers, marriage, or parenthood are generally eager to live the lives they have been preparing for. If they are suddenly struck by a potentially fatal illness or injury, they are likely to be extremely frustrated. Frustration may turn to rage, which can make them difficult hospital patients.

People who develop terminal illnesses, such as AIDS, in their twenties or thirties must face issues of death and dying at an age when they normally would be dealing with such issues of young adulthood as establishing an intimate relationship. Rather than having a long lifetime of losses as gradual preparation for the final loss of life, they find their entire world collapsing at once.

In middle age, most people realize more keenly than before that they are indeed going to die. Their bodies send them signals that they are not as young, agile, and hearty as they once were. More and more they think about how many years they may have left and of how to make the most of those years (Neugarten, 1967). Often—especially after the death of both parents—there is a new awareness of being the older generation next in line to die (Scharlach & Fredriksen, 1993). Middle-aged and older adults may prepare for death emotionally as well as in practical ways by making a will, planning their own funerals, and discussing their wishes with family and friends.

Older adults may have mixed feelings about the prospect of dying. Physical losses and other problems and losses of old age may diminish their pleasure in living and their will to live (McCue, 1995). Some older adults, especially after age 70, give up on achieving unfulfilled goals. Others push harder to do what they can with life in the time they have left. Many try to extend their remaining time by adopting healthier lifestyles or struggle to live even when they are profoundly ill (Cicirelli, 2002).

When they think of their impending death, some older adults express fear. Others, especially the devoutly religious, engage in what Kübler-Ross called *denial*. When asked what they imagine dying will be like, they compare it to falling asleep, an easy and painless transition to an afterlife. They do not talk about the process of dying itself or the declines that may precede it. For them, this approach may mute fear of dying (Cicirelli, 2002).

According to Erikson, older adults who resolve the final critical alternative of *integrity versus despair* (refer back to Chapter 18) achieve acceptance both of what they have done with their lives and of their impending death. One way to accomplish this resolution is through a *life review*, discussed later in this chapter. People who feel that their lives have been meaningful and who have adjusted to their losses may be better able to face death.

Special Losses

Especially difficult losses that may occur during adulthood are the deaths of a spouse, a parent, and a child. Less publicly noted is the loss of a potential offspring through miscarriage or stillbirth.

Surviving a Spouse

Because women tend to live longer than men and to be younger than their husbands, they are more likely to be widowed. They also tend to be widowed at

What's Your View?

- Try to imagine that you are terminally ill. What do you imagine your feelings would be? Would they be similar to or different from those described in the text with reference to your age group?

Lifemap CD

Have you thought about your own death? In the video "On Dying, at Age 72" video in Chapter 19 of your CD, an older man describes what he thinks would be the preferred way for his life to end.

Checkpoint

Can you . . .

✓ Discuss how people of different ages cope with death and bereavement?

Guidepost

6. What special challenges are involved in surviving a spouse, a parent, or a child, or in mourning a miscarriage?

Although widowed women may show their distress more openly, widowed men also feel their loss. Men are less likely to stay in touch with friends who could offer social support.

an earlier age. One-third of women lose their husbands by age 65, but it is not until 75 that an equal proportion of men lose their wives (Atchley, 1997).

The loss of a husband may be especially hard for a woman who has structured her life and her identity around pleasing or caring for her husband (Marks & Lambert, 1998). Such a woman has lost not only a companion but also an important, sometimes central, role (Lucas, Clark, Georgellis, & Diener, 2003). Although women may show their distress more openly, men also may feel they have lost their moorings (Aldwin & Levenson, 2001). Older widows are more likely than older widowers to stay in touch with friends from whom they receive social support (Kinsella & Velkoff, 2001).

The quality of the marital relationship that has been lost affects the degree to which widowhood affects mental health. In the CLOC study discussed earlier, widowed persons who had been highly dependent on their spouses tended to become more anxious and yearned more for their partners six months after the death than did those who had not been so dependent. Not surprisingly, those who had been especially close to their spouses also reported greater yearning (Carr et al., 2000).

The stress of widowhood may affect physical health. In a large-scale Finnish study, men who lost their wives within a 5-year period were 21 percent more likely to die within the same period than men who remained married, and widowed women were 10 percent more likely to die than nonwidowed women (Martikainen & Valkonen, 1996). As we discussed in earlier chapters, social relationships are related to good health. The loss of the protective "shield" of companionship may explain the strong likelihood that a widowed person will soon follow the spouse to the grave (Ray, 2004). However, the CLOC study suggests a more practical reason. After the death of a spouse, there may be no one to remind an older widow to take her pills or to make sure a widowed man adheres to a special diet. Those who received such reminders (say, from children or health workers) tended to improve in health habits and reported health (Williams, 2004).

Widowhood can create other practical problems. Widows whose husbands were chief breadwinners may experience economic hardship or fall into poverty (Hungerford, 2001). When a husband is widowed, he has to buy many household services a homemaker wife provided. When both spouses were employed, the loss of one income can be hard.

Ultimately, for women, especially, the distress of loss can be a catalyst for introspection and growth—for discovering submerged aspects of themselves and learning to stand on their own feet. More acutely aware of their own mortality, they may reevaluate their lives in a search for personal meaning. In the process, they may look back at their marriages more realistically. Some return to school or find new jobs (Lieberman, 1996).

With available women greatly outnumbering available men, elderly widowers are four times as likely to remarry as elderly widows (Carstensen & Pasupathi, 1993), typically within a year (Aldwin & Levenson, 2001). Many widows are not interested in remarriage (Talbott, 1998). Women usually can handle their household needs and may be reluctant to give up survivors' pension benefits or the freedom of living alone or to face the prospect of caring for an infirm husband, perhaps for the second time. An analysis of data from the CLOC study found that either widows or widowers are more likely to seek out a new romantic relationship if they have close, supportive friends, suggesting that the main benefit of many marriages in late life is companionship (Carr, 2004).

Losing a Parent in Adulthood

Little attention has been paid to the impact of a parent's death on an adult child. Today, with longer life expectancies, this loss normally occurs in middle age (Aldwin & Levenson, 2001). Thus, findings from the MIDUS study suggest, the loss of both parents in young adulthood is a nonnormative experience that may negatively affect mental or physical health (Marks, Bumpass, & Jun, 2004).

Of course, the loss of a parent at any time is not easy. In-depth interviews with 83 volunteers ages 35 to 60 found a majority of bereaved adult children still experiencing emotional distress—ranging from sadness and crying to depression and thoughts of suicide—after 1 to 5 years, especially following loss of a mother (Scharlach & Fredriksen, 1993). Still, the death of a parent can be a maturing experience. It can push adults into resolving important developmental issues: achieving a stronger sense of self and a more pressing, realistic awareness of their own mortality, along with a greater sense of responsibility, commitment, and attachment to others (M. S. Moss & Moss, 1989; Scharlach & Fredriksen, 1993; see Table 19-4).

The death of a parent often brings changes in other relationships. A bereaved adult child may assume more responsibility for the surviving parent and for keeping the family together (Aldwin & Levenson, 2001). The intense emotions of bereavement may draw siblings closer, or they may become alienated over differences that arose during the parent's final illness. A parent's death may free an adult child to spend more time and energy on rela-

Friendship is often a source of support and satisfaction for elderly widows.

tionships that were temporarily neglected to meet demands of caregiving. Or the death may free an adult child to shed a relationship that was being maintained to meet the parent's expectations (M. S. Moss & Moss, 1989; Scharlach & Fredriksen, 1993).

The death of a second parent can have especially great impact. The adult child may feel a sharpened sense of mortality now that the buffer of the older generation is gone (Aldwin & Levenson, 2001). This awareness can be an opportunity for growth, leading to a more mature outlook on life and a greater appreciation of the value of personal relationships (Scharlach & Frederiksen, 1993). Recognition of the finality of death and of the impossibility of saying anything more to the deceased parent motivates some people to resolve disturbances in their ties to the living while there is still time. Some people are moved to reconcile with their own adult children. Sometimes estranged siblings, realizing that the parent who provided a link between them is no longer there, try to mend the rift.

Losing a Child

In earlier times, it was not unusual for a parent to bury a child, as Louisa May Alcott's mother did. Today, with medical advances and the increase in life expectancy in industrialized countries, infant mortality has reached record lows, and a child who survives the first year of life is far more likely to live to old age.

A parent is rarely prepared emotionally for the death of a child. Such a death, no matter at what age, comes as a cruel, unnatural shock, an untimely event that, in the normal course of things, should not have happened. The parents may feel they

In the nineteenth century, it was not unusual for parents to bury a child. Today, infant and child mortality in industrialized countries has dropped dramatically.

Table 19-4	Self-reported Psychological Impacts of a Parent's Death on Adult Children		
Impacts		**Death of Mother (Percent)**	**Death of Father (Percent)**
Self-concept			
More "adult"		29	43
More self-confident		19	20
More responsible		11	4
Less mature		14	3
Other		8	17
No impact		19	12
Feelings about mortality			
Increased awareness of own mortality		30	29
More accepting of own death		19	10
Made concrete plans regarding own death		10	4
Increased fear of own death		10	18
Other		14	16
No impact		17	23
Religiosity			
More religious		26	29
Less religious		11	2
Other		3	10
No impact		60	59
Personal priorities			
Personal relationships more important		35	28
Simple pleasures more important		16	13
Personal happiness more important		10	7
Material possessions less important		5	8
Other		20	8
No impact		14	36
Work or career plans			
Left job		29	16
Adjusted goals		15	10
Changed plans due to family needs		5	6
Moved		4	10
Other		13	19
No impact		34	39

Source: Scharlach & Fredriksen, 1993, table 1, p. 311.

What's Your View?

- Have you lost a parent? a sibling? a spouse? a child? a friend? If not, which of these losses do you imagine would be hardest to bear, and why? If you have experienced more than one of these kinds of loss, how did your reactions differ?

- What advice would you give a friend about what to say—and what *not* to say—to a person in mourning?

have failed, no matter how much they loved and cared for the child, and they may find it hard to let go. If a marriage is strong, the couple may draw closer together, supporting each other in their shared loss. In other cases, the loss weakens and eventually destroys the marriage (Brandt, 1989). Parents, especially mothers, who have lost a child are at heightened risk of being hospitalized for mental illness (Li, Laursen, Precht, Olsen, & Mortensen, 2005). The stress of a child's loss may even hasten parents' death (Li, Precht, Mortensen, & Olsen, 2003).

Many parents hesitate to discuss a terminally ill child's impending death with the child, but those who do so tend to achieve a sense of closure that helps them cope after the loss. In 2001, a Swedish research team surveyed 449 Swedish parents who had lost a child to cancer four to nine years earlier. About one-third of the parents said they had talked with their children about their impending death, and none of these parents regretted having done so, whereas 27 percent of those who had not brought up the subject regretted it. Most likely to have regrets were parents who had sensed that their child was aware of his or her imminent death but had not spoken to the child about it, and a disproportionate number of these parents were still suffering from depression and anxiety (Kreicbergs, Baldimarsdóttir, Onelöv, Henter, & Steineck, 2004).

Although each bereaved parent must cope with grief in his or her own way, some have found that plunging into work, interests, and other relationships or joining a support group eases the pain. The Chilean writer Isabel Allende wrote a family memoir while sitting at the bedside of her comatose, dying daughter (refer back to Chapter 8 Focus vignette). Some well-meaning friends tell parents not to dwell on their loss; but remembering the child in a meaningful way may be exactly what they need to do.

Mourning a Miscarriage

At a Buddhist temple in Tokyo, small statues of infants accompanied by toys and gifts are left as offerings to Jizo, an enlightened being who is believed to watch over miscarried and aborted fetuses and eventually, through reincarnation, to guide them into a new life. The ritual of *mizuko kuyo,* a rite of apology and remembrance, is observed as a means of making amends to the aborted life (Orenstein, 2002).

The Japanese word *mizuko* means "water child." Japanese Buddhists believe that life flows into an organism gradually, like water, and a mizuko is somewhere on the continuum between life and death (Orenstein, 2002). In English, by contrast, there is no word for a miscarried or aborted fetus, nor any ritual of mourning. Families, friends, and health professionals tend to avoid talking about such losses, because they are often considered insignificant compared with the loss of a living child (Van, 2001). Grief can be more wrenching without social support.

How do prospective parents cope with the loss of a child they never knew? Because each person's or couple's experience of loss is unique, it is hard to generalize (Van, 2001). In one small study, eleven men whose child had died in utero reported being overcome with frustration and helplessness during and after the delivery, but several found relief in supporting their partners (Samuelsson, Radestad, & Segesten, 2001). In another study, grieving parents perceived their spouses and extended families as most helpful and their doctors as least helpful. Some bereaved parents benefited from a support group, and some not (DiMarco, Menke, & McNamara, 2001). Differences in the ways men and women grieve may be a source of tension and divisiveness in a couple's relationship (Caelli, Downie, & Letendre, 2002). Couples who have gone through the loss of a pregnancy may need extra-compassionate care during a later pregnancy (Caelli et al., 2002).

Medical, Legal, and Ethical Issues: The "Right to Die"

Do people have a right to die? If so, under what circumstances? Should a terminally ill person who wants to commit suicide be allowed or helped to do so? Should a doctor prescribe medicine that will relieve pain but may shorten the patient's life? What about giving a lethal injection to end a patient's suffering? Who decides that a life is not worth prolonging? These are some of the thorny moral, ethical, and legal questions that face individuals, families, physicians, and society—questions involving the quality of life and the nature and circumstances of death.

Suicide

Although suicide is no longer a crime in modern societies, there is still a stigma against it, based in part on religious prohibitions and in part on society's interest in preserving life. A person who expresses suicidal thoughts may be considered—often

Checkpoint
Can you . . .

✔ Describe specific challenges involved in losing a spouse?

✔ Tell ways in which an adult's loss of a spouse or parent can be a maturing experience?

✔ Explain why parents are rarely prepared emotionally for the death of a child?

✔ Discuss ways to help expectant parents cope with the loss of a pregnancy?

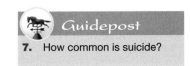

Guidepost

7. How common is suicide?

with good reason—mentally ill. On the other hand, a growing number of people consider a mature adult's deliberate choice of a time to end his or her life a rational decision and a right to be defended.

Suicide rates in the United States began declining in the late 1990s after a 25 percent rise from 1981 to 1997 (Sahyoun, Lentzner et al., 2001). Still, more than 30,000 people took their own lives in 2003, according to preliminary data, making suicide the eleventh leading cause of death and the third leading cause among 15- to 24-year-olds. The suicide rate in the United States—10.5 deaths per 100,000 population (Hoyert, Kung, & Smith, 2005)—is lower than in many other industrialized countries (Kinsella & Velkoff, 2001). Worldwide, suicide is the thirteenth leading cause of death (WHO, 2003a).

Many "accidental" overdoses of medication are actually suicides. Suicide is a leading cause of death in the United States.

Statistics probably understate the number of suicides, since many go unreported and some (such as traffic "accidents" and "accidental" medicinal overdoses) are not recognized as such. Also, the figures on suicides often do not include suicide *attempts*; an estimated 20 to 60 percent of people who commit suicide have tried before, and about 10 percent of people who attempt suicide will kill themselves within 10 years (Harvard Medical School, 2003b). A national study found that 60 percent of nonfatal self-inflicted injuries treated in U.S. hospital emergency rooms, especially among teenage girls and young women, are probable suicide attempts and 10 percent are possible attempts (Ikeda et al., 2002). (Teenage suicide is discussed in more depth in Chapter 11.)

In most nations, suicide rates rise with age and are higher among men than among women (Kinsella & Velkoff, 2001). In the United States, although more women than men attempt suicide, men are four times more likely to succeed (NCHS, 2004). That is because they tend to use more reliable methods, such as firearms, whereas women are equally likely to choose poisoning. An estimated 60 percent of completed suicides are by gunshot (Harvard Medical School, 2003b). White and Native American men have the highest suicide rates. Members of these two groups are approximately twice as likely to commit suicide as Hispanic American, African American, or Asian American men (NCHS, 2004).

By far the highest rate of suicide is among white men over age 50, who account for 30 percent of all suicides (Harvard Medical School, 2003b). The risk rises with age, particularly among men 85 and older (NCHS, 2004). Older people are more likely than younger people to be depressed and socially isolated, and if they try to commit suicide, they are more likely to succeed the first time (CDC, 2002b). Divorced and widowed men have high suicide rates at all ages. Suicide in older adults is associated with physical illness, family conflict, and financial troubles (Harvard Medical School, 2003b). Older African Americans are only one-third as likely to commit suicide as older white people (NCHS, 2004), perhaps in part because of religious commitment and in part because they may be accustomed to coping with hard knocks (NCHS, 1998; NIMH, 1999a). A family history of suicide and suicide attempts greatly raises the risk of suicide. An apparent hereditary vulnerability may be related to low activity of the mood- and impulse-regulating brain chemical serotonin in the prefrontal cortex, the seat of judgment, planning, and inhibition (Harvard Medical School, 2003b).

Although some people intent on suicide carefully conceal their plans, 8 out of 10 people who kill themselves give warning signs. These may include withdrawing from family or friends; talking about death, the hereafter, or suicide; giving away prized possessions; abusing drugs or alcohol; and personality changes, such as unusual anger, boredom, or apathy. People who are about to kill themselves may neglect their appearance, stay away from work or other customary activities, complain of physical problems when nothing is organically wrong, or sleep or eat much more or much less than usual. They often show signs of depression, such as unusual difficulty concentrating, loss of self-esteem, and feelings of helplessness, hopelessness, extreme anxiety, or panic (Harvard Medical School, 2003b; NIMH, 1999a).

Survivors of people who take their own lives have been called "suicide's other victims." Many blame themselves for failing to recognize the signs. They "obsessively replay the events leading up to the death, imagining how they could have prevented it and berating themselves for their failure to do so" (Goldman & Rothschild, in press). Because of the stigma attached to suicide, they often struggle with their emotions alone rather than share them with others who might understand.

Aid in Dying

In Evanston, Illinois, a 70-year-old man visited his 66-year-old wife, who was suffering from cancer and two strokes, in the hospital. Firing through a pillow to muffle the sound, he shot her in the heart to end her pain, then turned the handgun on himself. He left a long note explaining that they had planned their deaths together. "It appears to have been euthanasia," a hospital spokesman said (Wisby, 2001). In another Illinois case, a 77-year-old Oak Lawn man got a 20-year prison term after shooting dead his hospitalized wife, who had Parkinson's disease and was in the early stages of Alzheimer's disease ("Man, 77, pleads guilty to killing wife at hospital," 2003).

Euthanasia means "good death." These husbands' acts were examples of **active euthanasia** (sometimes called *mercy killing*), action taken directly and deliberately to shorten a life in order to end suffering or allow a terminally ill person to die with dignity. **Passive euthanasia** is withholding or discontinuing treatment that might extend the life of a terminally ill patient, such as medication, life-support systems, or feeding tubes. Active euthanasia is generally illegal; passive euthanasia, in some circumstances, is not. An important question regarding either form of euthanasia is whether it is *voluntary,* that is, whether it is done at the direct request, or to carry out the expressed wishes, of the person whose death results.

Assisted suicide—in which a physician or someone else helps a person bring about a self-inflicted death by, for example, prescribing or obtaining drugs or enabling a patient to inhale a deadly gas—commonly refers to situations in which people with incurable, terminal illnesses request help in ending their lives. Assisted suicide is still illegal in most places but in recent years has come to the forefront of public debate. It may be similar in principle to voluntary active euthanasia, in which, for example, a patient asks for, and receives, a lethal injection; but in assisted suicide the person who wants to die performs the actual deed.

All of these are forms of what is sometimes called *aid in dying* or *hastening death,* but their moral and ethical implications may differ and even their definitions often are debated.

Advance Directives In Louisa May Alcott's time and place, the idea of helping a suffering loved one hasten death was virtually unheard of. Changing attitudes toward aid in dying can be attributed largely to revulsion against technologies that keep patients alive against their will despite intense suffering, and sometimes even after the brain has, for all practical purposes, stopped functioning.

The United States Supreme Court, in the case of Nancy Cruzan, held that a person whose wishes are clearly known has a constitutional right to refuse or discontinue life-sustaining treatment (*Cruzan v. Director, Missouri Department of Health,* 1990)—in other words, to request passive euthanasia. A mentally competent person's

What's Your View?

- In your opinion, is the intentional ending of one's own life ever justified? Would you ever consider this option? If so, under what circumstances?

 Guidepost

8. Why are attitudes toward hastening death changing, and what concerns do such practices raise?

active euthanasia Deliberate action taken to shorten the life of a terminally ill person in order to end suffering or to allow death with dignity; also called *mercy killing.*

passive euthanasia Deliberate withholding or discontinuation of life-prolonging treatment of a terminally ill person in order to end suffering or allow death with dignity.

assisted suicide Suicide in which a physician or someone else helps a person take his or her own life.

BOX 19-2

Window on the World

Organ Donation: The Gift of Life

Snowboarder Chris Klug won a bronze medal in the Men's Parallel Giant Slalom event at the winter Olympics in Salt Lake City in February 2002—just 18 months after receiving a lifesaving liver transplant.

In 2004, 26,984 persons in the United States—a record high—received lifesaving transplants of donated organs and tissue, such as skin and bone marrow, an increase of close to 11 percent since 2003. The greater availability of donated organs and tissue is largely due to a rise in "living donation": donation of a single organ, usually the kidney or a portion of a liver or lung by a living person. Human beings have two kidneys but can lead healthy lives with only one. In 2004, nearly half of all donors—6,996—were living (OPTN, 2005; USDHHS, 2005), thanks to medical advances that make donation safer and more likely to succeed (USDHHS, 2002). Nearly two-thirds of living donors are related to the recipients by blood, and most of the others have personal relationships with the recipients, but some are complete strangers (Steinbrook, 2005). Deceased donors can give multiple organs that will improve or save the lives of several people (USDHHS, 2005).

Despite the increase in organ donation, there is a worldwide shortage of organs (West & Burr, 2002). In the United States about 16 people die every day—close to 6,000 each year—while waiting for transplants (Scientific Registry of Transplant Recipients, 2004). More than 87,000 are currently on the waiting list (OPTN, 2005). Organs are less likely to be rejected by the body of the recipient if they come from a donor of the same race or ethnicity; and some diseases of the kidney, heart, lung, pancreas, and liver are more common in certain racial and ethnic minorities than in the general population (USDHHS, 2002).

A major factor in the organ shortage is the refusal of families of potential donors to give consent. The decision to be a donor or to allow a deceased loved one to be a donor is not always an easy one. When one man collapsed and died of a brain aneurysm, his 16-year-old daughter initially opposed the idea but changed her mind when she thought about the possibility that another girl's father might be helped. Ultimately five people received transplants and a chance for life as a result of that one man's death (USDHHS, 2002).

Among the factors influencing denial of consent are misunderstanding of brain death, the timing and setting of the request, and the approach of the person making the request. Cultural attitudes also play a part (West & Burr, 2002). For example, the waiting list for African Americans is about twice as long as for other ethnic groups. Among African American women in the rural south, objections to donation seem related to religious beliefs and kinship ties (Wittig, 2001). In the United Kingdom, where the shortage of organs is particularly acute among Asian immigrants, Asians in the Glasgow, Scotland, region were generally unsympathetic to organ transplantation, especially after death, even when they understood the issues (Baines, Joseph, & Jindal, 2002). In India, most of the transplants that are done come from

---

advance directive (living will) Document specifying the type of care wanted by the maker in the event of an incapacitating or terminal illness.

wishes can be spelled out in advance in a document called an **advance directive,** which contains instructions for when and how to discontinue futile medical care. All 50 states have since legalized some form of advance directive or adopted other provisions governing the making of end-of-life decisions (APA Working Group on Assisted Suicide and End-of-Life Decision-making, 2005).

One type of directive is the *living will.* It may contain specific provisions with regard to circumstances in which treatment should be discontinued, what extraordinary measures—if any—should be taken to prolong life, and what kind of pain management is desired. A person also may specify, through a donor card or a signature on the back of his or her driver's license, that his or her organs be donated to someone in need of an organ transplant (see Box 19-2).

Some "living will" legislation applies only to terminally ill patients, not to those who are incapacitated by illness or injury but may live many years in severe pain. Nor do advance directives help many patients in comas or in a *persistent vegetative state,* in which, although technically alive, they have no awareness and only rudimentary brain functioning. Such situations can be covered by a **durable power of attorney,** which appoints another person to make decisions if the maker of the document becomes incompetent to do so. A number of states have adopted a simple form known as a *medical durable power of attorney* expressly for decisions about health care.

durable power of attorney Legal instrument that appoints an individual to make decisions in the event of another person's incapacitation.

The case of Terri Schiavo—a young woman diagnosed in a persistent vegetative state who had *not* left a written advance directive—erupted into a seven-year legal battle culminating in an unprecedented Congressional intervention in the judicial process because of a bitter disagreement between her husband and her parents over

—continued

living donors—again, because of moral, religious, and emotional constraints against donating organs of a brain-dead person (Chandra & Singh, 2001).

Culturally sensitive education may make a difference. An educational program among American Indian communities in the southwestern United States showed the need to change not only the attitudes of potential donors but also the stereotypes about Native Americans commonly held by health care providers who ask for the donations (Thomas, 2002). Interviews with Japanese, Korean, and Indian immigrants to the United States found vastly different views, not only about organ donation, but also about broader aspects of the medical experience, such as when to seek such assistance, the roles of doctors and nurses, how to talk with medical specialists, issues of privacy and disclosure, and end-of-life care (Andresen, 2001).

The National Organ Transplant Act regulates the procurement, distribution, and transplantation of scarce organs in the United States. Any healthy person of any age can be an organ donor—even a newborn baby. Donors under age 18 need parental consent. Adults who wish to be donors after death can express that wish by so indicating on their driver's licenses or filling out and carrying an organ donor card and informing their families, who may need to sign a consent form at the time of donation. The family does not pay the cost; it is paid by the recipient, usually through insurance or Medicare. Sale of human organs and tissues is illegal (USDHHS, 2002).

Organ donation by living donors poses some ethical issues. Medical ethicists say that "organs from living donors should be used only when the likelihood of success for the recipient [is] high, the risk to the donor [is] low, and true voluntary consent [is] obtained from all involved" (Ingelfinger, 2005, p. 449). Donors need to be informed about the risks of the surgery and about possible long-term effects (Ingelfinger, 2005). Donors are now openly solicited on the Internet and through advertising, raising questions about the potential for financial exploitation, inequitable allocation of organs, and possible violations of standards for donation (Steinbrook, 2005). The process for evaluating potential donors needs to be standardized, with independent counselors to make sure that the chance of success is great enough to justify the risks and to help donors make an informed choice (Truog, 2005).

What's Your View?

Would you donate an organ to a friend or family member who needed it? To a stranger? Upon your death? Why or why not?

Check It Out

For more information on this topic, go to http://www.organdonor.gov [a Web site of the U.S. Department of Health and Human Services, which gives basic facts and statistics about organ donation].

---

what her wishes had been and whether her condition was truly irreversible (Annas, 2005). Even with advance directives, many patients have undergone protracted, fruitless treatment against their expressed wishes. In a 5-year study of some 9,000 critically ill patients at five U.S. teaching hospitals, doctors were frequently unaware of patients' request not to be resuscitated in the event of cardiac arrest (The SUPPORT Principal Investigators, 1995).

Such findings led the American Medical Association to form a Task Force on Quality Care at the End of Life. Many hospitals now have ethics committees that create guidelines, review cases, and help doctors, patients, and their families with decisions about end-of-life care (Simpson, 1996); and a smaller number of hospitals employ full-time ethics consultants. A prospective randomized controlled two-year study of 551 patients in intensive care suggests that ethics consultations in difficult, value-laden situations can help resolve conflicts that might otherwise prolong non-beneficial or unwanted treatment (Schneiderman et al., 2003).

Assisted Suicide: Pros and Cons In the United States, assisted suicide is illegal in almost all states but often goes on covertly, without regulation. The American Medical Association opposes physician aid in dying as contrary to a practitioner's oath to "do no harm." Doctors are permitted to give drugs that may shorten a life if the purpose is to relieve pain (Gostin, 1997; Quill, Lo, & Brock, 1997), but some physicians refuse for reasons of personal or medical ethics (APA, 2001).

The *ethical* arguments *for* assisted suicide are based on the principles of autonomy and self-determination: that mentally competent persons should have the right to control the quality of their own lives and the timing and nature of their death. Proponents of assisted suicide place a high value on preserving the dignity and personhood of the dying human being. *Medical arguments* hold that a doctor is obligated to take all measures necessary to relieve suffering. Besides, in assisted suicide the patient is the one who takes the actual steps to end life. A *legal* argument is that legalizing assisted suicide would permit the regulation of practices that now occur anyway out of compassion for suffering patients. It is argued that adequate safeguards against abuse can be put in place through a combination of legislation and professional regulation (APA, 2001).

Some ethical and legal scholars go further: They favor legalizing *all* forms of *voluntary* euthanasia with safeguards against involuntary euthanasia. The key issue, according to these scholars, is not how death occurs but who makes the decision. They see no difference in principle between pulling the plug on a respirator or pulling out feeding tubes and giving a lethal injection or prescribing an overdose of pills at the patient's request. They maintain that aid in dying, if openly available, would reduce fear and helplessness by enabling patients to control their own fate (APA, 2001; Brock, 1992; R. A. Epstein, 1989; Orentlicher, 1996).

Ethical arguments *against* assisted suicide center on two principles: (1) the belief that taking a life, even with consent is wrong; and (2) concern for protection of the disadvantaged. Opponents of aid-in-dying point out that autonomy is often limited by poverty or disability or membership in a stigmatized social group, and they fear that persons in these categories may be subtly pressured into choosing suicide with cost containment as an underlying factor. Some patients may internalize this concern, insisting that they do not want their families to waste limited resources on their prolonged care. *Medical* arguments against assisted suicide include the possibility of misdiagnosis, the potential future availability of new treatments, the likelihood of incorrect prognosis, and the belief that helping someone die is incompatible with a physician's role as healer and that adequate safeguards are not possible. *Legal* arguments against assisted suicide include concerns about enforceability of such safeguards and also about lawsuits when family members disagree about the propriety of terminating a life (APA, 2001).

Because self-administered pills do not always work, some opponents contend that physician-assisted suicide would lead to voluntary active euthanasia (Groenewoud et al., 2000). The next step on the "slippery slope," some warn, would be involuntary euthanasia—not only for the terminally ill but also for others, such as people with disabilities, whose quality of life is perceived as diminished. They claim that people who want to die are often temporarily depressed and might change their minds with treatment or palliative care (APA, 2005; Butler, 1996; Hendin, 1994; Latimer, 1992; Quill et al., 1997; Simpson, 1996; Singer, 1988; Singer & Siegler, 1990).

Legalizing Physician Aid in Dying In September, 1996, a 66-year-old Australian man with advanced prostate cancer was the first person to die legally by assisted suicide. Under a law passed in the Northern Territory, he pressed a computer key that administered a lethal dose of barbiturates. In 1997 the law was repealed ("Australian Man," 1996; Voluntary Euthanasia Society, 2002).

Protestors against Oregon's assisted suicide law fear that it would lead to pressure on the disabled to end their lives, despite legal safeguards against abusing the law.

Since 1997, when a unanimous U.S. Supreme Court left regulation of physician aid in dying up to the states, measures to legalize assisted suicide for the terminally ill have been introduced in several states. So far Oregon is the only state to pass such a law, the Death with Dignity Act. In 1994, Oregonians voted to let mentally competent patients who have been told by two doctors that they have less than six months to live request a lethal prescription with strong safeguards to make sure that the request is serious and voluntary and that all other alternatives have been considered. The Oregon law survived a court challenge and a repeal referendum in 1997. In 2002 a federal district court overruled an attempt by U.S. Attorney General John Ashcroft to block the operation of the statute by making doctors criminally liable if they prescribe drugs to help patients end their lives. In 2005 the U.S. Supreme Court agreed to hear the administration's appeal (Greenhouse, 2005).

What has been the experience under the Oregon law? In its first seven years of operation, 238 terminally ill patients were reported to state health officials to have taken their lives under the act, 37 of them in 2004 (Schwartz, 2005). In an earlier study after two years of operation, physicians reported granting about one-sixth of the 221 requests for lethal prescriptions, but nearly half of these patients changed their minds and did not take the medications. Patients who received palliative interventions, such as control of pain or referral to a hospice program, were more likely to change their minds (Ganzini et al., 2000). Patients who requested and used lethal prescriptions tended to be more concerned about loss of autonomy or control of bodily functions than about fear of pain or financial loss (Chin, Hedberg, Higginson, & Fleming, 1999; Sullivan et al., 2000).

Active euthanasia remains illegal in the United States, even in Oregon, but not in the Netherlands, where in 2001 voluntary euthanasia was legalized for patients in a state of continuous, unbearable, and incurable suffering (Johnston, 2001; Osborn, 2002). In such cases, doctors can now inject a lethal dose of medication. Belgium followed suit the following year ("Belgium Legalises Euthanasia," 2002).

Before 2001, both assisted suicide and active euthanasia were technically illegal in the Netherlands, but physicians who engaged in these practices could avoid prosecution under strict conditions of reporting and government oversight (Simons, 1993). In 1995, 2.5 percent of deaths in the Netherlands resulted from euthanasia or assisted suicide (Van der Maas et al., 1996). Researchers found little evidence of a "slippery slope" and observed that Dutch doctors seemed to be practicing physician aid in dying "only reluctantly and under compelling circumstances" (Angell, 1996, p. 1677). Critics in the United States disagreed, claiming that doctors in the Netherlands had moved from assisted suicide for the terminally ill all the way to euthanasia for those with chronic illness or psychological distress and even, in some cases, to involuntary euthanasia (Hendin, Rutenfrans, & Zylicz, 1997).

End-of-Life Decisions and Cultural Attitudes It is hard to compare the experience of the Netherlands, which has a homogeneous population and universal national health coverage, with that of such a large, diverse country as the United States (APA, 2001; Griffiths, Bood, & Weyers, 1998). Nevertheless, with increasing numbers of Americans—3 out of 4 in a 2005 Gallup poll (Moore, 2005)—favoring euthanasia for a patient who is incurably ill and wants to die, some U.S. doctors have acceded to patients' requests for assistance in hastening death. A nationwide survey of 1,902 physicians whose specialties involve care of dying patients found that, of those who had received requests for help with suicide (18 percent) or lethal injections (11 percent), about 7 percent had complied at least once (Meier et al., 1998). On the other hand, in a survey in the United Kingdom, 80 percent of geriatric physicians—but only 52 percent of intensive care physicians—considered active voluntary euthanasia *never* ethically justified (Dickinson, Lancaster, Clark, Ahmedzai, & Noble, 2002).

The first representative study of end-of-life decisions in six European countries (Belgium, Denmark, Italy, the Netherlands, Sweden, and Switzerland) found important cultural differences. Questionnaires to be completed anonymously were sent to attending physicians in a random sample of deaths during a six-month period. In all six countries, physicians reported withholding or withdrawing life-prolonging treatment—most typically medication, followed by hydration or nutrition—but the frequency varied greatly, from 41 percent of deaths in Switzerland to 6 percent in Italy (Bosshard et al., 2005). Active forms of physician-assisted death were most prevalent in the Netherlands and Belgium. In these two countries as well as in Switzerland, end-of-life decisions were more frequently discussed with patients and relatives than in the other three countries (van der Heide et al., 2003).

Special end-of-life issues concern treatment of newborns with incurable conditions or very poor prognoses for quality of life. Forgoing or withdrawing life-prolonging treatment for newborns with no chance of survival and those born with severe brain abnormalities or extensive organ damage is now widely accepted medical practice (Verhagen & Sauer, 2005). Yet, here, too, cultural differences appear. In a study of physicians' self-reported practices in France, Germany, Italy, the Netherlands, Spain, Sweden, and the United Kingdom, the vast majority of neonatal practitioners in all seven countries had been involved at least once in decisions to withhold or not institute treatment. French, British, Dutch, and Swedish doctors were more likely to report clear-cut decisions such as withdrawal of ventilators. Only French and Dutch physicians acknowledged with significant frequency having administered drugs to end a newborn's life (Cuttini et al., 2000).

Active euthanasia of infants who would otherwise survive with unbearable pain or suffering remains illegal in the Netherlands, as elsewhere. Yet, as was the case with assisted suicide before enactment of the 2001 law, such deaths do occur there with a form of legal endorsement. Since 1998, 22 cases of euthanasia in newborns with very severe forms of spina bifida have been reported to Dutch authorities without prosecution. Guidelines developed by Groninen Hospital in Amsterdam in 2002 in cooperation with a district attorney permit doctors, with parental approval, to end the lives of newborns deemed to be in great pain from incurable disease or extreme deformities when the infant's medical team and independent doctors agree that there is no prospect for improvement. Four such deaths were reported in 2003; again, none were prosecuted (Verhagen & Sauer, 2005).

End-of-Life Options and Diversity Concerns One salutary result of the aid-in-dying controversy has been to call attention to the need for better palliative care and closer attention to patients' motivation and state of mind. A request for aid in dying can provide an opening to explore the reasons behind it. When doctors talk openly with patients about their physical and mental symptoms, their expectations, their fears and goals, their options for end-of-life care, their family concerns, and their need for meaning and quality of life, ways may be found to diminish these concerns without the taking of life (Bascom & Tolle, 2002). In terminally ill patients, the will to live can fluctuate greatly, so if aid in dying is contemplated, it is essential to ensure that the request is not just a passing one (Chochinov, Tataryn, Clinch, & Dudgeon, 1999). Sometimes a psychiatric consultation may discover an underlying disturbance masked by a seemingly rational request (Muskin, 1998). If lethal measures *are* taken, it is important that a physician be present to ensure that the death is as merciful and pain-free as possible (Nuland, 2000).

In the United States, with its ethnically diverse population, issues of social and cultural diversity need to be addressed in end-of-life decision making. Planning for death is inconsistent with traditional Navajo values, which avoid negative thinking and talk. Chinese families may seek to protect a dying person from unfavorable

What's Your View?

- Do you think assisted suicide should be legalized? If so, what safeguards should be provided? Would your answers be the same or different for voluntary active euthanasia? Do you see an ethical distinction between euthanasia and over-sedation of the terminally ill?

information, including knowledge of his or her impending death. Recent Mexican or Korean immigrants may believe less in individual autonomy than is customary in the dominant U.S. culture. Among some ethnic minorities, the value of longevity may take priority over health. African Americans and Hispanic Americans, for example, are more likely than European Americans to prefer life-sustaining treatment regardless of the state of the disease and of their educational level (APA Working Group on Assisted Suicide, 2005).

Issues of hastening death will become more pressing as the population ages. In years to come, both the courts and the public will be forced to come to terms with these issues as increasing numbers of people claim a right to die with dignity and with help.

Checkpoint
Can you . . .

✔ Explain why suicides are sometimes not recognized, and list some warning signs?

✔ Discuss the ethical, practical, and legal issues involved in advance directives, euthanasia, and assisted suicide?

Finding Meaning and Purpose in Life and Death

Guidepost
9. How can people overcome fear of dying and come to terms with death?

The central character in Leo Tolstoy's "The Death of Ivan Ilyich" is wracked by a fatal illness. Even greater than his physical suffering is his mental torment. He asks himself over and over what meaning there is to his agony, and he becomes convinced that his life has been without purpose and his death will be equally pointless. At the last minute, though, he experiences a spiritual revelation, a concern for his wife and son, which gives him a final moment of integrity and enables him to conquer his terror.

What Tolstoy dramatized in literature is being confirmed by research. In one study of 39 women whose average age was 76, those who saw the most purpose in life had the least fear of death (Durlak, 1973). Conversely, according to Kübler-Ross (1975), facing the reality of death is a key to living a meaningful life:

> It is the denial of death that is partially responsible for [people's] living empty, purposeless lives; for when you live as if you'll live forever, it becomes too easy to postpone the things you know that you must do. In contrast, when you fully understand that each day you awaken could be the last you have, you take the time that day to grow, to become more of who you really are, to reach out to other human beings. (p. 164)

Reviewing a Life

In Charles Dickens's *A Christmas Carol,* Scrooge changes his greedy, heartless ways after seeing ghostly visions of his past, his present, and his future death. In Akira Kurosawa's film *Ikiru* (To Live), a petty bureaucrat who discovers that he is dying of cancer looks back over the emptiness of his life and, in a final burst of energy, creates a meaningful legacy by pushing through a project for a children's park, which he has previously blocked. These fictional characters make their remaining time more purposeful through **life review,** a process of reminiscence that enables a person to see the significance of his or her life.

Life review can, of course, occur at any time. However, it may have special meaning in old age, when it can foster ego integrity—according to Erikson, the final critical task of the life span. As the end of their journey approaches, people may look back over their accomplishments and failures and ask themselves what their lives have meant. Awareness of mortality may be an impetus for reexamining values and seeing one's experiences

life review Reminiscence about one's life in order to see its significance.

Sharing memories evoked by a family photo album is one way to review a life. Life review can help people see important events in a new light and can motivate them to seek a sense of closure by rebuilding damaged relationships or completing unfinished tasks.

and actions in a new light. Some people find the will to complete unfinished tasks, such as reconciling with estranged family members or friends, and thus to achieve a satisfying sense of closure.

Not all memories are equally conducive to mental health and growth. Older people who use reminiscence for self-understanding show the strongest ego integrity, while those who entertain only pleasurable memories show less. Most poorly adjusted are those who keep recalling negative events and are obsessed with regret, hopelessness, and fear of death; their ego integrity has given way to despair (Sherman, 1993; Walasky, Whitbourne, & Nehrke, 1983–1984).

Life-review therapy can help focus the natural process of life review and make it more conscious, purposeful, and efficient (Butler, 1961; M. I. Lewis & Butler, 1974). Methods often used for uncovering memories in life-review therapy (which also may be used by individuals on their own) include writing or taping one's autobiography; constructing a family tree; talking about scrapbooks, photo albums, old letters, and other memorabilia; making a trip back to scenes of childhood and young adulthood; reunions with former classmates or colleagues or distant family members; describing ethnic traditions; and summing up one's life's work.

Development: A Lifelong Process

In his late seventies, the artist Pierre-Auguste Renoir had crippling arthritis and chronic bronchitis and had lost his wife. He spent his days in a wheelchair, and his pain was so great that he could not sleep through the night. He was unable to hold a palette or grip a brush: His brush had to be tied to his right hand. Yet he continued to produce brilliant paintings, full of color and vibrant life. Finally, stricken by pneumonia, he lay in bed, gazing at some anemones his attendant had picked. He gathered enough strength to sketch the form of these beautiful flowers, and then— just before he died—lay back and whispered, "I think I am beginning to understand something about it" (L. Hanson, 1968).

Even dying can be a developmental experience. As one health practitioner put it, ". . . there are things to be gained, accomplished in dying. Time with and for those whom we are close to, achieving a final and enduring sense of self-worth, and a readiness to let go are priceless elements of a good death" (Weinberger, 1999)—the kind of death Louisa May Alcott described in *Little Women*.

Checkpoint

Can you . . .

✔ Explain why life review can be especially helpful in old age and how it can help overcome fear of death?

✔ Tell what types of memories are most conducive to a life review?

✔ List several activities used in life review therapy?

✔ Tell how dying can be a developmental experience?

Refocus

Thinking back to the Focus vignette about Louisa May Alcott at the beginning of this chapter:

- How does Alcott's fictionalized description of the process of her sister "Beth's" dying illustrate attitudes and customs of her time and place?

- Did Beth seem to follow Kübler-Ross's stages of dying?

- How did her family deal with their grief?

- How did Beth and her family find meaning in her last months and days?

Within a limited life span, no person can realize all capabilities, gratify all desires, explore all interests, or experience all the richness that life has to offer. The tension between possibilities for growth and a finite time in which to do the growing defines human life. By choosing which possibilities to pursue and by continuing to follow them as far as possible, even up to the very end, each person contributes to the unfinished story of human development.

SUMMARY AND KEY TERMS

The Many Faces of Death

- Death has biological, social, cultural, historical, religious, legal, psychological, developmental, and ethical aspects.

Guidepost 1: How do attitudes and customs concerning death differ across cultures?

- Customs surrounding death and mourning vary greatly from one culture to another, depending on the society's view of the nature and consequences of death. Some modern customs have evolved from ancient beliefs and practices.

Guidepost 2: What are the implications of the "mortality revolution" in developed countries, and how does it affect care of the dying?

- Death rates dropped drastically during the twentieth century, especially in developed countries.
- Today three-quarters of deaths in the United States occur among the elderly, and the top causes of death are diseases that primarily affect older adults.
- As death became primarily a phenomenon of late adulthood, it became largely "invisible," and care of the dying took place in isolation, by professionals.
- There is now an upsurge of interest in understanding and dealing realistically and compassionately with death. Examples of this tendency are a growing interest in thanatology and increasing emphasis on hospice care and palliative care.

  thanatology *(713)*

  hospice care *(713)*

  palliative care *(713)*

Facing Death and Loss: Psychological Issues

Guidepost 3: How do people change as they approach death?

- People often undergo cognitive and functional declines shortly before death.
- Some people who come close to dying have "near-death" experiences.
- Elisabeth Kübler-Ross proposed five stages in coming to terms with dying: denial, anger, bargaining, depression, and acceptance. These stages, and their sequence, are not universal.

  terminal drop *(714)*

Guidepost 4: Is there a normal pattern of grieving?

- There is no universal pattern of grief. The most widely studied pattern moves from shock and disbelief to preoccupation with the memory of the dead person and finally to resolution. However, research has found wide variations and a great deal of resilience.

- Grief therapy may be indicated for persons who remain in a chronic state of grief.

  bereavement *(716)*

  grief *(716)*

  grief work *(716)*

  grief therapy *(718)*

Death and Bereavement Across the Life Span

Guidepost 5: How do attitudes and understandings about death and bereavement differ across the life span?

- Children's understanding of death develops gradually. Young children can better understand death if it is part of their own experience. Although children experience grief, as adults do, there are age-related reactions based on cognitive and emotional development.
- Although adolescents generally do not think much about death, violence and the threat of death are part of some adolescents' daily life. Adolescents tend to take needless risks.
- Realization and acceptance of the inevitability of death increase throughout adulthood.

Guidepost 6: What special challenges are involved in surviving a spouse, a parent, or a child, or in mourning a miscarriage?

- Women are more likely to be widowed, and widowed younger, than men, and may experience widowhood somewhat differently. Physical and mental health tend to decline after widowhood, but for some people widowhood can ultimately become a positive developmental experience.
- Today, loss of parents often occurs in middle age. Death of a parent can precipitate changes in the self and in relationships with others.
- The loss of a child can be especially difficult because it is no longer normative.
- Because miscarriage is not generally considered a significant loss in U.S. society, those who experience such losses are left to deal with a miscarriage in their own way.

Medical, Legal, and Ethical Issues: The "Right to Die"

Guidepost 7: How common is suicide?

- Although suicide is no longer illegal in modern societies, there is still a stigma attached to it. Some people maintain a "right to die," especially for people with long-term degenerative illness.
- Suicide is the eleventh leading cause of death in the United States and thirteenth worldwide. The number of suicides is probably underestimated.
- Suicide rates tend to rise with age and are more common among men than among women, though women are more likely to attempt suicide. The highest rate of

suicide in the United States is among elderly white men. It is often related to depression, isolation, and debilitating ailments.

$\mathcal{G}$uidepost 8: Why are attitudes toward hastening death changing, and what concerns do such practices raise?

- Euthanasia and assisted suicide involve controversial ethical, medical, and legal issues.
- To avoid unnecessary suffering through artificial prolongation of life, passive euthanasia is generally permitted with the patient's consent or with advance directives. However, such directives are not consistently followed. Most hospitals now have ethics committees to deal with decisions about end-of-life care.
- Active euthanasia and assisted suicide are generally illegal, but public support for physician aid in dying has increased. The state of Oregon has a law permitting physician-assisted-suicide for the terminally ill. The Netherlands and Belgium have legalized both euthanasia and assisted suicide.
- Forgoing or withdrawing treatment of newborns who cannot survive or who can do so only with extremely poor quality of life is becoming a common practice, especially in European countries.

- The aid-in-dying controversy has focused more attention on the need for better palliative care and understanding of patients' state of mind. Issues of social and cultural diversity also need to be considered.

active euthanasia *(729)*

passive euthanasia *(729)*

assisted suicide *(729)*

advance directive (living will) *(730)*

durable power of attorney *(730)*

Finding Meaning and Purpose in Life and Death

$\mathcal{G}$uidepost 9: How can people overcome fear of dying and come to terms with death?

- The more meaning and purpose people find in their lives, the less they tend to fear death.
- Life review can help people prepare for death and give them a last chance to complete unfinished tasks.
- Even dying can be a developmental experience.

life review *(735)*

Glossary

acceleration Approach to educating the gifted that moves them through the curriculum at an unusually rapid pace. (351)

accommodation Piaget's term for changes in a cognitive structure to include new information. (37)

achieving stage Second of Schaie's seven cognitive stages, in which young adults use knowledge to gain competence and independence. (491)

acquired immune deficiency syndrome (AIDS) Viral disease that undermines effective functioning of the immune system. (96)

acquisitive stage First of Schaie's seven cognitive stages, in which children and adolescents learn information and skills largely for their own sake or as preparation for participation in society. (491)

active engagement Personal involvement in schooling, work, family life, or other activity. (429)

active euthanasia Deliberate action taken to shorten the life of a terminally ill person in order to end suffering or to allow death with dignity; also called *mercy killing*. (729)

activities of daily living (ADLs) Essential activities that support survival, such as eating, dressing, bathing, and getting around the house. (646)

activity theory Theory of aging, proposed by Neugarten and others, which holds that in order to age successfully a person must remain as active as possible. (679)

acute medical conditions Illnesses that last a short time. (321)

adaptation Piaget's term for adjustment to new information about the environment. (37)

adolescence Developmental transition between childhood and adulthood entailing major physical, cognitive, and psychosocial changes. (397)

adolescent growth spurt Sharp increase in height and weight that precedes sexual maturity. (402)

adolescent rebellion Pattern of emotional turmoil, characteristic of a minority of adolescents, which may involve conflict with family, alienation from adult society, reckless behavior, and rejection of adult values. (453)

advance directive (living will) Document specifying the type of care wanted by the maker in the event of an incapacitating or terminal illness. (730)

affordances In the Gibsons' ecological theory of perception, the fit between a person's physical attributes and capabilities and characteristics of the environment. (145)

age-differentiated Describing a life structure in which primary roles—learning, working, and leisure—are based on age; typical in industrialized societies. Compare *age-integrated*. (578)

age-integrated Describing a life structure in which primary roles—learning, working, and leisure—are open to adults of all ages and can be interspersed throughout the life span. Compare *age-differentiated*. (579)

ageism Prejudice or discrimination against a person (most commonly an older person) based on age. (627)

age-related macular degeneration Condition in which the center of the retina gradually loses its ability to discern fine details; leading cause of irreversible visual impairment in older adults. (642)

alcoholism Chronic disease involving dependence on use of alcohol, causing interference with normal functioning and fulfillment of obligations. (480)

alleles Two or more alternative forms of a gene that can occupy the same position on paired chromosomes and affect the same trait. (68)

altruism Behavior intended to help others out of inner concern and without expectation of external reward; may involve self-denial or self-sacrifice. (302)

Alzheimer's disease Progressive, irreversible, degenerative brain disorder characterized by cognitive deterioration and loss of control of bodily functions, leading to death. (649)

ambiguous loss A loss that is not clearly defined or does not bring closure. (678)

ambivalent (resistant) attachment Pattern in which an infant becomes anxious before the primary caregiver leaves, is extremely upset during his or her absence, and both seeks and resists contact on his or her return. (206)

amyloid plaque Waxy chunks of insoluble tissue found in brains of persons with Alzheimer's disease. (651)

animism Tendency to attribute life to objects that are not alive. (251)

anorexia nervosa Eating disorder characterized by self-starvation. (409)

anoxia Lack of oxygen, which may cause brain damage. (114)

Apgar scale Standard measurement of a newborn's condition; it assesses appearance, pulse, grimace, activity, and respiration. (115)

art therapy Therapeutic approach that allows a person to express troubled feelings without words, using a variety of art materials and media. (383)

assimilation Piaget's term for incorporation of new information into an existing cognitive structure. (37)

assisted suicide Suicide in which a physician or someone else helps a person take his or her own life. (729)

asthma A chronic respiratory disease characterized by sudden attacks of coughing, wheezing, and difficulty in breathing. (323)

attachment Reciprocal, enduring tie between two people, especially between infant and caregiver, each of whom contributes to the quality of the relationship. (205)

attention-deficit/hyperactivity disorder (ADHD) Syndrome characterized by persistent inattention and distractibility, impulsivity, low tolerance for frustration, and inappropriate overactivity. (348)

authoritarian In Baumrind's terminology, parenting style emphasizing control and obedience. (300)

authoritative In Baumrind's terminology, parenting style blending respect for a child's individuality with an effort to instill social values. (300)

autism Pervasive developmental disorder of the brain, characterized by lack of normal social interaction, impaired communication and imagination, and a highly restricted range of activities and interests. (83)

autobiographical memory Memory of specific events in one's own life. (260)

autoimmunity Tendency of an aging body to mistake its own tissues for foreign invaders and to attack and destroy them. (634)

autonomy versus shame and doubt Erikson's second stage in psychosocial development, in which children achieve a

balance between self-determination and control by others. (214)

autosomes In humans, the 22 pairs of chromosomes not related to sexual differentiation. (66)

avoidant attachment Pattern in which an infant rarely cries when separated from the primary caregiver and avoids contact upon his or her return. (206)

balanced investment Pattern of retirement activity allocated among family, work, and leisure. (686)

basal metabolism Use of energy to maintain vital functions. (553)

basic trust versus basic mistrust Erikson's first crisis in psychosocial development, in which infants develop a sense of the reliability of people and objects. (205)

Bayley Scales of Infant Development Standardized test of infants' development. (156)

behavior therapy Therapeutic approach using principles of learning theory to encourage desired behaviors or eliminate undesired ones; also called *behavior modification*. (383)

behavioral genetics Quantitative study of relative hereditary and environmental influences on behavior. (75)

behaviorism Learning theory that emphasizes the predictable role of environment in causing observable behavior. (34)

behaviorist approach Approach to the study of cognitive development that is concerned with basic mechanics of learning. (153)

bereavement Loss, due to death, of someone to whom one feels close and the process of adjustment to the loss. (716)

bilingual Fluent in two languages. (345)

bilingual education System of teaching non–English-speaking children in their native language while they learn English, and later switching to all-English instruction. (345)

bioecological theory Bronfenbrenner's approach to understanding processes and contexts of human development. (41)

birth trauma Injury to newborn sustained at the time of birth. (118)

body image Descriptive and evaluative beliefs about one's appearance. (408)

brain growth spurts Periods of rapid brain growth and development. (133)

Brazelton Neonatal Behavioral Assessment Scale (NBAS) Neurological and behavioral test to measure neonate's responses to the environment. (115)

bulimia nervosa Eating disorder in which a person regularly eats huge quantities of food and then purges the body by laxatives, induced vomiting, fasting, or excessive exercise. (409)

bullying Aggression deliberately and persistently directed against a particular target, or victim, typically one who is weak, vulnerable, and defenseless. (379)

burnout Syndrome of emotional exhaustion and a sense that one can no longer accomplish anything on the job. (570)

canalization Limitation on variance of expression of certain inherited characteristics. (79)

caregiver burnout Condition of physical, mental, and emotional exhaustion affecting adults who provide continuous care for sick or aged persons. (613)

case study Study of a single subject, such as an individual or family. (47)

cataracts Cloudy or opaque areas in the lens of the eye, which cause blurred vision. (642)

cell death In brain development, the normal elimination of excess brain cells to achieve more efficient functioning. (135)

central executive In Baddeley's model, element of working memory that controls the processing of information. (258)

central nervous system Brain and spinal cord. (132)

centration In Piaget's theory, tendency of preoperational children to focus on one aspect of a situation and neglect others. (252)

cephalocaudal principle Principle that development proceeds in a head-to-tail direction; that is, that upper parts of the body develop before lower parts of the trunk. (85)

cesarean delivery Delivery of a baby by surgical removal from the uterus. (112)

child-directed speech (CDS) Form of speech often used in talking to babies or toddlers; includes slow, simplified speech, a high-pitched tone, exaggerated vowel sounds, short words and sentences, and much repetition; also called *parentese*. (185)

childhood depression Mood disorder characterized by such symptoms as a prolonged sense of friendlessness, inability to have fun or concentrate, fatigue, extreme activity or apathy, feelings of worthlessness, weight change, physical complaints, and thoughts of death or suicide. (382)

chromosomes Coils of DNA that consist of genes. (65)

chronic medical conditions Illnesses or impairments that persist for at least 3 months. (321)

chronosystem Bronfenbrenner's term for effects of time on other developmental systems. (43)

circular reactions Piaget's term for processes by which an infant learns to reproduce desired occurrences originally discovered by chance. (159)

class inclusion Understanding of the relationship between a whole and its parts. (326)

classical conditioning Learning based on association of a stimulus that does not ordinarily elicit a particular response with another stimulus that does elicit the response. (35)

code mixing Use of elements of two languages, sometimes in the same utterance, by young children in households where both languages are spoken. (185)

code switching Changing one's speech to match the situation, as in people who are bilingual. (185)

cognitive development Pattern of change in mental abilities, such as learning, attention, memory, language, thinking, reasoning, and creativity. (10)

cognitive neuroscience approach Approach to the study of cognitive development that links brain processes with cognitive ones. (167)

cognitive neuroscience Study of links between neural processes and cognitive abilities. (47)

cognitive perspective View that thought processes are central to cognitive development. (37)

cognitive reserve Hypothesized fund of energy that may enable a deteriorating brain to continue to function normally. (651)

cognitive-appraisal model Model of coping, proposed by Lazarus and Folkman, which holds that, on the basis of continuous appraisal of their relationship with the environment, people choose appropriate coping strategies to deal with situations that tax their normal resources. (675)

cognitive-stage theory Piaget's theory that children's cognitive development advances in a series of four stages involving qualitatively distinct types of mental operations. (37)

cohabitation Status of an unmarried couple who live together and maintain a sexual relationship. (526)

cohort A group of people born at about the same time. (19)

commitment Marcia's term for personal investment in an occupation or system of beliefs. (439)

committed compliance Kochanska's term for wholehearted obedience of a parent's orders without reminders or lapses. (217)

componential element Sternberg's term for the analytic aspect of intelligence. (334, 492)

conceptual knowledge Acquired interpretive understandings stored in long-term memory. (420)

concordant Term describing tendency of twins to share the same trait or disorder. (77)

concrete operations Third stage of Piagetian cognitive development (approximately from ages 7 to 12), during which children develop logical but not abstract thinking. (324)

conduct disorder (CD) Repetitive, persistent pattern of aggressive, antisocial behavior violating societal norms or the rights of others. (381)

conscience Internal standards of behavior, which usually control one's conduct and produce emotional discomfort when violated. (217)

conservation Piaget's term for awareness that two objects that are equal according to a certain measure remain equal in the face of perceptual alteration so long as nothing has been added to or taken away from either object. (253)

constructive play Play involving use of objects or materials to make something. (292)

contextual element Sternberg's term for the practical aspect of intelligence. (334, 492)

contextual perspective View of human development that sees the individual as inseparable from the social context. (40)

continuity theory Theory of aging, described by Atchley, which holds that in order to age successfully people must maintain a balance of continuity and change in both the internal and external structures of their lives. (680)

control group In an experiment, a group of people, similar to those in the experimental group, who do not receive the treatment under study. (50)

conventional morality (or morality of conventional role conformity) Second level in Kohlberg's theory of moral reasoning in which standards of authority figures are internalized. (422)

convergent thinking Thinking aimed at finding the one right answer to a problem. (350)

coping Adaptive thinking or behavior aimed at reducing or relieving stress that arises from harmful, threatening, or challenging conditions. (675)

coregulation Transitional stage in the control of behavior in which parents exercise general supervision and children exercise moment-to-moment self-regulation. (361)

corporal punishment Use of physical force with the intention of causing pain but not injury so as to correct or control behavior. (296)

correlational study Research design intended to discover whether a statistical relationship between variables exists. (48)

creativity Ability to see situations in a new way, to produce innovations, or to discern previously unidentified problems and find novel solutions. (350)

crisis Marcia's term for period of conscious decision making related to identity formation. (439)

critical period Specific time when a given event or its absence has the greatest impact on development. (21)

cross-modal transfer Ability to use information gained by one sense to guide another. (169)

cross-sectional study Study designed to assess age-related differences, in which people of different ages are assessed on one occasion. (53)

crystallized intelligence Type of intelligence, proposed by Horn and Cattell, involving the ability to remember and use learned information; it is largely dependent on education and cultural background. (573)

cultural bias Tendency of intelligence tests to include items calling for knowledge or skills more familiar or meaningful to some cultural groups than to others. (333)

culture A society's or group's total way of life, including customs, traditions, beliefs, values, language, and physical products—all learned behavior passed on from parents to children. (16)

culture-fair Describing an intelligence test that deals with experiences common to various cultures, in an attempt to avoid cultural bias. (334)

culture-free Describing an intelligence test that, if it were possible to design, would have no culturally linked content. (333)

culture-relevant Describing an intelligence test that would draw on and adjust for culturally related content. (334)

decenter In Piaget's terminology, to think simultaneously about several aspects of a situation. (252)

declarative knowledge Acquired factual knowledge stored in long-term memory. (420)

decoding Process of phonetic analysis by which a printed word is converted to spoken form before retrieval from long-term memory. (338)

deductive reasoning Type of logical reasoning that moves from a general premise about a class to a conclusion about a particular member or members of the class. (326)

deferred imitation Piaget's term for reproduction of an observed behavior after the passage of time by calling up a stored symbol of it. (163)

dementia Deterioration in cognitive and behavioral functioning due to physiological causes. (649)

Denver Developmental Screening Test Screening test given to children 1 month to 6 years old to determine whether they are developing normally. (142)

deoxyribonucleic acid (DNA) Chemical that carries inherited instructions for the development of all cellular forms of life. (65)

dependent variable In an experiment, the condition that may or may not change as a result of changes in the independent variable. (50)

depth perception Ability to perceive objects and surfaces three-dimensionally. (145)

developmental tasks In normative-stage theories, typical challenges that need to be mastered for successful adaptation to each stage of life. (514)

differentiation Process by which cells acquire specialized structure and function. (135)

"difficult" children Children with irritable temperament, irregular biological rhythms, and intense emotional responses. (199)

discipline Methods of molding children's character and of teaching them to exercise self-control and engage in acceptable behavior. (296)

disengagement theory Theory of aging, proposed by Cumming and Henry, which holds that successful aging is characterized by mutual withdrawal between the older person and society. (679)

dishabituation Increase in responsiveness after presentation of a new stimulus. (167)

disorganized-disoriented attachment Pattern in which an infant, after separation from the primary caregiver, shows contradictory behaviors upon his or her return. (206)

divergent thinking Thinking that produces a variety of fresh, diverse possibilities. (350)

dizygotic twins Twins conceived by the union of two different ova (or a single ovum that has split) with two different sperm cells; also called *fraternal twins*. (64)

dominant inheritance Pattern of inheritance in which, when a child receives different alleles, only the dominant one is expressed. (68)

Down syndrome Chromosomal disorder characterized by moderate-to-severe mental retardation and by such physical signs as a downward sloping skinfold at the inner corners of the eyes. (73)

drug therapy Administration of drugs to treat emotional or psychological disorders. (384)

dual representation hypothesis Proposal that children under the age of 3 have difficulty grasping spatial relationships because of the need to keep more than one mental representation in mind at the same time. (166)

dual-process model Model of cognitive functioning, proposed by Baltes, which identifies and seeks to measure two dimensions of intelligence: mechanics and pragmatics. (654)

durable power of attorney Legal instrument that appoints an individual to make decisions in the event of another person's incapacitation. (730)

dyslexia Developmental disorder in which reading achievement is substantially lower than predicted by IQ or age. (346)

early intervention Systematic process of providing services to help families meet young children's developmental needs. (157)

"easy" children Children with a generally happy temperament, regular biological rhythms, and a readiness to accept new experiences. (199)

ecological theory of perception Theory developed by Eleanor and James Gibson, which describes developing motor and perceptual abilities as interdependent parts of a functional system that guides behavior in varying contexts. (145)

ego integrity versus despair According to Erikson, the eighth and final stage of psychosocial development, in which people in late adulthood either achieve a sense of integrity of the self by accepting the lives they have lived, and thus accept death, or yield to despair that their lives cannot be relived. (674)

egocentrism Piaget's term for inability to consider another person's point of view; a characteristic of young children's thought. (197, 252)

ego-control Self-control. (517)

ego-resiliency Adaptability under potential sources of stress. (517)

elaboration Mnemonic strategy of making mental associations involving items to be remembered. (330)

elder abuse Maltreatment or neglect of dependent older persons, or violation of their personal rights. (693)

electronic fetal monitoring Mechanical monitoring of fetal heartbeat during labor and delivery. (112)

elicited imitation Research method in which infants or toddlers are induced to imitate a specific series of actions they have seen but not necessarily done before. (163)

embryonic stage Second stage of gestation (2 to 8 weeks), characterized by rapid growth and development of major body systems and organs. (89)

emergent literacy Preschoolers' development of skills, knowledge, and attitudes that underlie reading and writing. (268)

emerging adulthood Proposed transitional period between adolescence and adulthood, usually extending from the late teens through the midtwenties. (474)

emotional intelligence Salovey and Mayer's term for ability to understand and regulate emotions; an important component of effective, intelligent behavior. (494)

emotional maltreatment Action or inaction that may cause behavioral, cognitive, emotional, or mental disorders. (224)

emotion-focused coping In the cognitive-appraisal model, coping strategy directed toward managing the emotional response to a stressful situation so as to lessen its physical or psychological impact; sometimes called *palliative coping*. (675)

emotions Subjective reactions to experience that are associated with physiological and behavioral changes. (193)

empathy Ability to "put oneself in another person's place" and feel what the other person feels. (197)

empty nest Transitional phase of parenting following the last child's leaving the parents' home. (609)

encapsulation In Hoyer's terminology, progressive dedication of information processing and fluid thinking to specific knowledge systems, making knowledge more readily accessible. (574)

encoding Process by which information is prepared for long-term storage and later retrieval. (258)

English-immersion Approach to teaching English as a second language in which instruction is presented only in English. (345)

enrichment Approach to educating the gifted, which broadens and deepens knowledge and skills through extra activities, projects, field trips, or mentoring. (350)

enuresis Repeated urination in clothing or in bed. (242)

environment Totality of nonhereditary, or experiential, influences on development. (14)

episodic memory Long-term memory of specific experiences or events, linked to time and place. (259, 658)

equilibration Piaget's term for the tendency to seek a stable balance among cognitive elements. (37)

erectile dysfunction Inability of a man to achieve or maintain an erect penis sufficient for satisfactory sexual performance. (560)

ethnic gloss Overgeneralization about an ethnic or cultural group that obscures differences within the group. (18)

ethnic group A group united by ancestry, race, religion, language, and/or national origins, which contribute to a sense of shared identity. (17)

ethnographic study In-depth study of a culture, which uses a combination of methods including participant observation. (48)

ethology Study of distinctive adaptive behaviors of species of animals that have evolved to increase survival of the species. (40)

evolutionary psychology Application of Darwinian principles of natural selection and survival of the fittest to individual behavior. (40)

evolutionary/sociobiological perspective View of human development that focuses on evolutionary and biological bases of social behavior. (39)

executive stage Fourth of Schaie's seven cognitive stages, in which middle-aged people responsible for societal systems deal with complex relationships on several levels. (491)

exosystem Bronfenbrenner's term for linkages between two or more settings, one of which does not contain the child. (42)

experiential element   Sternberg's term for the insightful or creative aspect of intelligence. (334, 492)

experiment   Rigorously controlled, replicable procedure in which the researcher manipulates variables to assess the effect of one on the other. (50)

experimental group   In an experiment, the group receiving the treatment under study. (50)

explicit memory   Intentional and conscious memory, generally of facts, names, and events. (176)

extended family   Multigenerational kinship network of parents, children, and other relatives, sometimes living together in an extended-family household. (15)

external memory aids   Mnemonic strategies using something outside the person. (330)

family therapy   Psychological treatment in which a therapist sees the whole family together to analyze patterns of family functioning. (383)

family-focused lifestyle   Pattern of retirement activity that revolves around family, home, and companions. (686)

fast mapping   Process by which a child absorbs the meaning of a new word after hearing it once or twice in conversation. (265)

fertilization   Union of sperm and ovum to produce a zygote; also called *conception*. (63)

fetal alcohol syndrome (FAS)   Combination of mental, motor, and developmental abnormalities affecting the offspring of some women who drink heavily during pregnancy. (93)

fetal stage   Final stage of gestation (from 8 weeks to birth), characterized by increased differentiation of body parts and greatly enlarged body size. (89)

filial crisis   In Marcoen's terminology, normative development of middle age, in which adults learn to balance love and duty to their parents with autonomy within a two-way relationship. (612)

filial maturity   Stage of life, proposed by Marcoen and others, in which middle-aged children, as the outcome of a filial crisis, learn to accept and meet their parents' need to depend on them. (612)

fine motor skills   Physical skills that involve the small muscles and eye-hand coordination. (142, 242)

five-factor model   Theoretical model of personality, developed and tested by Costa and McCrae, based on the "Big Five" factors underlying clusters of related traits: neuroticism, extraversion, openness to experience, conscientiousness, and agreeableness. (515)

fluid intelligence   Type of intelligence, proposed by Horn and Cattell, which is applied to novel problems and is relatively independent of educational and cultural influences. (573)

foreclosure   Identity status, described by Marcia, in which a person who has not spent time considering alternatives (that is, has not been in crisis) is committed to other people's plans for his or her life. (439)

formal operations   Piaget's final stage of cognitive development, characterized by the ability to think abstractly. (416)

free radicals   Unstable, highly reactive atoms or molecules, formed during metabolism, which can cause internal bodily damage. (634)

functional age   Measure of a person's ability to function effectively in his or her physical and social environment in comparison with others of the same chronological age. (629)

functional play   Play involving repetitive muscular movements. (292)

gateway drugs   Drugs such as alcohol, tobacco, and marijuana, the use of which tends to lead to use of more addictive drugs. (412)

gender   Significance of being male or female. (203)

gender constancy   Awareness that one will always be male or female. Also called *sex-category constancy*. (287)

gender crossover   Gutmann's term for reversal of gender roles after the end of active parenting. (597)

gender identity   Awareness, developed in early childhood, that one is male or female. (284)

gender roles   Behaviors, interests, attitudes, skills, and traits that a culture considers appropriate for each sex; differs for males and females. (285)

gender stereotypes   Preconceived generalizations about male or female role behavior. (285)

gender-schema theory   Theory, proposed by Bem, that children socialize themselves in their gender roles by developing a mentally organized network of information about what it means to be male or female in a particular culture. (288)

gender-typing   Socialization process by which children, at an early age, learn appropriate gender roles. (204, 285)

generalized anxiety disorder   Anxiety not focused on any single target. (382)

generativity versus stagnation   Erikson's seventh stage of psychosocial development, in which the middle-aged adult develops a concern with establishing, guiding, and influencing the next generation or else experiences stagnation (a sense of inactivity or lifelessness). (589)

generativity   Erikson's term for concern of mature adults for establishing, guiding, and influencing the next generation. (589)

generic memory   Memory that produces scripts of familiar routines to guide behavior. (259)

genes   Small segments of DNA located in definite positions on particular chromosomes; functional units of heredity. (65)

genetic code   Sequence of bases within the DNA molecule; governs the formation of proteins that determine the structure and functions of living cells. (65)

genetic counseling   Clinical service that advises couples of their probable risk of having children with hereditary defects. (74)

genetic-programming theories   Theories that explain biological aging as resulting from a genetically determined developmental timetable. (633)

genotype   Genetic makeup of a person, containing both expressed and unexpressed characteristics. (69)

genotype-environment correlation   Tendency of certain genetic and environmental influences to reinforce each other; may be passive, reactive (evocative), or active. Also called *genotype-environment covariance*. (80)

genotype-environment interaction   The portion of phenotypic variation that results from the reactions of genetically different individuals to similar environmental conditions. (80)

geriatrics   Branch of medicine concerned with processes of aging and medical conditions associated with old age. (629)

germinal stage   First 2 weeks of prenatal development, characterized by rapid cell division, blastocyst formation, and implantation in the wall of the uterus. (85)

gerontology   Study of the aged and the process of aging. (629)

glaucoma   Irreversible damage to the optic nerve caused by increased pressure in the eye. (642)

goodness of fit Appropriateness of environmental demands and constraints to a child's temperament. (200)

grief Emotional response experienced in the early phases of bereavement. (716)

grief therapy Treatment to help the bereaved cope with loss. (718)

grief work Working out of psychological issues connected with grief. (716)

gross motor skills Physical skills that involve the large muscles. (142, 242)

guided participation Participation of an adult in a child's activity in a manner that helps to structure the activity and to bring the child's understanding of it closer to that of the adult. (176)

habituation Type of learning in which familiarity with a stimulus reduces, slows, or stops a response. (167)

handedness Preference for using a particular hand. (243)

haptic perception Ability to acquire information about properties of objects, such as size, weight, and texture, by handling them. (145)

Hayflick limit Genetically controlled limit, proposed by Hayflick, on the number of times cells can divide in members of a species. (636)

heredity Inborn characteristics inherited from the biological parents. (14)

heritability Statistical estimate of contribution of heredity to individual differences in a specific trait within a given population. (75)

heterozygous Possessing differing alleles for a trait. (68)

historical generation A group of people strongly influenced by a major historical event during their formative period. (19)

holophrase Single word that conveys a complete thought. (180)

Home Observation for Measurement of the Environment (HOME) Instrument to measure the influence of the home environment on children's cognitive growth. (157)

homozygous Possessing two identical alleles for a trait. (68)

horizontal décalage Piaget's term for inability to transfer learning about one type of conservation to other types, which causes a child to master different types of conservation tasks at different ages. (253)

hormone replacement therapy (HRT) Treatment with artificial estrogen, sometimes in combination with the hormone progesterone, to relieve or prevent symptoms caused by

decline in estrogen levels after menopause. (556)

hospice care Warm, personal patient- and family-centered care for a person with a terminal illness. (713)

hostile aggression Aggressive behavior intended to hurt another person. (303, 377)

human development Scientific study of processes of change and stability throughout the human life span. (7)

hypertension Chronically high blood pressure. (321, 561)

hypotheses Possible explanations for phenomena, used to predict the outcome of research. (29)

hypothetical-deductive reasoning Ability, believed by Piaget to accompany the stage of formal operations, to develop, consider, and test hypotheses. (417)

hysterectomy Surgical removal of the uterus. (565)

ideal self The self one would like to be. (280)

identification In Freudian theory, the process by which a young child adopts characteristics, beliefs, attitudes, values, and behaviors of the parent of the same sex. (287)

identity According to Erikson, a coherent conception of the self, made up of goals, values, and beliefs to which a person is solidly committed. (437)

identity accommodation Whitbourne's term for adjusting the self-concept to fit new experience. (594)

identity achievement Identity status, described by Marcia, that is characterized by commitment to choices made following a crisis, a period spent in exploring alternatives. (439)

identity assimilation Whitbourne's term for effort to fit new experience into an existing self-concept. (594)

identity diffusion Identity status, described by Marcia, that is characterized by absence of commitment and lack of serious consideration of alternatives. (439)

identity process model Whitbourne's model of identity development based on processes of assimilation and accommodation. (594)

identity statuses Marcia's term for states of ego development that depend on the presence or absence of crisis and commitment. (439)

identity style Whitbourne's term for a characteristic way of confronting, interpreting, and responding to experience. (594)

identity versus identity confusion Erikson's fifth stage of psychosocial development, in which an adolescent seeks to develop a coherent sense of self, including the role she or he is to play in society. Also called *identity versus role confusion.* (437)

imaginary audience Elkind's term for observer who exists only in an adolescent's mind and is as concerned with the adolescent's thoughts and actions as the adolescent is. (419)

implicit memory Unconscious recall, generally of habits and skills; sometimes called *procedural memory.* (176)

imprinting Instinctive form of learning in which, during a critical period in early development, a young animal forms an attachment to the first moving object it sees, usually the mother. (21)

incomplete dominance Pattern of inheritance in which a child receives two different alleles, resulting in partial expression of a trait. (72)

independent variable In an experiment, the condition over which the experimenter has direct control. (50)

individual differences Differences in characteristics, influences, or developmental outcomes. (14)

individual psychotherapy Psychological treatment in which a therapist sees a troubled person one-on-one. (383)

individuation Jung's term for emergence of the true self through balancing or integration of conflicting parts of the personality. (588)

inductive reasoning Type of logical reasoning that moves from particular observations about members of a class to a general conclusion about that class. (326)

inductive techniques Disciplinary techniques designed to induce desirable behavior by appealing to a child's sense of reason and fairness. (297)

industry versus inferiority Erikson's fourth stage of psychosocial development, in which children must learn the productive skills their culture requires or else face feelings of inferiority. (358)

infant mortality rate Proportion of babies born alive who die within the first year. (124)

infertility Inability to conceive after 12 months of trying. (486)

information-processing approach Approach to the study of cognitive development by observing and analyzing the mental processes involved in perceiving and handling information. (39, 167)

initiative versus guilt Erikson's third stage in psychosocial development, in which children balance the urge to pursue goals with moral reservations that may prevent carrying them out. (283)

instrumental activities of daily living (IADLs) Indicators of functional well-being and of the ability to live independently. (646)

instrumental aggression Aggressive behavior used as a means of achieving a goal. (303, 377)

integration Process by which neurons coordinate the activities of muscle groups. (135)

intelligent behavior Behavior that is goal oriented and adaptive to circumstances and conditions of life. (156)

interiority Neugarten's term for a concern with inner life (introversion or introspection), which usually appears in middle age. (590)

internalization During socialization, process by which children accept societal standards of conduct as their own. (215)

intimacy versus isolation Erikson's sixth stage of psychosocial development, in which young adults either make commitments to others or face a possible sense of isolation and self-absorption. (512)

invisible imitation Imitation with parts of one's body that one cannot see. (162)

IQ (intelligence quotient) tests Psychometric tests that seek to measure intelligence by comparing a test taker's performance with standardized norms. (156)

irreversibility Piaget's term for a preoperational child's failure to understand that an operation can go in two or more directions. (254)

Kaufman Assessment Battery for Children (KABC) Nontraditional individual intelligence test designed to provide fair assessments of minority children and children with disabilities. (336)

kinship care Care of children living without parents in the home of grandparents or other relatives, with or without a change of legal custody. (619)

laboratory observation Research method in which all participants are observed under the same controlled conditions. (46)

language Communication system based on words and grammar. (177)

language acquisition device (LAD) In Chomsky's terminology, an inborn mechanism that enables children to infer linguistic rules from the language they hear. (182)

lateralization Tendency of each of the brain's hemispheres to have specialized functions. (133)

learning disabilities (LDs) Disorders that interfere with specific aspects of learning and school achievement. (347)

learning perspective View of human development that holds that changes in behavior result from experience, or adaptation to the environment. (34)

legacy-creating stage Seventh of Schaie's seven cognitive stages, in which very old people prepare for death by recording their life stories, distributing possessions, and the like. (491)

life expectancy Age to which a person in a particular cohort is statistically likely to live (given his or her current age and health status), on the basis of average longevity of a population. (629)

life review Reminiscence about one's life in order to see its significance. (735)

life span The longest period that members of a species can live. (630)

life structure In Levinson's theory, the underlying pattern of a person's life at a given time, built on whatever aspects of life the person finds most important. (513)

lifelong learning Organized, sustained study by adults of all ages. (665)

life-span development Concept of human development as a lifelong process, which can be studied scientifically. (8)

linguistic speech Verbal expression designed to convey meaning. (180)

literacy (1) Ability to read and write. (186) (2) In an adult, ability to use printed and written information to function in society, achieve goals, and develop knowledge and potential. (504)

longevity Length of an individual's life. (630)

longitudinal study Study designed to assess changes in a sample over time. (53)

long-term memory Storage of virtually unlimited capacity that holds information for very long periods. (259)

low birth weight Weight of less than 5½ pounds (2,500 grams) at birth because of prematurity or being small for date. (119)

macrosystem Bronfenbrenner's term for a society's overall cultural patterns. (43)

mammography Diagnostic X-ray examination of the breasts. (565)

marital capital Financial and emotional benefits built up during a long-standing marriage, which tend to hold a couple together. (605)

maturation Unfolding of a natural sequence of physical and behavioral changes, including readiness to master new abilities. (14)

mechanics of intelligence In Baltes's dual-process model, the abilities to process information and solve problems, irrespective of content; the area of cognition in which there is often an age-related decline. (654)

mechanistic model Model that views human development as a series of passive, predictable responses to stimuli. (29)

menarche Girl's first menstruation. (403)

menopause Cessation of menstruation and of ability to bear children, typically around age 50. (555)

mental retardation Significantly subnormal cognitive functioning. (346)

mesosystem Bronfenbrenner's term for linkages between two or more microsystems. (42)

metabolism Conversion of food and oxygen into energy. (633)

metacognition Awareness of a person's own mental processes. (330)

Metamemory in Adulthood (MIA) Questionnaire designed to measure various aspects of adults' metamemory, including beliefs about their own memory and the selection and use of strategies for remembering. (661)

metamemory Understanding of processes of memory. (330)

microsystem Bronfenbrenner's term for a setting in which a child interacts with others on an everyday, face-to-face basis. (42)

midlife crisis In some normative-crisis models, stressful life period precipitated by the review and reevaluation of one's past, typically occurring in the early to middle forties. (592)

midlife review Introspective examination that often occurs in middle age, leading to reappraisal and revision of values and priorities. (593)

mnemonic strategies Techniques to aid memory. (330)

monozygotic twins Twins resulting from the division of a single zygote after fertilization; also called *identical twins*. (64)

moratorium Identity status, described by Marcia, in which a person is currently considering alternatives (in crisis) and seems headed for commitment. (439)

multifactorial transmission Combination of genetic and environmental factors to produce certain complex traits. (69)

mutations   Permanent alterations in genes or chromosomes that may produce harmful characteristics. (72)

mutual regulation   Process by which infant and caregiver communicate emotional states to each other and respond appropriately. (210)

myelination   Process of coating neural pathways with a fatty substance (myelin) that enables faster communication between cells. (136)

myopia   Nearsightedness. (553)

nativism   Theory that human beings have an inborn capacity for language acquisition. (182)

natural childbirth   Method of childbirth that seeks to prevent pain by eliminating the mother's fear through education about the physiology of reproduction and training in breathing and relaxation during delivery. (112)

natural selection   According to Darwin's theory of evolution, process by which characteristics that promote survival of a species are reproduced in successive generations, and characteristics that do not promote survival die out. (73)

naturalistic observation   Research method in which behavior is studied in natural settings without intervention or manipulation. (46)

neglect   Failure to meet a dependent's basic needs. (224)

neonatal jaundice   Condition in many newborn babies, caused by immaturity of liver and evidenced by yellowish appearance; can cause brain damage if not treated promptly. (114)

neonatal period   First 4 weeks of life, a time of transition from intrauterine dependency to independent existence. (113)

neonate   Newborn baby, up to 4 weeks old. (113)

neurofibrillary tangles   Twisted masses of protein fibers found in brains of persons with Alzheimer's disease. (651)

neurons   Nerve cells. (134)

niche-picking   Tendency of a person, especially after early childhood, to seek out environments compatible with his or her genotype. (80)

nonnormative   Characteristic of an unusual event that happens to a particular person or a typical event that happens at an unusual time of life. (19)

nonshared environmental effects   The unique environment in which each child grows up, consisting of distinctive

influences or influences that affect one child differently than another. (81)

normative   Characteristic of an event that occurs in a similar way for most people in a group. (14)

normative life events   In the timing-of-events model, commonly expected life experiences that occur at customary times. (514)

normative-stage models   Theoretical models that describe psychosocial development in terms of a definite sequence of age-related changes. (511)

nuclear family   Two-generational kinship, economic, and household unit consisting of one or two parents and their biological children, adopted children, or stepchildren. (15)

obesity   (1) Extreme overweight in relation to age, sex, height, and body type. (81)

object permanence   Piaget's term for the understanding that a person or object still exists when out of sight. (163)

observational learning   Learning through watching the behavior of others. (36)

obsessive-compulsive disorder (OCD)   Anxiety aroused by repetitive, intrusive thoughts, images, or impulses, often leading to compulsive ritual behaviors. (382)

open adoption   Adoption in which the birth parents and the adoptive parents know each other's identities and share infomation or have direct contact. (364)

operant conditioning   (1) Learning based on association of behavior with its consequences. (35) (2) Learning based on reinforcement or punishment. (154)

operational definition   Definition stated solely in terms of the operations or procedures used to produce or measure a phenomenon. (47)

oppositional defiant disorder (ODD)   Pattern of behavior, persisting into middle childhood, marked by negativity, hostility, and defiance. (381)

organismic model   Model that views human development as internally initiated by an active organism and as occurring in a sequence of qualitatively different stages. (30)

organization   (1) Mnemonic strategy of categorizing material to be remembered. (30) (2) Piaget's term for the creation of systems of knowledge. (37)

osteoporosis   Condition in which the bones become thin and brittle as a result of rapid calcium depletion. (564)

Otis-Lennon School Ability Test   Group intelligence test for kindergarten through twelfth grade. (332)

overt aggression   Aggression that is openly directed at its target. (304)

palliative care   Care aimed at relieving pain and suffering and allowing the terminally ill to die in peace, comfort, and dignity. (713)

Parkinson's disease   Progressive, irreversible degenerative neurological disorder, characterized by tremor, stiffness, slowed movement, and unstable posture. (649)

participant observation   Research method in which the observer lives with the people or participates in the activity being observed. (48)

parturition   Process of uterine, cervical, and other changes, usually lasting about two weeks preceding childbirth. (111)

passive euthanasia   Deliberate withholding or discontinuation of life-prolonging treatment of a terminally ill person in order to end suffering or allow death with dignity. (729)

perimenopause   Period of several years during which a woman experiences physiological changes that bring on menopause; also called *climacteric*. (553)

permissive   In Baumrind's terminology, parenting style emphasizing self-expression and self-regulation. (300)

personal fable   Elkind's term for conviction that one is special, unique, and not subject to the rules that govern the rest of the world. (419)

phenotype   Observable characteristics of a person. (69)

phonetic, or code-emphasis approach   Approach to teaching reading that emphasizes decoding of unfamiliar words. (338)

physical abuse   Action taken deliberately to endanger another person, involving potential bodily injury. (224)

physical development   Growth of body and brain, including patterns of change in sensory capacities, motor skills, and health. (10)

Piagetian approach   Approach to the study of cognitive development that describes qualitative stages in cognitive functioning. (153)

plasticity   (1) Modifiability of performance. (21) (2) Modifiability, or "molding," of the brain through experience. (137)

play therapy   Therapeutic approach in which a child plays freely while a therapist observes and occasionally comments, asks questions, or makes suggestions. (384)

polygenic inheritance   Pattern of inheritance in which multiple genes at different sites on chromosomes affect a complex trait. (69)

postconventional morality (or morality of autonomous moral principles) Third level of Kohlberg's theory of moral reasoning, in which people follow internally held moral principles and can decide among conflicting moral standards. (424)

postformal thought Mature type of thinking that relies on subjective experience and intuition as well as logic and is useful in dealing with ambiguity, uncertainty, inconsistency, contradiction, imperfection, and compromise. (489)

postmature Referring to a fetus not yet born as of 2 weeks after the due date or 42 weeks after the mother's last menstrual period. (119)

power assertion Disciplinary strategy designed to discourage undesirable behavior through physical or verbal enforcement of parental control. (297)

pragmatics (1) Set of linguistic rules that govern the use of language for communication. (337) (2) The practical knowledge needed to use language for communicative purposes. (266)

pragmatics of intelligence In Baltes's dual-process model, the dimension of intelligence that tends to grow with age and includes practical thinking, application of accumulated knowledge and skills, specialized expertise, professional productivity, and wisdom. (654)

preconventional morality First level of Kohlberg's theory of moral reasoning in which control is external and rules are obeyed in order to gain rewards or avoid punishment or out of self-interest. (422)

prejudice Unfavorable attitude toward members of certain groups outside one's own, especially racial or ethnic groups. (372)

prelinguistic speech Forerunner of linguistic speech; utterance of sounds that are not words. Includes crying, cooing, babbling, and accidental and deliberate imitation of sounds without understanding their meaning. (178)

premenstrual syndrome (PMS) Disorder producing symptoms of physical discomfort and emotional tension during the one to two weeks before a menstrual period. (484)

preoperational stage In Piaget's theory, the second major stage of cognitive development, in which children become more sophisticated in their use of symbolic thought but are not yet able to use logic. (248)

prepared childbirth Method of childbirth that uses instruction, breathing exercises, and social support to induce controlled physical responses to uterine contractions and reduce fear and pain. (112)

presbycusis Age-related, gradual loss of hearing, which accelerates after age 55, especially with regard to sounds at higher frequencies. (553)

presbyopia Age-related, progressive loss of the eyes' ability to focus on nearby objects due to loss of elasticity in the lens. (553)

pretend play Play involving imaginary people and situations; also called *fantasy play, dramatic play,* or *imaginative play.* (250, 292)

preterm (premature) infants Infants born before completing the thirty-seventh week of gestation. (119)

primary aging Gradual, inevitable process of bodily deterioration throughout the life span. (629)

primary sex characteristics Organs directly related to reproduction, which enlarge and mature during adolescence. (400)

priming Increase in ease of doing a task or remembering information as a result of a previous encounter with the task or information. (659)

private speech Talking aloud to oneself with no intent to communicate. (267)

problem-focused coping In the cognitive-appraisal model, coping strategy directed toward eliminating, managing, or improving a stressful situation. (675)

procedural knowledge Acquired skills stored in long-term memory. (420)

procedural memory Long-term memory of motor skills, habits, and ways of doing things, which often can be recalled without conscious effort; sometimes called *implicit memory.* (659)

prosocial behavior Any voluntary behavior intended to help others. (302)

protective factors Influences that reduce the impact of early stress or other potentially negative influences and tend to predict positive outcomes. (124, 386)

proximodistal principle Principle that development proceeds from within to without; that is, that parts of the body near the center develop before the extremities. (85)

psychoanalytic perspective View of human development as being shaped by unconscious forces. (32)

psychological aggression Verbal attacks on a child by a parent that may result in psychological harm. (299)

psychometric approach Approach to the study of cognitive development that seeks to measure the quantity of intelligence a person possesses. (153)

psychosexual development In Freudian theory, an unvarying sequence of stages of personality development during infancy, childhood, and adolescence, in which gratification shifts from the mouth to the anus and then to the genitals. (32)

psychosocial development (1) In Erikson's eight-stage theory, the socially and culturally influenced process of development of the ego, or self. (34) (2) Pattern of change in emotions, personality, and social relationships. (10)

puberty Process by which a person attains sexual maturity and the ability to reproduce. (397)

punishment In operant conditioning, a process that weakens and discourages repetition of a behavior. (35)

qualitative change Change in kind, structure, or organization, such as the change from nonverbal to verbal communication. (10)

qualitative research Research that focuses on "soft" data, such as subjective experiences, feelings, or beliefs. (44)

quantitative change Change in number or amount, such as in height, weight, or size of vocabulary. (10)

quantitative research Research that focuses on "hard" data and numerical or statistical measures. (43)

reaction range Potential variability, depending on environmental conditions, in the expression of a hereditary trait. (78)

real self The self one actually is. (280)

recall Ability to reproduce material from memory. (259)

recessive inheritance Pattern of inheritance in which a child receives identical recessive alleles, resulting in expression of a nondominant trait. (68)

recognition Ability to identify a previously encountered stimulus. (259)

reflective thinking Type of logical thinking that may emerge in adulthood, involving continuous, active evaluation of information and beliefs in the light of evidence and implications. (488)

reflex behaviors Automatic, involuntary, innate responses to stimulation. (137)

rehearsal Mnemonic strategy to keep an item in working memory through conscious repetition. (330)

reinforcement In operant conditioning, a process that strengthens and encourages repetition of a desired behavior. (35)

reintegrative stage Sixth of Schaie's seven cognitive stages, in which older adults choose to focus limited energy on tasks that have meaning to them. (491)

relational aggression Aggression aimed at damaging or interfering with another person's relationships, reputation, or psychological well-being; also called *covert* or *indirect aggression*. (304)

reorganizational stage Fifth of Schaie's seven cognitive stages, in which adults entering retirement reorganize their lives around nonwork-related activities. (491)

representational ability Piaget's term for capacity to store mental images or symbols of objects and events. (161)

representational mappings In neo-Piagetian terminology, second stage in development of self-definition, in which a child makes logical connections between aspects of the self but still sees these characteristics in all-or-nothing terms. (280)

representational systems In neo-Piagetian terminology, the third stage in development of self-definition, characterized by breadth, balance, and the integration and assessment of various aspects of the self. (357)

reserve capacity Ability of body organs and systems to put forth four to ten times as much effort as usual under acute stress; also called *organ reserve*. (640)

resilient children Children who weather adverse circumstances, function well despite challenges or threats, or bounce back from traumatic events. (386)

responsible stage Third of Schaie's seven cognitive stages, in which middle-aged people are concerned with long-range goals and practical problems related to their responsibility for others. (491)

retrieval Process by which information is accessed or recalled from memory storage. (258)

revolving door syndrome Tendency for young adults who have left home to return to their parents' household in times of financial, marital, or other trouble. (610)

risk factors Conditions that increase the likelihood of a negative developmental outcome. (16)

rough-and-tumble play Vigorous play involving wrestling, hitting, and chasing, often accompanied by laughing and screaming. (319)

sample Group of participants chosen to represent the entire population under study. (44)

sandwich generation Middle-aged adults squeezed by competing needs to raise or launch children and to care for elderly parents. (613)

scaffolding Temporary support to help a child master a task. (265)

schemes Piaget's term for organized patterns of behavior used in particular situations. (37, 159)

schizophrenia Mental disorder marked by loss of contact with reality; symptoms include hallucinations and delusions. (82)

school phobia Unrealistic fear of going to school; may be a form of *separation anxiety disorder* or *social phobia*. (382)

scientific method System of established principles and processes of scientific inquiry, which includes identifying a problem to be studied, formulating a hypothesis to be tested by research, collecting data, analyzing the data, and disseminating findings. (44)

script General remembered outline of a familiar, repeated event, used to guide behavior. (259)

secondary aging Aging processes that result from disease and bodily abuse and disuse and are often preventable. (629)

secondary sex characteristics Physiological signs of sexual maturation (such as breast development and growth of body hair) that do not involve the sex organs. (400)

secular trend Trend that can be seen only by observing several generations, such as the trend toward earlier attainment of adult height and sexual maturity, which began a century ago. (401)

secure attachment Pattern in which an infant cries or protests when the primary caregiver leaves and actively seeks out the caregiver upon his or her return. (206)

selective optimization with compensation (SOC) In Baltes's dual-process model, enhancing overall cognitive functioning by using stronger abilities to compensate for those that have weakened. (655)

self-awareness Realization that one's existence and functioning are separate from those of other people and things. (197)

self-concept Sense of self; descriptive and evaluative mental picture of one's abilities and traits. (213, 279)

self-conscious emotions Emotions, such as embarrassment, empathy, and envy, that depend on self-awareness. (197)

self-definition Cluster of characteristics used to describe oneself. (279)

self-efficacy Sense of one's own capability to master challenges and achieve goals. (36, 213)

self-esteem The judgment a person makes about his or her self-worth. (281)

self-evaluative emotions Emotions, such as pride, shame, and guilt, that depend on both self-awareness and knowledge of socially accepted standards of behavior. (197)

self-regulation A person's independent control of behavior to conform to understood social expectations. (217)

semantic memory Long-term memory of general factual knowledge, social customs, and language. (659)

senescence Period of the life span marked by declines in physical functioning usually associated with aging; begins at different ages for different people. (632)

sensitive periods Times in development when a person is particularly open to certain kinds of experiences. (21)

sensorimotor stage In Piaget's theory, first stage in cognitive development, during which infants learn through senses and motor activity. (159)

sensory memory Initial, brief, temporary storage of sensory information. (258, 658)

separation anxiety Distress shown by someone, typically an infant, when a familiar caregiver leaves. (208)

separation anxiety disorder Condition involving excessive, prolonged anxiety concerning separation from home or from people to whom a person is attached. (382)

sequential study Study design that combines cross-sectional and longitudinal techniques. (54)

seriation Ability to order items along a dimension. (325)

serious leisure Leisure activity requiring skill, attention, and commitment. (686)

sex chromosomes Pair of chromosomes that determine sex: XX in the normal human female, XY in the normal human male. (66)

sex-linked-inheritance Pattern of inheritance in which certain characteristics carried on the X chromosome inherited from the mother are transmitted differently to her male and female offspring. (72)

sexual abuse Physically or psychologically harmful sexual activity, or any sexual activity involving a child and an older person. (224)

sexual dysfunction Persistent disturbance in sexual desire or sexual response. (559)

sexual orientation Focus of consistent sexual, romantic, and affectionate interest, either heterosexual, homosexual, or bisexual. (443)

sexually transmitted diseases (STDs) Diseases spread by sexual contact. (448)

single representations In neo-Piagetian terminology, first stage in development of self-definition, in which children describe themselves in terms of individual, unconnected characteristics and in all-or-nothing terms. (280)

situational compliance Kochanska's term for obedience of a parent's orders only in the presence of signs of ongoing parental control. (217)

"slow-to-warm-up" children Children whose temperament is generally mild but who are hesitant about accepting new experiences. (199)

small-for-date (small-for-gestational age) infants Infants whose birth weight is less than that of 90 percent of babies of the same gestational age, as a result of slow fetal growth. (119)

social capital Family and community resources on which a person can draw. (341)

social clock Set of cultural norms or expectations for the times of life when certain important events, such as marriage, parenthood, entry into work, and retirement, should occur. (514)

social cognition Ability to understand that other people have mental states and to gauge their feelings and intentions. (197)

social cognitive theory Albert Bandura's expansion of social learning theory; holds that children learn gender roles through socialization. (289)

social construction Concept about the nature of reality based on societally shared perceptions or assumptions. (11)

social convoy theory Theory, proposed by Kahn and Antonucci, that people move through life surrounded by concentric circles of intimate relationships on which they rely for assistance, well-being, and social support. (602)

social interaction model Model, based on Vygotsky's sociocultural theory, which proposes that children construct autobiographical memories through conversation with adults about shared events. (262)

social learning theory Theory that behaviors are learned by observing and imitating models. Also called *social cognitive theory*. (36)

social phobia Extreme fear and/or avoidance of social situations. (382)

social promotion Policy of automatically promoting children even if they do not meet academic standards. (343)

social referencing Understanding an ambiguous situation by seeking out another person's perception of it. (211)

social-contextual approach Approach to the study of cognitive development by focusing on environmental influences, particularly parents and other caregivers. (167)

socialization Development of habits, skills, values, and motives shared by responsible, productive members of a society. (215)

sociocultural theory Vygotsky's theory of how contextual factors affect children's development. (38)

socioeconomic status (SES) Combination of economic and social factors describing an individual or family, including income, education, and occupation. (15)

socioemotional selectivity theory Theory, proposed by Carstensen, that people select social contacts on the basis of the changing relative importance of social interaction as a source of information, as an aid in developing and maintaining a self-concept, and as a source of emotional well-being. (602)

spermarche Boy's first ejaculation. (402)

spillover hypothesis Hypothesis that there is a positive correlation between intellectuality of work and of leisure activities because of a carryover of cognitive gains from work to leisure. (504)

spontaneous abortion Natural expulsion from the uterus of an embryo that cannot survive outside the womb; also called *miscarriage*. (89)

Stanford-Binet Intelligence Scale Individual intelligence test for ages 2 and up used to measure fluid reasoning, knowledge, quantitative reasoning, visual-spatial processing, and working memory. (263)

state of arousal An infant's physiological and behavioral status at a given moment in the periodic daily cycle of wakefulness, sleep, and activity. (116)

Sternberg Triarchic Abilities Test (STAT) Test that seeks to measure componential, experiential, and contextual intelligence. (335)

"still-face" paradigm Research procedure used to measure mutual regulation in infants 2 to 9 months old. (211)

storage Retention of information in memory for future use. (258)

Strange Situation Laboratory technique used to study infant attachment. (205)

stranger anxiety Wariness of strange people and places, shown by some infants during the second half of the first year. (208)

stressors Perceived environmental demands that may produce stress. (567)

substance abuse Repeated, harmful use of a substance, usually alcohol or other drugs. (411)

substance dependence Addiction (physical or psychological, or both) to a harmful substance. (411)

substantive complexity Degree to which a person's work requires thought and independent judgment. (503)

sudden infant death syndrome (SIDS) Sudden and unexplained death of an apparently healthy infant. (125)

survival curves Curves, plotted on a graph, showing percentages of a population that survive at each age level. (636)

symbolic function Piaget's term for ability to use mental representations (words, numbers, or images) to which a child has attached meaning. (250)

syntax Rules for forming sentences in a particular language. (181)

systems of action Increasingly complex combinations of motor skills, which permit a wider or more precise range of movement and more control of the environment. (142, 243)

tacit knowledge Sternberg's term for information that is not formally taught or openly expressed but is necessary to function successfully. (335, 493)

telegraphic speech Early form of sentence use consisting of only a few essential words. (180)

temperament Characteristic disposition, or style of approaching and reacting to situations. (64, 198)

teratogenic Capable of causing birth defects. (91)

terminal drop A frequently observed decline in cognitive abilities near the end of life. Also called *terminal decline*. (714)

thanatology Study of death and dying. (713)

theory Coherent set of logically related concepts that seeks to organize, explain, and predict data. (29)

theory of mind Awareness and understanding of mental processes. (254)

theory of multiple intelligences Gardner's theory that each person has several distinct forms of intelligence. (335)

timing-of-events model Theoretical model that describes adult psychosocial development as a response to the expected or unexpected occurrence and timing of important life events. (511)

trait models Theoretical models of personality development that focus on mental, emotional, temperamental, and behavioral traits, or attributes. (511)

transduction Piaget's term for a preoperational child's tendency to mentally link particular phenomena, whether or not there is logically a causal relationship. (250)

transitive inference Understanding of the relationship between two objects by knowing the relationship of each to a third object. (325)

triangular subtheory of love Sternberg's theory that patterns of love hinge on the balance among three elements: intimacy, passion, and commitment. (521)

triarchic theory of intelligence Sternberg's theory describing three types of intelligence: componential, experiential, and contextual. (334)

two-way (dual-language) learning Approach to second-language education in which English speakers and non-English speakers learn together in their own and each other's languages. (346)

typological models Theoretical models of personality development that identify broad personality types, or styles. (511)

ultrasound Prenatal medical procedure using high-frequency sound waves to detect the outline of a fetus and its movements, so as to determine whether a pregnancy is progressing normally. (90)

variable-rate theories Theories explaining biological aging as a result of processes that vary from person to person and are influenced by both the internal and the external environment; sometimes called *error theories*. (633)

violation-of-expectations Research method in which dishabituation to a stimulus that conflicts with experience is taken as evidence that an infant recognizes the new stimulus as surprising. (172)

visible imitation Imitation with parts of one's body that one can see. (162)

visual cliff Apparatus designed to give an illusion of depth and used to assess depth perception in infants. (145)

visual guidance The use of the eyes to guide the movement of the hands (or other parts of the body). (144)

visual preference Tendency of infants to spend more time looking at one sight than another. (168)

visual recognition memory Ability to distinguish a familiar visual stimulus from an unfamiliar one when shown both at the same time. (168)

visually based retrieval Process of retrieving the sound of a printed word upon seeing the word as a whole. (338)

vital capacity Amount of air that can be drawn in with a deep breath and expelled. (555)

Wechsler Adult Intelligence Scale (WAIS) Intelligence test for adults, which yields verbal and performance scores as well as a combined score. (653)

Wechsler Intelligence Scale for Children (WISC-III) Individual intelligence test for school-age children, which yields verbal and performance scores as well as a combined score. (332)

Wechsler Preschool and Primary Scale of Intelligence, Revised (WPPSI-III) Individual intelligence test for children ages 2½ to 7 that yields verbal and performance scores as well as a combined score. (263)

whole-language approach Approach to teaching reading that emphasizes visual retrieval and use of contextual clues. (338)

withdrawal of love Disciplinary strategy that involves ignoring, isolating, or showing dislike for a child. (297)

working memory Short-term storage of information being actively processed. (176, 258, 658)

zone of proximal development (ZPD) Vygotsky's term for the difference between what a child can do alone and what the child can do with help. (264)

zygote One-celled organism resulting from fertilization. (63)

Bibliography

AAP Committee on Nutrition. (2003). Prevention of pediatric overweight and obesity. *Pediatrics, 112,* 424–430.

Aaron, V., Parker, K. D., Ortega, S., & Calhoun, T. (1999). The extended family as a source of support among African Americans. *Challenge: A Journal of Research on African American Men, 10*(2), 23–36.

Abbott, R. D., White, L. R., Ross, G. W., Masaki, K. H., Curb, J. D., & Petrovitch, H. (2004). Walking and dementia in physically capable elderly men. *Journal of the American Medical Association, 292,* 1447–1453.

Abel, E. K. (1991). *Who cares for the elderly?* Philadelphia: Temple University Press.

Aber, J. L., Brown, J. L., & Jones, S. M. (2003). Developmental trajectories toward violence in middle childhood: Course, demographic differences, and response to school-based intervention. *Developmental Psychology, 39,* 324–348.

Abma, J. C., Chandra, A., Mosher, W. D., Peterson, L., & Piccinino, L. (1997). Fertility, family planning, and women's health: New data from the 1995 National Survey of Family Growth. *Vital Health Statistics, 23*(19). Washington, DC: National Center for Health Statistics.

Abma, J. C., Martinez, G. M., Mosher, W. D., & Dawson, B. S. (2004). Teenagers in the United States: Sexual activity, contraceptive use, and childbearing, 2002. *Vital Health Statistics, 23*(24), Washington, DC: National Center for Health Statistics.

Abramovitch, R., Corter, C., & Lando, B. (1979). Sibling interaction in the home. *Child Development, 50,* 997–1003.

Abramovitch, R., Corter, C., Pepler, D., & Stanhope, L. (1986). Sibling and peer interactions: A final follow-up and comparison. *Child Development, 57,* 217–229.

Abramovitch, R., Pepler, D., & Corter, C. (1982). Patterns of sibling interaction among preschool-age children. In M. E. Lamb (Ed.), *Sibling relationships: Their nature and significance across the lifespan.* Hillsdale, NJ: Erlbaum.

Abrams, J. (2004, December 15). U.S. says China forces abortions. Associated Press.

Abramson, T. A. (1995, Fall). From nonnormative to normative caregiving. *Dimensions: Newsletter of American Society on Aging,* pp. 1–2.

Achenbach, T. M., & Howell, C. T. (1993). Are American children's problems getting worse? A 13-year comparison. *Journal of the American Academy of Child and Adolescent Psychiatry, 32,* 1145–1154.

Achenbaum, W. A., & Bengtson, V. L. (1994). Re-engaging the disengagement theory of aging: On the history and assessment of theory development in gerontology. *The Gerontologist, 34,* 756–763.

Ackerman, B. P., Brown, E. D., & Izard, C. E. (2004). The relations between persistent poverty and contextual risk and children's behavior in elementary school. *Developmental Psychology, 40,* 367–377.

Ackerman, B. P., Kogos, J., Youngstrom, E., Schoff, K., & Izard, C. (1999). Family instability and the problem behaviors of children from economically disadvantaged families. *Developmental Psychology, 35*(1), 258–268.

Ackerman, M. J., Siu, B. L., Sturner, W. Q., Tester D. J., Valdivia, C. R., Makielski, J. C., & Towbin, J. A. (2001). Postmortem molecular analysis of SCN5A defects in sudden infant death syndrome. *Journal of the American Medical Association, 286,* 2264–2269.

Acosta, M. T., Arcos-Burgos, M., & Muenke, M. (2004). Attention deficit/hyperactivity disorder (ADHD): Complex phenotype, simple genotype? *Genetics in Medicine, 6,* 1–15.

ACT for Youth Upstate Center of Excellence. (2002). *Adolescent brain development. Research facts and findings.* [A collaboration of Cornell University, University of Rochester, and the NYS Center for School Safety.] [Online]. Available: http://www.human.cornell.edu/actforyouth. Access date: March 23, 2004.

AD2000 Collaborative Group. (2004). Long-term donepezil treatment in 565 patients with Alzheimer's disease (AD2000): Randomized double-blind trial. *The Lancet, 363,* 2105–2115.

Adam, E. K., Gunnar, M. R., & Tanaka, A. (2004). Adult attachment, parent emotion, and observed parenting behavior: Mediator and moderator models. *Child Development, 75,* 110–122.

Adams, B. N. (2004). Families and family study in international perspective. *Journal of Marriage and Family, 66,* 1076–1088.

Adams, C. (1991). Qualitative age differences in memory for text: A life-span developmental perspective. *Psychology and Aging, 6,* 323–336.

Adams, R. G. (1986). Friendship and aging. *Generations, 10*(4), 40–43.

Adams, R. G., & Allan, G. (1998). *Placing friendship in context.* Cambridge, MA: Cambridge University Press.

Adams, R., & Laursen, B. (2001). The organization and dynamics of adolescent conflict with parents and friends. *Journal of Marriage and the Family, 63,* 97–110.

Addis, M. E. & Mahalik, J. R. (2003). Men, masculinity, and the contexts of help seeking. *American Psychologist, 58,* 5–14.

Ades, P. A., Ballor, D. L., Ashikaga, T., Utton, J. L., & Nair, K. S. (1996). Weight training improves walking endurance in healthy elderly persons. *Annals of Internal Medicine, 124,* 568–572.

Adler, N. E., & Newman, K. (2002). Socioeconomic disparities in health: Pathways and policies. *Health Affairs, 21,* 60–76.

Adler, N. E., Ozer, E. J., & Tschann, J. (2003). Abortion among adolescents. *American Psychologist, 58,* 211–217.

Adler, P. A., & Adler, P. (1995). Dynamics of inclusion and exclusion in preadolescent cliques. *Social Psychology Quarterly, 58,* 145–162.

Administration on Aging. (2001). *A profile of older Americans: 2001.* Washington, DC: Author.

Administration on Aging. (2003a). *A profile of older Americans.* Washington, DC: U.S. Department of Health and Human Services.

Administration on Aging. (2003b, August 27). *Challenges of global aging.* (Fact sheet). Washington, DC: U.S. Department of Health and Human Services.

Adolph, K. E. (1997). Learning in the development of infant locomotion. *Monographs of the Society for Research in Child Development, 62*(3, Serial No. 251).

Adolph, K. E. (2000). Specificity of learning: Why infants fall over a veritable cliff. *Psychological Science, 11,* 290–295.

Adolph, K. E., & Eppler, M. A. (2002). Flexibility and specificity in infant motor skill acquisition. In J. Fagen & H. Hayne (Eds.), *Progress in infancy research* (vol. 2, pp. 121–167). Mahwah, NJ: Lawrence Erlbaum Associates.

Adolph, K. E., Vereijken, B., & Shrout, P. E. (2003). What changes in infant walking and why. *Child Development, 74,* 475–497.

Agency for Healthcare Research and Quality and the Centers for Disease Control. (2002). *Physical activity and older Americans: Benefits and strategies.* [Online]. Available: http://www.ahrq.gov/ppip/activity.htm

Aggarwal, S., Gollapudi, S., & Gupta, S. (1999). Increased TNF-alpha-induced apoptosis in lymphocytes from aged humans: Changes in TNF-alpha receptor expression and activation of caspases. *Journal of Immunology, 162,* 2154–2161.

Agoda, L. (1995). Minorities and ESRD. Review: African American study of kidney disease and hypertension clinical trials. *Nephrology News & Issues, 9,* 18–19.

Agosin, M. (1999). Pirate, conjurer, feminist. In J. Rodden (Ed.), *Conversations with Isabel Allende* (pp. 35–47). Austin: University of Texas Press.

Ahnert, L., & Lamb, M. E. (2003). Shared care: Establishing a balance between home and child care settings. *Child Development, 74,* 1044–1049.

Ahnert, L., Gunnar, M. R., Lamb, M. E., & Barthel, M. (2004). Transition to child care: Associations with infant-mother attachment, infant negative emotion and cortical elevation. *Child Development, 75,* 639–650.

Ahrons, C. R., & Tanner, J. L. (2003). Adult children and their fathers: Relationship changes

20 years after parental divorce. *Family Relations, 52,* 340–351.

Ainsworth, M. D. S. (1967). *Infancy in Uganda: Infant care and the growth of love.* Baltimore: Johns Hopkins University Press.

Ainsworth, M. D. S., Blehar, M. C., Waters, E., & Wall, S. (1978). *Patterns of attachment: A psychological study of the strange situation.* Hillsdale, NJ: Erlbaum.

Akutsu, H., Legge, G. E., Ross, J. A., & Schuebel, K. J. (1991). Psychophysics of reading: Effects of age-related changes in vision. *Journal of Gerontology: Psychological Sciences, 46*(6), P325–331.

Alaimo, K., Olson, C. M., & Frongillo, E. A. (2001). Food insufficiency and American school-aged children's cognitive, academic, and psychosocial development. *Pediatrics, 108,* 44–53.

Alan Guttmacher Institute (AGI). (1994). *Sex & America's teenagers.* New York: Author.

Alan Guttmacher Institute (AGI). (1999a). Facts in brief: Teen sex and pregnancy. [Online]. Available: http://www.agi_usa.org/pubs/fb_teen_sex.html#sfd. Access date: January 31, 2000.

Alan Guttmacher Institute (AGI). (1999b). Occasional report: Why is teenage pregnancy declining? The roles of abstinence, sexual activity and contraceptive use. [Online]. Available: http://www.agi_usa.org/pubs/or_teen_preg_decline.html. Access date: January 31, 2000.

Albright, M. (2003). *Madam Secretary: A memoir.* New York: Hyperion.

Alcott, L. M. (1929). *Little women.* New York: Saalfield. (Original work published 1868)

Aldwin, C. M., & Levenson, M. R. (2001). Stress, coping, and health at midlife: A developmental perspective. In M. E. Lachman (Ed.), *Handbook of midlife development* (pp. 188–214). New York: Wiley.

Alexander, K. L., Entwisle, D. R., & Dauber, S. L. (1993). First-grade classroom behavior: Its short- and long-term consequences for school performance. *Child Development, 64,* 801–814.

Aligne, C. A., & Stoddard, J. J. (1997). Tobacco and children: An economic evaluation of the medical effects of parental smoking. *Archives of Pediatric and Adolescent Medicine, 151,* 648–653.

Allen, G. L., & Ondracek, P. J. (1995). Age-sensitive cognitive abilities related to children's acquisition of spatial knowledge. *Developmental Psychology, 31,* 934–945.

Allen, J. P., & Philliber, S. (2001). Who benefits most from a broadly targeted prevention program? Differential efficacy across populations in the Teen Outreach Program. *Journal of Community Psychology, 29,* 637–655.

Allen, J. P., McElhaney, K. B., Land, D. J., Kuperminc, G. P., Moore, C. W., O'Beirner-Kelly, H., & Kilmer, S. L. (2003). A secure base in adolescence: Markers of attachment security in the mother-adolescent relationship. *Child Development, 74,* 292–307.

Allen, K. R., Blieszner, R., & Roberto, K. A. (2000). Families in the middle and later years:

A review and critique of research in the 1990s. *Journal of Marriage and the Family, 62,* 911–926.

Allende, I. (1995). *Paula.* (M. S. Peden, Trans.) New York: HarperCollins.

Almeida, D. M., & Horn, M. C. (2004). Is daily life more stressful during adulthood? In O. G. Brim, C. D. Riff, & R. C. Kessler (Eds.). *How healthy are we? A national study of well-being at midlife.* Chicago: University of Chicago Press.

Almeida, D. M., Maggs, J. L., & Galambos, N. L. (1993). Wives' employment hours and spousal participation in family work. *Journal of Family Psychology, 7,* 233–244.

Als, H., Duffy, F. H., McAnulty, G. B., Rivkin, M. J., Vajapeyam, S., Mulkern, R. V., Warfield, S. K., Huppi, P. S., Butler, S. C., Conneman, N., Fischer, C., and Eichenwald, E. C. (2004). Early experience alters brain function and structure. *Pediatrics, 113,* 846–857.

Alzheimer's disease: Recent progress and prospects. Part I. (2001, October). *The Harvard Mental Health Letter, 18*(4), 1–4.

Alzheimer's disease: Recent progress and prospects. Part III. (2001, December). *The Harvard Mental Health Letter, 18*(6), 1–4.

Alzheimer's Disease: The search for causes and treatments—Part I. (1998, August). *The Harvard Mental Health Letter, 15*(2).

Amato, P. R. (2000). The consequences of divorce for adults and children. *Journal of Marriage and the Family, 62,* 1269–1287.

Amato, P. R. (2003). Reconciling divergent perspectives: Judith Wallerstein, quantitative family research, and children of divorce. *Family Relations, 52,* 332–339.

Amato, P. R., & Booth, A. (1997). *A generation at risk: Growing up in an era of family upheaval.* Cambridge, MA: Harvard University Press.

Amato, P. R., & Cheadle, J. (2005). The long reach of divorce: Divorce and child well-being across three generations. *Journal of Marriage and Family, 67,* 191–206.

Amato, P. R., & Gilbreth, J. G. (1999). Nonresident fathers and children's well-being: A meta-analysis. *Journal of Marriage and the Family, 61,* 557–573.

Amato, P. R., Johnson, D. R., Booth, A., & Rogers, S. J. (2003). Continuity and change in marital quality between 1980 and 2000. *Journal of Marriage and Family, 65,* 1–22.

American Academy of Child & Adolescent Psychiatry. (2002). Children and the news. *Facts for Families* #67. [Online]. Retrieved April 24, 2005, from http://www.aacap.org/publications/factsfam/67.htm.

American Academy of Child & Adolescent Psychiatry. (2003). Talking to children about terrorism and war. *Facts for Families* #87. [Online]. Retrieved April 22, 2005, from http://www.aacap.org/publications/factsfam/87.htm.

American Academy of Child and Adolescent Psychiatry (AACAP). (1997). *Children's sleep problems.* [Fact sheet] No. 34.

American Academy of Pediatrics (AAP). (2004, September 30). *American Academy of Pedi-*

atrics (AAP) supports Institute of Medicine's (IOM) childhood obesity recommendations. Press release.

American Academy of Pediatrics (AAP) and Canadian Paediatric Society. (2000). Prevention and management of pain and stress in the neonate. *Pediatrics, 105*(2), 454–461.

American Academy of Pediatrics (AAP) Committee on Accident and Poison Prevention. (1988). Snowmobile statement. *Pediatrics, 82,* 798–799.

American Academy of Pediatrics (AAP) Committee on Adolescence and Committee on Early Childhood, Adoption, and Dependent Care. (2001). Care of adolescent parents and their children. *Pediatrics, 107,* 429–434.

American Academy of Pediatrics (AAP) Committee on Adolescence. (1994). Sexually transmitted diseases. *Pediatrics, 94,* 568–572.

American Academy of Pediatrics (AAP) Committee on Adolescence. (1999). Adolescent pregnancy. Current trends and issues: 1998. *Pediatrics, 103,* 516–520.

American Academy of Pediatrics (AAP) Committee on Adolescence. (2000). Suicide and suicide attempts in adolescents. *Pediatrics, 105*(4), 871–874.

American Academy of Pediatrics (AAP) Committee on Adolescence. (2003). Policy statement: Identifying and treating eating disorders. *Pediatrics, 111,* 204–211.

American Academy of Pediatrics (AAP) Committee on Bioethics. (2001). Ethical issues with genetic testing in pediatrics. *Pediatrics, 107*(6), 1451–1455.

American Academy of Pediatrics (AAP) Committee on Child Abuse and Neglect. (2001). Shaken baby syndrome: Rotational cranial injuries—Technical report. *Pediatrics, 108,* 206–210.

American Academy of Pediatrics (AAP) Committee on Children with Disabilities. (2001). The pediatrician's role in the diagnosis and management of autistic spectrum disorder in children. *Pediatrics, 107*(5), 1221–1226.

American Academy of Pediatrics (AAP) Committee on Children with Disabilities and Committee on Drugs. (1996). Medication for children with attentional disorders. *Pediatrics, 98,* 301–304.

American Academy of Pediatrics (AAP) Committee on Community Health Services. (1996). Health needs of homeless children and families. *Pediatrics, 88,* 789–791.

American Academy of Pediatrics (AAP) Committee on Drugs. (1994). The transfer of drugs and other chemicals into human milk. *Pediatrics, 93,* 137–150.

American Academy of Pediatrics (AAP) Committee on Drugs. (2000). Use of psychoactive medication during pregnancy and possible effects on the fetus and newborn. *Pediatrics, 105,* 880–887.

American Academy of Pediatrics (AAP) Committee on Environmental Health. (1997). Environmental tobacco smoke: A hazard to children. *Pediatrics, 99,* 639–642.

American Academy of Pediatrics (AAP) Committee on Environmental Health. (1998).

Screening for elevated blood lead levels. *Pediatrics, 101,* 1072–1078.

American Academy of Pediatrics (AAP) Committee on Fetus and Newborn and American College of Obstetricians and Gynecologists Committee on Obstetric Practice. (1996). Use and abuse of the Apgar score. *Pediatrics, 98,* 141–142.

American Academy of Pediatrics (AAP) Committee on Genetics. (1996). Newborn screening fact sheet. *Pediatrics, 98,* 1–29.

American Academy of Pediatrics (AAP) Committee on Genetics. (1999). Folic acid for the prevention of neural tube defects. *Pediatrics, 104,* 325–327.

American Academy of Pediatrics (AAP) Committee on Infectious Diseases. (2000). Recommended childhood immunization schedule—United States, January–December, 2000, *Pediatrics, 105,* 148.

American Academy of Pediatrics (AAP) Committee on Injury and Poison Prevention. (2001a). Bicycle helmets. *Pediatrics, 108*(4), 1030–1032.

American Academy of Pediatrics (AAP) Committee on Injury and Poison Prevention. (2001b). Injuries associated with infant walkers. *Pediatrics, 108*(3), 790–792.

American Academy of Pediatrics (AAP) Committee on Injury and Poison Prevention and Committee on Sports Medicine and Fitness. (1999). Policy statement: Trampolines at home, school, and recreational centers. *Pediatrics, 103,* 1053–1056.

American Academy of Pediatrics (AAP) Committee on Injury and Poison Prevention. (2000). Firearm-related injuries affecting the pediatric population. *Pediatrics, 105*(4), 888–895.

American Academy of Pediatrics (AAP) Committee on Nutrition. (1992a). Statement on cholesterol. *Pediatrics, 90,* 469–473.

American Academy of Pediatrics (AAP) Committee on Pediatric AIDS and Committee on Infectious Diseases. (1999). Issues related to human immunodeficiency virus transmission in schools, child care, medical settings, the home, and community. *Pediatrics, 104,* 318–324.

American Academy of Pediatrics (AAP) Committee on Pediatric AIDS. (2000). Education of children with human immunodeficiency virus infection. *Pediatrics, 105,* 1358–1360.

American Academy of Pediatrics (AAP) Committee on Pediatric Research. (2000). Race/ethnicity, gender, socioeconomic status—Research exploring their effects on child health: A subject review. *Pediatrics, 105,* 1349–1351.

American Academy of Pediatrics (AAP) Committee on Practice and Ambulatory Medicine and Section on Ophthalmology. (1996). Eye examination and vision screening in infants, children, and young adults. *Pediatrics, 98,* 153–157.

American Academy of Pediatrics (AAP) Committee on Practice and Ambulatory Medicine and Section on Ophthalmology. (2002). Use of photoscreening for children's vision screening. *Pediatrics, 109,* 524–525.

American Academy of Pediatrics (AAP) Committee on Psychosocial Aspects of Child and Family Health. (1992). The pediatrician and childhood bereavement. *Pediatrics, 89*(3), 516–518.

American Academy of Pediatrics (AAP) Committee on Psychosocial Aspects of Child and Family Health. (1998). Guidance for effective discipline. *Pediatrics, 101,* 723–728.

American Academy of Pediatrics (AAP) Committee on Psychosocial Aspects of Child and Family Health. (2000). The pediatrician and childhood bereavement. *Pediatrics, 105,* 445–447.

American Academy of Pediatrics (AAP) Committee on Psychosocial Aspects of Child and Family Health. (2002). Coparent or second-parent adoption by same-sex parents. *Pediatrics, 109,* 339–340.

American Academy of Pediatrics (AAP) Committee on Psychosocial Aspects of Child and Family Health and Committee on Adolescence. (2001). Sexuality education for children and adolescence. *Pediatrics, 108*(2), 498–502.

American Academy of Pediatrics (AAP) Committee on Public Education. (2001a). Media violence. *Pediatrics, 108,* 1222–1226.

American Academy of Pediatrics (AAP) Committee on Public Education (2001b). Policy statement: Children, adolescents, and television. *Pediatrics, 107,* 423–426.

American Academy of Pediatrics (AAP) Committee on Quality Improvement. (2002). Making Advances Against Jaundice in Infant Care (MAJIC). [Online]. Available: http://www/aap.org/visit/majic.htm. Access date: October 25, 2002.

American Academy of Pediatrics (AAP) Committee on Sports Medicine and Fitness. (1992). Fitness, activity, and sports participation in the preschool child. *Pediatrics, 90,* 1002–1004.

American Academy of Pediatrics (AAP) Committee on Sports Medicine and Fitness. (1997). Participation in boxing by children, adolescents, and young adults. *Pediatrics, 99,* 134–135.

American Academy of Pediatrics (AAP) Committee on Sports Medicine and Fitness. (1999). Human immunodeficiency virus and other blood-borne viral pathogens in the athletic setting. *Pediatrics, 104*(6), 1400–1403.

American Academy of Pediatrics (AAP) Committee on Sports Medicine and Fitness. (2000). Injuries in youth soccer: A subject review. *Pediatrics, 105*(3), 659–660.

American Academy of Pediatrics (AAP) Committee on Sports Medicine and Fitness. (2001). Risk of injury from baseball and softball in children. *Pediatrics, 107*(4), 782–784.

American Academy of Pediatrics (AAP) Committee on Substance Abuse and Committee on Children with Disabilities. (1993). Fetal alcohol syndrome and fetal alcohol effects. *Pediatrics, 91,* 1004–1006.

American Academy of Pediatrics (AAP) Committee on Substance Abuse. (2001). Tobacco's toll: Implications for the pediatrician. *Pediatrics, 107,* 794–798.

American Academy of Pediatrics (AAP) Section on Breastfeeding. (2005). Breastfeeding and the use of human milk. *Pediatrics, 115,* 496–506.

American Academy of Pediatrics (AAP) Task Force on Infant Positioning and SIDS. (1997). Does bed sharing affect the risk of SIDS? *Pediatrics, 100,* 272.

American Academy of Pediatrics (AAP) Task Force on Infant Sleep Position and Sudden Infant Death Syndrome. (2000). Changing concepts of sudden infant death syndrome: Implications for infant sleeping environment and sleep position. *Pediatrics, 105,* 650–656.

American Academy of Pediatrics (AAP) Work Group on Breastfeeding. (1997). Breastfeeding and the use of human milk. *Pediatrics, 100,* 1035–1039.

American Association of Retired Persons (AARP). (1993). *Abused elders or battered women?* Washington, DC: Author.

American Association of Retired Persons (AARP). (1995). *A profile of older Americans.* Washington, DC: Author.

American Association of University Women (AAUW) Educational Foundation. (1992). *The AAUW report: How schools shortchange girls.* Washington, DC: Author.

American Cancer Society. (2001). *Cancer facts and figures.* Atlanta: Author.

American College of Obstetricians and Gynecologists (ACOG). (2001a). Management of premenstrual syndrome. *Practice Bulletin.* Washington, DC: Author.

American College of Obstetricians and Gynecologists (ACOG). (2001b). Repeated miscarriage. *ACOG Education Pamphlet AP1000.* Washington, DC: Author.

American College of Obstetricians and Gynecologists. (2001, February). Management of recurrent early pregnancy loss. *ACOG Practice Bulletin,* No. 24.

American College of Obstetrics and Gynecology. (1994). *Exercise during pregnancy and the postpartum pregnancy* (Technical Bulletin No. 189). Washington, DC: Author.

American Diabetes Association. (1992). *Diabetes facts.* Alexandria, VA: Author.

American Heart Association (AHA). (1995). *Silent epidemic: The truth about women and heart disease.* Dallas: Author.

American Medical Association (AMA). (1992). *Diagnosis and treatment guidelines on elder abuse and neglect.* Chicago: Author.

American Medical Association. (1998). *Essential guide to menopause.* New York: Simon & Schuster.

American Psychiatric Association (APA). (1994). *Diagnostic and statistical manual of mental disorders* (4th ed.). Washington, DC: Author.

American Psychiatric Association (APA). (2000). *Diagnostic and Statistical Manual of Mental Disorders* (4th ed., Text Revision). Washington, DC: Author.

American Psychological Association and American Academy of Pediatrics. (1996).

Raising children to resist violence: What you can do [Online, Brochure]. Available: http:/www.apa.org/pubinfo/apaaap.html.

American Psychological Association Division 44/Committee on Lesbian, Gay, and Bisexual Concerns Joint Task Force on Guidelines for Psychotherapy with Lesbian, Gay, and Bisexual Clients. (2000). Guidelines for psychotherapy with lesbian, gay, and bisexual clients. *American Psychologist, 55,* 1440–1451.

American Psychological Association. (1997). Resolution on appropriate therapeutic responses to sexual orientation. In *Resolutions related to lesbian, gay, and bisexual interests.* Retrieved September 13, 2001, from http://www.apa.org/pi/reslgbc.html.

American Psychological Association. (2002). Ethical principles of psychologists and code of conduct. *American Psychologist, 57,* 1060–1073.

American Psychological Association. (undated). *Answers to your questions about sexual orientation and homosexuality* [Brochure]. Washington, DC: Author.

American Public Health Association. (2004). Disparities in infant mortality. Fact sheet. [Online]. Available: http://www.medscape.com/viewarticle/472721.

American Stroke Association. (2005). Learn to recognize a stroke. Retrieved May 23, 2005, from http://www.strokeassociation.org/presenter.jhtml?identifier=1020.

Americans on Values Follow-Up Survey, 1998. (1999). Washington, DC: Kaiser Family Foundation/Washington Post/Harvard University.

Ames, E. W. (1997). *The development of Romanian orphanage children adopted to Canada: Final report* (National Welfare Grants Program, Human Resources Development, Canada). Burnaby, BC, Canada: Simon Fraser University, Psychology Department.

Ammenheuser, M. M., Berenson, A. B., Babiak, A. E., Singleton, C. R., & Whorton, E. B. (1998). Frequencies of hprt mutant lymphocytes in marijuana-smoking. *Mutation Research, 403,* 55–64.

Amsel, E., Goodman, G., Savoie, D., & Clark, M. (1996). The development of reasoning about causal and noncausal influences on levers. *Child Development, 67,* 1624–1646.

Anastasi, A. (1988). *Psychological testing* (6th ed.). New York: Macmillan.

Anastasi, A., & Schaefer, C. E. (1971). Note on concepts of creativity and intelligence. *Journal of Creative Behavior, 3,* 113–116.

Anastasi, A., & Urbina, S. (1997). *Psychological testing* (7th ed.). Upper Saddle River, NJ: Prentice-Hall.

Andel, R., Crowe, M., Pedersen, N. L., Mortimer, J., Crimmins, E., Johansson, B., & Gatz, M. (2005). Complexity of work and risk of Alzheimer's disease: A population-based study of Swedish twins. *Journal of Gerontology, Psychological Sciences, 60B,* P251–P258.

Andersen, A. E. (1995). Eating disorders in males. In K. D. Brownell & C. G. Fairburn (Eds.), *Eating disorders and obesity: A comprehensive handbook* (pp. 177–187). New York: Guilford.

Andersen, R. E., Wadden, T. A., Bartlett, S. J., Zemel, B., Verde, T. J., & Franckowiak, S. C. (1999). Effects of lifestyle activity vs. structured aerobic exercise in obese women: A randomized trial. *Journal of the American Medical Association, 281,* 335–340.

Anderson, A. H., Clark, A., & Mullin, J. (1994). Interactive communication between children: Learning how to make language work in dialog. *Journal of Child Language, 21,* 439–463.

Anderson, C. (2000). *The impact of interactive violence on children.* Statement before the Senate Committee on Commerce, Science, and Transportation, 106th Congress, 1st session.

Anderson, C. A., Berkowitz, L., Donnerstein, E., Huesmann, L. R., Johnson, J. D., Linz, D., Malamuth, N. M., & Wartella, E. (2003). The influence of media violence on youth. *Psychological Science in the Public Interest, 4,* 367–377.

Anderson, D., & Anderson, R. (1999). The cost-effectiveness of home birth. *Journal of Nurse-Midwifery, 44*(1), 30–35.

Anderson, D. A., & Hamilton, M. (2005). Gender role stereotyping of parents in children's picture books: The invisible father. *Sex Roles, 52,* 145–151.

Anderson, D. R., Huston, A. C., Schmitt, K. L., Linebarger, D. L., & Wright, J. C. (2001). Early childhood television viewing and adolescent behavior. *Monographs of the Society for Research in Child Development,* Serial No. 264, *66*(1).

Anderson, M. (1992). *My Lord, what a morning.* Madison: University of Wisconsin Press.

Anderson, M., Kaufman, J., Simon, T. R., Barrios, L., Paulozzi, L., Ryan, G., Hammond, R., Modzeleski, W., Feucht, T., Potter, L., & the School-Associated Violent Deaths Study Group. (2001). School-associated violent deaths in the United States, 1994–1999. *Journal of the American Medical Association, 286*(21), 2695–2702.

Anderson, P., Doyle, L. W., and the Victorian Infant Collaborative Study Group. (2003). Neurobehavioral outcomes of school-age children born extremely low birth weight or very preterm in the 1990s. *Journal of the American Medical Association, 289,* 3264–3272.

Anderson, R. N. (2002). Deaths: Leading causes for 2000. *National Vital Statistics Reports, 50* (16). Hyattsville, MD: National Center for Health Statistics.

Anderson, R. N., & Smith, B. L. (2003). Deaths: Leading causes for 2001. *National Vital Statistics Reports, 52*(9). Hyattsville, MD: National Center for Health Statistics.

Anderson, R. N., & Smith, B. L. (2005). Deaths: Leading causes for 2002. *National Vital Statistics Reports, 53*(17). Hyattsville, MD: National Center for Health Statistics.

Anderson, S. E., Dallal, G. E., & Must, A. (2003). Relative weight and race influence average age at menarche: Results from two nationally representative surveys of U.S. girls studied 25 years apart. *Pediatrics, 111,* 844–850.

Anderson, W. F. (1998). Human gene therapy. *Nature, 392*(Suppl.), 25–30.

Anderssen N., Amlie, C., & Ytteroy, E. A. (2002). Outcomes for children with lesbian or gay parents: A review of studies from 1978 to 2000. *Scandinavian Journal of Psychology, 43,* 335–351.

Andrade, S. E., Gurwitz, J. H., Davis, R. L., Chan, K. A., Finkelstein, J. A., Fortman, K., McPhillips, H., Raebel, M. A., Roblin, D., Smith, D. H., Yood, M. U., Morse, A. N., & Platt, R. (2004). Prescription drug use in pregnancy. *American Journal of Obstetrics and Gynecology, 191,* 398–407.

Andresen, J. (2001). Cultural competence and health care: Japanese, Korean, and Indian patients in the United States. *Journal of Cultural Diversity, 8,* 109–121.

Andrews, N., Miller, E., Grant, A., Stowe, J., Osborne, V., & Taylor, B. (2004). Thimerosal exposure in infants and developmental disorders: A retrospective cohort study in the United Kingdom does not support a causal association. *Pediatrics, 114,* 584–591.

Angell, M. (1996). Euthanasia in the Netherlands—Good news or bad? *New England Journal of Medicine, 335,* 1676–1678.

Anisfeld, M. (1996). Only tongue protrusion modeling is matched by neonates. *Developmental Review, 16,* 149–161.

Ann Bancroft (1955–), explorer. (1999). Women in American history by Encyclopedia Britannica. [Online]. Available: http://www.britannica.com/women/articles/Bancroft_Ann.html. Access date: April 4, 2002.

Ann Bancroft, 1955–. (1998). National Women's Hall of Fame. [Online]. Available: http://www.jerseycity.k12.nj.us/womenshistory/bancroft.htm. Access date: April 4, 2002.

Ann Bancroft, explorer. (undated). [Online]. http://www.people/memphis.edu/~cbburr/gold/bancroft.htm. Access date: April 4, 2002.

Annas, G. J. (2005). "Culture of life" politics at the bedside—The case of Terri Shiavo. *New England Journal of Medicine.* [Online]. Retrieved from www.nejm.org on March 23, 2005.

Antonarakis, S. E., & Down Syndrome Collaborative Group. (1991). Parental origin of the extra chromosome in trisomy 21 as indicated by analysis of DNA polymorphisms. *New England Journal of Medicine, 324,* 872–876.

Antonio, A. L., Chang, M. J., Hakuta, K., Kenny, D. A., Levin, S., & Milem, J. F. (2004). Effects of racial diversity on complex thinking in college students. *Psychological Science, 15,* 507–510.

Antonucci, T. C. (1991). Attachment, social support, and coping with negative life events in mature adulthood. In E. M. Cummings, A. L. Greene, & K. H. Karraker (Eds.), *Life-span developmental psychology: Perspectives on stress and coping* (pp. 261–276). Hillsdale, NJ: Erlbaum.

Antonucci, T. C., & Akiyama, H. (1995). Convoys of social relations: Family and friendships within a life-span context. In R. Blieszner & V. Hilkevitch (Eds.), *Handbook of aging and the family* (pp. 355–371). Westport, CT: Greenwood Press.

Antonucci, T. C., Akiyama, H., & Merline, A. (2001). Dynamics of social relationships in midlife. In M. E. Lachman (Ed.), *Handbook of midlife development* (pp. 571–598). New York: Wiley.

Antonucci, T., & Akiyama, H. (1997). Concern with others at midlife: Care, comfort, or compromise? In M. E. Lachman & J. B. James (Eds.), *Multiple paths of midlife development* (pp. 145–169). Chicago: University of Chicago Press.

APA Online. (2001). End-of-life issues and care. Accessed 3/11/05. http://www.apa.org/pi/eol/arguments.html.

APA Working Group on Assisted Suicide and End-of-Life Decisions. (2005). Orientation to end-of-life decision making. APA Online. Accessed 2/7/05. http://www.apa.org/pi/aseol/section 1.html.

Apgar, V. (1953). A proposal for a new method of evaluation of the newborn infant. *Current Research in Anesthesia and Analgesia, 32,* 260–267.

Aquilino, W. S. (1996). The returning adult child and parental experience at midlife. In C. Ryff & M. M. Seltzer (Eds.), *The parental experience in midlife* (pp. 423–458). Chicago: University of Chicago Press.

Archer, S. L. (1993). Identity in relational contexts: A methodological proposal. In J. Kroger (Ed.), *Discussions on ego identity* (pp. 75–99). Hillsdale, NJ: Erlbaum.

Arcus, D., & Kagan, J. (1995). Temperament and craniofacial variation in the first two years. *Child Development, 66,* 1529–1540.

Arend, R., Gove, F., & Sroufe, L. A. (1979). Continuity of individual adaptation from infancy to kindergarten: A predictive study of ego resiliency and curiosity in preschoolers. *Child Development, 50,* 950–959.

Arias, E., MacDorman, M. F., Strobino, D. M., & Guyer, B. (2003). Annual summary of vital statistics—2002. *Pediatrics, 112,* 1215–1230.

Aries, P. (1962). *Centuries of childhood.* New York: Random House.

Arking, R., Novoseltsev, V., & Novoseltseva, J. (2004). The human life span is not that limited: The effect of multiple longevity phenotypes. *Journal of Gerontology: Biological Sciences, 59A,* 697–704.

Arlin, P. K. (1984). Adolescent and adult thought: A structural interpretation. In M. L. Commons, F. A. Richards, & C. Armon (Eds.), *Beyond formal operations* (pp. 258–271). New York: Praeger.

Arnett, J. J. (1999). Adolescent storm and stress, reconsidered. *American Psychologist, 54,* 317–326.

Arnett, J. J. (2000). Emerging adulthood: A theory of development from the late teens through the twenties. *American Psychologist, 55,* 469–480.

Arnett, J. J. (2004). *Emerging adulthood.* New York: Oxford University Press.

Arnold, D. S., & Whitehurst, G. J. (1994). Accelerating language development through picture book reading: A summary of dialogic reading and its effects. In D. K. Dickinson (Ed.), *Bridges to literacy: Children, families, and schools* (pp. 103–128). Oxford: Blackwell.

Arrich, J., Lalouschek, W., & Müllner, M. (2005). Influence of socioeconomic status on mortality after stroke: Retrospective cohort study. *Stroke, 36,* 310–314.

Ashe, A., & Rampersad, A. (1993). *Days of grace: A memoir.* New York: Ballantine.

Ashman, S. B., & Dawson, G. (2002). Maternal depression, infant psychobiological development, and risk for depression. In S. H. Goodman, & I. H. Gotlib (Eds.), *Children of depressed parents: Mechanisms of risk and implications for treatment* (pp. 37–58). Washington, DC: American Psychological Association.

Associated Press. (2004a, November 22). Boys have no place in politics: 4-year-old. AP Newswire.

Associated Press. (2004b, April 29). Mom in C-section case received probation: Woman originally charged with murder for delaying operation. [Online]. Available: http://www.msnbc.msn.com/id/4863415. Access date: June 8, 2004.

Associated Press. (2005, February 22). Britain starts gay civil unions this year, predicts 42,000. *Chicago Sun-Times,* p. 39.

Asthana, S., Bhasin, S., Butler, R. N., Fillit, H., Finkelstein, J., Harman, S. M., Holstein, L., Korenman, S. G., Matsumoto, A. M., Morley, J. E., Tsitouras, P., & Urban, R. (2004). Masculine vitality: Pros and cons of testosterone in treating the andropause. *Journal of Gerontology: Medical Sciences, 59A,* 461–466.

Astington, J. W. (1993). *The child's discovery of the mind.* Cambridge, MA: Harvard University Press.

Atchley, R. C. (1989). A continuity theory of normal aging. *The Gerontologist, 29,* 183–190.

Atchley, R. C. (1997). *Social forces and aging: An introduction to social gerontology* (8th ed.). Belmont, CA: Wadsworth.

Athansiou, M. S. (2001). Using consultation with a grandmother as an adjunct to play therapy. *Family Journal—Consulting and Therapy for Couples and Families, 9,* 445–449.

Australian man first in world to die with legal euthanasia. (1996, September 26). *The New York Times* (International Ed.), p. A5.

Ausubel, N. (1964). *The book of Jewish knowledge.* New York: Crown.

Autism-Part II. (2001, July). *The Harvard Mental Health Letter, 18*(1), 1–4.

Avis, N. E. (1999). Women's health at midlife. In S. L. Willis & J. D. Reid (Eds.), *Life in the middle: Psychological and social development in middle age* (pp. 105–146). San Diego: Academic Press.

Avolio, B. J., & Sosik, J. J. (1999). A life-span framework for assessing the impact of work on white-collar workers. In S. L. Willis & J. D. Reid (Eds.), *Life in the middle: Psychological and social development in middle age.* San Diego: Academic Press.

Aylward, G. P., Pfeiffer, S. I., Wright, A., & Verhulst, S. J. (1989). Outcome studies of low birth weight infants published in the last decade: A meta-analysis. *Journal of Pediatrics, 115,* 515–520.

Azar, B. (2002a, January). At the frontier of science. *Monitor on Psychology,* 40–41.

Azar, B. (2002b, March). Helping older adults get on the technology bandwagon. *Monitor on Psychology, 33*(3), [Online]. Available:

http://www.apa.org/monitor/mar02/helpingold.html. Access date: April 15, 2002.

Azuma, H. (1994). Two modes of cognitive socialization in Japan and the United States. In P. M. Greenfield & R. R. Cocking (Eds.), *Cross-cultural roots of minority child development* (pp. 275–284). Hillsdale, NJ: Erlbaum.

Babchuk, N. (1978–1979). Aging and primary relations. *International Journal of Aging and Human Development, 9*(2), 137–151.

Babu, A., & Hirschhorn, K. (1992). *A guide to human chromosome defects* (Birth Defects: Original Article Series, 28[2]). White Plains, NY: March of Dimes Birth Defects Foundation.

Bach, P. B., Schrag, D., Brawley, O. W., Galaznik, A., Yakren, S., & Begg, C. B. (2002). Survival of blacks and whites after a cancer diagnosis. *Journal of the American Medical Association, 287,* 2106–2113.

Baddeley, A. (1996). Exploring the central executive. *Quarterly Journal of Experimental Psychology: Human Experimental Psychology* (Special Issue: Working Memory), *49A,* 5–28.

Baddeley, A. (1998). Recent developments in working memory. *Current Opinion in Neurobiology, 8,* 234–238.

Baddeley, A. D. (1981). The concept of working memory: A view of its current state and probable future development. *Cognition, 10,* 17–23.

Baddeley, A. D. (1986). *Working memory.* London: Oxford University Press.

Baddeley, A. D. (1992). Working memory. *Science, 255,* 556–559.

Baer, J. S., Sampson, P. D., Barr, H. M., Connor, P. D., & Streissguth, A. P. (2003). A 21-year longitudinal analysis of the effects of prenatal alcohol exposure on young adult drinking. *Archives of General Psychiatry, 60,* 377–385.

Bagwell, C. L., Newcomb, A. F., & Bukowski, W. M. (1998). Preadolescent friendship and peer rejection as predictors of adult adjustment. *Child Development, 69,* 140–153.

Bailey, A., Le Couteur, A., Gottesman, I., & Bolton, P. (1995). Autism as a strongly genetic disorder: Evidence from a British twin study. *Psychological Medicine, 25,* 63–77.

Bailey, J. M., & Zucker, K. J. (1995). Childhood sex-typed behavior and sexual orientation: A conceptual analysis and quantitative review. *Developmental Psychology, 31,* 43–55.

Bailey, J. M., Dunne, M. P., & Martin, N. G. (2000). Genetic and environmental influences on sexual orientation and its correlates in an Australian twin sample. *Journal of Personality and Social Psychology, 78,* 524–536.

Baillargeon, R. (1994a). How do infants learn about the physical world? *Current Directions in Psychological Science, 3,* 133–140.

Baillargeon, R. (1994b). Physical reasoning in young infants: Seeking explanations for impossible events. *British Journal of Developmental Psychology, 12,* 9–33.

Baillargeon, R. (1999). Young infants' expectations about hidden objects. *Developmental Science, 2,* 115–132.

Baillargeon, R., & DeVos, J. (1991). Object permanence in young infants: Further evidence. *Child Development, 62,* 1227–1246.

Baines, L. S., Joseph, J. T., & Jindal, R. M. (2002). A public forum to promote organ donation amongst Asians: The Scottish initiative. *Transplant International, 15,* 124–131.

Baird, A. A., Gruber, S. A., Fein, D. A., Maas, L. C., Steingard, R. J., Renshaw, P. F., Cohen, B. M., & Yurgelon-Todd, D. A. (1999). Functional magnetic resonance imaging of facial affect recognition in children and adolescents. *Journal of the American Academy of Child and Adolescent Psychiatry, 38,* 195–199.

Baker, D. W., Sudano, J. J., Albert, J. M., Borawski, E. A., & Dor, A. (2001). Lack of health insurance and decline in overall health in late middle age. *New England Journal of Medicine, 345,* 1106–1112.

Baldwin, D. A., & Moses, L. J. (1996). The ontogeny of social information gathering. *Child Development, 67,* 1915–1939.

Balercia, G., Mosca, F., Mantero, F., Boscaro, M., Mancini, A., Ricciardo-Lamonica, G., & Littarru, G. (2004). Coenzyme q(10) supplementation in infertile men with idiopathic asthenozoospermia: An open, uncontrolled pilot study. *Fertility & Sterility, 81,* 93–98.

Balluz, L. S., Okoro, C. A., & Strine, T. W. (2004). Access to health-care preventive services among Hispanics and non-Hispanics—United States, 2001–2002. *Morbidity and Mortality Weekly Report, 53,* 937–941.

Balsis, S., Carpenter, B. D., & Storandt, M. (2005). Personality change precedes clinical diagnosis of dementia of the Alzheimer type. *Journal of Gerontology, Psychological Sciences, 60B,* P98–P101.

Baltes, P. B. (1987). Theoretical propositions of life-span development psychology: On the dynamics between growth and decline. *Developmental Psychology, 23*(5), 611–626.

Baltes, P. B. (1993). The aging mind: Potential and limits. *The Gerontologist, 33,* 580–594.

Baltes, P. B. (1997). On the incomplete architecture of human ontogeny: Selection, optimization, and compensation as foundation of developmental theory. *American Psychologist, 52,* 366–380.

Baltes, P. B., & Baltes, M. M. (1990). Psychological perspectives on successful aging: The model of selective optimization with compensation. In P. B. Baltes & M. M. Baltes (Eds.), *Successful aging: Perspectives from the behavioral sciences* (pp. 1–34). New York: Cambridge University Press.

Baltes, P. B., & Staudinger, U. M. (2000). Wisdom: A metaheuristic (pragmatic) to orchestrate mind and virtue toward excellence. *American Psychologist, 55,* 122–136.

Baltes, P. B., & Willis, S. L. (1982). Enhancement (plasticity) of intellectual functioning in old age: Penn State's Adult Development and Enrichment Project (ADEPT). In F. I. M. Craik & S. Trehub (Eds.), *Aging and cognitive processes* (pp. 353–389). New York: Plenum.

Baltes, P. B., Lindenberger, U., & Staudinger, U. M. (1998). Life-span theory in developmental psychology. In R. M. Lerner (Ed.), *Handbook of child psychology: Vol. 1. Theoretical models of human development* (pp. 1029–1143). New York: Wiley.

Baltes, P. B., Reese, H. W., & Lipsitt, L. (1980). Life-span developmental psychology. *Annual Review of Psychology, 31,* 65–110.

Baltes, P. B., Staudinger, U. M., Maercker, A., & Smith, J. (1995). People nominated as wise: A comparative study of wisdom-related knowledge. *Psychology and Aging, 10,* 155–166.

Bandura, A. (1977). *Social learning theory.* Englewood Cliffs, NJ: Prentice-Hall.

Bandura, A. (1986). *Social foundations of thought and action: A social cognitive theory.* Englewood Cliffs, NJ: Prentice-Hall.

Bandura, A. (1989). Social cognitive theory. In R. Vasta (Ed.), *Annals of child development.* Greenwich, CT: JAI.

Bandura, A. (1994). Self-efficacy. In V. S. Ramachaudran (Ed.), *Encyclopedia of human behavior* (Vol. 4, pp. 71–81). New York: Academic Press.

Bandura, A., Barbaranelli, C., Caprara, G. V., & Pastorelli, C. (1996). Multifaceted impact of self-efficacy beliefs on academic functioning. *Child Development, 67,* 1206–1222.

Bandura, A., Barbaranelli, C., Caprara, G. V., & Pastorelli, C. (2001). Self-efficacy beliefs as shapers of children's aspirations and career trajectories. *Child Development, 72*(1), 187–206.

Bandura, A., Ross, D., & Ross, S. A. (1961). Transmission of aggression through imitation of aggressive models. *Journal of Abnormal and Social Psychology, 63,* 575–582.

Bandura, A., Ross, D., & Ross, S. A. (1963). Imitation of film-mediated aggressive models. *Journal of Abnormal and Social Psychology, 66,* 3–11.

Banks, D. A., & Fossel, M. (1997). Telomeres, cancer, and aging: Altering the human life span. *Journal of the American Medical Association, 278,* 1345–1348.

Banks, E. (1989). Temperament and individuality: A study of Malay children. *American Journal of Orthopsychiatry, 59,* 390–397.

Barber, B. K. (1994). Cultural, family, and personal contexts of parent-adolescent conflict. *Journal of Marriage and the Family, 56,* 375–386.

Barber, B. L., & Eccles, J. S. (1992). Long-term influence of divorce and single parenting on adolescent family- and work-related values, behaviors, and aspirations. *Psychological Bulletin, 111*(1), 108–126.

Barfield, W., & Martin, J. (2004). Racial/ethnic trends in fetal mortality—United States, 1990–2000. *Morbidity and Mortality Weekly Report, 53,* 529–532.

Barinaga, M. (1998). Alzheimer's treatments that work now. *Science, 282,* 1030–1032.

Barkley, R. A. (1998a, February). How should attention deficit disorder be described? *Harvard Mental Health Letter,* p. 8.

Barkley, R. A. (1998b, September). Attention deficit hyperactivity disorder. *Scientific American,* pp. 66–71.

Barkley, R. A., Murphy, K. R., & Kwasnik, D. (1996). Motor vehicle competencies and risks in teens and young adults with attention deficit hyperactivity disorder. *Pediatrics, 98,* 1089–1095.

Barlow, S. E., & Dietz, W. H. (1998). Obesity evaluation and treatment: Expert committee recommendations [On-line]. *Pediatrics, 102*(3), e29. Available: http://www.pediatrics.org/cgi/content/full/102/3/e29

Barnes, J., Sutcliffe, A., Ponjaert, I., Loft, A., Wennerholm, U., Tarlatzis, V., & Bonduelle, M. (2003, July). The European study of 1,523 ICSI/IVF versus naturally conceived 5-year-old children and their families: Family functioning and socio-emotional development. Paper presented at conference of European Society of Human Reproduction and Embryology, Madrid.

Barnes, P. M., & Schoenborn, C. A. (2003). Physical activity among adults: United States, 2000. *Advance Data from Vital and Health Statistics,* No. 133. Hyattsville, MD: National Center for Health Statistics.

Barnett, R. (1985, March). *We've come a long way—but where are we and what are the rewards?* Paper presented at the conference on Women in Transition, New York University School of Continuing Education, Center for Career and Life Planning, New York, NY.

Barnett, R. C. (1997). Gender, employment, and psychological well-being: Historical and life-course perspectives. In M. E. Lachman & J. B. James (Eds.), *Multiple paths of midlife development* (pp. 325–343). Chicago: University of Chicago Press.

Barnett, R. C., & Hyde, J. S. (2001). Women, men, work, and family. *American Psychologist, 56,* 781–796.

Barnhart, M. A. (1992, Fall). Coping with the Methuselah syndrome. *Free Inquiry,* pp. 19–22.

Barrett-Connor, E., Hendrix, S., Ettinger, B., Wenger, N. K., Paoletti, R., Lenfant, C. J. M., & Pinn, V. W. (2002). Best clinical practices: Chapter 13. *International position paper on women's health and menopause: A comprehensive approach.* Washington, DC: National Heart, Lung, and Blood Institute.

Barry, B. K., & Carson, R. G. (2004). The consequences of resistance training for movement control in older adults. *Journal of Gerontology, Medical Sciences, 59A,* 730–754.

Bartoshuk, L. M., & Beauchamp, G. K. (1994). Chemical senses. *Annual Review of Psychology, 45,* 419–449.

Bascom, P. B., & Tolle, S. W. (2002). Responding to requests for physician-assisted suicide: "These are uncharted waters for both of us. . . ." *Journal of the American Medical Association, 288,* 91–98.

Bashore, T. R., Ridderinkhof, F., & van der Molen, M. W. (1998). The decline of cognitive processing speed in old age. *Current Directions in Psychological Science, 6,* 163–169.

Bassuk, E. L. (1991). Homeless families. *Scientific American, 265*(6), 66–74.

Bates, E., Bretherton, I., & Snyder, L. (1988). *From first words to grammar: Individual differences and dissociable mechanisms.* New York: Cambridge University Press.

Bates, E., O'Connell, B., & Shore, C. (1987). Language and communication in infancy. In

J. D. Osofsky (Ed.), *Handbook of infant development* (2nd ed.). New York: Wiley.

Bateson, M. C. (1984). *With a daughter's eye: A memoir of Margaret Mead and Gregory Bateson.* New York: William Morrow & Co.

Bauer, J. J., & McAdams, D. P. (2004). Growth goals, maturity, and well-being. *Developmental Psychology, 40,* 114–127.

Bauer, J. J., McAdams, D. P., & Sakaeda, A. R. (2005). Interpreting the good life: Growth memories in the lives of mature, happy people. *JPSP, 88,* 203–217.

Bauer, P. J. (1996). What do infants recall of their lives? Memory for specific events by 1- to 2-year-olds. *American Psychologist, 51,* 29–41.

Bauer, P. J. (2002). Long-term recall memory: Behavioral and neuro-developmental changes in the first 2 years of life. *Current Directions in Psychological Science, 11,* 137–141.

Bauer, P. J., Wenner, J. A., Dropik, P. L., & Wewerka, S. S. (2000). Parameters of remembering and forgetting in the transition from infancy to early childhood. *Monographs of the Society for Research in Child Development,* Serial No. 263, *65*(4). Malden, MA: Blackwell Publishers.

Bauer, P. J., Wiebe, S. A., Carver, L. J., Waters, J. M., & Nelson, C. A. (2003). Developments in long-term explicit memory late in the first year of life: Behavioral and electrophysiological indices. *Psychological Science, 14,* 629–635.

Baum, A., Cacioppo, J. T., Melamed, B. G., Gallant, S. J., & Travis, C. (1995). *Doing the right thing: A research plan for healthy living.* Washington, DC: American Psychological Association Science Directorate.

Baumer, E. P., & South, S. J. (2001). Community effects on youth sexual activity. *Journal of Marriage and the Family, 63,* 540–554.

Baumrind, D. (1971). Harmonious parents and their preschool children. *Developmental Psychology, 41,* 92–102.

Baumrind, D. (1989). Rearing competent children. In W. Damon (Ed.), *Child development today and tomorrow* (pp. 349–378). San Francisco: Jossey-Bass.

Baumrind, D. (1991). Parenting styles and adolescent development. In J. Brooks-Gunn, R. Lerner, & A. C. Peterson (Eds.), *The encyclopedia of adolescence* (pp. 746–758). New York: Garland.

Baumrind, D. (1996a). A blanket injunction against disciplinary use of spanking is not warranted by the data. *Pediatrics, 88,* 828–831.

Baumrind, D. (1996b). The discipline controversy revisited. *Family Relations, 45,* 405–414.

Baumrind, D., & Black, A. E. (1967). Socialization practices associated with dimensions of competence in preschool boys and girls. *Child Development, 38,* 291–327.

Baumrind, D., Larzelere, R. E., & Cowan, P. A. (2002). Ordinary physical punishment: Is it harmful? Comment on Gershoff (2002). *Psychological Bulletin, 128,* 580–589.

Bauserman, R. (2002). Child adjustment in joint-custody versus sole-custody arrangements: A meta-analytic review. *Journal of Family Psychology, 16,* 91–102.

Bayley, N. (1969). *Bayley Scales of Infant Development.* New York: Psychological Corporation.

Bayley, N. (1993). *Bayley Scales of Infant Development: II.* New York: Psychological Corporation.

Bayley, N. (2005). *Bayley Scales of Infant Development, Third Ed.* (Bayley-III). New York: Harcourt Brace.

Beall, A. E., & Sternberg, R. J. (1995). The social construction of love. *Journal of Social and Personal Relationships, 12*(3), 417–438.

Bearman, P. S., & Bruckner, H. (2001). Promising the future: Virginity pledges and first intercourse. *American Journal of Sociology, 106,* 859–913.

Bearman, P. S., & Moody, J. (2004). Suicide and friendships among American adolescents. *American Journal of Public Health, 94,* 89–95.

Becker, A. E., Grinspoon, S. K., Klibanski, A., & Herzog, D. B. (1999). Eating disorders. *New England Journal of Medicine, 340,* 1092–1098.

Becker, G. S. (1991). *A treatise on the family* (enlarged ed.). Cambridge, MA: Harvard University Press.

Becker, P. E., & Moen, P. (1999). Scaling back: Dual-earner couples' work-family strategies. *Journal of Marriage and the Family, 61,* 995–1007.

Bedford, V. H. (1995). Sibling relationships in middle and old age. In R. Blieszner & V. Hilkevitch (Eds.), *Handbook of aging and the family* (pp. 201–222). Westport, CT: Greenwood Press.

Behrman, R. E. (1992). *Nelson textbook of pediatrics* (13th ed.). Philadelphia: Saunders.

Beidel, D. C., & Turner, S. M. (1998). *Shy children, phobic adults: Nature and treatment of social phobia.* Washington, DC: American Psychological Association.

Bekedam, D. J., Engelsbe1, S., Mol, B. W., Buitendijk, S. E., & van der Pal-de Bruin, K. M. (2002). Male predominance in fetal distress during labor. *American Journal of Obstetrics and Gynecology, 187,* 1605–1607.

Belbin, R. M. (1967). Middle age: What happens to ability? In R. Owen (Ed.), *Middle age.* London: BBC.

Belgium legalises euthanasia. (2002, May 16). BBC-News online. Available: http://www.nvve.nl [Web site of the Dutch Voluntary Euthanasia Society].

Belizzi, M. (2002, May). *Obesity in children— What kind of future are we creating?* Presentation at the Fifty-Fifth World Health Assembly Technical Briefing, Geneva.

Bell, M. A., & Fox, N. A. (1992). The relations between frontal brain electrical activity and cognitive development during infancy. *Child Development, 63,* 1142–1163.

Bellafante, G. (2005, May 8). Even in gay circles, the women want the ring. *New York Times,* Section 9, pp. 1, 7.

Bellinger, D. (2004). Lead. *Pediatrics, 113,* 1016–1022.

Belsky, J. (1993). Etiology of child maltreatment: A developmental-ecological analysis. *Psychological Bulletin, 114,* 413–434.

Belsky, J., Fish, M., & Isabella, R. (1991). Continuity and discontinuity in infant negative and positive emotionality: Family antecedents and attachment consequences. *Developmental Psychology, 27,* 421–431.

Belsky, J., Jaffee, S. R., Caspi, A., Moffitt, T., & Silva, P. A. (2003). Intergenerational relationships in young adulthood and their life course, mental health, and personality correlates. *Journal of Family Psychology, 17,* 460–471.

Belsky, J., Jaffee, S., Hsieh, K., & Silva, P. A. (2001). Childrearing antecedents of intergenerational relations in young adulthood: A prospective study. *Developmental Psychology, 37,* 801–814.

Bem, S. L. (1983). Gender schema theory and its implications for child development: Raising gender-aschematic children in a gender-schematic society. *Signs, 8,* 598–616.

Bem, S. L. (1985). Androgyny and gender schema theory: A conceptual and empirical integration. In T. B. Sondregger (Ed.), *Nebraska Symposium on Motivation, 1984: Psychology and gender.* Lincoln: University of Nebraska Press.

Bem, S. L. (1993). *The lenses of gender: Transforming the debate on sexual inequality.* New Haven, CT: Yale University Press.

Benenson, J. F. (1993). Greater preference among females than males for dyadic interaction in early childhood. *Child Development, 64,* 544–555.

Benes, F. M., Turtle, M., Khan, Y., & Farol, P. (1994). Myelination of a key relay zone in the hippocampal formation occurs in the human brain during childhood, adolescence, and adulthood. *Archives of General Psychiatry, 51,* 447–484.

Bengtson, V. L. (2001). Beyond the nuclear family: The increasing importance of multigenerational bonds. *Journal of Marriage and Family, 63,* 1–16.

Bengtson, V. L., Rosenthal, C., & Burton, L. (1996). Paradoxes of families and aging. In R. H. Binstock & L. K. George (Eds.), *Handbook of aging and the social sciences* (pp. 253–282). San Diego: Academic Press.

Bengtson, V. L., Rosenthal, C. J., & Burton, L. M. (1990). Families and aging: Diversity and heterogeneity. In R. Binstock & L. George (Eds.), *Handbook of aging and the social sciences* (pp. 263–287). San Diego: Academic Press.

Benloucif, S., Orbeta, L., Ortiz, R., Janssen, I., Finkel, S. I., Bleiberg, J., & Zee, P. C. (2004). Morning or evening activity improves neuropsychological performance and subjective sleep quality in older adults. *Sleep, 27,* 1542–1551.

Benloucif, S., Zee, P. C., Orbeta, L., Ortiz, R., Janssen, I., Finkel, S., & Bleiberg, J. (2005). Nonagenarians and centarians in Switzerland, 1860–2001: A demographic analysis. *Journal of Epidemiology and Community Health, 59,* 31–37.

Benson, E. (2003). Intelligent intelligence testing. *Monitor on Psychology, 43*(2), 48–51.

Ben-Ze'ev A. (1997). Emotions and morality. *Journal of Value Inquiry, 31,* 195–212.

Berg, C. A., & Klaczynski, P. A. (1996). Practical intelligence and problem solving: Search for perspectives. In F. Blanchard-Fields & T. M. Hess (Eds.), *Perspectives on cognitive change in adulthood and aging* (pp. 323–357). New York: McGraw-Hill.

Bergeman, C. S., & Plomin, R. (1989). Genotype-environment interaction. In M. Bornstein & J. Bruner (Eds.), *Interaction in human development* (pp. 157–171). Hillsdale, NJ: Erlbaum.

Bergen, D. (2002). The role of pretend play in children's cognitive development. *Early Childhood Research & Practice, 4*(1). [Online]. Available: http://ecrp.uiuc.edu/v4n1/bergen.html.

Bergen, D., Reid, R., & Torelli, L. (2000). *Educating and caring for very young children: The infant-toddler curriculum*. Washington, DC: National Association for the Education of Young Children.

Berger, R. M., & Kelly, J. J. (1986). Working with homosexuals of the older population. *Social Casework, 67,* 203–210.

Bergman, I., & Burgess, A. (1980). *Ingrid Bergman: My story*. New York: Delacorte.

Bering, J. M., & Bjorklund, D. F. (2004). The natural emergence of reasoning ability about the afterlife as a developmental regularity. *Developmental Psychology, 40,* 217–233.

Berk, L. E. (1986a). Development of private speech among preschool children. *Early Child Development and Care, 24,* 113–136.

Berk, L. E. (1986b). Private speech: Learning out loud. *Psychology Today, 20*(5), 34–42.

Berk, L. E. (1992). Children's private speech: An overview of theory and the status of research. In R. M. Diaz & L. E. Berk (Eds.), *Private speech: From social interaction to self-regulation* (pp. 17–53). Hillsdale, NJ: Erlbaum.

Berk, L. E., & Garvin, R. A. (1984). Development of private speech among low-income Appalachian children. *Developmental Psychology, 20,* 271–286.

Berkman, L. F., & Glass, T. (2000). Social integration, social networks, social support, and health. In L. F. Berkman & I. Kawachi (Eds.), *Social epidemiology* (pp. 137–173). New York: Oxford University Press.

Berkowitz, G. S., Skovron, M. L., Lapinski, R. H., & Berkowitz, R. L. (1990). Delayed childbearing and the outcome of pregnancy. *New England Journal of Medicine, 322,* 659–664.

Berkowitz, R. I., Stallings, V. A., Maislin, G., & Stunkard, A. J. (2005). Growth of children at high risk of obesity during the first 6 y of life: Implications for prevention. *American Journal of Clinical Nutrition, 81,* 140–146.

Berkowitz, R. I., Wadden, T. A., Tershakovec, A. M., & Cronquist, J. L. (2003). Behavior therapy and sibutramine for the treatment of adolescent obesity: A randomized controlled trial. *Journal of the American Medical Association, 289,* 1805–1812.

Bernard, B. P. (Ed.). (1997). *Musculoskeletal disorders and workplace factors: A critical review of epidemiologic evidence for work-related musculoskeletal disorders of the neck, upper extremity, and low back*. Cincinnati, OH: National Institute for Occupational Safety and Health.

Berndt, T. J., & Perry, T. B. (1990). Distinctive features and effects of early adolescent friendships. In R. Montemayor, G. R. Adams, & T. P.

Gullotta (Eds.), *From childhood to adolescence: A transitional period?* Newbury Park, CA: Sage.

Bernhardt, P. C. (1997). Influences of serotonin and testosterone in aggression and dominance: Convergence with social psychology. *Current Directions in Psychological Science, 6,* 44–48.

Bernstein, A. M., Willcox, B. J., Tamaki, H., Kunishima, N., Suzuki, M., Willcox, D. C., Yoo, J. K., & Perls, T. T. (2004). First autopsy study of an Okinawan centenarian: Absence of many age-related diseases. *Journal of Gerontology: Medical Sciences, 59A,* 1195–1199.

Bernstein, N. (2004, March 7). Behind fall in pregnancy, a new teenage culture of restraint. *New York Times,* pp. 1, 36–37.

Berrick, J. D. (1998). When children cannot remain home: Foster family care and kinship care. *The Future of Children, 8,* 72–87.

Berrueta-Clement, J. R., Schweinhart, L. J., Barnett, W. S., & Weikart, D. P. (1987). The effects of early educational intervention on crime and delinquency in adolescence and early adulthood. In J. D. Burchard & S. N. Burchard (Eds.), *Primary prevention of psychopathology: Vol. 10. Prevention of delinquent behavior* (pp. 220–240). Newbury Park, CA: Sage.

Berrueta-Clement, J. R., Schweinhart, L. J., Barnett, W. S., Epstein, A. S., & Weikart, D. P. (1985). *Changed lives: The effects of the Perry Preschool Program on youths through age 19*. Ypsilanti, MI: High/Scope.

Berry, M., Dylla, D. J., Barth, R. P., & Needell, B. (1998). The role of open adoption in the adjustment of adopted children and their families. *Children and Youth Services Review, 20,* 151–171.

Berry, N., Jobanputra, V., & Pal, H. (2003). Molecular genetics of schizophrenia: A critical review. *Journal of Psychiatry and Neuroscience, 28,* 415–429.

Berry, R. J., Li, Z., Erickson, J. D., Li, S., Moore, C. A., Wang, H., Mulinare, J., Zhao, P., Wong, L.-Y. C., Gindler, J., Hong, S.-X., & Correa, A. for the China-U.S. Collaborative Project for Neural Tube Defect Prevention. (1999). Prevention of neural-tube defects with folic acid in China. *New England Journal of Medicine, 341,* 1485–1490.

Bertenthal, B. I., & Campos, J. J. (1987). New directions in the study of early experience. *Child Development, 58,* 560–567.

Bertenthal, B. I., Campos, J. J., & Barrett, K. C. (1984). Self-produced locomotion: An organizer of emotional, cognitive, and social development in infancy. In R. N. Emde & R. J. Harmon (Eds.), *Continuities and discontinuities in development*. New York: Plenum.

Bertenthal, B. I., Campos, J. J., & Kermoian, R. (1994). An epigenetic perspective on the development of self-produced locomotion and its consequences. *Current Directions in Psychological Science, 3*(5), 140–145.

Bertenthal, B. I., & Clifton, R. K. (1998). Perception and action. In W. Damon (Ed.-in-Chief) & D. Kuhn & R. S. Siegler (Vol. Eds.), *Handbook of child psychology, Vol. 2: Cognition, perception, and language* (pp. 51–102). New York: Wiley.

Bertram, L., Hiltunen, M., Parkinson, M., Ingelsson, M., Lange, C., Ramasamy, K., Mullin, K., Menon, R., Sampson, A. J., Hsiao, M., Elliott, K. J., Velicelebi, G., Moscarillo, T., Hyman, B. T., Wagner, S. L., Becker, K. D., Blacker, D., & Tanzi, R. E. (2005). Family-based association between Alzheimer's disease and variants in *UBQLN1*. *New England Journal of Medicine, 352,* 884–894.

Bespalova, I. N., & Buxbaum, J. D. (2003). Disease susceptibility genes for autism. *Annals of Medicine, 35,* 274–281.

Bethell, T. N. (2005, April). What's the big idea? There's more than one solution for Social Security. Here are nine ways to keep the system solvent. *AARP Bulletin,* pp. 22–26.

Beumont, P. J. V., Russell, J. D., & Touyz, S. W. (1993). Treatment of anorexia nervosa. *The Lancet, 341,* 1635–1640.

Beversdorf, D. Q., Manning, S. E., Anderson, S. L., Nordgren, R. E., Walters, S. E., Cooley, W. C., Gaelic, S. E., & Bauman, M. L., (2001, November 10–15). *Timing of prenatal stressors and autism*. Presentation at the 31st Annual Meeting of the Society for Neuroscience, San Diego.

Beyene, Y. (1986). Cultural significance and physiological manifestations of menopause: A biocultural analysis. *Culture, Medicine, and Psychiatry, 10,* 47–71.

Beyene, Y. (1989). *From menarche to menopause: Reproductive lives of peasant women in two cultures*. Albany: State University of New York Press.

Beyette, B. (1998, November 29). Carter keeps zest for life. *Chicago Sun-Times,* pp. A6–A7.

Bialystok, E., Craik, F. I. M., Klein, R., & Viswanathan, M. (2004). Bilingualism, aging, and cognitive control: Evidence from the Simon task. *Psychology and Aging, 19,* 290–303.

Bialystok, E., & Senman, L. (2004). Executive processes in appearance-reality tasks: The role of inhibition of attention and symbolic representation. *Child Development, 75,* 562–579.

Biason-Lauber, A., Konrad, D., Navratil, F., and Schoenle, E. J. (2004). A WNT4 mutation associated with Mullerian-duct regression and virilization in a 46, XX woman. *New England Journal of Medicine, 351,* 792–798.

Biegel, D. E. (1995). Caregiver burden. In G. E. Maddox (Ed.), *The encyclopedia of aging* (2nd ed., pp. 138–141). New York: Springer.

Bielby, D., & Papalia, D. (1975). Moral development and perceptual role-taking egocentrism: Their development and interrelationship across the lifespan. *International Journal of Aging and Human Development, 6*(4), 293–308.

Bienvenu. O. J., Nestadt, G., Samuels, J. F., Costa, P. T., Howard, W. T., & Eaton, W. W. (2001). Phobic, panic, and major depressive disorders and the five-factor model of personality. *Journal of Mental Diseases, 189,* 154–161.

Bierman, K. L., Smoot, D. L., & Aumiller, K. (1993). Characteristics of aggressive-rejected, aggressive (non-rejected), and rejected (nonaggressive) boys. *Child Development, 64,* 139–151.

Billet, S. (2001). Knowing in practice: Reconceptualising vocational expertise. *Learning & Instruction, 11,* 431–452.

Binstock, G. & Thornton, A. (2003). Separations, reconciliations, and living apart in cohabiting and marital units. *Journal of Marriage and Family, 65,* 432–443.

Binstock, R. H. (2004). Anti-aging medicine and research: A realm of conflict and profound societal implications. *Journal of Gerontology: Biological Sciences, 59A,* 523–533.

Birch, E. E., Garfield, S., Hoffman, D. R., Uauy, R. Birch, D. G. (2000). A randomized controlled trial of early dietary supply of long-chain polyunsaturated fatty acids and mental development in term infants. *Developmental Medicine & Child Neurology, 42,* 174–181.

Bird, K. (1990, November 12). The very model of an ex-president. *The Nation,* pp. 545, 560–564.

Bird, T. D. (2005). Genetic factors in Alzheimer's disease. *New England Journal of Medicine, 352,* 862–864.

Birmaher, B. (1998). Should we use antidepressant medications for children and adolescents with depressive disorders? *Psychopharmacology Bulletin, 34,* 35–39.

Birmaher, B., Ryan, N. D., Williamson, D. E., Brent, D. A., Kaufman, J., Dahl, R. E., Perel, J., & Nelson, B. (1996). Childhood and adolescent depression: A review of the past 10 years. *Journal of the American Academy of Child, 35,* 1427–1440.

Birren, J. E., Woods, A. M., & Williams, M. V. (1980). Behavioral slowing with age: Causes, organization, and consequences. In L. W. Poon (Ed.), *Aging in the 1980s.* Washington, DC: American Psychological Association.

Bishop, D. V. M., Price, T. S., Dale, P. S., & Plomin, R. (2003). Outcome of early language delay: II. Etiology of transient and persistent language difficulties. *Journal of Speech, Language, and Hearing Research, 46,* 561–575.

Bjork, J. M., Knutson, B., Fong, G. W., Caggiano, D. M., Bennett, S. M., & Hommer, D. W. (2004). Incentive-elicited brain activities in adolescents: Similarities and differences from young adults. *The Journal of Neuroscience, 24,* 1793–1802.

Bjorklund, D. F. (1997). The role of immaturity in human development. *Psychological Bulletin, 122,* 153–169.

Bjorklund, D. F., & Harnishfeger, K. K. (1990). The resources construct in cognitive development: Diverse sources of evidence and a theory of inefficient inhibition. *Developmental Review, 10,* 48–71.

Bjorklund, D. F., & Pellegrini, A. D. (2000). Child development and evolutionary psychology. *Child Development, 71*(6), 1687–1708.

Bjorklund, D. F., & Pellegrini, A. D. (2002). *The origins of human nature: Evolutionary developmental psychology.* Washington, DC: American Psychological Association.

Black, J. E. (1998). How a child builds its brain: Some lessons from animal studies of neural plasticity. *Preventive Medicine, 27,* 168–171.

Black, M. M., & Krishnakumar, A. (1998). Children in low-income, urban settings: Interventions to promote mental health and well-being. *American Psychologist, 53,* 636–646.

Black, R. E., Morris, S. S., & Bryce, J. (2003). Where and why are 10 million children dying each year? *The Lancet, 361,* 2226–2234.

Blackburn, J. A., Papalia-Finlay, D., Foye, B. F., & Serlin, R. C. (1988). Modifiability of figural relations performance among elderly adults. *Journal of Gerontology: Psychological Sciences, 43*(3), P87–89.

Blackman, A. (1998). *The seasons of her life: A biography of Madeleine Korbel Albright.* New York: Scribner.

Blagrove, M., Alexander, C., & Horne, J. A. (1995). The effects of chronic sleep reduction on the performance of cognitive tasks sensitive to sleep deprivation. *Applied Cognitive Psychology, 9,* 21–40.

Blair, C. (2002). School readiness: Integrating cognition and emotion in a neurobiological conceptualization of children's functioning at school entry. *American Psychologist, 57,* 111–127.

Blake, S. M., Ledsky, R., Goodenow, C., Sawyer, R., Lohrmann, D., & Windsor, R. (2003). Condom availability programs in Massachusetts high schools: Relationships with condom use and sexual behavior. *American Journal of Public Health, 93,* 955–962.

Blanchard-Fields, F., & Camp, C. J. (1990). Affect, individual differences, and real world problem solving across the adult life span. In T. Hess (Ed.), *Aging and cognition: Knowledge organization and utilization* (pp. 461–498). Amsterdam: North-Holland, Elsevier.

Blanchard-Fields, F., & Irion, J. (1987). Coping strategies from the perspective of two developmental markers: Age and social reasoning. *Journal of Genetic Psychology, 149,* 141–151.

Blanchard-Fields, F., & Norris, L. (1994). Causal attributions from adolescence through adulthood: Age differences, ego level, and generalized response style. *Aging and Cognition, 1,* 67–86.

Blanchard-Fields, F., Chen, Y., & Norris, L. (1997). Everyday problem solving across the adult life span: Influence of domain specificity and cognitive appraisal. *Psychology and Aging, 12,* 684–693.

Blanchard-Fields, F., Jahnke, H. C., & Camp, C. J. (1995). Age differences in problem solving style: The role of emotional salience. *Psychology and Aging, 10,* 173–180.

Blanchard-Fields, F., Stein, R., & Watson, T. L. (2004). Age differences in emotion-regulation strategies in handling everyday problems. *Journal of Gerontology: Psychological Sciences, 59B,* P261–P269.

Blieszner, R., Willis, S. L., & Baltes, P. B. (1981). Training research on induction ability: A short-term longitudinal study. *Journal of Applied Developmental Psychology, 2,* 247–265.

Block, J. (1971). *Lives through time.* Berkeley, CA: Bancroft.

Block, J. (1995a). A contrarian view of the Five-Factor approach to personality description. *Psychological Bulletin, 117,* 187–215.

Block, J. (1995b). Going beyond the five factors given: Rejoinder to Costa and McCrae (1995) and Goldberg and Saucier (1995). *Psychological Bulletin, 117,* 226–229.

Blood, M. R., & Rogers, J. (2004, June 10). Remembering Reagan: Confusion mixed with smiles in last years: Couldn't finish his jokes, but friends didn't mind. *Chicago Sun-Times,* p. 12.

Blood, T. (1997). *Madam secretary: A biography of Madeleine Albright.* New York: St. Martin's.

Bloom, B., Cohen, R. A., Vickerie, J. L., & Wondimu, E. A. (2003). Summary health statistics for U.S. children: National Health Interview Survey, 2001. *Vital and Health Statistics, 10*(216). Hyattsville, MD: National Center for Health Statistics.

Bloom, H. (Ed.). (1999). *A scholarly look at The Diary of Anne Frank.* Philadelphia: Chelsea.

Blum, N. J., Taubman, B., & Nemeth, N. (2003). Relationship between age at initiation of toilet training and duration of training: A prospective study. *Pediatrics, 111,* 810–814.

Blumenthal, J. A., Emery, C. F., Madden, D. J., Schniebolk, S., Walsh-Riddle, M., George, L. K., McKee, D. C., Higginbotham, M. B., Cobb, F. R., & Coleman, R. E. (1991). Long-term effects of exercise on psychological functioning in older men and women. *Journal of Gerontology, 46*(6), P352–361.

Boatman, D., Freeman, J., Vining, E., Pulsifer, M., Miglioretti, D., Minahan, R., Carson, B., Brandt, J., & McKhann, G. (1999). Language recovery after left hemispherectomy in children with late onset seizures. *Annals of Neurology, 46*(4), 579–586.

Bodkin, N. L., Alexander, T. M., Ortmeyer, H. K., Johnson, E., & Hansen, B. C. (2003). Mortality and morbidity in laboratory-maintained rhesus monkeys and effects of long-term dietary restriction. *Journal of Gerontology: Biological Sciences, 58A,* 212-219.

Bodrova, E., & Leong, D. J. (1998). Adult influences on play: The Vygotskian approach. In D. P. Fromberg & D. Bergen (Eds.), *Play from birth to twelve and beyond: Contexts, perspectives, and meanings* (pp. 277–282). New York: Garland.

Boerner, K., Schulz, R., & Horowitz, A. (2004). Positive aspects of caregiving and adaptation to bereavement. *Psychology and Aging, 19,* 668–675.

Boerner, K., Wortman, C. B., & Bonanno, G. A. (2005). Resilient or at risk? A 4-year study of older adults who initially showed high or low distress following conjugal loss. *Journal of Gerontology: Psychological Sciences, 60B,* P67–P73.

Bogg, T., & Roberts, B. W. (2004). Conscientiousness and health-related behaviors: A meta-analysis of the leading behavioral contributors to mortality. *Psychological Bulletin, 130,* 887–919.

Bograd, R., & Spilka, B. (1996). Self-disclosure and marital satisfaction in mid-life and latelife remarriages. *International Journal of Aging and Human Development, 42*(3), 161–172.

Bojczyk, K. E., & Corbetta, D. (2004). Object retrieval in the 1st year of life: Learning effects of task exposure and box transparency. *Developmental Psychology, 40,* 54–66.

Bolger, K. E., Patterson, C. J., Thompson, W. W., & Kupersmidt, J. B. (1995). Psychosocial adjustment among children experiencing persistent and intermittent family economic hardship. *Child Development, 66*, 1107–1129.

Bolla, K. I., Cadet, J. L., & London, E. D. (1998). The neuropsychiatry of chronic cocaine abuse. *Journal of Neuropsychiatry and Clinical Neuroscience, 10*, 280–289.

Bolla, K. I., Rothman, R., & Cadet, J. L. (1999). Dose-related neurobehavioral effects of chronic cocaine use. *Journal of Neuropsychiatry & Clinical Neurosciences, 11*, 361–369.

Bollinger, M. B. (2003). Involuntary smoking and asthma severity in children: Data from the Third National Health and Nutrition Examination Survey (NHANES III). *Pediatrics, 112*, 471.

Bonanno, G. A., Wortman, C. B., & Nesse, R. M. (2004). Prospective patterns of resilience and maladjustment during widowhood. *Psychology and Aging, 19*, 260–271.

Bonanno, G. A., Wortman, C. B., Lehman, D. R., Tweed, R. G., Haring, M., Sonnega, J., Carr, D., & Nesse, R. M. (2002). Resilience to loss and chronic grief: A prospective study from preloss to 18-month postloss. *Journal of Personality and Social Psychology*, 1150–1164.

Bond, C. A. (1989, September). A child prodigy from China wields a magical brush. *Smithsonian*, pp. 70–79.

Bonham, V. L., Warshauer-Baker, E., & Collins, F. S. (2005). Race and ethnicity in the genome era. *American Psychologist, 60*, 9–15.

Book, A. S., Starzyk, K. B., & Quinsey, V. L. (2001, November-December). The relationship between testosterone and aggression: A meta-analysis. *Aggression and Violent Behavior, 6*, 579–599.

Boosting brittle bones. (2004, May). *HealthNews*, p. 8.

Booth, A. E., & Waxman, S. (2002). Object names and object functions serve as cues to categories for infants. *Developmental Psychology, 38*, 948–957.

Booth-Kewley, S., Minagawa, R. Y., Shaffer, R. A., & Brodine, S. K. (2002). A behavioral intervention to prevent sexually transmitted diseases/human immunodeficiency virus in a Marine Corps sample. *Military Medicine, 167*, 145–150.

Borman G., Boulay, M., Kaplan, J., Rachuba, L., & Hewes, G. (1999, December 13). *Evaluating the long-term impact of multiple summer interventions on the reading skills of low-income, early-elementary students.* Preliminary report, Year 1. Center for Social Organization of Schools, Johns Hopkins University.

Bornstein, M., Kessen, W., & Weiskopf, S. (1976). The categories of hue in infancy. *Science, 191*, 201–202.

Bornstein, M. H. & Cote, L. R. with Maital, S., Painter, K., Park, S. Y., Pascual, L., Pecheux, M. G., Ruel, J., Venuti, P., and Vyt, A. (2004). Cross-linguistic analysis of vocabulary in young children: Spanish, Dutch, French, Hebrew, Italian, Korean, and American English. *Child Development, 75*, 1115–1139.

Bornstein, M. H., Haynes, O. M., O'Reilly, A. W., & Painter, K. (1996). Solitary and collaborative pretense play in early childhood: Sources of individual variation in the development of representational competence. *Child Development, 67*, 2910–2929.

Bornstein, M. H., Haynes, O. M., Pascual, L., Painter, K. M., & Galperin, C. (1999). Play in two societies: Pervasiveness of process, specificity of structure. *Child Development, 70*, 317–331.

Bornstein, M. H., & Sigman, M. D. (1986). Continuity in mental development from infancy. *Child Development, 57*, 251–274.

Bornstein, M. H., & Tamis-LeMonda, C. S. (1994). Antecedents of information processing skills in infants: Habituation, novelty responsiveness, and cross-modal transfer. *Infant Behavior and Development, 17*, 371–380.

Bornstein, M. H., Tamis-LeMonda, C. S., & Haynes, O. M. (1999). First words in the second year: Continuity, stability, and models of concurrent and predictive correspondence in vocabulary and verbal responsiveness across age and context. *Infant Behavior and Development, 22*, 65–85.

Borowsky, I. A., Ireland, M., & Resnick, M. D. (2001). Adolescent suicide attempts: Risks and protectors. *Pediatrics, 107*(3), 485–493.

Bortfield, H., Morgan, J. L., Golinkoff, R. M., & Rathbun, K. (2005). Mommy and me: Familiar names help launch babies into speech-stream segmentation. *Psychological Science, 16*, 298-304.

Bortz, W. M., II, & Wallace, D. H., & Wiley, D. (1999). Sexual function in 1,202 aging males: Differentiating aspects. *The Journals of Gerontology: Series A. Biological Sciences and Medical Sciences, 54*, M237–M241.

Bosch, J., Sullivan, S., Van Dyke, D. C., Su, H., Klockau, L., Nissen, K., Blewer, K., Weber, E., & Eberly, S. S. (2003). Promoting a healthy tomorrow here for children adopted from abroad. *Contemporary Pediatrics, 20*(2), 69–86.

Bosma, H., Peter, R., Siegrist, J., & Marmot, M. (1998). Two alternative job stress models and the risk of coronary heart disease. *American Journal of Public Health, 88*, 68–74.

Boss, P. (1999). *Ambiguous loss: Learning to live with unresolved grief.* Cambridge, MA: Harvard University Press.

Boss, P. (2004). Ambiguous loss research, theory, and practice: Reflections after 9/11. *Journal of Marriage and Family, 66*, 551–566.

Boss, P. G. (2002). Ambiguous loss: Working with families of the missing. *Family Processes, 41*, 14–17.

Boss, P., Beaulieu, L., Wieling, E., Turner, W., & LaCruz, S. (2003). Healing loss, ambiguity, and trauma: A community-based intervention with families of union workers missing after the 9/11 attacks in New York City. *Journal of Marital and Family Therapy, 29*, 455–467.

Bossé, R., Aldwin, C. M., Levenson, M. R., Spiro, A., & Mroczek, D. K. (1993). Change in social support after retirement: Longitudinal findings from the normative aging study. *Journal of Gerontology: Psychological Sciences, 48*, P210–217.

Bosshard, G., Nilstun, T., Bilsen, J., Norup, M., Miccinesi, G., vanDelden, J. J. M, Faisst, K., van der Heide, A., for the European End-of-Life (EURELD) Consortium. (2005). Forgoing treatment at the end of life in 6 European countries. *Archives of Internal Medicine, 165*, 401–407.

Bosworth, H. B., & Schaie, K. W. (1997). The relationship of social environment, social networks, and health outcomes in the Seattle Longitudinal Study: Two analytical approaches. *Journals of Gerontology: Psychological Sciences, 52B*, P197–P205.

Botwinick, J. (1984). *Aging and behavior* (3rd ed.). New York: Springer.

Bouchard, T. J. (1994). Genes, environment, and personality. *Science, 264*, 1700–1701.

Bouchard, T. J. (2004). Genetic influence on human psychological traits: A survey. *Current Directions in Psychological Science, 13*, 148–154.

Bouchey, H. A. & Furman, W. (2003). Dating and romantic experiences in adolescence. In G. R. Adams and M.D. Berzonsky. (eds.). *Blackwell handbook of adolescence* (pp. 313–329).

Boulé, N. G., Haddad, E., Kenny, G. P., Wells, G. A., & Sigal, R. J. (2001). Effects of exercise on glycemic control and body mass in type 2 diabetes mellitus: A meta-analysis of controlled clinical trials. *Journal of the American Medical Association, 286*, 1218–1227.

Boulton, M. J. (1995). Playground behaviour and peer interaction patterns of primary school boys classified as bullies, victims and not involved. *British Journal of Educational Psychology, 65*, 165–177.

Boulton, M. J., & Smith, P. K. (1994). Bully/victim problems in middle-school children: Stability, self-perceived competence, peer perception, and peer acceptance. *British Journal of Developmental Psychology, 12*, 315–329.

Boutin, P., Dina, C., Vasseur, F., Dubois, S. S., Corset, L., Seron, K., Bekris, L., Cabellon, J., Neve, B., Vasseur-Delannoy, V., Chikri, M., Charles, M. A., Clement, K., Lernmark, A., & Froguel, P. (2003). GAD2 on chromosome 10p12 is a candidate gene for human obesity. *Public Library of Science Biology, 1*(3), E68.

Bower, B. (1993). A child's theory of mind. *Science News, 144*, 40–42.

Bowlby, J. (1951). Maternal care and mental health. *Bulletin of the World Health Organization, 3*, 355–534.

Bowman, S. A., Gortmaker, S. L., Ebbeling, C. B., Pereira, M. A., Ludwig, D. S. (2004). Effects of fast food consumption on energy intake and diet quality among children in a national household survey. *Pediatrics, 113*, 112–118.

Boyles, S. (2002, January 27). Toxic landfills may boost birth defects. *WebMD Medical News*. [Online].

Brabant, S. (1994). An overlooked AIDS affected population: The elderly parent as caregiver. *Journal of Gerontological Social Work, 22*, 131–145.

Brabeck, M. M., & Shore, E. L. (2003). Gender differences in intellectual and moral development? The evidence refutes the claims. In

J. Demick and C. Andreoletti (eds.). *Handbook of adult development*. NY: Plenum Press.

Bracher, G., & Santow, M. (1999). Explaining trends in teenage childbearing in Sweden. *Studies in Family Planning, 30,* 169–182.

Bradford, J., & Ryan, C. (1991). Who are we: Health concerns of middle-aged lesbians. In J. W. B. Sang & A. Smith (Eds.), *Lesbians at midlife: The creative transition* (pp. 147–163). San Francisco: Spinsters.

Bradley, R. H. (1989). Home measurement of maternal responsiveness. In M. H. Bornstein (Ed.), *Maternal responsiveness: Characteristics and consequences* (New Directions for Child Development No. 43). San Francisco: Jossey-Bass.

Bradley, R. H., Corwyn, R. F., Burchinal, M., McAdoo, H. P., & Coll, C. G. (2001). The home environment of children in the United States: Part II: Relations with behavioral development through age thirteen. *Child Development, 72*(6), 1868–1886.

Bradley, R. H., Corwyn, R. F., McAdoo, H. P., & Coll, C. G. (2001). The home environment of children in the United States: Part I: Variation by age, ethnicity, and poverty status. *Child Development, 72*(6), 1844–1867.

Braine, M. (1976). Children's first word combinations. *Monographs of the Society for Research in Child Development, 41*(1, Serial No. 164).

Brambati, S. M., Termine, C., Ruffino, M., Stella, G., Fazio, F., Cappa, S. F., & Perani, D. (2004). Regional reductions of gray matter volume in familial dyslexia. *Neurology, 63,* 742–745.

Bramlett, M. D., & Mosher, W. D. (2001). *First marriage dissolution, divorce, and remarriage: United States.* (Advance data from vital and health statistics, no. 323). Hyattsville, MD: National Center for Health Statistics.

Bramlett, M. D., & Mosher, W. D. (2002). Cohabitation, marriage, divorce, and remarriage in the United States. *Vital Health Statistics, 23*(22). Hyattsville, MD: National Center for Health Statistics.

Brandt, B. (1989). A place for her death. *Humanistic Judaism, 17*(3), 83–85.

Bratton, S. C., & Ray, D. (2002). Humanistic play therapy. In D. J. Cain (Ed.), *Humanistic psychotherapies: Handbook of research and practice* (pp. 369–402). Washington, DC: American Psychological Association.

Braungart, J. M., Plomin, R., DeFries, J. C., & Fulker, D. W. (1992). Genetic influence on tester-rated infant temperament as assessed by Bayley's Infant Behavior Record: Nonadoptive and adoptive siblings and twins. *Developmental Psychology, 28,* 40–47.

Braungart-Rieker, J., Garwood, M. M., Powers, B. P., & Notaro, P. C. (1998). Infant affect and affect regulation during the still-face paradigm with mothers and fathers: The role of infant characteristics and parental sensitivity. *Developmental Psychology, 34*(6), 1428–1437.

Braungart-Rieker, J. M., Garwood, M. M., Powers, B. P., & Wang, X. (2001). Parental sensitivity, infant affect, and affect regulation: Predictors of later attachment. *Child Development, 72,* 252–270.

Bray, J. H. (1991). Psychosocial factors affecting custodial and visitation arrangements. *Behavioral Sciences and the Law, 9,* 419–437.

Bray, J. H., & Hetherington, E. M. (1993). Families in transition: Introduction and overview. *Journal of Family Psychology, 7,* 3–8.

Brazelton, T. B. (1973). *Neonatal behavioral assessment scale.* Philadelphia: Lippincott.

Brazelton, T. B. (1984). *Neonatal Behavioral Assessment Scale.* Philadelphia: Lippincott.

Brazelton, T. B., & Nugent, J. K. (1995). The Neonatal Behavioral Assessment Scale. Cambridge: Mac Keith Press.

Breier, J. I., Simos, P. G., Fletcher, J. M., Castillo, E. M., Zhang, W., & Papanicolaou, A. C. (2003). Abnormal activation of temporoparietal language areas during phonetic analysis in children with dyslexia. *Neuropsychology, 17,* 610–621.

Bremner, W. J., Vitiello, M. V., & Prinz, P. N. (1983). Loss of circadian rhythmicity in blood testosterone levels with aging in normal men. *Journal of Clinical Endocrinology and Metabolism, 56,* 1278–1281.

Brener, N., Lowry, R., Kann, L., Kolbe, L., Lenhherr, J., Janssen, R., & Jaffe, H. (2002). Trends in sexual risk behaviors among high school students—United States, 1991–2001. *Morbidity and Mortality Weekly Report, 51*(38), 856–859.

Brenneman, K., Massey, C., Machado, S. F., & Gelman, R. (1996). Young children's plans differ for writing and drawing. *Cognitive Development, 11,* 397–419.

Brenner, M. H. (1991). Health, productivity, and the economic environment: Dynamic role of socio-economic status. In G. Green & F. Baker (Eds.), *Work, health, and productivity* (pp. 241–255). New York: Oxford University Press.

Brenner, R. A., Simons-Morton, B. G., Bhaskar, B., Revenis, M., Das, A., & Clemens, J. D. (2003). Infant-parent bed sharing in an inner-city population. *Archives of Pediatrics and Adolescent Medicine, 57,* 33–39.

Brent, D. A., & Birmaher, B. (2002). Adolescent depression. *New England Journal of Medicine, 347,* 667–671.

Brent, R. L. & Weitzman, M. (2004). The current state of knowledge about the effects, risks, and science of children's environmental exposures. *Pediatrics, 113,* 1158–1166.

Bretherton, I. (1990). Communication patterns, internal working models, and the intergenerational transmission of attachment relationships. *Infant Mental Health Journal, 11*(3), 237–252.

Bretherton, I. (Ed.). (1984). *Symbolic play: The development of social understanding.* Orlando, FL: Academic.

Brezina, T. (1999). Teenage violence toward parents as an adaptation to family strain: Evidence from a national survey of male adolescents. *Youth & Society, 30,* 416–444.

Brim, O. G., Ryff, C. D., & Kessler, R. C. (2004). The MIDUS National Survey: An overview. In O. G. Brim, C. D. Ryff, & R. C. Kessler (Eds.), *How healthy are we? A national study of well-being at midlife.* Chicago: University of Chicago Press.

Briss, P. A., Sacks, J. J., Addiss, D. G., Kresnow, M., & O'Neil, J. (1994). A nationwide study of the risk of injury associated with day care center attendance. *Pediatrics, 93,* 364–368.

Brock, D. W. (1992, March–April). Voluntary active euthanasia. *Hastings Center Report,* pp. 10–22.

Broder, M. S., Kanouse, D. E., Mittman, B. S., & Bernstein, S. J. (2000). The appropriateness of recommendations for hysterectomy. *Obstetrics & Gynecology, 95,* 199–205.

Brody, G. H. (1998). Sibling relationship quality: Its causes and consequences. *Annual Review of Psychology, 49,* 1–24.

Brody, G. H. (2004). Siblings' direct and indirect contributions to child development. *Current Directions in Psychological Science, 13,* 124–126.

Brody, G. H., Flor, D. L., & Gibson, N. M. (1999). Linking maternal efficacy beliefs, developmental goals, parenting practices, and child competence in rural single-parent African American families. *Child Development, 70*(5), 1197–1208.

Brody, G. H., Ge, X., Conger, R., Gibbons, F. X., Murry, V. M., Gerrard, M., and Simons, R. L. (2001). The influence of neighborhood disadvantage, collective socialization, and parenting on African American children's affiliation with deviant peers. *Child Development, 72*(4), 1231–1246.

Brody, G. H., Kim, S., Murry, V. M., & Brown, A. C. (2004). Protective longitudinal paths linking child competence to behavioral problems among African American siblings. *Child Development, 75,* 455–467.

Brody, G. H., Stoneman, Z., & Flor, D. (1995). Linking family processes and academic competence among rural African American youths. *Journal of Marriage and the Family, 57,* 567–579.

Brody, G. H., Stoneman, Z., & Gauger, K. (1996). Parent-child relationships, family problem-solving behavior, and sibling relationship quality: The moderating role of sibling temperaments. *Child Development, 67,* 1289–1300.

Brody, J. E. (1995, June 28). Preventing birth defects even before pregnancy. *The New York Times,* p. C10.

Brody, L. R., Zelazo, P. R., & Chaika, H. (1984). Habituation-dishabituation to speech in the neonate. *Developmental Psychology, 20,* 114–119.

Brodzinsky, D. (1997). Infertility and adoption adjustment: Considerations and clinical issues. In S. R. Leiblum (Ed.), *Infertility: Psychological issues and counseling strategies* (pp. 246–262). New York: Wiley.

Broidy, L. M., Tremblay, R. E., Brame, B., Fergusson, D., Horwood, J. L., Laird, R., Moffitt, T. E., Nagin, D. S., Bates, J. E., Dodge, K. A., Loeber, R., Lyam, D. R., Pettit, G. S., & Vitaro, F. (2003). Developmental trajectories of childhood disruptive behaviors and adolescent delinquency: A six-site cross-national study. *Developmental Psychology, 39,* 222–245.

Bronfenbrenner, U. (1979). *The ecology of human development.* Cambridge, MA: Harvard University Press.

Bronfenbrenner, U. (1986). Ecology of the family as a context for human development: Research perspectives. *Developmental Psychology, 22,* 723–742.

Bronfenbrenner, U. (1994). Ecological models of human development. In T. Husen & T. N. Postlethwaite (Eds.), *International encyclopedia of education* (2nd ed., Vol. 3). Oxford: Pergamon Press/Elsevier Science.

Bronfenbrenner, U., & Morris, P. A. (1998). The ecology of developmental processes. In W. Damon (Series Ed.) & R. Lerner (Vol. Ed.), *Handbook of child psychology: Vol. 1. Theoretical models of human development* (5th ed., pp. 993–1028). New York: Wiley.

Bronner, E. (1999, January 22). Social promotion is bad; repeating a grade may be worse. *The New York Times* [Online]. Available: http://search. nytimes.com/search/daily/bin/fastweb?getdoc+site+site+13235+0+wAAA+social%7Epromotion

Bronstein, P. (1988). Father-child interaction: Implications for gender role socialization. In P. Bronstein & C. P. Cowan (Eds.), *Fatherhood today: Men's changing role in the family.* New York: Wiley.

Bronstein, P., Clauson, J., Stoll, M. F., & Abrams, C. L. (1993). Parenting behavior and children's social, psychological, and academic adjustment in diverse family structures. *Family Relations, 42,* 268–276.

Brooks, R., & Meltzoff, A. N. (2002). The importance of eyes: How infants interpret adult looking behavior. *Developmental Psychology, 38,* 958–966.

Brooks-Gunn, J. (2003). Do you believe in magic? What can we expect from early childhood intervention programs? *SRCD Social Policy Report, 17*(1).

Brooks-Gunn, J., Britto, P. R., & Brady, C. (1998). Struggling to make ends meet: Poverty and child development. In M. E. Lamb (Ed.), *Parenting and child development in "nontraditional" families* (pp. 279–304). Mahwah, NJ: Erlbaum.

Brooks-Gunn, J., & Duncan, G. J. (1997). The effects of poverty on children. *The Future of Children, 7,* 55–71.

Brooks-Gunn, J., Duncan, G. J., Leventhal, T., & Aber, J. L. (1997). Lessons learned and future directions for research on the neighborhoods in which children live. In J. Brooks-Gunn, G. J. Duncan, & J. L. Aber (Eds.), *Neighborhood poverty: Context and consequences for children* (Vol. 1, pp. 279–297). New York: Russell Sage Foundation.

Brooks-Gunn, J., Han, W.-J., & Waldfogel, J. (2002). Maternal employment and child cognitive outcomes in the first three years of life: The NICHD study of early child care. *Child Development, 73,* 1052–1072.

Brooks-Gunn, J., Klebanov, P. K., Liaw, F., & Spiker, D. (1993). Enhancing the development of low-birthweight, premature infants: Changes in cognition and behavior over the first three years. *Child Development, 64,* 736–753.

Brooks-Gunn, J., McCarton, C. M., Casey, P. H., et al. (1994). Early intervention in low-birthweight premature infants: Results through age 5 years from the Infant Health Development Program. *Journal of the American Medical Association, 272,* 1257–1262.

Broude, G. J. (1994). *Marriage, family, and relationships: A cross-cultural encyclopedia.* Santa Barbara, CA: ABC-CLIO.

Broude, G. J. (1995). *Growing up: A cross-cultural encyclopedia.* Santa Barbara, CA: ABC-CLIO.

Brown, A. L., Metz, K. E., & Campione, J. C. (1996). Social interaction and individual understanding in a community of learners: The influence of Piaget and Vygotsky. In A. Tryphon & J. Voneche (Eds), *Piaget-Vygotsky: The social genesis of thought* (pp. 145–170). Hove, England: Psychology/Erlbaum (UK) Taylor & Francis.

Brown, A. S., Begg, M. D., Gravenstein, S., Schaefer, C. A., Wyatt, R. J., Bresnahan, M., Babulas, V. P., & Susser, E. S. (2004). Serologic evidence of prenatal influence in the etiology of schizophrenia. *Archives of General Psychiatry, 61,* 774–780.

Brown, B. B., & Klute, C. (2003). Friendships, cliques, and crowds. In G. R. Adams and M. D. Berzonsky. (Eds.). *Blackwell handbook of adolescence* (pp. 330–348). Malden, MA: Blackwell.

Brown, B. B., Mounts, N., Lamborn, S. D., & Steinberg, L. (1993). Parenting practices and peer group affiliation in adolescence. *Child Development, 64,* 467–482.

Brown, J. L. (1987). Hunger in the U.S. *Scientific American, 256*(2), 37–41.

Brown, J. M. (1989). *Gandhi: Prisoner of hope.* New Haven: Yale University Press.

Brown, J. R., & Dunn, J. (1996). Continuities in emotion understanding from three to six years. *Child Development, 67,* 789–802.

Brown, J. T., & Stoudemire, A. (1983). Normal and pathological grief. *Journal of the American Medical Association, 250,* 378–382.

Brown, J. V., Bakeman, R., Coles, C. D., Platzman, K. A., and Lynch, M. E. (2004). Prenatal cocaine exposure: A comparison of 2-year-old children in parental and nonparental care. *Child Development, 75,* 1282–1295.

Brown, L. J., Wall, T. P., & Lazar, V. (2000). Trends in untreated caries in primary teeth of children 2 to 10 years old. *Journal of the American Dental Association, 131,* 93–100.

Brown, L. M., & Gilligan, C. (1990, April). *The psychology of women and the development of girls.* Paper presented at the Laurel-Harvard Conference on the Psychology of Women and the Education of Girls, Cleveland, OH.

Brown, N. M. (1990). Age and children in the Kalahari. *Health and Human Development Research, 1,* 26–30.

Brown, P. (1993, April 17). Motherhood past midnight. *New Scientist,* pp. 4–8.

Brown, S. L. (2004). Family structure and child well-being: The significance of parental cohabitation. *Journal of Marriage and Family, 66,* 351–367.

Brown, S. L., Bulanda, J. R., & Lee, G. R. (2005). The significance of nonmarital cohabitation: Marital status and mental health benefits among middle-aged and older adults. *Journal of Gerontology: Social Sciences, 60B,* S21–S29.

Brown, S. S. (1985). Can low birth weight be prevented? *Family Planning Perspectives, 17*(3), 112–118.

Browne, A., & Finkelhor, D. (1986). Impact of child sexual abuse: A review of research. *Psychological Bulletin 99*(1), 66–77.

Browning, C. R. (2002). The span of collective efficacy: Extending social disorganization theory to partner violence. *Journal of Marriage and Family, 64,* 833–850.

Brubaker, T. H. (1983). Introduction. In T. H. Brubaker (Ed.), *Family relationships in later life.* Beverly Hills, CA: Sage.

Brubaker, T. H. (Ed.). (1993). *Family relationships: Current and future directions.* Newbury Park, CA: Sage.

Bruck, M., & Ceci, S. J. (1997). The suggestibility of young children. *Current Directions in Psychological Science, 6,* 75–79.

Bruck, M., Ceci, S. J., & Hembrooke, H. (1998). Reliability and credibility of young children's reports: From research to policy and practice. *American Psychologist, 53,* 136–151.

Bruer, J. T. (2001). A critical and sensitive period primer. In D. B. Bailey, J. T. Bruer, F. J. Symons, & J. W. Lichtman (Eds.). *Critical thinking about critical periods: A series from the National Center for Early Development and Learning* (pp. 289–292). Baltimore, MD: Paul Brooks Publishing.

Bruner, A. B., Joffe, A., Duggan, A. K., Casella, J. F., & Brandt, J. (1996). Randomised study of cognitive effects of iron supplementation in non-anaemic iron-deficient adolescent girls. *Lancet, 348,* 992–996.

Bryant, B. K. (1987). Mental health, temperament, family, and friends: Perspectives on children's empathy and social perspective taking. In N. Eisenberg & J. Strayer (Eds.), *Empathy and its development* (pp. 245–270). Cambridge, UK: Cambridge University Press.

Bryce, J., Boschi-Pinto, C., Black, R. E., & the WHO Child Health Epidemiology Reference Group. (2005). WHO estimates of the causes of death in children. *Lancet, 365,* 1147–1152.

Buchanan, C. M., Eccles, J. S., & Becker, J. B. (1992). Are adolescents the victims of raging hormones?: Evidence for activational effects of hormones on moods and behavior at adolescence. *Psychological Bulletin, 111,* 62–107.

Buckner, J. C., Bassuk, E. L., Weinreb, L. F., & Brooks, M. G. (1999). Homelessness and its relation to the mental health and behavior of low-income school-age children. *Developmental Psychology, 35*(1), 246–257.

Budson, A. E., & Price, B. H. (2005). Memory dysfunction. *New England Journal of Medicine, 352,* 692–699.

Buhrmester, D. (1990). Intimacy of friendship, interpersonal competence, and adjustment during preadolescence and adolescence. *Child Development, 61,* 1101–1111.

Buhrmester, D. (1996). Need fulfillment, interpersonal competence, and the developmental contexts of early adolescent friendship. In W. M. Bukowski, A. F. Newcomb, & W. W. Hartup (Eds.), *The company they keep: Friendship in childhood and adolescence* (pp. 158–185). New York: Cambridge University Press.

Buhrmester, D., & Furman, W. (1990). Perceptions of sibling relationships during middle childhood and adolescence. *Child Development, 61,* 138–139.

Bulcroft, K., & O'Conner, M. (1986). The importance of dating relationships on quality of life for older persons. *Family Relations, 35,* 397–401.

Bulcroft, R. A., & Bulcroft, K. A. (1991). The nature and function of dating in later life. *Research on Aging, 13,* 244–260.

Bulkley, K., & Fisler, J. (2002). A decade of charter schools: From theory to practice. Philadelphia: Consortium for Policy Research in Education, Graduate School of Education, University of Pennsylvania.

Bumpass, L. L., & Lu, H.-H. (2000). Trends in cohabitation and implications for children's family contexts in the United States. *Population Studies, 54,* 29–41.

Bunikowski, R., Grimmer, I., Heiser, A., Metze, B., Schafer, A., & Obladen, M. (1998). Neurodevelopmental outcome after prenatal exposure to opiates. *European Journal of Pediatrics, 157,* 724–730.

Burchinal, M. R., Campbell, F. A., Bryant, D. M., Wasik, B. H., & Ramey, C. T. (1997). Early intervention and mediating processes in cognitive performance of children of low income African American families. *Child Development, 68,* 935–954.

Burchinal, M. R., Roberts, J. E., Nabors, L. A., & Bryant, D. M. (1996). Quality of center child care and infant cognitive and language development. *Child Development, 67,* 606–620.

Bureau of Labor Standards. (2000–2001, Winter). High-paying jobs requiring on-the-job training. *Occupational Outlook Quarterly.* [Online]. Available: http:/www.bls.gov/opub/ooq.htm.

Bureau of Labor Statistics. (1998). *Workers on flexible and shift schedules in 1997* (Suppl. to May 1997 Current Population Survey) [Online]. Available: http://www.bls.gov/news.release/flex.nws.htm.

Bureau of Labor Statistics. (2001). Industry at a glance. [Online] Available: http://www.bls.gov/iag/iaghome.htm.

Bureau of Labor Statistics. (2002a). Employment Characteristics of Families, 2001. *Current Population Survey* (USDL 02–175). Washington, DC: U. S. Department of Labor.

Bureau of Labor Statistics. (2002b). Table D-6: Employed persons by age and sex, seasonally adjusted. [Online]. Available: ftp://ftp.bls.gov/pub/suppl/empsit.cpseed6.txt. Access date: December 20, 2002.

Bureau of Labor Statistics. (2005a). Data on unemployment rate. [Online]. Retrieved February 16, 2005 from http://www.bls.gov/cps/home.htm.

Bureau of Labor Statistics. (2005b). *Women in the labor force: A databook.* [Online]. Retrieved May 19, 2005, from http://www.bls.gov/cps/wlf-databook2005.htm.

Burhans, K. K., & Dweck, C. S. (1995). Helplessness in early childhood: The role of contingent worth. *Child Development, 66,* 1719–1738.

Burke, D. M., & Shafto, M. A. (2004). Aging and language production. *Current Directions in Psychological Science, 13,* 81–84.

Burns, B. J., Phillips, S. D., Wagner, H. R., Barth, R. P., Kolko, D. J., Campbell, Y., & Landsverk, J. (2004). Mental health need and access to mental health services by youths involved with child welfare: A national survey. *Journal of the American Academy of Child & Adolescent Psychiatry, 43,* 960–970.

Burns, G. (1983). *How to live to be 100—or more: The ultimate diet, sex, and exercise book.* New York: Putnam.

Burton, L. C., Zolaniuk, B., Schulz, R., Jackson, S., & Hirsch, C. (2003). Transitions in spousal caregiving. *The Gerontologist, 43,* 230–241.

Bushnell, E. W., & Boudreau, J. P. (1993). Motor development and the mind: The potential role of motor abilities as a determinant of aspects of perceptual development. *Child Development, 64,* 1005–1021.

Busse, E. W. (1987). Primary and secondary aging. In G. L. Maddox (Ed.), *The encyclopedia of aging* (p. 534). New York: Springer.

Bussey, K., & Bandura, A. (1992). Self-regulatory mechanisms governing gender development. *Child Development, 63,* 1236–1250.

Bussey, K., & Bandura, A. (1999). Social cognitive theory of gender development and differentiation. *Psychological Review, 106,* 676–713.

Butler, R. (1961). Re-awakening interests. *Nursing Homes: Journal of the American Nursing Home Association, 10,* 8–19.

Butler, R. (1996). The dangers of physician-assisted suicide. *Geriatrics, 51,* 7.

Butler, R. N., Davis, R., Lewis, C. B., Nelson, M. E., & Strauss, E. (1998a). Physical fitness: Benefits of exercise for the older patient. 2. *Geriatrics 53,* 46, 49–52, 61–62.

Butler, R. N., Davis, R., Lewis, C. B., Nelson, M. E., & Strauss, E. (1998b). Physical fitness: How to help older patients live stronger and longer. 1. *Geriatrics, 53,* 26–28, 31–32, 39–40.

Butler, R. N., Sprott, R., Warner, H., Bland, J., Feuers, R., Forster, M., Fillit, H., Harman, M., Hewitt, M., Hyman, M., Johnson, K., Kligman, E., McClearn, G., Nelson, J., Richardson, A., Sonntag, W., Weindruch, R., & Wolf, N. (2004). Biomarkers of aging: From primitive organisms to humans. *Journal of Gerontology: Biological Sciences, 59A,* 560–567.

Byrne, M., Agerbo, E., Ewald, H., Eaton, W. W., & Mortensen, P. B. (2003). Parental age and risk of schizophrenia: A case-control study. *Archives of General Psychiatry, 60,* 673–678.

Byrnes, J. P., & Fox, N. A. (1998). The educational relevance of research in cognitive neuroscience. *Educational Psychology Review, 10,* 297–342.

Cabrera, N. J., Tamis-LeMonda, C. S., Bradley, R. H., Hofferth, S., & Lamb, M. E. (2000). Fatherhood in the twenty-first century. *Child Development, 71,* 127–136.

Cadman, C., Brewer, J. (2001). Emotional intelligence: A vital prerequisite for recruitment in nursing. *Journal of Nursing Management, 9,* 321–324.

Caelli, K., Downie, J., & Letendre, A. (2002). Parents' experiences of midwife-managed care following the loss of a baby in a previous pregnancy. *Journal of Advanced Nursing, 39,* 127–136.

Cain, W. S., Reid, F., & Stevens, J. C. (1990). Missing ingredients: Aging and the discrimination of flavor. *Journal of Nutrition for the Elderly, 9,* 3–15.

Caldwell, B. M., & Bradley, R. H. (1984). *Home Observation for Measurement of the Environment.* Unpublished manuscript, University of Arkansas at Little Rock.

Calkins, S. D., & Fox, N. A. (1992). The relations among infant temperament, security of attachment, and behavioral inhibition at twenty-four months. *Child Development, 63,* 1456–1472.

Camp, C. J. (1989). World-knowledge systems. In L. W. Poon, D. C. Rubin, & B. A. Wilson (Eds.), *Everyday cognition in adulthood and late life.* Cambridge, England: Cambridge University Press.

Camp, C. J., & McKitrick, L. A. (1989). The dialectics of remembering and forgetting across the adult lifespan. In D. Kramer & M. Bopp (Eds.), *Dialectics and contextualism in clinical and developmental psychology: Change, transformation, and the social context* (pp. 169–187). New York: Springer.

Camp, C. J., & McKitrick, L. A. (1992). Memory interventions in Alzheimer's-type dementia populations: Methodological and theoretical issues. In R. L. West & J. D. Sinnott (Eds.), *Everyday memory and aging: Current research and methodology* (pp. 155–172). New York: Springer-Verlag.

Camp, C. J., Doherty, K., Moody-Thomas, S., & Denney, N. W. (1989). Practical problem solving in adults: A comparison of problem types and scoring methods. In J. D. Sinnott (Ed.), *Everyday problem solving: Theory and applications* (pp. 211–228). New York: Praeger.

Camp, C. J., Foss, J. W., Stevens, A. B., Reichard, C. C., McKitrick, L. A., & O'Hanlon, A. M. (1993). Memory training in normal and demented populations: The E-I-E-I-O model. *Experimental Aging Research, 19,* 277–290.

Campbell, A., Shirley, L., & Candy, J. (2004). A longitudinal study of gender-related cognition and behaviour. *Developmental Science, 7,* 1–9.

Campbell, A., Shirley, L., Heywood, C., & Crook, C. (2000). Infants' visual preference for sex-congruent babies, children, toys, and activities: A longitudinal study. *British Journal of Developmental Psychology, 18,* 479–498.

Campbell, F. A., Pungello, E. P., Miller-Johnson, S., Burchinal, M., & Ramey, C. T. (2001). The development of cognitive and academic abilities: Growth curves from an early childhood education experiment. *Developmental Psychology, 37*(2), 231–242.

Campfield, L. A., Smith, F. J., & Burns, P. (1998, May 29). Strategies and potential molecular targets for obesity treatment. *Science, 280,* 1383–1387.

Campfield, L. A., Smith, F. J., Guisez, Y., Devos, R., & Burns, P. (1995). Recombinant mouse OB protein: Evidence for a peripheral signal linking adiposity and central neural networks. *Science, 269,* 546–549.

Campos, J., Bertenthal, B., & Benson, N. (1980, April). *Self-produced locomotion and the extraction of form invariance.* Paper presented at the meeting of the International Conference on Infant Studies, New Haven, CT.

Canfield, R. L., Henderson, C. R., Cory-Slechta, D. A., Cox, C., Jusko, T. A., & Lanphear, B. P. (April 17, 2003). Intellectual impairment in children with blood lead concentrations below 10 g per deciliter. *New England Journal of Medicine, 348,* 1517–1526.

Cantor, J. (1994). Confronting children's fright responses to mass media. In D. Zillman, J. Bryant, & A. C. Huston (Eds.), *Media, children, and the family: Social scientific, psychoanalytic, and clinical perspectives.* Hillsdale, NJ: Erlbaum.

Cao, A., Saba, L., Galanello, R., & Rosatelli, M. C. (1997). Molecular diagnosis and carrier screening for thalassemia. *Journal of the American Medical Association, 278,* 1273–1277.

Cao, X.-Y., Jiang, X.-M., Dou, Z.-H., Rakeman, M. A., Zhang, M.-L., O'Donnell, K., Ma, T., Amette, K., DeLong, N., & DeLong, G. R. (1994). Timing of vulnerability of the brain to iodine deficiency in endemic cretinism. *New England Journal of Medicine, 331,* 1739–1744.

Capaldi, D. M., Stoolmiller, M., Clark, S., & Owen, L. D. (2002). Heterosexual risk behaviors in at-risk young men from early adolescence to young adulthood: Prevalence, prediction, and association with STD contraction. *Developmental Psychology, 38,* 394–406.

Caplan, M., Vespo, J., Pedersen, J., & Hay, D. F. (1991). Conflict and its resolution in small groups of one- and two-year olds. *Child Development, 62,* 1513–1524.

Capon, N., Kuhn, D., & Carretero, M. (1989). Consumer reasoning. In J. D. Sinnott (Ed.), *Everyday problem solving: Theory and application* (pp. 153–174). New York: Praeger.

Caraballo, R. S., Giovino, G. A., Pechacek, T. F., Mowery, P. D., Richter, P. A., Strauss, W. J., Sharp, D. J., Eriksen, M. P., Pirkle, J. L., & Maurer, K. R. (1998). Racial and ethnic differences in serum cotinine levels of cigarette smokers. *Journal of the American Medical Association, 280,* 135–139.

Carbery, J., & Buhrmester, D. (1998). Friendship and need fulfillment during three phases of young adulthood. *Journal of Social & Personal Relationships, 15,* 393–409.

Carlson, E. A. (1998). A prospective longitudinal study of attachment disorganization/disorientation. *Child Development, 69*(4), 1107–1128.

Carlson, E. A., Sroufe, L. A., & Egeland, B. (2004). The construction of experience: A longitudinal study of representation and behavior. *Child Development, 75,* 66–83.

Carlson, S. M., & Taylor, M. (in press). Imaginary companions and impersonated characters: Sex differences in children's fantasy play. *Merrill-Palmer Quarterly.*

Carlson, S. M., Moses, L. J., & Hix, H. R. (1998). The role of inhibitory processes in young children's difficulties with deception and false belief. *Child Development, 69*(3), 672–691.

Carlson, S. M., Wong, A., Lemke, M., & Cosser, C. (2005). Gesture as a window in children's beginning understanding of false belief. *Child Development, 76,* 73–86.

Carmichael, M. (2004, January 26). In parts of Asia, sexism is ingrained and gender selection often means murder. No girls, please. *Newsweek,* p. 50.

Carpenter, D. (2004, May 16). An age-old issue: Some expect more lawsuits with half the work force 40 or older. *Chicago Sun-Times,* p. 45A.

Carr, D. (2004). The desire to date and remarry among older widows and widowers. *Journal of Marriage and Family, 66,* 1951–1968.

Carr, D., House, J. S., Kessler, R. C., Nesse, R. M., Sonnega, J., & Wortman, C. (2000). Marital quality and psychological adjustment to widowhood among older adults: A longitudinal analysis. *Journal of Gerontology: Social Sciences, 55B,* S197–S207.

Carraher, T. N., Schliemann, A. D., & Carraher, D. W. (1988). Mathematical concepts in everyday life. In G. B. Saxe and M. Gearhart (Eds.), Children's mathematics. *New Directions in Child Development, 41,* 71–87.

Carrel, L., & Willard, B. F. (2005). X-inactivation profile reveals extensive variability in X-linked gene expression in females. *Nature, 434,* 400–404.

Carroll-Pankhurst, C., & Mortimer, E. A. (2001). Sudden infant death syndrome, bed sharing, parental weight, and age at death. *Pediatrics, 107*(3), 530–536.

Carskadon, M. A., Acebo, C., Richardson, G. S., Tate, B. A., & Seifer, R. (1997). Long nights protocol: Access to circadian parameters in adolescents. *Journal of Biological Rhythms, 12,* 278–289.

Carstensen, L. L. (1991). Selectivity theory: Social activity in life-span context. In *Annual review of gerontology and geriatrics* (Vol. 11, pp. 195–217). New York: Springer.

Carstensen, L. L. (1995). Evidence for a life-span theory of socioemotional selectivity. *Current Directions in Psychological Science, 4,* 150–156.

Carstensen, L. L. (1996). Socioemotional selectivity: A life-span developmental account of social behavior. In M. R. Merrens & G. G. Brannigan (Eds.), *The developmental psychologists: Research adventures across the life span* (pp. 251–272). New York: McGraw-Hill.

Carstensen, L. L. (1999). Elderly show their emotional know-how. (Cited in *Science News, 155,* p. 374). Paper presented at the meeting of the American Psychological Society, Denver, CO.

Carstensen, L. L., & Pasupathi, M. (1993). Women of a certain age. In S. Matteo (Ed.), *Critical issues facing women in the '90s* (pp. 66–78). Boston: Northeastern University Press.

Carstensen, L. L., Graff, J., Levenson, R. W., & Gottman, J. M. (1996). Affect in intimate relationships: The development course of marriage. In C. Magai & S. H. McFadden (Eds.), *Handbook of emotion, adult development, and aging* (pp. 227–247). San Diego: Academic Press.

Carstensen, L. L., Gross, J., & Fung, H. (1997). The social context of emotion. *Annual Review of Geriatrics and Gerontology, 17,* 331.

Carstensen, L. L., Isaacowitz, D. M., & Charles, S. T. (1999). Taking time seriously: A theory of socioemotional selectivity. *American Psychologist, 54,* 165–181.

Carstensen, L. L., Pasupathi, M., Mayr, U., & Nesselroade, J. (2000). Emotional experience in everyday life across the adult life span. *Journal of Personality and Social Psychology, 79,* 644–655.

Carter Center. (1995, Winter). *Carter Center News,* pp. 1, 3, 4–6, 9.

Carter, J. (1975). *Why not the best?* Nashville, TN: Broadman.

Carter, J. (1998). *The virtues of aging.* New York: Ballantine.

Casaer, P. (1993). Old and new facts about perinatal brain development. *Journal of Child Psychology and Psychiatry, 34*(1), 101–109.

Case, R. (1985). *Intellectual development: Birth to adulthood.* Orlando, FL: Academic Press.

Case, R. (1992). Neo-Piagetian theories of child development. In R. Sternberg & C. Berg (Eds.), *Intellectual development.* New York: Cambridge University Press.

Case, R., & Okamoto, Y. (1996). The role of central conceptual structures in the development of children's thought. *Monographs of the Society for Research in Child Development, 61*(1–2, Serial No. 246).

Casey, B. M., McIntire, D. D., & Leveno, K. J. (2001). The continuing value of the Apgar score for the assessment of newborn infants. *New England Journal of Medicine, 344,* 467–471.

Casper, L. M. (1997). My daddy takes care of me: Fathers as care providers. *Current Population Reports* (P70–59). Washington, DC: U.S. Bureau of the Census.

Casper, L. M., & Bryson, K. R. (1998). *Coresident grandparents and their grandchildren: Grandparent maintained families* (Population Division Working Paper No. 26). Washington, DC: U.S. Bureau of the Census.

Caspi, A. (1998). Personality development across the life course. In W. Damon (Series Ed.) & N. Eisenberg (Vol. Ed.), *Handbook of child psychology: Vol. 3. Social, emotional, and personality development* (5th ed., pp. 311–388). New York: Wiley.

Caspi, A. (2000). The child is father of the man: Personality continuity from childhood to adulthood. *Journal of Personality and Social Psychology, 78,* 158–172.

Caspi, A., McClay, J., Moffitt, T. E., Mill, J., Martin, J., Craig, I. W., Taylor, A., & Poulton, R. (2002). Role of genotype in the cycle of violence in maltreated children. *Science, 297,* 851–854.

Caspi, A., & Silva, P. (1995). Temperamental qualities at age 3 predict personality traits in young adulthood: Longitudinal evidence from a birth cohort. *Child Development, 66,* 486–498.

Caspi, A., Sugden, K., Moffitt, T. E., Taylor, A., Craig, I. W., Harrington, H., McClay, J., Mill, J., Martin, J., Braithwaite, A., & Poulton, R. (2003). Influence of life stress on depression: Moderation by a polymorphism in the 5-HTT gene. *Science, 301,* 386–389.

Cassel, C. (1992). Ethics and the future of aging research: Promises and problems. *Generations, 16*(4), 61–65.

Cassidy, J. (1988). Child-mother attachment and the self in six-year-olds. *Child Development, 59,* 121–134.

Cassidy, J., & Hossler, A. (1992). State and federal definitions of the gifted: An update. *Gifted Child Quarterly, 15,* 46–53.

Cassidy, K. W., Werner, R. S., Rourke, M., Zubernis, L. S., & Balaraman, G. (2003). The relationship between psychological understanding and positive social behaviors. *Social Development, 12,* 198–221.

Cattell, R. B. (1965). *The scientific analysis of personality.* Baltimore: Penguin.

Cavanaugh, J. C., Kramer, D. A., Sinnott, J. D., Camp, C. J., & Markley, R. P. (1985). On missing links and such: Interfaces between cognitive research and everyday problem solving. *Human Development, 28,* 146–168.

Cavazanna-Calvo, M., Hacein-Bey, S., de Saint Basile, G., Gross, F., Yvon, E., Nusbaum, P., Selz, F., Hue, C., Certain, S., Casanova, J. L., Bousso, P., Deist, F. L., & Fischer, A. (2000). Gene therapy of human severe combined immunodeficiency (SCID)-X1 disease. *Science, 288,* 669–672.

Cawthon, R. M., Smith, K. R., O'Brien, E., Sivatchenko, A., & Kerber, R. A. (2003). Association between telomere length in blood and mortality in people aged 60 years or older. *The Lancet, 361,* 393–394.

CDC. (undated). Patterns of prescription drug use in the United States, 1988–1994. National Health and Nutrition Examination Survey.

Ceci, S., & Liker, J. (1986). A day at the races: A study of IQ, expertise, and cognitive complexity. *Journal of Experimental Psychology: General, 114,* 255–266.

Ceci, S. J. (1991). How much does schooling influence general intelligence and its cognitive components? A reassessment of the evidence. *Developmental Psychology, 27,* 703–722.

Ceci, S. J., & Bruck, M. (1993). Child witnesses: Translating research into policy. *Social Policy Report of the Society for Research in Child Development, 7*(3).

Ceci, S. J., & Williams, W. M. (1997). Schooling, intelligence, and income. *American Psychologist, 52*(10), 1105–1058.

Celis, W. (1990). More states are laying school paddle to rest. *New York Times,* pp. A1, B12.

Center for Education Reform. (2004, August 17). Comprehensive data discounts New York Times account; reveals charter schools performing at or above traditional schools. (CER Press Release). [Online]. Available: http://edreform. com/index.cfm?fuseAction=do-cument& documentID=1806. Access date: September 17, 2004.

Center for Effective Discipline. (2005). Facts about corporal punishment in Canada. Retrieved April 20, 2005, from http://www.stophitting. com/news.

Center for Weight and Health (2001). *Pediatric overweight: A review of the literature: Executive summary.* Berkeley, CA: University of California at Berkeley.

Center on Addiction and Substance Abuse at Columbia University (CASA). (1996, June). *Substance abuse and the American woman.* New York: Author.

Centers for Disease Control and Prevention (CDC). (2000a). *CDC's guidelines for school and community programs: Promoting lifelong physical activity.* [Online]. Available: http://www.cdc.gov/nccdphp/dash/phactaag. htm. Access date: May 26, 2000.

Centers for Disease Control and Prevention (CDC). (2000b). *Tracking the hidden epidemic: Trends in STDs in the U.S., 2000.* Washington, DC: Author.

Centers for Disease Control and Prevention (CDC). (2001a). *Assisted reproductive technology success rates: National summary and fertility clinic reports.* Atlanta, GA: Author.

Centers for Disease Control and Prevention (CDC). (2001b). *HIV/AIDS surveillance report, 13*(1).

Centers for Disease Control and Prevention (CDC). (2002a). Recent trends in mortality rates for four major cancers, by sex and race/ethnicity—United States, 1990–1998. *Morbidity and Mortality Weekly Report, 51,* 49–53.

Centers for Disease Control and Prevention (CDC) (2002b). Suicide in the United States. [Online]. Available: http://www.cdc.gov/ncipc/ factsheets/suifacts.htm.

Centers for Disease Control and Prevention. (CDC) (2003). *Second National Report on Human Exposure to Environmental Chemicals.* Atlanta, GA: Author.

Centers for Disease Control and Prevention (CDC). (2004). National, state, and urban area vaccination coverage among children aged 19–36 months—United States, 2003. *Morbidity and Mortality Weekly Report, 53,* 658–661.

Centre for Educational Research and Innovation. (2004). Education at a Glance: OECD indicators—2004. *Education and Skills, 2004*(14), 1–456.

Cepeda-Benito, A., Reynoso, J. T., & Erath, S. (2004). Meta-analysis of the efficacy of nicotine replacement therapy for smoking cessation: Differences between men and women. *Journal of Consulting and Clinical Psychology, 72,* 712–722.

Chafetz, M. D. (1992). *Smart for life.* New York: Penguin.

Chambers, R. A., Taylor, J. R., & Potenza, M. N. (2003). *American Journal of Psychiatry, 160,* 1041–1052.

Chambre, S. M. (1993). Volunteerism by elders: Past trends and future prospects. *The Gerontologist, 33,* 221–227.

Chan, R. W., Raboy, B., & Patterson, C. J. (1998). Psychosocial adjustment among children conceived via donor insemination by lesbian and heterosexual mothers. *Child Development, 69,* 443–457.

Chandra, H., & Singh, P. (2001). Organ transplantation: Present scenario and future strategies for transplant programme (specially cadaveric) in India: Socioadministrative respects. *Journal of the Indian Medical Association, 99,* 374–377.

Chao, A., Thun, M. J., Connell, C. J., McCullough, M. L., Jacobs, E. J., Fllanders, W. D., Rodriguez, C., Sinha, R., & Calle, E. E. (2005). Meat consumption and risk of colorectal cancer. *Journal of the American Medical Association, 293,* 172–182.

Chao, R. (1996). Chinese and European American mothers' beliefs about the role of parenting in children's school success. *Journal of Cross-Cultural Psychology, 27,* 403–423.

Chao, R. K. (1994). Beyond parental control and authoritarian parenting style: Understanding Chinese parenting through the cultural notion of training. *Child Development, 65,* 1111–1119.

Chao, R. K. (2001). Extending research on the consequences of parenting style for Chinese Americans and European Americans. *Child Development, 72,* 1832–1843.

Chapman, M., & Lindenberger, U. (1988). Functions, operations, and décalage in the development of transitivity. *Developmental Psychology, 24,* 542–551.

Chappell, N. L. (1991). Living arrangements and sources of caregiving. *Journal of Gerontology: Social Sciences, 46*(1), S1–8.

Charles, S. T., Reynolds, C. A., & Gatz, M. (2001). Age-related differences and change in positive and negative affect over 23 years. *Journal of Personality and Social Psychology, 80,* 136–151.

Charness, N., & Schultetus, R. S. (1999). Knowledge and expertise. In F. T. Durso, (Ed.), *Handbook of applied cognition* (pp. 57–81). Chichester, England: Wiley.

Chase-Lansdale, P. L., Moffitt, R. A., Lohman, B. J., Cherlin, A. J., Coley, R. L., Pittman, L. D., Rolf, J., & Votruba-Drzal, E. (2003). Mothers' transitions from welfare to work and the well-being of preschoolers and adolescents. *Science, 299*(5612), 1548–1552.

Chehab, F. F., Mounzih, K., Lu, R., & Lim, M. E. (1997, January 3). Early onset of reproductive function in normal female mice treated with leptin. *Science, 275,* 88–90.

Chen, A., & Rogan, W. J. (2004). Breastfeeding and the risk of postneonatal death in the United States. *Pediatrics, 113,* e435–e439.

Chen, C., & Stevenson, H. W. (1995). Motivation and mathematics achievement: A comparative study of Asian American, Caucasian American, and East Asian high school students. *Child Development, 66,* 1215–1234.

Chen, C. L., Weiss, N. S., Newcomb, P., Barlow, W., & White, E. (2002). Hormone replacement therapy in relation to breast cancer. *Journal of the American Medical Association, 287,* 734–741.

Chen, E., Matthews, K. A., & Boyce, W. T. (2002). Socioeconomic differences in children's health: How and why do these relationships change with age? *Psychological Bulletin, 128,* 295–329.

Chen, L., Baker S. P., Braver, E. R., & Li, G. (2000). Carrying passengers as a risk factor for crashes fatal to 16- and 17-year-old drivers. *Journal of the American Medical Association, 283*(12), 1578–1582.

Chen, W., Li, S., Cook, N. R., Rosner, B. A., Srinivasan, S. R., Boerwinkle, E., & Berenson, G. S. (2004). An autosomal genome scan for loci influencing longitudinal burden of body mass index from childhood to young adulthood in white sibships. The Bogalusa Heart Study. *International Journal of Obesity, 28,* 462–469.

Chen, X., Cen, G., Li, D., & He, Y. (2005). Social functioning and adjustment in Chinese children: The imprint of historical time. *Child Development, 76,* 182–195.

Chen, X., Hastings, P. D., Rubin, K. H., Chen, H., Cen, G., & Stewart, S. L. (1998). Child-rearing attitudes and behavioral inhibition in Chinese and Canadian toddlers: A cross-cultural study. *Developmental Psychology, 34*(4), 677–686.

Chen, X., Rubin, K. H., & Li, Z. (1995). Social functioning and adjustment in Chinese children: A longitudinal study. *Developmental Psychology, 31,* 531–539.

Chen, X., Rubin, K. H., & Sun, Y. (1992). Social reputation and peer relationships in Chinese and Canadian children: A cross-cultural study. *Child Development, 63,* 1336–1343.

Cherlin, A. (2004). The deinstitutionalization of American marriage. *Journal of Marriage and Family, 66,* 848–861.

Cherlin, A., & Furstenberg, F. F. (1986). *The new American grandparent.* New York: Basic Books.

Cherniss, C. (2002). Emotional intelligence and the good community. *American Journal of Community Psychology, 30,* 1–11.

Cherniss, C., & Adler, M. (2000). *Promoting emotional intelligence in organizations.* Alexandria, VA: American Society for Training & Development (ASTD).

Cherry, K. E., & Park, D. C. (1993). Individual differences and contextual variables influence spatial memory in younger and older adults. *Psychology and Aging, 8,* 517–526.

Chia, S. E., Shi, L. M., Chan, O. Y., Chew, S. K., & Foong, B. H. (2004). A population-based study on the association between parental occupations and some common birth defects in Singapore (1994–1998). *Journal of Occupational and Environmental Medicine, 46*(9), 916–923.

Childers, J. B., & Tomasello, M. (2002). Two-year-olds learn novel nouns, verbs, and conventional actions from massed or distributed exposures. *Developmental Psychology, 38,* 967–978.

Children's Defense Fund. (1998). *The state of America's children yearbook, 1998.* Washington, DC: Author.

Children's Defense Fund. (2004). *The state of America's children 2004.* Washington, DC: Author.

Chin, A. E., Hedberg, K., Higginson, G. K., & Fleming, D. W. (1999). Legalized physician-assisted suicide in Oregon: The first year's experience. *New England Journal of Medicine, 340,* 577–583.

Chipungu, S. S., & Bent-Goodley, T. B. (2004). Meeting the challenges of contemporary foster care. In David and Lucile Packard Foundation, Children, families, and foster care. *The Future of Children, 14*(1). Available: http://www. futureofchildren.org.

Chiriboga, C. A., Brust, J. C. M., Bateman, D., & Hauser, W. A. (1999). Dose-response effect of fetal cocaine exposure on newborn neurologic function. *Pediatrics, 103,* 79–85.

Chiriboga, D. A. (1997). Crisis, challenge, and stability in the middle years. In M. E. Lachman & J. B. James (Eds.), *Multiple paths of midlife development* (pp. 293–322). Chicago: University of Chicago Press.

Chivers, M. L., Rieger, G., Latty, E., & Bailey, J. M. (2004). A sex difference in the specificity of sexual arousal. *Psychological Science, 15,* 736–744.

Chochinov, H. M. (2002). Dignity-conserving care: A new model for palliative care: Helping the patient feel valued. *Journal of the American Medical Association, 287,* 2253–2260.

Chochinov, H. M., Hack, T., McClement, S., Harlos, M., & Kristjanson, L. (2002). Dignity in the terminally ill: A developing empirical model. *Social Science Medicine, 54,* 433–443.

Chochinov, H. M., Tataryn, D., Clinch, J. J., & Dudgeon, D. (1999). Will to live in the terminally ill. *Lancet, 354,* 816–819.

Chodirker, B. N., Cadrin, C., Davies, G. A. L., Summers, A. M., Wilson, R. D., Winsor, E. J. T., & Young, D. (2001, July). Canadian guidelines for prenatal diagnosis: Techniques of prenatal diagnosis. *JOGC Clinical Practice Guidelines,* No. 105.

Chomitz, V. R., Cheung, L. W. Y., & Lieberman, E. (1995). The role of lifestyle in preventing low birth weight. *The Future of Children, 5*(1), 121–138.

Chomsky, C. S. (1969). *The acquisition of syntax in children from five to ten.* Cambridge, MA: MIT Press.

Chomsky, N. (1957). *Syntactic structures.* The Hague: Mouton.

Chomsky, N. (1972). *Language and mind* (2nd ed.). New York: Harcourt Brace Jovanovich.

Chomsky, N. (1995). *The minimalist program.* Cambridge, MA: MIT Press.

Chorpita, B. P., & Barlow, D. H. (1998). The development of anxiety: The role of control in the early environment. *Psychological Bulletin, 124,* 3–21.

Christakis, D. A., Zimmerman, F. J., DiGiuseppe, D. L., & McCarty, C. A. (2004). Early television exposure and subsequent attentional problems in children. *Pediatrics, 113,* 708–713.

Christian, M. S., & Brent, R. L. (2001). Teratogen update: Evaluation of the reproductive and developmental risks of caffeine. *Teratology, 64*(1), 51–78.

Christie, J. F. (1991). *Psychological research on play: Connections with early literacy development.* Albany: State University of New York Press.

Christie, J. F. (1998). Play as a medium for literacy development. In D. P. Fromberg & D. Bergen (Eds.), *Play from birth to twelve and beyond: Contexts, perspectives, and meanings* (pp. 50–55). New York: Garland.

Chronis, A. M., Lahey, B. B., Pelham Jr., W. E., Kipp, H. L., Baumann, B. L., & Lee, S. S. (2003). Psychopathology and substance abuse in parents of young children with attention-deficit/hyperactivity disorder. *Journal of the American Academy of Child & Adolescent Psychiatry, 42,* 1424–1432.

Chu, S. Y., Barker, L. E., & Smith, P. J. (2004). Racial/ethnic disparities in preschool immunizations: United States, 1996-2001. *American Journal of Public Health, 94,* 973–977.

Chubb, N. H., Fertman, C. I., & Ross, J. L. (1997). Adolescent self-esteem and locus of control: A longitudinal study of gender and age differences. *Adolescence, 32,* 113–129.

Chugani, H. T. (1998). A critical period of brain development: Studies of cerebral glucose utilization with PET. *Preventive Medicine, 27,* 184–187.

Chugani, H. T., Behen, M. E., Muzik, O., Juhasz, C., Nagy, F., & Chugani, D. C. (2001). Local brain functional activity following early deprivation: A study of postinstitutionalized Romanian orphans. *NeuroImage, 14,* 1290–1301.

Chun, K. M., Organista, P. B., & Marin, G. (Eds.). (2002). *Acculturation: Advances in theory, measurement & applied research.* Washington, DC: American Psychological Association.

Cicchetti, D., & Toth, S. L. (1998). The development of depression in children and adolescents. *American Psychologist, 53,* 221–241.

Cicero, S., Curcio, P., Papageorghiou, A., Sonek, J., & Nicolaides, K. (2001). Absence of nasal bone in fetuses with trisomy 21 at 11–14 weeks of gestation: An observational study. *Lancet, 358,* 1665–1667.

Cicirelli, V. G. (1976). Family structure and interaction: Sibling effects on socialization. In M. F. McMillan & S. Henao (Eds.), *Child psychiatry: Treatment and research.* New York: Brunner/Mazel.

Cicirelli, V. G. (1977). Relationship of siblings to the elderly person's feelings and concerns. *Journal of Gerontology, 12*(3), 317–322.

Cicirelli, V. G. (1989). Feelings of attachment to siblings and well-being in later life. *Psychology and Aging, 4*(2), 211–216.

Cicirelli, V. G. (1994). Sibling relationships in cross-cultural perspective. *Journal of Marriage and the Family, 56,* 7–20.

Cicirelli, V. G. (1995). *Sibling relationships across the life span.* New York: Plenum Press.

Cicirelli, V. G. (Ed.). (2002). Older adults' views on death. New York: Springer.

Cillessen, A. H. N., & Mayeux, L. (2004). From censure to reinforcement: Developmental changes in the association between aggression and social status. *Child Development, 75,* 147–163.

Cirillo, D. J., Wallace, R. B., Rodabough, R. J., Greenland, P., LaCroix, A. Z., Limacher, M. C., & Larson, J. C. (2005). Effect of estrogen therapy on gallbladder disease. *Journal of the American Medical Association, 293,* 330–339.

Citizens for Equal Protection, Inc., Nebraska Advocates for Justice and Equality, Inc., & ACLU Nebraska v. Attorney General Jon C. Bruning & Governor Michael O. Johanns (2005, May 12). In the U.S. District Court for the District of Nebraska.

Citro, J., & Hermanson, S. (1999, March). *Assisted living in the United States* [Online]. Available: http://www.research.aarp.org/il/fs62r_assisted.html

Clark, A. G., Glanowski, S., Nielsen, R., Thomas, P. D., Kejariwal, A., Todd, M. A., Tanenbaum, D. M., Civello, D., Lu, F., Murphy, B., Ferriera, S., Wang, G., Zheng, X., White, T. J., Sninsky, J. J., Adams, M. D., & Cargill, M. (2003). Inferring nonneutral evolution from human-chimp-mouse orthologous gene trios. *Science, 302,* 1960–1963.

Clarke, S. C. (1995, March 22). Advance report of final divorce statistics, 1989 and 1990 (*Monthly Vital Statistics Report, 43*[9, Suppl.]). Hyattsville, MD: National Center for Health Statistics.

Clark-Plaskie, M., & Lachman, M. E. (1999). The sense of control in midlife. In S. L. Willis & J. D. Reid (Eds.), *Life in the middle* (pp. 181–208). San Diego: Academic Press.

Clausen, J. A. (1993). *American lives.* New York: Free Press.

Clavel-Chapelon, G., and the E3N-EPIC Group. (2002). Differential effects of reproductive factors on the risk of pre- and post-menopausal breast cancer: Results from a large cohort of French women. *British Journal of Cancer,* DOI 10.1038/sj/bjc/6600124.

Clay, R. A. (1998, July). Many managers frown on use of flexible work options [Online]. *APA Monitor, 29*(7). Available: http://www.apa.org/monitor/jul98/flex.html.

Clayton, E. W. (2003). Ethical, legal, and social implications of genomic medicine. *New England Journal of Medicine, 349,* 562–569.

Clearfield, M. W., & Mix, K. S. (1999). Number versus contour length in infants' discrimination of small visual sets. *Current Directions in Psychological Science, 10,* 408–411.

Cleary, P. D., Zaborski, L. B., & Ayanian, J. Z. (2004). Sex differences in health over the course of midlife. In O. G. Brim, C. E. Ryff, and R. C. Kessler (Eds.). How healthy are we? A national study of well-being at midlife. Chicago: University of Chicago Press.

Clément, K., Vaisse, C., Lahlou, N., Cabrol, S., Pelloux, V., Cassuto, D., Gourmelen, M., Dina, C., Chambaz, J., Lacorte, J.-M., Basdevant, A., Bougnères, P., Lebouc, Y., Froguel, P., & Guy-Grand, B. (1998). A mutation in the human leptin receptor gene causes obesity and pituitary dysfunction. *Nature, 392,* 398–401.

Clements, M. L., Stanley, S. M., & Markman, H. J. (2004). Before they said "I do": Discriminating among marital outcomes over 13 years. *Journal of Marriage and Family, 66,* 613–626.

Cleveland, H. H., & Wiebe, R. P. (2003). The moderation of adolescent-to-peer similarity in tobacco and alcohol use by school level of substance use. *Child Development, 74,* 279–291.

Clifton, R. K., Muir, D. W., Ashmead, D. H., & Clarkson, M. G. (1993). Is visually guided reaching in early infancy a myth? *Child Development, 64,* 1099–1110.

Climo, A. H., & Stewart, A. J. (2003). Eldercare and personality development in middle age. In J. Demick and C. Andreoletti (Eds.), *Handbook of adult development.* New York: Plenum Press.

Cnattingius, S., Bergstrom, R., Lipworth, L., & Kramer, M. S. (2000). Prepregnancy weight and the risk of adverse pregnancy outcomes. *New England Journal of Medicine, 338,* 147–152.

Cochran, S. D. (2001). Emerging issues in research on lesbians' and gay men's mental health: Does sexual orientation really matter? *American Psychologist, 56,* 931–947.

Coffey, C. E., Lucke, J. F., Saxton, J. A., Ratcliff, G., Unitas, L. J., Billig, B., & Bryan, N. (1998). Sex differences in brain aging: A quantitative magnetic resonance imaging study. *Archives of Neurology, 55,* 169–179.

Coffey, C. E., Saxton, J. A., Ratcliff, G., Bryan, R. N., & Lucke, J. F. (1999). Relation of education to brain size in normal aging: Implications for the reserve hypothesis. *Neurology, 53,* 189–196.

Cohan, C. L., & Kleinbaum, S. (2002). Toward a greater understanding of the cohabitation effect: Premarital cohabitation and marital communication. *Journal of Marriage and Family, 64,* 180–192.

Cohen, D. A., Nsuami, M., Martin, D. H., & Farley, T. A. (1999). Repeated school-based screening for sexually transmitted diseases: A feasible strategy for reaching adolescents. *Pediatrics, 104*(6), 1281–1285.

Cohen, L. B., & Amsel, L. B. (1998). Precursors to infants' perception of the causality of a simple event. *Infant Behavior and Development, 21,* 713–732.

Cohen, L. B., & Oakes, L. M. (1993). How infants perceive a simple causal event. *Developmental Psychology, 29,* 421–433.

Cohen, L. B., Rundell, L. J., Spellman, B. A., & Cashon, C. H. (1999). Infants' perception of causal chains. *Current Directions in Psychological Science, 10,* 412–418.

Cohen, R. A., & Bloom, B. (2005). Trends in health insurance and access to medical care for children under age 19 years: United States, 1998–2003. *Advance Data from Vital and Health Statistics,* No. 355. Hyattsville, MD: National Center for Health Statistics.

Cohen, S. (2004). Social relationships and health. *American Psychologist, 59,* 676–684.

Cohen, S., Doyle, W. J., Skoner, D. P., Rabin, B. S., & Gwaltney, Jr., J. M. (1997). Social ties and susceptibility to the common cold. *Journal of the American Medical Association, 277,* 1940–1944.

Cohen, S., Gottlieb, B., & Underwood, L. (2000). Social relationships and health. In S. Cohen, L. Underwood, & B. Gottlieb (Eds.), *Measuring and intervening in social support* (pp. 3–25). New York: Oxford University Press.

Cohler, B. J., Hostetler, A. J., & Boxer, A. M. (1998). Generativity, social context, and lived experience: Narratives of gay men in middle adulthood. In D. P. McAdams & E. de St. Aubin (Eds.), *Generativity and adult development* (pp. 265–309). Washington, DC: American Psychological Association.

Cohn, J. F., & Tronick, E. Z. (1983). Three-month-old infants' reaction to simulated maternal depression. *Child Development, 54,* 185–193.

Coie, J. D., & Dodge, K. A. (1998). Aggression and antisocial behavior. In W. Damon (Series Ed.) & N. Eisenberg (Vol. Ed.), *Handbook of child psychology: Vol. 3. Social, emotional, and personality development* (5th ed., pp. 780–862). New York: Wiley.

Coke, M. M. (1992). Correlates of life satisfaction among elderly African-Americans. *Journal of Gerontology: Psychological Sciences, 47*(5), P316–320.

Coke, M. M., & Twaite, J. A. (1995). *The black elderly: Satisfaction and quality of later life.* New York: Haworth.

Colapinto, J. (2000). *As nature made him: The boy who was raised as a girl.* New York: HarperCollins.

Colapinto, J. (2004, June 3). Gender gap: What were the real reasons behind David Reimer's suicide? *Medical Examiner.* [Online]. Available: http://slate.msn.com/id/2101678. Access date: December 13, 2004.

Colby, A., & Damon, W. (1992). *Some do care: Contemporary lives of moral commitment.* New York: Free Press.

Colby, A., Kohlberg, L., Gibbs, J., & Lieberman, M. (1983). A longitudinal study of moral development. *Monographs of the Society for Research in Child Development, 48*(1–2, Serial No. 200).

Colcombe, S. J., Erickson, K. I., Raz, N., Webb, A. G., Cohen, N. J., Mcauley, E., & Kramer, A. F. (2003). Aerobic fitness reduces brain tissue loss in aging humans *Journal of Gerontology: Medical Sciences, 58,* M176–M180.

Cole, M. (1998). *Cultural psychology: A once and future discipline.* Cambridge, MA: Belknap.

Cole, M., & Cole, S. R. (1989). *The development of children.* New York: Freeman.

Cole, P. M., Barrett, K. C., & Zahn-Waxler, C. (1992). Emotion displays in two-year-olds during mishaps. *Child Development, 63,* 314–324.

Cole, P. M., Bruschi, C. J., & Tamang, B. L. (2002). Cultural differences in children's emotional reactions to difficult situations. *Child Development, 73,* 983–996.

Coleman, J. S. (1988). Social capital in the creation of human capital. *American Journal of Sociology, 94*(Suppl. 95), S95–S120.

Coles, L. S. (2004). Demography of human supercentenarians. *Journal of Gerontology: Biological Sciences, 59A,* 579–586.

Coley, R. L. (2001). (In)visible men: Emerging research on low-income, unmarried, and minority fathers. *American Psychologist, 56,* 743–753.

Coley, R. L., Morris, J. E., & Hernandez, D. (2004). Out-of-school care and problem behavior trajectories among low-income adolescents: Individual, family, and neighborhood characteristics as added risks. *Child Development, 75,* 948–965.

Collier, V. P. (1995). Acquiring a second language for school. *Directions in Language and Education, 1*(4), 1–11.

Collins, N. L., & Miller, L. C. (1994). Self-disclosure and liking: A meta-analytic review. *Psychological Bulletin, 116*, 457–475.

Collins, W. A., Maccoby, E. E., Steinberg, L., Hetherington, E. M., & Bornstein, M. H. (2000). Contemporary research in parenting: The case for nature and nurture. *American Psychologist, 55*, 218–232.

Colombo, J. (1993). *Infant cognition: Predicting later intellectual functioning.* Thousand Oaks, CA: Sage.

Colombo, J. (2001). The development of visual attention in infancy. *Annual Review of Psychology, 52*, 337–367.

Colombo, J. (2002). Infant attention grows up: The emergence of a developmental cognitive neuroscience perspective. *Current Directions in Psychological Science, 11*,196–200.

Colombo, J., & Janowsky, J. S. (1998). A cognitive neuroscience approach to individual differences in infant cognition. In J. E. Richards (Ed.), *Cognitive neuroscience of attention* (pp. 363–391). Mahwah, NJ: Erlbaum.

Colombo, J., Kannass, K. N., Shaddy, D. J., Kundurthi, S., Maikranz, J. M., Anderson, C. J., Blaga, O. M., and Carlson, S. E. (2004). Maternal DHA and the development of attention in infancy and toddlerhood. *Child Development, 75*, 1254–1267.

Coltrane, S., & Adams, M. (1997). Work-family imagery and gender stereotypes: Television and the reproduction of difference. *Journal of Vocational Behavior, 50*, 323–347.

Commissioner's Office of Research and Evaluation and Head Start Bureau, Department of Health and Human Services. (2001). *Building their futures: How Early Head Start programs are enhancing the lives of infants and toddlers in low-income families. Summary report.* Washington, DC: Author.

Committee on Obstetric Practice. (2002). ACOG committee opinion: Exercise during pregnancy and the postpartum period. *International Journal of Gynaecology & Obstetrics, 77*(1), 79–81.

Compas, B. E., & Luecken, L. (2002). Psychological adjustment to breast cancer. *Current Directions in Psychological Science, 11*, 111–114.

Compton, W. M., Grant, B. F., Colliver, J. D., Glantz, M. D., & Stinson, F. S. (2004). Prevalence of marijuana use disorders in the United States 1991–1992 and 2001–2002. *Journal of the American Medical Association, 291*, 2114–2121.

Comuzzie, A. G., & Allison, D. B. (1998). The search for human obesity genes. *Science, 280*, 1374–1377.

Conel, J. L. (1959). *The postnatal development of the human cerebral cortex.* Cambridge, MA: Harvard University Press.

Conference Board. (1999, June 25). *Workplace education programs are benefiting U.S. corporations and workers* [Online, Press release]. Available: http://www.newswise.com/articles/1999/6/WEP.TCB.html.

Conger, R. C., Ge, X., Elder, G. H., Lorenz, F. O., & Simons, R. L. (1994). Economic stress, coercive family processes, and developmental problems of adolescents. *Child Development, 65*, 541–561.

Conger, R. D., & Elder, G. H., Jr. (1994). *Families in troubled times: Adapting to change in rural America.* New York: Aldine de Gruyter.

Conger, R. D., Conger, K. J., Elder, G. H., Jr., Lorenz, F. O., Simons, R. L. & Whitbeck, L. B. (1993). Family economic stress and adjustment of early adolescent girls. *Developmental Psychology, 29*, 206–219.

Congressional Budget Office. (2004a, November). Disability and retirement: The early exit of baby boomers from the labor force. [Online]. Retrieved February 14, 2005, from http://www.cbo.gov/showdoc.cfm?index=6018&sequence=0.

Congressional Budget Office. (2004b, May 12). Retirement age and the need for saving. *Economic and Budget Issue Brief.* [Online]. Retrieved February 14, 2005, from http://www.cbo.gov/showdoc.cfm?index=5419&sequence=0.

Congressional Budget Office. (2004c, March 18). The retirement prospects of the baby boomers. *Economic and Budget Issue Brief.* [Online]. Retrieved February 14, 2005, from http://www.cbo.gov/showdoc.cfm?index=5195&sequence=0.

Connidis, I. A., & Davies, L. (1992). Confidants and companions: Choices in later life. *Journal of Gerontology: Social Sciences, 47*(30), S115–122.

Constantino, J. N. (2003). Autistic traits in the general population: A twin study. *Archives of General Psychiatry, 60*, 524–530.

Conway, E. E. (1998). Nonaccidental head injury in infants: The shaken baby syndrome revisited. *Pediatric Annals, 27*, 677–690.

Cook, E. H., Courchesne, R., Lord, C., Cox, N. J., Yan, S., Lincoln, A., Haas, R., Courchesne, E., & Leventhal, B. L. (1997). Evidence of linkage between the serotonin transporter and autistic disorder. *Molecular Psychiatry, 2*, 247–250.

Cooper, H. (1989, November). Synthesis of research on homework. *Educational Leadership,* 85–91.

Cooper, H., Lindsay, J. J., Nye, B., & Greathouse, S. (1998). Relationships among attitudes about homework, amount of homework assigned and completed, and student achievement. *Journal of Educational Psychology, 90*, 70–83.

Cooper, H., Valentine, J. C., Nye, B., & Lindsay, J. J. (1999). Relationships between five after-school activities and academic achievement. *Journal of Educational Psychology, 91*(2), 369–378.

Cooper, K. L., & Gutmann, D. L. (1987). Gender identity and ego mastery style in middle-aged, pre- and post-empty nest women. *The Gerontologist, 27*(3), 347–352.

Cooper, R. P., & Aslin, R. N. (1990). Preference for infant-directed speech in the first month after birth. *Child Development, 61*, 1584–1595.

Cooper, R. S., Rotimi, C. N., & Ward, R. (1999, February). The puzzle of hypertension in African-Americans. *Scientific American,* pp. 56–63.

Coplan, R. J., Prakash, K., O'Neil, K., & Armer, M. (2004). Do you "want" to play? Distinguishing between conflicted-shyness and social disinterest in early childhood. *Developmental Psychology, 40*, 244–258.

Corbet, A., Long, W., Schumacher, R., Gerdes, J., Cotton, R., & the American Exosurf Neonatal Study Group 1. (1995). Double-blind developmental evaluation at 1-year corrected age of 597 premature infants with birth weights from 500 to 1350 grams enrolled in three placebo-controlled trials of prophylactic synthetic surfactant. *Journal of Pediatrics, 126,* S5–S12.

Corcoran, M., & Matsudaira, J. (2005). Is it getting harder to get ahead? Economic attainment in early adulthood for two cohorts. In R. A. Settersten, Jr., F. F. Furstenberg, Jr., & R. G. Rumbaut (Eds.), *On the frontier of adulthood: Theory, research, and public policy* (pp. 356–395). (John D. and Catherine T. MacArthur Foundation Series on Mental Health and Development, Research Network on Transitions to Adulthood and Public Policy.) Chicago: University of Chicago Press.

Cornelius, S. W., & Caspi, A. (1987). Everyday problem solving in adulthood and old age. *Psychology and Aging, 2,* 144–153.

Correa, A., Botto, L., Liu, V., Mulinare, J., & Erickson, J. D. (2003). Do multivitamin supplements attenuate the risk for diabetes-associated birth defects? *Pediatrics, 111,* 1146–1151.

Costa, P. T., Jr., & McCrae, R. R. (1980). Still stable after all these years: Personality as a key to some issues in adulthood and old age. In P. B. Baltes, Jr., & O. G. Brim (Eds.), *Lifespan development and behavior* (Vol. 3, pp. 65–102). New York: Academic Press.

Costa, P. T., Jr., & McCrae, R. R. (1988). Personality in adulthood: A six-year longitudinal study of self-reports and spouse ratings on the NEO Personality Inventory. *Journal of Personality and Social Psychology, 54,* 853–863.

Costa, P. T., Jr., & McCrae, R. R. (1994a). Set like plaster? Evidence for the stability of adult personality. In T. F. Heatherton & J. L. Weinberger (Eds.), *Can personality change?* (pp. 21–41). Washington, DC: American Psychological Association.

Costa, P. T., Jr., & McCrae, R. R. (1994b). Stability and change in personality from adolescence through adulthood. In C. F. Halverson, G. A. Kohnstamm, & R. P. Martin (Eds.), *The developing structure of temperament and personality from infancy to adulthood.* Hillsdale, NJ: Erlbaum.

Costa, P. T., Jr., & McCrae, R. R. (1996). Mood and personality in adulthood. In C. Magai & S. H. McFadden (Eds.), *Handbook of emotion, adult development, and aging* (pp. 369–383). San Diego: Academic Press.

Costa, P. T., Jr., McCrae, R. R., Zonderman, A. B., Barbano, H. E., Lebowitz, B., & Larson, D. M. (1986). Cross-sectional studies of personality in a national sample: 2. Stability in neuroticism, extraversion, and openness. *Psychology and Aging, 1,* 144–149.

Costello, E. J., Compton, S. N., Keeler, G., & Angold, A. (2003). Relationship between poverty and psychopathology: A natural experiment. *Journal of the American Medical Association, 290,* 2023–2029.

Costello, E. J., Mustillo, S., Erkanli, A., Keeler, G., & Angold, A. (2003). Prevalence and development of psychiatric disorders in childhood and adolescence. *Archives of General Psychiatry, 60,* 837–844.

Costello, S. (1990, December). Yani's monkeys: Lessons in form and freedom. *School Arts,* pp. 10–11.

Courchesne, E., Carper, R., & Akshoomoff, N. (2003). Evidence of brain overgrowth in the first year of life in autism. *Journal of the American Medical Association, 290,* 337–344.

Cowan, N., Nugent, L. D., Elliott, E. M., Ponomarev, I., & Saults, J. S. (1999). The role of attention in the development of short-term memory: Age differences in the verbal span of apprehension. *Child Development, 70,* 1082–1097.

Cox, J., Daniel, N., & Boston, B. O. (1985). *Educating able learners: Programs and promising practices.* Austin: University of Texas Press.

Cox, W. M., & Alm, R. (2005, February 28). Scientists are made, not born. *The New York Times,* p. A19.

Coyle, T. R., & Bjorklund, D. F. (1997). Age differences in, and consequences of, multiple and variable-strategy use on a multitrial sort-recall task. *Developmental Psychology, 33,* 372–380.

Craik, F. I. M., & Byrd, M. (1982). Aging and cognitive deficits: The role of attentional resources. In F. I. M. Craik & S. Trehub (Eds.), *Aging and cognitive processes* (pp. 191–221). New York: Plenum.

Craik, F. I. M., & Jennings, J. M. (1992). Human memory. In F. I. M. Craik & T. A. Salthouse (Eds.), *Handbook of aging and cognition* (pp. 51–110). Hillsdale, NJ: Erlbaum.

Craik, F. I. M., & Salthouse, T. A. (Eds.). (2000). *The handbook of aging and cognition* (2nd ed.). Mahwah, NJ: Erlbaum.

Crain-Thoreson, C., & Dale, P. S. (1992). Do early talkers become early readers? Linguistic precocity, preschool language, and emergent literacy. *Developmental Psychology, 28,* 421–429.

Creed, P. A., & Macintyre, S. R. (2001). The relative effects of deprivation of the latent and manifest benefits of employment on the well being of unemployed people. *Journal of Occupational Health Psychology, 6,* 324–331.

Crick, N. R., & Dodge, K. A. (1994). A review and reformulation of social information-processing mechanisms in children's social adjustment. *Psychological Bulletin, 115,* 74–101.

Crick, N. R., & Dodge, K. A. (1996). Social information-processing mechanisms in reactive and proactive aggression. *Child Development, 67,* 993–1002.

Crick, N. R., & Grotpeter, J. K. (1995). Relational aggression, gender, and social-psychological adjustment. *Child Development, 66,* 710–722.

Crick, N. R., Bigbee, M. A., & Howes, C. (1996). Gender differences in children's normative beliefs about aggression: How do I hurt thee? Let me count the ways. *Child Development, 67,* 1003–1014.

Crick, N. R., Casas, J. F., & Nelson, D. A. (2002). Toward a more comprehensive understanding of peer maltreatment: Studies of relational victimization. *Current Directions in Psychological Science, 11*(3), 98–101.

Crijnen, A. A. M., Achenbach, T. M., & Verhulst, F. C. (1999). Problems reported by parents of children in multiple cultures: The Child Behavior Checklist syndrome constructs. *American Journal of Psychiatry, 156,* 569–574.

Crockenberg, S. C. (2003). Rescuing the baby from the bathwater: How gender and temperament influence how child care affects child development. *Child Development, 74,* 1034–1038.

Crouter, A., & Larson, R. (Eds.). (1998). *Temporal rhythms in adolescence: Clocks, calendars, and the coordination of daily life* (New Directions in Child and Adolescent Development, No. 82). San Francisco: Jossey-Bass.

Crouter, A. C., & Manke, B. (1994). The changing American workplace: Implications for individuals and families. *Family Relations, 43,* 117–124.

Crouter, A. C., Helms-Erikson, H., Updegraff, K., & McHale, S. M. (1999). Conditions underlying parents' knowledge about children's daily lives in middle childhood: Between- and within-family comparisons. *Child Development, 70,* 246–259.

Crouter, A. C., MacDermid, S. M., McHale, S. M., & Perry-Jenkins, M. (1990). Parental monitoring and perception of children's school performance and conduct in dual- and single-earner families. *Developmental Psychology, 26,* 649–657.

Crouter, A. C., & McHale, S. M. (1993). Temporal rhythms in family life: Seasonal variation and the relation between parental work and family processes. *Developmental Psychology, 29,* 198–205.

Crow, J. F. (1993). How much do we know about spontaneous human mutation rates? *Environmental and Molecular Mutagenesis, 21,* 122–129.

Crow, J. F. (1995). Spontaneous mutation as a risk factor. *Experimental and Clinical Immunogenetics, 12*(3), 121–128.

Crow, J. F. (1999). The odds of losing at genetic roulette. *Nature, 397,* 293–294.

Crowe, M., Andel, R., Pedersen, N.L., Johansson, B., & Gatz, M. (2003). Does participation in leisure activities lead to reduced risk of Alzheimer's Disease? A prospective study of Swedish twins. *Journal of Gerontology: Psychological Sciences, 58B,* P249–P 255.

Crowley, S. L. (1993, October). Grandparents to the rescue. *AARP Bulletin,* pp. 1, 16–17.

Cruzan v. Director, Missouri Department of Health, 110 S. Ct. 2841 (1990).

Csikszentmihalyi, M. (1999). If we are so rich, why aren't we happy? *American Psychologist, 54,* 821–827.

Cumming, E., & Henry, W. (1961). *Growing old.* New York: Basic Books.

Cummings, E. M., Iannotti, R. J., & Zahn-Waxler, C. (1989). Aggression between peers in early childhood: Individual continuity and developmental change. *Child Development, 60,* 887–895.

Cummings, J. L. (2004). Alzheimer's disease. *New England Journal of Medicine, 351,* 56–67.

Cunniff, C., & the Committee on Genetics. (2004). Prenatal screening and diagnosis for pediatricians. *Pediatrics, 114,* 889–894.

Cunningham, A. S., Jelliffe, D. B., & Jelliffe, E. F. P. (1991). Breastfeeding and health in the 1980s: A global epidemiological review. *Journal of Pediatrics, 118,* 659–666.

Cunningham, F. G., & Leveno, K. J. (1995). Childbearing among older women—The message is cautiously optimistic. *New England Journal of Medicine, 333,* 1002–1004.

Curtin, S. C., & Park, M. M. (1999). Trends in the attendant, place, and timing of births, and in the use of obstetric interventions: United States, 1989–97 (*National Vital Statistics Reports, 47*[27]). Hyattsville, MD: National Center for Health Statistics.

Curtiss, S. (1977). *Genie.* New York: Academic Press.

Cutler, S. J. (1998, December). Senator/astronaut John Glenn shows what older persons can do. *Gerontology News,* p. 1.

Cuttini, M., Nadai, M., Kaminski, M., Hansen, G., de Leeuw, R., Lenoir, S., Persson, J., Rabagliato, M., Reid, M., de Vonderweid, U., Lenard, H. G., Orzalesi, M., & Saracci, R., for the EURONIC Study Group. (2000). End-of-life decisions in neonatal intensive care: Physicians' self-reported practices in seven European countries. *Lancet, 355,* 2112–2118.

Cutz, E., Perrin, D. G., Hackman, R., & Czegledy-Nagy, E. N. (1996). Maternal smoking and pulmonary neuroendocrine cells in sudden infant death syndrome. *Pediatrics, 88,* 668–672.

Cytrynbaum, S., Bluum, L., Patrick, R., Stein, J., Wadner, D., & Wilk, C. (1980). Midlife development: A personality and social systems perspective. In L. Poon (Ed.), *Aging in the 1980s.* Washington, DC: American Psychological Association.

Czaja, A. J., & Sharit, J. (1998). Ability-performance relationships as a function of age and task experience for a data entry task. *Journal of Experimental Psychology-Applied, 4,* 332–351.

Czeisler, C. A., Duffy, J. F., Shanahan, T. L., Brown, E. N., Mitchell, J. F., Rimmer, D. W., Ronda, J. M., Silva, E. J., Allan, J. S., Emens, J. S., Dijk, D., & Kronauer, R. E. (1999). Stability, precision, and near 24-hour period of the human circadian pacemaker. *Science, 284,* 2177–2181.

Daiute, C., Hartup, W. W., Sholl, W., & Zajac, R. (1993, March). *Peer collaboration and written language development: A study of friends and acquaintances.* Paper presented at the meeting of the Society for Research in Child Development, New Orleans, LA.

Dale, P. S., Price, T. S., Bishop, D. V. M., & Plomin, R. (2003). Outcomes of early language delay: I. Predicting persistent and transient language difficulties at 3 and 4 years. *Journal of Speech, Language, and Hearing Research, 46,* 544–560.

Dale, P. S., Simonoff, E., Bishop, D. V. M., Eley, T. C., Oliver, B., Price, T. S., Purcell, S., Stevenson, J., & Plomin, R. (1998). Genetic influence on language delay in two-year-old children. *Nature Neuroscience, 1,* 324–328.

Dan, A. J., & Bernhard, L. A. (1989). Menopause and other health issues for midlife women. In S. Hunter & M. Sundel (Eds.), *Midlife myths.* Newbury Park, CA: Sage.

Danesi, M. (1994). *Cool: The signs and meanings of adolescence.* Toronto: University of Toronto Press.

Dangour, A. D., Sibson, V. L., & Fletcher, A. E. (2004). Micronutrient supplementation in later life: Limited evidence for benefit. *Journal of Gerontology: Biological Sciences, 59A,* 659–673.

Darling, N., & Steinberg, L. (1993). Parenting style as context: An integrative model. *Psychological Bulletin, 113,* 487–496.

Darroch, J. E., Singh, S., Frost, J. J., & the Study Team. (2001). Differences in teenage pregnancy rates among five developed countries: The roles of sexual activity and contraceptive use. *Family Planning Perspectives, 33,* 244–250, 281.

Datar, A., & Sturm, R. (2004a). Childhood overweight and parent- and teacher-reported behavior problems. *Archives of Pediatric and Adolescent Medicine, 158,* 804–810.

Datar, A., & Sturm, R. (2004b). Physical education in elementary school and body mass index: Evidence from the Early Childhood Longitudinal Study. *American Journal of Public Health, 94,* 1501–1507.

Datar, A., Sturm, R., & Magnabosco, J. L. (2004). Childhood overweight and academic performance: National study of kindergartners and first-graders. *Obesity Research, 12,* 58–68.

David and Lucile Packard Foundation. (2004). Children, families, and foster care: Executive summary. *The Future of Children, 14*(1). Available: http://www.futureofchildren.org.

David, R. J., & Collins, J. W., Jr. (1997). Differing birth weight among infants of U.S.-born blacks, African-born blacks, and U.S.-born whites. *New England Journal of Medicine, 337,* 1209–1214.

Davidson, J. I. F. (1998). Language and play: Natural partners. In D. P. Fromberg & D. Bergen (Eds.), *Play from birth to twelve and beyond: Contexts, perspectives, and meanings* (pp. 175–183). New York: Garland.

Davidson, N. E. (1995). Hormone-replacement therapy—Breast versus heart versus bone. *New England Journal of Medicine, 332,* 1638–1639.

Davidson, P. W., Myers, G. J., & Weiss, B. (2004). Mercury exposure and child development outcomes. *Pediatrics, 113,* 1023–1029.

Davidson, R. J., & Fox, N. A. (1989). Frontal brain asymmetry predicts infants' response to maternal separation. *Journal of Abnormal Psychology, 948*(2), 58–64.

Davies, C., & Williams, D. (2002). *The grand-parent study 2002 report.* Washington, DC: AARP.

Davies, M., Stankov, L., Roberts, R. D. (1998). Emotional intelligence: In search of an elusive construct. *Journal of Personality and Social Psychology, 75,* 989–1015.

Davis, B. E., Moon, R. Y., Sachs, H. C., Ottolini, M. C. (1998). Effects of sleep position on infant motor development. *Pediatrics, 102,* 1135–1140.

Davis, M., & Emory, E. (1995). Sex differences in neonatal stress reactivity. *Child Development, 66,* 14–27.

Davis-Kean, P. E., & Sandler, H. M. (2001). A meta-analysis of measures of self-esteem for young children: A framework for future measures. *Child Development, 72,* 887–906.

Davison, K. K., & Birch, L. L. (2001). Weight status, parent reaction, and self-concept in five-year-old girls. *Pediatrics, 107,* 46–53.

Davison, K. K., Susman, E. J., & Birch, L. L. (2003). Percent body fat at age 5 predicts earlier pubertal development among girls at age 9. *Pediatrics, 111,* 815–821.

Dawson, D. A. (1991). Family structure and children's health and well-being: Data from the 1988 National Health Interview Survey on child health. *Journal of Marriage and the Family, 53,* 573–584.

Dawson, G., Frey, K., Panagiotides, H., Yamada, E., Hessl, D., & Osterling, J. (1999). Infants of depressed mothers exhibit atypical frontal electrical brain activity during interactions with mother and with a familiar nondepressed adult. *Child Development, 70,* 1058–1066.

Dawson, G., Klinger, L. G., Panagiotides, H., Hill, D., & Spieker, S. (1992). Frontal lobe activity and affective behavior of infants of mothers with depressive symptoms. *Child Development, 63,* 725–737.

Dawson-Hughes, B., Harris, S. S., Krall, E. A., & Dallal, G. E. (1997). Effect of calcium and vitamin D supplementation on bone density in men and women 65 years of age and older. *New England Journal of Medicine, 337,* 670–676.

Day, S. (1993, May). Why genes have a gender. *New Scientist, 138*(1874), 34–38.

de Castro, B. O., Veerman, J. W., Koops, W., Bosch, J. D., & Monshouwer, H. J. (2002). Hostile attribution of intent and aggressive behavior: A meta-analysis. *Child Development, 73,* 916–934.

Deary, I. J., & Der, G. (2005). Reaction time explains IQ's association with death. *Psychological Science, 16,* 64–69.

Deary, I. J., Leaper, S. A., Murray, A. D., Staff, R. T., & Whalley, L. J. (2003). Cerebral white matter abnormalities and lifetime cognitive change: A 67-year follow-up of the Scottish Mental survey of 1932. *Psychology and Aging, 18,* 140–148.

Deary, I. J., Whalley, L. J., & Starr, J. M. (2003). IQ at age 11 and longevity: Results from a follow-up of the Scottish Mental Survey 1932. In C. D. Finch, J.-M. Robine, & Y. Christen (Eds.), *Brain and longevity: Perspec-*

tives in longevity (pp. 153–164). Berlin: Springer.

DeBell, M., & Chapman, C. (2003). *Computer and Internet use by children and adolescents in 2001* (NCES 2004-014). Washington, DC: National Center for Education Statistics, U.S. Department of Education.

DeCasper, A. J., & Fifer, W. P. (1980). Of human bonding: Newborns prefer their mothers' voices. *Science, 208,* 1174–1176.

DeCasper, A. J., & Spence, M. J. (1986). Prenatal maternal speech influences newborns' perceptions of speech sounds. *Infant Behavior and Development, 9,* 133–150.

DeCasper, A. J., Lecanuet, J. P., Busnel, M. C., Granier-Deferre, C., & Maugeais, R. (1994). Fetal reactions to recurrent maternal speech. *Infant Behavior and Development, 17,* 159–164.

deGroot, L. C. P. M. G., Verheijden, M. W., deHenauw, S., Schroll, M., & van Staveren, W. A. for the SENECA Investigators. (2004). Lifestyle, nutritional status, health, and mortality in elderly people across Europe: A review of the longitudinal results of the SENECA study. *Journal of Gerontology: Medical Sciences, 59A,* 1277–1284.

DeHaan, L. G., & MacDermid, S. M. (1994). Is women's identity achievement associated with the expression of generativity? Examining identity and generativity in multiple roles. *Journal of Adult Development, 1,* 235–247.

Dekovic, M., & Janssens, J. M. A. M. (1992). Parents' child-rearing style and child's sociometric status. *Developmental Psychology, 28,* 925–932.

de la Chica, R. A., Ribas, I., Giraldo, J., Egozcue, J., & Fuster, C. (2005). Chromosomal instability in amniocytes from fetuses of mothers who smoke. *Journal of the American Medical Association, 293,* 1212–1222.

de Lange, T. (1998). Telomeres and senescence: Ending the debate. *Science, 279,* 334–335.

Del Carmen, R. D., Pedersen, F. A., Huffman, L. C., & Bryan, Y. E. (1993). Dyadic distress management predicts subsequent security of attachment. *Infant Behavior and Development, 16,* 131–147.

Delany, E., Delany, S., & Hearth, A. H. (1993). *The Delany sisters' first 100 years.* New York: Kodansha America.

DeLoache, J., & Gottlieb, A. (2000). If Dr. Spock were born in Bali: Raising a world of babies. In J. DeLoache & A. Gottlieb (Eds.), *A world of babies: Imagined childcare guides for seven societies* (pp. 1–27). New York: Cambridge University Press.

DeLoache, J. S. (2000). Dual representation and young children's use of scale models. *Child Development, 71,* 329–338.

DeLoache, J. S., Miller, K. F., & Pierroutsakos, S. L. (1998). Reasoning and problem solving. In D. Kuhn & R. S. Siegler (Eds.), *Handbook of Child Psychology: Vol. 2. Cognition, perception, and language* (5th ed., pp. 801–850). New York: Wiley.

DeLoache, J. S., Miller, K. F., & Rosengren, K. S. (1997). The credible shrinking room: Very young children's performance with symbolic and nonsymbolic relations. *Psychological Science, 8,* 308–313.

DeLoache, J. S., Pierroutsakos, S. L., & Uttal, D. H. (2003). The origins of pictorial competence. *Current Directions in Psychological Science, 12,* 114–118.

DeLoache, J. S., Pierroutsakos, S. L., Uttal, D. H., Rosengren, K. S., & Gottlieb, A. (1998). Grasping the nature of pictures. *Psychological Science, 9,* 205–210.

DeMaris, A., Benson, M. L., Fox, G. L, Hill, T., & VanWyk, J. (2003). Distal and proximal factors in domestic violence: A test of an integrated model. *Journal of Marriage and Family, 65,* 652–667.

Demo, D. H. (1991). A sociological perspective on parent-adolescent disagreements. In R. L. Paikoff (Ed.), *Shared views in the family during adolescence* (New Directions for Child Development, No. 51, pp. 111–118). San Francisco: Jossey-Bass.

Denham, M., Schell, L. M., Deane, G., Gallo, M. V., Ravenscroft, J., & DeCaprio, A. P., & the Akwesasne Task Force on the Environment. (2005). Relationship of lead, mercury, mirex, dichlorodiphenyldichloroethylene, hexachlorobenzene, and polychlorinated biphenyls to timing of menarche among Akwesasne Mohawk girls. *Pediatrics, 115*(2), e127–e134.

Denham, S. A., Blair, K. A., DeMulder, E., Levitas, J., Sawyer, K., Auerbach-Major, S., & Queenan, P. (2003). Preschool emotional competence: Pathway to social competence? *Child Development, 74,* 238–256.

Denney, N. W., & Palmer, A. M. (1981). Adult age differences on traditional and practical problem-solving measures. *Journal of Gerontology, 36*(3), 323–328.

Denney, N. W., & Pearce, K. A. (1989). A developmental study of practical problem solving in adults. *Psychology and Aging, 4*(4), 438–442.

Dennis, W. (1936). A bibliography of baby biographies. *Child Development, 7,* 71–73.

Denton, K., West, J., and Walston, J. (2003). *Reading—young children's achievement and classroom experiences: Findings from* The Condition of Education 2003. Washington, DC: National Center for Education Statistics.

Department of Commerce. (2002). *A nation online: How Americans are expanding their use of the Internet.* Washington, DC: Author.

Desai, M., Pratt, L. A., Lentzner, H., & Robinson, K. N. (2001). Trends in vision and hearing among older Americans. *Aging Trends,* No. 2. Hyattsville, MD: National Center for Health Statistics.

DeStefano, F., Bhasin, T. K., Thompson, W. W., Yeargin-Allsopp, M., and Boyle, C. (2004). Age at first measles-mumps-rubella vaccination in children with autism and school-matched control subjects: A population-based study in metropolitan Atlanta. *Pediatrics, 113,* 259–266.

Detrich, R., Phillips, R., & Durett, D. (2002). Critical issue: Dynamic debate—determining the evolving impact of charter schools. [Online]. North Central Regional Educational Laboratory. Available: http://www.ncrel.org/sdrs/areas/issues/envrnmnt/go/go800.htm.

Devaney, B., Johnson, A., Maynard, R., & Trenholm, C. (2002). *The evaluation of abstinence education programs funded under Title V, Section 510: Interim report.* Washington, DC: U.S. Department of Health and Human Services.

DeVoe, J. F., Peter, K., Kaufman, P., Miller, A., Noonan, M., Snuder, T. D., & Baum, K. (2004). *Indicators of school crime and safety: 2004* (NCES 2005-002/NCJ 205290). Washington, DC: U.S. Departments of Education and Justice.

de Vries, B. (1996). The understanding of friendship: An adult life course perspective. In C. Magai & S. H. McFadden (Eds.), *Handbook of emotion, adult development, and aging* (pp. 249–269). San Diego: Academic Press.

De Wolff, M. S., & van IJzendoorn, M. H. (1997). Sensitivity and attachment: A meta-analysis on parental antecedents of infant attachment. *Child Development, 68,* 571–591.

Dewey, K. G., Heinig, M. J., & Nommsen-Rivers, L. A. (1995). Differences in morbidity between breast-fed and formula-fed infants. *Journal of Pediatrics, 126,* 696–702.

Dey, A. N., Schiller, J. S., & Tai, D. A. (2004). Summary health statistics for U.S. children: National Health Interview Survey, 2002. *Vital Health Statistics 10* (221). Bethesda, MD: National Center for Health Statistics.

Deykin, E. Y., Alpert, J. J., & McNamara, J. J. (1985). A pilot study of the effect of exposure to child abuse or neglect on adolescent suicidal behavior. *American Journal of Psychiatry, 142*(11), 1299–1303.

Diamond, A. (1991). Neuropsychological insights into the meaning of object concept development. In S. Carey & R. Gelman (Eds.), *Epigenesis of mind* (pp. 67–110). Hillsdale, NJ: Erlbaum.

Diamond, L. M. (1998). Development of sexual orientation among adolescent and young adult women. *Developmental Psychology, 34*(5), 1085–1095.

Diamond, L. M. (2000). Sexual identity, attractions, and behavior among young sexual minority women over a 2-year period. *Developmental Psychology, 36,* 241–250.

Diamond, L. M. (2003). Was it a phase? Young women's relinquishment of lesbian/bisexual identities over a 5-year period. *Journal of Personality and Social Psychology, 84,* 352–364.

Diamond, L. M., & Savin-Williams, R. C. (2003). The intimate relationships of sexual-minority youths. In G. R. Adams & M. D. Berzonsky (Eds.), *Blackwell handbook of adolescence* (pp. 393–412). Malden, MA: Blackwell.

Diamond, M. C. (1988). *Enriching heredity.* New York: Free Press.

Diamond, M., & Sigmundson, H. K. (1997). Sex reassignment at birth: Long-term review and clinical implications. *Archives of Pediatric and Adolescent Medicine, 151,* 298–304.

Diamond, P., & Orszag, P. (2002). *Reducing benefits and subsidizing private accounts: An analysis of the plans proposed by the President's Commission to Strengthen Social Security.* Washington, DC: Center on Budget and Policy Priorities and the Century Foundation.

Diary of Anaïs Nin (1931–1934).

Dickinson, G. E., Lancaster, C. J., Clark, D., Ahmedzai, S. H., & Noble, W. (2002). U.K. physicians' attitudes toward active voluntary euthanasia and physician-assisted suicide. *Death Studies, 26,* 479–490.

Diehl, M., Willis, S. L., & Schaie, K. W. (1994). *Practical problem solving in older adults: Observational assessment and cognitive correlates.* Unpublished manuscript, Wayne State University, Detroit.

Dien, D. S. F. (1982). A Chinese perspective on Kohlberg's theory of moral development. *Developmental Review, 2,* 331–341.

Diener, E. (2000). Subjective well-being: The science of happiness and a proposal for a national index. *American Psychologist, 55,* 34–43.

DiFranza, J. R., Aligne, C. A., & Weitzman, M. (2004). Prenatal and postnatal environmental tobacco smoke exposure and children's health. *Pediatrics, 113,* 1007–1015.

Dillaway, H., & Broman, C. (2001). Race, class, and gender in marital satisfactions and divisions of household labor among dual-earner couples. *Journal of Family Issues, 22,* 309–327.

Dimant, R. J., & Bearison, D. J. (1991). Development of formal reasoning during successive peer interactions. *Developmental Psychology, 27,* 277–284.

DiMarco, M. A., Menke, E. M., & McNamara, T. (2001). Evaluating a support group for perinatal loss. *MCN American Journal of Maternal and Child Nursing, 26,* 135–140.

Ding, Y-C., Chi, H-C., Grady, D. L., Morishima, A., Kidd, J. R., Kidd, K. K., Flodman, P., Spence, M. A., Schuck, S., Swanson, J. M., Zhang, Y-P., & Moyzis, R. K. (2002). Evidence of positive selection acting at the human dopamine receptor D4 gene locus. *Proceedings of the National Academy of Science, 99,* 309–314.

Dingfelder, S. (2004). Programmed for psychopathology? Stress during pregnancy may increase children's risk for mental illness, researchers say. *Monitor on Psychology, 35*(2), 56–57.

DiPietro, J., Hilton, S., Hawkins, M., Costigan, K., & Pressman, E. (2002). Maternal stress and affect influences fetal neurobehavioral development. *Developmental Psychology, 38,* 659–668.

DiPietro, J. A. (2004). The role of prenatal maternal stress in child development. *Current Directions in Psychological Science, 13*(2), 71–74.

DiPietro, J. A., Caulfield, L. E., Costigan, K. A., Merialdi, M., Nguyen, R. H. N., Zavaleta, N., & Gurewitsch, E. D. (2004). Fetal neurobehavioral development: A tale of two cities. *Developmental Psychology, 40,* 445–456.

DiPietro, J. A., Hodgson, D. M., Costigan, K. A., Hilton, S. C., & Johnson, T. R. B. (1996). Fetal neurobehavioral development. *Child Development, 67,* 2553–2567.

Dishion, T. J., McCord, J., & Poulin, F. (1999). When intervention harms. *American Psychologist, 54,* 755–764.

Dixon, R. A., & Baltes, P. B. (1986). Toward lifespan research on the functions and pragmatics of intelligence. In R. J. Sternberg & R. K. Wagner (Eds.), *Practical intelligence: Nature and origins of competence in the everyday world* (pp. 203–235). New York: Cambridge University Press.

Dixon, R. A., & Hultsch, D. F. (1999). Intelligence and cognitive potential in late life. In J. C. Cavanaugh & S. K. Whitbourne (Eds.), *Gerontology: An interdisciplinary perspective.* New York: Oxford University Press.

Dixon, R. A., Hultsch, D. F., & Herzog, C. (1988). The metamemory in adulthood (MIA) questionnaire. *Psychopharmacology Bulletin, 24,* 671–688.

Dlugosz, L., Belanger, K., Helienbrand, K., Holfard, T. R., Leaderer, B., & Bracken, M. B. (1996). Maternal caffeine consumption and spontaneous abortion: A prospective cohort study. *Epidemiology, 7,* 250–255.

Dodge, K. A., Coie, J.D., Pettit, G. S., & Price, J. M. (1990). Peer status and aggression in boys' groups: Developmental and contextual analysis. *Child Development, 61,* 1289–1309.

Dodge, K. A., Pettit, G. S., & Bates, J. E. (1994). Socialization mediators of the relation between socioeconomic status and child conduct problems. *Child Development, 65,* 649–665.

Doherty, W. J., Kouneski, E. F., & Erickson, M. F. (1998). Responsible fathering: An overview and conceptual framework. *Journal of Marriage and the Family, 60,* 277–292.

Doka, K. J., & Mertz, M. E. (1988). The meaning and significance of greatgrandparenthood. *The Gerontologist, 28*(2), 192–197.

Dolan, M. A., & Hoffman, C. D. (1998). Determinants of divorce among women: A reexamination of critical influences. *Journal of Divorce & Remarriage, 28,* 97–106.

Donovan, W. L., Leavitt, L. A., & Walsh, R. O. (1998). Conflict and depression predict maternal sensitivity to infant cries. *Infant Behavior and Development, 21,* 505–517.

Dorris, M. (1989). *The broken cord.* New York: Harper & Row.

Dorsey, M. J., & Schneider, L. C. (2003). Improving asthma outcomes and self-management behaviors of inner-city children. *Pediatrics, 112,* 474.

Dougherty, T. M., & Haith, M. M. (1997). Infant expectations and reaction time as predictors of childhood speed of processing and IQ. *Developmental Psychology, 33,* 146–155.

Downey, D. B., & Condron, D. J. (2004). Playing well with others in kindergarten: The benefit of siblings at home. *Journal of Marriage and Family, 66,* 333–350.

Dozier, M., Stovall, K. C., Albus, K. E., & Bates, B. (2001). Attachment for infants in foster care: The role of caregiver state of mind. *Child Development, 72,* 1467–1477.

Dreher, M. C., Nugent, K., & Hudgins, R. (1994). Prenatal marijuana exposure and neonatal outcomes in Jamaica: An ethnographic study. *Pediatrics, 93,* 254–260.

Dreyfus, H. L. (1993–1994, Winter). What computers still can't do. *Key Reporter,* pp. 4–9.

Driscoll, I., McDaniel, M. A., & Guynn, M. J. (2005). Apolipoprotein E and prospective memory in normally aging adults. *Neuropsychology, 19,* 28–34.

Drug Policy Alliance. (2004, June 23). South Carolina v. McKnight. [Online]. Retrieved April 6, 2005 from http://www.drugpolicy.org/law/womenpregnan/mcknight.cfm.

Drumm, P., & Jackson, D. W. (1996). Developmental changes in questioning strategies during adolescence. *Journal of Adolescent Research, 11,* 285–305.

Drummond, S. P. A., Brown, G. G., Gillin, J. C., Stricker, J. L., Wong, E. C., & Buxton, R. B. (2000). Altered brain response to verbal learning following sleep deprivation. *Nature, 403,* 655–657.

Dubé, E. M., & Savin-Williams, R. C. (1999). Sexual identity development among ethnic sexual-minority youths. *Developmental Psychology, 35*(6), 1389–1398.

Dube, S. R., Anda, R. F., Felitti, V. J., Chapman, D. P., Williamson, D. F., & Giles, W. H. (2001). Childhood abuse, household dysfunction, and the risk of attempted suicide throughout the life span: Findings from the Adverse Childhood Experiences Study. *Journal of the American Medical Association, 286*(24), 3089–3096.

Dube, S. R., Felitti, V. J., Dong, M., Chapman, D. P., Giles, W. H. & Anda, R. F. (2003 March). Childhood abuse, neglect, and household dysfunction and the risk of illicit drug use: The Adverse Childhood Experiences Study. *Pediatrics, 111*(3), 564–572.

Dubowitz, H. (1999). The families of neglected children. In M. E. Lamb (Ed.), *Parenting and child development in "nontraditional" families* (pp. 327–345). Mahwah, NJ: Erlbaum.

Duenwald, M. (2003, July 15). After 25 years, new ideas in the prenatal test tube. *New York Times.* [Online]. Available: http://www.nytimes.com/2003/07/15/health/15IVF.html?ex1059274835&ei1&en21c6928d1811f348.

Duffy, P. H., Seng, J. E., Lewis, S. M., Mayhugh, M. A., Aidoo, A., Hattan, D. G., Casciano, D. A., & Feuers, R. J. (2001). The effects of different levels of dietary restriction on aging and survival in the Sprague-Dawley rat: Implications for chronic studies. *Aging, 13,* 263–272.

Duke, J., Huhman, M., & Heitzler, C. (2003). Physical activity levels among children aged 9–13 years—United States, 2002. *Morbidity and Mortality Weekly Report, 52,* 785–788.

Duncan, G. J., & Brooks-Gunn, J. (1997). Income effects across the life span: Integration and interpretation. In G. J. Duncan & J. Brooks-Gunn (Eds.), *Consequences of growing up poor* (pp. 596–610). New York: Russell Sage Foundation.

Dunham, P. J., Dunham, F., & Curwin, A. (1993). Joint-attentional states and lexical acquisition at 18 months. *Developmental Psychology, 29,* 827–831.

Dunlosky, J., & Hertzog, C. (1998). Aging and deficits in associative memory: What is the role of strategy production? *Psychology and Aging, 13,* 597–607.

Dunn, A. L., Marcus, B. H., Kampert, J. B., Garcia, M. E., Kohl, H. W., III, & Blair, S. N. (1999). Comparison of lifestyle and structured interventions to increase physical activity and cardiorespiratory fitness: A randomized trial. *Journal of the American Medical Association, 281,* 327–334.

Dunn, A. L., Trivedi, M. H., Kampert, J. B., Clark, C. G., & Chambliss, H. O. (2005). Exercise treatment for depression: Efficacy and dose response. *American Journal of Preventive Medicine, 28,* 1–8.

Dunn, J. (1991). Young children's understanding of other people: Evidence from observations within the family. In D. Frye & C. Moore (Eds.), *Children's theories of mind: Mental states and social understanding.* Hillsdale, NJ: Erlbaum.

Dunn, J. (1996). Sibling relationships and perceived self-competence: Patterns of stability between childhood and early adolescence. In A. J. Sameroff & M. M. Haith (Eds.), *The five to seven year shift: The age of reason and responsibility* (pp. 253–269). Chicago: University of Chicago Press.

Dunn, J., Brown, J., Slomkowski, C., Tesla, C., & Youngblade, L. (1991). Young children's understanding of other people's feelings and beliefs: Individual differences and antecedents. *Child Development, 62,* 1352–1366.

Dunn, J., & Hughes, C. (2001). "I got some swords and you're dead!": Violent fantasy, antisocial behavior, friendship, and moral sensibility in young children. *Child Development, 72,* 491–505.

Dunn, J., & Munn, P. (1985). Becoming a family member: Family conflict and the development of social understanding in the second year. *Child Development, 56,* 480–492.

Dunson, D. (2002). *Late breaking research session. Increasing infertility with increasing age: Good news and bad news for older couples.* Paper presented at 18th Annual Meeting of the European Society of Human Reproduction and Embryology, Vienna.

Dunson, D. B., Colombo, B., & Baird, D. D. (2002). Changes with age in the level and duration of fertility in the menstrual cycle. *Human Reproduction, 17,* 1399–1403.

DuPont, R. L. (1983). Phobias in children. *Journal of Pediatrics, 102,* 999–1002.

Durand, A. M. (1992). The safety of home birth: The Farm study. *American Journal of Public Health, 82,* 450–452.

DuRant, R. H., Smith, J. A., Kreiter, S. R., & Krowchuk, D. P. (1999). The relationship between early age of onset of initial substance use and engaging in multiple health risk behaviors among young adolescents. *Archives of Pediatrics & Adolescent Medicine, 153,* 286–291.

Durlak, J. A. (1973). Relationship between attitudes toward life and death among elderly women. *Developmental Psychology, 8*(1), 146.

Dush, C. M. K., Cohan, C. L., & Amato, P. R. (2003). The relationship between cohabitation and marital quality and stability: Change across cohorts? *Journal of Marriage and Family, 65,* 539–549.

Duskin, Rita. (1987). Haiku. In C. Spelius, Ed., *Sound and Light*. Deerfield, IL: Lakeshore Publishing.

Dwyer, T., Ponsonby, A. L., Blizzard, L., Newman, N. M., & Cochrane, J. A. (1995). The contribution of changes in the prevalence of prone sleeping position to the decline in sudden infant death syndrome in Tasmania. *Journal of the American Medical Association, 273,* 783–789.

Dychtwald, K., & Flower, J. (1990). *Age wave: How the most important trend of our time will change your future.* New York: Bantam.

Dykstra, P. A. (1995). Loneliness among the never and formerly married: The importance of supportive friendships and a desire for independence. *Journal of Gerontology: Social Sciences, 50B,* S321–329.

Early detection of Alzheimer's disease. (2002, August). *Harvard Mental Health Letter*, pp. 3–5.

Eastell, R. (1998). Treatment of postmenopausal osteoporosis. *New England Journal of Medicine, 338,* 736–746.

Eastman, F. (1965). John H. Glenn. In *The world book encyclopedia* (Vol. 8, pp. 214–214d). Chicago: Field Enterprises Educational Corporation.

Eating disorders—Part I. (1997, October). *The Harvard Mental Health Letter*, pp. 1–5.

Eating disorders—Part II. (1997, November). *The Harvard Mental Health Letter*, pp. 1–5.

Eber, G. B., Annest, J. L., Mercy, J. A., & Ryan, G. W. (2004). Nonfatal and fatal firearm-related injuries among children aged 14 years and younger: United States, 1993–2000. *Pediatrics, 113,* 1686–1692.

Eccles, A. (1982). *Obstetrics and gynaecology in Tudor and Stuart England.* Kent, OH: Kent State University Press.

Eccles, J. S., Wigfield, A., & Byrnes, J. (2003). Cognitive development in adolescence. In Weiner, I. B., (Ed.), *Handbook of psychology. Vol. 6: Developmental psychology.* Vol. Eds. R. M. Lerner, M. A. Easterbrooks, and J. Mistry. New York: John Wiley and Sons.

Echeland, Y., Epstein, D. J., St-Jacques, B., Shen, L., Mohler, J., McMahon, J. A., & McMahon, A. P. (1993). Sonic hedgehog, a member of a family of putative signality molecules, is implicated in the regulation of CNS polarity. *Cell, 75,* 1417–1430.

Eckerman, C. O., Davis, C. C., & Didow, S. M. (1989). Toddlers' emerging ways of achieving social coordination with a peer. *Child Development, 60,* 440–453.

Eckerman, C. O., & Didow, S. M. (1996). Nonverbal imitation and toddlers' mastery of verbal means of achieving coordinated action. *Developmental Psychology, 32,* 141–152.

Eckerman, C. O., & Stein, M. R. (1982). The toddler's emerging interactive skills. In K. H. Rubin & H. S. Ross (Eds.), *Peer relationships and social skills in childhood.* New York: Springer-Verlag.

Eden, G. F., Jones, K. M., Cappell, K., Gareau, L., Wood, F. B., Zeffiro, T. A., Dietz, N. A. E., Agnew, J. A., & Flowers, D. L. (2004). Neural changes following remediation in adult developmental dyslexia. *Neuron, 44,* 411–422.

Edwards, C. P. (1981). The comparative study of the development of moral judgment and reasoning. In R. Monroe, R. Monroe, & B. B. Whiting (Eds.), *Handbook of cross-cultural human development.* New York: Garland.

Edwards, C. P. (1994, April). *Cultural relativity meets best practice, or, anthropology and early education, a promising friendship.* Paper presented at the meeting of the American Educational Research Association, New Orleans.

Edwards, K. I. (1993). Obesity, anorexia, and bulimia. *Clinical Nutrition, 77,* 899–909.

Effective solutions for impotence. (1994, October). *Johns Hopkins Medical Letter: Health after 50,* pp. 2–3.

Egan, S. K., & Perry, D. G. (2001). Gender identity: A multidimensional analysis with implications for psychosocial adjustment. *Developmental Psychology, 37,* 451–463.

Egbuono, L., & Starfield, B. (1982). Child health and social status. *Pediatrics, 69,* 550–557.

Eggebeen, D. J., & Knoester, C. (2001). Does fatherhood matter for men? *Journal of Marriage and Family, 63,* 381–393.

Ehrensaft, M. K., Cohen, P., Brown, J., Smailes, E., Chen, H., & Johnson, J. G. (2003). Intergenerational transmission of partner violence: A 20-year prospective study. *Journal of Consulting and Clinical Psychology, 71,* 741–753.

Eimas, P., Siqueland, E., Jusczyk, P., & Vigorito, J. (1971). Speech perception in infants. *Science, 171,* 303–306.

Eisen, M., & Zellman, G. L. (1987). Changes in incidence of sexual intercourse of unmarried teenagers following a community-based sex education program. *Journal of Sex Research, 23*(4), 527–544.

Eisenberg, A. (April 5, 2001). A "smart" home, to avoid the nursing home. *The New York Times,* pp. G1, G6.

Eisenberg, A. R. (1996). The conflict talk of mothers and children: Patterns related to culture, SES, and gender of child. *Merrill-Palmer Quarterly, 42,* 438–452.

Eisenberg, L. (1995, Spring). Is the family obsolete? *Key Reporter,* pp. 1–5.

Eisenberg, N. (1992). *The caring child.* Cambridge, MA: Harvard University Press.

Eisenberg, N. (2000). Emotion, regulation, and moral development. *Annual Review of Psychology, 51,* 665–697.

Eisenberg, N., & Fabes, R. A. (1998). Prosocial development. In W. Damon (Series Ed.) & N. Eisenberg (Vol. Ed.), *Handbook of child psychology: Vol. 3. Social, emotional, and personality development* (5th ed., pp. 701–778). New York: Wiley.

Eisenberg, N., Fabes, R. A., Guthrie, I. K., & Reiser, M. (2000). Dispositional emotionality and regulation: Their role in predicting quality of social functioning. *Journal of Personality and Social Psychology, 78,* 136–157.

Eisenberg, N., Fabes, R. A., & Murphy, B. C. (1996). Parents' reactions to children's negative emotions: Relations to children's social competence and comforting behavior. *Child Development, 67,* 2227–2247.

Eisenberg, N., Fabes, R. A., Nyman, M., Bernzweig, J., & Pinuelas, A. (1994). The relations of emotionality and regulation to children's anger-related reactions. *Child Development, 65,* 109–128.

Eisenberg, N., Fabes, R. A., Schaller, M., & Miller, P. A. (1989). Sympathy and personal distress: Development, gender differences, and interrelations of indexes. In N. Eisenberg (Ed.), *Empathy and related emotional responses* (New Directions for Child Development No. 44). San Francisco: Jossey-Bass.

Eisenberg, N., Fabes, R. A., Shepard, S. A., Guthrie, I. K., Murphy, B. C., & Reiser, M. (1999). Parental reactions to children's negative emotions: Longitudinal relations to quality of children's social functioning. *Child Development, 70*(2), 513–534.

Eisenberg, N., Guthrie, I. K., Fabes, R. A., Reiser, M., Murphy, B. C., Holgren, R., Maszk, P., & Losoya, S. (1997). The relations of regulation and emotionality to resiliency and competent social functioning in elementary school children. *Child Development, 68,* 295–311.

Eisenberg, N., Guthrie, I. K., Murphy, B. C., Shepard, S. A., Cumberland, A., & Carlo, G. (1999). Consistency and development of prosocial dispositions: A longitudinal study. *Child Development, 70*(6), 1360–1372.

Eisenberg, N., Spinrad, T. L., Fabes, R. A., Reiser, M., Cumberland, A., Shepard, S. A., Valiente, C., Losoya, S. H., Guthrie, I. K., & Thompson, M. (2004). The relations of effortful control and impulsivity to children's resiliency and adjustment. *Child Development, 75,* 25–46.

Elbert, S. E. (1984). *A hunger for home: Louisa May Alcott and "Little Women."* Philadelphia: Temple University Press.

Elder, G. H., Jr. (1974). *Children of the Great Depression: Social change in life experience.* Chicago: University of Chicago Press.

Elder, G. H., Jr. (1998). The life course and human development. In W. Damon (Series Ed.) & R. M. Lerner (Vol. Ed.), *Handbook of child psychology: Vol. 1. Theoretical models of human development* (5th ed., pp. 939–9992). New York: Wiley.

Elia, J., Ambrosini, P. J., & Rapoport, J. L. (1999). Treatment of attention-deficit hyperactivity disorder. *New England Journal of Medicine, 340,* 780–788.

Elicker, J., Englund, M., & Sroufe, L. A. (1992). Predicting peer competence and peer relationships in childhood from early parent-child relationships. In R. Parke & G. Ladd (Eds.), *Family-peer relationships: Modes of linkage* (pp. 77–106). Hillsdale, NJ: Erlbaum.

Elkind, D. (1981). *The hurried child.* Reading, MA: Addison-Wesley.

Elkind, D. (1984). *All grown up and no place to go.* Reading, MA: Addison-Wesley.

Elkind, D. (1986). *The miseducation of children: Superkids at risk.* New York: Knopf.

Elkind, D. (1997). *Reinventing childhood: Raising and educating children in a changing world.* Rosemont, NJ: Modern Learning Press.

Elkind, D. (1998). *All grown up and no place to go.* Reading, MA: Perseus Books.

Ellickson, P. L., Orlando, M., Tucker, J. S., & Klein, D. J. (2004). From adolescence to young adulthood: Racial/ethnic disparities in smoking. *American Journal of Public Health, 94,* 293–299.

Elliott, D. S. (1993). Health enhancing and health compromising lifestyles. In S. G. Millstein, A. C. Petersen, & E. O. Nightingale (Eds.), *Promoting the health of adolescents: New directions for the twenty-first century.* New York: Oxford University Press.

Elliott, V. S. (2000, November 20). Doctors caught in middle of ADHD treatment controversy: Critics charge that medications are being both under- and overprescribed. *AMNews.* [Online]. Retrieved April 21, 2005, from http://www.ama-assn.org/amednews/2000/11/20/hlsb1120.htm.

Ellis, B. J., Bates, J. E., Dodge, K. A., Fergusson, D. M., Horwood, L. J., Pettit, G. S., & Woodward, L. (2003). Does father-absence place daughters at special risk for early sexual activity and teenage pregnancy? *Child Development, 74,* 801–821.

Ellis, B. J., & Garber, J. (2000). Psychosocial antecedents of variation in girls' pubertal timing: Maternal depression, stepfather presence, and marital family stress. *Child Development, 71*(2), 485–501.

Ellis, B. J., McFadyen-Ketchum, S., Dodge, K. A., Pettit, G. S., & Bates, J. E. (1999). Quality of early family relationships and individual differences in the timing of pubertal maturation in girls: A longitudinal test of an evolutionary model. *Journal of Personality and Social Psychology, 77,* 387–401.

Ellis, K. J., Abrams, S. A., & Wong, W. W. (1997). Body composition of a young, multiethnic female population. *American Journal of Clinical Nutrition, 65,* 724–731.

Eltzschig, H. K., Lieberman, E. S., & Camann, W. R. (2003). Regional anesthesia and analgesia for labor and delivery. *New England Journal of Medicine, 348,* 319–332.

Emde, R. N. (1992). Individual meaning and increasing complexity: Contributions of Sigmund Freud and René Spitz to developmental psychology. *Developmental Psychology, 28,* 347–359.

Emde, R. N., Plomin, R., Robinson, J., Corley, R., DeFries, J., Fulker, D. W., Reznick, J. S., Campos, J., Kagan, J., & Zahn-Waxler, C. (1992). Temperament, emotion, and cognition at 14 months: The MacArthur longitudinal twin study. *Child Development, 63,* 1437–1455.

Emmons, R. A., & McCullough, M. E. (2003). Counting blessings versus burdens: An experimental investigation of gratitude and subjective well-being in daily life. *JPSP, 84,* 377–389.

Emslie, G. J. (2004). *The Treatment of Adolescents with Depression Study (TADS): Primary safety outcomes.* Presentation at the New Clinical Drug Evaluation Unit conference, Phoenix, AZ.

Eng, P. M., Rimm, E. B., Fitzmaurice, G., & Kawachi, I. (2002). Social ties and change in social ties in relation to subsequent total and cause-specific mortality and coronary heart disease incidence in men. *American Journal of Epidemiology, 155,* 700–709.

Engels, H., Drouin, J., Zhu, W., & Kazmierski, J. F. (1998). Effects of low-impact, moderate-intensity exercise training with and without wrist weights on functional capacities and mood states in older adults. *Gerontology, 44,* 239–244.

Engle, P. L., & Breaux, C. (1998). Fathers' involvement with children: Perspectives from developing countries. *Social Policy Report, 12*(1), 1–21.

Enloe, C. F. (1980). How alcohol affects the developing fetus. *Nutrition Today, 15*(5), 12–15.

Eogan, M. A., Geary, M. P., O'Connell, M. P., & Keane, D. P. (2003). Effect of fetal sex on labour and delivery: Retrospective review. *British Medical Journal, 326,* 137.

Epel, E. S., Blackburn, E. H., Lin, J., Dhabhar, F. S., Adler, N. E., Morrow, J. D., & Cawthon, R. M. (2004). Accelerated telomere shortening in response to life stress. *Proceedings of the National Academy of Sciences, 101,* 17312–17315.

Epstein, R. A. (1989, Spring). Voluntary euthanasia. *Law School Record* (University of Chicago), pp. 8–13.

Erdley, C. A., Cain, K. M., Loomis, C. C., Dumas-Hines, F., & Dweck, C. S. (1997). Relations among children's social goals, implicit personality theories, and responses to social failure. *Developmental Psychology, 33,* 263–272.

Erikson, E. (1969). *Gandhi's Truth: On the origins of militant nonviolence.* New York: Norton.

Erikson, E. H. (1950). *Childhood and society.* New York: Norton.

Erikson, E. H. (1968). *Identity: Youth and crisis.* New York: Norton.

Erikson, E. H. (1973). The wider identity. In K. Erikson (Ed.), *In search of common ground: Conversations with Erik H. Erikson and Huey P. Newton.* New York: Norton.

Erikson, E. H. (1982). *The life cycle completed.* New York: Norton.

Erikson, E. H. (1985). *The life cycle completed* (paperback reprint ed.). New York: Norton.

Erikson, E. H., Erikson, J. M., & Kivnick, H. Q. (1986). *Vital involvement in old age: The experience of old age in our time.* New York: Norton.

Eriksson, P. S., Perfilieva, E., Björk-Eriksson, T., Alborn, A., Nordborg, C., Peterson, D. A., & Gage, F. H. (1998). Neurogenesis in the adult human hippocampus. *Nature Medicine, 4,* 1313–1317.

Eron, L. D. (1980). Prescription for reduction of aggression. *American Psychologist, 35,* 244–252.

Eron, L. D. (1982). Parent-child interaction, television violence, and aggression in children. *American Psychologist, 37,* 197–211.

Eron, L. D., & Huesmann, L. R. (1986). The role of television in the development of prosocial and antisocial behavior. In D. Olweus, J. Block, & M. Radke-Yarrow (Eds.), *The development of antisocial and prosocial behavior: Research, theories, and issues.* New York: Academic.

Ervin, R. B., Wright, J. D., Wang, C.-Y., & Kennedy-Stephenson, J. (2004). Dietary intake

of fats and fatty acids for the United States Population: 1999–2000. *Advance Data from Vital and Health Statistics, No. 348.* Hyattsville, MD: National Center for Health Statistics.

Escobar-Chaves, S. L., Tortolero, S. R., Markham, C. M., Low, B. J., Eitel, P., & Thickstun, P. (2005). Impact of the media on Adolescent Sexual Attitudes and Behaviors. *Pediatrics, 116,* 303–326.

Espeland, M. A., Gu, L., Masaki, K. H., Langer, R. D., Coker, L. H., Stefanick, M. L., Ockene, J., & Rapp, S. R., for the Women's Health Initiative Memory Study. (2005). Association between reported alcohol intake and cognition: Results from the Women's Health Initiative Memory Study. *American Journal of Epidemiology, 161,* 228–238.

Espeland, M. A., Rapp, S. R., Shumaker, S. A., Brunner, R., Manson, J. E., Sherwin, B. B., Hsia, J., Margolis, K. L., Hogan, P. E., Wallace, R., Dailey, M., Freeman, R., Hays, J. for the Women's Health Initiative Memory Study Investigators. (2004). Conjugated equine estrogens and global cognitive function in postmenopausal women: Women's Health Initiative Memory Study. Journal of the American Medical Association, 21, 2959–2968.

Esposito, K., Marfella, R., Ciotola, M., DiPalo, C., Giugliano, F., Giugliano, G., D'Armiento, M., D'Andrea, F., & Giugliano, D. (2004). Effects of a Mediterranean-style diet on endothelial dysfunction and markers of vascular inflammaion in the metabolic syndrome: A randomized trial. *Journal of the American Medical Association, 292,* 1440–1446.

Essex, M. J., & Nam, S. (1987). Marital status and loneliness among older women: The differential importance of close family and friends. *Journal of Marriage and the Family, 49,* 93–106.

Ettinger, B., Friedman, G. D., Bush, T., & Quesenberry, C. P. (1996). Reduced mortality associated with long-term postmenopausal estrogen therapy. *Obstetrics & Gynecology, 87,* 6–12.

Etzel, R. A. (2003). How environmental exposures influence the development and exacerbation of asthma. *Pediatrics, 112*(1), 233–239.

European Collaborative Study. (1994). Natural history of vertically acquired human immunodeficiency virus-1 infection. *Pediatrics, 94,* 815–819.

Evans, G. (1976). The older the sperm . . . *Ms., 4*(7), 48–49.

Evans, G. W. (2004). The environment of childhood poverty. *American Psychologist, 59,* 77–92.

Evans, G. W., & English, K. (2002). The environment of poverty: Multiple stressor exposure, psychophysiological stress, and socioemotional adjustment. *Child Development, 73,* 1238–1248.

Evans, J. (1994). *Caring for the caregiver: Body, mind and spirit.* New York: American Parkinson Disease Association.

Evert. J., Lawler, E., Bogan, H., & Perls, T. (2003). Morbidity profiles of centenarians: Survivors, delayers, and escapers. *Journal of Gerontology: Medical Sciences, 58A,* 232–237.

Evertsson, M., & Nermo, M. (2004). Dependence within families and the division of labor:

Comparing Sweden and the United States. *Journal of Marriage and Family, 66,* 1272–1286.

Eyre-Walker, A., & Keightley, P. D. (1999). High genomic deleterious rates in hominids. *Nature, 397,* 344–347.

Ezzati, M., & Lopez, A. D. (2004). Regional, disease specific patterns of smoking-attributable mortality in 2000. *Tobacco Control, 13,* 388–395.

Fabes, R. A., & Eisenberg, N. (1992). Young children's coping with interpersonal anger. *Child Development, 63,* 116–128.

Fabes, R. A., & Eisenberg, N. (1996). *An examination of age and sex differences in prosocial behavior and empathy.* Unpublished data, Arizona State University.

Fabes, R. A., Leonard, S. A., Kupanoff, K., & Martin, C. L. (2001). Parental coping with children's negative emotions: Relations with children's emotional and social responding. *Child Development, 72,* 907–920.

Fabes, R. A., Martin, C. L., & Hanish, L. D. (2003, May). Young children's play qualities in same-, other-, and mixed-gender peer groups. *Child Development, 74*(3), 921–932.

Fagot, B. I. (1997). Attachment, parenting, and peer interactions of toddler children. *Developmental Psychology, 33,* 489–499.

Fagot, B. I., & Leinbach, M. D. (1995). Gender knowledge in egalitarian and traditional families. *Sex Roles, 32,* 513–526.

Faison, S. (1997, August 17). Chinese happily break the "one child" rule. *The New York Times,* pp. 1, 10.

Faith, M. S., Berman, N., Heo, M., Pietrobelli, A., Gallagher, D., Epstein, L. H., Eiden, M. T., & Allison, D. B. (2001). Effects of contingent television on physical activity and television viewing in obese children. *Pediatrics, 107,* 1043–1048.

Falbo, T., & Polit, D. F. (1986). Quantitative review of the only child literature: Research evidence and theory development. *Psychological Bulletin, 100*(2), 176–189.

Falbo, T., & Poston, D. L. (1993). The academic, personality, and physical outcomes of only children in China. *Child Development, 64,* 18–35.

Falkner, D. (1995). *Great time coming: The life of Jackie Robinson, from baseball to Birmingham.* New York: Simon & Schuster.

Fantz, R. L. (1963). Pattern vision in newborn infants. *Science, 140,* 296–297.

Fantz, R. L. (1964). Visual experience in infants: Decreased attention to familiar patterns relative to novel ones. *Science, 146,* 668–670.

Fantz, R. L. (1965). Visual perception from birth as shown by pattern selectivity. In H. E. Whipple (Ed.), *New issues in infant development. Annals of the New York Academy of Science, 118,* 793–814.

Fantz, R. L., Fagen, J., & Miranda, S. B. (1975). Early visual selectivity. In L. Cohen & P. Salapatek (Eds.), *Infant perception: From sensation to cognition: Vol. 1. Basic visual processes* (pp. 249–341). New York: Academic Press.

Fantz, R. L., & Nevis, S. (1967). Pattern preferences and perceptual-cognitive development in early infancy. *Merrill-Palmer Quarterly, 13,* 77–108.

Farquhar, C. M., & Steiner, C. A. (2002). Hysterectomy rates in the United States 1990–1997. *Obstetrics & Gynecology, 99,* 229–234.

Farver, J. A. M., Kim, Y. K., & Lee, Y. (1995). Cultural differences in Korean- and Anglo-American preschoolers' social interaction and play behavior. *Child Development, 66,* 1088–1099.

Fawcett, G. M., Heise, L. L., Isita-Espejel, L., & Pick, S. (1999). Change community responses to wife abuse: A research and demonstration project in Iztacalco, Mexico. *American Psychologist, 54,* 41–49.

Fearon, P., O'Connell, P., Frangou, S., Aquino, P., Nosarti, C., Allin, M., Taylor, M., Stewart, A., Rifkin, L., & Murray, R. (2004). Brain volume in adult survivors of very low birth weight: A sibling-controlled study. *Pediatrics, 114,* 367–371.

Federal Glass Ceiling Commission. (1995). *Good for business: Making full use of the nation's human capital: The environmental scam.* Washington, DC: U.S. Department of Labor.

Federal Interagency Forum on Aging-Related Statistics. (2004). *Older Americans 2004: Key indicators of well-being.* Washington, DC: U.S. Government Printing Office.

Feingold, A., & Mazzella, R. (1998). Gender differences in body image are increasing. *Psychological Science, 9*(3), 190–195.

Feinleib, J. A., & Michael, R. T. (2000). Reported changes in sexual behavior in response to AIDS in the United States. In Laumann, E. O., & Michael, R. T. (Eds.), *Sex, love, and health in America: Private choices and public policies* (pp. 302–326). Chicago: University of Chicago Press.

Feldhusen, J. F. (1992). *Talent identification and development in education (TIDE).* Sarasota, FL: Center for Creative Learning.

Feldman, H. A., Goldstein, I., Hatzichristou, D. G., Krane, R. J., & McKinlay, J. B. (1994). Impotence and its medical and psychosocial correlates: Results of the Massachusetts Male Aging Study. *Journal of Urology, 151,* 54–61.

Felner, R. D., Brand, S., DuBois, D. L., Adan, A. M., Mulhall, P. F., & Evans, E. G. (1995). Socioeconomic disadvantage, proximal environmental experiences, and socioemotional and academic adjustment in early adolescence: Investigation of a mediated effect. *Child Development, 66,* 774–792.

Ferber, R. (1985). *Solve your child's sleep problems.* New York: Simon & Schuster.

Ferber, S. G. & Makhoul, I. R. (2004). The effect of skin-to-skin contact (Kangaroo Care) shortly after birth on the neurobehavioral responses of the term newborn: A randomized, controlled trial. *Pediatrics, 113,* 858–865.

Fernald, A., & O'Neill, D. K. (1993). Peekaboo across cultures: How mothers and infants play with voices, faces, and expectations. In K. MacDonald (Ed.), *Parent-child play* (pp. 259–285). Albany: State University of New York Press.

Fernald, A., Pinto, J. P., Swingley, D., Weinberg, A., & McRoberts, G. W. (1998). Rapid gains in speed of verbal processing by infants in the 2nd year. *Psychological Science, 9*(3), 228–231.

Fetal development: A psychobiological perspective (pp. 239–262). Hillsdale, NJ: Erlbaum.

Fiatarone, M. A., Marks, E. C., Ryan, N. D., Meredith, C. N., Lipsitz, L. A., & Evans, W. J. (1990). High-intensity strength training in nonagenarians: Effects on skeletal muscles. *Journal of the American Medical Association, 263,* 3029–3034.

Fiatarone, M. A., O'Neill, E. F., & Ryan, N. D. (1994). Exercise training and nutritional supplementation for physical frailty in very elderly people. *New England Journal of Medicine, 330,* 1769–1775.

Fiatarone, M. A., O'Neill, E. F., Ryan, N. D., Clements, K. M., Solares, G. R., Nelson, M. E., Roberts, S. B., Kehayias, J. J., Lipsitz, L. A., & Evans, W. J. (1994). Exercise training and nutritional supplementation for physical frailty in very elderly people. *New England Journal of Medicine, 330,* 1769–1775.

Field, A. E., Camargo, C. A., Taylor, B., Berkey, C. S., Roberts, S. B., & Colditz, G. A. (2001). Peer, parent, and media influence on the development of weight concerns and frequent dieting among preadolescent and adolescent girls and boys. *Pediatrics, 107*(1), 54–60.

Field, A. E., Cook, N. R., & Gillman, M. W. (2005). Weight status in childhood as a predictor of becoming overweight or hypertensive in early adulthood. *Obesity Research, 13,* 163–169.

Field, T. (1995). Infants of depressed mothers. *Infant Behavior and Development, 18,* 1–13.

Field, T. (1998a). Emotional care of the at-risk infant: Early interventions for infants of depressed mothers. *Pediatrics, 102,* 1305–1310.

Field, T. (1998b). Massage therapy effects. *American Psychologist, 53,* 1270–1281.

Field, T. (1998c). Maternal depression effects on infants and early intervention. *Preventive Medicine, 27,* 200–203.

Field, T., Diego, M., Hernandez-Reif, M., Schanberg, S., & Kuhn, C (2003). Depressed mothers who are "good interaction" partners versus those who are withdrawn or intrusive. *Infant Behavior & Development, 26,* 238–252.

Field, T., Fox, N. A., Pickens, J., Nawrocki, T., & Soutollo, D. (1995). Right frontal EEG activation in 3- to 6-month-old infants of depressed mothers. *Developmental Psychology, 31,* 358–363.

Field, T., Grizzle, N., Scafidi, F., Abrams, S., Richardson, S., Kuhn, C., & Schanberg, S. (1996). Massage therapy for infants of depressed mothers. *Infant Behavior and Development, 19,* 107–112.

Field, T., Hernandez-Reif, M., & Freedman, J. (2004). Stimulation programs for preterm infants. *Social Policy Report, 18*(1), 1–19.

Field, T. M. (1978). Interaction behaviors of primary versus secondary caretaker fathers. *Developmental Psychology, 14,* 183–184.

Field, T. M. (1986). Interventions for premature infants. *Journal of Pediatrics, 109*(1), 183–190.

Field, T. M., & Roopnarine, J. L. (1982). Infant-peer interaction. In T. M. Field, A. Huston, H. C. Quay, L. Troll, & G. Finley (Eds.), *Review of human development.* New York: Wiley.

Field, T. M., Sandberg, D., Garcia, R.,Vega-Lahr, N., Goldstein, S., & Guy, L. (1985). Pregnancy problems, postpartum depression, and early infant-mother interactions. *Developmental Psychology, 21,* 1152–1156.

Fields, J. (2003). Children's living arrangements and characteristics: March 2002. *Current Population Reports* (p. 20–547). Washington, DC: U.S. Bureau of the Census.

Fields, J. (2004). America's families and living arrangements: 2003. *Current Population Reports* (P20–553). Washington, DC: U.S. Census Bureau.

Fields, J., & Casper, L. (2001). *America's families and living arrangements: March 2000.* (Current Population Reports, P20–537). Washington, DC: U.S. Census Bureau.

Fields, J. M., & Smith, K. E. (1998, April). *Poverty, family structure, and child well-being: Indicators from the SIPP* (Population Division Working Paper No. 23, U.S. Bureau of the Census). Paper presented at the Annual Meeting of the Population Association of America, Chicago, IL.

Fields, L. E., Burt, V. L., Cutler, J. A., Hughes, J., Roccella, E. J., & Sorlie, P. (2004). The burden of adult hypertension in the United States 1999 to 2000: A rising tide. *Hypertension, 44,* 398.

Fifer, W. P., & Moon, C. M. (1995). The effects of fetal experience with sound. In J. P. Lecanuet, W. P. Fifer, N. A. Krasnegor, & W. P. Smotherman (Eds.), *Fetal development: A psychobiological perspective* (pp. 351–366). Hillsdale, NJ: Erlbaum.

Finch, C. E. (2001). Toward a biology of middle age. In M. E. Lachman (Ed.), *Handbook of midlife development* (pp. 77–108). New York: Wiley.

Fincham. F. D., Beach, S. H., & Davila, J. (2004). Forgiveness and conflict resolution in marriage. *Journal of Family Psychology, 18,* 72–81.

Finn, J. D., & Rock, D. A. (1997). Academic success among students at risk for dropout. *Journal of Applied Psychology, 82,* 221–234.

Finn, R. (1993, February 8). Arthur Ashe, tennis champion, dies of AIDS. *The New York Times,* pp. B1, B43.

First woman to both poles—Ann Bancroft. (1997). [Online]. Available: http://www.zplace.com/rhonda/abancroft. Access date: April 4, 2002.

Fiscella, K., Kitzman, H. J., Cole, R. E., Sidora, K. J., & Olds, D. (1998). Does child abuse predict adolescent pregnancy? *Pediatrics, 101,* 620–624.

Fischer, K. (1980). A theory of cognitive development: The control and construction of hierarchies of skills. *Psychological Review, 87,* 477–531.

Fischer K. W., & Pruyne, E. (2003). Reflective thinking in adulthood. In J. Demick & C. Andreoletti (Eds.) *Handbook of adult development.* New York: Plenum Press.

Fischer, K. W., & Rose, S. P. (1994). Dynamic development of coordination of components in brain and behavior: A framework for theory and research. In G. Dawson & K. W. Fischer (Eds.), *Human behavior and the developing brain* (pp. 3–66). New York: Guilford.

Fischer, K. W., & Rose, S. P. (1995, Fall). Concurrent cycles in the dynamic development of brain and behavior. *SRCD Newsletter,* pp. 3–4, 15–16.

Fisher, C. B., Hoagwood, K., Boyce, C., Duster, T., Frank, D. A., Grisso, T., Levine, R. J., Macklin, R., Spencer, M. B., Takanishi, R., Trimble, J. E., & Zayas, L. H. (2002). Research ethics for mental health science involving ethnic minority children and youth. *American Psychologist, 57,* 1024–1040.

Fisk, A. D., & Rogers, W. A. (2002). Psychology and aging: Enhancing the lives of an aging population. *Current Directions in Psychological Science, 11,* 107–110.

Fivush, R., Hudson, J., & Nelson, K. (1983). Children's long-term memory for a novel event: An exploratory study. *Merrill-Palmer Quarterly, 30,* 303–316.

Fivush, R., & Schwarzmeuller, A. (1998). Children remember childhood: Implications for childhood amnesia. *Applied Cognitive Psychology, 12,* 455–473.

Flavell, J. (1963). *The developmental psychology of Jean Piaget.* New York: Van Nostrand.

Flavell, J. H. (1970). Developmental studies of mediated memory. In H. W. Reese & L. P. Lipsitt (Eds.), *Advances in child development and behavior* (Vol. 5, pp. 181–211). New York: Academic.

Flavell, J. H. (1992). Cognitive development: Past, present, and future. *Developmental Psychology, 28,* 998–1005.

Flavell, J. H. (1993). Young children's understanding of thinking and consciousness. *Current Directions in Psychological Science, 2,* 40–43.

Flavell, J. H., Green, F. L., & Flavell, E. R. (1986). Development of knowledge about the appearance-reality distinction. *Monographs of the Society for Research in Child Development, 51* (1, Serial No. 212).

Flavell, J. H., Green, F. L., & Flavell, E. R. (1995). Young children's knowledge about thinking. *Monographs of the Society for Research in Child Development, 60*(1, Serial No. 243).

Flavell, J. H., Green, F. L., Flavell, E. R., & Grossman, J. B. (1997). The development of children's knowledge about inner speech. *Child Development, 68,* 39–47.

Flavell, J. H., Miller, P. H., & Miller, S. A. (1993). *Cognitive development.* Englewood Cliffs, NJ: Prentice-Hall.

Flavell, J. H., Miller, P. H., & Miller, S. A. (2002). *Cognitive development.* Englewood Cliffs, NJ: Prentice-Hall.

Fleeson, W. (2004). The quality of American life at the end of the century. In O. G. Brim, C. D. Ryff, & R. C. Kessler (Eds.), *How healthy are we? A national study of well-being at midlife.* Chicago: University of Chicago Press.

Flegal, K. M., Graubard, B. I., Williamson, D. F., & Gail, M. H. (2005). Excess deaths associated with underweight, overweight, and obesity. *Journal of the American Medical Association, 293,* 1861–1867.

Flint, M., & Samil, R. S. (1990). Cultural and subcultural meanings of the menopause. In M. Flint, F. Kronenberg, & W. Utian (Eds.), *Multidisciplinary perspectives on menopause* (pp. 134–148). New York: Annals of the New York Academy of Sciences.

Flores, G., Fuentes-Afflick, E., Barbot, O., Carter-Pokras, O., Claudio, L., Lara, M., McLaurin, J. A., Pachter, L., Gomez, F. R., Mendoza, F., Valdez, R. B., Villarruel, A. M., Zambrana, R. E., Greenberg, R., & Weitzman, M. (2002). The health of Latino children: Urgent priorities, unanswered questions, and a research agenda. *Journal of the American Medical Association, 288,* 82–90.

Flores, G., Olson, L, & Tomany-Korman, S. C. (2005). Racial and ethnic disparities in early childhood health and health care. *Pediatrics, 115,* e183–e193.

Fluoxetine-Bulimia Collaborative Study Group. (1992). Fluoxetine in the treatment of bulimia nervosa: A multicenter placebo-controlled, double-blind trial. *Archives of General Psychiatry, 49,* 139–147.

Flynn, J. R. (1984). The mean IQ of Americans: Massive gains 1932 to 1978. *Psychological Bulletin, 95,* 29–51.

Flynn, J. R. (1987). Massive IQ gains in 14 nations: What IQ tests really measure. *Psychological Bulletin, 101,* 171–191.

Foldvari, M., Clark, M., Laviolette, L. C., Bernstein, M. A., Kaliton, D., Castaneda, C., Pu, C. T., Hausdorff, J. M., Fielding, R. A., & Singh, M. A. (2000). Association of muscle power with functional status in community-dwelling elderly women. *Journal of Gerontology: Biological and Medical Sciences, 55,* M192–199.

Foley, D. J., & White, L. (2002). Dietary intake of antioxidants and risk of Alzheimer disease: Food for thought. *Journal of the American Medical Association, 287,* 3261–3263.

Folkman, S., & Lazarus, R. S. (1980). An analysis of coping in a middle-aged community sample. *Journal of Health and Social Behavior, 21,* 219–239.

Folkman, S., Lazarus, R. S., Pimley, S., & Novacek, J. (1987). Age differences in stress and coping processes. *Psychology and Aging, 2,* 171–184.

Fombonne, E. (2001). Is there an epidemic of autism? *Pediatrics, 107,* 411–412.

Fombonne, E. (2003). The prevalence of autism. *Journal of the American Medical Association, 289,* 87–89.

Fontanel, B., & d'Harcourt, C. (1997). *Babies, history, art and folklore.* New York: Abrams.

Ford, D. Y., & Harris, J. J., III. (1996). Perceptions and attitudes of black students toward school, achievement, and other educational variables. *Child Development, 67,* 1141–1152.

Ford, P. (April 10, 2002). In Europe, marriage is back. *Christian Science Monitor,* p. l.

Ford, R. P., Schluter, P. J., Mitchell, E. A., Taylor, B. J., Scragg, R., & Stewart, A. W. (1998). Heavy caffeine intake in pregnancy and sudden infant death syndrome (New Zealand Cot Death Study Group). *Archives of Disease in Childhood, 78*(1), 9–13.

Forteza, J. A., & Prieto, J. M. (1994). Aging and work behavior. In H. C. Triandis, M. D. Dunnette, & L. M. Hough (Eds.), *Handbook of industrial and organizational psychology* (pp. 447–483). Palo Alto, CA: Consulting Psychologists Press.

Fortner, M. R., Crouter, A. C., & McHale, S. M. (2004). Is parents' work involvement responsive to the quality of relationships with adolescent offspring? *Journal of Family Psychology, 18,* 530–538.

Foster, D. (1999). Isabel Allende unveiled. In J. Rodden (Ed.), *Conversations with Isabel Allende* (pp. 105–113). Austin: University of Texas Press.

Foundation Fighting Blindness. (2005). Macular Degeneration—Treatments. [Online]. Retrieved May 21, 2005, from http://www.blindness.org/disease/treatment detail.asp?typed=2&id=6.

Fowler, J. (1981). *Stages of faith: The psychology of human development and the quest for meaning.* New York: Harper & Row.

Fowler, J. W. (1989). Strength for the journey: Early childhood development in selfhood and faith. In D. A. Blazer, J. W. Fowler, K. J. Swick, A. S. Honig, P. J. Boone, B. M. Caldwell, R. A. Boone, & L. W. Barber (Eds.), *Faith development in early childhood* (pp. 1–63). New York: Sheed & Ward.

Fowler, M. G., Simpson, G. A., & Schoendorf, K. C. (1993). Families on the move and children's health care. *Pediatrics, 91,* 934–940.

Fox, M. A., Connolly, B. A., & Snyder, T. D. (2005). *Youth Indicators, 2005: Trends in the Well-Being of American Youth* (NCES 2005050). Washington, DC: National Center for Education Statistics.

Fox, M. K., Pac, S., Devaney, B., & Jankowski, L. (2004). Feeding Infants and Toddlers Study: What foods are infants and toddlers eating? *Journal of the American Dietetic Association, 104,* 22–30.

Fox, N. A., Kimmerly, N. L., & Schafer, W. D. (1991). Attachment to mother/attachment to father: A meta-analysis. *Child Development, 62,* 210–225.

Fox, N. C., Black, R. S., Gilman, S., Rossor, M. N., Griffith, S. G., Jenkins, L., & Koller, M. for the AN1792(QS-21)-201 Study Team. (2005). Effects of Aß immunization (AN1792) on MRI measures of cerebral volume in Alzheimer disease. *Neurology, 64,* 1563–1572.

Fraiberg, S. (1959). *The magic years.* New York: Scribner's.

Frank, A. (1958). *The diary of a young girl* (B. M. Mooyaart-Doubleday, Trans.). New York: Pocket.

Frank, A. (1995). *The diary of a young girl: The definitive edition* (O. H. Frank & M. Pressler, Eds.; S. Massotty, Trans.). New York: Doubleday.

Frank, D. A., Augustyn, M., Knight, W. G., Pell, T., & Zuckerman, B. (2001). Growth, development, and behavior in early childhood following prenatal cocaine exposure. *Journal of the American Medical Association, 285,* 1613–1625.

Frankenburg, W. K., Dodds, J., Archer, P., Bresnick, B., Maschka, P., Edelman, N., &

Shapiro, H. (1992). *Denver II training manual.* Denver: Denver Developmental Materials.

Frankenburg, W. K., Dodds, J. B., Fandal, A. W., Kazuk, E., & Cohrs, M. (1975). *The Denver Developmental Screening Test: Reference manual.* Denver: University of Colorado Medical Center.

Franz, C. E. (1997). Stability and change in the transition to midlife: A longitudinal study of midlife adults. In M. E. Lachman & J. B. James (Eds.), *Multiple paths of midlife development* (pp. 45–66). Chicago: University of Chicago Press.

Fraser, A. M., Brockert, J. F., & Ward, R. H. (1995). Association of young maternal age with adverse reproductive outcomes. *New England Journal of Medicine, 332*(17), 1113–1117.

Frazier, J. A., & Morrison, F. J. (1998). The influence of extended-year schooling on growth of achievement and perceived competence in early elementary school. *Child Development, 69,* 495–517.

Fredricks, J. A., & Eccles, J. S. (2002). Children's competence and value beliefs from childhood through adolescence: Growth trajectories in two male-sex-typed domains. *Developmental Psychology, 38,* 519–533.

Fredriksen, K., Rhodes, J., Reddy, R., & Way, N. (2004). Sleepless in Chicago: Tracking the effects of adolescent sleep loss during the middle-school years. *Child Development, 75,* 84–95.

Freeark, K., Rosenberg, E. B., Bornstein, J., Jozefowicz-Simbeni, D., Linkevich, M., & Lohnes, K. (2005). Gender differences and dynamics shaping the adoption life cycle: Review of the literature and recommendations. *American Journal of Orthopsychiatry, 75,* 86–101.

Freedman, J. (2004). Stimulation programs for preterm infants. *Social Policy Report, 18*(1), 1–19.

Freeman, C. (2004). *Trends in educational equity of girls & women: 2004* (NCES 2005016). Washington, DC: National Center for Education Statistics.

Freeman, D. (1983). *Margaret Mead and Samoa: The making and unmaking of an anthropological myth.* Cambridge, MA: Harvard University Press.

Freud, A. (1946). *The ego and the mechanisms of defense.* New York: International Universities Press.

Freud, S. (1942). On psychotherapy. In E. Jones (Ed.), *Collected papers.* London: Hogarth. (Original work published 1906).

Freud, S. (1953). *A general introduction to psychoanalysis* (J. Riviere, Trans.). New York: Perma-books (Original work published 1935).

Freud, S. (1964a). New introductory lectures on psycho-analysis. In J. Strachey (Ed. & Trans.), *The standard edition of the complete psychological works of Sigmund Freud* (Vol. 22). London: Hogarth (Original work published 1933).

Freud, S. (1964b). An outline of psychoanalysis. In J. Strachey (Ed. & Trans.), *The standard edition of the complete psychological works of Sigmund Freud* (Vol. 23). London: Hogarth (Original work published 1940).

Fried, P. A., & Smith, A. M. (2001). A literature review of the consequences of prenatal marijuana

exposure: An emerging theme of a deficiency in aspects of executive function. *Neurotoxicology and Teratology, 23,* 1–11.

Fried, P. A., Watkinson, B., & Willan, A. (1984). Marijuana use during pregnancy and decreased length of gestation. *American Journal of Obstetrics and Gynecology, 150,* 23–27.

Friedan, B. (1993). *The fountain of age.* New York: Simon & Schuster.

Friedland, R. P. (1993). Epidemiology, education, and the ecology of Alzheimer's disease. *Neurology, 43,* 246–249.

Friedman, H. S., & Markey, C. N. (2003). Paths to longevity in the highly intelligent Terman cohort. In C. E. Finch, J. Robine, J., & Y. Christen (Eds.), *Brain and longevity* (pp. 165–175). New York: Springer.

Friedman, H. S., Tucker, J. S., Schwartz, J. E., Martin, L. R., Tomlinson-Keasey, C., Wingard, D. L., & Criqui, M. H. (1995). Childhood conscientiousness and longevity: Health behaviors and cause of death. *Journal of Personality and Social Psychology, 68,* 696–703.

Friedman, H. S., Tucker, J. S., Schwartz, J. E., Tomlinson-Keasey, C., Martin, L. R., Wingard, D. L., & Criqui, M. H. (1995). Psychosocial and behavioral predictors of longevity. *American Psychologist, 50,* 69–78.

Friedman, H. S., Tucker, J. S., Tomlinson-Keasey, C., Schwartz, J. E., Martin, L. R., Wingard, D. L., & Criqui, M. H. (1993). Does childhood personality predict longevity? *Journal of Personality and Social Psychology, 65,* 176–185.

Friedman, L. J. (1999). *Identity's architect.* New York: Scribner.

Friedmann, P. D., Saitz, R., & Samet, J. H. (1998). Management of adults recovering from alcohol or other drug problems. *Journal of the American Medical Association, 279,* 1227–1231.

Friend, M., & Davis, T. L. (1993). Appearance reality distinction: Children's understanding of the physical and affective domains. *Developmental Psychology, 29,* 907–914.

Friend, R. A. (1991). Older lesbian and gay people: A theory of successful aging. In J. A. Lee (Ed.), *Gay midlife and maturity* (pp. 99–118). New York: Haworth.

Frith U. (1989). *Autism: Explaining the enigma.* Oxford: Basil Blackwell.

Fromkin, V., Krashen, S., Curtiss, S., Rigler, D., & Rigler, M. (1974). The development of language in Genie: Acquisition beyond the "critical period." *Brain and Language, 15*(9), 28–34.

Fromm, Erich. (1995). *The Sane Society.* New York. Rinehart.

Frydman, O., & Bryant, P. (1988). Sharing and the understanding of number equivalence by young children. *Cognitive Development, 3,* 323–339.

Fuchs, C. S., Stampfer, M. J., Colditz, G. A., Giovannucci, E. L., Manson, J. E., Kawachi, I., Hunter, D. J., Hankinson, S. E., Hennekens, C. H., Rosner, B., Speizer, F. E., & Willett, W. C. (1995). Alcohol consumption and mortality among women. *New England Journal of Medicine, 332,* 1245–1250.

Fujita, F., & Diener, E. (2005). Life satisfaction set point: Stability and change. *Journal of*

Personality and Social Psychology, 88, 158–164.

Fuligni, A. J. (1997). The academic achievement of adolescents from immigrant families: The roles of family background, attitudes, and behavior. *Child Development, 68,* 351–363.

Fuligni, A. J., & Eccles, J. S. (1993). Perceived parent-child relationships and early adolescents' orientation toward peers. *Developmental Psychology, 29,* 622–632.

Fuligni, A. J., Eccles, J. S., Barber, B. L., & Clements, P. (2001). Early adolescent peer orientation and adjustment during high school. *Developmental Psychology, 37*(1), 28–36.

Fuligni, A. J., & Stevenson, H. W. (1995). Time use and mathematics achievement among American, Chinese, and Japanese high school students. *Child Development, 66,* 830–842.

Fuligni, A. J., & Witkow, M. (2004). The postsecondary educational progress of youth from immigrant families. *Journal of Research on Adolescence, 14,* 159–183.

Fuligni, A. J., Yip, T., & Tseng, V. (2002). The impact of family obligation on the daily activities and psychological well-being of Chinese American adolescents. *Child Development, 73*(1), 302–314.

Fulton, R., & Owen, G. (1987–1988). Death and society in twentieth-century America: Special issue—Research in thanatology. *Omega: Journal of Death and Dying, 18,* 379–395.

Fung, H. H., Carstensen, L. L., & Lang, F. R. (2001). Age-related patterns in social networks among European-Americans and African-Americans: Implications for socioemotional selectivity across the life span. *International Journal of Aging and Human Development, 52,* 185–206.

Funk, J. B., & Bachman, D. D. (1996). Playing violent video and computer games and adolescent self-concept. *Journal of Communications, 46,* 19–32.

Furman, L., Taylor, G., Minich, N., & Hack, M. (2003). The effect of maternal milk on neonatal morbidity of very low-birth-weight infants. *Archives of Pediatrics and Adolescent Medicine, 157,* 66–71.

Furman, W. (1982). Children's friendships. In T. M. Field, A. Huston, H. C. Quay, L. Troll, & G. E. Finley (Eds.), *Review of human development.* New York: Wiley.

Furman, W., & Bierman, K. L. (1983). Developmental changes in young children's conception of friendship. *Child Development, 54,* 549–556.

Furman, W., & Buhrmester, D. (1985). Children's perceptions of the personal relationships in their social networks. *Developmental Psychology, 21,* 1016–1024.

Furman, W., & Wehner, E. A. (1997). Adolescent romantic relationships: A developmental perspective. In S. Shulman & A. Collins (Eds.). Romantic relationships in adolescence: Developmental perspectives. *New Directions for Child and Adolescent Development, 78,* 21–36.

Furrow, D. (1984). Social and private speech at two years. *Child Development, 55,* 355–362.

Furstenberg, F. F., Levine, J. A., & Brooks-Gunn, J. (1990). The children of teenage mothers: Patterns of early child bearing in two generations. *Family Planning Perspectives, 22*(2), 54–61.

Furstenberg, Jr., F. F., Rumbaut, R. G., & Setterstein, Jr., R. A. (2005). On the frontier of adulthood: Emerging themes and new directions. In R. A. Settersten, Jr., F. F. Furstenberg, Jr., & R. G. Rumbaut (Eds.), *On the frontier of adulthood: Theory, research, and public policy* (pp. 3–25). (John D. and Catherine T. MacArthur Foundation Series on Mental Health and Development, Research Network on Transitions to Adulthood and Public Policy.) Chicago: University of Chicago Press.

Furth, H. G., & Kane, S. R. (1992). Children constructing society: A new perspective on children at play. In H. McGurk (Ed.), *Childhood social development: Contemporary perspectives.* Hove: Erlbaum.

Fussell, E., & Furstenberg, F. (2005). The transition to adulthood during the twentieth century: Race, nativity, and gender. In R. A. Settersten, Jr., F. F. Furstenberg, Jr., & R. G. Rumbaut (Eds.), *On the frontier of adulthood: Theory, research, and public policy* (pp. 29–75). (John D. and Catherine T. MacArthur Foundation Series on Mental Health and Development, Research Network on Transitions to Adulthood and Public Policy.) Chicago: University of Chicago Press.

Fussell, E., & Gauthier, A. (2005). American women's transition to adulthood in comparative perspective. In R. A. Settersten, Jr., F. F. Furstenberg, Jr., & R. G. Rumbaut (Eds.), *On the frontier of adulthood: Theory, research, and public policy* (pp. 76–109). (John D. and Catherine T. MacArthur Foundation Series on Mental Health and Development, Research Network on Transitions to Adulthood and Public Policy.) Chicago: University of Chicago Press.

Gabbard, C. P. (1996). *Lifelong motor development* (2nd ed.). Madison, WI: Brown and Benchmark.

Gabhainn, S., & François, Y. (2000). Substance use. In C. Currie, K. Hurrelmann, W. Settertobulte, R. Smith, & J. Todd (Eds.), *Health behaviour in school-aged children: a WHO cross-national study (HBSC) international report* (pp. 97–114). WHO Policy Series: Healthy Policy for Children and Adolescents, Series No. 1.

Gabriel, T. (1996, January 7). High-tech pregnancies test hope's limit. *The New York Times,* pp. 1, 18–19.

Gaffney, M., Gamble, M., Costa, P., Holstrum, J., & Boyle, C. (2003). Infants tested for hearing loss—United States, 1999–2001. *Morbidity and Mortality Weekly Report, 51,* 981–984.

Galen, B. R., & Underwood, M. K. (1997). A developmental investigation of social aggression among children. *Developmental Psychology, 33,* 589–600.

Galinsky, E., Kim, S. S., & Bond, J. T. (2001). *Feeling overworked: When work becomes too much.* New York: Families and Work Institute.

Gallagher, W. (1993, May). Midlife myths. *The Atlantic Monthly,* pp. 51–68.

Gallagher-Thompson, D. (1995). Caregivers of chronically ill elders. In G. E. Maddox (Ed.), *The encyclopedia of aging* (pp. 141–144). New York: Springer.

Galli, R. L., Shukitt-Hale, B., Youdim, K. A., & Joseph, J. A. (2002). Fruit polyphenolics and brain aging: nutritional interventions targeting age-related neuronal and behavioral deficits. *Annals of the New York Academy of Science, 959,* 128–132.

Gallo, L. C., & Matthews, K. A. (2003). Understanding the association between socioeconomic status and physical health: Do negative emotions play a role? *Psychological Bulletin, 129,* 10–51.

Gallo, L. C., Troxel, W. M., Matthews, K. A., & Kuller, L. H. (2003). Marital status and quality in middle-aged women: Associations with levels and trajectories of cardiovascular risk factors. *Health Psychology, 22,* 453–463.

Galotti, K. M., Komatsu, L. K., & Voelz, S. (1997). Children's differential performance on deductive and inductive syllogisms. *Developmental Psychology, 33,* 70–78.

Gandhi, M. (1948). *Autobiography: The story of my experiments with truth.* New York: Dover.

Ganger, J. & Brent, M. R. (2004). Reexamining the vocabulary spurt. *Developmental Psychology, 40,* 621–632.

Gannon, P. J., Holloway, R. L., Broadfield, D. C., & Braun, A. R. (1998). Asymmetry of chimpanzee planum temporale: Humanlike pattern of Wernicke's brain language homolog. *Science, 279,* 22–222.

Gans, J. E. (1990). *America's adolescents: How healthy are they?* Chicago: American Medical Association.

Ganzini, L., Nelson, H. D., Schmidt, T. A., Kraemer, D. F., Delorit, M. A., & Lee, M. A. (2000). Physicians' experiences with the Oregon Death with Dignity Act. *New England Journal of Medicine, 342,* 557–563.

Garbarino, J., Dubrow, N., Kostelny, K., & Pardo, C. (1992). *Children in danger: Coping with the consequences of community violence.* San Francisco: Jossey-Bass.

Garbarino, J., Dubrow, N., Kostelny, K., & Pardo, C. (1998). *Children in danger: Coping with the consequences of community violence.* San Francisco: Jossey-Bass.

Garbarino, J., & Kostelny, K. (1993). Neighborhood and community influences on parenting. In T. Luster & L. Okagaki (Eds.), *Parenting: An ecological perspective* (pp. 203–226). Hillsdale, NJ: Erlbaum.

Garcia, M. M., Shaw, D. S., Winslow, E. B., & Yaggi, K. E. (2000). Destructive sibling conflict and the development of conduct problems in young boys. *Developmental Psychology, 36*(1), 44–53.

Gardiner, H. W. & Kosmitzki, C. (2005). *Lives across cultures: Cross-cultural human development.* Boston: Allyn & Bacon.

Gardner, H. (1986, Summer). Freud in three frames. *Daedalus,* 105–134.

Gardner, H. (1988). Creative lives and creative works: A synthetic scientific approach. In R. J. Sternberg (Ed.), *The nature of creativity: Contemporary psychological perspectives* (pp. 298–321). Cambridge, UK: Cambridge University Press.

Gardner, H. (1993). *Frames of mind: The theory of multiple intelligences.* New York: Basic. (Original work published 1983)

Gardner, H. (1995). Reflections on multiple intelligences: Myths and messages. *Phi Delta Kappan,* pp. 200–209.

Gardner, H. (1997). *Extraordinary minds: Portraits of exceptional individuals and an examination of our extraordinariness.* New York: Basic Books.

Gardner, H. (1998). Are there additional intelligences? In J. Kane (Ed.), *Education, information, and transformation: Essays on learning and thinking.* Englewood Cliffs, NJ: Prentice-Hall.

Gardner, M. (2002, Aug. 1). Meet the nanny—'Granny': Grandparents, says census, are nation's leading child-care providers. *Christian Science Monitor.* [Online]. Available: csmonitor.com

Garland, A. F., & Zigler, E. (1993). Adolescent suicide prevention: Current research and social policy implications. *American Psychologist, 48*(2), 169–182.

Garlick, D. (2003). Integrating brain science research with intelligence research. *Current Directions in Psychological Science, 12,* 185–192.

Garmon, L. C., Basinger, K. S., Gregg, V. R., & Gibbs, J. C. (1996). Gender differences in stage and expression of moral judgment. *Merrill-Palmer Quarterly, 42,* 418–437.

Garner, B. P. (1998). Play development from birth to age four. In D. P. Fromberg & D. Bergen (Eds.), *Play from birth to twelve and beyond: Contexts, perspectives, and meanings* (pp. 137–145). New York: Garland.

Garner, D. M. (1993). Pathogenesis of anorexia nervosa. *The Lancet, 341,* 1631–1635.

Garner, P. W., & Power, T. G. (1996). Preschoolers' emotional control in the disappointment paradigm and its relation to temperament, emotional knowledge, and family expressiveness. *Child Development, 67,* 1406–1419.

Gartstein, M. A., & Rothbart, M. K. (2003). Studying infant temperament via the Revised Infant Behavior Questionnaire. *Infant Behavior & Development, 26,* 64–86.

Gattis, K. S., Berns, S., Simpson, L. E., & Christensen, A. (2004). Birds of a feather or strange birds? Ties among personality dimensions, similarity, and marital quality. *Journal of Family Psychology, 18,* 564–574.

Gauderman, W. J., Avol, E., Gilliland, F., Vora, H., Thomas, D., Berhane, K., McConnell, R., Kuenzli, N., Lurmann, F., Rappaport, E., Margolis, H., Bates, D., & Peters, J. (2004). The effects of air pollution on lung development from 10 to 18 years of age. *New England Journal of Medicine, 351,* 1057–1067.

Gauthier, A. H., & Furstenberg, Jr., F. F. (2005). Historical trends in patterns of time use among young adults in developed countries. In R. A. Settersten, Jr., F. F. Furstenberg, Jr., & R. G. Rumbaut (Eds.), *On the frontier of adulthood: Theory, research, and public policy* (pp. 150–176). (John D. and Catherine T. MacArthur Foundation Series on Mental Health and Development, Research Network on Transitions to Adulthood and Public Policy.) Chicago: University of Chicago Press.

Gauvain, M. (1993). The development of spatial thinking in everyday activity. *Developmental Review, 13,* 92–121.

Gazzaniga, M. S. (Ed.). (2000). *The new cognitive neurosciences* (2nd ed.). Cambridge, MA: The MIT Press.

Ge, X., Conger, R. D., & Elder, G. H. (2001). Pubertal transition, stressful life events, and the emergence of gender differences in adolescent depressive symptoms. *Developmental Psychology, 37*(3), 404–417.

Geary, D. C. (1993). Mathematical disabilities: Cognitive, neuropsychological, and genetic components. *Psychological Bulletin, 114,* 345–362.

Geary, D. C. (1999). Evolution and developmental sex differences. *Current Directions in Psychological Science, 8*(4), 115–120.

Gecas, V., & Seff, M. A. (1990). Families and adolescents: A review of the 1980s. *Journal of Marriage and the Family, 52,* 941–958.

Geen, R. (2004). The evolution of kinship care: Policy and practice. In David and Lucile Packard Foundation, Children, families, and foster care. *The Future of Children, 14*(1). Available: http://www.futureofchildren.org.

Gelfand, D. M., & Teti, D. M. (1995, November). How does maternal depression affect children? *The Harvard Mental Health Letter,* p. 8.

Gelineau, K. (2004, December 28). 55-year-old has triplets for her daughter. *Associated Press.*

Gélis, J. (1991). *History of childbirth:* Fertility, pregnancy, and birth in early modern Europe. Boston: Northeastern University Press.

Gelman, R., & Gallistel, C. R. (1978). *The child's understanding of number.* Cambridge, MA: Harvard University Press.

Gelman, R., & Gallistel, C. R. (2004). Language and the origin of numerical concepts. *Science, 306,* 441–443.

Gelman, R., Spelke, E. S., & Meck, E. (1983). What preschoolers know about animate and inanimate objects. In D. R. Rogers & J. S. Sloboda (Eds.), *The acquisition of symbolic skills* (pp. 297–326). New York: Plenum.

Gendell, M., & Siegel, J. S. (1996). Trends in retirement age in the U.S., 1955–1993, by sex and race. *Journal of Gerontology: Social Sciences, 51B,* S132–139.

Genesee, F., Nicoladis, E., & Paradis, J. (1995). Language differentiation in early bilingual development. *Journal of Child Language, 22,* 611–631.

Genevay, B. (1986). Intimacy as we age. *Generations, 10*(4), 12–15.

Georganopoulou, D. G., Chang, I., Nam, J.-M., Thaxton, C. S., Mufson, E. J., Klein, W. L., & Mirkin, C. A. (2005). Nanoparticle-based detection in cerebral spinal fluid of a soluble pathogenic biomarker for Alzheimer's disease. *Proceedings of the National Academy of Sciences, 102,* 2273–2276.

George, C., Kaplan, N., & Main, M. (1985). *The Berkeley Adult Attachment Interview,* Unpublished protocol, Department of Psychology, University of California, Berkeley, CA.

George, T. P., & Hartmann, D. P. (1996). Friendship networks of unpopular, average, and popular children. *Child Development, 67,* 2301–2316.

Gershoff, E. T. (2002). Corporal punishment by parents and associated child behaviors and experiences: A meta-analytic and theoretical review. *Psychological Bulletin, 128,* 539–579.

Gertner, B. L., Rice, M. L., & Hadley, P. A. (1994). Influence of communicative competence on peer preferences in a preschool classroom. *Journal of Speech and Hearing Research, 37,* 913–923.

Gesell, A. (1929). Maturation and infant behavior patterns. *Psychological Review, 36,* 307–319.

Getzels, J. W. (1964). Creative thinking, problem-solving, and instruction. In *Yearbook of the National Society for the Study of Education* (Pt. 1, pp. 240–267). Chicago: University of Chicago Press.

Getzels, J. W. (1984, March). *Problem-finding in creativity in higher education* [The Fifth Rev. Charles F. Donovan, S. J., Lecture]. Boston College, School of Education, Boston, MA.

Getzels, J. W., & Jackson, P. W. (1962). *Creativity and intelligence: Explorations with gifted students.* New York: Wiley.

Getzels, J. W., & Jackson, P. W. (1963). The highly intelligent and the highly creative adolescent: A summary of some research findings. In C. W. Taylor & F. Baron (Eds.), *Scientific creativity: Its recognition and development* (pp. 161–172). New York: Wiley.

Ghetti, S., & Alexander, K. W. (2004). "If it happened, I would remember it": Strategic use of event memorability in the rejection of false autobiographical events. *Child Development, 75,* 542–561.

Giambra, L. M., & Arenberg, D. (1993). Adult age differences in forgetting sentences. *Psychology and Aging, 8,* 451–462.

Gibbs, J. C. (1991). Toward an integration of Kohlberg's and Hoffman's theories of moral development. In W. M. Kurtines & J. L. Gewirtz (Eds.), *Handbook of moral behavior and development: Advances in theory, research, and application,* Vol. 1. Hillsdale, NJ: Erlbaum.

Gibbs, J. C. (1995). The cognitive developmental perspective. In W. M. Kurtines & J. L. Gewirtz (Eds.), *Moral development: An introduction.* Boston: Allyn & Bacon.

Gibbs, J. C., Potter, G. B., Barriga, A. Q., & Liau, A. K. (1996). Developing the helping skills and prosocial motivation of aggressive adolescents in peer group programs. *Aggression and Violent Behavior, 1*(3), 283–305.

Gibbs, J. C., Potter, G. C., Goldstein, A. P., & Brendtro, L. K. (1998). How EQUIP programs help youth change. *Reclaiming Children and Youth, 7*(2), 117–122.

Gibbs, J. C., & Schnell, S. V. (1985). Moral development "versus" socialization. *American Psychologist, 40*(10), 1071–1080.

Gibbs, N. (1995, October 2). The EQ factor. *Time,* pp. 60–68.

Gibson, E. J. (1969). *Principles of perceptual learning and development.* New York: Appleton-Century-Crofts.

Gibson, E. J., & Pick, A. D. (2000). *An ecological approach to perceptual learning and development.* New York: Oxford University Press.

Gibson, E. J., & Walker, A. S. (1984). Development of knowledge of visual-tactual affordances of substance. *Child Development, 55,* 453–460.

Gibson, J. J. (1979). *The ecological approach to visual perception.* Boston: Houghton-Mifflin.

Gidwani, P. P., Sobol, A., DeJong, W., Perrin, J. M., & Gortmaker, S. L. (2002). Television viewing and initiation of smoking among youth. *Pediatrics, 110,* 505–508.

Gidycz, C. A., Hanson, K., & Layman, M. J. (1995). A prospective analysis of the relationships among sexual assault experiences: An extension of previous findings. *Psychology of Women Quarterly, 19,* 5–29.

Gielen, U., & Kelly, D. (1983, February). *Buddhist Ladakh: Psychological portrait of a nonviolent culture.* Paper presented at the Annual Meeting of the Society for Cross-Cultural Research: Washington, DC.

Gilbert, L. A. (1994). Current perspectives in dual-career families. *Current Directions in Psychological Science, 3,* 101–105.

Gilbert, W. M., Nesbitt, T. S., & Danielsen, B. (1999). Childbearing beyond age 40: Pregnancy outcome in 24,032 cases. *Obstetrics and Gynecology, 93,* 9–14.

Gilford, R. (1986). Marriages in later life. *Generations, 10*(4), 16–20.

Gill, B., & Schlossman, S. (1996). "A sin against childhood": Progressive education and the crusade to abolish homework, 1897–1941. *American Journal of Education, 105,* 27–66.

Gill, T. M., Allore, H. G., Holford, T. R, & Guo, Z. (2004). Hospitalization, restricted activity, and the development of disability among older persons. *Journal of the American Medical Association, 292,* 2115–2124.

Gill, T. M., Williams, C. S., Robison, J. T., & Tinetti, M. E. (1999). A population-based study of environmental hazards in the homes of older persons. *American Journal of Public Health, 89,* 553–556.

Gilligan, C. (1982). *In a different voice: Psychological theory and women's development.* Cambridge, MA: Harvard University Press.

Gilligan, C. (1987a). Adolescent development reconsidered. In E. E. Irwin (Ed.), *Adolescent social behavior and health.* San Francisco: Jossey-Bass.

Gilligan, C. (1987b). Moral orientation and moral development. In E. F. Kittay & D. T. Meyers (Eds.), *Women and moral theory* (pp. 19–33). Totowa, NJ: Rowman & Littlefield.

Gilligan, C., Murphy, J. M., & Tappan, M. B. (1990). Moral development beyond adolescence. In C. N. Alexander & E. J. Langer (Eds.), *Higher stages of human development* (pp. 208–228). New York: Oxford University Press.

Gillman, M. W., Cupples, L. A., Gagnon, D., Posner, B. M., Ellison, R. C., Castelli, W. P., & Wolf, P. A. (1995). Protective effects of fruit and vegetables on development of stroke in men. *Journal of the American Medical Association, 273,* 1113–1117.

Gilman, S., Koller, M., Black., R. S., Jenkins, L., Griffith, S. G., Fox, N. C., Eisner, L., Kirby, L., Rovira, B., Forette, F., & Orgogozo, J.-M. for the AN1792(QS-21)-201 Study Team. (2005). Clinical effects of Aß immunization (AN1792) in patients with AD in an interrupted trial. *Neurology, 64,* 1553–1562.

Ginsburg, G. S., & Bronstein, P. (1993). Family factors related to children's intrinsic/extrinsic motivational orientation and academic performance. *Child Development, 64,* 1461–1474.

Ginsburg, H., & Opper, S. (1979). *Piaget's theory of intellectual development* (2nd ed.). Englewood Cliffs, NJ: Prentice-Hall.

Ginsburg, H. P. (1997). Mathematics learning disabilities: A view from developmental psychology. *Journal of Learning Disabilities, 30,* 20–33.

Ginzburg, N. (1985). *The Little Virtues.* (D. Davis, Trans.). Manchester, England: Carcanet.

Giordano, P. C., Cernkovich, S. A., & DeMaris, A. (1993). The family and peer relations of black adolescents. *Journal of Marriage and the Family, 55,* 277–287.

Giovannucci, E., Rimm, E. B., Colditz, G. A., Stampfer, M. J., Ascherio, A., Chute, C. C., & Willett, W. C. (1993). A prospective study of dietary fat and risk of prostate cancer. *Journal of the National Cancer Institute, 85,* 1571–1579.

Gist, Y. J., & Hetzel, L. I. (2004). We the people: Aging in the United States. *Census 2000 Special Reports.* Washington, DC: U.S. Census Bureau.

Gitau, R., Cameron, A., Fisk, N. & Glover, V. (1998). Fetal exposure to maternal cortisol. *Lancet, 352,* 707–708.

Gjerdingen, D. (2003). The effectiveness of various postpartum depression treatments and the impact of antidepressant drugs on nursing infants. *Journal of American Board of Family Practice, 16,* 372–382.

Glantz, S. A., Kacirk, K. W., & McCulloch, C. (2004). Back to the future: Smoking in movies in 2002 compared with 1950 levels. *American Journal of Public Health, 94,* 261–263.

Glasgow, K. L., Dornbusch, S. M., Troyer, L., Steinberg, L., & Ritter, P. L. (1997). Parenting styles, adolescents' attributions, and educational outcomes in nine heterogeneous high schools. *Child Development, 68,* 507–529.

Glass, R. M. (2004). Treatment of adolescents with major depression: Contributions of a major trial. *Journal of the American Medical Association, 292,* 861–863

Glass, T. A., Seeman, T. E., Herzog, A. R., Kahn, R., & Berkman, L. F. (1995). Change in productive activity in late adulthood: MacArthur studies of successful aging. *Journal of Gerontology: Social Sciences, 50B,* S65–66.

Glasson, E. J., Bower, C., Petterson, B., de Klerk, N., Chaney, G., & Hallmayer, J. F. (2004). Perinatal factors and the development of autism: A population study. *Archives of General Psychiatry, 61,* 618–627.

Gleason, T. R., Sebanc, A. M., & Hartup, W. W. (2000). Imaginary companions of preschool children. *Developmental Psychology, 36,* 419–428.

Gleitman, L. R., Newport, E. L., & Gleitman, H. (1984). The current status of the motherese hypothesis. *Journal of Child Language, 11,* 43–79.

Glenn, N., & Marquardt, E. (2001). *Hooking up, hanging out, and hoping for Mr. Right: College women on dating and mating today.* New York: Institute for American Values.

Glick, J. E., & Van Hook, J. (2002). Parents' coresidence with adult children: Can immigration explain racial and ethnic variation? *Journal of Marriage and Family, 64,* 240–253.

Globe, D. R., Wu, J., Azen, S. P., Varma, R., & Los Angeles Latino Eye Study Group. (2004). The impact of visual impairment on self-reported visual functioning in Latinos: The Los Angeles Latino Eye Study. *Ophthalmology, 111,* 1141–1149.

Glover, M. J., Greenlund, K. J., Ayala, C., & Croft, J. B. (2005). Racial/ethnic disparities in prevalence, treatment, and control of hypertension—United States, 1999–2002. *Morbidity and Mortality Weekly Report, 54,* 7–9.

Goel, M. S., McCarthy, E. P., Phillips, R. S., & Wee, C. C. (2004). Obesity among US immigrant subgroups by duration of residence. *Journal of the American Medical Association, 292,* 2860–2867.

Goetz, P. J. (2003). The effects of bilingualism on theory of mind development. *Bilingualism: Language and Cognition, 6,* 1–15.

Gold, P. E., Cahill, L., & Wenk, G. L. (2002). Ginkgo biloba: A cognitive enhancer? *Psychological Science in the Public Interest, 3* (1), 3–11.

Goldberg, W. A., Greenberger, E., & Nagel, S. K. (1996). Employment and achievement: Mothers' work involvement in relation to children's achievement behaviors and mothers' parenting behaviors. *Child Development, 67,* 1512–1527.

Goldenberg, R. L., & Rouse, D. J. (1998). Prevention of premature labor. *New England Journal of Medicine, 339,* 313–320.

Goldin-Meadow, S., & Mylander, C. (1998). Spontaneous sign systems created by deaf children in two cultures. *Nature, 391,* 279–281.

Goldman, L., Falk, H., Landrigan, P. J., Balk, S. J., Reigart, J. R., and Etzel, R. A. (2004). Environmental pediatrics and its impact on government health policy. *Pediatrics, 113,* 1146–1157.

Goldman, L. L., & Rothschild, J. (in press). Healing the wounded with art therapy. In B. Danto (Ed.), *Bereavement and suicide.* Philadelphia: Charles Publishing.

Goldman, S. R., Petrosino, A. J., & Cognition and Technology Group at Vanderbilt. (1999). Design principles for instruction in content domains: Lessons from research on expertise and learning. In F. T. Durso, (Ed.), *Handbook of applied cognition* (pp. 595–627). Chichester, England: Wiley.

Goldstein, I., Padma-Nathan, H., Rosen, R. C., Steers, W. D., & Wicker, P. A., for the Sildenafil Study group. (1998). Oral sildenafil in the treatment of erectile dysfunction. *New England Journal of Medicine, 338,* 1397–1404.

Goleman, D. (1992, November 24). Anthropology goes looking in all the old places. *The New York Times*, p. B1.

Goleman, D. (1995). *Emotional intelligence: Why it can matter more than IQ.* New York: Bantam.

Goleman, D. (1998). *Working with emotional intelligence.* New York: Bantam.

Goleman, D. (2001). An EI-based theory of performance. In C. Cherniss & D. Goleman (Eds.), *The emotionally intelligent workplace: How to select for, measure, and improve emotional intelligence in individuals, groups, and organizations* (pp. 27–44). San Francisco: Jossey-Bass.

Golinkoff, R. M., Jacquet, R. C., Hirsh-Pasek, K., & Nandakumar, R. (1996). Lexical principles may underlie the learning of verbs. *Child Development, 67,* 3101–3119.

Golomb, C., & Galasso, L. (1995). Make believe and reality: Explorations of the imaginary realm. *Developmental Psychology, 31,* 800–810.

Golombok, S., Lycett, E., MacCallum, F., Jadva, V., Murray, C., Rust, J., Abdalla, H., Jenkins, J., & Margara, R. (2004). Parenting infants conceived by gamete donation. *Journal of Family Psychology, 18,* 443–452.

Golombok, S., MacCallum, F., & Goodman, E. (2001). The "test-tube" generation: Parent-child relationships and the psychological well-being of in vitro fertilization children at adolescence. *Child Development, 72,* 599–608.

Golombok, S., MacCallum, F., Goodman, E., & Rutter, M. (2002). Families with children conceived by donor insemination: A follow-up at age twelve. *Child Development, 73,* 952–968.

Golombok, S., Murray, C., Jadva, V., MacCallum, F., & Lycett, E. (2004). Families created through surrogacy arrangements: Parent-child relationships in the 1st year of life. *Developmental Psychology, 40,* 400–411.

Gonyea, J. G., Hudson, R. B., & Seltzer, G. B. (1990). Housing preferences of vulnerable elders in suburbia. *Journal of Housing for the Elderly, 7,* 79–95.

Gonzales, N. A., Cauce, A. M., & Mason, C. A. (1996). Interobserver agreement in the assessment of parental behavior and parent-adolescent conflict: African American mothers, daughters, and independent observers. *Child Development, 67,* 1483–1498.

Gonzalez, E., Kulkarni, H., Bolivar, H., Mangano, A., Sanchez, R., Catano, G., Nibbs, R. J., Freedman, B. I., Quinones, M. P., Bamshad, M. J., Murthy, K. K., Rovin, B. H., Bradley, W., Clark, R. A., Anderson, S. A., O'Connell, R. J., Agan, B. K., Ahuja, S. S., Bologna, R., Sen, L., Dolan, M. J., & Ahuja, S. K. (2005). The influence of *CCL3L1* gene-containing segmental duplications on HIV-1/AIDS susceptibility. *Science,* DOI 10.1126/science.1101160.

Gonzalez, P., Guzmàn, J. C., Partelow, L., Pahlke, E., Jocelyn, L., Kastberg, D., & Williams, T. (2004). *Highlights from the Trends in International Mathematics and Science Study (TIMSS) 2003* (NCES 2005-005). Washington, DC: National Center for Education Statistics.

Gooden, A. M. (2001). Gender representation in Notable Children's picture books: 1995–1999. *Sex Roles: A Journal of Research.* [Online]. Retrieved April 20, 2005 from http://www.find-articles.com/p/articles/mi m2294/is_2001_July/ai_81478076.

Goodman, G. S., Emery, R. E., & Haugaard, J. J. (1998). Developmental psychology and law: Divorce, child maltreatment, foster care, and adoption. In W. Damon (Series Ed.), I. E. Sigel, & K. A. Renninger (Vol. Eds.), *Handbook of child psychology* (Vol. 4, pp. 775–874). New York: Wiley.

Goodwyn, S. W., & Acredolo, L. P. (1998). Encouraging symbolic gestures: A new perspective on the relationship between gesture and speech. In J. M Iverson & S. Goldin-Meadow (Eds.), *The nature and functions of gesture in children's communication* (pp. 61–73). San Francisco: Jossey-Bass.

Gootman, E., & Herszenhorn, D. M. (2005, May 3). Getting smaller to improve the big picture. *New York Times.* [Online]. Retrieved May 3, 2005, from http://www.nytimes.com/1005/05/03/nyregion/03small.html.

Gopnik, A., Sobel, D. M., Schulz, L. E., & Glymour, C. (2001). Causal learning mechanisms in very young children: Two-, three-, and four-year-olds infer causal relations from patterns of variation and covariation. *Developmental Psychology, 37*(5), 620–629.

Gordon, I., Lask, B., Bryantwaugh, R., Christie, D., & Timini, S. (1997). Childhood onset anorexia nervosa: Towards identifying a biological substrate. *International Journal of Eating Disorders, 22*(2), 159–165.

Gordon, P. (2004). Numerical cognition without words: Evidence from Amazonia. *Science, 306,* 496–499.

Gorman, M. (1993). Help and self-help for older adults in developing countries. *Generations,* 17(4), 73–76.

Gortmaker, S. L., Hughes, M., Cervia, J., Brady, M., Johnson, G. M., Seage, G. R., Song, L. Y., Dankner, W. M., & Oleske, J. M. for the Pediatric AIDS Clinical Trial Group Protocol 219 Team. (2001). Effect of combination therapy including protease inhibitors on mortality among children and adolescents infected with HIV-1. *New England Journal of Medicine, 345*(21), 1522–1528.

Gortmaker, S. L., Must, A., Perrin, J. M., Sobol, A. M., & Dietz, W. H. (1993). Social and economic consequences of overweight in adolescence and young adulthood. *New England Journal of Medicine, 329,* 1008–1012.

Gostin, L. O. (1997). Deciding life and death in the courtroom: From Quinlan to Cruzan, Glucksberg, and Vacco—A brief history and analysis of constitutional protection of the "right to die." *Journal of the American Medical Association, 278,* 1523–1528.

Gottfredson, L. S., & Deary, I. J. (2004). Intelligence predicts health and longevity, but why? *Current Directions in Psychological Science, 13,* 1–4.

Gottfried, A. E., Fleming, J. S., & Gottfried, A. W. (1998). Role of cognitively stimulating home environment in children's academic intrinsic motivation: A longitudinal study. *Child Development, 69,* 1448–1460.

Gottlieb, G. (1991). Experiential canalization of behavioral development theory. *Developmental Psychology, 27*(1), 4–13.

Gottman, J. M., & Notarius, C. I. (2000). Decade review: Observing marital interaction. *Journal of Marriage and the Family, 62,* 927–947.

Goubet, N. & Clifton, R. K. (1998). Object and event representation in 6 1/2-month-old infants. *Developmental Psychology, 34,* 63–76.

Gould, E., Reeves, A. J., Graziano, M. S. A., & Gross, C. G. (1999). Neurogenesis in the neo-cortex of adult primates. *Science, 286,* 548–552.

Gould, M. S., Marrocco, F. A., Kleinman, M., Thomas, J. G., Mostkoff, K., Cote, J., & Davies, M. (2005). Evaluating iatrogenic risk of youth suicide screening programs: A randomized controlled trial. *Journal of the American Medical Association, 293,* 1635–1643.

Graber, J. A., Brooks-Gunn, J., & Warren, M. P. (1995). The antecedents of menarcheal age: Heredity, family environment, and stressful life events. *Child Development, 66,* 346–359.

Grady, D., Herrington, D., Bittner, V., Blumenthal, R., Davidson, M., Hlatky, M., Hsia, J., Hulley, S., Herd, Al., Khan, S., Newby, L. K., Waters, D., Vittinghoff, E., & Wenger, N. (2002). Cardiovascular disease outcomes during 6.8 years of hormone therapy: Heart and Estrogen/Progestin Replacement Study follow-up (HERS II). *Journal of the American Medical Association, 288,* 49–57.

Grant, B. F., Stinson, F. S., Dawson, D. A., Chou, S. P., Dufour, M. C., Compton, W., Pickering, R. P., & Kaplan, K. (2004). Prevalence and co-occurrence of substance use disorders and independent mood and anxiety disorders: Results from the National Epidemiologic Survey on Alcohol and Related Conditions. *Archives of General Psychiatry, 61,* 807–816.

Grant, B. F., Stinson, F. S., Hasin, D. S., Dawson, D. A., Chou, S. P., and Anderson, K. (2004). Immigration and lifetime prevalence of DSM-IV psychiatric disorders among Mexican Americans and non-Hispanic whites in the United States. *Archives of General Psychiatry, 61,* 1226–1233.

Grantham-McGregor, S., Powell, C., Walker, S., Chang, S., & Fletcher, P. (1994). The longterm follow-up of severely malnourished children who participated in an intervention program. *Child Development, 65,* 428–439.

Gray, M. R., & Steinberg, L. (1999). Unpacking authoritative parenting: Reassessing a multidimensional construct. *Journal of Marriage and the Family, 61,* 574–587.

Green, C. R., Tait, R. C., & Gallagher, R. M. (2005). The unequal burden of pain: Disparities and differences. *Pain Medicine, 8,* 1–2.

Greenberg, J., & Becker, M. (1988). Aging parents as family resources. *The Gerontologist, 28*(6), 786–790.

Greene, M. F. (2002). Outcomes of very low birth weight in young adults. *New England Journal of Medicine, 346*(3), 146–148.

Greene, M. L., & Way, N. (2005). Self-esteem trajectories among ethnic minority adolescents:

A growth curve analysis of the patterns and predictors of change. *Journal of Research on Adolescence, 15,* 151–178.

Greenfield, E. A., & Marks, N. F. (2004). Formal volunteering as a protective factor for older adults' psychological well-being. *Journal of Gerontology: Social Sciences, 59B,* S258–S264.

Greenfield, P. M., & Childs, C. P. (1978). Understanding sibling concepts: A developmental study of kin terms in Zinacanten. In P. R. Dasen, (Ed.), *Piagetian psychology* (pp. 335–358). New York: Gardner.

Greenhouse, L. (2000a, June 6). Justices reject visiting rights in divided case: Ruling favors mother over grandparents. *The New York Times* (national edition), pp. A1, A15.

Greenhouse, L. (2000b, February 29). Program of drug-testing pregnant women draws review by the Supreme Court. *The New York Times,* p. A12.

Greenhouse, L. (2005, February 23). Justices accept Oregon case weighing assisted suicide. *New York Times,* p. A1.

Greenstone, M., & Chay, K. (2003). The impact of air pollution on infant mortality: Evidence from geographic variation in pollution shocks induced by a recession. *Quarterly Journal of Economics, 118,* 1121–1167.

Gregg, E. W., Cauley, J. A., Stone, K., Tompson, T. J., Bauer, D. C., Cummings, S. R., Ensrud, K. E., for the Study of Osteopoorotic Fractures Research Group. (2003). Relationship of changes in physical activity and mortality among older women. *Journal of the American Medical Association, 289,* 2379–2386.

Gregg, E. W., Cheng, Y. J., Cadwell, B. L., Imperatore, G., Williams, D. E., Flegal, K. M., Narayan, K. M. V., & Williamson, D. F. (2005). Secular trends in cardiovascular disease risk factors according to body mass index in U.S. adults. *Journal of the American Medical Association, 293,* 1868–1874.

Greider, L. (2001, December). Hard times drive adult kids "home": Parents grapple with rules for "boomerangers." *AARP Bulletin,* pp. 3, 14.

Griffiths, J., Bood, A., & Weyers. H. (1998). *Euthanasia & law in the Netherlands.* Amsterdam: Amsterdam University Press.

Griffiths, M. D., & Hunt, N. (1998). Dependence on computer games by adolescents. *Psychology Report, 82,* 475–480.

Grigorenko, E. L., Meier, E., Lipka, J., Mohatt, G., Yanez, E., & Sternberg, R. J. (in press). The relationship between academic and practical intelligence: A case study of the tacit knowledge of Native American Yup'ik people in Alaska. *Learning and Individual Differences.*

Grigorinko, E. L., & Sternberg, R. J. (1998). Dynamic testing. *Psych Bulletin, 124,* 75–111.

Grigorenko, E. L., & Sternberg, R. J. (2001). Analytical, creative, and practical intelligence as predictors of self-reported adaptive functioning: A case study in Russia. *Intelligence, 29,* 57–73.

Grim, C. E., Cowley Jr., A. W., Hamet, P., Gaudet, D., Kaldunski, M. L., Kotchen, J. M., Krishnaswami, S., Pausova, Z., Roman, R., Tremblay, J., & Kotchen, T. A. (2005). Hyperaldosteronism and hypertension: Ethnic differences. *Hypertension, 45,* 1–7.

Grodstein, F. (1996). Postmenopausal estrogen and progestin use and the risk of cardiovascular disease. *New England Journal of Medicine, 335,* 453.

Groenewoud, J. H., van der Heide, A., Onwuteaka-Philipsen, B. D., Willems, D. L., van der Maas, P. J., & van der Wal, G. (2000). Clinical problems with the performance of euthanasia and physician-assisted suicide in the Netherlands. *New England Journal of Medicine, 342,* 551–556.

Grote, N. K., Clark, M. S., & Moore, A. (2004). Perceptions of injustice in family work: The role of psychological distress. *Journal of Family Psychology, 18,* 480–492.

Grotevant, H. D., McRoy, R. G., Elde, C. L., & Fravel, D. L. (1994). Adoptive family system dynamics: Variations by level of openness in the adoption. *Family Process, 33*(2), 125–146.

Grubman, S., Gross, E., Lerner- Weiss, N., Hernandez, M., McSherry, G. D., Hoyt, L. G., Boland, M., & Oleske, J. M. (1995). Older children and adolescents living with perinatally acquired human immunodeficiency virus. *Pediatrics, 95,* 657–663.

Grunberg, J. A. (Ed. Dir.), Kann, L., Kinchen, S. A., Williams, B., Ross, J. G., Lowry, R., & Kolbe, L. (2002, June 28). Youth risk behavior surveillance—United States, 2001. *MMWR Surveillance Summaries, 51*(SS04), 1–64.

Grusec, J. E., & Goodnow, J. J. (1994). Impact of parental discipline methods on the child's internalization of values: A reconceptualization of current points of view. *Developmental Psychology, 30,* 4–19.

Grusec, J. E., Goodnow, J. J., & Kuczynski, L. (2000). New directions in analyses of parenting contributions to children's acquisition of values. *Child Development, 71,* 205–211.

Guberman, S. R. (1996). The development of everyday mathematics in Brazilian children with limited formal education. *Child Development, 67,* 1609–1623.

Guerrero, L. (2001, April 25). Almost third of kids bullied or bullies: Health officials concerned either could lead to more aggressive behavior. *Chicago Sun-Times,* p. 28.

Guilford, J. P. (1956). Structure of intellect. *Psychological Bulletin, 53,* 267–293.

Guilford, J. P. (1959). Three faces of intellect. *American Psychologist, 14,* 469–479.

Guilford, J. P. (1960). Basic conceptual problems of the psychology of thinking. *Proceedings of the New York Academy of Sciences, 91,* 6–21.

Guilford, J. P. (1967). *The nature of human intelligence.* New York: McGraw-Hill.

Guilford, J. P. (1986). *Creative talents: Their nature, uses and development.* Buffalo, NY: Bearly.

Guilleminault, C., Palombini, L., Pelayo, R., & Chervin, R. D. (2003). Sleeping and sleep terrors in prepubertal children: What triggers them? *Pediatrics, 111,* pp. e17–e25.

Guillette, E. A., Meza, M. M., Aquilar, M. G., Soto, A. D., & Garcia, I. E. (1998). An anthropological approach to the evaluation of preschool children exposed to pesticides in Mexico. *Environmental Health Perspectives, 106,* 347–353.

Gullette, M. M. (1998). Midlife discourse in the twentieth-century United States: An essay on the sexuality, ideology, and politics of "middle-ageism." In R. A. Shweder (Ed.), *Welcome to middle age (and other cultural fictions)* (pp. 5–44). Chicago: University of Chicago Press.

Gullone, E. (2000). The development of normal fear: A century of research. *Clinical Psychology Review, 20,* 429–451.

Gunnar, M. R., Larson, M. C., Hertsgaard, L., Harris, M. L., & Brodersen, L. (1992). The stressfulness of separation among nine-month-old infants: Effects of social context variables and infant temperament. *Child Development, 63,* 290–303.

Gunnoe, M. L., & Hetherington, E. M. (2004). Stepchildren's perceptions of noncustodial mothers and noncustodial fathers: Differences in socioemotional involvement and associations with adolescent adjustment problems. *Journal of Family Psychology, 18,* 555–563.

Gunnoe, M. L., & Mariner, C. L. (1997). Toward a developmental-contextual model of the effects of parental spanking on children's aggression. *Archives of Pediatric and Adolescent Medicine, 151,* 768–775.

Gurung, R. A. R., Taylor, S. E., & Seeman, T. E. (2003). Accounting for changes in social support among married older adults: Insights from the MacArthur studies of successful aging. *Psychology and Aging, 18,* 487–496.

Gustafson, D., Lissner, L., Bengtsson, C., Björkelund, C., & Skoog, I. (2004). A 24-year follow-up of body mass index and cerebral atrophy. *Neurology, 63,* 1876–1881.

Gutmann, D. (1975). Parenting: A key to the comparative study of the life cycle. In N. Datan & L. H. Ginsberg (Eds.), *Life-span developmental psychology: Normative life crises.* New York: Academic Press.

Gutmann, D. (1977). The cross-cultural perspective: Notes toward a comparative psychology of aging. In J. E. Birren & K. W. Schaie (Eds.), *Handbook of the psychology of aging* (pp. 302–326). New York: Van Nostrand Reinhold.

Gutmann, D. (1985). The parental imperative revisited. In J. Meacham (Ed.), *Family and individual development.* Basel, Switzerland: Karger.

Gutmann, D. L. (1987). *Reclaimed powers; Toward a new psychology of men and women in later life.* New York: Basic Books.

Guyer, B., Hoyert, D. L., Martin, J. A., Ventura, S. J., MacDorman, M. F., & Strobino, D. M. (1999). Annual summary of vital statistics—1998. *Pediatrics, 104,* 1229–1246.

Guyer, B., Strobino, D. M., Ventura, S. J., & Singh, G. K. (1995). Annual summary of vital statistics—1994. *Pediatrics, 96,* 1029–1039.

Guzell, J. R., & Vernon-Feagans, L. (2004). Parental perceived control over caregiving and its relationship to parent-infant interaction. *Child Development, 75,* 134–146.

Haas, S. M., & Stafford, L. (1998). An initial examination of maintenance behaviors in gay and lesbian relationships. *Journal of Social and Personal Relationships, 15,* 846–855.

Haber, C. (2004). Life extension and history: The continual search for the Fountain of Youth. *Journal of Gerontology: Biological Sciences, 59A,* 515–522.

Hack, M., Flannery, D. J., Schluchter, M., Cartar, L., Borawski, E., & Klein, N. (2002). Outcomes in young adulthood for very low-birth-weight infants. *New England Journal of Medicine, 346*(3), 149–157.

Hack, M., Friedman, H., & Fanaroff, A. A. (1996). Outcomes of extremely low-birth-weight infants. *Pediatrics, 98,* 931–937.

Haddow, J. E., Palomaki, G. E., Allan, W. C., Williams, J. R., Knight, G. J., Gagnon, J., O'Heir, C. E., Mitchell, M. L., Hermos, R. J., Waisbren, S. E., Faix, J. D., & Klein, R. Z. (1999). Maternal thyroid deficiency during pregnancy and subsequent neuropsychological development of the child. *New England Journal of Medicine, 341,* 549–555.

Haden, C. A., & Fivush, F. (1996). Contextual variation in maternal conversational styles. *Merrill-Palmer Quarterly, 42,* 200–227.

Haden, C. A., Haine, R. A., & Fivush, R. (1997). Developing narrative structure in parent-child reminiscing across the preschool years. *Developmental Psychology, 33,* 295–307.

Haden, C. A., Ornstein, P. A., Eckerman, C. O., & Didow, S. M. (2001). Mother-child conversational interactions as events unfold: Linkages to subsequent remembering. *Child Development, 72*(4), 1016–1031.

Hagestad, G. O. (2000). *Intergenerational relations.* Paper prepared for the United Nations Economic Commission for Europe Conference on Generations and Gender, Geneva, July 3–5.

Haight, W. L., Wang, X., Fung, H. H., Williams, K., & Mintz, J. (1999). Universal, developmental, and variable aspects of young children's play: A cross-cultural comparison of pretending at home. *Child Development, 70*(6), 1477–1488.

Haith, M. M. (1986). Sensory and perceptual processes in early infancy. *Journal of Pediatrics, 109*(1), 158–171.

Haith, M. M. (1998). Who put the cog in infant cognition? Is rich interpretation too costly? *Infant Behavior and Development, 21*(2), 167–179.

Haith, M. M., & Benson, J. B. (1998). Infant cognition. In D. Kuhn & R. S. Siegler (Eds.), *Handbook of Child Psychology: Vol. 2. Cognition, perception, and language* (5th ed., pp. 199–254). New York: Wiley.

Hajat, A., Lucas, J. B., & Kington, R. (2000). Health outcomes among Hispanic subgroups: Data from National Health Interview Survey, 1992–1995. *Advance Data No. 310.* (PHS 2000–1250). Hyattsville, MD: National Center for Health Statistics.

Halaas, J. L., Gajiwala, K. S., Maffei, M., Cohen, S. L., Chait, B. T., Rabinowitz, D., Lallone, R. L., Burley, S. K., & Friedman, J. M. (1995). Weight reducing effects of the plasma protein encoded by the obese gene. *Science, 269,* 543–546.

Hale, S., Bronik, M. D., & Fry, A. F. (1997). Verbal and spatial working memory in schoolage children: Developmental differences in susceptibility to interference. *Developmental Psychology, 33,* 364–371.

Hall, D. G., & Graham, S. A. (1999). Lexical form class information guides word-to-object mapping in preschoolers. *Child Development, 70,* 78–91.

Hall, D. R., & Zhao, J. Z. (1995). Cohabitation in Canada: Testing the selectivity hypothesis. *Journal of Marriage and the Family, 57,* 421–427.

Hall, G. S. (1916). *Adolescence.* New York: Appleton. (Original work published 1904.)

Halpern, D. F. (1997). Sex differences in intelligence: Implications for education. *American Psychologist, 52*(10), 1091–1102.

Halterman, J. S., Aligne, A., Auinger, P., McBride, J. T., & Szilagyi, P. G. (2000). Inadequate therapy for asthma among children in the United States. *Pediatrics, 105*(1), 272–276.

Halterman, J. S., Kaczorowski, J. M., Aligne, A., Auinger, P., and Szilagyi, P. G. (2001). Iron deficiency and cognitive achievement among school-aged children and adolescence in the United States. *Pediatrics, 107*(6), 1381–1386.

Hamilton, B. E., Martin, J. A., & Sutton, P. D. (2004). Births: Preliminary data for 2003. *National Vital Statistics Reports, 53*(9). Hyattsville, MD: National Center for Health Statistics.

Hamm, J. V. (2000). Do birds of a feather flock together? The variable bases for African American, Asian American, and European American adolescents' selection of similar friends. *Developmental Psychology, 36*(2), 209–219.

Han, K. K., Soares, J. M., Jr., Haidar, M. A., de Lima, G. R., & Baracat, E. C. (2002). Benefits of soy isoflavene therapeutic regimen on menopausal symptoms. *Obstetrics & Gynecology, 99,* 389–394.

Hansen, D., Lou, H. C., & Olsen, J. (2000). Serious life events and congenital malformations: A national study with complete follow-up. *Lancet, 356,* 875–880.

Hanson, L. (1968). *Renoir: The man, the painter, and his world.* New York: Dodd, Mead.

Hara, H. (2002). Justifications for bullying among Japanese school children. *Asian Journal of Social Psychology, 5,* 197–204.

Hardy, R., Kuh, D., Langenberg, C., & Wadsworth, M. E. (2003). Birth weight, childhood social class, and change in adult blood pressure in the 1946 British birth cohort. *Lancet, 362,* 1178–1183.

Hardy-Brown, K., & Plomin, R. (1985). Infant communicative development: Evidence from adoptive and biological families for genetic and environmental influences on rate differences. *Developmental Psychology, 21,* 378–385.

Hardy-Brown, K., Plomin, R., & DeFries, J. C. (1981). Genetic and environmental influences on rate of communicative development in the first year of life. *Developmental Psychology, 17,* 704–717.

Harley, K., & Reese, E. (1999). Origins of autobiographical memory. *Developmental Psychology, 35,* 1338–1348.

Harlow, H. F., & Harlow, M. K. (1962). The effect of rearing conditions on behavior. *Bulletin of the Menninger Clinic, 26,* 213–224.

Harlow, H. F., & Zimmerman, R. R. (1959). Affectional responses in the infant monkey. *Science, 130,* 421–432.

Harman, S. M., & Blackman, M. R. (2004). Use of growth hormone for prevention of effects of aging. *Journal of Gerontology: Biological Sciences, 59A,* 652–658.

Harnishfeger, K. K., & Bjorklund, D. F. (1993). The ontogeny of inhibition mechanisms: A renewed approach to cognitive development. In M. L. Howe & R. P. Pasnak (Eds.), *Emerging themes in cognitive development* (Vol. 1, pp. 28–49). New York: Springer-Verlag.

Harnishfeger, K. K., & Pope, R. S. (1996). Intending to forget: The development of cognitive inhibition in directed forgetting. *Journal of Experimental Psychology, 62,* 292–315.

Harris, G. (1997). Development of taste perception and appetite regulation. In G. Bremner, A. Slater, & G. Butterworth (Eds.), *Infant development: Recent advances* (pp. 9–30). East Sussex, UK: Psychology Press.

Harris, G. (2005, March 3). Gene therapy is facing a crucial hearing. *New York Times.* [Online]. Retrieved March 3, 2005 from http://www.nytimes.com/2005/03/03/politics/03gene.html.

Harris, L. H., & Paltrow, L. (2003). The status of pregnant women and fetuses in U.S. criminal law. *Journal of the American Medical Association, 289,* 1697–1699.

Harris, P. L., Brown, E., Marriott, C., Whittall, S., & Harmer, S. (1991). Monsters, ghosts, and witches: Testing the limits of the fantasy-reality distinction in young children. In G. E. Butterworth, P. L. Harris, A. M. Leslie, & H. M. Wellman (Eds.), *Perspective on the child's theory of mind.* Oxford: Oxford University Press.

Harris, P. L., Olthof, T., Meerum Terwogt, M., & Hardman, C. (1987). Children's knowledge of situations that provoke emotion. *International Journal of Behavioral Development, 10,* 319–343.

Harrison, Y., & Horne, J. A. (1997). Sleep deprivation affects speech. *Sleep, 20,* 871–877.

Harrison, Y., & Horne, J. A. (2000a). Impact of sleep deprivation on decision making: A review. *Journal of Experimental Psychology, 6,* 236–249.

Harrison, Y., & Horne, J. A. (2000b). Sleep loss and temporal memory. *Quarterly Journal of Experimental Psychology: Human Experimental Psychology, 53A,* 271–279.

Harrison, Y., Horne, J. A., & Rothwell, A. (2000). Prefrontal neuropsychological effects of sleep deprivation in young adults—a model for healthy aging? *Sleep, 23,* 1067–1073.

Harrist, A. W., & Waugh, R. M. (2002). Dyadic synchrony: Its structure and function in children's development. *Developmental Review, 22,* 555–592.

Harrist, A. W., Zain, A. F., Bates, J. E., Dodge, K. A., & Pettit, G. S. (1997). Subtypes of social withdrawal in early childhood: Sociometric status and social-cognitive differences across four years. *Child Development, 68,* 278–294.

Hart, C. H., DeWolf, M., Wozniak, P., & Burts, D. C. (1992). Maternal and paternal disciplinary styles: Relations with preschoolers' playground behavioral orientation and peer status. *Child Development, 63,* 879–892.

Hart, C. H., Ladd, G. W., & Burleson, B. R. (1990). Children's expectations of the outcome of social strategies: Relations with sociometric status and maternal disciplinary style. *Child Development, 61*, 127–137.

Hart, D., Hofmann, V., Edelstein, W., & Keller, M. (1997). The relation of childhood personality types to adolescent behavior and development: A longitudinal study of Icelandic children. *Developmental Psychology, 33*, 195–205.

Hart, D., Southerland, N., & Atkins, R. (2003). Community service and adult development. In J. Demick & C. Andreoletti (Eds.), *Handbook of adult development* (pp. 585–597). New York: Plenum.

Hart, S., Field, T., del Valle, C., & Pelaez-Nogueras, M. (1998). Depressed mothers' interactions with their one-year-old infants. *Infant Behavior and Development, 21*, 519–525.

Harter, S. (1985a). Competence as a dimension of self-worth. In R. Leahy (Ed.), *The development of the self.* New York: Academic Press.

Harter, S. (1985b). *Manual for the Self-Perception Profile for Children.* Denver, CO: University of Denver.

Harter, S. (1990). Causes, correlates, and the functional role of global self-worth: A life-span perspective. In J. Kolligan & R. Sternberg (Eds.), *Competence considered: Perceptions of competence and incompetence across the life-span* (pp. 67–97). New Haven: Yale University Press.

Harter, S. (1993). Developmental changes in self-understanding across the 5 to 7 shift. In A. Sameroff & M. Haith (Eds.), *Reason and responsibility: The passage through childhood.* Chicago: University of Chicago Press.

Harter, S. (1996). Developmental changes in self-understanding across the 5 to 7 shift. In A. J. Sameroff & M. M. Haith (Eds.), *The five to seven year shift: The age of reason and responsibility* (pp. 207–235). Chicago: University of Chicago Press.

Harter, S. (1998). The development of self representations. In W. Damon (Series Ed.) & N. Eisenberg (Vol. Ed.), *Handbook of child psychology: Vol. 3. Social, emotional, and personality development* (5th ed., pp. 553–617). New York: Wiley.

Hartford, J. (1971). *Life prayer.*

Hartley, A. A., Speer, N. K., Jonides, J., Reuter-Lorenz, P. A., & Smith, E. E. (2001). Is the dissociability of working memory systems for name identity, visual-object identity, and spatial location maintained in old age? *Neuropsychology, 15*, 3–17.

Hartshorn, K., Rovee-Collier, C., Gerhardstein, P., Bhatt, R. S., Wondoloski, R. L., Klein, P., Gilch, J., Wurtzel, N., & Campos-de-Carvalho, M. (1998). The ontogeny of long-term memory over the first year-and-a-half of life. *Developmental Psychobiology, 32*, 69–89.

Hartup, W. W. (1989). Social relationships and their developmental significance. *American Psychologist, 44*, 120–126.

Hartup, W. W. (1992). Peer relations in early and middle childhood. In V. B. Van Hasselt & M. Hersen (Eds.), *Handbook of social*

development: A lifespan perspective (pp. 257–281). New York: Plenum.

Hartup, W. W. (1996a). The company they keep: Friendships and their developmental significance. *Child Development, 67*, 1–13.

Hartup, W. W. (1996b). Cooperation, close relationships, and cognitive development. In W. M. Bukowski, A. F. Newcomb, & W. W. Hartup (Eds.), *The company they keep: Friendship in childhood and adolescence* (pp. 213–237). New York: Cambridge University Press.

Hartup, W. W., & Stevens, N. (1999). Friendships and adaptation across the life span. *Current Directions in Psychological Science, 8*, 76–79.

Harvard Medical School. (2002a). The mind and the immune system—Part I. *The Harvard Mental Health Letter, 18*(10), pp. 1–3.

Harvard Medical School. (2002b, July). Treatment of bulimia and binge eating. *Harvard Mental Health Letter, 19*(1), pp. 1–4.

Harvard Medical School. (2003a, November). Alzheimer's disease: A progress report. *Harvard Mental Health Letter, 20*(5), 1–4.

Harvard Medical School. (2003b, May). Confronting suicide, Part I. *Harvard Mental Health Letter, 19*(11), 1–4.

Harvard Medical School. (2003c, June). Confronting suicide, Part II. *Harvard Mental Health Letter, 19*(12), 1–5.

Harvard Medical School. (2003d, September). Depression in old age. *Harvard Mental Health Letter, 20*(3), 5.

Harvard Medical School. (2004a, December). Children's fears and anxieties. *Harvard Mental Health Letter, 21*(6), 1–3.

Harvard Medical School. (2004b, April). Countering domestic violence. *Harvard Mental Health Letter, 20*(10), pp. 1–5.

Harvard Medical School. (2004c, October). Is obesity a mental health issue? *Harvard Mental Health Letter, 21*(4).

Harvard Medical School. (2004d, May). Women and depression: How biology and society may make women more vulnerable to mood disorders. *Harvard Mental Health Letter, 20*(11), 1–4.

Harvard Medical School. (2005, February). Dysthymia: Psychotherapists and patients confront the high cost of "low-grade" depression. *Harvard Mental Health Letter, 21*(8), 1–3.

Harvey, E. (1999). Short-term and long-term effects of early parental employment on children of the National Longitudinal Survey of Youth. *Developmental Psychology, 35*(2), 445–459.

Harvey, J. H., & Omarzu, J. (1997). Minding the close relationship. *Personality and Psychology Review, 1*, 224–240.

Harvey, J. H., & Pauwels, B. G. (1999). Recent developments in close-relationships theory. *Current Directions in Psychological Science, 8*(3), 93–95.

Harwood, R. L., Schoelmerich, A., Ventura-Cook, E., Schulze, P. A., & Wilson, S. P. (1996). Culture and class influences on Anglo and Puerto Rican mothers' beliefs regarding long-term socialization goals and child behavior. *Child Development, 67*, 2446–2461.

Hatano, G., Siegler, R. S., Richards, D. D., Inagaki, K., Stavy, R., & Wax, N. (1993). The development of biological knowledge: A multinational study. *Cognitive Development, 8*, 47–62.

Hatzichristou, C., & Hopf, D. (1996). A multiperspective comparison of peer sociometric status groups in childhood and adolescence. *Child Development, 67*, 1085–1102.

Hauck, F. R., Herman, S. M., Donovan, M., Iyasu, S., Moore, C. M., Donoghue, E., Kirschner, R. H., & Willinger, M. (2003). Sleep environment and the risk of sudden infant death syndrome in an urban population: The Chicago Infant Mortality Study. *Pediatrics, 111*, 1207–1214.

Haugaard, J. J. (1998). Is adoption a risk factor for the development of adjustment problems? *Clinical Psychology Review, 18*, 47–69.

Hawes, C., Phillips, C. D., Rose, M., Holan, S., & Sherman, M. (2003). A national survey of assisted living facilities. *The Gerontologist, 43*, 875–882.

Hawkins, J. D., Catalano, R. F., Kosterman, R., Abbott, R., & Hill, K. G. (1999). Preventing adolescent health-risk behaviors by strengthening protection during childhood. *Archives of Pediatrics and Adolescent Medicine, 153*, 226–234.

Hawkins, J. D., Catalano, R. F., & Miller, J. Y. (1992). Risk and protective factors for alcohol and other drug problems in adolescence and early adulthood: Implications for substance abuse programs. *Psychological Bulletin, 112*(1), 64–105.

Hay, D. (2003). Pathways to violence in the children of mothers who were depressed postpartum. *Developmental Psychology, 39*, 1083-1094.

Hay, D. F., Pedersen, J., & Nash, A. (1982). Dyadic interaction in the first year of life. In K. H. Rubin & H. S. Ross (Eds.), *Peer relationships and social skills in children.* New York: Springer.

Hayes, A., & Batshaw, M. L. (1993). Down syndrome. *Pediatric Clinics of North America, 40*, 523–535.

Hayflick, L. (1974). The strategy of senescence. *The Gerontologist, 14*(1), 37–45.

Hayflick, L. (1981). Intracellular determinants of aging. *Mechanisms of Aging and Development, 28*, 177.

Hayflick, L. (1994). *How and why we age.* New York: Ballantine.

Hayflick, L. (2004). "Anti-aging" is an oxymoron. *Journal of Gerontology: Biological Sciences, 59A*, 573–578.

Hayne, H., Barr, R., & Herbert, J. (2003). The effect of prior practice on memory reactivation and generalization. *Child Development, 74*, 1615–1627.

Hays, J., Ockene, J. K., Brunner, R. L., Kotchen, J. M., Manson, J. A. E., Patterson, R. E., Aragaki, A. K., Schumaker, S. A., Brzyski, R. G., LaCroix, A. Z., Granek, I. A., & Valanis, B. B., for the Women's Health Initiative Investigation. (2003, March 17). Effects of estrogen plus progestin on health-related quality of life. *New England Journal of*

Medicine, 348, [Online]. Available: http://www.nejm.org (10.1056/NEJMoa030311). Access date: March 20, 2003.

Hayward, M. D., Friedman, S., & Chen, H. (1996). Race inequalities in men's retirement. *Journal of Gerontology: Social Sciences, 51B,* S1–10.

Heath, S. B. (1989). Oral and literate tradition among black Americans living in poverty. *American Psychologist, 44,* 367–373.

Hebert, J. R., Hurley, T. G., Olendzki, B. C., Teas, J., Ma, Y., & Hampl, J. S. (1998). Nutritional and socioeconomic factors in relation to prostate cancer mortality: A cross-national study. *Journal of the National Cancer Institute, 90,* 1637–1647.

Hebert, L. E., Scherr, P. A., Bienias, J. L., Bennett, D. A., & Evans, D. A. (2003). Alzheimer disease in the U.S. population: Prevalence estimates using the 2000 census. *Archives of Neurology, 60,* 1119–1122.

Heckhausen, J. (2001). Adaptation and resilience in midlife. In M. E. Lachman (Ed.), *Handbook of midlife development* (pp. 345–394). New York: Wiley.

Heckhausen, J., Wrosch, C., & Fleeson, W. (2001). Developmental regulation before and after a developmental deadline: The sample case of biological clock for childbearing. *Psychology and Aging, 16,* 400–413.

Hedley, A. A., Ogden, C. L., Johnson, C. L., Carroll, M. D., Curtin, L. R., & Flegal, K. M. (2004). Prevalence of overweight and obesity among U.S. children, adolescents, and adults, 1999–2002. *Journal of the American Medical Association, 291,* 2847–2850.

Heijl, A., Leske, M. C., Bengtsson, B., Hyman, L., Bengtsson, B., & Hussein, M., for the Early Manifest Glaucoma Trial Group. (2002). Reduction of intraocular pressure and glaucoma progression: Results from the Early Manifest Glaucoma Trial. *Archives of Ophthalmology, 120,* 1268–1279.

Heilbronn, L. K., & Ravussin, E. (2003). Calorie restriction and aging: Review of the literature and implications for studies in humans. *American Journal of Clinical Nutrition, 78,* 361–369.

Heilbrunn, J. (1998, November 15). Frequent flier: A biography of Secretary of State Madeleine Albright. *The New York Times Book Review,* p. 12.

Heller, R. B., & Dobbs, A. R. (1993). Age differences in word finding in discourse and nondiscourse situations. *Psychology and Aging, 8,* 443–450.

Helms, H. M., Crouter, A. C., & McHale, S. M. (2003). Marital quality and spouses' marriage work with close friends and each other. *Journal of Marriage and Family, 65,* 963–977.

Helms, J. E. (1992). Why is there no study of cultural equivalence in standardized cognitive ability testing? *American Psychologist, 47,* 1083–1101.

Helms, J. E., Jernigan, M., & Macher, J. (2005). The meaning of race in psychology and how to change it: A methodological perspective. *American Psychologist, 60,* 27–36.

Helson, R. (1993). Comparing longitudinal studies of adult development: Toward a paradigm of tension between stability and change. In D. C. Funder, R. D. Parke, C. Tomlinson-Keasey, & K. Widaman (Eds.), *Studying lives through time: Personality and development* (pp. 93–120). Washington, DC: American Psychological Association.

Helson, R. (1997). The self in middle age. In M. E. Lachman & J. B. James (Eds.), *Multiple paths of midlife development* (pp. 21–43). Chicago: University of Chicago Press.

Helson, R., & Moane, G. (1987). Personality change in women from college to midlife. *Journal of Personality and Social Psychology, 53,* 176–186.

Helson, R., & Roberts, B. W. (1994). Ego development and personality change in adulthood. *Journal of Personality and Social Psychology, 66,* 911–920.

Helson, R., & Wink, P. (1992). Personality change in women from the early 40s to the early 50s. *Psychology and Aging, 7*(1), 46–55.

Helwig, C. C., & Jasiobedzka, U. (2001). The relation between law and morality: Children's reasoning about socially beneficial and unjust laws. *Child Development, 72,* 1382–1393.

Hemingway, H., Nicholson, A., Stafford, M., Roberts, R., & Marmot, M. (1997). The impact of socioeconomic status on health functioning as assessed by the SF-35 questionnaire: The Whitehall II Study. *American Journal of Public Health, 87,* 1484–1490.

Henderson, H. A., Marshall, P. J., Fox, N. A., & Rubin, K. H. (2004). Psychophysiological and behavioral evidence for varying forms and functions of nonsocial behavior in preschoolers. *Child Development, 75,* 251–263.

Hendin, H. (1994, December 16). Scared to death of dying. *The New York Times,* p. A39.

Hendin, H., Rutenfrans, C., & Zylicz, Z. (1997). Physician-assisted suicide and euthanasia in the Netherlands: Lessons from the Dutch. *Journal of the American Medical Association, 277,* 1720–1722.

Hendricks, J., & Cutler, S. J. (2004). Volunteerism and socioemotional selectivity in later life. *Journal of Gerontology: Social Sciences, 59B,* S251–S257.

Henker, F. O. (1981). Male climacteric. In J. G. Howells (Ed.), *Modern perspectives in the psychiatry of middle age.* New York: Brunner/Mazel.

Henrich, C. C., Brown, J. L., & Aber, J. L. (1999). Evaluating the effectiveness of school-based violence prevention: Developmental approaches. *Social Policy Report, SRCD, 13*(3).

Heraclitus, fragment (sixth century B.C.)

Herbig, B., Büssing, A., & Ewert, T. (2001). The role of tacit knowledge in the work context of nursing. *Journal of Advanced Nursing, 34,* 687–695.

Hernandez, D. J. (1997). Child development and the social demography of childhood. *Child Development, 68,* 149–169.

Hernandez, D. J. (2004, Summer). Demographic change and the life circumstances of immigrant families. In R. E. Behrman (Ed.), Children of immigrant families (pp. 17–48). The Future of Children, 14(2). [Online]. Available: http://www.futureofchildren.org. Access date: October 7, 2004.

Heron, J., Golding, J., and the ALSPAC Study Team. (2004). Thimerosal exposure in infants and developmental disorders: A prospective cohort study in the United Kingdom does not support a causal association. *Pediatrics, 114,* 577–583.

Herrmann, D. (1999). *Helen Keller: A Life.* Chicago: University of Chicago Press.

Herrmann, H. J., & Roberts, M. W. (1987). Preventive dental care: The role of the pediatrician. *Pediatrics, 80,* 107–110.

Hertenstein, M. J., & Campos, J. J. (2004). The retention effects of an adult's emotional displays on infant behavior. *Child Development, 75,* 595–613.

Hertzog, C. (1989). Influences of cognitive slowing on age differences in intelligence. *Developmental Psychology, 25*(4), 636–651.

Hertzog, C., Dixon, R. A., & Hultsch, D. F. (1990). Relationships between metamemory, memory predictions, and memory task performance in adults. *Psychology and Aging, 5*(2), 215–227.

Hertz-Pannier, L., Chiron, C., Jambaque, I., Renaux-Kieffer, V., Van de Moortele, P., Delalande, O., Fohlen, M., Brunelle, F., & Le Bihan, D. (2002). Late plasticity language in a child's nondominant hemisphere. A pre- and post-surgery fMRI study. *Brain, 125*(2), 361–372.

Herzog, A. R., Franks, M. M., Markus, H. R., & Holmberg, D. (1998). Activities and well-being in older age: Effects of self-concept and educational attainment. *Psychology and Aging, 13*(2), 179–185.

Herzog, D. B., Dorer, D. J., Keel, P. K., Selwyn, S. E., Ekeblad, E. R., Flores, A. T., Greenwood, D. N., Burwell, R. A., & Keller, M. B. (1999). Recovery and relapse in anorexia and bulimia nervosa: A 7.5-year follow-up study. *Journal of the American Academy of Child and Adolescent Psychiatry, 38,* 829–837.

Hess, T. M., Hinson, J. T., & Statham, J. A. (2004). Explicit and implicit stereotype activation effects on memory: Do age and awareness moderate the impact of priming? *Psychology and Aging, 19,* 495–505.

Hesso, N. A., & Fuentes, E. (2005). Ethnic differences in neonatal and postneonatal mortality. *Pediatrics, 115,* e44–e51.

Hetherington, E. M. (1987). Family relations six years after divorce. In K. Pasley & M. Ihinger-Tallman (Eds.), *Remarriage and parenting today: Research and theory.* New York: Guilford.

Hetherington, E. M., Bridges, M., & Insabella, G. M. (1998). What matters? What does not? Five perspectives on the association between marital transitions and children's adjustment. *American Psychologist, 53,* 167–184.

Hetherington, E. M., & Kelly, J. (2002). *For better or worse: Divorce reconsidered.* New York: Norton.

Hetherington, E. M., & Stanley-Hagan, M. (1999). The adjustment of children with divorced parents: A risk and resiliency perspective. *Journal of Child Psychology and Psychiatry, 40,* 129–140.

Hetherington, E. M., Stanley-Hagan, M., & Anderson, E. (1989). Marital transitions: A child's perspective. *American Psychologist, 44,* 303–312.

Hetzel, B. S. (1994). Iodine deficiency and fetal brain damage. *New England Journal of Medicine, 331,* 1770–1771.

Hetzel, L., & Smith, A. (2001). The 65 years and over population: 2000 (Census 2000 Brief C2KBR/01–10). Washington, DC: U.S. Census Bureau.

Heuveline, P. & Timberlake, J. M. (2004). The role of cohabitation in family formation: The United States in comparative perspective. *Journal of Marriage and Family, 66,* 1214–1230.

Hewlett, B. S. (1987). Intimate fathers: Patterns of paternal holding among Aka pygmies. In M. E. Lamb (Ed.), *The father's role: Cross-cultural perspectives* (pp. 295–330). Hillsdale, NJ: Erlbaum.

Hewlett, B. S. (1992). Husband-wife reciprocity and the father-infant relationship among Aka pygmies. In B. S. Hewlett (Ed.), *Father-child relations: Cultural and biosocial contexts* (pp. 153–176). New York: de Gruyter.

Hewlett, B. S., Lamb, M. E., Shannon, D., Leyendecker, B., & Schölmerich, A. (1998). Culture and early infancy among central African foragers and farmers. *Developmental Psychology, 34*(4), 653–661.

Heyman, R. E. & Slep, A. M. S. (2002). Do child abuse and interpersonal violence lead to adulthood family violence? *Journal of Marriage and Family, 64,* 864–870.

Hickling, A. K., & Wellman, H. M. (2001). The emergence of children's causal explanations and theories: Evidence from everyday conversations. *Developmental Psychology, 37*(5), 668–683.

Hickman, M., Roberts, C., & de Matos, M. G. (2000). Exercise and leisure time activities. In C. Currie, K. Hurrelmann, W. Settertobulte, R. Smith, & J. Todd (Eds.), *Health and health behaviour among young people.* WHO Policy Series: Healthy Policy for Children and Adolescents, Series No. 1. (pp. 73–82).

Hiedemann, B., Suhomilinova, O., & O'Rand, A. M. (1998). Economic independence, economic status, and empty nest in midlife marital disruption. *Journal of Marriage and the Family, 60,* 219–231.

Hill, D. A., Gridley, G., Cnattingius, S., Mellemkjaer, L., Linet, M., Adami, H.-O., Olsen, J. H., Nyren, O., & Fraumeni, J. F. (2003). Mortality and cancer incidence among individuals with Down syndrome. *Archives of Internal Medicine, 163,* 705–711.

Hill, N. E., & Taylor, L. C. (2004). Parental school involvement and children's academic achievement: Pragmatics and issues. *Current Directions in Psychological Science, 13,* 161–168.

Hill, P. C., & Pargament, K. I. (2003). Advances in the conceptualization and measurement of religion and spirituality: Implications for physical and mental health research. *American Psychologist, 58,* 64–74.

Hill, T. D., Angel, J. L., Ellison, C. G., & Angel, R. J. (2005). Religious attendance and mortality: An 8-year follow-up of older Mexican Americans. *Journal of Gerontology: Social Sciences, 60B,* S102–S109.

Hillier, L. (2002). "It's a catch-22": Same-sex-attracted young people on coming out to parents. In S. S. Feldman & D. A. Rosenthal, (Eds.), Talking sexuality. *New Directions for Child and Adolescent Development, 97,* 75–91.

Hillis, S. D., Anda, R. F., Dubè, S. R., Felitti, V. J., Marchbanks, P. A., & Marks, J. S. (2004). The association between adverse childhood experiences and adolescent pregnancy, long-term psychosocial consequences, and fetal death. *Pediatrics, 113,* 320–327.

Hilts, P. J. (1999, June 1). Life at age 100 is surprisingly healthy. *New York Times,* p. D7.

Hinds, D. A., Stuve, L. L., Nilsen, G. B., Halperin, E., Eskin, E., Ballinger, D. G., Frazer, K. A., & Cox, D. R. (2005). Whole-genome patterns of common DNA variation in three human populations. *Science, 307,* 1072–1079.

Hinds, T. S., West, W. L., Knight, E. M., & Harland, B. F. (1996). The effect of caffeine on pregnancy outcome variables. *Nutrition Reviews, 54,* 203–207.

Hines, A. M. (1997). Divorce-related transitions, adolescent development, and the role of the parent-child relationship: A review of the literature. *Journal of Marriage and the Family, 59,* 375–388.

Hines, M., Chiu, L., McAdams, L. A., Bentler, M. P., & Lipcamon, J. (1992). Cognition and the corpus callosum: Verbal fluency, visuospatial ability, language lateralization related to midsagittal surface areas of the corpus callosum. *Behavioral Neuroscience, 106,* 3–14.

Hingson, R., Heeren, T., Winter, M., & Wechsler, H. (2005). Magnitude of alcohol-related mortality and morbidity among U.S. college students ages 18–24: Changes from 1998–2001. *Annual Reviews, 26,* 259–279.

Hirsch, H. V., & Spinelli, D. N. (1970). Visual experience modifies distribution of horizontally and vertically oriented receptive fields in cats. *Science, 168,* 869–871.

Hirschl, T. A., Altobelli, J., & Rank, M. R. (2003). Does marriage increase the odds of affluence? Exploring the life course probabilities. *Journal of Marriage and Family, 65,* 927–938.

Hitchins, M. P., & Moore, G. E. (2002, May 9). Genomic imprinting in fetal growth and development. *Expert Reviews in Molecular Medicine.* [Online]. Retrieved April 6, 2005, from http://www.expertreviews.org/0200457Xh.htm.

Hitt, R., Young-Xu, Y., Perls, T. (1999). Centenarians: The older you get, the healthier you've been. *Lancet, 354,* 652.

Ho, C. S. -H., & Fuson, K. C. (1998). Children's knowledge of teen quantities as tens and ones: Comparisons of Chinese, British, and American kindergartners. *Journal of Educational Psychology, 90,* 536–544.

Ho, D. (1999, June 16). Midwestern living suits women to a ripe old age. *Chicago Sun-Times,* p. 26.

Ho, W. C. (1989). *Yani: The brush of innocence.* New York: Hudson Hills.

Hoban, T. F. (2004). Sleep and its disorders in children. *Seminars in Neurology, 24,* 327–340.

Hobson, J. A., & Silvestri, L. (1999, February). Parasomnias. *Harvard Mental Health Letter,* pp. 3–5.

Hodges, E. V. E., Boivin, M., Vitaro, F., & Bukowski, W. M. (1999). The power of friendship: Protection against an escalating cycle of peer victimization. *Developmental Psychology, 35,* 94–101.

Hoff, E. (2003). The specificity of environmental influence: Socioeconomic status affects early vocabulary development via maternal speech. *Child Development, 74,* 1368–1378.

Hofferth, S. L., & Jankuniene, Z. (2000, April 2). *Children's after-school activities.* Paper presented at biennial meeting of the Society for Research on Adolescence, Chicago.

Hofferth, S. L., & Sandberg, J. (1998). *Changes in American children's time, 1981–1997* (Report of the 1997 Panel Study of Income Dynamics, Child Development Supplement). Ann Arbor: University of Michigan Institute for Social Research.

Hoffman, H. J., & Hillman, L. S. (1992). Epidemiology of the sudden infant death syndrome: Maternal, neonatal, and postneonatal risk factors. *Clinics in Perinatology, 19,* 717–737.

Hoffman, M. L. (1970a). Conscience, personality, and socialization techniques. *Human Development, 13,* 90–126.

Hoffman, M. L. (1970b). Moral development. In P. H. Mussen (Ed.), *Carmichael's manual of child psychology* (Vol. 2, 3rd ed., pp. 261–360). New York: Wiley.

Hoffman, M. L. (1977). Sex differences in empathy and related behaviors. *Psychological Bulletin, 84,* 712–722.

Hoffman, M. L. (1998). Varieties of empathy-based guilt. In J. Bybee (Ed.), *Guilt and children* (pp. 91–112). San Diego: Academic.

Hoffrage, U., Weber, A., Hertwig, R., & Chase, V. M. (2003). How to keep children safe in traffic: Find the daredevils early. *Journal of Experimental Psychology: Applied, 9,* 249–260.

Hofman, P. L., Regan, F., Jackson, W. E., Jefferies, C., Knight, D. B., Robinson, E. M., & Cutfield, W. S. (2004). Premature birth and later insulin resistance. *New England Journal of Medicine, 351,* 2179–2186.

Hogge, W. A. (2003). The clinical use of karyotyping spontaneous abortions. *American Journal of Obstetrics and Gynecology, 189,* 397–402.

Holden, G. W., & Miller, P. C. (1999). Enduring and different: A meta-analysis of the similarity in parents' child rearing. *Psychological Bulletin, 125,* 223–254.

Holliday, R. (2004). The multiple and irreversible causes of aging. *Journal of Gerontology: Biological Sciences, 59A,* 568–572.

Holmes, T. H., & Rahe, R. H. (1976). The social readjustment rating scale. *Journal of Psychosomatic Research, 11,* 213.

Holowka, S., & Petitto, L. A. (2002). Left hemisphere cerebral specialization for babies while babbling. *Science, 297,* 1515.

Holstein, M. B., & Minkler, M. (2003). Self, society, and the "New Gerontology." *The Gerontologist, 43,* 787–796.

Holtzman, N. A., Murphy, P. D., Watson, M. S., & Barr, P. A. (1997). Predictive genetic testing: From basic research to clinical practice. *Science, 278,* 602–605.

Holtzman, R. E., Rebok, G. W., Saczynski, J. S. Kouzis, A. C., Doyle, K. W., & Eaton, W. W. (2004). Social network characteristics and cognition in middle-aged and older adults. *Journal of Gerontology: Psychological Sciences, 59B,* P278–P284.

Home, J. (1985). *Caregiving: Helping an aging loved one.* Washington, DC: AARP Books.

Honein, M. A., Paulozzi, L. J., Mathews, T. J., Erickson, J. D., & Wong, L.-Y. C. (2001). Impact of folic acid fortification of the U.S. food supply on the occurrence of neural tube defects. *Journal of the American Medical Association, 285,* 2981–2986.

Hood, B., Cole-Davies, V., & Dias, M. (2003). Looking and search measures of object knowledge in preschool children. *Developmental Psychology, 39,* 61–70.

Hopfensperger, J. (1996, April 15). Germany's fast track to a career. *Minneapolis Star-Tribune,* pp. A1, A6.

Hopkins, B., & Westra, T. (1988). Maternal handling and motor development: An intracultural study. *Genetic, Social and General Psychology Monographs, 14,* 377–420.

Hopkins, B., & Westra, T. (1990). Motor development, maternal expectations and the role of handling. *Infant Behavior and Development, 13,* 117–122.

Hopper, J. L., & Seeman, E. (1994). The bone density of female twins discordant for tobacco use. *New England Journal of Medicine, 330,* 387–392.

Horbar, J. D., Wright, E. C., Onstad, L., & the Members of the National Institute of Child Health and Human Development Neonatal Research Network. (1993). Decreasing mortality associated with the introduction of surfactant therapy: An observational study of neonates weighing 601 to 1300 grams at birth. *Pediatrics, 92,* 91–196.

Horn, I. B., Cheng, T. L., & Joseph, J. (2004). Discipline in the African American community: The impact of socioeconomic status on beliefs and practices. *Pediatrics, 113,* 1236–1241.

Horn, J. C., & Meer, J. (1987, May). The vintage years. *Psychology Today,* pp. 76–90.

Horn, J. L. (1967). Intelligence—Why it grows, why it declines. *Transaction, 5*(1), 23–31.

Horn, J. L. (1968). Organization of abilities and the development of intelligence. *Psychological Review, 75,* 242–259.

Horn, J. L. (1970). Organization of data on lifespan development of human abilities. In L. R. Goulet & P. B. Baltes (Eds.), *Life-span developmental psychology: Theory and research* (pp. 424–466). New York: Academic Press.

Horn, J. L. (1982a). The aging of human abilities. In B. B. Wolman (Ed.), *Handbook of developmental psychology* (pp. 847–870). Englewood Cliffs, NJ: Prentice-Hall.

Horn, J. L. (1982b). The theory of fluid and crystallized intelligence in relation to concepts of cognitive psychology and aging in adulthood. In F. I. M. Craik & S. Trehub (Eds.), *Aging and cognitive processes* (pp. 237–278). New York: Plenum.

Horn, J. L., & Donaldson, G. (1980). Cognitive development: 2. Adulthood development of human abilities. In O. G. Brim & J. Kagan (Eds.), *Constancy and change in human development.* Cambridge, MA: Harvard University Press.

Horn, J. L., & Hofer, S. M. (1992). Major abilities and development in the adult. In R. J. Sternberg & C. A. Berg (Eds.), *Intellectual development.* Cambridge, UK: Cambridge University Press.

Horn, L., & Berger, R. (2004). College persistence on the rise? Changes in 5-year completion and postsecondary persistence rates between 1994 and 2000 (NCES 2005-156). U.S. Department of Education, National Center for Education Statistics. Washington, DC: U.S. Government Printing Office.

Horne, J. (2000). Neuroscience: Images of lost sleep. *Nature, 403,* 605–606.

Horowitz, F. D. (2000). Child development and the PITS: Simple questions, complex answers, and developmental theory. *Child Development, 71*(1), 1–10.

Horton, R., & Shweder, R. A. (2004). Ethnic conservatism, psychological well-being, and the downside of mainstreaming: Generational differences. In O. G. Brim, C. D. Ryff, and R. C. Kessler (Eds.), *How healthy are we? A national study of well-being at midlife* (pp. 373–397). Chicago: University of Chicago Press.

Horvath, T. B., & Davis, K. L. (1990). Central nervous system disorders in aging. In E. L. Schneider & J. W. Rowe (Eds.), *The handbook of the biology of aging* (3rd ed., pp. 306–329). San Diego: Academic.

Horwitz, B., Rumsey, J. M., & Donohue, B. C. (1998). Functional connectivity of the angular gyrus in normal reading and dyslexia. *Proceedings of the National Academy of Sciences USA, 95,* 8939–8944.

Houston, D. K., Stevens, J., Cai, J., & Haines, P. S. (2005). Dairy, fruit, and vegetable intakes and functional limitations and disability in a biracial cohort: The Atherosclerosis Risk in Communities Study. *American Journal of Clinical Nutrition, 81,* 515–522.

Hoven, C. W., Mandell, D. J., & Duarte, C. S. (2003). Mental health of New York City public school children after 9/11: An epidemiological investigation. In S. Coates, J. L. Rosenthal, & D. L. Schechter (Eds.), *September 11: Trauma and human bonds.* Hillsdale, NJ: Analytic.

How to raise HDL. (2001, December). *University of California, Berkeley Wellness Letter, 18*(3), p. 3.

Howe, M. L. (2003). Memories from the cradle. *Current Directions in Psychological Science, 12,* 62–65.

Howe, M. L., & Courage, M. L. (1993). On resolving the enigma of infantile amnesia. *Psychological Bulletin, 113,* 305–326.

Howe, M. L., & Courage, M. L. (1997). The emergence and early development of autobiographical memory. *Psychological Review, 104,* 499–523.

Howes, C., & Matheson, C. C. (1992). Sequences in the development of competent play with peers: Social and social pretend play. *Developmental Psychology, 28,* 961–974.

Hoyer, W. J., & Rybash, J. M. (1994). Characterizing adult cognitive development. *Journal of Adult Development, 1*(1), 7–12.

Hoyert, D. L., Arias, E., Smith, B. L., Murphy, S. L., & Kochanek, K. D. (2001). Deaths: Final data for 1999. *National Vital Statistics Reports, 49*(8). Hyattsville, MD: National Center for Health Statistics.

Hoyert, D. L., Kochanek, K. D., & Murphy, S. L. (1999). Deaths: Final data for 1997. *National Vital Statistics Reports, 47*(19). Hyattsville, MD: National Center for Health Statistics.

Hoyert, D. L., Kung, H.-C., & Smith, B. L. (2005). Deaths: Preliminary data for 2003. *National Vital Statistics Reports, 53*(15). Hyattsville, MD: National Center for Health Statistics.

Hoyert, D. L., & Rosenberg, H. M. (1999). Mortality from Alzheimer's Disease: An update. *National Vital Statistics Reports, 47*(20). Hyattsville, MD: National Center for Health Statistics.

Hu, F. B., Li, T. Y., Colditz, G. A., Willett, W. C., & Manson, J. E. (2003). Television watching and other sedentary behaviors in relation to risk of obesity and type 2 diabetes mellitus in women. *Journal of the American Medical Association, 289,* 1785–1791.

Hu, F. B., Manson, J. E., Stampfer, M. J., Colditz, G., Liu, S., Solomon, C. G., & Willett, W. C. (2001). Diet, lifestyle, and the risk of type 2 diabetes mellitus in women. *New England Journal of Medicine, 345,* 790–797.

Hu, F. B., Willett, W. C., Li, T., Stampfer, M. J., Colditz, G. A., & Manson, J. E. (2004). Adiposity as compared with physical activity in predicting mortality among women. *New England Journal of Medicine, 351,* 2694–2703.

Hubbard, F. O. A., & van IJzendoorn, M. H. (1991). Maternal unresponsiveness and infant crying across the first 9 months: A naturalistic longitudinal study. *Infant Behavior and Development, 14,* 299–312.

Hudnall, C. E. (2001, November). "Grand" parents get help: Programs aid aging caregivers and youngsters. *AARP Bulletin,* pp. 9, 12–13.

Hudson, J. I., & Pope, H. G. (1990). Affective spectrum disorder: Does antidepressant response identify a family of disorders with a common pathophysiology? *American Journal of Psychiatry, 147*(5), 552–564.

Hudson, V. M., & den Boer, A. M. (2004). *Bare branches: Security implications of Asia's surplus male population.* Cambridge, MA: MIT Press.

Huesmann, L. R. (1986). Psychological processes promoting the relation between exposure to media violence and aggressive behavior by the viewer. *Journal of Social Issues, 42,* 125–139.

Huesmann, L. R., & Eron, L. D. (1984). Cognitive processes and the persistence of aggressive behavior. *Aggressive Behavior, 10,* 243–251.

Huesmann, L. R., Moise-Titus, J., Podolski, C. L., & Eron, L. (2003). Longitudinal relations between children's exposure to TV violence and their aggressive and violent behavior in young adulthood: 1977–1992. *Developmental Psychology, 39,* 201–221.

Hughes, I. A. (2004). Female development—all by default? *New England Journal of Medicine, 351,* 748–750.

Hughes, M. (1975). *Egocentrism in preschool children.* Unpublished doctoral dissertation, Edinburgh University, Edinburgh, Scotland.

Huizink, A., Robles de Medina, P., Mulder, E., Visser, G., & Buitelaar, J. (2002). Psychological measures of prenatal stress as predictors of infant temperament. *Journal of the American Academy of Child & Adolescent Psychiatry, 41,* 1078–1085.

Huizink, A. C., Mulder, E. J. H., & Buitelaar, J. K. (2004). Prenatal stress and risk for psychopathology: Specific effects or induction of general susceptibility? *Psychological Bulletin 130,* 80–114.

Hujoel, P. P., Bollen, A.-M., Noonan, C. J., & del Aguila, M. A. (2004). Antepartum dental radiography and infant low birth weight. *Journal of the American Medical Association, 291,* 1987–1993.

Hulley, S., Furberg, C., Barrett-Connor, E., Cauley, J., Grady, D., Haskell, W., Knopp, R., Lowery, M., Satterfield, S., Schrott, H., Vittinghoff, E., & Hunninghake, D. (2002). Noncardiovascular disease outcomes during 6.8 years of hormone therapy. *Journal of the American Medical Association, 288,* 58–66.

Hultsch, D. F. (1971). Organization and memory in adulthood. *Human Development, 14,* 16–29.

Humphrey, L. L. (1986). Structural analysis of parent-child relationships in eating disorders. *Journal of Abnormal Psychology, 95*(4), 395–402.

Humphreys, A. P., & Smith, P. K. (1984). Rough-and-tumble in preschool and playground. In P. K. Smith (Ed.), *Play in animals and humans.* Oxford: Blackwell.

Humphreys, G.W. (2002). Cognitive neuroscience. In H. Pashler, & D. Medin, (Eds.). *Steven's handbook of experimental psychology (3rd ed.), Vol. 2: Memory and cognitive processes* (pp. 77–112). New York: John Wiley & Sons, Inc.

Hungerford, T. L. (2001). The economic consequences of widowhood on elderly women in the United States and Germany. *The Gerontologist, 41,* 103–110.

Hunt, C. E. (1996). Prone sleeping in healthy infants and victims of sudden infant death syndrome. *Journal of Pediatrics, 128,* 594–596.

Huntsinger, C. S., & Jose, P. E. (1995). Chinese American and Caucasian American family interaction patterns in spatial rotation puzzle solutions. *Merrill-Palmer Quarterly, 41,* 471–496.

Huntsinger, C. S., Jose, P. E., & Larson, S. L. (1998). Do parent practices to encourage academic competence influence the social adjustment of young European American and Chinese American children? *Developmental Psychology, 34*(4), 747–756.

Huston, H. C., Duncan, G. J., Granger, R., Bos, J., McLoyd, V., Mistry, R., Crosby, D., Gibson, C., Magnuson, K., Romich, J., and Ventura, A. (2001). Work-based antipoverty programs for parents can enhance the performance and social behavior of children. *Child Development, 72*(1), 318–336.

Huth-Bocks, A. C., Levendossky, A. A., Bogat, G. A., & von Eye, A. (2004). The impact of maternal characteristics and contextual variables on infant-mother attachment. *Child Development, 75,* 480–496.

Huttenlocher, J. (1998). Language input and language growth. *Preventive Medicine, 27,* 195–199.

Huttenlocher, J., Haight, W., Bryk, A., Seltzer, M., & Lyons, T. (1991). Early vocabulary growth: Relation to language input and gender. *Developmental Psychology, 27,* 236–248.

Huttenlocher, J., Levine, S., & Vevea, J. (1998). Environmental input and cognitive growth: A study using time-period comparisons. *Child Development, 69,* 1012–1029.

Huttenlocher, J., Newcombe, N., & Vasilyeva, M. (1999). Spatial scaling in young children. *Psychological Science, 10,* 393–398.

Huttenlocher, J., Vasilyeva, M., Cymerman, E., & Levine, S. (2002). Language input and child syntax. *Cognitive Psychology, 45,* 337–374.

Huyck, M. H. (1990). Gender differences in aging. In J. E. Birren & K. W. Schaie (Eds.), *Handbook of the psychology of aging* (3rd ed., pp. 124–132). San Diego: Academic Press.

Huyck, M. H. (1995). Marriage and close relationships of the marital kind. In R. Blieszner & V. Hilkevitch (Eds.), *Handbook of aging and the family* (pp. 181–200). Westport, CT: Greenwood Press.

Huyck, M. H. (1999). Gender roles and gender identity in midlife. In S. L. Willis & J. D. Reid (Eds.), *Life in the middle: Psychological and social development in middle age* (pp. 209–232). New York: Academic.

Hwang, J., & Rothbart, M.K. (2003). Behavior genetics studies of infant temperament: Findings vary across parent-report instruments. *Infant Behavior & Development, 26,* 112–114.

Hwang, S. J., Beaty, T. H., Panny, S. R., Street, N. A., Joseph, J. M., Gordon, S., McIntosh, I., & Francomano, C. A. (1995). Association study of transforming growth factor alpha (TGFa) TaqI polymorphism and oral clefts: Indication of gene-environment interaction in a population-based sample of infants with birth defects. *American Journal of Epidemiology, 141,* 629–636.

Ialongo, N. S., Edelsohn, G., & Kellam, S. G. (2001). A further look at the prognostic power of young children's reports of depressed mood and feelings. *Child Development, 72,* 736–747.

Iervolino, A. C., Pike, A., Manke, B., Reiss, D., Hetherington, E. M., & Plomin, R. (2002). Genetic and environmental influences in adolescent peer socialization: Evidence from two genetically sensitive designs. *Child Development, 73*(1), 162–174.

Iglowstein, I., Jenni, O. G., Molinari, L., & Largo, R. H. (2003). Sleep duration from infancy to adolescence: Reference values and generational trends. *Pediatrics, 111,* 302–307.

Ikeda, R., Mahendra, R., Saltzman, L., Crosby, A., Willis, L., Mercy, J., Holmgreen, P., & Annest, J. L. (2002). Nonfatal self-inflicted injuries treated in hospital departments, United States, 2000. *Morbidity and Mortality Weekly Report 51,* 436–438.

Impagnatiello, F., Guidotti, A. R., Pesold, C., Dwivedi, Y., Caruncho, H., Pisu, M. G., Uzonov, D. P., Smalheiser, N. R., Davis, J. M., Pandey, G. N., Pappas, G. D., Tueting, P., Sharma, R. P., & Costa, E. (1998). A decrease of reelin expression as a putative vulnerability factor in schizophrenia. *Proceedings of the National Academy of Science, 95,* 15718–15723.

Infant Health and Development Program (IHDP). (1990). Enhancing the outcomes of low-birth-weight, premature infants. *Journal of the American Medical Association, 263*(22), 3035–3042.

Infante-Rivard, C., Fernández, A., Gauthier, R., David, M., & Rivard, G. E. (1993). Fetal loss associated with caffeine intake before and during pregnancy. *Journal of the American Medical Association, 270,* 2940–2943.

Ingelfinger, J. R. (2005). Risks and benefits to the living donor. *New England Journal of Medicine, 353,* 447–449.

Ingersoll, E. W., & Thoman, E. B. (1999). Sleep/wake states of preterm infants: Stability, developmental change, diurnal variation, and relation with caregiving activity. *Child Development, 70,* 1–10.

Ingersoll-Dayton, B., Neal, M. B., Ha, J., & Hammer, L. B. (2003). Redressing inequity in parent care among siblings. *Journal of Marriage and Family, 65,* 201–212.

Ingoldsby, B. B. (1995). Mate selection and marriage. In B. B. Ingoldsby & S. Smith (Eds.), *Families in multicultural perspective* (pp.143–160). New York: Guilford.

Ingram, J. L., Stodgell, C. S., Hyman, S. L., Figlewicz, D. A., Weitkamp, L. R., & Rodier, P. M. (2000). Discovery of allelic variants of HOXA1 and HOXB1: Genetic susceptibility to autism spectrum disorders. *Teratology, 62,* 393–406.

Institute of Medicine (IOM) National Academy of Sciences. (1993, November). *Assessing genetic risks: Implications for health and social policy.* Washington, DC: National Academy of Sciences.

International Agency for Cancer Research. (2002). Second-hand smoke carcinogenic to humans. Monographs Programme of the International Agency for Research on Cancer. Lyon, France: World Health Organization.

International Cesarean Awareness Network. (2003, March 5). Statistics: International cesarean and VBAC rates. [Online]. Available:

http://www.ican-online.org/resources.statistics3.htm. Access date: January 20, 2004.

International Human Genome Sequencing Consortium. (2004). Finishing the euchromatic sequence of the human genome. *Nature, 431,* 931–945.

International Longevity Center-USA. (2002). Is there an anti-aging medicine? ILC Workshop Report. On-line. Available at http://www.ilcusa.org

Isaacowitz, D. M., & Smith, J. (2003). Positive and negative affect in very old age. *Journal of Gerontology: Psychological Sciences, 58B,* P143–P152.

Isabella, R. A. (1993). Origins of attachment: Maternal interactive behavior across the first year. *Child Development, 64,* 605–621.

Ishii, N., Fujii, M., Hartman, P. S., Tsuda, M., Yasuda, K., Senoo-Matsuda, N., Yanase, S., Ayusawa, D., & Suzuki, K. (1998). A mutation in succinate dehydrogenase cytochrome b causes oxidative stress and ageing in nematodes. *Nature, 394,* 694–697.

ISLAT Working Group. (1998, July 31). ART into science: Regulation of fertility techniques. *Science, 281,* 651–652.

Iverson, J. M., & Goldin-Meadow, S. (1998). Why people gesture when they speak. *Nature, 396,* 228.

Ivy, G. O., MacLeod, C. M., Petit, T. L., & Markus, E. J. (1992). A physiological framework for perceptual and cognitive changes in aging. In F. I. M. Craik & T. A. Salthouse (Eds.), *Handbook of aging and cognition* (pp. 273–314). Hillsdale, NJ: Erlbaum.

Izard, C. E., Huebner, R. R., Resser, D., McGinness, G. C., & Dougherty, L. M. (1980). The young infant's ability to produce discrete emotional expressions. *Developmental Psychology, 16,* 132–140.

Jaccard, J., Blanton, H., & Dodge, T. (2005). Peer influences on risk behavior: An analysis of the effects of a close friend. *Developmental Psychology, 41,* 135–147.

Jaccard, J., & Dittus, P. J. (2000). Adolescent perceptions of maternal approval of birth control and sexual risk behavior. *American Journal of Public Health, 90,* 1426–1430.

Jacobsen, T., & Hofmann, V. (1997). Children's attachment representations: Longitudinal relations to school behavior and academic competency in middle childhood and adolescence. *Developmental Psychology, 33,* 703–710.

Jacobson, J. L., & Wille, D. E. (1986). The influence of attachment pattern on developmental changes in peer interaction from the toddler to the preschool period. *Child Development, 57,* 338–347.

Jacobson, M. W., Delis, D. C., Bondi, M. W., & Salmon, D. P. (2002). Do neuropsychological tests detect preclinical Alzheimer's disease?: Individual-test versus cognitive-discrepancy score analyses. *Neuropsychology, 16,* 132–139.

Jacques, E. (1967). The midlife crisis. In R. Owen (Ed.), *Middle age.* London: BBC.

Jaffee, S., & Hyde, J. S. (2000). Gender differences in moral orientation: A metaanalysis. *Psychological Bulletin, 126,* 703–725.

Jaffee, S. R., Caspim A., Moffitt, T. E., Polo-Tomas, M., Price, T. S., & Taylor, A. (2004). The limits of child effects: Evidence for genetically mediated child effects on corporal punishment but not on physical maltreatment. *Developmental Psychology, 40,* 1047–1058.

Jagasia, R., Grote, P., Westermann, B., & Conradt, B. (2005). DRP-1-mediated mitochondrial fragmentation during EGL-1-induced cell death in *C. elegans. Nature, 433,* 754–760.

Jagers, R. J., Bingham, K., & Hans, S. L. (1996). Socialization and social judgments among inner-city African-American kindergartners. *Child Development, 67,* 140–150.

Jain, T., Missmer, S. A., & Hornstein, M. D. (2004). Trends in embryo-transfer practice and in outcomes of the use of assisted reproductive technology in the United States. *New England Journal of Medicine, 350,* 1639–1645.

Jakicic, J. M., Marcus, B. H., Gallagher, K. I., Napolitano, M., & Lang, W. (2003). Effect of exercise duration and intensity on weight loss in overweight sedentary women: A randomized trial. *Journal of the American Medical Association, 290,* 1323–1330.

James, J. B., & Lewkowicz, C. J. (1997). Themes of power and affiliation across time. In M. E. Lachman & J. B. James (Eds.), *Multiple paths of midlife development* (pp. 109–143). Chicago: University of Chicago Press.

Jankowiak, W. (1992). Father-child relations in urban China. *Father-child relations: Cultural and bisocial contexts* (pp. 345–363). New York: de Gruyter.

Jankowski, J. J., Rose, S. A., & Feldman, J. F. (2001). Modifying the distribution of attention in infants. *Child Development, 72,* 339–351.

Janowsky, J. S., & Carper, R. (1996). Is there a neural basis for cognitive transitions in school-age children? In A. J. Sameroff & M. M. Haith (Eds.), *The five to seven year shift: The age of reason and responsibility* (pp. 33–56). Chicago: University of Chicago Press.

Janssen, I., Craig, W. M., Boyce, W. F., & Pickett, W. (2004). Associations between overweight and obesity with bullying behaviors in school-aged children. *Pediatrics, 113,* 1187–1194.

Japan in shock at school murder. (2004). June 2). BBC News. [Online]. Available: http://news.bbc.co.uk/go/pr/fr/-/1/hi/world/asia-pacific/3768983.stm. Access date: June 2, 2004.

Jarrell, R. H. (1998). Play and its influence on the development of young children's mathematical thinking. In D. P. Fromberg & D. Bergen (Eds.), *Play from birth to twelve and beyond: Contexts, perspectives, and meanings* (pp. 56–67). New York: Garland.

Jeffery, H. E., Megevand, M., & Page, M. (1999). Why the prone position is a risk factor for sudden infant death syndrome. *Pediatrics, 104,* 263–269.

Jeffords, J. M., & Daschle, T. (2001). Political issues in the genome era. *Science, 291,* 1249–1251.

Jenkins, J. M., Turrell, S. L., Kogushi, Y., Lollis, S., & Ross, H. S. (2003). A longitudinal investigation of the dynamics of mental state talk in families. *Child Development, 74,* 905–920.

Jensen, C. D., Block, G., Buffler, P., Ma, X., Selvin, S., & Month, S., representing the Northern California Childhood Leukemia Study Group. (2004). Maternal dietary risk factors in childhood acute lymphoblastic leukemia. *Cancer Causes and Control, 15,* 559–570.

Ji, B. T., Shu, X. O., Linet, M. S., Zheng, W., Wacholder, S., Gao, Y. T., Ying, D. M., & Jin, F. (1997). Paternal cigarette smoking and the risk of childhood cancer among offspring of nonsmoking mothers. *Journal of the National Cancer Institute, 89,* 238–244.

Jiao, S., Ji, G., & Jing, Q. (1996). Cognitive development of Chinese urban only children and children with siblings. *Child Development, 67,* 387–395.

Jimerson, S., Egeland, B., & Teo, A. (1999). A longitudinal study of achievement trajectories: Factors associated with change. *Journal of Educational Psychology, 91*(1), 116–126.

Jodl, K. M., Michael, A., Malanchuk, O., Eccles, J. S., & Sameroff, A. (2001). Parents' roles in shaping early adolescents' occupational aspirations. *Child Development, 72*(4), 1247–1265.

Johansson, B., Hofer, S. M., Allaire, J. C., Maldonado-Molina, M. M., Piccinin, A. M., Berg, S., Pedersen, N. L., & McClearn, G. E. (2004). Change in cognitive capabilities in the oldest old: The effects of proximity to death in genetically related individuals over a 6-year period. *Psychology and Aging, 19,* 145–156.

Johansson, G., Evans, G. W., Rydstedt, L. W., & Carrere, S. (1998). Job hassles and cardiovascular reaction patterns among urban bus drivers. *International Journal of Behavioral Medicine, 5,* 267–280.

Johnson, C. L. (1995). Cultural diversity in the late-life family. In R. Blieszner & V. Hilkevitch (Eds.), *Handbook of aging and the family* (pp. 307–331). Westport, CT: Greenwood Press.

Johnson, C. L., & Troll, L. E. (1994). Constraints and facilitators to friendships in late late life. *The Gerontologist, 34,* 79–87.

Johnson, D. J., Jaeger, E., Randolph, S. M., Cauce, A. M., Ward, J., & National Institute of Child Health and Human Development Early Child Care Research Network. (2003). Studying the effects of early child care experiences on the development of children of color in the United States. Toward a more inclusive research agenda. *Child Development, 74,* 1227–1244.

Johnson, D. W., Johnson, R. T., & Tjosvold, D. (2000). Constructive controversy: The value of intellectual opposition. In M. Deutsch & P. T. Coleman (Eds.), *The handbook of conflict resolution: Theory and practice* (pp. 65–85). San Francisco: Jossey-Bass.

Johnson, J. E. (1998). Play development from ages four to eight. In D. P. Fromberg & D. Bergen (Eds.), *Play from birth to twelve and beyond: Contexts, perspectives, and meanings* (pp. 145–153). New York: Garland.

Johnson, J., Canning, J., Kaneko, T., Pru, J. K., & Tilly, J. L. (2004). Germline stem cells and follicular renewal in the postnatal mammalian ovary. *Nature, 428*(6979), 145–150.

Johnson, J., Stewart, W., Hall, E., Fredlund, P., & Theorell, T. (1996). Long-term psychosocial work environment and cardiovascular mortality among Swedish men. *American Journal of Public Health, 86,* 324–331.

Johnson, J. G., Cohen, P., Smailes, E. M., Kasen, S., & Brook, J. S. (2002). Television viewing and aggressive behavior during adolescence and adulthood. *Science, 295,* 2468–2471.

Johnson, K. E., Scott, P., & Mervis, C. B. (1997). Development of children's understanding of basic-subordinate inclusion relations. *Developmental Psychology, 33,* 745–763.

Johnson, M. H. (1998). The neural basis of cognitive development. In D. Kuhn & R. S. Siegler (Eds.), *Handbook of child psychology: Vol. 2. Cognition, perception, and language* (5th ed., pp. 1–49). New York: Wiley.

Johnson, M. H. (1999). Developmental cognitive neuroscience. In M. Bennett, (Ed.), *Developmental psychology: Achievements and prospects* (pp. 147–164). Philadelphia, PA: Psychology Press/Taylor & Francis.

Johnson, M. H. (2001). Functional brain development during infancy. In G. Bremner, & A. Fogel (Eds.), *Handbooks of developmental psychology: Blackwell handbook of infant development* (pp. 169–190). Malden, MA: Blackwell Publishers.

Johnson, M. M. S. (1990). Age differences in decision making: A process methodology for examining strategic information processing. *Journal of Gerontology, Psychological Sciences, 45,* P75–78.

Johnson, M. M. S., Schmitt, F. A., & Everard, K. (1994). *Task driven strategies: The impact of age and information on decision-making performance.* Unpublished manuscript, University of Kentucky, Lexington.

Johnson, R. A., Hoffmann, J. P., & Gerstein, D. R. (1996). *The relationship between family structure and adolescent substance use* (DHHS Publication No. SMA 96-3086). Washington, DC: U.S. Department of Health and Human Services.

Johnson, S. J., & Rybash, J. M. (1993). A cognitive neuroscience perspective on age-related slowing: Developmental changes in the functional architecture. In J. Cerella, J. M. Rybash, W. J. Hoyer, & M. L. Commons (Eds.), *Adult information processing: Limits on loss* (pp. 143–175). San Diego: Academic Press.

Johnson, T. E. (1990). Age-1 mutants of Caenorhabditis elegans prolong life by modifying the Gompertz rate of aging. *Science, 229,* 908–912.

Johnston, J., & Ettema, J. S. (1982). *Positive images: Breaking stereotypes with children's television.* Newbury Park, CA: Sage.

Johnston, L. D., O'Malley, P. M., Bachman, J. G., & Schulenberg, J. E. (2004a, December 21). *Cigarette smoking among American teens continues to decline, but more slowly than in the past.* Ann Arbor, MI: University of Michigan News and Information Services. [Online]. Available: http://www.monitoringthefuture.org. Access date: December 22, 2004.

Johnston, L. D., O'Malley, P. M., Bachman, J. G., & Schulenberg, J. E. (2004b, December 21). *Overall teen drug use continues gradual decline; but use of inhalants rises.* Ann Arbor, MI: University of Michigan News and Information Services. [Online]. Available: http://www.monitoringthefuture.org. Access date: December 22, 2004.

Johnston, L. D., O'Malley, P. M., Bachman, J. G., & Schulenberg, J. E. (2005). *Monitoring the Future national results on adolescent drug use: Overview of key findings, 2004* (NIH Publication No. 05-5726). Bethesda, MD: National Institute on Drug Abuse.

Johnston, P. (2001, April 10). Dutch make euthanasia legal. *Chicago Sun-Times,* p. 22.

Joint United Nations Programme on HIV/AIDS and World Health Organization (UNAIDS/WHO). (2004). *AIDS epidemic update* (Publication No. UNAIDS/04.45E). Geneva: Author.

Jones, C. L., Tepperman, L., & Wilson, S. J. (1995). *The future of the family.* Englewood Cliffs, NJ: Prentice-Hall.

Jones, N. A., Field, T., Fox, N. A., Davalos, M., Lundy, B., & Hart, S. (1998). Newborns of mothers with depressive symptoms are physiologically less developed. *Infant Behavior & Development, 21*(3), 537–541.

Jones, N. A., Field, T., Fox, N. A., Lundy, B., & Davalos, M. (1997). *EEG activation in one-month-old infants of depressed mothers.* Unpublished manuscript, Touch Research Institute, University of Miami School of Medicine.

Jones, R. K., Purcell, A., Singh, S., & Finer, L. B. (2005). Adolescents' reports of parental knowledge of adolescents' use of sexual health services and their reactions to mandated parental notification for prescription contraception. *Journal of the American Medical Association, 293,* 340–348.

Jones, R. L. (2004). Biographies: Marian Anderson (1897–1993). *Afrocentric Voices in "Classical" Music.* [Online]. Available: http://www.afrovoices.com/anderson.html. Access date: November 18, 2004.

Jones, S. S. (1996). Imitation or exploration? Young infants' matching of adults' oral gestures. *Child Development, 67,* 1952–1969.

Jordan, B. (1993). *Birth in four cultures: A crosscultural investigation of childbirth in Yucatan, Holland, Sweden, and the United States* (4th ed.). Prospect Heights, IL: Waveland Press. (Original work published 1978).

Joshipura, K. J., Ascherio, A., Manson, J. E., Stampfer, M. H., Rim, E. B., Speizer, F. E., Hennekens, C. H., Spiegelman, D., & Willett, W. C. (1999). Fruit and vegetable intake in relation to risk of ischemic stroke. *Journal of the American Medical Association, 282,* 1233–1239.

Josselson, R. (2003). Revisions: Processes of development in midlife women. In J. Demick and C. Andreoletti (Eds.), *Handbook of adult development.* New York: Plenum Press.

Juffer, F., & van IJzendoorn, M. H. (2005). Behavior problems and mental health referrals of international adoptees. *Journal of the American Medical Association, 293,* 2501–2515.

Jung, C. G. (1933). *Modern man in search of a soul.* New York: Harcourt Brace.

Jung, C. G. (1953). The stages of life. In H. Read, M. Fordham, & G. Adler (Eds.), *Collected works* (Vol. 2). Princeton, NJ: Princeton University Press. (Original work published 1931).

Jung, C. G. (1966). Two essays on analytic psychology. In *Collected works* (Vol. 7). Princeton, NJ: Princeton University Press.

Jung, C. G. (1969). *The structure and dynamics of the psyche.* Princeton, NJ: Princeton University Press.

Jung, C. G. (1971). Aion: Phenomenology of the self (the ego, the shadow, the syzgy: Anima/animus). In J. Campbell (Ed.), *The portable Jung.* New York: Viking Penguin.

Jusczyk, P. W. (2003). The role of speech perception capacities in early language acquisition. In M. T. Banich & M. Mack (Eds.), *Mind, brain, and language: Multidisciplinary perspectives.* Mahwah, NJ: Erlbaum.

Jusczyk, P. W., & Hohne, E. A. (1997). Infants' memory for spoken words. *Science, 277,* 1984–1986.

Just, M. A., Cherkassky, V. L., Keller, T. A., & Minshew, N. J. (2004). Cortical activation and synchronization during sentence comprehension in high-functioning autism: Evidence of underconnectivity. *Brain, 127,* 1811–1821.

Juster, F. T., Ono. H., & Stafford, F. P. (2004). *Changing times of American youth: 1981–2003.* (Child Development Supplement). Ann Arbor, MI: University of Michigan Institute for Social Research.

Justice, B. (1994). Critical life events and the onset of illness. *Comprehensive Therapy, 20,* 232–238.

Juul-Dam, N., Townsend, J. & Courchesne, E. (2001). Prenatal, perinatal, and neonatal factors in autism, pervasive developmental disorder-not otherwise specified, and the general population. *Pediatrics, 107*(4), p. e63.

Kadhim, H., Kahn, A., & Sebire, G. (2003). High levels of immune protein in infant brain linked to SIDS. *American Academy of Neurology, 61,* 1256–1259.

Kagan, J. (1997). Temperament and the reactions to unfamiliarity. *Child Development, 68,* 139–143.

Kagan, J., & Snidman, N. (1991a). Infant predictors of inhibited and uninhibited behavioral profiles. *Psychological Science, 2,* 40–44.

Kagan, J., & Snidman, N. (1991b). Temperamental factors in human development. *American Psychologist, 46,* 856–862.

Kahn, R. L., & Antonucci, T. C. (1980). Convoys over the life course: Attachment, roles, and social support. In P. B. Baltes & O. G. Brim, Jr. (Eds.), *Life-span development and behavior* (pp. 253–286). New York: Academic Press.

Kail, R. (1991). Processing time declines exponentially during childhood and adolescence. *Developmental Psychology, 27,* 259–266.

Kail, R. (1997). Processing time, imagery, and spatial memory. *Journal of Experimental Child Psychology, 64,* 67–78.

Kail, R., & Park, Y. (1994). Processing time, articulation time, and memory span. *Journal of Experimental Child Psychology, 57,* 281–291.

Kaiser Family Foundation, Hoff, T., Greene, L., & Davis, J. (2003). *National survey of adolescents and young adults: Sexual health knowledge, attitudes and experiences.* Menlo Park, CA: Henry J. Kaiser Foundation.

Kalish, C. W. (1998). Young children's predictions of illness: Failure to recognize probabilistic cause. *Developmental Psychology, 34*(5), 1046–1058.

Kanaya, T., Scullin, M. H., & Ceci, S. J. (2003). The Flynn effect and U.S. policies: The impact of rising IQ scores on American society via mental retardation diagnoses. *American Psychologist, 58,* 778–790.

Kanetsuna, T., & Smith, P. K. (2002). Pupil insight into bullying and coping with bullying: A bi-national study in Japan and England. *Journal of School Violence, 1,* 5–29.

Kanoy, K., Ulku-Steiner, B., Cox, M., & Burchinal, M. (2003). Marital relationship and individual psychological characteristics that predict physical punishment of children. *Journal of Family Psychology, 17,* 20–28.

Kaplan, H., & Dove, H. (1987). Infant development among the Ache of East Paraguay. *Developmental Psychology, 23,* 190–198.

Kaplowitz, P. B., Oberfield, S. E., & the Drug and Therapeutics and Executive Committees of the Lawson Wilkins Pediatric Endocrine Society. (1999). Reexamination of the age limit for defining when puberty is precocious in girls in the United States: Implications for evaluation and treatment. *Pediatrics, 104,* 936–941.

Karafantis, D. M., & Levy, S. R. (2004). The role of children's lay theories about the malleability of human attributes in beliefs about and volunteering for disadvantaged groups. *Child Development, 75,* 236–250.

Karasik, D., Hannan, M. T., Cupples, L. A., Felson, D. T., & Kiel, D. P. (2004). Genetic contribution to biological aging: The Framingham study. *Journal of Gerontology: Biological Sciences, 59A,* 218–226.

Karney, B. R., & Bradbury, T. N. (1995). The longitudinal course of marital quality and stability: A review of theory, method, and research. *Psychological Bulletin, 118,* 3–34.

Katchadourian, H. (1987). *Fifty: Midlife in perspective.* New York: Freeman.

Katzman, R. (1993). Education and prevalence of Alzheimer's disease. *Neurology, 43,* 13–20.

Kaufman, A. S., & Kaufman, N. L. (1983). *Kaufman assessment battery for children: Administration and scoring manual.* Circle Pines, MN: American Guidance Service.

Kaufman, A. S., & Kaufman, N. L. (2003). *Kaufman Assessment Battery for Children* (2nd ed.). Circle Pines, MN: American Guidance Service.

Kaufman, P., Alt, M. N., & Chapman, C. (2001). *Dropout rates in the United States: 2000.* Washington, DC: National Center for Education Statistics.

Kaufman, P., Alt, M., & Chapman, C. (2004). *Dropout rates in the United States: 2001* (NCES 2005046). Washington, DC: National Center for Education Statistics.

Kaukinen, C. (2004). Status compatibility, physical violence, and emotional abuse in intimate relationships. *Journal of Marriage and Family, 66,* 452–471.

Kausler, D. H. (1990). Automaticity of encoding and episodic memory-processes. In E. A.

Lovelace (Ed.), *Aging and cognition: Mental processes, self-awareness, and interventions* (pp. 29–67). Amsterdam: North-Holland, Elsevier.

Kawachi, I., Colditz, G. A., Stampfer, M. J., Willett, W. C., Manson, J. E., Rosner, B., Speizer, F. E., & Hennekens, C. H. (1993). Smoking cessation and decreased risk of stroke in women. *Journal of the American Medical Association, 269,* 232–236.

Kaye, W. H., Weltzin, T. E., Hsu, L. K. G., & Bulik, C. M. (1991). An open trial of fluoxetine in patients with anorexia nervosa. *Journal of Clinical Psychiatry, 52,* 464–471.

Kazdin, A. E., & Benjet, C. (2003). Spanking children: Evidence and issues. *Current Directions in Psychological Science, 12,* 99–103.

Kearney, P. M., Whelton, M., Reynolds, K., Muntner, P., Whelton, P. K., & He, J. (2005). Global burden of hypertension: Analysis of worldwide data. *The Lancet, 365,* 217–223.

Keegan, C., Gross, S., Fisher, L., & Remez, S. (2004). Boomers at midlife: The AARP Life Stage Study executive summary. Wave 3. Washington, DC: American Association of Retired Persons.

Keegan, R. T. (1996). Creativity from childhood to adulthood: A difference of degree and not of kind. *New Directions for Child Development, 72,* 57–66.

Keegan, R. T., & Gruber, H. E. (1985). Charles Darwin's unpublished "Diary of an Infant": An early phase in his psychological work. In G. Eckardt, W. G. Bringmann, & L. Sprung (Eds.), *Contributions to a history of developmental psychology: International William T. Preyer Symposium* (pp. 127–145). Berlin, Germany: Walter de Gruyter.

Keel, P. K., Dorer, D. J., Eddy, K. T., Franko, D., Charatan, D. L., & Herzog, D. B. (2003). Predictors of mortality in eating disorders. *Archives of General Psychiatry, 60*(2), 179–183.

Keel, P. K., & Klump, K. L. (2003). Are eating disorders culture-bound syndromes? Implications for conceptualizing their etiology. *Psychological Bulletin, 129,* 747–769.

Keel, P. K., & Mitchell, J. E. (1997). Outcome in bulimia nervosa. *American Journal of Psychiatry, 154,* 313–321.

Keen, R. (2003). Representation of objects and events: Why do infants look so smart and toddlers look so dumb? *Current Directions in Psychological Science, 12,* 79–83.

Keenan, K., & Shaw, D. (1997). Developmental and social influences on young girls' early problem behavior. *Psychological Bulletin, 121*(1), 95–113.

Keightley, P. D., & Eyre-Walker, A. (2001). Response to Kondrashov. *Trends in Genetics, 17*(2), 77–78.

Kelleher, K. J., Casey, P. H., Bradley, R. H., Pope, S. K., Whiteside, L., Barrett, K. W., Swanson, M. E., & Kirby, R. S. (1993). Risk factors and outcomes for failure to thrive in low birth weight preterm infants. *Pediatrics, 91,* 941–948.

Keller, H. (1905). *The story of my life.* New York: Grosset & Dunlap. (Original work published 1903.)

Keller, H. (1920). *The world I live in.* New York: Century. (Original work published 1908.)

Keller, H. (1929). *The Bereaved.* New York: Leslie Fulenwider, Inc.

Keller, H. (2003). *The Story of My Life: The Restored Edition* (J. Berger, Ed.). New York: Norton.

Keller, M., Gummerum, M., Wang, T., & Lindsey, S. (2004). Understanding perspectives and emotions in contract violation: Development of deontic and moral reasoning. *Child Development, 75,* 614–635.

Kelley, M. L., Smith, T. S., Green, A. P., Berndt, A. E., & Rogers, M. C. (1998). Importance of fathers' parenting to African-American toddlers' social and cognitive development. *Infant Behavior & Development, 21,* 733–744.

Kellman, P. J., & Arterberry, M. E. (1998). *The cradle of knowledge: Development of perception in infancy.* Cambridge, MA: MIT.

Kellman, P. J., & Banks, M. S. (1998). Infant visual perception. In W. Damon (Ed.-in-Chief), D. Kuhn, & R. S. Siegler (Vol. Eds.), *Handbook of Child Psychology: Vol. 2. Cognition, perception, and language* (5th ed., pp. 103–146). New York: Wiley.

Kellogg, R. (1970). Understanding children's art. In P. Cramer (Ed.), *Readings in developmental psychology today.* Delmar, CA: CRM.

Kelly, A. M., Wall, M., Eisenberg, M., Story, M., & Neumark-Sztainer, D. (2004). High body satisfaction in adolescent girls: Association with demographic, socio-environmental, personal, and behavioral factors. *Journal of Adolescent Health, 34,* 129.

Kelly, J. B., & Emery, R. E. (2003). Children's adjustment following divorce: Risk and resiliency perspectives. *Family Relations, 52,* 352–362.

Kelly, J. R. (1987). *Peoria winter: Styles and resources in later life.* Lexington, MA: Lexington.

Kelly, J. R. (1994). Recreation and leisure. In A. Monk (Ed.), *The Columbia retirement handbook* (pp. 489–508). New York: Columbia University Press.

Kelly, J. R., Steinkamp, M., & Kelly, J. (1986). Later life leisure: How they play in Peoria. *The Gerontologist, 26,* 531–537.

Kemp. J. S., Unger, B., Wilkins, D., Psara, R. M., Ledbetter, T. L., Graham, M. A., Case, M., & Thach, B. T. (2000). Unsafe sleep practices and an analysis of bedsharing among infants dying suddenly and unexpectedly: Results of a four-year, population-based, death-scene investigation study of sudden infant death and related syndromes. *Pediatrics, 106*(3), e41.

Kemper, S., Thompson, M., & Marquis, J. (2001). Longitudinal change in language production: Effects of aging and dementia on grammatical complexity and propositional content. *Psychology and Aging, 16,* 600–614.

Kemper, T. L. (1994). Neuroanatomical and neuropathological changes during aging and dementia. In M. L. Albert & J. E. Knoefel (Eds.), *Clinical neurology of aging* (pp. 3–67). New York: Oxford University Press.

Kendler, K. S., MacLean, C., Neale, M., Kessler, R., Heath, A., & Eaves, L. (1991).

The genetic epidemiology of bulimia nervosa. *American Journal of Psychiatry, 148,* 1627–1637.

Kendler, K. S., Thornton, L. M., Gilman, S. E., & Kessler, R. C. (2000). Sexual orientation in a U.S. national sample of twin and nontwin sibling pairs. *American Journal of Psychiatry, 157,* 1843–1847.

Keppel, K. G., Pearcy, J. N., & Wagener, D. K. (2002). Trends in racial and ethnic-specific rates for the health status indicators: United States, 1990–1998. *Statistical Notes,* No. 23. Hyattsville, MD: National Center for Health Statistics.

Kernan, M. (1993, June). The object at hand. *Smithsonian,* pp. 14–16.

Kerns, K. A., Don, A., Mateer, C. A., & Streissguth, A. P. (1997). Cognitive deficits in nonretarded adults with fetal alcohol syndrome. *Journal of Learning Disabilities, 30,* 685–693.

Kessler, R. C., Berglund, P., Demler, O., Jin, R., Merikangas, K. R., & Walters, E. E. (2005). Lifetime prevalence and age-of-onset distributions of *DSM-IV* disorders in the National Comorbidity Survey Replication. *Archives of General Psychiatry, 62,* 593–602.

Kessler, R. C., Gilman, S. E., Thornton, L. M., & Kendler, K. S. (2004). Health, well-being, and social responsibility in the MIDUS twin and sibling subsamples. In O. G. Brim, C. D. Ryff, & R. Kessler (Eds.), *How healthy are we: A national study of well-being in midlife* (pp. 124–152). Chicago: University of Chicago Press.

Kestenbaum, R., & Gelman, S. A. (1995). Preschool children's identification and understanding of mixed emotions. *Cognitive Development, 10,* 443–458.

Keyes, C. L. M., & Ryff, C. D. (1998). Generativity in adult lives: Social structural contours and quality of life consequences. In D. P. McAdams & E. de St. Aubin (Eds.), *Generativity and adult development* (pp. 227–263). Washington, DC: American Psychological Association.

Keyes, C. L. M., & Ryff, C. D. (1999). Psychological well-being in midlife. In S. L. Willis & J. D. Reid (Eds.), *Life in the middle* (pp. 161–180). San Diego: Academic Press.

Keyes, C. L. M., & Shapiro, A. D. (2004). Social well-being in the United States: A descriptive epidemiology. In O. G. Brim, C. D. Ryff, and R. C. Kessler (Eds.), *How healthy are we? A national study of well-being at midlife* (pp. 350–372). Chicago: University of Chicago Press.

Khoury, M. J., McCabe, L. L., & McCabe, E. R. B. (2003). Population screening in the age of genomic medicine. *New England Journal of Medicine, 348,* 50–58.

Kiecolt-Glaser, J. K., & Glaser, R. (1999). Chronic stress and mortality among older adults. *Journal of the American Medical Association, 282,* 2259–2260.

Kiecolt-Glaser, J. K., & Glaser, R. (2001). Stress and immunity: Age enhances the risks. *Current Directions in Psychological Science, 10,* 18–21.

Kiefe, C. I., Williams, O. D., Weissman, N. W., Schreiner, P. J., Sidney, S., & Wallace, D. D. (2000). Changes in U.S. health care access in the 90s: Race and income differences from the CARDIA study. Coronary Artery Risk Development in Young Adults. *Ethnicity and Disease, 10,* 418–431.

Kiefer, K. M., Summer, L., & Shirey, L. (2001). What are the attitudes of young retirees and older workers? *Data Profiles: Young Retirees and Older Workers, 5.*

Kier, C., & Lewis, C. (1998). Preschool sibling interaction in separated and married families: Are same-sex pairs or older sisters more sociable? *Journal of Child Psychology and Psychiatry, 39,* 191–201.

Kiernan, K. (2002). Cohabitation in Western Europe: Trends, issues, and implications. In A. Booth & A. C. Crouter (Eds.), *Just living together: Implications of cohabitation on families, children, and social policy* (pp. 3–31). Mahwah, NJ: Erlbaum.

Killen, J. D., Robinson, T. N., Ammerman, S., Hayward, C., Rogers, J., Stone, C., Samuels, D., Levin, S. K., Green, S., & Schatzberg, A. F. (2004). Randomized clinical trial of the efficacy of bupropion combined with nicotine patch in the treatment of adolescent smokers. *Journal of Consulting and Clinical Psychology, 72,* 729–735.

Kim, J. E., & Moen, P. (2001). Moving into retirement: Preparation and transitions in late midlife. In M. E. Lachman (Ed.), *Handbook of midlife development* (pp. 487–527). New York: Wiley.

Kim, J. E., & Moen, P. (2002). Retirement transitions, gender, and psychological well-being: A life-course, ecological model. *Journal of Gerontology: Psychological Sciences, 57B,* P212–P222.

Kim, K. J., Conger, R. D., Elder, G. H., & Lorenz, F. O. (2003). Reciprocal influences between stressful life events and adolescent internalizing and externalizing problems. *Child Development, 74*(1), 127–143.

Kim, Y, S., Koh, Y.-J., & Leventhal, B. (2005). School bullying and suicidal risk in Korean middle school students. *Pediatrics, 115,* 357–363.

Kimball, M. M. (1986). Television and sex-role attitudes. In T. M. Williams (Ed.), *The impact of television: A natural experiment in three communities* (pp. 265–301). Orlando, FL: Academic Press.

Kim-Cohen, J., Caspi, A., Moffitt, T. E., Harrington, H., Milne, B. J., & Poulton, R. (2003). Prior juvenile diagnoses in adults with mental disorder: Developmental follow-back of a prospective-longitudinal cohort. *Archives of General Psychiatry, 60,* 709–717.

Kim-Cohen, J., Moffitt, T. E., Caspi, A., & Taylor, A. (2004). Genetic and environmental processes in young children's resilience and vulnerability to socioeconomic deprivation. *Child Development, 75,* 651–668.

Kim-Cohen, J., Moffitt, T. E., Taylor, A., Pawlby, S. J., & Caspi, A. (2005). Maternal depression and children's antisocial behavior: Nature and nurture effects. *Archives of General Psychiatry, 62,* 173–181.

Kimmel, D. (1990). *Adulthood and aging: An interdisciplinary, developmental view.* New York: Wiley.

Kimmel, D. C., & Sang, B. E. (1995). Lesbians and gay men in midlife. In A. R. D'Augelli & C. J. Patterson (Eds.), *Lesbian, gay, and bisexual identities over the lifespan: Psychological perspectives* (pp. 190–214). New York: Oxford University Press.

King, B. M. (1996). *Human sexuality today.* Englewood Cliffs, NJ: Prentice-Hall.

King, V. (2003). The legacy of a grandparent's divorce: Consequences for ties between grandparents and grandchildren. *Journal of Marriage and Family, 65,* 170–183.

King, W. J., MacKay, M., Sirnick, A., & The Canadian Shaken Baby Study Group. (2003). Shaken baby syndrome in Canada: Clinical characteristics and outcomes of hospital cases. *CMAJ* (Canadian Medical Association Journal), *168,* 155–159.

Kinney, H. C., Filiano, J. J., Sleeper, L. A., Mandell, F., Valdes-Dapena, M., & White, W. F. (1995). Decreased muscarinic receptor binding in the arcuate nucleus in Sudden Infant Death Syndrome. *Science, 269,* 1446–1450.

Kinsella, K., & Velkoff, V. A. (2001). *An aging world: 2001. U.S. Census Bureau, Series P95/01–1.* Washington, DC: U.S. Government Printing Office.

Kirby, D. (1997). *No easy answers: Research findings on programs to reduce teen pregnancy.* Washington, DC: National Campaign to Prevent Teen Pregnancy.

Kirby, S. E., Coleman, P. G., & Daley, D. (2004). Spirituality and well-being in frail and nonfrail older adults. *Journal of Gerontology: Psychological Sciences, 59B,* P123–P129.

Kisilevsky, B. S., Hains, S. M. J., Lee, K., Muir, D. W., Xu, F., Fu, G., Zhao, Z. Y., & Yang, R. L. (1998). The still-face effect in Chinese and Canadian 3- to 6-month-old infants. *Developmental Psychology, 34*(4), 629–639.

Kisilevsky, B. S., Hains, S. M. J., Lee, K., Xie, X., Huang, H., Ye, H. H., Zhang, K., & Wang, Z. (2003). Effects of experience on fetal voice recognition. *Psychological Science, 14,* 220–224.

Kisilevsky, B. S., Muir, D. W., & Low, J. A. (1992). Maturation of human fetal responses to vibroacoustic stimulation. *Child Development, 63,* 1497–1508.

Kistner, J., Eberstein, I. W., Quadagno, D., Sly, D., Sittig, L., Foster, K., Balthazor, M., Castro, R., & Osborne, M. (1997). Children's AIDS related knowledge and attitudes: Variations by grade, race, gender, socioeconomic status, and size of community. *AIDS Education and Prevention, 9,* 285–298.

Kitson, G. C., & Morgan, L. A. (1990). The multiple consequences of divorce: A decade review. *Journal of Marriage and Family Therapy, 52,* 913–924.

Kitzmann, K. M., Gaylord, N. K., Holt, A. R., & Kenny, E. D. (2003). Child witnesses to domestic violence: A meta-analytic review. *Journal of Counseling and Clinical Psychology, 71,* 339–352.

Kivett, V. R. (1991). Centrality of the grandfather role among older rural black and white men. *Journal of Gerontology: Social Sciences, 46*(5), S250–258.

Kivett, V. R. (1993). Racial comparisons of the grandmother role: Implications for strengthening the family support system of older Black women. *Family Relations, 42,* 165–172.

Kivett, V. R. (1996). The saliency of the grandmother—granddaughter relationship: Predictors of association. *Journal of Women & Aging, 8,* 25–39.

Kjerulff, K. H., Langenberg, P. W., & Rhodes, J. C. (2000). Effectiveness outcome of hysterectomy. *Obstetrics & Gynecology, 95,* 319–326.

Kjos, S. L., & Buchanan, T. A. (1999). Gestational diabetes mellitus. *New England Journal of Medicine, 341.*

Klaczynski, P. A., & Robinson, B. (2000). Personal theories, intellectual abiblity, and epistemological beliefs: Adult age differences in everyday reasoning biases. *Psychology and Aging, 15,* 400–416.

Klar, A. J. S. (1996). A single locus, RGHT, specifies preference for hand utilization in humans. In *Cold Spring Harbor Symposia on Quantitative Biology* (Vol. 61, pp. 59–65). Cold Spring Harbor, NY: Cold Spring Harbor Laboratory Press.

Klaus, M. H., & Kennell, J. H. (1997). The doula: An essential ingredient of childbirth rediscovered. *Acta Paediatrica, 86,* 1034–1036.

Klebanoff, M. A., Levine, R. J., DerSimonian, R., Clemens, J. D., & Wilkins, D. G. (1999). Maternal serum paraxanthine, a caffeine metabolite, and the risk of spontaneous abortion. *New England Journal of Medicine, 341,* 1639–1644.

Klebanov, P. K., Brooks-Gunn, J., McCarton, C., & McCormick, M. C. (1998). The contribution of neighborhood and family income to developmental test scores over the first three years of life. *Child Development, 69*(5), 1420–1436.

Klebanov, P. K., Brooks-Gunn, J., & McCormick, M. C. (2001). Maternal coping strategies and emotional distress: Results of an early intervention program for low birth weight young children. *Developmental Psychology, 37*(5), 654–667.

Kleiner, A., & Farris, E. (2002). *Internet access in U.S. public schools and classrooms: 1994–2001* (NCES 2002–018). Washington, DC: National Center for Education Statistics, U.S. Department of Education.

Kleiner, A., & Lewis, L. (2003). *Internet access in U.S. public schools and classrooms: 1994–2002* (NCES 2004-011). Washington, DC: National Center for Education Statistics.

Kleiner, B., Nolin, M. J., & Chapman, C. (2004). *Before- and after-school care, programs, and activities of children in kindergarten through eighth grade: 2001. Statistical analysis report* (NCES 2004–008). Washington, DC: National Center for Education Statistics.

Kline, D. W., Kline, T. J. B., Fozard, J. L., Kosnik, W., Schieber, F., & Sekuler, R. (1992). Vision, aging, and driving: The problems of older drivers. *Journal of Gerontology: Psychological Sciences, 47*(1), P27–34.

Kline, D. W., & Scialfa, C. T. (1996). Visual and auditory aging. In J. E. Birren & K. W. Schaie (Eds.), *Handbook of the psychology of aging* (pp. 191–208). San Diego: Academic Press.

Kline, G. H., Stanley, S. M., Markman, H. J., Olmos-Gallo, P. A., St. Peters, M., Whitton, S. W., & Prado, L. M. (2004). Timing is everything: Pre-engagement cohabitation and increased risk for poor marital outcomes. *Journal of Family Psychology, 18,* 311–318.

Kling, K. C., Hyde, J. S., Showers, C. J., & Buswell, B. N. (1999). Gender differences in self-esteem: A meta-analysis. *Psychological Bulletin, 125,* 470–500.

Klohnen, E. C., Vandewater, E., & Young, A. (1996). Negotiating the middle years: Ego-resiliency and successful midlife adjustment in women. *Psychology and Aging, 11,* 431–442.

Knoop, R. (1994). Relieving stress through value-rich work. *Journal of Social Psychology, 134,* 829–836.

Knoops, K. T. B., deGroot, L. C. P. G. M., Kromhout, D., Perrin, E., Moreiras,-Varela, O., Menotti, A., & van Staveren, W. A. (2004). Mediterranean diet, lifestyle factors, and 10-year mortality in elderly European men and women. Journal of the American Medical Association, 292, 1433–1439.

Knox, E. G. (2005). Childhood cancers and atmospheric carcinogens. *Journal of Epidemiology and Community Health, 59,* 101–105.

Knox, N. (2004, July 14). European gay-union trends influence U.S. debate: Lawmakers look to other nations. *USA Today.* [Online]. Available: http://www.keepmedia.com/pubs/USATODAY/2004/07/14/506463. Retrieved January 2, 2005.

Kochanek, K. D., Murphy, S. L., Anderson, R. N., & Scott, C. (2004). Deaths: Final data for 2002. *National Vital Statistics Reports, 53*(5). Hyattsville, MD: National Center for Health Statistics.

Kochanek, K. D., & Smith, B. L. (2004). Deaths: Preliminary data for 2002. *National Vital Statistics Reports, 52*(13). Hyattsville, MD: National Center for Health Statistics.

Kochanska, G. (1993). Toward a synthesis of parental socialization and child temperament in early development of conscience. *Child Development, 64,* 325–437.

Kochanska, G. (1995). Children's temperament, mothers' discipline, and security of attachment: Multiple pathways to emerging internalization. *Child Development, 66,* 597–615.

Kochanska, G. (1997a). Multiple pathways to conscience for children with different temperaments: From toddlerhood to age 5. *Developmental Psychology, 33,* 228–240.

Kochanska, G. (1997b). Mutually responsive orientation between mothers and their young children: Implications for early socialization. *Child Development, 68,* 94–112.

Kochanska, G. (2001). Emotional development in children with different attachment histories: The first three years. *Child Development, 72,* 474–490.

Kochanska, G. (2002). Mutually responsive orientation between mothers and their young children: A context for the early development of conscience. *Current Directions in Psychological Science, 11,* 191–195.

Kochanska, G., & Aksan, N. (1995). Mother-child positive affect, the quality of child compliance to requests and prohibitions, and maternal control as correlates of early internalization. *Child Development, 66,* 236–254.

Kochanska, G., Aksan, N., Knaack, A., & Rhines, H. M. (2004). Maternal parenting and children's conscience: Early security as moderator. *Child Development, 75,* 1229–1242.

Kochanska, G., Coy, K. C., & Murray, K. T. (2001). The development of self-regulation in the first four years of life. *Child Development, 72*(4), 1091–1111.

Kochanska, G., Friesenborg, A. E., Lange, L. A., & Martel, M. M. (2004). Parents' personality and infants' temperament as contibutors to their emerging relationship. *Journal of Personality and Social Psychology, 86,* 744–759.

Kochanska, G., Murray, K., & Coy, K. C. (1997). Inhibitory control as a contributor to conscience in childhood: From toddler to early school age. *Child Development, 68,* 263–277.

Kochanska, G., Tjebkes, T. L., & Forman, D. R. (1998). Children's emerging regulation of conduct: Restraint, compliance, and internalization from infancy to the second year. *Child Development, 69*(5), 1378–1389.

Kochenderfer, B. H., & Ladd, G. W. (1996). Peer victimization: Cause or consequence of school maladjustment? *Child Development, 67,* 1305–1317.

Koechlin, E., Basso, G., Pietrini, P., Panzer, S., & Grafman, J. (1999). The role of the anterior prefrontal cortex in human cognition. *Nature, 399,* 148–151.

Koechlin, E., Dehaene, S., & Mehler, J. (1997). Numerical transformations in five-month-old human infants. *Mathematical Cognition, 3,* 89–104.

Koenig, H. G. (1994). *Aging and God.* New York: Haworth.

Kogan., M. D., Alexander, G. R., Kotelchuck, M., MacDorman, M. F., Buekens, P., Martin, J. A., & Papiernik, E. (2000). Trends in twin birth outcomes and prenatal care utilization in the United States, 1981–1997. *Journal of the American Medical Association, 284,* 335–341.

Kogan, M. D., Martin, J. A., Alexander, G. R., Kotelchuck, M., Ventura, S. J., & Frigoletto, F. D. (1998). The changing pattern of prenatal care utilization in the United States, 1981–1995, using different prenatal care indices. *Journal of the American Medical Association, 279,* 1623–1628.

Kohlberg, L. (1966). A cognitive-developmental analysis of children's sex-role concepts and attitudes. In E. E. Maccoby (Ed.), *The development of sex differences.* Stanford, CA: Stanford University Press.

Kohlberg, L. (1969). Stage and sequence: The cognitive-developmental approach to socialization. In D. A. Goslin (Ed.), *Handbook of socialization theory and research.* Chicago: Rand McNally.

Kohlberg, L. (1973). Continuities in childhood and adult moral development revisited. In P. Baltes & K. W. Schaie (Eds.), *Life-span* developmental psychology: Personality and socialization (pp. 180–207). New York: Academic Press.

Kohlberg, L. (1981). Essays on moral development. San Francisco: Harper & Row.

Kohlberg, L., & Gilligan, C. (1971, Fall). The adolescent as a philosopher: The discovery of the self in a postconventional world. Daedalus, pp. 1051–1086.

Kohlberg, L., & Ryncarz, R. A. (1990). Beyond justice reasoning: Moral development and consideration of a seventh stage. In C. N. Alexander & E. J. Langer (Eds.), Higher stages of human development (pp. 191–207). New York: Oxford University Press.

Kohlberg, L., Yaeger, J., & Hjertholm, E. (1968). Private speech: Four studies and a review of theories. Child Development, 39, 691–736.

Kohn, M. L. (1980). Job complexity and adult personality. In N. J. Smelser & E. H. Erikson (Eds.), Themes of work and love in adulthood. Cambridge, MA: Harvard University Press.

Kohn, M. L., & Schooler, C. (1983). The cross-national universality of the interpretive model. In M. L. Kohn & C. Schooler (Eds.), Work and personality: An inquiry into the impact of social stratification (pp. 281–295). Norwood, NJ: Ablex.

Koivula, I., Sten, M., & Makela, P. H. (1999). Prognosis after community-acquired pneumonia in the elderly. Archives of Internal Medicine, 159, 1550–1555.

Kolata, G. (1999, March 9). Pushing limits of the human life span. The New York Times [Online]. Available: http://www.nytimes.com/library/national/science/030999sci-aging.html.

Kolata, G. (2003, February 18). Using genetic tests, Ashkenazi Jews vanquish a disease. The New York Times, pp. D1, D6.

Kolbert, E. (1994, January 11). Canadians curbing TV violence. The New York Times, pp. C15, C19.

Kopp, C. B. (1982). Antecedents of self-regulation. Developmental Psychology, 18, 199–214.

Kopp, C. B., & Kaler, S. R. (1989). Risk in infancy: Origins and implications. American Psychologist, 44(2), 224–230.

Kopp, C. B., & McCall, R. B. (1982). Predicting later mental performance for normal, at-risk, and handicapped infants. In P. B. Baltes & O. G. Brim (Eds.), Life-span development and behavior (Vol. 4). New York: Academic Press.

Koren, G., Pastuszak, A., & Ito, S. (1998). Drugs in pregnancy. New England Journal of Medicine, 338, 1128–1137.

Korner, A. (1996). Reliable individual differences in preterm infants' excitation management. Child Development, 67, 1793–1805.

Korner, A. F., Zeanah, C. H., Linden, J., Berkowitz, R. I., Kraemer, H. C., & Agras, W. S. (1985). The relationship between neonatal and later activity and temperament. Child Development, 56, 38–42.

Koropeckyj-Cox, T. (2002). Beyond parental status: Psychological well-being in middle and old age. Journal of Marriage and Family, 64, 957–971.

Korte, D., & Scaer, R. (1984). A good birth, a safe birth. New York: Bantam.

Kosnik, W., Winslow, L., Kline, D., Rasinski, K., & Sekuler, R. (1988). Visual changes in daily life throughout adulthood. Journal of Gerontology: Psychological Sciences, 43(3), P63–70.

Kosterman, R., Graham, J. W., Hawkins, J. D., Catalano, R. F., & Herrenkohl, T. I. (2001). Childhood risk factors for persistence of violence in the transition to adulthood: A social developmental perspective. Violence & Victims. Special Issue: Perspectives on Violence and Victimization, 16, 355–369.

Kotre, J. (1984). Outliving the self: Generativity and the interpretation of lives. Baltimore: Johns Hopkins University Press.

Kottak, C. P. (1994). Cultural anthropology. New York: McGraw-Hill.

Kowal, A. K., & Pike, L. B. (2004). Sibling influences on adolescents' attitudes toward safe sex practices. Family Relations, 53, 377–384.

Kozlowska, K., & Hanney, L. (1999). Family assessment and intervention using an interactive art exercise. Australia and New Zealand Journal of Family Therapy, 20(2), 61–69.

Kraaykamp, G. (2002). Trends and countertrends in sexual permissiveness: Three decades of attitude change in the Netherlands 1965–1995. Journal of Marriage and Family, 64, 225–239.

Kralovec, E., & Buell, J. (2000). The end of homework. Boston: Beacon.

Kramer, A. F., Hahn, S., McAuley, E., Cohen, N. J., Banich, M. T., Harrison, C., Chason, J., Boileau, R. A., Bardell, L., Colcombe, A., & Vakil, E. (1999). Ageing, fitness and neurocognitive function. Nature, 400, 418–419.

Kramer, D. A. (2003). The ontogeny of wisdom in its variations. In J. Demick & C. Andreolett (Eds.), Handbook of adult development (pp. 131–151). New York: Plenum Press.

Kranish, M. (2004, November 3). Gay marriage bans passed: Measures OK'd in all 11 states where eyed. Boston Globe. [Online]. Available: http://www.boston.com/news/nation/articles/2004/11/03/gay_marriage. Retrieved January 2, 2005.

Krause, N. (2004a). Common facets of religion, unique facets of religion, and life satisfaction among older African Americans. Journal of Gerontology: Social Sciences, 59B, S109–S117.

Krause, N. (2004b). Lifetime trauma, emotional support, and life satisfaction among older adults. The Gerontologist, 44, 615–623.

Krause, N., & Rook, K. S. (2003). Negative interaction in late life: Issues in the stability and generalizability of conflict across relationships. Journal of Gerontology: Psychological Sciences, 58B, P88–P99.

Krause, N., & Shaw, B. A. (2000). Role-specific feelings of control and mortality. Psychology and Aging, 15, 617–626.

Krauss, S., Concordet, J. P., & Ingham, P. W. (1993). A functionally conserved homolog of the Drosophila segment polarity gene hh is expressed in tissues with polarizing activity in zebra fish embryos. Cell, 75, 1431–1444.

Kravetz, J. D., & Federman, D. G. (2002). Cat-associated zoonoses. Archives of Internal Medicine, 162, 1945–1952.

Kreicbergs, U., Valdimarsdottir, U., Onelov, E., Henter, J., & Steineck, G. (2004). Talking about death with children who have severe malignant disease. New England Journal of Medicine, 351, 1175–1253.

Kreider, R. M. (2003). Adopted children and stepchildren: 2000. Census 2000 Special Reports. Washington, DC: U.S. Bureau of the Census.

Kreider, R. M. (2005). Number, timing, and duration of marriages and divorces: 2001. Household Economic Studies (P70–97). Washington, DC: U.S. Census Bureau.

Kreider, R. M., & Fields, J. M. (2002). Number, timing, and duration of marriages and divorces: Fall 1996. Current Population Reports, P70–80. Washington, DC: U.S. Census Bureau.

Kreijkamp-Kaspers, S., Kok, L., Grobbee, D. E., deHaan, E. H. F., Aleman, A., Lampe, J. W., & van der Schouw, Y. T. (2004). Effects of soy protein containing isoflavones on cognitive function, bone mineral density, and plasma lipids in postmenopausal women: A randomized controlled trial. Journal of the American Medical Association, 292, 65–74.

Kreutzer, M., Leonard, C., & Flavell, J. (1975). An interview study of children's knowledge about memory. Monographs of the Society for Research in Child Development, 40(1, Serial No. 159).

Krevans, J., & Gibbs, J. C. (1996). Parents' use of inductive discipline: Relations to children's empathy and prosocial behavior. Child Development, 67, 3263–3277.

Kristof, N. D. (1991, June 17). A mystery from China's census: Where have young girls gone? The New York Times, pp. A1, A8.

Kristof, N. D. (1993, July 21). Peasants of China discover new way to weed out girls. The New York Times, pp. A1, A6.

Kritchovski, S. B., Nicklas, B. J., Visser, M., Simonsick, E. M., Newman, A. B., Harris, T. B., Lange, E. M., Penninx, B. W., Goodpaster, B. H., Satterfield, S., Colbert, L. H., Rubin, S. M., & Pahor, M. (2005). Angiotensin—converting enzyme insertion—deletion genotype, exercise, and physical decline. Journal of the American Medical Association, 294, 691–698.

Kroenke, K., & Spitzer, R. L. (1998). Gender differences in the reporting of physical and somatoform symptoms. Psychosomatic Medicine, 60, 50–155.

Kroger, J. (1993). Ego identity: An overview. In J. Kroger (Ed.), Discussions on ego identity. Hillsdale, NJ: Erlbaum.

Kroger, J. (2003). Identity development during adolescence. In G. R. Adams and M. D. Berzonsky. (eds.). Blackwell handbook of adolescence (pp. 205–226). Malden, MA: Blackwell.

Kroger, J., & Haslett, S. J. (1991). A comparison of ego identity status transition pathways and change rates across five identity domains. International Journal of Aging and Human Development, 32, 303–330.

Krueger, A. B. (February 2003). Economic considerations and class size. The Economic Journal, 113, F34–F63.

Krueger, A. B., & Whitmore, D. M. (April 2000). The effect of attending a small class in the early grades on college-test taking and middle school test results: Evidence from Project STAR. NBER Working Paper No. W7656.

Kübler-Ross, E. (1969). *On death and dying.* New York: Macmillan.

Kübler-Ross, E. (1970). *On death and dying* [Paperback]. New York: Macmillan.

Kübler-Ross, E. (Ed.). (1975). *Death: The final stage of growth.* Englewood Cliffs, NJ: Prentice-Hall.

Kuczmarski, R. J., Ogden, C. L., Grummer-Strawn, L. M., Flegal, K. M., Guo, S. S., Wei, R., Mei, Z., Curtin, L. R., Roche, A. F., & Johnson, C. L. (2000). CDC growth charts: United States. *Advance Data,* No. 314. Centers for Disease Control and Prevention, U.S. Department of Health and Human Services.

Kuhl, P. K., Andruski, J. E., Chistovich, I. A., Chistovich, L. A., Kozhevnikova, E. V., Ryskina, V. L., Stolyarova, E. I., Sundberg, U., & Lacerda, F. (1997). Cross-language analysis of phonetic units in language addressed to infants. *Science, 277,* 684–686.

Kuhl, P. K., Williams, K. A., Lacerda, F., Stevens, K. N., & Lindblom, B. (1992). Linguistic experience alters phonetic perception in infants by 6 months of age. *Science, 255,* 606–608.

Kumar, C., & Puri, M. (1983). *Mahatma Gandhi: His life and influence.* New York: Franklin Watts.

Kupersmidt, J. B., & Coie, J. D. (1990). Preadolescent peer status, aggression, and school adjustment as predictors of externalizing problems in adolescence. *Child Development, 61,* 1350–1362.

Kurdek, L.A. (2004). Are gay and lesbian cohabiting couples really different from heterosexual married couples? *Journal of Marriage and Family, 66,* 880–900.

Kurjak, A., Kupesic, S., Matijevic, R., Kos, M., & Marton, U. (1999). First trimester malformation screening. *European Journal of Obstetrics, Gynecology, and Reproductive Biology (E4L), 85,* 93–96.

Kye, C., & Ryan, N. (1995). Pharmacologic treatment of child and adolescent depression. *Child and Adolescent Psychiatric Clinics of North America, 4,* 261–281.

La Sala, M. C. (1998). Coupled gay men, parents, and in-laws: Intergenerational disapproval and the need for a thick skin. *Families in Society, 79,* 585–595.

Labarere, J., Gelbert, Baudino, N., Ayral, A. S., Duc, C., Berchotteau, M., Bouchon, N., Schelstraete, C., Vittoz, J.-P., Francois, P., & Pons, J.-C. (2005). Efficacy of breastfeeding support provided by trained clinicians during an early, routine, preventive visit: A prospective, randomized, open trial of 226 mother-infant pairs. *Pediatrics, 115,* e139–e146.

Laberge, L., Tremblay, R. E., Vitaro, F., & Montplaisir, J. (2000). Development of parasomnias from childhood to early adolescence. *Pediatrics, 106,* 67–74.

Labouvie-Vief, G. (1985). Intelligence and cognition. In J. E. Birren & K. W. Schaie (Eds.), *Handbook of the psychology of aging* (pp. 500–530). New York: Van Nostrand Reinhold.

Labouvie-Vief, G. (1990a). Modes of knowledge and the organization of development. In M. L. Commons, L. Kohlberg, F. Richards, & J. Sinnott (Eds.), *Beyond formal operations: 2. Models and methods in the study of adult and adolescent thought.* New York: Praeger.

Labouvie-Vief, G. (1990b). Wisdom as integrated thought: Historical and development perspectives. In R. J. Sternberg (Ed.), *Wisdom: Its nature, origins, and development* (pp. 52–83). Cambridge, England: Cambridge University Press.

Labouvie-Vief, G., & Hakim-Larson, J. (1989). Developmental shifts in adult thought. In S. Hunter & M. Sundel (Eds.), *Midlife myths.* Newbury Park, CA: Sage.

Labouvie-Vief, G., Hakim-Larson, J., & Hobart, C. J. (1987). Age, ego level, and the life-span development of coping and defense processes. *Psychology and Aging, 2,* 286–293.

Labov, T. (1992). Social and language boundaries among adolescents. *American Speech, 67,* 339–366.

Lacey Jr., J. V., Mink, P. J., Lubin, J. H., Sherman, M. E., Troisi, R., Hartge, P., Schatzkin, A., & Schairer, C. (2002). Menopausal hormone replacement therapy and risk of ovarian cancer. *Journal of the American Medical Association, 288,* 334–341.

Lachman, J. L., & Lachman, R. (1980). Age and the actualization of knowledge. In L. W. Poon, J. L. Fozard, L. S. Cermak, D. Arenberg, & L. W. Thompson (Eds.), *New directions in memory and aging* (pp. 313–343). Hillsdale, NJ: Erlbaum.

Lachman, M. E. (2001). Introduction. In M. E. Lachman (Ed.), *Handbook of midlife development.* New York: Wiley.

Lachman, M. E. (2004). Development in midlife. *Annual Review of Psychology, 55,* 305–331.

Lachman, M. E., & Bertrand, R. M. (2001). Personality and the self in midlife. In M. E. Lachman (Ed.), *Handbook of midlife development* (pp. 279–309). New York: Wiley.

Lachman, M. E. & Firth, K. M. P. (2004). The adaptive value of feeling in control during midlife. In O. G. Brim, C. D. Ryff, & R. C. Kessler (Eds.), *How healthy are we? A national study of well-being at midlife.* Chicago: University of Chicago Press.

Lachman, M. E., & James, J. B. (1997). Charting the course of midlife development: An overview. In M. E. Lachman & J. B. James (Eds.), *Multiple paths of midlife development* (pp. 1–17). Chicago: University of Chicago Press.

Lachman, M. E., & Weaver, S. L. (1998). Sociodemographic variations in the sense of control by domain: Findings from the MacArthur Studies of Midlife. *Psychology and Aging, 13,* 553–562.

Ladd, G. W. (1996). Shifting ecologies during the 5 to 7 year period: Predicting children's adjustment during the transition to grade school. In A. J. Sameroff & M. M. Haith (Eds.), *The five to seven year shift: The age of reason and responsibility* (pp. 363–386). Chicago: University of Chicago Press.

Ladd, G. W., Birch, S. H., & Buhs, E. S. (1999). Children's social and scholastic lives in kindergarten: Related spheres of influence? *Child Development, 70,* 1373–1400.

LaFontana, K. M., & Cillessen, A. H. N. (2002). Children's perceptions of popular and unpopular peers: A multi-method assessment. *Developmental Psychology, 38,* 635–647.

Lagercrantz, H., & Slotkin, T. A. (1986). The "stress" of being born. *Scientific American, 254*(4), 100–107.

Laible, D. J., & Thompson, R. A. (1998). Attachment and emotional understanding in preschool children. *Developmental Psychology, 34*(5), 1038–1045.

Laible, D. J., & Thompson, R. A. (2002). Mother-child conflict in the toddler years: Lessons in emotion, morality, and relationships. *Child Development, 73,* 1187–1203.

Laird, R. D., Pettit, G. S., Bates, J. E., & Dodge, K. A. (2003). Parents' monitoring-relevant knowledge and adolescents' delinquent behavior: Evidence of correlated developmental changes and reciprocal influences. *Child Development, 74,* 752–768.

Lalonde, C. E., & Werker, J. F. (1995). Cognitive influences on cross-language speech perception in infancy. *Infant Behavior and Development, 18,* 459–475.

Lamb, M. E. (1981). The development of father-infant relationships. In M. E. Lamb (Ed.), *The role of the father in child development* (2nd ed.). New York: Wiley.

Lamb, M. E., Frodi, A. M., Frodi, M., & Hwang, C. P. (1982). Characteristics of maternal and paternal behavior in traditional and nontraditional Swedish families. *International Journal of Behavior Development, 5,* 131–151.

Lamberg, L. (1997). "Old and gray and full of sleep"? Not always. *Journal of the American Medical Association, 278,* 1302–1304.

Lamberts, S. W. J., van den Beld, A. W., & van der Lely, A. (1997). The endocrinology of aging. *Science, 278,* 419–424.

Lambeth, G. S., & Hallett, M. (2002). Promoting healthy decision making in relationships: Developmental interventions with young adults on college and university campuses. In C. L. & D. R. Atkinson (Eds.), *Counseling across the lifespan: Prevention and treatment* (pp. 209–226). Thousand Oaks, CA: Sage.

Lamborn, S. D., Mounts, N. S., Steinberg, L., & Dornbusch, S. M. (1991). Patterns of competence and adjustment among adolescents from authoritative, authoritarian, indulgent, and neglectful families. *Child Development, 62,* 1049–1065.

Landesman-Dwyer, S., & Emanuel, I. (1979). Smoking during pregnancy. *Teratology, 19,* 119–126.

Landi, F. F., Cesari, M., Onder, G., Lattanzio, F., Gravina, E. M., Bernabei, R., on behalf of the SilverNet-HC Study Group. (2004). Physical activity and mortality in frail, community-living elderly patients. *Journal of Gerontology: Medical Sciences, 59A,* M833–M837.

Landon, M. B., Hauth, J. C., Leveno, K. J., Spong, C. Y., Leindecker, S., Varner, M. W., Moawad, A. H., Caritis, S. N., Harper, M., Wapner, R. J., Sorokin, Y., Miodovnik, M., Carpenter, M., Peaceman, A. M., O'Sullivan, M. J., Sibai, B., Langer, O., Thorp, J. M., Ramin, S. M., Mercer, B. M., & Gabbe, S. G., for the National Institute of Child Health and Human Development Maternal-Fetal Medicine Units Network. (2004). Maternal and perinatal outcomes associated with a trial of labor after prior cesarean delivery. *New England Journal of Medicine, 351,* 2581–2589.

Landry, S. H., Smith, K. E., Swank, P. R., & Miller Loncar, C. L. (2000). Early maternal and child influences on children's later independent cognitive and social functioning. *Child Development, 71,* 358–375.

Landy, F. J. (1992, February). *Research on the use of fitness tests for police and fire fighting jobs.* Paper presented at the Second Annual Scientific Psychology Forum of the American Psychological Association, Washington, DC.

Landy, F. J. (1994, July–August). Mandatory retirement age: Serving the public welfare? *Psychological Science Agenda* (Science Directorate, American Psychological Association), pp. 10–11, 20.

Lane, H. (1976). *The wild boy of Aveyron.* Cambridge, MA: Harvard University Press.

Lang, F. R., & Carstensen, L, L. (1994). Close emotional relationships in late life: Further support for proactive aging in the social domain. *Psychology and Aging, 9,* 315–324.

Lang, F. R., & Carstensen, L. L. (1998). Social relationships and adaptation in later life. In A. S. Bellack & M. Hersen (Eds.), *Comprehensive clinical psychology* (pp. 55–72). Oxford: Pergamon.

Lang, F. R., Rieckmann, N., & Baltes, M. M. (2002). Adapting to aging losses: Do resources facilitate strategies of selection, compensation, and optimization in everyday functioning? *Journal of Gerontology: Psychological Sciences, 57B,* P501–P509.

Lange, G., MacKinnon, C. E., & Nida, R. E. (1989). Knowledge, strategy, and motivational contributions to preschool children's object recall. *Developmental Psychology, 25,* 772–779.

Lanphear, B. P., Aligne, C. A., Auinger, P., Weitzman, M., & Byrd, R. S. (2001). Residential exposure associated with asthma in U.S. children. *Pediatrics, 107,* 505–511.

Lansford, J. E., Dodge, K. A., Pettit, G. S., Bates, J. E., Crozier, J., & Kaplow, J. (2002). A 12-year prospective study of the long-term effects of early child physical maltreatment on psychological, behavioral, and academic problems in adolescence. *Archives of Pediatric and Adolescent Medicine, 156*(8), 824–830.

Lansford, J. E., Sherman, A. M., & Antonucci, T. C. (1998). Satisfaction with social networks: An examination of socioemotional selectivity. *Psychology and Aging, 13*(4), 544–552.

Lanting, C. I., Fidler, V., Huisman, M., Touwen, B. C. L., & Boersma, E. R. (1994). Neurological differences between 9-year-old children fed breast-milk or formula-milk as babies. *The Lancet, 334,* 1319–1322.

Lapham, E. V., Kozma, C., & Weiss, J. O. (1996). Genetic discrimination: Perspectives of consumers. *Science, 274,* 621–624.

Laquatra, J., & Chi, P. S. K. (1998, September). *Housing for an aging-in-place society.* Paper presented at the European Network for Housing Research Conference, Cardiff, Wales.

Larner, M. B., Stevenson, C. S., & Behrman, R. E. (1998). Protecting children from abuse and neglect: Analysis and recommendations. *The Future of Children, 8,* 4–22.

Larsen D. (1990, December–1991, January). Unplanned parenthood. *Modern Maturity,* pp. 32–36.

Larson, R. (1998). Implications for policy and practice: Getting adolescents, families, and communities in sync. In A. Crouter & R. Larson (Eds.), *Temporal rhythms in adolescence: Clocks, calendars, and the coordination of daily life* (New Directions in Child and Adolescent Development, No. 82, pp. 83–88). San Francisco: Jossey-Bass.

Larson, R., Mannell, R., & Zuzanek, J. (1986). Daily well being of older adults with friends and family. *Psychology and Aging, 1*(2), 117–126.

Larson, R., & Seepersad, S. (2003). Adolescents' leisure time in the United States: Partying, sports, and the American experiment. In S. Verma and R. Larson (Eds.), Examining adolescent leisure time across cultures: Developmental opportunities and risks. *New Directions for Child and Adolescent Development, 99,* 53–64.

Larson, R.W. (1997). The emergence of solitude as a constructive domain of experience in early adolescence. *Child Development, 68,* 80–93.

Larson, R.W., Moneta, G., Richards, M. H., & Wilson, S. (2002). Continuity, stability, and change in daily emotional experience across adolescence. *Child Development, 73,* 1151–1165.

Larson, R.W., Richards, M. H., Moneta, G., Holmbeck, G., & Duckett, E. (1996). Changes in adolescents' daily interactions with their families from ages 10 to 18: Disengagement and transformation. *Developmental Psychology, 32,* 744–754.

Larson, R.W., & Verma, S. (1999). How children and adolescents spend time across the world: Work, play, and developmental opportunities. *Psychological Bulletin, 125,* 701–736.

Larzalere, R. E. (2000). Child outcomes of nonabusive and customary physical punishment by parents: An updated literature review. *Clinical Child and Family Psychology Review, 3,* 199–221.

Lash, J. P. (1980). *Helen and teacher: The story of Helen Keller and Anne Sullivan Macy.* New York: Delacorte.

Latimer, E. J. (1992, February). Euthanasia: A physician's reflections. *Ontario Medical Review,* pp. 21–29.

Laucht, M., Esser, G., & Schmidt, M. H. (1994). Contrasting infant predictors of later cognitive functioning. *Journal of Child Psychology and Psychiatry, 35,* 649–652.

Laumann, E. O., Gagnon, J. H., Michael, R. T., & Michaels, S. (1994). *The social organization of sexuality: Sexual practices in the United States.* Chicago: University of Chicago Press.

Laumann, E. O., & Michael, R. T. (Eds.). (2000). *Sex, love, and health in America: Private choices and public policies.* Chicago: University of Chicago Press.

Laumann, E. O., Paik, A., & Rosen, R. C. (1999). Sexual dysfunction in the United States. *Journal of the American Medical Association, 281,* 537–544.

Laumann, E. O., Paik, A., & Rosen, R. C. (2000). Sexual dysfunction in the United States: Prevalence and predictors. In E. O. Laumann, & R. T. Michael, (Eds.), *Sex, love, and health in America: Private choices and public policies* (pp. 352–376). Chicago: University of Chicago Press.

Launer, L. J., Andersen, K., Dewey, M. E., Letenneur, L., Ott, A., Amaducci, L. A., Brayne, C., Copeland, J. R. M., Dartigues, J.-F., Kragh-Sorensen, P., Lobo, A., Martinez-Lage, J. M., Stijnen, T., & Hofman, A. (1999). Rates and risk factors for dementia and Alzheimer's disease: Results from EURODEM pooled analyses. *Neurology, 52,* 78–84.

Laursen, B. (1996). Closeness and conflict in adolescent peer relationships: Interdependence with friends and romantic partners. In W. M. Bukowski, A. F. Newcomb, & W. W. Hartup (Eds.), *The company they keep: Friendship in childhood and adolescence* (pp. 186–210). New York: Cambridge University Press.

Laursen, B., Coy, K. C., & Collins, W. A. (1998). Reconsidering changes in parent-child conflict across adolescence: A meta-analysis. *Child Development, 69,* 817–832.

Laursen, B., Pulkkinen, L., & Adams, R. (2002). The antecedents and correlates of agreeableness in adulthood. *Developmental Psychology, 38,* 591–603.

Lavee, Y. & Ben-Ari, A. (2004). Emotional expressiveness and neuroticism: Do they predict marital quality? *Journal of Marriage and Family, 18,* 620–627.

Lavie, C. J., Kuruvanka, T., Milani, R. V., Prasad, A., & Ventura, H. O. (2004). Exercise capacity in adult African-Americans referred for exercise stress testing: Is fitness affected by race? *Chest, 126,* 1962–1968.

Law, K. L., Stroud, L. R., LaGasse, L. L., Niaura, R., Liu, J., and Lester, B. (2003). Smoking during pregnancy and newborn neurobehavior. *Pediatrics, 111,* 1318–1323.

Layne, J. E., & Nelson, M. E. (1999). The effects of progressive resistance training on bone density: A review. *Medicine & Science in Sports & Exercise, 31,* 25–30.

Lazarus, R. S., & Folkman, S. (1984). *Stress, appraisal, and coping.* New York: Springer.

Le Bourdais, C., & LaPierre-Adamcyk, E. (2004). Changes in conjugal life in Canada: Is cohabitation progressively replacing marriage? *Journal of Marriage and Family, 66,* 929–942.

Leaper, C., Anderson, K. J., & Sanders, P. (1998). Moderators of gender effects on parents' talk to their children: A meta-analysis. *Developmental Psychology, 34*(1), 3–27.

Leaper, C., & Smith, T. E. (2004). A meta-analytic review of gender variations in children's language use: Talkativeness, affiliative speech, and assertive speech. *Developmental Psychology, 40,* 993–1027.

Leblanc, M., & Ritchie, M. (2001). A meta-analysis of play therapy outcomes. *Counseling Psychology Quarterly, 14,* 149–163.

Lecanuet, J. P., Granier-Deferre, C., & Busnel, M.-C. (1995). Human fetal auditory perception. In J. P. Lecanuet, W. P. Fifer, N. A. Krasnegor, & W. P. Smotherman (Eds.), *Fetal development: A psychobiological perspective* (pp. 239–262). Hillsdale, NJ: Erlbaum.

Lee, D. J., Gomez-Marin, O., Lam, B. L., & Zheng, D. D. (2004). Trends in hearing impairment in United States adults: The National Health Interview Survey, 1986–1995. *Journal of Gerontology: Medical Sciences, 59A,* 1186–1190.

Lee, F. R. (2004, July 3). Engineering more sons than daughters: Will it tip the scales toward war? *New York Times,* pp. A17, A19.

Lee, G. R., Dwyer, J. W., & Coward, R. T. (1993). Gender differences in parent care: Demographic factors and some gender preferences. *Journal of Gerontology: Social Sciences, 48,* S9–16.

Lee, G. R., Netzer, J. K., & Coward, R. T. (1995). Depression among older parents: The role of intergenerational exchange. *Journal of Marriage and the Family, 57,* 823–833.

Lee, J. (1998). Children, teachers, and the Internet. *Delta Kappa Gamma Bulletin, 64*(2), 5–9.

Lee, R. D. (2003). Rethinking the evolutionary theory of aging: Transfers, not births, shape senescence in social species. *Proceedings of the National Academy of Sciences, 100,* 9637–9642.

Leeman, L. W., Gibbs, J. C., & Fuller, D. (1993). Evaluation of a multi-component group treatment program for juvenile delinquents. *Aggressive Behavior, 19,* 281–292.

Lefkowitz, E. S., & Fingerman, K. L. (2003). Positive and negative emotional feelings and behaviors in mother-daughter ties in late life. *Journal of Family Psychology, 17,* 607–617.

Legerstee, M., & Varghese, J. (2001). The role of maternal affect mirroring on social expectancies in three-month-old infants. *Child Development, 72,* 1301–1313.

Lehman, S. (2005, March 4). At age 125, Brazilian woman has good memory, loves to talk. *Chicago Sun-Times,* p. 36.

Leibel, R. L. (1997). And finally, genes for human obesity. *Nature Genetics, 16,* 218–220.

Leichtman, M. D., & Ceci, S. J. (1995). The effects of stereotypes and suggestions on preschoolers' reports. *Developmental Psychology, 31,* 568–578.

Leigh, B. C. (1999). Peril, chance, adventure: Concepts of risk, alcohol use, and risky behavior in young adults. *Addiction, 94*(3), 371–383.

Leman, P. J., Ahmed, S., & Ozarow, L. (2005). Gender, gender relations, and the social dynamics of children's conversations. *Developmental Psychology, 41,* 64–74.

Lemke, M., Miller, D., Johnson, J., Krenze, T., Alvarez-Rojas, L., Kastberg, D., & Jocelyn, L. (2005). *Highlights from the 2003 International Adult Literacy and Lifeskills Survey (ALL) - Revised (NCES 2005–117).* Washington, DC: National Center for Education Statistics.

Lemke, M., Sen, A., Pahlke, E., Partelow, L., Miller, D., Williams, T., Kastberg, D., & Jocelyn, L. (2004). *International outcomes of learning in mathematics literacy and problem solving: PISA 2003. Results from the U.S. Perspective (NCES 2005–003).* Washington, DC: National Center for Education Statistics.

Lemon, B., Bengtson, V., & Peterson, J. (1972). An exploration of the activity theory of aging: Activity types and life satisfaction among in-movers to a retirement community. *Journal of Gerontology, 27*(4), 511–523.

Lenneberg, E. H. (1967). *Biological functions of language.* New York: Wiley.

Lenneberg, E. H. (1969). On explaining language. *Science, 164*(3880), 635–643.

Leone, J. M., Johnson, M. P., Cohan, C. L., & Lloyd, S. E. (2004). Consequences of male partner violence for low-income minority women. *Journal of Marriage and Family, 66,* 472–490.

Lerman, C., Caporaso, N. E., Audrain, J., Main, D., Bowman, E. D., Lockshin, B., Boyd, N. R., & Shields, P. G. (1999). Evidence suggesting the role of specific genetic factors in cigarette smoking. *Health Psychology, 18,* 14–20.

Lerner, J. V., & Galambos, N. L. (1985). Maternal role satisfaction, mother-child interaction, and child temperament: A process model. *Child Development, 21,* 1157–1164.

Lerner, M. J., Somers, D. G., Reid, D., Chiriboga, D., & Tierney, M. (1991). Adult children as caregivers: Egocentric biases in judgments of sibling contributions. *The Gerontologist, 31*(6), 746–755.

Lesch, K. P., Bengel, D., Heils, A., Sabol, S. Z., Greenberg, B. D., Petri, S., Benjamin, J., Müller, C. R., Hamer, D. H., & Murphy, D. L. (1996). Association of anxiety-related traits with a polymorphism in the serotonin transporter gene regulatory region. *Science, 274,* 1527–1531.

Lesgold, A. M. (1983). *Expert systems.* Paper represented at the Cognitive Science Meetings, Rochester, NY.

Lesgold, A., Glaser, R., Rubinson, H., Klopfer, D., Feltovich, P., & Wang, Y. (1988). Expertise in a complex skill: Diagnosing x-ray pictures. In M. T. H. Chi, R. Glaser, & M. J. Farr (Eds.), *The Nature of Expertise* (pp. 311–342). Hillsdale, NJ: Erlbaum.

Leslie, A. M. (1982). The perception of causality in infants. *Perception, 11,* 173–186.

Leslie, A. M. (1984). Spatiotemporal continuity and the perception of causality in infants. *Perception, 13,* 287–305.

Lester, B. M., & Boukydis, C. F. Z. (1985). *Infant crying: Theoretical and research perspectives.* New York: Plenum.

Lethbridge-Cejku, M., Schiller, J. S., & Bernadel, L. (2004). Summary health statistics for U.S. adults: National Health Interview Survey, 2002. *Vital and Health Statistics, 10*(222). Hyattsville, MD: National Center for Health Statistics.

LeVay, S. (1991). A difference in hypothalamic structure between heterosexual and homosexual men. *Science, 253,* 1034–1037.

Levenstein, S., Ackerman, S., Kiecolt-Glaser, J. K., & Dubois, A. (1999). Stress and peptic ulcer disease. *Journal of the American Medical Association, 281,* 10–11.

Leventhal, T., & Brooks-Gunn, J. (2000). The neighborhoods they live in: The effects of neighborhood residence on child and adolescent outcomes. *Psychological Bulletin, 126*(2), 309–337.

Levin, J. S., & Taylor, R. J. (1993). Gender and age differences in religiosity among black Americans. *The Gerontologist, 33*(1), 16–23.

Levin, J. S., Taylor, R. J., & Chatters, L. M. (1994). Race and gender differences in religiosity among older adults: Findings from four national surveys. *Journal of Gerontology: Social Sciences, 49,* S137–145.

Levine, R. (1980). Adulthood among the Gusii of Kenya. In N. J. Smelser & E. H. Erikson (Eds.), *Themes of work and love in adulthood* (pp. 77–104). Cambridge, MA: Harvard University Press.

LeVine, R. A. (1974). Parental goals: A cross-cultural view. *Teacher College Record, 76,* 226–239.

LeVine, R. A. (1989). Human parental care: Universal goals, cultural strategies, individual behavior. In R. A. LeVine, P. M. Miller, & M. M. West (Eds.), *Parental behavior in diverse societies* (pp. 3–12). San Francisco: Jossey-Bass.

LeVine, R. A. (1994). *Child care and culture: Lessons from Africa.* Cambridge, England: Cambridge University Press.

LeVine, R. A., & LeVine, S. (1998). Fertility and maturity in Africa: Gusii parents in middle adulthood. In R. A. Schweder (Ed.), *Welcome to middle age! (and other cultural fictions).* Chicago: University of Chicago Press.

Levine, S. C., Huttenlocher, J., Taylor, A., & Langrock, A. (1999). Early sex differences in spatial skill. *Developmental Psychology, 35*(4), 940–949.

Levinson, D. (1978). *The seasons of a man's life.* New York: Knopf.

Levinson, D. (1980). Toward a conception of the adult life course. In N. J. Smelser & E. H. Erikson (Eds.), *Themes of work and love in adulthood* (pp. 265–290). Cambridge, MA: Harvard University Press.

Levinson, D. (1986). A conception of adult development. *American Psychologist, 41,* 3–13.

Levinson, D. (1996). *The seasons of a woman's life.* New York: Knopf.

Levinson, W., & Altkorn, D. (1998). Primary prevention of postmenopausal osteoporosis. *Journal of the American Medical Association, 280,* 1821–1822.

Leviton, A., & Cowan, L. (2002). A review of the literature relating caffeine consumption by women to their risk of reproductive hazards. *Food & Chemical Toxicology, 40*(9), 1271–1310.

Levron, J., Aviram, A., Madgar, I., Livshits, A., Raviv, G., Bider, D., Hourwitz, A., Barkai, G., Goldman, B., & Mashiach, S. (1998, October). *High rate of chromosomal aneupoloidies in testicular spermatozoa retrieved from azoospermic patients undergoing testicular sperm extraction for in vitro fertilization.* Paper presented at the 16th World Congress on Fertility and Sterility and the 54th annual meeting of the American Society for Reproductive Medicine, San Francisco, CA.

Levy, B., & Langer, E. (1994). Aging free from negative stereotypes: Successful memory in China and among the American deaf. *Journal of Personality and Social Psychology, 66*, 989–997.

Levy, B. R. (2003). Mind matters: Cognitive and physical effects of aging self-stereotypes. *Journal of Gerontology: Psychological Sciences, 58B*, P203–P211.

Levy, G. D., & Carter, D. B. (1989). Gender schema, gender constancy, and gender-role knowledge: The roles of cognitive factors in preschoolers' gender-role stereotype attributions. *Developmental Psychology, 25*, 444–449.

Levy-Shiff, R. (1994). Individual and contextual correlates of marital change across the transition to parenthood. *Developmental Psychology, 30*, 591–601.

Levy-Shiff, R., Zoran, N., & Shulman, S. (1997). International and domestic adoption: Child, parents, and family adjustment. *International Journal of Behavioral Development, 20*, 109–129.

Lewinsohn, P. M., Gotlib, I. H., Lewinsohn, M., Seeley, J. R., & Allen, N. B. (1998). Gender differences in anxiety disorders and anxiety symptoms in adolescents. *Journal of Abnormal Psychology, 107*, 109–117.

Lewis, M. (1995). Self-conscious emotions. *American Scientist, 83*, 68–78.

Lewis, M. (1997). The self in self-conscious emotions. In S. G. Snodgrass & R. L. Thompson (Eds.), *The self across psychology: Self-recognition, self-awareness, and the self-concept* (Vol. 818). Annals of the New York Academy of Sciences. New York: The New York Academy of Sciences.

Lewis, M. (1998). Emotional competence and development. In D. Pushkar, W. Bukowski, A. E. Schwartzman, D. M. Stack, & D. R. White (Eds.), *Improving competence across the lifespan* (pp. 27–36). New York: Plenum.

Lewis, M., & Brooks, J. (1974). Self, other, and fear: Infants' reaction to people. In H. Lewis & L. Rosenblum (Eds.), *The origins of fear: The origins of behavior* (Vol. 2). New York: Wiley.

Lewis, M. I., & Butler, R. N. (1974). Life-review therapy: Putting memories to work in individual and group psychotherapy. *Geriatrics, 29*, 165–173.

Lewit, E., & Kerrebrock, N. (1997). Population-based growth stunting. *The Future of Children, 7*(2), 149–156.

Li, F., Harmer, P., Fisher, K. J., & McAuley, E. (2004). Tai Chi: Improving functional balance and predicting subsequent falls in older persons. *Medicine & Science in Sports & Exercise, 36*, 2046–2052.

Li, J., Laursen, T. M., Precht, D. H., Olsen, J., & Mortensen, P. B. (2005). Hospitalization for mental illness among parents after the death of a child. *New England Journal of Medicine, 352*, 1190–1196.

Li, J., Precht, D. H., Mortensen, P. B., & Olsen, J. (2003). Mortality in parents after death of a child in Denmark: A nationwide follow-up study. *The Lancet, 361*, 363–367.

Li, R., Darling, N., Maurice, E., Barker, L., & Grummer-Strawn, L. M. (2005). Breastfeeding rates in the United States by characteristics of the child, mother, or family: The 2002 National Immunization Survey. *Pediatrics, 115*, e31–e37.

Li, X., Li, S., Ulusoy, E., Chen, W., Srinivasan, S. R., & Berenson, G. S. (2004). Childhood adiposity as a predictor of cardiac mass in adulthood. *Circulation, 110*, 3488–3492.

Liaw, F., & Brooks-Gunn, J. (1993). Patterns of low-birth-weight children's cognitive development. *Developmental Psychology, 29*, 1024–1035.

Lieberman, M. (1996). *Doors close, doors open: Widows, grieving and growing.* New York: Putnam.

Liebman, B. (1995, June). A meat & potatoes man. *Nutrition Action Health Letter, 22*(5), 6–7.

Light, K. C., Girdler, S. S., Sherwood, A., Bragdon, E. E., Brownley, K. A., West, S. G., & Hinderliter, A. L. (1999). High stress responsivity predicts later blood pressure only in combination with positive family history and high life stress. *Hypertension, 33*, 1458–1464.

Light, L. L. (1990). Interactions between memory and language in old age. In J. E. Birren & K. W. Schaie (Eds.), *Handbook of the psychology of aging* (pp. 275–290). San Diego: Academic Press.

Lillard, A., & Curenton, S. (1999). Do young children understand what others feel, want, and know? *Young Children, 54*(5), 52–57.

Lillard, A. S. (1998). Ethnopsychologies: Cultural variations in theory of mind. *Psychological Bulletin, 123*, 3–33.

Lin, I., Goldman, N., Weinstein, M., Lin, Y., Gorrindo, T., & Seeman, T. (2003). Gender differences in adult childrens' support of their parents in Taiwan. *Journal of Marriage and Family, 65*, 184–200.

Lin, S., Hwang, S. A., Marshall, E. G., & Marion, D. (1998). Does paternal occupational lead exposure increase the risks of low birth weight or prematurity? *American Journal of Epidemiology, 148*, 173–181.

Lin, S. S., & Kelsey, J. L. (2000). Use of race and ethnicity in epidemiological research: Concepts, methodological issues, and suggestions for research. *Epidemiologic Reviews, 22*(2), 187–202.

Lin, Y., Seroude, L., & Benzer, S. (1998). Extended life-span and stress resistance in the Drosophila mutant methuselah. *Science, 282*, 943–946.

Lindbergh, Anne Morrow, *Gift from the Sea,* 1955.

Lindegren, M. L., Byers, R. H., Jr., Thomas, P., Davis, S. F., Caldwell, B., Rogers, M., Gwinn, M., Ward, J. W., & Fleming, P. L. (1999). Trends in perinatal transmission of HIV/AIDS in the United States. *Journal of the American Medical Association, 282*, 531–538.

Linder, K. (1990). *Functional literacy projects and project proposals: Selected examples.* Paris: United Nations Educational, Scientific, and Cultural Organization.

Lindsay, R., Gallagher, J. C., Kleerekoper, M., & Pickar, J. H. (2002). Effect of lower doses of conjugated equine estrogens with and without medroxyprogesterone acetate on bone in early postmenopausal women. *Journal of the American Medical Association, 287*, 2668–2676.

Lindwer, W. (1991). *The last seven months of Anne Frank* (A. Meersschaert, Trans.). New York: Pantheon.

Lino, M. (2001). *Expenditures on children by families, 2000 annual report* (Misc. Publication No. 1528–2000). Washington, DC: U.S. Department of Agriculture, Center for Nutrition Policy and Promotion.

Lissau, I., Overpeck, M. D., Ruan, J., Due, P., Holstein, B. E., Hediger, M. L., & Health Behaviours in School-Aged Children Obesity Working Group. (2004). Body mass index and overweight in adolescents in 13 European countries, Israel, and the Untied States. *Archives of Pediatric and Adolescent Medicine, 158*, 27–33.

Litovitz, T. L., Klein-Schwartz, W., Caravati, E. M., Youniss, J., Crouch, B., & Lee, S. (1999). Annual report of the American Association of Poison Control Centers Toxic Exposure Surveillance System. *American Journal of Emergency Medicine, 17*, 435–487.

Liu, J., Raine, A., Venables, P. H., Dalais, C., and Mednick, S. A. (2003). Malnutrition at age 3 years and lower cognitive ability at age 11 years. *Archives of Pediatric and Adolescent Medicine, 157*, 593–600.

Liu, S., Manson, J. E., Lee, I. M., Cole, S. R., Hennekens, C. H., Willett,W. C., & Buring, J. E. (2000). Fruit and vegetable intake and risk of cardiovascular disease: The Women's Health Study. *American Journal of Clinical Nutrition, 72*, 922–928.

Llagas, C., & Snyder, T. D. (April 2003). *Status and trends in the Education of Hispanics.* Washington, DC: National Center for Education Statistics.

Lloyd, J. J., & Anthony, J. C. (2003). Hanging out with the wrong crowd: How much difference can parents make in an urban environment? *Journal of Urban Health, 80*, 383–399.

Lloyd, T., Andon, M. B., Rollings, N., Martel, J. K., Landis, J. R., Demers, L. M., Eggli, D. F., Kieselhorst, K., & Kulin, H. E. (1993). Calcium supplementation and bone mineral density in adolescent girls. *Journal of the American Medical Association, 270*, 841–844.

Lloyd-Jones, D. M., Liu, K., Colangelo, L. A., Yan, L. L., Klein, L., Loria, C. M., Lewis, C. E., & Savage, P. (2004). Consistently stable body mass index and changes in risk factors associated with the metabolic syndrome. The CARDIA Study. *Circulation, 110,* III-772.

Lock, A., Young, A., Service, V., & Chandler, P. (1990). Some observations on the origin of the pointing gesture. In V. Volterra & C. J. Erting (Eds.), *From gesture to language in hearing and deaf children.* New York: Springer.

Lock, M. (1994). Menopause in cultural context. *Experimental Gerontology, 29,* 307–317.

Lock, M. (1998). Deconstructing the change: Female maturation in Japan and North America. In R. A. Shweder (Ed.), *Welcome to middle age (and other cultural fictions)* (pp. 45–74). Chicago: University of Chicago Press.

Lockwood, C. J. (2002). Predicting premature delivery—no easy task. *New England Journal of Medicine, 346,* 282–284.

Loeb, S., Fuller, B., Kagan, S. L., & Carrol, B. (2004). Child care in poor communities: Early learning effects of type, quality, and stability. *Child Development, 75,* 47–65.

Loewen, N., & Bancroft, A. (2001). *Four to the Pole: The American Women's Expedition to Antartica, 1992–1993.* North Haven, CT: Shoestring Press.

Lonczak, H. S., Abbott, R. D., Hawkins, J. D., Kosterman, R., & Catalano, R. F. (2002). Effects of the Seattle Social Development Project on sexual behavior, pregnancy, birth, and sexually transmitted disease. *Archives of Pediatric and Adolescent Medicine, 156,* 438–447.

Longino, C. F., & Earle, J. R. (1996). Who are the grandparents at century's end? *Generations, 20*(1), 13–16.

Longnecker, M. P., Klebanoff, M. A., Zhou, H., & Brock, J. W. (2001). Association between maternal serum concentration of the DDT metabolite DDE and preterm and small-for-gestational-age babies at birth. *Lancet, 358,* 110–114.

Lonigan, C. J., Burgess, S. R., & Anthony, J. L. (2000). Development of emergent literacy and early reading skills in preschool children: Evidence from a latent-variable longitudinal study. *Developmental Psychology, 36,* 593–613.

Lonigan, C. J., Fischel, J. E., Whitehurst, G. J., Arnold, D. S., & Valdez-Menchaca, M. C. (1992). The role of otitis media in the development of expressive language disorder. *Developmental Psychology, 28,* 430–440.

Looft, W. R. (1973). Socialization and personality: Contemporary psychological approaches. In P. B. Baltes & K. W. Schaie (Eds.), *Lifespan developmental psychology.* New York: Academic Press.

Lorenz, K. (1957). Comparative study of behavior. In C. H. Schiller (Ed.), *Instinctive behavior.* New York: International Universities Press.

Lorsbach, T. C., & Reimer, J. F. (1997). Developmental changes in the inhibition of previously relevant information. *Journal of Experimental Child Psychology, 64,* 317–342.

Love, J. M., Kisker, E. E., Ross, C. M., Schochet, P. Z., Brooks-Gunn, J., Paulsell, D., Boller, K., Constantine, J., Vogel, C., Fuligni, A. S., & Brady-Smith, C. (2002). *Making a difference in the lives of infants and toddlers and their families: The impacts of Early Head Start:*

Executive Summary. Washington, DC: U.S. Department of Health and Human Services.

Love, K. M. & Murdock, B. (2004). Attachment to parents and psychological well-being: An examination of young adult college students in intact families and stepfamilies. *Journal of Family Psychology, 18,* 600–608.

Lovelace, E. A. (1990). Basic concepts in cognition and aging. In E. A. Lovelace (Ed.), *Aging and cognition: Mental processes, self-awareness, and interventions* (pp. 1–28). Amsterdam: North-Holland, Elsevier.

Lowenthal, M., & Haven, C. (1968). Interaction and adaptation: Intimacy as a critical variable. *American Sociological Review, 33,* 20–30.

Lu, T., Pan, Y., Kao, S.-Y., Li, C., Cohane, I., Chan, J., & Yankner, B. A. (2004). Gene regulation and DNA damage in the ageing human brain. *Nature, 429,* 883–891.

Lubell, K. M., Swahn, M. H., Crosby, A. E., & Kegler, S. R. (2004). Methods of suicide among persons aged 10–19 years—United States, 1992–2001. *Morbidity and Mortality Weekly Report, 53,* 471–474.

Lucas, R. E., Clark, A. E., Georgellis, Y., & Diener, E. (2003). Reexamining adaptation and the set point model of happiness: Reactions to changes in marital status. *Journal of Personality and Social Psychology, 84,* 527–539.

Luecke-Aleksa, D., Anderson, D. R., Collins, P. A., & Schmitt, K. L. (1995). Gender constancy and television viewing. *Developmental Psychology, 31,* 773–780.

Lugaila, T. A. (1998). Marital status and living arrangements: March 1998 (update) *Current Population Reports* (pp. 20–514). Washington, DC: U.S. Bureau of the Census.

Lugaila, T. A. (2003). A child's day: 2000 (Selected indicators of child well-being). *Current Population Reports* (P70-89). Washington, DC: U.S. Census Bureau.

Luke, B., Mamelle, N., Keith, L., Munoz, F., Minogue, J., Papiernik, E., Johnson, T. R., & Timothy, R. B. (1995). The association between occupational factors and preterm birth: A United States nurses' study. *American Journal of Obstetrics and Gynecology, 173,* 849–862.

Luman, E. T., Barker, L., E., Shaw, K. M., McCauley, M. M., Buehler, J. W., & Pickering, L. K. (2005). Timeliness of childhood vaccinations in the United States: Days undervaccinated and number of vaccines delayed. *Journal of the American Medical Association, 293,* 1204–1211.

Lund, D. A. (1993a). Caregiving. In R. Kastenbaum (Ed.), *Encyclopedia of adult development* (pp. 57–63). Phoenix: Oryx.

Lund, D. A. (1993b). Widowhood: The coping response. In R. Kastenbaum (Ed.), *Encyclopedia of adult development* (pp. 537–541). Phoenix: Oryx.

Lundy, B., Field, T., & Pickens, J. (1996). Newborns of mothers with depressive symptoms are less expressive. *Infant Behavior and Development, 19,* 419–424.

Lundy, B. L. (2003). Father- and mother-infant face-to-face interactions: Differences in mind-related comments and infant attachment? *Infant Behavior & Development, 26,* 200–212.

Lundy, B. L., Jones, N. A., Field, T., Nearing, G., Davalos, M., Pietro, P. A., Schanberg, S., & Kuhn, C. (1999). Prenatal depression effects on neonates. *Infant Behavior and Development, 22,* 119–129.

Luszcz, M. A., & Bryan, J. (1999). Toward understanding age-related memory loss in late adulthood. *Gerontology, 45,* 2–9.

Luthar, S. S., & Latendresse, S. J. (2005). Children of the affluence: Challenges to well-being. *Current Directions in Psychological Science, 14,* 49–53.

Lyman, R. (1997, April 15). Michael Dorris dies at 52: Wrote of his son's suffering. *The New York Times,* p. C24.

Lynskey, M. T., Heath, A. C., Bucholz, K. K., Slutske, W. S., Madden, P. A. F., Nelson, E. C., Statham, D. J., & Martin, N. G. (2003). Escalation of drug use in early-onset cannabis users versus co-twin controls. *Journal of the American Medical Association, 289,* 427–433.

Lyon, T. D., & Saywitz, K. J. (1999). Young maltreated children's competence to take the oath. *Applied Developmental Science, 3*(1), 16–27.

Lyons-Ruth, K., Alpern, L., & Repacholi, B. (1993). Disorganized infant attachment classification and maternal psychosocial problems as predictors of hostile-aggressive behavior in the preschool classroom. *Child Development, 64,* 572–585.

Lytton, H., & Romney, D. M. (1991). Parents' differential socialization of boys and girls: A meta-analysis. *Psychological Bulletin, 109*(2), 267–296.

Lyytinen, P., Poikkeus, A., Laakso, M., Eklund, K., & Lyytinen, H. (2001). Language development and symbolic play in children with and without familial risk for dyslexia. *Journal of Speech, Language, and Hearing Research, 44,* 873–885.

Maccoby, E. (1980). *Social development.* New York: Harcourt Brace Jovanovich.

Maccoby, E. E. (1984). Middle childhood in the context of the family. In W. A. Collins (Ed.), *Development during middle childhood.* Washington, DC: National Academy.

Maccoby, E. E. (1988). Gender as a social category. *Developmental Psychology, 24,* 755–765.

Maccoby, E. E. (1990). Gender and relationships: A developmental account. *American Psychologist, 45*(11), 513–520.

Maccoby, E. E. (1992). The role of parents in the socialization of children: An historical overview. *Developmental Psychology, 28,* 1006–1017.

Maccoby, E. E. (1994). Commentary: Gender segregation in childhood. In C. Leaper (Ed.), *Childhood gender segregation: Causes and consequences* (New Directions for Child Development No. 65, pp. 87–97). San Francisco: Jossey-Bass.

Maccoby, E. E., & Lewis, C. C. (2003). Less day care or different day care? *Child Development, 74,* 1069–1075.

Maccoby, E. E., & Martin, J. A. (1983). Socialization in the context of the family: Parent-child interaction. In P. H. Mussen (Series Ed.)

& E. M. Hetherington (Vol. Ed.), *Handbook of child psychology: Vol. 4. Socialization, personality, and social development* (pp. 1–101). New York: Wiley.

MacDonald, R. K. (1983). *Louisa May Alcott.* Boston: Twayne.

MacDonald, W. L., & DeMaris, A. (1996). Parenting stepchildren and biological children. *Journal of Family Issues, 17,* 5–25.

Macfarlane, A. (1975). Olfaction in the development of social preferences in the human neonate. In *Parent-infant interaction* (CIBA Foundation Symposium No. 33). Amsterdam: Elsevier.

MacKinnon-Lewis, C., Starnes, R., Volling, B., & Johnson, S. (1997). Perceptions of parenting as predictors of boys' sibling and peer relations. *Developmental Psychology, 33,* 1024–1031.

Macmillan, C., Magder, L. S., Brouwers, P., Chase, C., Hittelman, J., Lasky, T., Malee, K., Mellins, C. A., & Velez-Borras, J. (2001). Head growth and neurodevelopment of infants born to HIV-1-infected drug-using women. *Neurology, 57,* 1402–1411.

MacMillan, H. M., Boyle, M. H., Wong, M. Y.-Y., Duku, E. K., Fleming, J. E., & Walsh, C. A. (1999). Slapping and spanking in childhood and its association with lifetime prevalence of psychiatric disorders in a general population sample. *Canadian Medical Association Journal, 161,* 805–809.

Macmillan, R., McMorris, B. J., & Kruttschnitt, C. (2004). Linked lives: Stability and change in maternal circumstances and trajectories of antisocial behavior in children. *Child Development, 75,* 205–220.

Madole, K. L., Oakes, L. M., & Cohen, L. B. (1993). Developmental changes in infants' attention to function and form-function correlations. *Cognitive Development, 8,* 189–209.

Madsen, K. M., Lauritsen, M. B., Pedersen, C. B., Thorsen, P. Plesner, A. M., Andersen, P. H., & Mortensen, P. B. (2003). Thimerosal and the occurrence of autism: Negative ecological evidence from the Danish population-based data. *Pediatrics, 112,* 604–606.

Mahoney, J. L. (2000). School extracurricular activity participation as a moderator in the development of antisocial patterns. *Child Development, 71*(2), 502–516.

Main, M. (1995). Recent studies in attachment: Overview, with selected implications for clinical work. In S. Goldberg, R. Muir, & J. Kerr (Eds.), *Attachment theory: Social, developmental, and clinical perspectives* (pp. 407–470). Hillsdale, NJ: Analytic Press.

Main, M., Kaplan, N., & Cassidy, J. (1985). Security in infancy, childhood and adulthood: A move to the level of representation. In I. Bretherton & E. Waters (Eds.), Growing points in attachment. *Monographs of the Society for Research in Child Development, 50*(1–20), 66–104.

Main, M., & Solomon, J. (1986). Discovery of an insecure, disorganized/disoriented attachment pattern: Procedures, findings, and implications for the classification of behavior. In M. Yogman & T. B. Brazelton (Eds.), *Affective development in infancy.* Norwood, NJ: Ablex.

Makino, M., Tsuboi, K., and Dennerstein, L. (2004). Prevalence of eating disorders: A comparison of Western and non-Western countries. *Medscape General Medicine, 6*(3). [Online]. Available: http://www.medscape.com/viewarticle/487413. Access date: 9/27/2004.

Makrides, M., Neumann, M., Simmer, K., Pater, J., & Gibson, R. (1995). Are long-chain polyunsaturated fatty acids essential nutrients in infancy? *The Lancet, 345,* 1463–1468.

Malaspina, D., Harlap, S., Fennig, S., Heiman, D., Nahon, D., Feldman, D., & Susser, E. S. (2001). Advancing paternal age and the risk of schizophrenia. *Archives of General Psychiatry, 58,* 361–371.

Malloy, M. H. (2004). SIDS—A syndrome in search of a cause. *New England Journal of Medicine, 351,* 957–959.

Man, 77, pleads guilty to killing wife at hospital. (2003, March 6). *Chicago Sun-Times,* p. 59.

Mandel, D. R., Jusczyk, P. W., & Pisoni, D. B. (1995). Infants' recognition of the sound patterns of their own names. *Psychological Science, 6*(5), 314–317.

Manders, M., deGroot, L. C. P. G. M., van Staveren, W. A., Woulters-Wesseling, W., Mulders, A. J. M. J., Schols, J. M. G. A., & Hoefnaagels, W. H. L. (2004). Effectiveness of nutritional supplements on cognitive functioning in elderly persons: A systematic review. *Journal of Gerontology: Medical Sciences, 59A,* 1041–1049.

Mandler, J. (1998). The rise and fall of semantic memory. In M. A. Conway, S. E. Gathercole, & C. Cornoldi (Eds.), *Theories of memory* (Vol. 2). East Sussex, England: Psychology Press.

Mandler, J. M., & McDonough, L. (1993). Concept formation in infancy. *Cognitive Development, 8,* 291–318.

Mandler, J. M., & McDonough, L. (1996). Drinking and driving don't mix: Inductive generalization in infancy. *Cognition, 59,* 307–335.

Mandler, J. M., & McDonough, L. (1998). Cognition across the life span: On developing a knowledge base in infancy. *Developmental Psychology. 34,* 1274–1288.

Manhardt, J., & Rescorla, L. (2002). Oral narrative skills of late talkers at ages 8 and 9. *Applied Psycholinguistics, 23,* 1–21.

Manlove, J., Ryan, S., & Franzetta, K. (2003). Patterns of contraceptive use within teenagers' first sexual relationships. *Perspectives on Sexual and Reproductive Health, 35,* 246–255.

Mannell, R. (1993). High investment activity and life satisfaction: Commitment, serious leisure, and flow in the daily lives of older adults. In J. Kelly (Ed.), *Activity and aging.* Newbury Park, CA: Sage.

Manning, W. D. (2004). Children and stability of cohabiting couples. *Journal of Marriage and Family, 66,* 674–689.

Manson, J. E., & Martin, K. A. (2001). Postmenopausal hormone-replacement therapy. *New England Journal of Medicine, 345,* 34–40.

March of Dimes Birth Defects Foundation. (1987). *Genetic counseling: A public health information booklet* (Rev. ed.). White Plains, NY: Author.

March of Dimes Birth Defects Foundation. (2004a). *Cocaine use during pregnancy.* Fact sheet. [Online]. Available: http://www.marchofdimes.com/professionals/681_1169.asp. Access date: October 29, 2004.

March of Dimes Birth Defects Foundation. (2004b). *Marijuana: What you need to know.* [Online]. Available: http://www.marchofdimes.com/pnhec/159_4427.asp. Access date: October 29, 2004.

March of Dimes Foundation. (2002). *Toxoplasmosis.* (Fact Sheet). Wilkes-Barre, PA: Author.

Marcia, J. E. (1966). Development and validation of ego identity status. *Journal of Personality and Social Psychology, 3*(5), 551–558.

Marcia, J. E. (1979, June). *Identity status in late adolescence: Description and some clinical implications.* Address given at symposium on identity development, Rijksuniversitat Groningen, Netherlands.

Marcia, J. E. (1980). Identity in adolescence. In J. Adelson (Ed.), *Handbook of adolescent psychology.* New York: Wiley.

Marcia, J. E. (1993). The relational roots of identity. In J. Kroger (Ed.), *Discussions on ego identity* (pp. 101–120). Hillsdale, NJ: Erlbaum.

Marcoen, A. (1995). Filial maturity of middle-aged adult children in the context of parent care: Model and measures. *Journal of Adult Development, 2,* 125–136.

Marcon, R. A. (1999). Differential impact of preschool models on development and early learning of inner-city children: A three-cohort study. *Developmental Psychology, 35*(2), 358–375.

Marcus, G. F., Vijayan, S., Rao, S. B., & Vishton, P. M. (1999). Rule learning by seven-month-old infants. *Science, 283,* 77–80.

Mariani, M. (Summer 2001). Distance learning in postsecondary education: Learning whenever, wherever. *Occupational Outlook Quarterly,* 1–10.

Markoff, J. (1992, October 12). Miscarriages tied to chip factories. *The New York Times,* pp. A1, D2.

Marks, N. (1998). Does it hurt to care? Caregiving, work-family conflict, and midlife well-being. *Journal of Marriage and the Family, 60,* 951–956.

Marks, N. F. (1996). Caregiving across the lifespan: National prevalence and predictors. *Family Relations, 45,* 27–36.

Marks, N. F., Bumpass, L. L., & Jun, H. (2004). Family roles and well-being during the middle life course. In O. G. Brim, C. D. Ryff, and R. C. Kessler (Eds.), *How healthy are we? A national study of well-being at midlife* (pp. 514–549). Chicago: University of Chicago Press.

Marks, N. F., & Lambert, J. D. (1998). Marital status continuity and change among young and midlife adults. *Journal of Family Issues, 19,* 652–686.

Markus, H. R., Ryff, C. D., Curhan, K. B., & Palmersheim, K. A. (2004). In their own words: Well-being at midlife among high school-educated and college-educated adults.

In O. G. Brim, C. D. Ryff, and R. C. Kessler (Eds.), *How healthy are we? A national study of well-being at midlife* (pp. 273–319). Chicago: University of Chicago Press.

Marlow, N., Wolke, D., Bracewell, M. A., & Samara, M., for the EPICure Study Group. (2005). Neurologic and developmental disability at six years of age after extremely preterm birth. *New England Journal of Medicine, 352,* 9–19.

Marmot, M. G., & Fuhrer, R. (2004). Socioeconomic position and health across midlife. In O G. Brim, C. D. Ryff, and R. C. Kessler (Eds.). *How healthy are we? A national study of well-being at midlife.* Chicago: University of Chicago Press.

Marshall, N. L. (2004). The quality of early child care and children's development. *Current Directions in Psychological Science, 13,* 165–168.

Marshall, T. A., Levy, S. M., Broffitt, B., Warren, J. J., Eichenberger-Gilmore, J. M., Burns, T. L., and Stumbo, P. J. (2003). Dental caries and beverage consumption in young children. *Pediatrics, 112,* e184–e191.

Marsiske, M., Lang, F. R., Baltes, P. B., & Baltes, M. M. (1995). Selective optimization with compensation: Life-span perspectives on successful human development. In R. A. Dixon & L. Backman (Eds.), *Compensating for psychological deficits and declines: Managing losses and promoting gains* (pp. 35–79). Mahwah, NJ: Erlbaum.

Martikainen, P., & Valkonen, T. (1996). Mortality after the death of a spouse: Rates and causes of death in a large Finnish cohort. *American Journal of Public Health, 86,* 1087–1093.

Martin, C. L., Eisenbud, L., & Rose, H. (1995). Children's gender-based reasoning about toys. *Child Development, 66,* 1453–1471.

Martin, C. L., & Halverson, C. F. (1981). A schematic processing model of sex typing and stereotyping in children. *Child Development, 52,* 1119–1134.

Martin, C. L., & Ruble, D. (2004). Children's search for gender cues: Cognitive perspectives on gender development. *Current Directions in Psychological Science, 13,* 67–70.

Martin, J. A., Hamilton, B. E., Sutton, P. D., Ventura, S. J., Menacker, F., & Munson, M. L. (2003). Births: Final data for 2002. *National Vital Statistics Reports, 52*(10). Hyattsville, MD: National Center for Health Statistics.

Martin, J. A., Hamilton, B. E., Ventura, S. J., Menacker, F., & Park, M. M. (2002). Births: Final Data for 2000. *National Vital Statistics Reports, 50*(5). Hyattsville, MD: National Center for Health Statistics.

Martin, J. A., Kochanek, K. D., Strobino, D. M., Guyer, B., & MacDorman, M. F. (2005). Annual summary of vital statistics—2003. *Pediatrics, 115,* 619–634.

Martin, L. G. (1988). The aging of Asia. *Journal of Gerontology: Social Sciences, 43*(4), S99–113.

Martin, L. R., Friedman, H. S., Tucker, J. S., Tomlinson-Keasey, C., Criqui, M. H., &

Schwartz, J. E. (2002). A life course perspective on childhood cheerfulness and its relation to mortality risk. *Personality and Social Psychology Bulletin, 28,* 1155–1165.

Martin, P., Hagberg, B., & Poon, L. W. (1997). Predictors of loneliness in centenarians: A parallel study. *Journal of Cross-Cultural Gerontology, 12,* 203–224.

Martin, R., Noyes, J., Wisenbaker, J., & Huttunen, M. (2000). Prediction of early childhood negative emotionality and inhibition from maternal distress during pregnancy. *Merrill-Palmer Quarterly, 45,* 370–391.

Martínez-González, M. A., Gual, P., Lahortiga, F., Alonso, Y., de Irala-Estévez, J., & Cervera, S. (2003). Parental factors, mass media influences, and the onset of eating disorders in a prospective population-based cohort. *Pediatrics, 111,* 315–320.

Marwick, C. (1997). Health care leaders form drug policy group. *Journal of the American Medical Association, 278,* 378.

Marwick, C. (1998). Physician leadership on national drug policy finds addiction treatment works. *Journal of the American Medical Association, 279,* 1149–1150.

Maslach, C. (2003). Job burnout: New directions in research and intervention. *Current Directions in Psychological Science, 12*(5), 189–192.

Maslow, A. (1968). *Toward a psychology of living.* Princeton, NJ: Van Nostrand Reinhold.

Mason, J. A., & Herrmann, K. R. (1998). Universal infant hearing screening by automated auditory brainstem response measurement. *Pediatrics, 101,* 221–228.

Masse, L. C., & Tremblay, R. E. (1997). Behavior of boys in kindergarten and the onset of substance use during adolescence. *Archives of General Psychiatry, 54,* 62–68.

Masten, A., Best, K., & Garmezy, N. (1990). Resilience and development: Contributions from the study of children who overcome adversity. *Development and Psychopathology, 2,* 425–444.

Masten, A. S. (2001). Ordinary magic: Resilience processes in development. *American Psychologist, 56,* 227–238.

Masten, A. S., & Coatsworth, J. D. (1998). The development of competence in favorable and unfavorable environments: Lessons from research on successful children. *American Psychologist, 53,* 205–220.

Masters, W. H., & Johnson, V. E. (1966). *Human sexual response.* Boston: Little, Brown.

Masters, W. H., & Johnson, V. E. (1981). Sex and the aging process. *Journal of the American Geriatrics Society, 29,* 385–390.

Mathews, T. J., Menacker, F., & MacDorman, M. F. (2003). Infant mortality statistics from the 2001 period linked birth/infant death data set. *National Vital Statistics Reports, 52*(2). Hyattsville, MD: National Center for Health Statistics.

Matthews, S. H. (1995). Gender and the division of filial responsibility between lone sisters and their brothers. *Journal of Gerontology: Social Sciences, 50B,* S312–320.

Maurer, D., Stager, C. L., & Mondloch, C. J. (1999). Cross-modal transfer of shape is difficult to demonstrate in one-month-olds. *Child Development, 70,* 1047–1057.

Maynard, A. E. (2002). Cultural teaching: The development of teaching skills in Maya sibling interactions. *Child Development, 73,* 969–982.

Mazzeo, R. S., Cavanaugh, P., Evans, W. J., Fiatarone, M., Hagberg, J., McAuley, E., & Startzell, J. (1998). ACSM position stand on exercise and physical activity for older adults. *Medicine & Science in Sports & Exercise, 30,* 992–1008.

McAdams, D. (1993). *The stories we live by.* New York: Morrow.

McAdams, D. P. (2001). Generativity in midlife. In M. E. Lachman (Ed.), *Handbook of midlife development* (pp. 395–443). New York: Wiley.

McAdams, D. P., & de St. Aubin, E. (1992). A theory of generativity and its assessment through self-report, behavioral acts, and narrative themes in autobiography. *Journal of Personality and Social Psychology, 62,* 1003–1015.

McAdams, D. P., de St. Aubin, E., & Logan, R. L. (1993). Generativity among young, midlife, and older adults. *Psychology and Aging, 8,* 221–230.

McAdams, D. P., Diamond, A., de St. Aubin, E., & Mansfield, E. (1997). Stories of commitment: The psychosocial construction of generative lives. *Journal of Personality and Social Psychology, 72,* 678–694.

McCall, R. B., & Carriger, M. S. (1993). A meta-analysis of infant habituation and recognition memory performance as predictors of later IQ. *Child Development, 64,* 57–79.

McCallum, K. E., & Bruton, J. R. (2003). The continuum of care in the treatment of eating disorders. *Primary Psychiatry, 10*(6), 48–54.

McCartney, N., Hicks, A. L., Martin, J., & Webber, C. E. (1996). A longitudinal trial of weight training in the elderly: Continued improvements in year 2. *The Journals of Gerontology: Series A: Biological Sciences and Medical Sciences, 51,* B425–B433.

McCarton, C. M., Brooks-Gunn, J.,Wallace, I. F., Bauer, C. R., Bennett, F. C., Bernbaum, J. C., Broyles, S., Casey, P. H., McCormick, M. C., Scott, D. T., Tyson, J., Tonascia, J., & Meinert, C. L., for the Infant Health and Development Program Research Group. (1997). Results at age 8 years of early intervention for low-birth-weight premature infants. *Journal of the American Medical Association, 277,* 126–132.

McCartt, A. T. (2001). Graduated driver licensing systems: Reducing crashes among teenage drivers. *Journal of the American Medical Association, 286,* 1631–1632.

McCarty, M. E., Clifton, R. K., Ashmead, D. H., Lee, P., & Goubet, N. (2001). How infants use vision for grasping objects. *Child Development, 72,* 973–987.

McClearn, G. E., Johansson, B., Berg, S., Pedersen, N. L., Ahern, F., Petrill, S. A., & Plomin, R. (1997). Substantial genetic influence on cognitive abilities in twins 80 or more years old. *Science, 276,* 1560–1563.

McClintock, M. K., & Herdt, G. (1996). Rethinking puberty: The development of sexual attraction. *Current Directions in Psychological Science, 5*(6), 178–183.

McCord, J. (1996). Unintended consequences of punishment. *Pediatrics, 88,* 832–834.

McCormick, M. C., McCarton, C., Brooks-Gunn, J., Belt, P., & Gross, R. T. (1998). The infant health and development program: Interim summary. *Journal of Developmental and Behavioral Pediatrics, 19,* 359–371.

McCoy, A. R., & Reynolds, A. J. (1999). Grade retention and school performance: An extended investigation. *Journal of School Psychology, 37,* 273–298.

McCrae, R. R. (2002). Cross-cultural research on the five-factor model of personality. In W. J. Lonner, D. L. Dinnel, S. A. Hayes, & D. N. Sattler (Eds.), *Online readings in psychology and culture* (Unit 6, Chapter 1). Bellingham, WA: Center for Cross-Cultural Research, Western Washington University.

McCrae, R. R., & Costa, P. T. (1994). The stability of personality: Observations and evaluations. *Current Directions in Psychological Science, 3*(6), 173–175.

McCrae, R. R., & Costa, P. T., Jr. (1984). *Emerging lives, enduring dispositions.* Boston: Little, Brown.

McCrae, R. R., Costa, P. T., Jr., & Busch, C. M. (1986). Evaluating comprehensiveness in personality systems: The California Q-set and the five factor model. *Journal of Personality, 54,* 430–446.

McCrae, R. R., Costa, P. T., Jr., Ostendorf, F., Angleitner, A., Hebríčková, M., Avia, M. D., Sanz, J., Sánchez-Bernardos, M. L., Kusdil, M. E., Woodfield, R., Saunders, P. R., & Smith, P. B. (2000). Nature over nurture: Temperament, personality, and lifespan development. *Journal of Personality and Social Psychology, 78,* 173–186.

McCue, J. D. (1995). The naturalness of dying. *Journal of the American Medical Association, 273,* 1039–1043.

McDaniel, M. A., Maier, S. F., & Einstein, G. O. (2002). "Brain-specific" nutrients: A memory cure? *Psychological Science in the Public Interest, 3*(1), 12–38.

McFall, S., & Miller, B. H. (1992). Caregiver burden and nursing home admission of frail elderly patients. *Journal of Gerontology: Social Sciences, 47,* S73–79.

McFarland, R. A., Tune, G. B., & Welford, A. (1964). On the driving of automobiles by older people. *Journal of Gerontology, 19,* 190–197.

McGauhey, P. J., Starfield, B., Alexander, C., & Ensminget, M. E. (1991). Social environment and vulnerability of low birth weight children: A social-epidemiological perspective. *Pediatrics, 88,* 943–953.

McGee, R., Partridge, F., Williams, S., & Silva, P. A. (1991). A twelve-year follow-up of preschool hyperactive children. *Journal of the American Academy of Child and Adolescent Psychiatry, 30,* 224–232.

McGruder, H. F., Greenlund, K. J., Croft, J. B., & Zheng, Z. J. (2005, January 14). Differences in disability among black and white stroke survivors—United States, 2000–2001. *Morbidity and Mortality Weekly Report, 54*(01), 3–6.

McGue, M. (1993). From proteins to cognitions: The behavioral genetics of alcoholism. In R. P. Plomin & G. E. McClearn (Eds.), *Nature, nurture, and psychology.* Washington, DC: American Psychological Association.

McGue, M. (1997). The democracy of the genes. *Nature, 388,* 417–418.

McGuffin, P., Owen, M. J., & Farmer, A. E. (1995). Genetic basis of schizophrenia. *The Lancet, 346,* 678–682.

McGuffin, P., Riley, B., & Plomin, R. (2001). Toward behavioral genomics. *Science, 291,* 1232, 1249.

McGuigan, F. & Salmon, K. (2004). The time to talk: The influence of the timing of adult-child talk on children's event memory. *Child Development, 75,* 669–686.

McGuire, P. A. (1998, July). Wanted: Workers with flexibility for 21st century jobs [Online]. *APA Monitor Online, 29*(7). Available: http://www.apa.org/monitor/jul98/factor.html.

McHale, S. M., Kim, J., Whiteman, S., & Crouter, A. C. (2004). Links between sex-typed time use in middle childhood and gender development in early adolescence. *Developmental Psychology, 40,* 868–881.

McHale, S. M., Updegraff, K. A., Helms-Erikson, H., & Crouter, A. C. (2001). Sibling influences on gender development in middle childhood and early adolescence: A longitudinal study. *Developmental Psychology, 37,* 115–125.

McKay, N. Y. (1992). Introduction. In M. Anderson, *My Lord, what a morning* (pp. ix–xxxiii). Madison: University of Wisconsin Press.

McKenna, J. J., & Mosko, S. (1993). Evolution and infant sleep: An experimental study of infant-parent co-sleeping and its implications for SIDS. *Acta Paediatrica, 389*(Suppl.), 31–36.

McKenna, J. J., Mosko, S. S., & Richard, C. A. (1997). Bedsharing promotes breastfeeding. *Pediatrics, 100,* 214–219.

McKitrick, L. A., Camp, C. J., & Black, F. W. (1992). Prospective memory intervention in Alzheimer's disease. *Journal of Gerontology: Psychological Sciences, 47*(5), P337–343.

McKusick, V. A. (2001). The anatomy of the human genome. *Journal of the American Medical Association, 286*(18), 2289–2295.

McLanahan, S., & Sandefur, G. (1994). *Growing up with a single parent.* Cambridge, MA: Harvard University Press.

McLeskey, J., Lancaster, M., & Grizzle, K. L. (1995). Learning disabilities and grade retention: A review of issues with recommendations for practice. *Learning Disabilities Research & Practice, 10,* 120–128.

McLoyd, V. C. (1990). The impact of economic hardship on black families and children: Psychological distress, parenting, and socioemotional development. *Child Development, 61,* 311–346.

McLoyd, V. C. (1998). Socioeconomic disadvantage and child development. *American Psychologist, 53,* 185–204.

McLoyd, V. C., Jayaratne, T. E., Ceballo, R., & Borquez, J. (1994). Unemployment and work interruption among African American single mothers: Effects on parenting and adolescent socioemotional functioning. *Child Development, 65,* 562–589.

McLoyd, V. C., & Smith, J. (2002). Physical discipline and behavior problems in African American, European American, and Hispanic children: Emotional support as a moderator. *Journal of Marriage and Family, 64,* 40–53.

McNeilly-Choque, M. K., Hart, C. H., Robinson, C. C., Nelson, L. J., & Olsen, S. F. (1996). Overt and relational aggression on the playground: Correspondence among different informants. *Journal of Research in Childhood Education, 11,* 47–67.

McNicholas, J., & Collis, G. M. (2001). Children's representations of pets in their social networks. *Child: Care, Health, & Development, 27,* 279–294.

McQuillan, J., Greil, A. L., White, L., & Jacob, M. C. (2003). Frustrated fertility: Infertility and psychological distress among women. *Journal of Marriage and Family, 65,* 1007–1018.

McTiernan, A., Kooperberg, C., White, E., Wilcox, S., Coates, R., Adams-Campbell, L. L., Woods, N., & Ockene, J. (2003). Recreational physical activity and the risk of breast cancer in postmenopausal women: The Women's Health Initiative Cohort Study. *Journal of the American Medical Association, 290,* 1331–1336.

Mead, M. (1928). *Coming of age in Samoa.* New York: Morrow.

Mead, M. (1930). *Growing up in New Guinea.* New York: Blue Ribbon.

Mead, M. (1935). *Sex and temperament in three primitive societies.* New York: Morrow.

Mead, M. (1972). *Blackberry winter: My earlier years.* New York: Morrow.

Mears, B. (2005, March 1). High court: Juvenile death penalty unconstitutional: Slim majority cites 'evolving standards' in American society. CNN.com. [Online]. Retrieved March 30, 2005, from http://cnn.com./2005/LAW/03/01/scotus.death.penalty.

Measelle, J. R., Ablow, J. C., Cowan, P. A., & Cowan, C. P. (1998). Assessing young children's view of their academic, social, and emotional lives: An evaluation of the self-perception scales of the Berkeley Puppet Interview. *Child Development, 69,* 1556–1576.

Mednick, S. C., Nakayama, K., Cantero, J. L., Atienza, M., Levin, A. A., Pathak, N., & Stickgold, R. (2002). The restorative effect of naps on perceptual deterioration. *Nature Neuroscience, 5,* 677–681.

Meeks, J. J., Weiss, J., & Jameson, J. L. (2003, May). Dax1 is required for testis formation. *Nature Genetics, 34,* 32–33.

Meier, D. (1995). *The power of their ideas.* Boston: Beacon.

Meier, D. E., Emmons, C.-A., Wallenstein, S., Quill, T., Morrison, R. S., & Cassel, C. (1998). A national survey of physician-assisted suicide and euthanasia in the United States. *New England Journal of Medicine, 338,* 1193–1201.

Meier, R. (1991, January–February). Language acquisition by deaf children. *American Scientist, 79,* 60–70.

Meins, E. (1998). The effects of security of attachment and maternal attribution of meaning on children's linguistic acquisitional style. *Infant Behavior and Development, 21,* 237–252.

Meis, P. J., Klebanoff, M., Thom, E., Dombrowski, M. P., Sibai, B., Moawad, A. H., Spong, C. Y., Hauth, J. C., Miodovnik, M., Varner, M. W., Leveno, K. J., Caritis, S. N., Iams, J. D., Wapner, R. J., Conway, D., O'-Sullivan, M. J., Carpenter, M., Mercer, B., Ramin, S. M., Thorp, J. M., Peaceman, A. M., Gabbe, S., & National Institute of Child Health and Human Development Maternal-Fetal Medicine Units Network. (2003). Prevention of recurrent preterm delivery by 17 alpha-hydroxyprogesterone caproate. *New England Journal of Medicine, 348,* 2379–2385.

Melson, G. F. (1998). The role of companion animals in human development. In D. D. Wilson & D. C. Turner (Eds.), *Companion animals in human health* (pp. 219–236). Thousand Oaks, CA: Sage.

Meltzoff, A. N., & Moore, M. K. (1983). Newborn infants imitate adult facial gestures. *Child Development, 54,* 702–709.

Meltzoff, A. N., & Moore, M. K. (1989). Imitation in newborn infants: Exploring the range of gestures imitated and the underlying mechanisms. *Developmental Psychology, 25,* 954–962.

Meltzoff, A. N., & Moore, M. K. (1994). Imitation, memory, and the representation of persons. *Infant Behavior and Development, 17,* 83–99.

Meltzoff, A. N., & Moore, M. K. (1998). Object representation, identity, and the paradox of early permanence: Steps toward a new framework. *Infant Behavior & Development, 21,* 201–235.

Menacker, F., Martin, J. A., MacDorman, M. F., & Ventura, S. J. (2004). Births to 10–14 year-old mothers, 1990–2002: Trends and health outcomes. *National Vital Statistics Reports, 53*(7). Hyattsville, MD: National Center for Health Statistics.

Menec, V. H. (2003). The relation between everyday activities and successful aging: A 6-year longitudinal study. *Journal of Gerontology: Social Sciences, 58B,* S74–S82.

Mennella, J. A., & Beauchamp, G. K. (1996a). The early development of human flavor preferences. In E. D. Capaldi (Ed.), *Why we eat what we eat: The psychology of eating* (pp. 83–112). Washington, DC: American Psychological Association.

Mennella, J. A., & Beauchamp, G. K. (1996b). The human infant's response to vanilla flavors in mother's milk and formula. *Infant Behavior and Development, 19,* 13–19.

Mennella, J. A., & Beauchamp, G. K. (2002). Flavor experiences during formula feeding are related to preferences during childhood. *Early Human Development, 68,* 71–82.

Menon, U. (2001). Middle adulthood in cultural perspective: The imagined and the experienced in three cultures. In M. E. Lachman (Ed.), *Handbook of midlife development* (pp. 40–74). New York: Wiley.

Ment, L. R., Vohr, B., Allan, W., Katz, K. H., Schneider, K. C., Westerveld, M., Duncan, C. C., & Makuch, R. W. (2003). Changes in cognitive function over time in very low-birth-weight infants. *Journal of the American Medical Association, 289,* 705–711.

Merrill, S. S., & Verbrugge, L. M. (1999). Health and disease in midlife. In S. L. Willis & J. D. Reid (Eds.), *Life in the middle: Psychological and social development in middle age* (pp. 78–103). San Diego: Academic Press.

Merva, M., & Fowles, R. (1992). *Effects of diminished economic opportunities on social stress: Heart attacks, strokes, and crime* [Briefing paper]. Washington, DC: Economic Policy Institute.

Messinger, D. S., Bauer, C. R., Das, A., Seifer, R., Lester, B. M., Lagasse, L. L., Wright, L. L., Shankaran, S., Bada, H.S., Smeriglio, V. L., Langer, J. C., Beeghly, M., and Poole, W. K. (2004). The maternal lifestyle study: Cognitive, motor, and behavioral outcomes of cocaine-exposed and opiate-exposed infants through three years of age. *Pediatrics, 113,* 1677–1685.

Meyer, B. J. F., Russo, C., & Talbot, A. (1995). Discourse comprehension and problem solving: Decisions about the treatment of breast cancer by women across the life-span. *Psychology in Aging, 10,* 84–103.

Michael, R. T., Gagnon, J. H., Laumann, E. O., & Kolata, G. (1994). *Sex in America: A definitive survey.* Boston: Little, Brown.

Miedzian, M. (1991). *Boys will be boys: Breaking the link between masculinity and violence.* New York: Doubleday.

Milberger, S., Biederman, J., Faraone, S. V., Chen, L., & Jones, J. (1996). Is maternal smoking during pregnancy a risk factor for attention hyperactivity disorder in children? *American Journal of Psychiatry, 153,* 1138–1142.

Milgram, N. W., Head, E., Zicker, S. C., Ikeda-Douglas, C. J., Murphey, H., Muggenburg, B., Siwak, C., Tapp, D., & Cotman, C. W. (2005). Learning ability in aged beagle dogs is preserved by behavioral enrichment and dietary fortification: A two-year longitudinal study. *Neurobiology of Aging, 26,* 77–90.

Milkie, M. A, & Peltola, P. (1999). Playing all the roles: Gender and the work-family balancing act. *Journal of Marriage and the Family, 61,* 476–490.

Milkie, M. A., Mattingly, M. J., Nomaguchi, S. M., Bianchi, S. M., & Robinson, J. P. (2004). The time squeeze: Parental statuses and feelings about time with children. *Journal of Marriage and Family, 66,* 739–761.

Miller, K. F., Smith, C. M., Zhu, J., & Zhang, H. (1995). Preschool origins of cross-national differences in mathematical competence: The role of number-naming systems. *Psychological Science, 6,* 56–60.

Miller, K., & Kohn, M. (1983). The reciprocal effects of job condition and the intellectuality of leisure-time activities. In M. L. Kohn & C. Schooler (Eds.), *Work and personality: An inquiry into the impact of social stratification* (pp. 217–241). Norwood, NJ: Ablex.

Miller, W. R., & Thoresen, C. E. (2003) Spirituality, religion, and health. *American Psychologist, 58,* 24–35.

Miller-Kovach, K. (2003). Childhood and adolescent obesity: A review of the scientific literature. Weight Watchers International: Unpublished ms.

Mills, D. L., Cofley-Corina, S. A., & Neville, H. J. (1997). Language comprehension and cerebral specialization from 13 to 20 months. *Developmental Neuropsychology, 13,* 397–445.

Mills, J. L., & England, L. (2001). Food fortification to prevent neural tube defects: Is it working? *Journal of the American Medical Association, 285,* 3022–3033.

Mills, J. L., Holmes, L. B., Aarons, I. H., Simpson, J. L., Brown, Z. A., Jovanovic-Peterson, L. G., Conley, M. R., Graubard, B. I., Knopp, R. H., & Metzger, B. E. (1993). Moderate caffeine use and the risk of spontaneous abortion and intrauterine growth retardation. *Journal of the American Medical Association, 269,* 593–597.

Milunsky, A. (1992). *Heredity and your family's health.* Baltimore: Johns Hopkins University Press.

Minkler, M., & Fuller-Thomson, E. (2005). African American grandparents raising grandchildren: A national study using the Census 2000 American Community Survey. *Journal of Gerontology: Social Sciences, 60B,* S82–S92.

Minnesota explorer Ann Bancroft. (2002). Minnesota Public Radio. [Online]. http://news.mpr.org/programs/midmorning. Access date: February 20, 2002.

Mintz, T. H. (2005). Linguistic and conceptual influences on adjective acquisition in 24- to 36-month-olds. *Developmental Psychology, 41,* 17–29.

Miserandino, M. (1996). Children who do well in school: Individual differences in perceived competence and autonomy in above-average children. *Journal of Educational Psychology, 88*(2), 203–214.

Misra, D. P., & Guyer, B. (1998). Benefits and limitations of prenatal care: From counting visits to measuring content. *Journal of the American Medical Association, 279,* 1661–1662.

Mistry, R. S., Vandewater, E. A., Huston, A. C., & McLoyd, V. (2002). Economic well-being and children's social adjustment: The role of family process in an ethnically diverse low-income sample. *Child Development, 73,* 935–951.

Mitchell, B. A.,Wister, A. V., & Burch, T. K. (1989). The family environment and leaving the parental home. *Journal of Marriage and the Family, 51,* 605–613.

Mitchell, V., & Helson, R. (1990). Women's prime of life: Is it the 50s? *Psychology of Women Quarterly, 16,* 331–347.

Mitka, M. (2004). Improvement seen in U.S. immunization rates. *Journal of the American Medical Association, 292,* 1167.

Mix, K. S., Huttenlocher, J., & Levine, S. C. (2002). Multiple cues for quantification in infancy: Is number one of them? *Psychological Bulletin, 128,* 278–294.

Mix, K. S., Levine, S. C., & Huttenlocher, J. (1999). Early fraction calculation ability. *Developmental Psychology, 35,* 164–174.

Miyake, K., Chen, S., & Campos, J. (1985). Infants' temperament, mothers' mode of interaction and attachment in Japan: An interim report. In I. Bretherton & E. Waters (Eds.), Growing points of attachment theory and research. *Monographs of the Society for Research in Child Development, 50*(1–2, Serial No. 109), 276–297.

Mlot, C. (1998). Probing the biology of emotion. *Science, 280*, 1005–1007.

Moen, P., Dempster-McClain, D., & Williams, R. M., Jr. (1992). Successful aging: A lifecourse perspective on women's multiple roles and health. *American Journal of Sociology, 97*, 1612–1638.

Moen, P., Kim, J. E., & Hofmeister, H. (2001). Couples' work/retirement transitions, gender, and marital quality. *Social Psychology Quarterly, 64*, 55–71.

Moen, P., & Wethington, E. (1999). Midlife development in a life course context. In S. L. Willis & J. D. Reid (Eds.), *Life in the middle: Psychological and social development in middle age* (pp. 1–23). San Diego: Academic Press.

Moffitt, T. E. (1993). Adolescent-limited and life-course persistent antisocial behavior: A developmental taxonomy. *Psychological Review, 100*, 674–701.

Moffitt, T. E., Caspi, A., Belsky, J., & Silva, P. A. (1992). Childhood experience and the onset of menarche: A test of a sociobiological model. *Child Development, 63*, 47–58.

Mokdad, A. H., Bowman, B. A., Ford, E. S., Vinicor, F., Marks, J. S., & Koplan, J. P. (2001). The continuing epidemics of obesity and diabetes in the United States. *Journal of the American Medical Association, 286*, 1195–1200.

Mokdad, A. H., Ford, E. S., Bowman, B. A., Dietz,W. H.,Vinicor, F., Bales,V. S., & Marks, J. S. (2003). Prevalence of obesity, diabetes, and obesity-related health risk factors, 2001. *Journal of the American Medical Association, 289*, 76–79.

Mokdad, A. H., Marks, J. S., Stroup, D. F., & Gerberding, J. L. (2005). Correction: Actual causes of death in the United States, 2000. *Journal of the American Medical Association, 293*, 293–294.

Molina, B. S. G., & Chassin, L. (1996). The parent-adolescent relationship at puberty: Hispanic ethnicity and parent alcoholism as moderators. *Developmental Psychology, 32*, 675–686.

Molina, B. S. G., & Pelham Jr., W. E. (2003). Childhood predictors of adolescent substance use in a longitudinal study of children with ADHD. *Journal of Abnormal Psychology, 112*, 497–507.

Moline, M. L., & Zendell, S. M. (2000). Evaluating and managing premenstrual syndrome. Medscape General Medicine, 2. Accessed online 12/27/04. http://www.medscape.com/viewarticle/408913_print.

Mollenkopf, J., Waters, M. C., Holdaway, J., & Kasinitz, P. (2005). The ever-winding path: Ethnic and racial diversity in the transition to adulthood. In R. A. Settersten, Jr., F. F. Furstenberg, Jr., & R. G. Rumbaut (Eds.), *On the frontier of adulthood: Theory, research, and public policy* (pp. 454–497). (John D. and Catherine T. MacArthur Foundation Series on Mental Health and Development, Research Network on Transitions to Adulthood and Public Policy.) Chicago: University of Chicago Press.

Mondschein, E. R., Adolph, K. E., & Tamis-Lemonda, C. S. (2000). Gender bias in mothers' expectations about infant crawling. *Journal of Experimental Child Psychology. Special Issue on Gender, 77*, 304–316.

Money, J., & Ehrhardt, A. A. (1972). *Man and woman/Boy and girl.* Baltimore: Johns Hopkins University Press.

Monk, T. H. (2000). What can the chronobiologist do to help the shift worker? *Journal of Biological Rhythms, 15*, 86–94.

Montague, D. P. F., & Walker-Andrews, A. S. (2001). Peekaboo: A new look at infants' perception of emotion expressions. *Developmental Psychology, 37*, 826–838.

Montaldo, C. (2005). About death penalty for juveniles. [Online]. Retrieved May 5, 2005, from http://crime.about.com/od/juvenile/i/juvenile death 2.htm.

Montenegro, X. P. (2004). *The divorce experience: A study of divorce at midlife and beyond.* Washington, DC: American Association of Retired Persons.

Montgomery, M. J., & Cote, J. E. (2003). College as a transition to adulthood. In G. R. Adams and M. D. Berzonsky (eds.). Blackwell *Handbook of adolescence.* Malden, MA: Blackwell Publishing.

Moon, C., Cooper, R. P., & Fifer, W. P. (1993). Two-day-olds prefer their native language. *Infant Behavior and Development, 16*, 495–500.

Moon, C., & Fifer, W. P. (1990, April). *Newborns prefer a prenatal version of mother's voice.* Paper presented at the biannual meeting of the International Society of Infant Studies, Montreal, Canada.

Mooney-Somers, J., & Golombok, S, (2000). Children of lesbian mothers: From the 1970s to the new millennium. *Sexual & Relationship Therapy, 15*, 121–126.

Moore, D. W. (2005, May 17). Three in four Americans support euthanasia: Significantly less support for doctor-assisted suicide. The Gallup Organization. [Online]. Retrieved May 24, 2005, http://www.gallup.com/poll/content/login.aspx?ci=16333.

Moore, M. J., Moir, P., & Patrick, M. M. (2004). *The state of aging and health in America 2004.* Washington, DC: Centers for Disease Control and Prevention and Merck Institute of Aging & Health.

Moore, S. E., Cole, T. J., Poskitt, E. M. E., Sonko, B. J., Whitehead, R. G., McGregor, I. A., & Prentice, A. M. (1997). Season of birth predicts mortality in rural Gambia. *Nature, 388*, 434.

Morelli, G. A., Rogoff, B., Oppenheim, D., & Goldsmith, D. (1992). Cultural variation in infants' sleeping arrangements: Questions of independence. *Developmental Psychology, 28*, 604–613.

Morgan, B., Maybery, M., & Durkin, K. (2003). Weak central coherence, poor joint attention, and low verbal ability: Independent deficits in early autism. *Developmental Psychology, 39*, 646–656.

Morgan, W. J., Crain, E. F., Gruchalla, R. S., O'Connor, G. T., Kattan, M., Evans, R., Stout, J., Malindzak, G., Smartt, E., Plaut, M., Walter, M., Vaughan, B., & Mitchell, H. for the Inner-City Asthma Study Group. (2004). Results of a home-based environmental intervention among urban children with asthma. *New England Journal of Medicine, 351*, 1068–1080.

Morin, C. M., Colecchi, C., Stone, J., Sood, R., & Brink, D. (1999). Behavioral and pharmacological therapies for late-life insomnia: A randomized controlled trial. *Journal of the American Medical Association, 281*, 991–999.

Morison, P., & Masten, A. S. (1991). Peer reputation in middle childhood as a predictor of adaptation in adolescence: A seven-year follow-up. *Child Development, 62*, 991–1007.

Morison, S. J., Ames, E. W., & Chisholm, K. (1995). The development of children adopted from Romanian orphanages. *Merrill-Palmer Quarterly Journal of Developmental Psychology, 41*, 411–430.

Morison, S. J., & Ellwood, A.-L. (2000). Resiliency in the aftermath of deprivation: A second look at the development of Romanian orphanage children. *Merrill-Palmer Quarterly, 46*, 717–737.

Morris, M. C. (2004). Diet and Alzheimer's Disease: What the evidence shows. *Medscape General Medicine, 6*, 1–5.

Morris, M. C., Evans, D. A., Bienias, J. L., Tangney, C. C., & Wilson, R. S. (2002). Vitamin E and cognitive decline in older persons. *Archives of Neurology, 59*, 1125–1132.

Morris, R. D., Stuebing, K. K., Fletcher, J. M., Shaywitz, S. E., Lyon, G. R., Shankweiler, D. P., Katz, L., Francis, D. J., & Shaywitz, B. A. (1998). Subtypes of reading disability: Variability around a phonological core. *Journal of Educational Psychology, 90*, 347–373.

Morrison, D. R., & Cherlin, A. J. (1995). The divorce process and young children's well-being: A prospective analysis. *Journal of Marriage and the Family, 57*, 800–812.

Morrow, D. G., Menard, W. W. E., Stine-Morrow, E. A. L., Teller, T., & Bryant, D. (2001). The influence of expertise and task factors on age differences in pilot communication. *Psychology and Aging, 16*, 31–46.

Morse, J. M., & Field, P. A. (1995). *Qualitative research methods for health professionals.* Thousand Oaks, CA: Sage.

Mortensen, E. L., Michaelson, K. F., Sanders, S. A., & Reinisch, J. M. (2002). The association between duration of breastfeeding and adult intelligence. *Journal of the American Medical Association, 287*, 2365–2371.

Mortimer, J. A., Gosche, K. M., Riley, K. P., Markesbery, W. R., & Snowdon, D. A. (2004). Delayed recall, hippocampal volume and Alzheimer's neuropathology: Findings from the Nun Study. *Neurology, 62*, 428–432.

Mortimer, J. A., Snowdon, D. A., & Markesbery, W. R. (2002). Head circumference, education, and risk of dementia: Findings from the Nun Study. *Journal of Clinical and Experimental Neuropsychology, 25*, 671–679.

Morton, K. R., Worthley, J. S., Nitch, S. R., Lamberton, H. H., Loo, L. K., & Testerman, J. K. (2000). Integration of cognition and emotion: A postformal operations model of physician-patient interaction. *Journal of Adult Development, 7*, 151–160.

Mosca, L., Collins, P., Harrington, D. M., Mendelsohn, M. E., Pasternak, R. C., Robertson, R. M., Schen K-Gustafsson, K., Smith, S. C., Jr., Taubert, K. A., & Wenger, N. K., (2001). Hormone therapy and cardiovascular disease: A statement for healthcare professionals from the American Heart Association. *Circulation, 104*, 499–503.

Mosconi, L. Tsui, W.-H., De Santi, S., Li, J., Rusinek, H., Convit, A., Li, Y., Boppana, M., & de Leon, M. J. (2005). Reduced hippocampal metabolism in MCI and ADO Automated FDG-PET image analysis. *Neurology, 64*, 1860–1867.

Moscovitch, M., & Winocur, G. (1992). The neuropsychology of memory and aging. In F. I. M. Craik & T. A. Salthouse (Eds.), *Handbook of aging and cognition* (pp. 315–372). Hillsdale, NJ: Erlbaum.

Moses, L. J., Baldwin, D. A., Rosicky, J. G., & Tidball, G. (2001). Evidence for referential understanding in the emotions domain at twelve and eighteen months. *Child Development, 72*, 718–735.

Mosier, C. E., & Rogoff, B. (2003). Privileged treatment of toddlers: Cultural aspects of individual choice and responsibility. *Developmental Psychology, 39*, 1047–1060.

Moskovitz, J., Bar-Noy, S., Williams, W. M., Requena, J., Berlett, B. S., & Stadtman, E. R. (2001). Methionine sulfoxide reductase (MsrA) is a regulator of antioxidant defense and lifespan in mammals. *Proceedings of the National Academy of Sciences, 98*, 12920–12925.

Moskow-McKenzie, D., & Manheimer, R. J. (1994). *A planning guide to organize educational programs for older adults.* Asheville, NC: University Publications, UNCA.

Moss, E., & St-Laurent, D. (2001). Attachment at school age and academic performance. *Developmental Psychology, 37*, 863–874.

Moss, M. H. (2003). Trends in childhood asthma: Prevalence, health care utilization, and mortality. *Pediatrics, 112*, 479.

Moss, M. S., & Moss, S. Z. (1989). The death of a parent. In R. A. Kalish (Ed.), *Midlife loss: Coping strategies.* Newbury Park, CA: Sage.

Mounts, N. S., & Steinberg, L. (1995). An ecological analysis of peer influence on adolescent grade point average and drug use. *Developmental Psychology, 31*, 915–922.

Mouw, T. (2005). Sequences of early adult transition: A look at variability and consequences. In R. A. Settersten, Jr., F. F. Furstenberg, Jr., & R. G. Rumbaut (Eds.), *On the frontier of adulthood: Theory, research, and public policy* (pp. 256–291). (John D. and Catherine T. MacArthur Foundation Series on Mental Health and Development, Research Network on Transitions to Adulthood and Public Policy.) Chicago: University of Chicago Press.

Mroczek, D. K. (2004). Positive and negative affect at midlife. In O. G. Brim, C. D. Ryff, and R. C. Kessler (Eds.), How healthy are we? A national study of well-being at midlife. (pp. 205–226). Chicago: University of Chicago Press.

Mroczek, D. K., & Kolarz, C. M. (1998). The effect of age on positive and negative affect: A developmental perspective on happiness. *Journal of Personality and Social Psychology, 75*(5), 1333–1349.

Mroczek, D. K., & Spiro, A. (2005). Change in life satisfaction during adulthood: Findings from the Veterans Affairs Normative Aging Study. *Journal of Personality and Social Psychology, 88*, 189–202.

Msall, M. S. E. (2004). Developmental vulnerability and resilience in extremely preterm infants. *Journal of the American Medical Association, 292*, 2399–2401.

MTA Cooperative Group. (1999). A 14-month randomized clinical trial of treatment strategies for attention-deficit/hyperactivity disorder. *Archives of General Psychiatry, 56*, 1073–1986.

MTA Cooperative Group. (2004a). National Institute of Mental Health multimodal treatment study of ADHD follow-up: Changes in effectiveness and growth after the end of treatment. *Pediatrics, 113*, 762–769.

MTA Cooperative Group. (2004b). National Institute of Mental Health multimodal treatment study of ADHD follow-up: 24-month outcomes of treatment strategies for attention-deficit/hyperactivity disorder. *Pediatrics, 113*, 754–769.

Mueller, T. I., Kohn, R., Leventhal, N., Leon, A. C., Solomon, D., Coryell, W., Endicott, J., Alexopoulos, G. S., & Keller, M. B. (2004). The course of depression in elderly patients. *American Journal of Psychiatry, 12*, 22–29.

Mullan, D., & Currie, C. (2000). Socioeconomic equalities in adolescent health. In C. Currie, K. Hurrelmann, W. Settertobulte, R. Smith, & J. Todd (Eds.), *Health and health behaviour among young people: a WHO cross-national study (HBSC) international report* (pp. 65–72). WHO Policy Series: Healthy Policy for Children and Adolescents, Series No. 1.

Müller, M. (1998). *Anne Frank: The biography.* New York: Holt.

Mulrine, A. (2004, February 2). Coming of age in ancient times. *U.S. News & World Report.* [Online]. Retrieved March 31, 2004, from http://www.usnews.com/usnews/culture/articles/040202/2child.htm.

Mumme, D. L., & Fernald, A. (2003). The infant as onlooker: Learning from emotional reactions observed in a television scenario, *Child Development, 74*, 221–237.

Munakata, Y. (2001). Task-dependency in infant behavior: Toward an understanding of the processes underlying cognitive development. In F. Lacerda, C. von Hofsten, & M. Heimann (Eds.), *Emerging cognitive abilities in early infancy.* Hillsdale, NJ: Erlbaum.

Munakata, Y., McClelland, J. L., Johnson, M. J., & Siegler, R. S. (1997). Rethinking infant knowledge: Toward an adaptive process account of successes and failures in object permanence tasks. *Psychological Review, 104*, 686–714.

Munson, M. L., & Sutton, P. O. (2004). Births, marriages, divorces, and deaths: Provisional data for 2003. *National Vital Statistics Reports, 52*(22). Hyattsville, MD: National Center for Health Statistics.

Muntner, P., He, J., Cutler, J. A., Wildman, R. P., & Whelton, P. K. (2004, May 5). Trends in blood pressure among children and adolescents. *Journal of the American Medical Association, 291*, 2107–2113.

Murachver, T., Pipe, M., Gordon, R., Owens, J. L., & Fivush, R. (1996). Do, show, and tell: Children's event memories acquired through direct experience, observation, and stories. *Child Development, 67*, 3029–3044.

Murchison, C., & Langer, S. (1927). Tiedemann's observations on the development of the mental facilities of children. *Journal of Genetic Psychology, 34*, 205–230.

Muris, P., Merckelbach, H., & Collaris, R. (1997). Common childhood fears and their origins. *Behaviour Research and Therapy, 35*, 929–937.

Murphy, C. M., & Bootzin, R. R. (1973). Active and passive participation in the contact desensitization of snake fear in children. *Behavior Therapy, 4*, 203–211.

Murphy, G. C., & Athanasou, J. (1999). The effect of unemployment on mental health. *Journal of Occupational and Organizational Psychology, 72*, 83–99.

Murray, M. L., deVries, C. S., and Wong, I. C. K. (2004). A drug utilisation study of antidepressants in children and adolescents using the General Practice Research data base. *Archives of the Diseases of Children, 89*, 1098–1102.

Musick, K. (2002). Planned and unplanned childbearing among unmarried women. *Journal of Marriage and Family, 64*, 915–929.

Musick, M. A., Herzog, A. R., & House, J. S. (1999). Volunteering and mortality among older adults: Findings from a national sample. *Journal of Gerontology: Psychological Sciences, 54B*, S173–S180.

Muskin, P. R. (1998). The request to die. Role for a psychodynamic perspective on physician-assisted suicide. *Journal of the American Medical Association, 279*, 323–328.

Must, A., Jacques, P. F., Dallal, G. E., Bajema, C. J., & Dietz, W. H. (1992). Long-term morbidity and mortality of overweight adolescents: A follow-up of the Harvard Growth Study of 1922 to 1935. *New England Journal of Medicine, 327*(19), 1350–1355.

Mustanski, B. S., DuPree, M. G., Nievergelt, C. M., Bocklandt, S., Schork, N. J., & Hamer, D. H. (2005). A genomewide scan of male sexual orientation. *Human Genetics, 116*, 272–278.

Mustillo, S., Worthman, C., Erkanli, A., Keeler, G., Angold, A., & Costello, E. J. (2003). Obesity and psychiatric disorder: Developmental trajectories. *Pediatrics, 111,* 851–859.

Muter, V., Hulme, C., Snowling, M. J., & Stevenson, J. (2004). Phonemes, rimes, vocabulary, and grammatical skill as foundations of early reading development: Evidence from a longitudinal study. *Developmental Psychology, 40,* 665–681.

Myers, D., & Diener, E. (1995). Who is happy? *Psychological Science, 6,* 10–19.

Myers, D. G. (2000). The funds, friends, and faith of happy people. *American Psychologist, 55,* 56–67.

Myers, D. G., & Diener, E. (1996). The pursuit of happiness. *Scientific American, 274,* 54–56.

Myers, J. E., & Perrin, N. (1993). Grandparents affected by parental divorce: A population at risk? *Journal of Counseling and Development, 72,* 62–66.

Myerson, J., Shealy, D., & Stern, M. B. (Eds.). (1987). *The selected letters of Louisa May Alcott.* Boston: Little, Brown.

Mykityshyn, A. L., Fisk, A. D., & Rogers, W. A. (in press). Learning to use a home medical device: Mediating age-related differences with training. *Human Factors.*

Naeye, R. L., & Peters, E. C. (1984). Mental development of children whose mothers smoked during pregnancy. *Obstetrics and Gynecology, 64,* 601.

Nagaoka, J., & Roderick, M. (April 2004). Ending social promotion: The effects of retention. Chicago: Consortium on Chicago School Research.

Naito, M., & Miura, H. (2001). Japanese children's numerical competencies: Age- and schooling-related influences on the development of number concepts and addition skills. *Developmental Psychology, 37,* 217–230.

Nakonezny, P. A., Shull, R. D., & Rodgers, J. L. (1995). The effect of no-fault divorce rate across the 50 states and its relation to income, education, and religiosity. *Journal of Marriage and the Family, 57,* 477–488.

Nansel, T. R., Overpeck, M., Pilla, R. S., Ruan, W. J., Simons-Morton, B., & Scheidt, P. (2001). Bullying behaviors among U.S. youth: Prevalence and association with psychosocial adjustment. *Journal of the American Medical Association, 285,* 2094–2100.

Nash, J. M. (1997, February 3). Fertile minds. *Time,* pp. 49–56.

Nathanielsz, P. W. (1995). The role of basic science in preventing low birth weight. *The Future of Our Children, 5*(1), 57–70.

National Association of Educational Progress: The Nation's Report Card. (2004). *America's charter schools: Results from the NAEP 2003 Pilot Study* (NCES 2005-456). Jessup, MD: U.S. Department of Education.

National Center for Biotechnology Information. (2002). Genes and disease. [Online] Available: http://www.ncbi.nlm.nih.gov/disease.

National Center for Education Statistics (NCES). (1999). *The condition of education, 1999* (NCES 1999-022). Washington, DC: U.S. Government Printing Office.

National Center for Education Statistics (NCES). (2001). *The condition of education 2001* (NCES 2001-072). Washington, DC: U.S. Government Printing Office.

National Center for Education Statistics (NCES). (2003). *The condition of education, 2003* (Publication No. 2003–067). Washington, DC: Author.

National Center for Education Statistics (NCES). (2003). *The condition of education 2003* (NCES 2003-067). Washington, DC: U.S. Department of Education.

National Center for Education Statistics (NCES). (2004a). *The condition of education 2004* (NCES 2004-077). Washington, DC: U.S. Department of Education.

National Center for Education Statistics. (2004b, August). English language learner students in U.S. public schools: 1994 and 2000. Issue Brief (NCES 2004-035). Washington, DC: Author.

National Center for Education Statistics (NCES). (2004c). *The nation's report card: America's charter school report* (NCES 2005-456). Washington, DC: Author.

National Center for Education Statistics. (2005a). Children born in 2001—First results from the base year of Early Childhood Longitudinal Study, Birth Cohort (ECLS-B). [Online]. Retrieved November 19, 2004 from http://nces.ed.gov/pubs2005/children/index.asp.

National Center for Education Statistics. (2005b). *The condition of education 2005* (NCES 2005-094). Washington, DC: U.S. Government Printing Office.

National Center for Education Statistics. (2005c). Postsecondary participation rates by sex and race/ethnicity: 1974-2003. *Issue Brief* (NCES 2005-028). Jessup, MD: Author.

National Center for Health Statistics (NCHS). (1994). Advance report of final natality statistics, 1992 (*Monthly Vital Statistics Report, 43*[5, Suppl.]). Hyattsville, MD: U.S. Public Health Service.

National Center for Health Statistics (NCHS). (1998). *Health, United States, 1998 with socioeconomic status and health chartbook.* Hyattsville, MD: Author.

National Center for Health Statistics (NCHS). (2001). *Health, United States, 2001 with Urban and Rural Health Chartbook.* (PHS) 2001–1232. Hyattsville, MD: Author.

National Center for Health Statistics (NCHS). (2003). *Health, United States, 2003.* Hyattsville, MD: Author.

National Center for Health Statistics (NCHS). (2004). *Health, United States, 2004 with chartbook on trends in the health of Americans* (DHHS Publication No. 2004–1232). Hyattsville, MD: National Center for Health Statistics.

National Center for Health Statistics (NCHS). (2004). *Health, United States, 2004 with chartbook on trends in the health of Americans* (DHHS Publication No. 2004-1232). Hyattsville, MD: Author.

National Center for Injury Prevention and Control (NCIPC) (2001). *2001 United States suicide: Ages 15–19, all races, both sexes* (Web-based injury statistics query and reporting system) [Online]. Available: http://www.cdc.gov/ncipc. Access date: May 7, 2004.

National Center for Injury Prevention and Control (NCIPC) (2004). *Fact sheet: Teen drivers* [Online]. Available: http://www.cdc.gov/ncipc. Access date: May 7, 2004.

National Center for Learning Disabilities. (2004a). *Dyslexia: Learning disabilities in reading.* Fact sheet. [Online]. Available: http://www.ld.org/LDInfoZone/InfoZone_FactSheet_Dyslexia.cfm. Access date: May 30, 2004.

National Center for Learning Disabilities. (2004b). *LD at a glance.* Fact sheet. [Online]. Available: http://www.ld.org/LDInfoZone/InfoZone_FactSheet_LD.cfm. Access date: May 30, 2004.

National Center on Elder Abuse & Westat, Inc. (1998). *National Elder Abuse Incidence Study: Executive summary.* Washington, DC: American Public Human Services Association.

National Center on Shaken Baby Syndrome. (2000). SBS questions. [Online]. Available: http://www.dontshake.com/sbsquestions.html.

National Child Abuse and Neglect Data System (NCANDS). (2001). *Child maltreatment 1999.* [Online]. Available: http://www.calib.com/nccanch/pubs.factsheets/canstats.cfm. Access date: April 8, 2002.

National Children's Study. (2004, November 16). National Children's Study releases study plan and locations. [Online]. Retrieved from http://www.nationalchildrensstudy.gov/research/study plan/index.cfm on April 3, 2005.

National Clearinghouse on Child Abuse and Neglect Information (NCCANI). (2004a). Child abuse and neglect fatalities: Statistics and interventions. Washington, DC: Author.

National Clearinghouse on Child Abuse and Neglect Information (NCCANI). (2004b). Long-term consequences of child abuse and neglect. Washington, DC: Author. [Online]. Available: http://nccanch.acf.hhs.gov/pubs/factsheets/long term consequences.cfm. Access date: October 5, 2004.

National Coalition for the Homeless. (2002, September). *How many people experience homelessness?* NCH Fact Sheet 2. Washington, DC: Author.

National Coalition for the Homeless. (2004, May). *Who is homeless?* NCH Fact Sheet 3. Washington, DC: Author.

National Commission for the Protection of Human Subjects of Biomedical and Behavioral Research. (1978). *Report.* Washington, DC: Author.

National Committee for Citizens in Education (NCCE). (1986, Winter Holiday). Don't be afraid to start a suicide prevention program in your school. *Network for Public Schools,* pp. 1, 4.

National Council on Aging. (2000, March). *Myths and Realities 2000 survey results.* Washington, DC: Author.

National Council on the Aging. (2002). American perceptions of aging in the 21st century: The NCOA's Continuing Study of the Myths and Realities of Aging (2002 update). Washington, DC: Author.

National Enuresis Society. (1995). *Enuresis.* [Fact sheet].

National High Blood Pressure Education Program Working Group on High Blood Pressure in Children and Adolescents. (2004). The fourth report on the diagnosis, evaluation, and treatment of high blood pressure in children and adolescents. *Pediatrics, 114*(2-Supp.), 555–576.

National Highway Traffic Safety Administration. (2003). *Traffic safety facts 2002: Young drivers.* Washington, DC: Author.

National Hospice and Palliative Care Organization. (2002). *NHPCO Facts and Figures.* Alexandria, VA: Author.

National Institute of Child Health and Development (NICHD). (1997; updated 1/12/00). *Sudden Infant Death Syndrome.* [Fact sheet] [Online]. Available: http://www.nichd.nih.gov/sids/sids_fact.html. Access date: January 30, 2001.

National Institute of Mental Health (NIMH). (1999a, April). *Suicide facts* [Online]. Washington, DC: Author. Available: http://www.nimh.nih.gov/research/suifact.htm.

National Institute of Mental Health (NIMH). (1999b, June 1). *Older adults: Depression and suicide facts* [Online]. Washington, DC: Author. Available: http:www.nimh.hin.gov/publicat/elderlydepsuicide.htm.

National Institute of Mental Health (NIMH). (2001a). *Helping children and adolescents cope with violence and disasters: Fact sheet* (NIH Publication No., 01-3518). Bethesda, MD: Author.

National Institute of Mental Health (NIMH). (2001b). *Teenage brain: A work in progress.* Available: http://www.nimh.gov/publicat/teenbrain.cfm. Access date: March 11, 2004.

National Institute of Neurological Disorders and Stroke. (1999, November 10). *Autism* [Fact sheet]. (NIH Publication No. 96–1877.) Bethesda, MD: National Institutes of Health.

National Institute on Aging (NIA). (1980). *Senility: Myth or madness.* Washington, DC: U.S. Government Printing Office.

National Institute on Aging (NIA). (1993). *Bound for good health: A collection of Age Pages.* Washington, DC: U.S. Government Printing Office.

National Institute on Aging (NIA). (1994). *Age page: Sexuality in later life.* Washington, DC: U.S. Government Printing Office.

National Institute on Aging (NIA). (1995). *Don't take it easy—exercise.* Washington, DC: U.S. Government Printing Office.

National Institute on Alcohol Abuse and Alcoholism (NIAAA). (1996, July). *Alcohol alert* (No. 33-1996 [PH 366]). Bethesda, MD: Author.

National Institute on Alcohol Abuse and Alcoholism (NIAAA). (1998, January). *Alcohol Alert,* No. 39-1998. Rockville, MD: Author.

National Institute on Alcohol Abuse and Alcoholism (NIAAA). (2002). *A call to action: Changing the culture of drinking at U.S. colleges.* Washington, DC: Author.

National Institutes of Health (NIH). (1992, December 7–9). Impotence (*NIH Consensus Statement, 10*[4]). Washington, DC: U.S. Government Printing Office.

National Institutes of Health Consensus Development Panel. (2001). National Institutes of Health Consensus Development conference statement: Phenylketonuria screening and management. October 16–18, 2000. *Pediatrics, 108*(4). 972–982.

National Library of Medicine. (2003a). Medical Encyclopedia: Antisocial personality disorder. [Online]. Retrieved April 23, 2005, from http://www.nlm.nih.gov/medlineplus/ency/article/000921.htm.

National Library of Medicine. (2003b). Medical Encyclopedia: Conduct disorder. [Online]. Retrieved April 23, 2005, from http://www.nlm.nih.gov/medlineplus/ency/article/000919.htm.

National Library of Medicine. (2004). Medical Encyclopedia: Oppositional defiant disorder. [Online]. Retrieved April 23, 2005, from http://www.nlm.nih.gov/medlineplus/ency/article/001537.htm.

National Parents' Resource Institute for Drug Education. (1999, September 8). *PRIDE surveys, 1998–99 national summary: Grades 6–12.* Bowling Green, KY: Author.

National Reading Panel. (2000). *Report of the National Reading Panel: Teaching children to read: An evidence-based assessment of the scientific research literature on reading and its implications for reading instruction: Reports of the subgroups.* Washington, DC: National Institute of Child Health and Human Development.

National Research Council (NRC). (1993a). *Losing generations: Adolescents in high-risk settings.* Washington, DC: National Academy Press.

National Research Council (NRC). (1993b). *Understanding child abuse and neglect.* Washington, DC: National Academy Press.

National Research Council (NRC). (1998). *Work-related musculoskeletal disorders: A review of the evidence.* Washington, DC: National Academy Press.

National Research Council (NRC). (2001). *Musculoskeletal disorders and the workplace: Low back and upper extremities.* Washington, DC: National Academy Press.

National Sleep Foundation. (2001). *2001 Sleep in America poll.* [Online]. Available: http://www.sleepfoundation.org/publications/2001poll.html. Access date: October 18, 2002.

National Television Violence Study. (1995). *Scientific Papers: 1994–1995.* Studio City, CA: Mediascope.

National Television Violence Study: Key findings and recommendations. (1996, March). *Young Children, 51*(3), 54–55.

Nawrot, T. S., Staessen, J. A., Gardner, J. P., & Aviv, A. (2004). Telomere length and possible link to X chromosome. *The Lancet, 363,* 507–510.

NCES Digest of Education Statistics (2001). [Online] Available: http://nces.ed.gov/pubsearch/pubsinfo.asp?pubid_2002130.

Needleman, H. L., Riess, J. A., Tobin, M. J., Biesecker, G. E., & Greenhouse, J. B. (1996). Bone lead levels and delinquent behavior. *Journal of the American Medical Association, 275,* 363–369.

Nef, S. Verma-Kurvari, S., Merenmies, J., Vassallt, J.-D., Efstratiadis, A., Accili, D., & Parada, L. F. (2003). Testis determination requires insulin receptor family function in mice. *Nature, 426,* 291–295.

Neimeyer, R. A. (2000). Searching for the meaning of meaning: Grief therapy and the process of reconstruction. *Death Studies, 24,* 541–558.

Neisser, U. (1976). General, academic, and artificial intelligence. In L. Resnick (Ed.), *Human intelligence: Perspectives on its theory and measurement* (pp. 179–189). Norwood, NJ: Ablex.

Neisser, U., Boodoo, G., Bouchard, T. J., Jr., Boykin, A. W., Brody, N., Ceci, S. J., Halpern, D. F., Loehlin, J. C., Perloff, R., Sternberg, R. J., & Urbina, S. (1996). Intelligence: Knowns and unknowns. *American Psychologist, 51*(2), 77–101.

Neitzel, C., & Stright, A. D. (2003). Relations between parents' scaffolding and children's academic self-regulation: Establishing a foundation of self-regulatory competence. *Journal of Family Psychology, 17,* 147–159.

Nelson, C. A. (1995). The ontogeny of human memory: A cognitive neuroscience perspective. *Developmental Psychology, 31,* 723–738.

Nelson, C. A., & Monk, C. S. (2001). The use of event-related potentials in the study of cognitive development. In C. A. Nelson & M. Luciana (Eds.), *Handbook of developmental cognitive neuroscience* (pp. 125–136). Cambridge, MA: MIT Press.

Nelson, C. A., Monk, C. S., Lin, J., Carver, L. J., Thomas, K. M., & Truwit, C. L. (2000). Functional neuroanatomy of spatial working memory in children. *Developmental Psychology, 36,* 109–116.

Nelson, J. (1994, December 18). Motive behind Carter's missions spark debate. *Chicago Sun-Times,* p. 40.

Nelson, K. (1992). Emergence of autobiographical memory at age 4. *Human Development, 35,* 172–177.

Nelson, K. (1993a). Events, narrative, memory: What develops? In C. Nelson (Ed.), *Memory and affect in development: The Minnesota Symposia on Child Psychology* (Vol. 26, pp. 1–24). Hillsdale, NJ: Erlbaum.

Nelson, K. (1993b). The psychological and social origins of autobiographical memory. *Psychological Science, 47,* 7–14.

Nelson, K. B., Dambrosia, J. M., Ting, T. Y., & Grether, J. K. (1996). Uncertain value of electronic fetal monitoring in predicting cerebral palsy. *New England Journal of Medicine, 334,* 613–618.

Nelson, L. J., & Marshall, M. F. (1998). *Ethical and legal analyses of three coercive policies aimed at substance abuse by pregnant women.*

Report published by the Robert Wood Johnson Substance Abuse Policy Research Foundation.

Nelson, M. E., Fiatarone, M. A., Morganti, C. M., Trice, I., Greenberg, R. A., & Evans, W. J. (1994). Effects of high-intensity strength training on multiple risk factors for osteoporotic fractures: A randomized controlled trial. *Journal of the American Medical Association, 272*, 1909–1914.

Neporent, L. (1999, January 12). Balancing exercises keep injuries at bay. *The New York Times*, p. D8.

Neppl, T. K., & Murray, A. D. (1997). Social dominance and play patterns among preschoolers: Gender comparisons. *Sex Roles, 36*, 381–393.

Ness, J., Ahmed, A., & Aronow, W. S. (2004). Demographics and payment characteristics of nursing home residents in the United States: A 23-year trend. *Journal of Gerontology: Medical Sciences, 59A*, 1213–1217.

Netherlands State Institute for War Documentation. (1989). *The diary of Anne Frank: The critical edition* (D. Barnouw & G. van der Stroom, Eds.; A. J. Pomerans & B. M. Mooyaart-Doubleday, Trans.). New York: Doubleday.

Neugarten, B. L. (1967). The awareness of middle age. In R. Owen (Ed.), *Middle age*. London: BBC.

Neugarten, B. L. (1968). Adult personality: Toward a psychology of the life cycle. In B. Neugarten (Ed.), *Middle age and aging*. Chicago: University of Chicago Press.

Neugarten, B. L. (1977). Personality and aging. In J. E. Birren & K. W. Schaie (Eds.), *Handbook of the psychology of aging and the social sciences*. New York: Van Nostrand Reinhold.

Neugarten, B. L., Havighurst, R., & Tobin, S. (1968). Personality and patterns of aging. In B. Neugarten (Ed.), *Middle age and aging*. Chicago: University of Chicago Press.

Neugarten, B. L., Moore, J. W., & Lowe, J. C. (1965). Age norms, age constraints, and adult socialization. *American Journal of Sociology, 70*, 710–717.

Neugarten, B. L., & Neugarten, D. A. (1987, May). The changing meanings of age. *Psychology Today*, pp. 29–33.

Neugebauer, R., Hoek, H. W., & Susser, E. (1999). Prenatal exposure to wartime famine and development of antisocial personality disorder in early adulthood. *Journal of the American Medical Association, 282*, 455–462.

Neville, H. J., & Bavelier, D. (1998). Neural organization and plasticity of language. *Current Opinion in Neurobiology, 8*(2), 254–258.

Newacheck, P. W., & Halfon, N. (2000). Prevalence, impact, and trends in childhood disability due to asthma. *Archives of Pediatrics and Adolescent Medicine, 154*, 287–293.

Newacheck, P. W., Stoddard, J. J., & McManus, M. (1993). Ethnocultural variations in the prevalence and impact of childhood chronic conditions. *Pediatrics, 91*, 1031–1047.

Newacheck, P. W., Strickland, B., Shonkoff, J. P., Perrin, J. M., McPherson, M., McManus, M., Lauver, C., Fox, H., & Arango, P. (1998). An epidemiologic profile of children with special health care needs. *Pediatrics, 102*, 117–123.

Newcomb, A. F., & Bagwell, C. L. (1995). Children's friendship relations: A meta-analytic review. *Psychological Bulletin, 117*(2), 306–347.

Newcomb, A. F., Bukowski, W. M., & Pattee, L. (1993). Children's peer relations: A meta-analytic review of popular, rejected, neglected, controversial, and average sociometric status. *Psychological Bulletin, 113*, 99–128.

Newman, A. J., Bavelier, D., Corina, D., Jezzard, P., & Neville, H. J. (2002). A critical period for right hemisphere recruitment in American Sign Language processing. *Nature Neuroscience, 5*(1), 76–80.

Newman, D. L., Caspi, A., Moffitt, T. E., & Silva, P. A. (1997). Antecedents of adult interpersonal functioning: Effects of individual differences in age 3 temperament. *Developmental Psychology, 33*, 206–217.

Newman, J. (1995). How breast milk protects newborns. *Scientific American, 273*, 76–79.

Newman, S. (2003). The living conditions of elderly Americans. *The Gerontologist, 43*, 99–109.

Newport, E., & Meier, R. (1985). The acquisition of American Sign Language. In D. Slobin (Ed.), *The cross-linguistic study of language acquisition* (Vol. 1, pp. 881–938). Hillsdale, NJ: Erlbaum.

Newport, E. L. (1991). Contrasting conceptions of the critical period for language. In S. Carey & R. Gelman (Eds.), *The epigenesis of mind: Essays on biology and cognition*. Hillsdale, NJ: Erlbaum.

Newport, E. L., Bavelier, D., & Neville, H. J. (2001). Critical thinking about critical periods: Perspectives on a critical period for language acquisition. In E. Dupoux, Emmanuel (Ed.), *Language, brain, and cognitive development: Essays in honor of Jacques Mehler* (pp. 481–502). Cambridge, MA: The MIT Press.

Newschaffer, C. J., Falb, M. D., & Gurney, J. G. (2005). National autism prevalence trends from United States special education data. *Pediatrics, 115*, e277–e282.

Newsweek Poll. (2000). *Post super Tuesday/gays and lesbians (United States)*. Storrs, CT: Roper Center for Public Opinion Research.

Newswise. (2004, November 16). High stress doubles risk of painful periods. [Online]. Available: http://www.newswise.com/p/articles/view/508336. Access date: November 18, 2004.

NFO Research, Inc. (1999). *AARP/Modern Maturity sexuality survey: Summary of findings*. [Online]. Available: http://research.aarp.org/health/mmsexsurvey1.html.

NICHD Early Child Care Research Network. (1997). The effects of infant child care on infant-mother attachment security: Results of the NICHD study of early child care. *Child Development, 68*, 860–879.

NICHD Early Child Care Research Network. (1998a). Early child care and self-control, compliance and problem behavior at twenty-four and thirty-six months. *Child Development, 69*, 1145–1170.

NICHD Early Child Care Research Network. (1998b). Relations between family predictors and child outcomes: Are they weaker for children in child care? *Developmental Psychology, 34*, 1119–1128.

NICHD Early Child Care Research Network. (1998c, November). *When childcare classrooms meet recommended guidelines for quality*. Paper presented at the meeting of the National Association for the Education of Young People.

NICHD Early Child Care Research Network. (1999a). Child outcomes when child care center classes meet recommended standards for quality. *American Journal of Public Health, 89*, 1072–1077.

NICHD Early Child Care Research Network. (1999b). Chronicity of maternal depressive symptoms, maternal sensitivity, and child functioning at 36 months. *Developmental Psychology, 35*, 1297–1310.

NICHD Early Child Care Research Network. (2000). The relation of child care to cognitive and language development. *Child Development, 71*, 960–980.

NICHD Early Child Care Research Network. (2001a). Child care and children's peer interaction at 24 and 36 months: The NICHD Study of Early Child Care. *Child Development, 72*, 1478–1500.

NICHD Early Child Care Research Network. (2001b). Child-care and family predictors of preschool attachment and stability from infancy. *Developmental Psychology, 37*, 847–862.

NICHD Early Child Care Research Network. (2002). Child-care structure → process → outcome: Direct and indirect effects of childcare quality on young children's development. *Psychological Science, 13*, 199–206.

NICHD Early Child Care Research Network. (2003). Does amount of time spent in child care predict socioemotional adjustment during the transition to kindergarten? *Child Development, 74*, 976–1005.

NICHD Early Child Care Research Network. (2004a). Are child developmental outcomes related to before- and after-school care arrangement? Results from the NICHD Study of Early Child Care. *Child Development 75*, 280–295.

NICHD Early Child Care Research Network. (2004b). Does class size in first grade relate to children's academic and social performance or observed classroom processes? *Developmental Psychology, 40*, 651–664.

NICHD Early Child Care Research Network. (2005). Predicting individual differences in attention, memory, and planning in first graders from experiences at home, child care, and school. *Developmental Psychology, 41*, 99–114.

NICHD Early Child Care Research Network & Duncan, G. J. (2003). Modeling the impacts of child care quality on children's preschool cognitive development. *Child Development, 74*, 1454–1475.

Nielsen, K., McSherry, G., Petru, A., Frederick, T., Wara, D., Bryson, Y., Martin, N., Hutto, C., Ammann, A. J., Grubman, S., Oleske, J., & Scott, G. B. (1997). A descriptive survey of pediatric human immunodeficiency virus-infected, long-term survivors [Online]. *Pediatrics, 99*. Available: http://www.pediatrics.org/cgi/content/full/99/4/e4.

Nielsen, M., Dissanayake, C., & Kashima, Y. (2003). A longitudinal investigation of self-other discrimination and the emergence of mirror self-recognition. *Infant Behavior & Development, 26*, 213–226.

NIH Consensus Development Panel on Osteoporosis Prevention, Diagnosis, and Therapy. (2001). Osteoporosis prevention, diagnosis, and therapy. *Journal of the American Medical Association, 285*, 785–794.

Nin, A. (1971). *The Diaries of Anaïs Nin* (Vol. IV). New York: Harcourt.

Nisan, M., & Kohlberg, L. (1982). Universality and variation in moral judgment: A longitudinal and cross-sectional study in Turkey. *Child Development, 53*, 865–876.

Nisbett, R. E. (1998). Race, genetics, and IQ. In C. Jencks & M. Phillips (Eds.), *The Black-White test score gap* (pp. 86–102). Washington, DC: Brookings Institution.

Nishimura, H., Hashikawa, K., Doi, K., Iwaki, T., Watanabe, Y., Kusuoka, H., Nishimura, T., & Kubo, T. (1999). Sign language 'heard' in the auditory cortex. *Nature, 397*, 116.

Niskar, A. S., Kieszak, S. M., Holmes, A., Esteban, E., Rubin, C., & Brody D. J. (1998). Prevalence of hearing loss among children 6 to 19 years of age: The Third National Health and Nutrition Examination Survey. *Journal of the American Medical Association, 279*, 1071–1075.

Nix, R. L., Pinderhughes, E. E., Dodge, K. A., Bates, J. E., Pettit, G. S., & McFadyen-Ketchum, S. A. (1999). The relation between mothers' hostile attribution tendencies and children's externalizing behavior problems: The mediating role of mothers' harsh discipline practices. *Child Development, 70*(4), 896–909.

Nixon, K., & Crews, F. T. (2004). Temporally specific burst in cell proliferation increases hippocampal neurogenesis in protracted abstinence from alcohol. *Journal of Neuroscience, 24*, 9714-9722.

Nobre, A. C., & Plunkett, K. (1997). The neural system of language: Structure and development. *Current Opinion in Neurobiology, 7*, 262–268.

Noël, P. H., Williams, J. W., Unutzer, J., Worchel, J., Lee, S., Cornell, J., Katon, W., Harpole, L. H., & Hunkeler, E. (2004). Depression and comorbid illness in elderly primary care patients: Impact on multiple domains of health status and well-being. *Annals of Family Medicine, 2*, 555–562.

Nojima, M. (1994). Japan's approach to continuing education for senior citizens. *Educational Gerontology, 20*, 463–471.

Nomaguchi, K. M. & Milkie, M. A. (2003). Costs and rewards of children: The effects of becoming a parent on adults' lives. *Journal of Marriage and Family, 65*, 356–374.

Noone, K. (2000). Ann Bancroft, polar explorer. *My Prime Time.* [Online]. Available: http://www.myprimetime.com/misc/bae_abpro/index.shtml. Access date: April 4, 2002.

Norton, A. J., & Moorman, J. E. (1987). Current trends in marriage and divorce among American women. *Journal of Marriage and the Family, 49*(1), 3–14.

Notzon, F. C., Komarov, Y. M., Ermakov, S. P., Sempos, C. T., Marks, J. S., & Sempos, E. V. (1998). Causes of declining life expectancy in Russia. *Journal of the American Medical Association, 279*, 793–800.

Nourot, P. M. (1998). Sociodramatic play: Pretending together. In D. P. Fromberg & D. Bergen (Eds.), *Play from birth to twelve and beyond: Contexts, perspectives, and meanings* (pp. 378–391). New York: Garland.

Nozyce, M., Hittelman, J., Muenz, L., Durako, S. J., Fischer, M. L., & Willoughby, A. (1994). Effect of perinatally acquired human immunodeficiency virus infection on neurodevelopment in children during the first two years of life. *Pediatrics, 94*, 883–891.

Nugent, J. K., Keefer, C., O'Brien, S., Johnson, L., & Blanchard, Y. (2005). The Newborn Behavioral Observation System. Brazelton Institute, Children's Hospital, Boston.

Nugent, J. K., Lester, B. M., Greene, S. M., Wieczorek-Deering, D., & O'Mahony, P. (1996). The effects of maternal alcohol consumption and cigarette smoking during pregnancy on acoustic cry analysis. *Child Development, 67*, 1806–1815.

Nugent, T. (1999, September). At risk: 4 million students with asthma: Quick access to rescue inhalers critical for school children. *AAP News*, pp. 1, 10.

Nuland, S. B. (2000). Physician-assisted suicide and euthanasia in practice. *New England Journal of Medicine, 342*, 583–584.

Nurnberg, H. G., Hensley, P. L., Gelenberg, A. J., Fava, M., Lauriello, J., & Paine, S. (2003). Treatment of antidepressant-associated sexual dysfunction with sildenafil. *Journal of the American Medical Association, 289*, 56–64.

Nurnberger, J. I., Foroud, T., Flury, L., Su, J., Meyer, E. T., Hu, K., Crowe, R., Edenberg, H., Goate, A., Bierut, L., Reich, T., Schuckit, M., & Reich, W. (2001). Evidence for a locus on chromosome 1 that influences vulnerability to alcoholism and affective disorder. *American Journal of Psychiatry, 158*, 718–724.

Nussbaum, R. L. (1998). Putting the parkin into Parkinson's. *Nature, 392*, 544–545.

O'Brien, C. M., & Jeffery, H. E. (2002). Sleep deprivation, disorganization and fragmentation during opiate withdrawal in newborns. *Pediatric Child Health, 38*, 66–71.

O'Connor, B. P., & Vallerand, R. J. (1998). Psychological adjustment variables as predictors of mortality among nursing home residents. *Psychology and Aging, 13*(3), 368–374.

O'Connor, T., Heron, J., Golding, J., Beveridge, M., & Glover, V. (2002). Maternal antenatal anxiety and children's behavioural/emotional problems at 4 years. *British Journal of Psychiatry, 180*, 502–508.

O'Neill, G., Summer, L, & Shirey, L. (1999). Hearing loss: A growing problem that affects quality of life. Washington, DC: National Academy on an Aging Society.

O'Rahilly, S. (1998). Life without leptin. *Nature, 392*, 330–331.

O'Sullivan, J. T., Howe, M. L., & Marche, T. A. (1996). Children's beliefs about long-term retention. *Child Development, 67*, 2989–3009.

Oakes, L. M. (1994). Development of infants' use of continuity cues in their perception of causality. *Developmental Psychology, 30*, 869–879.

Oakes, L. M., Coppage, D. J., & Dingel, A. (1997). By land or by sea: The role of perceptual similarity in infants' categorization of animals. *Developmental Psychology, 33*, 396–407.

Oakes, L. M., & Madole, K. L. (2000). The future of infant categorization research: A process-oriented approach. *Child Development, 71*, 119–126.

Ochsner, K. N., & Lieberman, M. D. (2001). The emergence of social cognitive neuroscience. *American Psychologist, 56*, 717–734.

Offer, D. (1987). In defense of adolescents. *Journal of the American Medical Association, 257*, 3407–3408.

Offer, D., & Church, R. B. (1991). Generation gap. In R. M. Lerner, A. C. Petersen, & J. Brooks-Gunn (Eds.), *Encyclopedia of adolescence* (pp. 397–399). New York: Garland.

Offer, D., Kaiz, M., Ostrov, E., & Albert, D. B. (2002). Continuity in family constellation. *Adolescent and Family Health, 3*, 3–8.

Offer, D., Offer, M. K., & Ostrov, E. (2004). *Regular guys: 34 years beyond adolescence.* Dordrecht, Netherlands: Kluwer Academic.

Offer, D., Ostrov, E., & Howard, K. I. (1989). Adolescence: What is normal? *American Journal of Diseases of Children, 143*, 731–736.

Offer, D., Ostrov, E., Howard, K. I., & Atkinson, R. (1988). *The teenage world: Adolescents' self-image in ten countries.* New York: Plenum.

Offer, D., & Schonert-Reichl, K. A. (1992). Debunking the myths of adolescence: Findings from recent research. *Journal of the American Academy of Child and Adolescent Psychiatry, 31*, 1003–1014.

Office of Minority Health, Centers for Disease Control and Prevention. (2005). Health disparities experienced by black or African Americans—United States. *Morbidity and Mortality Weekly Report, 54*, 1–3.

Offit, P. A., Quarles, J., Gerber, M. A., Hackett, C. J., Marcuse, E. K., Kollman, T. R., Gellin, B. G., & Landry, S. (2002). Addressing parents' concerns: Do multiple vaccines overwhelm or weaken the infant's immune system? *Pediatrics, 109*, 124–129.

Ogden, C. L., Flegal, K. M., Carroll, M. D., & Johnson, C. L. (2002). Prevalence and trends in overweight among US children and adolescents, 1999–2000. *Journal of the American Medical Association, 288*, 1728–1732.

Ogden, C. L., Fryar, C. D., Carroll, M. D., & Flegal, K. M. (2004). Mean body weight, height, and body mass index, United States 1960–2002. Advance data from *Vital and Health Statistics*, No. 347. Hyattsville, MD: National Center for Health Statistics.

Okamoto, K. & Tanaka, Y. (2004). Subjective usefulness and 6-year mortality risks among elderly persons in Japan. *Journal of Gerontology: Psychological Sciences, 59B*, P246–P249.

Olds, D. L., Henderson, C. R., & Tatelbaum, R. (1994a). Intellectual impairment in children of women who smoke cigarettes during pregnancy. *Pediatrics, 93*, 221–227.

Olds, D. L., Henderson, C. R., & Tatelbaum, R. (1994b). Prevention of intellectual impairment in children of women who smoke cigarettes during pregnancy. *Pediatrics, 93,* 228–233.

Ollendick, T. H., Yang, B., King, N. J., Dong, Q., & Akande, A. (1996). Fears in American, Australian, Chinese, and Nigerian children and adolescents: A crosscultural study. *Journal of Child Psychology and Psychiatry, 37,* 213–220.

Olmsted, P. P., & Weikart, D. P. (Eds.). (1994). *Family speak: Early childhood care and education in eleven countries.* Ypsilanti, MI: High/Scope.

Olshansky, S. J., Carnes, B. A., & Desesquelles, A. (2001). Prospects for human longevity. *Science, 291*(5508), 1491–1492.

Olshansky, S. J. Hayflick, L., & Carnes, B. A. (2002a). No truth to the fountain of youth. *Scientific American, 286,* 92–95.

Olshansky, S. J., Hayflick, L., & Carnes, B. A. (2002b). The truth about human aging. *Scientific American.* [Online]. Available: http://www.sciam.com/explorations/ 2002/051302aging. Access date: August 23, 2002.

Olshansky, S. J., Hayflick, L., & Perls, T. T. (2004). Anti-aging medicine: The hype and the reality—Part I. *Journal of Gerontology: Biological Sciences, 59A,* 513–514.

Olshansky, S. J., Passaro, D. J., Hershow, R. C., Layden, J., Carnes, B. A., Brody, J., Hayflick, L., Butler, R. N., Allison, D. B., & Ludwig, D. S. (2005). A potential decline in life expectancy in the United States in the 21st century. *New England Journal of Medicine, 352,* 1138–1145.

Olthof, T., Schouten, A., Kuiper, H., Stegge, H., & Jennekens-Schinkel, A. (2000). Shame and guilt in children: Differential situational antecedents and experiential correlates. *British Journal of Developmental Psychology, 18,* 51–64.

Olweus, D. (1995). Bullying or peer abuse at school: Facts and intervention. *Current Directions in Psychological Science, 4,* 196–200.

Orbuch, T. L., House, J. S., Mero, R. P., & Webster, P. S. (1996). Marital quality over the life course. *Social Psychology Quarterly, 59,* 162–171.

Orenstein, P. (2002, April 21). Mourning my miscarriage. Available: http://www.NYTimes.com.

Orentlicher, D. (1996). The legalization of physician-assisted suicide. *New England Journal of Medicine, 335,* 663–667.

Organ Procurement & Transplantation Network (OPTN). (2005). Data. [Online]. Retrieved from http://www.optn.org/data/ on March 27, 2005.

Organisation for Economic Cooperation and Development. (2004). Education at a glance: OECD indicators—2004. *Education & Skills, 2004* (14), 1–456.

Organization for Economic Co-Operation and Development. (1998). *Maintaining prosperity in an ageing society.* Paris: Author.

Oropesa, R. S. & Landale, N. S. (2004). The future of marriage and Hispanics. *Journal of Marriage and Family, 66,* 901–920.

Orr, W. C., & Sohal, R. S. (1994). Extension of life-span by overexpression of superoxide dimutase and catylase in drosphila melanogaster. *Science, 263,* 1128–1130.

Osborn, A. (2002, April 1). Mercy killing now legal in Netherlands. *The Guardian.* [Online]. Available: http://www.nvve.ni/english/info/euth.legal_guardian01-04-02.htm. Access date: July 31, 2002.

Osgood, D. W., Ruth, G., Eccles, J., Jacobs, J., & Barber, B. (2005). Six paths to adulthood: Fast starters, parents without careers, educated partners, educated singles, working singles, and slow starters. In R. A. Settersten, Jr., F. F. Furstenberg, Jr., & R. G. Rumbaut (Eds.), *On the frontier of adulthood: Theory, research, and public policy* (pp. 320–355). (John D. and Catherine T. MacArthur Foundation Series on Mental Health and Development, Research Network on Transitions to Adulthood and Public Policy.) Chicago: University of Chicago Press.

Oshima, S. (1996, July 5). Japan: Feeling the strains of an aging population. *Science,* pp. 44–45.

Oshima-Takane, Y., Goodz, E., & Derevensky, J. L. (1996). Birth order effects on early language development: Do secondborn children learn from overheard speech? *Child Development, 67,* 621–634.

Ossorio, P., & Duster, T. (2005). Race and genetics: Controversies in biomedical, behavioral, and forensic sciences. *American Psychologist, 60,* 115–128.

Ostir, G. V., Ottenbacher, K. J., & Markides, K. S. (2004). Onset of frailty in older adults and the protective role of positive affect. *Psychology and Aging, 19,* 402–408.

Otsuka, R., Watanabe, H., Hirata, K., Tokai, K., Muro, T., Yoshiyama, M., Takeuchi, K., & Yoshikawa, J. (2001). Acute effects of passive smoking on the coronary circulation in healthy young adults. *Journal of the American Medical Association, 286,* 436–441.

Ott, A., Slooter, A. J. C., Hofman, A., Van Harskamp, F.,Witteman, J. C. M., Van Broeckhoven, C., Van Duijn, C. M., & Breteler, M. M. B. (1998). Smoking and risk of dementia and Alzheimer's disease in a population-based cohort study. *Lancet, 351,* 1840–1843.

Otten, M. W., Teutsch, S. M., Williamson, D. F., & Marks, J. S. (1990). The effect of known risk factors on the excess mortality of black adults in the United States. *Journal of the American Medical Association, 263*(6), 845–850.

Owen, C. G., Whincup, P. H., Odoki, K., Gilg, J. A., & Cook, D. G. (2002). Infant feeding and blood cholesterol: A study in adolescents and a systematic review. *Pediatrics, 110,* 597–608.

Owens, R. E. (1996). *Language development* (4th ed.). Boston: Allyn and Bacon.

Ozick, C. (2003, June 16 & 23). What Helen Keller saw: The making of a writer. *New Yorker,* pp. 188–196.

Padden, C. A. (1996). Early bilingual lives of deaf children. In I. Parasnis (Ed.), *Cultural and language diversity and the deaf experience* (pp. 99–116). New York: Cambridge University Press.

Padilla, A. M., Lindholm, K. J., Chen, A., Durán, R., Hakuta, K., Lambert, W., & Tucker, G. R. (1991). The English-only movement: Myths, reality, and implications for psychology. *American Psychologist, 46*(2), 120–130.

Padovani, A., Borroni, B., Colciaghi, F., Pettenati, C., Cottini, E., Agosti, C., Lenzi, G. L., Caltagirone C., Trabucchi, M., Cattabeni, F., & Di Luca, M. (2002). Abnormalities in the pattern of platelet amyloid precursor protein forms in patients with mild cognitive impairment and Alzheimer disease. *Archives of Neurology, 59,* 71–75.

Palella, F. J., Delaney, K. M., Moorman, A. C., Loveless, M. O., Fuhrer, J., Satten, G. A., Aschman, D. J., Holmberg, S. D., & the HIV Outpatient Study investigators. (1998). Declining morbidity and mortality among patients with advanced human immunodeficiency virus infection. *New England Journal of Medicine, 358,* 853–860.

Pally, R. (1997). How brain development is shaped by genetic and environmental factors. *International Journal of Psychoanalysis, 78,* 587–593.

Pamuk, E., Makuc, D., Heck, K., Reuben, C., & Lochner, K. (1998). Socioeconomic status and health chartbook. In *Health, United States, 1998.* Hyattsville, MD: National Center for Health Statistics.

Panigrahy, A., Filiano, J., Sleeper, L. A., Mandell, F., Vales-Dapena, M., Krous, H. F., Rava, L. A., Foley, E., White, W. F., & Kinney, H. C. (2000). Decreased serotonergic receptor binding in rhombic lip-derived regions of the medulla oblongata in the sudden infant death syndrome. *Journal of Neuropathology and Experimental Neurology, 59,* 377–384.

Papalia, D. (1972). The status of several conservation abilities across the lifespan. *Human Development, 15,* 229–243.

Papernow, P. (1993). *Becoming a stepfamily: Patterns of development in remarried families.* San Francisco: Jossey-Bass.

Parasuraman, R., Greenwood, P. M., & Sunderland, T. (2002). The Apolilpoprotein E gene, attention, and brain function. *Neuropsychology, 16,* 254–274.

Park, S., Belsky, J., Putnam, S., & Crnic, K. (1997). Infant emotionality, parenting, and 3-year inhibition: Exploring stability and lawful discontinuity in a male sample. *Developmental Psychology, 33,* 218–227.

Parke, R. D. (2004). The Society for Research in Child Development at 70: Progress and promise. *Child Development, 75,* 1–24.

Parke, R. D., & Buriel, R. (1998). Socialization in the family: Ethnic and ecological perspectives. In W. Damon (Series Ed.) & N. Eisenberg (Vol. Ed.), *Handbook of child psychology: Vol. 3. Social, emotional, and personality development* (5th ed., pp. 463–552). New York: Wiley.

Parke, R. D., Coltrane, S., Duffy, S., Buriel, R., Dennis, J., Powers, J., French, S., & Widaman, K. F., (2004). Economic stress, parenting, and child adjustment in Mexican American and European American families. *Child Development, 75,* 1632–1656.

Parke, R. D., Grossman, K., & Tinsley, R. (1981). Father-mother-infant interaction in the newborn period: A German-American comparison. In T. M. Field, A. M. Sostek, P. Viete, & P. H. Leideman (Eds.), *Culture and early interaction*. Hillsdale, NJ: Erlbaum.

Parke, R. D., Ornstein, P. A., Rieser, J. J., & Zahn-Waxler, C. (1994). The past as prologue: An overview of a century of developmental psychology. In R. D. Parke, P. A. Ornstein, J. J. Rieser, & C. Zahn-Waxler (Eds.), *A century of developmental psychology* (pp. 1–70). Washington, DC: American Psychological Association.

Parker, J. G., & Asher, S. R. (1987). Peer relations and later personal adjustment: Are low-accepted children at risk? *Psychological Bulletin, 102*, 357–389.

Parker, L., Pearce, M. S., Dickinson, H. O., Aitkin, M., & Craft, A. W. (1999). Stillbirths among offspring of male radiation workers at Sellafield nuclear reprocessing plant. *Lancet, 354*, 1407–1414.

Parker, S. K., Schwartz, B., Todd, J., & Pickering, L. K. (2004). Thimerosal-containing vaccines and autistic spectrum disorder: A critical review of published original data. *Pediatrics, 114*, 793–804.

Parkes, T. L., Elia, A. J., Dickinson, D., Hilliker, A. J., Phillips, J. P., & Boulianne, G. L. (1998). Extension of Drosophila lifespan by overexpression of human SOD1 in motorneurons. *Nature Genetics, 19*, 171–174.

Parnes, H. S., & Sommers, D. G. (1994). Shunning retirement: Work experience of men in their seventies and early eighties. *Journal of Gerontology: Social Sciences, 49*, S117–124.

Parrish, K. M., Holt, V. L., Easterling, T. R., Connell, F. A., & LeGerfo, J. P. (1994). Effect of changes in maternal age, parity, and birth weight distribution on primary cesarean delivery rates. *Journal of the American Medical Association, 271*, 443–447.

Parten, M. B. (1932). Social play among preschool children. Journal of Abnormal and Social *Psychology, 27*, 243–269.

Pascarella, E. T., Edison, M. I., Nora, A., Hagedorn, L. S., & Terenzini, P. T. (1998). Does work inhibit cognitive development during college? *Educational Evaluation and Policy Analysis, 20*, 75–93.

Pasterski, V. L., Geffner, M. E., Brain, C., Hindmarsh, P., Brook, C., & Hines, M. (2005). Prenatal hormones and postnatal socialization by parents as determinants of male-typical toy play in girls with congenital adrenal hyperplasia. *Child Development, 76*, 264–278.

Pastor, P. N., Makuc, D. M., Reuben, C., & Xia, H. (2002). Chartbook on trends in the health of Americans. In *Health, United States, 2002*. Hyattsville, MD: National Center for Health Statistics.

Pasupathi, M., Staudinger U. M., & Baltes, P. B. (2001). Seeds of wisdom: Adolescents' knowledge and judgment about difficult life problems. *Developmental Psychology, 37*(3), 351–361.

Patel, H., Rosengren, A., & Ekman, I. (2004). Symptoms in acute coronary syndromes: Does sex make a difference? *American Heart Journal, 148*, 27–33.

Patenaude, A. F., Guttmacher, A. E., & Collins, F. S. (2002). Genetic testing and psychology: New roles, new responsibilities. *American Psychologist, 57*, 271–282.

Patrick, K., Norman, G. J., Calfas, K. J., Sallis, J. F., Zabinski, M. F., Rupp, J., & Cella, J. (2004). Diet, physical activity, and sedentary behaviors as risk factors for overweight in adolescence. *Archives of Pediatric Adolescent Medicine, 158*, 385–390.

Patterson, C. J. (1992). Children of lesbian and gay parents. *Child Development, 63*, 1025–1042.

Patterson, C. J. (1995a). Lesbian mothers, gay fathers, and their children. In A. R. D'Augelli & C. J. Patterson (Eds.), *Lesbian, gay, and bisexual identities over the lifespan: Psychological perspectives* (pp. 293–320). New York: Oxford University Press.

Patterson, C. J. (1995b). Sexual orientation and human development: An overview. *Developmental Psychology, 31*, 3–11.

Patterson, C. J. (1997). Children of gay and lesbian parents. In T. H. Ollendick & R. J. Prinz (Eds.), *Advances in clinical child psychology* (Vol. 19, pp. 235–282). New York: Plenum.

Patterson, G. R., DeBaryshe, B. D., & Ramsey, E. (1989). A developmental perspective on antisocial behavior. *American Psychologist, 44*(2), 329–335.

Patterson, G. R., Reid, J. B., & Dishion, T. J. (1992). *Antisocial boys*. Eugene, OR: Castalia.

Pauen, S. (2002). Evidence for knowledge-based category discrimination in infancy. *Child Development, 73*, 1016–1033.

Paul, E. L. (1997). A longitudinal analysis of midlife interpersonal relationships and well-being. In M. E. Lachman & J. B. James (Eds.), *Multiple paths of midlife development* (pp. 171–206). Chicago: University of Chicago Press.

Pearce, M. J., Jones, S. M., Schwab-Stone, M. E., & Ruchkin, V. (2003). The protective effects of religiousness and parent involvement on the development of conduct problems among youth exposed to violence. *Child Development, 74*, 1682–1696.

Pearman, A., & Storandt, M. (2004). Predictors of subjective memory in older adults. *Journal of Gerontology: Psychological Sciences, 59B*, P4–P6.

Pearson, H. (2002, February 12). Study refines breast cancer risks. *Nature Science Update.* [Online]. Available: http://www.nature.com/nsu/020211/020211–8. html. Access date: February 19, 2002.

Pearson, J. D., Morell, C. H., Gordon-Salant, S., Brant, L. J., Metter, E. J., Klein, L., & Fozard, J. L. (1995). Gender differences in a longitudinal study of age-associated hearing loss. *Journal of the Acoustical Society of America, 97*, 1196–1205.

Peeters, A., Barendregt, J. J.,Willekens, F., Mackenbach, J. P., Al Mamun, A., & Bonneux, L., for NEDCOM, the Netherlands

Epidemiology and Demography Compression of Morbidity Research Group (2003). Obesity in adulthood and its consequences for life expectancy. *Annals of Internal Medicine, 138*, 24–32.

Peisner-Feinberg, E. S., Burchinal, M. R., Clifford, R. M., Culkin, M. L., Howes, C., Kagan, S. L., & Yazejian, N. (2001). The relation of preschool child-care quality to children's cognitive and social developmental trajectories through second grade. *Child Development, 72*, 1534–1553.

Pellegrini, A. D. (1998). Rough-and-tumble play from childhood through adolescence. In D. P. Fromberg & D. Bergen (Eds.), *Play from birth to twelve and beyond: Contexts, perspectives, and meanings* (pp. 401–408). New York: Garland.

Pellegrini, A. D., & Long, J. D. (2002). A longitudinal study of bullying, dominance, and victimization during the transition from primary school through secondary school. *British Journal of Developmental Psychology, 20*, 259–280.

Pellegrini, A. D., Kato, K., Blatchford, P., & Baines E. (2002). A short-term longitudinal study of children's playground games across the first year of school: Implications for social competence and adjustment to school. *American Educational Research Journal, 39*, 991–1015.

Pellegrini, A. D., & Smith, P. K. (1998). Physical activity play: The nature and function of a neglected aspect of play. *Child Development, 69*, 577–598.

Pelleymounter, N. A., Cullen, M. J., Baker, M. B., Hecht, R., Winters, D., Boone, T., & Collins, F. (1995). Effects of the obese gene product on body regulation in ob/ob mice. *Science, 269*, 540–543.

Pellicano, E., & Rhodes, G. (2003). Holistic processing of faces in preschool children and adults. *Psychological Science, 14*, 618–622.

Penning, M. J. (1998). In the middle: Parental caregiving in the context of other roles. *Journal of Gerontology: Social Sciences, 53B*, S188–S197.

Pennington, B. F., Moon, J., Edgin, J., Stedron, J., & Nadel, L. (2003). The neuropsychology of Down Syndrome: Evidence for hippocampal dysfunction. *Child Development, 74*, 75–93.

Penninx, B. W. J. H., Guralnik, J. M., Ferrucci, L., Simonsick, E. M., Deeg, D. J. H., & Wallace, R. B. (1998). Depressive symptoms and physical decline in community-dwelling older persons. *Journal of the American Medical Association, 279*, 1720–1726.

Pennisi, E. (1998). Single gene controls fruit fly life-span. *Science, 282*, 856.

Peplau, L. A. (2003). Human sexuality: How do men and women differ? *Current Directions in Psychological Science, 12*(2), 37–40.

Pepper, S. C. (1942). *World hypotheses*. Berkeley: University of California Press.

Pepper, S. C. (1961). *World hypotheses*. Berkeley: University of California Press.

Pereira, M. A. Kartashov, A. I., Ebbeling, C. B., Van Horn, L., Slattery, M. L., Jacobs, Jr., D. R., & Ludwig, D. S. (2005). Fast-food habits, weight gain, and insulin resistance (the

CARDIA study): 15-year prospective analysis. *Lancet, 365,* 36–42.

Perera, F. P., Rauh, V., Whyatt, R. M., Tsai, W.-Y., Bernert, J. T., Tu, Y.-H., Andrews, H., Ramirez, J., Qu, L., & Tang, D. (2004). Molecular evidence of an interaction between prenatal environmental exposures and birth outcomes in a multiethnic population. *Environmental Health Perspectives, 112,* 626–630.

Perera, F. P., Tang, D., Tu, Y.-H., Cruz, L. A., Borjas, M., Bernert, T., & Whyatt, R. M. (2004). Biomarkers in maternal and newborn blood indicate heightened fetal susceptibility to procarcinogenic DNA damage. *Environmental Health Perspectives, 112,* 1133–1136.

Perera, V. (1995). Surviving affliction. [Online.] Available: http://www.metroactive.com/papers/metro/12.14.95/allende-9550.html. Access date: April 1, 2002.

Pérez-Stable, E. J., Herrera, B., Jacob, P., III, & Benowitz, N. L. (1998). Nicotine metabolism and intake in black and white smokers. *Journal of the American Medical Association, 280,* 152–156.

Perlmutter, M., Kaplan, M., & Nyquist, L. (1990). Development of adaptive competence in adulthood. *Human Development, 33,* 185–197.

Perls, T., Kunkel, L. M., & Puca, A. (2002a). The genetics of aging. *Current Opinion in Genetics and Development, 12,* 362–369.

Perls, T., Kunkel, L. M., & Puca, A. A. (2002b). The genetics of exceptional human longevity. *Journal of the American Geriatric Society, 50,* 359–368.

Perls, T. T. (2004). Anti-aging quackery: Human growth hormone and tricks of the trade—More dangerous than ever. *Journal of Gerontology: Biological Sciences, 59A,* 682–691.

Perls, T. T., Alpert, L., & Fretts, R. C. (1997). Middle-aged mothers live longer. *Nature, 389,* 133.

Perls, T. T., Hutter-Silver, M., & Lauerman, J. F. (1999). *Living to 100: Lessons in living to your maximum potential at any age.* New York: Basic Books.

Perls, T. T., Wilmoth, J., Levenson, R., Drinkwater, M., Cohen, M., Bogan, H., Joyce, E., Brewster, S., Kunkel, L., & Puca, A. (2002). Life-long sustained mortality advantage of siblings of centenarians. *Proceedings of the National Academy of Sciences, 99,* 8442–8447.

Perozynski, L., & Kramer, L. (1999). Parental beliefs about managing sibling conflict. *Developmental Psychology, 35,* 489–499.

Perrin, E. C. and the Committee on Psychosocial Aspects of Child and Family Health. (2002). Technical report: Coparent or second-parent adoption by same-sex parents. *Pediatrics, 109*(2), 341–344.

Perrucci, C. C., Perrucci, R., & Targ, D. B. (1988). *Plant closings.* New York: Aldine.

Perry, W. G. (1970). *Forms of intellectual and ethical development in the college years.* New York: Holt.

Pérusse, L., Chagnon, Y. C., Weisnagel, J., & Bouchard, C. (1999). The human obesity gene map: The 1998 update. *Obesity Research, 7,* 111–129.

Pesonen, A., Raikkonen, K, Keltikangas-Jarvinen, L., Strandberg, T., & Jarvenpaa, A. (2003). Parental perception of infant temperament: Does parents' joint attachment matter? *Infant Behavior & Development, 26,* 167–182.

Peter D. Hart Research Associates. (1999). *The new face of retirement.* Washington, DC: Author.

Peter, K., & Horn, L. (2005). *Gender differences in participation and completion of undergraduate education and how they have changed over time* (NCES 2005-169). Washington, DC: U.S. Government Printing Office.

Peters, R. D., Kloeppel, A. E., Fox, E., Thomas, M. L., Thorne, D. R., Sing, H. C., & Balwinski, S. M. (1994). *Effects of partial and total sleep deprivation on driving performance.* Washington, DC: Federal Highway Administration.

Peters, V., Liu, K.-L., Dominguez, K., Frederick, T., Melville, S., Hsu, H.-W., Ortiz, I., Rakusan, T., Gill, B., & Thomas, P. (2003). Missed opportunities for perinatal HIV prevention among HIV-exposed infants born 1996–2000, Pediatric Spectrum of HIV Disease Cohort. *Pediatrics, 111,* 1186–1191.

Petersen, A. C. (1993). Presidential address: Creating adolescents: The role of context and process in developmental transitions. *Journal of Research on Adolescents, 3*(1), 1–18.

Petersen, A. C., Compas, B. E., Brooks-Gunn, J., Stemmler, M., Ey, S., & Grant, K. E. (1993). Depression in adolescence. *American Psychologist, 48*(2), 155–168.

Petersen, R. C., Thomas, R. G., Grundman, M., Bennett, D., Doody, R., Ferris, S., Galasko, D., Jin, S., Kaye, J., Levey, A., Pfeiffer, E., Sano, M., van Dyck, C. H., & Thal, L. J. for the Alzheimer's Disease Cooperative Study Group. (2005). Vitamin E and donepezil for the treatment of mild cognitive impairment. *New England Journal of Medicine, 352,* 2379–2388.

Peterson, B. E. (2002). Longitudinal analysis of midlife generativity, intergenerational roles, and caregiving. *Psychology and Aging, 17,* 161–168.

Peterson, C., & McCabe, A. (1994). A social interactionist account of developing decontextualized narrative skill. *Developmental Psychology, 30,* 937–948.

Peterson, J. L., Moore, K. A., & Furstenberg, F. F., Jr. (1991). Television viewing and early initiation of sexual intercourse: Is there a link? *Journal of Homosexuality, 21,* 93–118.

Peterson, J. T. (1993). Generalized extended family exchange: A case from the Philippines. *Journal of Marriage and the Family, 55*(3), 570–584.

Peterson, K. (2005, April 14). Same-sex unions—A constitutional race. *Stateline.org.* Retrieved May 13, 2005 from http://www.stateline.org/live/ViewPage.action?siteNodeId=137&languageId=1&contentId=20695.

Petitti, D. B. (2002). Hormone replacement therapy for prevention: More evidence, more pessimism. *Journal of the American Medical Association, 288,* 99–101.

Petitto, L. A., Katerelos, M., Levy, B., Gauna, K., Tetrault, K., & Ferraro, V. (2001). Bilingual signed and spoken language acquisition from birth: Implications for mechanisms underlying bilingual language acquisition. *Journal of Child Language, 28,* 1–44.

Petitto, L. A., & Kovelman, I. (2003). The bilingual paradox: How signing-speaking bilingual children help us to resolve it and teach us about the brain's mechanisms underlying all language acquisition. *Learning Languages, 8,* 5–18.

Petitto, L. A., & Marentette, P. F. (1991). Babbling in the manual mode: Evidence for the ontogeny of language. *Science, 251,* 1493–1495.

Petrill, S. A., Lipton, P. A., Hewitt, J. K., Plomin, R., Cherny, S. S., Corley, R., and DeFries, J. C. (2004). Genetic and environmental contributions to general cognitive ability through the first 16 years of life. *Developmental Psychology, 40,* 805–812.

Pettit, G. S., Bates, J. E., & Dodge, K. A. (1997). Supportive parenting, ecological context, and children's adjustment: A seven-year longitudinal study. *Child Development, 68,* 908–923.

Pharaoh, P. D. P., Antoniou, A., Bobrow, M., Zimmern, R. L., Easton, D. F., & Ponder, B. A. J. (2002). Polygenic susceptibility to breast cancer and implications for prevention. *Nature Genetics, 31,* 33–36.

Phelan, E. A., Williams, B., Penninx, B. W. J. H., LoGerfo, J. P. & Leveille, S. G. (2004). Activities of daily living function and disability in older adults in a randomized trial of the Health Enhancement Program. *Journal of Geronotology: Medical Sciences, 59A,* 838–843.

Philipp, B. L., Merewood, A., Miller, L. W., Chawla, N., Murphy-Smith, M. M., Gomes, J. S., Cimo, S., & Cook, J. T. (2001). Baby-friendly hospital initiative improves breastfeeding initiation rates in a U.S. hospital setting. *Pediatrics, 108*(3), 677–681.

Phillips, D. F. (1998). Reproductive medicine experts till an increasingly fertile field. *Journal of the American Medical Association, 280,* 1893–1895.

Phinney, J. S. (1998). Stages of ethnic identity development in minority group adolescents. In R. E. Muuss & H. D. Porton (Eds.), *Adolescent behavior and society: A book of readings* (pp. 271–280). Boston: McGraw-Hill.

Piaget, J. (1929). *The child's conception of the world.* New York: Harcourt Brace.

Piaget, J. (1932). *The moral judgment of the child.* New York: Harcourt Brace.

Piaget, J. (1951). *Play, dreams, and imitation* (C. Gattegno & F. M. Hodgson, Trans.). New York: Norton.

Piaget, J. (1952). *The origins of intelligence in children.* New York: International Universities Press. (Original work published 1936).

Piaget, J. (1962). *The language and thought of the child* (M. Gabain, Trans.). Cleveland, OH: Meridian. (Original work published 1923.)

Piaget, J. (1964). *Six psychological studies.* New York: Vintage.

Piaget, J. (1969). *The child's conception of time* (A. J. Pomerans, Trans.). London: Routledge & Kegan Paul.

Piaget, J. (1972). Intellectual evolution from adolescence to adulthood. *Human Development, 15*, 1–12.

Piaget, J., & Inhelder, B. (1967). *The child's conception of space.* New York: Norton.

Piaget. J., & Inhelder, B. (1969). *The psychology of the child.* New York: Basic Books.

Pianezza, M. L., Sellers, E. M., & Tyndale, R. F. (1998). Nicotine metabolism defect reduces smoking. *Nature, 393*, 750.

Pickering, L. K., Granoff, D. M., Erickson, J. R., Mason, M. L., Cordle, C. T., Schaller, J. P., Winship, T. R., Paule, C. L., & Hilty, M. D. (1998). Modulation of the immune system by human milk and infant formula containing nucleotides. *Pediatrics, 101*, 242–249.

Pickett, W., Streight, S., Simpson, K., & Brison, R. J. (2003). Injuries experienced by infant children: A population-based epidemiological analysis. *Pediatrics, 111*, e365–e370.

Pierce, K. M., Hamm, J. V., & Vandell, D. L. (1999). Experiences in after-school programs and children's adjustment in first-grade classrooms. *Child Development, 70*(3), 756–767.

Pillemer, K., & Suitor, J. J. (1991). "Will I ever escape my child's problems?" Effects of adult children's problems on elderly parents. *Journal of Marriage and the Family, 53*, 585–594.

Pillow, B. H., & Henrichon, A. J. (1996). There's more to the picture than meets the eye: Young children's difficulty understanding biased interpretation. *Child Development, 67*, 803–819.

Pimentel, E. E., & Liu, J. (2004). Exploring nonnormative coresidence in urban China: Living with wives' parents. *Journal of Marriage and Family, 66*, 821–836.

Piña, J. A. (1999). The "uncontrollable" rebel. In J. Rodden (Ed.), *Conversations with Isabel Allende* (pp. 167–200). Austin: University of Texas Press.

Pines, M. (1981). The civilizing of Genie. *Psychology Today, 15*(9), 28–34.

Pinzone-Glover, H. A., Gidycz, C. A., & Jacobs, C. D. (1998). An acquaintance rape prevention program: Effects on attitudes toward women, rape-related attitudes, and perceptions of rape scenarios. *Psychology of Women Quarterly, 22*, 605–621.

Pleck, J. H. (1997). Paternal involvement: Levels, sources, and consequences. In M. E. Lamb et al. (Eds.), *The role of the father in child development* (3rd ed., pp. 66–103). New York: Wiley.

Plemons, J., Willis, S., & Baltes, P. (1978). Modifiability of fluid intelligence in aging: A short-term longitudinal training approach. *Journal of Gerontology, 33*(2), 224–231.

Plomin, R. (1990). The role of inheritance in behavior. *Science, 248*, 183–188.

Plomin, R. (1996). Nature and nurture. In M. R. Merrens & G. G. Brannigan (Eds.), *The developmental psychologist: Research adventures across the life span* (pp. 3–19). New York: McGraw-Hill.

Plomin, R., & Crabbe, J. (2000). DNA. *Psychological Bulletin, 126*(6), 806–828.

Plomin, R., & Daniels, D. (1987). Why are children in the same family so different from one another? *Behavioral and Brain Sciences, 10*, 1–16.

Plomin, R., & DeFries, J. C. (1999). The genetics of cognitive abilities and disabilities. In S. J. Ceci & W. M. Williams (Eds.), *The nature nurture debate: The essential readings* (pp. 178–195). Malden, MA: Blackwell.

Plomin, R., Owen, M. J., & McGuffin, P. (1994). The genetic bases of behavior. *Science, 264*, 1733–1739.

Plomin, R., & Rutter, M. (1998). Child development, molecular genetics, and what to do with genes once they are found. *Child Development, 69*(4), 1223–1242.

Plotkin, S. A., Katz, M., & Cordero, J. F. (1999). The eradication of rubella. *Journal specialization? Child Development, 72*, 691–695.

Polit, D. F., & Falbo, T. (1987). Only children and personality development: A quantitative review. *Journal of Marriage and the Family, 49*, 309–325.

Pollock, L. A. (1983). *Forgotten children.* Cambridge, England: Cambridge University Press.

Pomerantz, E. M., & Saxon, J. L. (2001). Conceptions of ability as stable and selfevaluative processes: A longitudinal examination. *Child Development, 72*, 152–173.

Pong, S. L. (1997). Family structure, school context, and eighth-grade math and reading achievement. *Journal of Marriage and the Family, 59*, 734–746.

Pong, S., Dronkers, J., & Hampden-Thompson, G. (2003). Family policies and children's school achievement in single- versus two-parent families. *Journal of Marriage and the Family, 65*, 681–699.

Poon, L. W. (1985). Differences in human memory with aging: Nature, causes, and clinical implications. In J. E. Birren & K. W. Schaie (Eds.), *Handbook of the psychology of aging* (pp. 427–462). New York: Van Nostrand Reinhold.

Pope, A. W., Bierman, K. L., & Mumma, G. H. (1991). Aggression, hyperactivity, and inattention-immaturity: Behavior dimensions associated with peer rejection in elementary school boys. *Developmental Psychology, 27*, 663–671.

Popenoe, D., & Whitehead, B. D. (1999). *Should we live together? What young adults need to know about cohabitation before marriage.* New Brunswick: National Marriage Project Rutgers, State University of New Jersey.

Popenoe, D., & Whitehead, B. D. (2003). *The state of our unions 2003: The social health of marriage in America.* Piscataway, NJ: The National Marriage Project.

Popenoe, D., & Whitehead, B. D. (Eds.) (2004). *The state of our unions 2004: The social health of marriage in America.* Piscataway, NJ: The National Marriage Project, Rutgers University.

Population Reference Bureau. (2005). Human population: Fundamentals of growth; World health. [Online]. Retrieved April 11, 2005 from http://www.prb.org/Content/NavigationMenu/PRB/Educators/Human_Population/Health2/World_Health1.htm.

Porcino, J. (1993, April–May). Designs for living. *Modern Maturity*, pp. 24–33.

Porter, E., & Walsh, M. W. (2005, February 9). Retirement turns into a rest stop as benefits dwindle. *New York Times*. [Online]. Retrieved February 9, 2005, from http://www.nytimes.com/2005/02/09/business/09retire.html.

Portwood, S. G., & Repucci, N. D. (1996). Adults' impact on the suggestibility of preschoolers' recollections. *Journal of Applied Developmental Psychology, 17*, 175–198.

Posada, G., Gao, Y., Wu, F., Posada, R., Tascon, M., Schoelmerich, A., Sagi, A., Kondo-Ikemura, K., Haaland, W., & Synnevaag, B. (1995). The secure-base phenomenon across cultures: Children's behavior, mothers' preferences, and experts' concepts. In E. Waters, B. E. Vaughn, G. Posada, & K. Kondo-Ikemura (Eds.), Caregiving, cultural, and cognitive perspectives on secure-base behavior and working models: New growing points of attachment theory and research (pp. 27–48). *Monographs of the Society for Research in Child Development, 60*(2–3, Serial No. 244).

Posner, J. K., & Vandell, D. L. (1999). After-school activities and the development of low income urban children: A longitudinal study. *Developmental Psychology, 35*(3), 868–879.

Posner, M. L., & DiGirolamo, G. J. (2000). Cognitive neuroscience: Origins and promise. *Psychological Bulletin, 126*(6), 873–889.

Post, S. G. (1994). Ethical commentary: Genetic testing for Alzheimer's disease. *Alzheimer Disease and Associated Disorders, 8*, 66–67.

Povinelli, D. J., & Giambrone, S. (2001). Reasoning about beliefs: A human specialization? *Child Development, 72*, 691–695.

Powell, L. H., Shahabi, L., & Thoresen, C. E. (2003). Religion and spirituality: Linkages to physical health. *American Psychologist, 58*, 36–52.

Powell, M. B., & Thomson, D. M. (1996). Children's memory of an occurrence of a repeated event: Effects of age, repetition, and retention interval across three question types. *Child Development, 67*, 1988–2004.

Powlishta, K. K., Serbin, L. A., Doyle, A. B., & White, D. R. (1994). Gender, ethnic, and body type biases: The generality of prejudice in childhood. *Developmental Psychology, 30*, 526–536.

Pratt, M. (1999). Benefits of lifestyle activity vs. structured exercise. *Journal of the American Medical Association, 281*, 375–376.

President's Commission to Strengthen Social Security. (2001). *Strengthening Social Security and creating personal wealth for all Americans.* Executive summary.

Preston, S. H. (2005). Deadweight?—The influence of obesity on longevity. *New England Journal of Medicine, 352*, 1135–1137.

Previti, D. & Amato, P. R. (2003). Why stay married? Rewards, barriers, and marital stability. *Journal of Marriage and the Family, 65*, 561–573.

Price, T. S., Simonoff, E., Waldman, I., Asherson, P., & Plomin, R. (2001). Hyperactivity in preschool children is highly heritable. *Journal of the American Academy of Child & Adolescent Psychiatry, 40*(12), 1362–1364.

Princiotta, D., Bielick, S., & Chapman, C. (2004). *1.1 million homeschooled students in the United States in 2003* (NCES 2004–115). Washington, DC: National Center for Education Statistics.

Prockop, D. J. (1998). The genetic trail of osteoporosis. *New England Journal of Medicine, 338,* 1061–1062.

Proctor, B. D., & Dalaker, J. (2003). *Poverty in the United States: 2002* (Current Population Reports, Series P60–222). Washington, DC: U.S. Government Printing Office.

ProEnglish (2002). *The status of bilingual education.* Fact sheet. [Online]. Available: http://www.proenglish.org/issues/education/bes tatus.html. Access date: May 30, 2004.

Prohaska, T. R., Leventhal, E. A., Leventhal, H., & Keller, M. L. (1985). Health practices and illness cognition in young, middle-aged, and elderly adults. *Journal of Gerontology, 40,* 569–578.

Pruchno, R., & Johnson, K. W. (1996). Research on grandparenting: Current studies and future needs. *Generations, 20*(1), 65–70.

Puca, A. A., Daly, M. J., Brewster, S. J., Matise, T. C., Barrett, J., SheapDrinkwater, M., Kang, S., Joyce, E., Nicoli, J., Benson, E., Kunkel, L. M., & Perls, T. (2001). A genomewide scan for linkage to human exceptional longevity identifies a locus on chromosome 4. *Proceedings of the National Academy of Science, 28,* 10505–10508.

Pulkkinen, L. (1996). Female and male personality styles: A typological and developmental analysis. *Journal of Personality and Social Psychology, 70,* 1288–1306.

Purcell, J. H. (1995). Gifted education at a crossroads: The program status study. *Gifted Child Quarterly, 39*(2), 57–65.

Putallaz, M., & Bierman, K. L. (Eds.). (2004). *Aggression, antisocial behavior, and violence among girls: A developmental perspective.* New York: Guilford.

Putney, N. M., & Bengtson, V. L. (2001). Families, intergenerational relationships, and kinkeeping in midlife. In M. E. Lachman (Ed.), *Handbook of midlife development* (pp. 528–570). New York: Wiley.

Quadrel, M. J., Fischoff, B., & Davis, W. (1993). Adolescent (in)vulnerability. *American Psychologist, 48,* 102–116.

Quattrin, T., Liu, E., Shaw, N., Shine, B., & Chiang, E. (2005). Obese children who are referred to the pediatric oncologist: Characteristics and outcome. *Pediatrics, 115,* 348–351.

Quill, T. E., Lo, B., & Brock, D. W. (1997). Palliative options of the last resort. *Journal of the American Medical Association, 278,* 2099–2104.

Quinn, P. C., Eimas, P. D., & Rosenkrantz, S. L. (1993). Evidence for representations of perceptually similar natural categories by 3-month-old and 4-month-old infants. *Perception, 22,* 463–475.

Rabbitt, P., Diggle, P., Holland, F., & McInnes, L. (2004). Practice and drop-out effects during a 17-year longitudinal study of cognitive aging. *Journal of Gerontology: Psychological Sciences, 59B,* 84–P97.

Rabbitt, P., Watson, P., Donlan, C., McInnes, L., Horan, M., Pendleton, N., & Clague, J.

(2002). Effects of death within 11 years on cognitive performance in old age. *Psychology and Aging, 17,* 468–481.

Rabiner, D., & Coie, J. (1989). Effect of expectancy induction on rejected peers' acceptance by unfamiliar peers. *Developmental Psychology, 25,* 450–457.

Raffaelli, M., & Crockett, L. J. (2003). Sexual risk-taking in adolescence: The role of self-regulation and attraction to risk. *Developmental Psychology, 39,* 1036–1046.

Rafferty, Y., & Shinn, M. (1991). Impact of homelessness on children. *American Psychologist, 46*(11), 1170–1179.

Ragland, D. R., Satariano, W. A., & MacLeod, K. E. (2004). Reasons given by older people for limitation or avoidance of driving. *The Gerontologist, 44,* 237–244.

Raine, A., Mellingen, K., Liu, J., Venables, P., & Mednick, S. (2003). Effects of environmental enrichment at ages 3–5 years in schizotypal personality and antisocial behavior at ages 17 and 23 years. *American Journal of Psychiatry, 160,* 1627–1635.

Rakoczy, H., Tomasello, M., and Striano. T. (2004). Young children know that trying is not pretending: A test of the "behaving-as-if" construal of children's early concept of pretense. *Developmental Psychology, 40,* 388–399.

Rall, L. C., Meydani, S. N., Kehayias, B. D. H., Dawson-Hughes, B., & Roubenoff, R. (1996). The effect of progressive resistance training in rheumatoid arthritis. *Arthritis and Rheumatism, 39,* 415–426.

Ram, A., & Ross, H. S. (2001). Problem solving, contention, and struggle: How siblings resolve a conflict of interests. *Child Development, 72,* 1710–1722.

Ramey, C. T., & Campbell, F. A. (1991). Poverty, early childhood education, and academic competence. In A. Huston (Ed.), *Children reared in poverty* (pp. 190–221). Cambridge, England: Cambridge University Press.

Ramey, C. T., Campbell, F. A., Burchinal, M., Skinner, M. L., Gardner, D. M., & Ramey, S. L. (2000). Persistent effects of early childhood education on high-risk children and their mothers. *Applied Developmental Science, 4*(1), 2–14.

Ramey, C. T., & Ramey, S. L. (1996). Early intervention: Optimizing development for children with disabilities and risk conditions. In M. Wolraich (Ed.), *Disorders of development and learning: A practical guide to assessment and management* (2nd ed., pp. 141–158). Philadelphia: Mosby.

Ramey, C. T., & Ramey, S. L. (1998a). Early intervention and early experience. *American Psychologist, 53,* 109–120.

Ramey, C. T., & Ramey, S. L. (1998b). Prevention of intellectual disabilities: Early interventions to improve cognitive development. *Preventive Medicine, 21,* 224–232.

Ramey, S. L. (1999). Head Start and preschool education: Toward continued improvement. *American Psychologist, 54,* 344–346.

Ramey, S. L., & Ramey, C. T. (1992). Early educational intervention with disadvantaged

children—To what effect? *Applied and Preventive Psychology, 1,* 131–140.

Ramirez, J. M. (2003). Hormones and aggression in childhood and adolescence. *Aggression and Violent Behavior, 8,* 621–644.

Ramoz, N., Reichert, J. G., Smith, C. J., Silverman, J. M., Bespalova, I. N., Davis, K. L., & Buxbaum, J. D. (2004). Linkage and association of the mitochondrial aspartate/glutamate carrier SLC25A12 gene with autism. *American Journal of Psychiatry, 161,* 662–669.

Rampersad, A. (1997). *Jackie Robinson: A biography.* New York: Knopf.

Ramsey, P. G., & Lasquade, C. (1996). Preschool children's entry attempts. *Journal of Applied Developmental Psychology, 17,* 135–150.

Randall, D. (2005). *Corporal punishment in school.* FamilyEducation.com. [Online]. Retrieved April 20, 2005, from http://www.familyeducation.com/article/0,1120,1–3980,00.html.

Rao, R., & Georgieff, M. K. (2000). Early nutrition and brain development. *The effects of early adversity on neurobehavioral development. The Minnesota Symposia on Child Psychology* (Vol. 31, pp. 1–30). Mahwah, NJ: Lawrence Erlbaum Associates.

Rapin, I. (1997). Autism. *New England Journal of Medicine, 337,* 97–104.

Rapp, S. R., Espeland, M. A., Shumaker, S. A., Henderson, V. W., Brunner, R. L., Manson, J. E., Gass, M. L. S., Stefanisk, M. L., Lane, D. S., Hays, J., Johnson, K. C., Coker, L. H., Dailey, M., Bowen, D., for the WHIMIS Investigators. (2003). Effects of estrogen plus progestin on global cognitive function in post-menopausal women: The Women's Health Initiative Memory Study: A randomized controlled trial. *Journal of the American Medical Association,* 2663–2672.

Rask-Nissilä, L., Jokinen, E., Terho, P., Tammi, A., Lapinleimu, H., Ronnemaa, T., Viikari, J., Seppanen, R., Korhonen, T., Tuominen, J., Valimaki, I., & Simell, O. (2000). Neurological development of 5-year-old children receiving a low-saturated fat, low-cholesterol diet since infancy. *Journal of the American Medical Association, 284*(8), 993–1000.

Rathbun, A., West, J., & Germino-Hausken, E. (2004). From kindergarten through third grade: Children's beginning school experiences (NCES 2004–007). Washington, DC: National Center for Education Statistics.

Ratner, H. H., & Foley, M. A. (1997, April). *Children's collaborative learning: Reconstructions of the other in the self.* Paper presented at the meeting of the Society for Research in Child Development, Washington, DC.

Rauh, V. A., Whyatt, R. M., Garfinkel, R., Andrews, H., Hoepner, L., Reyes, A., Diaz, D., Camann, D., & Perera, F. P. (2004). Developmental effects of exposure to environmental tobacco smoke and material hardship among inner-city children. *Neurotoxicology and Teratology, 26,* 373–385.

Raver, C. C. (2002). Emotions matter: Making the case for the role of young children's emotional development for early school readiness. *Social Policy Report, 16*(3).

Ray, O. (2004). How the mind hurts and heals the body. *American Psychologist, 59,* 29–40.

Redding, R. E., Harmon, R. J., & Morgan, G. A. (1990). Maternal depression and infants' mastery behaviors. *Infant Behavior and Development, 113,* 391–396.

Reed, T., Dick, D. M., Uniacke, S. K., Foroud, T., & Nichols, W. C. (2004). Genomewide scan for a healthy aging phenotype provides support for a locus near D4S1564 promoting healthy aging. *Journal of Gerontology: Biological Sciences, 59A,* 227–232.

Reese, E. (1995). Predicting children's literacy from mother-child conversations. *Cognitive Development, 10,* 381–405.

Reese, E., & Cox, A. (1999). Quality of adult book reading affects children's emergent literacy. *Developmental Psychology, 35,* 20–28.

Reese, E., & Fivush, R. (1993). Parental styles of talking about the past. *Developmental Psychology, 29,* 596–606.

Reese, E., Haden, C., & Fivush, R. (1993). Mother-child conversations about the past: Relationships of style and memory over time. *Cognitive Development, 8,* 403–430.

Reeves, M. J., & Rafferty, A. P. (2005). Healthy lifestyle characteristics among adults in the United States, 2000. *Archives of Internal Medicine, 165,* 854–857.

Reid, J. D. (1995). Development in late life: Older lesbian and gay life. In A. R. D'Augelli & C. J. Patterson (Eds.), *Lesbian, gay, and bisexual identities over the lifespan: Psychological perspectives* (pp. 215–240). New York: Oxford University Press.

Reid, J. D., & Willis, S. K. (1999). Middle age: New thoughts, new directions. In S. L. Willis & J. D. Reid (Eds.), *Life in the middle* (pp. 272–289). San Diego: Academic Press.

Reid, J. R., Patterson, G. R., & Loeber, R. (1982). The abused child: Victim, instigator, or innocent bystander? In D. J. Berstein (Ed.), *Response structure and organization.* Lincoln: University of Nebraska Press.

Reijo, R., Alagappan, R. K., Patrizio, P., & Page, D. C. (1996). Severe oligozoospermia resulting from deletions of azoospermia factor gene on Y chromosome. *The Lancet, 347,* 1290–1293.

Reilly, J. J., Jackson, D. M., Montgomery, C., Kelly, L. A., Slater, C., Grant, S., & Paton, J. Y. (2004). Total energy expenditure and physical activity in young Scottish children: Mixed longitudinal study. *Lancet, 363,* 211–212.

Reiner, W. (2000, May 12). Cloacal exstrophy: A happenstance model for androgen imprinting. Presentation at the meeting of the Pediatric Endocrine Society, Boston.

Reiner, W. G., & Gearhart, J. P. (2004). Discordant sexual identity in some genetic males with cloacal exstrophy assigned to female sex at birth. *New England Journal of Medicine, 350*(4), 333–341.

Reis, H. T., & Patrick, B. C. (1996). Attachment and intimacy: Component processes. In E. T. Higgins & A. Kruglanski (Eds.), *Social psychology: Handbook of basic principles* (pp. 523–563). New York: Guilford.

Reisberg, B., Doody, R., Stoffler, A., Schmitt, F., Ferris, S., & Mobius, H. J. (2003). Memantine in moderate-to-severe Alzheimer's Disease. *New England Journal of Medicine, 348,* 1333–1341.

Reiss, A. L., Abrams, M. T., Singer, H. S., Ross, J. L., & Denckla, M. B. (1996). Brain development, gender and IQ in children: A volumetric imaging study. *Brain, 119,* 1763–1774.

Reitzes, D. C., & Mutran, E. J. (2002). Self-concept as the organization of roles: Importance, centrality, and balance. *Sociological Quarterly, 43,* 647–667.

Reitzes, D. C., & Mutran, E. J. (2004). Grandparenthood: Factors influencing frequency of grandparent-grandchildren contact and role satisfaction. *Journal of Gerontology: Social Sciences,* S9–S16.

Remafedi, G., French, S., Story, M., Resnick, M.D., & Blum, R. (1998). The relationship between suicide risk and sexual orientation: Results of a population-based study. *American Journal of Public Health, 88,* 57–60.

Remafedi, G., Resnick, M., Blum, R., & Harris, L. (1992). Demography of sexual orientation in adolescents. *Pediatrics, 89,* 714–721.

Remez, L. (2000). Oral sex among adolescents: Is it sex or is it abstinence? *Family Planning Perspectives, 32,* 298–304.

Research Unit on Pediatric Psychopharmacology Anxiety Study Group. (2001). Fluvoxamine for the treatment of anxiety disorder in children and adolescents. *New England Journal of Medicine, 344,* 1279–1285.

Resnick, L. B. (1989). Developing mathematical knowledge. *American Psychologist, 44,* 162–169.

Resnick, M. D., Bearman, P. S., Blum, R. W., Bauman, K. E., Harris, K. M., Jones, J., Tabor, J., Beuhring, T., Sieving, R. E., Shew, M., Ireland, M., Bearinger, L. H., & Udry, J. R. (1997). Protecting adolescents from harm: Findings from the National Longitudinal Study on Adolescent Health. *Journal of the American Medical Association, 278,* 823–832.

Rest, J., Narvaez, D., Bebeau, M. J., & Thoma, S. J. (1999). *Postconventional moral thinking.* Mahwah, NJ: Erlbaum.

Rest, J. R. (1975). Longitudinal study of the Defining Issues Test of moral judgment: A strategy for analyzing developmental change. *Developmental Psychology, 11,* 738–748.

Rest, J. R., Deemer, D., Barnett, R., Spickelmier, J., & Volker, J. (1986). Life experiences and developmental pathways. In J. R. Rest (Ed.), *Moral development: Advances in theory and research.* New York: Praeger.

Restak, R. (1984). *The brain.* New York: Bantam.

Reuter-Lorenz, P. A., Jonides, J., Smith, E. E., Hartley, A., Miller, A., Marshuetz, C., & Koeppe, R. A. (2000). Age differences in the frontal lateralization of verbal and spatial working memory revealed by PET. *Journal of Cognitive Neuroscience, 12,* 174–187.

Reuter-Lorenz, P. A., Stanczak, L., & Miller, A. (1999). Neural recruitment and cognitive aging: Two hemispheres are better than one especially as you age. *Psychological Science, 10,* 494–500.

Reuters. (2004a). Canada first country to ban sale of baby walkers.

Reuters. (2004b). Senate passes Unborn Victims Bill. *New York Times.* [Online]. Available: http://www.nytimes.com/reuters/politics/politics-congress-unborn.html?ex=1081399302&ei=1&en=636394338d275008. Access date: March 29, 2004.

Reynolds, A. J. (1994). Effects of a preschool plus follow-on intervention for children at risk. *Developmental Psychology, 30,* 787–804.

Reynolds, A. J., & Robertson, D. L. (2003). School-based early intervention and later child maltreatment in the Chicago Longitudinal Study. *Child Development, 74,* 3–26.

Reynolds, A. J., & Temple, J. A. (1998). Extended early childhood intervention and school achievement: Age thirteen findings from the Chicago Longitudinal Study. *Child Development, 69,* 231–246.

Reynolds, A. J., Temple, J. A., Robertson, D. L., & Mann, E. A. (2001). Long-term effects of an early childhood intervention on educational achievement and juvenile arrest. *Journal of the American Medical Association, 285,* 2339–2346.

Reynolds, C. F., III, Buysse, D. J., & Kupfer, D. J. (1999). Treating insomnia in older adults: Taking a long-term view. *Journal of the American Medical Association, 281,* 1034–1035.

Reynolds, M. A., Schieve, L. A., Martin, J. A., Jeng, G., & Macaluso, M. (2003). Trends in multiple births conceived using assisted reproductive technology, United States, 1997–2000. *Pediatrics, 111,* 1159–1166.

Reznick, J. S., Chawarska, K., & Betts, S. (2000). The development of visual expectations in the first year. *Child Development, 71,* 1191–1204.

Ricciuti, H. N. (1999). Single parenthood and school readiness in white, black, and Hispanic 6- and 7-year-olds. *Journal of Family Psychology, 13,* 450–465.

Ricciuti, H. N. (2004). Single parenthood, achievement, and problem behavior in white, black, and Hispanic children. *Journal of Educational Research, 97,* 196–206.

Rice, C., Koinis, D., Sullivan, K., Tager-Flusberg, H., & Winner, E. (1997). When 3-year-olds pass the appearance-reality test. *Developmental Psychology, 33,* 54–61.

Rice, M., Oetting, J. B., Marquis, J., Bode, J., & Pae, S. (1994). Frequency of input effects on SLI children's word comprehension. *Journal of Speech and Hearing Research, 37,* 106–122.

Rice, M. L. (1989). Children's language acquisition. *American Psychologist, 44*(2), 149–156.

Rice, M. L., Hadley, P. A., & Alexander, A. L. (1993). Social biases toward children with speech and language impairments: A correlative causal model of language limitations. *Applied Psycholinguistics, 14,* 445–471.

Rice, M. L., Huston, A. C., Truglio, R., & Wright, J. (1990). Words from "Sesame Street": Learning vocabulary while viewing. *Developmental Psychology, 26,* 421–428.

Richards, M. H., Boxer, A. M., Petersen, A. C., & Albrecht, R. (1990). Relation of weight to body image in pubertal girls and boys from two communities. *Developmental Psychology, 26,* 313–321.

Richards, T. L., Dager, S. R., Corina, D., Serafini, S., Heide, A. C., Steury, K., Strauss, W., Hayes, C. E., Abbott, R. D., Craft, S., Shaw, D., Posse, S., & Berninger, V. W. (1999). Dyslexic children have abnormal brain lactate response to reading-related language tasks. *American Journal of Neuroradiology, 20,* 1393–1398.

Richardson, C. R., Kriska, A. M., Lantz, P. M., & Hayward, R. A. (2004). Physical activity and mortality across cardiovascular disease risk groups. *Medicine and Science in Sports and Exercise, 36,* 1923–1929.

Richardson, J. (1995). *Achieving gender equality in families: The role of males* (Innocenti Global Seminar, Summary Report). Florence, Italy: UNICEF International Child Development Centre, Spedale degli Innocenti.

Riddle, R. D., Johnson, R. L., Laufer, E., & Tabin, C. (1993). Sonic hedgehog mediates the polarizing activity of the ZPA. *Cell, 75,* 1401–1416.

Rideout, V. J., Vandewater, E. A., & Wartella, E. A. (2003). *Zero to six: Electronic media in the lives of infants, toddlers and preschoolers.* A Kaiser Family Foundation Report.

Riediger, M., Freund, A. M., & Baltes, P. B. (2005). Managing life through personal goals: Intergoal facilitation and intensity of goal pursuit in younger and older adults. *Journal of Gerontology: Psychological Sciences, 60B,* P84–P91.

Riemann, M. K., & Kanstrup Hansen, I. L. (2000). Effects on the fetus of exercise in pregnancy. *Scandinavian Journal of Medicine & Science in Sports. 10*(1), 12–19.

Rifkin, J. (1998, May 5). Creating the "perfect" human. *Chicago Sun-Times,* p. 29.

Riis, J., Baron, J., Loewenstein, G., Jepson, C., Fagerlin, A., & Ubel, P. A. (2005). Ignorance of hedonic adaptation to hemodialysis: A study using ecological momentary assessment. *Journal of Experimental Psychology: General, 134,* 3–4.

Riley, K. P., Snowdon, D. A., Desrosiers, M. F., & Markesbery, W. R. (2005). Early life linguistic ability, late life cognitive function, and neuropathology: Findings from the Nun Study. *Neurobiology of Aging, 26,* 341–347.

Riley, M. W. (1994). Aging and society: Past, present, and future. *The Gerontologist, 34,* 436–446.

Rimm, E. B., Ascherio, A., Giovannucci, E., Spiegelman, D., Stampfer, M. J., & Willett, W. C. (1996). Vegetable, fruit, and cereal fiber intake and risk of coronary heart disease among men. *Journal of the American Medical Association, 275,* 447–451.

Rimm, E. B., & Stampfer, M. J. (2004). Diet, lifestyle, and longevity—the next steps? *Journal of the American Medical Association, 292,* 1490–1492.

Rios-Ellis, B., Bellamy, L., & Shoji, J. (2000). An examination of specific types of *ijime*

within Japanese schools. *School Psychology International, 21,* 227–241.

Ripple, C. H., Gilliam, W. S., Chanana, N., & Zigler, E. (1999). Will fifty cooks spoil the broth? The debate over entrusting Head Start to the states. *American Psychologist, 54,* 327–343.

Risks of hormone use continue to emerge: Ongoing analyses strengthen case against menopausal hormone therapy. (2004, May). *HealthNews,* p. 3.

Ritchie, L., Crawford, P., Woodward-Lopez, G., Ivey, S., Masch, M., & Ikeda, J. (2001). *Prevention of childhood overweight: What should be done?* Berkeley, CA: Center for Weight and Health, U.C. Berkeley.

Ritter, J. (1999, November 23). Scientists close in on DNA code. *Chicago Sun-Times,* p. 7.

Rivera, J. A., Sotres-Alvarez, D., Habicht, J.-P., Shamah, T., & Villalpando, S. (2004). Impact of the Mexican Program for Education, Health and Nutrition (Progresa) on rates of growth and anemia in infants and young children. *Journal of the American Medical Association, 291,* 2563–2570.

Rivera, S. M., Wakeley, A., & Langer, J. (1999). The drawbridge phenomenon: Representational reasoning or perceptual preference? *Developmental Psychology, 35*(2), 427–435.

Rizzo, T. A., Metzger, B. E., Dooley, S. L., & Cho, N. H. (1997). Early malnutrition and child neurobehavioral development: Insights from the study of children of diabetic mothers. *Child Development, 68,* 26–38.

Robbins, A., & Wilner, A. (Eds.) (2001). *Quarterlife crisis: The unique challenges of life in your twenties.* New York: Putnam.

Roberts, B. W., & Del Vecchio, W. F. (2000). The rank-order consistency of personality traits from childhood to old age: A quantitative review of longitudinal studies. *Psychological Bulletin, 126,* 3–25.

Roberts, B. W., Caspi, A., & Moffitt, T. E. (2003). Work experiences and personality development in young adulthood. *Journal of Personality and Social Psychology, 84,* 582–593.

Roberts, G. C., Block, J. H., & Block, J. (1984). Continuity and change in parents' child-rearing practices. *Child Development, 55,* 586–597.

Robin, D. J., Berthier, N. E., & Clifton, R. K. (1996). Infants' predictive reaching for moving objects in the dark. *Developmental Psychology, 32,* 824–835.

Robine, J., & Michel, P. (2004). Looking forward to a general theory on population aging. *Journal of Gerontology: Medical Sciences, 59,* M590–M597.

Robins, R. W., John, O. P., Caspi, A., Moffitt, T. E., & Stouthamer-Loeber, M. (1996). Resilient, overcontrolled, and undercontrolled boys: Three replicable personality types. *Journal of Personality and Social Psychology, 70,* 157–171.

Robinson, J. (as told to A. Duckett). (1995). *I never had it made.* Hopewell, NJ: Ecco.

Robinson, L. C., & Blanton, P. W. (1993). Marital strengths in enduring marriages. *Family Relations, 42,* 38–45.

Robinson, S. (1996). *Stealing home.* New York: HarperCollins.

Robinson, S. D., Rosenberg, H. J., & Farrell, M. P. (1999). The midlife crisis revisited. In S. L. Willis & J. D. Reid (Eds.), *Life in the middle: Psychological and social development in middle age* (pp. 47–77). San Diego, CA: Academic.

Robinson, T. N., Wilde, M. L., Navracruz, L. C., Haydel, K. F., & Varady, A. (2001). Effects of reducing children's television and video game use on aggressive behavior: A randomized controlled trial. *Archives of Pediatric and Adolescent Medicine, 155,* 17–23.

Rochat, P., Querido, J. G., & Striano, T. (1999). Emerging sensitivity to the timing and structure of proto conversations in early infancy. *Developmental Psychology, 35,* 950–957.

Rochat, P., & Striano, T. (2002). Who's in the mirror? Self-other discrimination in specular images by four- and nine-month-old infants. *Child Development, 73,* 35–46.

Rockwood, K., Howlett, S. E., MacKnight, C., Beattie, B. L., Bergman, H., Hebert, R., Hogan, D. B., Wolfson, C., & McDowell, I. (2004). Prevalence, attributes, and outcomes of fitness and frailty in community-dwelling older adults: Report from the Canadian Study of Health and Aging. *Journal of Gerontology: Medical Sciences, 59A,* 1310–1317.

Rodden, J. (Ed.). (1999). *Conversations with Isabel Allende.* Austin: University of Texas Press.

Roderick, M., Engel, M., & Nagaoka, J. (2003). *Ending social promotion: Results from Summer Bridge.* Chicago: Consortium on Chicago School Research.

Rodier, P. M. (2000, February). The early origins of autism. *Scientific American,* pp. 56–63.

Rodin, J., & Ickovics, J. (1990). Women's health: Review and research agenda as we approach the 21st century. *American Psychologist, 45,* 1018–1034.

Rodkin, P. C., Farmer, T. W., Pearl, R., & Van Acker, R. (2000). Heterogeneity of popular boys: Antisocial and prosocial configurations. *Developmental Psychology, 36*(1), 14–24.

Rodriguez, C., Patel, A.V., Calle, E. E., Jacob, E. J., & Thun, M. J. (2001). Estrogen replacement therapy and ovarian cancer mortality in a large prospective study of U.S. women. *Journal of the American Medical Association, 285,* 1460–1465.

Rogan, W. J., Dietrich, K. N., Ware, J. H., Dockery, D. W., Salganik, M., Radcliffe, J., Jones, R. L., Ragan, N. B., Chisolm Jr., J. J., & Rhoads, G. G., for the Treatment of Lead-Exposed Children Trial Group. (2001). The effect of chelation therapy with succimer on neuropsychological development in children exposed to lead. *New England Journal of Medicine, 344,* 1421–1426.

Rogers, A. R. (2003). Economics and the evolution of life histories. *Proceedings of the National Academy of Sciences, 100,* 9114–9115.

Rogers, C. R. (1961). *On becoming a person.* Boston: Houghton Mifflin.

Rogers, R. G. (1995). Marriage, sex and mortality. *Journal of Marriage and the Family, 57,* 515–526.

Rogers, S. J. (2004). Dollars, dependency, and divorce: Four perspectives on the role of wives' income. *Journal of Marriage and Family, 66,* 59–74.

Rogers, W. A., Meyer, B., Walker, N., & Fisk, A. D. (1998). Functional limitations to daily living tasks in the aged: A focus group analysis. *Human Factors, 40,* 111–125.

Rogler, L. H. (2002). Historical generations and psychology: The case of the Great Depression and World War II. *American Psychologist, 57*(12), 1013–1023.

Rogoff, B., Mistry, J., Göncü, A., & Mosier, C. (1993). Guided participation in cultural activity by toddlers and caregivers. *Monographs of the Society for Research in Child Development, 58*(8, Serial No. 236).

Rogoff, B., & Morelli, G. (1989). Perspectives on children's development from cultural psychology. *American Psychologist, 44,* 343–348.

Roisman, G. I., Masten, A. S., Coatsworth, J. D., & Tellegen, A. (2004). Salient and emerging developmental tasks in the transition to adulthood. *Child Development, 75,* 123–133.

Rolls, B. J., Engell, D., & Birch, L. L. (2000). Serving portion size influences 5-year-old but not 3-year-old children's food intake. *Journal of the American Dietetic Association, 100,* 232–234.

Rome-Flanders, T., Cronk, C., & Gourde, C. (1995). Maternal scaffolding in mother-infant games and its relationship to language development: A longitudinal study. *First Language, 15,* 339–355.

Ronca, A. E., & Alberts, J. R. (1995). Maternal contributions to fetal experience and the transition from prenatal to postnatal life. In J. P. Lecanuet, W. P. Fifer, N. A. Krasnegor, & W. P. Smotherman (Eds.), *Fetal development: A psychobiological perspective* (pp. 331–350). Hillsdale, NJ: Erlbaum.

Rönnlund, M., Nyberg, L., Bäckman, L., & Nilsson, L.-G. (2005). Stability, growth, and decline in adult life span development of declarative memory: Cross-sectional and longitudinal data from a population-based study. *Psychology and Aging, 20,* 3–18.

Roopnarine, J., & Honig, A. S. (1985, September). The unpopular child. *Young Children,* pp. 59–64.

Roopnarine, J. L., Hooper, F. H., Ahmeduzzaman, M., & Pollack, B. (1993). Gentle play partners: Mother-child and father-child play in New Delhi, India. In K. MacDonald (Ed.), *Parent-child play* (pp. 287–304). Albany: State University of New York Press.

Roopnarine, J. L., Talokder, E., Jain, D., Josh, P., & Srivastav, P. (1992). Personal well-being, kinship ties, and mother-infant and father-infant interactions in single-wage and dual-wage families in New Delhi, India. *Journal of Marriage and the Family, 54,* 293–301.

Rosamond, W. D., Chambless, L. E., Folsom, A. R., Cooper, L. S., Conwill, D. E., Clegg, L., Wang, C.-H., & Heiss, G. (1998). Trends in the incidence of myocardial infarction and in mortality due to coronary heart disease, 1987 to 1994. *New England Journal of Medicine, 339,* 861–867.

Rose, A. J. & Asher, S. R., (2004). Children's strategies and goals in response to help-giving and help-seeking tasks within a friendship. *Child Development, 75,* 749–763.

Rose, S. A. (1994). Relation between physical growth and information processing in infants born in India. *Child Development, 65,* 889–902.

Rose, S. A., & Feldman, J. F. (1995). Prediction of IQ and specific cognitive abilities at 11 years from infancy measures. *Developmental Psychology, 31,* 685–696.

Rose, S. A., & Feldman, J. F. (1997). Memory and speed: Their role in the relation of infant information processing to later IQ. *Child Development, 68,* 630–641.

Rose, S. A., & Feldman, J. F. (2000). The relation of very low birth weight to basic cognitive skills in infancy and childhood. In CA. Nelson (Ed.), The effects of early adversity on neurobehavioral development. *The Minnesota Symposia on Child Psychology* (Vol. 31, pp. 31–59). Mahwah, NJ: Lawrence Erlbaum Associates.

Rose, S. A., Feldman, J. F., & Jankowski, J. J. (2001). Attention and recognition memory in the 1st year of life: A longitudinal study of preterm and full-term infants. *Developmental Psychology, 37,* 135–151.

Rose, S. A., Feldman, J. F., & Jankowski, J. J. (2002). Processing speed in the 1st year of life: A longitudinal study of preterm and full-term infants. *Developmental Psychology, 38,* 895–902.

Rosenberg, S. D., Rosenberg, H. J., & Farrell, M. P. (1999). The midlife crisis revisited. In S. L. Willis & J. D. Reid (Eds.), *Life in the middle* (pp. 47–73). San Diego: Academic Press.

Rosenblum, G. D., & Lewis, M. (1999). The relations among body image, physical attractiveness, and body mass in adolescence. *Child Development, 70,* 50–64.

Rosenblum, K. L., McDonough, S., Muzik, M., Miller, A., & Sameroff, A. (2002). Maternal representations of the infant: Associations with infant response to the still face. *Child Development, 73,* 999–1015.

Rosenbluth, S. C., & Steil, J. M. (1995). Predictors of intimacy for women in heterosexual and homosexual couples. *Journal of Social and Personal Relationships, 12*(2), 163–175.

Rosenfeld, D. (1999). Identity work among lesbian and gay elderly. *Journal of Aging Studies, 13,* 121–144.

Rosengren, K. S., Gelman, S. A., Kalish, C. W., & McCormick, M. (1991). As time goes by: Children's early understanding of growth in animals. *Child Development, 62,* 1302–1320.

Rosenthal, C. J., Martin-Matthews, A., & Matthews, S. H. (1996). Caught in the middle? Occupancy in multiple roles and help to parents in a national probability sample of Canadian adults. *Journal of Gerontology: Social Sciences, 51B,* S274–S283.

Rosenthal, E. (1998, November 1). For one-child policy, China rethinks iron hand. *The New York Times,* pp. 1, 20.

Rosenthal, E. (2003, July 20). Bias for boys leads to sale of baby girls in China. *New York Times,* sec. 1, p. 6, col. 3.

Rosenthal, R., & Vandell, D. L. (1996). Quality of care at school-aged child-care programs: Regulatable features, observed experiences, child perspectives, and parent perspectives. *Child Development, 67,* 2434–2445.

Ross, C. E., Mirowsky, J., & Goldsteen, K. (1990). The impact of the family on health: A decade in review. *Journal of Marriage and the Family, 52,* 1059–1078.

Ross, G., Lipper, E. G., & Auld, P. A. M. (1991). Educational status and school-related abilities of very low birth weight premature children. *Pediatrics, 8,* 1125–1134.

Ross, H. S. (1996). Negotiating principles of entitlement in sibling property disputes. *Developmental Psychology, 32,* 90–101.

Rossi, A. S. (2004). The menopausal transition and aging process. In O. G. Brim, C. D. Ryff, and R. C. Kessler (Eds.), *How healthy are we? A national study of well-being at midlife.* Chicago: University of Chicago Press.

Rossi, R. (1996, August 30). Small schools under microscope. *Chicago Sun-Times,* p. 24.

Rotenberg, K. J., & Eisenberg, N. (1997). Developmental differences in the understanding of and reaction to others' inhibition of emotional expression. *Developmental Psychology, 33,* 526–537.

Roth, G. S., Lane, M. A., Ingram, D. K., Mattison, J. A., Elahi, D., Tobin, J. D., Muller, D., & Metter, E. J. (2002). Biomarkers of caloric restriction may predict longevity in humans. *Science, 297,* 811.

Rothbart, M. K., Ahadi, S. A., & Evans, D. E. (2000). Temperament and personality: Origins and outcomes. *Journal of Personality and Social Psychology, 78,* 122–135.

Rothbart, M. K., Ahadi, S. A., Hershey, K. L., & Fisher, P. (2001). Investigations of temperament at three to seven years: The Children's Behavior Questionnaire. *Child Development, 72,* 1394–1408.

Rothbart, M. K., & Hwang, J. (2002). Measuring infant temperament. *Infant Behavior & Development, 130,* 1–4.

Rotheram-Borus, M. J., & Futterman, D. (2000). Promoting early detection of human immunodeficiency virus infection among adolescents. *Archives of Pediatric and Adolescent Medicine, 154,* 435–439.

Rothermund, K., & Brandtstadter, J. (2003). Coping with deficits and losses in later life: From compensatory action to accommodation. *Psychology and Aging, 18,* 896–905.

Rouse, C., Brooks-Gunn, J., & McLanahan, S. (2005). Introducing the issue. *The Future of Children, 15*(1), 5–14.

Roush, W. (1995). Arguing over why Johnny can't read. *Science, 267,* 1896–1898.

Rovee-Collier, C. (1996). Shifting the focus from what to why. *Infant Behavior and Development, 19,* 385–400.

Rovee-Collier, C. (1999). The development of infant memory. *Current Directions in Psychological Science, 8,* 80–85.

Rowe, J. W., & Kahn, R. L. (1997). Successful aging. *The Gerontologist, 37,* 433–440.

Rowland, A. S., Umbach, D. M., Stallone, L., Naftel, J., Bohlig, E. M., & Sandler, D. P. (2002). Prevalence of medication treatment for attention-deficit hyperactivity disorder among elementary school children in Johnston County, North Carolina. *American Journal of Public Health, 92,* 231–234.

Rubin, D. H., Erickson, C. J., San Agustin, M., Cleary, S. D., Allen, J. K., & Cohen, P. (1996). Cognitive and academic functioning of homeless children compared with housed children. *Pediatrics, 97,* 289–294.

Rubin, D. H., Krasilnikoff, P. A., Leventhal, J. M., Weile, B., & Berget, A. (1986, August 23). Effect of passive smoking on birth-weight. *The Lancet,* pp. 415–417.

Rubin, K. H., Bukowski, W., & Parker, J. G. (1998). Peer interactions, relationships, and groups. In W. Damon (Series Ed.) & N. Eisenberg (Vol. Ed.), *Handbook of child psychology: Vol. 3. Social, emotional, and personality development* (5th ed., pp. 619–700). New York: Wiley.

Rubin, K. H., Fein, G. G., & Vandenberg, B. (1983). Play. In P. H. Mussen (Series Ed.) & E. M. Hetherington (Vol. Ed.), *Handbook of child psychology: Vol. 4. Socialization, personality, and social development* (pp. 694–774). New York: Wiley.

Rubinstein, R. L., Alexander, B. B., Goodman, M., & Luborsky, M. (1991). Key relationships of never married, childless older women: A cultural analysis. *Journal of Gerontology: Social Sciences, 46,* S270–277.

Ruble, D. N., & Dweck, C. S. (1995). Self-conceptions, person conceptions, and their development. In N. Eisenberg, (Ed.), *Social development: Review of personality and social psychology* (pp. 109–139). Thousand Oaks, CA: Sage.

Ruble, D. N., & Martin, C. L. (1998). Gender development. In W. Damon (Series Ed.) & N. Eisenberg (Vol. Ed.), *Handbook of child psychology: Vol. 3. Social, emotional, and personality development* (5th ed., pp. 933–1016). New York: Wiley.

Rudman, D., Axel, G. F., Hoskote, S. N., Gergans, G. A., Lalitha, P. Y., Goldberg, A. F., Schlenker, R. A., Cohn, L., Rudman, I. W., & Mattson, D. E. (1990). Effects of human growth hormone in men over 60 years old. *New England Journal of Medicine, 323*(1), 1–6.

Rudolph, K. D., Lambert, S. F., Clark, A. G., & Kurlakowsky, K. D. (2001). Negotiating the transition to middle school: The role of self-regulatory processes. *Child Development, 72*(3), 929–946.

Rueter, M. A., & Conger, R. D. (1995). Antecedents of parent-adolescent disagreements. *Journal of Marriage and the Family, 57,* 435–448.

Ruffman, T., Slade, L., & Crowe, E. (2002). The relation between children's and mothers' mental state language and theory-of-mind understanding. *Child Development, 73,* 734–751.

Ruitenberg, A., van Swieten, J. C., Witteman, J. C., Mehta, K. M., van Duijn, C. M., Hofman, A., & Breteler, M. M. (2002). Alcohol consumption and risk of dementia: The Rotterdam Study. *Lancet, 359,* 281–286.

Ruiz, F., & Tanaka, K. (2001). The *ijime* phenomenon and Japan: Overarching consideration for cross-cultural studies. *Psychologia: An International Journal of Psychology in the Orient, 44,* 128–138.

Rutland, A. F., & Campbell, R. N. (1996). The relevance of Vygotsky's theory of the "zone of proximal development" to the assessment of children with intellectual disabilities. *Journal of Intellectual Disability Research, 40,* 151–158.

Rutledge, T., Reis, S. T., Olson, M., Owens, J., Kelsey, S. F., Pepine, C. J., Mankad, S., Rogers, W. J., Merz, C. N. B., Sopko, G., Cornell, C. E., Sharaf, B., & Matthews, K. A. (2004). Social networks are associated with lower mortality rates among women with suspected coronary disease: The National Heart, Lung, and Blood Institute-sponsored Women's Ischemia Syndrome Evaluation Study. *Psychosomatic Medicine, 66,* 882–888.

Rutter, M. (2002). Nature, nurture, and development: From evangelism through science toward policy and practice. *Child Development, 73,* 1–21.

Rutter, M. (2003). Commentary: Causal processes leading to antisocial behavior. *Developmental Psychology, 39,* 372–378.

Rutter, M., Caspi, A., Fergusson, D., Horwood, L. J., Goodman, R., Maughan B., Moffitt, T. E., Meltzer, H., & Carroll, J. (2004). Sex differences in developmental reading disability: New findings from 4 epidemiological studies. *Journal of the American Medical Association, 291,* 2007–2012.

Rutter, M., & the English and Romanian Adoptees (ERA) Study Team. (1998). Developmental catch-up, and deficit, following adoption after severe global early privation. *Journal of Child Psychology and Psychiatry, 39,* 465–476.

Rutter, M., O'Connor, T. G., and the English and Romanian Adoptees (ERA) Study Team. (2004). Are there biological programming effects for psychological development? Findings from a study of Romanian adoptees. *Developmental Psychology, 40,* 81–94.

Ryan, A. (2001). The peer group as a context for the development of young adolescent motivation and achievement. *Child Development, 72*(4), 1135–1150.

Ryan, A. S. (1997). The resurgence of breastfeeding in the United States. *Pediatrics, 99.* [Online]. Available: http://www.pediatrics.org/cgi/content/full/99/4/e12.

Ryan, A. S., Wenjun, Z., & Acosta, A. (2002). Breastfeeding continues to increase into the new millennium. *Pediatrics, 110,* 1103–1109.

Ryan, V., & Needham, C. (2001). Nondirective play therapy with children experiencing psychic trauma. *Clinical Child Psychology and Psychiatry* (special issue), *6,* 437–453.

Rybash, J. M., Hoyer, W. J., & Roodin, P. A. (1986). *Adult cognition and aging: Developmental changes in processing, knowing, and thinking.* New York: Pergamon.

Ryff, C. D. (1995). Psychological well-being in adult life. *Current Directions in Psychological Science, 4,* 99–104.

Ryff, C. D., & Keyes, C. L. M. (1995). The structure of psychological well-being revisited. *Journal of Personality and Social Psychology, 69,* 719–727.

Ryff, C. D., Keyes, C. L., & Hughes, D. L. (2004). Psychological well-being in MIDUS: Profiles of ethnic/racial diversity and life-course uniformity. In O. G. Brim, C. D. Ryff, and R. C. Kessler (Eds.), *How healthy are we? A national study of well-being at midlife* (pp. 398–424). Chicago: University of Chicago Press.

Ryff, C. D., & Seltzer, M. M. (1995). Family relations and individual development in adulthood and aging. In R. Blieszner & V. Hilkevitch (Eds.), *Handbook of aging and the family* (pp. 95–113). Westport, CT: Greenwood Press.

Ryff, C. D., & Singer, B. (1998). Middle age and well-being. *Encyclopedia of Mental Health, 2,* 707–719.

Ryff, C. D, Singer, B. H., & Palmersheim, K. A. (2004). Social inequalities in health and well-being: The role of relational and religious protective factors. In O. G. Brim, C. D. Ryff, and R. C. Kessler (Eds.). *How healthy are we? A national study of well-being at midlife.* Chicago: University of Chicago Press.

Rymer, R. (1993). *An abused child: Flight from silence.* New York: HarperCollins.

Saarni, C., Mumme, D. L., & Campos, J. J. (1998). Emotional development: Action, communication, and understanding. In W. Damon (Series Ed.) & N. Eisenberg (Vol. Ed.), *Handbook of child psychology: Vol. 3. Social, emotional, and personality development* (5th ed., pp. 237–309). New York: Wiley.

Sabbagh, M. A., & Baldwin, D. A. (2001). Learning words from knowledgeable versus ignorant speakers: Links between preschoolers' theory of mind and semantic development. *Child Development, 72*(4), 1054–1070.

Sabol, S. Z., Nelson, M. L., Fisher, C., Gunzerath, L., Brody, C. L., Hu, S., Sirota, L. A., Marcus, S. E., Greenberg, B. D., Lucas, F. R., IV, Benjamin, J., Murphy, D. L., & Hamer, D. H. (1999). A genetic association for cigarette smoking behavior. *Health Psychology, 18,* 7–13.

Sachs, B. P., Kobelin, C., Castro, M. A., & Frigoletto, F. (1999). The risks of lowering the cesarean-delivery rate. *New England Journal of Medicine, 340,* 54–57.

Sadeh, A., Raviv, A., & Gruber, R. (2000). Sleep patterns and sleep disruptions in school age children. *Developmental Psychology, 36*(3), 291–301.

Saffran, J. R. & Thiessen, E.D. (2003). Pattern induction by infant language learners. *Developmental Psychology, 39,* 484–494.

Sahyoun, N. R., Lentzner, H., Hoyert, D., & Robinson, K. N. (2001). Trends in causes of death among the elderly. *Aging Trends, No. 1.* Hyattsville, MD: National Center for Health Statistics.

Sahyoun, N. R., Pratt, L. A., Lentzner, H., Dey, A., & Robinson, K. N. (2001). The changing profile of nursing home residents: 1985–1997. *Aging Trends*, No. 4.

Saigal, S., Hoult, L. A., Streiner, D. L., Stoskopf, B. L., & Rosenbaum, P. L. (2000). School difficulties at adolescence in a regional cohort of children who were extremely low birth weight. *Pediatrics, 105,* 325–331.

Saigal, S., Stoskopf, B. L., Streiner, D. L., & Burrows, E. (2001). Physical growth and current health status of infants who were of extremely low birth weight and controls at adolescence. *Pediatrics, 108*(2), 407–415.

Salihu, H. M., Shumpert, M. N., Slay, M., Kirby, R. S., & Alexander, G. R. (2003). Childbearing beyond maternal age 50 and fetal outcomes in the United States. *Obstetrics and Gynecology, 102,* 1006–1014.

Salisbury, A., Law, K., LaGasse, L., & Lester, B. (2003). Maternal-fetal attachment. *Journal of the American Medical Association, 289,* 1701.

Salovey, P., Rothman, A. J., Detweiler, J. B., & Steward, W. T. (2000). Emotional states and physical health. *American Psychologist, 55,* 110–121.

Salthouse, T. A. (1984). Effects of age and typing skill. *Journal of Experimental Psychology: General, 113,* 345–371.

Salthouse, T. A. (1985). Anticipatory processing in transcription typing. *Journal of Applied Psychology, 70,* 264–271.

Salthouse, T. A. (1991). *Theoretical perspectives on cognitive aging.* Hillsdale, NJ: Erlbaum.

Salthouse, T. A., Fristoe, N., McGuthry, K. E., & Hambrick, D. Z. (1998). Relation of task switching to speed, age, and fluid intelligence. *Psychology and Aging, 13,* 445–461.

Salthouse, T. A., & Maurer, T. J. (1996). Aging, job performance, and career development. In J. E. Birren & K. W. Schaie (Eds.), *Handbook of the psychology of aging* (pp. 353–364). San Diego: Academic Press.

Samdal, O., & Dür, W. (2000). The school environment and the health of adolescents. In C. Currie, K. Hurrelmann, W. Settertobulte, R. Smith, & J. Todd (Eds.), *Health and health behaviour among young people: a WHO crossnational study (HBSC) international report* (pp. 49–64). WHO Policy Series: Healthy Policy for Children and Adolescents, Series No. 1.

Sampson, R. J. (1997). The embeddedness of child and adolescent development: A community-level perspective on urban violence. In J. McCord (Ed.), *Violence and childhood in the inner city* (pp. 31–77). Cambridge, England: Cambridge University Press.

Samuelsson, M., Radestad, I., & Segesten, K. (2001). A waste of life: Fathers' experience of losing a child before birth. *Birth, 28,* 124–130.

Sandberg, S., Järvenpää, S., Penttinen, A., Paton, J. Y., & McCann, D. C. (2004). Asthma exacerbations in children immediately following stressful life events: A Cox's hierarchical regression. *Thorax, 59,* 1046–1051.

Sandefur, G., Eggerling-Boeck, J., & Park, H. (2005). Off to a good start? Postsecondary education and early adult life. In R. A. Settersten, Jr., F. F. Furstenberg, Jr., & R. G. Rumbaut (Eds.), *On the frontier of adulthood: Theory, research, and public policy* (pp. 292–319). (John D. and Catherine T. MacArthur Foundation Series on Mental Health and Development, Research Network on Transitions to Adulthood and Public Policy.) Chicago: University of Chicago Press.

Sandler, D. P., Everson, R. B., Wilcox, A. J., & Browder, J. P. (1985). Cancer risk in adulthood from early life exposure to parents' smoking. *American Journal of Public Health, 75,* 487–492.

Sandler, W., Meir, I., Padden, C., & Aronoff, M. (2005). The emergence of grammar: Systematic structure in a new language. *Proceedings of the National Academy of Sciences, 102,* 2661–2665.

Sandnabba, H. K., & Ahlberg, C. (1999). Parents' attitudes and expectations about children's cross-gender behavior. *Sex Roles, 40,* 249–263.

Sandstrom, M. J., & Coie, J. D. (1999). A developmental perspective on peer rejection: Mechanisms of stability and change. *Child Development, 70*(4), 955–966.

Sankar, P., Cho. M. K., Condit, C. M., Hunt, L. M., Koenig, B., Marshall, P., Lee, S., & Spicer, P. (2004). Genetic research and health disparities. *Journal of the American Medical Association, 291,* 2985–2989.

Santer, L. J., & Stocking, C. B. (1991). Safety practices and living conditions of low-income urban families. *Pediatrics, 88,* 111–118.

Santos, F., & Ingrassia, R. (August 18, 2002). The face of homelessness has changed: Family surge at shelters. *New York Daily News.* Available at www.nationalhomeless.org/housing/familiesarticle.html.

Santos, I. S., Victora, C. G., Huttly, S., & Carvalhal, J. B. (1998). Caffeine intake and low birth weight: A population-based case-control study. *American Journal of Epidemiology, 147,* 620–627.

Sapienza, C. (1990, October). Parental imprinting of genes. *Scientific American,* pp. 52–60.

Sapolsky, R. M. (1992). Stress and neuroendocrine changes during aging. *Generations, 16*(4), 35–38.

Sapp, F., Lee, K., & Muir, D. (2000). Three-year-olds' difficulty with the appearance-reality distinction: Is it real or apparent? *Developmental Psychology, 36,* 547–560.

Sarkisian, N., & Gerstel, N. (2004). Explaining the gender gap in help to parents: The importance of employment. *Journal of Marriage and Family, 66,* 431–451.

Satariano, W. A., MacLeod, K.E., Cohn, T. E., & Ragland, D. R. (2004). Problems with vision associated with limitations of avoidance of driving in older populations. *Journal of Gerontology: Social Sciences, 59B,* S281–S286.

Satcher, D. (2001). *Women and smoking: A report of the Surgeon General.* Washington, DC: Department of Health and Human Services.

Satz, P. (1993). Brain reserve capacity on symptom onset after brain injury: A formulation and review of evidence for threshold theory. *Neuropsychology, 7,* 273–295.

Saudino, K. J. (2003a). Parent ratings of infant temperament: Lessons from twin studies. *Infant Behavior & Development, 26,* 100–107.

Saudino, K. J. (2003b). The need to consider contrast effects in parent-rated temperament. *Infant Behavior & Development, 26,* 118–120.

Saudino, K. J., Wertz, A. E., Gagne, J. R., & Chawla, S. (2004). Night and day: Are siblings as different in temperament as parents say they are? *Journal of Personality and Social Psychology, 87,* 698–706.

Savage, S. L., & Au, T. K. (1996). What word learners do when input contradicts the mutual exclusivity assumption. *Child Development, 67,* 3120–3134.

Savic, I., Berglund, H., Gulyas, B., & Roland, P. (2001). Smelling of odorous sex hormone-like compounds causes sex-differentiated hypothalamic activations in humans. *Neuron, 31,* 661–668.

Savic, I., Berglund, H., & Lindström, P. (2005). Brain response to putative pheromones in homosexual men. *Proceedings of the National Academy of Sciences, 102,* 7356–7361.

Sawicki, M. B. (2005, March 16). *Collision course: The Bush budget and Social Security.* EPI Briefing Paper #156. Retrieved April 28, 2005, from http://www.epinet.org/content.cfm/bp156.

Saxe, G. B., Guberman, S. R., & Gearhart, M. (1987). Social processes in early number development. *Monographs of the Society for Research in Child Development, 52*(216).

Scandinavian Simvastatin Survival Study Group. (1994). Randomized trial of cholesterol lowering in 4444 patients with coronary heart disease: The Scandinavian Simvastatin Survival Study (4S). *The Lancet, 344,* 1383–1389.

Scarborough, H. S. (1990). Very early language deficits in dyslexic children. *Child Development, 61,* 1728–1743.

Scariati, P. D., Grummer-Strawn, L. M., & Fein, S. B. (1997). A longitudinal analysis of infant morbidity and the extent of breastfeeding in the United States. *Pediatrics, 99,* e5.

Scarr, S. (1992). Developmental theories for the 1990s: Development and individual differences. *Child Development, 63,* 1–19.

Scarr, S. (1997b). Why child care has little impact on most children's development. *Current Directions in Psychological Science, 6*(5), 143–148.

Scarr, S., & McCartney, K. (1983). How people make their own environments: A theory of genotype environment effects. *Child Development, 54,* 424–435.

Schacter, D. L. (1999). The seven sins of memory: Insights from psychology and cognitive neuroscience. *American Psychologist, 54,* 182–203.

Schafer, G. (2005). Infants can learn decontextualized words before their first birthday. *Child Development, 76,* 87-96.

Schaie, K. W. (1977–1978). Toward a stage theory of adult cognitive development. *Journal of Aging and Human Development, 8*(2), 129–138.

Schaie, K. W. (1983). The Seattle Longitudinal Study: A twenty-one-year investigation of psychometric intelligence. In K. W. Schaie (Ed.), *Longitudinal studies of adult personality development* (pp. 64–155). New York: Guilford.

Schaie, K. W. (1984). Midlife influences upon intellectual functioning in old age. *International Journal of Behavioral Development, 7,* 463–478.

Schaie, K. W. (1990). Intellectual development in adulthood. In J. E. Birren & K. W. Schaie (Eds.), *Handbook of the psychology of aging* (pp. 291–309). San Diego: Academic Press.

Schaie, K. W. (1994). The course of adult intellectual development. *American Psychologist, 49*(4), 304–313.

Schaie, K. W. (1996a). Intellectual development in adulthood. In J. E. Birren & K. W. Schaie (Eds.), *Handbook of the psychology of aging* (4th ed., pp. 266–286). San Diego: Academic Press.

Schaie, K. W. (1996b). *Intellectual development in adulthood: The Seattle Longitudinal Study.* Cambridge, England: Cambridge University Press.

Schaie, K. W. (2005). *Developmental influences on adult intelligence: The Seattle Longitudinal Study.* New York: Oxford University Press.

Schaie, K. W., & Hertzog, C. (1983). Fourteen-year cohort sequential analyses of adult intellectual development. *Developmental Psychology, 19*(4), 531–543.

Schaie, K. W., & Willis, S. L. (1986). Can decline in adult intellectual functioning be reversed? *Developmental Psychology, 22,* 223–232.

Schaie, K. W., & Willis, S. L. (1991). Adult personality and psychomotor performance: Cross-sectional and longitudinal analysis. *Journal of Gerontology, 46*(6), P275–284.

Schaie, K. W., & Willis, S. L. (1996). Psychometric intelligence and aging. In F. Blanchard-Fields & T. M. Hess (Eds.), *Perspectives on cognitive change in adulthood and aging* (pp. 293–322). New York: McGraw-Hill.

Schaie, K. W., & Willis, S. L. (2000). A stage theory model of adult cognitive development revisited. In B. Rubinstein, M. Moss, & M. Kleban (Eds.). *The many dimensions of aging: Essays in honor of M. Powell Lawton* (pp. 173–191). New York: Springer.

Schairer, C., Lubin, J., Troisi, R., Sturgeon, S., Brinton, L., & Hoover, R. (2000). Menopausal estrogen and estrogen-progestin replacement therapy and breast cancer risk. *Journal of the American Medical Association, 283,* 485–491.

Schanberg, S. M., & Field, T. M. (1987). Sensory deprivation illness and supplemental stimulation in the rat pup and preterm human neonate. *Child Development, 58,* 1431–1447.

Schardt, D. (1995, June). For men only. *Nutrition Action Health Letter, 22*(5), 4–7.

Scharf, M., Mayseless, O., & Kivenson-Baron, I. (2004). Adolescents' attachment representations and developmental tasks in emerging adulthood. *Developmental Psychology, 40,* 430–444.

Scharlach, A. E., & Fredriksen, K. I. (1993). Reactions to the death of a parent during midlife. *Omega, 27,* 307–319.

Schauble, L. (1996). The development of scientific reasoning in knowledge-rich contexts. *Developmental Psychology, 32,* 102–119.

Schaubroeck, J., Jones, J. R., & Xie, J. L. (2001). Individual differences in utilizing control to cope with job demands: Effects on susceptibility to infectious disease. *Journal of Applied Psychology, 86,* 265–278.

Schaumberg, D. A., Mendes, F., Balaram, M., Dana, M. R., Sparrow, D., & Hu, H. (2004). Accumulated lead exposure and risk of age-related cataract in men. *Journal of the American Medical Association, 292,* 2750–2754.

Scheers, N. J., Rutherford, G. W., & Kemp, J. S. (2003). Where should infants sleep? A comparison of risk for suffocation of infants sleeping in cribs, adult beds, and other sleeping locations. *Pediatrics, 112,* 883–889.

Scheidt, P., Overpeck, M. D., Wyatt, W., & Aszmann, A. (2000). In C. Currie, K. Hurrelmann, W. Settertobulte, R. Smith, & J. Todd (Eds.), *Health and health behaviour among young people: a WHO cross-national study (HBSC) international report* (pp. 24–38). WHO Policy Series: Healthy Policy for Children and Adolescents, Series No. 1.

Schemo, D. J. (2004, August 19). Charter schools lagging behind, test scores show. *New York Times,* pp. A1, A16.

Scher, M. S., Richardson, G. A., & Day, N. L., (2000). Effects of prenatal crack/cocaine and other drug exposure on electroencephalographic sleep studies at birth and one year. *Pediatrics, 105,* 39–48.

Schieve, L. A., Meikle, S. F., Ferre, C., Peterson, H. B., Jeng, G., & Wilcox, L. S. (2002). Low- and very low-birth-weight in infants conceived with use of assisted reproductive technology. *New England Journal of Medicine, 346,* 731–737.

Schiller, J. S., & Bernadel, L. (2004). Summary health statistics for the U.S. population: National Health Interview Survey, 2002. *Vital and Health Statistics, 10*(220). Hyattsville, MD: National Center for Health Statistics.

Schlegel, A., & Barry, H. (1991). *Adolescence: An anthropological inquiry.* New York: Free Press.

Schmidt, P. J., Nieman, L. K., Danaceau, M. A., Adams, L. F., & Rubinow, D. R. (1998). Differential behavioral effects of gonadal steroids in women with and in those without premenstrual syndrome. *New England Journal of Medicine, 338,* 209–216.

Schmitt, B. D. (1997). Nocturnal enuresis. *Pediatrics in Review, 18,* 183–190.

Schmitz, S., Saudino, K. J., Plomin, R., Fulker, D. W., & DeFries, J. C. (1996). Genetic and environmental influences on temperament in middle childhood: Analyses of teacher and tester ratings. *Child Development, 67,* 409–422.

Schmuckler, M. A., & Fairhall, J. L. (2001). Visual-proprioceptive intermodal perception using point light displays. *Child Development, 72,* 949–962.

Schnall, P. L., Pieper, C., Schwartz, J. E., Karasek, R. A., Schlussel, Y., Devereaux, R. B., Ganau, A., Alderman, M.,Warren, K., & Pickering, T. G. (1990). The relationship between "job strain," workplace diastolic blood pressure, and left ventricular mass index: Results of a case-control study. *Journal of the American Medical Association, 263,* 1929–1935.

Schneider, B. H., Atkinson, L., & Tardif, C. (2001). Child-parent attachment and children's peer relations: A quantitative review. *Developmental Psychology, 37,* 86–100.

Schneider, E. L. (1992). Biological theories of aging. *Generations, 16*(4), 7–10.

Schneider, M. (2002). *Do school facilities affect academic outcomes?* Washington, DC: National Clearinghouse for Educational Facilities.

Schneiderman, L. J., Gilmer, T., Teetzel, H. D., Dugan, D. O., Blustein, J., Cranford, R., Briggs, K. B., Komatsu, G. I., Goodman-Crews, P., Cohn, F., & Young, E. W. D. (2003). Effects of ethics consultations on non-beneficial life-sustaining treatments in the intensive care setting: A randomized controlled trial. *Journal of the American Medical Association, 290,* 1166–1172.

Schoenborn, C. A. (2004). Marital status and health: United States, 1999–2002. *Advance Data from Vital and Health Statistics,* No. 351. Hyattsville, MD: National Center for Health Statistics.

Schoeni, R., & Ross, K. (2005). Maternal assistance from families during the transition to adulthood. In R. A. Settersten, Jr., F. F. Furstenberg, Jr., & R. G. Rumbaut (Eds.), *On the frontier of adulthood: Theory, research, and public policy* (396–416). (John D. and Catherine T. MacArthur Foundation Series on Mental Health and Development, Research Network on Transitions to Adulthood and Public Policy.) Chicago: University of Chicago Press.

Scholten, C. M. (1985). *Childbearing in American society: 1650–1850.* New York: New York University Press.

Schonfeld, D. J., Johnson, S. R., Perrin, E. C., O'Hare, L. L., & Cicchetti, D. V. (1993). Understanding of acquired immunodeficiency syndrome by elementary school children—A developmental survey. *Pediatrics, 92,* 389–395.

Schonfield, D. (1974). Translations in gerontology—From lab to life: Utilizing information. *American Psychologist, 29,* 228–236.

Schooler, C. (1984). Psychological effects of complex environments during the life-span: A review and theory. *Intelligence, 8,* 259–281.

Schooler, C. (1990). Psychosocial factors and effective cognitive functioning in adulthood. In J. E. Burren & K. W. Schaie (Eds.), *The handbook of aging* (pp. 347–358). San Diego: Academic Press.

Schore, A. N. (1994). *Affect regulation and the origin of the self: The neurobiology of emotional development.* Hillsdale, NJ: Erlbaum.

Schreiber, J. B., Robins, M., Striegel-Moore, R., Obarzanek, E., Morrison, J. A., & Wright, D. J. (1996). Weight modification efforts reported by preadolescent girls. *Pediatrics, 96,* 63–70.

Schulenberg, J., O'Malley, P., Backman, J., & Johnston, L. (2005). Early adult transitions and their relation to well-being and substance use. In R. A. Settersten, Jr., F. F. Furstenberg, Jr., &

R. G. Rumbaut (Eds.), *On the frontier of adult-hood: Theory, research, and public policy* (pp.417–453). (John D. and Catherine T. MacArthur Foundation Series on Mental Health and Development, Research Network on Transitions to Adulthood and Public Policy.) Chicago: University of Chicago Press.

Schulz, M. S., Cowan, P. A., Cowan, C. P., & Brennan, R. T. (2004). Coming home upset: Gender, marital satisfaction, and the daily spillover of workday experience into couple interactions. *Journal of Family Psychology, 18,* 250–263.

Schulz, R. (1978). *A psychology of death, dying, and bereavement.* Reading, MA: Addison-Wesley.

Schulz, R., & Beach, S. R. (1999). Caregiving as a risk factor for mortality: The Caregiver Health Effects Study. *Journal of the American Medical Association, 282,* 2215–2219.

Schulz, R., & Heckhausen, J. (1996). A life-span model of successful aging. *American Psychologist, 51,* 702–714.

Schulz, R, & Martire, L. M. (2004). Family caregiving of persons with dementia: Preva-lence, health effects, and support strategies. *American Journal of Geriatric Psychiatry, 12,* 240–249.

Schumann, J. (1997). The view from elsewhere: Why there can be no best method for teaching a second language. *The Clarion: Magazine of the European Second Language Acquisition, 3*(1), 23–24.

Schwartz, D., Chang, L., & Farver, J. M. (2001). Correlates of victimization in Chinese children's peer groups. *Developmental Psychology, 37*(4), 520–532.

Schwartz, D., Dodge, K. A., Pettit, G. S., & Bates, J. E. & The Conduct Problems Pre-vention Research Group (2000). Friendship as a moderating factor in the pathway between early harsh home environment and later victim-ization in the peer group. *Developmental Psychology, 36*(5), 646–662.

Schwartz, D., McFadyen-Ketchum, S. A., Dodge, K. A., Pettit, G. S., & Bates, J. E. (1998). Peer group victimization as a predictor of children's behavior problems at home and in school. *Development and Psychopathology, 10,* 87–99.

Schwartz, J. (2004). Air pollution and children's health. *Pediatrics, 113,* 1037–1043.

Schwartz, J. (2005, March 21). New openness in deciding when and how to die. *New York Times,* p. A1.

Schwartz, L. L. (2003). A nightmare for King Solomon: The new reproductive technologies. *Journal of Family Psychology, 17,* 292–237.

Schweinhart, L. J., Barnes, H. V., & Weikart, D. P. (1993). *Significant benefits: The High/Scope Perry Preschool Study through age 27* (Monographs of the High/Scope Educational Research Foundation No. 10). Ypsilanti, MI: High/Scope.

Schwimmer, J. B., Burwinkle, T. M., Varni, J. W. (2003 April). Health-related quality of life of severely obese children and adolescents. *Journal of the American Medical Association, 289*(14), 1813–1819.

Scientific Registry of Transplant Recipients. (2004). Fast facts about transplants, July 1, 2003-June 30, 2004. [Online]. Retrieved from http://www.ustransplant.org/csr0105/facts.php on March 15, 2005.

Scott, G., & Ni, H. (2004). Access to health care among Hispanic/Latino children: United States, 1998–2001. *Advance Data from Vital and Health Statistics,* No. 344. Hyattsville, MD: National Center for Health Statistics.

Scott, J. (1998). Changing attitudes to sexual morality: A cross-national comparison. *Sociol-ogy, 32,* 815–845.

Sedlak, A. J., & Broadhurst, D. D. (1996). *Ex-ecutive summary of the third national incidence study of child abuse and neglect* (NIS-3). Washington, DC: U.S. Department of Health and Human Services.

Seeman, E. Dubin, L. F., & Seeman, M. (2003). Religiosity/spirituality and health: A critical re-view of the evidence for biological pathways. *American Psychologist, 58,* 53–63.

Seftor, N. S., & Turner, S. E. (2002). Back to school: Federal student aid policy and adult col-lege enrollment. *Journal of Human Resources, 37,* 336–352.

Segerstrom, S. C., & Miller, G. E. (2004). Psychological stress and the human immune system: A meta-analytic study of 30 years of inquiry. *Psychological Bulletin, 130,* 601–630.

Seidler, A., Neinhaus, A., Bernhardt, T., Kauppinen, T., Elo, A. L., & Frolich, L. (2004). Psychosocial work factors and demen-tia. *Occupational and Environmental Medicine, 61,* 962–971.

Seifer, R. (2003). Twin studies, biases of parents, and biases of researchers. *Infant Behavior & Development, 26,* 115–117.

Seifer, R., Schiller, M., Sameroff, A. J., Resnick, S., & Riordan, K. (1996). Attach-ment, maternal sensitivity, and infant tempera-ment during the first year of life. *Developmental Psychology, 32,* 12–25.

Seiner, S. H., & Gelfand, D. M. (1995). Effects of mother's simulated withdrawal and de-pressed affect on mother-toddler interactions. *Child Development, 60,* 1519–1528.

Seitz, V. (1990). Intervention programs for im-poverished children: A comparison of educa-tional and family support models. *Annals of Child Development, 7,* 73–103.

Selkoe, D. J. (1991). The molecular pathology of Alzheimer's disease. *Neuron, 6*(4), 487–498.

Selkoe, D. J. (1992). Aging brain, aging mind. *Scientific American, 267,* 135–142.

Sellers, E. M. (1998). Pharmacogenetics and eth-noracial differences in smoking. *Journal of the American Medical Association, 280,* 179–180.

Selman, R. L. (1980). *The growth of interper-sonal understanding: Developmental and clini-cal analyses.* New York: Academic.

Selman, R. L., & Selman, A. P. (1979, April). Children's ideas about friendship: A new the-ory. *Psychology Today,* pp. 71–80.

Seltzer, J. A. (2000). Families formed outside of marriage. *Journal of Marriage and the Family, 62,* 1247–1268.

Seltzer, J. A. (2004). Cohabitation in the United States and Britain: demography, kinship, and

the future. *Journal of Marriage and Family, 66,* 921–928.

Seminara, S. B., Messager, S., Chatzidaki, E. E., Thresher, R. R., Acierno Jr., J. S., Shagoury, J. K., Bo-Abbas, Y., Kuohung, W., Schwinof, K. M., Hendrick, A. G., Zahn, D., Dixon, J., Kaiser, U. B., Slaugenhaupt, S. A., Gusella, J. F., O'Rahilly, S., Carlton, M. B. L., Crowley Jr., W. F., Aparicio, S. A. J. R., & Colledge, W. H. (2003). The GPR54 gene as a regulator of puberty. *New England Journal of Medicine, 349,* 1614–1627.

Sen, A., Partelow, L., & Miller, D. C. (2005). *Comparative indicators of education in the United States and other G8 countries: 2004* (NCES 2005-021). Washington, DC: National Center for Education Statistics.

Senghas, A., & Coppola, M. (2001). Children creating language: How Nicaraguan sign lan-guage acquired a spatial grammar. *Psychologi-cal Science, 12,* 323–328.

Senghas, A., Kita, S., & Ozyürek, A. (2004). Children creating core properties of language: Evidence from an emerging sign language in Nicaragua. *Science, 305,* 1779–1782.

Serbin, L. A., Moller, L. C., Gulko, J., Powlishta, K. K., & Colburne, K. A. (1994). The emergence of gender segregation in tod-dler playgroups. In C. Leaper (Ed.), *Childhood gender segregation: Causes and consequences* (*New Directions for Child Development No. 65,* pp. 7–17). San Francisco: Jossey-Bass.

Serbin, L., Poulin-Dubois, D., Colburne, K. A., Sen, M., & Eichstedt. J. A. (2001). Gender stereotyping in infancy: Visual preferences for knowledge of gender-stereotyped toys in the second year. *International Journal of Behav-ioral Development, 25,* 7–15.

Serres, L. (2001). Morphological changes of the human hippocampal formation from midgesta-tion to early childhood. In C. A. Nelson & M. Luciana (Eds.), *Handbook of developmental cognitive neuroscience* (pp. 45–58). Cambridge, MA: MIT Press.

Seshadri, S., Beiser, A., Selhub, J., Jacques, P. F., Rosenberg, I. H., D'Agostino, R. B., Wilson, P. W., & Wolf, P. A. (2002). Plasma homocysteine as a risk factor for dementia and Alzheimer's disease. *New England Journal of Medicine, 346,* 476–483.

Sethi, A., Mischel, W., Aber, J. L., Shoda, Y., & Rodriguez, M. L. (2000). The role of strategic attention deployment in development of selfregulation: Predicting preschoolers' de-lay of gratification from mother-toddler inter-actions. *Developmental Psychology, 36,* 767–777.

Settersten, Jr., R. A. (2005). Social policy and the transition to adulthood: Toward stronger in-stitutions and individual capacities. In R. A. Settersten, Jr., F. F. Furstenberg, Jr., & R. G. Rumbaut (Eds.), *On the frontier of adulthood: Theory, research, and public policy* (534–560). Chicago: University of Chicago Press.

Sexton, A. (1966). Little girl, my string bean, my lovely woman. *The complete poems: Anne Sex-ton.* New York: Houghton Mifflin, 1981.

Seybold, K. S., & Hill, P. C. (2001). The role of religion and spirituality in mental and physical health. *Current Directions in Psychological Science, 10,* 21–24.

Shanahan, M. J., & Flaherty, B. P. (2001). Dynamic patterns of time use in adolescence. *Child Development, 72*(2), 385–401.

Shanahan, M., Porfeli, E., & Mortimer, J. (2005). Subjective age identity and the transition to adulthood: When do adolescents become adults? In R. A. Settersten, Jr., F. F. Furstenberg, Jr., & R. G. Rumbaut (Eds.), *On the frontier of adulthood: Theory, research, and public policy* (pp. 225–255). (John D. and Catherine T. MacArthur Foundation Series on Mental Health and Development, Research Network on Transitions to Adulthood and Public Policy.) Chicago: University of Chicago Press.

Shankaran, S., Das, A., Bauer, C. R., Bada, H. S., Lester, B., Wright, L. L., and Smeriglio, V. (2004). Association between patterns of maternal substance use and infant birth weight, length, and head circumference. *Pediatrics, 114,* e226–e234.

Shannon, J. D., Tamis-LeMonda, C. S., London, K., & Cabrera, N. (2002). Beyond rough and tumble: Low income fathers' interactions and children's cognitive development at 24 months. *Parenting: Science & Practice, 2*(2), 77–104.

Shannon, M. (2000). Ingestion of toxic substances by children. *New England Journal of Medicine, 342,* 186–191.

Shapiro, P. (1994, November). My house is your house: Advance planning can ease the way when parents move in with adult kids. *AARP Bulletin,* p. 2.

Sharma, A. R., McGue, M. K., & Benson, P. L. (1996a). The emotional and behavioral adjustment of United States adopted adolescents, Part I: An overview. *Children and Youth Services Review, 18,* 83–100.

Sharma, A. R., McGue, M. K., & Benson, P. L. (1996b). The emotional and behavioral adjustment of United States adopted adolescents, Part II: Age at adoption. *Children and Youth Services Review, 18,* 101–114.

Shatz, M., & Gelman, R. (1973). The development of communication skills: Modifications in the speech of young children as a function of listener. *Monographs of the Society for Research in Child Development, 38*(5, Serial No. 152).

Shaw, B. A., Krause, N., Chatters, L. M., Connell, C. M., & Ingersoll-Dayton, B. (2004). Emotional support from parents early in life, aging, and health. *Psychology and Aging, 19,* 4–12.

Shaywitz, S. (2003). *Overcoming dyslexia: A new and complete science-based program for overcoming reading problems at any level.* New York: Knopf.

Shaywitz, S. E. (1998). Current concepts: Dyslexia. *New England Journal of Medicine, 338,* 307–312.

Shaywitz, S. E., Shaywitz, B. A., Pugh, K. R., Fulbright, R. K., Constable, R. T.,Mencl, W. E., Shankweiler, D. P., Liberman, A. M., Skudlarski, P., Fletcher, J. M., Katz, L., Marchione, K. E., Lacadie, C., Gatenby, C., & Gore, J. C. (1998). Functional disruption in the organization of the brain for reading in dyslexia. *Proceedings of the National Academy of Sciences of the United States of America, 95,* 2636–2641.

Shea, K. M., Little, R. E., & the ALSPAC Study Team (1997). Is there an association between preconceptual paternal X-ray exposure and birth outcome? *American Journal of Epidemiology, 145,* 546–551.

Shea, S., Basch, C. E., Stein, A. D., Contento, I. R., Irigoyen, M., & Zybert, P. (1993). Is there a relationship between dietary fat and stature or growth in children three to five years of age? *Pediatrics, 92,* 579–586.

Shedlock, D. J., & Cornelius, S. W. (2003). Psychological approaches to wisdom and its development. In J. Demick & C. Andreolett (Eds.), *Handbook of adult development* (pp. 153–167). New York: Plenum Press.

Sheldon, K. M., & Kasser, T. (2001). Getting older, getting better? Personal strivings and psychological maturity across the life span. *Developmental Psychology, 37,* 491–501.

Shepherd, J., Cobbe, S. M., Ford, I., Isles, C. G., Lorimer, A. R., MacFarlane, P. W., McKillop, J. H., & Packard, C. J. (1995). Prevention of coronary heart disease with pravastatin in men with hypercholesterolemia. *New England Journal of Medicine, 333,* 1301–1307.

Sherman, E. (1993). Mental health and successful adaptation in late life. *Generations, 17*(1), 43–46.

Shields, M. K., & Behrman, R. E. (2004). Children of immigrant families: Analysis and recommendations. In R. E. Behrman (Ed.), *Children of immigrant families* (pp. 4–15). *The Future of Children, 14*(2). [Online]. Available: http://www.futureofchildren.org. Access date: October 8, 2004.

Shields. A. E., Comstock, C., & Weiss, K. B. (2004). Variations in asthma by race/ethnicity among children enrolled in a state Medicaid program. *Pediatrics, 113,* 496–504.

Shiono, P. H., & Behrman, R. E. (1995). Low birth weight: Analysis and recommendations. *The Future of Children, 5*(1), 4–18.

Shoghi-Jadid, K., Small, G. W., Agdeppa, E. D., Kepe, V., Ercoli, L. M., Siddarth, P., Read, S., Satyamurthy, N., Petric, A., Huang, S. C., & Barrio, J. R. (2002). Localization of neurofibrillary tangles and beta-amyloid plaques in the brains of living patients with Alzheimer disease. *American Journal of Geriatric Psychiatry, 10,* 24–35.

Shonkoff, J., & Phillips, D. (2000). Growing up in child care. In I. Shonkoff & D. Phillips (Eds.), *From neurons to neighborhoods* (pp. 297–327). Washington, DC: National Research Council/Institute of Medicine.

Should you take estrogen to prevent osteoporosis? (1994, August). *Johns Hopkins Medical Letter: Health after 50,* pp. 4–5.

Shuey, K., & Hardy, M.A. (2003). Assistance to aging parents and parents-in-law: Does lineage affect family allocation decisions? *Journal of Marriage and Family, 65,* 418-431.

Shulik, R. N. (1988). Faith development in older adults. *Educational Gerontology, 14,* 291–301.

Shulman, S., Scharf, M., Lumer, D., & Maurer, O. (2001). Parental divorce and young adult children's romantic relationships: Resolution of the divorce experience. *American Journal of Orthopsychiatry, 71,* 473–478.

Shumaker, S. A., Legault, C., Kuller, L., Rapp, S. R., Thal, L., Lane, D. S., Fillit, H., Stefanick, M. L., Hendrix, S. L., Lewis, C. E., Masaki, K., Coker, L. H. for the Women's Health Initiative Memory Study Investigators. (2004). Conjugated equine estrogens and incidence of probable dementia and mild cognitive impairment in postmenopausal women: Women's Health Initiative Memory Study. *Journal of the American Medical Association, 291,* 2947–2958.

Shumaker, S. A., Legault, C., Rapp, S. R., Thal, L., Wallace, R. B., Ockene, J. K., Hendrix, S. L., Jones, B. N., Assaf, A. R., Jackson, R. D., Kotchen, J. M., Wassertheil-Smoller, S., Wactawski-Wende, J., for the WHIMS Investigators. (2003). Estrogen plus progestin and the incidence of dementia and mild cognitive impairment in postmenopausal women: The Women's Health Initiative Memory Study: A randomized controlled trial. *Journal of the American Medical Association, 289,* 2651–2662.

Shwe, H. I., & Markman, E. M. (1997). Young children's appreciation of the mental impact of their communicative signals. *Developmental Psychology, 33*(4), 630–636.

Sick, W. T., Perfetti, C. A., Jin, Z., & Tan, L. H. (2004). Biological abnormality of impaired reading is constrained by culture. *Nature, 431,* 71–76.

Siegal, M., & Peterson, C. C. (1998). Preschoolers' understanding of lies and innocent and negligent mistakes. *Developmental Psychology, 34*(2), 332–341.

Siegel, A. C., & Burton, R. V. (1999). Effects of baby walkers on motor and mental development in human infants. *Journal of Developmental and Behavioral Pediatrics, 20,* 355–361.

Siegler, I. C. (1997). Promoting health and minimizing stress in midlife. In M. E. Lachman & J. B. James (Eds.), *Multiple paths of midlife development* (pp. 241–255). Chicago: University of Chicago Press.

Siegler, I. C., & Brummett, B. H. (2000). Associations among NEO personality assessments and well-being at midlife: Facet-level analyses. *Psychology and Aging, 15,* 710–714.

Siegler, R. S. (1998). *Children's thinking* (3rd ed.). Upper Saddle River, NJ: Prentice-Hall.

Siegler, R. S., & Booth, J. L. (2004). Development of numerical estimation in young children. *Child Development, 75,* 428–444.

Siegler, R. S., & Opfer, J. E. (2003). The development of numerical estimation: Evidence for multiple representations of numerical quantity. *Psychological Science, 14,* 237–243.

Siegler, R. S., & Richards, D. (1982). The development of intelligence. In R. Sternberg (Ed.), *Handbook of human intelligence.* London: Cambridge University Press.

Siegrist, J. (1996). Adverse health effects of high-effort/low-reward conditions. *Journal of Occupational Health Psychology, 1*(1), 27–41.

Sieving, R. E., McNeely, C. S., & Blum, R. W. (2000). Maternal expectations, mother-child connectedness, and adolescent sexual debut.

Archives of Pediatric & Adolescent Medicine, 154, 809–816.

Sieving, R. E., Oliphant, J. A., & Blum, R. W. (2002). Adolescent sexual behavior and sexual health. *Pediatrics in Review, 23,* 407–416.

Sigelman, C., Alfeld-Liro, C., Derenowski, E., Durazo, O., Woods, T., Maddock, A., & Mukai, T. (1996). Mexican American and Anglo American children's responsiveness to a theory-centered AIDS education program. *Child Development, 67,* 253–266.

Sigman, M., Cohen, S. E., & Beckwith, L. (1997). Why does infant attention predict adolescent intelligence? *Infant Behavior and Development, 20,* 133–140.

Signorello, L. B., Nordmark, A., Granath, F., Blot, W. J., McLaughlin, J. K., Anneren, G., Lundgren, S., Ekbom, A., Rane, A., & Cnattingius, S. (2001). Caffeine metabolism and the risk of spontaneous abortion of normal karyotype fetuses. *Obstetrics & Gynecology, 98*(6), 1059–1066.

Silberner, J. (2005), July 9). Labels on erectile dysfunction drugs to contain new warnings. [Online]. Retrieved from http://www.npr.org/templates/story/story.php?story Id=4736996.

Silver, M. H., Bubrick, E., Jilinskaia, E., & Perls, T. T. (1998, August). Is there a centenarian personality? Paper presented at the annual meeting of the American Psychological Association, San Francisco.

Silver, M. H., Jininskaia, E., & Perls, T. T. (2001). Cognitive functional status of age-confirmed centenarians in a population-based study. *Journal of Gerontology: Psychological Sciences, 56B,* P134–140.

Silverberg, S. B. (1996). Parents' well-being as their children transition to adolescence. In C. Ryff & M. M. Seltzer (Eds.), *The parental experience in midlife* (pp. 215–254). Chicago: University of Chicago Press.

Silverman, W. K., La Greca, A. M., & Wasserstein, S. (1995). What do children worry about? Worries and their relation to anxiety. *Child Development, 66,* 671–686.

Silvern, S. B. (1998). Educational implications of play with computers. In D. P. Fromberg & D. Bergen (Eds.), *Play from birth to twelve and beyond: Contexts, perspectives, and meanings* (pp. 530–536). New York: Garland.

Silverstein, M., & Bengtson, V. L. (1997). Intergenerational solidarity and the structure of adult child-parent relationships in American families. *American Journal of Sociology, 103,* 429–460.

Silverstein, M., & Long, J. D. (1998). Trajectories of grandparents' perceived solidarity with adult grandchildren: A growth curve analysis over 23 years. *Journal of Marriage and the Family, 60,* 912–923.

Simmons, R. G., Blyth, D. A., & McKinney, K. L. (1983). The social and psychological effect of puberty on white females. In J. Brooks-Gunn & A. C. Petersen (Eds.), *Girls at puberty: Biological and psychological perspectives.* New York: Plenum.

Simon, T. J., Hespos, S. J., & Rochat, P. (1995). Do infants understand simple arithmetic: A replication of Wynn (1992). *Cognitive Development, 10,* 253–269.

Simons, M. (1993, February 10). Dutch parliament approves law permitting euthanasia. *The New York Times,* p. A10.

Simons, R. L., Chao, W., Conger, R. D., & Elder, G. H. (2001). Quality of parenting as mediator of the effect of childhood defiance on adolescent friendship choices and delinquency: A growth curve analysis. *Journal of Marriage and the Family, 63,* 63–79.

Simons, R. L., Lin, K.-H., & Gordon, L. C. (1998). Socialization in the family of origin and male dating violence: A prospective study. *Journal of Marriage and the Family, 60,* 467–478.

Simonton, D. K. (1989). The swan-song phenomenon: Last-works effects for 172 classical composers. *Psychology and Aging, 4,* 42–47.

Simonton, D. K. (1990). Creativity and wisdom in aging. In J. E. Birren & K. W. Schaie (Eds.), *Handbook of the psychology of aging* (pp. 320–329). New York: Academic Press.

Simonton, D. K. (1998). Career paths and creative lives: A theoretical perspective on late life potential. In C. E. Adams-Price (Ed.)., *Creativity and successful aging.* New York: Springer.

Simonton, D. K. (2000a). Creative development as acquired expertise: Theoretical issues and an empirical test. *Developmental Review, 20,* 283–318.

Simonton, D. K. (2000b). Creativity: Cognitive, personal, developmental, and social aspects. *American Psychologist, 55,* 151–158.

Simpson, G. A., Bloom, B., Cohen, R. A., Blumberg, S., & Bourdon, K. H. (2005). U.S. children with emotional and behavioral difficulties: Data from the 2001, 2002, and 2003 National Health Interview Surveys. *Advance Date form Vital and Health Statistics,* No. 360. Hyattsville, MD: National Center for Health Statistics.

Simpson, G. A., & Fowler, M. G. (1994). Geographic mobility and children's emotional/behavioral adjustment and school functioning. *Pediatrics, 93,* 303–309.

Simpson, K. H. (1996). Alternatives to physician-assisted suicide. *Humanistic Judaism, 24*(4), 21–23.

Singer, D. G., & Singer, J. L. (1990). *The house of make-believe: Play and the developing imagination.* Cambridge, MA: Harvard University Press.

Singer, J. L., & Singer, D. G. (1981). *Television, imagination, and aggression: A study of preschoolers.* Hillsdale, NJ: Erlbaum.

Singer, J. L., & Singer, D. G. (1998). *Barney & Friends* as entertainment and education: Evaluating the quality and effectiveness of a television series for preschool children. In J. K. Asamen & G. L. Berry (Eds.), *Research paradigms, television, and social behavior* (pp. 305–367). Thousand Oaks, CA: Sage.

Singer, P. A. (1988, June 1). Should doctors kill patients? *Canadian Medical Association Journal, 138,* 1000–1001.

Singer, T., Lindenberger, U., & Baltes, P. B. (2003). Plasticity of memory for new learning in very old age: A story of major loss? *Psychology and Aging, 18,* 306–317.

Singer, T., Verhaeghen, P., Ghisletta, P., Lindenberger, U., & Baltes, P. B. (2003). The fate of cognition in very old age: Six-year longitudinal findings in the Berlin Aging Study (BASE). *Psychology and Aging, 18,* 318–331.

Singh, K. K., Barroga, C. F., Hughes, M. D., Chen, J., Raskino, C., McKinney, R. E., & Spector, S. A. (2003, November 15). Genetic influence of CCR5, CCR2, and SDF1 variants on human immunodeficiency virus 1 (HIV-1)-related disease progression and neurological impairment, in children with symptomatic HIV-1 infection. *Journal of Infectious Disease, 188*(10), 1461–1472.

Singh, S., Wulf, D., Samara, R., & Cuca, Y. P. (2000). Gender differences in the timing of first intercourse: Data from 14 countries. *International Family Planning Perspectives, Part 1, 26,* 21–28.

Singhal, A., Cole, T. J., Fewtrell, M., & Lucas, A. (2004). Breastmilk feeding and lipoprotein profile in adolescents born preterm: Follow-up of a prospective randomised study. *Lancet, 363,* 1571–1578.

Singletary, K. W., & Gapstur, S. M. (2001). Alcohol and breast cancer: Review of epidemiologic and experimental evidence and potential mechanisms. *Journal of the American Medical Association, 286,* 2143–2151.

Sinnott, J. (1996). The developmental approach: Postformal thought as adaptive intelligence. In F. Blanchard-Fields & T. M. Hess (Eds.), *Perspectives on cognitive change in adulthood and aging* (pp. 358–386). New York: McGraw-Hill.

Sinnott, J. D. (1984). Postformal reasoning: The relativistic stage. In M. L. Commons, F. A. Richards, & C. Armon (Eds.), *Beyond formal operations: Late adolescence and adult cognitive development* (pp. 357–380). New York: Praeger.

Sinnott, J. D. (1989a). A model for solution of ill-structured problems: Implications for everyday and abstract problem-solving. In J. D. Sinnott (Ed.), *Everyday problem solving: Theory and applications* (pp. 72–99). New York: Praeger.

Sinnott, J. D. (1989b). Life-span relativistic postformal thought: Methodology and data from everyday problem–solving studies. In M. L. Commons, J. D. Sinnott, F. A. Richards, & C. Armon (Eds.), *Adult development: Vol. 1. Comparison and application of developmental models* (pp. 239–278). New York: Praeger.

Sinnott, J. D. (1991). Limits to problem solving: Emotion, intention, goal clarity, health and other factors in postformal thought. In J. D. Sinnott & J. C. Cavanaugh (Eds.), *Bridging paradigms: Positive development in adulthood and cognitive aging* (pp. 169–202). New York: Praeger.

Sinnott, J. D. (1998). *The development of logic in adulthood: Postformal thought and its applications.* New York: Plenum.

Sinnott, J. D. (2003). Postformal thought and adult development. In J. Demick and C. Andreoletti (Eds.). *Handbook of adult development.* NY: Plenum Press.

Siris, E. S., Miller, P. D., Barrett-Connor, E., Faulkner, K. G., Wehren, L. E., Abbott, T. A.,

Berger, M. L., Santora, A. C., & Sherwood, L. M. (2001). Identification and fracture outcomes of undiagnosed low bone mineral density in postmenopausal women: Results from the National Osteoporosis Risk Assessment. *Journal of the American Medical Association, 286*, 2815–2822.

Sjostrom, K., Valentin, L., Thelin, T., & Marsal, K. (1997). Maternal anxiety in late pregnancy and fetal hemodynamics. *European Journal of Obstetrics and Gynecology, 74*, 149–155.

Skadberg, B. T., Morild, I., & Markestad, T. (1998). Abandoning prone sleeping: Effects on the risk of sudden infant death syndrome. *Journal of Pediatrics, 132*, 234–239.

Skinner, B. F. (1938). *The behavior of organisms: An experimental approach.* New York: Appleton-Century.

Skinner, B. F. (1957). *Verbal behavior.* New York: Appleton-Century-Crofts.

Skinner, D. (1989). The socialization of gender identity: Observations from Nepal. In J. Valsiner (Ed.), *Child development in cultural context* (pp. 181–192). Toronto: Hogrefe & Huber.

Skoe, E. E., & Diessner, R. E. (1994). Ethic of care, justice, identity, and gender: An extension and replication. *Merrill-Palmer Quarterly, 40*, 272–289.

Skoe, E. E., & Gooden, A. (1993). Ethics of care and real-life moral dilemma content in male and female early adolescents. *Journal of Early Adolescence, 13*(2), 154–167.

Skolnick, A. A. (1993). "Female athlete triad" risk for women. *Journal of the American Medical Association, 270*, 921–923.

Slade, A., Belsky, J., Aber, J. L., & Phelps, J. L. (1999). Mothers' representation of their relationships with their toddlers: Links to adult attachment and observed mothering. *Developmental Psychology, 35*, 611–619.

Slap, G. B., Vorters, D. F., Chaudhuri, S., & Centor, R. M. (1989). Risk factors for attempted suicide during adolescence. *Pediatrics, 84*, 762–772.

Slemenda, C. W. (1994). Cigarettes and the skeleton. *New England Journal of Medicine, 330*, 430–431.

Sliwinski, M., & Buschke, H. (1999). Cross-sectional and longitudinal relationships among age, cognition, and processing speed. *Psychology and Aging, 14*, 18–33.

Sloan, R. P., & Bagiella, E. (2002). Claims about religious involvement and health outcomes. *Annals of Behavioral Medicine, 24*, 14–21.

Slobin, D. (1971). Universals of grammatical development in children. In W. Levett & G. B. Flores d'Arcais (Eds.), *Advances in psycholinguistic research.* Amsterdam: New Holland.

Slobin, D. (1973). Cognitive prerequisites for the acquisition of language. In C. Ferguson & D. Slobin (Eds.), *Studies of child language development.* New York: Holt, Rinehart, & Winston.

Slobin, D. (1983). Universal and particular in the acquisition of grammar. In E. Wanner & L. Gleitman (Eds.), *Language acquisition: The state of the art.* Cambridge, England: Cambridge University Press.

Sly, R. M. (2000). Decreases in asthma mortality in the United States. *Annals of Allergy, Asthma, and Immunology, 85*, 121–127.

Small, B. J., Fratiglioni, L., von Strauss, E., & Bäckman, L. (2003). Terminal decline and cognitive performance in very old age: Does cause of death matter? *Psychology and Aging, 18*, 193–202.

Small, B. J., Hertzog, C., Hultsch, D. F., & Dixon, R. A. (2003). Stability and change in adult personality over 6 years: Findings from the Victoria Longitudinal Study. *Journal of Gerontology: Psychological Sciences, 58B*, P166–P176.

Small, G. W., Rabins, P. V., Barry, P. P., Buckholtz, N. S., DeKosky, S. T., Ferris, S. H., Finkel, S. I., Gwyther, L. P., Khachaturian, Z. S., Lebowitz, B. D., McRae, T. D., Morris, J. C., Oakley, F., Schneider, L. S., Streim, J. E., Sunderland, T., Teri, L. A., & Tune, L. E. (1997). Diagnosis and treatment of Alzheimer's Disease and related disorders: Consensus statement of the American Association for Geriatric Psychiatry, the Alzheimer's Association, and the American Geriatrics Society. *Journal of the American Medical Association, 278*, 1363–1371.

Small, M. Y. (1990). *Cognitive development.* New York: Harcourt Brace.

Smedje, J., Broman, J. E., & Hetta, J. (1999). Parents' reports of disturbed sleep in 5–7-year-old Swedish children. *Acta Paediatrica, 88*, 858–865.

Smedley, A., & Smedley, B. D. (2005). Race as biology is fiction, racism as a social problem is real: Anthropological and historical perspectives on the social construction of race. *American Psychologist, 60*, 16–26.

Smedley, B. D., Stith, A. Y., & Nelson, A. R. (Eds.). (2002). *Unequal treatment: Confronting racial and ethnic disparities in health care.* Washington, DC: National Academy Press.

Smetana, J. G., Metzger, A., & Campione-Barr, N. (2004). African American late adolescents' relationships with parents: Developmental transitions and longitudinal patterns. *Child Development, 75*, 932–947.

Smilansky, S. (1968). *The effects of sociodramatic play on disadvantaged preschool children.* New York: Wiley.

Smith, A. D., & Earles, J. L. (1996). Memory changes in normal aging. In F. Blanchard-Fields & T. M. Hess (Eds.), *Perspectives on cognitive change in adulthood and aging* (pp. 165–191). New York: McGraw-Hill.

Smith, B. A., & Blass, E. M. (1996). Taste-mediated calming in premature, preterm, and full-term human infants. *Developmental Psychology, 32*, 1084–1089.

Smith, E. A. (2001). The role of tacit and explicit knowledge in the workplace. *Journal of Knowledge Management, 5*, 311–321.

Smith, E. E., Geva, A., Jonides, J., Miller, A., Reuter-Lorenz, P., & Koeppe, R. A. (2001). The neural basis of task-switching in working memory: Effects of performance and aging. *Proceedings of the National Academy of Science USA, 98*, 2095–2100.

Smith, G. C. S., Pell, J. P., Cameron, A. D., & Dobbie, R. (2002). Risk of perinatal death associated with labor after previous cesarean delivery in uncomplicated term pregnancies. *Journal of the American Medical Association, 287*, 2684–2690.

Smith, G. C. S., Wood, A. M., Pell, J. P., White, I. R., Crossley, J. A., & Dobbie, R. (2004). Second-trimester maternal serum levels of alpha-fetoprotein and the subsequent risk of Sudden Infant Death Syndrome. *New England Journal of Medicine, 351*, 978–986.

Smith, J., & Baltes, P. B. (1990). Wisdom-related knowledge: Age/cohort differences in response to life planning problems. *Developmental Psychology, 26*(3), 494–505.

Smith, K. (2002). Who's minding the kids? Child care arrangements: Spring 1997. *Current Population Reports,* P70–86. Washington, DC: U.S. Census Bureau.

Smith, K. A., Fairburn, C. G., & Cowen, P. J. (1999). Symptomatic release in bulimia nervosa following acute tryptophan depletion. *Archives of General Psychiatry (72C), 56*(2), 171–176.

Smith, P. K., & Levan, S. (1995). Perceptions and experiences of bullying in younger pupils. *British Journal of Educational Psychology, 65*, 489–500.

Smith, R. B., & Brown, R. A. (1997). The impact of social support on gay male couples. *Journal of Homosexuality, 33*, 39–61.

Smith, T. W. (2003). *American sexual behavior: Trends, socio-demographic differences, and risk behavior* (GSS Topical Report No. 25). Chicago: National Opinion Research Center, University of Chicago.

Smith, T. W. (2005). Generation gaps in attitudes and values from the 1970s to the 1990s. In R. A. Settersten, Jr., F. F. Furstenberg, Jr., & R. G. Rumbaut (Eds.), *On the frontier of adulthood: Theory, research, and public policy* (pp. 177–221). (John D. and Catherine T. MacArthur Foundation Series on Mental Health and Development, Research Network on Transitions to Adulthood and Public Policy.) Chicago: University of Chicago Press.

Smith-Khuri, E., Iachan, R., Scheidt, P. C., Overpeck, M. D., Gabhainn, S. N., Pickett, W., & Harel, Y. (2004). A cross-national study of violence-related behaviors in adolescents. *Archives of Pediatrics and Adolescent Medicine, 158*, 539–544.

Smith-Warner, S. A., Spiegelman, D., Yaun, S., van den Brandt, P. A., Folsom, A. R., Goldbohm, A., Graham, S., Holmberg, L., Howe, G. R., Marshall, J. R., Miller, A. B., Potter, M. D., Speizer, F. E., Willett, W. C., Wolk, A., & Hunter, D. J. (1998). Alcohol and breast cancer in women: A pooled analysis of cohort studies. *Journal of the American Medical Association, 279*, 535–540.

Smotherman, W. P., & Robinson, S. R. (1995). Tracing developmental trajectories into the prenatal period. In J. P. Lecanuet, W. P. Fifer, N. A. Krasnegor, & W. P. Smotherman (Eds.), *Fetal development: A psychobiological perspective* (pp. 15–32). Hillsdale, NJ: Erlbaum.

Smotherman, W. P., & Robinson, S. R. (1996). The development of behavior before birth. *Developmental Psychology, 32,* 425–434.

Snarey, J. R. (1985). Cross-cultural universality of social-moral development: A critical review of Kohlbergian research. *Psychological Bulletin, 97,* 202–232.

Snow, C. E. (1990). The development of definitional skill. *Journal of Child Language, 17,* 697–710.

Snow, C. E. (1993). Families as social contexts for literacy development. In C. Daiute (Ed.), *The development of literacy through social interaction* (New Directions for Child Development No. 61, pp. 11–24). San Francisco: Jossey-Bass.

Snow, M. E., Jacklin, C. N., & Maccoby, E. E. (1983). Sex-of-child differences in father-child interaction at one year of age. *Child Development, 54,* 227–232.

Snyder, H. N. (2000). *Special analyses of FBI serious violent crimes data.* Pittsburgh, PA: National Center for Juvenile Justice.

Snyder, J., Cramer, A., Afrank, J., & Patterson, G. R. (2005). The contributions of ineffective discipline and parental hostile attributions of child misbehavior to the development of conduct problems at home and school. *Developmental Psychology, 41,* 30–41.

Snyder, J., West, L., Stockemer, V., Gibbons, S., & Almquist-Parks, L. (1996). A social learning model of peer choice in the natural environment. *Journal of Applied Developmental Psychology, 17,* 215–237.

Snyder, T. D., & Hoffman, C. M. (2001). *Digest of Education Statistics, 2000.* NCES 2001-034. Washington, DC: National Center for Education Statistics.

Snyder, T. D., & Hoffman, C. M. (2002). *Digest of Education Statistics 2001.* Washington, DC: National Center for Education Statistics.

Snyder, T. D., & Hoffman, C. M. (2003). *Digest of education statistics, 2002* (Publication No. NCES 2003-060). Washington, DC: Author.

Society for Assisted Reproductive Technology, The American Fertility Society. (1993). Assisted reproductive technology in the United States and Canada: 1991 results from the Society for Assisted Reproductive Technology generated from The American Fertility Society Registry. *Fertility and Sterility, 59,* 956–962.

Society for Assisted Reproductive Technology and the American Society for Reproductive Medicine. (2002). Assisted reproductive technology in the United States: 1998 results generated from the American Society for Reproductive Medicine/Society for Assisted Reproductive Technology Registry. *Fertility & Sterility, 77*(1), 18–31.

Society for Research in Child Development. (1996). Ethical standards for research with children. In *Directory of members* (pp. 337–339). Ann Arbor, MI: Author.

Sokol, R. J., Delaney-Black, V., and Nordstrom, B. (2003). Fetal alcohol spectrum disorder, *Journal of the American Medical Association, 209,* 2996–2999.

Soldz, S., & Vaillant, G. E. (1998). A 50-year longitudinal study of defense use among inner city men: A validation of the DSM-IV defense axis. *Journal of Nervous and Mental Disease, 186,* 104–111.

Solomon, P. R., Adams, F., Silver, A., Zimmer, J., & DeVeaux, R. (2002). Ginkgo for memory enhancement: A randomized controlled trial. *Journal of the American Medical Association, 288,* 835–840.

Solomon, P. R., Hirschoff, A., Kelly, B., Relin, M., Brush, M., DeVeaux, R. D., & Pendlebury, W. W. (1998). A 7-minute neurocognitive screening battery highly sensitive to Alzheimer's disease. *Archives of Neurology, 55,* 349–355.

Solomon, S. E., Rothblum, E. D., & Balsam, K. F. (2004). Pioneers in partnership: lesbian and gay male couples in civil unions compared with those not in civil unions and married heterosexual siblings. *Journal of Family Psychology, 18,* 275–286.

Solowij, N., Stephens, R. S., Roffman, R. A., Babor, T., Kadden, R. Miller, M., Christiansen, K., McRee, B., & Vendetti, J. for the Marijuana Treatment Research Group. (2002). Cognitive functioning of long-term heavy cannabis users seeking treatment. *Journal of the American Medical Association, 287,* 1123–1131.

Sondergaard, C., Henriksen, T. B., Obel, C., & Wisborg, K. (2001). Smoking during pregnancy and infantile colic. *Pediatrics, 108*(2), 342–346.

Sood, B., Delaney-Black, V., Covington, C., Nordstrom-Klee, B., Ager, J., Templin, T., Janisse, J., Martier, S., & Sokol, R. J. (2001). Prenatal alcohol exposure and childhood behavior at age 6 to 7 years: I. Dose-response effect. *Pediatrics, 108*(8), e461–462.

Sophian, C. (1988). Early developments in children's understanding of numbers: Inferences about numerosity and one-to-one correspondence. *Child Development, 59,* 1397–1414.

Sophian, C., Garyantes, D., & Chang, C. (1997). When three is less than two: Early developments in children's understanding of fractional quantities. *Developmental Psychology, 33,* 731–744.

Sophian, C., & Wood, A. (1997). Proportional reasoning in young children: The parts and the whole of it. *Journal of Educational Psychology, 89,* 309–317.

Sophian, C., Wood, A., & Vong, K. I. (1995). Making numbers count: The early development of numerical inferences. *Developmental Psychology, 31,* 263–273.

Sorof, J. M., Lai, D., Turner, J., Poffenbarger, T., & Portman, R. J. (2004). Overweight, ethnicity, and the prevalence of hypertension in school-aged children. *Pediatrics, 113.* 475–482.

Sowell, E. R., Thompson, P. M., Welcome, S. E., Henkenius, A. L., Toga, A. W., & Peterson, B. S. (2003). Cortical abnormalities in children and adolescents with attention-deficit hyperactivity disorder. *Lancet, 362,* 1699–1701.

Spady, D. W., Saunders. D. L., Schopflocher, D. P., & Svenson, L. W. (2004). Patterns for injury in childhood: A population-based approach. *Pediatrics, 113,* 522–529.

Spalding, J. J. (1977). Carter, James Earl, Jr. In W. H. Nault (Ed.), *The 1977 World Book Year-book* (pp. 542–547). Chicago: Field Enterprises Educational Corporation.

Speece, M. W., & Brent, S. B. (1984). Children's understanding of death: A review of three components of a death concept. *Child Development, 55,* 1671–1686.

Spelke, E. (1994). Initial knowledge: Six suggestions. *Cognition, 50,* 431–445.

Spelke, E. S. (1998). Nativism, empiricism, and the origins of knowledge. *Infant Behavior and Development, 21*(2), 181–200.

Spence, A. P. (1989). *Biology of human aging.* Englewood Cliffs, NJ: Prentice-Hall.

Sperling, M. A. (2004). Prematurity—A window of opportunity? *New England Journal of Medicine, 351,* 2229–2231.

Spieker, S. J., Nelson, D. C., Petras, A., Jolley, S. N., & Barnard, K. E. (2003). Joint influence of child care and infant attachment security for cognitive and language outcomes of low-income toddlers. *Infant Behavior & Development, 26,* 326–344.

Spinrad, T. L., Eisenberg, N., Harris, E., Hanish, L., Fabes, R. A., Kupanoff, K., Ringwald, S., & Holmes, J. (2004). The relation of children's everyday nonsocial peer play behavior to their emotionality, regulation, and social functioning. *Developmental Psychology, 40,* 67–80.

Spirduso, W. W., & MacRae, P. G. (1990). Motor performance and aging. In J. E. Birren & K. W. Schaie (Eds.), *Psychology of aging* (3rd ed., pp. 183–200). New York: Academic Press.

Spiro, A., III (2001). Health in midlife: Toward a life-span view. In M. E. Lachman (Ed.), *Handbook of midlife development* (pp. 156–187). New York: Wiley.

Spitz, R. A. (1945). Hospitalism: An inquiry into the genesis of psychiatric conditioning in early childhood. In D. Fenschel et al. (Eds.), *Psychoanalytic studies of the child* (Vol. 1, pp. 53–74). New York: International Universities Press.

Spitz, R. A. (1946). Hospitalism: A follow-up report. In D. Fenschel et al. (Eds.), *Psychoanalytic studies of the child* (Vol. 1, pp. 113–117). New York: International Universities Press.

Spohr, H. L., Willms, J., & Steinhausen, H.-C. (1993). Prenatal alcohol exposure and longterm developmental consequences. *The Lancet, 341,* 907–910.

Spoto, D. (1997). *Notorious: The life of Ingrid Bergman.* New York: HarperCollins.

Springer, M. V., McIntosh, A. R., Winocur, G., & Grady, C. L. (2005). The relation between brain activity during memory tasks and years of education in young and older adults. *Neuropsychology, 19,* 181–192.

Squire, L. R. (1992). Memory and the hippocampus: A synthesis of findings with rats, monkeys, and humans. *Psychological Review, 99,* 195–231.

Squire, L. R. (1994). Declarative and nondeclarative memory: Multiple brain systems supporting learning and memory. In D. L. Schacter & E. Tulving (Eds.), *Memory systems 1994* (pp. 203–232). Cambridge, MA: MIT Press.

Srivastava, S., John. O. P., Gosling, S. D., & Potter, J. (2003). Development of personality in early and middle adulthood: Set like plaster or persistent change? *Journal of Personality and Social Psychology, 84,* 1041–1053.

Sroufe, L. A. (1997). *Emotional development.* Cambridge, England: Cambridge University Press.

Sroufe, L. A., Bennett, C., Englund, M., Urban, J., & Shulman, S. (1993). The significance of gender boundaries in preadolescence: Contemporary correlates and antecedents of boundary violation and maintenance. *Child Development, 64,* 455–466.

Sroufe, L. A., Carlson, E., & Shulman, S. (1993). Individuals in relationships: Development from infancy through adolescence. In D. C. Funder, R. D. Parke, C. Tomlinson-Keasey, & K. Widaman (Eds.), *Studying lives through time: Personality and development* (pp. 315–342). Washington, DC: American Psychological Association.

Stadtman, E. R. (1992). Protein oxidation and aging. *Science, 257,* 1220–1224.

Stamler, J., Dyer, A. R., Shekelle, R. B., Neaton, J., & Stamler, R. (1993). Relationship of baseline major risk factors to coronary and all-cause mortality, and to longevity: Findings from long-term follow-up of Chicago cohorts. *Cardiology, 82*(2–3), 191–222.

Standley, J. M. (1998). Strategies to improve outcomes in critical care—The effect of music and multimodal stimulation on responses of premature infants in neonatal intensive care. *Pediatric Nursing, 24,* 532–538.

Stapleton, S. (1998, May 11). Asthma rates hit epidemic numbers; experts wonder why [Online]. *American Medical News, 41*(18). Available: http://www.ama-assn.org/special/asthma/newsline/special/epidem.htm.

Staplin, L., Lococo, K., Byington, S., & Harkey, D. (2001a). *Guidelines and recommendations to accommodate older drivers and pedestrians.* McLean, VA: Office of Safety and Traffic Operations, Federal Highway Administration.

Staplin, L., Lococo, K., Byington, S., & Harkey, D. (2001b). *Highway design handbook for older drivers and pedestrians.* McLean, VA: Office of Safety and Traffic Operations, Federal Highway Administration.

Starfield, B. (1991). Childhood morbidity: Comparisons, clusters, and trends. *Pediatrics, 88,* 519–526.

Starr, J. M., Deary, I. J., Lemmon, H., & Whalley L. J. (2000). Mental ability age 11 years and health status age 77 years. *Age and Ageing, 29,* 523–528.

Staub, E. (1996). Cultural-societal roots of violence: The examples of genocidal violence and of contemporary youth violence in the United States. *American Psychologist, 51,* 117–132.

Stauder, J. E. A., Molenaar, P. C. M., & Van der Molen, M. W. (1993). Scalp topography of event-related brain potentials and cognitive transition during childhood. *Child Development, 64,* 769–788.

Staudinger, U. M., & Baltes, P. B. (1996). Interactive minds: A facilitative setting for wisdom-related performance? *Journal of Personality and Social Psychology, 71,* 746–762.

Staudinger, U. M., & Bluck, S. (2001). A view of midlife development from life-span theory. In M. E. Lachman (Ed.), *Handbook of midlife development* (pp. 3–39). New York: Wiley.

Staudinger, U. M., Fleeson, W., & Baltes, P. B. (1999). Predictors of subjective physical health and global well-being: Similarities and differences between the United States and Germany. *Journal of Personality and Social Psychology, 76,* 305–319.

Staudinger, U. M., Smith, J., & Baltes, P. B. (1992). Wisdom-related knowledge in a life review task: Age differences and the role of professional specialization. *Psychology and Aging, 7,* 271–281.

Steinbach, U. (1992). Social networks, institutionalization, and mortality among elderly people in the United States. *Journal of Gerontology: Social Sciences, 47*(4), S183–190.

Steinberg, L. (1988). Reciprocal relation between parent-child distance and pubertal maturation. *Developmental Psychology, 24,* 122–128.

Steinberg, L. (2000, January 19). *Should juvenile offenders be tried as adults? A developmental perspective on changing legal policies.* Paper presented as part of a Congressional Research Briefing entitled "Juvenile Crime: Causes and Consequences." Washington, DC.

Steinberg, L., & Darling, N. (1994). The broader context of social influence in adolescence. In R. Silberstein & E. Todt (Eds.), *Adolescence in context.* New York: Springer.

Steinberg, L., Dornbusch, S. M., & Brown, B. B. (1992). Ethnic differences in adolescent achievement: An ecological perspective. *American Psychologist, 47,* 723–729.

Steinberg, L., & Scott, E. S. (2003). Less guilty by reason of adolescence: Developmental immaturity, diminished responsibility, and the juvenile death penalty. *American Psychologist, 58,* 1009–1018.

Steinbrook, R. (2005). Public solicitation of organ donors. *New England Journal of Medicine, 353,* 441–444.

Stennes, L. M., Burch, M. M., Sen, M. G., & Bauer, P. J. (2005). A longitudinal study of gendered vocabulary and communicative action in young children. *Developmental Psychology, 41,* 75–88.

Stern, M. B. (1950). *Louisa May Alcott.* Norman: University of Oklahoma Press.

Sternbach, H. (1998). Age-associated testosterone decline in men: Clinical issues for psychiatry. *American Journal of Psychiatry, 155,* 1310–1318.

Sternberg, R. J. (1985a). *Beyond IQ: A triarchic theory of human intelligence.* New York: Cambridge University Press.

Sternberg, R. J. (1986). A triangular theory of love. *Psychological Review, 93,* 119–135.

Sternberg, R. J. (1987, September 23). The use and misuse of intelligence testing: Misunderstanding meaning, users over-rely on scores. *Education Week,* pp. 22, 28.

Sternberg, R. J. (1990). Wisdom and its relations to intelligence and creativity. In R. J. Sternberg (Ed.), *Wisdom: Its nature, origins, and development* (pp. 142–159). Cambridge: Cambridge University Press.

Sternberg, R. J. (1993). *Sternberg Triarchic Abilities Test.* Unpublished manuscript.

Sternberg, R. J. (1995). Love as a story. *Journal of Social and Personal Relationships, 12*(4), 541–546.

Sternberg, R. J. (1997). The concept of intelligence and its role in lifelong learning and success. *American Psychologist, 52,* 1030–1037.

Sternberg, R. J. (1998). A balance theory of wisdom. *Review of General Psychology, 2,* 347–365.

Sternberg, R. J. (1998a). *Cupid's arrow.* New York: Cambridge University Press.

Sternberg, R. J. (1998b). *Love is a story.* New York: Oxford University Press.

Sternberg, R. J. (2004). Culture and intelligence. *American Psychologist, 59,* 325–338.

Sternberg, R. J. (in press). A duplex theory of love. In R. J. Sternberg & M. L. Barnes (Eds.), *The psychology of love* (2nd ed.). New Haven: Yale University Press.

Sternberg, R. J., & Clinkenbeard, P. (1995). A triarchic view of identifying, teaching, and assessing gifted children. *Roeper Review, 17,* 255–260.

Sternberg, R. J., Forsythe, G. B., Hedlund, J., Horvath, J. A., Wagner, R. K., Williams, W. M., Snook, S. A., & Grigorenko, E. L. (2000). *Practical intelligence in everyday life.* New York: Cambridge University Press.

Sternberg, R. J., Grigorenko, E. L., & Kidd, K. K. (2005). Intelligence, race, and genetics. *American Psychologist, 60,* 46–59.

Sternberg, R. J., Grigorenko, E. L., & Oh, S. (2001). The development of intelligence at midlife. In M. E. Lachman (Ed.), *Handbook of midlife development* (pp. 217–247). New York: Wiley.

Sternberg, R. J., Hojjat, M., & Barnes, M. L. (2001). Empirical aspects of a theory of love as a story. *European Journal of Personality, 15,* 1–20.

Sternberg, R. J., & Horvath, J. A. (1998). Cognitive conceptions of expertise and their relations to giftedness. In R. C. Friedman & K. B. Rogers (Eds.), *Talent in context: Historical and social perspectives on giftedness* (pp. 177–191). Washington, DC: American Psychological Association.

Sternberg, R. J., & Lubart, T. I. (1995). *Defying the crowd: Cultivating creativity in a culture of conformity.* NY: Free Press.

Sternberg, R. J., Nokes, K., Geissler, P. W., Prince, R., Okatcha, F., Bundy, D. A., & Grigorenko, E. L. (2001). The relationship between academic and practical intelligence: A case study in Kenya. *Intelligence, 29,* 401–418.

Sternberg, R. J., Torff, B., & Grigorenko, E. L. (1998). Teaching triarchically improves school achievement. *Journal of Educational Psychology, 90*(3), 374–384.

Sternberg, R. J., & Wagner, R. K. (1989). Individual differences in practical knowledge, and its acquisition. In P. L. Ackerman, R. J. Sternberg, & R. Glaser (Eds.), *Learning and individual differences* (pp. 255–278). New York: Freeman.

Sternberg, R. J., & Wagner, R. K. (1993). The g-ocentric view of intelligence and job performance is wrong. *Current Directions in Psychological Science, 2*(1), 1–4.

Sternberg, R. J., Wagner, R. K., Williams, W. M., & Horvath, J. A. (1995). Testing common sense. *American Psychologist, 50,* 912–927.

Sterns, H. L., & Huyck, M. H. (2001). The role of work in midlife. In M. E. Lachman (Ed.), *Handbook of midlife development* (pp. 447–486). New York: Wiley.

Steunenberg, B., Twisk, J. W. R., Beekman, A. T. F., Deeg, D. J. H., & Kerkof, A. J. F. M. (2005). Stability and change of neuroticism in aging. *Journal of Gerontology: Psychological Sciences, 60B,* P27–P33.

Stevens, J. C., Cain, W. S., Demarque, A., & Ruthruff, A. M. (1991). On the discrimination of missing ingredients: Aging and salt flavor. *Appetite, 16,* 129–140.

Stevens, J. C., Cruz, L. A., Hoffman, J. M., & Patterson, M. Q. (1995). Taste sensitivity and aging: High incidence of decline revealed by repeated threshold measures. *Chemical Senses, 20,* 451–459.

Stevenson, H. W. (1995). Mathematics achievement of American students: First in the world by the year 2000? In C. A. Nelson (Ed.), *The Minnesota Symposia on Child Psychology: Vol. 28. Basic and applied perspectives on learning, cognition, and development* (pp. 131–149). Mahwah, NJ: Erlbaum.

Stevenson, H. W., Chen, C., & Lee, S. Y. (1993). Mathematics achievement of Chinese, Japanese, and American children: Ten years later. *Science, 258* (5081), 53–58.

Stevenson, H. W., Lee, S., Chen, C., & Lummis, M. (1990). Mathematics achievement of children in China and the United States. *Child Development, 61,* 1053–1066.

Stevenson, H. W., Lee, S. Y., Chen, C., Stigler, J. W., Hsu, C. C., & Kitamura, S. (1990). Contexts of achievement: A study of American, Chinese, and Japanese children. *Monographs of the Society for Research in Child Development, 55*(1–2, Serial No. 221).

Stevenson-Hinde, J., & Shouldice, A. (1996). Fearfulness: Developmental consistency. In A. J. Sameroff & M. M. Haith (Eds.), *The five to seven year shift: The age of reason and responsibility* (pp. 237–252). Chicago: University of Chicago Press.

Steward, M. S., & Steward, D. S. (1996). Interviewing young children about body touch and handling. *Monographs of the Society for Research in Child Development, 61*(4–5, Serial No. 248).

Stewart, A. J., & Ostrove, J. M. (1998). Women's personality in middle age: Gender, history, and midcourse correction. *American Psychologist, 53,* 1185–1194.

Stewart, A. J., & Vandewater, E. A. (1998). The course of generativity. In D. P. McAdams & D. de St. Aubin (Eds.), *Generativity and adult development: How and why we care for the next generation.* Washington, DC: American Psychological Association.

Stewart, A. J., & Vandewater, E. A. (1999). "If I had to do it over again . . . ": Midlife review, midlife corrections, and women's well-being in midlife. *Journal of Personality and Social Psychology, 76,* 270–283.

Stewart, I. C. (1994, January 29). Two-part message [Letter to the editor]. *The New York Times,* p. A18.

Stice, E., & Bearman, K. (2001). Body image and eating disturbances prospectively predict increases in depressive symptoms in adolescent girls: A growth curve analysis. *Developmental Psychology, 37*(5), 597–607.

Stice, E., Presnell, K., & Bearman, S. K. (2001). Relation of early menarche to depression, eating disorders, substance abuse, and comorbid psychopathology among adolescent girls. *Developmental Psychology, 37,* 608–619.

Stick, S. M., Burton, P. R., Gurrin, L., Sly, P. D., & LeSouëf, P. N. (1996). Effects of maternal smoking during pregnancy and a family history of asthma on respiratory function in newborn infants. *The Lancet, 348,* 1060–1064.

Stipek, D. (2002). At what age should children enter kindergarten? A question for policy makers and parents. *SRCD Social Policy Report, 16*(2), 1–16.

Stipek, D., & Byler, P. (2001). Academic achievement and social behaviors associated with age of entry into kindergarten. *Journal of Applied Developmental Psychology, 22,* 175–189.

Stipek, D. J., Gralinski, H., & Kopp, C. B. (1990). Self-concept development in the toddler years. *Developmental Psychology, 26,* 972–977.

Stock, G., & Callahan, D. (2004). Point-counterpoint: Would doubling the human life span be a net positive or negative for us either as individuals or as a society? *Journal of Gerontology: Biological Sciences, 59A,* 554–559.

Stoecker, J. J., Colombo, J., Frick, J. E., & Allen, J. R. (1998). Long- and short-looking infants' recognition of symmetrica and asymmetrical forms. *Journal of Experimental Child Psychology, 71,* 63–78.

Stoelhorst, M. S. J., Rijken, M., Martens, S. E., Brand, R., den Ouden, A. L., Wit, J.-M., & Veen, S., on behalf of the Leiden Follow-up Project on Prematurity. (2005). Changes in neonatology: Comparison of two cohorts of very preterm infants (gestational age <32 weeks): The Project on Preterm and Small for Gestational Age Infants 1983 and the Leiden Follow-up Project on Prematurity 1996–1997. *Pediatrics, 115,* 396–405.

Stoll, B. J., Hansen, N. I., Adams-Chapman, I., Fanaroff, A. A., Hintz, S. R., Vohr, B., & Higgins, R. D., for the National Institute of Child Health and Human Development Neonatal Research Network. (2004). Neurodevelopmental and growth impairment among extremely low-birth-weight infants with neonatal infection. *Journal of the American Medical Association, 292,* 2357–2365.

Stones, M. J., & Kozma, A. (1996). Activity, exercise, and behavior. In J. E. Birren & K. W. Schaie (Eds.), *Handbook of the psychology of aging* (4th ed., pp. 338–352). San Diego: Academic Press.

Strasburger, V. C., & Donnerstein, E. (1999). Children, adolescents, and the media: Issues and solutions. *Pediatrics, 103,* 129–139.

Strassberg, Z., Dodge, K. A., Pettit, G. S., & Bates, J. E. (1994). Spanking in the home and children's subsequent aggression toward kindergarten peers. *Development and Psychopathology, 6,* 445–461.

Straus, M. A. (1994a). *Beating the devil out of them: Corporal punishment in American families.* San Francisco, CA: Jossey-Bass.

Straus, M. A. (1994b). Should the use of corporal punishment by parents be considered child abuse? In M. A. Mason & E. Gambrill (Eds.), *Debating children's lives: Current controversies on children and adolescents* (pp. 196–222). Newbury Park, CA: Sage.

Straus, M. A. (1999). The benefits of avoiding corporal punishment: New and more definitive evidence. Submitted for publication in K. C. Blaine (Ed.), *Raising America's Children.*

Straus, M. A., & Field, C. J. (2003). Psychological aggression by American parents: National data on prevalence, chronicity, and severity. *Journal of Marriage and Family, 65,* 795–808.

Straus, M. A., & Paschall, M. J. (1999, July). *Corporal punishment by mothers and children's cognitive development: A longitudinal study of two age cohorts.* Paper presented at the Sixth International Family Violence Research Conference, University of New Hampshire, Durham, NH.

Straus, M. A., & Stewart, J. H. (1999). Corporal punishment by American parents: National data on prevalence, chronicity, severity, and duration, in relation to child and family characteristics. *Clinical Child and Family Psychology Review, 2*(2), 55–70.

Straus, M. A., Sugarman, D. B., & Giles-Sims, J. (1997). Spanking by parents and subsequent antisocial behavior of children. *Archives of Pediatric and Adolescent Medicine, 151,* 761–767.

Strawbridge, W. J., & Wallhagen, M. I. (1991). Impact of family conflict on adult child caregivers. *The Gerontologist, 31*(6), 770–777.

Streissguth, A. P., Aase, J. M., Clarren, S. K., Randels, S. P., LaDue, R. A., & Smith, D. F. (1991). Fetal alcohol syndrome in adolescents and adults. *Journal of the American Medical Association, 265,* 1961–1967.

Streissguth, A. P., Bookstein, F. L., Barr, H. M., Sampson, P. D., O'Malley, K., Young, J. K. (2004). Risk factors for adverse life outcomes in fetal alcohol syndrome and fetal alcohol effects. *Journal of Developmental & Behavioral Pediatrics, 25,* 228–238.

Streissguth, A. P., Martin, D. C., Barr, H. M., Sandman, B. M., Kirchner, G. L., & Darby, B. L. (1984). Intrauterine alcohol and nicotine exposure: Attention and reaction time in 4-year-old children. *Developmental Psychology, 20,* 533–541.

Striano, T. (2004). Direction of regard and the still-face effect in the first year: Does intention matter? *Child Development, 75,* 468–479.

Strobel, A., Camoin, T. I. L., Ozata, M., & Strosberg, A. D. (1998). A leptin missense mutation associated with hypogonadism and morbid obesity. *Nature Genetics, 18,* 213–215.

Stroebe, M., Gergen, M. M., Gergen, K. J., & Stroebe, W. (1992). Broken hearts or broken bonds: Love and death in historical perspective. *American Psychologist, 47*(10), 1205–1212.

Strömland, K., & Hellström, A. (1996). Fetal alcohol syndrome—An ophthalmological and socioeducational prospective study. *Pediatrics, 97*, 845–850.

Stuart, J. (1991). Introduction. In Z. Zhensun & A. Low, *A young painter: The life and paintings of Wang Yani—China's extraordinary young artist* (pp. 6–7). New York: Scholastic.

Stuck, A. E., Egger, M., Hammer, A., Minder, C. E., & Beck, J. C. (2002). Home visits to prevent nursing home admission and functional decline in elderly people: Systematic review and meta-regression analysis. *Journal of the American Medical Association, 287*, 1022–1028.

Sturges, J. W., & Sturges, L. V. (1998). In vivo systematic desensitization in a single-session treatment of an 11-year-old girl's elevator phobia. *Child & Family Behavior Therapy, 20*, 55–62.

Sturm, R. (2002). The effects of obesity, smoking, and drinking on medical problems and costs. *Health Affairs, 21*, 245–253.

Subramanian, G., Adams, M. D., Venter, J. C., & Broder, S. (2001). Implications of the human genome for understanding human biology and medicine. *Journal of the American Medical Association, 26*(18), 2296–2307.

Substance Abuse and Mental Health Services Administration (SAMHSA). (2001). *Summary of findings from the 2000 National Household Survey on Drug Abuse.* NHSDA Series H-13, DHHS Publication No. (SMA) 01-3549. Rockville, MD: Office of Applied Studies.

Substance Abuse and Mental Health Services Administration (SAMHSA). (2004a, October 22). Alcohol dependence or abuse and age at first use. *The NSDUH Report.* [Online]. Available: http://oas.samhsa.gov/2k4/ageDependence/ageDependence.htm. Access date: December 18, 2004.

Substance Abuse and Mental Health Services Administration (SAMHSA). (2004b). *Results from the 2003 National Survey on Drug Use & Health: National findings* (Office of Applied Studies, NSDUH Series H-25, DHHS Publication No. SMA 04-3964). Rockville, MD: U.S. Department of Health and Human Services.

Suddendorf, T. (2003). Early representational insight: 24-month-olds can use a photo to find an object in the world. *Child Development, 74*, 896–904.

Sue, S., & Okazaki, S. (1990). Asian-American educational achievements: A phenomenon in search of an explanation. *American Psychologist, 45*(8), 913–920.

Suicide—Part I. (1996, November). *The Harvard Mental Health Letter*, pp. 1–5.

Suitor, J. J., & Pillemer, K. (1993). Support and interpersonal stress in the social networks of married daughters caring for parents with dementia. *Journal of Gerontology: Social Sciences, 41*(1), S1–8.

Suitor, J. J., Pillemer, K., Keeton, S., & Robison, J. (1995). Aged parents and aging children: Determinants of relationship quality. In R. Blieszner & V. Hilkevitch (Eds.), *Handbook of*

aging and the family (pp. 223–242). Westport, CT: Greenwood Press.

Sullivan, A. D., Hedberg, K., & Fleming, D. W. (2000). Legalized physician-assisted suicide in Oregon: the second year. *New England Journal of Medicine, 342*, 598–604.

Sullivan, P. F., Bulik, C. M., Fear, J. L., & Pickering, A. (1998). Outcome of anorexia nervosa: A case-control study. *American Journal of Psychiatry, 155*, 939–946.

Sum, A., Kirsch, I., & Taggart, R. (2002). *The twin challenges of mediocrity and inequality: Literacy in the U.S. from an international perspective.* Princeton, NJ: Policy Information Center, Educational Testing Service.

Sun, Y. (2001). Family environment and adolescents' well-being before and after parents' marital disruption. *Journal of Marriage and the Family, 63*, 697–713.

Suomi, S., & Harlow, H. (1972). Social rehabilitation of isolate-reared monkeys. *Developmental Psychology, 6*, 487–496.

Surkan, P. J., Stephansson, O., Dickman, P. W., & Cnattingius, S. (2004). Previous preterm and small-for-gestational-age births and the subsequent risk of stillbirth. *New England Journal of Medicine, 350*, 777–785.

Susman, E. J., Dorn, L. D., & Schiefelbein, V. L. (2003). Puberty, sexuality, and health. In I. Weiner (Ed.) and R. M. Lerner, M. A. Easterbrooks, & J. Mistry (Vol. Eds.), *Handbook of Psychology. Vol. 6: Developmental Psychology* (295–324). Hoboken, NJ: Wiley.

Susman-Stillman, A., Kalkoske, M., Egeland, B., & Waldman, I. (1996). Infant temperament and maternal sensitivity as predictors of attachment security. *Infant Behavior and Development, 19*, 33–47.

Sutcliffe, A., Loft, A., Wennerholm, U. B., Tarlatzis, V., & Bonduelle, M. (2003, July). The European study of 1,523 ICSI/IVF versus naturally conceived 5-year-old children and their families: Physical development at five years. Paper presented at conference of European Society of Human Reproduction and Embryology, Madrid.

Suzuki, L. A., & Valencia, R. R. (1997). Race-ethnicity and measured intelligence: Educational implications. *American Psychologist, 52*, 1103–1114.

Swain, I. U., Zelazo, P. R., & Clifton, R. K. (1993). Newborn infants' memory for speech sounds retained over 24 hours. *Developmental Psychology, 29*, 312–323.

Swallen, K. C., Reither, E. N., Haas, S. A., & Meier, A. M. (2005). Overweight, obesity, and health-related quality of life among adolescents: The National Longitudinal Study of Adolescent Health. *Pediatrics, 115*, 340–347.

Swan, S. H., Kruse, R. L., Liu, F., Barr, D. B., Drobnis, E. Z., Redmon, J. B., Wang, C., Brazil, C., Overstreet, J. W., and Study for Future Families Research Group. (2003). Semen quality in relation to biomarkers of pesticide exposure. *Environmental Health Perspectives, 111*, 1478–1484.

Swanson, H. L. (1999). What develops in working memory? *Developmental Psychology, 35*, 986–1000.

Swanston, H. Y., Tebbutt, J. S., O'Toole, B. I., & Oates, R. K. (1997). Sexually abused children 5 years after presentation: A case-control study. *Pediatrics, 100*, 600–608.

Swarr, A. E., & Richards, M. H. (1996). Longitudinal effects of adolescent girls' pubertal development, perceptions of pubertal timing, and parental relations on eating problems. *Developmental Psychology, 32*, 636–646.

Swedo, S., Rettew, D. C., Kuppenheimer, M., Lum, D., Dolan, S., & Goldberger, E. (1991). Can adolescent suicide attemptors be distinguished from at-risk adolescents? *Pediatrics, 88*(3), 620–629.

Sweeney, M. M. & Phillips, J. A. (2004). Understanding racial differences in marital disruption: Recent trends and explanations. *Journal of Marriage and Family, 66*, 639–650.

Szaflarski, J. P., Holland, S. K., Schmithorst, V. J., & Weber-Byars, A. (2004). An fMRI study of cerebral language lateralization in 121 children and adults. Paper presented at the 56th Annual Meeting of the American Academy of Neurology, San Francisco, CA.

Szatmari, P. (1999). Heterogeneity and the genetics of autism. *Journal of Psychiatry and Neuroscience, 24*, 159–165.

Szinovacz, M. E. (1998). Grandparents today: A demographic profile. *The Gerontologist, 38*, 37–52.

Szkrybalo, J., & Ruble, D. N. (1999). "God made me a girl": Sex category constancy judgments and explanations revisited. *Developmental Psychology, 35*, 392–403.

Talbott, M. M. (1998). Older widows' attitudes towards men and remarriage. *Journal of Aging Studies, 12*, 429–449.

Tamburro, R. F., Gordon, P. L., D'Apolito, J. P., & Howard, S. C. (2004). Unsafe and violent behavior in commercials aired during televised major sporting events. *Pediatrics, 114*, 694–698.

Tamis-LeMonda, C. S., Bornstein, M. H., & Baumwell, L. (2001). Maternal responsiveness and children's achievement of language milestones. *Child Development, 72*(3), 748–767.

Tanda, G., Pontieri, F. E., & DiChiara, G. (1997). Cannabinoid and heroin activation of mesolimbic dopamine transmission by a common N1 opioid receptor mechanism. *Science, 276*, 2048–2050.

Tang, Y.-P., Shimizu, E., Dube, G. R., Rampon, C., Kerchner, G. A., Zhuo, M., Liu, G., & Tsien, J. Z. (1999). Genetic enhancement of learning and memory in mice. *Nature, 401*(6748), 63–68.

Tanner, M. D. (2001, October 18). Testimony before the President's Commission to Strengthen Social Security. Washington, DC.

Tao, K.-T. (1998). An overview of only child family mental health in China. *Psychiatry and Clinical Neurosciences, 52*(Suppl.), S206–S211.

Tarabulsy, G. M., Provost, M. A., Deslandes, J., St-Laurent, D., Moss, E., Lemelin, E., Bernier, A., & Dassylva, J. (2003). Individual differences in infant still-face response at 6 months. *Infant Behavior & Development, 26*, 421–438.

Tarnowski, A. C., & Antonucci, T. C. (1998, June 21). Adjustment to retirement: The influence of social relations. Paper presented at the SPSSI Convention, Ann Arbor, MI.

Taubes, G. (1998, May 29). As obesity rates rise, experts struggle to explain why. *Science, 280,* 1367–1368.

Taveras, E. M., Capra, A. M., Braveman, P. A., Jensvold, N. G., Escobar, G. J., & Lieu, T. A. (2003). Clinician support and psychosocial risk factors associated with breastfeeding discontinuation. *Pediatrics, 112,* 108–115.

Taylor, M. (1997). The role of creative control and culture in children's fantasy/reality judgments. *Child Development, 68,* 1015–1017.

Taylor, M., & Carlson, S. M. (1997). The relation between individual differences in fantasy and theory of mind. *Child Development, 68,* 436–455.

Taylor, M., Carlson, S. M., Maring, B. L., Gerow, L., & Charley, C. M. (2004). The characteristics and correlates of fantasy in school-age children: Imaginary companions, impersonation, and social understanding. *Developmental Psychology, 40,* 1173–1187.

Taylor, M., Cartwright, B. S., & Carlson, S. M. (1993). A developmental investigation of children's imaginary companions. *Developmental Psychology, 28,* 276–285.

Taylor, M. G. (1996). The development of children's beliefs about social and biological aspects of gender differences. *Child Development, 67,* 1555–1571.

Taylor, R. D., & Roberts, D. (1995). Kinship support in maternal and adolescent well-being in economically disadvantaged African-American families. *Child Development, 66,* 1585–1597.

Teachman, J. (2003a). Childhood living arrangements and the formation of coresidential unions. *Journal of Marriage and Family, 65,* 507–524.

Teachman, J. (2003b). Premarital sex, premarital cohabitation, and the risk of subsequent marital dissolution among women. *Journal of Marriage and Family, 65,* 444–455.

Teachman, J. D., Tedrow, L. M., & Crowder, K. D. (2000). The changing demography of America's families. *Journal of Marriage and Family, 62,* 1234–1246.

Techner, D. (1994, February 6). *Death and dying.* Seminar presentation for candidates in Leadership Program, International Institute for Secular Humanistic Judaism, Farmington Hills, MI.

Teller, D. Y., & Bornstein, M. H. (1987). Infant color vision and color perception. In P. Salapatek & L. B. Cohen (Eds.), *Handbook of infant perception: Vol. 1. From sensation to perception* (pp. 185–236). Orlando, FL: Academic Press.

Temple, J. A., Reynolds, A. J., & Miedel, W. T. (2000). Can early intervention prevent high school dropout? Evidence from the Chicago Child-Parent Centers. *Urban Education, 35*(1), 31–57.

Tennyson, Alfred, Lord (1850). "In Memoriam A. H. H., Canto 54."

Termine, N. T., & Izard, C. E. (1988). Infants' responses to their mothers' expressions of joy and sadness. *Developmental Psychology, 24,* 223–229.

Terry, D. F., Wilcox, M. A., McCormick, M. A., & Perls, T. T. (2004). Cardiovascular disease delay in centenarian offspring. *Journal of Gerontology: Medical Sciences, 59A,* 385–389.

Tesman, J. R., & Hills, A. (1994). Developmental effects of lead exposure in children. *Social Policy Report of the Society for Research in Child Development, 8*(3), 1–16.

Teti, D. M., & Ablard, K. E. (1989). Security of attachment and infant-sibling relationships: A laboratory study. *Child Development, 60,* 1519–1528.

Teti, D. M., Gelfand, D. M., Messinger, D. S., & Isabella, R. (1995). Maternal depression and the quality of early attachment: An examination of infants, preschoolers, and their mothers. *Developmental Psychology, 31,* 364–376.

Thabes, V. (1997). A survey analysis of women's long-term, postdivorce adjustment. *Journal of Divorce & Remarriage, 27,* 163–175.

Thal, D., Tobias, S., & Morrison, D. (1991). Language and gesture in late talkers: A one-year follow-up. *Journal of Speech and Hearing Research, 34,* 604–612.

Thapar, A., Fowler, T., Rice, F., Scourfield, J., van den Bree, M., Thomas, H., Harold, G., & Hay, D. (2003). Maternal smoking during pregnancy and attention deficit hyperactivity disorder symptoms in offspring. *American Journal of Psychiatry, 160,* 1985–1989.

Tharp, R. G. (1989). Psychocultural variables and constants: Effects on teaching and learning in schools. *American Psychologist, 44,* 349–359.

The breast cancer genes. (1994, December). *Harvard Women's Health Watch,* p. 1.

The Breastfeeding and HIV International Transmission Study Group. (2004). Late postnatal transmission of HIV-1 in breast-fed children: An individual patient data meta-analysis. *Journal of Infectious Diseases, 189,* 2154–2166.

The Early College High School Initiative. (undated). [Online]. Available: http://www.earlycolleges.org. Access date: March 31, 2004.

The SUPPORT Principal Investigators. (1995). A controlled trial to improve care for seriously ill hospitalized patients: The Study to Understand Prognoses and Preferences for Outcomes and Risks of Treatments (SUPPORT). *Journal of the American Medical Association, 274,* 1591–1598.

Thelen, E. (1995). Motor development: A new synthesis. *American Psychologist, 50*(2), 79–95.

Thelen, E., & Fisher, D. M. (1982). Newborn stepping: An explanation for a "disappearing" reflex. *Developmental Psychology, 18,* 760–775.

Thelen E., & Fisher, D. M. (1983). The organization of spontaneous leg movements in newborn infants. *Journal of Motor Behavior, 15,* 353–377.

Theodore, A. D., Chang, J. J., Runyan, D. K., Hunter, W. M., Bangdiwala, S. I., & Agans, R. (2005). Epidemiological features of the physical and sexual maltreatment of children in the Carolinas. *Pediatrics, 115,* 331–337.

Thomas, A., & Chess, S. (1977). *Temperament and development.* New York: Brunner/Mazel.

Thomas, A., & Chess, S. (1984). Genesis and evolution of behavioral disorders: From infancy to early adult life. *American Journal of Orthopsychiatry, 141*(1), 1–9.

Thomas, A., Chess, S., & Birch, H. G. (1968). *Temperament and behavior disorders in children.* New York: New York University Press.

Thomas, C. (2002). Development of a culturally sensitive, locality-based program to increase kidney donation. *Advances in Renal Replacement Therapy, 9,* 54–56.

Thomas, C. R., Holzer, C. E., & Wall, J. (2002). The Island Youth Programs: Community interventions for reducing youth violence and delinquency. In L. T. Flaherty (Ed.), *Adolescent psychiatry: Developmental and clinical studies, Vol. 26. Annals of the American Society for Adolescent Psychiatry* (pp. 125–143). Hillsdale, NJ: Analytic Press.

Thomas, M. (2005, March 14). At age 69, her career is just taking off: Shows how far flight attendants have come. *Chicago Sun-Times,* p. 3.

Thomas, R. M. (1996). *Comparing theories of child development* (4th ed.). Pacific Grove, CA: Brooks-Cole.

Thomas, S. P. (1997). Psychosocial correlates of women's self-rated physical health in middle adulthood. In M. E. Lachman & J. B. James (Eds.), *Multiple paths of midlife development* (pp. 257–291). Chicago: University of Chicago Press.

Thomas, W. P., & Collier, V. P. (1997). *School effectiveness for language minority students.* Washington, DC: National Clearinghouse for Bilingual Education.

Thomas, W. P., & Collier, V. P. (1998). Two languages are better than one. *Educational Leadership, 55*(4), 23–28.

Thompson, R. A. (1990). Vulnerability in research: A developmental perspective on research risk. *Child Development, 61,* 1–16.

Thompson, R. A. (1991). Emotional regulation and emotional development. *Educational Psychology Review, 3,* 269–307.

Thompson, R. A. (1998). Early sociopersonality development. In W. Damon (Series Ed.) & N. Eisenberg (Vol. Ed.), *Handbook of child psychology: Vol. 3. Social, emotional, and personality development* (4th ed., pp. 25–104). New York: Wiley.

Thompson, R. A. (2001). Development in the first years of life. In R. E. Behrman (Ed.). Caring for infants and children. *The Future of Children, 11,* 21–33.

Thomson, E., Mosley, J., Hanson, T. L., & McLanahan, S. S. (2001). Remarriage, cohabitation, and changes in mothering behavior. *Journal of Marriage and Family, 63,* 370–380.

Thorne, A., & Michaelieu, Q. (1996). Situating adolescent gender and self-esteem with personal memories. *Child Development, 67,* 1374–1390.

Thornton, W. J. L., & Dumke, H. A. (2005). Age differences in everyday problem-solving and decision-making effectiveness: A meta-analytic review. *Psychology and Aging, 20,* 85–99.

Thurstone, L. L. (1938). Primary mental abilities. *Psychometric Monographs,* No. 1.

Tice, J. A., Ettinger, B., Ensrud, K., Wallace, R., Blackwell, T., & Cummings, S. R. (2003). Phytoestrogen supplements for the treatment of hot flashes: The Isoflavone Clover Extract (ICE) Study: A randomized controlled trial. *Journal of the American Medical Association, 290,* 207–214.

Tiedemann, D. (1897). *Beobachtungen ber die entwickelung der seelenfhigkeiten bei kindern* (Record of an infant's life). Altenburg, Germany: Oscar Bonde. (Original work published 1787.)

Tilvis, R. S., Kahonen-Vare, M. H., Jolkkonen, J., Valvanne, J., Pitkala, K. H., & Stradnberg, T. E. (2004). Predictors of cognitive decline and mortality of aged people over a 10-year period. *Journal of Gerontology: Medical Sciences, 59A,* 268–274.

Tincoff, R., & Jusczyk, P. W. (1999). Some beginnings of word comprehension in 6-month-olds. *Psychological Science, 10,* 172–177.

Tisdale, S. (1988). The mother. *Hippocrates,* 2(3), 64–72.

Tolan, P. H., Gorman-Smith, D., & Henry, D. B. (2003). The developmental ecology of urban males' youth violence. *Developmental Psychology, 39,* 274–291.

Tomashek, K. M., Hsia, J., & Iyasu, S. (2003). Trends in postneonatal mortality attributable to injury, United States, 1988–1998. *Pediatrics, 111,* 1215–1218.

Torrance, E. P. (1966). *The Torrance Tests of Creative Thinking: Technical-norms manual (Research ed.).* Princeton, NJ: Personnel Press.

Torrance, E. P. (1974). *The Torrance Tests of Creative Thinking: Technical-norms manual.* Bensonville, IL: Scholastic Testing Service.

Torrance, E. P. (1988). The nature of creativity as manifest in its testing. In R. J. Sternberg (Ed.), *The nature of creativity: Contemporary psychological perspectives* (pp. 43–75). Cambridge, UK: Cambridge University Press.

Torrance, E. P., & Ball, O. E. (1984). *Torrance Tests of Creative Thinking: Streamlined (revised) manual, Figural A and B.* Bensonville, IL: Scholastic Testing Service.

Towers Perrin. (2004). Back to the future: Redefining retirement in the 21st century. [Online]. Retrieved from http://www.towersperrin.com/hrservices/webcache/towers/United States/publications/Reports/Redefining_Retirement/2002_redefining_ret.pdf.

Townsend, N. W. (1997). Men, migration, and households in Botswana: An exploration of connections over time and space. *Journal of Southern African Studies, 23,* 405–420.

Trautner, H. M., Ruble, D. N., Cyphers, L., Kirsten, B., Behrendt, R., & Hartmann, P. (2003). *Rigidity and flexibility of gender stereotypes in childhood: Developmental or differential?* Manuscript submitted for publication.

Travis, J. (1996, January 6). Obesity researchers feast on two scoops. *Science News,* p. 6.

Travis, J. M. J. (2004). The evolution of programmed death in a spatially structured population. *Journal of Gerontology: Biological Sciences, 59A,* 301–305.

Treas, J. (1995, May). Older Americans in the 1990s and beyond. *Population Bulletin, 50*(2). Washington, DC: Population Reference Bureau.

Treatment for Adolescents with Depression Study (TADS) Team. (2004). Fluoxetine, cognitive-behavioral therapy, and their combination for adolescents with depression: Treatment of Adolescent with Depression Study (TADS) randomized controlled trial. *Journal of the American Medical Association, 292,* 807–820.

Trimble, C. L., Genkinger, J. M., Burke, A. E., Helzlsouer, K. J., Diener-West, M., Comstock, G. W., & Alberg, A. J. (2005). Active and passive cigarette smoking and the risk of cervical neoplasia. *Obstetrics & Gynecology, 105,* 174–181.

Trimble, J. E., & Dickson, R. (in press). Ethnic gloss. In C. B. Fisher & R. M. Lerner (Eds.), *Applied developmental science: An encyclopedia of research, policies, and programs.* Thousand Oaks, CA: Sage.

Troiano, R. P. (2002). Physical inactivity among young people. *New England Journal of Medicine, 347,* 706–707.

Troll, L. E. (1985). *Early and middle adulthood* (2nd ed.). Monterey, CA: Brooks/Cole.

Troll, L. E., & Fingerman, K. L. (1996). Connections between parents and their adult children. In C. Magai & S. H. McFadden (Eds.), *Handbook of emotion, adult development, and aging* (pp. 185–205). San Diego: Academic Press.

Tronick, E. (1972). Stimulus control and the growth of the infant's visual field. *Perception and Psychophysics, 11,* 373–375.

Tronick, E., Als, H., Adamson, L.,Wise, S., & Brazelton, T. B. (1978). The infant's response to entrapment between contradictory messages in face-to-face interaction. *American Academy of Child Psychiatry, 17,* 1–13.

Tronick, E. Z. (1980). On the primacy of social skills. In D. B. Sawin, L. O. Walker, & J. H. Penticuff (Eds.), *The exceptional infant: Psychosocial risk in infant environment transactions.* New York: Brunner/Mazel.

Tronick, E. Z. (1989). Emotions and emotional communication in infants. *American Psychologist, 44*(2), 112–119.

Tronick, E. Z., Morelli, G. A., & Ivey, P. (1992). The Efe forager infant and toddler's pattern of social relationships: Multiple and simultaneous. *Developmental Psychology, 28,* 568–577.

Troseth, G. L. (2003). TV Guide: 2-year-old children learn to use video as a source of information. *Developmental Psychology, 39,* 140–150.

Troseth, G. L., & DeLoache, J. S. (1998). The medium can obscure the message: Young children's understanding of video. *Child Development, 69,* 950–965.

Trotter, R. J. (1986, August). Profile: Robert J. Sternberg: Three heads are better than one. *Psychology Today,* pp. 56–62.

Trottier, G., Srivastava, L., & Walker, C. (1999). Etiology of infantile autism: A review of recent advances in genetic and neurobiological research. *Journal of Psychiatry and Neuroscience, 24,* 103–115.

True, M. M., Pisani, L., & Oumar, F. (2001). Infant-mother attachment among the Dogon of Mali. *Child Development, 72,* 1451–1466.

Truog, R. D. (2005). The ethics of organ donation by living donors. *New England Journal of Medicine, 353,* 444–446.

Tsai, J., & Floyd, R. L. (2004). Alcohol consumption among women who are pregnant or who might become pregnant—United States, 2002. *Morbidity and Mortality Weekly Report, 53*(50), 1178–1181.

Tsao, F. M., Liu, H. M., and Kuhl, P. K. (2004). Speech perception in infancy predicts language development in the second year of life: A longitudinal study. *Child Development, 75,* 1067–1084.

Tschann, J., Johnston, J. R., & Wallerstein, J. S. (1989). Resources, stressors, and attachment as predictors of adult adjustment after divorce: A longitudinal study. *Journal of Marriage and Family Therapy, 51,* 1033–1046.

Tseng, V. (2004). Family interdependence and academic adjustment in college youth from immigrant and U.S.-born families. *Child Development, 75,* 966–983.

Tucker, J. S., & Friedman, H. S. (1996). Emotion, personality, and health. In C. Magai, & S. H. McFadden (Eds.), *Handbook of emotion, adult development, and aging* (pp. 307–326). San Diego: Academic Press.

Tucker, M. B., & Mitchell-Kernan, C. (1998). Psychological well-being and perceived marital opportunity among single African American, Latina and White women. *Journal of Comparative Family Studies, 29,* 57–72.

Tucker, M. B., Taylor, R. J., & Mitchell-Kernan, C. (1993). Marriage and romantic involvement among aged African Americans. *Journal of Gerontology: Social Sciences, 48,* S123–132.

Turati, C., Simion, F., Milani, I., & Umilta, C. (2002). Newborns' preference for faces: What is crucial? *Developmental Psychology, 38,* 875–882.

Turiel, E. (1998). The development of morality. In W. Damon (Series Ed.) & N. Eisenberg (Vol. Ed.), *Handbook of child psychology: Vol. 3. Social, emotional, and personality development* (4th ed., pp. 863–932). New York: Wiley.

Turkheimer, E., Haley, A., Waldron, J., D'Onofrio, B., & Gottesman, I. I. (2003). Socioeconomic status modifies heritability of IQ in young children. *Psychological Science, 14,* 623–628.

Turner, C. F., Ku, L., Rogers, S. M., Lindberg, L. D., Pleck, J. H., & Sonenstein, F. L. (1998). Adolescent sexual behavior, drug use, and violence: Increased reporting with computer survey technology. *Science, 280,* 867–873.

Turner, P. J., & Gervai, J. (1995). A multidimensional study of gender typing in preschool children and their parents: Personality, attitudes, preferences, behavior, and cultural differences. *Developmental Psychology, 31,* 759–772.

Tuulio-Henriksson, A., Haukka, J., Partonen, T., Varilo, T., Paunio, T., Ekelund, J., Cannon, T. D., Meyer, J. M., & Lonnqvist, J. (2002). Heritability and number of quantitative trait loci of neurocognitive functions in families with schizophrenia. *American Journal of Medical Genetics, 114*(5), 483–490.

Twenge, J. M. (2000). The age of anxiety? Birth cohort change in anxiety and neuroticism,

1952–1993. *Journal of Personality and Social Psychology, 79,* 1007–1021.

Twenge, J. M., Campbell, W. K., & Foster, C. A. (2003). Parenthood and marital satsifaction: A meta-analytic review. *Journal of Marriage and Family, 65,* 574–583.

Tygiel, J. (1983). Baseball's great experiment: Jackie Robinson and his legacy. New York: Oxford University Press.

Tygiel, J. (Ed.). (1997). *The Jackie Robinson reader.* New York: Dutton.

U.S. Bureau of the Census. (1991a). *Household and family characteristics, March 1991* (Publication No. AP-20-458). Washington, DC: U.S. Government Printing Office.

U.S. Bureau of the Census. (1991b). *1990 census of population and housing.* Washington, DC: Data User Service Division.

U.S. Bureau of the Census. (1992). *Marital status and living arrangements: March 1991* (Current Population Reports, Series P-20-461). Washington, DC: U.S. Government Printing Office.

U.S. Bureau of the Census. (1993). *Sixty-five plus in America.* Washington, DC: U.S. Government Printing Office.

U.S. Cancer Statistics Working Group. (2004). United States Cancer Statistics: 2001 Incidence and Mortality. Atlanta: Centers for Disease Control and National Cancer Institute.

U.S. Census Bureau, (1930). *Population in the United States: Population characteristics.* January, 1930. Washington, DC: U.S. Government Printing Office.

U.S. Census Bureau. (2000, November). Resident population estimates of the United States by age and sex. Washington, DC: Author.

U.S. Census Bureau. (2001). *The 65 years and over population: 2000.* Washington, DC: Author.

U.S. Census Bureau. (2002). Grandparents living with own grandchildren under 18 years old and responsibility for own grandchildren. Table PCT015 of the Census 2001 Supplementary Survey. Retrieved November 12, 2002, from http://factfinder.census.gov/servlet/BasicFactsServlet.

U.S. Census Bureau, (2003a). *Population in the United States: Population characteristics.* June, 2002. Washington, DC: U.S. Government Printing Office.

U.S. Census Bureau. (2003b). Table 010. Infant mortality rates and deaths, and life expectancy at birth, by sex. International Data Base. Available: http://www.census.gov/cgi-bin/ipc.agggen.

U.S. Conference of Mayors. (2003). *A status report on hunger and homelessness in America's cities: 2003.* Washington, DC: Author.

U.S. Department of Agriculture. (1999). *Household food security in the United States 1995–1998.* Washington, DC: Author.

U.S. Department of Agriculture & U.S. Department of Health and Human Services. (2000). *Dietary guidelines for Americans* (5th ed.), USDA Home and Garden Bulletin No. 232. Washington, DC: U.S. Department of Agriculture.

U.S. Department of Agriculture and U.S. Department of Health and Human Services (USDHHS). (2005). *Dietary guidelines for Americans, 2005.* Washington, DC: U.S. Government Printing Office.

U.S. Department of Commerce. (1996). *Statistical abstract of the United States, 1996.* Washington, DC: U.S. Government Printing Office.

U.S. Department of Education. (1992). *Dropout rates in the U.S., 1991* (Publication No. NCES 92-129). Washington, DC: U.S. Government Printing Office.

U.S. Department of Health and Human Services (USDHHS). (1992). *Health, United States, 1991, and Prevention Profile* (DHHS Publication No. PHS 92-1232). Washington, DC: U.S. Government Printing Office.

U.S. Department of Health and Human Services (USDHHS). (1996a). *Health, United States, 1995* (DHHS Publication No. PHS 96-1232). Washington, DC: U.S. Government Printing Office.

U.S. Department of Health and Human Services (USDHHS). (1996b). *HHS releases study of relationship between family structure and adolescent substance abuse* [Press release, online]. Available: http://www.hhs.gov

U.S. Department of Health and Human Services (USDHHS). (1999a). *Blending perspectives and building common ground: A report to Congress on substance abuse and child protection.* Washington, DC: U.S. Government Printing Office.

U.S. Department of Health and Human Services (USDHHS). (1999b). *Mental health: A report of the Surgeon General*—Rockville, MD: U.S. Department of Health and Human Services, Substance Abuse and Mental Health Services Administration, National Institutes of Health, National Institute of Mental Health.

U.S. Department of Health and Human Services (USDHHS). (2000, December 6). *Statistics on child care help* (HHS Press Release). [Online] 10 paragraphs. Available: http://www.hhs.gov/search/press.html. Access date: December 6, 2000.

U.S. Department of Health and Human Services (USDHHS). (2002). "Gift of life" donation initiative fact sheet. [Online]. Available: http://www.organdonor.gov

U.S. Department of Health and Human Services (USDHHS). (2003a). State-funded prekindergarten: What the evidence shows. http://aspe.hhs.gov/hsp/state-funded-pre-k/index.htm

U.S. Department of Health and Human Services (USDHHS). (2003b). Strengthening Head Start: What the evidence shows. http://aspe.hhs.gov/hsp/StrengthenHeadStart03/index.htm

U.S. Department of Health and Human Services (USDHHS). (2004). [Online]. Child maltreatment 2002. Accessed: http://www.acf.hhs.gov/programs/cb/publications/cm02/index.htm.

U.S. Department of Health and Human Services (USDHHS). (2005, March 29). New high set for organ transplants: Nearly 27,000 individuals received transplants last year.

(News release). [Online]. Available: http://www.hhs.gov/news.

U.S. Environmental Protection Agency. (1994). *Setting the record straight: Secondhand smoke is a preventable health risk* (EPA Publication No. 402-F-94-005). Washington, DC: U.S. Government Printing Office.

U.S. Preventive Services Task Force. (2002). *Screening for breast cancer: Recommendations and rationale.* Rockville, MD: Agency for Healthcare Research and Quality. [Online]. Available: http://www.ahrq.gov/clinic/3rduspstf/breastcancer/brcanrr.htm

Uhlenberg, P. (1988). Aging and the social significance of cohorts. In J. E. Birren & V. L. Bengtson (Eds.), *Emergent theories of aging* (pp. 405–425). New York: Springer.

Uhlenberg, P., Cooney, T., & Boyd, R. (1990). Divorce for women after midlife. *Journal of Gerontology, 45*(1), 53–61.

Uitterlinden, A. G., Burger, H., Huang, Q., Yue, F., McGuigan, F. E. A., Grant, S. F. A., van Leeuwen, J. P. T., Pols, H. A. P., & Ralston, S. H. (1998). Relation of alleles of the collagen type Ia1 gene to bone density and the risk of osteoporitic fractures in postmenopausal women. *New England Journal of Medicine, 33,* 1016–1021.

Uller, C., Carey, S., Huntley-Fenner, G., & Klatt, L. (1999). What representations might underlie infant numerical knowledge? *Cognitive Development, 14,* 1–36.

Umberger, F. G., & Van Reenen, J. S. (1995). Thumb sucking management: A review. *International Journal of Orofacial Myology, 21,* 41–47.

Umberson, D., Anderson, K. L., Williams, K., & Chen, M. D. (2003). Relationship dynamics, emotion state, and domestic violence. *Journal of Marriage and Family, 65,* 233–247.

UNAIDS. (2000). UNAIDS/WHO-AIDS epidemic update—December 2000. Geneva: UNAIDS. [Online]. Available: http://www.unaids.org/epidemic_update/index.html. Access date: May 21, 2002.

Underwood, M. K., Schockner, A. E., & Hurley, J. C. (2001). Children's responses to same- and other-gender peers: An experimental investigation with 8-, 10-, and 12-year-olds. *Developmental Psychology, 37,* 362–372.

UNESCO. (2004). *Education for All Global Monitoring Report 2005—The quality imperative.* [Online]. Available: http://www.unesco.org/education/GMR2005/press. Access date: November 10, 2004.

UNICEF. (2002). Official summary of The State of the World's Children 2002. [Online]. Available: http://www.unicef.org/pubsgen/sowc02summary/index.html. Access date: September 19, 2002.

UNICEF. (2003). *Social monitor 2003.* Florence, Italy: Innocenti Social Monitor, UNICEF Innocenti Research Centre.

United Nations International Labor Organization (UNILO). (1993). *Job stress: The 20th-century disease.* New York: United Nations.

University of Virginia Health System. (2004). How chromosome abnormalities happen: Meiosis, mitosis, maternal age, environment. [Online]. Available: http://www.healthsystem.

virginia.edu/UVAHealth/peds_genetics/
happen.cfm. Access date: September 16, 2004.

Urban Institute. (2000). *A new look at home-lessness in America.* Washington, DC: Author.

Utiger, R. D. (1998). A pill for impotence. *New England Journal of Medicine, 338,* 1458–1459.

Vaillant, G. E. (1977). *Adaptation to life.* Boston: Little, Brown.

Vaillant, G. E. (1989). The evolution of defense mechanisms during the middle years. In J. M. Oldman & R. S. Liebert (Eds.), *The middle years.* New Haven: Yale University Press.

Vaillant, G. E. (1993). *The wisdom of the ego.* Cambridge, MA: Harvard University Press.

Vaillant, G. E. (2000). Adaptive mental mechanisms: Their role in a positive psychology. *American Psychologist, 55,* 89–98.

Vaillant, G. E., Meyer, S. E., Mukamal, K., & Soldz, S. (1998). Are social supports in late midlife a cause or a result of successful physical aging? *Psychological Medicine, 28*(5), 1159–1168.

Vaillant, G., & Mukamal, K. (2001). Successful aging. *American Journal of Psychiatry, 158,* 839–847.

Vainio, S., Heikkiia, M., Kispert, A., Chin, N., & McMahon, A. P. (1999). Female development in mammals is regulated by Wnt-4 signalling. *Nature, 397,* 405–409.

Valeski, T. N., & Stipek, D. J. (2001). Young children's feelings about school. *Child Development, 72*(4), 1198–1213.

van den Boom, D. C. (1989). Neonatal irritability and the development of attachment. In G. A. Kohnstamm, J. E. Bates, & M. K. Rothbart (Eds.), *Temperament in childhood* (pp. 299–318). Chichester, England: Wiley.

van den Boom, D. C. (1994). The influence of temperament and mothering on attachment and exploration: An experimental manipulation of sensitive responsiveness among lower-class mothers with irritable infants. *Child Development, 65,* 1457–1477.

van der Heide, A., Deliens, L., Faisst, K., Nilstun, T., Norup, M., Paci, E., van der Wei, G, & van der Maas, P. J. on behalf of the EURELD consortium. (2003). End-of-life decision making in six European countries: Descriptive study. *Lancet, 362,* 345–350.

Van der Maas, P. J., Van der Wal, G., Haverkate, I., De Graeff, C. L. M., Kester, J. G. C., Onwuteaka-Philipsen, B. D., Van der Heide, A., Bosma, J. M., & Willems, D. L. (1996). Euthanasia, physician-assisted suicide, and other medical practices involving the end of life in the Netherlands, 1990–1995. *New England Journal of Medicine, 335,* 1699–1705.

Van Dongen, H. P. A., Maislin, G., Mullington, J. M., & Dinges, D. F. (2003). The cumulative cost of additional wakefulness: Dose-response effects on neurobehavioral functions and sleep physiology from chronic sleep restriction and total sleep deprivation. *Sleep, 26,* 117–126.

van Dyk, D. (2005, January 24). Parlez-vous twixter? *Time,* p. 50.

van Gelder, B. M., Tijhuis, M. A. R., Kalmijn, S., Giampaoli, S., Nissinen, A., & Krombout, D. (2004). Physical activity in relation to cognitive decline in elderly men. *American Academy of Neurology, 63,* 2316–2321.

van Gils, C. H., Peeters, P. H. M., Bueno-de-Mesquita, H. B., Boshuizen, H. C., Lahmann, P. H., Clavel-Chapelon, F., Thiébaut, A., Kesse, E., Sieri, S., Palli, D., Tumino, R., Panico, S., Vineis, P., Gonzalez, C. A., Ardanaz, E., Sánchez, M.-J., Amiano, P., Navarro, C., Quirós, J. R., Key, T. J., Allen, N., Khaw, K.-T., Bingham, S. A., Psaltopoulou, T., Koliva, M., Trichopoulou, A., Nagel, G., Linseisen, J., Boeing, H., Berglund, G., Wirfält, E., Hallmans, G., Lenner, P., Overvad, K., Tjonneland, A., Olsen, A., Lund, E., Engeset, D., Alsaker, E., Norat, T., Kaaks, R., Slimani, N., & Riboli, E. (2005). Consumption of vegetables and fruits and risk of breast cancer. *Journal of the American Medical Association, 293,* 183–193.

Van Heuvelen, M. J., Kempen, G. I., Ormel, J., & Rispens, P. (1998). Physical fitness related to age and physical activity in older persons. *Medicine & Science in Sports and Exercise, 30,* 434–441.

van Hooren, S. A. H., Valentijn, S. A. M., Bosma, H., Ponds, R. W. H. M., van Boxtel, M. P. J. & Jolles, J. (2005). Relation between health status and cognitive functioning: A 6-year follow-up of the Maastricht Aging Study. *Journal of Gerontology: Psychological Sciences, 60B,* P57–P60.

van IJzendoorn, M. H. (1995). Adult attachment representations, parental responsiveness, and infant attachment: A meta-analysis on the predictive validity of the Adult Attachment Interview. *Psychological Bulletin, 117*(3), 387–403.

van IJzendoorn, M. H., & Kroonenberg, P. M. (1988). Cross-cultural patterns of attachment: A meta-analysis of the strange situation. *Child Development, 59,* 147–156.

van IJzendoorn, M. H., & Sagi, A. (1997). Crosscultural patterns of attachment: Universal and contextual dimensions. In J. Cassidy & P. Shaver (Eds.), *Handbook on attachment theory and research.* New York: Guilford Press.

van IJzendoorn, M. H., & Sagi, A. (1999). Crosscultural patterns of attachment: Universal and contextual dimensions. In J. Cassidy & P. R. Shaver (Eds.), *Handbook of attachment: Theory, research, and clinical applications* (pp. 713–734). New York: Guilford.

van IJzendoorn, M. H., Schuengel, C., & Bakermans-Kranenburg, M. J. (1999). Disorganized attachment in early childhood: Meta-analysis of precursors, concomitants, and sequelae. *Development and Psychopathology, 11,* 225–250.

van IJzendoorn, M. H., Vereijken, C.M. J. L., Bakermans-Kranenburg, M. J., & Riksen-Walraven, J. M. (2004). Assessing attachment security with the Attachment Q Sort: Meta-analytic evidence for the validity of the observer AQS. *Child Development, 75,* 1188.

van Lieshout, C. F. M., Haselager, G. J. T., Riksen-Walraven, J. M., & van Aken, M. A. G. (1995, April). Personality development in middle childhood. In D. Hart (Chair), *The contribution of childhood personality to adolescent competence: Insights from longitudinal studies from three societies.* Symposium conducted at the Biennial Meeting of the Society for Research in Child Development, Indianapolis, IN.

van Noord-Zaadstra, B. M., Looman, C. W., Alsbach, H., Habbema, J. D., te Velde, E. R., & Karbaat, J. (1991). Delayed childbearing: Effect of age on fecundity and outcome of pregnancy. *British Medical Journal, 302,* 1361–1365.

Van Praag, H., Schinder, A. F., Christie, B. R., Toni, N., Palmer, T. D., & Gage, F. H. (2002). Functional neurogenesis in the adult hippocampus. *Nature, 415,* 1030–1034.

Van, P. (2001). Breaking the silence of African American women: Healing after pregnancy loss. *Health Care Women International, 22,* 229–243.

Vandell, D. L. (2000). Parents, peer groups, and other socializing influences. *Developmental Psychology, 36,* 699–710.

Vandell, D. L., & Bailey, M. D. (1992). Conflicts between siblings. In C. U. Shantz & W. W. Hartup (Eds.), *Conflict in child and adolescent development* (pp. 242–269). New York: Cambridge University Press.

Vandell, D. L., & Ramanan, J. (1992). Effects of early and recent maternal employment on children from low-income families. *Child Development, 63,* 938–949.

Vandewater, E. A., Ostrove, J. M., & Stewart, A. J. (1997). Predicting women's well-being in midlife: The importance of personality development and social role involvements. *Journal of Personality and Social Psychology, 72,* 1147–1160.

VanSolinge, H., & Henkens, K. (2005). Couples' adjustment to retirement: A multi-actor panel study. *Journal of Gerontology: Social Sciences, 60B,* S11–S20.

Vargas, C. M., Kramarow, F. A., & Yellowitz, J. A. (2001). The oral health of older Americans. *Aging Trends,* No. 3. Hyattsville, MD: National Center for Health Statistics.

Vargha-Khadem, F., Gadian, D. G., Watkins, K. E., Connelly, A., Van Paesschen, W., & Mishkin, M. (1997). Differential effects of early hippocampal pathology on episodic and semantic memory. *Science, 277,* 376–380.

Varma, R., Fraser-Bell, S., Tan, S., Klein, R., Azen, S. P., & Los Angeles Latino Eye Study Group. (2004). Prevalence of age-related macular degeneration in Latinos: The Los Angeles Latino Eye Study. *Ophthalmology, 111,* 1288–1297.

Varma, R., Paz, S. H., Azen, S. P., Klein, R., Globe, D., Torres, M., Shufelt, C., Preston-Martin, S., & Los Angeles Latino Eye Study Group. (2004). The Los Angeles Latino Eye Study: Design, methods, and baseline data. *Ophthalmology, 111,* 1121–1131.

Varma, R., Torres, M., & Los Angeles Latino Eye Study Group. (2004). Prevalence of lens opacities in Latinos: The Los Angeles Latino Eye Study. *Ophthalmology, 111,* 1449–1456.

Varma, R., Torres, M., Peña, F., Klein, R., Azen, S. P., & Los Angeles Latino Eye Study Group. (2004). Prevalence of diabetic retinopathy in adult Latinos: The Los Angeles

Latino Eye Study. *Ophthalmology, 111,* 1298–1306.

Varma, R., Ying-Lai, M., Francis, B. A., Nguyen, B. B.-T., Deneen, J., Wilson, M. R., Azen, S. P., & Los Angeles Latino Eye Study Group. (2004). Prevalence of open-angle glaucoma and ocular hypertension in Latinos: The Los Angeles Latino Eye Study. *Ophthalmology, 111,* 1439–1448.

Varma, R., Ying-Lai, M., Klein, R., Azen, S. P., & Los Angeles Latino Eye Study Group. (2004). Prevalence and risk indicators of visual impairment and blindness in Latinos: The Los Angeles Latino Eye Study. *Ophthalmology, 111,* 1132–1140.

Vartanian, L. R., & Powlishta, K. K. (1996). A longitudinal examination of the social-cognitive foundations of adolescent egocentrism. *Journal of Early Adolescence, 16,* 157–178.

Vartanian, T. P., & McNamara, J. M. (2002). Older women in poverty: The impact of midlife factors. *Journal of Marriage and Family, 64,* 532–548.

Vasilyeva, M. & Huttenlocher, J. (2004). Early development of scaling ability. *Developmental Psychology, 40,* 682–690.

Vaswani, M., & Kapur, S. (2001). Genetic basis of schizophrenia: trinucleotide repeats. *An update Progress in Neuro-Psychopharmacology & Biological Psychiatry, 25*(6), 1187–1201.

Vaughn, B. E., Stevenson-Hinde, J., Waters, E., Kotsaftis, A., Lefever, G. B., Shouldice, A., Trudel, M., & Belsky, J. (1992). Attachment security and temperament in infancy and early childhood: Some conceptual clarifications. *Developmental Psychology, 28,* 463–473.

Vaupel, J. W., Carey, J. R., Christensen, K., Johnson, T. E., Yashin, A. I., Holm, N. V., Iachine, I. A., Kannisto, V., Khazaeli, A. A., Liedo, P., Longo, V. D., Zeng, Y., Manton, K. G., & Curtsinger, J. W. (1998). Biodemographic trajectories of longevity. *Science, 280,* 855–860.

Vecchiotti, S. (2003). Kindergarten: An overlooked educational policy priority. *SRCD Social Policy Report, 17*(2), 1–19.

Ventura, S. J., Abma, J. C., Mosher, W. D., & Henshaw, S. (2004). Estimated pregnancy rates for the United States, 1990–2000: An update. *National Vital Statistics Reports, 52*(23). Hyattsville, MD: National Center for Health Statistics.

Ventura, S. J., Hamilton, B. E., Mathews, T. J., & Chandra, A. (2003). Trends and variations in smoking during pregnancy and low birth weight: Evidence from the birth certificate 1990–2000. *Pediatrics, 111,* 1176–1180.

Ventura, S. J., Martin, J. A., Curtin, S. C., Menacker, F., & Hamilton, B. E. (2001). Births: Final data for 1999. *National Vital Statistics Reports, 49*(1). Hyattsville, MD: National Center for Health Statistics.

Ventura, S. J., Mathews, T. J., & Curtin, S. C. (1999). Declines in teenage birth rates 1991–1998: Update of national and state trends. *National Vital Statistics Reports, 47*(6). Hyattsville, MD: National Center for Health Statistics.

Vercruyssen, M. (1997). Movement control and speed of behavior. In A. D. Fisk & W. A. Rogers (Eds.), *Handbook of human factors and the older adult* (pp. 55–86). San Diego: Academic Press, Inc.

Vereecken, C., & Maes, L. (2000). Eating habits, dental care and dieting. In C. Currie, K. Hurrelmann, W. Settertobulte, R. Smith, & J. Todd (Eds.), *Health and health behaviour among young people: a WHO cross-national study (HBSC) international report* (pp. 83–96). WHO Policy Series: Healthy Policy for Children and Adolescents, Series No. 1.

Verhaeghen, P., Marcoen, A., & Goossens, L. (1992). Improving memory performance in the aged through mnemonic training: A meta-analytic study. *Psychology and Aging, 7*(2), 242–251.

Verhagen, E., & Sauer, P. J. J. (2005). The Groningen Protocol—Euthanasia in severely ill newborns. *New England Journal of Medicine, 352,* 959–962.

Verlinsky, Y., Rechitsky, S., Verlinsky, O., Masciangelo, C., Lederer, K., and Kuliev, A. (2002). Preimplantation diagnosis for early-onset Alzheimer disease caused by V717L mutation. *Journal of the American Medical Association, 287,* 1018–1021.

Verma, S., & Larson, R. (2003). Editors' notes. In S. Verma and R. Larson (Eds.), Examining adolescent leisure time across cultures: Developmental opportunities and risks. *New Directions for Child and Adolescent Development, 99,* 1–7.

Verschueren, K., Buyck, P., & Marcoen, A. (2001). Self-representations and socioemotional competence in young children: A 3-year longitudinal study. *Developmental Psychology, 37,* 126–134.

Verschueren, K., Marcoen, A., & Schoefs, V. (1996). The internal working model of the self, attachment, and competence in five-year-olds. *Child Development, 67,* 2493–2511.

Verschuren, W. M. M., Jacobs, D. R., Bloemberg, B. P. M., Kromhout, D., Menotti, A., Aravanis, C., Blackburn, H., Buzina, R., Dontas, A. S., Fidanza, F., Karvonen, M. J., Nedeljkovic, S., Nissinen, A., & Toshima, H. (1995). Serum total cholesterol and long-term coronary heart disease mortality in different cultures. *Journal of the American Medical Association, 274,* 131–136.

Vgontzas, A. N., & Kales, A. (1999). Sleep and its disorders. *Annual Review of Medicine, 50,* 387–400.

Vink, T., Hinney, A., van Elburg, A. A., van Goozen, S. H. M., Sandkuijl, L. A., Sinke, R. J., Herpertz-Dahlmann, B.-M., Hebebrand, J., Remschmidt, H., van Engeland, H., & Adan, R. A. H. (2001). Association between an agouti-related protein gene polymorphism and anorexia nervosa. *Molecular Psychiatry, 6,* 325–328.

Vinokur, A. D., Schul, Y., Vuori, J., & Price, R. H. (2000). Two years after a job loss: Long-term impact of the JOBS program on reemployment and mental health. *Journal of Occupational Health Psychology, 5,* 32–47.

Vita, A. J., Terry, R. B., Hubert, H. B., & Fries, J. F. (1998). Aging, health risk, and cumulative disability. *New England Journal of Medicine, 338,* 1035–1041.

Vitaliano, P. P., Zhang, J., & Scanlan, J. M. (2003). Is caregiving hazardous to one's physical health? A meta-analysis. *Psychological Bulletin, 129,* 946–972.

Vitaro, F., Tremblay, R. E., Kerr, M., Pagani, L., & Bukowski, W. M. (1997). Disruptiveness, friends' characteristics, and delinquency in early adolescence: A test of two competing models of development. *Child Development, 68,* 676–689.

Voluntary Euthanasia Society. (2002). In depth: Factsheets. Australia. [Online]. Available: http://www.ves.org.uk/DpFS_Aust.html

Vondra, J. I., & Barnett, D. (1999). A typical attachment in infancy and early childhood among children at developmental risk. *Monographs of the Society for Research in Child Development, Serial No. 258, 64*(3).

Vosniadou, S. (1987). Children and metaphors. *Child Development, 58,* 870–885.

Votruba-Drzal, E., Coley, R. L., & Chase-Lansdale, P. L. (2004). Child care and low-income children's development: Direct and moderated effects. *Child Development, 75,* 296–312.

Voydanoff, P. (1987). *Work and family life.* Newbury Park, CA: Sage.

Voydanoff, P. (1990). Economic distress and family relations: A review of the eighties. *Journal of Marriage and the Family, 52,* 1099–1115.

Voydanoff, P. (2004). The effects of work demands and resources on work-to-family conflict and facilitation. *Journal of Marriage and Family, 66,* 398–412.

Vrijheld, M., Dolk, H., Armstrong, B., Abramsky, L., Bianchi, F., Fazarinc, I., Garne, E., Ide, R., Nelen, V., Robert, E., Scott, J. E. S., Stone, D., & Tenconi, R. (2002). Chromosomal congenital anomalies and residence near hazardous waste landfill sites. *Lancet, 359,* 320–322.

Vuchinich, S., Angelelli, J., & Gatherum, A. (1996). Context and development in family problem solving with preadolescent children. *Child Development, 67,* 1276–1288.

Vygotsky, L. S. (1956). *Selected psychological investigations.* Moscow: Izdstel'sto Akademii Pedagogicheskikh Nauk USSR.

Vygotsky, L. S. (1962). *Thought and language.* Cambridge, MA: MIT Press. (Original work published 1934).

Vygotsky, L. S. (1978). *Mind in society: The development of higher psychological processes.* Cambridge, MA: Harvard University Press.

Wade, N. (2001, Aug. 24). Human genome now appears more complicated after all. *The New York Times,* p. A13.

Wagner, C. L., Katikaneni, L. D., Cox, T. H., & Ryan, R. M. (1998). The impact of prenatal drug exposure on the neonate. *Obstetrics and Gynecology Clinics of North America, 25,* 169–194.

Wagner, R. K., & Sternberg, R. J. (1985). Practical intelligence in real-world pursuits: The role of tacit knowledge. *Journal of Personality and Social Psychology, 49,* 436–458.

Wagner, R. K., & Sternberg, R. J. (1986). Tacit knowledge and intelligence in the everyday world. In R. J. Sternberg & R. K. Wagner (Eds.), *Practical intelligence: Nature and origins of competence in the everyday world.* Cambridge, UK: Cambridge University Press.

Wahlbeck, K., Forsen, T., Osmond, C., Barker, D. J. P., & Erikkson, J. G. (2001). Association of schizophrenia with low maternal body mass index, small size at birth, and thinness during childhood. *Archives of General Psychiatry, 58,* 48–55.

Wainright, J. L., Russell, S. T., & Patterson, C. J. (2004). Psychosocial adjustment, school outcomes, and romantic relationships of adolescents with same-sex parents. *Child Development, 75,* 1886–1898.

Waisbren, S. E., Albers, S., Amato, S., Ampola, M., Brewster, T. G., Demmer, L., Eaton, R. B., Greenstein, R., Korson, M., Larson, C., Marsden, D., Msall, M., Naylor, E. W., Pueschel, S., Seashore, M., Shih, V. E., & Levy, H. L. (2003). Effect of expanded newborn screening for biochemical disorders on child outcomes and parental stress. *Journal of the American Medical Association, 290,* 2564–2572.

Waite, L. J., & Joyner, K. (2000). Emotional and physical satisfaction with sex in married, cohabiting, and dating sexual unions: Do men and women differ? In Laumann, E. O., & Michael, R. T. (Eds.), *Sex, love, and health in America: Private choices and public policies* (pp. 239–269). Chicago: University of Chicago Press.

Wakefield, M., Reid, Y., Roberts, L., Mullins, R., & Gillies, P. (1998). Smoking and smoking cessation among men whose partners are pregnant: A qualitative study. *Social Science and Medicine, 47,* 657–664.

Wakschlag, L. S., Lahey, B. B., Loeber, R., Green, S. M., Gordon, R. A., & Leventhal, B. L. (1997). Maternal smoking during pregnancy and the risk of conduct disorder in boys. *Archives of General Psychiatry, 54,* 670–676.

Walasky, M., Whitbourne, S. K., & Nehrke, M. F. (1983–1984). Construction and validation of an ego-integrity status interview. *International Journal of Aging and Human Development, 81,* 61–72.

Waldman, I. D. (1996). Aggressive boys' hostile perceptual and response biases: The role of attention and impulsivity. *Child Development, 67,* 1015–1033.

Waldstein, S. R. (2003). The relation of hypertension to cognitive function. *Current Directions in Psychological Sciences, 12,* 9–12.

Walfish, S., Antonovsky, A., & Maoz, B. (1984). Relationship between biological changes and symptoms and health and behavior during the climacteric. *Maturitas, 6,* 9–17.

Walk, R. D., & Gibson, E. J. (1961). A comparative and analytical study of visual depth perception. *Psychology Monographs, 75*(15).

Walker, L. (1995). Sexism in Kohlberg's moral psychology? In W. M. Kurtines & J. L. Gewirtz (Eds.), *Moral development: An introduction* (pp. 83–107). Boston: Allyn and Bacon.

Walker, L. E. (1999). Psychology and domestic violence around the world. *American Psychologist, 54,* 21–29.

Walker, L. J. (1984). Sex differences in the development of moral reasoning: A critical review. *Child Development, 55,* 677–691.

Walker, L. J., & Taylor, J. H. (1991). Family interactions and the development of moral reasoning. *Child Development, 62,* 264–283.

Walker, M. P., Brakefield, T., Morgan, A., Hobson, J. A., & Stickgold, R. (2002). Practice with sleep makes perfect: Sleep-dependent motor skill learning. *Neuron, 35,* 205–211.

Walker, W. R., Skowronski, J. J., & Thompson, C. P. (2003). Life is pleasant—and memory helps to keep it that way! *Review of General Psychology, 7,* 203–210.

Wallace, D. C. (1992). Mitochondrial genetics: A paradigm for aging and degenerative diseases? *Science, 256,* 628–632.

Wallerstein, J., & Corbin, S. B. (1999). The child and the vicissitudes of divorce. In R. M. Galatzer-Levy & L. Kraus (Eds.), *The scientific basis of child custody decisions* (pp. 73–95). New York: Wiley.

Wallerstein, J. S., Lewis, J. M., & Blakeslee, S. (2000). *The unexpected legacy of divorce: A 25-year landmark study.* New York: Hyperion.

Wallhagen, M. I., Strawbridge, W. J., Cohen, R. D., & Kaplan, G. A. (1997). An increasing prevalence of hearing impairment and associated risk factors over three decades of the Alameda County Study. *American Journal of Public Health, 87,* 440–442.

Wallhagen, M. I., Strawbridge, W. J., Shema, S. J., & Kaplan, G. A. (2004). Impact of self-assessed hearing loss on a spouse: A longitudinal analysis of couples. *Journal of Gerontology: Social Sciences, 59,* S190–S196.

Walls, C., & Zarit, S. (1991). Informal support from black churches and well-being of elderly blacks. *The Gerontologist, 31,* 490–495.

Walma van der Molen, J. (2004). Violence and suffering in television news: Toward a broader conception of harmful television content for children. *Pediatrics, 113,* 1771–1775.

Walsh, D. A., & Hershey, D. A. (1993). Mental models and the maintenance of complex problem solving skills into old age. In J. Cerella & W. Hoyer (Eds.), *Adult information processing: Limits on loss* (pp. 553–584). New York: Academic Press.

Walston, J. T., & West, J. (2004). *Full-day and half-day kindergarten in the United States: Findings from the Early Childhood Longitudinal Study, Kindergarten Class of 1998–99* (NCES 2004–078). Washington, DC: National Center for Education Statistics.

Wang, D. E. (2003). Risk profiles of adolescent girls who were victims of dating violence. *Adolescence, 38,* 1–14.

Wang, L., Wang, X., Wang, W., Chen, C., Ronnennberg, A. G., Guang, W., Huang, A., Fang, Z., Zang, T., Wang, L., & Xu, X. (2004). Stress and dysmenorrhea: A population-based prospective study. *Occupational and Environmental Medicine, 61,* 1021–1026.

Wang, Q. (2004). The emergence of cultural self-constructs: Autobiographical memory and self-description in European American and Chinese children. *Developmental Psychology, 40,* 3–15.

Wannamethee, S. G., Shaper, A. G., Whincup, P. H., & Walker, M. (1995). Smoking cessation and the risk of stroke in middle-aged men. *Journal of the American Medical Association, 274,* 155–160.

Ward, R. A., & Spitze, G. D. (2004). Marital implications of parent-adult child coresidence: A longitudinal view. *Journal of Gerontology: Social Sciences, 59B,* S2–S8.

Wardle, J., Robb, K. A., Johnson, F., Griffith, J., Brunner, E., Power, C., & Tovée, M. (2004). Socioeconomic variation in attitudes to eating and weight in female adolescents. *Health Psychology, 23,* 275–282.

Warner, H. R. (2004). Current status of efforts to measure and modulate the biological rate of aging. *Journal of Gerontology: Biological Sciences, 59A,* 692–696.

Warr, P. (1994). Age and employment. In H. C. Triandis, M. D. Dunnette, & L. M. Hough (Eds.), *Handbook of industrial and organizational psychology* (Vol. 4, pp. 485–550). Palo Alto, CA: Consulting Psychologists Press.

Warren, J. A., & Johnson, P. J. (1995). The impact of workplace support on work-family role strain. *Family Relations, 44,* 163–169.

Wasik, B. H., Ramey, C. T., Bryant, D. M., & Sparling, J. J. (1990). A longitudinal study of two early intervention strategies: Project CARE. *Child Development, 61,* 1682–1696.

Wassertheil-Smoller, S., Hendrix, S. L., Limacher, M., Heiss, G., Kooperberg, C., Baird, A., Kotchen, T., Curb, J. D., Black, H., Rossouw, J. E., Aragaki, A., Safford, M., Stein, E., Laowattana, S., Mysiw, W. J., for the WHI Investigators. (2003). Effects of estrogen plus progestin on stroke in postmenopausal women: The Women's Health Initiative: A randomized trial. *Journal of the American Medical Association, 289,* 2673–2684.

Watamura, S. E., Donzella, B., Alwin, J., & Gunnar, M. R. (2003). Morning-to-afternoon increases in cortisol concentrations for infants and toddlers at child care: Age differences and behavioral correlates. *Child Development, 74,* 1006–1020.

Waters, E., & Deane, K. E. (1985). Defining and assessing individual differences in attachment relationships: Q-methodology and the organization of behavior in infancy and early childhood. *Monographs of the Society for Research in Child Development, 50,* 41–65.

Waters, E., Wippman, J., & Sroufe, L. A. (1979). Attachment, positive affect, and competence in the peer group: Two studies in construct validation. *Child Development, 50,* 821–829.

Waters, K. A., Gonzalez, A., Jean, C., Morielli, A., & Brouillette, R. T. (1996). Face-straight-down and face-near-straight-down positions in healthy prone-sleeping infants. *Journal of Pediatrics, 128,* 616–625.

Watson, A. C., Nixon, C. L., Wilson, A., & Capage, L. (1999). Social interaction skills and theory of mind in young children. *Developmental Psychology, 35*(2), 386–391.

Watson, J. B., & Rayner, R. (1920). Conditioned emotional reactions. *Journal of Experimental Psychology, 3,* 1–14.

Watts, D. H. (2002). Management of human immunodeficiency virus infection in pregnancy. *New England Journal of Medicine, 346,* 1879–1891.

Weese-Mayer, D. E., Berry-Kravis, E. M., Maher, B. S., Silvestri, J. M., Curran, M. E., & Marazita, M. L. (2003). Sudden infant death syndrome: Association with a promoter polymorphism of the serotonin transporter gene. *American Journal of Medical Genetics, 117A,* 268–274.

Weese-Mayer, D. E., Berry-Kravis, E. M., Zhou, L., Maher, B. S., Curran, M. E., Silvestri, J. M., & Marazita, M. L. (2004). Sudden Infant Death Syndrome: Case-control frequency differences at genes pertinent to autonomic nervous system embryological development. *Pediatric Research, 56,* 391–395.

Weg, R. B. (1989). Sensuality/sexuality of the middle years. In S. Hunter & M. Sundel (Eds.), *Midlife myths.* Newbury Park, CA: Sage.

Wegman, M. E. (1992). Annual summary of vital statistics—1991. *Pediatrics, 90,* 835–845.

Wegman, M. E. (1994). Annual summary of vital statistics—1993. *Pediatrics, 94,* 792–803.

Wegman, M. E. (1999). Foreign aid, international organizations, and the world's children. *Pediatrics, 103*(3), 646–654.

Weinberg, M. K., & Tronick, E. Z. (1996). Infant affective reactions to the resumption of maternal interaction after still face. *Child Development, 67,* 905–914.

Weinberger, B., Anwar, M., Hegyi, T., Hiatt, M., Koons, A., & Paneth, N. (2000). Antecedents and neonatal consequences of low Apgar scores in preterm newborns. *Archives of Pediatric and Adolescent Medicine, 154,* 294–300.

Weinberger, D. R. (2001, March 10). A brain too young for good judgment. *The New York Times.* [Online]. Available: http://www.nytimes.com/2001/03/10/opinion/10WEIN.html?ex_9852503 09&ei_1&en_995bc03f7a8c7207.

Weinberger, J. (1999, May 18). Enlightening conversation [Letter to the editor]. *The New York Times,* p. F3.

Weindruch, R., & Walford, R. L. (1988). *The retardation of aging and disease by dietary restriction.* Springfield, IL: Thomas.

Weinreb, L., Wehler, C., Perloff, J., Scott, R., Hosmer, D., Sagor, L., and Gundersen, C. (2002). Hunger: Its impact on children's health and mental health. *Pediatrics, 110,* 816.

Weinstein, A. R., Sesso, H. D., Lee, I. M., Cook, N. R., Manson, J. E., Buring, J. E., & Gaziano, J. M. (2004). Relationship of physical activity vs body mass index with type 2 diabetes in women. *Journal of the American Medical Association, 292,* 1188–1194.

Weinstock, H., Berman, S., & Cates Jr., W. (2004). Sexually transmitted diseases among American youth: Incidence and prevalence estimates, 2000. *Perspectives on Sexual and Reproductive Health, 36,* 6–10.

Weisner, T. S. (1993). Ethnographic and ecocultural perspectives on sibling relationships. In Z. Stoneman & P. W. Berman (Eds.), *The effects of mental retardation, visibility, and illness on sibling relationships* (pp. 51–83). Baltimore, MD: Brooks.

Weiss, B., Amler, S., & Amler, R. W. (2004). Pesticides. *Pediatrics, 113,* 1030–1036.

Weiss, B., Dodge, K. A., Bates, J. E., & Pettit, G. S. (1992). Some consequences of early harsh discipline: Child aggression and a maladaptive social information processing style. *Child Development, 63,* 1321–1335.

Weissman, M. M., Warner, V., Wickramaratne, P. J., & Kandel, D. B. (1999). Maternal smoking during pregnancy and psychopathology in offspring followed to adulthood. *Journal of the American Academy of Child and Adolescent Psychiatry, 38,* 892–899.

Weisz, J. R., Weiss, B., Han, S. S., Granger, D. A., & Morton, T. (1995). Effects of psychotherapy with children and adolescents revisited: A meta-analysis of treatment outcome studies. *Psychological Bulletin, 117*(3), 450–468.

Weitzman, M., Gortmaker, S., & Sobol, A. (1992). Maternal smoking and behavior problems of children. *Pediatrics, 90,* 342–349.

Welch-Ross, M. K. (1997). Mother-child participation in conversation about the past: Relationships to preschoolers' theory of mind. *Developmental Psychology, 33*(4), 618–629.

Welch-Ross, M. K., & Schmidt, C. R. (1996). Gender-schema development and children's story memory: Evidence for a developmental model. *Child Development, 67,* 820–835.

Weller, C. E. (2005, April). *Social Security privatization: The mother of all unfunded mandates.* Washington, DC: Center for American Progress.

Wellman, H. M., & Cross, D. (2001). Theory of mind and conceptual change. *Child Development, 72,* 702–707.

Wellman, H. M., Cross, D., & Watson, J. (2001). Meta-analysis of theory-of-mind development: The truth about false belief. *Child Development, 72,* 655–684.

Wellman, H. M., & Gelman, S. A. (1998). Knowledge acquisition in foundational domains. In W. Damon (Series Ed.), D. Kuhn, & R. S. Siegler (Vol. Eds.), *Handbook of child psychology: Vol. 2. Cognition, perception, and language* (5th ed., pp. 523–573). New York: Wiley.

Wellman, H. M., & Liu, D. (2004). Scaling theory-of-mind tasks. *Child Development, 75,* 523–541.

Wellman, H. M., & Woolley, J. D. (1990). From simple desires to ordinary beliefs: The early development of everyday psychology. *Cognition, 35,* 245–275.

Wells, G. (1985). Preschool literacy-related activities and success in school. In D. R. Olson, N. Torrence, & A. Hilyard (Eds.), *Literacy, language, and learning* (pp. 229–255). New York: Cambridge University Press.

Wender, P. H. (1995). *Attention-deficit hyperactivity disorder in adults.* New York: Oxford University Press.

Wennerholm, U. B., & Bergh, C. (2000). Obstetric outcome and follow-up of children born after in-vitro fertilization (IVF). *Human Fertility, 3*(1), 52–64.

Wentworth, N., Benson, J. B., & Haith, M. M. (2000). The development of infants' reaches for stationary and moving targets. *Child Development, 71,* 576–601.

Wenzel, D. (1990). *Ann Bancroft: On top of the world.* Minneapolis: Dillon.

Werker, J. F. (1989). Becoming a native listener. *American Scientist, 77,* 54–59.

Werker, J. F., Pegg, J. E., & McLeod, P. J. (1994). A cross-language investigation of infant preference for infant-directed communication. *Infant Behavior and Development, 17,* 323–333.

Werner, E., & Smith, R. S. (2001). *Journeys from childhood to midlife.* Ithaca: Cornell University Press.

Werner, E., Bierman, L., French, F. E., Simonian, K., Conner, A., Smith, R., & Campbell, M. (1968). Reproductive and environmental casualties: A report on the 10-year follow-up of the children of the Kauai pregnancy study. *Pediatrics, 42,* 112–127.

Werner, E. E. (1985). Stress and protective factors in children's lives. In A. R. Nichol (Ed.), *Longitudinal studies in child psychology and psychiatry.* New York: Wiley.

Werner, E. E. (1987, July 15). *Vulnerability and resiliency: A longitudinal study of Asian Americans from birth to age 30.* Invited address at the Ninth Biennial Meeting of the International Society for the Study of Behavioral Development, Tokyo, Japan.

Werner, E. E. (1989). Children of the garden island. *Scientific American, 260*(4), 106–111.

Werner, E. E. (1993). Risk and resilience in individuals with learning disabilities: Lessons learned from the Kauai longitudinal study. *Learning Disabilities Research and Practice, 8,* 28–34.

Werner, E. E. (1995). Resilience in development. *Current Directions in Psychological Science, 4*(3), 81–85.

Wessel, T. R., Arant, C. B., Olson. M. B., Johnson, B. D., Reis, S. E., Sharaf, B. L., Shaw, L. J., Handberg, E., Sopko, G., Kelsey, S. F., Pepine, C. J., & Merz, C. N. B. (2004). Relationship of physical fitness vs. body mass index with coronary artery disease and cardiovascular events in women. *Journal of the American Medical Association, 292,* 1179–1187.

West, R., & Burr, G. (2002). Why families deny consent to organ donation. *Australian Critical Care, 15,* 27–32.

West, R. L. (1996). An application of prefrontal cortex function theory to cognitive aging. *Psychological Bulletin, 120,* 272–292.

West, R. L., & Yassuda, M. S. (2004). Aging and memory control beliefs: Performance in relation to goal setting and memory self-evaluation. *Journal of Gerontology: Psychological Sciences, 59B,* P56–P65.

Westen, D. (1998). The scientific legacy of Sigmund Freud: Toward a psychodynamically informed psychological science. *Psychological Bulletin, 124,* 333–371.

Wethington, E., Kessler, R. C., & Pixley, J. E. (2004). Turning points in adulthood. In O. G. Brim, C. D. Ryff, and R. C. Kessler (Eds.), *How healthy are we? A national study of well-being at midlife* (pp. 586–613). Chicago: University of Chicago Press.

Weuve, J., Kang, J. H., Manson, J. E., Breteler, M. M. B., Ware, J. H., & Grodstein, F. (2004). Physical activity, including walking, and cognitive function in older women. *Journal of the American Medical Association, 292,* 1454–1461.

Whalen, C. K., Jamner, L. D., Henker, B., Delfino, R. J., & Lozano, J. M. (2002). The ADHD spectrum and everyday life: Experience sampling of adolescent moods, activities, smoking, and drinking. *Child Development, 73,* 209–228.

Whalley, L. J., & Deary, I. J. (2001). Longitudinal cohort study of childhood IQ and survival up to age 76. *British Medical Journal, 322,* 819.

Whalley, L. J., Starr, J. M., Athawes, R., Hunter, D., Pattie, A., & Deary, I. J. (2000). Childhood mental ability and dementia. *Neurology, 55,* 1455–1459.

What is Elderhostel? (2005). [Online]. Retrieved from www.elderhostel.org/about/whatis.asp on March 11, 2005.

Whisman, M. A., Uebelacker, L. A., & Weinstock, L. M. (2004). Psychopathology and marital satisfaction: The importance of evaluating both partners. *Journal of Consulting and Clinical Psychology, 72,* 830–838.

Whitaker, R. C., Wright, J. A., Pepe, M. S., Seidel, K. D., & Dietz, W. H. (1997). Predicting obesity in young adulthood from childhood and parental obesity. *New England Journal of Medicine, 337,* 869–873.

Whitbourne, S. K. (1987). Personality development in adulthood and old age: Relationships among identity style, health, and well-being. In K. W. Schaie (Ed.), *Annual review of gerontology and geriatrics* (pp. 189–216). New York: Springer.

Whitbourne, S. K. (1996). *The aging individual: Physical and psychological perspectives.* New York: Springer.

Whitbourne, S. K. (1999). Physical changes. In J. C. Cavanaugh & S. K. Whitbourne (Eds.). *Gerontology: An interdisciplinary perspective* (pp. 91–122). New York: Oxford University Press.

Whitbourne, S. K. (2001). The physical aging process in midlife: Interactions with psychological and sociocultural factors. In M. E. Lachman (Ed.), *Handbook of midlife development* (pp. 109–155). New York: Wiley.

Whitbourne, S. K., & Connolly, L. A. (1999). The developing self in midlife. In S. L. Willis & J. D. Reid (Eds.), *Life in the middle: Psychological and social development in middle age* (pp. 25–45). San Diego: Academic Press.

White, A. (2001). Alcohol and adolescent brain development. [Online]. Available: http://www.duke.edu/~amwhite/alc_adik_pf.html.

Whitehead, B. D., & Popenoe, D. (2003). Marriage and children: Coming together again? Executive summary. In Popenoe, D., & Whitehead, B. D. (Eds.), *The state of our unions: The social health of marriage in America* (pp. 6–18). Piscataway, NJ: The National Marriage Project, Rutgers University.

Whitehurst, G. J., & Lonigan, C. J. (1998). Child development and emergent literacy. *Child Development, 69,* 848–872.

Whitehurst, G. J., Falco, F. L., Lonigan, C. J., Fischel, J. E., DeBaryshe, B. D., Valdez-Menchaca, M. D., & Caufield, M. (1988). Accelerating language development through picture book reading. *Developmental Psychology, 24,* 552–559.

Whyatt, R. M., Rauh, V., Barr, D. B., Camann, D. E., Andrews, H. F., Garfinkel, R., Hoepner, L. A., Diaz, D., Dietrich, J., Reyes, A. Tang, D., Kinney, P. L., & Perera, F. P. (in press). Prenatal insecticide exposures, birth weight and length among an urban minority cohort.

Wickelgren, I. (1996, July 5). For the cortex, neuron loss may be less than thought. *Science,* pp. 48–50.

Wickelgren, I. (1998, May 29). Obesity: How big a problem? *Science, 280,* 1364–1367.

Wiggins, S., Whyte, P., Higgins, M., Adams, S., et al. (1992). The psychological consequences of predictive testing for Huntington's disease. *New England Journal of Medicine, 327,* 1401–1405.

Wilcox, A. J., Weinberg, C. R., & Baird, D. D. (1995). Timing of sexual intercourse in relation to ovulation: Effects on the probability of conception, survival of the pregnancy, and sex of the baby. *New England Journal of Medicine, 333,* 1563–1565.

Wilcox, A. J., Weinberg, C. R., O'Connor, J. F., Baird, D. D., Schlatterer, J. P., Canfield, R. E., Armstrong, E. G., & Nisula, B. C. (1988). Incidence of early loss of pregnancy. *New England Journal of Medicine, 319,* 189–194.

Wilens, T. E., Faraone, S. V., & Biederman, J. (2004). Attention-Deficit Hyperactivity Disorder in adults. *Journal of the American Medical Association, 292,* 619–623.

Willcox, B. J., Yano, K., Chen, R., Willcox, D. C., Rodriguez, B. L., Masaki, K. H., Donlon, T., Tanaka, B., & Curb, J. D. (2004). How much should we eat? The association between energy intake and mortality in a 36-year follow-up study of Japanese-American men. *Journal of Gerontology: Biological Sciences, 59A,* 789–795.

Willett, W. C. (1994). Diet and health: What should we eat? *Science, 264,* 532–537.

Willett, W. C., Colditz, G., & Stampfer, M. (2000). Postmenopausal estrogens—opposed, unopposed, or none of the above. *Journal of the American Medical Association, 283,* 534–535.

Willett, W. C., Hunter, D. J., Stampfer, M. J., Colditz, G., Manson, J. E., Spiegelman, D., Rosner, B., Hennekens, C. H., & Spiezer, F. E. (1992). Dietary fat and fiber in relation to risk of breast cancer. *Journal of the American Medical Association, 268,* 2037–2044.

Willett, W. C., Stampfer, M. J., Colditz, G. A., Rosner, B. A., & Speizer, F. E. (1990). Relation of meat, fat, and fiber intake to the risk of colon cancer in a prospective study among women. *New England Journal of Medicine, 323,* 1664–1672.

Williams, G. (1991, October–November). Flaming out on the job: How to recognize when it's all too much. *Modern Maturity,* pp. 26–29.

Williams, G. J. (2001). The clinical significance of visual-verbal processing in evaluating children with potential learning-related visual problems. *Journal of Optometric Vision Development, 32*(2), 107–110.

Williams, J., Wake, M., Hesketh, K., Maher, E., & Waters, E. (2005). Health-related quality of life of overweight and obese children. *Journal of the American Medical Association, 293,* 70–76.

Williams, K. (2004). The transition to widowhood and the social regulation of health: Consequences for health and health risk behavior. *Journal of Gerontology: Social Sciences, 59B,* S343–S349.

Williams, M. E. (1995). *The American Geriatric Society's complete guide to aging and health.* New York: Harmony.

Willinger, M., Hoffman, H. T., & Hartford, R. B. (1994). Infant sleep position and risk for sudden infant death syndrome: Report of meeting held January 13 and 14, 1994. *Pediatrics, 93,* 814–819.

Willis, S. L. (1990). Current issues in cognitive training research. In E. A. Lovelace (Ed.), *Aging and cognition: Mental processes, self-awareness, and intervention* (pp. 263–280). Amsterdam: North-Holland, Elsevier.

Willis, S. L., Blieszner, R., & Baltes, P. B. (1981). Intellectual training research in aging: Modification of performance on the fluid ability of figural relations. *Journal of Educational Psychology, 73,* 41–50.

Willis, S. L., Jay, G. M., Diehl, M., & Marsiske, M. (1992). Longitudinal change and prediction of everyday task competence in the elderly. *Research on Aging, 14,* 68–91.

Willis, S. L., & Nesselroade, C. S. (1990). Long-term effects of fluid ability training in old-old age. *Developmental Psychology, 26,* 905–910.

Willis, S. L., & Reid, J. D. (1999). *Life in the middle.* San Diego: Academic Press.

Willis, S. L., & Schaie, K. W. (1986a). Practical intelligence in later adulthood. In R. J. Sternberg & R. K. Wagner (Eds.), *Practical intelligence: Nature and origins of competence in the everyday world* (pp. 236–268). New York: Cambridge University Press.

Willis, S. L., & Schaie, K. W. (1986b). Training the elderly on the ability factors of spatial orientation and inductive reasoning. *Psychology and Aging, 2,* 239–247.

Willis, S. L., & Schaie, K. W. (1999). Intellectual functioning in midlife. In S. L. Willis & J. D. Reid (Eds.), *Life in the middle: Psychological and social development in middle age* (pp. 233–247). San Diego: Academic Press.

Willis, S. L., Schaie, K. W., Yanling, Z., Kennett, J., Intrieri, B., & Persaud, A. (1998). *Longitudinal studies of practical intelligence.* University Park: Pennsylvania State University.

Willson, A. E., Shuey, K. M., & Elder, G. H. (2003). Ambivalence in the relationship of adult children to aging parents and in-laws. *Journal of Marriage and Family, 65,* 1055–1072.

Wilmoth, J., & Koso, G. (2002). Does marital history count? Marital status and wealth outcomes among preretirement adults. *Journal of Marriage and Family, 64,* 254–268.

Wilmoth, J. R. (2000). Demography of longevity: Past, present, and future trends. *Experimental Gerontology, 35,* 1111–1129.

Wilmoth, J. R., Deegan, L. J., Lundstrom, H., & Horiuchi, S. (2000). Increase of maximum life-span in Sweden, 1861–1999. *Science, 289,* 2366–2368.

Wilson, E. O. (1975). *Sociobiology: The new synthesis.* Cambridge, MA: Belknap Press of Harvard University Press.

Wilson, K., & Ryan, V. (2001). Helping parents by working with their children in individual child therapy. *Child and Family Social Work* (special issue), 6, 209–217.

Wilson, R. S. (2005). Mental challenge in the workplace and risk of dementia in old age: Is there a connection? *Occupational and Environmental Medicine, 62,* 72–73.

Wilson, R. S., Beckett, L. A., Barnes, L. L., Schneider, J. A., Bach, J., Evans, D. A., & Bennett, D. A. (2002). Individual differences in rates of change in cognitive abilities of older persons. *Psychology and Aging, 17,* 179–193.

Wilson, R. S., & Bennett, D. A. (2003). Cognitive activity and risk of Alzheimer's Disease. *Current Directions in Psychological Science, 12,* 87–91.

Wilson, R. S., Mendes de Leon, C. F., Bienias, J. L., Evans, D. A., & Bennett, D. A. (2004). Personality and mortality in old age. *Journal of Gerontology: Psychological Sciences, 59B,* P110–P116.

Wilson, S. J., Lipsey, M. W., & Derzon, J. H. (2003). The effects of school-based intervention programs on aggressive behavior: A meta-analysis. *Journal of Consulting and Clinical Psychology, 71,* 136–149.

Winefield, A. H. (1995). Unemployment: Its psychological costs. In C. L. Cooper & I. T. Robertson (Eds.), *International review of industrial and organizational psychology* (pp. 169–212). Chichester, England: Wiley.

Wingfield, A., & Stine, E. A. L. (1989). Modeling memory processes: Research and theory on memory and aging. In G. C. Gilmore, P. J. Whitehouse, & M. L. Wykle (Eds.), *Memory, aging, and dementia: Theory, assessment, and treatment* (pp. 4–40). New York: Springer.

Wingfield, A., Tun, P. A., & McCoy, S. L. (2005). Hearing loss in older adulthood: What it is and how it interacts with cognitive performance. *Current Directions in Psychological Science, 14,* 144–148.

Wink, P., & Dillon, M. (2003). Religiousness, spirituality, and psychosocial functioning in late adulthood: Findings from a longitudinal study. *Psychology and Aging, 18,* 916–924.

Winner, E. (1997). Exceptionally high intelligence and schooling. *American Psychologist, 52*(10), 1070–1081.

Wisby, G. (2001, Sept. 27). Husband kills wife, himself in hospital. *Chicago Sun-Times,* p. 18.

Witteman, P. A. (1993, February 15). A man of fire and grace: Arthur Ashe, 1943–1993. *Time,* p. 70.

Wittig, D. R. (2001). Organ donation beliefs of African American women residing in a small southern community. *Journal of Transcultural Nursing, 12,* 203–210.

Wittstein, I. S., Thiemann, D. R., Lima, J. A. C., Baughman, K. L., Schulman, S. P., Gerstenblith, G., Wu, K. C., Rade, J. J., Bivalacqua, T. J., & Champion, H. C. (2005). Neurohumoral features of myocardial stunning due to sudden emotional stress. *New England Journal of Medicine, 352,* 539–548.

Wolchik, S. A., Sandler, I. N., Millsap, R. E., Plummer, B. A., Greene, S. M., Anderson, E. R., Dawson-McClure, S. R., Hipke, K., & Haine, R. A. (2002). Six-year follow-up of preventive interventions for children of divorce: A randomized controlled trial. *Journal of the American Medical Association, 288,* 1874–1881.

Wolf, M. (1968). *The house of Lim.* Englewood Cliffs, NJ: Prentice-Hall.

Wolfe, D. A., Edwards, B., Manion, I., & Koverola, C. (1988). Early intervention for parents at risk of child abuse and neglect: A preliminary investigation. *Journal of Consulting and Clinical Psychology, 56,* 40–47.

Wolfe, L. (2004). Should parents speak with a dying child about impending death? *New England Journal of Medicine, 351,* 1251–1253.

Wolff, J. L., & Agree, E. M. (2004). Depression among recipients of informal care: The effects of reciprocity, respect, and adequacy of support. *Journal of Gerontology: Psychological Sciences, 59B,* S173–S180.

Wolff, P. H. (1963). Observations on the early development of smiling. In B. M. Foss (Ed.), *Determinants of infant behavior* (Vol. 2). London: Methuen.

Wolff, P. H. (1969). The natural history of crying and other vocalizations in early infancy. In B. M. Foss (Ed.), *Determinants of infant behavior* (Vol. 4). London: Methuen.

Wolf-Maier, K., Cooper, R. S., Banegas, J. R., Giampaoli, S., Hense, H., Joffres, M., Kastarinen, M., Poulter, N., Primatesta, P., Rodriguez-Artalejo, F., Steggmayr, B., Thamm, M., Tuomilehto, J., Vanuzzo, D., & Vescio, F. (2003). Hypertension prevalence and blood pressure levels in 6 European countries, Canada, and the United States. *Journal of the American Medical Association, 289,* 2363–2369.

Women in History. (2004). *Marian Anderson biography.* Lakewood, OH: Lakewood Public Library. [Online]. Available: http://www.lkwdpl.org/wihohio/ande-mar.htm. Access date: November 18, 2004.

Wong, C. A., Scavone, B. M., Peaceman, A. M., McCarthy, R. J., Sullivan, J. T., Diaz, N. T., Yaghmour, E., Marcus, R.-J. L., Sherwani, S. S., Sproviero, M. T., Yilmaz, M., Patel, R., Robles, C., & Grouper, S. (2005). The risk of cesarean delivery with neuraxial analgesia given early versus late in labor. *New England Journal of Medicine, 352,* 655–665.

Wong, C.K., Murray, M.L., Camilleri-Novak, D., & Stephens, P. (2004). Increased prescribing trends of paediatric psychtropic medications. *Archives of the Diseases of Children, 89,* 1131–1132.

Wood, D. (1980). Teaching the young child: Some relationships between social interaction, language, and thought. In D. Olson (Ed.), *The social foundations of language and thought.* New York: Norton.

Wood, D., Bruner, J., & Ross, G. (1976). The role of tutoring in problem solving. *Journal of Child Psychiatry and Psychology, 17,* 89–100.

Wood, R. M., & Gustafson, G. E. (2001). Infant crying and adults' anticipated caregiving responses: Acoustic and contextual influences. *Child Development, 72,* 1287–1300.

Woodruff, T. J., Axelrad, D. A., Kyle, A. D., Nweke, O., Miller, G. G., and Hurley, B. J. (2004). Trends in environmentally related childhood illnesses. *Pediatrics, 113,* 1133–1140.

Woodward, A. L., Markman, E. M., & Fitzsimmons, C. M. (1994). Rapid word learning in 13- and 18-month olds. *Developmental Psychology, 30,* 553–566.

Woodward, S. A., McManis, M. H., Kagan, J., Deldin, P., Snidman, N., Lewis, M., & Kahn, V. (2001). Infant temperament and the brainstem auditory evoked response in later childhood. *Developmental Psychology, 37,* 533–538.

Woolley, J. D. (1997). Thinking about fantasy: Are children fundamentally different thinkers and believers from adults? *Child Development, 68*(6), 991–1011.

Woolley, J. D., & Boerger, E. A. (2002). Development of beliefs about the origins and controllability of dreams. *Developmental Psychology, 38*(1), 24–41.

Woolley, J. D., & Bruell, M. J. (1996). Young children's awareness of the origins of their mental representations. *Developmental Psychology, 32,* 335–346.

Wooten, J. (1995, January 29). The conciliator. *The New York Times Magazine,* pp. 28–33.

World Health Organization (WHO). (1998). *Obesity: Preventing and managing the global epidemic.* Geneva: Author.

World Health Organization (WHO). (2000, June 4). *WHO issues new healthy life expectancy rankings: Japan number one in new "healthy life" system.* (Press release). Washington, DC: Author.

World Health Organization (WHO). (2002a). *Move for Health.* Geneva: Author.

World Health Organization (WHO). (2002b). *Toward health with justice: Litigation and public inquiries as tools for tobacco control.* Geneva: World Health Organization.

World Health Organization (WHO). (2003a). *Causes of death: Global, regional and country-specific estimates of death by cause, age and sex.* Retrieved from http://www.who.int/mip/2003/other_documents/en/causesofdeath.pdf on March 25, 2005.

World Health Organization (WHO). (2003b). *Facts and figures: The world health report 2003–Shaping the future.* [Online]. Retrieved from http://www.who.int/whr.2003.en/Facts and Figures-en.pdf on March 18, 2005.

Wortman, C. B., & Silver, R. C. (1989). The myths of coping with loss. *Journal of Consulting and Clinical Psychology, 57*(3), 349–357.

Wright, A. L. (1983). A cross-cultural comparison of menopausal symptoms. *Medical Anthropology, 7,* 20–35.

Wright, J. C., Huston, A. C., Murphy, K. C., St. Peters, M., Pinon, M., Scantlin, R., & Kotler, J. (2001). The relations of early television viewing to school readiness and vocabulary of children from low-income families: The Early Window Project. *Child Development, 72*(5), 1347–1366.

Wright, J. T., Waterson, E. J., Barrison, I. G., Toplis, P. J., Lewis, I. G., Gordon, M. G., MacRae, K. D., Morris, N. F., & Murray Lyon, I. M. (1983, March 26). Alcohol consumption, pregnancy, and low birth weight. *The Lancet,* pp. 663–665.

Wright, V. C., Schieve, L. A., Reynolds, M. A., & Jeng, G. (2003). *Assisted Reproductive Technology Surveillance—United States, 2000.* Division of Reproductive Health, National Center for Chronic Disease Prevention and Health Promotion. [Online]. Available: http://www.cdc.gov/reprod.

Writing Group for the Women's Health Initiative Investigators. (2002). Risks and benefits of estrogen plus progestin in healthy postmenopausal women: Principal results from the Women's Health Initiative randomized controlled trial. *Journal of the American Medical Association, 288,* 321–333.

Wrosch, C., & Heckhausen, J. (1999). Control processes before and after passing a developmental deadline: Activation and deactivation of intimate relationship goals. *Journal of Personality and Social Psychology, 77,* 415–427.

Wu, T., Mendola, P., & Buck, G. M. (2002). Ethnic differences in the presence of secondary sex characteristics and menarche among U.S. girls: The Third National Health and Nutrition Survey, 1988–1994. *Pediatrics, 11,* 752–757.

Wu, Z. (1999). Premarital cohabitation and the timing of first marriage. *Canadian Review of Sociology and Anthropology, 36,* 109–127.

Wu, Z., & Hart, R. (2002). The effects of marital and nonmarital union transition on health. *Journal of Marriage and Family, 64,* 420–432.

WuDunn, S. (1997, January 14). Korean women still feel demands to bear a son. *The New York Times* (International Ed.), p. A3.

Wulczyn, F. (2004). Family reunification. In David and Lucile Packard Foundation, Children, families, and foster care. *The Future of Children, 14*(1). Available: http://www.futureofchildren.org.

Wykle, M. L., & Musil, C. M. (1993). Mental health of older persons: Social and cultural factors. *Generations, 17*(1), 7–12.

Wynn, K. (1992). Evidence against empiricist accounts of the origins of numerical knowledge. *Mind and Language, 7,* 315–332.

Wynn, K. (1996). Infants' individuation and enumeration of actions. *Psychological Science, 7,* 164–169.

Wynn, K. (2000). Findings of addition and subtraction in infants are robust and consistent: Reply to Wakeley, Rivera, and Langer. *Child Development, 71,* 1535–1536.

Yamada, H. (2004). Japanese mothers' views of young children's areas of personal discretion. *Child Development, 75,* 164–179.

Yan, L. L., Liu, K., Matthews, K. A., Daviglus, M. L., Ferguson, T. F., & Kiefe, C. I. (2003). Psychosocial factors and risk of hypertension: The Coronary Artery Risk Development in Young Adults (CARDIA) study. *Journal of the American Medical Association, 290,* 2138.

Yang, B., Ollendick, T. H., Dong, Q., Xia, Y., & Lin, L. (1995). Only children and children with siblings in the People's Republic of China: Levels of fear, anxiety, and depression. *Child Development, 66,* 1301–1311.

Yardley, J. (2005, January 31). Fearing future, China starts to give girls their due. *New York Times.* [Online]. Retrieved February 1, 2005, from http://www.nytimes.com/2005/01/31/international/asia/31china.html.

Yazigi, R. A., Odem, R. R., & Polakoski, K. L. (1991). Demonstration of specific binding of cocaine to human spermatozoa. *Journal of the American Medical Association, 266,* 1956–1959.

Yeargin-Allsopp, M., Rice, C., Karapurkar, T., Doernberg, N., Boyle, C., & Murphy, C. (2003). Prevalence of autism in a U.S. metropolitan area. *Journal of the American Medical Association, 289,* 49–55.

Yeung, W. J., Sandberg, J. F., Davis-Kean, P. E., & Hofferth, S. L. (2001). Children's time with fathers in intact families. *Journal of Marriage and Family, 63,* 136–154.

Yingling, C. D. (2001). Neural mechanisms of unconscious cognitive processing. *Clinical Neurophysiology, 112*(1), 157–158.

Yokota, F., & Thompson, K. M. (2000). Violence in G-rated animated films. *Journal of the American Medical Association, 283,* 2716–2720.

Yoshikawa, H. (1994). Prevention as cumulative protection: Effects of early family support and education on chronic delinquency and its risks. *Psychological Bulletin, 115*(1), 28–54.

Young, L. R., & Nestle, M. (2002). The contribution of expanding portion sizes to the US obesity epidemic. *American Journal of Public Health, 92,* 246–249.

Youngblade, L. M., & Belsky, J. (1992). Parent-child antecedents of 5-year-olds' close friendships: A longitudinal analysis. *Developmental Psychology, 28,* 700–713.

Youth violence: A report of the Surgeon General. (2001, January). [Online]. Available: http://www.surgeongeneral.gov/library/youthviolence/default.htm.

Yu, S. M., Huang, Z. J., & Singh, G. K. (2004). Health status and health services utilization among U.S. Chinese, Asian Indian, Filipino, and other Asian/Pacific Islander children. *Pediatrics, 113*(1), 101–107.

Yunger, J. L., Carver, P. R., & Perry, D. G. (2004). Does gender identity influence children's psychological well-being? *Developmental Psychology, 40,* 572–582.

Yurgelon-Todd, D. (2002). *Inside the teen brain.* [Online]. Available: http://www.pbs.org/wgbh/pages/frontline/shows/teenbrain/interviews/todd.html.

Zahn-Waxler, C., Friedman, R. J., Cole, P. M., Mizuta, I., & Hiruma, N. (1996). Japanese and U.S. preschool children's responses to conflict and distress. *Child Development, 67,* 2462–2477.

Zahn-Waxler, C., Radke-Yarrow, M.,Wagner, E., & Chapman, M. (1992). Development of concern for others. *Developmental Psychology, 28,* 126–136.

Zametkin, A. J. (1995). Attention-deficit disorder: Born to be hyperactive. *Journal of the American Medical Association, 273*(23), 1871–1874.

Zametkin, A. J., & Ernst, M. (1999). Problems in the management of Attention-Deficit-Hyperactivity Disorder. *New England Journal of Medicine, 340,* 40–46.

Zandhi, P. P., Carlson, M. C., Plassman, B. L., Welsh-Bohmer. K. A., Mayer, L. S., Steffens, D. C., & Breitner, J. C. S., for the Cache County Memory Study Investigators. (2002). Hormone replacement therapy and incidence of Alzheimer disease in older women: The Cache County Study. *Journal of the American Medical Association, 288,* 2123–2129.

Zarbatany, L., Hartmann, D. P., & Rankin, D. B. (1990). The psychological functions of preadolescent peer activities. *Child Development, 61,* 1067–1080.

Zeedyk, M. S., Wallace, L., & Spry, L. (2002). Stop, look, listen, and think? What young children really do when crossing the road. *Accident Analysis and Prevention, 34*(1), 43–50.

Zelazo, P. D., Müller, U., Frye, D., & Marcovitch, S. (2003). The development of executive function in early childhood. *Monographs of the Society for Research in Child Development, 68*(3, Serial No. 274).

Zelazo, P. R., Kearsley, R. B., & Stack, D. M. (1995). Mental representations for visual sequences: Increased speed of central processing from 22 to 32 months. *Intelligence, 20,* 41–63.

Zeskind, P. S., & Stephens, L. E. (2004). Maternal selective serotonin reuptake inhibitor use during pregnancy and newborn neurobehavior. *Pediatrics, 11,* 368–375.

Zhang, J., Meikle, S., Grainger, D. A., & Trumble, A. (2002). Multifetal pregnancy in older women and perinatal outcomes. *Fertility and Sterility, 78,* 562–568.

Zhang, Q. F. (2004). Economic transition and new patterns of parent-adult child coresidence in China. *Journal of Marriage and Family, 66,* 1232–1245.

Zhang, Y., Proenca, R., Maffei, M., Barone, M., Leopold, L., & Friedman, J. M., (1994). Positional cloning of the mouse obese gene in its human homologue. *Nature, 372,* 425–431.

Zhao, Y. (2002, May 29). Cultural divide over parental discipline. *The New York Times.* [Online]. Available: www.nytimes.com/2002/05/29/

nyregion/29DISC.html?ex_1023674535&ei_1&
en_5eeaee8e940eee1a.

Zhensun, Z., & Low, A. (1991). *A young painter: The life and paintings of Wang Yani—China's extraordinary young artist.* New York: Scholastic.

Zhou, Q., Eisenberg, N., Wang, Y., & Reiser, M. (2004). Chinese children's effortful control and dispositional anger/frustration: Relations to parenting styles and children's social functioning. *Developmental Psychology, 40,* 352–366.

Zhu, B.-P., Rolfs, R. T., Nangle, B. E., & Horan, J. M. (1999). Effect of the interval between pregnancies on perinatal outcomes. *New England Journal of Medicine, 340,* 589–594.

Zigler, E. (1998). School should begin at age 3 years for American children. *Journal of Developmental and Behavioral Pediatrics, 19,* 37–38.

Zigler, E., & Styfco, S. J. (1993). Using research and theory to justify and inform Head Start expansion. *Social Policy Report of the Society for Research in Child Development, 7*(2).

Zigler, E., & Styfco, S. J. (1994). Head Start: Criticisms in a constructive context. *American Psychologist, 49*(2), 127–132.

Zigler, E., & Styfco, S. J. (2001). Extended childhood intervention prepares children for school and beyond. *Journal of the American Medical Association, 285,* 2378.

Zigler, E., Taussig, C., & Black, K. (1992). Early childhood intervention: A promising preventative for juvenile delinquency. *American Psychologist, 47,* 997–1006.

Zigler, E. F. (1987). Formal schooling for four-year-olds? *North American Psychologist, 42*(3), 254–260.

Zimmerman, B. J., Bandura, A., & Martinez-Pons, M. (1992). Self-motivation for academic attainment: The role of self-efficacy beliefs and personal goal setting. *American Educational Research Journal, 29,* 663–676.

Zito, J. M., Safer, D. J., dosReis, S., Gardner. J. F., Magder, L., Soeken, K., Boles, M., Lynch, F., & Riddle, M. A. (2003). Psychotropic practice patterns for youth: A 10-year perspective. *Archives of Pediatrics and Adolescent Medicine, 57,* 17–25.

Zizza, C., Siega-Riz, A. M., & Popkin, B. M. (2001). Significant increase in young adults' snacking between 1977–1978 and 1994–1996 represents a cause for concern! *Preventive Medicine, 32,* 303–310.

Zubenko, G. S., Maher, B., Hughes, III, H. B., Zubenko, W. N., Stiffler, J. S., Kaplan, B. B., & Marazita, M. L. (2003). Genome-wide linkage survey for genetic loci that influence the development of depressive disorders in families with recurrent, early-onset, major depression. *American Journal of Medical Genetics Part B: Neuropsychiatric Genetics, 123B*(1), 1–18.

Zucker, A. N., Ostrove, J. M., & Stewart, A. J. (2002). College-educated women's personality development in adulthood: Perceptions and age differences. *Psychology and Aging, 17,* 236–244.

Zuckerman, B. S., & Beardslee, W. R. (1987). Maternal depression: A concern for pediatricians. *Pediatrics, 79,* 110–117.

Acknowledgments

Text and Line Arts Credits

Chapter 1

Opening quote: Heraclitus, fragment (sixth century B.C.). In *The Collected Wisdom of Heraclitus,* transl. by Brooks Haxton. New York: Viking Press, 2001.

Fig. 1-1: Hernandez, D. J. (2004). Demographics changes and the life circumstances of immigrant families. In R. E. Behrman (Ed.), Children of immigrant families (pp. 17–48). The Future of Children, 14(2). Woodrow Wilson School of Public and International Affairs. Used with permission. Data from Population Projections Program, Population Division, U.S. Census Bureau, issued January 18, 2000.

Chapter 2

Opening quote: Charles Sanders Peirce, *Collected Papers,* vol. 5, edited by Charles Hartshorne and Paul Weiss. Cambridge: Harvard University Press, 1934.

Fig. 2-1: From *Development of Children* by Michael Cole and Shelia R. Cole. © 1989 by Michael Cole and Shelia R. Cole. Used with permission of Worth Publishers.

Chapter 3

Opening quote: Anne Sexton, "Little Girl, My String Bean, My Lovely Woman" (1966). *The Complete Poems of Anne Sexton.* Boston: Houghton-Mifflin, 1981.

Pg. 61: Excerpt from "Little Girl, My Stringbean, My Lovely Woman" from *Live or Die* by Anne Sexton. Copyright © 1966 by Anne Sexton. Reprinted by permission of Houghton Mifflin Company and Sll/Sterling Lord Literistic, Inc. All rights reserved.

Fig. 3-7 From *A Child's World,* 8th edition by Diane E. Papalia, Sally Wendkos Olds, Ruth Duskin Feldman. Copyright © 1998 The McGraw-Hill Companies. Reproduced with permission of The McGraw-Hill Companies.

Table 3-2: From *Choices, Not Chances* by Aubrey Milunsky, M. D., table 32, p. 122. Copyright © 1977, 1989 by Aubrey Milunsky, M. D. Used with permission from Lippincott, Williams & Wilkins

Chapter 4

Opening quote: Selma Fraiberg, *The Magic Years.* New York: Scribner's, 1959.

Fig. 4-1: From H. Lagercrantz and T. A. Slotkin, "The 'stress' of being born," *Scientific American,* 254(4), 1986, pp. 100–107. Art by Patricia J. Wynne. Reprinted by permission of Patricia J. Wynne.

Fig. 4-2: From Wegman, M. E. (1996) From "Infant mortality: Some international comparisons," *Pediatrics,* Vol. 98, pp. 1020–1027. Copyright 1996. Reprinted with permission.

Fig. 4-5: From W. Maxwell Cowan, "The Development of the Brain." Copyright © 1979 Scientific American. Reprinted with permission.

Table 4-1: Adapted from V. Apgar, "A proposal for a new method of evaluation of the newborn infant," pp. 260–267, *Current Research in Anesthesia and Analgesia,* 32, 1953. Reprinted with permission of Lippincott, Williams & Wilkins.

Table 4-3 From *A Child's World,* 9th edition by Diane E. Papalia, Sally Wendkos Olds, Ruth Duskin Feldman. Copyright © 2000 The McGraw-Hill Companies. Reproduced with permission of The McGraw-Hill Companies.

Chapter 5

Opening quote: Alfred, Lord Tennyson, *In Memoriam,* Canto 54 (1850).

Fig. 5-2: From C. Rovee-Collier-Collier & K. Boller, "Current theory and research on infant learning and memory: Application to early intervention" in *Infants and Young Children,* Vol. 7, No. 3, p. 7. Copyright © 1995 Aspen Publishers, Inc. Reprinted by permission of Lippincott, Williams & Wilkins.

Fig. 5-4: From R. Baillargeon and J. DeVos, "Object permanence in young infants: Further evidence," pp. 1227–1246 in *Child Development,* Vol. 62, 1991. © Society for Research in Child Development. Reprinted with permission from the Society for Research and Child Development.

Fig. 5-5: Figure from Hood, Cole-Davies, & Dias, 2003. Looking and search measures of object knowledge in preschool children. *Developmental Psychology,* 39, 61–70. Copyright © 2003 by the American Psychological Association. Reproduced with permission.

Fig. 5-6: From R. Baillargeon, "How do infants learn about the physical world?" in *Current Directions in Psychological Science,* Vol. 3, No. 5, 1994, pp. 133–139. Reprinted by permission of Blackwell Publishers.

Table 5-2 From *A Child's World,* 10th edition by Diane E. Papalia, Sally Wendkos Olds, Ruth Duskin Feldman. Copyright © 2005 The McGraw-Hill Companies. Reproduced with permission of The McGraw-Hill Companies.

Chapter 6

Opening quote: John Hartford, "Life Prayer" (1971). Copyright, Flying Fish Records.

Pg. 191: From J. Hartford, "Life Prayer." Copyright © 1968 by Ensign Music Corporation.

Table 6-1 From L. A. Sroufe, "Socioemotional development" in *Handbook of Infant Development* by J. Osofsky. Copyright © 1979. This material used by permission of John Wiley & Sons, Inc.

Table 6-5 From *A Child's World,* 9th edition by Diane E. Papalia, Sally Wendkos Olds, Ruth Duskin Feldman. Copyright © 2000 The McGraw-Hill Companies. Reproduced with permission of The McGraw-Hill Companies.

Table 6-6 From *A Child's World,* 9th edition by Diane E. Papalia, Sally Wendkos Olds, Ruth Duskin Feldman. Copyright © 2000 The McGraw-Hill Companies. Reproduced with permission of The McGraw-Hill Companies.

Chapter 7

Opening quote: Adam Gottlob Oehlenschlager, *Aladdin, or The Wonderful Lamp,* transl. by Theodore Martin (1857).

Fig. 7-1: Reprinted with the permission of Simon & Schuster Adult Publishing Group from *Solve Your Child's Sleep Problems* by Richard Ferber. Copyright © 1985 by Richard Ferber, M. D.

p. 246 Fig. for Box 7-1: Children's Defense Fund. (2004). *The State of America's Children 2004.* Washington, DC: Author. Reprinted with permission.

Fig. 7-2 From *Analyzing Children's Art* by Rhoda Kellogg. Copyright © 1969, 1970 by Rhoda Kellogg. Reproduced with permission of The McGraw-Hill Companies.

Fig. 7-3 From *A Child's World,* 10th edition by Diane E. Papalia, Sally Wendkos Olds, Ruth Duskin Feldman, fig. 10-1, p. 270. Copyright © 2000 The McGraw-Hill Companies. Reproduced with permission of The McGraw-Hill Companies.

Tables 7-1, 7-4, 7-5 From *A Child's World,* 9th edition by Diane E. Papalia, Sally Wendkos Olds, Ruth Duskin Feldman. Copyright © 2000 The McGraw-Hill Companies. Reproduced with permission of The McGraw-Hill Companies.

Chapter 8

Opening quote: Michel de Montaigne, *Essays* (transl. by Charles Cotton).

Table 8-2: Table adapted from M. B. Parten, "Social play among preschool children" in *Journal of Abnormal and Social Psychology,* 27, 1943, pp. 3243–269. Used with permission.

Chapter 9

Opening quote: Natalia Ginzburg, *The Little Virtues,* transl. by Dick Davis. New York: Little, Brown, & Co., 1985.

Table 9-3: From M. L. Hoffman, "Moral development" in *Carmichael's Manual of Child Psychology,* Vol. 2, edited by P. H. Mussen, pp. 261–380. Copyright © 1970 John Wiley & Sons, Inc. Reprinted with permission of John Wiley & Sons, Inc.

Chapter 10

Table 10-3: From Masten & Coatsworth, "Characteristics of Resilient Children and Adolescents" in *American Psychologist, 53,*

of Child and Family Health. The Pediatrician and Childhood Bereavement. *Pediatrics*. 2000; 105:446. Used with permission.

Table 19-4: Reprinted from *Omega*, Vol. 27, A. E. Scharlach & K. I. Frederiksen, "Reactions to the death of a parent during midlife," table 1, p. 311. Copyright © 1993, with permission from Elsevier.

Photo Credits

Chapter 1

Part Opener: ©Walter Hodges/Corbis Images; **p. 3(left):** ©Richard Hutchings/PhotoEdit; **p. 3(right):** ©Bob Daemmrich/Image Works; **Chapter Opener:** ©Richard Hutching/PhotoEdit; **p. 5:** ©By permission of the British Library.; **p. 9:** ©Bob Daemmrich/PhotoEdit; **p. 11:** ©Zhang Yanhui/Sovfoto/Eastfoto; **p. 15:** ©Blair Seitz/Photo Researchers; **p. 18:** ©David Cannon/Getty Images; **p. 19:** ©Erika Stone; **p. 20:** ©John Vachon/Library of Congress; **p. 21:** ©Nina Leen/TimePix; **p. 22:** ©Don Smetzer/PhotoEdit

Chapter 2

Opener: ©Bob Daemmrich/Image Works; **p. 27:** ©Bettmann/Corbis Images; **p. 30:** ©Robin Nelson/PhotoEdit; **p. 32:** ©Mary Evans Picture Library/Sigmund Freud Copyrights; **p. 34:** ©Bettmann/Corbis Images; **p. 36:** ©Image Source Limited/Index Stock Imagery; **p. 37:** ©Bill Anderson/Photo Researchers; **p. 38:** A. R. Luria/Dr. Michael Cole, Laboratory of Human Cognition, University of California, San Diego; **p. 40:** ©Richard Hutchings/Photo Researchers; **p. 46:** ©Laura Dwight/PhotoEdit; **p. 51:** ©Miguel Gandert/Corbis Images

Chapter 3

Part Opener: ©Bob Krist/Corbis Images; **p. 59(left):** ©Barbara Peacock/Getty Images; **p. 59(center left):** ©Camille Tokerud/Getty Images; **p. 59(center right):** ©PhotoDisc; **p. 59(right):** ©Brand X/Getty Images; **Chapter Opener:** ©Barbara Peacock/Getty Images; **p. 64:** ©Pascal Goetgheluck/Photo Researchers; **p. 69:** ©David Young-Wolff/PhotoEdit; **p. 74:** ©Ellen Senisi/Image Works; **p. 78:** ©T. K. Wanstal/Image Works; **p. 80:** ©Anthony Jalandoni; **p. 82:** ©Rosanne Olson/Getty Images; **p. 83:** ©Ellen Senisi/Image Works; **p. 86(1 mo., 7 wks., 7 mo., 8 mo.):** ©Petit Format/Nestle/Science Source/Photo Researchers; **p. 86(3 mo.):** ©Lennart Nilsson/Albert Bonniers Forlag AB, A CHILD IS BORN, Dell Publishing Company; **p. 86(4 mo):** ©J. S. Allen/Daily Telegraph/International Stock; **p. 86(5 mo.):** ©James Stevenson/Photo Researchers; **p. 87(6 mo.):** ©Lennart Nilsson/Albert Bonniers Forlag AB; **p. 87(9 mo.):** ©Ronn Maratea/International Stock; **p. 90:** ©Billy E. Barnes/PhotoEdit; **p. 92:** ©Macduff Everton/Corbis Images; **p. 94:** ©George Steinmetz; **p. 99:** ©Arlene Collins/Image Works

Chapter 4

Opener: ©Camille Tokerud/Getty Images; **p. 107:** ©Library of Congress; **p. 110:** ©Margaret Miller/Photo Researchers; **p. 113:** ©Viviane Moos/Corbis Images; **p. 114:** ©Joseph Nettis/Stock Boston; **p. 120:** ©David Young-Wolff/PhotoEdit; **p. 121:** ©Chuck Savage/Corbis Images; **p. 123:** ©Mike Teruya/Free Spirit Photography; **p. 128:** ©Saturn Stills/Photo Researchers; **p. 130:** ©Myrleen Ferguson Cate/PhotoEdit; **p. 132:** ©Dennis MacDonald/PhotoEdit; **p. 138(top left):** ©Astier/Photo Researchers; **p. 138(top center):** ©Lew Merrim/Photo Researchers; **p. 138(top right, bottom left):** ©Laura Dwight; **p. 138(bottom center, bottom right):** ©Elizabeth Crews; **p. 141(left):** ©Kevin Delgado; **p. 141(center):** ©Elizabeth Crews; **p. 141(right):** ©Jennie Woodcock/Corbis Images; **p. 145:** ©Innervisions; **p. 146:** ©Steve Maines/Stock Boston

Chapter 5

Opener: ©PhotoDisc; **p. 151:** ©Courtesy Department Library Services, American Museum of Natural History, Neg. No. 32799; **p. 154:** ©Mary Ellen Mark; **p. 155:** Courtesy, Carolyn Rovee-Collier; **p. 157:** ©PhotoDisc; **p. 163:** ©Enrico Ferorelli; **p. 168:** ©James Kilkelly; **p. 165:** ©Doug Goodman/Photo Researchers; **p. 171:** ©Peter Southwick/Stock Boston; **p. 179:** ©PhotoDisc; **p. 182:** ©Michael Newman/PhotoEdit; **p. 185:** ©Rubberball; **p. 186:** ©Digital Vision; **p. 164:** ©Brand X Pictures

Chapter 6

Opener: ©Brand X/Getty Images; **p. 191:** ©Ken Heyman/Woodfin Camp; **p. 195:** ©Digital Stock; **p. 196:** ©Laura Dwight; **p. 199:** Courtesy, Ruth Duskin Feldman; **p. 200:** ©Michael Newman/PhotoEdit; **p. 202:** Harlow Primate Laboratory, University of Wisconsin; **p. 203:** ©Rubberball/Punchstock; **p. 204:** ©LWA-Dann Tardif/Corbis Images; **p. 205:** ©Jonathan Finlay; **p. 208:** ©Michael Newman/PhotoEdit; **p. 209:** ©PhotoDisc; **p. 214:** Courtesy, Dr. Michael Lewis; **p. 215:** ©PhotoDisc; **p. 219:** ©Eastcott/Image Works; **p. 222:** ©Paul Conklin/PhotoDisc; **p. 227:** ©Janet Fries

Chapter 7

Part Opener: ©Stephen Simpson/Getty Images; **p. 233(left):** ©Bob Daemmrich/Stock Boston; **p. 233(right):** ©CLEO Photo/Index Stock Imagery; **Chapter Opener:** ©Bob Daemmrich/Stock Boston; **p. 235:** ©Cynthia Johnson/Getty Images; **p. 238:** ©David Young-Wolff/PhotoEdit; **p. 243a:** ©Laura Dwight; **p. 243b:** ©PhotoDisc; **p. 243c:** ©Miro Vintoni/Stock Boston; **p. 247:** ©Dennis MacDonald /PhotoEdit; **p. 248:** ©Tony Freeman/PhotoEdit; **p. 250:** ©Erika Stone; **p. 256:** ©AP/Wide World Photos; **p. 261:** ©Creatas; **p. 262:** ©Robert Brenner/PhotoEdit; **p. 265:** ©Erika Stone; **p. 269:** ©Ellen Senisi/Image Works; **p. 270:** ©David Young-Wolff/PhotoEdit

Chapter 8

Opener: ©CLEO Photo/Index Stock Imagery; **p. 277:** ©AP/Wide World Photos; **p. 279:** ©Laura Dwight/PhotoEdit; **p. 281:** ©Nancy Richmond/Image Works; **p. 285:** ©Leanna Rathkelly/Getty Images; **p. 288(both):** ©Sandra Lipsitz Bem; **p. 292:** ©David Young-Wolff/PhotoEdit; **p. 295:** ©Michael Newman/PhotoEdit; **p. 299:** ©Myrleen Ferguson Cate/PhotoEdit; **p. 303(top):** ©Margaret Miller/Photo Researchers; **p. 303(bottom):** ©Sybil Shackman; **p. 305:** ©AP/Wide World Photos; **p. 307:** ©Nita Winter

Chapter 9

Part Opener: ©Bill Bachmann/Photo Network; **p. 313(left):** ©Michael Newman/PhotoEdit; **p. 313(right):** ©Digital Vision; **Chapter Opener:** ©Michael Newman/PhotoEdit; **p. 315:** ©AP/Wide World Photos; **p. 319:** ©David Young-Wolff/PhotoEdit; **p. 323:** ©Susan Van Etten/PhotoEdit; **p. 324:** ©Bob Daemmrich/Stock Boston; **p. 327:** ©Laura Dwight; **p. 331:** ©David Lassman/Image Works; **p. 335, p. 339:** ©PhotoDisc; **p. 340:** ©Laura Dwight/PhotoEdit; **p. 344:** ©Peter Dublin/Stock Boston; **p. 345:** ©Bob Daemmrich/Image Works; **p. 347:** ©Richard Orton; **p. 349(top):** ©Allan Tannenbaum/Image Works; **p. 349(bottom):** ©Michael Newman/PhotoEdit

Chapter 10

Opener: ©Digital Vision; **p. 355:** ©Bettmann/Corbis Images; **p. 358:** ©Michael Justice/Image Works; **p. 360:** ©Laura Dwight/PhotoEdit; **p. 365:** ©Myrleen Ferguson Cate/PhotoEdit; **p. 366:** ©C. Boretz/Image Works; **p. 369:** ©Amy Etra/PhotoEdit; **p. 370:** ©James R. Holland/Stock Boston; **p. 372:** ©Mindy E. Klarman/Photo Researchers; **p. 374:** ©Dallas & John Heaton/Stock Boston; **p. 375:** ©Erika Stone; **p. 379:** ©Jonathan Nourok/PhotoEdit; **p. 380:** ©David Young-Wolff/PhotoEdit; **p. 384:** ©Michael Newman/PhotoEdit

Chapter 11

Part Opener: ©Bob Daemmrich/Image Works; **p. 393(left):** ©Michael J. Doolittle/Image Works; **p. 393(right):** ©Arthur Tilley/Getty Images; **Chapter Opener:** ©Michael J. Doolittle/Image Works; **p. 395:** ©Culver Pictures; **p. 398:** ©AP/Wide World Photos; **p. 402:** ©Michael Newman/PhotoEdit; **p. 407:** ©David Young-Wolff/PhotoEdit; **p. 409:** ©Richard Nowitz/Photo Researchers; **p. 412, p. 414:** ©PhotoDisc; **p. 419:** ©Laura Dwight; **p. 426:** ©EyeWire; **p. 427:** ©Erika Stone; **p. 428:** ©David Young-Wolff/PhotoEdit; **p. 431:** ©Dennis MacDonald/PhotoEdit

Chapter 12

Opener: ©Arthur Tilley/Getty Images; **p. 435:** ©AP/Wide World Photos; **p. 438:** ©Miro Vintoniv/Stock Boston; **p. 441:** ©Bob Daemmrich/Image Works; **p. 443:** ©Getty

Name Index

Bhasin, T. K., 128
Bialystok, E., 257, 657
Bianchi, S. M., 536
Biason-Lauber, A., 67
Biederman, J., 95
Biegel, D. E., 613, 615
Bielby, D., 495
Bielick, S., 343
Bienias, J. L., 650, 673
Bienvenu, O. J., 516
Bierman, K. L., 95, 373
Biesecker, G. E., 248
Bigbee, M. A., 377
Billet, S., 575
Binstock, G., 528, 635
Birch, D. G., 131
Birch, E. E., 82
Birch, H. G., 82, 199
Birch, L. L., 239, 399
Birch, S. H., 272
Bird, T. D., 651, 652, 669, 670
Birmaher, B., 383, 413, 414
Birren, J. E., 553
Bishop, D. V. M., 268
Björkelund, C., 640
Bjorklund, D. F., 40, 162, 332, 721
Black, F. W., 653
Black, J. E., 137, 139
Black, K., 464
Black, M. M., 16
Black, R. E., 124, 130, 139
Blackburn, J. A., 662
Blackman, A., 585
Blackman, M. R., 635
Blagrove, M., 477
Blair, C., 123, 272
Blake, S. M., 447
Blakeslee, S., 158
Blanchard-Fields, F., 116, 491, 656, 673, 676, 677
Blanchard, Y., 116
Blanco, Kathleen, 290
Blanton, H., 459
Blanton, P. W., 609
Blass, E. M., 140
Blatchford, B., 319, 372
Blehar, M. C., 205, 206
Blieszner, R., 609, 662
Blizzard, L., 126
Block, J., 361, 593
Block, Jack, 517
Blood, M. R., 650
Blood, T., 585, 586
Bloom, B., 240, 381
Bloom, H., 395
Bluck, S., 23, 550, 601, 615
Blum, N. J., 214
Blum, R., 415, 443, 445
Blumberg, S., 381
Blumenthal, J. A., 647
Blyth, D. A., 403
Boatman, D., 22
Bode, J., 268
Bodkin, N. L., 637
Bodrova, E., 294
Boerger, E. A., 255
Boerner, K., 698, 717, 719
Boersma, E. R., 131
Bogan, H., 639

Bogat, G. A., 210
Bogg, T., 516, 673
Bohlig, E. M., 348
Boivin, M., 380
Bojczyk, K. E., 165
Bolger, K. E., 362
Bolla, K. I., 480
Bollen, A. -M., 100
Bollinger, M. B., 323
Bolton, P., 84
Bonanno, G. A., 698, 717, 719
Bond, C. A., 235
Bond, J. T., 569
Bondi, M. W., 652
Bonduelle, M., 488
Bonham, V. L., 18
Bood, A., 733
Boodoo, G., 82, 264, 332
Book, A. D., 286
Booth, A., 366, 532
Booth, A. E., 172, 328
Booth-Kewley, S., 486
Borawski, E. A., 562
Borman, G., 343
Bornstein, M., 77, 141, 156, 161, 168, 170, 177, 180, 184, 185, 364, 461
Borowsky, I. A., 415
Borquez, J., 457
Bortfield, H., 178
Bortz, W. M., II, 645
Bos, J., 341
Bosch, J., 364, 365
Bosma, H., 569
Boss, Pauline, 678, 718
Bossé, R., 695
Bosshard, G., 734
Boston, B. O., 351
Bosworth, H. B., 695
Botto, L., 98
Botwinick, J., 654
Bouchard, C., 82
Bouchard, T. J., 81, 516, 648
Bouchard, T. J., Jr., 264
Bouchey, H. A., 460, 461
Boudreau, J. P., 141, 145
Boukydis, C. F. Z., 178
Boulay, M., 343
Boulé, N. G., 477
Boulton, M. J., 380
Bourdon, K. H., 381
Boutin, P., 82
Bower, B., 254
Bowlby, John, 30, 40, 205, 206
Bowman, B. A., 476
Bowman, S. A., 320
Boxer, A. M., 408, 596
Boyce, W. F., 380
Boyce, W. T., 245
Boyd, P., 607
Boyle, C., 128
Boyles, S., 99
Brabant, S., 701
Brabeck, M. M., 499
Bracewell, M. A., 121
Bracher, G., 450
Bradbury, T. N., 697
Bradford, J., 607
Bradley, R. H., 157, 158, 158t
Brady, C., 362

Braine, M., 180, 181
Brakefield, T., 477
Brame, B., 377, 462
Bramlett, M. D., 528, 533, 605
Brandley, R. H., 203
Brandstädter, J., 682
Brandt, B., 726
Brandt, J., 407
Bratton, S. C., 384
Braun, A. R., 182
Braungart, J. M., 200
Braungart-Riecker, J., 207, 211
Braungart-Rieker, J. M., 207, 211
Braveman, P. A., 131
Braver, E. R., 414
Bray, J. H., 364, 366, 369
Brazelton, T. Berry, 116, 121, 211
Breaux, C., 203
Breier, J. I., 348
Bremner, W. J., 645
Brendtro, L. K., 465
Brener, N., 445, 446, 447
Brennan, R. T., 537
Brenner, R. A., 118
Brent, D. A., 413, 414
Brent, M. R., 180
Brent, R. L., 95
Brent. R. L., 247
Brent, S. B., 719
Bretherton, I., 180, 210, 292
Brewer, J., 494
Brim, O. G., 549
Brink, D., 644
Brison, R. J., 127
Britto, P. R., 362
Broadfield, D., 182
Broadfield, D. C., 182
Broadhurst, D. D., 225
Brock, D. W., 99, 731, 732
Brock, J. W., 99
Brockert, J. F., 99
Broder, M. S., 76, 565
Broder, S., 76
Brodersen, L., 208
Brodine, S. K., 486
Brody, G. H., 218, 341, 363, 371
Brody, L. R., 140
Brodzinsky, D., 364
Broffitt, B., 240
Broidy, L. M., 377, 462
Broman, C., 537
Broman, J. E., 241
Bronfenbrenner, Urie, 30, 41, 42, 43, 220, 360, 461
Bronner, E., 343
Bronstein, P., 204, 341
Brook, J. S., 463
Brooks-Gunn, J., 16, 122–123, 159, 220
Brooks, J., 214
Brooks, R., 169
Broude, G., 109, 117, 118, 130, 240, 328, 406, 529
Brouillette, R. T., 126
Browder, J. P., 100
Brown, A. C., 363
Brown, A. L., 416
Brown, A. S., 83
Brown, B. B., 428, 458, 459, 460, 461
Brown, E., 256
Brown, E. D., 363

Brown, J., 257
Brown, J. L., 377
Brown, J. M., 440, 547–548
Brown, J. R., 283
Brown, J. T., 716
Brown, J. V., 96
Brown, N. M., 15
Brown, P., 99
Brown, R. A., 608
Brown, S. L., 456, 602, 604, 605
Brown, S. S., 120
Brown-Sequard, Charles Edouard, 635
Browne, A., 228
Brubaker, T. H., 696
Bruck, M., 259
Bruckner, H., 448
Bruell, M. J., 259
Bruer, J. T., 21, 139
Brummett, B. H., 599
Bruner, A. B., 407
Bruner, J., 265
Bruning, J. C., 526
Bruschi, C. J., 194, 359
Brust, C. J. M., 96
Bruton, J. R., 410
Bryan, J., 660
Bryan, R. N., 640
Bryan, Y. E., 207
Bryant, B. K., 158, 360
Bryant, D. M., 221, 264
Bryant, P., 328
Bryantwaugh, R., 409
Bryce, J., 124, 130
Bryk, A., 185
Bryson, K. R., 618
Bubrick, E, 639
Buchanan, C. M., 399
Buck, G. M., 401
Budson, A. E., 658, 660, 661
Buell, J., 342
Buhrmester, D., 376, 457, 459
Buhs, E. S., 272
Buitelaar, J., 98
Buitendijk, S. E., 117
Bukowski, W. M., 293, 373, 376, 380, 464
Bulanda, J. R., 602, 604
Bulcroft, K. A., 699
Bulik, C. M., 410, 411
Bulkley, K., 343
Bumpass, L. L., 528, 604, 725
Bunikowski, R., 96
Burch, M. M., 204
Burchinal, M., 157, 158, 159, 220, 221, 264
Burgess, A., 509
Burgess, S. R., 268
Burglund, H., 402
Burhans, K. K., 281, 282
Buriel, R., 361, 537, 539
Burke, D. M., 659
Burns, B. J., 226
Burns, George, 682
Burr, G., 730
Burrows, E., 121
Burton, L. C., 95, 698
Burton, L. M., 615
Burton, P. R., 95
Burton, R. V., 143
Burwinkle, T. M., 320

Busch, C. M., 516
Buschke, H., 657
Bushnel, M. -C., 91
Bushnell, E. W., 141, 145
Busnel, M. C., 178
Busse, E. W., 629
Bussey, K., 288, 289, 290
Bûssing, A., 494
Buswell, B. N., 441
Butler, R. N., 635, 647, 732, 736
Buyck, P., 281
Buysse, D. J., 644
Byington, S., 641
Byler, P., 272
Byrd, M., 660
Byrd, R. S., 323
Byrne, M., 100
Byrnes, J., 416, 426
Byrnes, J. P., 47

Cabrera, N. J., 203
Cacioppo, J. T., 568
Cadet, J. L., 480
Cadman, C., 494
Caelli, K., 727
Cahill, L., 635
Cai, J., 648
Cain, K. M., 282, 359
Cain, W. S., 553
Caldwell, B. M., 157, 158t
Calhoun, T., 15
Calkins, S. D., 210
Callahan, D., 637
Calle, E. E., 566
Cameron, A., 98, 112
Camilleri-Novak, D., 384
Camoin, T. I. L., 399
Camp, C. J., 653, 656, 659, 660, 676
Campbell, A., 204, 285
Campbell, F. A., 158, 159, 264
Campbell, R. N., 337
Campbell, W. K., 536
Campfield, L. A., 476
Campione-Barr, N., 455
Campione, J. C., 416
Campos, J. J., 143, 207, 211, 213, 359
Candy, J., 285
Canfield, R. L., 248
Canning, J., 63
Cao, A., 74
Cao, X. -Y., 92
Capaldi, D. M., 446
Caplan, M., 219
Capon, N., 656
Cappell, K., 348
Capra, A. M., 131
Caprara, G. V., 340, 430
Capute, R., 177
Caraballo, R. S., 482
Caravati, E. M., 245
Carey, S., 174
Carlson, E. A., 206, 210, 294
Carlson, S. M., 255
Carnes, B. A., 635, 637
Carpenter, D., 650, 685
Carper, R., 83, 330
Carr, D., 724
Carrel, L., 67

Carretero, M., 656
Carriger, M. S., 156, 168, 169, 170, 171
Carrol, B., 223
Carrol-Pankhurst, C., 223
Carroll, M. D., 238, 317, 407
Carroll-Pankhurst, C., 118
Carskadon, M. A., 407
Carson, R. G., 643, 644
Carstensen, Laura, 598, 602, 620, 673, 680, 681,
    694, 695, 696, 697, 724
Carter, Jimmy, 585, 669, 670, 671, 674, 675,
    678, 686, 696
Carter, Rosalynn, 686, 696
Cartwright, B. S., 294
Carvalhal, J. B., 95
Carver, L. J., 163, 175
Carver, P. R., 289, 372
Casaer, P., 132, 133, 133f
Casals, Pablo, 335
Case, R., 38, 280, 328, 416
Casella, J. F., 407
Casey, B. M., 115
Cashon, C. H., 171
Casper, L., 203, 528, 618
Caspi, A., 16, 200, 212, 264, 388, 517, 568,
    611, 656
Caspim, A., 225
Cassel, C., 637
Cassidy, J., 210, 281, 350, 520
Cassidy, K. W., 257
Castillo, E. M., 348
Castro, M. A., 112
Catalano, R. F., 412, 464
Cattell, R. B., 573–574
Cauce, A. M., 49
Cavanaugh, J. C., 659
Cavazanna-Calvo, M., 76
Cawthon, R. M., 633
Ceausescu, Nicolae, 139
Ceballo, R., 457
Ceci, S. J., 259, 332, 333, 346
Celis, W., 226
Cen, G., 374, 375
Centor, R. M., 415
Cepeda-Benito, A., 479
Cernkovich, S. A., 454
Chafetz, M. D., 660
Chagnon, Y. C., 82
Chaika, H., 140
Chambers, R. A., 405, 411
Chambliss, H. O., 649
Chan, R. W., 369
Chandler, P., 179
Chandra, A., 94
Chandra, H., 94, 731
Chang, C., 328
Chang, J. J., 224
Chang, L., 380
Chao, R. K., 344
Chao, W., 464, 476
Chapieski, S., 215
Chapman, C., 343, 344, 406, 429
Chapman, M., 326
Chappell, N. L., 689
Charles, S. T., 602, 674
Charley, C. M., 294
Charness, N., 575
Chase-Lansdale, P. L., 224, 341

Chase, V. M., 245
Chassin, L., 454, 455
Chatters, L. M., 649, 678
Chaudhuri, S., 415
Chawarska, K., 171
Chawla, S., 82
Chay, K., 124
Cheadle, J., 367
Chehab, F. F., 399
Chen, A., 130, 320, 345
Chen, C., 344, 428
Chen, C. L., 566
Chen, E., 245
Chen, H., 685
Chen, L., 95, 414
Chen, M. D., 532
Chen, S., 207
Chen, W., 82
Chen, X., 201, 374, 375
Chen, Y., 656, 676
Cherkassky, V. L., 84
Cherlin, A., 341, 527, 528, 529, 530, 535, 539, 618, 703
Cherniss, C., 494
Cherry, K. E., 658
Chervin, R. D., 241
Chess, S., 82, 198, 199, 199t, 200
Cheung, L. W. Y., 120
Chi, H-C., 349
Chi, P. S. K., 692
Chia, S. E., 100
Chiang, E., 239
Childers, J. B., 180
Childs, C. P., 49
Chin, A. E., 67, 733
Chin, N., 67
Chipungu, S. S., 227
Chiriboga, C. A., 96
Chiriboga, D., 592, 609, 615
Chisholm, K., 139
Chistovich, L. A., 185, 186
Chiu, L., 286
Chivers, M. L., 444
Cho, M. K., 474
Cho, N. H., 98
Chochinov, H. M., 713, 734
Chodriker, C., 101t
Chomitz, V. R., 120
Chomsky, C. S., 266, 337
Chomsky, Noam, 181, 182, 187
Chorpita, B. P., 382
Chou, S. P., 564
Christakis, D. A., 169
Christensen, A., 516, 522
Christian, M. S., 95
Christie, D., 409
Christie, J. F., 294
Chronis, A. M., 348
Chu, S. Y., 128
Chubb, N. H., 441
Chugani, D. C., 139
Chugani, H. T., 137
Chun, K. M., 18
Church, R. B., 452, 453
Cicchetti, D., 383, 413
Cicero, S., 101t
Cicirelli, V. G., 370, 615, 702, 723
Cillessen, A. H. N., 373, 377

Cirillo, D. J., 566
Citro, J., 692
Clark, A., 337
Clark, A. E., 724
Clark, A. G., 76, 383, 531
Clark, C. G., 649
Clark, D., 733
Clark, M., 325
Clark, M. S., 538
Clark-Plaskie, M., 552
Clark, S., 446
Clarke, S. C., 605
Clarke-Stewart, K. A., 221
Clarkson, M. G., 144
Clausen, J. A., 53, 518
Clavel-Chapelton, G., 565
Clay, R. A., 503
Clayton, E. W., 76, 77
Clearfield, M. W., 174
Cleary, P. D., 564
Clemens, J. D., 95
Clément, K., 399
Clements, M. L., 533
Cleveland, H. H., 413
Clifford, R. M., 220
Clifton, R. K., 144, 144–145, 145, 165, 169, 175
Climo, A. H., 613, 615
Clinch, J. J., 734
Clinkenbeard, P., 335
Clinton, Bill, 16, 586
Cnattingius, S., 95, 122
Coatsworth, J. D., 373, 387t, 388, 514, 518
Cochran, S. D., 523
Cochrane, J. A., 126
Coffey, C. E., 640
Cofley-Corina, S. A., 184
Cohan, C. L., 528, 532, 533
Cohen, D. A., 450
Cohen, L. B., 171, 172
Cohen, P., 463, 533, 553
Cohen, R. A., 240, 381
Cohen, S., 483
Cohen, S. E., 171
Cohler, B. J., 596
Cohn, J. F., 211
Cohn, T. E., 642
Cohrs, M., 142
Coie, J. D., 42, 362, 373, 377, 379, 461
Coke, M. M., 678
Colapinto, John, 287
Colburne, K. A., 204
Colby, A., 424, 576, 597
Colcombe, S. J., 640
Colditz, G. A., 562, 566
Cole-Davies, V., 173–174, 173f
Cole, M., 334
Cole, P. M., 194, 212, 359
Cole, R. E., 228
Colecchi, C., 644
Coleman, J. S., 341
Coleman, P. G., 678
Coles, C. D., 96
Coles, L. S., 96, 636, 638, 639
Coley, R. L., 224, 341, 457, 536
Coll, C. G., 157
Collier, V. P., 345, 346
Collins, F. S., 18, 76, 288
Collins, J. W., Jr., 120

Collins, N. L., 520
Collins, W. A., 77, 78, 80, 455, 461
Collis, G. M., 371
Colliver J. D., 480
Colombo, B., 486
Colombo, J., 156, 168, 169, 170, 171
Coltrane, S., 291
Compas, B. E., 568
Compton, S. N., 52
Comuzzie, A. G., 476
Concordet, J. P., 85
Conel, J. L., 134
Conger, R. D., 20, 413, 455, 464
Connell, C. M., 649
Connell, F. A., 112
Connidis, I. A., 702
Connolly, B. A., 500
Connolly, L. A., 593, 594
Connor, P. D., 93
Conpton, W. M., 480
Conradt, B., 633
Constantino, J. N., 84
Conway, E. E., 127
Cook, D. G., 131
Cook, E. H., 131
Cook, N. R., 321
Cooney, T., 607
Cooper, H., 342
Cooper, K. L., 597, 609
Cooper, R. P., 91, 140, 186
Cooper, R. S., 563
Coplan, R. J., 293
Coppage, D. J., 172
Copper, P., 186
Coppola, M., 183
Corbet, A., 121
Corbetta, D., 165
Corbin, S. B., 367
Corcoran, M., 503
Cordero, J. F., 98
Corina, D., 22, 348
Cornelius, S. W., 656, 663, 665
Correa, A., 98
Corwyn, R. F., 157
Cory-Slechta, D. R., 248
Cosser, C., 255
Costa, P. T., Jr., 588, 671, 672, 674
Costa, Paul T., 515, 516, 518
Costello, E. J., 52, 382, 383
Costello, S., 235
Costigan, K. A., 90, 98
Côté, J. E., 500, 502
Cote, L. R., 180
Courage, M. L., 260
Courchesne, E., 83, 84
Cowan, C. P., 537
Cowan, L., 95
Cowan, P. A., 281, 537
Coward, R. T., 701
Cowen, P. J., 410
Cowley Jr., A. W., 563
Cox, A., 186
Cox, D. R., 564
Cox, J., 351
Cox, T. H., 96
Cox, W. M., 501t
Coy, K. C., 217, 455
Coyle, T. R., 330

DiMarco, M. A., 727
Ding, Y. -C., 349
Dingel, A., 172
Dinges, D. F., 478
Dingfelder, S., 98
DiPietro, J. A., 90, 98
Dishion, T. J., 464
Dissanayake, C., 214
Dittus, P. J., 446
Dixon, R. A., 578, 661, 663
Dlugosz, L., 95
Dobbie, R., 112
Dobbs, A. R., 659
Dodds, J. B., 142
Dodge, K. A., 228, 293, 373, 377, 378, 379,
        401, 461, 464
Dodge, T., 459
Doherty, K., 656
Doherty, W. J., 203
Doi, K., 184
Doka, K. J., 703
Dolan, M. A., 533
Don, A., 94
Dong, M., 228
Dong, Q., 385
Donnerstein, E., 448
D'Onofrio, B., 333
Donohue, B. C., 348
Donovan, W. L., 212
Donzella, B., 220
Dooley, S. A., 98
Dooley, S. L., 98
Dorn, L. D., 399
Dornbusch, S. M., 428, 455
Dorris, M., 61, 62
Dorsey, M. J., 323
Dougherty, L. M., 195
Dougherty, T. M., 171
Dove, H., 146
Downie, J., 727
Doyle, A. B., 372
Doyle, L. W., 121
Doyle, W. J., 483
Dozier, M., 210
Dreher, M. C., 95
Dreyfus, H. L., 575
Dronkers, J., 368
Dropik, P. L., 163, 175
Drouin, J., 643
Drumm, P., 421
Drumond, S. P. A., 478
Duarte, C. S., 385
Dubé, E. M., 445
Dube, S. R., 228
Dubin, L. F., 678
Dubowitz, H., 225
Dubrow, N., 385
Duckett, E., 454
Dudgeon, D., 734
Due, P., 408
Duenwald, M., 488
Duffy, P. H., 637
Duggan, A. K., 407
Dukakis, Michael, 586
Duke, J., 319, 320
Dumas-Hines, F., 282, 359
Dumke, H., 656
Duncan, G. J., 223, 341, 362, 720

Dunham, F., 184
Dunham, P. J., 184
Dunlosky, J., 660
Dunn, A. L., 477, 649
Dunn, J., 218, 257, 283, 370
Dunson, D. B., 486, 487
Dür, W., 429
Duran, R., 345
Durand, A. M., 110
Durant, R. H., 413
Durett, D., 343
Durkin, K., 84
Durlak, J. A., 735
Dush, C. M. K., 528
Duskin, Rita, 669
Duster, T., 18
Dweck, C. S., 282, 359
Dwyer, T., 126
Dychtwald, K., 641
Dykstra, P. A., 700
Dylla, D. J., 364

Earle, J. R., 618
Earles, J. L., 658, 659, 660
Easterling, T. R., 112
Eastman, F., 625
Eaton, W. W., 83, 516
Ebbeling, C. B., 320
Eber, G. B., 385
Eberstein, I. W., 322
Eccles, A., 109
Eccles, J., 518, 519
Eccles, J. S., 358, 362, 399, 416, 426, 428,
        430, 455, 456
Echeland, Y., 85
Eckerman, C. O., 219, 261
Edelsohn, G., 383
Edelstein, W., 517
Eden, G. F., 348
Edgin, J., 74
Edison, M. I., 504
Edwards, B., 226
Edwards, K. I., 410, 425
Egan, S. K., 285
Egbuono, L., 245
Egeland, B., 208, 210, 426
Eggebeen, D. J., 536
Egger, M., 690
Eggerling-Boeck, J., 519
Egozcue, C., 94
Ehrensaft, M. K., 533
Ehrhardt, A., 287
Eimas, P. D., 140, 172
Einstein, Albert, 335, 347
Einstein, G. O., 635
Eisen, M., 450
Eisenberg, A., 641
Eisenberg, A. R., 359, 360
Eisenberg, L., 538
Eisenberg, M., 408
Eisenberg, N., 193, 194, 217, 218, 284
Eisenbud, L., 289
Eklund, K., 268
Elbert, S. E., 709
Elde, C. L., 364
Elder, Glen H., Jr., 20, 413, 464, 611
Elia, J., 348, 349
Elicker, J., 209

Elkind, D., 11
Elkind, David, 11, 270, 384, 416–417, 421,
        433, 437
Ellickson, P. L., 413
Elliott, D. S., 464
Elliott, V. S., 348
Ellis, B. J., 401, 402, 403, 446
Ellis, K. J., 317
Ellison, C. G., 678
Ellwood, A. -L., 139
Eltzschig, H. K., 113
Emanuel, I., 95
Emde, R. N., 200
Emery, R. E., 364, 366, 367
Emmons, R. A., 599
Emory, E., 204
Emslie, G. J., 414
Eng, P. M., 695
Engel, D., 239
Engel, M., 343
Engels, H., 643
Engelsbel, S., 117
England, L., 92
Engle, P. L., 203
English, K., 139, 362
Englund, M., 209, 373
Enloe, C. F., 62
Ensminget, M. E., 122
Entwisle, D. R., 339
Eogan, M. A., 117
Epel, E. S., 569, 633
Eppler, M. A., 144, 145, 146
Epstein, A. S., 271
Epstein, R. A., 732
Erath, S., 479
Erdley, C. A., 282, 359
Erdrich, L., 62
Erickson, J. D., 92, 98
Erickson, M. F., 203
Ericksson, J. G., 83
Erikson, Erik, 30, 31, 32, 34, 57, 191, 192, 204,
        204–205, 205, 206, 214, 229, 283, 284,
        371, 437, 438, 439, 466, 512, 514, 588,
        589, 594, 595, 601, 663, 669, 674
Erikson, J. M., 674
Eriksson, P. S., 135, 641
Ernst, M., 348
Eron, L., 378, 379
Ervin, R. B., 475, 476
Escobar-Chavez, S. L., 448
Eskin, E, 564
Espeland, M. A., 566, 649
Esposito, K., 648
Esser, G., 171
Essex, M. J., 699
Ettema, J. S., 291
Ettinger, B., 564, 566
Etzel, R. A., 323
Evans, D. A., 563, 650, 673
Evans, D. E., 198, 199, 208
Evans, G., 100
Evans, G. W., 16, 341, 362, 570
Evans. J., 614
Everard, K., 656
Everson, R. B., 100
Evert, J., 639
Evertsson, M., 537
Ewald, H., 83

Hultsch, D. F., 660, 661
Humphrey, L. L., 410
Humphreys, A. P., 319
Humphreys, G. W., 47
Hungerford, T. L., 724
Hunt, C. E., 126
Hunt, N., 379
Huntley-Fenner, G., 174
Huntsinger, C. S., 344
Hurley, B. J., 348, 349
Hurley, J. C., 285
Hurwitz, 720
Huston, A. C., 269, 362, 378
Huston, H. C., 341
Huth-Bocks, A. C., 210
Huttenlocher, J., 174, 185, 250, 266, 284,
   328, 333
Hutter-Silver, M., 639
Huttly, S., 95
Huttunen, M., 98
Huyck, M. H., 597, 605, 696, 699
Hwang, C. P., 203
Hwang, J., 200
Hwang, S. A., 100
Hwang, S. J., 91, 100, 200, 203
Hyde, J. S., 441, 499, 536, 537

Ialongo, N. S., 383
Ickovics, J., 482, 483
Iglowstein, I., 240, 406
Ikeda, R., 728
Iliescue, Adriana, 98
Impagnatiello, F., 83
Infante-Rivard, C., 95
Ingelfinger, J. R., 731
Ingersoll-Dayton, B., 615, 649
Ingersoll, E. W., 116, 121
Ingham, P. W., 85
Ingoldsby, B. B., 529
Ingram, J. L., 73
Inhelder, B., 253, 329
Ireland, M., 415
Irion, J., 676
Isabella, R., 200, 207
Ishii, N., 637
Isita-Espejel, L., 533
Issacowitz, D. M., 602, 673, 674
Itard, Jean Marc Gaspard, 5–6, 6
Ito, S., 93
Iverson, J. M., 179
Ivey, P., 201
Ivy, G. O., 660
Iyasu, S., 127
Izard, Carroll, 195, 211, 363, 388

Jaccard, J., 446, 459
Jacklin, C. N., 204
Jackson, D. W., 421
Jackson, P. W., 350
Jackson, S., 698
Jacob, M. C., 486
Jacob, P., III, 482
Jacobs, C. D., 523
Jacobs, J., 518, 519
Jacobsen, T., 209
Jacobson, J. L., 209
Jacques, Elliott, 592

Jacques, P. F., 320
Jacquet. R. C., 265
Jadva, V., 489
Jaeger, E., 17, 18, 173, 224
Jaffee, S., 225, 499, 519, 611
Jagasia, R., 633
Jahnke, H. C., 676
Jain, D., 203
Jain, T., 64
Jakicic, J. M., 477
James, J. B., 587, 597
Jameson, J. L., 67
Jamner, L. D., 349
Jankowiak, W., 203
Jankowski, J. J., 121, 169, 171
Jankowski, L., 132
Jankuniene, Z., 362
Janowski, J. S., 171
Janowsky, J. S., 330
Janssen, I., 380
Janssens, J. M. A. M, 373
Jarrell, R. H., 291
Järvenpää, S., 210, 323
Jasiobedzka, U., 424
Jay, G. M., 662
Jayaratne, T. E., 457
Jean, C., 126
Jeffery, H. E., 96, 126
Jeffords, J. M., 76, 77
Jeng, G., 64, 488
Jenkins, J. M., 257
Jennekens-Schinkel, A., 359
Jenni, O. G., 240, 406
Jennings, J. M., 658, 660
Jensen, C. D., 92
Jernigan, M., 18, 51
Jezzard, P., 22
Jilinskaia, E., 639
Jimerson, S., 426
Jin, Z., 348
Jindal, R. M., 730
Jobanputra, V., 83
Jocelyn, L., 342
Jodl, K. M., 430
Joffe, A., 407
Johannes, M. O., 526
Johansson, B., 651, 713, 714
Johansson, G., 570
John, O. P., 516, 517
Johnson, C. L., 238, 696, 700
Johnson, D. J., 15, 17, 18, 97, 173, 224
Johnson, D. R., 532
Johnson, D. W., 416
Johnson, E., 637
Johnson, J., 63, 569
Johnson, J. E., 292, 294
Johnson, J. G., 463
Johnson, K. E., 326
Johnson, K. W., 703
Johnson, L., 116
Johnson, M. H., 22, 175, 258
Johnson, M. J., 175
Johnson, M. M. S., 656
Johnson, M. P., 532, 533
Johnson, P. J., 537
Johnson, R. A., 412
Johnson, R. L., 85

Johnson, R. T., 416
Johnson, S. J., 554
Johnson, S. R., 322
Johnson, T. E., 637
Johnson, T. R. B., 90
Johnson, V. E., 557, 645
Johnston, J., 291
Johnston, J. R., 539
Johnston, L., 519
Johnston, L. D., 411, 412, 413, 473, 733
Jokinen, E., 239
Jolley, S. N., 223
Jones, A. K., 447
Jones, C. L., 605
Jones, J., 95
Jones, J. R., 570
Jones, K. M., 348
Jones, N. A., 212
Jones, R. L., 355
Jones, S. M., 377, 463
Jones, S. S., 162
Jonides, J., 660
Jordan, B., 109
Jose, P. E., 344
Joseph, J. A., 640, 663
Joseph, J. T., 730
Josh, P., 203
Joshipura, K. J., 648
Josselson, R., 591, 597, 598
Juffer, F., 365
Jun, H., 725
Jung, Carl G., 588, 589, 597, 663, 680
Jusczyk, P., 140
Jusczyk, P. W., 140, 178, 181
Just, M. A., 84
Juster, F. T., 319, 344, 360, 454
Juul-Dam, N., 84

Kaban, 158, 158t
Kacirk, K. W., 413
Kaczorowski, J. M., 407
Kadhim, H., 126
Kagan, J., 223
Kagan, Jerome, 201
Kagan, S. L., 223
Kahn, A., 126
Kahn, R. L., 602, 620, 679, 681, 695
Kahn, Y., 137
Kail, R., 330
Kaiser, Henry J., 170
Kaiz, M., 453
Kaldunski, M. L., 563
Kaler, S. R., 156
Kales, A., 241, 242
Kalish, C. W., 251
Kalkoske, M., 208
Kampert, J. B., 649
Kanaya, T., 346
Kandel, D. B., 95
Kane, 294
Kanetsuna, T., 380
Kann, L., 398
Kannass, K. N., 169
Kanouse, D. E., 565
Kanstrup Hansen, I. L., 92
Kaplan, G. A., 553, 643
Kaplan, H., 146

Kaplan, J., 343
Kaplan, M., 656
Kaplan, N., 210, 520
Kaplowitz, P. B., 400
Kapur, S., 83
Karafantis, D. M., 359, 373
Karasik, D., 636
Karney, B. R., 697
Kasen, S., 463
Kashima, Y., 214
Kasinitz, P., 519
Kasser, T., 602, 674
Kastberg, D., 342
Katchadourian, H., 553, 556, 639
Katerolos, M., 185
Katikaneni, L. D., 96
Kato, K., 319, 372
Katz, M., 98
Katzman, R., 49
Kaufman, A. S., 336
Kaufman, J., 384
Kaufman, N. L., 336
Kaufman, P., 429
Kaukinen, C., 533
Kausler, D. H., 658, 659
Kawachi, I., 695
Kaye, W. H., 410
Kazdin, M., 299
Kazmierski, J. F., 643
Kazuk, E., 142
Keane, D. P., 117
Kearney, P. M., 561
Kearsley, R. B., 168, 169
Keefer, C., 116
Keegan, C., 551
Keegan, R. T., 151, 152, 576
Keel, P. K., 409, 410
Keeler, G., 52
Keen, R., 174
Keenan, K., 204, 284
Keeton, S., 701
Kegler, S. R., 415
Kehayias, B. D. H, 647
Keightly, P. D., 73
Kellam, S. G., 383
Kelleher, K. J., 123
Keller, Helen, 107, 107–108, 110,
        112, 124, 139, 143, 146,
        172, 220
Keller, M., 84, 329, 517, 676
Keller, T. A., 84
Kelley, M. L., 203, 204
Kellman, P. J., 141
Kelly, A. M., 408
Kelly, D., 425, 496
Kelly, J., 686
Kelly, J. B., 366, 367
Kelly, J. J., 699
Kelly, J. R., 680, 686
Kelsey, J. L., 18
Keltikangas-Järvinen, L., 210
Kemoian,, 143
Kemp, J. S., 118, 126
Kempen, G. I., 643
Kemper, S., 660
Kemper, T. L., 640
Kendler, K. S., 410

Keneko, T., 63
Kennedy, Robert, 348
Kennedy-Stephenson, J., 475, 476
Kennell, J. H., 113
Kenny, G. P., 477, 533
Keppel, K. G., 482, 563
Kerber, R. A., 633
Kerkhof, A. J. F. M., 672
Kermoian, C., 143
Kerns, K. A., 94
Kerr, M., 464
Kerrebrock, N., 239
Kessen, W., 141
Kessler, R. C., 549, 570
Kestenbaum, R., 283
Keyes, C. L. M., 595, 596, 598, 599,
        600, 601
Khan, Y., 137
Khoury, M. J., 76, 77
Kidd, J. R., 349
Kidd, K. K., 17, 75, 156, 349
Kiecolt-Glaser, J. K., 633, 638, 697
Kiefe, C, I., 482
Kiefer, K. M., 685
Kiel, D. P., 636
Kiernan, K., 527
Kieszak, S. M., 323
Killen, J. D., 413
Kim-Cohen, J., 16, 212, 264, 381
Kim, J., 371
Kim, J. E., 579, 684, 685, 686, 690
Kim, K. J., 20
Kim, S., 363
Kim, S. S., 569
Kim. Y. S., 380
Kimball, M. M., 291
Kimmel, D., 699
Kimmel, D. C., 607, 608
Kimmerly, M. L., 207
Kimmerly, N. L., 207
King, B. M., 370, 443, 486, 487, 557
King, Martin Luther, Jr., 549
King, N. J., 385
King, V., 618
King, W. J., 127
Kington, R., 564
Kinney, H. C., 126
Kinsella, K., 612, 613, 615, 616, 617, 618, 627,
        628, 630, 631, 638, 682, 683, 684, 688,
        689, 690, 692, 696, 697, 698, 701,
        724, 728
Kipp, H. L., 348
Kirby, D., 450, 451
Kirby, R. S., 99
Kirby, S. E., 678
Kirsch, I., 505
Kisilevsky, B. S., 91, 211
Kisker, E. E., 271
Kispert, A., 67
Kistner, J., 322
Kita, S., 183
Kitamura, S., 344
Kitson, G. C., 539
Kitzman, J. H., 228
Kitzmann, K. M., 533
Kivenson-Baron, I., 514, 519, 520
Kivett, V. R., 617

Kivnick, H. Q., 34, 674
Kjelurff, K. H., 565
Klaczynski, P. A., 490, 656, 657
Klatt, L., 174
Klaus, M. H., 113
Klebanoff, M. A., 95, 99
Klebanov, P. K., 123
Kleerekoper, M., 566
Klein, D. J., 413
Klein, R., 563, 657
Klein-Schwartz, W., 245
Kleinbaum, S., 528
Kleiner, A., 344, 349
Kleiner, B., 406
Klibanski, A., 407, 409
Kline, D. W., 553, 642
Kline, G. H., 528, 642
Kling, K. C., 441
Klohnen, E. C., 593
Klump, K. L., 410
Klute, C., 458, 459, 460
Knaack, A., 218
Knight, E. M., 95
Knight, W. G., 96
Knoester, C., 536
Knoops, K. T. B., 648
Knox, E. G., 99
Knox, N., 526
Kobelin, C., 112
Kochanek, K. D., 64, 124, 125, 126, 127, 324,
        474, 482, 514, 563, 564
Kochanska, G., 194, 209, 210, 215, 217,
        218, 516
Kochenderfer, B. H., 382
Koechlin, E., 174, 504
Koenig, H. G., 497
Kogan, M. D., 102
Kogos, J., 388
Kogushi, Y., 257
Koh, Y. -J., 380
Kohlberg, L., 267, 329
Kohlberg, Lawrence, 286, 287, 288, 289,
        416, 421, 422–425, 433, 489,
        495–496, 498
Kohn, M. L., 503, 504
Koinis, D., 256
Koivula, L., 640
Kolarz, C. M., 673, 675
Kolata, G., 74, 523, 525, 637
Komatsu, L. K., 326
Konachek, K. D., 561
Konrad, D., 67
Koops, W., 377
Kopp, C. B., 156, 214, 215, 217
Koren, G., 93
Korner, A., 200
Koropeckyj-Cox, T., 701, 702
Korte, D., 110
Kos, M., 101t
Kosmitzki, C., 109, 146, 328, 416, 523, 525,
        528, 529, 537
Kosnik, W., 553
Koso, G., 605
Kostelny, K., 226, 385
Kosterman, R., 464
Kotchen, J. M., 563
Kotchen, T. A., 563

Michaelieu, Q., 441
Michaels, S., 523, 525
Michaelson, K. F., 131
Michel, P., 646
Miedel, W. T., 343
Miedzian, M., 290
Milani, I., 168
Milani, R. V., 563
Milberger, S., 95
Milgram, N. W., 641
Miller, A., 211, 250, 661
Miller, B. H., 689, 690
Miller, D. C., 269, 339, 342
Miller, G. E., 568
Miller, G. G., 348, 349
Miller, J. Y., 412
Miller, K., 504
Miller, K. F., 166, 250, 252
Miller-Kovach, K., 321
Miller, L. C., 520
Miller, L. W., 131
Miller Loncar, C. L., 265
Miller, P. A., 284
Miller, P. H., 182, 254, 326, 330
Miller, S. A., 182, 254, 326, 330
Miller, W. R., 678
Mills, D. L., 184
Mills, J. L., 92, 95
Milunsky, A., 71t
Minagawa, R. Y., 486
Minder, C. E., 690
Minich, N., 120
Minkler, M., 618, 679
Minshew, N. J., 84
Mintz, T. H., 180
Miranda, S. B., 168
Mischel, W., 217
Miserandino, M., 340
Misra, D. P., 103
Missmer, S. A., 64
Mistry, J., 176
Mistry, R., 341
Mistry, R. S., 362
Mitchell-Kernan, C., 524, 699
Mitchell, V., 597, 609
Mitka, M., 128
Mittman, B. S., 565
Mix, K. S., 174, 328
Miyake, K., 207
Mlot, C., 197, 198
Moane, G., 513, 597
Moen, P., 537, 549, 579, 587,
    593, 680, 684, 685,
    686, 690
Moffitt, R. A., 341
Moffitt, T., 16, 200, 225, 264, 388,
    464, 611
Moffitt, T. E, 517, 519
Moir, P., 645, 646, 648
Moise-Titus, J., 378
Mokdad, A. H., 475, 476
Mol, B. W., 117
Molennar, P. C. M., 328
Molina, B. S. G., 349, 454, 455
Molinari, L., 240, 406
Moline, M. L., 485
Mollenkopf, J., 519
Mondloch, C. J., 169
Mondschein, E. R., 142, 204

Moneta, G., 453
Money, J., 287
Monk, C. S., 175, 258
Monk, T. H., 175, 477
Monshouwer, H. J., 377
Montague, D. F. P., 211
Montenegro, X. P., 606
Montessori, Maria, 269
Montgomery, M. J., 500, 502
Montplaisir, J., 241
Moody, J., 415
Moody-Thomas, S., 656
Moon, C., 140
Moon, C. M., 74, 91
Moon, J., 74
Moon, R. Y., 126
Mooney-Somers, J., 369, 370
Moore, A., 538
Moore, D. W., 733
Moore, G. E., 73
Moore, J. W., 514
Moore, K. A., 448
Moore, M. J., 645, 646, 648
Moore, M. Keith, 162, 163, 173
Moore, S. E., 92
Moorman, J. E., 606
Morelli, G. A., 49, 118, 126, 201
Morgan, A., 477
Morgan, B., 84
Morgan, G. A., 212
Morgan, J. L., 178
Morgan, L. A., 539
Morgan W. J., 323
Morielli, A., 126
Morin, C. M., 644
Morishima, A., 349
Morison, P., 373
Morison, S. J., 139
Morris, J. E., 457
Morris, M. C., 651, 653
Morris, P. A., 41, 348
Morris, S. S., 124, 130
Morrison, F. J., 272
Morrow, D. G., 575
Morse, J. M., 44
Mortensen, E. L., 131
Mortenson, P. B., 83, 726
Mortimer, E. A., 118
Mortimer, J., 473, 649, 661
Morton, K. R., 491
Morton, T., 383
Mosconi, L., 652
Moscovitch, M., 660
Mosely, J., 369
Moses, L. J., 212, 255
Mosher, W. D., 446, 451, 528,
    533, 605
Mosier, C., 176, 215, 216
Mosko, S., 118
Moskovitz, J., 634
Moskow-McKenzie, D., 665
Moss, E., 210
Moss, M. H., 323
Moss, M. S., 725
Moss, S. Z., 725
Mounts, N. S., 455, 461, 464
Mounzih, K., 399
Mouw, T., 499, 518, 519, 610
Moyzis, R. K., 349

Mroczek, D. K., 598, 599, 673, 674, 675,
    695, 714
Msall, M. S. E., 121
Mueller, T. I., 649
Muenke, M., 348
Muir, D. W., 91, 144, 256
Mukamal, K., 629, 695
Mulder, E., 98
Mulinaire, J., 98
Mullan, D., 405
Müller, M., 395
Müller, U., 258
Mullin, J., 337
Mullington, J. M., 478
Mullins, R., 100
Müllner, M., 562
Mulrine, A., 11
Mumma, G. H., 373
Mumme, D. L., 213, 359
Munakata, Y., 175
Munn, P., 218
Munson, M. L., 365
Muntner, P., 321
Murachver, T., 260
Murchison, C., 7
Murdoch, B., 369
Murphy, B. C., 194
Murphy, G. C., 570
Murphy, J. M., 499
Murphy, K. C., 269
Murphy, K. R., 349
Murphy. P. D., 76
Murphy, S. L., 124, 324, 474, 482, 561,
    563, 564
Murray, A. D., 640
Murray, C., 489
Murray, K., 217
Murray, M. L., 217, 384
Murry, V. M., 363
Musick, K., 534
Musick, M. A., 680
Musil, C. M., 648, 649, 675
Muskin, P. R., 734
Must, A., 320, 400, 403, 408
Mustillo, S., 320
Muter, V., 268
Mutran, E. J., 616
Muzik, M., 211
Myers, D. G., 520, 529, 598, 599
Myers, G. J., 100
Myers, J. E., 618
Myerson, J., 709, 710
Mykityshyn, A. L., 665
Mylander, C., 183

Nabors, L., 221
Nadel, L., 74
Naeye, R. L., 95
Naftel, J., 348
Nagaoka, J., 343
Nagel, S. K., 341
Nair, K. S., 643
Nakonezny, P. A., 538
Nam, S., 699
Nandakumar, R., 265
Nangle, B. E., 120
Nansel, T. R., 380
Napolitano, M., 477
Nash, A., 219

Santos, I. S., 95
Santow, M., 450
Sanz, J., 516
Sapienza, C., 73
Sapolsky, R. M., 568
Sapp, F., 256
Sarkisian, N., 613
Satariano, W. A., 642
Satcher, D., 448, 450, 483
Satz, P., 640
Saudino, K. J., 82, 200
Sauer, P. J. J., 734
Saunders, D. L., 324
Saunders, P. R., 516
Savage, S. L., 266
Savic, I., 402, 444
Savin-Williams, R. C., 444, 445
Savoie, D., 325
Sawicki, M. B., 688
Saxe, G. B., 252
Saxton, J. A., 640
Scaer, R., 110
Scanlan, J. M., 613
Scarborough, H. S., 268
Scariati, P. D., 130
Scarr, S., 80, 81, 221, 223
Schacter, D. L., 39, 47
Schaefer, C. E., 350
Schaefer, W. D., 207
Schafer, G., 185
Schafer, W. D., 207
Schaie, K. Warner, 8, 491–492, 522, 571,
      571–572, 574, 581, 652, 653, 654, 655,
      656, 662, 663, 673, 695
Schaller, M., 284
Schanberg, S., 121
Scharf, M., 367, 514, 519, 520
Scharlach, A. E., 723, 725
Schaubroeck, J., 569
Schaumberg, D. A., 642
Scheers, N. J., 118, 126
Scheidt, P. C., 405, 406
Schell, L. M., 403
Schemo, D. J., 343
Scher, M. S., 96
Scherr, P. A., 650
Schiavo, Terry, 730
Schiefelbein, V. L., 399
Schieve, L. A., 64, 488
Schiller, J. S., 245, 323, 348, 562
Schiller, M., 208
Schlegel, A., 453
Schlossman, S., 342
Schmidt, Lars, 510
Schmidt, M. H., 171
Schmidt, P. J., 485
Schmithorst, V. J., 133
Schmitt, F. A., 656
Schmitt, K. L., 288
Schmitz, S., 82, 200
Schmuckler, M. A., 169
Schnall, P. L., 569
Schneider, B. H., 210
Schneider, E. L., 633, 634, 636
Schneider, L. C., 323
Schneider, M., 343
Schneiderman, L. J., 731
Schnell, S. V., 425

Schockner, A. E., 285
Schoefs, V., 209, 281
Schoelmerich, A., 218
Schoenborn, C. A., 477, 484
Schoendorf, K. C., 384
Schoeni, R., 499
Schoenle, E. J., 67
Schoff, K., 388
Schölmerich, A., 202
Scholten, C. M., 109, 110
Schonert-Reichl, K. A., 398
Schonfeld, D. J., 322
Schonfield, D., 659
Schopflocher, D. P., 324
Schore, A. N., 197
Schouten, A., 359
Schuck, S., 349
Schuebel, K. J., 642
Schuengel, C., 206
Schulenberg, J., 519
Schulenberg, J. E., 411, 412, 413,
      473, 481
Schulz, L. E., 250
Schulz, M. S., 537
Schulz, R., 613, 614, 679, 697,
      698, 716
Schulze, P. A., 218
Schwartz, B., 128
Schwartz, D., 380
Schwartz, J., 246
Schwartz, J. E., 672, 733
Schwartz, L. L., 489
Schwarzmueller, A., 260
Schweder, R. A., 601
Schweinhart, L. J., 271, 451, 465
Schwimmer, J. B., 320
Scialfa, C. T., 553, 642
Scott, C., 324, 474, 482, 563, 564
Scott, E., 403, 404, 464
Scott, G., 247
Scott, J., 523
Scott, P., 326
Scourfield, J., 349
Scullin, M. H., 346
Sebanc, A. M., 294
Sebire, G., 126
Sedlak, A. J., 225
Seeley, J. R., 382
Seeman, E., 478, 678
Seeman, M., 678
Seeman, T. E., 697
Seepersad, S., 454
Seff, M. A., 457
Seftor, N. S., 500
Segerstrom, S. C., 568
Segesten, K., 727
Seidler, A, 581, 649
Seifer, R., 200, 208, 407
Seigler, R. S., 251
Sekuler, R., 553
Selkoe, D. J., 640
Sellers, E. M., 482
Selman, A. P., 376
Selman, Robert, 376
Seltzer, G. B., 688
Seltzer, J. A., 368, 527, 528
Seltzer, M., 185
Seltzer, M. M., 701

Selznick, David, 509
Seminara, S. B., 399
Sen, A., 269, 342
Sen, M. G., 204, 339
Senghas, A., 183
Senman, L., 257
Serafini, S., 348
Serbin, L., 204
Serbin, L. A., 372
Serlin, R. C., 662
Seroude, L., 637
Service, V., 179
Sethi, A., 217
Settersten, R. A., Jr., 473, 505
Seybold, K. S., 678
Seyle, Hans, 567
Shaddy, D. J., 169
Shaffer, R. A., 486
Shafto, M. A., 659
Shahabi, L., 678
Shamah, T., 92, 132
Shanahan, M., 473
Shanahan, M. J., 430
Shankaran, S., 94, 96
Shannon, D., 202, 203
Shannon, M., 245
Shaper, A. G., 479
Shapiro, A. D., 598, 601, 690
Sharit, J., 685
Sharma, A. R., 364
Shatz, M., 266
Shaw, B. A, 649, 679
Shaw, D., 204, 284, 348
Shaw, N., 239
Shaywitz, S. E., 347, 348
Shea, K. M., 100, 239
Shealy, D., 709, 710
Shedlock, D. J., 663, 665
Sheldon, K. M., 602, 674
Shema, S. J., 643
Shepherd, J., 476
Sherman, A. M., 694
Sherman, M., 692
Shields, Brooke, 212
Shields, M. K., 17
Shine, B., 239
Shinn, M., 246
Shiono, P. H., 101, 103, 120
Shirey, L., 641, 685
Shirley, L., 204, 285
Shoda, Y., 217
Shoghi-Jadid, K., 652
Shoji, J., 380
Sholl, W., 339
Shonkoff, J., 220, 221
Shonkoff, J. P., 322
Shore, C., 177, 177t, 179
Shore, E. L., 499
Showers, C. J., 441
Shuey, K. M., 611, 612, 613
Shufelt, C., 563
Shukitt-Hale, B., 640, 663
Shull, R. D., 538
Shulman, S., 210, 365, 367, 373
Shultetus, R. S., 575
Shumpert, M. N., 99
Shwe, H. I., 181
Sibson, V. L., 635

Willan, A., 95
Willard, B. F., 67
Willcox, B. J., 637
Wille, D. E., 209
Willett, W. C., 476, 562, 566
Williams, B., 648
Williams, C. S., 644
Williams, D., 616, 617
Williams, G. J., 39
Williams, J., 94, 320
Williams, K., 532, 724
Williams, K. A., 179
Williams, M. V., 554
Williams, R. M., 680
Williams, Robin, 348
Williams, S., 349
Williams, T., 342
Williams, W. M., 332, 333, 493
Williams, William Carlos, 653
Williamson, D. F., 477, 563
Willinger, M., 126
Willis, S. K., 593
Willis, S. L., 549, 571, 574, 654, 662,
    663, 673
Willson, A. E., 611, 612
Wilmoth, J. R., 605, 630, 636, 639
Wilner,, A., 592
Wilson, E. O., 39, 57
Wilson, K., 384
Wilson, M. R., 563
Wilson, R. S., 381, 651, 673
Wilson, S., 453
Wilson, S. J., 380, 605
Wilson, S. P., 218
Winfrey, Oprah, 16
Wingfield, A., 658
Wink, P., 597, 678
Winkow, M., 17
Winner, E., 256, 351
Winocur, G., 661
Winter, M., 479
Wippman, J., 209
Wisborg, K., 94
Wisby, G., 729
Wise, S., 211
Wisenbacker, J., 98
Witkow, M., 430
Witteman, P. A., 471–472
Wittig, D. R., 730
Wittstein, I. S., 568
Wlikins, D. G., 95
Wolchik, S. A., 366
Wolf, M., 497
Wolf-Maier, K., 562
Wolfe, D. A., 226
Wolfe, L., 720, 722
Wolff, J. L., 693
Wolff, Kaspar Friedrich, 63
Wolff, P. H., 117, 195
Wolke, D., 121

Wondimu, E. A., 240
Wong, A., 255
Wong, C. A., 113
Wong, C. K., 384
Wong, I. C. K., 384
Wong, L. -Y. C., 92
Wong, L.-Y. C., 92
Wong, W. W., 317
Wood, A., 259, 328
Wood, D., 265
Wood, F. B., 348
Wood, R. M., 195
Woodfield, R., 516
Woodruff, T. J., 247, 323, 348, 349
Woods, A. M., 553
Woods, Margo N., 558
Woods, Tiger, 18
Woodward, A. L., 180
Woodward, S. A., 201
Woolley, J. D., 255, 259
Wooten, J., 669
Worthman, C., 320
Wortman, C. B., 698, 716, 717
Wright, A., 122
Wright, A. L., 95, 558
Wright, J., 269
Wright J. A., 239
Wright, J. D., 475, 476
Wright, Steven, 49
Wright, V. C., 64, 488
Wrosch, C., 593
Wu, F., 208
Wu, T., 401
Wu, Z., 484, 563
WuDunn, S., 682
Wulczyn, F., 227
Wulf, D., 445
Wyatt, W., 405
Wykle, M. L., 648, 649, 675
Wynn, Karen, 174

Xia, H., 474
Xie, J. L., 570

Yaeger, J., 267
Yan, L. L., 562
Yang, B., 385
Yassuda, M. S., 662
Yazigi, R. A., 100
Yeargin-Allsopp, M., 83, 128
Yellowitz, J. A., 648
Yeung, W. J., 536
Ying-Lai, M., 563
Yingling, C. D., 39
Yip, T., 454
Yokota, F., 378
Yoshikawa, H., 464
Youdim, K. A., 640, 663
Young, A., 179

Young, L. R., 476
Young-Xu, Y., 639
Youngblade, L. M., 209, 257
Youngstrom, E., 388
Ytteroy, E. A., 369
Yu, S. M., 247
Yunger, J. L., 289, 372

Zaborski, L. B., 564
Zahn-Waxler, C., 31, 212
Zain, A. F., 293
Zajac, R., 339
Zametkin, A. J., 348
Zandhi, P. P., 566
Zarbatany, L., 372
Zarit, S., 678
Zee, P. C., 638
Zeedyk, M. S., 245
Zeffiro, T. A., 348
Zelazo, P. D., 258
Zelazo, P. R., 140, 168, 169
Zellman, G. L., 450
Zendell, S. M., 485
Zeskind, P. S., 93
Zhang, H., 252
Zhang, J., 99, 613
Zhang, Q. F., 683
Zhang, W., 348
Zhang, Y., 476
Zhang, Y-P., 349
Zhao, J. Z., 528
Zheng, D. D., 643
Zheng, Z. J., 563
Zhensun, Z., 235, 236
Zhou, H., 99
Zhou, Q., 359
Zhu, B. -P., 120
Zhu, J., 252
Zhu, W., 643
Zigler, E., 415, 464
Zigler, E. F., 270, 271
Zimmer, J., 635
Zimmerman, B. J., 340, 426
Zimmerman, F. J., 169
Zimmerman, R. R., 202
Zito, J. M., 384
Zizza, C., 476
Zolaniuk, B., 698
Zonderman, A. B., 515
Zoran, N., 365
Zubenko, G. S., 474
Zubernis, L. S., 257
Zucker, A. N., 595
Zucker, K. J., 444
Zuckerman, B., 96
Zuckerman, B. S., 212
Zuckerman, W. R., 121
Zuzanek, J., 700
Zylicz, Z., 733

Subject Index

Eqypt, obesity in, 238
Erectile dysfunction, 560
Eriksonian theory, 204–205, 358
  autonomy vs. shame and doubt, 33t, 214, 229
  basic trust vs. basic mistrust, 33t, 204–205, 229, 370
  ego integrity vs. despair, 674
  generativity vs. stagnation, 33t, 588–589
  identity vs. confusion, 33t
  identity vs. identity confusion, 437–440
  industry vs. inferiority, 358
  initiative vs. guilt, 33t, 283–284
  integrity vs. despair, 33t
  intimacy vs. isolation, 33t, 512–513
Eskimos. *See* Alaskan Natives
Estonia, 405
Ethics, research, 55–56
Ethnic gloss, definition, 18
Ethnic group, definition, 17
Ethnic groups. *See also* Race
  diversity within, 17, 18
  and identity formation, 441–442
  inclusion in research, 18–19
Ethnicity, as social construction, 18
Ethnographic studies, 48, 48t
Ethology, 40
European Collaborative Study, 323
European cultures, 257. *See also* under individual countries
  AIDS in, 485
  cohabitation, 526, 527
  end-of-life decisions in, 733–734
  and homosexuality, 523
  marriage, 529
  onset of puberty, 401
  overweight in, 476
  same-sex marriage, 526
  self in, 280–281
  sex education, 450
  sexual mores, 523
Euthanasia, 729, 731–734, 738
  ethical concerns, 732
Evolutionary perspective, 30t, 32, 39, 40
Evolutionary psychology, 40
Exercise, and pregnancy, 92
Exosystem, 42–43, 42f
Experiential element, of intelligence, 492
Experiment, definition, 50
Experimental designs, 50–52
Experimental group, 50
Experimental research designs, 48t
Expertise, and intelligence, 574–575
Explicit memory, 175
Extended family, 15
External memory aids, 330, 331t
Eyes. *See* Vision problems
Eyewitnesses, children as, 259, 261

Failure to thrive, 194
Faith, 496, 497
Fallopian tube, 88f
Falls, preventing, safety checklist, 644t
False beliefs, 255–256
Families, characteristics of abusive, 225
Family, 15, 20. *See also* Parenting
  role, in adolescence, 452–453, 453–457
  role in gender development, 290
  role in identity formation, 440, 442

role, in late adulthood, 695–696, 700–701
role, in moral development, 425
role, in psychosocial development, 201–204
role, in young adulthood, 519–520
single-parent, 203
Family conflict, in adolescence, 454–457
Family-focused lifestyle, 686
Family science, 9
Family structure, 363–371, 455–457
  adoptive families, 364–365
  developing countries, 370
  and divorce, 365–367
  dual-income, 536–537, 542
  gay parents, 364
  multigenerational, 695–696
  and sibling relationships, 370–371
  single-parent families, 363f, 367–368, 368f
  stepfamilies, 368–369
  United States, 523–524
Family studies, 76
Family therapy, 383
Family Transitions Project, 20
FAS (fetal alcohol syndrome), 61–62, 93–94
FASD (fetal alcohol spectrum disorder), 93
Fathers, 203
  and adolescent development, 401–402
  and prenatal development, 100
  role of, 535–536
  as single parents, 364, 367
Fearfulness, early childhood, 305–306
Fears, childhood, 306t, 382, 384–386, 387
Federal Glass Ceiling Commission, 570
Federal Interagency Forum on Aging-Related Statistics, 628, 631, 642, 646, 658, 665, 685, 687, 688, 689, 696, 698–699
Feral children, 5–6
Fertility rates, 535
Fertility treatments, 486–487, 488, 489
Fertilization, 63–64, 88f
Fetal alcohol syndrome (FAS), 61–62, 93–94, 206
Fetal blood sampling, 101t
Fetal development. *See* Prenatal development
Fetal mortality, 102, 103
Fetal stage, 86–87, 89–91
Fetoscopy, 101t
Fidelity, 438
Field experiments, 51, 52
Filial crisis, 612
Filial maturity, 612
Filipino Americans
  mother's age at first birth, 535t
  prenatal care, late, 102f
Fine motor skills, 142, 242, 243
Finland, 405
  corporal punishment, 298
  infant mortality rate, 125f
  teen pregnancy, 450
Five-factor trait model, 515–517, 515f
Fluid intelligence, 573–574
Fluoxetine-Bulimia Collaborative Study Group, 410
Fontanels, 114
Food and Drug Administration (FDA), 652
Foreclosure, identity, 439
Formal operations, 33t, 416–418, 487
  definition, 416
Foster care, 227
Fragile X syndrome, 73t

France, 405
  education, 500
  infant mortality rate, 125f
  teen pregnancy, 450
Freudian theory, 32–33
Friendship, stages of, 376t
Friendships
  adolescence, 458–459
  early childhood, 307, 309, 311
  in late adulthood, 699–700
  middle adulthood, 599, 608
  middle childhood, 374, 375–376
  young adulthood, 520
Functional age, 629
Functional play, 292

Gallistel, C. R., 174
Gaslight (film), 508
Gay marriage, 526
Gays and lesbians, 525–526, 525–526
  adolescent, 443–445
  and AIDS, 485
  in late adulthood, 699
  in middle adulthood, 607–608, 620–621
  negative attitudes about, 523
  as parents, 364
  and suicide, 415
Gender, 476
  and aggression, 303–304
  and child abuse, 224
  and depression, 413
  discrimination, 503, 570
  division of labor, 537–538, 542
  and education, 500, 501t
  and genetic disorders, 71f, 72
  and health, 482–483, 564–567
  and identity formation, 597–598
  and life expectancy, 630
  and living arrangements, in retirement, 689f
  and moral reasoning, 498–499
  and parenting, 535–536
  and personality development, 512, 513, 516
  and physical development, 317
  and play, 295
  and relationships, 602
  and school achievement, 428
  and self-esteem, 441
  and sexual behavior, 446
  and sexuality, 445
  and stress, 570
  and suicide, 415
  wage gap, 503
Gender constancy, 287–288
Gender crossover, 597
Gender development, 285–291, 310
  biological approaches, 285, 286–287, 286t
  cognitive approaches, 287–289
  and peer groups, 372
  psychoanalytic approach, 286t, 287
  social cognitive approach, 286t
  socialization and, 289–291
Gender differences, 284–285
  body image, in adolescence, 408
  bullying, 380
  in identity formation, 440–441
  in moral development, 425
  in play, 319

HPV (human papilloma virus), 448, 449t
HRT (hormone replacement therapy), 556, 566
Huhot people, 203
Human capital, 16
Human development
  basic concepts, 9–10
  definition, 7
  study of, 7–9
Hungary, 405
Huntington's disease, 71
Hurried child, 384
Hypertension, 561, 563
  in late adulthood, 646
  in middle childhood, 321
Hypothesis, definition, 29
Hypothetical-deductive reasoning, 416–418
  definition, 417
Hysterectomy, 565

Iceland, corporal punishment, 298
Id, 32
Ideal self, 280
Identity accommodation, 594
Identity achievement, 439–440
Identity assimilation, 594
Identity crisis, 439
Identity, definition, 437
Identity diffusion, 439
Identity formation, 437–445, 466
  and gender, 597–598
  gender differences, 440–441
  identity process model, 594–595
  middle adulthood, 593–594, 620
  sexual, 442–445
Identity process model, 594–595
Identity-status interview, 439t
Identity statuses, 439, 594
  factors associated with, 440t
Identity style, 594
Identity vs. identity confusion, 33t, 437–438
Ifaluk atoll people, 201
Illiteracy, adult, 504–505
Illness. See also Death and bereavement; Health
  maternal, and prenatal development, 96, 97–98
  in middle adulthood, 561–562
  mother-to-child transmission, 131
Imaginary audience, 419
Imaginary companions, 294–295
Imaginative play, 293–294
Imitation, and cognitive development, 162–163,
    248, 250
Immaturity, adaptive nature of, 40, 41
Immigrants, 17, 18
  acculturation of, 18
Immunization, 127–128, 244
Implicit memory, 175
Impotence, 560
Imprinting, 21
In vitro fertilization, 488, 489
Income, neighborhood, 16
Independent variable, 50
India, 176, 203
  childbirth in, 113
  gender roles in, 290
  play in, 319
Indians, American, 164. See American Indians
Individual differences, 14
Individual psychotherapy, 383
Individuation, 588

Indonesia, 240
Inductive reasoning, 326
  definition, 326
  middle childhood, 325t, 326
Inductive techniques, of discipline, 297,
    298, 361
Industry vs. inferiority, 33t, 358
Infancy
  developmental issues in, 204–213
  fears in, 306t
  major developments in, 12, 12t
Infant amnesia, 154, 155
Infant Health Development Program (IHDP),
    122–123
Infant mortality, 124–127, 147–148
  causes of, 125–127
  definition, 124
  and homelessness, 246
  and race, 125
  reducing, 124, 125
  risk factors, 124
Infant mortality rate, definition, 124
Infant mortality rates, in industrialized
    countries, 125f
Infants
  cognitive development, 156–158
  developmental testing, 156
  feeding, 130–131
  fostering competence, 158f
  growth and development, 128–132
  nutrition, 130–132
Infertility, 486–487, 488, 489
Information-processing theory, 30t, 39
  adolescence, 420–421
  causality, 171–172
  early childhood, 258–269
  infancy, 167–175
  and intelligence, 169, 170–171
  late adulthood, 657
  middle childhood, 329–330
Informed consent, 55
Inheritance, genetic, 68–69. See also Heredity
  sex-linked, 72
Initiative vs. guilt, 33t, 283–284
Injuries, death from, 126, 244–245
Inner Mongolia, 203
Innate learning mechanisms, 173
Institute of Medicine (IOM), 77
Instrumental aggression, 303, 377, 378
Insurance, health, 245
Integration, neuronal, 135
Integrative thought, 575, 576
Intelligence
  age-related changes, 493
  correlation with early abilities, 188
  and creativity, 578
  early childhood, 263–265
  emotional, 494–495
  and expertise, 574–575
  fluid vs. crystallized, 573–574
  and heredity, 82, 333
  and information processing, 169, 170–171
  in late adulthood, 653–655
  and longevity, 657–658
  measuring, 156, 170–171, 187, 188, 332–337,
    493–494, 653–655
  middle adulthood, 571–574
  reaction range, 79f
  theories of, 653–654

theory of multiple, 335
  triarchic theory of, 334–335, 492–493
Intelligence quotient (IQ)
  correlation with early abilities, 170–171
  and culture, 333
  and early intervention programs, 158
  and longevity, 658
  and nutrition, 240
  parental, 264
  and race, 333
  tests, 156, 263–265, 332–334, 350, 653–654
Intelligence tests, 332–337, 352
  and creativity, 350
  dynamic, 336–337
  IQ (intelligence quotient). See Intelligence
    quotient (IQ)
  and multiple intelligences, 334–337
Intelligent behavior, 156
Interiority, 590
Internalization, 215, 216
International Agency for Cancer
    Research, 478
International Cesarean Awareness
    Network, 112
International Covenant on Civil and Political
    Rights, 404
International Human Genome Sequencing
    Consortium, 2004, 76
International Longevity Center, Mount Sinai
    School of Medicine, 635, 637
Internet
  education, 500
  use, in school, 343–344
  violence, 379
Interpersonal intelligence, 336t
Interviews, 45
Intimacy vs. isolation, 33t, 512–513
Intimate relationships, 520–522, 541
Intrapersonal intelligence, 336t
Inuit. See Alaskan Natives
Invisible imitation, 162
Iran, 164, 398
Ireland, 405
  infant mortality rate, 125f
  school violence, 462
  sexual mores, 523
Irish Americans, 296
Irreversibility, concept of, 249t, 254
Islam, 398
Isolette, 121
Israel, 207, 251, 405
  adoption in, 365
  corporal punishment, 298
  family relationships, 519–520
  infant mortality rate, 125f
Italian Americans, 71f
Italy
  education, 500
  infant mortality rate, 125f
  teen pregnancy, 450

Jamaica
  childrearing practices, 146
  malnutrition, 239–240
Japan, 207
  aggression in, 304–305
  bullying in, 380
  child abuse, 226
  childrearing practices, 118, 164, 257–258

Private speech, 267
Problem-focused coping, 675
Procedural knowledge, 420
Procedural memory, 659
Prodigy, child, 235
ProEnglish, 346
Professional degrees awarded, by
    gender, 501t
Project CARE, 158
Project Head Start, 270–271
Prosocial behavior, 302–303
    middle childhood, 359–360
Protective factors, and stress, 386
Proximodistal principle, 84, 128–129
Psychoanalysis, 32
Psychoanalytic perspective, 30t, 31, 32, 32–33
Psychological aggression, 299–300
Psychometric approach, to cognitive develop-
    ment, 156–159, 332–334
Psychopathology
    and heredity, 83–84
    and maternal nutrition, 92
Psychosexual development, 32
Psychosexual stages, 33t
Psychosexual theory, 30t, 286t
Psychosocial development, 10, 34
    in adolescence, 434–467
    in early childhood, 276–311
    and emotions, 193–198
    and the family, 201–204
    foundations of, 193–201
    highlights, of infants' and toddlers', 194t
    in late adulthood, 668–705
    in middle adulthood, 583–621
    in middle childhood, 354–390
    normative-stage models, 511–514, 588–591
    young adulthood, 508–544
Psychosocial stages, 33t
Psychosocial theory, 30t
Puberty, 399–403, 432
    definition, 397
    influences, on onset, 401–402
Puerto Ricans, 563–564
    health, 601
    infant mortality, 125
    mother's age at first birth, 535t
    prenatal care, late, 102f
Punishment, 35–36

Qualitative change, 10
Qualitative research, 44
Quantitative change, 10
Quantitative research, 43–44
Questionnaires, 45

Race
    and adoption, 364, 365
    and AIDS, 485
    and body image, 408
    and drug abuse, 479
    and education, 500
    and end-of-life decisions, 735
    and family relationships, 368f, 454, 455
    and health, 247, 482, 563, 601
    and identity formation, 441–442
    and infant mortality, 125, 246
    and IQ scores, 333
    and late prenatal care, 102f
    and life expectancy, 632f

    and low birth weight, 120, 120t
    mother's age at first birth, 534–535, 535t
    and onset of puberty, 401
    and poverty, 363
    and retirement income, 687
    and school achievement, 428
    and sensory impairment, 642
    and sexual behavior, 445
    and single-parent families, 203
    as social construction, 18
    social impact of, 18
    and teenage motherhood, 451
Racism, 435–436, 471–472
Radcliffe College, 596, 598
Random assignment, 50–51
Rape
    acquaintance, 523
    adolescent victims, 447
Reaction range, 78–79
    and intelligence, 79f
Reading skills, 337
Reading, to children, 186
Real self, 280
Reality principle, 32
Reasoning
    hypothetical-deductive, 416–418
    middle childhood, 325t, 326, 329, 352
Recall, 259
Recessive inheritance, 68, 71, 72
Recognition, 259
Reflective thinking, 488, 489
Reflex behaviors, 137
Reflexes, 137
    early human, 138t, 144
Rehearsal, 330, 331t
Reinforcement, 35–36
    and family discipline, 296–297
Relational aggression, 304
Relationships. *See* Marriage
    and gender, 602
    and health, 483–484, 601, 695
Reliability, 47
Religion, 496, 497
    and life satisfaction, 599
    and sexual mores, 523
    and well-being, 678
Representational ability, 161, 165–166
Representational mappings, 280
Representational systems, 357
Reproductive system. *See also* Pregnancy;
    Sexuality
    changes, in midlife, 555–558, 555t
Research designs, 47–48
    basic, 49–52
    case studies, 47, 48
    developmental, 52–54
    experimental, 50–52
Research, ethics of, 55–56
Research methods, 43–55
    data collection, 31, 44–46
    qualitative vs. quanitative, 43–44
    sampling, 44
    and sex research, 442–443
    and theoretical perspectives, 43
Reserve capacity, 640
Resilient children, 386, 387–388
Resistant attachment, 206
Respite care, 614
Reticent play, 293t

Retirement, 579–580, 683–688
    income in, 687–688
    life after, 685–686
    living arrangements in, 688–692
Retrieval, of memory, 258
Reuters, 97, 143
Revolving door syndrome, 610–611
Righs to die issues, 727–733
Rights, civil, vs. fetal welfare, 96, 97
Risk factors, definition, 16
Risk-taking behavior, 419–420. *See also* Drunk
    driving; Substance abuse
    sexual, 446–447
Ritalin, 349, 384
Rituals, coming of age, 397
Romania
    adopted children from, 365
    corporal punishment, 298
Romantic love, 521–522, 530
Rooting reflex, 138t
Rothbart Infant Behavior Questionnaire
    (IBQ), 199
Rough-and-tumble play, 319
Royal Dramatic School, Stockholm, 508
Rubella virus, 97–98
Russia, 164, 405
    education, 500

Salt Lake City, 176, 216
Same-sex marriage, 526
SAMHSA (Substance Abuse and Mental Health
    Services Administration), 412, 478, 479,
    480, 481
Sample, definition, 44
Sampling, 44
Sandwich generation, 613, 614
Scaffolding, 164, 265
Scandinavian Simvastatin Survival Study
    Group, 476
Schema, 288
Schemes, 37, 159
Schizophrenia
    and heredity, 83
    and maternal nutrition, 92
School achievement, influences on, 340–345,
    353, 362, 427–429
School environment, 342–344, 428–429
School phobia, 382
School to Work Opportunities Act, 431
School violence, 380, 384, 462
Schools. *See* Education
Scientific method, 44
Scotland, 239, 405
Script, 259
Seattle Longitudinal Study, 522, 571–572, 652,
    655–656, 662
Secondary aging, 629
Secondary sex characteristics, 400, 401t
Secular trend, 401
Secure attachment, 206, 207t
Selective attention, 331, 332
Selective organization with compensation (SOC),
    655, 681
Self
    ideal, 280
    real, 280
Self-awareness
    emergence of, 214
    and emotion, 197

Stress
  and caregiving, 613–615
  coping with, 386, 387–388
  in middle adulthood, 567–571
  in middle childhood, 384–388
  occupational, 569–570
  during pregnancy, 98
  stressful life events, 568t
  and unemployment, 570–571
Stressors, 567
Stroke, warning signs of, 646t
Sub-Saharan Africa, 485, 505
Substance abuse, 479–481
  in adolescence, 398
  definition, 411
  in pregnancy, 93–96
  risk factors, 412
  and suicide, 415
Substance Abuse and Mental Health Services
    Administration (SAMSA), 412, 478,
    479, 480, 481
Substance dependence, in adolescence, 411–413
Substantive complexity, 503
Suicide, 414, 415, 727–729
  assisted, 729, 731–734, 738
Superego, 32
Support groups, parent, 226
SUPPORT Principal Investigators, 731
Supreme Court
  South Carolina, 96
  United States, 96
Surgeon General's Report on Youth Violence, 463
Survival curves, 636
Survival of the fittest, 39
Swaddling, 146
Sweden, 203, 405
  corporal punishment, 298
  infant mortality rate, 125f
  school violence, 462
  sexual mores, 523
  stillbirth, 122
  teen pregnancy, 450
Swimming reflex, 138t
Switzerland, 405
Symbolic function, 248, 249t, 250
Symbols. *See* Symbolic function
Syntax, 181
Syphilis, 449t
Systematic desensitization, 305, 306
Systems of action, 142, 243

Tabula rasa, 29
Tacit knowledge, 335, 493–494
  definition, 493
Tahiti, child abuse, 226
Taste, sense of, 140, 553
Tay-Sachs disease, 70t, 71
Teen Outreach Program, 451
Teen pregnancy, worldwide, 450, 451
Teenage motherhood, 120, 452
Teenagers. *See* Adolescence; Adolescents
Telegraphic speech, 180–181
Television
  and cognitive development, 170
  and gender development, 290–291
Temperament, 64, 198–201, 229
  and child care adjustment, 220
  and culture, 200, 201
  definition, 198

and goodness of fit, 200–201
  measuring, 199–200
  role of, 208
  stability of, 200
Temperamental patterns, 199t
Temple University, 404
Teratogenic, 91
Teratogens. *See* Prenatal development, and ma-
    ternal drug use; Prenatal development,
    and maternal illness
Terminal drop, 714
Terrible twos, 215, 215t, 216
Terrorism, 385, 386, 387
Testimony, of children, 259, 261
Testing, psychometric, 156–159, 263–265
  influences, on IQ scores, 264
Testosterone replacement therapy, 557, 558
Thailand, childbirth in, 109
Thanatology, 712
Theoretical perspectives, 31
  major, 3
Theories, of development, 30t
Theory, definition, 29
Theory of mind, 84, 257
  development of, 257–258
  in preoperational stage, 249t, 254–258
Time use, in adolescence, 453–454
Timing-of-events models, 511, 512t
Timing, of influences. *See* Critical periods;
    Sensitive periods
Tobacco use, 413
Toddlerhood
  developmental issues in, 213–218, 229
  fears in, 306t
  major developments in, 12, 12t, 13
Toddlers, developmental testing, 156–157
Tonic reflex, 138t
TOP (Teen Outreach Program), 451
Torrance Tests of Creative Thinking, 350
Touch, sense of, 140
Toxoplasmosis, 98
Traditional learning theory, 30t
Trait models, 511, 512t
  five-factor, 515–517, 515f
Transduction, 250
Transitive inference, 325–326
Transracial adoption, 364, 365
Trauma, age-related reactions to, 385t
Treatment for Adolescents with Depression
    Study (TADS) Team, 414
Triangular subtheory of love, 521
Triarchic theory of intelligence (Sternberg),
    334–335, 492–493
Trichomoniasis, 449t
Trust vs. mistrust, 33t, 204–205, 229, 370
Tsunami, Southeast Asia December 2004, 718
Tufts University School of Medicine, 559
Turkey, 176
Turn of the Screw (film), 508
Turner syndrome, 73t
Twin studies, 76, 77, 78
  on autism, 84
  on child abuse, 225
Two-way learning, 346
Typological models, 511, 512t, 517

U.S. Preventative Services Task Force, 565
Ukraine, corporal punishment, 298
Ultrasound, 90, 101t

Umbilical cord sampling, 101t
UNAIDS, 97, 323, 485, 486f
Unbilical cord, 88f
Unemployment, 570–571
UNESCO, 339, 505
UNICEF, 119, 124, 239
  Press Centre, 128
United Kingdom, 319, 370, 405, 500
  bullying in, 380
  childrearing practices, 146
  infant mortality rate, 125f
  obesity in, 476
  psychopharmacological therapy, 384
  sexual mores, 523
  teen pregnancy, 450
United Nations, 131, 505
  Convention on the Rights of Children,
    298, 404
  Principles for Older Persons, 694t
United Nations International Labor Organization
    (UNILO), 569
United States, 207
  aging population, 628–629
  childrearing practices, 257
  cohabitation, 527–528
  father's role, 203
  infant mortality rate, 125f
  self, and culture, 280–281
  violence in, 226
United States Cancer Statistics Working
    Group, 483
University of California at Berkeley, 8, 53, 503
  Oakland (Adolescent) Growth Study, 8, 20
University of Iowa, 8
University of Minnesota, 8
University of Montreal, 164
University of Pennslyvania, 27, 76
University of Virginia Health System, 73
University of Virginia School of Law, 404
USA TODAY/CNN/Gallup polls, 526
Utah, 176, 216

Validity, 47
Variable-rate theories, of aging, 632–633, 632t,
    633–634, 634, 635, 636
Variables, 50
Viagra, 560
Victorian Infant Collaborative Study Group, 121
Video games, 379
Violation-of-expectations, 172–175
  evaluating, 174–175
Violence
  domestic, 298, 532, 533. *See also* Elder
    abuse
  in the media, 385, 386
  school, 380, 384, 462. *See also* Bullying
  youth, 462–463
Visible imitation, 162
Vision problems, 322–323
  in late adulthood, 641t, 642
  in midlife, 552–553
Visual abilities, measuring, 171
Visual cliff, 145
Visual guidance, 144
Visual perception, 168
Visual preference, 168
Visual recognition memory, 168
Visually-based retrieval, 338
Vital capacity, 555

Vocabulary development, 184–185, 265–266
  middle childhood, 337
  teenage, 421, 422
Vocalization, early, 178
Vocational training, 431

Wages, gender gap, 503
Wales, 405
Walkers, baby, 143
Walking reflex, 138t, 144
Washington, D.C., 176–177
Waters and Dean Attachment Q-set (AQS),
    207–208
Wechsler Adult Intelligence Scale (WAIS), 571
  and older adults, 653–654
Wechsler Intelligence Scale for Children
    (WISC-III), 332
Wechsler Preschool and Primary Scale of
    Intelligence, Revised (WPPSI-III), 263
West India, childrearing practices, 146
West Side Story (play), 460
Wharton School of Business, 27
Whites
  body image, in adolescence, 408
  family structure, 368f
  genetic disorders in, 71t
  low birth weight babies, 120t
  mother's age at first birth, 535t
  onset of puberty, 401
  physical development, 317
  and poverty, 363
  school achievement, 428
  teenage motherhood, 451
  vision problems, 322
Whole-language approach, to reading, 338
Widowhood, 698

Wilderness Inquiry, 316
Wisdom, 663–665
With a Daughter's Eye (Bateson), 191, 192
Withdrawal of love, 297
Witnesses, children as, 259
Woman Called Golda (film), 508
Women. *See also* Gender
  in the workforce, 570
Work
  and cognitive development, 580–581
  in late adulthood, 684–685
  in middle adulthood, 578–581, 583
  retirement, 579–580, 683–688
  stress at, 569–570
  unemployment, 570–571
Workforce, entering, 503–505
Working memory, 176, 258, 658
Working parents, 219–220
  dual-income families, 536–538
  effects, on children, 220, 361–362, 456–457
World Health Organization (WHO), 405, 406,
    476, 477, 485, 486f, 632, 646, 728
World Trade Center attacks, 385, 569, 718
World Wide Web, 343–344
WPPSI-III (Wechsler Preschool and Primary
    Scale of Intelligence, Revised), 263
Writing Group for the Women's Health Initiative
    Investigators, 566–567
Writing skills, 338–339

Xxx chromosomal abnormality, 73t
Xyy chromosomal abnormality, 73t

Yale University, 8
Young adulthood, 468–507
  alcohol and drug use, 479–481

  cognitive development, 487, 487–507
  cohabitation, 526–528, 541
  education, 499–503, 507
  emerging adulthood, 473–474
  friendships, 520
  health in, 474–487, 506
  infertility, 486–487
  major developments in, 13t
  marriage, 523–524, 528–534, 541–542
  menstrual disorders, 484–485
  moral reasoning, 488, 489, 495–499, 506–507
  nutrition in, 474–475
  obesity, 476–477
  parenthood, 534–536
  paths to, 518–520
  personality development, 511–514, 540–541
  physical activity, 477
  physical development, 474–484
  postformal thought, 489–491
  psychosocial development, 508–544
  reflective thinking, 488, 489
  role of parents in, 519–520
  sexuality, 484–487, 506, 522–523
  singlehood, 524–525, 541
  sleep needs, 477–478
  STDs (sexually transmitted diseases), 485–486
  workforce, entering, 503–505
Young adults, 467
Youth violence, 462–463
  myths about, 463
Yucatan, 146

Zinacantan, Mexico, 216
Zone of proximal development (ZPD), 264, 336
Zuni people, 240
Zygote, 63